DATE DUE

FOURTH EDITION

WILLS, TRUSTS, AND ESTATE ADMINISTRATION FOR THE PARALEGAL

FOURTH EDITION

WILLS, TRUSTS, AND ESTATE ADMINISTRATION FOR THE PARALEGAL

DENNIS R. HOWER
University of Minnesota

West Publishing Company

- Minneapolis/St. Paul ■ New York
- Los Angeles ■ San Francisco

Copyeditor: Patricia Lewis
Text and Cover Designer: Lois Stanfield, LightSource Images
Composition: Parkwood Composition

WEST'S COMMITMENT TO THE ENVIRONMENT

In 1906, West Publishing Company began recycling materials left over from the production of books. This began a tradition of efficient and responsible use of resources. Today, 100% of our legal bound volumes are printed on acid-free, recycled paper consisting of 50% new paper pulp and 50% paper that has undergone a de-inking process. We also use vegetable-based inks to print all of our books. West recycles nearly 22,650,000 pounds of scrap paper annually—the equivalent of 187,500 trees. Since the 1960s, West has devised ways to capture and recycle waste inks, solvents, oils, and vapors created in the printing process. We also recycle plastics of all kinds, wood, glass, corrugated cardboard, and batteries, and have eliminated the use of polystyrene book packaging. We at West are proud of the longevity and the scope of our commitment to the environment.

West pocket parts and advance sheets are printed on recyclable paper and can be collected and recycled with newspapers. Staples do not have to be removed. Bound volumes can be recycled after removing the cover.

Production, Prepress, Printing and Binding by West Publishing Company.

TEXT IS PRINTED ON 10% POST
CONSUMER RECYCLED PAPER

British Library Cataloguing-in-Publication Data. A catalogue record for this book is available from the British Library.

Copyright ©1979, 1985, 1991   By WEST PUBLISHING COMPANY
Copyright ©1996   By WEST PUBLISHING COMPANY
**   610 Opperman Drive**
**   P.O. Box 64526**
**   St. Paul, MN 55164-0526**

LIBRARY OF CONGRESS CATALOGING-IN-PUBLICATION DATA

Hower, Dennis R.
    Wills, trusts, and estate administration for the paralegal/
Dennis R. Hower.—4th ed.
        p.   cm.
    Includes index.
    ISBN 0-314-06114-2 (hard : alk. paper).—ISBN 0-314-06482-6 (soft : alk. paper)
    1. Wills—United States. 2. Trusts and trustees—United States. 3. Probate law and practice—United States. 4. Legal assistants—United States—Handbooks, manuals, etc. I. Title.
    KF755.H68   1996
346.7305'4—dc20
[347.30654]   95-32140
                                                                            CIP

With love and affection to my wife, Audrey, whose patience, support, and assistance in preparing the manuscript made the completion of this edition possible, and also to my sisters, Rhonnie and Debbie—family is everything.

CONTENTS IN BRIEF

CONTENTS

PREFACE

Over the past twenty-five years, the performance of qualified and competent paralegals (legal assistants) has raised their status and established their work as a new and unique type of legal professional. The economic benefits paralegals bring both to their employers (supervising attorneys) and to the firm's clients have proven their need and value. It is no surprise, therefore, that their vocation has become one of the fastest growing professions in the current decade.

The goal of the fourth edition of *Wills, Trusts, and Estate Administration* is to continue to provide a textbook that explains the basic, practical, everyday duties of a paralegal in these fields of law and prepares paralegals, such as yourself, to confidently undertake and successfully accomplish these tasks. After using the text and obtaining work experience, you will attain the level of competence that will enable you to perform your work with confidence and continue the success and uphold the standards that your profession demands.

The text is written primarily for paralegals, but others such as trust officers and personal representatives appointed to administer the estate of a deceased person have also found it useful. The text identifies the responsibilities and duties that a paralegal can perform under the supervision of an attorney when drafting a will or trust or assisting with the administration of a decedent's estate. The fourth edition provides a review of the terminology and general principles of law that are basic for drafting wills and trusts, or planning and administering an estate, and identifies the participants and the duties they must perform in these legal areas. Next, a chronological treatment of the step-by-step procedures required to complete the will and trust drafts and the administration of a decedent's estate is presented, including sample drafts and the executed forms needed to administer the estate. Updated federal and state tax information and the appropriate tax forms are also discussed. The final chapter addresses the ethical standards and guidelines that currently govern the conduct of legal assistants practicing in wills, trusts, and estate administration.

The author is indebted to the American Law Institute for granting permission to cite numerous sections of the Restatement (Second) or (Third) on Trusts, and to the National Conference of Commissioners on Uniform State Laws and the American Bar Association for permission to include the Uniform Probate Code in this text.

CHAPTER ORGANIZATION

To help students obtain confidence and proficiency, each chapter of the fourth edition contains the following features:

- *Objectives*. The objectives focus students on what they will have learned upon completion of the chapter.
- *Scope of the chapter*. The scope identifies and lists, in order, the topics to be discussed within the chapter.
- *Terminology*. Key terms are printed in boldface type and are defined in the margin at their first appearance. Mini-glossary Boxes are used to group multiple definitions on a page. Key terms are also listed at the end of each chapter and defined in a comprehensive end-of-text glossary.
- *Examples, hypothetical situations, sample state statutes and legal forms, exhibits, checklists, drafted documents, and actual cases*. These are interspersed throughout the chapters to help the students understand the concepts and procedures discussed.
- *Assignments*. Frequent assignments within the chapters require students to apply the chapter's legal concepts or to perform tasks required of a practicing paralegal.
- *Checklists*. Checklists that collect relevant client data and information are included in the text, and *"What You Do"* lists in the Estate Administration chapter emphasize and clarify the actual procedures and specific tasks the paralegal student must master to attain confidence and competency.
- *Ethical Issues*. These are found throughout the text to call attention to important ethical concerns that are relevant to the procedures discussed within the individual chapters.
- *Review Questions*. New questions have been added at the end of each chapter and updated to correspond to the changes in content within the chapters. These help students review key chapter concepts.
- *Case Problems*. These actual cases and hypothetical problems have been added at the end of the chapters to enable the students to verify what they have learned and apply it to a specific problem or task discussed in the chapter.

CHANGES IN THE FOURTH EDITION

Some of the major changes in the fourth edition include the following:

- *Terminology*. Treatment of terminology has been revised for emphasis and clarity. Key terms are printed in boldface type, defined in the margins or Mini-glossary Boxes, listed at the end of each chapter, and included in the expanded glossary at the end of the text.
- *Case references*. More than 125 new case references have been added to the chapters to illustrate important points of law, and additional cases have been cited in the Case Problems at the end of the chapters to give students experience in reading and applying actual cases to the legal topics and concepts presented in the text.
- *Statutes*. State statutes have been added or updated that identify the variations in state laws and emphasize the need for paralegals to master the statutes of the state in which they live and practice.
- *State-by-state charts*. Numerous new charts show differences among all 50 states on topics such as Eligibility Requirements for Personal Representatives (Chapter 3) and Effects of Marriage on a Pre-Existing Will (Chapter 4).
- *Sample clauses and documents*. Sample clauses included in wills and trusts are presented with the corresponding discussion in the chapters, and frequently the entire will or trust document with comments is illustrated.

- *Examples*. Hypothetical examples illustrating the use of essential terminology and explaining complicated legal concepts are found throughout the chapters.
- *Legal forms*. Legal forms from various U.P.C. and non-U.P.C. states have been added within the chapters, and executed estate administration forms, including the essential tax forms, are included in Appendix A.
- *Checklists*. The checklists used for collecting data and information for drafting wills, trusts, or an estate plan have been expanded and updated.
- *Ethics*. This vital topic, formerly in an appendix, is now expanded into a new Chapter 15, giving the topic the importance it deserves. New margin notations (Ethical Issues) integrate ethical concerns within the chapter material.
- *Estate planning*. Estate planning coverage is expanded and is now a new chapter that explains the need for and purpose of an estate plan, including relevant tax consequences and the procedures used in creating the plan.
- *Small estates*. In-depth coverage of the administration of small estates is included in Chapter 12.
- *Living trusts*. Coverage of this popular trust has also been increased and now includes drafts of both revocable and irrevocable living trusts.
- *Right to die laws and advance medical directives*. A significant new section on this topic in Chapter 7 includes a discussion and copies of the following directives: a Living Will, a Health Care Proxy, and a Durable Power of Attorney for Health Care.
- *Tax laws have been updated.*
- *Historical coverage is deleted or greatly condensed.*
- *Examples of the problems and concerns of single parents have been added.*
- *The text has been reorganized based on reviewers' feedback:*
  - Coverage of sources of law, formerly in Chapter 1, has been omitted.
  - The new Chapter 1 now includes a discussion of the purpose of a will (previously in Chapter 5).
  - The chapter on Property (Chapter 2) now precedes the chapter on the Participants and the Proper Court (Chapter 3).
  - The hypothetical dialogue of a paralegal, attorney, and executor discussing a typical estate administration case has been moved from Chapter 2 to Chapter 11, "Personal Representatives."
  - Coverage has been streamlined, and unnecessary detail and repetition have been greatly reduced for a more concise, clear presentation.

EXTENSIVE TEACHING PACKAGE

- The **Instructor's Manual with Test Bank and Transparency Masters**, prepared by Virginia Noonan, Northern Essex Community College, contains detailed lecture outlines, teaching suggestions, answers to the text questions and assignments, a test bank, and transparency masters.
- The **Study Guide** contains chapter outlines, review questions, and additional practice exercises.
- **State-specific supplements** are available for California, Florida, New York, and Texas. These supplements provide summaries of state law where it differs from the text discussion. State-specific forms are also provided.
  - The California Supplement, prepared by Mark Milker, Southern California College of Business and Law.

- The Florida Supplement, prepared by Kathryn Cobb, Brevard Community College.
- The New York Supplement, prepared by Gina-Marie Reitano, St. John's University.
- The Texas Supplement, prepared by Gene Silverblatt, Central Texas College.

- **Instructor's Manual and Test Bank on disk.** The complete Instructor's Manual is available on disk for your convenience in testing and organizing.

- ***Strategies and Tips for Paralegal Educators,*** by Anita Tebbe of Johnson County Community College, provides teaching strategies specifically designed for the paralegal educator. It concentrates on how to teach and is organized in terms of three parts of paralegal education: the Who—students and teachers; the What—goals and objectives; and the How—methods of instruction, evaluation, and other aspects of teaching. One copy of this pamphlet is available to qualified adopters.

- **WESTLAW,** West's on-line computerized legal research system, offers students "hands-on" experience with a system commonly used in law offices. Qualified adopters can receive 10 free hours of WESTLAW. WESTLAW can be accessed with Macintosh and IBM PCs and compatibles. A modem is required.

- **WESTMATE Tutorial** (for DOS and Windows) is an interactive tutorial for WESTMATE software that introduces students to WESTLAW capabilities. WEST-MATE guides students through basic WESTLAW commands at their own pace using a personal computer. It is available free to qualified adopters.

- **Paralegal Video Library** includes:
    - "The Drama of the Law II: Paralegal Issues" Videotape. This series of five separate dramatizations is intended to stimulate classroom discussion about various issues and problems faced by paralegals on the job today. Each dramatization is approximately five to seven minutes. Topics include intake interview, human error, strategic information, client confidentiality, and unauthorized practice. The scripts were written by John Osborne, author of *The Paper Chase* and are professionally produced.
    - "I Never Said I Was a Lawyer" Paralegal Ethics Videotape uses a variety of scenarios to inspire discussion and give students experience in dealing with ethical dilemmas. Topics include the unauthorized practice of law, identification of paralegals as nonlawyers, waiver of client's rights through breaches of confidentiality, and lack of attorney supervision. "Situation analysis," how to evaluate an ethical situation and decide on the proper course of action, is also covered. The tape was created by the Colorado Bar Association Committee on Legal Assistants but is non-state-specific and will be useful in all paralegal programs.
    - "The Making of a Case" Videotape is narrated by Richard Dysart, star of the former popular T.V. program *L.A. Law*. In this introduction to law library materials and legal research, a case is followed from the court system to the law library shelf. This gives a better understanding of what case law is, why it is important, and how cases are published.
    - "West's Legal Research" Videotapes teach the basis and rationale for legal research. The three types of legal research tools—Primary Tools, Secondary Tools, and Finding Tools—are covered. Topics like case law reporters, digests, computer assistance, statutes, special searches, and CD-ROM libraries are included. The nine segments are contained on two tapes.

ACKNOWLEDGMENTS

Special thanks is given to the following individuals at West Publishing who made my work and life a lot easier: Elizabeth Hannan, acquisitions editor; Patty Bryant, developmental editor; Lisa Gunderman, production editor; Pat Lewis, copyeditor; and Karen Laird, promotion manager.

Special appreciation is extended to the following reviewers of the manuscript for their thoughtful and valuable comments and suggestions for the fourth edition:

- Lisa Ann Duncan
Central Carolina Community College, North Carolina
- Paul D. Guymon
California State University, San Bernardino
- Susan W. Harrell
University of West Florida
- Cynthia Baker Lauber
Denver Paralegal Institute
Community College of Aurora
- Dorothy B. Moore
Broward Community College, Florida
- Virginia C. Noonan
Northern Essex Community College, Massachusetts
- Gina-Marie Reitano
St. John's University, New York
- Francisco R. Wong
City College of San Francisco, California

CHAPTER ONE

THE PURPOSE AND NEED FOR A WILL

OBJECTIVES

After completing this chapter, you should be able to:

- Understand and explain the reasons why a high percentage of Americans die without a will.

- Begin to identify and become familiar with the basic terminology of wills and trusts.

- Recognize and explain the function and purpose of wills.

- Begin to identify and contrast the procedures and outcomes when property is passed by testacy versus intestacy.

- Begin to recognize the terms used to identify the persons who make, manage, administer, or benefit from wills, trusts, and a deceased person's estate.

- Identify examples of instances where a person may not need a will.

SCOPE OF THE CHAPTER

This chapter begins with a brief explanation of why so few people in this country die with wills. The terminology associated with the law of wills, trusts, and estate administration is introduced as you begin the process of mastering the terms and legal concepts essential to the practice of law in these areas. A discussion on the purpose and use of wills and the necessity of having a will, also called a testament, concludes this chapter.

AN INTRODUCTION TO WILLS

Will
The legally enforceable written declaration of a person's intended distribution of property after death.

Less than one-third of all citizens of the United States die having made and signed a **will**—the written declaration of a person's intended distribution of property after death. That means that the vast majority have no say in the way the property they have accumulated over a lifetime will pass after they die. In some states, financial planners are recommending that individuals make a will as soon as they reach majority age, 18 in most states. No matter how young or old we are, everyone owns property of some sort, and most individuals want to determine to whom this property will pass after they die. Why then do so few people make wills? Some put off making a will because they do not want to discuss or face their mortality; others are reluctant to discuss their property and finances with "strangers"; some procrastinate, then die prematurely due to an accident or sudden unexpected illness; and some cite the cost as their reason (although attorneys generally charge minimal fees for preparing simple wills). It seems that no matter how much effort is expended encouraging Americans to make a will, the majority is not influenced or convinced.

Statutory Requirements

Another reason so many people die without wills is that not everyone can make a will. To begin with, state laws impose restrictions on the makers of wills and on the procedures for creating a valid will. Through its legislature, every state passes laws, called **statutes,** that determine the **testamentary capacity** (e.g., age and sanity) requirements for a person to make a will. Testamentary capacity means the maker or **testator** must be old enough (at least 18) and be of **"sound mind"** at the time the will is made. Therefore people who are under 18 or who are not mentally well (lacking a "sound mind") cannot make a valid will.

In the case of *Matter of Yett's Estate,* 44 Or.App. 709, 606 P.2d 1174 (1980), a will was challenged on the ground that the testator lacked testamentary capacity. The court held that in deciding whether the maker of a will had testamentary capacity, great weight is accorded the testimony of attesting witnesses who were

---

MINI-GLOSSARY BOX

Statutes	**Testamentary capacity**	**Testator**	**Sound mind**
Laws passed by state and federal legislatures.	Age and sanity (sound mind) requirements for a person to make a will.	A man who makes and/or dies with a will.	Having the mental ability to make a will.

present at the execution of the will. It is the decedent's capacity at that time, not the general condition over a span of time that determines testamentary capacity. In this instance, the evidence indicated that the decedent had this capacity even though she was suffering from a malignant brain tumor. The court also ruled that the evidence failed to establish that the decedent's illness (the tumor) had caused insane delusions that resulted in a decreased share of her estate passing to the contestant of the will. Accordingly, the court ruled that the will was valid.

State statutes also establish formal requirements for the creation and **execution of a valid will**; e.g., most wills must be written, signed by the maker, and attested to by two or three witnesses. To be properly executed, a will must conform to the laws of the state in which it is made. Each state enacts (passes) its own laws on the execution of wills, and these laws are not always the same. Laws differ, for example, on the method of writing that may be used (e.g., whether the will may be handwritten or **holographic,** typed, audiotaped, or videotaped) and on the placement of the testator's signature (e.g., whether it must be on every page, only at the end of the will, or simply anywhere on the will). Individuals who are unfamiliar with the laws of their state and try to create their own wills often make mistakes or omissions concerning their property, naming their **beneficiaries,** or attempting to satisfy the requirements for a will. The result may be an unintended, undesirable, or invalid will. As a trained and experienced paralegal, you will need to learn and master the laws of your state, so that you can explain the statutory requirements, terminology, and procedures associated with wills and help clients execute a valid and meaningful will that accurately fulfills their intent and desires.

Execution of a valid will
The writing and signing by the testator and the attesting and signing by two or more witnesses of the will to establish its validity.

Holographic will
A completely handwritten and signed will that requires no witnesses.

Beneficiary (of a will)
A person to whom the decedent's property is given or distributed.

Basic Terminology Related to Wills

Before proceeding further, it will be helpful to present some basic terminology related to wills and estates. Exhibit 1.1 explains the terms that are used to indicate whether a person died with a will or not.

The following terms relate to the actual making of a will:

- *Execute.* To perform or complete.

Exhibit 1.1   Testacy versus Intestacy

Decedent

(the deceased or person who dies)

With a will / \ Without a will

- Testacy. Death with a will.
- Testate. Any person who makes and/or dies with a will.
- Testator. A man who makes and/or dies with a will.
- Testatrix. A woman who makes and/or dies with a will.

- Intestacy. Death without a will.
- Intestate. Any person who dies without a will. The decedent's property passes to heirs (real property) or next-of-kin (personal property). See the text discussion.

The common practice today is to use the term *testator* for both sexes, so this text will refer to any person (man or woman) who makes and dies with a will as a *testator*.

- *Execution of a will.* The writing and signing of a will by the testator and the attesting and signing of the will by two or more witnesses.
- *Witnesses.* Two or more persons who attest (acknowledge a testator's intent, capacity, and signature on a will) and also sign the will.

Other important terms relate to the administration of the decedent's estate:

- *Estate.* The variety of property items accumulated during a person's lifetime and owned at the time of death.
- *Property.* Anything subject to ownership; classified as real property or personal property.
    - *Real Property.* Land, buildings, and things permanently attached to them.
    - *Personal Property.* Any property that is not real property.
- *Estate administration.* The process of appointing a personal representative (executor or administrator) to collect, preserve, manage, and inventory the decedent's estate; notifying creditors to present their claims; paying all the decedent's debts and death taxes due; and distributing the remaining estate according to the will or to state law if the decedent died intestate.
- *Probate.* Often used synonymously with estate administration. For example, the phrase "to avoid probate" means to avoid the process and procedures of estate administration.
- *Probate court.* The court that has jurisdiction (authority) over the handling or administration of a decedent's estate and the distribution of the property; also called Surrogate's or Orphan's Court.
- *Personal representative.* The person (man or woman) who is nominated by a will, or appointed by the probate court when there is no will, to manage the estate of the decedent and distribute the estate assets according to the will or the law. A personal representative includes:
    - *Executor/executrix.* The man or woman named in the will to carry out its provisions, i.e., administer the decedent's estate.
    - *Administrator/administratrix.* The man or woman appointed by the probate court to administer the decedent's estate when there is no will.

The types and titles of personal representatives are discussed in Chapter 11.

The following terms are used to refer to the recipients of the decedent's property:

- *Beneficiary.* In the broadest sense, any person to whom the decedent's property is given or distributed. It can include a legatee, devisee, heir, or next-of-kin. Traditionally, a beneficiary is a person who receives the personal property of the decedent. This definition for beneficiaries will be used throughout the remaining chapters.
- Will terms:
    - *Devisee.* A person who receives a gift of real property under a will; or as defined by the Uniform Probate Code, the person who receives a gift of either real or personal property.
    - *Legatee.* A person who receives a gift of personal property under a will.
- Intestate terms:
    - *Heir.* A person who receives the real property of an intestate; it is incorrect to refer to a person receiving property under a will as an heir.
    - *Next-of-kin.* A person who receives the personal property of an intestate.

THE PURPOSE OF WILLS

The primary function of a will is to allow individuals to distribute their property any way they choose. A will gives the testator the opportunity to accurately describe the property owned at death and to designate to whom that property is to be distributed. Since **probate courts** closely scrutinize the language of the will to determine the testator's true intent, it is of paramount importance that no word or sentence within the will create a contradiction, ambiguity, or mistaken interpretation that could cause confusion that would change the testator's plan or, worse, invalidate the will.

Example: In an early provision of her handwritten will, Thelma Parker leaves "all my antique furniture to my best friend, Maude Thompson." Later in the will, Thelma states that she wants the furniture to go to her only daughter, Betsy. Then, in the final clause of the will, she selects five pieces of this furniture to be given to her housekeeper. Because of all these contradictions, the court could declare the will invalid.

Since the language and individual words in a will and the context in which these words are used are major factors in determining the testator's intent, it is essential that the will be carefully constructed so that the testator's plan for the distribution of the estate property is readily identifiable. The court in the case of *Richland Trust Co. v. Becvar,* 44 Ohio St.2d 219, 339 N.E.2d 830 (1975) stated: "The function of the court in a will construction case is to determine and apply the testatrix's intention, as expressed in the language of the whole will, read in the light of the circumstances surrounding its execution."

Without a will, the statutes of the decedent's domicile (home) state will determine to whom the decedent's property will be distributed with the exception that **real property,** i.e., land, buildings (house, cottage, apartment, or office building), and the like, will be distributed according to the laws of the state in which the property is located. One of your major tasks and responsibilities will be to prepare drafts of the will and review them carefully with the client *to ensure that the final draft contains complete, accurate, and clearly understandable language to enable readers, especially the probate court, to agree on the meaning of the will and the client's intent.*

The will takes effect only when the testator dies. This is because all wills are **ambulatory,** i.e., they can be revoked and are subject to change anytime before death. While living, the testator can review and modify the will as often as he wishes at anytime and in any way by adding, deleting, or changing gifts, beneficiaries, clauses of the will, or fiduciaries (see further discussion in this chapter under Appointment of Guardians). Also, the testator can sell or dispose of any property listed in the will before death. If the modification is a simple change, e.g., adding a new gift, a **codicil** or amendment to the will is sufficient. If numerous or major modifications are needed, a new will should be executed.

In no particular order of importance, the next paragraphs discuss some of the reasons for making a will.

Funeral and Burial Arrangements

One reason to make a will is that it provides an opportunity to preplan one's funeral and burial. After planning the funeral with a funeral director (including

Probate court
The court that has jurisdiction (authority) over the probate of wills and the administration of the decedent's estate.

Real property
Land, buildings, and things permanently attached to them.

ETHICAL ISSUE

Ambulatory
Subject to being revoked and changed anytime before death, e.g., a will is ambulatory.

Codicil
A written amendment to the will that changes but does not invalidate it.

costs and arrangements for a casket, church service, and a reception) and purchasing a burial plot, a testator can insert these plans into the will and make them known to family members. Preplanning the funeral and burial takes a heavy burden off the grieving family, both economically and emotionally, that alone is worth the expense of the will. If the testator prefers to be cremated, she can show a will containing the cremation plan to family members; then, if there are any objections, they can be resolved prior to the testator's death to ensure that her wishes will be carried out. Again, preplanning with a funeral director would be wise. Other than the decedent, the following persons generally have priority in deciding on funeral and burial arrangements including cremation: the surviving spouse, an adult child, a parent, an adult sibling, the decedent's guardian, and any other authorized or obligated person, e.g., a personal representative or medical examiner.

In reality, all such preplanning may be an exercise in futility, either because the will is not found until after the testator has been buried, or because the family simply disobeys or ignores the instructions. Often the family makes final decisions concerning the disposal of the testator's body and the type of funeral or service. All too frequently, serious disagreements arise over such questions as whether there should be a burial or cremation, a denominational religious or nondenominational service, an open or closed casket, and the like.

Example: Fred has told his family he wants to be cremated when he dies. After his death, Fred's family, for religious reasons, decides to have him buried in the family plot. Often the decedent's wishes are not followed, as in this example.

Sometimes the testator's family disregards the funeral plans outlined in the will because the arrangements are too elaborate, too expensive, or unreasonable.

Examples: John wants to be cremated and have his ashes flown to Paris and spread from the top of the Eiffel Tower. Bill wants a horse-drawn carriage, a hundred-member band, and an all-night party. Honoring such requests may deplete the estate and create additional hardships for survivors.

Even though the funeral and burial arrangements are often made by someone other than the personal representative (such as a surviving spouse or other family member), the cost of all "reasonable" expenses is paid as a priority debt of the decedent's estate according to state law, as will be discussed in detail in later chapters. It will be your job to keep accurate records of the costs and *remind the personal representative so that these expenses remain "reasonable."* Personal representatives are liable to the estate if they allow these costs to become excessive due to their neglect.

In addition to allowing a decedent to personally plan the funeral and burial, a will can provide an opportunity for organ donations. If the testator wishes to donate his organs or remains for transplant or medical research, he should obtain a donor card from the National Kidney Foundation, Inc., as well as mention the organ donation in the will. The card is available at most hospitals and mortuaries and must be signed by the testator and two witnesses to be legal. Some states also provide a notation for an organ donation (gift) on the face or the back of the driver's license (see Exhibit 1.2).

ETHICAL ISSUE →

Apportionment clause
A clause in a will that allocates the tax burden among the residuary estate and the beneficiaries of the will.

Apportionment for Death Taxes

By adding an appropriate **apportionment clause** to the will, the testator can determine the source from which death taxes (federal and state estate taxes and

Exhibit 1.2 Donor Card from the National Kidney Foundation and Driver's License

A Public Service Agency

Pursuant to the Uniform Anatomical Gift Act.
I hereby elect upon my death the following option(s):

A ___ To donate any organ or parts

B ___ To donate a pacemaker (date implanted _____)

C ___ To donate parts or organs listed _____

_____

D ___ To not donate any organs, parts or pacemaker.

_____
SIGNATURE   DATE
DL 290   (REV 5/92)

NOTICE

If you are at least 18, you may designate on your driver license or I.D. card a donation of any needed organs, tissues or pacemaker for medical transplantation.   Under the Uniform Anatomical Gift Act (Sec. 7150, Health & Safety Code) donation takes effect upon your death.
NEXT OF KIN (OPTIONAL)

NAME _____

ADDRESS _____

TELEPHONE NO. _____

---DETACH HERE---

IMPORTANT INSTRUCTION

To make a donation, fill out this card and put the "DONOR" dot on the front of your license or I.D. card as shown below. The card should be carried with your license or I.D. card. If you change your mind complete a new card and remove the dot. Whole Body donations require separate arrangement.

To refuse to donate, fill out this card and carry it with your license or I.D. card. Do not use the dot.

DMV CALIFORNIA
Driver License

DONOR   DONOR DOT

---DETACH HERE---

Additional information regarding the Donor program may be obtained by writing or calling The Gift of Life:

National Kidney Foundation of Southern California
- 5777 West Century Blvd.
  Suite 395
  Los Angeles, CA 90045-7404
  1/800 747-5527
- 2320 Fifth Avenue
  Suite 206
  San Diego, CA 92101-1633
  (619) 235-8280

Southern California
- 17050 Bushard Street
  Suite 202
  Fountain Valley, CA 92708
  (714) 962-7675

Northern California
- 553 Pilgrim Drive
  Suite C
  Foster City, CA 94404
  (415) 349-5111

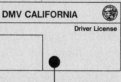

For further information consult your physician or
☐ Yes, I have discussed my wishes with my family.
This is a legal document under the Anatomical Gift Act or similar laws.

_____   _____
Witness   Witness

_____   _____
City and State   Date Signed

_____   _____
Date of Birth of Donor   Signature of Donor

of each other:
Signed by the donor and the following two witnesses in the presence

UNIFORM DONOR CARD

Here's all you have to do...

1. **Designate your wishes by filling out the card, and sign it in front of two witnesses**

2. **Discuss your wishes with your family and give them the top half of the card**

3. **Carry the bottom half of the card in your wallet**

ORGAN DONATION...The **GIFT** of Life!

THE NATIONAL KIDNEY FOUNDATION
Please detach and give this portion of the card to your family.

This is to inform you that, should the occasion ever arise, I would like to be an organ and tissue donor. Please see that my wishes are carried out by informing the attending medical personnel that I have indicated my wishes to become a donor.
Thank you.

_____
SIGNATURE   DATE
For further information write or call:
THE NATIONAL KIDNEY FOUNDATION
30 East 33rd Street, New York, NY 10016
(800) 622-9010

UNIFORM DONOR CARD

of _____
                                        (print or type name of donor)
In the hope that I may help others, I hereby make this anatomical gift, if medically acceptable, to take effect upon my death. The words and marks below indicate my wishes.
I give: (a) _____ any needed organs or parts
        (b) _____ only the following organs or parts

_____
                                        (specify the organ(s), tissue(s) or part(s)
for the purposes of transplantation, therapy, medical research or education;
        (c) _____ my body for anatomical study if needed.

Limitations or special wishes, if any: _____

state inheritance taxes) will be paid. Unless the will contains an unambiguous apportionment clause, state law determines the method of apportionment. Some states place the burden of estate and inheritance taxes on the **residuary estate** of the will as is commonly done with creditors' claims. The following is an example of an apportionment clause from West's McKinney's Forms, ESP, § 7:412:

> I direct that all estate, inheritance, succession and transfer taxes and other death duties, including any interest or penalties thereon, imposed or payable by reason of my death upon or in respect of any property passing under my will and required to be included in my gross estate for the purpose of such taxes, shall be paid out of my residuary estate as an administration expense and shall not be apportioned. (Reprinted with permission from West's McKinney's Forms, Copyright ©, by West Publishing Company.)

Many other states apportion state and federal death taxes among the various persons (**legatees** or beneficiaries) on a **pro rata** basis (see New York's Estate Powers & Trusts Law § 2–1.8).

The advantage of having the testator make the apportionment decision rather than leaving it to state law is that customarily the property included in the will's residue clause is left to the surviving spouse and children. If this property is the primary or sole source of payment of creditors' claims and death taxes, *these family members may be unintentionally placed in a hardship situation by this major oversight*. It is your responsibility to recognize this mistake and bring it to your supervising attorney's attention. The attorney will explain its significance to the client and then obtain permission for you to redraft this provision of the will.

The Uniform Estate Tax Apportionment Act of 1958 (Revised 1964), which apportions state and federal death taxes on all beneficiaries on a pro rata basis, has been adopted in some states and is incorporated in the Uniform Probate Code § 3–916(a)(b). Remember, though, that if a will contains an apportionment clause, that clause overrides any apportionment method established by state statute. Without a will that includes the provision, the statute of the decedent's domicile state applies.

Property Distributions

With a will, the testator can avoid many ill-advised and awkward property distributions. Consider the following example:

Example: Jacob Weizman dies intestate, without a will, leaving as his only heirs, five daughters, each of whom is married and has children of her own. Jacob's only estate assets consist of three farms (each farm is located in Jacob's domicile state and each is worth $200,000) and $100,000 cash in various banks. Jacob's domicile (home) state statute, like the law in most other states, would divide his assets equally among his five daughters. Dividing the cash would be easy—each daughter would receive $20,000. The three farms, however, would go to the five daughters in the form of co-ownership called **tenancy in common,** which allows each co-owner (each daughter) to have an undivided, equal interest in each farm and the right to equal possession of the entire premises of each farm. As a tenant in common, each daughter, on her death, can pass her equal interest (one-fifth) of each farm to the beneficiaries she names in her will; if she dies intestate, her state law will determine who receives her one-fifth interest.

This example could be made even more complex: e.g., two of the daughters might want to live on the farms, while the others want to sell them; one or more

---

Residuary estate
The remaining assets (residue) of the decedent's estate after all debts have been paid and all other gifts in the will are distributed.

Legatee
A person who receives a gift of personal property under a will.

Pro rata
According to a certain rate or percentage.

ETHICAL ISSUE ▶

Tenancy in common
The ownership of an undivided interest of real or personal property by two or more persons without the right of survivorship, which allows each owner's interest to be passed to his or her heirs upon death.

of the daughters might divorce and remarry; or some of the daughters might die before their father (Jacob). The point is clear: disregarding the serious personality conflicts that might occur, the occupation and management problems of the property alone would be impossible.

Jacob could have avoided this unfortunate situation if he had discussed his assets with his daughters, so that, as a family, they could identify possible options and arrive at a compromise they could accept. In this way, Jacob's original plan to treat the daughters equally could be accomplished harmoniously, and the solution could be included in his will.

⚏ ASSIGNMENT 1.1

Review the facts in the Jacob Weizman example above. Draw up three different plans that could be used as part of Jacob's will to transfer the three farms and the $100,000 to his five daughters in equal shares.

Provisions for Family Members

With a will, the testator can appropriately provide for a surviving spouse and the special needs of individual children. In most cases, the surviving spouse receives the majority of the testator's estate. By following certain procedures and including specific provisions in wills and trusts, death taxes, especially federal and state estate taxes, can be reduced, thereby maximizing the portion of the testator's estate that family members receive. This tax reduction could be lost if the decedent dies intestate. For a complete discussion of these problems and tax concerns, see Chapter 10.

If the decedent were to die intestate leaving a spouse and minor children, the **intestate succession statutes** of most states would leave much of the estate property to the spouse and children as **tenants in common.** Because the children are minors, a court would need to appoint a **guardian** (see Appointment of Guardians below) to handle any property in which they have an interest. In such a case, the guardian's appointment could cause the surviving spouse additional expense and needless delay if the property had to be sold promptly, e.g., to provide funds for the family's necessary living expenses. For this reason, it is often best to leave the decedent's estate solely to the surviving spouse without minor children becoming co-owners. This can be accomplished using a will.

The only person a testator cannot disinherit is a surviving spouse because the spouse has a statutory right to a share of the decedent spouse's estate. This is

MINI-GLOSSARY BOX

Intestate succession statutes
Laws passed in each state establishing the manner in which a decedent's property will be distributed when death occurs without a valid will.

Tenants in common
Two or more persons who own property in a tenancy in common.

Guardian
The person or institution named by the maker of a will or appointed by the court when there is no will to care for the person and/or property of a minor or a handicapped or incompetent person.

Spouse's statutory, forced or elective share
The spouse's statutory right to choose a share of the decedent spouse's estate instead of inheriting under the provisions of the decedent's will.

called the surviving **spouse's statutory, forced or elective share.** Every state has some provision for the benefit of the surviving spouse that makes it impossible for the deceased to leave the surviving spouse nothing. On the other hand, a decedent who dies testate can disinherit children. Of course, this happens at times, but more commonly, the testator wants the children to receive unequal shares of the estate to meet their different needs (see the examples below).

Examples: In her will:

1. Kristin Neilsen leaves her entire estate to her three children equally.
2. Kristin Neilsen leaves the majority of her estate to her handicapped child and only a few nominal gifts to her other two children.
3. Kristin Neilsen intentionally and specifically states that one, two, or all three of her children (naming them) are not to receive any assets of her estate.

In the above examples, if the decedent, Kristin Neilsen, dies intestate, the children's special needs won't be met, but none of them will be disinherited. All the children will receive equal shares.

Numerous other problems concerning family members' inheritance rights are discussed in detail in Chapter 7.

Appointment of Guardians

Heir
A person, including a spouse, who is entitled by statute to the real property of an intestate decedent. Under the Uniform Probate Code, a person entitled to real or personal property of the intestate.

Fiduciary duty
A duty or responsibility required of a fiduciary that arises out of a position of loyalty, trust, and confidence.

Adoptive parent
A person who legally adopts another individual, usually a child.

With a will, a testator can appoint guardians for minor or **incompetent persons.** Guardians appointed by the court are either **personal guardians** or **property guardians.** Both guardians are a type of **fiduciary,** a person in a position of trust who controls and manages property exclusively for the benefit of others. Fiduciaries include guardians acting for minors or incompetent persons, trustees acting for the beneficiaries of the trust, and personal representatives acting for the beneficiaries of the will or for **heirs** when there is no will. The fiduciary is required to give absolute loyalty to the beneficiary or minor in carrying out **fiduciary duties,** i.e., all dealings concerning the property held in trust.

A personal guardian is an adult who has custody, control, and responsibility for the care of the minor child until the child reaches the age of majority, usually 18. If the decedent (testator) is survived by the other natural or **adoptive parent,** that parent by law immediately becomes the personal guardian of the minor. An attempt by the testator to appoint some other person as the minor's guardian is not valid or binding, see Tex. Prob. Code § 109(a).

This situation frequently occurs when married couples divorce and one of the former spouses is given custody of the minor children of the marriage. If the custodial spouse dies while the children are still minors, often he or she leaves a will naming a personal guardian who is not the other natural parent (the former spouse). The appointment of a personal guardian is discussed in detail with examples and cases in Chapter 7.

On the other hand, when there is no other surviving natural parent, the appointment of a personal guardian in the custodial parent's will is generally upheld by the court, and any further hearing on custody is unnecessary, see Mass. Gen. Laws Ann. ch. 201 § 3.

When parents die without a will, the probate court must select both a personal and a property guardian based on what is "in the best interests of the child." Usually, the court appoints a family member who may or may not have been the choice of the decedent. Without a will, the appointment of a guardian can lead to a time-consuming and expensive contest in probate court between relatives. Unfortunately, the dispute often has lasting harmful effects on the children.

Example: Tal Anderson dies intestate. Tal had often talked to Cathy Merrill and Cathy's spouse, Tal's close friends, about his desire to have Cathy and her spouse "take care of my children if I should die." Even though Cathy and her spouse informed the probate court of Tal's wishes and their willingness to be the guardians, the probate court would most likely appoint blood relatives of Tal who agree to be the guardians.

Example: The only blood relative of Rachel Weinstein, age 27, is her grandmother, age 70. Because of her grandmother's age and uncertain health, Rachel asked her close friend, Susan Steindorf, if she would be the guardian of her 8-year-old daughter. Susan agrees, but Rachel dies intestate. The probate court would likely appoint the grandmother guardian if she is willing to serve even though she was not Rachel's choice.

Unlike the case of the personal guardian, the surviving natural or adoptive parent or the person appointed by the testator's will is not automatically appointed the property guardian for the decedent's minor or incompetent children. Such people may be appointed and often are, but the decision is made by the probate court, which appoints the guardian.

The property guardian can be a natural person or a legal person such as a corporation, bank, or trust department. The property guardian's responsibility is to take exclusive control of and manage the property inherited by a minor or incompetent person in order to preserve and increase its value. The guardian must perform the management and investment functions according to strict standards set by the court and state law. These standards cannot be changed, broadened, or made less rigid by the terms of a will even if that was the testator's intent.

A property guardian for an incompetent person whom the probate court has found to be incapable of managing property is sometimes called a **conservator.** Typically, conservators are appointed in situations, such as aging or illnesses like Alzheimer's disease, in which people are under a legal disability making them physically or mentally incapable of managing their property assets. States usually require that a guardian or conservator be appointed whenever a minor or incompetent person owns property, obtained through inheritance or otherwise, that is greater than petty cash.

Property guardians are discussed further in Chapter 7.

Creation of Testamentary Trusts

With a will, a testator can create a **testamentary trust,** i.e., a trust within the will. A **trust** is a legal agreement in which one person (the **settlor**) transfers **legal**

Conservator
An individual or trust institution appointed by a court to care for and manage property, specifically, the substantial inheritance of an incompetent person or minor.
Trust
A right of property, real or personal, held by one person (trustee) for the benefit of another (beneficiary).

MINI-GLOSSARY BOX

Testamentary trust
A trust created in a will. It becomes operative only after death.

Settlor
A person who creates a trust; also called donor, grantor, creator, or trustor.

Legal title
The form of ownership of

trust property held by the trustee giving the trustee the right to control the property.

Trustee
The person or institution named by the maker of a will or a settlor of a trust to administer property for

the benefit of another according to provisions in a testamentary trust or an *inter vivos* trust.

Beneficiary (of a trust)
The person or institution holding equitable title to whom the trustee distributes the income earned

from the trust property and, depending on the terms of the trust, even the trust property itself.

Equitable title
A right of the party to whom it (the equitable or beneficial title) belongs to the benefits of the trust.

title (ownership) to one or more persons (the **trustee** or trustees) who hold and manage the property for one or more **beneficiaries** who receive the **equitable title** that gives them the right to the benefits of the trust. The settlor gives up possession, control, and ownership of the property to the trustee who is specifically instructed by the trust terms how the trust is to be managed and the trust property invested so that income produced (profits) can be distributed to the beneficiaries. All three positions (settlor, trustee, and beneficiary) can be held by the same person, but the fundamental characteristic of a trust, i.e., the splitting of title into legal title (transferred to the trustee) and equitable title (given to the beneficiary), requires that no one person can be the sole trustee and the sole beneficiary since that person would hold both titles, merging them and invalidating the attempt to create a trust. The solution to this problem is to have either co-trustees or co-beneficiaries so the "splitting title" requirement is satisfied.

Examples:

1. A trust is not created if the settlor, Mike Ford, names himself as both the sole trustee and the sole beneficiary.

2. A trust is created if the settlor, Mike Ford, names himself sole trustee and Carley Brown and himself as co-beneficiaries.

3. A trust is created if the settlor, Mike Ford, names Carley Brown and himself as co-trustees and himself as sole beneficiary.

Trusts can be created either during the life of the settlor (***inter vivos*** or **living trusts**) or as part of the testator-settlor's will (testamentary trusts); the latter take effect only on death. One of the most common uses of a testamentary trust is the **bypass trust** (also called Trust B of an A-B trust, credit shelter trust, exemption equivalent trust, and residuary trust) established for the benefit of a surviving spouse. By limiting the surviving spouse's right to the **principal** of the trust, the property is not included in the estate of the surviving spouse when he dies; thus, it avoids **federal estate tax.** By reducing federal taxes in this manner, more of the estate property is free to pass to future beneficiaries, usually the children (see the detailed discussion in Chapter 10). If a person dies without a will (intestate), this tax advantage would be lost.

Another common reason for creating testamentary or *inter vivos* trusts is to counter and avoid the rigid control and expense of a property guardianship for minors or conservators for incompetents. Through the terms of these trusts, the

MINI-GLOSSARY BOX

Inter vivos (living) trust
A trust created by a maker (settlor) during the maker's lifetime. It becomes operative during the lifetime of the maker.

Bypass (residuary) trust
A testamentary trust established for the benefit of a surviving spouse.

Principal
In trust law, the capital or property of a trust, as opposed to the income, which is the fruit of the capital.

Federal estate tax
A tax imposed on the transfer of the taxable estate and not on any particular legacy, devise, or distributive share.

trustee can be given flexible management powers without the probate court involvement, delays, and expense that accompany a guardianship. The following examples illustrate the advantages of trusts.

Example: In a trust, trustee Edward Benson can be given discretion to choose among accumulating trust income, distributing income, or even distributing the principal of the trust for the benefit of one or more beneficiaries. The stricter regulations imposed on a property guardian would not grant this freedom.

Example: After reviewing the pros and cons of wills, trusts, and guardianships, spouses, Beverly and Howard Mayberry, who have two minor children, decide on the following: Because he has a terminal illness, Howard drafts and executes his will leaving his entire estate to his surviving spouse, Beverly, confident that she will provide for their minor children and eventually transfer the balance of the property to them in her own will. Since no property is left to the minor children, guardianships (with their corresponding control and expense) are avoided. In the event that Beverly dies first, Howard adds a contingent testamentary trust, leaving his estate to the trust for the benefit of his minor children.

Other reasons for the creation of trusts include the following:

- Trusts are used to provide professional management of the trust property for those beneficiaries (including a settlor-beneficiary) who do not have the time, inclination, or skill to manage the property themselves or are no longer able to do so.
- Trusts allow the settlors to maintain control of the trust property throughout life and even after death. The duration of a **private trust** is limited by the legal doctrine called the Rule Against Perpetuities (discussed in Chapter 7). **Public (charitable) trusts** are not limited in time.
- Trusts can prevent spendthrift beneficiaries from recklessly depleting the trust fund and can also prevent their creditors from obtaining the trust principal on demand for the payment of debts.
- Trusts can save taxes and avoid probate expenses if properly established.

A complete discussion of the formation, drafting, and types of trusts, including the popular living trust, is included in Chapters 8 and 9.

Private trust
A trust created for the financial benefit of a designated person or class of persons, clearly identified by the terms of the trust.

Public (charitable) trust
A trust established for the social benefit either of the public at large or the community.

Appointment of Personal Representative

With a will, the testator has the authority to name a **personal representative (executor** or **executrix),** the person who administers the decedent's estate and

MINI-GLOSSARY BOX

Personal representative
The person who administers the decedent's estate and either carries out the terms of the will or follows the appropriate intestate succession statute in distributing the estate.

Executor
A man named in the will by the maker to be the personal representative of the decedent's estate and to carry out the provisions of the will.

Executrix
A woman named in the will by the maker to be the personal representative of the decedent's estate and to carry out the provisions of the will.

carries out the terms of the will. Personal representative is the term the Uniform Probate Code uses to designate the individual chosen by the testator to administer the estate; the traditional terms for this person are executor, if the individual is a man, and executrix, if a woman. Throughout the remaining chapters of this book, the words *personal representative* will be used to identify the person named in the will to carry out its terms.

Like trustees and guardians, the personal representative is a fiduciary who owes fiduciary duties (trust, loyalty, and the like) to the recipients of the testator's estate, e.g., the beneficiaries and devisees. To acquire the authority and powers of the position, a personal representative must be appointed by the appropriate court, which most states call the probate court. Generally, the court appoints the person nominated by the testator in the will unless that person is not qualified under state law. A typical list of persons who are not qualified appears in Texas Probate Code § 78. The list includes:

1. Minors.
2. Incompetent persons.
3. A person convicted of a felony.
4. A nonresident who has failed to appoint a resident agent to accept service of process.
5. A nonresident corporation that is not authorized to act as a fiduciary in the state.
6. A person whom the court finds "unsuitable."

Example: Carry Swanson's will names Jack Daniels to be the personal representative. Because of previous associations, Carry's family and heirs feel extremely hostile toward Jack. The hostility of beneficiaries toward a nominated personal representative does not ordinarily or automatically disqualify the person as "unsuitable." See *Matter of Petty's Estate,* 227 Kan. 697, 608 P.2d 987 (1980), where the court refused to appoint the nominee because the hostility could lead to unnecessary difficulties and expenses for the estate.

Caveat: If a testator appoints a personal representative and also in the will selects an attorney to assist the personal representative with the estate administration, the estate is not legally bound to this selection. For assistance in handling the decedent's estate, personal representatives have the right to select any attorney of their own choice. *It is a violation of the Code of Ethics for the attorney or paralegal to suggest that they be named in the will for such purpose.*

ETHICAL ISSUE ▶

The various types of personal representatives and the important role they play in administering the decedent's estate are discussed in Chapters 11 and 12.

Without a will, none of the testator's appointments, procedures, or opportunities occur. If the decedent dies intestate, a person called the **administrator,** or using the same Uniform Probate Code term, the personal representative, is appointed by the probate court to administer the estate and distribute the decedent's property according to state law. Usually, this law is called the intestate succession statute, but its provisions vary from state to state. The decedent-intestate's domicile and the location of the decedent's property will determine how and to whom the property of the intestate will be distributed. Chapter 4 of this text discusses death with a will (testacy) and death without a will (intestacy) in more detail.

Administrator
The man appointed by the probate court to administer the decedent's estate when there is no will.
Administratrix
The woman appointed by the probate court to administer the decedent's estate when there is no will.

WILL SUBSTITUTES

In some cases it may not be absolutely necessary to have a will, but the decision should be made only after consultation with an attorney knowledgeable about estate planning, unless the person owns no property at all. It may be possible, especially in the cases of small estates, to employ "will substitutes" instead of a will to distribute a decedent's estate. Examples of will substitutes include (1) joint tenancy, (2) life insurance, (3) *inter vivos* trusts, and (4) *inter vivos* gifts. The value and kinds of property owned by the client deserve paramount consideration in deciding whether a will should be executed.

- Joint tenancy:

Example: Jean and her fiancé, Bill, own a house in joint tenancy valued at $90,000. They have $1,200 in a joint checking account and $4,000 in a joint savings account. They each own other separate property. Both Jean and Bill are salaried employees and contributed equal sums to purchase the home and to the checking and savings accounts. Jean dies without a will. As the sole surviving joint tenant, Bill will receive all the joint property, which was the couple's intent. Jean's individual or separate property has to go through probate. The tax consequences in such cases will be discussed in the tax chapter (see Chapter 14). A more complex problem could result, however, if the unmarried couple, Jean and Bill, were to die in a common accident and both die intestate.

- Life insurance:

Example: As another example of a will substitute, assume that Mary, a single parent, had only one major asset, a $100,000 life insurance policy through a group plan with premiums paid by her employer. Her son, Mike, is named as sole beneficiary. At Mary's death without a will, Mike will receive the proceeds of the life insurance policy.The proceeds are not declared as income or as a gift to Mike, so no income or gift tax is owed (see Chapter 10).

- *Inter vivos* (living) trust:

Example: Serena owns an apartment building valued at $300,000. During her lifetime she places this property in trust (*inter vivos* trust), naming her brother, Reginald, trustee, and two friends, Vaughn and Renee, beneficiaries. In the trust instrument, Serena directs the trustee to pay the income from the trust property—the apartment building—to the beneficiaries, Vaughn and Renee, during their lifetimes and, at the death of the last of the two to survive, to convey the apartment building and land to the children of Renee (Christopher and Ann) as tenants in common. Even if Serena dies intestate, the disposition of the trust income and the trust property will be determined by the *inter vivos* trust instrument. Any remaining property in Serena's estate at her death will be distributed according to the provisions of her will or according to the state intestate succession statute. For a more complete discussion of the use of an *inter vivos* (living) trust as a substitute for a will, see Chapter 9.

- *Inter vivos* gift:

Example: Anyone may dispose of property during a lifetime simply by giving it away (*inter vivos* gift). During his lifetime, Sherman gives to his relatives and friends $100,000 in cash, $50,000 in stocks and bonds, a pickup truck, and his collection of Chinese figurines. These gifts are executed (completed), and there are no strings attached, i.e., Sherman retains no right to demand the return of the gifts. Gift taxes may be due and payable on the *inter vivos* gifts if Sherman exceeds the $10,000 per donee annual exclusion. For a complete discussion of the gift tax laws, see Chapters 10 and 14.

Checklist for Whether a Will Is Needed

The following checklist will help you determine a client's need, or your own need, for a will. To determine whether a person needs a will, the following questions must be answered:

1. What property does the client own?
2. In what form of ownership, e.g., severalty (sole ownership), joint tenancy, or tenancy in common, is the property held?
3. Is the client aware of the intestate succession statute that determines who would take her property if the client died without a will? Would the client be content with these persons receiving the property, or does the client desire to leave the property to someone else, e.g., a close friend or institutions such as a church or a charity?
4. Is the client aware that probate files are open to the public?
5. Are specific items of property, real or personal, to be left to certain devisees?
6. Does the client have any special instructions for funeral and burial arrangements or for the donation of organs or the client's body for medical or educational reasons?
7. Does the client wish to establish a testamentary trust for the purpose of maintaining an income for an elderly parent, minor child, or spendthrift relative?
8. Is there a need for a guardian to be appointed over property or the person of minor children?
9. Does the client want to appoint a personal representative (executor or executrix) to handle the administration of the estate?
10. Has the client considered the possible tax consequences to the estate with and without a will? To the beneficiaries, devisees, or heirs?
11. Does the client want any taxes owed, including state inheritance taxes, to be paid out of estate assets?
12. What powers and authority does the client wish to bestow on the personal representative (executor), guardian, or trustee?
13. If the client is married and the client and the spouse were to die in a common accident, have the consequences to their respective estates been considered?
14. Does the client want to avoid the probate process and its corresponding expenses and delays?

THE NEED FOR A WILL—A CONCLUSION

In summary, there are numerous reasons why so many Americans die without a will. They include:

1. Some people, by statute, cannot make a valid will, e.g., minors and incompetent persons.

2. Everyone does not need a will. Some people have limited or no property, others have no heirs (and believe they have no need), and some are satisfied with the "will" their state makes for them, i.e., the intestate succession statute.

3. Some attempt to create a will, but it is declared invalid by the probate court due to improper execution.

4. Some procrastinate too long or simply don't bother.

5. Some use "will substitutes" instead of wills to distribute the decedent's estate.

As Chapter 2 explains, the need for a will is determined by the kind of property the individual possesses and the form of the possessor's ownership.

KEY TERMS

Will	Residuary estate	Personal guardian	*Inter Vivos* (living)
Statutes	(also called	Property guardian	trust
Testamentary	residue)	Fiduciary	Bypass (residuary)
capacity	Legatee	Heir	trust
Testator	Pro rata	Fiduciary duty	Principal
Sound mind	Tenancy in common	Adoptive parent	Federal estate tax
Execution of a valid	Intestate succession	Conservator	Private trust
will	statutes	Testamentary trust	Public (charitable)
Holographic will	Tenants in common	Trust	trust
Beneficiary (of a	Guardian	Settlor	Personal
will)	Spouse's statutory,	Legal title	representative
Probate court	forced or elective	Trustee	Executor
Real property	share	Beneficiary (of a	Executrix
Ambulatory	Incompetent person	trust)	Administrator
Codicil		Equitable title	Administratrix
Apportionment			
clause			

REVIEW QUESTIONS

1. Explain the reasons why so many Americans die without wills.
2. What does it mean to say the maker of a will has testamentary capacity?
3. List your state's statutory requirements for the execution of a will. How does your state's requirements for a valid will differ from those of other states?
4. Because the terminology included in this chapter is essential to your understanding of legal concepts and procedures presented in future chapters and your practice in the fields of wills, trusts, and estates, write out your own definition of each key term in this chapter. Are your definitions essentially the same as those in the text?
5. Can a will be changed or revoked? Explain.
6. List and explain the various reasons or purposes for making a will.
7. Identify four examples of "will substitutes" and discuss how each might possibly be used to eliminate the need for a will.

CASE PROBLEMS

Problem 1

Erik Larson handwrote a three-page will in pencil. At the end of the business day, he took the will to an attorney and asked that it be typed. Since Erik mentioned that he was leaving on a vacation and would be out-of-state for one week, the paralegal for the firm asked if he would like to sign the handwritten (holographic) will. Erik did sign the will, but he also stated that he would return after his trip to sign "his will," i.e., the typed will. While on vacation, Erik became ill and died. Answer the following:

A. Is a signed holographic will a valid will in your state?

B. Are witnesses required for a holographic will?

C. Should the executed holographic will operate as Erik's will pending the execution of the typewritten will? Explain. See and compare *In re Cosgrove's Estate,* 290 Mich. 258, 287 N.W. 456 (1939).

Problem 2

Otto Halverson died testate. He was survived by twenty-seven nieces and nephews. Otto had had little formal education and had not learned how to write his signature; therefore, he signed his name with a mark, i.e., an "X." Otto's nieces and nephews challenged the validity of his will. They claimed the will had been improperly executed because he signed with an "X."

A. Is a testator's mark, i.e., an "X," sufficient to satisfy the signature requirement for a valid will in your state? Cite the statute or case law.

B. In your opinion, if there is no statute or case law on this issue in your state, how should your state court decide this issue? See and compare *In re Estate of Hobelsberger, 85 S.D. 282, 181 N.W.2d 455 (1970).*

CHAPTER TWO

THE CONCEPT OF PROPERTY RELATING TO WILLS, TRUSTS, AND ESTATE ADMINISTRATION

OBJECTIVES

After completing this chapter, you should be able to:

- Identify, explain, and classify the various kinds of property, such as real and personal property or probate and nonprobate property.

- Recognize and understand the terminology associated with property law.

- Distinguish the various forms of ownership of real and personal property and explain the requirements for their creation and the methods of transferring them.

- Understand and explain why courts do not favor the creation of joint tenancies between parties other than spouses.

- Identify the community property states and differentiate between community and separate property.

- Explain the kinds, methods of creation, and characteristics of estates in real property.

SCOPE OF THE CHAPTER

Everyone owns some kind of property, e.g., a home, car, savings and checking accounts, appliances, clothes, jewelry, or stocks and bonds. The owner of certain property called probate property (discussed below) has the opportunity to transfer it while living by gift, sale, or trust. After the owner dies, property can be passed by will, trust, or inheritance according to state law. Without property, a will is unnecessary, and a trust cannot be created. Thus, property is the essential component that establishes the need for and use of wills and trusts. You must fully understand the law of property and its terminology before you can discuss drafts of wills or trusts and the administration of an estate with clients. This chapter introduces the terminology of the law of property, explains its association with wills, trusts, and estate administration, and discusses the related statutes and court decisions. Also introduced are the ways or forms in which property can be owned; each form of ownership is identified, defined, and explained. Estates in real property (freeholds and leaseholds) are also covered.

PROPERTY: TERMINOLOGY AND CLASSIFICATION

Property is anything subject to ownership. It is classified as either real property or personal property.

Real Property

Real property (also called realty or real estate) is property that is immovable, fixed, or permanent. It includes:

- Land.
- Structures affixed to the land such as houses, apartment buildings, condominiums, and office buildings.
- Objects attached to the land and buildings called fixtures.
- Some things growing on the land.

Owners of real property also have rights to airspace above their land and to the earth below it, including any minerals in the earth.

Fixtures

Fixture
Real property that may have once been personal property but now is permanently attached to land or buildings.

A **fixture** is real property that may once have been personal property but now is permanently attached to land or buildings. An example of a fixture growing on land is a tree; however, growing crops that are annually cultivated like corn, wheat, and vegetables are not fixtures. They are considered to be personal property. Carpeting nailed to the floor and a built-in dishwasher are examples of fixtures in buildings.

State courts apply three tests—annexation, adaptation, and intention—to determine if personal property has been converted into a fixture:

1. Annexation means that the personal property has been affixed or annexed to the real property.

2. *Adaptation* means that the personal property has been adapted to the use or purpose of the real estate. The court asks whether the property is necessary or beneficial to the function or enjoyment of the real estate.

3. In most states, however, the *intention* of the person who annexed the personal property to the real property has been the controlling test for determining the existence of a fixture.

Courts throughout the country vary substantially on what constitutes a fixture, but generally, though not always, doors, fences, windows, stoves, refrigerators, electric lights, wall to wall carpeting, and the like are held to be fixtures. Compare the following cases:

- *Mortgage Bond Co. v. Stephens,* 181 Okl. 419, 74 P.2d 361 (1937), in which the court held that a refrigerator was a fixture.
- *Andrews v. First Realty Corp.,* 6 Cal.App.2d 407, 44 P.2d 628 (1935), in which the court held that a refrigerator was personal property.

Tenants often install fixtures on property they are renting. A tenant farmer raising chickens may build a shed to shelter them or install gasoline tanks to avoid long drives to town for fuel; a tenant renting an apartment may add carpeting, bookshelves, and a door knocker for comfort and convenience. Previously, any such items a tenant attached to the real estate could not be removed when the tenant vacated. Today, however, tenants may remove property they have attached to real estate if the property falls under one of three exceptions, known as tenant's fixtures:

1. *Trade fixtures.* Property placed on the land or in a building to help the tenant carry on a trade or business.
   Examples: Smokehouse, machinery, barber chairs, greenhouse, pipe organ.
2. *Agricultural fixtures.* Property annexed by the tenant for farming purposes.
   Examples: Wooden silo, toolshed, henhouse, hay carrier, irrigation plant.
3. *Domestic fixtures.* Property attached by the tenant to make an apartment more comfortable or convenient.
   Examples: Carpeting, dishwasher, clothes dryer, gas stove, bookshelves.

ASSIGNMENT 2.1

Henry recently sold his movie theater to Helma. Which of the following items are fixtures (real property) that now belong to Helma? Give reasons for your answers.

Seats in the auditorium	Popcorn machine	Furnace in the building
Computers in the office	Movie projector	Telephones in the building
Carpeting in the theater	Movie film	Mirrors in the restrooms

Transfers of Real Property

When real property is transferred by gift or sale, the title or ownership is conveyed to the donee or buyer by a written formal document called a *deed.* Some of the more important terms associated with transfers of real property include the following:

- *Transfer.* An act by which the title to property is conveyed from one party to another. A party may be an individual, a corporation, or the government.
- *Conveyance.* Any transfer by deed or will of legal or equitable title (see below) to real property from one party to another.
- *Disposition.* The parting with, transfer of, or conveyance of property.
- *Grantor.* The person who conveys (transfers) real property to another.
- *Grantee.* The person to whom real property is conveyed.

Example: Abner conveys Blackacre, a farm, by deed to his friend, Charles. Abner is the grantor; Charles is the grantee.

- *Deed.* A written, signed, and delivered legal document that transfers title or ownership of real property such as land or buildings.
- *Title.* The right to and evidence of ownership of real or personal property.
- *Legal title.* A title that is complete, perfect, and enforceable in a court of law, granting the holder the right of ownership and possession.
- *Equitable title.* A party who has equitable title has the right to have the legal title transferred to him. For instance, a person who purchases a house through a mortgage has equitable title and is in possession of the house while paying off the installments on the mortgage to the legal title owner, e.g., the bank. Once the last payment is made, legal title will be transferred to the possessor by the delivery of a deed.
- *Interest.* The terms "interest" and "title" are not synonymous. An interest entitles a person to some right in the property, but that right may be less than title or ownership. For example, a renter has an interest in the apartment that she leases, but not the title. The owner (usually the landlord) has title.
- *Vest.* To deliver full title and possession of land. State law automatically passes (vests) title to the decedent's real property to the beneficiaries of the will or to the heirs if the decedent dies without a will. The title to the real property is passed (vested) "subject to" the right of the personal representative to devest or take away the property in order to pay claims of the decedent's creditors (see Cal. Prob. Code § 7000 and Texas Prob. Code § 37).
- *Devest* or *divest.* To withdraw or take away title from the possessor.

The following example illustrates the use of these terms.

Example: Valerie agrees to buy Richard's cottage. At the closing, Richard *transfers legal title* to the cottage by the *conveyance* of a *deed* to Valerie. Since Richard is the person (seller) who transfers *real property* (the cottage) to another (Valerie, the buyer), Richard is also the *grantor*. Valerie is the *grantee*. Clearly, Valerie has an *interest* in the cottage, and in this case, her interest is the *ownership (title)* of the cottage. If Valerie financed the purchase of the cottage by obtaining a mortgage from a bank, Valerie has the *equitable title* and the bank has the *legal title* until the mortgage is paid. One year later Valerie dies in a car accident without having made a will. Title to real property (the cottage) owned by the decedent (Valerie) *vests* in her heirs the moment she dies. If Valerie had substantial debts, her personal representative may have a right to *devest* (take away) the property from the heirs and sell it to pay creditors' claims.

Personal Property

Personal property, also referred to as "chattels personal," is movable property. It is everything subject to ownership that is not real estate and includes such items as clothing, household furnishings, stocks, money, contract rights, and life insurance. A **chattel** is an item of personal property.

Unlike real property, which passes directly to the decedent's beneficiaries or heirs, under state law, title to the decedent's personal property passes to the personal representative (executor or administrator) appointed to handle the administration of the decedent's estate. If creditors must be paid, generally the decedent's personal property is used to obtain the necessary funds.

Personal property can be subdivided into two categories:

1. *Tangible personal property.* Property that has a physical existence, i.e., it can be touched and is movable.

Examples:

Merchandise	Animals	Tools
Clothing	Household goods	Furniture
Appliances	Jewelry	Works of art
Books	China	Stamp/coin collections
Television sets	Cars	Boats
Airplane	RVs	Computers

2. *Intangible personal property.* Property that has no physical existence, i.e., it cannot be touched. Although such property has little or no value in itself, it establishes and represents the right to receive something of value. The ownership of intangible property is established by various documents, such as bank statements, stock or bond certificates, and written contracts for life insurance and annuities.

Intangible personal property also includes a chose in action, a right to personal property that the owner does not possess but does have a right of action for, e.g, a right to receive payment of a debt or to sue for damages for another's negligence.

Examples: A ten dollar bill is just a piece of paper, but it represents the right to receive property worth ten dollars. A promissory note by itself has no value, but it represents the right to receive payment from a debtor. The ten dollar bill and the promissory note are intangible personal property. Other examples of intangible personal property include the following:

Cash	Savings and checking accounts
Profit sharing plans	Shares of corporate stock
Annuities	Corporate and government bonds
Pension plans	Negotiable instruments (checks and promissory notes)
Life insurance proceeds	
Patent rights	Government benefits such as Social Security and veterans' benefits
Copyrights	
Trademarks	Individual retirement accounts
Royalties	Claims against another person for debts, property damage, personal injury, or wrongful death

Chattel
Generally, any item of personal property.

🏛 ASSIGNMENT 2.2

Classify each of the following items by placing a mark (X) in the most appropriate column.

Item	Real Property	Tangible Personal Property	Intangible Personal Property
Car			
Cash in checking account			
Right to renew apartment lease			
House			
Life insurance proceeds			
Furniture			
Stocks and bonds			
Furnace			
Personal injury lawsuit			
Clothing			
Dishwasher (built-in)			
Dishwasher (portable)			
Mobile home on wheels			
Houseboat			
Tax refund check			
Television roof antenna			
Bookcase			
Trees on land			
Gun collection			
Corn growing on farm			

You will play a major role in helping the personal representative find, collect, preserve, appraise, and liquidate or distribute the decedent's personal assets. These tasks will be discussed in more detail in future chapters. In addition, you will have to list all the decedent's assets and classify them as real property or (tangible or intangible) personal property. Since an accurate classification is essential to the administration of the estate, you must learn to distinguish the different types of property and *be sure to verify your classification with your supervising attorney.*

ETHICAL ISSUE ▸

Probate Property or Probate Estate

All decedents own one or both of the two types of property (real and personal). Together, they are often called the decedent's estate. An estate (also called a gross estate) is all the property, real and personal, owned by any living person, or all the assets owned by a decedent at the time of death.

Example: Jana Bronowski is single. She owns her own home, furnishings, household goods, and clothing. She has money in savings and checking accounts, stocks and bonds, and valuable jewelry. She also owns a lake cottage with a boat and motor. All these property items, real and personal, constitute Jana's estate or gross estate.

Not all property owned by the decedent can be passed by will, however. The only type of property a testator can distribute through a will is probate property, which is also referred to as probate assets, the probate estate, or simply the estate.

Probate property is all real or personal property that the decedent owned either individually as a single or sole owner, called ownership in **severalty,** or as a co-

Severalty
Ownership of property held by one person only.

owner with another person or persons in the form of ownership called tenancy in common. Probate property is subject to estate administration by the personal representative (executor or administrator) according to the terms of the will or, if the decedent died intestate, according to the appropriate state intestate succession statute.

Example: LaShanna Morgan owns her house, car, furniture, and savings account in severalty; i.e., she is the sole owner of each of these items of property. LaShanna also equally owns a boat and a condominium with her best friend Sarah as tenants in common. If LaShanna dies and her debts and taxes due are paid, all of this property, including her one-half interest in the boat and the condominium as a tenant in common, would be probate property and would pass to her named beneficiaries or devisees if she has a will or to her heirs if she died intestate.

The following probate property is subject to creditors' claims:

- Real property owned in severalty (single ownership) or in a tenancy in common.
- Personal property owned in severalty or in a tenancy in common.
- Life insurance proceeds payable to the estate or a policy in which the decedent retained the **incidents of ownership** (see the discussion in Chapter 10).
- Debts owed the decedent for mortgages, promissory notes, contracts for deed, loans, rents, stock dividends, income tax refunds, interest, royalties, and copyrights.
- Gain from the sale of a business.
- Social Security, Railroad Retirement, and Veterans Administration benefits.
- Civil lawsuit for money damages.
- Testamentary trusts and living trusts not registered as owned by the trustee.

Incidents of ownership
The right of the insured or her estate to the economic benefits of the life insurance policy.

Nonprobate Property (Nonprobate Assets)

Nonprobate property is real or personal property that is not part of the decedent's estate. For that reason, a decedent's nonprobate property is:

- Not distributed according to the decedent's will.
- Not distributed according to intestate succession statutes if there is no will.
- Not subject to administration (probate) of the decedent's estate.
- Not subject to a spouse's claims.
- Not subject to claims of the decedent's creditors.

But nonprobate property is part of the decedent's *gross estate* for federal and state death tax purposes, i.e., it is subject to federal and state estate taxes and state inheritance tax.

Various methods are available to convert real and personal property into nonprobate assets, e.g., placing property into trusts or joint tenancy. Therefore, nonprobate property includes the following:

- Real and personal property owned and held in joint tenancy with the right of survivorship.
- Real and personal property transferred to living (*inter vivos*) trusts that are registered as owned by the trustee.
- Money placed in a bank account as a *Totten trust.*

■ Proceeds of a life insurance policy payable to a named beneficiary (recipient of the money) and not to the decedent's estate.

■ Employment benefits contracts that contain a named beneficiary such as profit sharing plans, pension plans, group life insurance, 401(k) plans, employee stock ownership plans (ESOPs), and Keogh plans.

■ Annuity contracts with a named beneficiary.

■ Individual retirement accounts (IRAs) with a named beneficiary.

■ U.S. savings bonds payable on death to a beneficiary other than the decedent's estate.

■ Annual gifts of less than $10,000 per donee (the person receiving the gift). Spouses can give a total of $20,000 annually to each donee without paying federal gift tax, but a gift tax return must be filed with the IRS.

Operation of law
Rights pass to a person by the application of the established rules of law, without the act, knowledge, or cooperation of the person.

Each of these types of nonprobate property goes directly to the named beneficiary or the surviving joint tenant(s) by **operation of law.** If the decedent's entire estate consists of nonprobate property, there is no need for estate administration (probate). Even though nonprobate property avoids the probate process, you must identify and keep accurate records of each item for the preparation of federal and state estate taxes and state inheritance tax returns. For a detailed discussion, see Chapter 14.

STATUTES GOVERNING THE PASSAGE OF PROPERTY

The law of property is mostly statutory law. States have the power to enact statutes governing the passage of property from one generation to another or from the deceased to someone in his own generation. The states derive such power from their right, under the U.S. Constitution, to levy and collect taxes and from their duty to protect the citizenry.

Example: If Jane Doe dies owning property including her house (real property) and items of personal property such as her household furniture and small savings and checking accounts, what are the respective rights of Jane Doe and her creditors?

As an owner of an estate, a citizen such as Jane Doe has the right to have her property distributed as she wishes, so long as those desires do not conflict with the rights of others, e.g., a spouse, children, or creditors. Generally, a spouse cannot be disinherited, and minor children are entitled to support.

Every decedent's creditors have the right to be compensated for their claims, and the state by statute establishes procedures whereby the creditor may make a claim against the decedent's estate whether or not the decedent has made a will.

Generally, each state requires careful recording of all activity involving a decedent's estate so that it can fairly and accurately calculate the amount of tax that should be taken from the estate of the decedent. Here the state becomes a "creditor"; the estate may owe the state a death tax (see Chapter 14).

Descent and distribution
Refers to the distribution by intestate succession statutes.

The state protects the decedent's rights by enacting statutes to ensure that each person will be allowed to make a will. If someone dies without a will, the state's statutes also provide for distribution of the property to those whom the decedent would probably have chosen if the decedent had made a will. These are called **descent and distribution** or *intestate succession statutes.* Exhibit 2.1 is the intestate succession statute of New York (for further discussion, see Chapter 4).

Exhibit 2.1 New York State's Intestate Succession Statute

N.Y. Estates Powers and Trusts Law § 4–1.1 (McKinney 1992)
Descent and Distribution of a Decedent's Estate

The property of a decedent not disposed of by will shall be distributed as provided in this section. In computing said distribution, debts, administration expenses and reasonable funeral expenses shall be deducted but all estate taxes shall be disregarded, except that nothing contained herein relieves a distributee from contributing to all such taxes the amounts apportioned against him or her under 2–1.8. Distribution shall then be as follows:

(a) If a decedent is survived by:

(1) A spouse and **issue,** fifty thousand dollars and one-half of the residue to the spouse, and the balance thereof to the issue by representation.

(2) A spouse and no issue, the whole to the spouse.

(3) Issue and no spouse, the whole to the issue, by representation.

(4) One or both parents, and no spouse and no issue, the whole to the surviving parent or parents.

(5) Issue of parents, and no spouse, issue or parent, the whole to the issue of the parents, by representation.

(6) One or more grandparents or the issue of grandparents (as hereinafter defined), and no spouse, issue, parent or issue of parents, one-half to the surviving paternal grandparent or grandparents, or if neither of them survives the decedent, to their issue, by representation, and the other one-half to the surviving maternal grandparent or grandparents, or if neither of them survives the decedent, to their issue, by representation; provided that if the decedent was not survived by a grandparent or grandparents on one side or by the issue of such grandparents, the whole to the surviving grandparent or grandparents on the other side, or if neither of them survives the decedent, to their issue, by representation, in the same manner as the one-half. For the purposes of this subparagraph, issue of grandparents shall not include issue more remote than grandchildren of such grandparents.

(7) Great-grandchildren of grandparents, and no spouse, issue, parent, issue of parents, grandparent, children of grandparents or grandchildren of grandparents, one-half to the great-grandchildren of the paternal grandparents, per capita, and the other one-half to the great-grandchildren of the maternal grandparents, **per capita**; provided that if the decedent was not survived by great-grandchildren of grandparents on one side, the whole to the great-grandchildren of grandparents on the other side, in the same manner as the one-half.

(b) For all purposes of this section, decedent's relatives of the **half blood** shall be treated as if they were relatives of the whole blood.

(c) **Distributees** of the decedent, conceived before his or her death but born alive thereafter, take as if they were born in his or her lifetime.

(d) The right of an adopted child to take a **distributive share** and the **right of succession** to the estate of an adopted child continue as provided in the domestic relations law.

(e) A distributive share passing to a surviving spouse under this section is in lieu of any right of **dower** to which such spouse may be entitled.

MINI-GLOSSARY BOX

Issue
All persons who have descended from a common ancestor; a broader term than "children."

Per capita
A distribution of property based on giving equal shares to all those entitled to the intestate's estate.

Half blood
A term denoting the degree of relationship that exists between those who have the same mother or the same father, but not both parents in common.

Distributee
The person to whom personal property of the intestate decedent is distributed (orthodox terminology).

Distributive share
A recipient's portion of property left by a decedent who died intestate, as determined by state intestate succession laws.

Right of succession
The right of an heir or successor to share in a decedent's estate, determined by degree of kinship.

Dower
At common law, the wife's right to a life estate in one-third of the real property her husband owned during the marriage.

🏛 ASSIGNMENT 2.3

1. Define the following new words contained in the New York statute (Exhibit 2.1) by using the Glossary at the end of this book (all these terms will be defined and discussed in later chapters): *dower, right of succession, distributees, issue, distributive share, per capita, residue, half blood,* and *adopted child.*
2. List seven types of property interests that are not part of the decedent's probate estate.

FORMS OF PROPERTY OWNERSHIP

Various forms of property ownership exist, ranging from one person holding the entire interest in an item of real or personal property to situations where two or more persons share concurrent ownership rights as co-owners (co-tenants). The most common forms of property ownership are *tenancy in severalty* (individual ownership) and *concurrent ownership* (joint tenancy, tenancy in common, tenancy by the entirety, and community property). The term "tenant" or "tenancy," which is used to describe severalty and some of the types of concurrent ownership, is synonymous with "owner" or "ownership." Exhibit 2.2 summarizes the forms of property ownership.

Tenancy in Severalty—Ownership by One Person

Tenancy in severalty (ownership in severalty, or individual ownership) means that one person is the sole owner of real property, such as land, or personal property, such as a car. As an individual, the owner in severalty has absolute ownership of the real or personal property with exclusive rights, privileges, and interests in it. The owner may voluntarily dispose of the property while living, either by gift or sale, or may dispose of it at death through a will. If no such **disposition** has taken place at the time of death, the property remains in the owner's estate and passes to certain specified takers under intestate succession statutes.

Disposition
The parting with, transfer of, or conveyance of property.

   Example: John buys Joe's car. The title is transferred to John. John is the sole owner of the car. He owns it in severalty.

   Example: Mary is given a ring by her aunt. Once delivered, the ring belongs to Mary, solely. She owns it in severalty.

   Example: Uncle Henry died. In his will, he left his lake cottage to his niece, Kathy. Kathy owns the real property in severalty.

Exhibit 2.2   Forms of Property Ownership

Real or personal property can be owned:		
By one person (individual ownership)	or	By two or more persons (concurrent ownership)
• Tenancy in severalty		• Joint tenancy
		• Tenancy in common
		• Tenancy by the entirety
		• Community property

Example:

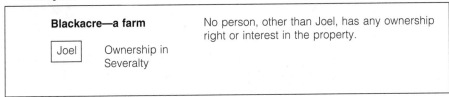

Blackacre—a farm

| Joel | Ownership in Severalty |

No person, other than Joel, has any ownership right or interest in the property.

Forms of Concurrent Ownership—Ownership by Two or More Persons

Situations where ownership rights in property are shared by more than one person are forms of concurrent ownership. The most common forms of such multiple ownership are joint tenancy, tenancy in common, tenancy by the entirety, and community property.

Joint Tenancy

Joint tenancy is the ownership of real or personal property by two or more persons (called the joint tenants) who obtain the property by gift, purchase, or inheritance. The unique and distinguishing characteristic of a joint tenancy is the **right of survivorship.** On the death of one joint tenant, the right of survivorship passes the decedent's interest in the property automatically to the surviving joint tenants by operation of law, with the last surviving joint tenant entitled to the whole property.

Example:

Blackacre—a farm

| Eno | Ruth | → Ruth dies → | Eno |

Blackacre

Eno and Ruth are joint tenants who concurrently own Blackacre. Ruth dies. Eno owns the undivided whole property in severalty (single ownership).

The farm goes directly to Eno *without* passing through Ruth's estate. Even if Ruth had a will, the will would not affect property owned as joint tenants.

In order for a joint tenancy to be created, common law requires "four unities": unity of time, unity of title, unity of interest, and unity of possession. According to common law, a simple conveyance of property to two or more persons as joint tenants does not necessarily create a joint tenancy unless the four unities also exist. The decision in *Cleaver v. Long,* 69 Ohio L. Abs. 488, 126 N.E.2d 479 (1955), supports the common law rules for the creation of a joint tenancy; in this case, the court said that all tenants must:

- Have the same interest in land with respect to duration of the estate (unity of interest).
- Acquire their interest by the same title (unity of title).
- Receive a vesting of the estate of joint tenancy at the same time (unity of time).
- Take their right to possession of the estate at the same time (unity of possession).

Cleaver involved a quitclaim deed, to which husband and wife were both grantors and grantees; the deed created a joint tenancy for them with the right of

Joint tenancy
Ownership of real or personal property by two or more persons, called joint tenants, with the right of survivorship.

Right of survivorship
Passes the decedent joint tenant's interest in property automatically to the surviving joint tenant(s) by operation of law.

survivorship. The court ruled that the deed was valid as long as the four unities under common law were present. The next paragraphs discuss the common law definitions of these "unities" in more detail.

Unity of Time. For unity of time to exist, joint tenant owners must take their interests in the property at the same time. To satisfy this requirement, the joint tenants must receive their interest in the property together.

Example: In most states, a single conveyance of property from Mary to Amy and Betty as joint tenants dated July 15, 1995, would create a joint tenancy. If, however, Mary were to convey the property to Amy and Betty as joint tenants in a single transfer taking effect on different dates, Amy receiving an interest on July 15, 1995, and Betty receiving an interest a day later, then the conveyance would fail in its attempt to create the interest desired, and a tenancy in common would exist between Amy and Betty. Some states require an express statement creating a joint tenancy and avoiding a tenancy in common (see the discussion below).

🏛 ASSIGNMENT 2.4

Howard conveys a farm, Blackacre, by deed to "Brown and Jones as joint tenants and not as tenants in common." What form of ownership is presumed in your state by this conveyance?

Unity of Title. For unity of title to exist, the tenancy must be created and the tenants must receive their title (ownership rights) from a single source, e.g., the same will or deed.

Example: When Mary, in a single deed, transfers property to Amy and Betty as joint tenants, unity of title exists and a joint tenancy is created. On the other hand, when Mary transfers property to Amy and Betty by will *and* deed, respectively, or by more than one deed, the use of multiple instruments of transfer fails to meet this (i.e., unity of title) requirement, and the result is the creation of a tenancy in common between Amy and Betty.

Some states do not allow the creation of a joint tenancy wherein the grantor names herself and another or others as joint tenants. For example, if Brown conveys a farm, Blackacre, which he inherited and now solely owns, to "Conrad and himself (Brown) as joint tenants with the right of survivorship," a joint tenancy, generally, does not result because of the lack of unities of time and title. The parties do not receive their interest in the property simultaneously since Brown already owned the farm, nor do they receive their title from one document since Brown received his title through inheritance.

To create a joint tenancy between an existing owner of the property (Brown) and one or more persons, Brown must first transfer a deed to the property to a third person, called the **straw man** (Jones); then, by a second deed, Jones, the straw man, immediately reconveys the property back to the original owner (Brown) and the new co-owner (Conrad) as joint tenants with the right of survivorship. The prevailing view in the majority of states today, however, is that, as in the *Cleaver* case, Brown can convey the farm from himself to "himself and Conrad" and create a valid joint tenancy.

Straw man
A person used to create a joint tenancy of real property between the existing owner of the property and one or more other persons.

ASSIGNMENT 2.5

Determine whether your state statute would allow an existing owner to create a joint tenancy as Brown did in the last example by conveying the farm to "himself and Conrad."

Unity of Interest. For unity of interest to exist, each tenant must have an interest in the property identical with that of the other tenants; the interests must be of the same quantity and duration, e.g., fee simple estate or life estate.

Example: If Mary were to convey property to Amy, Betty, and Carol as joint tenant owners each holding an equal life interest, a joint tenancy would be created. But if Mary instead had given Amy and Carol each one-sixth shares of the ownership rights and Betty a two-thirds share, then the unity of interest requirement would not be met, and Amy, Betty, and Carol would own the property as tenants in common and not joint tenants, even though the conveyance specified that they were to be joint tenants.

ASSIGNMENT 2.6

If Keller attempted to create a joint tenancy by transferring his farm, Blackacre, by deed to three friends, Hudson, Daniels, and Miller, he would fail if he transferred a life estate to Hudson and fee simple estates to Daniels and Miller. What form of ownership has Keller created?

Unity of Possession. To have unity of possession, each joint tenant must own and hold the same undivided possession of the whole property held in joint tenancy. As part of the group that owns all the property, each joint tenant has an equal right to possess the entire property and share equally in the profits derived from the property, e.g., the sale of crops or livestock.

Example:

Blackacre—a farm 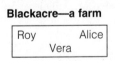	Alice, Roy, and Vera are joint tenants, and each has the right to possess the whole property concurrently with the other co-tenants. None has the right to exclude the others from possession of all or any part of the property, and each has the right to share in profits derived from the use of the farm.

Example: A conveyance of a farm, Blackacre, from Mary to "Amy and Betty as joint tenants with the right of survivorship," with no restrictions on the amount of their respective possession rights would successfully create joint tenancy ownership. In contrast, if Mary instead had attempted to limit the possession rights of either Amy or Betty ("to Amy and Betty as joint tenants, with only Betty having the right to possess Blackacre"), the transfer would fail to create a joint tenancy for want of the possession unity, and Amy and Betty would be tenants in common.

SUMMARY EXAMPLE: Williams conveys a farm to A, B, and C as joint tenants on June 1, 1995 (unity of time), by a single deed (unity of title). Each co-owner receives a one-third undivided interest (unity of interest) of the whole property, and each has an equal right to possession of the whole (unity of possession). All four unities are present. Therefore, a valid joint tenancy has been created if Williams has complied with other state statutory requirements, e.g., used language indicating that he desired to create a joint tenancy, such as "to A, B, and C as joint tenants and not as tenants in common." If any of the four "unities" is not included in the conveyance of the property, the form of ownership created is *not* a joint tenancy but is instead a tenancy in common (see the discussion below).

⚚ ASSIGNMENT 2.7

1. If Robert Green owned a farm in your state and died leaving by will the farm to "my three sons, Roger, John, and James as joint owners with equal shares," what form of ownership would the three sons have? Go to your state statutes and look up forms of ownership, specifically joint tenancy. Then answer according to the laws of your state.
2. If Robert Green in the problem above had devised the farm "to my three sons, Roger, John, and James as joint tenants and not tenants in common," would a joint tenancy be created according to the laws of your state?
3. Joyce, age 21, and Ellen, age 20, are sisters. When Aunt Mary dies, she leaves her country home "to Joyce immediately and to Ellen on her twenty-first birthday, as joint tenants with the right of survivorship." What form of ownership has Aunt Mary created?

The legal document in Exhibit 2.3, a deed, is executed to illustrate the creation of a joint tenancy with the required four unities. Notice that the conveyance reads "to Roger L. Green, John M. Green, and James R. Green, grantees as joint tenants" and not as tenants in common. In some states, this language is necessary to create the joint tenancy. Since Roger, John, and James receive their co-ownership at the same time (August 1, 1994—the date on the deed); by the same legal document (the deed); with the same undivided interest in the whole (equal interest); and with the right to possess the entire property (equal possession), all four unity requirements are satisfied.

Undivided interest
A right to an undivided portion of property that is owned by one of two or more joint tenants or tenants in common before the property is divided (partitioned).

Severance
The destruction of a joint tenancy by one of the joint tenants transferring while alive his interest in real property to another person by deed, thereby creating a tenancy in common with the new owner and the other remaining joint tenant(s).

⚚ ASSIGNMENT 2.8

Assume you own the house in which you now live. Using your state form, draft a deed conveying the house to your two best friends as joint tenants. Draft a second deed conveying the house to your friends as tenants in common.

Besides the four unities, certain other characteristics distinguish joint tenancy from tenancy in common and other forms of co-ownership. They include the following:

- Right of survivorship.
- **Undivided interest.**
- **Severance.**

Right of Survivorship.　　When a joint tenant dies, the surviving joint tenants receive the interest of the deceased, i.e., the undivided part, with nothing passing

Exhibit 2.3   Sample Deed Showing Creation of a Joint Tenancy

∕MD FORM No. 5–M WARRANTY DEED   Minnesota Uniform Conveyancing Blanks (1978)   Miller-Davis Co., MPLS

Individual(s) to Joint Tenants

No delinquent taxes and transfer entered; Certificate of
Real Estate Value (   ) filed (   ) not required
Certificate of Real Estate Value No. _____
_____ , 19_____

                                                        County Auditor

by _____
                                                        Deputy

STATE DEED TAX DUE HEREON: $ __282.70__
Date: __August 1_____ , 19 94____

(reserved for recording data)

FOR VALUABLE CONSIDERATION, _____
__Henry J. Smith and Sara M. Smith,   husband and wife_____ , Grantor(s),
                                                        (MARITAL STATUS)

hereby convey(s) and warrant(s) to _____
__Roger L. Green, John M. Green, and James R. Green__ , Grantees as joint
tenants, real property in ____Brownstad_____ County, Minnesota, described as follows:

        Lot 4, Block 12, Moser's Addition to Fairview Village

(if more space is needed, continue on back)

together with all hereditaments and appurtenances belonging thereto, subject to the following exceptions:

Affix Deed Tax Stamp Here

/S/ Sara M. Smith

/S/ Henry J. Smith

STATE OF MINNESOTA

COUNTY OF _Brownstad_____ } ss.

The foregoing instrument was acknowledged before me this _1st_ day of _August_____ , 19 94_____,
by _Henry J. Smith and Sara M. Smith, husband and wife_____
                                                        ,Grantor(s).

NOTARIAL STAMP OR SEAL (OR OTHER TITLE OR RANK)

/S/ Mary A. Williams

SIGNATURE OF PERSON TAKING ACKNOWLEDGMENT

My commission expires on:
August 4, 1995

Tax Statements for the real property described in this instrument should
be sent to (Include name and address of Grantee):

THIS INSTRUMENT WAS DRAFTED BY (NAME AND ADDRESS):

Dean T. Anderson
Plaza Bank Building
Minneapolis, MN 55455

Roger L. Green
1400 River Street
Minneapolis, MN 55455

Source: Miller/Davis Company, Minneapolis, Minnesota.

to the heirs or devisees of the decedent. The deceased joint tenant's ownership rights pass directly to the other living co-tenants under the *right of survivorship*. Each joint tenant has this right of survivorship, which prevents a joint tenant from transferring property by a will. If all the joint tenants die except one, the remaining joint tenant owns the property in *severalty,* which means that the joint tenancy is destroyed and the lone survivor owns the property solely.

Undivided Interest.   Joint tenants are entitled to the equal use, enjoyment, control, and possession of the property since they have an equal and undivided identical interest in the same property. Each joint tenant is considered to be the owner of the whole property and also of an undivided part. The undivided interest means that no joint tenant can say she owns a specific or individual part of the property. If a joint tenant did own a particular portion of the property, it would be owned as a single owner, in *severalty,* not as a co-owner, *joint tenant.* (See the example and further discussion under Tenancy in Common.)

⚏ ASSIGNMENT 2.9

1. Which of the following items of property can be owned in a joint tenancy?

Stocks	House
Bonds	Cottage
Art	Condominium
Jewelry	Boat
Car	Contents of a safe deposit box

2. Conchita and Emilio are not related by blood or marriage. All of the items in Question 1 are either given, sold, or willed to Conchita and Emilio as joint tenants with the right of survivorship. Emilio dies owing many debts. Do his creditors have any claim against the property? Can Emilio will any of the property to his spouse and family? When Emilio dies, who owns the property? What form of ownership is created by Emilio's death?

Severance.   While alive, each joint tenant has the right of severance, i.e., an act of severing, separating, or partitioning real property. Severance occurs when a joint tenant owner conveys his equal interest in the property during his lifetime, thereby destroying one of the four essential unities and terminating the joint tenancy. Such an "*inter vivos*" conveyance, i.e., a transfer of interest while the joint owner is alive, is the *only* way a joint tenancy can be severed. Severance of real property is accomplished by transferring a deed. When a joint tenancy is severed in this manner, the remaining joint tenants and the new tenant are tenants in common, with the new tenant having no right of survivorship. (See the examples below.)

   Example: To illustrate joint tenancy ownership, suppose X dies, willing a farm to A and B as joint tenants. If during their lifetimes neither A nor B conveys his interest in the farm by deed to another person and A dies, B becomes the sole owner (*in severalty*) of the farm through right of survivorship.

X	wills	A and B	A dies	B owns property
	$\rightarrow$	⏜	$\rightarrow$	in severalty
decedent	property	joint tenants		

Assume that X dies and wills the farm to A, B, and C as joint tenants. C later conveys, by deed, an undivided one-third interest in the farm to D. This conveyance, as a severance, terminates the joint tenancy between (A and B) and (C) and creates a tenancy in common form of ownership between (A and B) and (D). Since they have done nothing to change (sever) their form of ownership, a joint tenancy still remains between A and B. Therefore, if A were to die having made no conveyance of an interest, B would receive A's interest in the farm through right of survivorship. The result would then be that B and D would own the farm as tenants in common, B owning a two-thirds interest and D owning a one-third interest of the whole property. The unities of time, title, and interest having been destroyed, only the unity of possession remains.

Example:

X	wills	A, B, C	C	to D
→	→	→	→	
dies	property	joint tenants	conveys his ⅓ interest and severs the joint tenancy	

Result: A and B own a two-thirds interest in the farm, and they remain joint tenants (each owns a one-third undivided interest). A tenancy in common now exists between (A and B) and (D), who owns the other one-third.

Then:

A	B takes A's ⅓ interest	B and D are tenants in common
→	→	⅔ interest for B
dies	as surviving joint tenant	⅓ interest for D

As tenants in common, on the death of either B or D, the decedent's interest in the farm passes by will or inheritance to his devisees or heirs (see the discussion of tenancy in common below).

ASSIGNMENT 2.10

Apply the previous illustration to the following cases and then answer the questions.

Case 1. Alice died, providing in her will that her farm, Blackacre, should be conveyed to her three nephews, Able, Baker, and Charlie, as joint tenants. Able is married and has eleven children; Baker is divorced and has two children; Charlie is a bachelor. Able dies, and his will leaves all his property to his wife, Agnes. Who owns Blackacre? What form or forms of ownership exist between the owners?

Case 2. Continue with the facts of Case 1 except Abel sold and deeded his interest in Blackacre to Dolan, and Charlie gave and deeded his interest to Elaine, his girlfriend. Who owns Blackacre? What form or forms of ownership exist between the owners? What happens to Baker's interest in the property when he dies? Does Able's wife, Agnes, have any interest in Blackacre?

Creating a Joint Tenancy.   Today, state statute determines whether a joint tenancy is legally created. Most states recognize a joint tenancy, but they vary in the express language they require to create it. The required wording and the intent of the creator of the joint tenancy determine whether a binding joint tenancy is established. For example, if Harold Wong wants to give his lake cottage to his two children, Sue and James, he may satisfy the statutes in most states by writing in the deed of conveyance "to my two children, Sue Wong and James Wong as Joint Tenants." Other states require more, such as ". . . as Joint Tenants with the right of survivorship" or, as some documents are written today, ". . . as Joint Tenants with the right of survivorship and not as Tenants in Common" (see the Illinois statute below). A few states like Louisiana and Kentucky have no joint tenancy with survivorship rights. See the forms of ownership by state in Exhibit 2.4.

Another problem is that some states have a preference for certain forms of co-ownership of property. At one time, common law preferred the creation of a joint tenancy over the creation of a tenancy in common when an instrument of conveyance was unclear concerning which of these two interests was intended by the grantor. Today the reverse is generally true, and by statute, when the intention of the parties is not clear, tenancy in common is presumed and preferred over a joint tenancy in most states since the legislatures believe the decedent's property should pass to heirs or devisees and not to surviving joint tenants. An example of one such statute is Minn. Stat. Ann. § 500.19(2), *Construction of grants and devises.* The decision in *Short v. Milby,* 31 Del.Ch. 49, 64 A.2d 36 (1949), illustrates the current preference. In this case, the court stated, "Joint tenancies are not favored and can only be created by clear and definite language not reasonably capable of any different construction."

Unless the parties have shown an express intent in a will or deed to create a joint tenancy, the law today presumes that a tenancy in common has been created. For this reason, when a joint tenancy is desired, it is important to be very cautious in wording the instrument of conveyance. For example, a deed or will should read: "To Adam and James as joint tenants and not as tenants in common" (see Chapter 6 on drafting wills). Notice the wording required to create a joint tenancy in the states of New York and Illinois:

N.Y. Estates Powers & Trusts Law § 6–2.2 (McKinney 1991)
The law provides that a grant of an estate (interest in property) to two or more persons "creates in them a tenancy in common, unless expressly declared to be in joint tenancy."

Former Ill. Rev. Stat. ch. 76, § 1 (1966) [now S.H.A. 765 ILCS 1005/1 (1993)]
The law states that the deed of conveyance must expressly provide that the property interest is granted "not in tenancy in common but in joint tenancy."

▦ ASSIGNMENT 2.11

Using your state's codes, find and cite appropriate statutes, if any, that determine the form of ownership that would be created by the following conveyances by deed: (1) "to A and B jointly," (2) "to A and B as joint owners," (3) "to A and B equally," (4) "to A or to B," (5) "to A and to B." If your statutes or case law do not address this problem, find a statute from another state that does. Find and cite your state statute that determines the required wording to create a joint tenancy or a tenancy in common.

Advantages and Disadvantages of Joint Tenancy.   When working with clients, you will discover that they frequently have created joint tenancies with spouses and others. When reviewing the following advantages and disadvantages

Exhibit 2.4 Forms of Ownership by State

By One Person	By Two or More Persons			
Tenancy in severalty	Tenancy in Common	Joint Tenancy	Tenancy by the Entirety	Community Property
All states	All states	All states except as follows: 　Alaska—for personal property only 　Kentucky—no right of survivorship 　Louisiana—not recognized 　Ohio—called survivorship tenancy 　Oregon—equivalent only if language reads "not as tenants in common but with the right of survivorship" 　South Carolina—for real property and some types of personal property 　Texas—for real property only	Alaska, Arkansas, Delaware, Florida, Hawaii, Kentucky, Maryland, Massachusetts, Mississippi, Missouri, New Jersey, Oklahoma, Pennsylvania, Rhode Island, Tennessee, Vermont, Virginia, West Virginia, Wyoming Indiana, Michigan, New York, North Carolina, Ohio, Oregon, Utah—for real property only Washington—no right of survivorship	Arizona, California, Idaho, Louisiana, Nevada, New Mexico, Texas, Washington Wisconsin—recognizes marital property equivalent of community property

with the client, *you must be careful not to attempt to respond to questions that seek legal advice or interpretations.* All such questions *must* be referred to your supervising attorney.

▶ **ETHICAL ISSUE**

Advantages of a joint tenancy:

- Because of the right of survivorship, on the death of a joint tenant, title passes automatically to the surviving joint tenant(s).
- No probate proceedings with their corresponding expense and delay are necessary or required for the surviving joint tenant(s) to acquire title.
- Title passes to the surviving joint tenant(s) free of the claims of the decedent's creditors unless the joint tenancy was created to defraud creditors. The decedent's real estate may be subject to certain creditors' claims such as mortgages, taxes, and liens, e.g., a mechanic's lien for work or improvements to the property that have not been paid.
- If the joint tenants are husband and wife, no federal gift tax is owed because of the unlimited marital gift tax deduction (this may also be true for state gift tax concerns). See the discussion in Chapters 10 and 14.
- If property located in other (foreign) states is in a joint tenancy, ancillary administration may be avoided.
- Joint tenancy of personal property, e.g., joint bank accounts that are properly and legally created to establish the right of survivorship for the named co-owners, can provide immediate cash for family needs on the death of a spouse or parent. You must be careful to ensure the account is correctly created, e.g., all signature cards executed and state statutory requirements met.

■ Creating a joint tenancy is fast and inexpensive, whereas probate and the cost of creating a trust and paying its continuing trustee's fees are expensive.

Disadvantages of a joint tenancy:

■ The person who creates the joint tenancy no longer has complete control of the property.

Example: Shirley is a single parent who has a teenage son, Zachary. Shirley owns a house in her name only. Aware that she can avoid the expense of probate by placing her house in joint tenancy, Shirley executes a deed creating a joint tenancy of the house with Zachary. A wonderful job opportunity becomes available in another state, and Shirley must immediately sell the house. Because Zachary is a minor and cannot convey real property, a court must appoint a guardian to represent and protect Zachary's interest in the house. This loss of control may cause Shirley to lose the employment opportunity.

■ The creation and severance of a joint tenancy are sometimes complicated and burdensome especially in terms of federal income, estate, and gift tax consequences.

■ The surviving joint tenant may not have been the intended beneficiary.

Example: In the preceding example, if Shirley died after creating the joint tenancy with Zachary, he would own the house. If Zachary was killed in a car accident a year later while still owning the house, the house will pass to his heir, his father, if living, which may not be a result that Shirley would have intended.

Example: Sally, a single parent, intends to leave certain property to her children when she dies, but her parents need additional income for their care and medical expenses that the property would produce. Expecting to outlive her parents, Sally puts the property in joint tenancy with her parents. Sally dies in an accident. The property is now her parents to do with as they wish. Sally's intent has been subverted.

■ The step-up in basis for full value of the proceeds is lost. See the discussion in Chapter 10.

■ Other examples of problems created by joint tenancy follow.

Example: Robbie, age 19, wants to buy a car, but he is unable to obtain a loan to finance the purchase. His parents agree to cosign the promissory note required by the bank for the loan. The parents also list themselves as joint tenancy owners with Robbie on the title of the car. While driving the new car, Robbie is the sole cause of an accident in which the driver of the other car is seriously injured. The injured driver sues Robbie and his parents. If the injured driver wins the case and receives a judgment of $450,000 in damages, she can collect the money damages from the personal assets of Robbie's parents if they are not adequately insured.

Example: A married couple, H and W, want to avoid probate and see no reason to have individual wills, so they place all their real and personal property (including their home, cars, checking and savings accounts, stocks and bonds) in joint tenancy. When one of them dies, the title to all of the property will go to the surviving spouse because of the right of survivorship. However, if both spouses die in a common accident, for example, a plane crash, then the property will have to go through probate, and if they have no wills when the accident occurs, their property will be transferred to their heirs according to their state's intestate succession laws, which may be a distribution very different from what they wanted or intended.

Tenancy in Common

Tenancy in common is a form of concurrent ownership of real or personal property by two or more persons called tenants in common. Each tenant owns separate undivided interests in the property with the "unity" of possession. The tenants' interests may be equal or unequal. The "unity" of possession establishes each tenant's equal right to take and possess the whole property in common with the other co-tenants, and each is entitled to share proportionately in the profits derived from the property. A tenancy in common differs from a joint tenancy in several important ways, including the following:

▪ The undivided interest of the joint tenants *must* be equal; for tenants in common, it may be equal or unequal. Thus, when there are two tenants in common, each may own one-half of the property, i.e., an equal interest, or one may own three-fourths of the property and the other one-fourth, i.e., an unequal interest. Neither owns a specific portion of the property, because each has an undivided interest in the entire property.

Example: X may expressly create a tenancy in common in the following way:

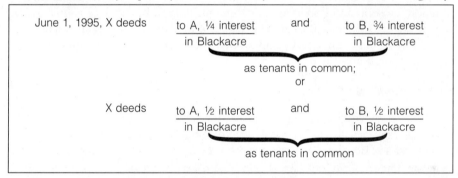

▪ The creation of a joint tenancy must include the "four unities" (time, title, interest, and possession); a tenancy in common requires only "unity of possession."

▪ Property held in joint tenancy does not go through estate administration (probate) when a joint tenant dies; property held in a tenancy in common does.

▪ The distinguishing characteristic of a joint tenancy is the right of survivorship; there is *no* right of survivorship in a tenancy in common. Therefore, unlike a joint tenancy, when a tenant in common dies, the decedent's interest goes to an heir or as directed in a will, and it is subject to estate administration.

Example: Jeff Morrow dies with a will. In the will, he gives a one-half interest in his original Picasso painting to his only living relative, his nephew Charles Morrow. Jeff gives the other half of the ownership rights in the painting to his two close friends, Mike Flaherty and Dave Rossi, equally. Charles, Mike, and Dave are co-owners of the Picasso painting as tenants in common. If Mike Flaherty should die, his one-fourth interest in the painting would be transferred according to his will, if he has one, or to his heir (closest blood relative, if he is not married) according to state law.

Not only may tenants in common own different interests in terms of quantity and duration, but they may receive their interests from different parties through different instruments of conveyance at different times. Nevertheless, they retain an undivided interest in the property unless it is merged or severed.

Creating a Tenancy in Common. A tenancy in common may be expressly created as in the deed in Exhibit 2.5, but as previously mentioned, a tenancy in common is also created when a person making a conveyance (grantor) fails to use the terminology required to establish a joint tenancy. In addition, once a joint tenancy is validly established, if one of the joint tenants makes an *inter vivos* conveyance by deed to another person, the joint tenancy is severed, and a tenancy in common is created for the new owner (see the examples below).

Example: Most states today prefer the establishment of tenancy in common over a joint tenancy. Therefore, if William Kennedy dies providing in his will that Blackacre is to go "to my sons, Joseph and Robert jointly in equal shares," the real property will pass to the two sons as tenants in common in states with such a preference. Note that the conveyance did not contain an explicit statement saying that a "joint tenancy" was to be created.

Example: In another case, suppose William Kennedy creates a valid joint tenancy by providing in his will that Blackacre should go "to my sons, Joseph and Robert, as joint tenants with the right of survivorship and not as tenants in common." Joseph and Robert are joint tenants. Robert, by deed, sells his interest in Blackacre to Charles Brown. The result is that the original joint tenancy is severed by Robert's *inter vivos* conveyance and a tenancy in common is created between Joseph and Charles.

ASSIGNMENT 2.12

1. If Michael conveys one-third of his farm, Blackacre, to Fred on August 15, 1995, and the remaining two-thirds to Bob on September 20, 1995, what form of ownership will Fred and Bob have according to the statutes or case law in your state?
2. If Peter and Mary are joint tenants, and Peter gives his interest in the property to Paul by a valid conveyance, what form of ownership exists according to your state law?

The state of New York, by statute, handles the transfer of property to two or more persons in the following way:

N.Y. Estates Powers & Trusts Law § 6–2.2 (McKinney 1991),
When Estate Is in Common, in Joint Tenancy or by the Entirety:

(a) A disposition of property to two or more persons creates in them a tenancy in common, unless expressly declared to be a joint tenancy.

(b) A disposition of real property to a husband and wife creates in them a tenancy by the entirety [see below], unless expressly declared to be a joint tenancy or a tenancy in common.

(c) A disposition of real property to persons who are not legally married to one another but who are described in the disposition as husband and wife creates in them a joint tenancy, unless expressly declared to be a tenancy in common.

(d) A disposition of property to two or more persons as executors, trustees or guardians creates in them a joint tenancy.

(e) Property passing in intestacy to two or more persons is taken by them as tenants in common.

Example: Phyllis, a resident of New York, dies without leaving a will. Her husband, Martin, has died a year earlier. She leaves a house, which had been in

Exhibit 2.5 Sample Deed Showing Creation of a Tenancy in Common

M/D Form No. 1-M—WARRANTY DEED   Minnesota Uniform Conveyancing Blanks (1978)   Miller-Davis Co., Minneapolis
Individual (s) to Individual (s)

No delinquent taxes and transfer entered; Certificate
of Real Estate Value (   ) filed (   ) not required
Certificate of Real Estate Value No. _____
_____, 19 ____

_____
                                    County Auditor

by _____
                                    Deputy

STATE DEED TAX DUE HEREON: $ ___282.70___

Date: ___September 12___, 19 _95_

(reserved for recording data)

FOR VALUABLE CONSIDERATION, _____
_____David L. Smith and Sally J. Smith,____husband and wife_____, Grantor (s),
                                          (marital status)
hereby convey (s) and warrant (s) to _Warren P. Jones and Mary S. Jones,_____
_____husband and wife as tenants in common_____, Grantee (s),
real property in _____Lowry_____ County, Minnesota, described as follows:

Lot Two (2), Block Five (5), Samuel's Addition to Lake Park

(if more space is needed, continue on back)
together with all hereditaments and appurtenances belonging thereto, subject to the following exceptions:

___/S/ Sally J. Smith_____

Affix Deed Tax Stamp Here

___/S/ David L. Smith_____

STATE OF MINNESOTA   }
                        } ss.
COUNTY OF _Lowry_____   }

The foregoing instrument was acknowledged before me this ___12th___ day of _September_, 19 _95_,
by ___David L. Smith and Sally J. Smith, husband and wife_____
_____, Grantor (s).

NOTARIAL STAMP OR SEAL (OR OTHER TITLE OR RANK)

___/S/ Janice S. Brown_____
SIGNATURE OF PERSON TAKING ACKNOWLEDGMENT

Tax Statements for the real property described in this instrument should
be sent to (Include name and address of Grantee):

My commission expires on:
June 4, 1998

THIS INSTRUMENT WAS DRAFTED BY (NAME AND ADDRESS)

Dean T. Anderson
Plaza Bank Building
Minneapolis, MN 55455

Mary S. Jones
1704 Northland Road
St. Paul, MN 55243

Source: Miller/Davis Company, Minneapolis, Minnesota.

her name only, and no debts. The law of descent and distribution of the state of New York entitles their children, Joan and Jack, to take the house in tenancy in common.

🏛 ASSIGNMENT 2.13

1. If Susan Sowles, a resident of New York, died without a will, owning a lakeshore cottage in upstate New York, and her only heirs were her three children, what form of ownership of the cottage would result for the benefit of the three children?
2. If Mary Main, also a resident of New York, died leaving a will transferring her homestead to her two nephews, who were the executors of her estate, what form of ownership would exist between the nephews? Cite the section and subdivision in New York Estates, Powers, and Trusts Law where this information is found.

Transferring an Interest.   Each tenant in common may transfer an interest by gift, will, or sale or may pledge it as security for a loan. When a tenant in common dies without having conveyed her share of the property, it goes to her devisees or heirs. The *right of survivorship* that accompanies a joint tenant interest does not exist with a tenancy in common.

Example: A, B, and C each own an undivided one-third interest in property as tenants in common. Upon A's death *intestate,* A's interest in the property will pass by descent to his heirs and not automatically go to B and C.

Concurrent Ownership of Blackacre			
A, B, and C are tenants in common			
A	B	C	A dies
⅓ interest	⅓ interest	⅓ interest	

Result: A's heirs receive A's one-third interest (by descent). (A's heirs and B and C are tenants in common.)

If A died testate (with a will) in the above example, his will determines how and to whom his interest in Blackacre will be distributed. Such a testamentary transfer is not possible in a joint tenancy. If one is attempted in a joint tenancy, the provision in the will is not followed since the property held in joint tenancy is automatically transferred to the surviving joint tenant.

🏛 ASSIGNMENT 2.14

Abner, Boswell, and Clarence are owners of Blackacre as joint tenants. Clarence sells his interest and delivers a deed to Boswell. Abner gives his interest to Ruth by delivering a deed. What form of ownership exists? Name the owners and the amount of their interests. Explain what would happen to Boswell's interest if he died testate or intestate.

When a tenant in common disposes of an interest by gift, sale, or will, the new owner is also a tenant in common with the remaining co-tenants in common. Tenancy in common is destroyed by merger, i.e., when entire ownership rights vest in (pass to) one person or by severance when the property is partitioned.

Example: A and B are tenants in common. A purchases B's interest by deed. A now has merged the property and is the sole owner of the property *in severalty*.

Undivided Interest.   As mentioned previously in the discussion of joint tenancy, an undivided interest is a right to an undivided portion of property that is owned by one of two or more *tenants in common* or joint tenants before the property is divided (partitioned). A farm, including the buildings (house, barn, etc.), the personal property (tractor, other machinery, and livestock), and the land itself, owned in joint tenancy or tenancy in common creates an *undivided interest* for each co-tenant. In a practical sense this means that each co-owner has a right or interest in the entire farm, but cannot claim a specific portion of the property, e.g., the house or the livestock, as the co-owner's own individual property. After partition, each person (co-owner) owns the apportioned part of the property in severalty, i.e., in single ownership. (See the example below and the subsequent discussion of partition).

Example:

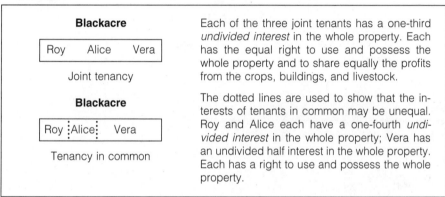

Blackacre	Each of the three joint tenants has a one-third *undivided interest* in the whole property. Each has the equal right to use and possess the whole property and to share equally the profits from the crops, buildings, and livestock.
Roy Alice Vera	
Joint tenancy	

Blackacre	The dotted lines are used to show that the interests of tenants in common may be unequal. Roy and Alice each have a one-fourth *undivided interest* in the whole property; Vera has an undivided half interest in the whole property. Each has a right to use and possess the whole property.
Roy ⁞Alice⁞ Vera	
Tenancy in common	

Partition.   One way to cause severance is for a joint tenant or tenant in common to ask the court to **partition** the property. Partition is the division of real property held by joint tenants or tenants in common into distinct and separate portions so that the individuals may hold the property in severalty, i.e., in single ownership. A partition can occur by a voluntary agreement of the co-owners, or it can be made by the court. If the co-owners cannot agree on a division, any one of the owners can petition the court for partition, which, in most cases, can force the sale of the property. The owners then split the proceeds. In some states, a court-ordered partition is not allowed for property in joint tenancy.

Once joint tenancy or tenancy in common property has been partitioned, severance results, and the former co-tenants each own a portion of the property in severalty. Joint tenancy property will be partitioned into equal parts; tenancy in common property will be partitioned into equal or unequal parts. (The example is shown on the following page.)

Partition
The division of real property held by joint tenants or tenants in common into separate portions so that the individuals may hold the property in severalty, i.e., in single ownership.

Tenancy by the Entirety
Tenancy by the entirety is an estate available only to a husband and wife. It is essentially a special form of "joint tenancy" modified by the common law theory that husband and wife are one person. Therefore, in addition to the four unities of time, title, interest, and possession required for joint tenancy, tenancy by the entirety requires a fifth unity—the unity of person, i.e., a husband and wife are one.

Unlike an ordinary joint tenancy, neither husband nor wife in a tenancy by the entirety can mortgage, sell, or give the property to another or sever the tenancy

Tenancy by the entirety
A form of joint tenancy available only to a husband and wife; it also has the right of survivorship.

Example: If a concurrently owned farm, Blackacre, is partitioned, it is divided into separate parts:

PARTITION—JOINT TENANCY		PARTITION—TENANCY IN COMMON	
Blackacre		**Blackacre**	
Before Partition	**After Partition**	**Before Partition**	**After Partition**
Roy Alice Vera	Roy | Alice | Vera	Roy	Roy
			Alice
Joint tenancy Equal parts (cannot be unequal)	Each owns the divided property as a single owner, i.e., in *severalty*.	Alice	Alice
			Alice
		Vera	Vera
		Tenancy in common Unequal parts (could be equal)	Roy ⅕ Alice ⅗ Vera ⅕

without the written and signed consent of the other spouse. Because it imposes such restrictions on the transfer of property, some states have abolished tenancy by the entirety as being against public policy. Consequently, tenancy by the entirety is not recognized in all states (see Exhibit 2.4).

The states that allow tenancy by the entirety differ in the wording they require in the deed or will that creates the tenancy. In some states, unless the deed or will provides differently, a conveyance to a husband and wife automatically creates a tenancy by the entirety. Other states require that the conveyance include explicit language, e.g., to husband and wife "as tenants by the entirety with the right of survivorship." Any conveyance without the exact words may result in the creation of a joint tenancy or tenancy in common.

Example: A will states: "I hereby give and devise my farm, Blackacre, to Jim and Trudy Lozano, husband and wife, in tenancy by the entirety." But if the will had been worded "I hereby give and devise my farm, Blackacre, to Jim and Trudy Lozano, husband and wife, with the right of survivorship," the devise might have been interpreted to be a tenancy by the entirety in some states or a joint tenancy in other states. In the latter case, it could be severed and individually transferred by one of the joint tenants.

Most statutes concerning tenancy by the entirety are worded like the New York statute (N.Y. Estates Powers & Trusts Law § 6–2.2 [McKinney 1991]):

A disposition of real property to a husband and wife creates in them a tenancy by the entirety, unless expressly declared to be a joint tenancy or a tenancy in common.

But court interpretations of similar statutory language seem to vary among the states.

The predominant and distinguishing feature of both joint tenancy and tenancy by the entirety is the *right of survivorship,* which, on the death of one spouse, passes sole ownership of the property in severalty to the surviving spouse. Neither spouse can terminate the estate by individually selling or giving property by deed to another person during the spouse's lifetime or passing it by will after death.

Example: William and Margaret, husband and wife, own property as tenants by the entirety. William dies and wills all his property to his son by a previous marriage. The son does not receive any interest in the tenancy by the entirety property because of Margaret's right of survivorship. Margaret owns the property in severalty (single ownership).

Only if both spouses consent can the property be sold or given to another. Unless both husband and wife join in (i.e., sign) the conveyance, it is invalid. This characteristic distinguishes tenancy by the entirety from joint tenancy since joint tenants can transfer their interest (by deed) without obtaining the permission of the other joint tenants.

In addition, a creditor of one spouse cannot foreclose on property held in tenancy by the entirety or enforce a judgment (court decision) against it, and a judgment against one spouse is not a claim (lien) against the property (see N.Y. Estates Powers & Trusts Law § 6–2.2). On the other hand, a judgment against both spouses can become a lien against the property, and a creditor can foreclose.

In New York and Massachusetts, the unity of person in a tenancy by the entirety is terminated by a divorce (dissolution). The divorced couple become tenants in common of the property with each former spouse owning a one-half interest in the property (see N.Y. Estates Powers & Trusts Law § 6–2.2, note 135). Unlike a divorce, a legal separation does not terminate a tenancy by the entirety in most states.

Some commentators have argued that the common law tenancy by the entirety should be abolished for policy reasons. First, property owned in this form is not subject to the claims of creditors of a deceased tenant (spouse); second, the specific language that creates this form of ownership is not always clear; and finally, when marital problems and disagreements arise, the mutual consent required to transfer property held in tenancy by the entirety may be difficult to obtain.

ASSIGNMENT 2.15

1. John and May are married and live in your state. The deed conveying their property states: "to John A. Kowalski and May F. Kowalski, husband and wife, as joint tenants and not as tenants in common." (a) Would this conveyance create a tenancy by the entirety in your state? (b) Cite your state statute, if any.
2. What five unities are necessary for the establishment of a tenancy by the entirety? Explain each one.
3. Which unity exists in tenancy by the entirety but not in joint tenancy?
4. Select a state that recognizes tenancy by the entirety (possibly your own state) and identify the type of tenancy created by the following conveyances according to the courts of that state. Each conveyance is to husband and wife with wording as indicated.

	Joint Tenancy	Tenancy by the Entirety	Tenancy in Common

- "as tenants by the entirety"
- "as tenants by the entirety with the right of survivorship"
- "with the right of survivorship"
- "as joint tenants"
- "as tenants in common"
- no other words, just to "husband and wife"

Community Property

In the United States originally eight southern and western states (Arizona, California, Idaho, Louisiana, Nevada, New Mexico, Texas, and Washington) statutorily adopted the form of ownership by spouses known as **community property.** Wisconsin, the only state to adopt the Uniform Marital Property Act, which is essentially the same as the community property system, joined the other eight states in 1986. The theory behind community property ownership is that a husband and wife should share equally in the property acquired by their joint efforts during marriage. Therefore, each spouse is considered to own half of all property that is acquired during a marriage even though one spouse may have earned considerably less than the other or even nothing at all. Community property law is set entirely by state statute. The statutes vary considerably among the nine states.

Community property states recognize two kinds of property: **separate property** and community property. Separate property is property that the husband or wife owned prior to their marriage or acquired during marriage by inheritance, will, or gift. Separate property is entirely under the management and control of the spouse to whom it belongs no matter how it was acquired, and it is completely free from all interest and claim on the part of the other spouse. Either spouse may, without the consent of the other, dispose of separate property by gift, sale, or will; mortgage it; or replace it with other property, with the newly acquired property also being separate property. A typical statute is former Cal. Prob. Code § 20 (now §§ 6100 and 6101):

> Every person of sound mind, over the age of 18 years, may dispose of his or her separate property, real and personal, by will. . . .

If the spouses agree, however, they can treat separately owned property as community property. All other property acquired by either spouse during the marriage in any manner is *presumed* to be *community property* (see La. Civ. Code art. 2340). The presumption may be rebutted by valid evidence that proves the property is separate property.

In determining whether a married couple's property is separate or community property, the following factors should be considered:

- Whether the property was acquired by either spouse before or after their marriage.
- The language and date of the conveyance (deed or will).

Community property
All property, other than property received by gift or inheritance, acquired by either spouse during marriage is considered to belong to both spouses equally in the nine community property states.

Separate property
Property that the husband or wife owned prior to their marriage or acquired during marriage by inheritance, will, or gift.

▪ The intent of the grantor, if the conveyance was made by deed, or of the testator(trix) if made by will.

▪ Whether the property was given as a gift to one or both spouses.

▪ Whether the property was inherited by one or both spouses.

▪ Whether separate property of a spouse was sold or exchanged for other separate property, or whether the purpose of the sale was to use the proceeds for community purposes.

▪ The purpose and use of property acquired or obtained by the married couple.

Examples:

1. In a community property state, when a deed conveys property to a husband and wife, it is community property.

2. On the other hand, a deed that expressly states that the property is the separate property of either husband or wife creates a conclusion that it is indeed the separate property of that person.

3. A married woman's father dies, conveying property in his will to her. Such property is separate property belonging to the woman.

4. If a married woman's father dies intestate, i.e., without a will, and she is her father's only heir, she will receive his property as her own separate property.

5. An employer gives $1,000 to a married man living in California, and the man's wife claims the money is salary. The employer gives testimony as evidence, establishing that the $1,000 was a gift. Therefore, it becomes part of the husband's separate property.

Characteristics of Community Property.   Formerly, a husband had sole control over community property and could convey or mortgage it without his wife's consent. Today, the community property states have enacted statutes requiring the signatures of both spouses with any transfer or mortgage of community property.

Since each spouse owns one-half of the community property, on the death of either (in the majority of the community property states), the surviving spouse is entitled to his or her one-half of the community property (see Cal. Prob. Code § 100). The decedent's will, if one exists, or the state's statutes determine the disposition of the decedent's remaining half. Under no circumstances can either spouse dispose of more than one-half of the community property by will. A typical community property state statute illustrating the disposition of such property is former Cal. Prob. Code § 201 (now §§ 6101 and 6401):

> Upon the death of either husband or wife, one-half of the community property belongs to the surviving spouse; the other half is subject to the testamentary disposition of the decedent, and in the absence thereof goes to the surviving spouse, subject to the provisions of sections 202 and 203 of this code.

The statutes of the community property states differ on the division and distribution of property in cases involving intestacy, divorce, creditors' claims, commingling, and a new category of property created by these statutes called "quasi-community property." Each topic is discussed in more detail in the following paragraphs.

Intestacy.   In most community property states, depending on the length of the marriage, when a spouse dies intestate, all of the decedent's community property passes to the surviving spouse but only a smaller share of the separate property [see Cal. Prob. Code § 6401 (a) & (c), but compare Texas Prob. Code § 45 where a surviving spouse may not be entitled to all of the property and La. Civ. Code art. 890]. See also the case *In re Salvini's Estate,* 65 Wash. 2d 442, 397 P.2d 811 (1964), in which the court ruled a gift of store property to the deceased prior to her death was community property to which, after her death, her husband was entitled to an interest.

Divorce.   In a divorce, the division of community property varies in community property states. If a married couple is divorced, the court generally divides the community property so that each party receives an equal share (see Cal. Civ. Code § 4800). Other states, such as Arizona, allow the court to use its discretion in deciding how to divide community property "equitably" (see Ariz. Rev. Stat. § 25–318). In most community property states, even without divorce, spouses may at any time enter into an agreement dissolving the community relationship and divide the property. The share each spouse receives after the negotiations is then his or her separate property.

Creditors' Claims.   The classification of property as community or separate also affects claims of creditors. In some community property states, e.g., Arizona and Washington, a creditor of one spouse can attach only that spouse's separate property (see *Nationwide Resources Corp. v. Massabni,* 143 Ariz. 460 694 P.2d 290 [App. 1984] and *Nichols Hills Bank v. McCool,* 104 Wash.2d 78, 701 P.2d 1114 [1985]).

In the *Massabni* case, the court acknowledged that in community property states, all property acquired by either spouse during marriage is presumed to be community property and that a spouse's separate property can be transmuted (changed into) community property by agreement, gift, or commingling. In this complex case, however, the court held that the property in question was the husband's separate property and therefore that a judgment creditor of the husband could **garnish,** make a claim against, only this separate property to satisfy the debt, but could not make a claim against the community property for the husband's individual debt.

In the *Nichols* case, the court ruled that "although one spouse's interest in community property can be reached (and used) to satisfy a tort judgment," a bank (the creditor) could not enforce a loan guaranty agreement signed only by the husband against his interest in the community property since the wife had neither signed nor ratified the agreement. The state of Washington statute requires consent of both spouses before a gift or transfer of community property can be legally enforced.

Other community property states allow creditors with community debts to satisfy their claims against the community property of the spouses and creditors with separate debts to satisfy their claims first against the individual spouse's separate property and then, if the debt is not paid in full, to collect the remainder of the debt from community property.

Commingling.   Another concern of spouses in community property states is the problem of commingled separate and community property. When extensive

Garnish
Make a claim against.
Garnishment
A three-party statutory proceeding in which a judgment creditor may demand that an employer who owes wages to an employee (the judgment debtor) pay these wages to the creditor to satisfy the creditor's claim against the employee (debtor).

commingling occurs and it becomes impossible to identify the separate property, the presumption is that the commingled property is community property. To overcome this presumption, each spouse must keep complete and accurate records of how the property was obtained, as well as its purpose and use.

Quasi-community Property. Property that is acquired outside a community property state and then moved into it or that is owned by spouses who have moved into a community property state is called **quasi-community property.** If the newcomer dies *domiciled* in the community property state, the presumption discussed earlier still stands; i.e., all of the decedent's property that is not separate property as defined by the current domicile state is community property. On the other hand, if the newcomer's domicile is considered to be the former, non-community property state, the presumption can be rebutted and reversed. Conversely, when spouses move from a community property state to a non-community property state, the community property obtained while they lived in the community property state is not automatically converted into separate property solely by the change of domicile. When your clients are spouses seeking your assistance, *you must not forget to inquire about their state residences throughout their marriage.*

Community property states have abolished the form of co-ownership called a tenancy by the entirety, but usually they continue to allow spouses to own property in a joint tenancy. See Exhibit 2.6 for a summary and comparison of forms of concurrent ownership.

Commingling
Combining community and separate property, e.g., into the same account or by using both to acquire a different item of property.

Quasi-community property
Property that is acquired outside a community property state and then moved into it or that is owned by spouses who have moved into a community property state.

ETHICAL ISSUE ◀ ··········

🏛 ASSIGNMENT 2.16

1. John and Mary Doe live in a community property state. John dies. John and Mary owned the following property: a house in joint tenancy; two cars in both names; a camper given to John by his father; savings and checking accounts in both names; a boat purchased by Mary before their marriage; and furniture and household goods, a stereo, and television sets purchased during their marriage. Which of this property can John transfer or convey in his will?
2. Doug died, providing in his will, "I give and devise Blackacre to my best friends, Jim, Carl, and Alan, as joint tenants with the right of survivorship and not as tenants in common." What form of ownership is created for Doug's three friends? Is it a concurrent ownership?
3. In the question above, Alan is married and has two children; Jim is married and has six children; Carl is single. Alan's will leaves all his property to his wife. Carl, who wants to move out of state, finds a buyer for his interest in Blackacre and sells the property, transferring by deed the title to the buyer, Jeff. Six months later, on his way to work, Alan is killed in an automobile accident. (a) Who owns Blackacre? (b) What form of ownership exists? (c) What effect did Jeff's purchase have on the ownership before the accident? (d) Why would a court prefer the creation of a tenancy in common over a joint tenancy in the hypothetical case in Question 2?

🏛 ASSIGNMENT 2.17

If possible, obtain your own family documents and determine the forms of ownership in which your family property is held, e.g., house, stocks, bonds, savings account.

Exhibit 2.6   Summary and Comparison of Forms of Concurrent Ownership—Two or More Persons

Form of Ownership	Joint Tenancy	Tenancy in Common	Tenancy by Entirety	Community Property
Formation: By deed—gift or sale or by will	Yes	Yes	Yes	No—by operation of law
Owners: Two or more named in conveyance	Yes	Yes	Two only—must be husband and wife	Two only—must be husband and wife by operation of law
Right of survivorship	Yes	No	Yes	No
Unity of interest: Undivided and equal shares	Yes	Undivided but shares may be equal or unequal	Undivided but husband and wife as a unit own the property	Yes—of the community property
Unity of possession	Yes	Yes	Yes	Yes
Right of partition	Yes—but not in all states	Yes	No—except if spouses divorce	No—except if spouses divorce
Probate or nonprobate	Nonprobate	Probate	Nonprobate	Probate
Right to sell or give by deed a co-owner's interest in the property	Yes	Yes	No	No—of the community property
Creditors of individual co-owner may attach co-owner's interest in the property	Yes	Yes	No—only creditors of both husband and wife	Yes—but only separate property in Arizona and Washington

ESTATES IN REAL PROPERTY

The law of real property divides the rights of ownership in real property into two categories: *freehold estates* and *leasehold estates*. The categories are distinguished by the extent and duration of the individual's interest. In other words, freeholds and leaseholds in real property are classified according to how long and how much an interest a person has in realty. Exhibit 2.7 illustrates the classification of estates that will be discussed.

Freehold Estates

Fee Simple Estate or Fee Simple Absolute

The vast majority of all real property, including houses, apartment and office buildings, and farms, is owned as a fee simple estate. A **fee simple estate,** also known as a fee simple absolute, an estate in fee, or simply as a fee, is the largest, best, and most extensive estate possible. An individual holding a fee estate has an absolute, unqualified, and unlimited interest in the real property. This means the fee estate is not subject to any restrictions and the owner is entitled to all rights and privileges associated with the property. There is no limit on the estate's duration or on the owner's method of disposition. The owner has the unconditional power to dispose of the property during his lifetime by deed and after

Fee simple estate
An estate that is the largest, best, and most extensive estate possible. Also known as a fee simple absolute, an estate in fee, or simply a fee.

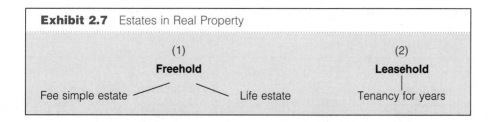

Exhibit 2.7   Estates in Real Property

(1)	(2)
Freehold	**Leasehold**
Fee simple estate — Life estate	Tenancy for years

death by will; if the owner dies intestate, the property descends (passes) to his heirs (see the statute and discussion below). Section 44–6–20 of the Georgia Code Annotated defines the estate as follows:

> An absolute or fee simple estate is one in which the owner is entitled to the entire property with unconditional power of disposition during his life and which descends to his heirs and legal representatives upon his death intestate.

In most states no special language is needed to establish a fee simple estate. Every conveyance is presumed to create a fee simple estate unless the conveyance expressly states an intent to create another type of estate such as a smaller estate or an estate of limited duration.

Characteristics of a Fee Simple Estate.   The following are characteristics of a fee simple estate:

- *A fee simple estate is transferable during life.*

Example: Jane Doe owns a farm, Blackacre, in fee simple. While living, she can sell the farm or give it away by transferring the title to the real property as a fee simple estate to another person by conveying (delivering) a deed. Jane Doe sells Blackacre by deed to Tom Brown:

	SALE			
Jane Doe			**Tom Brown**	Tom now has a fee simple estate in the farm.
Blackacre	sells ——→ by deed	to	Blackacre	
Estate in fee simple				

Jane Doe gives Blackacre to Tom Brown by delivering the deed to the farm to Tom:

	GIFT			
Jane Doe			**Tom Brown**	Tom now has a fee simple estate in the farm.
Blackacre	gives ——→ by deed	to	Blackacre	
Estate in fee simple				

- *A fee simple estate is transferable by will.*

Example: Jane Doe owns Blackacre in fee simple. In her will she gives the farm, Blackacre, to her niece, Sheila Johnson. When Jane dies, Sheila will own Blackacre as a fee simple estate:

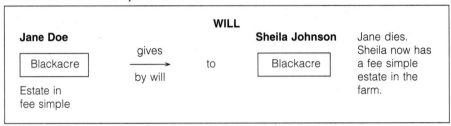

- *A fee simple estate descends to heirs if not transferred through a will.*

Example: Jane Doe owns Blackacre in fee simple and dies intestate. The state in which the farm is located will generally determine which of Jane's heirs are entitled to the farm in fee simple.

ASSIGNMENT 2.18

Assume Blackacre in the above example is located in your state. Jane Doe dies intestate owning Blackacre, the family home, in her name only. She is survived by a husband, three children, her father, and two brothers. According to your state law, who owns Blackacre?

- *A fee simple estate is subject to the rights of the owner's surviving spouse.*

Example: Jane Doe owns Blackacre. She dies. Whether Jane dies testate or intestate, her surviving spouse, John, is entitled to an interest in Jane's property. The current rights one spouse has in the decedent spouse's estate are discussed below.

- *A fee simple estate is subject to claims from creditors of the fee owner both before and after the owner's death.*

Example: Jane Doe owns Blackacre in fee simple. Jane owes Sam Bender $10,000, which is now due for payment. If Jane cannot pay this debt to Sam using her other assets, she may have to sell or mortgage Blackacre in order to satisfy the debt.

Creating and Transferring a Fee Simple Estate. Under common law, a fee simple estate could be created in only one way. The fee owner was required to convey the title to real property by deed or will using the words "to A *and his heirs.*" (The letter A stands for the name of a person.) The words *and his heirs* create a fee simple absolute estate for A and were the only words allowed by common law to create this estate. Times have changed, however, and currently, the words " to A and his heirs" are infrequently used to create a fee simple estate. Today a fee simple estate can be created by any words that indicate an intent to convey absolute ownership, e.g., "to A in fee simple," "to A forever," or simply, "I give the land to A." Generally, whenever any real estate, e.g., a house, is purchased, the buyer becomes the fee owner.

Example: Steven Brown buys a business including the land and building in which the business operates. When the current fee owner, Janet Williams, transfers the deed to Steve, he becomes the sole owner of the property *in severalty* and holds the real property in a *fee simple estate.* The transfer of the deed accomplishes the following: (1) Steven now holds legal title to the property; (2) Steven, as sole owner, owns the property *in severalty*—single ownership; (3) Steven receives a *fee simple estate* in the realty since this is the estate Janet held and transferred to Steven by deed. All the rights associated with a fee owner are now Steven's.

Example: Susan and David Martin contract to buy a house from Stan Williams. When Stan delivers the deed to the real property (house) thereby transferring legal title to the Martins, the deeds reads "to Susan Martin and David Martin, husband and wife as joint tenants in fee simple." Susan and David own the property as joint tenants with a fee simple estate. They are the fee owners.

Keeping in mind the characteristics of joint tenancy ownership and fee simple estates, the following summary of the principles of law applies:

- A fee simple estate allows the fee owner, while alive, the right to sell or give the property to another. But since the property is held in joint tenancy by a husband and wife, both joint tenants must join in the conveyance (sale or gift) to pass the title to the new owner(s). Thus, both Susan and David (in the previous example) must sign a deed transferring their house to another as part of a sales contract or as a gift.

- Although another characteristic of a fee simple estate allows a fee owner to transfer the property through a will, neither Susan nor David can will her or his interest in the house to another because they are joint tenants and a joint tenancy has the right of survivorship; i.e., when a joint tenant dies, the decedent's interest automatically passes to the surviving joint tenant by operation of law. Thus, the survivor of Susan or David would hold a fee simple estate as a single owner and could therefore transfer the estate by will, but while both are alive, neither can pass the property by a testamentary disposition until after the death of the first joint tenant.

⚜ ASSIGNMENT 2.19

Zachary, a Montana farmer, deeds 20 acres of his land to his daughter, Catherine, in fee simple when she becomes engaged to Frank. Catherine marries Frank, and they have two children. Upon Catherine's death, Frank claims that he, and not the children, is the owner of the land as a joint tenant with the right of survivorship. Is Frank's claim correct? Explain.

Life Estate

A **life estate** in real property is another type of freehold estate in which an individual, called the **life tenant,** holds an ownership interest in the property that lasts either for the lifetime of that individual or for the life of another person. If the life estate is created for the life of a person other than the life tenant, then it is known as an estate *pur autre vie.*

The next paragraphs discuss the characteristics of life estates and examine some property law concepts associated with them including future interests (reversion and remainder), dower and curtesy, a spouse's elective rights, and waste.

Characteristics of a Life Estate. The characteristics of a life estate can be summarized as follows:

MINI-GLOSSARY BOX

Life estate
A freehold estate in which a person, called the life tenant, holds an interest in land during his own or someone else's lifetime.

Life tenant
The person holding a life estate.

Pur autre vie
An estate lasting for the life of a person other than the life tenant.

■ *A life estate may last for the lifetime of the original owner (the person who conveys the estate).*

Example: Sam conveys Blackacre by a deed to "Shirley for the life of Sam." Shirley has a life estate based on Sam's lifetime. Shirley is the life tenant. Since real property is being conveyed, Sam is the grantor and Shirley is the grantee.

■ *A life estate may last for the lifetime of the person enjoying the estate (the person to whom the estate is conveyed).*

Example: Sam conveys Blackacre by a deed to "Shirley for life." Shirley receives a life estate based on her own lifetime.

■ *A life estate may last for the lifetime of a third person, called an estate pur autre vie.*

Example: Sam conveys Blackacre by a deed to "Shirley for the life of Julie." Shirley has a life estate based on Julie's lifetime.

■ *A life estate can be created by deed or will.*

Example: Sam sells Blackacre to "Shirley for life" and delivers a deed to her at the closing.

Example: Sam gives Blackacre to "Shirley for life" in his will.

■ *Unlike a fee simple estate, a life estate cannot be transferred by will.*

Example: Shirley, a life tenant, could not transfer her life estate to another person through her will.

■ *Life tenants while living may convey their interests in the property by sale or gift to a third person, however.*

Example: Shirley, a life tenant, sells her lifetime interest in Blackacre to Laverne. When Shirley gives a deed to Laverne, Laverne becomes the new life tenant and holds the property until Shirley dies. Shirley can sell only her interest in Blackacre, i.e., her life interest or life estate. Since a life tenant's death is inevitable but uncertain and it terminates the life estate, finding a buyer for a life estate is difficult and uncommon.

■ *Upon the death of the life tenant, the life estate terminates, and no interest remains to be passed to heirs or by will; nor can it be probated or be subject to creditors' claims.* The property returns (reverts) to the person who created the life estate by conveying the property by deed or will.

Example: Sam conveys Blackacre by a deed to "Shirley for life." Shirley dies. The property is returned to Sam (see the discussion below).

Future Interests—Reversion and Remainder. Whenever a grantor, who owns a fee simple estate in real property, creates a life estate, one of two results occurs:

1. At the time of the creation of the life estate, the grantor retains a reversion or reversionary interest.

2. Alternatively, at the time of the creation of the life estate, a future remainder interest is also created within the same conveyance. The person who receives the future remainder is called the remainderman.

Each of these possibilities is discussed in the next paragraphs.

Reversion.   A **reversion** or **reversionary interest** is the interest or right a **grantor** alone has to the return of real property, at present in the possession of another (the **grantee**), upon the termination of the grantee's preceding estate. A reversion exists only when the grantor holding a fee simple estate conveys an interest in property by deed or will that is less than the entire fee simple estate.

When a life estate is created and a reversion is retained, the following rules apply:

- The grantor is the only person entitled to a reversion.
- The grantor is entitled to the reversion (return) of the property, when the grantee's estate terminates (ends).
- The grantor, while alive, can transfer the reversion by deed or will.
- If the grantor dies first, the reversion is not lost because the right to the reversion can be transferred by the grantor's will to beneficiaries; or if the grantor dies without a will, the right to the reversion can be inherited by the grantor's heirs.
- The real property that reverts (returns) does not go through the probate process of the life tenant's estate and is not subject to tax or creditors' claims (see Chapter 10).

The following example explains the grantor's right to a reversion or reversionary interest:

Example: Peter Nokamura owns a farm, Blackacre, in fee simple. Peter conveys (transfers) the farm by a deed to "Reiko Yoshida for life." Peter is the grantor who retains a reversion in the farm. Reiko receives a life estate (which is the preceding estate) and is both the grantee and life tenant. Reiko's life estate gives her the right to use and possess Blackacre or to convey her life estate to another for her own lifetime. When Reiko dies, the life estate ends, and the farm, because of the reversion, automatically reverts (returns) to the grantor, Peter, without going through probate. If Peter dies before Reiko, then his reversion in the

---

MINI-GLOSSARY BOX

Reversion or reversionary interest
The interest in real property that a grantor retains when a conveyance of the property by deed or by will transfers an estate smaller than what the grantor owns, e.g., when the grantor has a fee simple estate and conveys to the grantee a life estate. At some future time the real property reverts back to the grantor.

Grantor
The person who makes a conveyance (transfer) of real property to another.

Grantee
The person to whom a conveyance of real property is made.

property passes (reverts) to Peter's estate, and Peter's will, if he has one, or state intestate succession statutes, if he has no will, determine which of Peter's devisees or heirs will receive the property. Exhibit 2.8 diagrams a reversion of this example.

☗ ASSIGNMENT 2.20

Jane Smallwood owns a lake cottage. In a deed she conveys the cottage "to my father, Brent Smallwood, for life, then to my sister, Sue Smallwood for life." Jane outlives her father but dies before her sister, Sue. Is Brent a life tenant? Who gets the property when he dies? What interest does Sue have at the time of Jane's conveyance? Explain what will happen to the property, and why, after the death of Sue.

Remainder
A future estate in real property that takes effect on the termination of a prior estate created by the same instrument at the same time.

Remainderman
A person entitled to the future fee simple estate after a particular smaller estate, e.g., a life estate, has expired.

Remainder. A **remainder** is a future estate in real property that will take effect on the termination of a prior estate created by the same instrument at the same time. A grantor who owns a fee simple estate in real property can create a life estate for one person and, in the same conveyance and at the same time, transfer the future fee simple estate to another person by deed. When the life tenant dies, the property passes to the future fee owner who is called the **remainderman.** This term is used for any person (man or woman) who receives the future estate.

Example: Bill Maxwell conveys Blackacre by deed "to James Maxwell for life, then to Mary Wilson and her heirs" or "to James Maxwell for life, then to Mary Wilson." Result: By the same conveyance and at the same time, James receives a life estate and Mary receives a future fee simple estate. When James dies, the property does *not* revert to the grantor, Bill, but instead passes as a fee

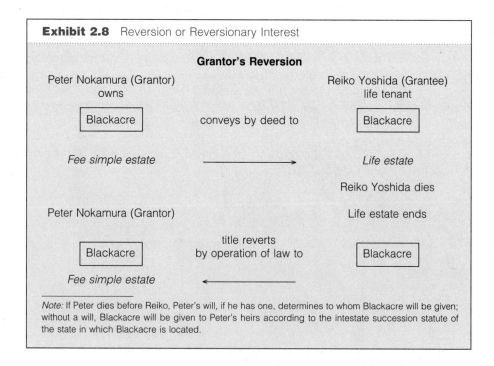

Exhibit 2.8   Reversion or Reversionary Interest

Grantor's Reversion

Peter Nokamura (Grantor) owns

Blackacre

conveys by deed to

Reiko Yoshida (Grantee) life tenant

Blackacre

Fee simple estate ⟶ *Life estate*

Reiko Yoshida dies

Peter Nokamura (Grantor)

Life estate ends

Blackacre

title reverts by operation of law to

Blackacre

Fee simple estate ⟵

Note: If Peter dies before Reiko, Peter's will, if he has one, determines to whom Blackacre will be given; without a will, Blackacre will be given to Peter's heirs according to the intestate succession statute of the state in which Blackacre is located.

simple estate to Mary. Since he has a fee simple estate and conveys the property by deed or will giving a fee simple estate to Mary, Bill terminates his grantor's right to a reversion in Blackacre. Once Mary becomes the fee owner, she is entitled to do with the property as she pleases, i.e., sell it, give it to another, or convey it after death through her will. The same result would have occurred if Bill had conveyed Blackacre "to James Maxwell for life, then to Mary Wilson forever," or "to Mary Wilson in fee simple." In such cases, where a person, other than the grantor, is entitled to the remainder of an estate in real property after another prior estate has expired, the person (Mary) is called the remainderman. Exhibit 2.9 presents a diagram of this example.

🏛 ASSIGNMENT 2.21

According to your own state laws, what kind of an estate in real property would Mary Williams receive if her Uncle Charles deeded a farm to her in the following ways? (1) "to Mary"; (2) "to Mary and her heirs"; (3) "to Mary in fee"; (4) "to Mary forever"; (5) "to Mary for life"; (6) "to Mary for the life of Helen"; (7) "to Mary for as long as I live."

Dower and Curtesy.   Property law in America is derived from the English common law. The rights of spouses in each other's real property, called rights of dower and **curtesy,** developed through the common law system. Under common law, at the time of marriage, a wife was given dower rights to provide her with the means of support after her husband's death. Specifically, dower was the surviving wife's (widow's) right to a life estate in one-third of all the real property her husband owned during the marriage. Similarly, the husband was given curtesy rights to his wife's real property. Curtesy was the right of the surviving husband (widower) to a life estate in all of his wife's real property owned during

Curtesy
The right of the surviving husband to a life estate in all of his wife's real property owned during the marriage, but only if the married couple had a child born alive.

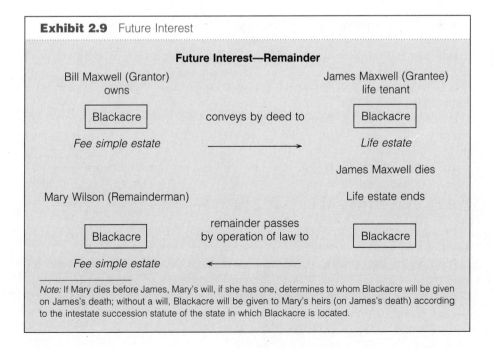

Exhibit 2.9 Future Interest

Future Interest—Remainder

Bill Maxwell (Grantor)
owns

Blackacre

Fee simple estate

conveys by deed to ⟶

James Maxwell (Grantee)
life tenant

Blackacre

Life estate

James Maxwell dies

Life estate ends

Mary Wilson (Remainderman)

Blackacre

Fee simple estate

remainder passes
by operation of law to ⟵

Blackacre

Note: If Mary dies before James, Mary's will, if she has one, determines to whom Blackacre will be given on James's death; without a will, Blackacre will be given to Mary's heirs (on James's death) according to the intestate succession statute of the state in which Blackacre is located.

the marriage, but only if the married couple had a child born alive. Under common law, the wife's dower right terminated if:

- She was divorced from her husband when he died; a legal separation did not terminate dower, however.
- Her husband held his real property in joint tenancy with another person; however, if the real property was held by the husband in a tenancy in common, his share was subject to his wife's dower right.

Dower and curtesy applied whether or not the decedent died testate, i.e., the surviving spouse had a right to a life estate in real property.

Both dower and curtesy have undergone numerous changes in every state. Most states (including the states that have adopted the Uniform Probate Code) have replaced dower and curtesy with statutes establishing a surviving spouse's right to a share, often called an elective or forced share, of the entire estate (both real and personal property) in cases where the decedent spouse's will makes unreasonable or inadequate provisions for the surviving spouse. A few states have retained their own versions of dower and curtesy rights, though with major modifications. Some states grant equivalent rights or shares to both spouses under the term "dower" (see Mass. Gen. Laws Ann. ch. 189 § 1). Even though this state uses the term "dower," it is not the same as common law dower; e.g., in Massachusetts "dower" is restricted to land owned by the decedent spouse at death. Other states have enacted "statutory" dower and curtesy where dower is not available if the decedent spouse dies intestate since the surviving spouse is an heir (see 20 Pa. Stat. Ann. § 2105). In these states, a conveyance of real property owned by one spouse requires written consent by the other spouse to release the dower or curtesy interest in the property. Despite these variations, the states that retain dower and curtesy agree on the following:

- Dower and curtesy occur only on the death of a spouse.
- Dower and curtesy apply even if the decedent died testate.
- Common law rules on the termination of dower and curtesy in the event of divorce and joint tenancy (see above) are retained.
- Written consent is necessary by the spouses to release their dower or curtesy rights in property.
- Dower and curtesy cannot and do not exist in community property states where the surviving spouse generally receives at least one-half of the community property.
- Dower and curtesy are exempt from the claims of the creditors of the decedent spouse or the decedent spouse's estate except for liens and encumbrances such as mortgages and judgments (see Mass. Gen. Laws Ann. ch. 189 § 1).

Policy reasons for replacing dower and curtesy include (1) the inadequate support they provide a surviving spouse under the common law rules; (2) the complications that occur in transferring or clearing title to real property, i.e., the passing of a free and legal title to the land for the benefit of prospective purchasers or for future heirs or devisees; and (3) the fact that they transfer only real property, and many estates contain only personal property, such as stocks and life insurance.

MINI-GLOSSARY BOX

Right of election
The right of a surviving husband or wife to choose to take, under the decedent's state law, his or her statutory share in preference to the provision made in the deceased spouse's will.

Election or forced share statute
The statute that grants the surviving spouse the election or choice.

Spouse's Right to Election or Elective Share. Most states give a surviving spouse a statutory right to avoid being disinherited by the will of the decedent spouse. The right is established by a statute that allows the surviving spouse to choose between the provision made by the deceased spouse's will and the prescribed share set by state statute. This choice is called the spouse's right to an election. The statute granting the **right of election** to take "against the will" is called an **"election"** or a **"forced share" statute,** and the property acquired by the selection is called the spouse's forced share, elective share, or statutory share. A case that illustrates the surviving spouse's right to an election is *Matter of Estate of Cole,* 200 N.J.Super. 396, 491 A.2d 770 (1984), in which the spouse elected to take her share but the court had the right to fix the value of the share and to relieve the spouse from responsibility of estate and inheritance taxes, which was the court's decision in this case.

If the choice is to elect "against the will," the spouse waives the will, renounces it, and takes what the state provides, thereby forfeiting any further claims to property under the will. The choice of the will or elective share must be made within the time period set by statute, usually six to nine months after the initiation of probate proceedings or the death of the decedent spouse.

States vary substantially in the amount a surviving spouse receives by statute. Some states determine the amount by their own version of "statutory dower"; a few set the amount by their intestate succession statute; others allow their method of "dower" and have an "elective right" statute. Most states, however, grant one-third to one-half of the decedent's estate to the surviving spouse. Sections 2–202 and 2–203 of the Uniform Probate Code set the spouse's elective share at the amount equal to the value of the elective-share percentage of the augmented estate, determined by the length of time the spouse and the decedent were married to each other, in accordance with the following schedule:

If the decedent and the spouse were married to each other:	The elective-share percentage is:
Less than 1 year	Supplemental Amount Only.
1 year but less than 2 years	3% of the augmented estate.
2 years but less than 3 years	6% of the augmented estate.
3 years but less than 4 years	9% of the augmented estate.
4 years but less than 5 years	12% of the augmented estate.
5 years but less than 6 years	15% of the augmented estate.
6 years but less than 7 years	18% of the augmented estate.
7 years but less than 8 years	21% of the augmented estate.
8 years but less than 9 years	24% of the augmented estate.
9 years but less than 10 years	27% of the augmented estate.
10 years but less than 11 years	30% of the augmented estate.

11 years but less than 12 years ....34% of the augmented estate.
12 years but less than 13 years ....38% of the augmented estate.
13 years but less than 14 years ....42% of the augmented estate.
14 years but less than 15 years ....46% of the augmented estate.
15 years or more ....50% of the augmented estate.

Augmented estate
The value of all the decedent's property that consists of the sum of four components (see Glossary), reduced by funeral and administration expenses, homestead allowance, family allowances, exempt property, and enforceable creditors' claims.

Note: in any situation, a $50,000 minimum elective-share is granted for the support of the surviving spouse, see U.P.C. § 2–202(b). The **augmented estate** consists of the value of all property, whether real or personal, tangible or intangible, wherever situated, that constitutes the sum of four components (1) the decedent's net probate estate; (2) the decedent's nonprobate transfers to others; (3) the decedent's nonprobate transfers to the surviving spouse; (4) the surviving spouse's net assets and nonprobate transfers to others, reduced by funeral and administration expenses, homestead allowance, family allowances, exempt property, and enforceable creditors' claims, see U.P.C. §§ 2–202 through 2–207. Exhibit 2.10 summarizes the spouse's elective share in all fifty states.

Waste
Any act or omission that does permanent damage to real property or unreasonably changes its character or value.

Waste.   While in possession of real property, a life tenant has the absolute right to possess and use the property. However, because of the future reversion and remainder interests of grantors and remaindermen, the tenant is under a duty to exercise reasonable and prudent care to protect and preserve the property and is required by law not to cause or commit **"waste."** Waste is a legal term referring to "any act or omission that does permanent damage to the real property or unreasonably changes its character or value." Therefore, waste occurs when a life tenant permits any unreasonable or unauthorized use or neglect of the real property that causes permanent physical damage, decreases the property's value, and detrimentally affects the persons entitled to the future interest, i.e., reversion and remainder interests. Specific examples of waste include:

- The failure to make necessary repairs in a building.
- Cutting and selling all trees on timberland.
- Strip-mining, removing, and selling minerals from the land.
- Neglecting to heat a house in winter causing major damage to the plumbing.

If guilty of waste, the life tenant may be subject to a lawsuit for damages, an injunction from an equity court, or—the extreme remedy—forfeiture (termination) of the tenant's life estate. Because forfeiture is such a severe remedy, most courts are reluctant to find waste. In addition, state court decisions are inconsistent in determining what constitutes waste. A case involving waste that illustrates the limits placed on a life tenant concerning mineral rights is *Nutter v. Stockton,* 626 P.2d 861 (Okl. 1981).

Leasehold Estates

Various types of leasehold estates exist including tenancy at will, tenancy at sufferance, and tenancy from month to month. This text will examine only one example, however, a tenancy or estate for years. For a more complete discussion, see textbooks on real property [e.g., William E. Burby, *Real Property,* 3d ed. (St. Paul: West Publishing Co., 1965), p. 123].

Exhibit 2.10   Summary of Spouse's Elective Share by State

Alabama	One-third of decedent's estate
Alaska	One-third of decedent's estate
Arizona	One-half of community property (community property law)
Arkansas	Dower or curtesy interest
California	One-half of community or quasi-community property (community property law)
Colorado	One-half of the augmented estate
Connecticut	One-third of decedent's estate for life
Delaware	One-third of the elective estate
Florida	Thirty percent of net estate
Georgia	One year's support during estate administration
Hawaii	One-third of net estate
Idaho	One-half of augmented quasi-community property; one-half of community property (community property law)
Illinois	One-third of estate if surviving descendant(s); one-half if no surviving descendant(s)
Indiana	One-half of net estate if surviving spouse is first spouse of decedent; if not, separate rules apply and share is limited
Iowa	Intestate share
Kansas	Elective-share percentage of the augmented estate
Kentucky	Dower right
Louisiana	One-half of community property (community property law)
Maine	One-third of the augmented estate
Maryland	One-third of net estate if surviving issue; one-half if no surviving issue
Massachusetts	One-third of estate if surviving issue; $25,000 plus life estate in one-half of remaining estate if surviving kindred but no issue; $25,000 plus one-half of remaining estate if no surviving kindred or issue
Michigan	One-half of intestate share, reduced by one-half of the value of all property received from decedent other than by testate or intestate succession
Minnesota	Elective-share percentage of the augmented estate
Mississippi	Intestate share not to exceed one-half of the estate
Missouri	One-half of estate if no lineal descendants or one-third if lineal descendants, reduced by the value of all property derived by spouse from decedent
Montana	One-third of the augmented estate
Nebraska	One-half of the augmented estate
Nevada	One-half of community property (community property law)
New Hampshire	One-third of estate if surviving issue; $10,000 of personalty and realty each plus one-half of remaining estate if surviving parent or sibling but no issue; $10,000 plus $2,000 for each year of marriage to decedent plus one-half of remaining estate if no issue, parent, or sibling
New Jersey	One-third of the augmented estate
New Mexico	One-half of community property (community property law)
New York	The greater of $50,000 or one-third of net estate
North Carolina	Intestate share
North Dakota	One-third of the augmented estate
Ohio	Intestate share not to exceed one-half of net estate; one-third if two or more surviving children or their lineal issue
Oklahoma	One-half of all property acquired during marriage by the joint industry of the husband and wife
Oregon	One-fourth of net estate
Pennsylvania	One-third of decedent's estate
Rhode Island	Life estate as provided by intestacy law
South Carolina	One-third of decedent's estate
South Dakota	The greater of $100,000 or one-third of the augmented estate
Tennessee	One-third of net estate
Texas	One-half of community property (community property law)
Utah	One-third of the augmented estate multiplied by a fraction

Exhibit 2.10	Summary of Spouse's Elective Share by State—*continued*
Vermont	Dower or courtesy interest
Virginia	One-third of the augmented estate if surviving children or their descendants; one-half if no surviving children or their descendants
Washington	One-half of community property (community property law)
West Virginia	Percentage of the augmented estate (3% for spouses married for one year to 50% for spouses married more than 15 years)
Wisconsin	One-half of the deferred marital property and one-half of the augmented estate
Wyoming	One-half of estate if no surviving issue or if spouse is also a parent of any surviving issue; one-fourth if spouse is not the parent of any surviving issue

Tenancy for Years

A tenancy or estate for years creates an interest in real property that will last for the period designated, e.g., a tenancy for 10 years. Such a tenancy is created and terminates according to its own terms. No notice to terminate is required.

Example: John Kellar owns a farm, Blackacre, in fee simple. John conveys the farm by deed to "Maude Owens for 20 years." Maude holds Blackacre as a tenancy for 20 years. She has the right to use, possess, or even to sell her *interest* in the property. At the end of the 20-year period, however, Maude's interest ends, and the property reverts to John because of the grantor's reversionary interest. A tenancy for years may include a lease, but it must be clear that ownership to real property is conveyed for the stated time period and not just rights to possession.

🏛 ASSIGNMENT 2.22

On the basis of the above discussion, and after reviewing freehold estates, answer the following questions.

Amy conveys by deed her lake cottage to "Clare for life, then to Maxine for 20 years, then to Elizabeth and her heirs."

1. What kind of estate does Clare have?
2. Who receives the property when Clare dies?
3. If Maxine dies before Clare dies, who receives the property on Clare's death?
4. Does Amy have a reversionary interest in the property? Explain.
5. What interest does Elizabeth hold?
6. Two remaindermen are involved in the conveyance. Who are they and why are they so classified?
7. Do Elizabeth's heirs have any interest in the property by this conveyance?

Leaseholds, such as the tenancy for years, also include the standard landlord-tenant relationships. If Harold signs a lease, i.e., a contract to take possession of real property for a specified time period while agreeing to pay rent while in possession, such a contract creates the estate called the tenancy for years. It is not the function of this text to review in depth this area of contract and property law, but it is important to identify where the landlord-tenant relationship fits into the terminology and legal concepts previously discussed. Confusion between such terms as landlord-tenant and joint tenancy, tenancy in common, tenancy by the entirety, and tenancy for years must be avoided.

KEY TERMS

Fixture	Right of succession	Garnish	Grantor
Chattel	Dower	Garnishment	Grantee
Severalty	Disposition	Commingling	Remainder
Incidents of ownership	Joint tenancy	Quasi-community property	Remainderman
Operation of law	Right of survivorship	Fee simple estate	Curtesy
Descent and distribution	Straw man	Life estate	Right of election
Issue	Undivided interest	Life tenant	Election or forced share statute
Per capita	Severance	*Pur autre vie*	Augmented estate
Half blood	Partition	Reversion or reversionary interest	Waste
Distributee	Tenancy by the entirety		
Distributive share	Community property		
	Separate property		

REVIEW QUESTIONS

1. How does real property differ from personal property?
2. In whom and when does the real and personal property of the decedent vest (pass)?
3. What are the three tests state courts use to determine if property is a fixture?
4. What are trade fixtures? List three examples.
5. Write out your own definition of each key term in this chapter. Are your definitions essentially the same as those in the text?
6. How do tangible and intangible personal property differ?
7. What items of property are classified as probate property and what items are nonprobate property?
8. What is the significance of property being classified as probate or nonprobate property in terms of the need for probate, creditors' claims, and payment of federal and state estate and death taxes?
9. What are the four common law "unities" required for the creation of a joint tenancy?
10. How does a joint tenancy differ from both a tenancy in common and a tenancy by the entirety?
11. How many states are community property states? List them.
12. In a community property state, what property is separate property and what is community property?
13. What is a fee simple estate and what are its characteristics?
14. Concerning future interests in real property, what are the differences between a reversion and a remainder?
15. How does dower differ from curtesy and why have most states replaced them with a spouse's right to elect "against a will"?
16. What responsibilities does a life tenant have concerning the problem of "waste"? Give an example of waste.

CASE PROBLEMS

Problem 1

A client of the law firm where you work as a paralegal, and with whom you have become acquainted, calls you at your home to discuss and ask your advice about the following matter. The client wants to change the form of ownership in a cottage she currently owns in severalty to either a joint tenancy or a tenancy in common with her two adult children and herself. She tells you her main concern is that she does not want her children's spouses to "ever have any interest in the cottage," and she wants your advice as to how she can obtain this result. Because of your experience, you feel you know the answer to the question. How should you respond to her request? Is this an ethical issue or concern for you as a paralegal? Explain.

Problem 2

When he died, Abner Huntington owned a magnificent and expensive home well known for its beautiful landscaping and flower gardens. In his will, he gave his children "all household furnishings, equipment, decorations, and appliances." The home was sold to a famous entertainer who claimed the children had improperly removed certain fixtures from the house and the premises. The property removed included garden statues, lighting fixtures, a pipe organ, metal decorative birds around the swimming pool, and inside the house, a large statue of Pegasus, the flying horse. Most of these property items could be easily removed.

A. In your opinion, are these items fixtures? Explain.

B. Read the case *Paul v. First National Bank of Cincinnati,* 52 Ohio Misc. 77, 369 N.E.2d 488 (1976). In that case, the court ruled that items similar to those in the example were all fixtures. Do you agree?

CHAPTER THREE

THE PARTICIPANTS AND THE PROPER COURT

OBJECTIVES

After completing this chapter, you should be able to:

- Identify the participants who are essential for drafting wills and trusts and for administering the estate of a decedent and explain their basic functions.
- Identify the proper court that supervises the administration and distribution of a decedent's estate.
- Explain what is meant by jurisdiction.
- Identify the various elements of jurisdiction required by a specific court, such as the probate court.
- Determine the proper place (county/state) to commence probate proceedings of a decedent's estate.
- Recognize the necessity for establishing a second or ancillary administration of a decedent's estate when property of the decedent is located in another state.

OUTLINE

SCOPE OF THE CHAPTER

Many different participants are involved in the drafting of wills and trusts and the administration of estates. This chapter reviews the basic functions of these participants and describes the role of the proper court, often called the probate court, in the administration of an estate. Important terms associated with the selection and function of the court, such as probate, jurisdiction, domicile, venue, and ancillary administration, are defined and explained in the second half of the chapter.

THE PARTICIPANTS

The following people are involved in the preparation of wills and trusts and the administration of a decedent's estate: the personal representative of the estate, an attorney, a paralegal, the probate court (judge), the registrar, and the clerk. We begin our discussion by examining the functions of each of these participants.

The Personal Representative

The personal representative is a person or corporate institution, such as a bank or trust department, appointed by a proper court, usually the probate court, to administer the estate of a decedent who died with or without a will. As a fiduciary, a person who serves in a position of utmost trust and loyalty, a personal representative has obligations called "fiduciary duties" to act in good faith solely for the benefit of another person. Trustees, guardians, and conservators are three other types of fiduciaries commonly appointed by will. Personal representatives act for the beneficiaries of the estate; trustees act for beneficiaries of trusts; guardians act for minors; and conservators act for incompetent persons.

In most cases, before executing the final draft of the will, the testator asks the prospective personal representative if he is willing to serve. Even if the person agrees, he has a right to change his mind later and reject the position before being appointed or resign the position after being formally appointed by the probate court.

Most personal representatives are family members or friends who accept their appointment. The knowledge that the court and professional assistance (an attorney and you, the paralegal) are available to help complete the necessary tasks can help reluctant personal representatives overcome their anxiety about dealing with matters that are unfamiliar to them.

Appropriate Terminology

If the personal representative named in the will is a man, he is also traditionally or commonly called the executor; if a woman, she is the executrix.

Example: Howard dies with a will. He names his sister, Nanette, as his personal representative to administer his estate and distribute his property according to the terms of his will. Nanette is Howard's personal representative or executrix. If Howard had named the First National Bank's trust department as his personal representative to administer his estate, the bank would be his personal representative or executor.

If there is no will, the court appoints the personal representative, traditionally called an administrator (man) or administratrix (woman).

Example: Howard dies without a will. The probate court appoints his sister, Nanette, to oversee the distribution of his estate to his heirs as determined by state law. Nanette is Howard's personal representative or administratrix.

Generally, executors and administrators perform similar duties, face similar liabilities, and hold similar powers. Most states now use the term *personal representative* instead of executor or administrator, and this practice will be followed here. Throughout this book, any person (man or woman) who administers the estate of a decedent will be referred to as a personal representative, whether the decedent died with or without a will. The various types of personal representatives and the fiduciary duties they perform are discussed in detail in Chapter 11.

The Role of the Personal Representative

Although state statutes often grant numerous fiduciary powers to personal representatives, usually the powers are limited to those stated explicitly in the will or incorporated into the will by reference to a statute authorizing them. As an example, see Section 3–715 of the Uniform Probate Code, which lists twenty-seven transactions the personal representative can perform. You should review these functions carefully.

Generally, the role of the personal representative is:

- To probate the will or petition for estate administration when there is no will.
- To collect, protect, preserve, and manage the probate estate of the decedent.
- To publish notice to creditors to submit their claims by a specific date.
- To pay all federal and state taxes and approved creditor claims.
- To distribute the remaining assets to the beneficiaries named in the will or to the decedent's heirs if no will exists.
- To refrain from engaging in acts of self-dealing, often referred to as the duty of loyalty; e.g., *the personal representative cannot borrow, sell, or buy estate property. It may be appropriate for you to remind the personal representative of this duty.*   **ETHICAL ISSUE** ◄
- To commence a civil lawsuit for claims on behalf of the estate or to defend the estate against claims brought by creditors or disgruntled family members.
- *To keep all collected estate assets separate from the personal representative's own assets,* i.e., to not commingle these assets.   **ETHICAL ISSUE** ◄
- *To not delegate the management of the probate estate or these fiduciary duties to others.* Obviously, this does not prevent the personal representative from selecting and hiring professional advisers, e.g., an attorney and a paralegal, to help perform these duties.   **ETHICAL ISSUE** ◄

Circumstances may arise that make the personal representative's task more difficult. Problems that may occur include the following:

- A beneficiary cannot be found.
- An heir or beneficiary challenges the personal representative's authority to act or appointment and proposes an alternate candidate.
- Someone contests the will.
- Someone challenges the personal representative's payment to creditors or distributions to beneficiaries or heirs.

The court will ultimately resolve these problems, but they may cause lengthy delays in the estate administration and add considerable expense that depletes the assets of the estate.

The personal representative distributes only the probate property of the decedent's estate, i.e., the assets that are disposed of by will or that descend as intestate property. The personal representative does not have administrative power to distribute nonprobate property such as jointly owned property, the proceeds from an insurance policy payable to a named beneficiary other than the decedent's estate, and the like. Statutes generally require that the personal representative report all the property (probate and nonprobate) in the estate for tax purposes. These tax requirements will be discussed in Chapter 14.

Pre-Probate Duties of the Personal Representative

Neither this list of the personal representative's duties nor the lists in the following sections are intended to be all-inclusive. Not only do these duties vary from state to state, but many aspects of estate administration depend on the provisions of the will, if one exists, and the amount and nature of the assets the decedent owned. The personal representative will generally perform these tasks with the advice of an attorney and your assistance, which will be discussed in more detail in Chapters 11 and 12. The following are the main tasks of the personal representative prior to probate:

1. Upon request, assist with anatomical gifts and funeral arrangements. Obtain copies of the death certificate from the funeral director.
2. Hire an attorney to represent the estate and to help with its administration.
3. Find and review any existing will.
4. Contact all of the decedent's financial advisers to obtain information about business records, papers, keys to a safe deposit box, and the like.
5. Convene a conference of family members and other interested persons to discuss the provisions of the will or intestate laws, election rights, immediate financial needs, maintenance, and similar matters. Advise a surviving spouse of the right to obtain his or her own attorney and elect against the will. Determine whether fiduciaries (guardians or conservators) are needed for minors and incompetent persons.
6. Locate and notify witnesses of the testator's death.
7. Discontinue the telephone and other utilities if advantageous and notify the post office to forward mail to the address of the personal representative. Stop newspaper and other deliveries.
8. Determine the appropriate probate proceedings—solemn (formal) or common (informal). See the discussion in Chapters 12 and 13.

Probate Duties prior to Appointment as Personal Representative

The personal representative is expected to file all required legal documents, petitions, and accounts, as discussed in detail in Chapters 11 and 12. Before being formally appointed, the personal representative should attend to the following:

1. Petition for probate of the will or for general administration if there is no will and, in either case, for appointment of the personal representative (out-of-state property may require ancillary administration, see later discussion in this chapter).
2. Give notice of the decedent's death and notice of the date for the hearing to probate the will and for appointment of the personal representative to beneficiaries, heirs, creditors, and other interested persons.
3. Notify the surviving spouse and minor children of their rights.

Estate Administration Duties from Appointment to Closing of the Estate
The personal representative will perform the following tasks in administering the estate:

1. Obtain from the court the **Letters Testamentary** or **Letters of Administration** that establish the authority of the personal representative and file an oath of office as personal representative. Letters are one-page certificates of appointment authorizing the personal representative to act on behalf of the decedent's estate in performing the tasks of estate administration.

2. Arrange for a **bond** with **surety** if necessary.

3. Apply for an Employer Identification Number (Form SS–4).

4. Open an estate bank (checking) account.

5. Open the decedent's safe deposit box.

6. Defend the estate against will contests.

7. Discuss the need for survivors to draft or rewrite their own wills and review their health and life insurance.

8. Protect, collect, and preserve assets:

   a. Find and review all documents, records, and papers (e.g., business records, checkbooks, tax returns, pension plans, insurance policies) concerning the decedent's financial affairs. Notify local banks of the decedent's death and request information on accounts or an unknown safe deposit box.

   b. Take possession of all personal property not set aside for the spouse and/or minor children and transfer all cash from such sources as savings and checking accounts, life insurance payable to the estate, and dividends from securities into the new estate checking account.

   c. Inspect the condition of all real estate and review all written documents, including promissory notes, leases, mortgages, and deeds. Arrange for security, management, and collection of rents and pay insurance premiums, rent, and other obligations.

   d. Determine the form of ownership of all real and personal property.

   e. Protect both real and personal property with adequate and appropriate kinds of insurance coverage (obtain confirmation in writing) and keep all property in reasonable repair. Place valuable personal property in a new estate safe deposit box or vault.

MINI-GLOSSARY BOX

Letters Testamentary
The formal instrument of authority and appointment given to a personal representative (executor) by the proper court to carry out the administration of the decedent's estate according to the terms of a will.

Letters of Administration
The formal instrument of authority and appointment given to a personal representative (administrator) by the proper court to carry out the administration of the decedent's estate according to the proper state intestate succession statute.

Bond
A certificate whereby a surety company promises to pay money if the personal representative of a deceased fails to faithfully perform the duties of administering the decedent's estate.

Surety
An individual or company that, at the request of another, such as a personal representative, agrees to pay money in the amount of a bond in the event that the personal representative fails to faithfully perform his duties.

f. Collect information on all nonprobate assets to be used later in preparing tax returns, e.g., property in joint tenancy or trusts and other assets designated for a named beneficiary (e.g., life insurance, IRA, and pension plans).

g. Collect all debts including family debts owed to the decedent and place the funds in the estate account. Contact the decedent's employer and collect any amounts owed to the decedent such as unpaid salary, bonus, and vacation pay. Make sure the decedent was not involved in any pending litigation. If the decedent or the estate is entitled to sue others, e.g., debtors and the like, then the personal representative must perform these tasks.

h. File claims for any Social Security, veterans' pension benefits, and the like to which the decedent's estate is entitled.

i. Determine whether the decedent made any gifts for which a gift tax return must be filed.

j. Determine whether ancillary administration of out-of-state assets is necessary and make appropriate arrangements for such administration when required (see the discussion under Ancillary Administration later in the chapter).

9. Ascertain whether the decedent owned any business (sole proprietorship or partnership) and determine whether the business should be liquidated, sold, or continued. Arrange proper management for the business as needed.

10. Review all securities (stocks and bonds) and collect all interest and dividends, make decisions on proper investments, and determine whether any of these assets will have to be liquidated to pay administration expenses, taxes, or creditors' claims.

11. Once the assets are determined and collected, inventory and make arrangements to have all assets appraised according to their value at the date of the decedent's death or the alternate evaluation date.

12. Distribute family allowances, including support and maintenance to the surviving spouse and/or minor children, as determined by statute.

13. Examine all claims made against the estate; determine their reasonableness, timeliness, validity, and priority; defend the estate against any improper claims.

14. Defend the estate against any litigation filed against it.

15. Pay all allowed claims against the estate according to their statutory priority.

16. Prepare and file all necessary federal and state tax returns and pay all taxes due.

17. Terminate the ancillary administration, if one exists, and pay any debts or taxes due.

18. Obtain and keep detailed records of all receipts (income) and vouchers for all disbursements (expenses and debt payments) and prepare all necessary data for the final accounting, listing assets, receipts, disbursements, and sales (if any), noting any gains or losses, and providing a reconciliation of beginning and ending balances.

19. Obtain court approval of attorney's and personal representative's fees.

20. Distribute proper title to remaining assets of the estate to beneficiaries according to the will or to heirs according to the intestate statute.

21. After the final accounting, obtain approval of the settlement of the estate and a discharge of the personal representative by order of the court.

22. Cancel the personal representative's bond, if one was necessary, with the surety (bonding) company and close the estate.

The Attorney

In many cases the personal representative appointed by the decedent will lack the knowledge, experience, or expertise to handle the complexities of estate administration. For this reason, the personal representative generally requests the assistance of an attorney. Once the attorney is hired, you also will begin your tasks.

Potential ethical problems, of which you, too, must be aware, arise for the supervising attorney who is hired to draft the will *whenever the following occur:*

ETHICAL ISSUE

1. The attorney or her family is named a beneficiary of the will. The case of *In re Estate of Peterson,* 283 Mn. 446, 168 N.W.2d 502 (1969) illustrates this problem.

> Grace Peterson, a 74-year-old spinster asked her attorney, Chester Gustafson, to draft her will. Over a period of five years, the attorney prepared six wills or codicils for Peterson with the last will leaving her entire estate to Gustafson's children. Peterson died, and Gustafson sought to have the last will probated.
>
> ■ Issue: Is a will valid when the entire estate is left to the family of the attorney who drew the will?
> ■ Decision: No, said the Minnesota Supreme Court. The will was a product of the attorney's undue influence and cannot be probated.

Comment: Rule 1.15 of the Model Rules of Professional Conduct (see Chapter 15) specifically states:

> A lawyer shall not prepare an instrument giving the lawyer, or a person related to the lawyer as parent, child, sibling, or spouse, any substantial gift from a client, including a testamentary gift, *except* where the client is related to the donee.

Example: Attorney John Edwards drafts a will for Elizabeth Thompson, the mother of John's wife, Sarah Edwards. In the will, Elizabeth leaves her lake cottage in Maine to her daughter, Sarah Edwards. This gift would be ethically acceptable.

2. The attorney is appointed in the will to be the personal representative.
3. The attorney is named in the will as the testator's choice to assist the personal representative.

Situations 2 and 3 both raise a serious ethical issue. In each case, the appointment would be financially rewarding to the attorney, especially when the compensation is a percentage of the estate. For this reason, *the attorney or paralegal must not solicit or suggest either appointment to the client.*

ETHICAL ISSUE

Comment: The Model Code of Professional Responsibility (the predecessor to the Model Rules discussed in Chapter 15) stated:

> A lawyer should not consciously influence a client to name [the lawyer] as executor, trustee, or lawyer in an instrument. In those cases where the client wishes to name the lawyer as such, care should be taken by the lawyer to avoid even the appearance of impropriety.

A leading case on these issues is *State v. Gulbankian,* 54 Wis.2d 605, 196 N.W.2d 733 (1972), in which the Wisconsin Supreme Court stated:

It is clear an attorney cannot solicit either directly or by any indirect means a direction of a testator that he or a member of his firm be named executor or be employed as an attorney to probate the estate. . . . An attorney, merely because he drafts a will, has no preferential claim to probate it.

A lawyer must not only avoid solicitation but also the appearance of solicitation so as not to damage the confidence the public has in the legal profession.

The Wisconsin court added that a lawyer may draft a will that names him as executor *if* that is the *unprompted* intent of the client. The court also observed that testators rarely name the attorney who drafts the will to be their personal representative or to assist the personal representative.

Furthermore, even when the will recommends an attorney to assist in probating the estate, that attorney may not be the one to do so. The personal representative of the estate has the sole discretion to select the attorney and is under no obligation to choose one named in the will.

Having been retained to help the personal representative settle an estate, the attorney has a duty to inform the beneficiaries or heirs of the estate that the attorney works for the estate while advising the personal representative and not individually for them. In case of conflict, such as when named beneficiaries to the will want to sue the estate, they must hire their own attorney. *They cannot retain the attorney who is representing the estate because that would create a conflict of interest for the attorney.* The attorney, like the personal representative, has a fiduciary responsibility, a basic duty of loyalty to the client (the estate), and cannot become involved in a situation where a conflict may develop or where the attorney has a personal interest in the outcome of the proceedings.

ETHICAL ISSUE ▶

🏛 ASSIGNMENT 3.1

Sharon, the personal representative of her father's estate, hires Tamara Colby, an attorney, to help administer the estate. The will names all of Sharon's brothers and sisters beneficiaries except Charles. Charles intends to contest the will. Answer the following questions yes or no and explain your position according to your own state's statutory code for wills *and* the Code of Ethics (see Chapter 15).

1. Could Charles hire Tamara to represent him in the will contest?
2. If Tamara and Sharon's father were business partners, could Tamara accept the position offered by Sharon?
3. Could the attorney who drafted the will act as the attorney for the estate?
4. Charles owns his own business. On occasion, he has retained Tamara to handle various legal problems for the business. The business has no legal actions pending at this time. Could Tamara accept the position offered by Sharon?

The Paralegal or Legal Assistant

As the legal assistant, you must act under the direction and supervision of an attorney and cannot give legal advice. Many tasks must be performed when drafting wills and trusts and administering decedents' estates, but not all of them must be handled personally by an attorney. As the attorney's assistant, you will perform many tasks and assist in many others.

The specific duties you will perform when assisting the attorney and the personal representative in estate administration will be discussed in later chapters.

The next paragraphs provide a brief overview of your tasks in wills, trusts, and estate administration.

Wills

Your tasks concerning wills include the following:

1. Collect all data and information necessary for making a client's will, including helping the client complete questionnaires and handling all communication (phone calls, letter writing, and interviews) to obtain the required information.

2. After reviewing the client's financial information, discuss with the attorney the contents of the will. You should be prepared to discuss such topics as the need to incorporate trusts; tax considerations, including methods of reducing taxes; the identification and clarification of all assets; and the beneficiaries to whom the property is to be distributed according to the client's wishes.

3. Prepare a preliminary draft of the will.

4. Review the draft with your attorney and the client and make any corrections, additions, deletions, or modifications necessary to avoid inconsistencies and ensure that the will reflects the wishes of the client.

5. Assist in the execution of the final draft of the will.

Trusts

The following are your main tasks in relation to trusts:

1. Obtain from the client data and information needed for the creation of a trust (e.g., the purpose of the trust, parties, property to be transferred, powers of the trustee, distributions of income and principal, and tax considerations).

2. Draft a preliminary trust.

3. Review the preliminary draft with your supervising attorney and the client and make corrections, additions, deletions, or modifications as necessary.

4. Assist in the final execution of the trust.

Estate Administration

Your *pre-probate tasks* in estate administration generally include the following:

1. Locate the will, if one exists.

2. Set up a family conference and notify all family members and beneficiaries or heirs.

3. Assist in reviewing the will or intestacy procedures with the family and beneficiaries of the will or the heirs of the intestate.

4. Explain the **"tickler" system** and probate procedures.

5. Set up the "tickler" with the personal representative and prepare for the maintenance and monitoring of the procedures (e.g., dates for filing, correspondence, and filing of documents).

> **Tickler system**
> A chronological list of all the important steps and dates in the stages of the administration of the decedent's estate.
>
> **ETHICAL ISSUE** ◄

Probate tasks include the following:

1. Help locate, collect, preserve, and maintain assets and ensure that *estate assets are not commingled with other assets of the law firm.*

2. Handle communication (phone calls, letter writing, and personal interviews) with parties holding assets (e.g., insurance companies, banks), creditors, beneficiaries, and heirs. *None of your communications may contain legal advice, and any information you receive must remain confidential.*

> **ETHICAL ISSUE** ◄

3. Assist in preparing preliminary drafts of legal documents (forms) associated with administration.

4. Maintain records of all collected assets (filing of documents, creditors' claims, and the like).

5. Prepare an inventory and appraisal of all probate assets and also list all nonprobate property and its value for federal and state death tax purposes.

6. Prepare preliminary drafts of final estate accounts and necessary tax returns.

7. Record the payment of debts and taxes due.

8. File legal documents (from the original petition to the final account).

9. File tax returns after review with the attorney.

Your handling of such tasks frees the attorney from the time-consuming but important details of estate administration, thus decreasing the cost of legal services. You are responsible for seeing that these matters move smoothly and chronologically. By doing so, you can handle queries that do not involve the dispensing of legal advice and can indirectly improve attorney-client rapport by allowing the attorney more time to advise the client. The ethical conduct required of paralegals when performing these tasks under the supervision of an attorney is discussed in Chapter 15 and throughout the text. Exhibit 3.1 summarizes the duties a paralegal can and cannot perform.

Exhibit 3.1 Duties and Functions a Paralegal with Proper Supervision Can or Cannot Perform

Duties/Functions	Paralegal Can Perform	Paralegal Cannot Perform
Accept an employment (client) contract.		X
Establish your legal fees with a client when working for a firm.		X
Interview a client to gather relevant data needed for drafting wills, trusts, and estate administration forms.	X	
Prepare questionnaires for estate planning and checklists for wills and trusts.	X	
Give legal advice on estate planning, e.g., gifts, taxes.		X
Perform legal research.	X	
Draft preliminary wills, trusts, and estate documents.	X	
Verify that the creation and execution of all documents and estate administration procedures comply with state statutes.	X	
Assist in the final execution of the will or trust.	X	
Set up and explain to appropriate parties the "tickler" system used in probate.	X	
Handle communication (phone calls, correspondence, interviews, etc.) with the decedent's family, beneficiaries, heirs, and creditors.	X	
Perform legal advocacy (represent a client before a court in a will contest).*		X
Identify and keep records of all probate property for preparing the estate inventory.	X	
File legal documents for probate and estate administration.	X	
Determine if federal and state death taxes are due and execute tax returns.	X	

*Exceptions currently allow paralegals or other nonlawyers to act on behalf of a client in a few situations, e.g., appeals at Social Security hearings.

The Probate Court

Another participant with an essential role in the administration of a decedent's estate is the judge. The words *court* and *judge* are frequently used synonymously in statutes and in legal writings. As a courtesy, the judge who presides over a court is referred to as "the court." Throughout the remaining chapters of this text, the words will be used interchangeably. Chapters 11 and 12 discuss the role of the court in greater detail. In many states, the court that handles estate administration is called the probate court, but in some states, this court is called a Surrogate, Orphan's, or Chancery Court. In a few states, the court is part of the state's regular judicial system, e.g., a district, circuit, county, or superior court. The usual designation, probate court, will be used throughout this text. Exhibit 3.2 identifies the name of the appropriate court in each state.

In general, once the probate court has jurisdiction, its function is to ensure that the personal representative properly administers the estate so that (1) the homestead exemption, exempt property, family allowances, and maintenance are granted; (2) creditors who have valid claims are paid; (3) taxes owed are paid; (4) the remaining property is distributed to the rightful beneficiaries according to the testator's wishes as expressed in the provisions of the will if a will exists or, in the alternative, according to the controlling state intestate succession statute; and (5) disputes that may arise in the course of the administration of the estate are settled. By approving the will or identifying the decedent's rightful heirs according to statute, the probate court establishes clear title to the property distributed to the beneficiaries of the will or to the heirs. Terminology relating to the functions of the probate court will be covered in a later section of this chapter.

The Registrar

An officer of the probate court, known as the Probate **Registrar,** Surrogate, or Register of Wills, depending on the state, acts on behalf and in place of the court. The Registrar may be a judge but more often is a person designated by the judge to perform functions of the court in certain probate proceedings, e.g., common, independent, or informal proceedings in Uniform Probate Code states. Although Registrars cannot, by statute, give legal advice, they can answer questions about

Registrar
A person designated by the judge to perform the functions of the court in informal proceedings.

Exhibit 3.2 State Courts Having Jurisdiction over Wills and Distribution of Decedents' Estates

Probate court	AL, AR, CT, GA, ME, MA, MI, MN, NH, RI, SC, VT
Probate division of circuit court	IL, MO
Probate court or district court	NM
Probate division of court of common pleas	OH
Surrogate's court	NJ, NY
Orphan's court	MD, PA
Chancery court	MS
Register's court	DE
District court	CO, ID, IA, KS, KY, LA, MT, NV, UT, WY
District or county court	OK
Circuit court	FL, HI, IN, OR, SD, VA, WI
County court	NE, ND, TN, TX, WV
Superior court	AK, AZ, CA, NC, WA

forms and procedures that are common concerns for paralegals working in estate administration.

The Clerk or Court Administrator

Clerk
An administrative assistant to the court who receives and files documents and keeps records of court proceedings.

The **clerk** (of the probate court) is an administrative assistant to the court (judge). The clerk administers oaths and authenticates and certifies copies of instruments, documents, and records of the court. Like the Registrar, the court clerk in the county of the decedent's domicile state cannot give legal advice, but both are essential and extremely helpful sources of information about probate procedures and the execution of the required forms. Because your county may follow "local customs" in administering decedents' estates, you should contact the Registrar or clerk and become familiar with their procedures. Since you will file all forms and other documents with these officers of the court, you will find their help invaluable in assuring that your forms are complete and accurate.

🏛 ASSIGNMENT 3.2

1. If May B. Brown was appointed executrix of her mother's estate, did her mother die intestate or testate?
2. Does either an executor(trix) or administrator(trix) have the duty to collect money from insurance policies naming a specific person as the beneficiary? Do they have this duty if the beneficiary predeceased the decedent?
3. To whom is a personal representative responsible?
4. Look up the sections in your state's statutes describing the appointment and duties of the personal representative. Cite the sections.

TERMINOLOGY RELATED TO PROBATE COURT PROCEEDINGS

Because probate court proceedings are an essential part of estate administration, you need to become familiar with the basic terminology related to probate. Jurisdiction, domicile, venue, and ancillary administration are all important aspects of probate proceedings.

Probate

Probate (of a will)
The procedure by which a document is presented to the court to confirm it is a valid will.
Probate proceedings
The process of distributing the estate of a person who died testate or intestate; includes all other matters over which probate courts have jurisdiction.

Originally, the term **probate** referred to a proceeding in the appropriate court to prove that a certain document was a will. To prove a will means to acknowledge its existence and validity as the properly executed last will of a decedent. A will that is proved is said to be admitted to probate. Initially an adjective, *probate* today is commonly used as a noun meaning **probate proceedings,** which expands the definition and use of the term *probate* to include the process of distributing the estate of a person who died testate or intestate and includes all other matters over which probate courts have jurisdiction. Sometimes the term *probate* is also used to refer to the completion of the entire administration of the decedent's estate, including such matters as the settlement of a dispute concerning a will. Such suits, known as will contests—for example, a contest between two beneficiaries who claim that the same item of property was willed to each of them—may arise after the will is admitted to probate. Further discussion concerning the actual procedures of probate versus estate administration are included in Chapter 12.

Jurisdiction

Jurisdiction is the authority by which a particular court is empowered by statute to hear and decide a certain kind of case and to have its decision enforced. As mentioned previously, the court that has authority (jurisdiction) over wills and the administration of decedents' estates is often called the probate court.

In general, the jurisdiction of a probate court extends to the administration and distribution of a decedent's estate, including the primary function of proving that a certain legal document is a will. The powers and duties of the probate court are set out in the statutes or constitution of each state. A former statute on the subject is New Mexico's:

> *N. Mex. Comp. Laws § 16–4–10* Jurisdiction of the Probate Court
> The probate courts have concurrent [i.e., the same] jurisdiction with the district courts [i.e., the general trial court] of: (A) The probate of last wills and testaments, the granting, repealing, and revoking of letters testamentary and of administration, the appointment and removal of estate representatives, the settlement and allowance of accounts of estate representatives, and the determination of heirship; and (B) The hearing and determination of all controversies respecting wills, the right of executorship and administration, the duties, accounts, and settlements of estate representatives and any order, judgment, or decree of the probate courts with reference to those matters of which the probate courts have exclusive original jurisdiction.

Note that in this statute the probate court operates at the level of the district court. In other words, in New Mexico the probate court is a division of the state district courts instead of a separate court. In other states, the probate court may be a division of a system of courts (e.g., of the county courts, as in certain counties of Oregon) or a separate court (as in New York, where it is called the Surrogate's Court, or in Pennsylvania, where it is called the Orphan's Court).

Note also that the New Mexico statute enumerates the powers of the probate court. It may make orders or decrees (decisions) respecting wills and estate administration, but the court's jurisdiction is limited to these areas. No other state court has the power to assess the validity of a decedent's will or to decide matters concerning the estate. Although the probate court's jurisdiction is limited to powers given it by statutory law, it has "superior" jurisdiction in the matters on which it rules; that is, its decisions can be overruled only by the highest state court, often called the state supreme court.

Domicile

Domicile (legal home) has been defined as the place a person has adopted as her permanent home (place of habitation), and to which the person intends to return when absent. A probate court has jurisdiction over decedents who were domiciles, i.e., legal residents, of its territory. The terms *domicile* and *residence* are often confused and frequently used interchangeably, but they are distinguishable. **Domicile** is the legal home, the fixed permanent place of dwelling, whereas **residence** is a temporary place of dwelling. Therefore, a temporary

Jurisdiction
The authority by which a particular court is empowered by statute to decide a certain kind of case and to have its decision enforced.

Domicile
The legal home where a person has a true, fixed, and permanent place of dwelling and to which the person intends to return when absent.
Residence
The dwelling in which one temporarily lives or resides.

residence, such as a summer home, is not a domicile. A person can have only one domicile but could have more than one residence.

Example: Sam's permanent home is in Dayton, Ohio. He spends every winter at his condominium in Miami and two weeks each summer at a friend's cottage on Cape Cod. All three places are Sam's residences, but only the home in Dayton is his domicile.

Domicile, not residence, determines venue (see the next section). A permanent legal address is determined by where one lives, banks, goes to church, buys license plates, pays taxes, and votes. If an uncertainty does arise, e.g., if a person abandons his domicile in one place and has not yet taken up another before dying, probate proceedings are usually conducted in the county where the assets of the decedent's estate are located. Some cases and examples will illustrate how a court determines a person's domicile.

In the case of *Application of Winkler,* 171 A.D.2d 474 567, N.Y.S.2d 53 (1991), the court held that a person's domicile is "determined by the conduct of the person and all the surrounding circumstances which may be proven by acts and declarations." Documentation, such as a person's voting records, passport, marriage certificate, and driver's license, as well as witnesses' testimony can also be used to verify a person's true intention as to domicile. In the case of *In re Estate of Elson,* 120 Ill.App 3d 649, 76 Ill. Dec. 237, 458 N.E.2d 637, (1983), the court was asked to decide whether Illinois or Pennsylvania was the true and intended domicile of the decedent. The court stated:

1. "Domicile" has been defined as the place where a person has her true, permanent home to which she intends to return whenever she is absent.

2. "Domicile" is a continuing thing, and from the moment a person is born she must, at all times, have a domicile.

3. A person can have only one "domicile," and once a domicile is established, it continues until a new one is actually acquired.

4. To effect a "change of domicile," there must be actual abandonment of the first domicile, coupled with intent not to return to it, and physical presence must be established in another place with intention of making the last-acquired residence a permanent home.

5. "Domicile" is largely a matter of intention and, hence, is primarily a question of fact.

6. Once a "domicile" is established, it is presumed to continue, and the burden of proof in such cases rests on the party who attempts to establish that change in domicile occurred.

7. Very slight circumstances often decide questions of "domicile," and the determination is made based on the preponderance of evidence in favor of some particular place as a domicile and depends upon facts and circumstances of the particular case.

In reaching a decision, the court considered various actions of the decedent: in particular, when the decedent left Illinois five or six days prior to her death, she took most of her personal possessions with her, closed her bank accounts in Illinois, and established new accounts in Delaware near her new home in Pennsylvania. In addition, in an unmailed letter she penned the day before her death, she wrote that she had "moved to Pennsylvania." The court found that this evidence was sufficient to support a finding that the decedent intended to abandon her Illinois domicile permanently and acquire a permanent domicile in Pennsylvania, despite other evidence that she intended to stay in Pennsylvania for only one year and planned to return to Illinos.

Example: Whitney legally resides, i.e., is domiciled, in Kennebec County, Augusta, Maine. The probate court of Kennebec County in Maine would be the proper court to probate her will. Whitney moves her household goods from Augusta to Hartford, Connecticut, but dies before establishing legal residence there. If she still owned land in Augusta, the probate court of Kennebec County would remain the proper court to probate her will.

Example: Allisson owns real estate in more than one state, i.e., a house in Ohio, a farm in Kentucky, and a cottage in Minnesota, but only one residence is her domicile. Since the house in Ohio is Allisson's permanent address and Ohio is the state where she pays taxes, votes, and has a driver's license, Ohio would be Allisson's domicile state.

Venue

Venue is the particular place (either city or county) where a court having jurisdiction may hear and decide a case. Venue and jurisdiction are not interchangeable, although they are closely related. "Jurisdiction" is abstract, denoting the power or authority of a court to act; "venue" is concrete, denoting the physical place of a trial. "Venue" approximates the definition of territorial jurisdiction and will be used throughout this text to signify the location of the proper court, usually the county within a specific state.

In determining which probate court is the proper one to handle the decedent's estate, the question of the court's jurisdiction is primary. After that has been resolved, the question of venue arises. Usually, venue corresponds to the decedent's place of domicile (legal abode) or to the decedent's residence at death. In other words, the proper venue (place) for the probate administration of the estate of a deceased state resident is usually the county in which the decedent was domiciled at his death. The venue for out-of-state residents is generally the county in which the nonresident left property.

Example: Harold Wickes was living in Cook County, Chicago, Illinois, at the time of his death. The administration of his estate will be supervised by the probate (circuit) court of Cook County. Thus, the venue in this instance is Cook County. "Change of venue" means transferring the location of the court proceedings; a change of venue may be granted if a devisee of the will shows a good reason for the transfer to another location. If Harold's will gave a farm located in Gogebic County, Michigan, to his cousin, and the cousin could prove that Harold's actual domicile was Gogebic County, the venue of the probate proceedings would be changed to that county.

Example: Ralph Schollander wrote a will three years ago identifying himself as a resident "of the . . . County of Marion, State of Indiana." Last year he moved to St. Joseph County (Indiana) to live with his sister. Should Ralph die in St. Joseph County, venue for the probate of his will would be a question for the probate court of Marion County to decide. The court would have to consider, among other things, whether Ralph intended to give up permanent legal residence in Marion County and establish it in St. Joseph County (i.e., to remain there indefinitely).

An example of statutory regulation of venue is former Cal. Prob. Code § 301 (West 1956), Jurisdiction and Venue (now §§ 7050 and 7051):

Venue
The particular place, city or county, where a court having jurisdiction may hear and decide a case.

Wills must be proved and letters testamentary or of administration granted and administration of estates of decedent had, in the superior court:

(1) Of the county of which the decedent was a resident at the time of his death, wherever he may have died:

(2) Of the county in which the decedent died, leaving estate therein, he not being a resident of the state;

(3) Of any county in which he leaves estate, the decedent not being a resident of the state at the time of his death and having died out of the state or without leaving estate in the county in which he died; in either of which cases when the estate is in more than one county, the superior court of the county in which a petition for letters testamentary or of administration is first filed has exclusive jurisdiction of the administration of the estate. [Compare Uniform Probate Code § 1–303.]

In addition to its value in determining the venue of a probate proceeding, the fact of the decedent's domicile aids the court in establishing ***in rem* jurisdiction** over the estate's probate assets. Similarly, when two or more states are involved in the probate of a single will, the state that can claim the testator as its citizen will collect the greater share of the state inheritance or estate taxes. The fact of domicile controls not only the state's power to levy taxes, but also its right to collect taxes on the decedent's property passed by will. Therefore, the tax liability of an estate may vary noticeably, depending on the inheritance tax demands, if any, of the state in which the estate assets are situated.

Ancillary Administration or Ancillary Probate Administration

If at death the decedent-testator owns any real property (e.g., cottage, condominium, vacation home) in a state other than his domicile state and, in some cases, any tangible personal property in another state, his will must be admitted to probate in each state where the real property is located. These separate or secondary court proceedings are known as ancillary probate administration or simply **ancillary administration.** Ancillary administration is necessary because the court in the county of the decedent's domicile has no jurisdiction over real property located in another state, often referred to as the **"foreign state."** Furthermore, by admitting the will to probate in each state and holding ancillary administration there, any local creditors of the decedent are protected. The court in the case of *First National Bank of Brush, Colo. v. Blessing,* 231 Mo. App. 288, 98 S.W.2d 149 (1936), provided a good explanation of ancillary administration:

> It seems to be well-settled law that the administration of the estate of a person who dies owning property in different states may be had in each of the states dealing with the property of the estate having a local situs [location] therein. Administration in the state where a person is domiciled at the time of his death is deemed the principal or primary administration and is ordinarily termed the "domiciliary administration"; and, in the state other than where he is domiciled where he has property, the administration is termed "ancillary" or "auxiliary." Administration either in the state of the decedent's domicile or the state other than the decedent's domicile in which he left property affects persons and things within that state only.

Thus, when a person dies leaving real property in more than one state, not only are separate domiciliary and ancillary administrations required, but the property is administered under the laws of the state where it is located.

***In rem* jurisdiction**
The authority of the court over the decedent's property.

Ancillary administration
Additional administration used to dispose of and distribute that portion of the decedent's estate located in a state other than the decedent's domicile state.

Foreign state
Any state other than the decedent's domicile state.

Usually, the testator or the court of the state of domicile appoints a person, called an **ancillary administrator(trix),** to handle the administration in each state where the decedent's assets are located. Some states allow the personal representative of the domiciliary state to administer the ancillary proceedings. In such cases, the personal representative is also the ancillary administrator. However, state law often requires the ancillary administrator to be a resident of that state, thereby increasing the expense of ancillary administration. Exceptions are sometimes made to allow nonresident family members (e.g., the spouse of the testator) to serve as ancillary administrators, but at the same time, the court must take care to safeguard the rights of the creditors of the decedent who live in the foreign state. Section 3–203(g) of the Uniform Probate Code gives the domiciliary personal representative priority in being appointed the ancillary administrator. See Exhibit 3.3 for the various state requirements for personal representatives who want to be appointed the ancillary administrator in the foreign state. Consider the following examples.

Ancillary administrator(trix)
The personal representative appointed by the court to distribute that part of a decedent's estate located in a state other than the decedent's domicile state.

Exhibit 3.3 State Eligibility Requirements for Personal Representatives

Age Requirement

Over 18: AZ, CA, CT, DE, FL, GA, HI, ID, IL, IN, IA, KS, KY, LA, ME, MD, MA, MI, MN, MS, MO, NV, NH, NJ, NM, NY, NC, ND, OH, OK, OR, PA, RI, SC, SD, TN, TX, VT, VA, WA, WV, WI, WY
Over 19: AL
Over 21: AK, AR, CO, MT, NE, UT

Unsuitability Disqualifications

Legal disqualifications:
■ Felony or infamous crime conviction: AL, AR, DE, FL, IL, IN, LA, MD, MS, MO, NV, NY, NC, OK, OR, SD, TX, WA
■ Disbarred from practice of law: OR
■ Misdemeanor involving "moral turpitude": WA
Capacity disqualifications:
■ Mentally incapacitated: DE
■ Disabled: IL
■ Incapacitated: IN
■ Mentally ill, retarded, an alcoholic, or a spendthrift: IA
■ Bad moral character: LA
■ Mentally incompetent: MD
■ Not having "proper capacity": MA
■ Not of sound mind: MS, MO, WA
■ Decreed incompetent: NV, NC, OK, OR, SD, TX
■ Incompetent: NY

Nonresident Requirements

■ Nonresident must be approved by judge or consent to the jurisdiction of the state's court: HI, ID, MN, NH, PA
■ Nonresident must appoint a specific person for service of process including probate judge, secretary of state, court surrogate, register, or clerk of court: AR, CT, DE, NJ, TN, WV
■ Nonresident must appoint resident agent for service of process: IL, IN, KY, LA, ME, MD, MA, MI, MO, NC, OK, RI, SC, SD, TX, VT, WA, WI, WY
■ Nonresident must serve with co-administrator or resident fiduciary: or state prefers resident only: IA, MS, NV, TN, VA, WY
■ Nonresident may or can be executor only if named in will or if a spouse, child, parent, or relative of the decedent: FL, KS, KY, OH, VT, WV
■ All other states not listed allow the appointment of nonresidents

Example: Lina resides in Virginia and owns a summer cottage in North Carolina. Several years ago she mortgaged the cottage to a bank in Raleigh. Should she die without having paid the mortgage, the bank would have no notice of her death even though it is an "interested party" by virtue of being her creditor. For this reason, an ancillary administration of her North Carolina property is necessary. In North Carolina the ancillary administrator must be over 18, not declared incompetent or convicted of a felony, and, if a nonresident, must designate a resident agent for service of process.

Example: North Dakota is Benjamin's domicile. Most of his assets are in North Dakota, but he has a winter home in Georgia. In his will Benjamin appoints his wife, Alesha, his personal representative. Under Georgia law, Alesha could also be appointed ancillary administratrix to administer the assets in Georgia including the winter home.

The ancillary administration in the foreign state generally includes the following procedures:

1. Acceptance by the foreign state court of the will admitted to probate in the decedent-testator's domicile state.

2. Issuance of letters of authority, e.g., Letters Ancillary Testamentary, to the ancillary administrator that permit the real property to be transferred to the designated devisee named in the will if all creditors of the testator in the foreign state have been paid.

3. If any inheritance or estate taxes are imposed by the foreign state, these taxes must be paid to that state and not to the testator's domicile state.

If the decedent died intestate, then the persons entitled to the decedent's real property in the foreign state will be determined by that state's intestate succession statute. However, generally, all of the decedent's personal property, wherever located, will pass to the persons entitled to it according to the decedent's domicile state's intestate succession statute. Specific tasks of paralegals concerning ancillary administration are discussed in Chapter 12.

KEY TERMS

Letters testamentary	Tickler system	Jurisdiction	Ancillary
Letters of	Registrar	Domicile	administration
administration	Clerk	Residence	Foreign state
Bond	Probate (of a will)	Venue	Ancillary
Surety	Probate proceedings	*In rem* jurisdiction	administrator(trix)

REVIEW QUESTIONS

1. A personal representative is a fiduciary. What does that mean?
2. Who may act as a personal representative?
3. Why is a personal representative sometimes called an executor or an administrator?
4. What are Letters Testamentary and Letters of Administration and how do they differ?
5. Summarize the duties of a personal representative.
6. What are three ethical problems an attorney and paralegal face when drafting a client's will?
7. What are the general duties a paralegal may perform concerning wills, trusts, and estate administration?
8. What other titles besides probate court do states use to identify the court that supervises the administration of the decedent's estate?
9. How do the functions of a registrar and a court clerk differ?

10. Why are the terms *probate* and *probate proceedings* often confused? Explain.
11. Are domicile and venue the same thing? Explain.

CASE PROBLEMS

Problem 1

Alberto Gomez owns real and personal property in three states, California, New Mexico, and New York. Alberto is 102 years old and has outlived his only spouse and their three children. When he dies intestate, Alberto has no surviving family, i.e., blood relatives. Answer the following:

A. What facts would be required for you to determine Alberto's domicile state?
B. What is the difference between Alberto's domicile and his residence?
C. Where would the proper venue be for Alberto's estate administration?
D. If a conflict arises over which of two or three states is the decedent's domicile, how does the Uniform Probate Code resolve the problem? See U.P.C. § 3–202 and *Riley v. New York Trust Co.,* 315 U.S. 343, 62 S.Ct. 608, 86 L.Ed. 885 (1942).
E. Which state would determine how Alberto's property would be inherited? Caveat: Discuss both real and personal property. For personal property, see *Howard v. Reynolds,* 30 Ohio St.2d 214, 283 N.E.2d 629 (1972).

Problem 2

Maura Hanlon, legally a resident of Amarillo, Texas, dies while traveling in Waterford, Ireland. Maura owns a house in Amarillo and an apartment building in Tulsa, Oklahoma. Answer and explain each of the following:

A. In which state should Maura's will be probated?
B. Is an ancillary administration necessary in this case?
C. Whether Maura dies testate or intestate, is an ancillary administration still necessary?
D. What are the eligibility requirements for appointment of an ancillary administrator in the foreign state in this case?
E. Find and cite the section of the Uniform Probate Code that gives the domiciliary personal representative priority to be appointed the ancillary administrator.

12. When is an ancillary administration necessary and what is its purpose?
13. Who is authorized to act as an ancillary administrator in your state?

CHAPTER FOUR

THE LAW OF SUCCESSION: DEATH TESTATE OR INTESTATE

OBJECTIVES

After completing this chapter, you should be able to:

- Recognize, understand, and use the basic terms associated with testacy and intestacy.
- Understand the difference between orthodox (traditional) and U.P.C. terminology for gifts made by will, for persons named to receive such property, and for property conveyed according to intestate succession statutes.
- Read a will and identify the parties and gifts using both orthodox (traditional) and U.P.C. terminology.
- Recognize and identify lineal and collateral relationships and know the difference between them as they relate to the right to inherit a decedent's property under intestate succession law.
- Interpret state intestate succession statutes and determine who is entitled to receive what property under such laws.
- Know the difference between relationship to the decedent by consanguinity (by blood) and by affinity (by marriage) as it relates to the right to inherit a decedent's property under intestate succession laws.
- Understand the difference between the right of heirs of an intestate to take their share of the estate per capita or per stirpes.
- Understand the process of escheat (the right of the state to take the decedent's property).

OUTLINE

Scope of the Chapter

Death with a Will—Testacy
  Terminology Relating to Wills
  Types of Distributions—Gifts Made in a Will

Illustrating the Use of Testate Terminology
  The Facts

Death without a Will—Intestacy
  Terminology Relating to Intestacy
  Intestate Succession Laws

Inheritance Rights of Family Members
  Rights of a Surviving Spouse
  Effect of Divorce and Marriage on a Spouse's Rights
  Rights of Children (Issue)
  Additional Rights or Protection for a Surviving Spouse
    and Children

Illustrating the Use of Intestate Terminology
  The Facts

Advantages and Disadvantages of Having a Will
  Advantages of a Will
  Disadvantages of a Will

SCOPE OF THE CHAPTER

Chapters 1 and 2 defined the basic terms associated with death with a will (testacy) and death without a will (intestacy) and identified the fiduciaries (personal representative, executor, administrator, trustee, and guardian) who are named in a will or appointed by the probate court. By now you are familiar with these and other terms such as decedent, intestate, and testator or testatrix. If your memory needs refreshing, review these terms in the opening chapters.

Before the specific procedures for drafting wills and trusts and completing the forms necessary for the administration of a decedent's estate can be understood and executed, you will need to add still more terms to your basic vocabulary. This chapter explains the terms associated with the persons and proceedings involved in the laws of succession. The laws of succession deal with the ways property of a deceased person who dies with or without a will is distributed and to whom. Next, two sets of terminology, orthodox (traditional) and the Uniform Probate Code, that are used in practice and by legal writers are identified, defined, and discussed. Both will be used throughout the remainder of the text.

First to be discussed are terms related to testacy—death with a will. A sample will is included with an illustrative review of the terminology. Next, terms that relate to death without a will—intestacy—are discussed, and the use of intestate terminology is also illustrated. The chapter concludes with a list of the advantages and disadvantages of wills.

DEATH WITH A WILL—TESTACY

When death occurs, it is necessary to determine whether the decedent died testate or intestate. These terms refer to death with a valid will **(testacy)** or without a valid will **(intestacy).** The difference in the way and to whom property is distributed between testacy and intestacy is significant whenever the decedent's will is challenged, for example, in a **will contest.** If the challenge is successful and the will is declared invalid, the state intestate succession statute determines who receives the decedent's property. These recipients may be entirely different than those individuals named by the maker of the will.

When a will exists, your training, experience, and investigatory skills should enable you to determine, with verification by your supervising attorney, whether the will is valid, e.g., whether it was properly formed and executed. If it is not valid, you must be able to analyze and accurately apply your state's intestate succession statute to determine to whom the property will be distributed. Even when a will exists, its distribution provisions may not dispose of some probate property; for example, the will may not include a residuary clause. In such cases, the forgotten, overlooked, or excluded property not disposed of by the will passes instead according to the proper state's intestate succession statute. Before learning how to collect the requisite information and prepare the preliminary draft of a client's will, you must understand certain basic terms.

Terminology Relating to Wills

In general, two different sets of terminology are used in dealing with wills:

Testacy
Death with a valid will.
Intestacy
Death without a valid will.
Will contest
Litigation to overturn a decedent's will.

Uniform Probate Code (U.P.C.)

A uniform law available for adoption by the states to modernize and improve the efficiency of the administration of a decedent's estate.

■ *Orthodox or traditional terminology.* Orthodox terminology refers to the traditional words relating to wills and probate matters, which were used universally before the adoption into law of the **Uniform Probate Code (U.P.C.).**

■ *Uniform Probate Code (U.P.C.) terminology.* The Uniform Probate Code has presented for adoption an alternative plan for procedures and new terminology for wills and estate administration. Close to half of the states have either adopted or modified the U.P.C. or use the terminology it recommends. Most states use a combination of U.P.C. and orthodox terminology. The following states have adopted the Uniform Probate Code: Alaska, Arizona, Colorado, Florida, Hawaii, Idaho, Kentucky, Maine, Michigan, Minnesota, Montana, Nebraska, New Mexico, North Dakota, and Utah. Exhibit 4.1 lists both the traditional and the U.P.C. terms used in testacy and intestacy cases.

Wills can be divided into four basic types and a separate document called a living will:

1. *Holographic (also called an olographic) will.* A holographic will is a will written in the maker's own handwriting. About half of the states and the U.P.C. allow holographic wills, and generally, such wills do not require witnesses to be valid (see Exhibit 4.2). In the case of *In re Mulkins' Estate,* 17 Ariz. App. 179, 496 P.2d 605 (1972), the court held that the handwritten words by the decedent on a publisher's will form was a valid holographic will. Many states require some or all of the following for a holographic will to be valid:

Exhibit 4.1 Orthodox (Traditional) and U.P.C. Terminology Compared

Testacy Terminology	Orthodox	U.P.C.
Person appointed to administer an estate when there is a will	Executor (man) Executrix (woman)	Personal representative
Gift of money by will	Legacy	Devise
Gift of personal property by will (other than money)	Bequest	Devise
Gift of real property by will	Devise	Devise
Recipient of money by will	Legatee	Devisee
Recipient of personal property by will (other than money)	Beneficiary	Devisee
Recipient of real property by will	Devisee	Devisee

Intestacy Terminology	Orthodox	U.P.C.
Person appointed to administer an estate when there is no will	Administrator (man) Administratrix (woman)	Personal representative
Person entitled by statute to real property of intestate	Heir or heir-at-law	Heir
Person entitled by statute to personal property of intestate	Distributee or next-of-kin	Heir
Passage of an intestate's property to the state when the decedent has no surviving blood relatives (kin)	Escheat	Escheat

Testacy or Intestacy Terminology	Orthodox	U.P.C.
Person, other than creditors, entitled to the real or personal property of a decedent by will or through intestate succession	No all-inclusive word	Successor
Person, other than a creditor or purchaser, who has actually received real or personal property from the decedent's personal representative	No all-inclusive word	Distributee

- The will must be dated.
- The will must be "entirely" handwritten by the testator.
- The testator must have a clear intent to make a will.
- The testator's signature must be placed in a specific part of the will, e.g., at the "foot" or end of the will.

Typewritten wills are not recognized as holographic wills in the United States.

2. *Nuncupative (oral) will.* A **nuncupative will** is an oral will spoken in the presence of witnesses; such a will is valid only under exceptional circumstances, such as the impending death of the person "speaking" the will. Nuncupative wills are prohibited in some states (see Exhibit 4.2), but when they are allowed, they can generally pass only a limited amount of personal property of the speaker-testator. Some states allow nuncupative (oral) wills such as soldiers' and sailors' wills made during military service in time of war, but a few states do not require formal hostilities; see Va. Code § 64.1–53; and N.Y. E.P.T.L. 3–2.2(b). The Uniform Probate Code does not allow oral wills (U.P.C. § 2–502). At the present time, an oral statement on a tape recording intended to be a will is not a valid will, as illustrated by the decision in *Matter of Reed's Estate,* 672 P.2d 829 (Wyo. 1983).

Nuncupative will
An oral will.

3. *Statutory Will.* A **statutory will** fulfills all the state's mandatory formal requirements for a will including:

- The will must be written or typed.
- The will must be signed by the testator.
- The will must be formally attested to and signed by two or three witnesses.

Statutory will
A fill-in-the-blanks type of will that is authorized by statute in a few states.

It is a "fill-in-the-blanks" type of will that is authorized by statute in the testator's domicile state. California, Louisiana, Maine, Michigan, and Wisconsin have developed their own unique statutory wills (see Exhibits 4.2, 6.8, and 6.9). Two other states, Massachusetts and New Mexico, have adopted the Uniform Statutory Will Act. Exhibit 4.3 shows the Uniform Statutory Will established by the act.

Uniform Statutory Will Act

a. In the Uniform Statutory Will Act form, the maker of the will fills in blanks naming herself or himself as testator and the appropriate fiduciaries, i.e., personal representative, guardians, and trustees, as needed. The remainder of the form includes the testimonium clause which the testator signs and dates, the attestation clause which the two attending witnesses sign, and the self proved notarization clause signed, dated, and sealed by the notary public.

b. Provisions for the dispositions of the testator's property are not included on the form but instead all such provisions are incorporated by reference to the Act. The following are provisions of the Act: If the sole survivor of the testator is the surviving spouse, such spouse receives the entire estate. If the survivors are the spouse and children, then the surviving spouse receives the homestead and the greater of one-half of the remainder of the estate or $300,000. After the spouse's share is determined, the remaining balance of the estate is placed in a trust which pays the income of the trust to the spouse for life and then distributes the remainder to the children. If there is no surviving spouse but there are children, they receive the entire estate in equal shares with the share of any minor children placed in a trust.

Exhibit 4.2 Types of Valid Wills by State

	Holographic	Nuncupative	State's Statutory Will Form	Uniform Statutory Will Act
Alabama	Prohibited (2)	Prohibited		
Alaska	Valid	1,5		
Arizona	Valid	Prohibited		
Arkansas	Valid	Prohibited		
California	Valid	Prohibited	X	
Colorado	Valid	Prohibited		
Connecticut	Prohibited	Prohibited		
Delaware	Prohibited	Prohibited		
Florida	Prohibited (2)	Prohibited		
Georgia	Prohibited	3, 5		
Hawaii	Prohibited	Prohibited		
Idaho	Valid	Prohibited		
Illinois	Prohibited	Prohibited		
Indiana	Prohibited (2)	4, 5		
Iowa	Prohibited	Prohibited		
Kansas	Prohibited	3, 5		
Kentucky	Valid	Prohibited		
Louisiana	Valid	Prohibited	X	
Maine	Valid	Prohibited	X	
Maryland	Prohibited (1)	Prohibited		
Massachusetts	Prohibited	1		X
Michigan	Valid	Prohibited	X	
Minnesota	Prohibited	Prohibited		
Mississippi	Valid	3, 5		
Missouri	Prohibited	4, 5		
Montana	Valid	Prohibited		
Nebraska	Valid	Prohibited		
Nevada	Valid	3, 5		
New Hampshire	Prohibited	5		
New Jersey	Valid	Prohibited		
New Mexico	Prohibited	Prohibited		X
New York	Prohibited (1)	1		
North Carolina	Valid	3, 5		
North Dakota	Valid	Prohibited		
Ohio	Prohibited	3, 5		
Oklahoma	Valid	1, 5		
Oregon	Prohibited	Prohibited		
Pennsylvania	Valid	Prohibited		
Rhode Island	Prohibited	Prohibited		
South Carolina	Prohibited	Prohibited		
South Dakota	Valid	1, 4, 5		
Tennessee	Valid	4, 5		
Texas	Valid	3, 5		
Utah	Valid	Prohibited		
Vermont	Prohibited	5		
Virginia	Valid	1		
Washington	Prohibited	1, 3, 5		
West Virginia	Valid	1		
Wisconsin	Prohibited	Prohibited	X	
Wyoming	Valid	Prohibited		

1. Prohibited except for mariners at sea or for military exceptions, e.g., armed forces members in actual service or during armed conflict.
2. Prohibited unless it meets execution requirements, e.g., witnesses.
3. Applies to anyone during their last illness.
4. Applies to anyone in imminent peril of death and who dies from that peril.
5. Prohibited unless declared in the presence of witnesses, reduced to writing, and/or probated within statutory time periods.

Exhibit 4.3   Uniform Statutory Will

....

I, _____ , of the City of _____ , and State of _____ , declare this to be my Last Will and hereby revoke all of my prior wills and codicils.

1. I direct that my testamentary estate be disposed of in accordance with the _____ Uniform Statutory Will Act, as in effect on the date of execution of this will.

2. I appoint _____ as personal representative of my estate under this will. If a trust becomes applicable under the provision of the Act, I appoint _____ as trustee hereunder. If either of them does not serve, or at any time ceases to serve, in either capacity, I appoint _____ to serve in the vacant capacity or capacities. I appoint _____ as guardian and conservator of my minor children.

I, _____ , the testator, sign my name to this instrument this _____ day of _____ , 19 _____ , and being first duly sworn, do hereby declare to the undersigned authority that I sign and execute this instrument as my Last Will and that I (sign it willingly) (willingly direct another to sign for me) (cross out the one of these two alternatives that is inapplicable), that I execute it as my free and voluntary act for the purposes therein expressed, and that I am 18 years of age or older, of sound mind, and under no constraint or undue influence.

_____ Testator

We, _____ and _____ the witnesses, sign our names to this instrument, being first duly sworn, and do hereby declare to the undersigned authority that the testator signs and executes this instrument as (his) (her) (cross out the inapplicable word or phrase in each of these instances), and that each of us, in the presence and hearing of the testator, hereby signs this will as witness to the testator's signing, and that to the best of our knowledge the testator is 18 years of age or older, of sound mind, and under no constraint or undue influence.

_____ Witness

_____ Witness

State of _____

County of _____

Subscribed, sworn to and acknowledged before me by _____ , the testator, and subscribed and sworn to before me by _____ and _____ , witnesses, this _____ day of _____ , 19 _____ .

(Seal)   (Signed) _____

_____
(Notary public)

_____

Source: The Judge Advocate General's School, U.S. Army, JA 262, Legal Assistance Wills Guide (2–29; 2–30) (May 1993).

---

c. Some variations can be made in the Uniform Statutory Will such as allowing the testator to include specific legacies within the Uniform Will and to determine the duration of the testamentary trust and the distribution of the trust income or principal. Also the Uniform Will makes it possible for spouses with large estates to shelter 1.2 million dollars of combined assets from federal estate taxation by incorporating appropriate trust provisions into the Uniform Statutory Will.

4. *Joint or mutual will.* When one document is made the will of two persons (usually spouses) and is jointly signed by them, a joint will is created. The joint

will is probated twice—on the death of each spouse. Mutual wills are the separate wills of two persons who make identical reciprocal provisions in each will. Many problems are created by these wills, especially when one co-maker dies and the other decides to make a different will or wishes to revoke the original joint or mutual will. Most attorneys do not recommend or use joint or mutual wills.

Living will. A **living will** is generally a separate legal document from the standard will. The living will governs the withholding or withdrawal of life-sustaining treatment from the maker of this will in the event of an incurable or irreversible condition that will cause death within a short time, and the maker is no longer able to make decisions regarding her medical treatment. For further discussion and an example of a living will, see Chapter 7.

Living will

A document, separate from a will, that expresses a person's wish to be allowed to die a natural death and not be kept alive by artificial means.

Types of Dispositions—Gifts Made in a Will

A will's dispositions are the various ways property is conveyed by the will. Dispositions include gifts that are called bequests, legacies, or devises.

Bequest, Legacy, or Devise

In traditional terminology, a bequest or legacy is a gift of personal property, and a devise is a gift of real property. When the gifts are made by a will, they are called a specific legacy or a specific devise. In cases in which a testator has mistakenly used the wrong term in connection with real or personal estate property, e.g., "I bequeath my home to my daughter, Sarah," or "I devise my books and paintings to my son, Benjamin," the courts have consistently upheld such gifts because of the unmistakable intention of the testator. Therefore, the terms may be used interchangeably or applied to either real or personal property if the context of the will clearly indicates that such was the testator's intention. The states that have adopted the Uniform Probate Code use one term, *devise,* to include all gifts of real or personal property by will. The next paragraphs explain the following categories of dispositions of a will: specific legacy, specific devise, demonstrative legacy, general legacy, and residuary legacy or devise.

Specific Legacy. A specific legacy (also called a specific bequest or, in states that have adopted the Uniform Probate Code, a specific devise) is a gift of a particular item of personal property or a gift of a class of property in a will.

Examples: In his will, John Williams states:

1. "I give my 1994 Buick to my daughter, Marilyn Williams, if she survives me."

2. "I give my gun and stamp collections to my son, Henry Williams, if he survives me."

3. "I give my grand piano and all my sheet music to my niece, Linda Anderson, if she survives me."

4. "I give one-half of all of the rest of my tangible personal property, that has not otherwise been specifically mentioned heretofore in this will, to my spouse, Elizabeth Williams, if she survives me. If my said spouse, Elizabeth Williams, does not survive me, I give the above-mentioned property to my children, Marilyn Williams and Henry Williams, in equal shares." (This is an example of a gift of a class of property.)

Specific Devise.   A specific devise is a gift of real property in a will. In states that have adopted the Uniform Probate Code, a specific devise includes a gift of real or personal property in a will.

Real property is land or buildings owned by the decedent (testator) in sever-alty, i.e., single ownership, or as a co-owner in a tenancy in common. Unlike title to personal property, which passes to the personal representative (executor or administrator) upon the testator's death, the title to real property passes directly to the heirs or devisees when death occurs. The personal representative has the right to devest (take away) the real property from the heirs or devisees and sell it, either according to the terms of the will or by an order from the court, when it is necessary to pay creditors' claims or death taxes. However, in most states, personal property of the decedent is the primary source of the funds required to pay these estate debts (see the discussion below).

Example: In his will, John Williams states: "I give my homestead at 4645 Fair Hills Lane, City of Bloomingdale, County of Nobles, State of Indiana, and legally described as "Lot 7, Block 4, of Hillstrom's Addition to Stone Valley" to my spouse, Elizabeth Williams, if she survives me. If she fails to survive me, I give the hereinbefore described homestead to my son, Henry Williams, if he survives me."

Demonstrative Legacy.   A demonstrative legacy is a gift of a specific monetary amount to be paid from the proceeds of the sale of a particular item of property or from some identifiable fund.

Examples: In his will, John Williams states:

1. "I give $2,000 to be paid from the *sale* of my U.S. savings bonds to my nephew, Daniel Anderson, if he survives me."

2. "I give $5,000 to be paid out of my savings account on deposit in First State Bank, 1204 Main Street, City of Redwood Falls, County of Morgan, State of Oregon, to my niece, Linda Anderson, if she survives me."

A demonstrative legacy differs from a specific legacy in that if the fund from which the demonstrative legacy is to be paid has diminished or is nonexistent when the testator dies, it can come out of estate funds the same as a general legacy. A demonstrative legacy differs from a general legacy in that it is not subject to unpaid debts as a general legacy is, but instead is used to pay the debts like a specific legacy (see the discussion of abatement below).

Because demonstrative legacies are similar to both specific legacies and general legacies in some respects, distinguishing between them can be difficult and lead to confusion. Therefore, drafters seldom include demonstrative legacies in wills. The court in the case of *In re Jeffcott's Estate,* 186 So.2d 80 (Fla.App. 1966), identifies and distinguishes general and demonstrative legacies.

General Legacy.   A general legacy (also called a pecuniary bequest) is a gift of a fixed amount of money from the general assets of the estate or an amount of money derived from a source established in the estate by a calculated formula.

Examples: In his will, John Williams states:

1. "I give the sum of $20,000 to my niece, Linda Anderson, if she survives me."

2. "I give one-half of all the value of the stock I own at the time of my death to my daughter, Marilyn Williams, if she survives me." (Calculations are necessary to determine the actual amount Marilyn will receive.)

Residuary Legacy or Devise.   A gift of all the testator's personal property not otherwise effectively disposed of by a will is a residuary legacy, and a gift of all the real property not disposed of is a residuary devise.

A residuary clause distributes the remaining assets (the residue) of the decedent's (testator's) estate after all other gifts in the will have been distributed. A residuary clause is the most important clause in a will because it generally passes the bulk of the decedent's estate after the payment of debts, taxes, and costs of administration and the distribution of specific, demonstrative, and general legacies. It is essential that every will include a residuary clause; otherwise all remaining assets, whether inadvertently overlooked, omitted, forgotten, or acquired after execution of the current will, will pass through intestate succession statutes. Clearly, this would not reflect the intent of the will's maker since it defeats the will's purpose.

Example: In his will, John Williams states: "I give all the rest, residue, and remainder of my estate, including all real and personal property wherever located that is not previously disposed of by this will, to my wife, Elizabeth Williams, if she survives me. If she does not survive me, I give this, my residuary estate, to my children, Marilyn Williams and Henry Williams, in equal shares."

If the decedent does not include any specific, demonstrative, or general legacies in the will, a gift by John Williams that states "I give all my real and personal property to my daughter, Marilyn Williams" acts as a residuary clause.

If any beneficiaries of the will, especially those named in the residuary clause, predecease the testator, the will should be reviewed and new beneficiaries added to avoid having the property in that clause pass through intestate succession. These changes can be accomplished by adding a codicil to the will or by including successor beneficiaries in the residuary clause.

Another important function of the residuary clause is that after any intestate property of the decedent, it serves as the next, and generally the major, source of payment of the decedent's debts, death taxes, and funeral, burial, and administration expenses. If property (funds) from the residue is insufficient to pay these debts and taxes, other gifts in the will are used to satisfy these obligations (see Abatement below).

Ademption, Lapses, and Abatement
The gifts (legacies or devises) distributed by will can be affected by ademption, lapses, and abatement.

Ademption

The intentional act of the testator to revoke, recall, or cancel a gift made through the will.

Ademption.   **Ademption** is the intentional act of the testator to revoke, recall, or cancel a gift made through the will or to satisfy the beneficiary by executing (delivering) the gift while living or substituting a different item for the gift. As a result, the beneficiary or devisee does not receive the gift through the will, nor does other property of the estate pass to the beneficiary or devisee as a substitute for the "adeemed" gift, unless the testator so indicated in the will. Of the three types of legacies or devises, only the specific legacy (or specific devise) is subject to ademption.

Ademption can occur by extinction or by satisfaction. Ademption by extinction occurs when the property is either nonexisting (destroyed by storm, fire, and the like) at the time of the testator's death or is given or sold by the testator to someone other than the person named in the will.

Examples:

1. In her will, Elizabeth has named Arnold to receive her champion thorough-bred racehorse, Secretary. Secretary dies before Elizabeth. The gift of the horse is "adeemed" by extinction.

2. In her will, Elizabeth has named Arnold to receive the horse, but she sells the horse before she dies. Again, the gift of the horse is "adeemed."

See *Shriners Hospital v. Stahl,* 610 S.W.2d 147 (Tex. 1980), in which the court ruled that a specific devise of property was "adeemed" when the testatrix sold the property before her death, and the proceeds of the sale passed under the residuary clause of her will.

Ademption by satisfaction occurs when the testator, while living, gives the gift to the named beneficiary in the will with the intent that the gift will not be replaced.

Example: In her will, Elizabeth has named Benedict to receive her Renoir painting. Elizabeth decides to give Benedict the painting on his birthday. When she delivers the painting to him, Elizabeth satisfies this specific legacy by ademption.

The following former California statute now combined in §§ 6174 and 6409 illustrates the ademption procedure:

Cal. Prob. Code § 1050   Gift before Death

A gift before death shall be considered as an ademption of a bequest or devise of the property given; but such gift shall not be taken as an advancement to an heir or as an ademption of a general legacy unless such intention is expressed by the testator in the grant or otherwise in writing, or unless the donee acknowledges it in writing to be such. [Compare U.P.C. §§ 2–606 and 2–609.]

Lapses.   A **lapse** is the failure to pass a gift in a will because the beneficiary (legatee) or devisee dies before the testator. This causes the gift in the will to lapse and to fall into the residue of the estate *unless* the will provides for an alternate beneficiary or a statute provides for the gift's distribution. Such a state statute, called an antilapse statute, provides that the gift goes to the decedent beneficiary's children or heirs who survive the testator. The antilapse statutes of Illinois, Mississippi, and Texas only pass the gift to the beneficiary's heirs when the beneficiary is the child of the testator. Most states have expanded the eligible beneficiaries who can receive the gift according to their statute, but no state includes the spouse of a beneficiary who dies prior to the testator. Section 2–603 of the Uniform Probate Code allows the antilapse statute to apply to gifts given to grandparents of the testator. If a testator wants to avoid the application of an antilapse statute, the words in the following clause would accomplish that end:

> "I give my Picasso painting to my daughter, Irene Benson, if she shall survive me."

If Irene dies before the testator, an antilapse statute would not apply for the benefit of Irene's children or heirs. Instead the gift, e.g., the Picasso painting, becomes part of the residue of the estate and is passed to the persons named as beneficiaries in the residuary clause of the will.

On the other hand, if the testator wants a successor to receive the gift if the beneficiary predeceases the testator, the clause would state:

> ". . . to Irene Benson, if she survives me, if she does not survive me, to my son, Howard Benson."

Lapses
Failure to distribute a gift in a will because the beneficiary or devisee dies before the testator.

Abatement

The process of determining the order in which gifts made by the testator in the will shall be applied to the payment of the decedent-testator's debts, taxes, and expenses.

Abatement.   **Abatement** is the process of determining the order in which gifts (legacies and devises) made by the testator in the will shall be applied to the payment of the decedent-testator's debts, taxes, and expenses. If required, such payments may and most assuredly will cause the gifts made in the will to be reduced or even eliminated. The need for abatement arises when there are insufficient assets in the testator's estate to pay all the decedent's death taxes, funeral, burial, and administration expenses, and other creditors' claims that must be paid before the remaining estate is distributed to beneficiaries and devisees. State statutes list the order in which the various assets and categories of gifts (legacies and devises) are used to pay these debts and taxes: first, any intestate property not disposed of by the will; second, residuary assets; third, general legacies and devises; fourth, demonstrative legacies; and last, specific legacies and devises.

Example: In the examples earlier in this chapter, John Williams made specific legacies (his car, gun and stamp collections, piano and sheet music, and all of the rest of his tangible personal property); a specific devise (his home); demonstrative legacies (sums of money from the sale of bonds or from an identifiable fund); general legacies (cash and money from a calculated source); and a final residuary gift. John dies. Before any of the property listed in the will can be distributed, John's debts, expenses, and taxes due must be paid. The gifts made in the will, with the exception of the homestead, are used according to the priority order of payment listed in the preceding paragraph.

This arrangement or ranking of testamentary gifts into a certain order to be used for the payment of debts is called **marshaling the assets** of the estate, and the assets used for payment are said to "abate." Generally, personal property is the source of the funds used to pay debts, but, if necessary, real property must be devested from devisees or heirs by the personal representative and sold to pay the decedent's creditors. In a few states, the decedent's personal property in all categories must be used first before any real property is used to pay debts and taxes due (see Mass. Gen. Laws Ann. ch. 202 § 1). Other states only require that all personal property in each category be used for payments prior to the use of real property within the category (see Tex. Prob. Code § 322B). Today, the prevailing trend is to use gifts of real and personal property within the same category equally; see Cal. Prob. Code § 10000; N.Y. E.P.T.L. § 13–1.3(b); and U.P.C. § 3–902. When property within each category "abates" to pay decedent's debts, the gifts are used for payment on a prorated basis.

Marshaling the assets

The arrangement or ranking of testamentary gifts into a certain order to be used for the payment of debts.

Example: Sydney makes the following testamentary gifts: $2,000 cash to Rita, a homestead valued at $45,000 to Ralph, and the residue (valued at $8,000) to Peter. Expenses, debts, and taxes amount to $12,000. The residue assets would first be applied to payment of expenses, debts, and taxes. Thus, Peter would lose all his $8,000. Second, the general gift, i.e., the sum of money left to Rita ($2,000) would be applied. Rita would lose all her $2,000. Third, Ralph would be required to pay the remaining deficiency of $2,000, or, depending on the state, the homestead may have to be sold and $2,000 of the proceeds of the sale used to pay the deficiency. Ralph would get the remainder of the proceeds of the sale. If a spouse survives the decedent, however, the spouse will receive the statutory share of the decedent's estate before any of the other named devisees receive their gifts through the will.

Example: Oscar dies, leaving an estate valued at $175,000. It consists of a homestead owned in his own name valued at $100,000, $30,000 in cash in a savings account, $30,000 in stocks and bonds, and $15,000 in household furnishings. Oscar leaves his home and $10,000 in cash to his spouse, Evelyn. He leaves $10,000 in cash to his nephew, Phil, and $10,000 to his niece, Trudy. The administration and funeral expenses, death taxes, and creditors' claims (debts) amount to $60,000. Thus, since these obligations must be paid first (have priority), only $115,000 remains to be distributed among the named devisees.

In the example of Oscar's will, above, because not enough assets remain in the estate to distribute the assets as Oscar intended (specified in the will), the state statute on abatement will determine which devisees get what property. If Oscar's estate were probated in California, it would have to adhere to the California abatement statute. This statute is typical of other state laws that determine the order of payment when the decedent's assets are insufficient:

> *Cal. Prob. Code § 21402*   Order of Abatement.
> (a) Shares of beneficiaries abate in the following order:
> (1) Property not disposed of by the instrument.
> (2) Residuary gifts.
> (3) General gifts to persons other than the transferor's relatives.
> (4) General gifts to the transferor's relatives.
> (5) Specific gifts to persons other than the transferor's relatives.
> (6) Specific gifts to the transferor's relatives.
> (b) For purposes of this section, a "relative" of the transferor is a person to whom property would pass from the transferor under Section 6401 or 6402 (intestate succession) if the transferor died intestate and there were no other person having priority.

ILLUSTRATING THE USE OF TESTATE TERMINOLOGY

To better understand the meaning and usage of the terms discussed above, read the following facts and the will in Exhibit 4.4.

The Facts

Sheila M. Swanson, desiring that all the property she owns be distributed at death according to her wishes, draws up a will specifying the persons to whom the property in her estate shall be distributed and which items of real and personal property will go to each person. She leaves a fur coat along with all her other clothing to a sister, Myrtle Jones. Sheila also gives $20,000 to each of her children living at her death. To a close cousin, John Stewart, Sheila leaves her one acre of land in Northern County. The sum of $100,000 is left in trust for her surviving grandchildren, to be administered by Glen Howard of the Fullservice Bank. The rest of her estate is given to her husband, Frank, but if he does not survive her, then her surviving children receive the property in equal shares. In the event that Sheila and her husband die at the same time (as in a common accident) before her children are adults, she appoints her sister, Myrtle, to take care of them. Viola Larson is named to oversee the management and distribution of the estate according to the dictates of the will, which is signed and witnessed by Charles Larson and Althea Gibbons.

Exhibit 4.4   Last Will and Testament of Sheila M. Swanson

I, Sheila M. Swanson, of the City of Winslow, in the County of Northern, and State of Maine, being of sound mind and memory, and not acting under duress, menace, fraud, or undue influence of any person whatsoever, do make, publish, and declare this instrument to be my Last Will and Testament. I do hereby cancel, revoke, and annul all former wills and testaments or codicils.

First: I direct that my valid debts, funeral, and burial expenses be paid out of my estate as soon after my death as can conveniently be done;

Specific legacy	→
Specific devise	→
General legacy	→
Demonstrative legacy	→
Residuary legacy or devise	→

Second: I give my fur coat and all other personal clothing to my sister, Myrtle Jones;

Third: I give my one acre of land with the following legal description, "Lot 1, Block 4, Brauer Addition," located in Northern County to my cousin, John Stewart, and his heirs;

Fourth: I give $20,000 to each of my children living at my death;

Fifth: I give $100,000 from the sale of my Picasso painting entitled "Self Portrait" to Mr. Glen Howard of the Fullservice Bank to hold in trust for the benefit of my grandchildren. See attached testamentary trust. (For an example of such trusts, see Chapter 9.)

Sixth: All the rest, residue, and remainder of my estate, real and personal of any kind, of which I die possessed or to which I am entitled at the time of my death, I give to my husband, Frank, if he survives me, and if he does not survive me, or we die in a common accident, I give this my residuary estate to my children that survive me in equal shares;

Seventh: In the event of a common accident in which both my husband and I die, I nominate and appoint my sister, Myrtle Jones, to be the personal and property guardian over any of my minor children living at the time of our deaths;

Eighth: Finally, I nominate and appoint Viola Larson to be the executrix of this my last will and testament and direct that she not be required to give any bond or security for the proper discharge of her duties.

IN TESTIMONY WHEREOF I hereunto set my hand and seal on this _____ day of _____ , in the Year Nineteen Hundred and _____ .

[Signature]   *Sheila M. Swanson*
[Address]   *11712 Sundown Avenue*

The foregoing instrument, consisting of two pages, including this page, was, at the date hereof, signed, sealed, published, and declared by Sheila M. Swanson, the testatrix above named, at _____ in the State of _____ as and for her last will and testament, in our presence, who, in her presence, at her request, and in the presence of each other hereunto set our names as witnesses.

Names
Althea Gibbons
_____
Witness

Addresses
4656 Gaywood Drive
_____

Charles Larson
_____
Witness

401 Elm Street
_____

[Signed by two witnesses]

Review of Terminology

If Ms. Swanson dies now, her death will occur *testate* because she has left a will. For her will to have validity as a written legal document directing the distribution and disposition of an estate on death, it must be *executed* carefully to comply with the requirements established by statutes or common law controlling *testate succession*. The fact that Mr. Larson and Ms. Gibbons were *attesting* and *subscribing witnesses* to the will is an example of such statutory control.

Because Sheila Swanson as *testatrix* can change her mind and dispose of her estate prior to death in any manner she chooses, she might execute a *codicil,* i.e., a written modification of the will that, while not canceling the will, could add to, delete from, or otherwise change various provisions to keep them up-to-date with Sheila's wishes. She also retains the option to cancel or destroy the will and either to substitute a new one in its place or to decide never to make a new will, in which event she would die *intestate.*

The *beneficiaries* under the will are Sheila's children and grandchildren living at her death, her sister Myrtle, cousin John, and husband Frank; these are the persons to whom she intends to leave her estate. Before any of the interests pass to these recipients, the will must be *probated,* declared by a court to be a valid testamentary disposition. This procedure for approving a will and overseeing its administration is discussed in detail in later chapters.

The following discussion illustrates the use of both the orthodox and the U.P.C. terminology. The first term listed is the orthodox term; the corresponding U.P.C. term is placed in parentheses.

The distribution of Sheila's one acre of land is a *devise,* the gift of real property by will, and its taker, cousin John, is a *devisee* (or *successor*). Sheila devised the land to him. The $20,000 to be received by Sheila's surviving children, a gift of money, is a *legacy* (*devise*), Sheila's children being the *legatees* (*devisees* or *successors*) of this gift of money. Myrtle, because she is receiving personal property under the will, is a *beneficiary* (*devisee* or *successor*), but the distribution of the fur coat and other clothing to her, since it is not money, is known as a *bequest* (*devise*). Sheila bequeathed (devised) the clothing to her. Although it is important to keep the latter distinction in mind, in modern practice the terms *bequest* and *legacy* are used interchangeably. Generally, if the orthodox terms such as "bequeath" or "bequest" are used in a will, they stand for a gift of any personal property, including money. In preparing wills today, however, most attorneys prefer to use the phrase "I give" in place of the words "I bequeath" or "I devise."

The $100,000 earmarked for the grandchildren constitutes a *testamentary trust* (i.e., a trust created by the will) with Mr. Howard of the bank as its administrator, the *trustee.* Since Viola Larson has been named to handle the estate, she is its *executrix* (*personal representative*). Had Viola's husband, Charles, been given the responsibility instead, he would be the *executor* (*personal representative*) of the estate. Sheila's sister, Myrtle, has a role beyond that of a *beneficiary* (*successor*). As the person designated to care for the testatrix's minor children at her death, if Sheila's husband, Frank, is also deceased, Myrtle is a *guardian* for Sheila's children.

⚖ ASSIGNMENT 4.1

Read the following will, then answer the questions at the end.

LAST WILL AND TESTAMENT OF JOHN L. JONES

I, John L. Jones, of the City of _____ , in the County of _____ and State of _____ , being of sound and disposing mind and memory, and not acting under duress, menace, fraud, or undue influence of any person what-soever, do make, publish, and declare this instrument to be my Last Will and Testa-ment. I do hereby cancel, revoke, and annul all former wills and testaments or codicils made by me at any time.

First: I direct that my debts, funeral, and burial expenses be paid out of my estate as soon after my death as can be conveniently be done.

Second: I give to my son, James, my diamond ring and all my other personal jewelry.

Third: I give to my said son, James, the sum of five thousand dollars.

Fourth: All the rest, residue and remainder of my estate, real and personal, of what-soever character and wheresoever situated, of which I die seized or possessed or to which I am in any way entitled at the time of my death, I give to my wife, Mary, if she survives me, and if my said wife is not living at the time of my death or we both should die in a common accident, I give this my residuary estate to my son, James.

Fifth: I nominate and appoint Bill Brown to be the executor of this my last Will and Testament, and I direct that my said executor shall not be required to give any bond or security for the proper discharge of his duties.

    IN TESTIMONY WHEREOF I hereunto set my hand and seal on this _____ day of _____ , in the Year Nineteen Hundred and _____ .

            [*Signature*] _____

            [*Address*] _____

    The foregoing instrument, consisting of two pages, including this page, was, at the date hereof, signed, sealed, published, and declared by JOHN L. JONES, the testator above named, at _____ in the State of _____ as and for his Last Will and Testament, in our presence, who, in his presence, at his request, and in the presence of each other have hereunto set our names as witnesses.

            Names   Addresses

_____   _____

_____   _____

                             [*Signed by two witnesses*]

1. Who is the testator?
2. Is there a testatrix?
3. Did John Jones die testate or intestate?
4. Does the document name a guardian or trustee?
5. Is the document a will or a codicil?
6. What is the diamond ring given to James called according to the U.P.C.?
7. Is a devisee named in the will?
8. Who are the beneficiaries named in the will?
9. Who is the personal representative?
10. Is there an executrix?
11. Does the document contain a testamentary trust?
12. Has the will been attested and subscribed?
13. Is this an example of a nuncupative will?
14. How many witnesses are required to sign this will according to your state statute?

DEATH WITHOUT A WILL—INTESTACY

A person who dies without a will dies intestate. He is called the intestate. In all states, the distribution of an intestate's estate is determined by state law called the intestate succession statute. Such statutes, in effect, write the will the decedent failed to make by directing the distribution of the intestate's property to the heirs. Each state has its own specific statutes and court decisions that cover and control intestacy. These laws and decisions vary substantially from state to state and determine the identity of the heirs, rights of family members, guardianship of minor children, procedures and rules for the administration of the estate, appointment of the personal representative or administrator, and the disposition of the estate property to the surviving spouse and blood relatives of the intestate. The controlling statutes are those of the state in which the intestate had her domicile *and* the states where any real property is located.

Example: Sandra lives in Nebraska where she owns a house, is registered to vote, has her driver's license, and pays state income tax. Collectively, these factors determine that Nebraska is Sandra's true legal home—her domicile. She also owns real property in other states, i.e., a cottage in Wisconsin and a condominium in Florida. If Sandra dies intestate, Nebraska's statutes will determine how and by whom her house and personal property will be inherited; however, Wisconsin's statutes will decide who receives the cottage, and Florida's law, the condominium.

Through study, research, and experience, you must become knowledgeable of your state's intestate statute so that you can accurately explain and apply its provisions to the estate of the deceased.

Terminology Relating to Intestacy

The following terms are associated with the persons and proceedings involved in the law of intestate succession:

- *Kindred.* Kindred refers to persons related to one another by blood. The persons are also referred to as kin or next-of-kin.
- *Consanguinity.* Consanguinity refers to persons who are related by blood through at least one common ancestor.

Example: A child, grandchild, grandparent, aunt, uncle, cousin, and the like related to the decedent through a common ancestor. Janice Rule is the granddaughter of Elliot Sanderson. She is related to her grandfather by consanguinity (blood).

- *Affinity.* Affinity refers to persons who are related by marriage. They include stepchildren, father- or mother-in-law, and brother- or sister-in-law. Since only blood relatives can inherit from the intestate's estate, none of the individuals related by affinity (except for a surviving spouse) can inherit from the intestate under the laws of intestate succession.

Example: In Exhibit 4.5, Nathan's wife is related to Joe by affinity. She cannot inherit from Joe under intestate succession laws. The decedent and the person related to him by affinity have no common blood ancestor. This rule, of course, does not apply to the spouse of the decedent even though husband and wife are related solely by marriage (by affinity).

- *Ascendant or ancestor.* An ascendant or ancestor is a claimant to an intestate's share who is related to the decedent in an ascending lineal or collateral blood line.

Exhibit 4.5   Examples of Lineal and Collateral Relationships

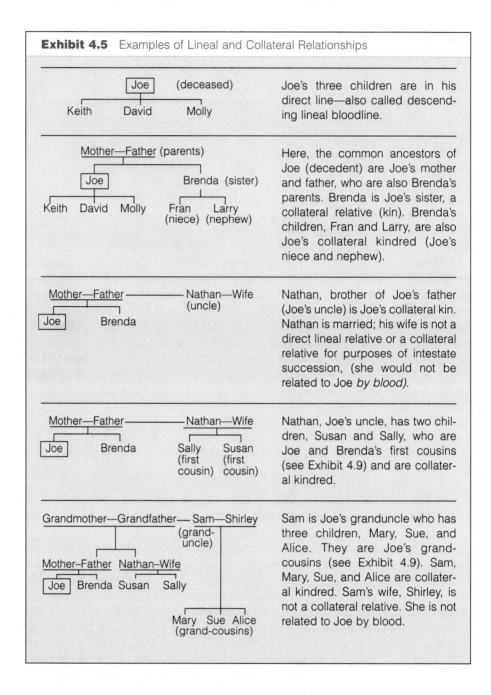

Joe's three children are in his direct line—also called descending lineal bloodline.

Here, the common ancestors of Joe (decedent) are Joe's mother and father, who are also Brenda's parents. Brenda is Joe's sister, a collateral relative (kin). Brenda's children, Fran and Larry, are also Joe's collateral kindred (Joe's niece and nephew).

Nathan, brother of Joe's father (Joe's uncle) is Joe's collateral kin. Nathan is married; his wife is not a direct lineal relative or a collateral relative for purposes of intestate succession, (she would not be related to Joe *by blood).*

Nathan, Joe's uncle, has two children, Susan and Sally, who are Joe and Brenda's first cousins (see Exhibit 4.9) and are collateral kindred.

Sam is Joe's granduncle who has three children, Mary, Sue, and Alice. They are Joe's grand-cousins (see Exhibit 4.9). Sam, Mary, Sue, and Alice are collateral kindred. Sam's wife, Shirley, is not a collateral relative. She is not related to Joe by blood.

Example: The parent of a decedent is a lineal ancestor. The sister of a decedent is a collateral relative.

- *Descendant.* A descendant is a claimant to an intestate's share who is related to the decedent in a descending lineal or collateral blood line.

Example: The child of a decedent is a lineal descendant. A niece is a collateral descendant.

- *Lineal.* As a noun, a lineal is a person related to an intestate decedent in a direct line either upward in an ascending bloodline (e.g., parents, grandparents, or great-grandparents) or downward in a descending bloodline (e.g., children, grandchildren, or great-grandchildren). See Exhibits 4.5, 4.6, and 4.9. Lineal consanguinity exists between persons when one is descended (or ascended) in a direct line from the other, e.g., a father to a son.

▪ *Collateral.* As a noun, in intestate terminology, a collateral is a person not in a direct line of lineal ascent or descent who traces a kinship relationship to an intestate decedent through a common ancestor (e.g., brothers, sisters, aunts, uncles, nieces, nephews, cousins, and other such relatives), forming a collateral line of relationship (see Exhibits 4.5, 4.7, and 4.9). Collateral consanguinity exists between persons who have the same ancestors, but who do not descend or ascend from each other, e.g., brother, uncle, or nephew.

▪ *Half blood.* Half blood is the degree of relationship that exists between persons who have the same mother or the same father in common, but not both parents.

Example: Luis and Carlos are half brothers. They are related to each other through only one common ancestor, i.e., they have the same father but not the same mother. Carlos's daughter would be Luis's half niece. Most state statutes, including the U.P.C. § 2–107, allow half blood and whole blood kindred to receive an equal share of the intestate's estate (see Cal. Prob. Code § 6406; Iowa Code Ann. § 633.219; Mass. Gen. Law Ann. ch. 190 § 4; Mich. Stat. Ann. § 700.109; N.J. Stat. Ann. § 3B: 5–7; and N.Y. E.P.T.L. § 4–1.1[b]). Other states give the half blood

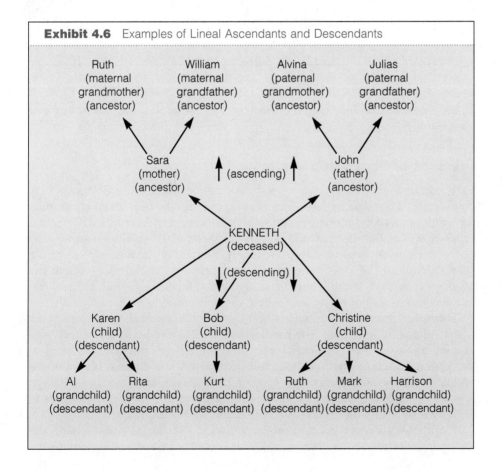

Exhibit 4.6 Examples of Lineal Ascendants and Descendants

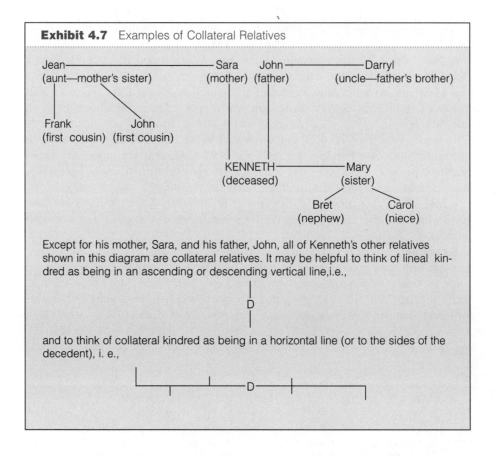

Exhibit 4.7 Examples of Collateral Relatives

Except for his mother, Sara, and his father, John, all of Kenneth's other relatives shown in this diagram are collateral relatives. It may be helpful to think of lineal kindred as being in an ascending or descending vertical line, i.e.,

and to think of collateral kindred as being in a horizontal line (or to the sides of the decedent), i. e.,

kindred only half as much as a whole blood (see Fla. Stat. Ann. § 732.105 and Va. Code § 64.1–2).

Intestate Succession Laws

Each state has enacted its own intestate succession statute. These statutes vary considerably from state to state. They provide rules for the descent and determine the distribution of the probate property of the decedent. An important distinction exists, however, between real and personal property that involves the application of the intestate succession statute. Generally, the law of the intestate's domicile state determines the inheritance of personal property regardless of where the property is located. On the other hand, real estate passes according to the intestate succession statute of the state where the real property is located.

Example: Rosa Sanchez owns a house in South Dakota, her domicile state, and a cottage in Minnesota. She has furniture in both the home and the cottage and savings accounts in banks in both states. If Rosa dies intestate, the intestate succession statute of South Dakota will determine the recipients of her house and all of her personal property, including her furniture and savings account in Minnesota. The real property in Minnesota—the cottage—however, will pass to the recipient according to Minnesota's intestate succession law.

Nonprobate property, such as property held in joint tenancy and tenancy by the entirety, is affected neither by a will nor by intestate succession statutes but instead passes automatically, due to the right of survivorship, to the surviving co-owners.

Some of the terms used in intestate statutes to identify heirs and methods of distributing the intestate's property include "issue," "per capita," "per stirpes," and distribution "by representation." The term "issue" refers to all of the lineal descendants from a common ancestor. The law of intestate succession rests on two basic principles:

1. The intestate's property does not pass to all members of the class of persons defined as "issue" but only to persons closest in line to the intestate, e.g., generally children take before grandchildren.

2. The heirs can only be persons who survive the intestate; they must be living at the time of the intestate's death. A deceased person's "estate" cannot be an heir. Thus, if an intestate's child dies before the intestate, neither the child nor the child's estate is an heir. However, the deceased child's children living at the time of the intestate's death would be heirs. See the discussion and examples below.

An intestate's estate is distributed by one of two statutory methods: *per capita distribution* or *per stirpes distribution*.

Per Capita Distribution

"Per capita" distribution means "equal to each person" or "by the heads." Per capita distribution is a method of dividing an intestate estate by giving an equal share to a number of persons all of whom are related to the decedent in the same degree of relationship (same-generation ascendants or descendants). See *Martin v. Beatty*, 253 Iowa 1237, 115 N.W.2d 706 (1962), in which the court ruled that the beneficiaries take their interests in the property per capita and not per stirpes as determined by the testator's words and intent.

Example: Howard dies intestate, and his only heirs are his children, Betty, Sue, and Joe. The three children would receive equal shares in Howard's estate per capita.

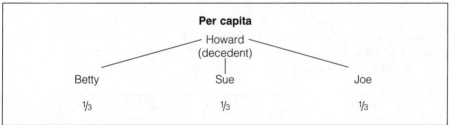

Per capita

Howard (decedent)

Betty — Sue — Joe

1/3 — 1/3 — 1/3

Example: Continuing with the above case, suppose not all of the heirs are of the same generation because one or more heirs in a class (generation) has predeceased Howard. Then, each living "head" of a descendant's line takes equally, per capita. For example, suppose Betty dies before Howard and has two surviving children, Bob and Sally, Howard's grandchildren. Per capita distribution in this case would be determined by counting the number of heirs that "head" each descendant's line (since Betty is dead, Bob and Sally "head" her line; Sue and Joe "head" their lines); therefore, there are four (4) heirs, and each would receive an equal one-fourth of Howard's estate per capita.

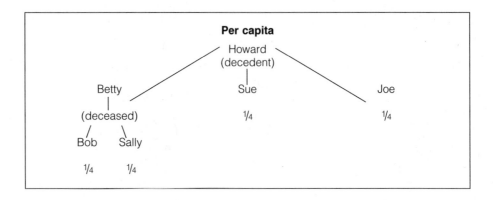

Right of Representation

When Betty died and was survived by her two children, Bob and Sally, the principle of **representation** gives Betty's children, Bob and Sally, the share in Howard's estate that Betty would have taken if she had survived Howard. All states allow distribution by representation, although some states limit it among collateral heirs, see and compare Uniform Probate Code § 2–103(4).

Per Stirpes Distribution

"Per stirpes" distribution means by representation. Using the principle of representation, per stirpes distribution is the method of dividing an intestate estate where a class or group of heirs takes the share to which their deceased parent would have been entitled had he lived; thus, the heirs take by their right of representing their ancestor (parent) and not as so many individuals. A majority of the states employ this method. In per stirpes distribution, the heirs are related to the intestate in different degrees of relationship (intergenerational ascendants or descendants) with some heirs having predeceased the intestate. The descendants of such persons receive their shares through the predeceased heir by representation. Using the per stirpes method, the intestate's estate is divided into as many equal shares as the decedent has children (1) who are living or (2) who are already dead but have living descendants. The living children of any deceased parent take their parent's share per stirpes, by right of representation.

    Example: Returning to the previous example, a per stirpes distribution would be as follows:

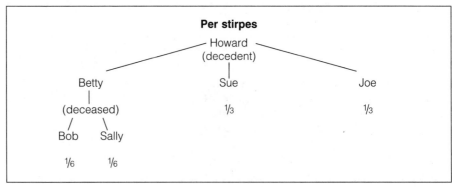

Right of representation
The right of a child to receive the share of an intestate's property that the child's deceased parent would have received if the parent was still living.

Per stirpes
A distribution of property that depends upon the relationship to the intestate of those entitled to the estate.

Method: Divide the estate into equal shares based on the living children and the children who have died but have living descendants. There are three (3) shares. Thus, Sue and Joe each receive one-third of the estate, and Bob and Sally receive their mother's (Betty's) one-third share equally by right of representation. Bob and Sally each receive a one-sixth share.

An example, of a statute regulating per capita and per stirpes rights to an intestate's estate is Idaho Code § 15–2–103 (1979) on the share of heirs other than a surviving spouse:

> The part of the intestate estate not passing to the surviving spouse under Idaho Code § 15–2–102 of this part, or the entire intestate estate if there is no surviving spouse, passes as follows:
>
> (a) To the issue of the decedent; if they all are of the same degree of kinship to the decedent they take equally [per capita], but if of unequal degree, then those of more remote degree take by representation [per stirpes].

Example: Mary, a widow, has three children—Jim, Nora, and Kathryn. Jim is married and has two children—Matt and Colleen. Nora is single. Kathryn also was married and had three children—Charles, Darlene, and Elaine. Kathryn died of cancer two years ago. Now Mary dies. (Refer to Exhibit 4.8). If Mary dies intestate, leaving an estate valued at $225,000 after payment of debts, taxes, and all other expenses, and her only surviving relatives are two of her three adult children and her five grandchildren (three of whom are the children of her deceased daughter, Kathryn), her estate would be distributed according to the Idaho statute as follows:

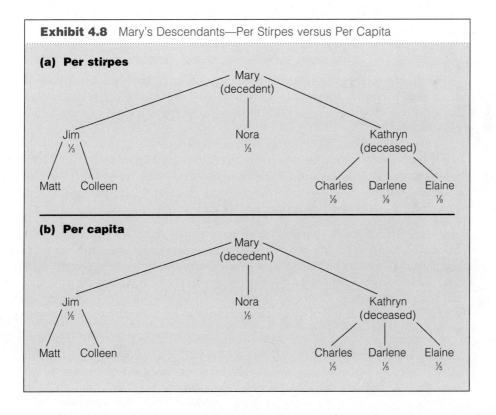

Exhibit 4.8 Mary's Descendants—Per Stirpes versus Per Capita

(a) Per stirpes

Mary (decedent)

Jim ⅓ — Matt, Colleen

Nora ⅓

Kathryn (deceased) — Charles ⅑, Darlene ⅑, Elaine ⅑

(b) Per capita

Mary (decedent)

Jim ⅕ — Matt, Colleen

Nora ⅕

Kathryn (deceased) — Charles ⅕, Darlene ⅕, Elaine ⅕

- $75,000 to Jim (son) per capita—a one-third interest.
- $75,000 to Nora (daughter) per capita—a one-third interest.
- $25,000 to Charles (grandchild) per stirpes—a one-ninth interest.
- $25,000 to Darlene (grandchild) per stirpes—a one-ninth interest.
- $25,000 to Elaine (grandchild) per stirpes—a one-ninth interest.

If Kathryn had still been alive at her mother's death, she would have taken a per capita share of $75,000 (one-third of the total estate). Since Kathryn was deceased at her mother's death, Kathryn's children receive Kathryn's share through Kathryn, taking per stirpes. This means that Kathryn's share was divided equally among her children, each child taking a third of their mother's share. Each took only one-ninth of the total estate, whereas the two children of the decedent, Mary, each took one-third. The three children of Kathryn take per stirpes (by right of representation), i.e., they "represent" their mother. The other two grandchildren of the decedent receive nothing because their father, Jim, who was the son of the decedent, Mary, survived his mother. If Mary had died with a will and left her estate to her then living children and to the issue of any deceased child of hers per capita, then Mary's estate would be distributed as follows: Jim, Nora, Charles, Darlene, and Elaine would each receive $45,000. See Exhibit 4.8.

Degree of Relationship

The **degree of relationship** is a method of determining which collateral relatives or heirs will inherit from an intestate. When a person dies intestate, most state statutes and the U.P.C. pass the decedent's estate in the following order:

1. First to surviving spouse and lineal descendants (children), but if none, then to:

2. Other lineal descendants such as grandchildren or great-grandchildren, but if none, then to:

3. Lineal ascendants (ancestors) such as parents or grandparents, but if none, then to:

4. Collateral relatives who are lineal descendants of the decedent's parents such as brothers and sisters and their children who come before aunts, uncles, and cousins, and whose degree of relationship determines their inheritance rights (see Exhibit 4.9.)

5. Other next-of-kin, blood relatives of the decedent.

6. If there are none of the above, the decedent's property passes to the state by escheat, the right of the state to title of an intestate's property when no spouse or kindred survive the intestate. Reminder: real property would pass by escheat to the state in which the real property is located.

In determining which collateral heirs receive the intestate's property to the exclusion of other collateral heirs, it is often necessary to ascertain the degree of relationship between the decedent and the particular heirs in question. Most states and the U.P.C. limit collateral heirs to the next-of-kin, i.e., to the collateral relatives of the decedent who are lineal descendants of the decedent's grandparents. These potential heirs are determined according to either the civil law or the common law as follows:

- *Civil law computation.* Under the civil law method, the degree of relationship is determined by first counting up from the decedent-intestate to the *closest common ancestor* to both the decedent and the possible *heir,* and then counting

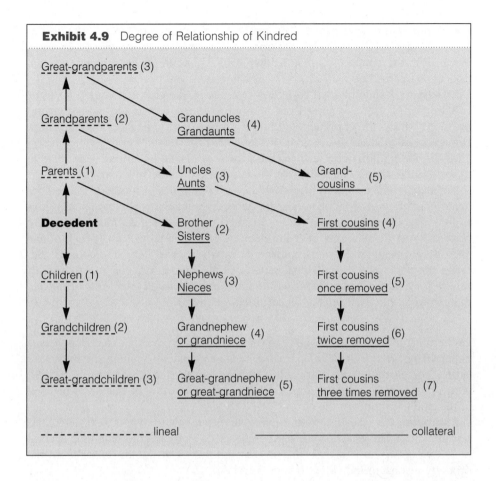

Exhibit 4.9 Degree of Relationship of Kindred

down to the heir (see Exhibit 4.9). When counting, the decedent is excluded, and the possible heir is included.

Example: Using Exhibit 4.9 to determine the degree of relationship of a grandnephew, Jeffrey, to the decedent-intestate, Marilyn, count up to her parents (1), the closest common ancestor to both Marilyn and Jeffrey, and then down through brothers and sisters (2) and nephews and nieces (3), to Jeffrey, the grand-nephew (4). Thus, the grandnephew, Jeffrey, is related to the decedent in the fourth degree.

Similarly, a first cousin is also related in the fourth degree, i.e., parents (1), grandparents (2), uncles and aunts (3), to first cousins (4).

In states that follow the civil law computation, the collateral heir who is related to the decedent-intestate in the lowest degree (smallest number) receives the property to the exclusion of the other collateral heirs. If several collateral heirs are related in equal degree, they all share equally; thus, in the example above, Jeffrey and Marilyn's first cousin would receive equal shares. However, some states specify that in case of a degree tie between collateral heirs, those related through the closest common ancestor take to the exclusion of the others; see Calif. Prob. Code § 6402(f); Mass. Gen. Laws Ann. ch. 190, § 3(6). Thus, in the example above, although Jeffrey and a first cousin of Marilyn's are both in the fourth degree, Jeffrey would receive her property since he was related through her parents while the first cousin was related through her grandparents.

■ *Common law computation.* This method computes the degree of relationship as the greater number of steps (1) from the intestate up to the closest ancestor or (2) from the common ancestor down to the possible collateral heir (see Ga. Code Ann. § 53–4–2).

Example: Using the Marilyn-Jeffrey case above, the closest common ancestor is Marilyn's parent. Counting from Marilyn to the parent is (1), and from the parent to Jeffrey, the grandnephew, is (3). Thus, (3) is the degree of relationship. However, calculating the degree of Marilyn's first cousin using their common ancestor, the grandparent, leads to the degree of (2); i.e., counting from Marilyn to the grandparent is (2) and from the grandparent to the first cousin is (2).

No matter which system, the civil law or common law method, is used for determining degrees for collaterals, the decedent-intestate's property usually goes to the "nearest surviving kin" as established by state statutes. Most states give preference to descendants over ancestors, e.g., children over parents; brothers and sisters over grandparents; and nephews and nieces over first cousins. Because the variations in individual state laws are numerous, *you must carefully review your state's laws with the supervising attorney when they must be applied to determine a client's interest in an intestate's estate.*

Escheat

Escheat is the passing of property to the state when an intestate decedent leaves no surviving spouse or blood (kindred) relatives entitled to inherit the intestate's estate. For example, see Maryland's escheat statute (Md. Code Ann. § 3–105), which passes the intestate's property to the county board of education to be used in the public schools of the county.

Example: Bob dies intestate, leaving an estate valued at $100,000. There are no surviving relatives. The property "escheats" to the state; the state enjoys complete ownership and can use the property as it sees fit; it can sell or lease the property just as an individual owner could do.

ETHICAL ISSUE

Escheat
The passage of an intestate's property to the state when there are no surviving blood relatives or a spouse.

⚖ ASSIGNMENT 4.2

Armond died in Great Falls, Montana. Either by choice or through oversight, he had neither married nor drawn a will. At his death, Armond had the following blood relatives surviving him:
  ■ A brother, Niles, living in Sacramento, California.
  ■ A sister, Lorraine, living in London, England.
  ■ A niece, Francine, living in Fridley, Minnesota, and a nephew, Frank, living in Albany, New Mexico, both children of Armond's deceased brother, Harry.
  ■ A mother, Lila, who lived with Armond.
  ■ A grandfather, Alonzo, Lila's father, living in Cleveland, Ohio.
  ■ An aunt, Rose, Lila's sister, living in Bangor, Maine.
  ■ A first cousin, Judy, Rose's daughter, living in Lawrence, Kansas.
Answer the following questions:
1. Who of Armond's surviving blood relatives are lineal descendants?
2. Who of Armond's surviving blood relatives are lineal ascendants?
3. Who of Armond's surviving blood relatives are collaterals? What are their degrees of relationship?
4. What is the order of inheritance of Armond's surviving relatives in your state? Which heir receives property to the exclusion of others?
5. Do any of Armond's kindred receive his property per stirpes or per capita?

6. If Francine and Judy are Armond's only surviving relatives when he dies intestate, who receives his property according to your state statute? If Francine is dead but her son, Fred, and Judy are living when Armond dies, who receives the property?
7. Beginning with Alonzo, diagram a family tree for Armond's family.

General Rules of Distribution under State Intestate Succession Statutes

As we have emphasized throughout this discussion, intestate succession statutes vary from state to state. Nevertheless, many states do have similar rules on which surviving relatives will inherit an intestate's estate. The following scenarios illustrate some of these general rules of distribution. If the decedent-intestate is survived by:

- A surviving spouse and no blood relatives: The spouse receives the entire estate.
- A surviving spouse and children all born to the surviving spouse and the deceased: The spouse receives a lump sum of money (ranging from $5,000 to $150,000 depending on the state) and an additional portion (usually one-half) of the estate. The children receive the remainder of the estate to be distributed equally.
- A surviving spouse and children, some or all of whom are not the children of the surviving spouse: The estate is divided equally between the spouse and the children. If there is more than one child, the children's half is divided equally among the children.
- A surviving spouse, no children, but surviving parents: In most states, the surviving spouse gets everything; in other states, the spouse receives a lump sum ranging from $5,000 to $150,000 plus one-half of the remaining estate, and the parents receive the other half.
- A surviving spouse, no children and no parents, but brothers and sisters: In the majority of states, the surviving spouse receives everything; in other states, the spouse receives a lump sum ranging from $25,000 to $200,000 plus one-half of the remaining estate, and the brothers and sisters receive the other half equally.
- No surviving spouse and no children: The parents receive the property followed by brothers and sisters, then their children and other collateral heirs.
- No spouse or kindred (blood relatives): The state receives the property by escheat.

Exhibit 4.10 is an example of a state (Wisconsin) intestate succession statute.

☷ ASSIGNMENT 4.3

Molly Brown dies intestate in Wisconsin, her domicile. She had three children, Curly, Betty, and Moe. Curly and Betty each have two children. Curly's two daughters are Judy and Jody; Betty's two sons are Bobby and Billy. Moe died six months before Molly, and he had three children, Mark, Luke, and John. Answer the following according to Wisconsin law and your own state statutes:
1. Who receives Molly's property?
2. What portion does each recipient receive?
3. In Wisconsin is the inheritance per stirpes or per capita? Explain. Which method is used in your own state?
4. Does any of Molly's property escheat to the state of Wisconsin?

INHERITANCE RIGHTS OF FAMILY MEMBERS

Upon the death of a major "breadwinner" in the family, i.e., a spouse or the single parent, the distraught surviving family members may face a financial crisis. This section examines the inheritance rights of a surviving spouse and children.

Rights of a Surviving Spouse

In the case of a testate decedent, the rights of a surviving spouse to the decedent spouse's property usually are determined by the decedent spouse's will. When the decedent spouse dies without a will, the surviving spouse's right to part of the intestate spouse's estate is determined by state statute and by which family members, e.g., children, parents, brothers and sisters, and other kindred, outlive the intestate. For examples of the rights of surviving spouses under state statutes, see the New York and Wisconsin statutes in Exhibits 2.1 and 4.10.

Exhibit 4.10   Wisconsin's Intestate Succession Statute

852.01. Basic rules for intestate succession
(1) Who are heirs. The net estate of a decedent which the decedent has not disposed of by will, whether the decedent dies without a will, or with a will which does not completely dispose of the decedent's estate, passes to the decedent's surviving heirs as follows:
(a) To the spouse:
1. If there are no surviving issue of the decedent, or if the surviving issue are all issue of the surviving spouse and the decedent, the entire estate.
2. If there are surviving issue one or more of whom are not issue of the surviving spouse, one-half of that portion of the decedent's net estate not disposed of by will consisting of decedent's property other than marital property and other than property described under 861.02(1).
(b) To the issue, the share of the estate not passing to the spouse under part (a), or the entire estate if there is no surviving spouse; if the issue are all in the same degree of kinship to the decedent they take equally, but if they are of unequal degree then those of more remote degrees take by representation.
(c) If there is no surviving spouse or issue, to the parents.
(d) If there is no surviving spouse, issue or parent, to the brothers and sisters and the issue of any deceased brother or sister by representation.
(e) If there is no survivng spouse, issue, parent or brother or sister, to the issue of brothers and sisters; if such issue are all in the same degree of kinship to the decedent they take equally, but if they are of unequal degree then those of more remote degrees take by representation.
(f) If there is no surviving spouse, issue, parent or issue of a parent, to the grandparents.
(g) If there is no surviving spouse, issue, parent, issue of a parent, or grandparent, to the intestate's next of kin in equal degree.

(2) Requirement that heir survive decedent for a certain time. If any person who would otherwise be an heir under sub. (1) dies within 72 hours of the time of death of the decedent, the net estate not disposed of by will passes under this section as if that person had predeceased the decedent. If the time of death of the decedent or of the person who would otherwise be an heir, or the times of death of both, cannot be determined, and it cannot be established that the person who would otherwise be an heir has survived the decedent by at least 72 hours, it is presumed that the person died within 72 hours of the decedent's death. In computing time for purposes of this subsection, local standard time at the place of death of the decedent is used.

(3) Escheat. If there are no heirs of the decedent under subs. (1) and (2), the net estate escheats to the state to be added to the capital of the school fund.

Surviving Spouse's Elective Share

To protect a surviving spouse from being disinherited, a married person is limited in disposing of property in that a surviving spouse cannot be completely excluded. In other words, a testator is permitted in a will to disinherit anyone except a surviving spouse. The decision in *Solomon v. Dunlap*, 372 So.2d 218 (Fla. App. 1st. Dist., 1979), illustrates this point. In this case, the testator had made a will leaving his entire estate to his two sons of a previous marriage. After making the will, he married for the second time but did not change the will before he died. His current surviving spouse petitioned the court for her share in the testator's estate as a pretermitted (omitted) spouse. The court granted her the share to which she was entitled by state (Florida) statute which was one-half of the net value of the testator's estate.

Most states offer a surviving spouse the choice or election of taking the benefits in the will or renouncing the provisions made in the will for the surviving spouse (thereby forfeiting, i.e., giving up, all benefits from the will) and *electing* a statutory share of a certain minimum portion of the deceased spouse's estate. Often the elective share of the surviving spouse is the same amount the spouse would have received if the decedent spouse had died intestate. Generally, the surviving spouse will choose whichever share is greater. As noted in Chapter 2, this elective right has replaced the common law provisions of dower and curtesy, which have been either abolished or materially altered in most states (see U.P.C. § 2–112). Because the personal representative of the decedent spouse's estate is required to determine the amount of the marital deduction on the federal estate tax return, the spouse's election must be made within nine (9) months of death. If no election is made, the surviving spouse is required to take the share provided under the decedent spouse's will. The election is made when the spouse gives written notice to the personal representative and files the notice with the probate court. See Exhibit 4.11 for an example of a notice. The amount of the decedent's property that passes to the spouse as the elective share, excluding a life estate interest, qualifies for the estate tax marital deduction (see the discussion in Chapter 10).

This right of election does not apply if the surviving spouse has previously waived the right to the elective share by signing an antenuptial agreement. Also, in some states like New York, a surviving spouse can be prohibited from the election if the spouse "abandoned" the deceased spouse prior to the latter's death or failed to provide required support for the deceased spouse for any period up to death (see N.Y. E.P.T.L. §§ 5–1.1 and 5–1.2). Indiana, North Carolina, Pennsylvania, and Virginia have similar statutes.

In some states, a surviving spouse's elective share grants the spouse an ownership share in *all* property owned during the decedent spouse's lifetime. In these states, which include Florida, Indiana, Iowa, Kansas, Maine, Maryland, Minnesota, Missouri, Nebraska, Pennsylvania, and Utah, *both* spouses' signatures are necessary on any deed, mortgage, or contract to sell the property. In other states, a surviving spouse may be limited to the property that the decedent spouse owned at death. In these states, which include Alaska, Colorado, Connecticut, Georgia, Mississippi, New York, North Dakota, Oklahoma, Oregon, South Dakota, and Wyoming, the surviving spouse has no claim on property sold or gifted during the decedent spouse's lifetime without the surviving spouse's signature.

Exhibit 4.11 Notice of Election of Surviving Spouse

SURROGATE'S COURT: COUNTY OF _____

_____

In the Matter of the Estate of

_____ ,

Deceased.

NOTICE OF ELECTION

File No. _____

TO: [*Insert name of fiduciary and clerk of court*]

    1. I, _____ , am the surviving spouse of _____ , who died a domiciliary of the County of _____ , and the State of New York, on _____ , 19 _____ .

    2. The said decedent left a certain Last Will and Testament dated the _____ day of _____ , 19 _____ , which was probated in the Surrogate's Court of the County of _____ , New York, on the _____ day of _____ , 19 _____ , and Letters Testamentary were issued to _____ as Executor on _____ , 19 _____ .

    3. I, _____ , the surviving spouse of _____ , deceased, do hereby exercise the personal right of election given to me pursuant to the provisions of Section 5–1.1 of the New York Estates, Powers and Trusts Law, and I do hereby elect to take my elective share pursuant to the provisions of the New York Estates, Powers and Trusts Law.

    IN WITNESS WHEREOF, I have hereunto set my hand and seal this _____ day of _____ , 19 _____ .

[*Acknowledgment*]

_____ L.S.

Source: West's McKinney's Forms, ESP, § 7:499. Reprinted with permission from West's McKinney's Forms, Copyright ©, by West Publishing Company.

Effect of Divorce and Marriage on a Spouse's Rights

If the testator obtains a divorce (or annulment) *after* executing a will, the effect on the will is determined by state law. In a few states, the divorce may revoke the will (see Ga. Code Ann. § 53–2–76), with the result that the testator's property passes by intestacy and the former spouse is excluded from any inheritance. In most states, by statute or case law, a divorce revokes only the provisions that benefit the former spouse, not the will itself (see Exhibit 4.12 and U.P.C. §§ 2–802 and 2–804). The decision in *Matter of Seymour's Estate,* 93 N.M. 328, 600 P.2d 274 (1979) illustrates this position (for further discussion, see Chapter 5). A legal separation that does not terminate the spouse's marital status does not revoke a will's provisions for the benefit of a spouse; see Calif. Prob. Code § 6122(d) and U.P.C. § 2–802.

A testator's subsequent marriage after creating a will may have the effect of revoking the will; see Conn. Gen. Stat. Ann. § 45a–257; Ky. Rev. Stat. Ann. § 394.090; R. I. Gen. Laws § 33–5–9; and Exhibit 4.13. Since the majority of states, excluding the community property states, allow a statutory share to a surviving spouse who elects against a decedent spouse's will, some of these states often have no "marriage revocation law" since the new spouse is covered by the election right. A number of states, including states that have adopted the Uniform Probate Code, give the new spouse an amount equal to the intestate share of the decedent spouse's estate unless it can be shown that the omission was intentional or that the testator provided for the surviving spouse outside the will in a way

---

Exhibit 4.12 Consequence of Divorce on Preexisting Will

Revokes the entire will:
  Connecticut
  Georgia
Does not affect provisions of the will:
  Louisiana
  Mississippi
  New Hampshire
  Vermont
Revokes all the will provisions pertaining to the former spouse:
  All remaining states not listed above

---

that is clearly a substitute for the provisions (bequests) of the will (see U.P.C. § 2–301). See also the discussion in Chapter 5.

Rights of Children (Issue)

Issue

All persons who have descended from a common ancestor are the issue of that ancestor. Issue is a broader term than children and, as it is normally used in wills, includes all blood descendants of the ancestor, not just lineal descendants, such as children, grandchildren, and great-grandchildren; see *In re Wolf's Estate,* 98 N.J.Super. 89, 236 A.2d 166 (1967). Formerly, the term included only legitimate issue, but in *Reed v. Campbell,* 476 U.S. 852, 106 S.Ct. 2234, 90 L.Ed.2d 858 (1986), the U.S. Supreme Court prohibited unjustified discrimination against children born out of wedlock. In some states, such as New York, a nonmarital (illegitimate) child shares in the intestate estate of the child's father; see N.Y. E.P.T.L.

Exhibit 4.13 Consequence of Marriage on Preexisting Will

Revokes the entire will:
  Connecticut
  Georgia
  Kansas
  Kentucky
  Maryland (marriage followed by the birth, adoption, or legitimation of a child by the testator, provided the child or the child's descendant survives the testator)
  Oregon
  Rhode Island
  South Dakota
  Tennessee (marriage and birth of a child)
  West Virginia
  Wisconsin
Revokes all the will provisions pertaining to the former spouse:
  Nevada
  Washington
Does not revoke the will:
  All remaining states not listed above

4–1.2(a)(2)(c). In trusts in Massachusetts, the word "issue," which formerly meant legitimate children, today includes all biological descendants unless the settlor clearly expresses a different intent; see *Powers v. Wilkinson,* 399 Mass. 650, 506 N.E.2d 842 (1987). In addition, many states' intestacy statutes have established that an adopted child is "issue" of the adoptive parents, giving the child the same rights, including inheritance rights, as the adoptive parents' natural children. The next paragraphs discuss the rights of children in the following order: natural children, adopted children, nonmarital (illegitimate) children, and pretermitted (omitted) children.

Natural Children

A natural child is a child by birth of a mother and the biological father, as distinguished from a child by adoption. In addition, if a married woman gives birth to a child, her husband is presumed to be the father of the child. Although most testators leave all or most of their property to their surviving spouse, state intestate statutes differ sharply from those testamentary provisions. Under these statutes, whenever a spouse *and* child(ren) survive the intestate, the spouse generally receives one-third to one-half of the intestate's estate with the remainder to the child or children equally; alternatively, the surviving spouse receives a lump sum amount of the estate plus half of the remainder, with the child(ren) receiving the other half. In either case, this distribution of a decedent's estate is substantially different from what the usual testator's will provides. Therefore, except for specific bequests (gifts) to named children, most natural and, as we shall see, adopted children receive the estate of their parents when the second parent dies. Obviously, this is not the case in single-parent families, since the parent who dies testate generally leaves the entire estate to the children. When the single parent or the second parent-spouse dies intestate, the natural children are the first-in-line heirs and inherit the entire estate, except that a deceased child's share will pass per stirpes, by right of representation, to that child's issue.

Parents are not required to leave anything to their children. Nevertheless, excluding children from sharing in an estate is best accomplished by inserting a clause in the will to the effect that the testator or testatrix has intentionally made no provision for a certain named child. In the event that no specific exclusion is stated in the will, the child may ultimately receive a share despite the testator's intention as a result of an omitted child statute (see the discussion below).

Divorce and remarriage often have a detrimental effect on the rights and opportunities of natural or adopted children to inherit by will or by law.

Example: If William and Marilyn are divorced when William dies, he almost certainly will not leave his estate to Marilyn (if he did, it could then pass from her to their children, Sally and Joe, when Marilyn dies). Suppose William moved to another state after losing custody of the children upon the divorce (dissolution); by now he may have lost interest in the children, thereby disinheriting them. In addition, William may have remarried prior to his death; frequently, divorced fathers do *not* provide for children of a former marriage in their wills. Therefore, only if William died intestate would Sally and Joe share in their father's estate, but their interest would be diminished by the inheritance rights of William's new spouse.

In divorce decrees, the spouses may agree by stipulation that the spouse who is obligated to pay child support will make a will leaving a portion of the estate to the child(ren) or name the child(ren) as beneficiaries of a life insurance policy.

Such insurance policies and the survivor's benefits from Social Security may terminate the need for continuing child support after the death of the parent making support payments.

Adopted Children

Adoption is a legal process whereby state statutes terminate a child's legal rights and duties toward his natural parents and substitute similar rights and duties toward the adoptive parents. The state statutes are inconsistent in determining the inheritance rights of adopted children or adoptive parents. The modern trend is to treat the adopted child as a natural child of the adoptive parents and not as the child of her former natural parents for all legal purposes including inheritance. The states that have adopted U.P.C. § 2–114 and the Uniform Adoption Act have followed this trend (these states include Arkansas, Montana, New Mexico, North Dakota, Ohio, and Oklahoma). Consider the following examples:

Example: Karen Wilson's son, Ron, is adopted by Scott and Shirley Mikulski. The adopted child, Ron, has the right to inherit from either of the adoptive parents, Scott or Shirley, when they die intestate, and they have the right to inherit from Ron. However, Ron will no longer inherit from his natural mother, Karen, nor will she inherit from Ron when one of them is the first to die.

Example: If, instead, Karen Wilson marries Fred Maxwell and Fred adopts Ron, Ron will have the right to inherit from his natural mother, Karen, and from his adoptive parent, Fred, and they, in turn, will have a right to inherit from Ron.

Note: Not all states follow the procedures described in these examples. Several states allow adopted children to inherit from their biological kindred; see Ala. Code § 43–8–48; La. Civ. Code art. 214; Tex. Fam. Code § 15.07; and Wyo. Stat. § 2–4–107. Since a testator can leave an estate to anyone, with the exception that a surviving spouse cannot be disinherited, the adoption rules apply only to intestacy cases. When a testator has an adopted child whom he wants to treat equally as a natural child, a clause such as the following should be added to the will to avoid confusion:

Sample Clause
For the purpose of this will, the words "issue," "child," or "children" used within this will describing the relationship of a person or class of persons to another shall refer both to persons who are related by blood and also to any person whose relationship is acquired by adoption.

Adults can also be adopted. When this occurs, the purpose is generally to allow the adopted adult to inherit, or take by will, from the adopting person. The case *In re Adult Anonymous II,* 88 A.D.2d 30, 452 N.Y.S.2d 198 (1982), in which a gay lover was adopted, is an example of adoption for inheritance purposes. Adult adoptions may only affect the inheritance rights of the immediate parties.

Nonmarital (Illegitimate) Children

A **nonmarital child** is a child born to parents who are not married to each other. The child is said to be born out of lawful wedlock. A nonmarital child's inheritance rights are now governed by state statute. Generally, they hold that the child has the right to inherit from and through the child's mother, but the statutes vary about the rights of the child to inherit from the father. However, since the U.S. Supreme Court's decision in *Trimble v. Gordon,* 430 U.S. 762, 97 S.Ct. 1459, 52 L.Ed.2d 31 (1977), established that a nonmarital (illegitimate) child

Nonmarital (illegitimate) child
A child born to parents who are not married.

has a constitutional right to inherit from her father, most states have amended their statutes to avoid unjustified discrimination against nonmarital children. Some states continue to control the right of inheritance from the biological father by requiring either (1) an acknowledgment by the man that he is the father of the child or (2) convincing evidence in a civil paternity lawsuit that the man is the father of the child. Whenever either of these requirements is met, the nonmarital child has the right to inherit from the father; see Cal. Prob. Code § 6408(a); and U.P.C. § 2–114.

Reversing the roles, most states allow parents and their relatives to inherit from their nonmarital (illegitimate) children who die intestate without issue (children). However, the father must establish appropriate proof of paternity; see Ga. Code § 53–4–5 and Tex. Prob. Code § 42, and compare U.P.C. § 2–114(c), in which the father must have treated the child as his and supported the child. Some states, like New York, have passed legislation preventing a parent from inheriting from a child whom the parent abandoned or failed to support during minority; see N.Y. E.P.T.L. § 4–1.4.

Pretermitted (Omitted) Children

Pretermitted (omitted) child

A child omitted in a parent's will.

Unlike a surviving spouse, children can be disinherited by their parents if the omission is intentional. A **pretermitted child** is a child omitted in a will by a parent. If a parent unintentionally does not mention a child or make provision for a child in the will, and that child was either living at the date of the will's execution or was born thereafter, a statute may provide that the child, or the issue of a deceased child, shall receive a share in the estate as though the parent-testator had died intestate. The decision in *Crump's Estate v. Freeman,* 614 P.2d 1096 (Okl. 1980), illustrates this position. The court held that the omitted child (in the case) should receive the same share of the estate that the child would have taken if the testator had died intestate "unless the omission was intentional and not caused by accident or mistake." Most states have statutes that allow a child not named in the will to receive a share of the parent's estate. The Uniform Probate Code and other state statutes, however, include only children who were born after the will was executed; see U.P.C. § 2–302 which limits the amount to the omitted child to an equal amount that is given to other children. Other states cover children born before or after the execution of the will; see Mass. Gen. Laws Ann. ch. 191, § 20. For an adopted child, the date of the adoption rather than the date of birth is controlling. An example of a state statute on the pretermitted child's right to inherit is Wis. Stat. Ann. § 853.25(5).

Under a pretermitted statute, a testator, while living, must either (1) make some settlement or give an equal share of property to the omitted child (or grandchild, if the child is dead and there is a grandchild) by way of advancement; (2) after death, name the child as a beneficiary in the will; *or* (3) make it clear in the will that the omission of the child was intentional. Thus, a parent can give a child little or nothing through a will but must do so expressly; if the child is not mentioned at all in the will, the assumption is that the omission was inadvertent and not intended. The testator should include a specific clause in the will to establish a clear intent concerning pretermitted or omitted children.

Sample Disinheritance Clause

I have intentionally not provided in this will for my daughter, Elizabeth May Johnson, and for my son, Robert Jay Johnson, and these omissions are not caused by accident or mistake.

Section 2–101(b) of the Uniform Probate Code officially recognizes the right of the testator to disinherit any heir, except a surviving spouse, by specifically excluding the named person or class of persons in the will.

Additional Rights or Protection for a Surviving Spouse and Children

In addition to the specific rights of a surviving spouse and children discussed above, these family members may receive benefits from a decedent spouse's estate that are not determined by the decedent's will or the state intestate succession statute. These benefits, established by other specific statutes, include the homestead exemption, homestead allowance, family or "widow's" support or allowance, and exempt property. They take priority not only over the decedent's will or the intestacy laws but also over creditors' claims against the decedent's estate.

Homestead Exemption

In most states, statutes protect a family that owns their house from eviction by creditors by allowing the head of the household or family to designate a house and land as the homestead. This **homestead exemption** is free from claims and execution by creditors regardless of the amount of the household's debt.

The **homestead** is defined as the house and adjoining land occupied by the owner (decedent) as a home. The amount of land comprising the homestead may be limited in acreage by statute. For example, in Kansas a rural homestead is limited to 160 acres and an urban homestead to one acre. The following Minnesota statutes define a homestead, identify its area limits, and explain its descent to surviving family members:

Homestead exemption
A statute that protects a family from eviction from their home by creditors.

Homestead
The house and adjoining land occupied by the owner (decedent) as a home.

Minn. Stat. Ann. § 510.01 Homestead Defined; Exempt; Exception
The house owned and occupied by a debtor as his dwelling place, together with the land upon which it is situated to the amount of area and value hereinafter limited and defined, shall constitute the homestead of such debtor and his family, and be exempt from seizure or sale under legal process on account of any debts not lawfully charged thereon in writing, except such as are incurred for work or materials furnished in the construction, repair, or improvement of such homestead, or for services performed by laborers or servants.

Minn. Stat. Ann. § 510.02 Area and value; how limited
The homestead may include any quantity of land not exceeding 160 acres, and not included in the laid out or platted portion of any city. If the homestead is within the laid out or platted portion of a city, its area must not exceed one-half of an acre. The value of the homestead exemption, whether the exemption is claimed jointly or individually, may not exceed $200,000 or, if the homestead is used primarily for agricultural purposes, $500,000, exclusive of the limitations set forth in section 510.05.

Minn. Stat. Ann. § 524.2–402 Descent of Homestead
(a) If there is a surviving spouse, the homestead, including a manufactured home which is the family residence, descends free from any testamentary or other disposition of it to which the spouse has not consented in writing or as provided by law, as follows:
   (1) if there is no surviving descendant of decedent, to the spouse; or
   (2) if there are surviving descendants of decedent, then to the spouse for the term of the spouse's natural life and the remainder in equal shares to the decedent's descendants by representation.
   (b) If there is no surviving spouse and the homestead has not been disposed of by will it descends as other real estate.

(c) If the homestead passes by descent or will to the spouse or decedent's descendants, it is exempt from all debts which were not valid charges on it at the time of decedent's death except that the homestead is subject to a claim filed pursuant to section 246.53 for state hospital care or 256B.15 for medical assistance benefits. If the homestead passes to a person other than a spouse or decedent's descendants, it is subject to the payment of the items mentioned in section 524.2–101. No lien or other charge against a homestead so exempted is enforceable in the probate court, but the claimant may enforce the lien or charge by an appropriate action in the district court.

(d) For purposes of this section, except as provided in section 524.2–301, the surviving spouse is deemed to consent to any testamentary or other disposition of the homestead to which the spouse has not previously consented in writing unless the spouse files in the manner provided in section 524.2–211, paragraph (f), a petition that asserts the homestead rights provided to the spouse by this section.

It is common practice for spouses (husband and wife) to have title to their home in the joint tenancy form of ownership. When such is the case and one of the spouses dies without a will, the transfer of the homestead is not affected. As previously mentioned, the decedent's interest in jointly owned property of any kind, real or personal, automatically passes to the surviving joint tenant as a result of the right of survivorship. Thus, in the case of a homestead, when a husband dies, owning a home in joint tenancy with his wife, the house belongs to the wife automatically whether his death has taken place with a will or without. Because it is not affected by either intestate succession statutes or wills, jointly owned property is an example of *nonprobate property* (see Chapter 12).

To illustrate the passage of a homestead upon the intestate death of its owner, consider the following assignment.

🏛 ASSIGNMENT 4.4

Henry and Wilma are husband and wife. They have been married for the past 32 years, and Henry owns their house in his name only. Henry suddenly dies without having executed a will, leaving surviving his widow, Wilma; two children, Abby and Beth; and six grandchildren: Cindy and Daniel, Abby's children; Elaine and Fred, Beth's children; and George and Ida, children of Henry's already deceased child, Stanley. The house, in which Henry and Wilma lived, has a lien against it for partial nonpayment of 1994 property taxes and a 30-year mortgage with 5 years remaining. According to your state laws, how, to whom, and in what shares will the house descend? Is the descent of the homestead free from claims against it?

If both spouses are living, most states provide that the homestead cannot be sold without the consent and signature of each spouse.

Homestead Allowance

Homestead allowance
A statute that provides a modest cash award for the benefit of a surviving spouse or minor children; it is a priority payment to them and is not subject to creditors' claims.

Instead of a homestead exemption, some states provide a modest cash award called a **homestead allowance** for the benefit of a surviving spouse or minor children. This allowance is also not subject to creditors' claims and is a priority payment made to the surviving spouse or children in addition to any property passing to them by the provisions of a will, by intestate succession, or by a surviving spouse's election rights; see U.P.C. § 2–402.

Exempt Property

Many states and the Uniform Probate Code also exempt from creditors' claims a certain amount of the decedent's personal property up to a specific dollar amount, which is given to the surviving spouse and/or children. The property is often limited to household furniture, appliances, furnishings, automobiles, and personal effects, and the number of items in the various categories that constitute the **exempt property** can also be limited, e.g., one car; see Ala. Code § 43–8–111; R. I. Gen. Laws § 33–10–1; Va. Code § 64.1–151.2; and U.P.C. § 2–403. Under the Uniform Probate Code, all of the exempt property goes to the surviving spouse; it goes to the children only if there is no surviving spouse. Sections 271, 272, and 278 of the Texas Probate Code allow either minor or adult children to receive exempt property. In cases in which the decedent did not own any qualifying exempt personal property, state laws may provide for a modest cash allowance in place of the property; see Tex. Prob. Code §§ 273–277. Exempt property is identified in the following statute:

Minn. Stat. Ann. § 524.2–403 Exempt Property

(a) If there is a surviving spouse, then, in addition to the homestead and family allowance, the surviving spouse is entitled from the estate to:

(1) property not exceeding $10,000 in value in excess of any security interests therein, in household furniture, furnishings, appliances, and personal effects, subject to an award of sentimental value property under section 525.152; and

(2) one automobile, if any, without regard to value.

(b) If there is no surviving spouse, the decedent's children are entitled jointly to the same property as provided in paragraph (a).

(c) If encumbered chattels are selected and the value in excess of security interests, plus that of other exempt property, is less than $10,000, or if there is not $10,000 worth of exempt property in the estate, the surviving spouse or children are entitled to other personal property of the estate, if any, to the extent necessary to make up the $10,000 value.

(d) Rights to exempt property and assets needed to make up a deficiency of exempt property have priority over all claims against the estate, but the right to any assets to make up a deficiency of exempt property abates as necessary to permit earlier payment of the family allowance.

(e) The rights granted by this section are in addition to any benefit or share passing to the surviving spouse or children by the decedent's will, unless otherwise provided by intestate succession or by way of elective share.

Family or "Widow's" Allowance

During the administration of the decedent spouse's estate, most states give the probate court the power to award the surviving spouse and/or minor children the exempt personal property (see discussion above) *and* a monthly cash allowance for their maintenance and support; see Ariz. Rev. Stat. Ann. § 14–2404; Conn. Gen. Stat. Ann. § 45a–320; Ore. Rev. Stat. § 114.015; and U.P.C. § 2–404. The amount of the award varies, but the award may be terminated by the death of a recipient or remarriage of the surviving spouse, as illustrated by the case of *Hamrick v. Bonner,* 182 Ga.App. 76, 354 S.E.2d 687 (1987). The decedent's will cannot defeat this **"family" allowance** even if the decedent disinherited them, and it, too, is exempt from creditors' claims.

The following statute provides an example of such an allowance:

Exempt property
The decedent's personal property up to a specific dollar amount that is given to the surviving spouse and/or minor children and is exempt from creditors' claims.

Family allowance
A statute that allows the court to award to the surviving spouse and/or minor children some of the decedent's personal property and a monthly cash allowance for their maintenance and support.

Minn. Stat. Ann. § 524.2–404   Family Allowance

(a) In addition to the right to the homestead and exempt property, the decedent's surviving spouse and minor children whom the decedent was obligated to support, and children who were in fact being supported by the decedent, shall be allowed a reasonable family allowance in money out of the estate for their maintenance as follows:

(1) for one year if the estate is inadequate to discharge allowed claims; or

(2) for 18 months if the estate is adequate to discharge allowed claims.

(b) The amount of the family allowance may be determined by the personal representative in an amount not to exceed $1,500 per month.

(c) The family allowance is payable to the surviving spouse, if living; otherwise to the children, their guardian or conservator, or persons having their care and custody.

(d) The family allowance is exempt from and has priority over all claims.

(e) The family allowance is not chargeable against any benefit or share passing to the surviving spouse or children by the will of the decedent unless otherwise provided, by intestate succession or by way of elective share. The death of any person entitled to family allowance does not terminate the right of that person to the allowance.

(f) The personal representative or an interested person aggrieved by any determination, payment, proposed payment, or failure to act under this section may petition the court for appropriate relief, which may include a family allowance other than that which the personal representative determined or could have determined.

See also Chapter 12 on family allowances.

☰ ASSIGNMENT 4.5

Benjamin and Christy, husband and wife, have been married ten years. They have three minor children, Andrew, Shannon, and Lincoln. Benjamin is killed in an airplane mishap. He has no will, and his wife and children survive him. Christy has been advised that probate might be lengthy. Benjamin's estate encompasses (a) a $100,000 house; (b) household furnishings, clothing, and other like items valued at $20,000; (c) additional items of personal property amounting to $15,000; (d) a $10,000 family car. Christy estimates that upkeep for the family during probate of her husband's estate will cost $400 per month. At death, Benjamin's estate had $200,000 in assets and $5,000 in liabilities.

As an exercise in how to analyze a state statute, answer the following according to the family allowance and exempt property procedures under the Minnesota law, mentioned above.

1. From what source and how much can Christy seek as the allowance and exempt property granted a surviving spouse?
2. Will Benjamin's children be entitled to receive the allowance, and if so, when?
3. Does the family allowance or exempt property in this case include the car?
4. Will the family receive a sum of money to maintain it for the balance of the time it takes to administer Benjamin's estate? If so, for how long? If not, why not?
5. Check to see if your state has a family allowance statute. If it does, answer the questions above according to your own state laws.

On the descent of other property, Minn. Stat. Ann. § 524.2–101 states that subject to the family allowances that are granted in cases of both testacy and intestacy, the first items paid out of the estate are the expenses of probate administration, followed by funeral expenses, debts and taxes under federal law, then expenses of the last illness, debts and taxes under state law, and finally all allowed creditors' claims. The balance of the estate, both real and personal property, descends and is distributed as follows:

Minn. Stat. Ann. § 524.2–102   Share of the Spouse

The intestate share of a decedent's surviving spouse is:

(1) the entire intestate estate if:

(i) no descendant of the decedent survives the decedent; or

(ii) all of the decedent's surviving descendants are also descendants of the surviving spouse and there is no other descendant of the surviving spouse who survives the decedent;

(2) the first $150,000 plus one-half of any balance of the intestate estate, if all of the decedent's surviving descendants are also descendants of the surviving spouse and the surviving spouse has one or more surviving descendants who are not descendants of the decedent, or if one or more of the decedent's surviving descendants are not descendants of the surviving spouse.

Minn. Stat. Ann. § 524.2–103   Share of Heirs Other Than Surviving Spouse

Any part of the intestate estate not passing to the decedent's surviving spouse under section 524.2–102, or the entire intestate estate if there is no surviving spouse, passes in the following order to the individuals designated below who survive the decedent:

(1) to the decedent's descendants by representation;

(2) if there is no surviving descendant, to the decedent's parents equally if both survive, or to the surviving parent;

(3) if there is no surviving descendant or parent, to the descendants of the decedent's parents or either of them by representation;

(4) if there is no surviving descendant, parent, or descendant of a parent, but the decedent is survived by one or more grandparents or descendants of grandparents, half of the estate passes to the decedent's paternal grandparents equally if both survive, or to the surviving paternal grandparent, or to the descendants of the decedent's paternal grandparents or either of them if both are deceased, the descendants taking by representation; and the other half passes to the decedent's maternal relatives in the same manner; but if there is no surviving grandparent or descendant of a grandparent on either the paternal or the maternal side, the entire estate passes to the decedent's relatives on the other side in the same manner as the half;

(5) if there is no surviving descendant, parent, descendant of a parent, grandparent, or descendant of a grandparent, to the next of kin in equal degree, except that when there are two or more collateral kindred in equal degree claiming through different ancestors, those who claim through the nearest ancestor shall take to the exclusion of those claiming through an ancestor more remote.

Finally, if neither a spouse nor any kindred survives the intestate, the estate passes to the state by the process of *escheat*. Personal property *escheats* to the state of the decedent's domicile at death as does real property located in that state. Real property situated outside the state of the decedent's domicile escheats to the state of its location.

ILLUSTRATING THE USE OF INTESTATE TERMINOLOGY

The following situation illustrates the meaning and use of the terminology used in cases of intestacy.

The Facts

Toby Smith has died without executing a will. Surviving him are Sally Smith, Toby's present wife; Wylie Smith and Margo Smith Tyler, children by his marriage to Sally; John Smith, an adopted son; Bob Smith, his brother; Sue Smith, his sister; Doris Smith, his mother; Kay and Mary Tyler, Margo's children; Bert and Thad Smith, Wylie's nonmarital (illegitimate) children; Rosey Thorn, Sally's daughter by a previous marriage; Tom Johnson, a foster child living with the Smiths; Jane Carson, a woman Toby had lived with, but not married; and Carol Stuart, Toby's former wife. Frank Malcolm was named administrator by the probate court to handle the affairs of Toby's estate.

Review of Terminology

Toby Smith died *intestate* because he left no will directing the distribution of his estate at his death. His situation of having died without a will is known as *intestacy,* and Toby, as the decedent, is the *intestate.* What, how, and to whom the various items of property in his estate pass on his death are controlled by *intestate succession statutes,* state laws governing the process by which intestate estates are administered. In effect, they write the "will" when the decedent fails to write one. In this case, the statutes of Toby's home state will be referred to for this purpose.

Various blood relatives, ranked in order of closeness to the intestate, in addition to the decedent's spouse, are the *successors, distributees,* or *heirs* who receive a portion of the decedent's estate. The class of individuals entitled to share in the distribution of an *intestate* estate are called *heirs.* Under the Uniform Probate Code, an heir may receive either real or personal property, or both. Confusion exists in the terminology used to describe the manner in which property passes from an intestate. Under the orthodox terminology, an *heir* is one entitled to inherit the decedent's real property, and a *distributee* or *next-of-kin* is one entitled to inherit the decedent's personal property. However, these words are frequently used interchangeably.

All persons mentioned in the situation above who survived Toby, including his adopted son John, are potential *successors, distributees,* or *heirs,* except Rosey Thorn, Tom Johnson, Jane Carson, and Carol Stuart, who are not blood relatives and do not trace their relationship to Toby through *consanguinity.* His mother, Doris, is an *ascendant* possessing an interest in the estate through a direct upward bloodline as an ascending *lineal ancestor.* Wylie, Margo, Bert, Thad, Kay, and Mary, Toby's children and grandchildren, being in a direct bloodline downward as descending lineals, are his *descendants.* Bob and Sue, his brother and sister, are not direct blood *lineals,* but instead trace their relationship to him through their mother, Doris, as a common ancestor. They are *collaterals* in a collateral relationship line to Toby.

Toby's adopted son, John Smith, would be entitled to share in the estate equally with Toby's natural children in virtually all states today by statute. An example of one such statute is former Cal. Prob. Code § 257 (now § 6408):

> An adopted child shall be deemed a descendant of one who has adopted him, the same as a natural child, for all purposes of succession by, from, or through the adopting parent the same as a natural parent. An adopted child does not succeed to the estate of a natural parent when the relationship between them has been severed by adoption, nor does such natural parent succeed to the estate of such adopted child, nor does such adopted child succeed to the estate of a relative of the natural parent, nor does any relative of the natural parent succeed to the estate of the adopted child.

Statutes such as these entitle adopted children to inherit from their adoptive parents on the same basis that natural children have for inheritance—lineal descent. At the same time, adopted children are precluded from inheritance from their natural parents. The law declares the latter relationship null and void and treats it as though it had never existed.

The inheritance rights of a child whose natural parent dies and whose surviving parent remarries and the new spouse legally adopts the child are sometimes delineated by statute:

> *Conn. Gen. Stat. Ann. § 45a–731* Effects of Final Decree of Adoption—Surviving Rights
> A final decree of adoption whether issued by a court of this state or a court of any other jurisdiction shall have the following effect in this state: . . .
>   (8) Notwithstanding the provisions of subdivisions (1) and (7) when one of the genetic parents of a minor child has died and the surviving parent has remarried subsequent to such parent's death, adoption of such child by the person with whom such remarriage is contracted shall not affect the rights of such child to inherit from or through the deceased parent . . . .

Depending on the statutes of Toby's domicile state, Wylie's nonmarital children, Bert and Thad, may or may not inherit from Toby, but such inheritance is possible only if Wylie dies before Toby. Most state statutes would allow Bert and Thad to inherit their mother's share of Toby's estate by representation. Tom Johnson, the foster child living with the Smiths, would not inherit from Toby.

🏛 ASSIGNMENT 4.6

After Louis's father died, his mother remarried; her second husband legally adopted Louis as his son. Three weeks later, the brother of Louis's natural father died intestate, leaving no surviving children. Louis wishes to claim a part of his uncle's estate. Is he entitled? Cite statutory authority from the state of Connecticut. If this situation had occurred in your state, what statute(s) would control it?

In most states, all the successors (heirs) in the same degree of relationship to the intestate share equally through *per capita* distribution. If Toby had died leaving only his children as surviving heirs, then Wylie, Margo, and John would each receive one-third of his estate per capita, a distribution equally divided among the heirs standing in the same degree of relationship to the intestate.

Example:

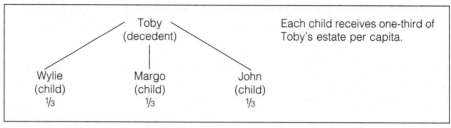

The same is true if only his grandchildren are living and Toby's domicile state statutes allow nonmarital children to inherit from their grandparent.

Example:

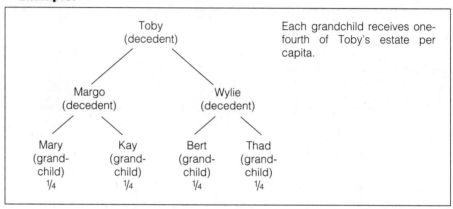

The same is true if only his brother and sister survive his death.

Example:

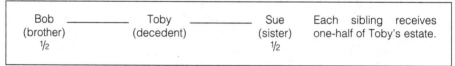

If only the grandchildren survive Toby, then Mary, Kay, Bert, and Thad each receive one-fourth of their grandfather's estate. If only Toby's brother and sister survive, Bob and Sue split their brother's estate equally.

A different result is reached when a successor (heir) predeceases the intestate decedent. If Wylie had died before her father, then when Toby died, his grandchildren through Wylie (Bert and Thad) would receive their mother's share of their grandfather's estate through the dead parent, Wylie, by right of representation (*per stirpes*) to be divided equally between them. If only Toby's natural daughter, Margo, his adopted son, John, and two of his grandchildren, Bert and Thad, survived him, this distribution per stirpes results in Margo's receiving one-third and John receiving one-third of their father's estate, and Bert and Thad each receiving one-sixth of their grandfather's estate, sharing equally the one-third interest their mother, Wylie, would have received had she survived her father, Toby.

Example:

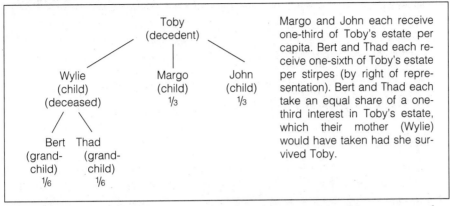

Toby
(decedent)

Wylie
(child)
(deceased)

Margo
(child)
⅓

John
(child)
⅓

Bert
(grand-
child)
⅙

Thad
(grand-
child)
⅙

Margo and John each receive one-third of Toby's estate per capita. Bert and Thad each receive one-sixth of Toby's estate per stirpes (by right of representation). Bert and Thad each take an equal share of a one-third interest in Toby's estate, which their mother (Wylie) would have taken had she survived Toby.

If Toby died without the above-named persons surviving him, or any other relatives entitled to inherit his estate, the property *escheats* to the state. The state acquires title to the intestate's property by the process of escheat.

Since Frank Malcolm has been appointed to handle the distribution of Toby's estate, he is the *administrator* of the estate functioning under the supervision of the probate court. If, however, Frank's sister, Karen (or any other woman), had been appointed by the probate court, she would be the *administratrix* of Toby's estate, performing the same duties.

ASSIGNMENT 4.7

Mary Worth died without a will, leaving the following relatives surviving her: a husband, Atkinson, from her present marriage; an adopted daughter, Lana; a foster son, Thomas; two sisters, Faith and Nadine, and a brother, Thor; her mother, Theresa, and father, Lorenzo; her mother-in-law, Islodean; Atkinson's sister, Cynthia; an aunt, Rose, and an uncle, Oscar; two nephews, Donnie and Kevin, sons of her deceased brother, William; a niece, Diane, daughter of her deceased sister, Sharon; a grandson, David, son of her deceased daughter, Denise; a granddaughter, Luella, daughter of her deceased daughter, Nancy; and Manny, a husband by a prior marriage whom she divorced.

1. Who is the intestate?
2. Who is the administrator or administratrix?
3. Name the laws that govern the passage of the decedent's estate.
4. Find and cite the state statute that would determine the passage of Mary's estate in your state.
5. Name the decedent's lineal relatives who are ascendants and descendants.
6. Name the collaterals related to the decedent.
7. List all the potential successors (heirs) of the decedent.
8. Name the relationship that entitles the persons in question 7 to possibly share in the decedent's estate.
9. List relatives who might be excluded from receiving any of the decedent's property.
10. How are the persons in question 9 related to the decedent?

11. Name relatives who might receive their share of the decedent's estate per capita.
12. Name relatives who might receive their share of the decedent's estate per stirpes.
13. What would happen if the decedent had no surviving spouse or relatives?
14. Diagram a family tree for Mary and her relatives.

ADVANTAGES AND DISADVANTAGES OF HAVING A WILL

Advantages of a Will

The history of descent and distribution (intestate) statutes proves that the individual's execution of a valid will avoids many of the legal problems that may accompany an intestate's estate.

Most individuals want to have a say in the distribution of their estate. By writing a will, a person can designate how and to whom all property owned, real and personal, is to be distributed after death. When no will exists, an estate will be distributed according to the state's intestate succession statutes. The decedent's orally transmitted wishes, even if known, would not be upheld by the courts without a will. Intestate succession statutes do not take into consideration the financial status of the decedent's relatives.

Example: Harry and Sharon are the adult children and only surviving heirs of their father, Dennis. Harry is wealthy; Sharon is destitute. If Dennis dies intestate, his estate will be divided equally between his two children. A will could have provided for a larger gift to Sharon and a smaller gift, or none at all, to Harry.

Without a will, distribution of the estate under intestate succession statutes may result in the apportionment of the estate to persons to whom the decedent might not wish to devise anything, while others whom the decedent might wish to share in the estate receive nothing.

Example: John dies intestate. During the last four years of his life, John had constantly fought over family matters with one of his brothers, Harold. John did not intend to leave any of his property to Harold, but procrastinated in writing a will and died before executing one. John's only heirs were Harold and two other brothers, Mark and Luke. All three surviving brothers would inherit John's property in equal shares.

In the last example, John had on numerous occasions voiced his intent to leave his entire estate to his church and to the Memorial Heart Hospital. Unless John transferred his property to these recipients as *inter vivos* gifts while he lived *or* named the church and the hospital as beneficiaries or devisees in a valid will, his intentions would be frustrated.

Many if not most decedents wish to choose the recipients of their property and to distribute the property according to the relative need or worthiness of the chosen recipients. The decedent may wish to reward faithful long-term employees or others with a testamentary gift.

Example: For the past five years, Maria has been an invalid and confined to a wheelchair. Her constant companion and friend is Sandra. If, after her death, Maria wishes to leave a gift of property from her estate to Sandra, the only way she can accomplish this purpose is through a will. Because Sandra is not Maria's heir, Sandra will not receive any property if Maria dies intestate.

Another advantage of having a will is that the testator has the opportunity to select the person who will be the personal representative (executor or executrix). At the same time, the testator can give the named executor or executrix special powers relating to the estate, for example, the power to sell any property owned by the decedent, the authority to settle claims, and the right to distribute the residue of the estate.

A will also gives a person the opportunity to create testamentary trusts and to appoint trustees whose function it is to administer the trusts established by the will. The powers of the trustee are set forth in the will, but must conform to statutory guidelines (for a discussion of trusts, see Chapters 8 and 9). In a will, the testator can also nominate a personal guardian to care for any minor children, subject to the approval of the probate court, and a property guardian to manage the property inherited by the minor. The personal guardian and the property guardian may or may not be the same person.

In addition, the decedent's estate may benefit from certain tax advantages when there is a will, and a will may diminish the transfer taxes levied against devisees. Skillful estate planning incorporated into the decedent's will can utilize techniques that minimize the amount of death taxes payable upon the death of a testator (see Chapter 14).

Disadvantages of a Will

A person who dies leaving a will does more of a favor to his beneficiaries than a person who dies without one. Nevertheless, property transferred by will is subject to scrutiny by a probate court before it may pass to the beneficiaries or devisees. The objective of this process is to locate all the heirs, to determine if the testator actually owned more or fewer assets than are mentioned in the will, and to satisfy creditors of the estate whose valid claims legally precede the rights of the beneficiaries or devisees. The probating of a will, however, can be a time-consuming and expensive process, often causing the most inconvenience to those whom the testator intended to benefit.

Simply having a will does not remove the problems accompanying the transfer of ownership from decedent to beneficiary. It is possible for a properly executed and published will to languish in probate until the decedent's estate has dwindled to a fraction of its original size; fees paid to the probate attorney, personal representative (executor or executrix), appraisers, accountant, and other personnel all come out of the decedent's property. Not to be forgotten are the tax revenue agencies, the largest and most insistent "creditors." These Treasury Departments of the state and federal governments appear at all probate proceedings to claim inheritance and estate taxes; in some states, the decedent's assets are frozen for a time by order of the state inheritance tax division, so that it may collect taxes due.

Why does it take so long to probate a will? Bureaucracy, as much as expense, gives the probate process a bad name. The transfer of even a small estate may require the signing of dozens of forms and involve perhaps hundreds of subprocesses, such as the appraisal of real estate mentioned in the will. In addition, the chronic congestion of probate court calendars (remember that an estate is not finished until declared settled by a probate judge) causes lengthy delays.

Fortunately, there is a way for you to help the testator bypass many of the hazards of probate while still having a will. *Proper advance planning* by the property owner (estate planning) goes a long way toward eliminating complications that may result in the property being tied up for years while the beneficiaries wait. Estate planning might be compared to preventive medicine. Its task is to prevent future difficulties by the present application of legal and financial expertise to the testator's wishes. A testator might wish to leave property to named beneficiaries but know nothing of the possibility of making nontestamentary (not subject to probate) dispositions such as *inter vivos* transactions, which could prove more advantageous to those beneficiaries. (See *inter vivos* trusts, Chapter 9). The duty of your supervising attorney is to make sure that the client is aware of the estate planning options available, and your responsibility is to make the best use of them in drafting the will and trust, so that the testator's property changes ownership with a minimum of friction, expense, and delay.

Having a will enables a person to devise property in virtually any way; the testator or testatrix may give more to a favorite child or a close friend than intestate succession statutes would allow. There are, however, instances in which "the law's own estate plan" (intestate succession statutes' plan of distribution) works just as well as a will.

- A person who dies without a will, leaving the state to apportion the property, actually does more good to the heirs than the person who dies with a will that does not stand the test of time (becomes obsolete by the time the testator dies) or contains so many uncertainties that it may cause extensive (and expensive) will contests.

ETHICAL ISSUE ▶
- *A will drafted by an attorney or a paralegal who has little or no experience with probate matters (e.g., a family friend who happens to be a lawyer or paralegal) may turn out to be a poor instrument when the testator dies.* For example, devises may be awarded to persons to whom the testator did not want to give anything.

- Persons who try to cut corners by obtaining a will at the lowest possible price may find themselves with a will that is too general; it hardly fits the testator's needs or wishes apart from some basic dispositions.

- On the other hand, a person who insists that the attorney draft a complex will should think twice if the estate is small or the devisees few. The possibility of something highly unusual happening that the complex will would take care of (e.g., the deaths of the spouse and all the devisees before the death of the testator) would hardly justify the necessity of paying an increased fee.

The point is that it is disadvantageous to have an ill-fitting, poorly drafted, or inadequate will; in such cases, having no will may be better than having a defective one.

🏛 ASSIGNMENT 4.8

1. Review § 1–201 of the U.P.C. in Appendix C on general definitions. Does your state's code have a separate section on such definitions? Note any differences from those presented in this text.
2. Does every eligible member of your family have a will? Why or why not? Should they? If a member of your family has no will, list reasons why that person should have a will.
3. Secure a copy of someone's will (e.g., spouse, parent) or a sample will from a law library and identify as many of the terms defined in this chapter as possible.

4. Roy Hallet had not made a will before he died. His survivors included a wife, Ida; three children, Nancy, Marie, and Bart; a sister, Carmela; a brother-in-law, Roger (Carmela's husband); a niece, Melanie; two second cousins, Bernie and Barbara. Roy's property included the family house, which was in his name only; several pieces of antique furniture, which he was refinishing; five U.S. savings bonds with a face value of $1,000 each; and a diamond valued at $15,000. Which of his relatives would receive Roy's property according to the intestate succession statute of your state?

KEY TERMS

Testacy	Living will	Degree of	Homestead
Intestacy	Ademption	relationship	exemption
Will contest	Lapses	Escheat	Homestead
Uniform Probate	Abatement	Nonmarital	Homestead
Code (U.P.C.)	Marshaling the assets	(illegitimate) child	allowance
Nuncupative will	Right of representation	Pretermitted	Exempt property
Statutory will	Per stirpes	(omitted) child	Family allowance

REVIEW QUESTIONS

1. What is a will contest? If the contestant of a will is successful and the will is declared invalid, what law determines how and to whom the intestate's in-state and out-of-state real and personal property is distributed?
2. Review the comparison of orthodox and U.P.C. terminology in Exhibit 4.1. How do the meanings of the terms *heir* and *devisee* differ between the two sets of terminology?
3. What are four types of basic wills? Define and explain each one.
4. Explain the differences between (A) a bequest and a devise; (B) a specific legacy and a specific devise; (C) a demonstrative legacy and a general legacy; and (D) a residuary legacy and a residuary devise.
5. What does it mean when a gift in a will is adeemed or lapses?
6. When there are insufficient assets in the testator's estate to pay all debts, taxes, and expenses, what is the order of abatement of the decedent's assets including legacies and devises?
7. How does per capita distribution differ from per stirpes distribution in intestacy cases?
8. Which computation method, the civil law method or the common law method, do you prefer to determine the degree of relationship of collateral heirs? Explain.
9. What does the term *escheat* mean? When does escheat occur?
10. Why is it generally impossible for a testator to disinherit his or her surviving spouse? Explain.
11. What effect does a divorce or a marriage have on a preexisting will?
12. What are the inheritance rights of an adopted child; a stepchild; a nonmarital child; and a pretermitted child?
13. How does a homestead exemption differ from a homestead allowance? How do family allowances differ from exempt property?
14. What are the advantages and disadvantages of a will?

CASE PROBLEMS

Problem 1

Emmett Tomas, a bachelor, makes the following testamentary gifts: a house valued at $110,000 to his best friend, Roxanne Rudin; furniture and household appliances worth $8,000 to Roxanne; a television and stereo system worth $2,500 to his nephew, Roland Tomas; a 1994 Toyota Camry worth $15,000 to his only brother, William Tomas; a gift of $10,000 to his sister-in-law, Sally Tomas, to be paid out of his savings account in Metro State Bank in his hometown; a gift of $5,000 to his church; and a residue gift of his remaining property, which is all personal property worth $22,000, to the American Cancer Society.

A. Place each gift in the appropriate disposition category:

    Specific devise
    Specific legacy
    Residuary legacy
    General legacy
    Demonstrative legacy

B. After his death, Emmett's expenses, debts, and taxes amount to $50,000 and none of his assets pass outside his will as intestate property. Explain how Emmett's testamentary gifts are used to pay his obligations according to the abatement process.

C. If William dies before Emmett and no successor beneficiary is named to receive the Toyota before Emmett dies, what happens to this gift and how does it abate?

D. If the law in Emmett's domicile state "abates" a decedent's property within each disposition category and uses the property for payment of debts on a prorated basis, how much, if any, of the specific legacies does each beneficiary get to keep after the $50,000 obligation is paid? See *Matter of the Estate of Wales,* 727 P.2d 536 (1986).

Problem 2

The following diagram shows the interest each descendant would receive in Howard's estate. All descendants are living except as noted.

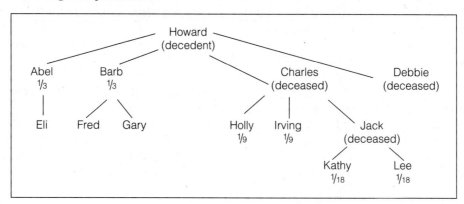

A. Is the distribution method per capita or per stirpes? See *Godwin v. Marvel,* 55 Del. 1, 99 A.2d 354 (1953), and *Estate of Morton,* 48 N.J. 42, 222 A.2d 185 (1966).

B. Explain how the shares of Abel and Barb are determined.

C. Eli, Fred, and Gary do not receive an interest. Why not? Explain.

D. Explain the calculation of the shares of Kathy and Lee.

E. If Debbie was married, would her surviving husband receive an interest? Explain.

CHAPTER FIVE

WILLS: VALIDITY REQUIREMENTS, MODIFICATION, REVOCATION, AND CONTESTS

OBJECTIVES

After completing this chapter, you should be able to:

- Use the terminology associated with the validity, modification, and revocation of wills.
- Recognize the formal requirements for a valid will and verify that a client's will has satisfied all those requirements.
- Interpret statutes and statutory language so that you can apply the statutes to problems presented by a client's will.
- Understand the legal requirements for modifying an existing will and know how to avoid errors in making modifications.

OUTLINE

SCOPE OF THE CHAPTER

Executing, modifying, and revoking wills must be done according to certain statutory guidelines. This chapter presents the terms relating to execution, modification, and revocation and then discusses the basic requirements for the creation of a valid will. Next the ways an existing will can be changed or modified are covered, as are the procedures for demonstrating the intention of a testator or testatrix to revoke a will. The chapter concludes with a discussion of will contests—the proper persons to contest the legality of a will and the grounds for commencing a will contest.

STATUTORY REQUIREMENTS FOR CREATING A VALID WILL

A will is a legally enforceable, written declaration of a person's intended distribution of property after death. Because a will is "ambulatory," i.e., subject to change, the declaration is revocable during the testator's lifetime and is operative only upon death. Each state passes legislation that controls the right and power of a person to execute a will, and these statutes and subsequent case law (court decisions) establish the procedure that must be followed. The following are examples of state statutes concerned with the requirements for testamentary capacity and the proper execution of a will.

> *20 Pa. Stat. Ann. § 2501* Who May Make a Will—Testamentary Capacity
> Any person 18 or more years of age who is of sound mind may make a will.
>
> *Minn. Stat. Ann. § 524.2–502* Execution: Witnessed Wills
> Except as provided in sections 524.2–506 and 524.2–513, a will must be:
>   (1) in writing;
>   (2) signed by the testator or in the testator's name by some other individual in the testator's conscious presence and by the testator's direction; and
>   (3) signed by at least two individuals, each of whom signed within a reasonable time after he or she witnessed either the signing of the will as described in clause (2) or the testator's acknowledgment of that signature or acknowledgment of the will.

⚖ ASSIGNMENT 5.1

Mike Hasper is 17 years old. He handwrites and signs a will leaving all his property to his brother, Matthew. There are no witnesses to the will. At age 23, Mike is killed while driving a car. Mike's only other living relative is his mother, Mary. Answer the following questions according to your own state laws:
1. Is Mike's will valid? Explain.
2. Does Mike's holographic will need witnesses? Must it be dated?
3. What formal requirements for the proper execution of a will are lacking?
4. If both Mary and Matthew claim Mike's estate, who prevails? Explain.

The importance of learning your own state's requirements for making a valid will cannot be overstated. At the same time, even though state statutes regulating the preparation and execution of wills are far from uniform and vary widely, they do share some basic similarities. All of them require wills to comply with certain formalities in order to prevent fraud and uncertainty. Commonly, the following are required for a properly executed will: (1) the maker must have testamentary capacity; (2) the will must satisfy certain formal requirements; (3) the will must be signed and dated; and (4) the will must be witnessed.

Intent of the Testator

For a will to be declared a legal document that can transfer a decedent's estate after death, the maker must have testamentary intent; that is, the testator must establish that the written document currently operates as his last will. The document is a valid will only if the maker possesses the required *animus testandi,* the intention to make a will with the express purpose of disposing of property upon death—but not before, as illustrated by the case of *Faith v. Singleton,* 286 Ark. 403, 692 S.W.2d 239 (1985). The testator's intent is revealed from the form, general language, and particular words used in the will itself. Many courts, however, also look at the surrounding circumstances in determining testamentary intent, e.g., the comments and activities of a person who is terminally ill, the collection and placement of important papers in a safe location, and comments made by a person about distribution plans after death. The absence of the ceremonial declaration "this is my last will" often creates doubt about whether a will is intended (see *Matter of Griffin's Will,* 81 A.D.2d 735, 439 N.Y.S.2d 492 [1981], in which the court ruled that because the testatrix, Griffin, did not declare or publish to the witnesses that she intended a document they signed to be her will, the document was not entitled to be probated). Courts have often ruled, however, that a document need not be labeled a "will" to be a valid testamentary instrument. In the case of *Estate of Logan's,* 489 Pa. 29, 413 A.2d 681 (1980), a paper stating, "I give all my monies and estates to my sister Lillian," was declared a will and probated.

Caveat: With the exception of "statutory" wills, which have been adopted in a few states (see the detailed discussion in Chapter 6), writing one's own will or using printed will forms to avoid the expense of an attorney may be foolhardy. Even worse, it may end in the creation of a document that fails to satisfy the statutory requirements for a legal will regardless of the good intentions of the maker.

Capacity of the Testator

As we saw in Chapter 1, testamentary capacity is necessary for the creation of a valid will. In all states, a testator must be of majority age (usually 18) and sane to have testamentary capacity (see U.P.C. § 2–501). State statutes and court decisions have established, however, that a member of the armed forces or a married person can make a valid will even if under the age of majority (see Texas Prob. Code § 57 and Iowa Code § 599.1). Sanity is the "soundness of mind" that enables a person to have sufficient mental capacity to create a valid will. In general, a testator must meet the following test for testamentary capacity (sound mind):

- The testator must remember and be aware of the persons who are the "**natural objects** of his or her bounty"—usually family members but also persons for whom the testator has affection.

Natural objects of the testator's bounty
Family members and other persons, e.g., friends, and institutions, e.g., charitable or religious organizations, for whom the testator has affection.

■ The testator must know and be aware of the kind, extent, and nature of the property to be distributed.

■ The testator must formulate a plan, e.g., a will, for disposing of the property to the intended beneficiaries, i.e., family and friends, and understand the effect of the dispositions of the plan.

The Oklahoma case *In the Matter of the Estate of Lacy,* 431 P.2d 366 (Okl. 1967), illustrates the application of this test. The court stated, "A person has 'testamentary capacity' when his mind and memory are such that he knows in a general way the character and extent of his property, understands his relationship to the objects of his bounty and those who ought to be in his mind on occasion of making his will, and comprehends the nature and effect of the testamentary act."

This test for "sound mind," which was formed in case law instead of statutes, relates to the testator's ability, not to his actual knowledge of details. Still a testator must be able to hold these facts in mind long enough to make a rational judgment. Such capacity is needed only at the time of making and executing the will. Even though a person has a low level of intelligence or suffers from a mental illness or senility, it does not mean the person automatically lacks testamentary capacity. The individual case and circumstances must be investigated and judged on the basis of the test, as established in cases such as *Estate of Wrigley,* 104 Ill.App.3rd. 1008, 60 Ill.Dec. 757, 433 N.E.2d 995 (1982). Case law has consistently held that neither eccentricities or peculiarities of the will nor uncleanliness, slovenliness, neglect of person and clothing, and offensive and disgusting habits of a testator constitute an "unsound mind."

Insane delusions
A person with a disordered mind who imagines facts to exist for which there is no evidence.

Lucid interval
A temporary restoration to sanity during which an incompetent person has sufficient intelligence and judgment to make a valid will.

A common question when determining testamentary capacity is whether a person suffering "delusions" lacks such capacity. Some courts have held that a testator suffering delusions is not mentally competent. Most have decided that the presence of **insane delusions** is not inconsistent with testamentary capacity, if the delusions are of such a nature that they cannot reasonably have affected the dispositions made by a will. The testimony of witnesses to the will is often critical in court decisions on "delusions" as noted in *Yett's* case in Chapter 1. See also *Matter of Coleman's Estate,* 1 Hawaii App. 136, 615 P.2d 760 (1980), in which the court held that during a **"lucid interval,"** a mentally ill person can execute a valid will.

In will contest cases, Section 3–407 of the Uniform Probate Code places the burden of proof of the lack of the testator's capacity on the contestant—the person contesting the will (this was the decision in the *Matter of the Estate of Lacy,* cited above). Some states, however, place the burden of proof of the testator's "sound mind" on the proponent—the person who submits or delivers the will to the court—as in the case of *Croucher v. Croucher,* 660 S.W.2d 55 (Tex. 1983). The procedures generally followed to satisfy the burden of proof and establish testamentary capacity (i.e., sound mind) include:

■ The filing of the will.
■ The witnesses' testimony or affidavits acknowledging the proper formal procedures required for a valid will and the testator's rational behavior and comments *at the time of the execution of the will.*
■ The order of the probate court admitting the probate of the will.

Then, during the contest of the will, others, in addition to the witnesses, may testify concerning the testator's "sound mind." Family members, the testator's personal physician, and other medical care providers may testify, for example. Since this determination of testamentary capacity is a "fact issue," the decision of capacity or lack thereof is generally left to a jury or the court. As a paralegal, if you are asked to witness a will, you must make your judgment of the testator's capacity at the time of the execution of the will with the understanding that *if the testator obviously lacks capacity you should not sign the will.*

ETHICAL ISSUE

⛩ ASSIGNMENT 5.2

1. Billy Budd, age 18, inherited an estate valued at $150,000 from his father. Billy wants his property to go to his dog, Snoopy. Therefore, Billy executes a formal written will leaving all his property to his dog and providing that when the dog dies, the remaining property is to be given to the Animal Humane Society. At age 20, while walking on the railroad tracks, Billy is killed by a train. Billy's only living relative, his mother, claims his estate. Was Billy's will valid in your state when he died? Who would receive Billy's estate according to the law in your state?

2. Bradford is not married and has no heirs besides his sisters, Katherine and Clara, with whom he lives and who are completely dependent on him for support. Upon his death, he wills his entire estate of $100,000 to the American Lung Association, making it necessary for his sisters to live on welfare payments. Would Katherine and Clara have grounds on which to challenge the will by alleging that Bradford lacked the capacity to make a valid will? Answer the question according to your state's laws.

Formal Requirements of a Will

In addition to being made by a person with testamentary capacity, a will must be executed in accordance with certain formal requirements to be valid.

A Written Will

By either statute or case law, a majority of the states require a will to be in writing to be valid (see U.P.C. § 2–502). Generally, a will must be either typed, printed, or handwritten to fulfill the requirement. A completely handwritten, or holographic, will is valid in some states, but it must meet all other formal requirements (except the requirement of witnesses' signatures) unless otherwise provided by statute. Section 133.090(1) of the Nevada Revised Statute provides:

> A holographic will is one that is entirely written, dated, and signed by the hand of the testator himself. It is subject to no other form, and may be made in or out of this state and need not be witnessed.

Currently, twenty-seven states allow holographic wills, but the details of the requirements differ from state to state. In the case of *In re Estate of Cunningham,* 198 N.J.Super. 484, 487 A.2d 777 (1984), the court did not require a holographic will to be completely handwritten. Instead, the court held that all that is required to admit the writing to probate as a holographic will is that the signature and material provisions in the will be in the handwriting of the testator. Some states require the will to be signed and dated in the testator's handwriting, but compare U.P.C. § 2–502, which does not require a holographic will to be dated (see Exhibit 4.2 in Chapter 4). The courts have held that an audio tape recording of an oral statement cannot be probated as a will.

⚏ **ASSIGNMENT 5.3**

Jim Brown executed an instrument in his own handwriting, in which he wrote: "To whom it may concern. When I die, I sign everything I own over to my best friend, Sarah Williams." Signed and dated: Jim Brown, August 13, 1994. Mr. Brown was a bachelor. Two witnesses also signed the instrument. Would this document be considered a valid will? Were the witnesses necessary for this will? Answer these questions according to your own state statutes or case law.

A few states allow oral wills under specific conditions. An oral will is called a nuncupative will. It is usually made during a terminal illness in the presence of witnesses or during military service in time of war. When allowed by statute, oral wills generally can pass only personal property. If a nuncupative will is reduced to a writing by the still living testator or by disinterested witnesses (usually two are required) who can attest to the decedent's oral declaration within a statutory time period (e.g., ten to thirty days) after it was spoken, it may be probated. The following are examples of statutes that recognize nuncupative wills under special conditions:

> *Tex. Prob. Code Ann. § 64 (Vernon 1980)* Capacity to Make a Nuncupative Will
> Any person who is competent to make a last will and testament may dispose of his personal property by a nuncupative will made under the conditions and limitations prescribed in this Code.

> *Tex. Prob. Code Ann. § 65 (Vernon 1980)* Requisites of a Nuncupative Will
> No nuncupative will shall be established unless it be made in the time of the last sickness of the deceased, at his home or where he has resided for ten days or more next pre-ceding the date of such will, except when the deceased is taken sick away from home and dies before he returns to such home; nor when the value exceeds Thirty Dollars, unless it be proved by three credible witnesses that the testator called on a person to take notice or bear testimony that such is his will, or words of like import. [For com-parison, see U.P.C. § 2–502, which requires a will to be written.]

Texas allows nuncupative wills under specific circumstances, however, it al-lows such wills to transfer only personal property—not real property—and often only a limited monetary amount of personal property. Therefore, nuncupative wills play a minimal role in actual estate proceedings. The Uniform Probate Code does not allow oral wills.

⚏ **ASSIGNMENT 5.4**

Helen Anderson is dying of cancer at the county hospital. In the presence of her doctor and two nurses, Helen, who has no written will, announces that it is her intent to leave her entire estate to her favorite niece, Alice Marble. She asks those present to act as witnesses of her intention and oral declaration. Helen's only other living relative is another niece, Carla Bergen, whom Helen states she wishes to disinherit. Later that day, Helen dies. According to your own state statutes, would Alice be entitled to Helen's estate? Are nuncupative wills on the "deathbed" of the speaker-decedent valid in the majority of the states?

Signature of the Testator

A will must ordinarily be signed by its maker. However, because of illness or illiteracy, the mere making of a mark, e.g., an "X" or an initial, can suffice in some situations. See *In re Mangeris's Estate,* 55 Cal.App.3d 76, 127 Cal.Rptr. 438 (1976), where the court ruled that a signature by mark is permitted (but other statutory requirements were not met), and *Mitchell v. Mitchell,* 245 Ga. 291, 264 S.E.2d 222 (1980), where an "X" was allowed when directed and intended to be a signature, thereby authenticating the will. Also, a New York statute, N.Y. E.P.T.L. § 3–2.1(n.70), requires that a will bear the testator's signature or some mark, symbol, or inscription that can be regarded as the testator's signature. The court in the case *In re Romaniw's Will,* 163 Misc. 481, 296 N.Y.S. 925 (1937), ruled that a printed or typewritten signature of the testator has been sustained as a valid subscription, but said it should be resorted to only in extreme cases. In addition, in all states a person other than the testator may sign the maker's name to the will in her presence, but such signing must occur at the express direction of the maker, given in a clear manner. The express direction must precede the signing.

Example: If Mary, the wife of Sam, signs his name on his will for Sam, her signing alone does not validate the will. Sam must direct or request that she sign for him. The case of *Matter of Kelly's Estate,* 99 N.M. 482, 660 P.2d 124 (App. 1983), illustrates this requirement. The court ruled that another person who signs the testator's name on the will must be directed by the testator and that two witnesses must attest to the request and the substitute's signature; since those requirements were not met in this case, the will was not admitted to probate.

Courts have also consistently held that subsequent ratification of a prior signed will by a substitute person is not sufficient to reinstate a prior will. On the other hand, at his request, the hand of the testator may be guided by another to aid in the signing. All wills should also be dated in the testator's handwriting, but it is somewhat perplexing that this is not a common requirement except in the holographic wills that are recognized in some states. In the case of *Randall v. Salvation Army,* 100 Nev. 466, 686 P.2d 241 (1984), the court ruled that "the fact a two page instrument bears more than one date does not necessarily make its date uncertain or otherwise prevent it from being probated as a holographic will."

The placement of the testator's signature has created a lot of controversy. In most cases, the maker's signature need not be at the end of the will if it can be shown that the intention to authenticate the will was present. See *In re Estate of Carroll,* 192 Ill. App.3d 202, 139 Ill. Dec. 265, 548 N.E.2d 650 (1989), in which the Illinois court ruled it is immaterial where the signature is written in the will so long as there was intent to authenticate. However, some states insist that the testator's signature appear at the end of the will. Under New York law, the testator's signature marks "the end of the will"; see N.Y. E.P.T.L. § 3–2.1. Accordingly, the New York court in the case of the *Will of Winters,* 302 N.Y. 666, 98 N.E.2d 477 (1951), held the testator must sign at the end of the will. Therefore, testators domiciled in the state of New York should not sign the bottom of each page of their will. The Kansas Supreme Court took a similar position in the case of the *Matter of Reed's Estate,* 229 Kan. 431, 625 P.2d 447 (1981), where the court held that a will must be signed at the end by the testator in order for it to be probated. But compare the comment to U.P.C.§ 2–502, which states that if the testator "writes his name in the body of the will, and intends it to be his signature, this would satisfy the statute" and the will can be probated. Because the proper place for a signature varies from state to state, the statutes of the state that has jurisdiction over the decedent's estate must be checked.

A lengthy will of several pages must be carefully drafted and typed to prevent unscrupulous persons from inserting additional words, names, or even pages into the will. To ensure that there is no opportunity to alter the will, each page should be numbered; no spaces on any page should be large enough for additions or modifications; and the total number of pages should be specifically identified in an attestation clause that states: "The foregoing last will and testament consisting of eight pages, including this page, etc. . . . ." In some states (but not New York), when a will consists of multiple pages, it might be wise for the maker to sign or initial each page; however, all states have routinely validated wills that are signed only on the last page (but compare the *Randall* case previously cited).

⚏ ASSIGNMENT 5.5

1. Michael Shain was 85 years old and suffered from arthritis. He asked that a will be drawn for him. The will was delivered to Michael's hospital room, and in the presence of three witnesses, he said, "This is my last will. I want my property to be distributed according to its provisions." Michael did not sign the will or direct anyone to sign for him. Does this document fulfill the requirements for a valid will in your state based on statute or case law? Compare your answer with Ohio Rev. Code § 2107.03.

2. Viola Carter drew a will satisfying all other statutory requirements of her state, but she signed the eight-page document on the first page only. Would her will be valid in your state? Cite the controlling law and then see U.P.C. § 2–502, Tex. Prob. Code § 59, and Ga. Code Ann. § 53–2–40, and compare 20 Pa. Stat. Ann. § 2502.

3. If Viola had asked Jane to sign Viola's name for her on all eight pages, would her will be valid in your state? Cite the controlling law.

4. If Viola had a twenty-page will and page five was missing when she signed the will, would the will or any part of the will be valid in your state? Cite the controlling law and review *Matter of Griffin's Will,* discussed previously, and compare it to *In re Beale's Estate,* 15 Wis.2d 546, 113 N.W.2d 380 (1962).

5. If Viola misspelled her name or used a nickname when she signed her will, would her will be valid in your state? Cite the controlling law. Compare your answer with 72 ALR 2d 1267 and 98 ALR 2d 841.

6. Viola writes, "I, Viola Carter, leave my property to Phyllis Meyer," but does not sign after the statement. Does the fact that Viola wrote out her name in the statement constitute a "signature"? See *In re Estate of Cunningham,* previously cited, and *McNair's Estate,* 72 S.D. 604, 38 N.W.2d 449 (1949).

Signatures of Witnesses

The purpose of witnesses is to validate that the document declared to be a will was freely and intentionally signed by the testator. As the court explained in *Ferguson v. Ferguson,* 187 Va. 581, 47 S.E.2d 346 (1948), the function of the witnesses' subscription "is to establish and prove the genuineness of the testator's signature." The witnesses are not required to read the will or even to be told its contents, but they must be made aware that what they are signing is the testator's will.

Statutes provide that to be valid a will must be signed in the maker's presence by two or three competent witnesses (but compare U.P.C. § 2–502, which also allows the testator to acknowledge to the witnesses that she signed the will). A will is not valid without witnesses unless it is a holographic will or, as we shall see, a self-proved will (a will in which the testator's and witnesses' signatures are acknowledged before a *notary public*). State statutes establish the required number of witnesses; all states require two witnesses, except Vermont, which requires three witnesses (see Exhibit 5.1). In addition, the witnesses must be competent, i.e., capable of testifying as to the facts of execution of the will and the mental capacity of the testator. Various factors help determine the **competency of a witness,** although age does not appear to be one of them. The minimum age to be a witness is below the age of majority in some states. The following seven questions must be answered in order to assess competency. The list also helps identify who is and who is not an appropriate witness.

Competent witness
A person who is legally capable and suitable to act as a witness to a will.

- *Is the witness capable of testifying as to the facts of the execution of the will?* (See the next example.)
- *Is the witness able, by legal standards, to testify as to the mental capacity of the testator?*

Example: Sam Jones attests (witnesses) and **subscribes** (signs) Greg Hartman's will. Sam is acquainted with Greg, knows the document is Greg's last will, remembers and can relate the facts of the execution of the will, i.e., declaring and signing by Greg, and can testify to Greg's mental capacity. Thus, Sam is a competent (capable) witness.

Subscribe (a will)
To sign a will.

- *When is the competency of the witness required?* If the witness is incompetent at the execution of the will but later becomes competent to testify, the will is invalid.

Example: Stephen Hart is intoxicated. He is asked to witness Kevin Hanson's will. Stephen signs his name unaware of what he is signing. Later, when sober, Stephen is told he witnessed and subscribed Kevin's will. The witness's competence must exist at the time of the execution of the will. The will is not valid.

Conversely, if the witness is competent at the time a will is attested, subsequent incompetency does not invalidate the will. See Mass. Gen. Laws Ann. ch. 191 § 3.

Example: Stanley Novak attests and subscribes Allan Sheppard's will. Five years later Stanley becomes mentally ill and is hospitalized. Stanley's later insanity would not affect the validity of Allan's will. The purpose of the statutory requirement that a will be witnessed by a competent person is that such a person might later be required to testify that the deceased testator was of sound and disposing mind and memory at the time of the will's execution.

- *Is an "interested witness," i.e., a beneficiary, devisee, or successor who is named in a will, a competent witness?*

Example: In his will, Daniel Kane gives a valuable ring to Margaret Wilson. Margaret is one of the witnesses and subscribers to the execution of Daniel's will. She is a competent witness. However, Margaret's act of attesting a will in which she is named a devisee may cost her the ring because she is an **interested witness**—a witness who is also a beneficiary of the will. If there are two other witnesses, the gift to Margaret is valid. If she is one of only two witnesses, however, the gift to Margaret is void, in some states, even though she remains a competent witness. Finally, under some state statutes such as the Tennessee statute below, Margaret may be able to retain the gift even if she is one of only two

Interested witness
A person who is a beneficiary and a witness of the same will.

Exhibit 5.1   Formal Requirements for a Valid Will by State

	Age	Testamentary Capacity	Testator's Signature Required	Witnesses
Alabama	18	1	Yes	2
Alaska	18	2	Yes	2
Arizona	18	2, 3, 4	Yes	2
Arkansas	18	1	Yes (6)	2
California	18	1	Yes	2
Colorado	18	1, 2	Yes	2
Connecticut	18	1	Yes	2
Delaware	18	1	Yes	2
Florida	18	1	Yes (6)	2
Georgia	14	1	Yes	2
Hawaii	18	1	Yes	2
Idaho	18	1	Yes	2
Illinois	18	1	Yes	2
Indiana	18	1	Yes	2
Iowa	18	1	Yes	2
Kansas	18	1	Yes (6)	2
Kentucky	18	1	Yes	2
Louisiana	16	1	Yes (7)	2
Maine	18	1	Yes	2
Maryland	18	1	Yes	2
Massachusetts	18	1	Yes	2
Michigan	18	1	Yes	2
Minnesota	18	1	Yes	2
Mississippi	18	1	Yes	2
Missouri	18	1	Yes	2
Montana	18	1	Yes	2
Nebraska	18	1	Yes	2
Nevada	18	1	Yes	2
New Hampshire	18	1	Yes	2
New Jersey	18	1	Yes	2
New Mexico	18	1	Yes	2
New York	18	1	Yes (6)	2
North Carolina	18	1	Yes	2
North Dakota	18	1	Yes	2
Ohio	18	1, 5	Yes (6)	2
Oklahoma	18	1	Yes (6)	2
Oregon	18	1	Yes	2
Pennsylvania	18	1	Yes (6)	2
Rhode Island	18	1	Yes	2
South Carolina	18	1	Yes	2
South Dakota	18	1	Yes	2
Tennessee	18	1	Yes	2
Texas	18	1	Yes	2
Utah	18	1	Yes	2
Vermont	18	1	Yes	3
Virginia	18	1	Yes	2
Washington	18	1	Yes	2
West Virginia	18	1	Yes	2
Wisconsin	18	1	Yes	2
Wyoming	19	1	Yes	2

1. Sound mind; mentally competent; or legally competent.
2. Capable of understanding the nature of the act.
3. Recognize the nature and character of property owned.
4. Understand relationship to heirs.
5. Not under restraint.
6. Signature at end of will.
7. Signature at end of each separate page of will.

witnesses because if she is an heir, she would receive her intestate's share within the limits of the value of the gift she was to receive through the will. See U.P.C. § 2–505, which also provides that a will is valid even if it is attested by an interested witness.

The following is a typical state statute that addresses itself to this problem:

Tenn. Code Ann. § 32–1–103 (1984)   Witness—Who May Act:

(a) Any person competent to be a witness generally in this state may act as attesting witness to a will.

(b) No will is invalidated because attested by an interested witness, but any interested witness shall, unless the will is also attested by two (2) disinterested witnesses, forfeit so much of the provisions therein made for him as the aggregate exceeds in value, as of the date of the testator's death, what he would have received had the testator died intestate. . . .

This statute is typical of many in states that have not enacted the Uniform Probate Code. Here the witness is compelled to relinquish part or all of the will's devise to him or her (compare U.P.C. § 2–505).

■ *Can the personal representative (executor) or trustee named in the will also act as a competent witness?* The prevailing view is that a person named as personal representative (executor) or trustee in a will, if not a beneficiary or devisee of the will, is not disqualified from acting as a proper witness to a will. The basis for the rule is the opinion that an executor (or court-appointed administrator) does not have a direct interest in the will by virtue of the duty to see that the testator's wishes are carried out, even though the executor claims a personal representative's fee from the estate. The fact that an executor's interest is not "pecuniary, legal and immediate," as is a beneficiary's, qualifies the executor to be a witness.

Example: Fred Johnson names Robert Olson executor of his will. Robert also attests and subscribes the will. Most states consider Robert a competent witness. (Check your own state to see if it follows the majority view.)

■ *Is a person disqualified as a competent witness because the testator owes her a debt?* Generally, a creditor is competent to act as a witness as long as no bequest or devise other than the debt owed is mentioned in the will.

Example: In her will, Janet Martin provides that all her approved debts, funeral expenses, and taxes should be paid out of assets of her estate. Marian Cooper is a creditor of Janet's. No other provisions in the will mention Marian. When Marian attests and subscribes the will, she does so as a competent witness.

■ *According to the sample Tennessee statute quoted above, can an heir, who would be entitled to inherit if the decedent died intestate, named a beneficiary or devisee in a will receive the gift from the decedent's estate if the heir witnesses the will?* Could such an heir and devisee validly attest to and subscribe a will *and* receive property from it?

Example: Howard is Adam's son. As Adam's heir, Howard is entitled to inherit property from Adam if Adam dies intestate. Adam, however, has a will. In it, Adam has named Howard as a beneficiary or devisee to receive a considerable amount of the estate. Unfortunately, Howard and only one other person have attested and subscribed the will. Is Howard a competent witness? Is Howard allowed to receive any of his father's estate? Answer: In Tennessee, Howard would be a competent witness, unlike some beneficiary- or devisee-attesters. In addition, he could receive property from his father's estate, but in an amount no greater than what he would receive according to the state intestate succession statute. The reason behind this and similar provisions is to enable the witness to maintain objectivity. Monetarily, it may be to the advantage of the beneficiary- or devisee-attester to have the will admitted to probate; therefore, he might be tempted to testify falsely about it in order to achieve this end. On the other hand, if the will is denied probate (i.e., if the testator is declared intestate), an heir would take from the estate anyway; therefore, the amount of the bequest or devise is limited in order to reduce the possibility of perjury.

As a reminder, good legal practice dictates that a beneficiary or devisee, although competent to act as a witness, should never be a witness to a will from which the beneficiary or devisee benefits, since the bequest or devise (gift of real or personal property) may be voided or may possibly invalidate the entire will. The laws of some states provide that an interested party who acts as one of the required witnesses to a will is not a competent witness, and therefore, the will is not legally binding. It is also unwise for the attorney drafting a client's will to act as a witness. Although no statute forbids an attorney from being a witness, this is seldom done since any challenge to the will could require the attorney to cease representing the estate if the attorney is likely to be called as a witness in the will contest. *A paralegal acting as a witness could run into the same ethical problem.* However, compare the Model Rules of Professional Conduct Rule 3.7, which appears to allow an attorney who was also a witness to turn the will contest over to another member of the law firm and to resume acting as attorney for the estate after the will is proved (accepted).

ETHICAL ISSUE

In summary, it is best that a witness be both acquainted with the testator and a disinterested witness.

𒀭 ASSIGNMENT 5.6

Answer the following according to your own state laws:
1. Can an heir of an intestate, who becomes a beneficiary or devisee when the intestate makes a will, be a competent witness?
2. In such a case, can the heir-devisee or heir-beneficiary receive any property from the decedent testator?
3. Linda is Sara's daughter and only heir. Sara dies testate; through her will, she leaves Linda the following property: a diamond ring valued at $2,500; silverware worth $750; an $1,800 fur coat; and a lake cottage appraised at $25,000. The rest of Sara's estate is given to charity. The total value of the estate after deducting expenses, debts, and taxes is $100,000. Linda, and Sara's best friend, Sylvia, witness and sign the will. In Tennessee, is Linda a competent witness? In your state is Linda competent? In your state would Linda be entitled to receive any of her mother's estate? If so, how much? In your state, what effect does Linda's signature as a witness have on the validity of the will?
4. Determine whether the following persons can act as competent witnesses in your state: (a) a minor, (b) the attorney drafting the will, (c) the spouse of the testator, (d) the personal representative (executor) not named a devisee, (e) a parent of the testator, (f) a creditor of the testator, (g) the probate judge, (h) a spouse of a beneficiary or devisee named in the will.
5. If you are drafting your own will, should the age of an adult witness (person over 18) have any bearing on whether you choose a witness younger or older than yourself? Explain.

In most states the witnesses to the will must sign in the conscious presence of the testator or testatrix (see Conn. Gen. Stat. Ann. § 45a–251, but compare U.P.C. § 2–502 where presence is not required). In a few states, the witnesses do not necessarily have to sign in one another's presence so long as they both were present when the testator signed the will. In common practice, however, subscribing (signing) by witnesses is accomplished in the presence of both the maker of the will and each other. The signatures of the witnesses attest to the act of signing by the testator, his age and sound mind, and that they themselves signed in his presence. In addition, some states require that the addresses of the witnesses be given. Although witnesses need not know the contents of a will, they usually must be aware that what they have subscribed is a will. To help resolve doubts that the testator and the witnesses were present together when all signatures were made, they all should sign with the same pen. For an example of a standard attestation clause used in drafting a will, see Exhibit 5.2.

In summary, the individual state's statutory requirements concerning the maker of the will (testator), witnesses, and signatures vary substantially and may or may not require any or all of the following:

- The will must be written.
- Usually two and sometimes three witnesses are required (see Exhibit 5.1).
- The testator must declare (publish) to the witnesses that the document is her will (this is called publication) and request that they sign it (see N.Y. E.P.T.L. § 3–2.1[a] [3], [4]). **Publication,** as the term is used in the law of wills, is the declaration or act of the testator at the time of execution of a will that manifests intent that the document is a will; any communication made to witnesses by word, sign, motion, or conduct is sufficient to constitute a publication. This was the definition of publication upheld by the court in the *Estate of Kelly* case cited

Publication
In the law of wills, the formal declaration made by a testator at the time of signing a will that it is her last will and testament.

Exhibit 5.2   Sample Signature and Attestation Clauses

Signature Clause

I, Jane C. Doe, have signed this my last will and testament consisting of ten (10) typewritten pages including this page, on June 15, 1994.

_____
Jane C. Doe, Testatrix

Attestation Clause

We certify that in our presence on the date appearing above the testatrix, __[name]__ , signed the foregoing instrument and acknowledged and declared it to be her will, that at her request and in her presence and in the presence of each other, we haved signed our names below as witnesses, and that we believe her to be eighteen (18) years of age or more, of sound mind, and under no constraint or undue influence.

_____   residing at   _____
(Witness)   (Address)

_____   residing at   _____
(Witness)   (Address)

_____
Note: Although an attestation clause is not required, all states recommend its use.

previously. But see and compare *Matter of Estate of Polda,* 349 N.W.2d 11 (N.D. 1984). Publication is becoming an unnecessary formality in many states, and it is not required under the Uniform Probate Code.

- The testator must sign the will in the presence of the witnesses.
- The testator's signature must be at the end of the will.
- The witnesses must see the testator sign the will, or the testator must acknowledge in their presence that the signature on the will is his (see Cal. Prob. Code § 6110[c] or N.Y. E.P.T.L. § 3–2.1[a] [2]).
- The witnesses must sign (subscribe) in the presence of the testator and/or at the testator's request (see *In re Estate of Graham,* 295 N.W.2d 414 [Iowa 1980]).
- The witnesses must sign in each other's presence (see Ky. Rev. Stat. Ann. § 394.040 or Fla. Stat. Ann. § 732.502). But the placement of the witnesses' signatures may vary according to individual state laws, as noted in the cases cited previously.

The modern way to resolve these problems is to include signature and attestation clauses, which state that all the formalities listed above have been properly performed (see Exhibit 5.2).

For the most part, statutes have not established many qualifications for attesting witnesses; e.g., in many states, there are no age requirements for witnesses, but they must be competent as previously discussed. When choosing attesting witnesses, good practice would be to choose adult, mature, literate witnesses who are younger than the testator and acquainted with her. If not acquainted, such witnesses should engage in conversation with the testator prior to the execution of the will to establish some rapport and most importantly to reassure the attesting witnesses that the testator exhibits both testamentary intent and capacity should they later be asked to verify these requirements in court.

ASSIGNMENT 5.7

David Erickson executes a will and declares to three competent witnesses, "This is my last will and testament." In the will, Erickson leaves part of his estate to Allan Potter, who is also a witness to the will. Answer the following questions according to your state's law:

1. Must the witnesses know the contents of Erickson's will before they attest and subscribe their names to the document in order for it to be valid?
2. Can Potter receive his benefit from the will?
3. Is the will valid?

MODIFICATION OF AN EXISTING WILL—CODICIL

Because people are living longer, many years may pass between the date a will is executed and the death of the maker of the will. During that time, the testator's wishes concerning the beneficiaries or devisees of the estate assets may dramatically change, as may the potential beneficiaries themselves. For example, the testator's decisions may be influenced by the birth, death, adoption, divorce, marriage, or legal separation of family members or by a change in their financial standing. The testator's property may no longer be the same due to additions, sales, gifts, or a change in value. As a result of such changes, it may become necessary to revise the testator's original will. The most appropriate way to accomplish major and needed changes in a will is by executing a new, updated will and revoking the original.

The most common method of changing provisions in a will, however, is a codicil, a separate amendment modifying parts of an existing will. Any number of codicils may be executed. A codicil may alter one clause in the will and leave the rest unchanged and enforceable, or it can replace the former will entirely. Most states require that a codicil satisfy the same formalities prescribed for the execution of a valid will, such as the signature of the testator and the attestation with signatures by a specified number of witnesses. The codicil should also incorporate the preexisting will by reference. The **incorporation by reference** ensures that the provisions of the prior will remain intact except for the modifications of the codicil and that the actual date of the testator's new modified will is now the date of the codicil. This date will be important if the probate court is presented with more than one will, each of which is purported to be the testator's last will. Since the testator's most recent will is presumed to be the valid will proclaiming his final wishes, the date on the codicil is critical to the court's decision. See *Estate of Krukenberg,* 77 Nev. 226, 361 P.2d 537 (1961).

One important outcome of a codicil's incorporation by reference is **republication,** i.e., the revival or restoration of the will. Even a will that was defectively executed (e.g., the will had only one witness) or a will that had been revoked is restored with a properly executed codicil. See N.Y. E.P.T.L. § 3–4.6(b); *In re Knecht's Estate,* 341 Pa. 292, 19 A.2d 111 (1941), in which the court ruled that a duly executed codicil operates as a republication of the original will so as to "make it speak as of the date of the codicil"; and *In re Erbach's Estate,* 41 Wis.2d 335, 164 N.W.2d 238 (1969), which identifies the requirements for a validly executed codicil to incorporate language of another document by reference. New York and Louisiana do not allow a will to "incorporate by reference" a nontestamentary writing (memorandum).

Crossing out a clause of a will and writing in a new provision (called **interlineation)** does not create a proper or valid codicil or new will because such an action changes the effect of the original will but does not meet the statutory requirements for a valid codicil. In other words, the will, prior to interlineation, was executed validly with respect to attestation, signature, and the like, but that validity does not apply to the will in its interlineated state. The will and codicil must meet the formal requirements of the maker's state statutes (see N.Y. E.P.T.L. § 3–4.1[a]).

Drafting codicils and example clauses of wills are discussed in Chapter 7. An example of a codicil in which the testator has modified his original will by deleting one of its provisions is shown in Exhibit 5.3.

Codicils or new wills may also be used to update an older, and now inappropriate, will. For example, a testator has previously designated her father, age 60, to be guardian of her minor sons, ages 8 and 16. Five years have passed, and the father has had a heart attack and is confined to a wheelchair. A codicil could be executed to change the guardian from the father to the elder son—now a 21-year-old adult.

Incorporation by reference
The method of making one document a part of another separate document by referring to the former in the latter and declaring that the former shall be considered part of the latter.

Republication
The reexecution, revival, or restoration by a testator of a will that had previously been revoked.

Interlineation
The act of writing between the lines of an instrument.

🏛 ASSIGNMENT 5.8

On July 15, 1994, Colleen Shannon executes a will. In one of its provisions, she leaves a $50,000 diamond brooch to Susan Slade, a lifelong friend. Sometime afterward,

---

Exhibit 5.3   Sample Codicil

[The facts: Henry Hamilton executed a will on June 1, 1990. One provision of the will gives his gun collection to his son, John; another gives his faithful employee, Joe Spencer, $10,000; and a third provision transfers a valuable painting to an art museum. In 1994, John lost an arm in a hunting accident. That same year, Joe Spencer died, and the painting was destroyed in a fire. Henry therefore executes the following first codicil to his will.]

CODICIL

I, Henry Hamilton, of River City, Cornstalk County, State of A, do make, publish, and declare this to be the first codicil to my last will and testament, executed June 1, 1990.

First: Whereas in Article IV in my said last will and testament, I gave my gun collection to my son, John; and whereas my said son is no longer able to use said gun collection due to a hunting accident, I hereby give said gun collection to my son, Edwin Hamilton.

Second: Whereas in Article V, I gave $10,000 to my employee, Joseph Spencer; and wheras my said employee has died, I give said $10,000 to his wife, Renee Spencer.

Third: Whereas, I gave my original Matisse painting, "Flower Market," to the Art Museum of River City; and said painting has been destroyed, I hereby revoke said gift.

Fourth: Except as modified by this codicil, in all other respects, I ratify, confirm, and republish all of the provisions of my said last will and testament dated June 1, 1990.

IN WITNESS WHEREOF, I have hereunto set my hand to this, the first Codicil to my Last Will and Testament, dated this 26th day of February, 1995.

Henry Hamilton
2114 Oak Street

THIS INSTRUMENT, bearing the signature of the above-named Testator, was by him on the date thereof willingly signed, published, and declared by him to be a Codicil to his Last Will and Testament, in our presence, who, at his request and in his presence, and in the presence of each other, we believing him to be of sound mind and under no constraint or undue influence, have hereunto subscribed our names as attesting witnesses.

Mary Ann Garrity   residing at   *9341 Silverman Avenue*

Lawrence Escrach   residing at   *87 Coronada Circle*

Susan and Colleen have a falling out. No longer wanting Susan to receive the brooch, Colleen crosses out Susan's name from the will and writes in Diane Pylkas as the new beneficiary. A short time later, after having won $100,000 on a television quiz show, Colleen adds a page to her will giving the prize money to Patty Barron. According to your state's law, are the changes Colleen made to her will valid? Draft a codicil making these changes.

REVOCATION AND REJECTION OF A WILL

A will is operative only after the testator or testatrix dies. Until then, it is ambulatory, i.e., revocable and subject to change. A will can be changed or revoked at any time before death, and testators often do change their wills many times by codicil or by writing new wills. Whenever the maker of the will changes the way estate property is to be distributed upon death, revocation results, and it terminates the existence of a will. Revocation may be accomplished in three ways:

1. Revocation by physical act.
2. Revocation by operation of law.
3. Revocation by subsequent writing.

Revocation by Physical Act

The following are examples of revocation by a physical act:

- Keri Wilson terminates her existing will by purposely burning it.
- Steven Wong terminates his will by tearing it in half.
- Kendra Espinoza writes the word "canceled" across each page of her will, thereby terminating it.
- Jack Miles uses a pen to cross out all clauses of his will, thus terminating it.
- Sally Smallwood, suffering from frostbite on both hands, asks Julie Adams to burn Sally's will. Julie, in the presence of her husband, Sam Adams, and under specific directions by Sally, burns the will.

All these deliberate physical acts, i.e., burning, tearing, canceling, obliterating, or otherwise destroying a will, or directing and consenting to have another person do the same, allow the maker to revoke the will. The case of *In re Will of Bonner*, 17 N.Y.2d 9, 266 N.Y.S.2d 971, 214 N.E.2d 154 (1966), illustrates a revocation of a will by deliberate act:

> A will of Merritt Bonner that had been cut-in-two was found after his death. The executors named in the severed will offered it for probate, and the decedent's father opposed the petition to admit the will on the grounds that the will had been revoked. The court ruled that cutting a will in two was an act of revocation that canceled the will.

When destruction is by another person, the direction and consent of the testator and the fact of such destruction must comply with the state statute regulating the revocation of a will by destruction by a person other than the testator. Some states require such destruction to be witnessed by two persons, neither of whom is the destroyer; others require only that the destruction be at the direction and with the consent of the testator. The following Pennsylvania statute is typical of state statutes outlining procedures for the revocation of wills:

> *20 Pa. Stat. Ann. § 2505* Revocation of a Will
> No will or codicil in writing, or any part thereof, can be revoked or altered otherwise than:
> (1) *Will or codicil* By some other will or codicil in writing;
> (2) *Other writing* By some other writing declaring the same, executed and proved in the manner required of wills; or
> (3) *Act to the document* By being burnt, torn, canceled, obliterated, or destroyed, with the intent and for the purpose of revocation, by the testator himself or by another person in his presence and by his express direction. If such act is done by any person other than the testator, the direction of the testator must be proved by the oaths or affirmations of two competent witnesses [compare U.P.C. § 2–507].

At times, statutory language, as in the above example, needs to be defined. The "intent" to terminate an existing will is apparent from the testator's acts.

Clearly, if one physically destroys or obliterates a will or directs others to do the same, the revocation is intentional. When the destruction is done by another person at the direction of the testator, such direction often must be proved by the oaths or affirmation of two "competent" witnesses.

Lost Wills

Sometimes a will cannot be found even though individuals acknowledge it existed. A lost will that cannot be found is not necessarily considered to be a will that has been revoked by a physical act. Many states have statutes or allow case law to decide whether a "lost will" can be probated. With or without a statute, courts require "clear and convincing proof" of a lost will, as in the case of *In re Thompson's Estate,* 214 Neb. 899, 336 N.W.2d 590 (1983), where a second will revoked the original but the second will could not be found. Thus, the required standard of "clear and convincing proof" was not met, and the original will was probated. State laws vary on the question of whether a "lost will" is revoked or can be probated. The decision is generally based on the following:

- Proof that the will was properly executed.
- Proof that while the will was under the control of the decedent-testator, she did not expressly revoke it.
- Proof of the contents of the will.

One method of satisfying the "proof of execution" requirement is to have the two or three witnesses to the lost will, if available, testify that the "lost" will was "published" and signed by the testator. Depending on the circumstances, a true and complete copy of the lost will may or may not be admitted to probate. Consider the following examples:

Example: Martina Martinez's will is properly executed and left in her attorney's office. Martina dies and her will cannot be found. The state statute requires two witnesses to testify concerning the "lost will," but only one witness is discovered. The result could be the same as in the famous lost will case, *Howard Hughes Medical Institute v. Gavin,* 96 Nev. 905, 621 P.2d 489 (1980). There the court denied probate because the statute governing lost wills required evidence from two witnesses and only one witness was found.

Example: Peter Wheaton properly executes a will in 1990. During the last five years, Peter has frequently mentioned to his attorney, beneficiaries, and devisees that he is happy with his estate plans and keeps his will at home. He has shown his family the contents of his will. When Peter dies, the will cannot be found. Any statutory presumption that this will is revoked by physical act can be opposed and refuted by the facts, e.g., the will was under the control of the decedent-testator. See *Matter of Estate of Travers,* 121 Ariz. 282, 589 P.2d 1314 (App. 1978), in which the court ruled that the evidence supported the trial court's finding in a will contest that the will had been destroyed by the testator with intent to revoke. If the other issues, such as proper execution of the will and no expressed revocations by the testator while the will was under his control, are resolved, then a lost will can be probated if its contents are satisfactorily proved.

Example: Boris Decker properly executed his will. When he died, his will could not be found. The attorney who drafted the will retained a photocopy of the original will. This copy could be used as evidence to prove the contents of the will (see *Matter of Estate of Wheadon,* 579 P.2d 930 [Utah 1978], but compare the case of *In re Will of Sage,* 76 Misc.2d 676, 351 N.Y.S. 2d 930 [1974], in which the court disapproved the use of a photocopy in place of the original will).

Case law has generally held that in will contests involving lost or misplaced wills, the burden of proof is on the proponent of the lost will to prove that the testator did not intentionally revoke the lost, misplaced, or destroyed will during his lifetime. This was the position of the Supreme Court of Nevada in the case of *In the Matter of Estate of Irvine*, 101 Nev. 698, 710 P.2d 1366 (1985). In *Barksdale v. Pendergrass*, 294 Ala. 526, 319 So.2d 267 (1975), another case in which the original will could not be found, the court stated that the burden was on the proponent alleging a lost will to establish (1) the existence of a will; (2) the loss or destruction of the will; (3) the nonrevocation of the will by the testatrix; and (4) the contents of the will. The court affirmed the jury's decision that the original will was either lost, misplaced, or destroyed but not with the testatrix's intent.

Finally, a lost will may be found after the administration of a decedent's estate is completed. In that case, if the will is offered for probate and a request to reopen the administration is made, the following factors apply:

- The request may be barred by a statute of limitations. Some states like Texas have a four-year limit after death (see Texas Prob. Code § 73[a]); others like California have no time limit (see Cal. Prob. Code § 8000, and compare U.P.C. § 3–108).

- Generally, creditors, banks, trustees or guardians of property, and "good faith" purchasers of estate property are exonerated and protected by the previous estate administration; see Texas Prob. Code § 73(b).

- In some states, however, beneficiaries, devisees, or heirs are subject to the distribution provisions of the new will; see U.P.C. § 3–1008.

Revocation by Operation of Law

A will can be revoked wholly or partially by the following:

- By marriage.
- By divorce.

A will can be revoked by other than a deliberate physical act on the part of the maker or another person. A state statute may automatically revoke or amend a will without the testator knowing of or agreeing to the revocation. For example, by **operation of law,** a will is often affected by the marriage or divorce of the testator or testatrix. If the testator marries after executing a will, it is revoked in some states by operation of law, and the testator's property passes by intestacy. Under U.P.C. § 2–508, a subsequent marriage does not revoke a will. The surviving spouse receives an intestate share of the decedent spouse's estate, and the rest of the estate passes under the will (see U.P.C. § 2–301). Further, if a maker is divorced after executing a will, all provisions in favor of the maker's former spouse are generally revoked by similar operation leaving the rest of the will intact. This is especially true whenever the divorce decree contains a property settlement between the spouses. Note that although the subsequent marriage of the maker of the will may revoke it entirely in some states, a divorce (dissolution) after a will has been drawn revokes only the provisions affecting the divorced (former) spouse. For the effects of divorce and marriage on an existing will in all states, see Exhibits 4.12 and 4.13. An example of a state statute explaining the effect of marriage on an existing will follows:

Operation of law Rights pass to a person by the application of the established rules of law, without the act, knowledge, or cooperation of the person.

> *Ky. Rev. Stat. Ann. § 394.090* Marriage Revokes Will—Exception
> Every will shall be revoked by the marriage of the person who made the will, except:

(1) A will made in exercise of a power of appointment when the estate thereby appointed would not, in default of such appointment, pass to the heir, personal representative, or next of kin of the person who made the will;

(2) A will that expressly provides that it is intended that a subsequent marriage shall not revoke the will;

(3) A will that expressly provides for the person who later becomes the spouse of the deceased and is married to the testator on the date of death. [Compare U.P.C. § 2–301.]

🏛 ASSIGNMENT 5.9

Harold and Maude are close friends. Maude has drawn her will leaving half her estate to Harold and the other half to charity. If, subsequently, Harold and Maude marry, would Maude's will be revoked by operation of law in Kentucky? What would your answer be according to the laws of your own state? Would the charity receive half of Maude's estate in your state?

The following Pennsylvania statute addresses itself to the effect of a divorce on an existing will:

20 Pa. Stat. Ann. § 2507 Modification by Circumstances
Wills shall be modified upon the occurrence of any of the following circumstances, among others:
. . .

(2) Divorce. If the testator is divorced from the bonds of matrimony after making a will, any provision in the will in favor of or relating to his spouse so divorced shall thereby become ineffective for all purposes unless it appears from the will that the provision was intended to survive the divorce. . . . [Compare U.P.C. § 2–802.]

🏛 ASSIGNMENT 5.10

Frank and Eleanor are single and both have their own wills. Then Frank and Eleanor marry. Both execute new wills. Subsequently, the couple obtains a divorce. Answer the following according to the statutes of your state:

1. What effect did the marriage have on the wills Frank and Eleanor made before marrying?
2. What effect does their divorce have on the former spouses' wills?

Revocation by Subsequent Writing

Both of the following are examples of a revocation of a will by subsequent writing:

- Samantha Nguyen writes a new will.
- Lee Shapiro adds a new codicil to her will.

A current will can be expressly revoked only by a written document validly executed with the same formalities as a will. The law is well settled that the last will or codicil (from the standpoint of time) executed with the same formalities required for a written will, i.e., dated and signed by the testator and attested and subscribed by witnesses, is the valid will of the decedent. This is usually the decision of the courts whenever more than one will or codicil is discovered after the death of a testator.

A revoked will is usually destroyed, but it may be advisable to retain the former will when the testator's testamentary capacity is questionable or there is a possibility of a will contest. The reason for keeping the will is that the revocation of the earlier will may turn out to be dependent on the validity of the later will. Possibly, too, the testator may change her mind and decide she prefers the terms of the earlier will. If the later will is held invalid, it may be possible and appropriate to probate the earlier will. An example of a statute concerned with the retention and validity of an earlier will is 20 Pa. Stat. Ann. § 2506:

> If, after the making of any will, the testator shall execute a later will which expressly or by necessary implication revokes the earlier will, the revocation of the later will shall not revive the earlier will, unless the revocation is in writing and declares the intention of the testator to revive the earlier will, or unless, after such revocation, the earlier will shall be reexecuted. Oral republication of itself shall be ineffective to revive a will. [Compare U.P.C. § 2–509.]

Example: In 1992, Richard makes a will leaving $4,000 to his niece, Myrrha. In 1995, he revokes but does not destroy the will and writes a new one, leaving $2,000 to Myrrha and $2,000 to her sister, Melisande. Later, Melisande marries someone of whom Richard does not approve; he destroys the latter will, intending to revive the former one, but dies before accomplishing this. In the eyes of the law, Richard died intestate. Myrrha would not be entitled to the $4,000 devise because the old will was rendered ineffective by Richard's deliberate revocation of it. The second will was revoked when Richard destroyed it, but this revocation does not revive the first will.

ASSIGNMENT 5.11

1. In the above example, would Myrrha be entitled to the $4,000 legacy or devise in your state?
2. Would Myrrha be entitled to the $4,000 devise under the Uniform Probate Code?

The current will is often kept in either a safe deposit box or another place of safekeeping maintained by the testator. Some major problems may arise, however, if the will is placed in a safe deposit box (see Chapter 7). Other common storage places for wills are a lawyer's safe or a bank vault. Sometimes wills are filed with the proper court, e.g., the probate court.

WILL CONTESTS

A will contest is a lawsuit that challenges the validity of an existing will. The suit is brought by a person claiming an interest, i.e., some right, in a decedent's estate. State statutes vary regarding when a hearing on a will contest must occur. In the *Tobin* case discussed below, the Illinois court allowed a niece who was not given notice to contest the will eighteen years after the will was admitted to probate. Usually, the hearing is prior to or shortly after a will is admitted to probate by the court. Before the hearing, the contesting party files an affidavit of objection to the petition for probate listing the grounds for the objection.

Who Can Contest a Will

Standing
The requirement that a person stands to lose a pecuniary interest in a decedent's estate if a will is allowed.

Very few wills are contested, and most contests are unsuccessful. Only a person who has "standing" may make an objection to the probate court and request that a will offered for probate be rejected. A person with **standing** is someone who stands to lose a pecuniary interest, i.e., a share of the decedent's estate, if a will is allowed, such as a spouse, heir, or devisee of an earlier will. The person who contests the will has the burden of proving his objection by "clear and convincing evidence," a standard that is more than a mere preponderance of the evidence (the civil law standard) but less than beyond a reasonable doubt (the criminal law standard). Generally, creditors are not proper contestants since they can pursue their claims in a separate lawsuit in civil court. If probate is denied, i.e., the will is successfully contested and declared invalid by the probate court, then the decedent's estate passes according to intestate succession laws, and all belongings are distributed as if the decedent had left no will. This rule is the reason that an heir who would inherit when the decedent is declared intestate has standing, i.e., the right to contest the will.

Most states have a statute of limitations, i.e., a limited time period during which the contestant must file the appropriate documents to contest the will. If the time limit is not strictly followed, the opportunity to contest the will is lost regardless of the validity of the contestant's challenge.

ASSIGNMENT 5.12

Harry is not mentioned in the will of his father, George. In their domiciliary state, Harry receives a share of his father's estate if George dies intestate. George's will provides that half his estate goes to his wife, Helen, and the remaining half goes to charity. As an heir, Harry contests the will and establishes his right to inherit the property in the case of intestacy. According to your state's laws, is Harry entitled to contest the will? Would this will contest succeed? If Harry wins the case, how much of his father's estate does he receive in your state?

ASSIGNMENT 5.13

Joan is named beneficiary or devisee in her Aunt Grace's will, dated April 10, 1990. In 1994 Grace executes a new will, which states that it revokes all prior wills and codicils. Joan is not mentioned in the new will. Joan establishes that the will dated April 1990 has been properly executed while the will written in 1994 was witnessed by two persons named as beneficiaries or devisees in the will. According to your state's laws, is Joan a proper will contestant? Would Joan's contest succeed? Explain.

Grounds for Contesting a Will

The probate court may refuse to accept a will that has been presented to it for approval for several reasons. In some of those cases, the court finds legitimate grounds for a successful will contest. The following are grounds for contesting a will:

- *The will is not properly executed.*

Examples: (1) John writes but does not sign his will. (2) John writes and signs the will, but it is not witnessed. (3) John writes and signs the will, but the witnesses are not competent (review the discussion on competency in this chapter).

■ *No notice of the probate of a will is given to heirs or creditors.*

Example: John's estate is administered and distributed without notice of the proceedings being given to one of John's sons or to a creditor. The requirement of notice is illustrated by *In re Estate of Tobin,* 152 Ill.App.3d 965, 105 Ill.Dec. 891, 505 N.E.2d 17 (1987). In that case, the court ruled that a niece, who was an heir of the decedent but did not receive notice, was entitled to contest the will.

■ *The will is forged.*

Examples: (1) John's signature is copied and written by another. (2) John's written (holographic) will is a forgery. Handwriting experts could be retained to determine authenticity.

■ *The testator lacks testamentary capacity.*

Examples: (1) John is a minor. (2) John is of "unsound mind." He is mentally ill or mentally retarded and lacks knowledge and understanding of the nature and extent of his property and of the persons who are the natural objects of his bounty at the time of the execution of the will. In the case *In re Stitt's Estate,* 93 Ariz. 302, 380 P.2d 601 (1963), which involved a will contest, the court stated that "in determining testamentary capacity, the law is concerned only with the testator's state of mind at the time of the execution of the will." As previously discussed, the Uniform Probate Code places the burden of proof on the contestant to establish the testator's lack of mental or testamentary capacity, i.e., a sound mind; see U.P.C. § 3–407.

■ *The will has been revoked.*

Examples: (1) John has written a new will. (2) John has destroyed or canceled his existing will. (3) John has married or been divorced since writing his will.

■ *The testator is induced by fraud to write or change the will.*

Examples: (1) John is tricked into leaving his estate to his nephew who causes John to believe erroneously that his only other heir is dead. (2) John disinherits his daughter after being told erroneously by his son that the daughter hates John.

In order for a probate court to refuse a will on the grounds that the testator was deceived into making it, the contestant must prove (1) that a beneficiary of the will actually led the testator into an erroneous belief concerning the disposition of the property (as in the first example above, where John's nephew caused him to believe his only other heir was dead) and (2) that the testator, believing the false statement to be true, relied on it and wrote a will accordingly. (If John did not believe his nephew, but nevertheless wrote a will favoring the nephew over the other heir, the court would allow the will to be probated and disregard the claim of fraud. The testator's acting in reliance on the beneficiary's willful misrepresentation is essential.)

■ *The will contains* material *mistakes, contradictions, or ambiguities.*

Examples: (1) John's will leaves the same items of property to different persons. (2) John's will is written so ambiguously that it is impossible to determine his intent. (3) John did not know he was signing a will.

A material mistake is one that alters the substance or matter of the provision in which it appears. If John had given his automobile to Eugene and to Eloise in the same will, both gifts to take effect at the same time, John's mistake would be material; it would alter the bequest itself. Without further evidence to show which beneficiary John intended to have the automobile, the probate court would hold the gift invalid. Although a probate court does not have the power to rewrite (re-form) the will in its entirety, the court may strike down individual provisions on the ground that the testator's wishes concerning the bequests or devises therein cannot be determined; the remaining portions of the will would then be admitted. A mistake may or may not invalidate a will. If the mistake is material, e.g., a mistake as to the document signed, then the will is invalid.

Example: John signs a document believing it to be his will, when in fact it is his wife's will.

If the mistake is a simple drafting error, e.g., the will lists the address of the testator as 4711 Fair Hills Avenue instead of 4771, the will would not be declared void.

▪ *The testator is forced by duress or persuaded by undue influence to sign the will.* The contestant in this situation alleges the testator did not execute the will independently or voluntarily.

Examples: (1) John is forced by physical threats to himself or his family to sign the will. (2) John is influenced by another with whom John had a close personal (confidential) relationship to include that person in his will while excluding his rightful beneficiaries or devisees, e.g., his spouse and children. (3) John makes a will leaving a substantial amount of his estate to his housekeeper, Mary, who also signs the will as one of the two required witnesses. As previously discussed, some states presume that there was undue influence in this case, while other states may declare the will invalid because Mary is an "interested witness" or at least deny her the benefits she would receive through John's will while not invalidating the entire will.

In the above examples, John may have written and executed a proper will and observed the required formalities of the law of wills in his state, yet the probate court could hold the will invalid because John's free will to dispose of the property according to his own wishes has been taken away. To create a valid will, the requisite testamentary intent must be present. A will is invalid if obtained through physical or mental influence that destroys the freedom of choice and intent of its maker. Threatening the maker or members of her immediate family with violence to force the execution of a will constitutes duress and physical coercion—factors that invalidate the will. Substituting another's wishes in place of the maker's is another example of the use of coercion in drawing a will. Although not physical in nature as with duress, nor apparent from the appearance of the will as with mistake, undue or extraordinary influence on the mind of the maker can also render the will invalid.

A will might be disallowed because of both fraud and undue influence, as illustrated by the case of *Cook v. Loftus*, 414 N.E.2d 581 (Ind.App. 1981), in which a beneficiary of a new will falsely told the testator that the beneficiaries under his prior will planned to put him in a nursing home. The court upheld the prior will.

The presence of undue influence is especially difficult to determine for there are as many kinds of undue influence as there are personalities. The probate court must consider the testator, the person who allegedly exerted the undue influence, and the circumstances. The court may infer undue influence if the testator ignores blood relatives and names, as beneficiary, a nonrelative who is in constant close contact with the testator and thus in a position to unduly influence her. Nevertheless, undue influence must still be proven.

Example: A nurse or friend caring for the deceased at the time of death is named beneficiary to the exclusion of all family members. See *In re Estate of Price,* 223 Neb. 12, 388 N.W.2d 72 (1986), in which the court found that in this instance there had been no undue influence. See also the case of *Succession of Bacot,* 502 So.2d 1118 (La.App. 1987), in which the court upheld a devise of the decedent's estate to a homosexual lover instead of to the family.

In some states, a presumption of undue influence is raised if a contestant (opponent) of the will shows (1) that a confidential relationship (doctor, attorney, legal assistant, priest or minister, fiduciary) allowed the alleged influencer an opportunity to control the testamentary act; (2) that the maker's weakened physical and mental condition easily permitted a subversion of free will; (3) that the influencer actively participated in preparing the will; or (4) that the influencer unduly profited as a beneficiary or devisee under the provisions of the will. *Note:* In most states, not to mention the canons of professional ethics, *a lawyer or paralegal who is intended to be a beneficiary or devisee under a will must refrain from drafting and designing the will.* Rule 1.8(c) of the Model Rules of Professional Conduct specifically states:

◄ ETHICAL ISSUE

> A lawyer [or paralegal] shall not prepare an instrument giving the lawyer or a person related to the lawyer as parent, child, sibling, or spouse, any substantial gift from a client, including a testamentary gift, except when the client is related to the donee.

But see *In re Conduct of Tonkon,* 292 Or. 660, 642 P.2d 660 (1982), where the attorney (Tonkon) represented his client (testator) for many years and the client's final will left Tonkon a gift of $75,000. Even though Tonkon did not advise the client to consult another attorney, the Oregon Supreme Court held he did not violate the Code of Ethics. As an attorney or paralegal in a situation like Tonkon's, the following are other procedures you could and should use to avoid this ethical problem:

1. Refuse to draft the will.
2. Insist another attorney of the client's choice draft the will but not an associate or partner from your law firm. See Model Rule 1.10(a).
3. Fully disclose the Code of Conduct to your client.
4. Make sure you do not in any way suggest or encourage the gift and that the client originated the bequest.
5. Make sure the $75,000 was not the major asset of the estate.

🏛 ASSIGNMENT 5.14

Review the resolutions of the ethical problem above; then answer the following:
1. You are asked to draft a client's will that includes a gift to you as in the *Tonkon* case. What should you do if the client is so near death there is no time to obtain another attorney?
2. Could you argue the gift is appropriate because you are a "close personal friend" of the client and, therefore, "a natural object of the testator's bounty"?

Prima facie
At first sight; on the face of it. A fact presumed to be true unless disproved by evidence to the contrary.

The burden of proving undue influence, fraud, duress, mistake, or revocation is generally on the contestant (the person challenging the will), and, as mentioned earlier, the proof must be "clear and convincing" (see U.P.C. § 3–407). Once the contestant has established sufficient evidence of the truth of the case that can be disproved only by evidence to the contrary, i.e., the contestant has established a **prima facie** case, the burden of establishing evidence to the contrary shifts to the proponent of the will. The proponent now carries the primary responsibility for establishing the validity of the will. Exhibit 5.4 illustrates the method of contesting a will in the state of New York.

In Terrorem or "No Contest" Clause—A Forfeiture Clause

People who have wills are concerned about will contests even though very few contests are successful. If the maker of a will fulfills all requirements for

---

Exhibit 5.4   Objection to Probating a Will

Surrogate's Court: County of _____

In the Matter of the Objections to Probate against   Objections to Probate
the Last Will and Testament of _____ ,   File No. _____
Deceased.

_____ , a distributee objects to the probate of the instrument propounded herein as the last will and testament of _____ , late of the County of _____ , deceased, upon the following grounds:
   First: That the alleged will was not duly executed by the said _____ , deceased, that she did not publish the same as her will in presence of the witnesses whose names are subscribed thereto, that she did not request the said two witnesses to be witnesses thereto, and that the said alleged witnesses did not sign as witnesses in her presence or in the presence of each other.
   Second: That on the _____ day of _____ , 19 _____ , the said decedent, _____ , was not of sound mind or memory and was not mentally capable of making a will.
   Third: That the said paper writing was not freely or voluntarily made or executed by the said _____ , as her last will and testament, but that the said paper writing purporting to be her will was obtained and the subscription and publication thereof if it was in fact subscribed or published by her, were procured by fraud and undue influence practiced upon the decedent by _____ and _____ , the principal legatees and devisees named in said paper, or by some other person or persons acting in concert or privity with them, whose name or names are at the present time unknown to this contestant.
   Fourth: A trial by jury of the issues raised by this answer is hereby demanded.
   Wherefore, the above named contestant prays that this proceeding may be dismissed, with costs.

                                        _____
                                        Attorney for Objecting Distributee
                                        P.O. Address
                                        Tel. No.

[*Verification*]

This form is used in New York when an interested party (beneficiary, distributee, or heir at law) objects to the acceptance and probate of a will.

Source: West's McKinney's Forms, ESP, § 7:523. Reprinted with permission from West's McKinney's Form, Copyright ©, by West Publishing Company.

a valid will and executes it correctly, the probate court will uphold it. Nevertheless, any will is open to a will contest whether by well-intentioned persons or unscrupulous ones. Even though the contest has no merit, the cost of this potential litigation may be so high that a settlement is reached, giving the would-be contestants part of the estate even though this was not the intent of the testator.

In anticipation that an omitted family member or disgruntled heir may contest the will, the testator may attempt to prevent a will contest by such person by including in the will a "no contest" or **"in terrorem" clause.** Such clauses state that if a beneficiary or devisee named in the will disputes the validity of the will, objects to the probate of the will, or challenges the dispositions, i.e., the kind and amount of the gifts that pass to the named persons listed in the will, that contestant will forfeit all benefits of the will. Some states, e.g., Indiana, declare such in terrorem clauses void; some, e.g., New York and Wyoming, strictly enforce the clause; others disregard the clause if the contestant had "probable cause" to commence the will contest. See N.Y. E.P.T.L. § 3–3.5 and *Dainton v. Watson,* 658 P.2d 79 (Wyo. 1983), in which the court ruled that "a no contest or in terrorem clause in the will, which required forfeiture of the bequest to the [beneficiary] as a result of the beneficiary's unsuccessful will contest, was valid and did not violate public policy." The following is an example of an in terrorem clause:

> If any beneficiary or devisee under this will opposes or challenges the probate of this will or any of its provisions in any manner whatsoever, then in such event the benefit or share of my estate given to such beneficiary or devisee under this will is hereby canceled and forfeited, and in such event, I give such respective benefit or share to [name of successor].

In terrorem clause
A clause in a will that if a beneficiary of the will objects to probate or challenges the will's distributions, that contestant forfeits all benefits of the will.

KEY TERMS

Natural objects of the testator's bounty	Competent witness	Incorporation by reference	Operation of law
	Subscribe (a will)		Standing
	Interested witness	Republication	Prima facie
Insane delusions	Publication	Interlineation	In terrorem clause
Lucid interval			

REVIEW QUESTIONS

1. Who may make a valid will?
2. Can an attorney or a paralegal prepare and draft a will for a client who is of unsound mind? Explain.
3. What are the statutory or formal requirements for executing a will?
4. What are the signature requirements, e.g., types of signatures or placement of signatures, for testators and witnesses?
5. How is a witness determined to be competent?
6. Can an attorney or a paralegal be a competent witness to a will? Should they be witnesses?
7. Is an attestation clause required in every will? Explain.
8. In what three ways can a will be revoked? Explain.
9. Under what circumstances can a "lost will" be probated?
10. Only a person with "standing" can contest a will. What does this mean?
11. What are the appropriate reasons or grounds for contesting a will? Explain.
12. Are in terrorem clauses in a will enforced in your state? Cite the appropriate statute or case law.

CASE PROBLEMS

Problem 1

Bill Jorgenson is terminally ill. Suppose Bill's son, Harold, convinces his father that Cheryl Jorgenson, Bill's wife and Harold's mother, is initiating institutional commitment proceedings against Bill. In fact, that is not true. Nevertheless, Bill changes his will because of this allegation and leaves everything to Harold. According to your state's law, what are the grounds for contesting a will? Which grounds can Cheryl use to contest Bill's will? What other rights does Cheryl have if the will is declared valid? See the *Cook* case previously cited.

Problem 2

A will was drafted for Melinda Wadsworth. Melinda's attorney, Malcolm Edwards, was present when she signed the will. Malcolm then signed as one of the attesting witnesses. It was Malcolm's intent to have Jaclene Morgan, a paralegal working for his law firm, be the second required witness. However, Jaclene was out of the office when Melinda and Malcolm signed the will. When Jaclene returned, Melinda had left the office. Malcolm showed the will to Jaclene, informed her that it was Melinda's will and signature, and asked Jaclene to witness and sign the will. Instead of immediately signing the will, Jaclene first called Melinda and verified that it was Melinda's will and signature. Then, Jaclene signed as a witness to the will.

A. Is the above procedure for executing a will proper? Explain.

B. Would this will be valid in your state? Cite the statute. See *Matter of Will of Jefferson,* 349 So.2d 1032 (Miss. 1977).

CHAPTER SIX

PREPARING TO DRAFT A WILL: CHECKLISTS AND THE CONFERENCE WITH THE CLIENT

OBJECTIVES

After completing this chapter, you should be able to:

- Collect and assimilate the relevant facts in preparation for the preliminary drafting of a will.

- Identify, explain, and interpret the sources of law, e.g., common law, statutes, and the like, that determine the validity of a will.

- Develop and use checklists to elicit the information necessary for the preliminary draft of a will.

- Ensure that all necessary pertinent information is obtained accurately and completely via appropriate checklists.

- Recognize when additional information is needed.

OUTLINE

SCOPE OF THE CHAPTER

This chapter is concerned with the procedures preliminary to making a will. A will must be prepared with meticulous care according to the standards prescribed by case law and state statutes. Nevertheless, a drafter can fail to execute a valid and appropriate will if necessary and proper information has not been elicited from the client and certain rules of practice have not been followed.

The chapter begins with the initial meeting with the client. Then it addresses the use of checklists for gathering facts that pertain to how and to whom the client's property is to be transferred, how tax burdens can be minimized, and how one can provide for miscellaneous problems that arise. Definitions and examples of terms used in the checklists precede the individual lists. Examples of checklists to use with a client in preparing to draft a will are supplied. You must learn to develop checklists and questionnaires appropriate for each situation. Next comes a discussion of some pitfalls in preparing the rough draft of a will. Guidelines for making the document a purposeful, legally enforceable, and unimpeachable testamentary disposition are presented.

THE CONFERENCE WITH THE CLIENT: INITIAL INTERVIEW, CHECKLISTS, AND OTHER MATTERS

When you and the attorney meet with a client to discuss preliminary matters prior to drafting a will, you will need to obtain information about the client's financial and family picture, e.g., who and where relatives and friends are, the extent of property holdings, the existence of creditors, and the like. To obtain the necessary data, checklists must be developed.

While assisting the attorney in formulating an appropriate will for a client, you will need to develop interviewing, data collecting, negotiating, drafting, and counseling skills to help clients overcome the normal reluctance that most people have in discussing family relationships and financial matters. By being positive, cooperative, reassuring, informative, and professional in appearance and demeanor, you can help the client overcome this reluctance and understand that his best interests will be served by an open, frank, and complete discussion of financial data and information. You should also assure the client that strict confidentiality of all matters concerning family and finances will be maintained. Once a client seeking a will or an estate plan hires your supervising attorney, your work as a legal assistant will commence.

Initial Interview

The development of a will begins with an initial and lengthy interview of the client by the attorney. Assuming a "comfort" level has been reached and the client is willing to be open and frank about financial data in front of others, you will be asked to attend the interview. Your first task will be to help the client identify all facts, data, and information needed to create a draft of the will. You must develop checklists and questionnaires or expand, amend, or modify existing copies of these documents and thoroughly review them with the client to ensure that they elicit the information necessary for the draft. Exhibits 6.1, 6.2, and 6.5 through 6.8 are examples of the checklists that will enable you to obtain the requisite information.

You will need the following information concerning the client's financial affairs and family relationships: names, addresses, domicile, and marital status of the client and family members. A chart showing the family tree should be drawn. It should identify adopted and nonmarital (illegitimate) children and include the general health of all family members. Assets and liabilities should be listed. Beneficiaries, including charities, should be named, and the assets to be transferred to them should be identified and valued. All fiduciaries, e.g., personal representatives, trustees, guardians, or conservators, should be named. All known creditors and the amounts of the debts owed to them should be listed. Finally, the specific wishes of the client for disposition of the estate should be determined and carefully considered in order to anticipate, counter, or prevent potential will contests by disgruntled family members who may receive nominal gifts of the estate or be completely disinherited.

Once the checklists have been executed and the questionnaires answered, you will review them with the client to ensure they are complete and accurate. Then you can discuss how best to achieve the specific objectives of the client. In addition, one of the more important tasks the attorney undertakes is to help the client reduce death taxes. The attorney should familiarize the client with the taxes imposed on a decedent's estate and give legal advice, *something you must not do,* on how to minimize them. This can be accomplished by reducing the decedent's gross estate through lifetime gifts and increasing the potential deductions from the gross estate such as the marital and charitable deductions. Finally, the client should be informed of the necessity of making decisions about how best to achieve an effective, valid distribution of her estate, at death, in a manner of her own choosing.

ETHICAL ISSUE

If it is obviously apparent that a person lacks mental capacity—a sound mind—the attorney and paralegal cannot accept employment. On the other hand, the lawyer and paralegal should not be judgmental about the client's plans for the will, even if they are eccentric. The paralegal should be helpful and encourage the client to carefully consider, examine, analyze, and determine her true feelings toward beneficiaries and the distributions planned for them. The attorney and paralegal can help the client focus on whether the will should distribute the testator's estate (1) on the basis of a property distribution plan in which the closest family members receive the greater share and other relatives and friends a lesser amount, (2) on the basis of family need, or (3) a combination of these two. Some clients may adopt an unduly submissive or subordinate attitude toward their attorney or the paralegal and may even suggest or request that the attorney or you advise them as to what they should do with their estate property. *This request must be adamantly denied to avoid unethical consequences.*

ETHICAL ISSUE

ETHICAL ISSUE

After the interview, you should prepare optional drafts of the will distribution plans for consideration and review by the client. The plans should include comparisons of their tax consequences and other expenses including attorney's fees. The drafts should then be summarized and explained in plain language to the client so that any modifications can be noted and incorporated into the appropriate selected draft. Once the client is satisfied with the changes, the final will is prepared and properly executed. While avoiding improper solicitation, you should recommend periodic reviews of the will as necessary whenever the client's marital status (divorce or marriage), domicile, or the law changes, or additional children are born or adopted.

Using Checklists to Obtain Basic Data

The following discussion illustrates the development and use of checklists, which are helpful in assembling the data necessary to draft a will appropriate to the individual needs of the client. Definitions and examples of terms used within the checklists precede the individual lists. In addition to being used during the formation of the will, the information will be helpful in determining the proper venue for probating the estate as well as for locating the beneficiaries and devisees and the assets of the deceased. The client should be given a copy of each checklist before the conference so that he can gather the information requested. The client should not attempt to complete the checklists alone, however, but should obtain the assistance of family members and financial advisers. You will also assist in obtaining the information. *Remember that if a previously drawn will of the client exists, a copy of it must be obtained.*

▸ **ETHICAL ISSUE**

The purpose of checklists is to ensure that accurate, complete, and requisite information is obtained. As you review each checklist, you will need to interpret the collected data and recognize when supplementary information is needed.

The sample checklists in this chapter are (1) Family Data, (2) Family Advisers, (3) Assets, (4) Liabilities, (5) Life Insurance Policies, and (6) Locations of Important Documents. In Chapter 7 you will be asked to draft your own will from these sample checklists or from those you develop for yourself. The same or similar checklists will be used to establish an estate plan in Chapter 10. In specific instances, additional or supplementary checklists may be needed, and you will be asked to produce them.

Terminology Relating to Family Data Checklists

The following are terms you are likely to encounter when preparing a family data checklist:

Advancement
Money or property given by a parent while living to a child in anticipation of the share that child will inherit from the parent's estate and in advance of the proper time for receipt of such property.

■ *Advancement.* An **advancement** is money or property given by a parent to a child in anticipation of the share that child will inherit from the parent's estate and in advance of the proper time for receipt of such property. It is intended to be deducted from the share of the parent's estate that the child eventually receives after the parent's death.

Example: Shirley Wilson has 100 shares of valuable stock. Under intestate succession laws, Shirley's only daughter would be entitled to the 100 shares. While alive, Shirley gives her daughter 50 shares. The 50 shares would be considered an advancement unless Shirley dies testate or other evidence is presented that rebuts the advancement presumption. The laws of most states require that a written confirmation of an advancement must exist on the date of the donor's death. The rule of advancement generally applies when there is no will.

Antenuptial (prenuptial) contract or agreement
A contract made by a man and woman before their marriage or in contemplation of that marriage whereby the property rights of either or both the prospective husband or wife are determined.

■ *Antenuptial contract.* An **antenuptial (prenuptial) contract** is a contract made by a man and woman before their marriage or in contemplation of that marriage whereby the property rights of either or both the prospective husband and wife are determined. The agreement resolves issues such as the division of property after death or due to failure of the marriage resulting in divorce or legal separation. The provisions and validity of such agreements vary from state to state. Some states have adopted the Uniform Premarital Agreement Act that establishes the formalities of execution and revocation of the agreement.

Example: John and Mary are contemplating marriage. Both are elderly, and each has two children from a prior marriage. Their first spouses are now deceased. Before their marriage, John and Mary agree in writing to retain all property that each owned separately for the benefit of their respective children. Sometimes spouses agree after marriage to execute a contract that accomplishes the same result for their respective children. These are called **postnuptial contracts or agreements.** See *Friedlander v. Friedlander,* 80 Wash.2d 293, 494 P.2d 208 (1972).

■ *Disinheritance.* Disinheritance is the act by which the owner of an estate specifically deprives another, who would otherwise be the owner's legal heir, from receiving the estate.

Example: Susan York specifically states in her will that "I, intentionally and with full knowledge, leave nothing to my son, Leonard, from the assets of my estate." *Note:* Compare this to the "no contest" (in terrorem) clause in Chapter 5.

■ *Life estate.* A life estate is an interest in real property, e.g., land and buildings, for a lifetime, either the lifetime of the person holding the estate or of some other person. A person who holds a life estate, called the life tenant, possesses and is entitled to use the real property only during the lifetime of the person specified by the will that granted the life estate.

Example: Barry receives a life estate in a lake cottage through his uncle's will. Barry may use and possess the cottage until he dies.

■ *Spendthrift.* A spendthrift is one who spends money unwisely and wastefully.

Example: George wastes the estate left him by his father by drinking, gambling, idleness, and the like.

Checklist for Family Data

As a paralegal, part of your investigatory duties will include collecting complete information concerning your client, the client's family, and the beneficiaries or devisees to be named in the will. Your tasks should include obtaining the following:

■ The full names, addresses, and phone numbers of the participants: the maker of the will, the beneficiaries or devisees, the executor (or executrix), the witnesses, the guardians, and the trustee, if any.

■ The age of the maker, beneficiaries, and devisees.

■ The marital status of the maker, beneficiaries, and devisees.

■ The relationship of each participant to the client.

■ The mental and physical health of the client and the client's spouse.

■ The financial status (worth) of the client and the client's spouse and family, and the nature of any business in which the client has an interest.

■ Family affairs, including tensions, possible mistreatment of the client and the source of such mistreatment, debts owed the maker by family members, advancements (property previously transferred) given to some members, spendthrifts, persons incapable of handling their own financial affairs who may need a trustee, and other pertinent matters.

Using a checklist like the one in Exhibit 6.1, you can collect and organize the family data.

The Need for Supplementary Data. In some instances, information provided by the checklist will not be adequate to inform the attorney of all the client's needs or desires in disposing of property. As an observant practitioner, you should note situations likely to lead to specific devises (gifts) and should further

Postnuptial contract or agreement
A contract made by spouses after marriage whereby the property rights of either or both spouses are determined.

Exhibit 6.1 Family Data

CHECKLIST: FAMILY DATA

Client
Name: _____
Alias or a/k/a: _____
Telephone number: Home _____ Other _____
Social Security number: _____
Date of birth: _____ City, State _____
Marital status: _____ Maiden name _____
Date of marriage: _____ City, State _____
Date of divorce: _____ City, State _____
Date of death: _____ City, State _____
Present health: _____
Occupation/business: _____
Name of employer: _____ Telephone _____
Employer address: _____

Family Members (use additional sheets as necessary) (Spouse, children, grandchildren, parents, other dependents, relatives, and beneficiaries)
Name: _____
Relationship: _____
Telephone number: Home _____ Other _____
Address: _____
Date of birth: _____ City, State _____
Marital status: _____ Maiden name _____
Date of death: _____ City, State _____
Present health: _____

Domicile of Client	**Address**	**City**	**County**	**State**
Home:				
Other residences (homes, cottages, etc.):				
Prior residences over past 10 years, especially if in a community property state:				

Business
Name of business: _____
Business address: _____
Telephone number: _____
Type of business (purpose): _____
Form of ownership (interest):
  Sole proprietor: _____
  Partner: _____
  Limited partner: _____
  Corporation: _____
  Other: _____

Family Concerns
Antenuptial or postnuptial agreements: _____

Exhibit 6.1 Family Data—*continued*

....

Previous marriages: _____
   Children of
   previous
   marriages: _____
Settlement information
   (child support,
   maintenance, etc.): _____
Divorce or legal
   separation: _____
Special dependency
   cases:
   Handicapped child,
   parent, relative: _____
Mental disability: _____
Emotional problems: _____

Trusts
   Spendthrift child: _____
   Life estate to be
   transferred: _____
   Potential inheritance: _____

Persons to be disinherited (specific reasons listed below):
_____
_____

Advancements (property previously transferred before client's death):
_____
_____

Names and Addresses of Potential Fiduciaries and Successors
   Personal representative
   (Executor/trix): _____
   Successor: _____
   Guardian for minor children: _____
   Successor: _____
   Trustees: _____
   Successor: _____

---

pursue these matters with the client after first bringing them to the attention of the supervising attorney. *You should not discuss any circumstances or suggest resolutions to problems that may involve giving legal advice.*

◄ ETHICAL ISSUE

Example: Suppose that George Samson, the client, indicated he had been previously married and had two children by that marriage. The paralegal would have to determine (1) whether the former spouse and children are still living; (2) whether a satisfactory property settlement and child support agreement were reached by all interested parties in the prior marriage, and the terms of those agreements; and (3) whether the client intends to leave any part of his estate to his former wife and children of that marriage.

Example: Suppose the client, George, has an invalid mother who is 75 years old. He has been supporting his mother for the past 15 years and wants to continue this support for her lifetime. The original checklist has only the information that the client's mother is alive and currently an invalid. Questions you put to the client could obtain additional information about his mother and the method by which George wishes to maintain support for her in case he should die first, *but legal advice must come from the attorney.*

ETHICAL ISSUE ....➤

Example: Suppose George does not want any of his estate to go to his brother, Henry. The reasons for this decision and the manner in which George's intent can be manifested in his will must be discussed with the client under the supervision of the attorney.

Example: Suppose that in completing the checklist, George comes to the question of advancements and remembers he gave his youngest son $500 to buy a used motorbike last year. Like most people, George is not sure what an advancement is. This concept must be reviewed and explained. You could explain

ETHICAL ISSUE ....➤

this term and probable results or outcomes; *however, any counseling or legal advice must come from the attorney* during the conference with the client.

The checklists help you to draw out general information and to clarify the client's intentions. If additional data about specific matters and details to be incorporated into the future will must be obtained, you must perform that task.

Checklist for Family Advisers

A list of the names of the client's advisers is helpful in obtaining information about the names of creditors or debtors and the location of the client's assets, personal records and documents, beneficiaries, successors, or even the previous will (see Exhibit 6.2).

Terminology Relating to Assets and Liabilities Checklists

The following terms relating to assets may appear in your assets and liabilities checklist:

- *Dividend.* The share of profits or property to which the owners of a business are entitled; e.g., stockholders are entitled to dividends authorized by a corporation in proportion to the number of shares of the corporation's stock owned by each stockholder.

Exhibit 6.2 Family Advisers

CHECKLIST: FAMILY ADVISERS

	Name	Address	Telephone Number
Accountant:			
Appraiser:			
Attorney:			
Banker:			
Doctor:			
Insurance agent:			
Financial planner:			
Stockbroker:			
Pastor or other religious leader:			
Others:			

- *Fair market value.* The fair market value is the monetary amount that an item of property, e.g., a house, would bring if sold on the open market. Usually, it is the price agreed to by a willing seller and a willing buyer, neither party being compelled to offer a price above or below the average price for such an item.

  Example: Fred Morley offers $120,000 to buy Sam Hacker's house. Houses of this type usually command a price of at least $120,000. Sam accepts Fred's offer. The fair market value of the house is $120,000.

- *Homestead.* A homestead is the family home and the adjoining land (within statutory limits) where the head of the family lives; it is the family's fixed place of residence. Most states allow the head of the family to exempt the homestead from claims and executions by creditors.

Terms relating to miscellaneous property include the following:

- *Copyright.* A government grant to an author of an exclusive right to publish, reprint, and sell a manuscript for a period of the life of the author plus fifty years after the author's death for works written after January 1, 1978.
- *Patent.* A government grant to an inventor of an exclusive right to make, use, and sell an invention for a nonrenewable period of seventeen years.
- *Royalty.* A payment made to an author, composer, or inventor by a company that has been licensed to publish or manufacture the manuscript or invention of that author, composer, or inventor.
- *Receivables.* Receivables are debts (such as promissory notes and the like) established in the course of business that are due from others at present or due within a certain time period.

The following terms describe liabilities you are likely to encounter:

- *Contract for deed.* An agreement or contract to sell real property on an installment basis. On payment of the last installment, the title to the property is transferred by delivery of the deed to the purchaser (see Exhibit 6.3).
- *Installment purchase.* The purchase of goods on credit whereby the purchaser pays for them over a period of time. The purchaser (in the case of a small-loan purchase) immediately obtains the title, or ownership, of the purchase; the seller retains a security interest until the purchaser has paid the full price.
- *Mortgage.* A mortgage is a contract by which a person pledges property to another as security in order to obtain a loan.

  Example: Debbie Johnson obtains a $70,000 mortgage from her bank as a loan in order to finance the purchase of a house costing $90,000.

- *Mortgagor.* The person who mortgages property; the borrower.
- *Mortgagee.* The person to whom property is mortgaged; the lender.

  Example: Debbie Johnson in the example above would be the mortgagor (borrower), and the bank would be the mortgagee (lender).

- *Promissory note.* A promissory note is a promise in writing to pay a certain sum of money at a future time to a specific person. Exhibit 6.4 shows a typical promissory note.

Checklists for Assets and Liabilities

Next, checklists reviewing all assets and liabilities of the client should be developed, and they should include the form of ownership in which the assets are held, e.g., whether each is solely owned or concurrently owned, such as a homestead

Exhibit 6.3 Sample Contract for Deed

CONTRACT FOR DEED   **Form No. 54-M**   Minnesota Uniform Conveyancing Blanks (1978) Miller-Davis Co., Minneapolis
Individual Seller

No delinquent taxes and transfer entered;
Certificate of Real Estate Value
(   )filed   (   )not required
_____ , 19____ .

_____
County Auditor

By _____
Deputy

(reserved for mortgage registry tax payment data)

(reserved for recording data)

MORTGAGE REGISTRY TAX DUE HEREON:

$_____

Date: _____ , 19____

THIS CONTRACT FOR DEED is made on the above date by _____

_____ , _____
(marital status)

Seller (whether one or more), and _____

_____ , Purchaser (whether one or more).

Seller and Purchaser agree to the following terms:

1. PROPERTY DESCRIPTION. Seller hereby sells, and Purchaser hereby buys, real property in _____ County, Minnesota, described as follows:

together with all hereditaments and appurtenances belonging thereto (the Property).

2. TITLE. Seller warrants that title to the Property is, on the date of this contract, subject only to the following exceptions:
   (a) Covenants, conditions, restrictions, declarations and easements of record, if any;
   (b) Reservations of minerals or mineral rights by the State of Minnesota, if any;
   (c) Building, zoning and subdivision laws and regulations;
   (d) The lien of real estate taxes and installments of special assessments which are payable by Purchaser pursuant to paragraph 6 of this contract; and
   (e) The following liens or encumbrances:

3. DELIVERY OF DEED AND EVIDENCE OF TITLE. Upon Purchaser's prompt and full performance of this contract, Seller shall:
   (a) Execute, acknowledge and deliver to Purchaser a _____ Deed, in recordable form, conveying marketable title to the Property to Purchaser, subject only to the following exceptions:
      (i) Those exceptions referred to in paragraph 2(a), (b), (c) and (d) of this contract;
      (ii) Liens, encumbrances, adverse claims or other matters which Purchaser has created, suffered or permitted to accrue after the date of this contract; and

---

Exhibit 6.3 Sample Contract for Deed—*continued*

....

(iii) The following liens or encumbrances:

; and

(b) Deliver to Purchaser the abstract of title to the Property or, if the title is registered, the owner's duplicate certificate of title.

4. PURCHASE PRICE. Purchaser shall pay to Seller, at _____
_____ , the sum of
_____ ($_____) ,
as and for the purchase price for the Property, payable as follows:

5. PREPAYMENT. Unless otherwise provided in this contract, Purchaser shall have the right to fully or partially prepay this contract at any time without penalty. Any partial prepayment shall be applied first to payment of amounts then due under this contract, including unpaid accrued interest, and the balance shall be applied to the principal installments to be paid in the inverse order of their maturity. Partial prepayment shall not postpone the due date of the installments to be paid pursuant to this contract or change the amount of such installments.

6. REAL ESTATE TAXES AND ASSESSMENTS. Purchaser shall pay, before penalty accrues, all real estate taxes and installments of special assessments assessed against the Property which are due and payable in the year 19___ and in all subsequent years. Real estate taxes and installments of special assessments which are due and payable in the year in which this contract is dated shall be paid as follows:

Seller warrants that the real estate taxes and installments of special assessments which were due and payable in the years preceding the year in which this contract is dated are paid in full.

7. PROPERTY INSURANCE.
   (a) INSURED RISKS AND AMOUNT. Purchaser shall keep all buildings, improvements and fixtures now or later located on or a part of the Property insured against loss by fire, extended coverage perils, vandalism, malicious mischief and, if applicable, steam boiler explosion for at least the amount of _____
   If any of the buildings, improvements or fixtures are located in a federally designated flood prone area, and if flood insurance is available for that area, Purchaser shall procure and maintain flood insurance in amounts reasonably satisfactory to Seller.
   (b) OTHER TERMS. The insurance policy shall contain a loss payable clause in favor of Seller which provides that Seller's right to recover under the insurance shall not be impaired by any acts or omissions of Purchaser or Seller, and that Seller shall otherwise be afforded all rights and privileges customarily provided a mortgagee under the so-called standard mortgage clause.
   (c) NOTICE OF DAMAGE. In the event of damage to the Property by fire or other casualty, Purchaser shall promptly give notice of such damage to Seller and the insurance company.

8. DAMAGE TO THE PROPERTY.
   (a) APPLICATION OF INSURANCE PROCEEDS. If the Property is damaged by fire or other casualty, the insurance proceeds paid on account of such damage shall be applied to payment of the amounts payable by Purchaser under this contract, even if such amounts are not then due to be paid, unless Purchaser makes a permitted election described in the next paragraph. Such amounts shall be first applied to unpaid accrued interest and next to the installments to be paid as provided in this contract in the inverse order of their maturity. Such payment shall not postpone the due date of the installments to be paid pursuant to this contract or change the amount of such installments. The balance of insurance proceeds, if any, shall be the property of Purchaser.

Exhibit 6.3   Sample Contract for Deed—*continued*

(b) PURCHASER'S ELECTION TO REBUILD. If Purchaser is not in default under this contract, or after curing any such default, and if the mortgagees in any prior mortgages and sellers in any prior contracts for deed do not require otherwise, Purchaser may elect to have that portion of such insurance proceeds necessary to repair, replace or restore the damaged Property (the repair work) deposited in escrow with a bank or title insurance company qualified to do business in the State of Minnesota, or such other party as may be mutually agreeable to Seller and Purchaser. The election may only be made by written notice to Seller within sixty days after the damage occurs. Also, the election will only be permitted if the plans and specifications and contracts for the repair work are approved by Seller, which approval Seller shall not unreasonably withhold or delay. If such a permitted election is made by Purchaser, Seller and Purchaser shall jointly deposit, when paid, such insurance proceeds into such escrow. If such insurance proceeds are insufficient for the repair work, Purchaser shall, before the commencement of the repair work, deposit into such escrow sufficient additional money to insure the full payment for the repair work. Even if the insurance proceeds are unavailable or are insuffficient to pay the cost of the repair work, Purchaser shall at all times be responsible to pay the full cost of the repair work. All escrowed funds shall be disbursed by the escrowee in accordance with generally accepted sound construction disbursement procedures. The costs incurred or to be incurred on account of such escrow shall be deposited by Purchaser into such escrow before the commencement of the repair work. Purchaser shall complete the repair work as soon as reasonably possible and in a good and workmanlike manner, and in any event the repair work shall be completed by Purchaser within one year after the damage occurs. If, following the completion of and payment for the repair work, there remain any undisbursed escrow funds, such funds shall be applied to payment of the amounts payable by Purchaser under this contract in accordance with paragraph 8 (a) above.

9. INJURY OR DAMAGE OCCURRING ON THE PROPERTY.
(a) LIABILITY. Seller shall be free from liability and claims for damages by reason of injuries occurring on or after the date of this contract to any person or persons or property while on or about the Property. Purchaser shall defend and indemnify Seller from all liability, loss, costs and obligations, including reasonable attorneys' fees, on account of or arising out of any such injuries. However, Purchaser shall have no liability or obligation to Seller for such injuries which are caused by the negligence or intentional wrongful acts or omissions of Seller.
(b) LIABILITY INSURANCE. Purchaser shall, at Purchaser's own expense, procure and maintain liability insurance against claims for bodily injury, death and property damage occurring on or about the Property in amounts reasonably satisfactory to Seller and naming Seller as an additional insured.

10. INSURANCE, GENERALLY. The insurance which Purchaser is required to procure and maintain pursuant to paragraphs 7 and 9 of this contract shall be issued by an insurance company or companies licensed to do business in the State of Minnesota and acceptable to Seller. The insurance shall be maintained by Purchaser at all times while any amount remains unpaid under this contract. The insurance policies shall provide for not less than ten days written notice to Seller before cancellation, non-renewal, termination or change in coverage, and Purchaser shall deliver to Seller a duplicate original or certificate of such insurance policy or policies.

11. CONDEMNATION. If all or any part of the Property is taken in condemnation proceedings instituted under power of eminent domain or is conveyed in lieu thereof under threat of condemnation, the money paid pursuant to such condemnation or conveyance in lieu thereof shall be applied to payment of the amounts payable by Purchaser under this contract, even if such amounts are not then due to be paid. Such amounts shall be applied first to unpaid accrued interest and next to the installments to be paid as provided in this contract in the inverse order of their maturity. Such payment shall not postpone the due date of the installments to be paid pursuant to this contract or change the amount of such installments. The balance, if any, shall be the property of Purchaser.

12. WASTE, REPAIR AND LIENS. Purchaser shall not remove or demolish any buildings, improvements or fixtures now or later located on or a part of the Property, nor shall Purchaser commit or allow waste of the Property. Purchaser shall maintain the Property in good condition and repair. Purchaser shall not create or permit to accrue liens or adverse claims against the Property which constitute a lien or claim against Seller's interest in the Property. Purchaser shall pay to Seller all amounts, costs and expenses, including reasonable attorneys' fees, incurred by Seller to remove any such liens or adverse claims.

13. DEED AND MORTGAGE REGISTRY TAXES. Seller shall, upon Purchaser's full performance of this contract, pay the deed tax due upon the recording or filing of the deed to be delivered by Seller to Purchaser. The mortgage registry tax due upon the recording or filing of this contract shall be paid by the party who records or files this contract; however, this provision shall not impair the right of Seller to collect from Purchaser the amount of such tax actually paid by Seller as provided in the applicable law governing default and service of notice of termination of this contract.

14. NOTICE OF ASSIGNMENT. If either Seller or Purchaser assigns their interest in the Property, a copy of such assignment shall promptly be furnished to the non-assigning party.

15. PROTECTION OF INTERESTS. If Purchaser fails to pay any sum of money required under the terms of this contract or fails to perform any of Purchaser's obligations as set forth in this contract, Seller may, at Seller's option, pay the same or cause the same to be performed, or both, and the amounts so paid by Seller and the cost of such performance shall be payable at once, with interest at the rate stated in paragraph 4 of this contract, as an additional amount due Seller under this contract.

If there now exists, or if Seller hereafter creates, suffers or permits to accrue, any mortgage, contract for deed, lien or encumbrance against the Property which is not herein expressly assumed by Purchaser, and provided Purchaser is not in default under this contract, Seller shall timely pay all amounts due thereon, and if Seller fails to do so, Purchaser may, at Purchaser's option, pay any such delinquent amounts and deduct the amounts paid from the installment(s) next coming due under this contract.

16. DEFAULT. The time of performance by Purchaser of the terms of this contract is an essential part of this contract. Should Purchaser fail to timely perform any of the terms of this contract, Seller may, at Seller's option, elect to declare this contract cancelled and terminated by notice to Purchaser in accordance with applicable law. All right, title and interest acquired under this contract by Purchaser shall then cease and terminate, and all improvements made upon the Property and all payments made by Purchaser pursuant to this contract shall belong to Seller as liquidated damages for breach of this contract. Neither the extension of the time for payment of any sum of money to be paid hereunder nor any waiver by Seller of Seller's rights to declare this contract forfeited by reason of any breach shall in any manner affect Seller's right to cancel this contract because of defaults subsequently occurring, and no extension of time shall be valid unless agreed to in writing. After service of notice of default and failure to cure such default within the period allowed by law, Purchaser shall, upon demand, surrender possession of the Property to Seller, but Purchaser shall be entitled to possession of the Property until the expiration of such period.

17. BINDING EFFECT. The terms of this contract shall run with the land and bind the parties hereto and their successors in interest.

Exhibit 6.3   Sample Contract for Deed—*continued*

18. HEADINGS. Headings of the paragraphs of this contract are for convenience only and do not define, limit or construe the contents of such paragraphs.

19. ASSESSMENTS BY OWNERS' ASSOCIATION. If the Property is subject to a recorded declaration providing for assessments to be levied against the Property by any owners' association, which assessments may become a lien against the Property if not paid, then:
   (a) Purchaser shall promptly pay, when due, all assessments imposed by the owners' association or other governing body as required by the provisions of the declaration or other related documents; and
   (b) So long as the owners' association maintains a master or blanket policy of insurance against fire, extended coverage perils and such other hazards and in such amounts as are required by this contract, then:
      (i) Purchaser's obligation in this contract to maintain hazard insurance coverage on the Property is satisfied; and
      (ii) The provisions in paragraph 8 of this contract regarding application of insurance proceeds shall be superceded by the provisions of the declaration or other related documents; and
      (iii) In the event of a distribution of insurance proceeds in lieu of restoration or repair following an insured casualty loss to the Property, any such proceeds payable to Purchaser are hereby assigned and shall be paid to Seller for application to the sum secured by this contract, with the excess, if any, paid to Purchaser.

20. ADDITIONAL TERMS:

SELLER(S)   PURCHASER(S)

_____   _____

_____   _____

_____   _____

_____   _____

State of Minnesota   } *ss.*

County of _____

The foregoing instrument was acknowledged before me this ____ day of _____ , 19___ , by _____ .

NOTARIAL STAMP OR SEAL (OR OTHER TITLE OR RANK)

SIGNATURE OF NOTARY PUBLIC OR OTHER OFFICIAL

State of Minnesota   } *ss.*

County of _____

The foregoing instrument was acknowledged before me this ____ day of _____ , 19___ , by _____ .

NOTARIAL STAMP OR SEAL (OR OTHER TITLE OR RANK)

SIGNATURE OF NOTARY PUBLIC OR OTHER OFFICIAL

Tax Statements for the real property described in this instrument should be sent to.

THIS INSTRUMENT WAS DRAFTED BY (NAME AND ADDRESS)

FAILURE TO RECORD OR FILE THIS CONTRACT FOR DEED MAY GIVE OTHER PARTIES PRIORITY OVER PURCHASER'S INTEREST IN THE PROPERTY.

Source: Miller/Davis Company, Minneapolis, Minn.

in joint tenancy between a husband and wife. Such listings should include the following information:

- *Real property,* including the legal description and estimated fair market value of the homestead, all other land, and business buildings. Determine whether the property is owned individually in severalty or concurrently in joint tenancy, tenancy in common, or as community property (see Chapter 2). Check the location of the property. If it is outside the client's home state, ancillary administration might be necessary.

- *Tangible personal property,* including personal effects and clothing of considerable value, furniture and household goods, automobiles, boats, jewelry, antiques, art and stamp collections, and other miscellaneous items.

- Other items of personal property such as savings and checking accounts, safe deposit box, stocks and bonds, cash on hand, promissory notes receivable, mortgages, patents, and copyrights.

- Insurance policies, including life, disability, health and accident, hospitalization, and annuities, must be scrutinized to determine how and to whom payments are to be made upon the client's death.

- Employee benefits like Social Security, veterans' benefits, pension plans, profit-sharing plans, death benefits, stock options, and all other claims to which the client's estate or successors may be entitled.

- Business interests in a corporation, partnership, or sole proprietorship, with complete details about the client's interest, rights, and responsibilities therein.

- All debts owed by the client, including outstanding mortgages, promissory notes payable, business debts, payments owed on contracts for deeds, and accounts with a stockbroker.

- Interest and duties in trust assets (property transferred, beneficiary, trustee, trust agreement) or estates of others, including powers of appointment (a power to dispose of property not owned by the holder of the power), which the decedent may hold by virtue of being given this power by another's will or trust. A general power of appointment held by the decedent is taxable to the decedent's estate.

Using checklists like those in Exhibits 6.5 and 6.6, you can collect and organize the data on the client's assets and liabilities.

Exhibit 6.4 Sample Promissory Note

$200.00   Date _January 13, 1995_

_____Sixty days_____ after date __I__ promise to pay

to the order of _____John Jones_____

__Two hundred and no/100 --__

Payable at __First Northwestern Bank__ with interest at _11_ %

                                    Sandy Brown

Exhibit 6.5   Assets

CHECKLIST: ASSETS

List the item (by name), the estimated fair market value of the property owned, the location, the form of ownership, e.g., single ownership by husband (H) or wife (W), joint tenancy (J), tenancy in common (T), or community property (C) for each item, and the beneficiary or beneficiaries (Bene.).

	Item	Value	Location	Form of Ownership (H/W/J/T/C)	Bene.
Cash					
Cash and checking accounts:					
Savings accounts:					
Money market accounts:					
Certificates of deposit:					
Stocks and Bonds					
Stocks (Name and no. of shares):					
Stock options:					
U.S. government bonds:					
Municipal bonds:					
Mutual funds:					
Other:					
Real Property					
Residential (homestead):					
Business building:					
Recreational (summer cottage):					
Foreign real estate:					
Other:					
Personal Property					
Furniture and household goods:					
Furs and jewelry:					
Automobiles (model and year):					
(1)					
(2)					
Collections (art, guns, coins, stamps, antiques, etc.):					
Other vehicles (boats, trailers, campers, snowmobiles, motorbikes, etc.):					
Wearing apparel and personal effects:					
Other:					
Business Interests					
Sole proprietorship:					
Partnership:					
Limited partnership:					
Corporation:					
Buy-sell agreements:					
Other:					

Exhibit 6.5 Assets—continued

Receivables
Promissory notes
(payable to client): _____
Contract for deed (client
is seller): _____
Other: _____

**Employee, Corporate,
and Other Benefits**
Pension plan: _____
Stock bonus: _____
Profit-sharing plan: _____
401(k) plan: _____
Individual retirement
account (I.R.A.): _____
Health insurance
Accident and health: _____
Medical and surgical: _____
Hospitalization: _____
Social Security: _____
Union benefits: _____
Railroad retirement
benefits: _____
Veterans' benefits: _____
Fraternal organization
benefits: _____

Interests in Trusts
Power of Appointment
(General or Special) _____
Insurance and
Annuities
(See Exhibit 6.7)
Straight life, universal
life, or term: _____
Endowment or annuity: _____
Group life insurance: _____

Miscellaneous Property
Patents: _____
Copyrights: _____
Royalties: _____
Other: _____
TOTAL ASSETS (value): _____

ASSIGNMENT 6.1

Your law firm's client is heavily invested in the bond and stock markets. As a paralegal for the firm, you have been asked to collect the necessary data concerning the extent and value of the client's holdings. Due to the client's extensive holdings, you will need a more detailed checklist than the one shown in Exhibit 6.5. You have been asked to include the number of shares, ownership, date of purchase and cost basis, and current market value for all stocks, bonds, and mutual funds owned by the client. Draft an appropriate checklist.

If the client has substantial stock holdings, a separate sheet listing the holdings should be attached to the assets checklist. Also, some of the items listed may be difficult to value, e.g., an art collection, certain clothing, and business interests. You may find it necessary to communicate, with the client's assistance, with financial advisers and other experts in specific fields, e.g., an art collector and appraiser, to obtain the necessary information. If the assets of the estate include certain property, such as a patent, collections other than art, or hobby equipment, whose value may be difficult to estimate accurately, you should ask the client to suggest potential buyers or appraisers for these items. A separate list of this information should be made.

Terminology Relating to Life Insurance Policies Checklist

The life insurance policies checklist may include the following terms:

- *Life insurance.* Life insurance is a contract, a legally binding agreement, by which one party (the insurance company) promises to pay another (the policyholder or designated beneficiary) a certain sum of money if the policyholder sustains a specific loss (e.g., death or total disability). For this protection the policyholder makes a payment called a premium on a regular basis, usually annually, to the insurance company. Life insurance includes term, ordinary (whole or straight) life, and universal life insurance (see Chapter 10).

Exhibit 6.6 Liabilities

CHECKLIST: LIABILITIES

List the item, its location, the estimated value of each debt, the parties indebted, i.e., husband (H), wife (W), or both (B), and the creditor.

Type of Liability	Item	Value	Location	Form of Liability (H/W/B)	Creditor
Promissory notes (to banks, loan companies, individuals, etc.):					
Mortgages—on real property:					
Payment on contracts for deed:					
Charge accounts and installment purchases:					
Automobile loans:					
Credit card charges:					
Loans on insurance policies:					
Business debts:					
Enforceable pledges to charitable and religious organizations:					
Taxes owed:					
TOTAL LIABILITIES (value):					

- *Annuity.* An annuity is a fixed sum to be paid at regular intervals, such as annually, for either a certain or indefinite period, as for a stated number of years or for life.

- *Primary beneficiary.* The primary beneficiary is the person who has a superior claim over all others to the benefits of a life insurance contract. The policyholder selects the primary beneficiary.

- *Secondary (contingent) beneficiary.* The secondary beneficiary is the person selected by the policyholder as a successor to the benefits of a life insurance policy whenever the proceeds of the policy are not paid to the primary beneficiary.

- *Cash surrender value.* In ordinary (straight) life insurance, the cash surrender value is the cash reserve that increases (builds) each year the policy remains in force as a minimum savings feature. After the policy has been in force for a period specified by the insurer (company), the policyholder may borrow an amount not to exceed the cash value.

- *Premium.* The sum paid or agreed to be paid annually by the insured person (policyholder) to the insurance company (insurer) as the consideration for the insurance contract.

- *Settlement option.* A settlement option is one of a number of alternatives that parties to an insurance contract agree to follow to discharge their agreement.

Checklist for Life Insurance Policies

Exhibit 6.5 (Assets) includes basic information about the existence and types of life insurance owned by the client. If necessary, more detailed information about such policies must be compiled. This is an example of an instance in which you must develop a checklist within a checklist. Exhibit 6.7 shows a checklist for gathering information on the client's life insurance policies. Information on the insurance policies of the client's spouse and children should also be obtained.

Example: Charles Rivera is the named primary beneficiary of his deceased parent's life insurance policy. The policy gives Charles the option of receiving payment in a lump sum or in a monthly payment over a period of years. The option selected by Charles acts as a discharge of the contract.

ASSIGNMENT 6.2

John Smith owned a straight life insurance policy with the Life Assurance Company of Kingstown with $50,000 as its face value. John named his wife, Mary Smith, as his primary beneficiary and his son, William Smith, as the secondary beneficiary. The cash value of the policy at the time of John's death is $8,700. The year before John's death, he obtained a $2,500 loan on his insurance from the insurance company at 5 percent interest. When John died, a $1,200 balance, including interest, was unpaid on the loan. To whom will the life insurance be paid? How much will the beneficiary receive?

Checklist for Important Documents

You should collect all documents involving the client's property and business interests for review with the attorney. These documents may include stock certificates and options, contracts, deeds, receivables, insurance policies, gift tax returns, income tax returns for the past three years (the Internal Revenue Service can challenge the accuracy of a taxpayer's income tax return for the three pre-

Exhibit 6.7 Life Insurance Policies

CHECKLIST: LIFE INSURANCE DATA

Policyholder (owner): _____
Insured: _____
Insurance agent: _____ Phone: _____

	Company 1	Company 2	Company 3	Company 4	Totals
Name/Policy no.					
Location of policy					
Type of insurance					
Face or death value					
Dividends					
Annual premium					
Cash (surrender) value					
Loan on cash value					
Primary beneficiaries					
Secondary beneficiaries					
Settlement option Installment					
Annuity					
Others					

vious taxable years, although if fraud is involved, the statute of limitations does not apply; see I.R.C. § 6531 [1939]), divorce decrees and alimony or child support payments or other property settlements from a previous marriage, antenuptial agreements, mortgages, *inter vivos* (between living persons) trust agreements in which the client is either the donor or beneficiary, and any existing will the client may have. Exhibit 6.8 is a sample checklist for gathering information about the existence and location of these important documents.

ASSIGNMENT 6.3

Using the above checklists as a guide, develop and fill in the checklists necessary for preparing a preliminary draft of your own will or the will of some member of your family, e.g., a spouse, parent, brother, or sister. Organize the data according to your checklists, taking into account assets, liabilities, family data, location of records, lists of documents needed, and advisers or sources of required information. Indicate what additional facts, if any, are needed.

PRELIMINARY TAX ADVICE AND OTHER MATTERS

At the conference with the client, in addition to eliciting information by means of the checklists, the attorney or the supervised paralegal should explain the tax consequences of dying in terms understandable to the client. Resolving tax problems under the supervision of an attorney is an important function of a paralegal. Chapter 14 of this text identifies and defines the various types of taxes (both state and federal), explains how the basic tax regulations are applied to analytical problems, and demonstrates the necessary tax calculations. Therefore, Chapter 14 must be reviewed before you can perform the duties outlined below during the conference.

At the conference the following matters should be explained and discussed. Some of these items are discussed in more detail in later chapters.

- For smaller estates, the importance of considering joint tenancy ownership to avoid a portion of administration expenses. Guard against overemphasizing the advantages of this form of property ownership, however, since transferring property into joint tenancy may involve a gift tax and a loss of control over the property, making it impossible to sell the property later without the joint co-owner's consent.
- How the federal estate tax can be reduced by using the marital and charitable deductions to which a client's estate is entitled.
- The use of certain *inter vivos* gifts or trusts to lower administration expenses and death taxes by reducing the client's gross estate.
- Whether the client wants taxes on the estate paid from estate funds or whether the individual beneficiaries or devisees are to pay taxes on their shares.

During the conference you should clarify other pertinent matters for the client and determine the client's desires in a number of situations. Particularly important are the spouse's right of election and the children's right to inherit.

Spouse's Right of Election

The client should be informed that a married person is limited in disposing of property since a surviving spouse may not be completely excluded. Most states offer a surviving spouse the right to renounce the will and elect a statutory share of a certain minimum portion of the deceased spouse's estate, thus invalidating an exclusion from the will. Therefore, your state's right of election should be explained to the client. A typical state statute involving this matter is N.C. Gen. Stat. Ann. § 30–1, which allows a surviving spouse to take an elective share equal to the intestate share (but compare U.P.C. §§ 2–202 and 2–203).

For more on this topic, see Chapter 4.

Examples: John Evans dies testate and leaves his surviving spouse, Bette (1) *all* his property; (2) *some* of his property; (3) *nothing*—he disinherits Bette. In Case 1, Bette would receive through John's will all his property as his sole successor. In Case 2, Bette would have the election (statutory) right to take either through John's will or by statute. Usually, she would choose whichever was the

Exhibit 6.8 Locations of Important Documents

CHECKLIST: RECORDS OR DOCUMENTS (COPIES)

List the applicable documents' location or comment on missing items. Use additional sheets as necessary. If any documents are kept in a safe deposit box, list its location and where the key may be found.

Checklists   Location
   Checklists: _____

Personal Data (Client and Family Members)
   Birth certificate: _____
   Social Security card: _____
   Medicare card: _____
   Marriage certificate: _____
   Separation agreement: _____
   Divorce decree: _____
   Antenuptial agreement: _____
   Postnuptial agreement: _____
   Adoption papers: _____
   Naturalization papers: _____
   Passports: _____
   Military records: _____
   Death certificate: _____
   Other: _____ _____

Real Property
   Abstracts of title: _____
   Deeds: _____
   Contracts for deed: _____
   Leases: _____
   Appraisals: _____
   Property tax valuation notices: _____
   Other: _____ _____

Personal Property
   Titles/registrations for:
     Automobiles: _____
     Recreational vehicles: _____
     Trailers: _____
     Boats: _____
     Airplanes: _____
   Other: _____ _____

Cash, Stocks, and Bonds
   Bank account statements: _____
   Investment account statements: _____
   Certificates of deposit: _____
   Bonds and other debentures: _____
   Stock certificates: _____
   Other: _____ _____

Miscellaneous Property
   Patent agreements: _____
   Copyright agreements: _____
   Royalty agreements: _____
   Promissory notes: _____
   Other: _____ _____

Exhibit 6.8   Locations of Important Documents—*continued*

Business Interests
 Partnership agreements: _____
 Limited partnership agreements: _____
 Franchise agreements: _____
 Buy-sell agreements: _____
 Corporation documents:
  Charter: _____
  Bylaws: _____
  Stock certificates: _____
  Stock options: _____
 Other: _____   _____

Retirement Plans
 Pension plan: _____
 Profit sharing plan: _____
 401(k) plan: _____
 Keogh plan: _____
 Individual retirement accounts: _____
 Other: _____   _____

Interests in Trusts
 Trust agreements: _____
 Declaration of trust: _____
 Powers of appointment: _____
 Other: _____   _____

Insurance Policies
 Life insurance: _____
 Annuity contracts: _____
 Accident insurance: _____
 Health insurance: _____
 Disability insurance: _____
 Title insurance: _____
 Homeowner's insurance: _____
 Mortgage insurance: _____
 Automobile insurance: _____
 Other: _____   _____

Liabilities
 Promissory notes: _____
 Mortgages on real property: _____
 Contracts for deed: _____
 Loans on insurance policies: _____
 Installment purchases:
  Automobile loans: _____
  Credit card charges: _____
 Business debts: _____
 Other: _____   _____

Miscellaneous (specify)
 Credit cards: _____
 Other: _____   _____

Tax Returns
 Federal income tax (3 years):   _____
 State income tax (3 years):   _____
 Federal gift tax (all years):   _____

Exhibit 6.8 Locations of Important Documents—*continued*

Current Will or Codicil
Original (client): _____
Original (spouse): _____
Letter of Last Instructions: _____

Safe Deposit Box and Key Location _____

---

greater. She cannot take both. In Case 3, John would fail in his attempt to disinherit his wife since in most states she is entitled to the statutory share, which she would naturally choose.

ASSIGNMENT 6.4

If John Evans were domiciled in your state and attempted through his will to leave all, some, or none of his property to his surviving spouse, how would your state handle each conveyance? Cite and explain your statute.

ASSIGNMENT 6.5

1. Jerry and Audrey Maxwell are husband and wife. They have no children. If upon Audrey's death Jerry were to choose to take the surviving spouse's elective share according to your state's statute, how much of Audrey's property would Jerry receive?
2. In another example, Jerry and Audrey have had five children—Marty, Mike, Marc, Mary, and Michelle. Marc died in a childhood accident; all the other children are married and have two children of their own. Upon Jerry's death, what would be Audrey's share if she elected against the will based on your state's statute?
3. In a third case, Jerry and Audrey have one child, Marty, who is married and has three children. Marty dies in an industrial accident. Then Jerry dies one year later. Audrey elects against the will. What will be her statutory share according to your own state statute?

Children's Right to Inherit

It should be made clear to the client that parents are not required to leave anything to their children. Nevertheless, if children are to be excluded from sharing in a parent's estate, it is best accomplished by inserting a clause in the will to the effect that the parent has intentionally made no provision for a certain named child. When a child is not specifically excluded in the will, the child may ultimately receive a share as a result of a state's Pretermitted (Omitted) Child Statute, despite the parent's intent to disinherit. Most parents, however, have no intention of disinheriting their children, but they may wish to pass their estates to their children in unequal proportions because of the children's different financial status.

🏛 ASSIGNMENT 6.6

In completing the family data checklist illustrated earlier in this chapter, William Richardson, age 68, the prospective testator, indicates that of his four adult children, Duane, James, Amy, and Beth, and one minor child, Susan, age 17, only Amy has consistently shown an interest in her father's health and welfare. Therefore, William intends to leave his entire estate to Amy. Answer the following according to your own state laws:

1. Can William disinherit his three adult children other than Amy? If so, how could this be done?
2. Can William disinherit his minor child, Susan? Explain.
3. If Duane, one of William's adult children, is physically handicapped or mentally retarded, can William disinherit him? Explain.
4. William stated in a clause in his will, "Because of their mistreatment of me, I intentionally disinherit all my other children, Duane, James, and Beth, and leave my entire estate to Amy." Susan is not mentioned, yet the words *all my other children* are included in the will. After William dies, Susan and the other adult children, Duane, James, and Beth, contest their father's will. Who prevails according to your state laws?

GUIDELINES FOR PREPARING A WILL

In addition to discussing with the client facts pertinent to the valid and effective drafting of a will, you must follow general rules for drafting a will to ensure its effectiveness and validity and to decrease the likelihood that persons claiming an interest in the decedent's estate might challenge it in a will contest. Following are guidelines for drafting a valid testamentary document. They provide a convenient checklist of good construction habits to develop in preparation for the execution of a will. Actual drafting assignments will be included in Chapter 7.

Guideline 1: Avoid Using Printed Forms

Printed forms are seldom used. They may not fill the special needs of the testator and may cause problems. For instance, if part of the form is printed, part is typed, and part is handwritten, a will contest based on forgery could result. An alteration of any kind in a will usually casts doubt on whether the altered section is the work of the testator or of some other person who placed it in the will unknown to the testator. *Note:* The state "statutory will" forms available in California, Louisiana, Maine, Michigan, and Wisconsin are a major exception to the caveat on using printed or computerized forms. These are printed forms with written instructions to the maker of the will, and they require choices that must be made on the form; see Cal. Prob. Code §§ 6220–6226 and Mich. Stat. Ann. § 700.123c and compare the California and Wisconsin statutory wills in Exhibit 6.9 and 6.10.

Another problem is that words on printed forms are often crossed out or deleted by ink or type. Sometimes corrections or changes are written on the forms. In such cases, the question arises as to who made these changes and the reason for them. Thus, the validity of the will is in jeopardy.

A third problem is that printed forms are written in generalities and therefore do not address the specific problems or objectives of the testator. Property may be inadvertently omitted, intended beneficiaries or devisees may be excluded, and tax advantages may be overlooked.

Example: Louise Pendleton, using a printed will form, forgot to include a residuary clause leaving the residue or remainder of her estate to a named person. Louise had made a number of specific gifts to relatives and friends, but the bulk of her estate was in the residue. Since Louise used a printed form and no residuary clause was included, the residue of her estate would pass by intestate succession statutes.

ASSIGNMENT 6.7

In the example above, if Louise had only two relatives, Peter, a nephew, and Clara, a grandparent, how and to whom would Louise's residuary estate be transferred according to your state laws?

Guideline 2: Use One Word Processor and Typeface

Among the good habits to develop in constructing wills is to use the same word processor and typeface for the entire testament. Using different typefaces makes it appear that someone other than the testator has inserted provisions. In addition, the typist should not leave blank spaces in the will, which might make possible the addition of words or names or even an entire page. Such procedures help ensure that the decedent's heirs will have a measure of protection against persons who would change the will to benefit themselves.

Example: Michael intends to leave the bulk and residue of his considerable estate to three friends—Mary Brown, Adam Korkowski, and Stanley Weskoskowitz. Because of the length of Stanley's last name, the typist of the will left a long

---

Exhibit 6.9 California Statutory Will

CALIFORNIA STATUTORY WILL OF

_____

Print Your Full Name

1. Will. This is my Will. I revoke all prior Wills and codicils.

2. Specific Gift of Personal Residence. (Optional – use only if you want to give your personal residence to a different person or persons than you give the balance of your assets to under paragraph 5 below). I give my interest in my principal personal residence at the time of my death (subject to mortgages and liens) as follows: (Select one choice only and sign in the box after your choice.)

a. _Choice One:_ All to my spouse, if my spouse survives me; otherwise to my descendants (my children and the descendants of my children) who survive me.

b. _Choice Two:_ Nothing to my spouse; all to my descendants (my children and the descendants of my children) who survive me.

c. _Choice Three:_ All to the following person if he or she survives me: (Insert the name of the person):

_____

d. _Choice Four:_ Equally among the following persons who survive me: (Insert the names of two or more persons):

_____
_____
_____

WOLCOTTS FORM 1665—CALIFORNIA STATUTORY WILL—Rev. 12-92 (price class 2)   Page 1   ©1992 WOLCOTTS FORMS, INC.

Exhibit 6.9   California Statutory Will—*continued*

3. Specific Gift of Automobiles, Household and Personal Effects. (Optional – use only if you want to give automobiles and household and personal effects to a different person or persons than you give the balance of your assets to under paragraph 5 below). I give all of my automobiles (subject to loans), furniture, furnishings, household items, clothing, jewelry, and other tangible articles of a personal nature at the time of my death as follows: (Select one choice only and sign in the box after your choice.)

   a. <u>Choice One:</u> All to my spouse, if my spouse survives me; otherwise to my descendants (my children and the descendants of my children) who survive me.

   b. <u>Choice Two:</u> Nothing to my spouse; all to my descendants (my children and the descendants of my children) who survive me.

   c. <u>Choice Three:</u> All to the following person if he or she survives me: (Insert the name of the person):

   d. <u>Choice Four:</u> Equally among the following persons who survive me: (Insert the names of two or more persons):

_____

_____

_____

4. Specific Gifts of Cash. (Optional) I make the following cash gifts to the persons named below who survive me, or to the named charity, and I sign my name in the box after each gift. If I don't sign in the box, I do not make a gift. (Sign in the box after each gift you make.)

Name of Person or Charity to receive gift (name one only – please print)	Amount of Cash Gift
	Sign your name in this box to make this gift.
Name of Person or Charity to receive gift (name one only – please print)	Amount of Cash Gift
	Sign your name in this box to make this gift.
Name of Person or Charity to receive gift (name one only – please print)	Amount of Cash Gift
	Sign your name in this box to make this gift.
Name of Person or Charity to receive gift (name one only – please print)	Amount of Cash Gift
	Sign your name in this box to make this gift.
Name of Person or Charity to receive gift (name one only – please print)	Amount of Cash Gift
	Sign your name in this box to make this gift.

5. Balance of My Assets. Except for the specific gifts made in paragraphs 2, 3 and 4 above, I give the balance of my assets as follows: (Select <u>one</u> choice only and sign in the box after your choice. If I sign in more than one box or if I don't sign in any box, the court will distribute my assets as if I did not make a Will).

   a. <u>Choice One:</u> All to my spouse, if my spouse survives me; otherwise to my descendants (my children and the descendants of my children) who survive me.

   b. <u>Choice Two:</u> Nothing to my spouse; all to my descendants (my children and the descendants of my children) who survive me.

   c. <u>Choice Three:</u> All to the following person if he or she survives me: (Insert the name of the person):

_____

   d. <u>Choice Four:</u> Equally among the following persons who survive me: (Insert the names of two or more persons):

_____

_____

_____

6. Guardian of the Child's Person. If I have a child under age 18 and the child does not have a living parent at my death, I nominate the individual named below as First Choice as guardian of the person of such child (to raise the child). If the First Choice does not serve, then I nominate the Second Choice, and then the Third Choice, to serve. Only an individual (not a bank or trust company) may serve.

Name of First Choice for Guardian of the Person	Name of Second Choice for Guardian of the Person

Name of Third Choice for Guardian of the Person

Exhibit 6.9 California Statutory Will—*continued*

7. Special Provision of Property of Persons Under Age 25. (Optional – Unless you use this paragraph, assets that go to a child or other person who is <u>under</u> age 18 may be given to the parent of the person, or to the guardian named in paragraph 6 above as guardian of the person until age 18, and the court will require a bond; and assets that go to a child or other person who is age 18 or older will be given outright to the person. By using this paragraph you may provide that a custodian will hold the assets for the person until the person reaches any age between 18 and 25 which you choose). If a beneficiary of this Will is between age 18 and 25, I nominate the individual or bank or trust company named below as First Choice as custodian of the property. If the First Choice does not serve, then I nominate the Second Choice, and then the Third Choice, to serve.

Name of First Choice for Custodian of Assets	Name of Second Choice for Custodian of Assets

Name of Third Choice for Custodian of Assets

Insert any age between 18 and 25 as the age for the person to receive the property: (If you do not choose an age, age 18 will apply.) . . . .

8. I nominate the individual or bank or trust company named below as First Choice as executor. If the First Choice does not serve, then I nominate the Second Choice, and then the Third Choice, to serve.

Name of First Choice for Executor	Name of Second Choice for Executor

Name of Third Choice for Executor

9. Bond. My signature in this box means a bond is <u>not</u> required for any person named as executor. A bond may be required if I do not sign in this box:
No bond shall be required.

(Notice: You must sign this Will in the presence of two (2) adult witnesses. The witnesses must sign their names in your presence and in each other's presence. You must first read to them the following two sentences.)

This is my Will. I ask the persons who sign below to be my witnesses.

Signed on _____ at

(date)

_____ , California.

(city)

Signature of Maker of Will

(Notice to Witnesses: Two (2) adults must sign as witnesses. Each witness must read the following clause before signing. The witnesses should not receive assets under this Will.)

Each of us declares under penalty of perjury under the laws of the State of California that the following is true and correct:

a. On the date written below the maker of this Will declared to us that this instrument was the maker's Will and requested us to act as witnesses to it;

b. We understand this is the maker's Will;

c. The maker signed this Will in our presence, all of us being present at the same time;

d. We now, at the maker's request, and in the maker's and in each other's presence, sign below as witnesses;

e. We believe the maker is of sound mind and memory;

f. We believe that this Will was not procured by duress, menace, fraud or undue influence;

g. The maker is age 18 or older; and

h. Each of us is now age 18 or older, is a competent witness, and resides at the address set forth after his or her name.

Dated: _____ , _____

Signature of Witness	Signature of Witness

Print name here: | Print name here:

Residence Address: | Residence Address:

AT LEAST TWO WITNESSES <u>MUST</u> SIGN. NOTARIZATION ALONE IS NOT SUFFICIENT.

The following sections of the law are included for reference.

DEFINITIONS AND RULES OF CONSTRUCTION
[Marginal numbers are the California Probate Code Sections.]

6200. Unless the provision or context clearly requires otherwise, these definitions and rules of construction govern the construction of this Chapter. [Statutory will.]

6201. "**Testator**" means a person choosing to adopt a California statutory will.

6202. "**Spouse**" means the testator's husband or wife at the time the testator signs a California statutory will.

6203. "**Executor**" means both the person so designated in a California statutory will and any other person acting at any time as the executor or administrator under a California statutory will.

6204. "**Trustee**" means both the person so designated in a California statutory will and any other person acting at any time as the trustee under a California statutory will.

6205. "**Descendants**" mean children, grandchildren, and their lineal descendants of all generations with the relationship of parent and child at each generation being determined as provided in Section 6152. A reference to "descendants" in the plural includes a single descendant where the context so requires.

6206. A reference in a California statutory will to the "Uniform Gifts to Minors Act of any state" or the "Uniform Transfers to Minors Act of any state" includes both the Uniform Gifts to Minors Act of any state and Uniform Transfers to Minors Act of any state. A reference to a "custodian" means the person so designated in a California statutory will or any other person acting at any time as a custodian under a Uniform Gifts to Minors Act or Uniform Transfers to Minors Act.

6207. Masculine pronouns include the feminine, and plural and singular words include each other, where appropriate.

6208. (a) If a California statutory will states that a person shall perform an act, the person is required to perform that act.

(b) If a California statutory will states that a person may do an act, the person's decision to do or not to do the act shall be made in the exercise of the person's fiduciary powers.

6209. Whenever a distribution under a California statutory will is to be made to a person's descendants, the property shall be divided into as many equal shares as there are then living descendants of the nearest degree of living descendants and deceased descendants of that same degree who leave descendants then living, and each living descendant of the nearest degree shall receive one share and the share of each deceased descendant of that same degree shall be divided among his or her descendants in the same manner.

6210. "**Person**" includes individuals and institutions.

6211. Reference to a person "if living" or who "survives me" means a person who survives the decedent by 120 hours. A person who fails to survive the decedent by 120 hours is deemed to have predeceased the decedent for the purpose of a California statutory will, and the beneficiaries are determined accordingly. If it cannot be established by clear and convincing evidence that a person who would otherwise be a beneficiary has survived the decedent by 120 hours, it is deemed that the person failed to survive for the required period. The requirement of this section that a person who survives the decedent must survive the decedent by 120 hours does not apply if the application of this 120 hour survival requirement would result in the escheat of property to the state.

Source: Wolcotts Forms, available at most stationery or office supply stores or by calling 1(800) 421–2220.

Exhibit 6.10   Wisconsin Basic Will

Signature of Testator ....

WISCONSIN BASIC WILL OF

....
(Insert Your Name)

Article 1. Declaration.

This is my will and I revoke any prior wills and codicils (additions to prior wills).

Article 2. Disposition of My Property

2.1   PERSONAL, RECREATIONAL AND HOUSEHOLD ITEMS. Except as provided in paragraph 2.2, I give all my furniture, furnishings, household items, recreational equipment, personal automobiles and personal effects to my spouse, if living; otherwise they shall be divided equally among my children who survive me.

2.2   GIFTS TO PERSONS OR CHARITIES. I make the following gifts to the persons or charities in the cash amount stated in words (. . . . . . Dollars) and figures ($ . . . . . .) or of the property described. I SIGN IN EACH BOX USED. I WRITE THE WORDS "NOT USED" IN THE REMAINING BOXES. If I fail to sign opposite any gift, then no gift is made. If the person mentioned does not survive me or if the charity does not accept the gift, then no gift is made.

FULL NAME OF PERSON OR CHARITY TO RECEIVE GIFT. (Name only one. Please print.)	AMOUNT OF CASH GIFT OR DESCRIPTION OF PROPERTY.	SIGNATURE OF TESTATOR.
		....
FULL NAME OF PERSON OR CHARITY TO RECEIVE GIFT. (Name only one. Please print.)	AMOUNT OF CASH GIFT OR DESCRIPTION OF PROPERTY.	SIGNATURE OF TESTATOR.
		....
FULL NAME OF PERSON OR CHARITY TO RECEIVE GIFT. (Name only one. Please print.)	AMOUNT OF CASH GIFT OR DESCRIPTION OF PROPERTY.	SIGNATURE OF TESTATOR.
		....
FULL NAME OF PERSON OR CHARITY TO RECEIVE GIFT. (Name only one. Please print.)	AMOUNT OF CASH GIFT OR DESCRIPTION OF PROPERTY.	SIGNATURE OF TESTATOR.
		....
FULL NAME OF PERSON OR CHARITY TO RECEIVE GIFT. (Name only one. Please print.)	AMOUNT OF CASH GIFT OR DESCRIPTION OF PROPERTY.	SIGNATURE OF TESTATOR.
		....

Exhibit 6.10 Wisconsin Basic Will—*continued*

2.3 ALL OTHER ASSETS (MY "RESIDUARY ESTATE"). I adopt only one Property Disposition Clause in this paragraph by writing my signature on the line next to the title of the Property Disposition Clause I wish to adopt. I SIGN ON ONLY ONE LINE. I WRITE THE WORDS "NOT USED" ON THE REMAINING LINE. If I sign on more than one line or if I fail to sign on any line, the property will go under Property Disposition Clause (b) and I realize that means the property will be distributed as if I did not make a will in accordance with Chapter 852 of the Wisconsin Statutes.

PROPERTY DISPOSITION CLAUSES *(Select one.)*

(a) TO MY SPOUSE IF LIVING; IF NOT LIVING, THEN TO MY CHILDREN AND THE DESCENDANTS OF ANY DECEASED CHILD BY RIGHT OF REPRESENTATION. ....

(b) TO BE DISTRIBUTED AS IF I DID NOT HAVE A WILL. ....

Article 3. Nominations of Personal Represenative and Guardian

3.1 PERSONAL REPRESENTATIVE. *(Name at least one.)*
I nominate the person or institution named in the first box of this paragraph to serve as my personal representative. If that person or institution does not serve, then I nominate the others to serve in the order I list them in the other boxes. I confer upon my personal representative the authority to do and perform any act which he or she determines is in the best interest of the estate, with no limitations. This provision shall be given the broadest possible construction. This authority includes, but is not limited to, the power to borrow money, pledge assets, vote stocks and participate in reorganizations, to sell or exchange real or personal property, and to invest funds and retain securities without any limitation by law for investments by fiduciaries.

FIRST PERSONAL REPRESENTATIVE

SECOND PERSONAL REPRESENTATIVE

THIRD PERSONAL REPRESENTATIVE

3.2 GUARDIAN. *(If you have a child under 18 years of age, you should name at least one guardian of the child.)*
If my spouse dies before I do or if for any other reason a guardian is needed for any child of mine, then I nominate the person named in the first box of this paragraph to serve as guardian of the person and estate of that child. If the person does not serve, then I nominate the person named in the second box of this paragraph to serve as guardian of that child.

FIRST GUARDIAN

SECOND GUARDIAN

Signature of Testator ....

Exhibit 6.10   Wisconsin Basic Will—*continued*

3.3   BOND.
My signature in this box means I request that a bond, as set by law, be required for each individual personal representative or guardian named in this will. IF I DO NOT SIGN IN THIS BOX, I REQUEST THAT A BOND NOT BE REQUIRED FOR ANY OF THOSE PERSONS.

I sign my name to this Wisconsin Basic Will on . . . . (date), at . . . . (city), ... (state).

. . . .
Signature of Testator

STATEMENT OF WITNESSES *(You must use two adult witnesses.)*

EACH OF US DECLARES THAT THE TESTATOR SIGNED THIS WISCONSIN BASIC WILL IN OUR PRESENCE, ALL OF US BEING PRESENT AT THE SAME TIME, AND WE NOW, AT THE TESTATOR'S REQUEST, IN THE TESTATOR'S PRESENCE AND IN THE PRESENCE OF EACH OTHER, SIGN BELOW AS WITNESSES, DECLARING THAT THE TESTATOR APPEARS TO BE OF SOUND MIND AND UNDER NO UNDUE INFLUENCE.

Signature . . . .   Residence Address: . . . .
Print Name
Here: . . . .

Signature . . . .   Residence Address: . . . .
Print Name
Here: . . . .

. . . .
Signature of Testator

Source: Wisconsin Legal Blank Co., Inc.

space at the end of one line of the will and started Stanley's name on the next line. Michael's residuary clause reads:

> "I give and bequeath all the rest, residue and remainder of my property to Mary Brown, Adam Korkowski, _____
> and Stanley Weskoskowitz share and share alike."

Joe Blitz typed his name in the empty space left on the line after Adam Korkowski's name. Unless the addition is detected and deleted before Michael's death, Joe may become a residuary beneficiary or devisee of Michael's will.

Example: Paul has typed a six-page will. Before it is witnessed and signed, his brother, Robert, adds an extra page to the will in which most of Paul's estate passes to Robert. Even if Paul does not notice the additional page, he could have protected himself by signing each of the original pages and stating in the attestation clause that the will contained only six pages.

Another advantage of typing the entire will is that uncertainties so often found in holographic (handwritten) wills due to the illegible handwriting of the testator can be avoided. Typed wills are easier to read and errors are more readily identified than in handwritten wills. However, typed wills prove disadvantageous if the will is contested because of forgery or undue influence, or if a question arises concerning the testator's knowledge of the contents of the will; if the testator had written a holographic will, it would defeat these contentions.

Example: Joan is elderly and suffering from severe arthritis. She is concerned that her signature on the will may be contested as a forgery. What procedures might be followed to avert the foreseeable will contest? (1) Joan might identify her affliction within the will's provisions so all interested parties have notice of her infirmity. A will contest on the grounds of forgery requires that many persons testify to the genuineness of the writing; the testatrix's own declaration as to the reason for her unusual signature would eliminate the need for calling a great number of witnesses and provide direct evidence in the matter. (2) A better procedure is to have Joan write in her own hand the testimonium clause so that, if necessary, a handwriting expert could compare and identify the validity of Joan's signature. (3) The best procedure would be to have her personal physician witness the will so that, if called on to testify, the physician could explain the reason for the shaky signature.

Guideline 3: Use Clear Wording

The will must be written so that the testator's intent is clear. Chapter 7 will discuss the drafting of a will and give sample clauses or provisions illustrating the step-by-step formation of a will. Our immediate concerns are the uncertainties, ambiguities, and alterations that the testator must avoid. The will should be clear and understandable.

Example: Marcia's will provides: (1) I give my diamond ring to my best friend, Florence Williams. (2) I give $5,000 to my faithful employee, Steven Newell. (3) *All my personal property* I leave to my beloved son and only heir, Kevin. A conflict such as this in which the testator apparently leaves the same gifts to different persons may result in a will contest.

Guideline 4: Use Simple Language

As noted in Chapter 4, the Uniform Probate Code has attempted to resolve the confusion surrounding the terminology used to identify gifts transferred through a will and the recipients of such gifts. Because the traditional terms "bequest," "legacy," and "devise" have been used interchangeably, much confusion has resulted. The proper way to handle this problem today is to use phrases such as "I *give* my diamond to my daughter, Marilyn," rather than "I *bequeath* my ring, etc." Using simple, easily recognizable terms is the better practice in will construction.

Guideline 5: Consider Placing Small Estates in Joint Tenancy

In most cases, small estates may be placed in joint tenancy, one of the most common ways to avoid probate, so that administrative procedures and expenses can be kept to a minimum. In certain cases, a will may be unnecessary because of the nature of a joint tenancy.

Guideline 6: Sign the Will According to State Guidelines, but Do Not Sign Copies

The original will must be signed and should always be dated. If the will consists of multiple pages, all pages of the original should be signed or initialed except in states such as New York that require the signature to be only at the end of the will. If copies are made, they should not be signed. Having too many original executed wills in existence is dangerous because it increases the possibility of will contests. All copies that are executed (signed and witnessed) must be presented in court, or the law presumes that the will was revoked. Therefore you should make copies of the original will before it is signed. Give one to the personal representative and another to the spouse, if he or she is not the personal representative, and explain where the original will is located.

ASSIGNMENT 6.8

Joyce's original will cannot be found. A photocopy with Joyce's signature has been located, however. According to the laws of your state, would the copy be a valid testament? See Wheadon case previously cited in Chapter 5.

Guideline 7: Include a Residuary Clause

The testator's entire estate must be transferred. This requires employing a residuary (or residue) clause like the following (for another example of such a clause, see Chapter 7):

> I give the residue of my estate, consisting of all property that I can dispose of by will and not effectively disposed of by the preceding articles of this will, as follows:

Guideline 8: Choose Witnesses with Care

To improve the probability that the witnesses will be available when the will is probated, it is good practice to have the will witnessed by individuals who are younger than the testator and who live in the same county. Also, the witnesses should not be beneficiaries or devisees of the will. If the testator's mental capacity might be questioned, the testator's physician should be one of the witnesses (see the previous discussion and examples of who may be a competent witness in Chapter 5). Some states now provide for attestation clauses that result in "self-proved" wills (see Chapter 7); these clauses eliminate the need for witnesses.

Guideline 9: Tell Witnesses What Might Be Expected of Them

The witnesses should be informed that what they are witnessing is the testator's will and that they may be called on to testify to that fact in court. They need not read the will, however, nor be informed of its contents before they sign as witnesses.

Guideline 10: Do Not Make Additions After Execution

No words should be added after execution (writing, signing, and publishing the will). Words added to the will below the testator's signature some time after execution generally do not revoke or affect the validity of the entire will. The will (above the testator's signature) is valid because the will was signed at its end at the time of execution. The maker's signature indicates that the will is complete up to the point where the signature is placed. For this reason, statutes in some states require the signature at the end or "foot" of the will. Words added after execution, whether above or below the testator's signature, may be denied execution since technically they do not form part of the will, whether or not a statute requires that the will be signed at the end. The solution would be to reexecute the will including the added provisions before the signature and to make sure the new will includes a clause revoking all previous wills and codicils.

🏛 ASSIGNMENT 6.9

After executing and signing her will, Laura writes the following beneath her signature: "All of the provisions of my will previously mentioned shall take effect after my death unless my son, Randall, predeceases me." What effect, if any, would such an alteration have on Laura's will in your state?

Guideline 11: Use a Codicil for Minor Changes

When only a few minor changes are needed, for example, the elimination or addition of a gift, a codicil should be used.

Guideline 12: Avoid Erasures and Corrections

Great care should be taken to avoid all erasures and corrections in the drafting of a will. When a page is found to contain an error, the entire page should be retyped. Where, because of time and circumstances, it is necessary to use an altered page, the testator should approve it by signing or initialing the alteration in the margin of the page. The witnesses should also sign in the margin to indicate that the alteration was made prior to execution of the will. It is a good idea also to identify the corrections made in the attestation clause.

Guideline 13: Word Conditions Carefully to Avoid Ambiguity

Attaching a condition to a devise may change the effect of the gift quite apart from the testator's wishes. The drafter should recognize the importance of correct wording. A conditional devise is one that takes effect, or continues in effect, according to the happening of some future event. A **condition precedent** is one in which a specified event must occur before the interest vests in (passes to) the named devisee. A *condition subsequent* is one in which an estate that is already vested in a named devisee will not continue to be vested in that devisee unless a specified event occurs. If it does not occur, the devisee will be divested of the estate, i.e., the devisee will not continue to receive the interest.

Condition precedent
A condition or specific event that must occur before an agreement or obligation becomes binding.

Conditions Precedent

When a decedent devises property with a condition precedent attached, title (ownership) in the property does not vest until the stated event (condition) occurs. The devisee must perform some act *before* (precedent to) ownership of the devise will vest in the devisee.

Example: Andrew devises Blackacre "to Ralph when he marries Florence." Ownership of Blackacre will vest in Ralph only if and when Ralph marries Florence. If the marriage never occurs, the ownership of property will never pass to Ralph but will pass to another person named in the will or, if no one is named, will revert to the testator or his heirs by operation of law.

Example: Andrew makes a gift of $20,000 "to Renee when she receives her college degree."

Example: Andrew devises Blackacre "to Saul at such time as he comes back to Texas to live and takes possession of Blackacre." (Saul is living in California at the time the will is drafted.) The will may provide that the condition precedent be an act performed by the testator or by another person.

Example: Andrew gives "the automobile owned by me at the time of my death to my son, Chris." Andrew might buy and sell many cars prior to his death. However, only that car owned by Andrew at his death will go to Chris. If Andrew does not own a car at his death, Chris is out of luck; he will get no car.

Example: Andrew makes a gift of $30,000 "to the person who is taking care of me at death." The person taking care of Andrew at his death may be different from the one taking care of him at the time he drafts the will. The fact that Andrew may not now know the identity of his devisee does not invalidate the devise. The identity of the "person who is taking care of me at my death" is ascertainable. Whoever that person is would be entitled to the $30,000 gift.

Caution must be taken to prevent vague conditions from being inserted into a will. The last example illustrates a potential problem. At his death, Andrew may have several people caring for him, e.g., his niece, with whom he lives; a nephew who helps dress and feed Andrew; his doctor, who visits him routinely; and a physical therapist who daily helps Andrew exercise.

When a decedent-testator places a condition precedent on a gift, the condition may fail because it is regarded as socially unacceptable.

Example: Andrew makes a gift of $1,000,000 "to my daughter Rachael, if she divorces the man to whom she is now married."

Conditions Subsequent

A **condition subsequent** is one in which the nonhappening of the event or a violation (breach) of a condition will terminate an estate that has already vested. If an estate vests in (passes to) the devisee when the will becomes operative but is subject to being divested on the future happening or nonhappening of an event or on a breach, the condition is subsequent. If the event occurs or fails to occur, or if a specified condition is breached, the devisee will be divested of ownership of the devise (property) by "operation of law." This is also called *defeasance*.

Example: Ralph devises Blackacre "to my wife, Tina, to hold while she remains a widow." The estate vests in Tina upon the death of her husband, Ralph, and will be divested on Tina's remarriage.

Example: Sara devises her summer home "to my daughter, Rose, but if Rose fails to return to the family home within five years, then to my son, Waldo." The devise vests in Rose upon her mother's death. If Rose does not return to the family home within five years from the date of Sara's death, Rose will then be divested of the estate, and it will vest in Waldo. Waldo's potential future estate is not subject to divestment (i.e., not subject to any condition) but is a *fee simple absolute*.

In theory, the defeasance occurs by operation of law; in practice it occurs after a court action has been brought. If the devisee who has been divested of ownership in the property is in actual physical possession of the property, it will nearly always be necessary for the grantor, the grantor's heirs, or another person named by the grantor to retake or recover ownership of the property after the defeasance to (1) exercise a right of reentry (this must be a positive physical act of reentering the land) and (2) bring an action in **ejectment** in court to regain possession of the property.

Generally, the determination of whether a condition is precedent or subsequent will depend on the intention of the testator as interpreted from the language of the will in light of the circumstances. The particular expression used is not conclusive. Because the law prefers a vested estate, the presumption of courts favors a condition subsequent rather than a condition precedent. Therefore, the courts will construe ambiguous testamentary language as a condition subsequent rather than a condition precedent. The reason for this is that a vested estate is more marketable, i.e., it can be sold or conveyed more easily.

Condition subsequent
A condition that will continue or terminate an existing agreement if the condition does or does not occur.

Ejectment
An action (a lawsuit brought in a court) for the recovery of the possession of land.

Guideline 14: Include Full Data on Beneficiaries and Devisees

The full names, addresses, and relationship to the testator of the beneficiaries and devisees under the will must be correctly written. This avoids uncertainty as to whom the assets are to be transferred. When the beneficiary or devisee is a charitable corporation, the corporate name and address should be given.

Guideline 15: Give the Client a Rough Draft

A rough draft of the will should be presented to the client to be scrutinized so that the client may make deletions or additions.

KEY TERMS

Advancement
Antenuptial (prenuptial)
   contract or
   agreement

Postnuptial contract
   or agreement

Condition precedent
Condition
   subsequent

Ejectment

REVIEW QUESTIONS

1. What procedures would you recommend to put a new client at ease and overcome his reluctance when you need to elicit confidential family and financial information for the preparation of legal documents such as wills?
2. Are there additional checklists you require to obtain the necessary information for drafting wills?
3. What would you add to the checklists in the text to make them more comprehensive and useful?
4. Diagram your family tree beginning with your grandparents and including all their descendants.
5. What are some of the tax issues and rights of the surviving spouse and children that the attorney and paralegal discuss at the family conference?
6. Which states have statutory wills? What are statutory wills?
7. What is the distinction between a condition precedent and a condition subsequent?
8. What are the guidelines recommended for the preparation of wills?
9. Are there any other guidelines for preparing wills you would add to those in the text?
10. What are the advantages of a typewritten will over a holographic will?

CASE PROBLEMS

Problem 1

Liza Mills owns a considerable amount of personal property. She is an only child, and her parents and other blood relatives are all deceased. Liza's lesbian domestic partner is Alecia Browning. Liza is dying of AIDS.

A. If Liza dies intestate, to whom will her property pass?
B. List three suggestions you could make to Liza that would enable her to ensure that her property will go to Alecia.
C. If Liza had a brother who survived her, would your suggestions successfully negate, prohibit, or disallow any claim he might make to obtain her property?

Problem 2

Based on the guidelines for drafting a will, point out as many errors in the following sample will as you can.

LAST WILL AND TESTAMENT OF
Ben Brady

1. I, <u>Ben Brady</u>, declare this my last will and testament.

2. I direct that my debts be paid out of my estate.
3. I give my son, George, my ~~two~~ *three* rings, ~~10~~ *8* guns, clothing and all my other personal property.
4. I give my beloved wife, Sarah, my interest in our home that we own jointly; all the money (cash) I have in savings and checking at our local bank; and, if she does not remarry, my interest in the summer cottage I own with my brother.
5. I request that no bond be required of my executor.
6. If my wife does not survive me, I request that ~~Robert Brown~~ *Jerry Clark* be executor of this will, and he be appointed guardian of any minor children of mine.

IN WITNESS WHEREOF, I set my hand to this my last will and testament.

Date: _____   *Ben Brady* _____

The will above contains many mistakes. Some of them are: No residence of the testator, Ben Brady, is given; numbers are changed in the bequest to George, e.g., two rings to three rings, 10 guns to 8 guns; the full names and addresses of the beneficiaries and devisees are not listed; conflicting benefits are bestowed, e.g., *all* my personal property to George, then giving money to his wife, Sarah; no residuary clause is included; an attempt is made to pass joint tenancy property by will; there is no named original executor (-trix); con- fusion exists in the appointment of Robert Brown, whose name is apparently deleted and replaced by Jerry Clark; no date is on the will; there are no attesting signatures of witnesses; and Ben cannot appoint a guardian of the minor children of Ben and Sarah, if Sarah outlives Ben.

CHAPTER SEVEN

DRAFTING AND EXECUTING A VALID, LEGAL WILL

OBJECTIVES

After completing this chapter, you should be able to:

- Identify and understand the terminology used in preparing a will.
- Analyze the data collected and make sure the information conforms to the client's objectives in preparation for the drafting of the will.
- Apply the appropriate state statutes that affect the valid construction of a will.
- Draft a preliminary will, for the supervising attorney to review, that is free from errors of construction that might invalidate the will or lead to a will contest.
- Explain the purpose and function of a self-proving affidavit, living will, health care proxy, and durable power of attorney.

OUTLINE

SCOPE OF THE CHAPTER

This chapter covers the procedures involved in drafting a preliminary will, an important task of the paralegal. Exhibit 7.1 outlines these procedures. Next the contents of a standard will are discussed, and samples of a preliminary will and worksheets are provided. Sample clauses used in drafting a will and statutes that pertain to such clauses are examined, as are some other documents that are not part of a standard will but are related to it. These include a self-proving affidavit, letter of last instructions, and right-to-die directives such as a living will, health care proxy, and a durable power of attorney.

CONTENTS OF A STANDARD WILL

We now turn to the drafting of a formal will. A standard will has the following clauses or provisions:

1. Introductory or exordium and publication clause.
2. General revocatory clause.
3. Provision for payment of debts and funeral expenses.
4. Instructions for funeral and burial.
5. Specific testamentary gifts.
6. Provision for residue of estate.
7. Appointment of the personal representative, i.e., an executor or executrix.
8. Appointment of a personal and/or property guardian.
9. Simultaneous death.
10. Testamentary trust clause.
11. Testimonium clause.
12. Testator's signature.
13. Attestation clause of witnesses.
14. Witnesses' signatures and addresses.

The next sections discuss each of these clauses and provisions in detail, along with relevant statutes and sample clauses.

In addition, the following documents, which are not part of a standard will but are related to it, are identified and discussed:

1. Self-proving provision or affidavit or self-proved will.
2. Letter of last instructions.
3. Living will.
4. Health care proxy.
5. Durable power of attorney for health care.

1. Introductory or Exordium and Publication Clause

The **exordium clause** identifies the maker of the will and states or declares the maker's intention that the provisions in this written document be followed after death. To be valid and enforceable, the document must appear to be a will or testamentary in nature. The introductory clause should also include the address, city, county, and state of its maker (helping to determine domicile for probate proceedings); any alias or other name by which the maker is known (often written "a/k/a"—also known as) so that all property owned by the maker can be

Exordium clause
The beginning or introductory clause of a will.

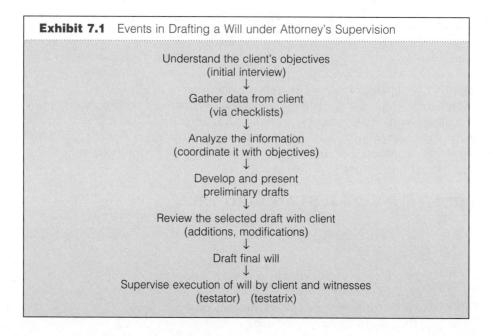

Exhibit 7.1   Events in Drafting a Will under Attorney's Supervision

Understand the client's objectives
(initial interview)
↓
Gather data from client
(via checklists)
↓
Analyze the information
(coordinate it with objectives)
↓
Develop and present
preliminary drafts
↓
Review the selected draft with client
(additions, modifications)
↓
Draft final will
↓
Supervise execution of will by client and witnesses
(testator)   (testatrix)

identified, located, and properly transferred or eventually distributed; and a statement of the maker's capacity and freedom from undue influence.

Sample Exordium Clause:

Last Will and Testament of Rowley D. Morse. I, Rowley D. Morse, also known as R. David Morse, of 4607 Elmors Drive, City of Middleton, County of Heather, and State of Iowa, being of sound mind and not acting under undue influence of any person whomsoever, do make, publish, and declare this document to be my last will and testament.

The purpose of the exordium clause is to declare to the public the following: (1) the identity of the testator, (2) that the testator has the intent and capacity to create a will, (3) that the document is the testator's last will, and (4) the location of the testator's principal residence (city, county, and state) or domicile, which enables the personal representative to determine which state has the proper authority to tax the testator's property and which court has jurisdiction over the administration of the decedent-testator's estate.

ASSIGNMENT 7.1

1. Examine the following exordium clause: "Being of sound mind and body, I, D. E. Pearson, of 2914 Columba Street, Bloomington, dispose of the following property by will: . . . ."
   a. Is this adequate for the purposes of an exordium clause? Why or why not?
   b. Could any word or phrase be misinterpreted so as to prevent the document's admission to probate?
   c. Redraft the parts of the clause likely to cause difficulty. If necessary, include information not found in the original clause and explain the reasons for including it.
2. Tom Hardy lives in Zuma, Arizona. He owns a cottage in Wisconsin and has a savings and checking account in Zuma. The deed to the cottage is written to "Thomas William Hardy," and both bank accounts are in the name, Tom W. Hardy. Draft an appropriate exordium clause for Tom and explain your reasons for the draft.

2. General Revocatory Clause

A decedent's new will generally revokes an earlier will. State statutes vary on the requirements necessary for a new will to revoke a prior will. Some require a specific statement saying that the new will revokes the prior will; in most states, however, a prior will is automatically revoked when the maker writes, dates, and signs a new will. The testamentary document last in time also supersedes existing codicils attached to previous wills. The safest way to ensure revocation by a new will is to include a **revocatory clause** as part of the exordium clause. For example: "I hereby revoke all prior wills and codicils made by me, and declare this to be my last will and testament." Review Chapter 5 on the revocation of wills.

Revocatory clause
A clause or statement in a will that revokes all prior wills and codicils.

⚏ ASSIGNMENT 7.2

1. Henry Howard has a will. He then writes, signs, dates, and has witnessed by two other individuals a document changing one gift made in the will from his son, Harold, to his daughter, Helen. Answer the following according to your state statutes: Does this revision revoke Henry's original will? Is such a change legal? Is this a valid codicil?

2. In 1990, Leah Olson made a will leaving half her estate to her husband, Albert, one-fourth to their son, Lloyd, and one-fourth to their daughter, Lynda. (a) Draft such a provision for the will. If in 1995 Leah decides to change her will to leave equal shares to each of the above-named persons, how should this be done? Redraft the provisions in (a) to illustrate this change. Does your revision legally revoke Leah's 1990 will?

3. Provision for Payment of Debts and Funeral Expenses

The maker of a will often directs the named personal representative or executor to pay all debts, administration expenses, and expenses for the last illness, funeral, and burial out of estate funds before the decedent's property is distributed. These duties are automatic responsibilities of the personal representative of the estate, however, and need not be embodied in a formal clause. The phrasing of the debt payment clause can also present a danger. For example, if the clause reads "I direct my personal representative or executor to pay all of my valid debts and administration expenses out of the residue of my estate," and the decedent-testator was personally liable for a debt such as a mortgage on the decedent's home, the specific devisee of the home in the will could require that the mortgage be paid out of the residue (according to the rules of abatement). Many states avoid this problem by statute, unless the decedent's will specifically states otherwise; see Cal. Prob. Code § 21131; Mass. Gen. Laws Ann. ch.191 § 23; N.Y. E.P.T.L. § 3–3.6; and U.P.C. § 2–607. A more appropriate clause is the following.

Sample Debt Payment Clause:
I direct my personal representative (executor), hereinafter named, to pay the debts, administration expenses, and expenses for my last illness, funeral, and burial out of my estate as soon as possible after my will is admitted to probate.

The inclusion of a clause in the testator's will that requires payment of debts and administration expense from the estate can lead to a deduction from federal estate or income taxes for those payments (see I.R.C. §§ 2053 and 212).

The cost of funeral and burial expenses has escalated dramatically in the past decade. When the burden of making the necessary arrangements falls on the bereaved family, emotions often play a part in their financial decisions concerning, for example, the casket, flowers, headstone, reception, and religious service. To alleviate this unpleasant burden, many people prearrange and pay for their funeral and burial prior to death. You should discuss this sensitive but responsible option with the client and suggest possible methods of accomplishing it; e.g., the client could open a bank savings account covering the estimated cost of a client-selected casket, headstone, reception, and so on, or execute a simple trust agreement with a funeral home in which the money for these expenses would be held in trust by the funeral director until the client's death. Some state statutes establish monetary limits for the funeral and burial expenses. If the decedent has many creditors and the personal representative overspends the reasonable limit, the personal representative is liable for this breach of fiduciary duty, and the court can order that the personal representative pay damages to the estate.

⚖ ASSIGNMENT 7.3

1. Check your own state statutes and determine the priority of payment of decedent's debts in your state (compare U.P.C. §§ 3–805 and 3–807).
2. In writing his will, Quincy Rudd included a clause directing his executor to pay the debts owed by him at the time of his death from the residue of the estate. Draft a clause for Quincy's will to this effect. Explain the hardship that your draft may cause if the residuary clause is the sole provision in a testator's will that provides for the surviving spouse and children.
3. Draft a clause for Quincy Rudd's will that identifies how any estate taxes owed by his estate will be paid.

4. Instructions for Funeral and Burial

A simple clause such as the following may be included in a will to inform the decedent's family of the previous plans or instructions the deceased has made for her funeral:

Sample Clause:

I direct that my funeral is to be conducted according to my written instructions that are on file at the Benson Funeral Home, 1404 Second Avenue, City of Cedar Falls, County of Polk, State of Iowa. The said written instructions are hereby incorporated into and made part of this will.

The testator should give a copy of these instructions to family members and the named personal representative.

Including funeral and burial instructions in a will may be futile, however, not only because the will may not be found in time, but also because in many states the desires of the decedent's surviving spouse or next-of-kin legally supersede any such instructions by the decedent. A conflict between the wishes of the family and the testator may also arise when the testator desires to be cremated. Concerning cremation, a testator can simply add a clause in the will that states:

Sample Clause:

At my death, I direct that my body be taken to the Nielson Chapel and Crematory, that my remains be cremated, and that my ashes be spread over Lake Minnetonka in Minnesota.

Another challenge to burial instructions may occur when the testator desires to donate his body for educational or medical purposes (e.g., to an organ transplant bank), but the nearest relatives object. To resolve questions associated with the giving of anatomical gifts, the Uniform Anatomical Gift Act, which has been adopted in all fifty states, provides that the maker may legally determine in a will the disposition of all or any part of the body for organ transplant, medical research, or educational purposes. Although the wording of the act has been modified in some states, it substantively regulates who may be a donor and a donee, the manner of executing, delivering, and amending the gift, and the rights and duties of the parties. A sample clause follows:

Sample Clause:

I hereby direct my personal representative (executor) upon my death to see that my body be delivered to the State University Medical School to be used for educational purposes.

In addition to a provision in a will, under the Uniform Anatomical Gift Act, any person may donate organs by a donor card or other document that becomes legally enforceable once the signatures of the donor and two attesting and subscribing witnesses are obtained. See Exhibit 1.2 for a card and comments. Whenever the testator intends to donate his body or organs for transplants or medical research, he should carry a written expression of those wishes, such as a donor card, on his person at all times. Otherwise, by the time the will is located and read, his body may already have been cremated or buried, or the organs to be donated may not be useful for transplants.

If a potential organ donor has taken no action during her lifetime to make a gift of body organs, only specific relatives have the ability to make a gift of the decedent's organs (absent any evidence of a contrary decision by the decedent). The following are excerpts of typical state statutes concerning anatomical gifts and the relatives of the decedent who are allowed to make the gifts:

Fla. Stat. Ann. § 732.912 Persons Who May Make an Anatomical Gift

(1) Any person who may make a will may give all or part of his body for any purpose specified . . . , the gift to take effect upon death.

(2) In the order of priority stated and in the absence of actual notice of contrary indications by the decedent or actual notice of opposition by a member of the same or a prior class, any of the following persons may give all or any part of the decedent's body for any purpose specified . . . :

(a) The spouse of the decedent;

(b) An adult son or daughter of the decedent;

(c) Either parent of the decedent;

(d) An adult brother or sister of the decedent;

(e) A guardian of the person of the decedent at the time of his death; or

(f) A representative ad litem . . . .

(3) If the donee has actual notice of contrary indications by the decedent or objection of an adult son or daughter or actual notice that a gift by a member of a class is opposed by a member of the same or a prior class, the donee shall not accept the gift.

(4) The persons authorized by subsection (2) may make the gift after the decedent's death or immediately before the decedent's death.

(5) A gift of all or part of a body authorizes any examination necessary to assure medical acceptability of the gift for the purposes intended.

(6) The rights of the donee created by the gift are paramount to the rights of others except as provided by § 732.917.

Fla. Stat. Ann. § 732.913 Persons Who May Become Donees; Purposes for Which Anatomical Gifts May Be Made

The following persons may become donees of gifts of bodies or parts of them for the purposes stated:

(1) Any hospital, surgeon, or physician for medical or dental education or research, advancement of medical or dental science, therapy, or transplantation.

(2) Any accredited medical or dental school, college or university for education, research, advancement of medical or dental science, or therapy.

(3) Any bank or storage facility for medical or dental education, research, advancement of medical or dental science, therapy, or transplantation.

(4) Any individual specified by name for therapy or transplantation needed by him.

ASSIGNMENT 7.4

1. Margaret is dying. She is unconscious and in a coma from which her doctors do not expect her to recover. Margaret's family is aware that another patient is seeking a kidney transplant, and the doctors have informed the family that Margaret could be a successful donor. Margaret's husband and children are in favor of donating Margaret's kidneys after her death; Margaret's parents are opposed. How would this conflict be resolved in Florida? In your state?
2. Claudia's will does not contain an anatomical gift clause. She thinks it would be a good idea to leave her eyes to the State Society for the Prevention of Blindness eye bank. Draft such a provision for the revised will she is writing.
3. Claudia realizes that her family may hold the funeral and burial before reading her will and the provision mentioned above. What should she do to prevent this potential problem?

5. Specific Testamentary Gifts

It is important to remember that under the orthodox system of terminology "legacies" are gifts of money, "bequests" are gifts of personal property, and "devises" are gifts of real property. Nevertheless, these terms are often used interchangeably. Under U.P.C. terminology, the disposition of both real and personal property under a will is called a devise. Both sets of terminology are used in this section of the text.

One of the most important functions of a will is the determination of "what goes to whom." To prevent family arguments over specific items of a decedent's estate, the will should provide for the disposition of property as its maker chooses. The maker may have many reasons for leaving specific property to certain individuals. These gifts must be made before the maker transfers the remaining assets in a residuary clause. Marital deduction provisions (discussed in Chapters 10 and 14) must also be stated before the residue is transferred. For example, John Harrington has three sons. His will provides:

Sample Clause:

I give the sum of Two Thousand Dollars ($2,000) to my son, James L. Harrington; my diamond ring to my son, Thomas J. Harrington; and my collection of guns and rifles to my son, Harold L. Harrington. If any of my three sons predecease me, the gift designated for that son shall pass into the residue of my estate. All my sons' addresses are currently the same as my own.

I give the land that I own in the County of Adams, State of Iowa, legally described as follows: Lot 17, Block 8, consisting of twenty acres, known as Stonybroke, according to the plat filed with the Registrar of Titles in and for the County of Adams, State of Iowa, to my wife, Jeanine Harrington, as fee owner in severalty if she survives me, if not, I give the aforementioned land, legally described above, known as Stonybroke, to my three sons equally as tenants in common. Also, I give all my automobiles and articles of personal and household goods to my wife, Jeanine Harrington, to do with as she sees fit if she survives me, if not, I give the aforementioned property to my three sons equally.

An important point to recall is that a will is ambulatory (not yet operative), so regardless of a clause like the above, its maker is free before death to destroy the will or give away or sell any property constituting a specific gift in the will. Any intentional act of the testator that cancels a gift in the will, such as the destruction, sale, or gift of the property to another person, is called ademption. In such cases, the testamentary gift is adeemed (taken away by the process of ademption), and the beneficiary or devisee is not entitled to receive the property unless a substitute for the gift is mentioned in the will. Ademption has the same result as if the maker had formally canceled the gift.

Example: In the clause above, if the diamond ring left to Thomas and the gun collection left to Harold are not in John Harrington's estate at his death, then the two sons do not receive their specific bequests or devises.

🏛 ASSIGNMENT 7.5

1. Roger's will provides, in part: "To my daughter, Nadine, I give 100 shares of common stock in the Hopewell Corporation, if she survives me." What kind of gift is this? If Roger owns 75 shares of common stock in the Hopewell Corporation at the time of his death, would Nadine be entitled to them plus the fair market value of 25 shares? Why or why not?
2. Lillian wishes to leave her antique rosewood furniture to her daughters, Kimberly and Ellen. Draft a provision in Lillian's will for this gift (bequest or devise).
3. At Lillian's death Kimberly and Ellen are living in separate houses. They cannot agree on dividing the furniture. Could Lillian's will have been written so as to avoid the dispute? If necessary, redraft your provision to illustrate.
4. "To my son, Gerald, I leave 30 acres of land in Marsh County." What kind of devise is this? Is it defeasible (see the Glossary)? Why or why not? If it is, redraft the provision to illustrate the testator's wishes in a valid devise.

In most states, statutes have established procedures for the disposition of the tangible personal property, other than money, that remains after the testator has made specific testamentary gifts (see U.P.C. § 2–513). The testator is allowed to write a separate "memorandum" or letter of instruction "in the handwriting of the testator or signed by the testator." The memorandum describes the property, item by item, and the beneficiary or devisee who is to receive it with "reasonable certainty." The following sample will clause identifies the separate memorandum that lists the decedent's tangible personal property and names the beneficiary who is to receive each item listed.

Sample Clause:

I give my tangible personal property to the beneficiaries and devisees named herein, in accordance with any written list or memorandum which is signed and dated by me and is incorporated by reference in this will, and which is prepared in accordance with the provisions of [add appropriate state statute]. The most recent written list shall control if there are inconsistent dispositions. I give all tangible personal property not disposed of by the provisions of any such written list or memorandum to my wife if she survives me, or if she does not survive me, I give such property in equal shares to my children who survive me.

Such statutes allow the testator who owns numerous items of tangible personal property, such as antiques, jewelry, art objects, stamp or coin collections, and the like, to identify and list the property and the beneficiaries and devisees to whom it is to be given on a separate memorandum or letter from the will. The testator can then easily add to or modify this memorandum or letter without having to revoke the will and draft a new one.

The complications that can arise, e.g., family problems, make it necessary to draft the will carefully to satisfy the purposes and intentions of the client. Provisions for a surviving spouse must be determined and carefully written. An attempt by the testator to disinherit a spouse will generally fail since, as previously discussed, the surviving spouse is entitled to a statutory elective share of the decedent-testator's estate. Additional complications occur when the testator has been married more than once and two or more sets of children are potential beneficiaries or devisees. The rule that the testator may favor or exclude anyone in the will still applies, but so does the rule that a spouse cannot be disinherited. Children, however, can be disinherited according to the wishes of the testator. The following illustrates a typical family problem that could affect the validity of a will.

Example: A man divorces his first wife, with whom he had two children, remarries, and has a child by his second wife. His will, written during the first marriage, leaves half his estate to the wife and children of the first marriage and says nothing of the second wife or her child. Should he die without revising his will, his estate may be distributed as if he had died intestate, since the will may be revoked by "operation of law" by some state statutes. For example, in states that have adopted the Uniform Probate Code, his divorce revokes the provisions of the will that benefit his first wife (U.P.C. §§ 2–802 and 2–804); in others, remarriage or remarriage and the birth of issue may revoke a will. The result of such revocation is the same as if the testator died without a will, i.e., intestate. In such a case, the second wife and all his children will take under the state intestate succession statute; the first wife will be entitled to nothing.

During will construction, problems may arise concerning the client's children, e.g., natural, adopted, nonmarital, and stepchildren, when the client attempts to identify the persons to be included or excluded in the will. Words such as "issue," "heirs," "descendants," and, of course, "child" or "children," are often ambiguous or misleading. In the statutes of most states, the terms just mentioned include natural and adopted children of the testator, exclude stepchildren, and may vary concerning nonmarital children. To resolve these problems, the following clause should be used if it matches the client's wishes:

Sample Clause:

As used in this will, words such as "issue," "child," and "children," describing a person or class of persons by relationship to another, shall refer to persons who are related by blood and also to persons who are related by adoption.

If the testator wishes to make a provision for stepchildren, that intention must be expressly stated in the will. Understanding the law of wills and careful drafting are necessary to resolve such problems.

🏛 ASSIGNMENT 7.6

Harold Wilson is currently married to his second wife, Cheryl. They have two teenage children, James and Barbara. Previously, Harold was married to and later divorced from Margaret Wilson. Harold and Margaret were married for ten years and also had two children, Wilbur and Maude. The following is an excerpt from a will written by Harold when he was married to Margaret.

Article IV
I give all my personal effects, including books, art objects, jewelry, furnishings, and other tangible items, to my wife, Margaret, and children, Wilbur and Maude, to be divided equally, as determined by my executrix.

Article V
I give the sum of two thousand dollars ($2,000) to my secretary, Jerome Davis, if he is employed by me at the time of my death.

Article VI
I give the sum of ten thousand dollars ($10,000) to be divided equally to my children, if they survive me, or if they do not survive me, then to my issue who survive me, per stirpes.

Article VII
I give the sum of five thousand dollars ($5,000) and all stocks, bonds, and debentures which I shall hold at the time of my death to my wife, if she survives me, or if she does not survive me, to my children who survive me in equal shares.

Answer the following questions and draft appropriate clauses to change or modify Harold's will as requested:

1. If Harold and his first wife, Margaret, as part of their divorce agreement, had a fair and complete property settlement between themselves and for the benefit of their two children, Wilbur and Maude, could Harold exclude these three members of his first family from the benefits of his current will according to your state laws? Draft the necessary provisions in Harold's will that would exclude all three members of his first family.

2. Suppose in the example above that Maude is now married and has a son, Thomas, who is Harold's grandson. Thomas is physically handicapped. According to your state's laws, could Harold exclude Thomas from his will? Could Harold include Thomas, but exclude Maude? Draft sample will provisions that accomplish these purposes if allowed by your state statutes.

3. Suppose that, while married, Harold and Margaret had adopted a daughter, Marjory. At the time of the divorce, Marjory had requested that she be allowed to live with her father, Harold. The request was granted. In your state, what are the rights of an adopted child to inherit from either of the adoptive parents? Because

of his affection for Marjory, Harold wants half of his entire estate to go to her with the remaining half to be split equally by his current wife, Cheryl, and his two natural minor children, James and Barbara. Would such a provision be legal in your state? If so, draft the appropriate provision(s).

4. While married to his first wife, Margaret, Harold fathered an illegitimate son, Charles. Although their relationship is known by all, Harold has never acknowledged in writing that he is Charles's father.

a. According to your state's laws, what rights would an illegitimate child (Charles) have in his father's (Harold's) estate?

b. Must a provision be included in Harold's will in order to exclude Charles?

c. If Harold had acknowledged Charles as his son in writing or in any requisite statutory manner, could Charles claim a share in Harold's estate even though he (Charles) was not mentioned in the will?

d. Can any children, natural, adopted, or nonmarital (illegitimate), demand or claim a share of their parent's estate when they are not mentioned in their parent's will? What are the rights of stepchildren?

e. Can property from an estate be willed to some of the testator's children while other children are disinherited? If so, draft such a provision in Harold's will including James, Barbara, and Marjory but excluding Wilbur and Maude.

5. A different complication would result if the facts in the Harold Wilson case were changed as follows: Instead of Harold and his second wife, Cheryl, having two children, they are childless. If Harold were to die testate and leave his entire estate to Cheryl, on Cheryl's subsequent death her relatives may receive the entire estate to the exclusion of Harold's children by his first wife. Harold wants to leave his estate to Cheryl if she survives him, but he also wants to provide for his two children, Wilbur and Maude. How could this be accomplished? Draft at least two clauses, one of which includes a life estate that would allow Harold to ensure that all or part of his estate would be received by his children upon the death of either Harold or Cheryl.

6. Suppose that Harold Wilson was injured in an automobile accident, crippling him for life. He decided to leave his entire estate to his faithful nurse, Agnes, who had cared for him continuously since the year of the accident. According to your state laws, can Harold leave his estate to his nurse, excluding his wife and children?

7. If the beneficiaries, legatees, or devisees in Articles IV and V, i.e., Margaret, Wilbur, and Maude in Article IV and Jerome Davis in Article V, die before Harold, who will receive the gifts designated for them in this will? Draft additions to each clause that could resolve this problem.

6. Provision for Residue of Estate

Residuary clause
A clause in a will that disposes of the remaining assets (residue) of the decedent's estate after all debts and gifts in the will are satisfied.

The **residuary clause** allows the maker to transfer the remaining property of an estate that has not been specifically given to devisees. This includes any additional property that may come into the estate after the will has been executed or after the maker's death. Generally, the bulk of an estate falls within the residue, which is usually the source for paying all taxes, debts, and expenses of the decedent. Remember: Always name an alternate or successor residuary beneficiary. The following is an example of a residuary clause:

Sample Clause:

I give all the rest, or residue of my estate, consisting of all property I can dispose of by will and not effectively disposed of by the preceding articles of this will, to my surviving spouse, if she survives me, but if she does not survive me, to my children in equal shares. I direct my personal representative, hereinafter named, to pay out of this my residuary estate, all estate, income, and inheritance taxes, all valid debts, and expenses of my last illness, funeral, and burial, and those incurred in the administration of my estate (see U.P.C. §§ 3–805, 3–807, and 3–902).

When the residue is insufficient to meet priority obligations of the estate, e.g., debts, taxes, and expenses, payment must come from legacies or devises made in the will. The *abatement* process will determine the order in which property in the estate will be applied to the payment of such obligations causing some gifts to be diminished or totally abolished. Consequently, state statutes that control the abatement process must be checked (see U.P.C. § 3–902).

Some residuary clauses are simple, leaving everything to one person. Others are complex, with lengthy provisions concerning the establishment of testamentary trusts and the powers and duties of the named trustee. In either case, the will's maker must remember that if the named residuary beneficiaries or devisees should predecease the maker, there would be no one to receive the residue, so all or part of it will be distributed according to appropriate state intestate succession statutes. Thus, the residuary clause must be carefully drafted to cover potential problems caused by the sequence of deaths of named devisees and must list alternative or successor beneficiaries or devisees.

Finally, it is important to keep in mind that without a residuary clause or in any circumstances in which some or all of the decedent's estate passes by intestacy, there are no specific or general legacies or devises. Therefore, the estate's net assets or income are divided among the heirs on a pro rata basis. An example of a case in which the decedent died testate but the will contained an invalid residuary clause, thereby causing the property not disposed of to pass by the state's intestate succession statute, is *Estate of Cancik,* 12 Ill.App.3d 113, 76 Ill.Dec. 659, 459 N.E.2d 296 (1984).

⚜ ASSIGNMENT 7.7

1. Suppose in the John Harrington example in which James received $2,000, Thomas the diamond ring, and Harold the gun collection, the testator, John Harrington, added the following provision, "all the residue of my estate I leave to my wife, Jeanine Harrington." The residue is valued at $10,000. If John died and left debts and expenses amounting to $11,000, how would his testamentary gifts abate according to your state's laws?
2. In the Harrington case, if Jeanine, the residual beneficiary, predeceases John, the testator, and he has not named a successor residual beneficiary, all the assets included in the residue will pass according to the intestate succession statute. Check to see how this problem is handled in your state.
3. Draft a residuary clause for John Harrington containing a successor residual beneficiary.

A typical state statute that determines the transfer of the decedent's residual assets is:

Cal. Prob. Code § 21105 Residuary Disposition
Except as provided by Sections 1386.1 and 1386.2 of the Civil Code relating to powers of appointment, a devise of the residue of the testator's real property, or a bequest of the residue of the testator's personal property, passes all of the real or personal property,

as the case may be, which he was entitled to devise or bequeath at the time of his death, not otherwise effectually devised or bequeathed by his will. [Compare U.P.C. §§ 3–902 and 3–906.]

7. Appointment of the Personal Representative

To acquire the powers and authority of a personal representative, a person must be appointed by a court (e.g., the probate judge or, for informal proceedings, a registrar). Generally, unless the person is unqualified, the court approves and appoints the personal representative named in the will. Since personal representatives are fiduciaries who are entrusted with the assets and property of others (the decedent), they must be intelligent, organized, honest, and loyal to the beneficiaries or devisees of the estate while performing all estate administration tasks. They must also be capable of engaging in business transactions or making contracts such as selling assets. Therefore, they should not be minors, incompetent persons, felons, or persons who have or *may have a conflict of interest, e.g., an attorney or paralegal who drafts a will and who influences a client to also name him as the personal representative* (see U.P.C. § 3–203 and Tex. Prob. Code § 78).

ETHICAL ISSUE

State statutes often enumerate the powers granted a personal representative or trustee. The testator, however, may want to list certain specific powers and duties to help the personal representative facilitate the administration of the estate. Giving the personal representative the power to sell one's property, for instance, saves time and perhaps money; otherwise, the personal representative would have to obtain permission from the probate court for such a sale. Such permission is called a *license to sell*. When the estate requires detailed handling, it is best that the testator direct the personal representative's course of action. For example, promissory notes payable to the testator should be collected by the personal representative. Unless the testator mentions collection on such notes in the letter of instructions, the personal representative might overlook this detail, with the result that the probate court might hold the personal representative liable. In addition, just as a contingent devisee should always be named in the event the original devisee predeceases the maker, a contingent or alternate personal representative should also be selected in case the original one may be unable or unwilling to serve in that capacity (for an example of a statute on executor's and administrator's powers and duties, see Wash. Rev. Code Ann. § 11.48.010 and compare U.P.C. §§ 3–701 and 3–703).

Sample Clause:

I nominate my son, Marvin Jameson, as personal representative of this will and my estate and authorize him to (among other powers) sell at public or private sale any real or personal property of my estate. If Marvin Jameson predeceases me, fails to qualify, or ceases to act as my personal representative for any reason, I nominate my daughter, Myrtle B. Jameson, as successor personal representative with all powers hereinbefore mentioned, and I request that my personal representative be permitted to serve without bond or surety thereon. [See the detailed discussion of bond and surety in Chapter 11.]

A typical statute on the time for commencing the personal representative's duties is the following North Dakota law.

N.D. Cent. Code § 30.1–18–01 Time of Accrual of Duties and Powers

The duties and powers of a personal representative commence upon his appointment. The powers of a personal representative relate back in time to give acts by the person appointed which are beneficial to the estate occurring prior to appointment the same effect as those occurring thereafter. Prior to appointment a person named executor in a will may carry out written instructions of the decedent relating to his body, funeral, and burial arrangements. A personal representative may ratify and accept acts on behalf of the estate done by others, where the acts would have been proper for a personal representative.

The personal representative (executor or executrix) appointed is responsible for collecting and preserving the estate assets, paying all allowed debts of the decedent, as well as estate expenses and taxes, and distributing the balance to devisees named in the will (see U.P.C. § 3–703). The procedures for appointing the personal representative are discussed in Chapters 11 and 12.

It is important that you be able to interpret statutory language correctly. A phrase in the North Dakota statute above, "The powers of a personal representative relate back in time," refers to the fact that although personal representatives do not have authority to handle the administration of the estate until qualified, they do possess limited authority (e.g., to preserve the assets of the estate before the personal representatives can be duly qualified), a universal though unwritten rule that several states, including U.P.C. states, have incorporated into their probate codes. Formal qualification of the personal representative requires a hearing before a probate judge, registrar, or clerk of the court, an order signed by the judge, and issuance of documents called Letters Testamentary or Letters of Administration (see Chapter 11), which officially authorize the named personal representative to commence the administration.

The cost of selecting and utilizing fiduciaries such as personal representatives, trustees, or attorneys handling an estate is governed by state law. In some states, such as New York, California, and Iowa, personal representatives are paid commissions (fees) according to a sliding scale based on the monetary value of the estate or trust. The statutory fees paid personal representatives in those states are as follows:

- California: Up to 4 percent of first $15,000; 3 percent on next $85,000; 2 percent on next $900,000; 1 percent on next $9,000,000; 0.5 percent on next $15,000,000; and a "reasonable rate" for anything over $25,000,000.
- Iowa: Up to 6 percent of first $1,000; 4 percent on next $4,000; and 2 percent on anything over $5,000.
- New York: 5 percent of first $100,000; 4 percent on next $200,000; 3 percent on next $700,000; 2.5 percent of next $4,000,000; and 2 percent on anything over $5,000,000.

New York also uses such scales to compensate trustees, while California uses them for personal representatives and attorneys but not for trustees. Formerly, state bar associations established minimum attorney fee schedules based on the size of the estate. But the U.S. Supreme Court in *Goldfarb v. Virginia State Bar,* 421 U.S. 773, 95 S.Ct. 2004, 44 L.Ed.2d 572 (1975), ruled that such minimum fee schedules were prohibited by antitrust laws as a method of price fixing. Currently, the trend is to use "reasonable compensation" rather than the size of the estate to determine fees. Today, almost half of the states and the Uniform Probate Code establish "reasonable compensation" for personal representatives (executors or administrators); see U.P.C. § 3–719. Custom and local practice play a major part in determining what constitutes "reasonable compensation."

8. Appointment of a Personal and/or Property Guardian

A parent has a statutory obligation to support children until they reach majority. The law establishes two types of guardianships: a personal guardian and a property guardian. Whenever the testator has minor or physically or mentally handicapped children and the other parent is deceased or unable to care for them, a personal guardian should be named in the will to ensure proper care of the children after the testator's death. Otherwise, if there is no will, the court is required to determine who shall have custody and/or *guardianship of the person* i.e., the child or the incompetent).

Example: Bryan dies testate. He had sole custody of his minor daughter, Kate. Bryan's wife had died several years earlier. Bryan's brother, Gerald, with whom Bryan and Kate had lived for a number of years, and Kate's maternal grandmother both claim to be a more fitting guardian for the child. The probate court must choose between the two if Bryan's will fails to name a guardian. Either Bryan or his wife could have prevented the unpleasantness resulting from this guardianship proceeding by naming in their wills a guardian of the person, and of the property, for Kate.

The testator should also appoint a *guardian of the property* or conservator to manage property left to minor or incompetent children. If such an appointment is not made, the probate court must do so. The testator should empower the property guardian or conservator to hold, accumulate, and manage the funds and property for incapacitated or minor devisees or beneficiaries under a trust for the duration of their minority or incapacity (compare U.P.C. §§ 5–209, 5–309, and 5–401). The personal guardian and the property guardian may or may not be the same person. The following is an example of a clause appointing a personal and property guardian:

Sample Clause:

I nominate Francine E. Richter as personal and property guardian of my minor child, Debra G. Thorsby, and empower her with the right to have care, custody, and control of said minor child, and to collect, invest, and manage, without court approval, any property passing to said minor child by this will. I direct that the guardian shall not be required to give any bond or other surety in connection with qualifying or acting in this capacity. The guardian may use the income from the property for the support, education, and well-being of said child and distribute the principal balance to her upon her 25th birthday or her marriage, whichever occurs first. In the event Francine E. Richter fails to qualify or is unable, or unwilling, or ceases to act as guardian, I nominate William B. Kruger to serve in her place as successor personal and property guardian with all the hereinbefore mentioned powers.

A statute granting testamentary appointment of a guardian is *Tex. Prob. Code Ann. § 676(d),* Guardians of Minors:

The surviving parent of a minor may, by will or written declaration, appoint any qualified person to be guardian of the person of his or her children after the death of such parent; and, if not disqualified, such person shall be entitled to be appointed guardian of their estate after the death of such parent, upon compliance with the provision of this Code.

A statute that treats the order of preference for the appointment of a guardian is *Ind.Code § 29-3-5-5,* Consideration for Appointment of Guardian; Order of Consideration; Priorities:

Sec. 5 (a) The following are entitled to consideration for appointment as a guardian under section 4 of this chapter in the order listed:

(1) A person designated in a durable power of attorney.

(2) The spouse of an incapacitated person.

(3) An adult child of an incapacitated person.

(4) A parent of an incapacitated person, or a person nominated by will of a deceased parent of an incapacitated person or by any writing signed by a parent of an incapacitated person and attested to by at least two (2) witnesses.

(5) Any person related to an incapacitated person by blood or marriage with whom the incapacitated person has resided for more than six (6) months before the filing of the petition.

(6) A person nominated by the incapacitated person who is caring for or paying for the care of the incapacitated person.

(b) With respect to persons having equal priority, the court shall select the person it considers best qualified to serve as guardian. The court, acting in the best interest of the incapacitated person or minor, may pass over a person having priority and appoint a person having a lower priority or no priority under this section.

A controversial and often stressful situation arises whenever a single parent attempts to appoint a guardian for a child in a will and specifically excludes from the appointment the other natural parent. The surviving natural parent, without regard to marital status, has the right to custody of the child and to be the guardian unless the parent is found to be unfit. The custodial parent cannot change the rights of the surviving parent (see Minn. Stat. Ann. § 525.6155).

Example: In her will, Sandra, the custodial parent, selects her sister, Ruth, to be the personal guardian of Sandra's minor son, William. Sandra also states that she does not want her former husband, Roy, who is the father of William, to obtain custody of William. Upon Sandra's death, the court would appoint Roy the personal guardian unless he was unwilling or unfit.

ASSIGNMENT 7.8

Rhoda's husband, Steven Clark, has a will, leaving his estate equally to Rhoda and their three-year-old adopted daughter, Karen, who has muscular dystrophy.

1. Draft a provision to be added to Steven's will that more adequately protects Karen's interest in her father's estate.

2. If Rhoda remarries and dies intestate five years after Steven's death, would her new husband or Karen's maternal grandparents have a statutory preference to the appointment of guardian for Karen in the state of Indiana? In your own state?

9. Simultaneous Death

Most states have enacted statutes that govern the distribution of a decedent-testator's property when there is insufficient evidence to determine if a beneficiary survived the testator. Because of the frequent occurrence of these inheritance and distribution problems whenever two people, such as a married couple or a parent and adult child, die at the same time in a common accident, nearly all states have adopted the Uniform Simultaneous Death Act. The act provides that where the inheritance of property depends on the priority of death of the decedents, and there is no sufficient evidence that the decedents have died other than simultaneously, the property of each decedent involved shall be distributed as if he or she had survived the other (see U.P.C. § 2–104). This provision can be added to the decedent's will. A typical state statute is *Conn. Gen. Stat. Ann. § 45a–440*, Simultaneous Death; Disposition of Property:

> (a) When no sufficient evidence of survivorship. When the title to property or the devolution thereof depends upon priority of death and there is no sufficient evidence that the persons have died otherwise than simultaneously, the property of each person shall be disposed of as if he had survived, except as provided otherwise in this section.

Example: Margaret and her daughter, Mary, are at home asleep. Gas leaks into the house causing an explosion that destroys the house and kills Margaret and Mary. Margaret's will named Mary as her sole beneficiary, but in the event of Mary's death before Margaret, the property was to pass to Margaret's brother, Adam. The will contained a **simultaneous death clause** that allowed the property to go to Adam instead of possibly passing into Mary's estate.

The Uniform Simultaneous Death Act has also resolved the following problem. If two individuals owning property in joint tenancy die simultaneously under circumstances in which it cannot be determined who died first, the property is divided equally and distributed to the beneficiaries named in the residuary clause of their respective wills. In the previous example, if Margaret and Mary owned a house in joint tenancy and they died simultaneously in a plane crash, half of the value of the house would pass to Margaret's brother, and the other half would pass to Mary's beneficiaries or heirs depending on whether she died testate or intestate.

Unfortunately, the act can result in a significant financial loss to surviving beneficiaries and devisees, because the act implies that if there is adequate proof of the sequence of deaths, the surviving beneficiary, no matter how long that person survives, will be entitled to the property passed by will from the first decedent's estate. For example, suppose a wife, who died a few days after her husband in a common accident, was the sole beneficiary of her husband's will; then, after his estate is taxed and debts are paid, the residue would be added to the wife's estate, where it would be taxed again. Most states, including those that have adopted the Uniform Probate Code, have eliminated this problem by adding a "delay clause" to the simultaneous death provision that requires that to qualify as a surviving beneficiary, a person must survive the first decedent in the common accident by at least 120 days. If the beneficiary does not survive the decedent-testator by 120 days, the beneficiary does not receive the property through the will. Caution: A delay clause that exceeds 180 days will disqualify a bequest to the spouse for the marital deduction (see U.S.C.A. § 2056[b] [3]; Federal Tax Regulations, § 20:2056). The following is a sample clause, taken from West's McKinney's Forms, ESP, § 7:255, that can be used to resolve the "delay" problem:

> *Sample Clause:*
> In the event that my said wife shall die within a period of [six] months (180 days) after the date of my death, my said wife shall be deemed to have predeceased me, and all provisions contained herein for her benefit shall be cancelled and my estate shall be administered and the assets of my estate distributed as though I had died immediately after the death of my said wife. (Reprinted with permission from West's McKinney's Forms, Copyright ©, by West Publishing Co.)

In cases involving intestacy and simultaneous deaths, Section 47 of the Texas Probate Code establishes a "delay" period of 120 hours (5 days) that must pass

Simultaneous death clause

A clause in a will that determines the distribution of property in the event there is no evidence as to the priority of time of death of the testator and another, usually the testator's spouse.

in order for an heir to "survive" and inherit from the intestate. If the heir does not survive the intestate by the 5 days, the beneficiary is considered to have predeceased the intestate, and none of the intestate's property will be passed to the beneficiary. The U.P.C. § 2–104 has the same provision.

Although the Uniform Simultaneous Death Act is the most common provision for directing how a testator's property will be distributed, i.e., that the beneficiary in the will predeceased the testator, a different presumption of death can be established in the will by an appropriate provision. For example, when estate planning for spouses is an important consideration, it is common to provide that the spouse with the smaller estate is determined to survive in the event of simultaneous death.

🏛 ASSIGNMENT 7.9

Ruth and Edmund Barnet, husband and wife, live in Connecticut. Edmund's will gives his country house to Ruth, if she should survive him, but if she does not, to his sister, Estelle. Ruth's will gives her collection of antiques to Edmund, if he should survive her, but if he does not, to her brother, Keith. Ruth and Edmund die simultaneously in an automobile collision. Answer these questions according to your own state laws:

1. Who inherits which property?
2. Would your answer differ if Ruth had died one day later than Edmund? Is there "sufficient evidence" to prevent the Connecticut statute above from operating?
3. If Ruth receives injuries in the accident and dies 90 days afterward, would she be entitled to receive Edmund's gift? Would Estelle?

10. Testamentary Trust Clause

Occasionally, a person wishes to transfer ownership of property to another without giving the recipient full power over the designated property. A method generally used to accomplish this is a *trust* (see Chapters 8 and 9). As previously defined, a trust is the conveyance of legal title to property to a person, the *trustee,* with the understanding that the trustee holds, manages, and controls the property for the benefit or use of another person, the beneficiary (or *cestui que trust*).

Attorneys handle the drafting of any trusts their clients wish to establish. The immediate focus here is on trusts contained in wills. You must be aware of the reasons for establishing such trusts and understand the basic principles involved in their creation. This knowledge provides a foundation for intelligently and competently assisting the attorney in drafting and executing testamentary trusts.

The following characteristics common to trusts established in a will are generally essential to their validity: (1) a settlor, (2) a trustee, (3) a beneficiary, (4) a remainderman (may be the same person as the beneficiary), (5) property, and (6) terms of the trust.

Trusts are useful for several purposes (see also Chapters 8 and 9). Estate taxes may be saved by transferring property to children and grandchildren. For example, a settlor can place property in a trust with the income therefrom paid to a child during the latter's lifetime, and the trust property transferred to the child's own children (settlor's grandchildren) on the child's death. The tax consequences of such a trust are discussed in Chapter 14 under "generation-skipping" transfers.

The **Rule Against Perpetuities,** a common law rule that originated in England centuries ago, affects the validity and duration of all private noncharitable trusts.

Rule Against Perpetuities
A rule that fixes the time within which a future interest must vest (pass). The estate must vest (pass) within a time limited by a life or lives then in being and 21 years thereafter, together with the period of gestation.

Since the rule does not affect charitable trusts, such trusts have an unlimited duration. The rule regulates the creation of future interests and holds that to be valid, title to property must vest (that is, some beneficiary must get full and unrestricted possession and control over the property) no later than 21 years together with the period of gestation after the death of some life or lives in being (a living person or persons) named in the instrument (e.g., a will) that transferred the property.

The Rule Against Perpetuities has an important bearing on testamentary trusts that prevents testator-settlors from controlling property long after they are dead. Because public policy, as enunciated in the rule, opposes the accumulation and monopolizing of property and income over many generations, the maker of a will may not create a trust that lasts longer than 21 years together with the period of gestation after the life of a named person. The life of such a person is referred to as a "life in being" when the trust is created. To illustrate: A settlor of property currently without children cannot create a testamentary trust for grandchildren (children's children, neither of which class is yet born), since there is no "life in being" at the time of the creation of the trust. The trust is void because of the rule. On the other hand, if the settlor were to create a trust leaving property at death in trust to a daughter now living—the "life in being"—and on her death to the daughter's children, the trust would be legal since the duration of the trust would be measured by the life of the daughter. The trust terminates no later than 21 years after her death, at which time her child or children would receive the trust property. If the daughter were to die childless, the trust property would revert (return) immediately to the settlor or the settlor's beneficiaries or heirs. Most states have enacted the rule into statutory law.

The following Iowa law exemplifies state statutes on the Rule Against Perpetuities:

Iowa Code Ann. § 558.68   Perpetuities
1. A nonvested interest in property is not valid unless it must vest, if at all, within twenty-one years after one or more lives in being at the creation of the interest and any relevant period of gestation.

Sample Clause:
All the remainder of my estate, I give to the Fourth Western Bank to hold in trust, invest, reinvest, and distribute the net income accruing from the date of my death, for the benefit of my son, Jeremy, for life, and the remainder to such child or children of him who reach the age of 18 years.

To avoid running afoul of the Rule Against Perpetuities in will drafting is difficult, as evidenced by the great number of lawsuits brought by persons alleging that certain trust provisions violate the rule. For this reason, you must go over the perpetuities statute of the state where the trust is to take effect in detail to ensure that the trust harmonizes with it.

The above-quoted Iowa statute, for example, holds the effective time of a trust to be the remaining length of the lives of persons named in the instrument, plus 21 years, plus nine months (the "usual period of gestation"—this provision provides for persons not yet born at the time of the trust execution). The trust set up in the sample clause could last for the rest of the life of Jeremy (the life in being) and continue for 21 years and nine months. The clause, then, falls within the limits set by the Rule Against Perpetuities.

11. Testimonium Clause

The **testimonium clause** contains a statement by the maker of the will that it has been freely signed and that a request has been made of the proper number of witnesses to do the same.

Since the testimonium clause does not contain any new information and in most instances only repeats what the testator has stated in the opening paragraphs, it would appear to be expendable. Although each state demands that the will conform to standards regarding writing, signing by the testator, and witnessing, no state statute prescribes a form for the testimonium clause. Likewise, the use of a seal to indicate the identity of the testator or the substitution of L.S. (Lieu of Seal; set in place of a seal) is largely disregarded by will-drafters, although there are adherents to the practice. The following is an example of a testimonium clause:

Testimonium clause
A clause in a will in which the maker states that she has freely signed and dated the will and requests the proper number of witnesses to do the same.

Sample Clause:

In Witness Whereof, I, the undersigned testator (trix), do hereby declare that I willingly sign and execute this instrument as my last will consisting of _____ pages, including this page, on this _____ day of _____ , 19 _____ , at City of _____ , County of _____ , State of _____ , in the presence of the witnesses whose names appear hereafter.

_____

Testator(trix)

A typical statute on this matter is *N.J. Stat. Ann. § 3A:3–2,* Formal Requisites of a Will:

Except as provided . . . this title, a will to be valid shall be in writing and signed by the testator, which signature shall be made by the testator or the making thereof acknowledged by him, and such writing declared to be his last will, in the presence of 2 witnesses present at the same time, who shall subscribe their names thereto, as witnesses, in the presence of the testator.

ASSIGNMENT 7.10

After reading a copy of a will prepared for him by an attorney, Owen decides that he does not like the antiquated language of the testimonium clause. He erases it and writes the following clause in its place.

At the time this will was executed, the testator knew of and fully complied with the statutes of this state relating to the execution of wills.

/S/ _____
(*Testator*)

Witnessed this same day, April 13, 19 _____ .

/S/ _____
(*Witness*)

/S/ _____
(*Witness*)

1. Would this clause serve in lieu of the traditionally worded testimonium clause? Why or why not?
2. Point out potential difficulties caused by this testimonium clause when the will's executor offers the document for probate. Are there any words or omissions likely to be challenged in a will contest? Why?
3. If necessary, add to or modify the clause to make it conform both to the requirements of the law and to Owen's desire to modernize its language.

12. Testator's Signature

For a will to be valid, its maker must sign, make a mark, or direct another to sign. In most states, the signature must be witnessed by two or more persons acting as attesting witnesses. The date, either in the beginning, within, or at the end of the will, is essential. Without it, it may be impossible to prove that the will is the last (in time) made by the testator.

A typical statute on the execution of a will is *Cal. Prob. Code § 6110,* Necessity of Writing; Other Requirements:

(a) Except as provided in this part, a will shall be in writing and satisfy the requirements of this section.

(b) The will shall be signed either (1) by the testator or (2) in the testator's name by some other person in the testator's presence and by the testator's direction.

(c) The will shall be witnessed by being signed by at least two persons each of whom (1) being present at the same time, witnessed either the signing of the will or the testator's acknowledgment of the signature or of the will and (2) understand that the instrument they sign is the testator's will. [Compare U.P.C. § 2–502.]

Example: Walter typewrites his will. He puts his signature at the beginning of it, but types his name at the end. In some states, e.g., New York, the will may not be valid for lack of a proper signature in the proper place.

Example: Dora signs her will in the presence of three witnesses. She had not said directly to them that the document was her will, but gave them to understand that the document contained her wishes for the distribution of her property after death. Dora has complied with the required declaration of testator in the California statute.

Example: Luke writes a will but neglects to date it. Previously, he had made a will but had decided to discard it. He did not destroy the former will. Both documents are found after his death. The latter will may not supersede the former or prevail over it for lack of evidence that it was written at a later time.

⚖ ASSIGNMENT 7.11

Edith wishes to make a will, but she is partially paralyzed and cannot write her name. Her nephew, Arthur, agrees to draw up the will and to witness the X she will make in place of her name. The clause preceding the signature follows.

I, the testatrix, Edith B. Pendergast, on this 19th day of March, 1963, subscribe my name to this will.

_____

I, Arthur G. Pendergast, have witnessed this mark made by Edith B. Pendergast who affixed it in lieu of her signature.

_____

1. Do these clauses fulfill your state's statutory requirements for signature by the testator? Why or why not?
2. If necessary, add to or modify the clauses to make them conform to your answer in question 1 (compare U.P.C. § 2–502).

13. Attestation Clause of Witnesses

Witnesses must state that they have attested the maker's signature on the will; ordinarily, they sign a clause to this effect. As in the case of the testimonium clause, each state has legislation requiring subscription by witnesses, although none prescribes the words or form to be used to accomplish this. The traditional form of the **attestation clause,** like the familiarly worded testimonium clause, is illustrated below.

Attestation clause
Witnesses to a will state that they have attested the maker's signature and that they have subscribed (signed) a clause in the will to this effect.

Sample Clause:
The above and foregoing instrument, consisting of three (3) typewritten pages including this page, was on the date hereof, signed by _____ , the testator herein named and published and declared by him to be his last will and testament, in our presence, and we at his request and in his presence and in the presence of each other, have hereunto signed our names as witnesses and believe the testator to be over 18 years of age, of sound mind, and under no constraint or undue influence.

_____ address _____
(Witness)

_____ address _____
(Witness)

ASSIGNMENT 7.12

"We, the undersigned, declare that Lyman Jarrett validly signed and executed this will. We sign at his request, all of us signing in each other's presence."
1. Does such a clause comply with statutory requirements? Why or why not?
2. If necessary, add to or modify the clause to make it conform to the statutory requirements.

14. Witnesses' Signatures and Addresses

Only the original copy of the will is signed. Copies should be made before the original is signed. All states require that at least two witnesses sign the will, except

Vermont, which requires three witnesses' signatures. Witnesses should sign using the same pen as the testator.

Example:

	Address
Pamela C. Hunter	*111 Wheelock Drive*
Fredrick G. Burns	*2307 Ayleshire Avenue*
Marshall Jayner	*417 Kenyan Place*

ASSIGNMENT 7.13

You are a paralegal and also a notary public. At the execution of a will, while you are discussing the procedures with the attorney, the testator inadvertently signs the will, and now he wants you to notarize it. What would you have the testator do to resolve this problem?

ASSIGNMENT 7.14

Herman Sharp wrote his will, aided by Joel Prentis, a notary public. After Herman's signature, Joel wrote, "I hereby certify that this is the last will and testament of Herman Sharp. (signed) Joel A. Prentis, Notary Public. My commission expires 12/31/98. (Seal.)"

Herman had his cousin, Pearl, witness the will and intended to ask another cousin to witness it but died before accomplishing this. Is the will valid? What validates or invalidates it? What would have been a better procedure for Joel to follow?

SAMPLE PRELIMINARY WILL

Exhibit 7.2 shows a sample worksheet for preparing to draft a client's will, and a draft of the will itself drawn from the information on the worksheet is on p. 222.

In our hypothetical situation, Leona Bayn Farrell wishes to make a will. She is married and has a husband, Oren, and four children, Randolph, Jonathan, Daria, and Thomas. Her estate consists of both real and personal property, all of which she acquired prior to the marriage or as testamentary gifts to her alone (i.e., it is separate property). Leona lives in Arizona, a community property state, so she may dispose by will only half of the community property acquired by herself and her husband while they are married.

ASSIGNMENT 7.15

Peter Rice Cochran wishes to make a will. He is currently unmarried, having been divorced from Viola Leigh after a five-year marriage during which two children, Nancy and Jean, were born. His estate consists of both real and personal property, namely, a townhouse; household goods; automobile; checking account of $587; certificate of

Exhibit 7.2 Sample Worksheet for Drafting a Will

Client's Name: Leona Bayn Farrell (also known as Leona Alice Bayn)

Address: 913 Garth Avenue, City Santa Maria, County Harkness, State Arizona (if more than one) 17 Mesa Grande, Dorado, New Mexico.

Permanent Residence (Domicile): 913 Garth Avenue, Harkness County, Santa Maria.

Funeral and Burial Directions: I direct that my kidneys be delivered, immediately upon my death, without autopsy having been performed, to the Dorado State School of Medicine, 403 Alamoreal Street, Dorado, New Mexico, to be used for educational purposes.

Method (source of payments of debts and all taxes): I direct that my executor pay all my expenses, debts, and taxes from the residue of my estate.

Specific Gifts
Personal Property (community property)
Beneficiary: Oren Johnstone Farrell   Contingent beneficiary: Children
Relationship: Husband   Relationship: Sons and daughters
Item: Share of community property consisting of household furnishing, cloth-
   ing, jewelry, books, and other personal effects.

Method: Legacy

Personal property
Beneficiary: Randolph Bayn Farrell   Contingent beneficiary: Ella Gamble Dean

Relationship: Son   Relationship: Niece
Item: The Buick automobile that I own, serial number 70–5015–63–9229

Present location: At my permanent residence, 913 Garth Avenue

Method: Legacy

Personal Property
Beneficiary: Oren Johnstone Farrell   Contingent beneficiary: Jonathan Bayn Farrell

Relationship: Husband   Relationship: Son
Item: All the farm equipment located at Siete Rios

Method: Legacy

Personal Property
Beneficiary: Jonathan Bayn Farrell   Contingent beneficiary: Angela Bayn Rodgers

Relationship: Son   Relationship: Niece
Item: All the horses and riding equipment located at Vallejo Grande
Method: Legacy

Real Property: Ranch—"Vallejo Grande"

Beneficiary: Jonathan Bayn Farrell   Contingent beneficiary: Angela Bayn Rodgers

Relationship: Son   Relationship: Niece
Legal description of "Vallejo Grande": "The West half of Section 12, being 320 acres more or less, Township 4 North, Range 28 West of the 4th Principal Meridian, according to the United States Government survey."

Location: County: Almedo State: New Mexico

Amount of interest: Fee simple

Method: Fee simple devise

Exhibit 7.2   Sample Worksheet for Drafting a Will—*continued*

Real Property: Farm—"Siete Rios"

Beneficiary: Oren Johnstone Farrell   Contingent beneficiary: Daria Eileen Farrell

Relationship: Husband   Relationship: Daughter

Location: County: Dorado   State New Mexico

Legal description of "Siete Rios": "The Southwest Quarter of Section 13, being 160 acres more or less, Township 4 North, Range 28 West of the 4th Principal Meridian, according to the United States Government survey."

Amount of Interest: Fee simple

Method: Fee simple devise

Residue

Beneficiary: Daria Eileen Farrell   Contingent beneficiary: Randolph Bayn Farrell

Relationship: Daughter   Relationship: Son

Interest given: Legacy or devise; if any residue remains after payment of debts, expenses, and taxes

Name and Address of Executor: Randolph Bayn Farrell
119 Golden Valley Road,
Santa Maria, Arizona

Contingent (Successor) Executor: Farmers National Bank,
Santa Maria, Arizona

Powers of Executor: To sell publicly or privately all or part of my residual property to carry on the operations of "Vallejo Grande" and "Siete Rios" until the dispositions thereof are complete

Trusts

Trustee: Carl A. Woodward, Farmers National Bank, Santa Maria, Arizona

Property: $75,000 (cash)

Location: Farmers National Bank, Account #922160

Duration of trust (life, years, etc.): For the life of my son, Thomas Earl Farrell

Remainder: First United Methodist Church of Waco, Texas

Trustee's powers

Investment: To invest and reinvest the corpus

Management: To distribute the earned income for the benefit of Thomas Earl Farrell

Payment of income: Quarterly if possible; at least semiannually

Payment of principal: At the trustee's discretion or at the request of Thomas Earl Farrell's natural or legal personal guardian

Power of sale: N/A

Special Provisions: Both principal and interest may be used for education, training, and maintenance of Thomas Earl Farrell. If guardian and trustee disagree, guardian's opinion is to prevail.

Guardians

Guardian of person: Hal August Rodgers, husband of my niece, Angela Bayne Rodgers

Name and address: 366 Rector Avenue, County of Harkness, City of Santa Maria, Arizona

Ward: Thomas Earl Farrell   Successor Guardian: Randolph Bayn Farrell

Bond: None required

Guardian of property: Randolph Bayn Farrell, my son

Exhibit 7.2 Sample Worksheet for Drafting a Will—*continued*

Name and address: 119 Golden Valley Road, County of Harkness, City of Santa Maria, Arizona

Ward: Thomas Earl Farrell   Successor Guardian: Hal August Rodgers

Bond: None required

Common Disaster Provision: If any beneficiary under this will and I should die under circumstances which make it impossible to determine the order of deaths, I shall be deemed to have predeceased them. In the event that my husband and I die in a common accident, I give all the property that would otherwise have passed to him under this will to my children in equal shares.

Witnesses
Name and Addresses: Raymond Meador, Route 34, White Plains, Arizona
Philip Harston, 1661 N. 3rd Street, Santa Maria, Arizona
Mildred Wagoner, Route 7, Adolphus, Arizona

General Notes
Location—safe deposit box: Leona and Oren Farrell, joint tenants, Farmers National Bank

Location where will shall be placed: In the custody of Frank R. Goad, Attorney-at-law

Will prepared by: Joyce Bell, paralegal assistant under supervision of attorney Judith K. Larson

Date: July 18, 1995

---

deposit of $7,000; insurance policy on his life, payable to his brother, Desmond Cochran, $10,000; 100 shares of Xerox Corporation stock; savings account of $10,525.

1. Make a preliminary outline of a will for Peter Cochran using the form suggested by the Leona Farrell example. Make up facts in the testator's life (e.g., devisees who are not named above, testamentary trusts to be created) if you wish.

2. Using the will of Leona Farrell on p. 222 as a guide, write a will for Peter Cochran. (Assume the testator lives in your state. Be sure to consult the probate laws of your state before drafting the will.)

ADDITIONAL NONTESTAMENTARY DOCUMENTS

Several other documents are not part of the formal will itself, but are related to it. Depending on the circumstances, the client may require some or all of the documents discussed in the next paragraphs.

1. Self-Proving Provision or Affidavit or Self-Proved Will

Some states have adopted a statute that provides an option for the "proving" (establishing the authenticity) of a will. This is accomplished by an acknowledgment of the testator and with affidavits (statements under oath) of the witnesses to the will. The acknowledgment and affidavits are made before an officer authorized to administer oaths by the state, e.g., a **notary public,** and can be signed either at the time of the execution of the will or at any subsequent date during the lifetime of the testator and witnesses. The document recites that the

Notary Public
A person authorized by the state whose function is to administer oaths, certify documents and deeds, and attest to the authenticity of signatures.

LAST WILL AND TESTAMENT
OF
LEONA BAYN FARRELL

Exordium clause →

Revocatory clause →

I, Leona Bayn Farrell, a/k/a (also known as) Leona Alice Bayn, residing at 913 Garth Avenue, City of Santa Maria, County of Harkness, State of Arizona, being of sound and disposing mind and memory, and not acting under undue influence of any person whomsoever, make, publish, and declare this document to be my last will and testament, and expressly revoke any prior wills and codicils, and make this my will.

Article I

Payment of debts, expenses, and taxes →

I direct my personal representative hereinafter named, to pay my debts, and expenses for my last illness, funeral, and burial out of the residue of my estate. I further direct my personal representative to pay out of my residuary estate all estate, income, and inheritance taxes assessed against my taxable estate or the recipients thereof, whether passing by this will or by other means, without contribution or reimbursement from any person.

Article II

Organ donation →

I direct my personal representative to notify the Dorado State School of Medicine, 403 Alamoreal Street, Dorado, New Mexico, of my death, so that it may receive the gift of my kidneys to use for medical or educational purposes. I further request that no autopsy or embalming be performed upon my body unless ordered by the aforesaid school.

Article III

Burial →

I direct my personal representative, after having completed the gift in Article II, to deliver my body to be interred in my family lot in the Paz de Christo cemetery, (Address) _____ , (City) _____ , (County) _____ , State of _____ .

Article IV

I give that portion of our community property which I own, consisting of household furnishings, clothing, jewelry, books, and personal effects of every kind used about my home or person to my husband, Oren Johnstone Farrell, to do with as he sees fit, if he survives me; if he does not survive me, to my children that survive me in shares of substantially equal value, per stirpes.

Article V

Specific legacies →

I give the Buick automobile which I own, serial number 70–5015–63–9229, to my son, Randolph Bayn Farrell, if he survives me. If he does not survive me, I give said Buick automobile to my niece, Ella Gamble Dean.

Article VI

I give all the farming equipment located at my farm, "Siete Rios," hereinafter legally described, to my husband, Oren Johnstone Farrell, if he survives me. If he does not survive me, I give said farming equipment to my son, Jonathan Bayn Farrell.

Article VII

I give all the horses and riding equipment located at my ranch, "Vallejo Grande," to my son, Jonathan Bayn Farrell, if he survives me. If he does not survive me, I give said horses and said equipment to my niece, Angela Bayn Rodgers.

Article VIII

Specific devises →

I give my ranch, "Vallejo Grande," in Almedo county, New Mexico, legally described "The West half of Section 12, being 320 acres more or less, Township 4 North, Range 28 West of the 4th Principal Meridian, according to the United States Government survey," to my son, Jonathan Bayn Farrell, in fee simple if he survives me. If he does not survive me, I give said ranch in fee simple to my niece, Angela Bayn Rodgers.

Article IX

I give my farm, "Siete Rios," in Dorado County, New Mexico, legally described: "The Southwest Quarter of Section 13, being 160 acres more or less, Township 4 North, Range 28 West of the 4th Principal Meridian, according to the United States Government survey," to my husband, Oren Johnstone Farrell, in fee simple if he survives me. If he does not survive me, I give said farm in fee simple to my daughter, Daria Eileen Farrell.

Article X

I give to Carl A. Woodward of Farmers National Bank, Santa Maria, Arizona, the sum of $75,000 to hold in trust for the life of my son, Thomas Earl Farrell. The trustee shall invest and reinvest the corpus of said trust and distribute the income earned thereby for the benefit of Thomas Earl Farrell at least semiannually, or, if possible, quarterly. Payment of the principal shall be made at the discretion of the trustee or at the request of Thomas Earl Farrell's natural or legal personal guardian, but if the trustee and the personal guardian cannot agree on the dispensing of the principal, the personal guardian's word shall be conclusive in the situation. Upon the death of my son, Thomas Earl Farrell, the remainder of the trust property, if any, is to be given to the First United Methodist Church of Waco, Texas. *— Testamentary trust*

Article XI

I nominate as personal guardian of my minor son, Thomas Earl Farrell, Hal August Rodgers, the husband of my niece, Angela Bayn Rodgers.

I nominate as property guardian of my minor son, Thomas Earl Farrell, Randolph Bayn Farrell, my oldest son.

If either guardian becomes disabled or declines to serve, I nominate the other to serve in the former's capacity as well as the capacity in which he is presently serving. *— Appointment of personal and property guardians and successors*

I direct that bond be required of neither of said guardians for the performance of the duties of their respective offices. *— No bond required*

Article XII

I give the residue of my estate, after the payment of debts and expenses, as mentioned in Article I, and after transfer of my community property mentioned in Article IV, subject to the laws of this state regarding community property, to my daughter, Daria Eileen Farrell, if she survives me. If she does not survive me, I give said residue to my son, Randolph Bayn Farrell. *— Residuary clause*

Article XIII

In the event that my husband, Oren Johnstone Farrell, and I die under such circumstances that it is difficult or impossible to determine who died first, it shall be presumed that my husband predeceased me. *— Simultaneous death clause*

Article XIV

I nominate my son, Randolph Bayn Farrell of 119 Golden Valley Road, Santa Maria, Arizona, to be personal representative of this will, and to serve without bond. *— Nomination of personal representative; no bond required*

If Randolph Bayne Farrell does not survive me or does not qualify as personal representative, I nominate Farmers National Bank, a national banking institution located in Santa Maria, Arizona, to be successor personal representative of this will. *— Nomination of successor personal representative*

My personal representative shall have the power to sell publicly or privately all or part of the residue of my property in the event that such sale will become necessary for the payment of debts, taxes, or expenses; to carry on the operations of "Vallejo Grande" and "Siete Rios" until the testamentary dispositions thereof are complete; and to settle all valid claims against my estate. *— Powers of personal representative*

I freely and willingly subscribe my name to this will consisting of three pages on this 18th day of July, 1995, at Santa Maria, County of Harkness, State of Arizona, in the presence of these witnesses: Raymond Meador, Philip Harston, and Mildred Wagoner, each of whom I have requested to subscribe their names in my presence and in the presence of all the others. *— Testimonium clause*

/S/ Leona Bayn Farrell *— Signature of testatrix*

On the last date shown above, Leona Bayn Farrell, known to us to be the person whose signature appears at the end of this will, declared to us, the undersigned, that the foregoing instrument was her will. She then signed the will in our presence; at her request, we now sign our names in her presence and the presence of each other. *— Attestation clause*

Names	Addresses
_____ (Witness)	_____
_____ (Witness)	_____

— Signatures of witnesses (only two required)

testator is of sound mind and that the testator and the subscribing witnesses (most states require two witnesses) followed the required formalities for the proper and legal execution of the will. The testator and the witnesses sign the document in the presence of a notary public or other public official.

The form for the acknowledgment and affidavit of self-proved wills is provided in § 2–504 of the Uniform Probate Code. An example appears in Exhibit 7.3

The self-proving provision or affidavit signed and sealed by a notary public at the end of the will is *not* required to validate the will. However, if it is added to the will and executed, it makes it unnecessary to produce witnesses to testify when probating the will. The execution of the affidavit supplies the requisite evidence to admit the will to probate, but the affidavit does not waive the formal requirements for a valid will such as the written form, the signature of the testator, and the signatures of the attesting witnesses, nor does it prevent a will contest on legitimate grounds such as duress, fraud, undue influence, revocation, or lack of testamentary capacity of the testator.

Exhibit 7.3 Sample Self-Proving Affidavit

The State of _____
County of _____

We, the undersigned, _____ , _____ , and _____ , the Testator and the witnesses, respectively, whose names are signed to the attached or foregoing instrument, consisting of _____ type-written pages, including this page, being first duly sworn, do hereby declare to the undersigned authority that the Testator signed and executed the instrument as his last will and testament, that he signed willingly (or directed another to sign it for him), that he executed it as his free and voluntary act for the purposes herein expressed; and that each of the witnesses, in the presence and hearing of the Testator, signed the will as witnesses, and that to the best of their knowledge the Testator was at the time 18 or more years of age, of sound mind, and under no constraint or undue influence.

_____
Testator

_____
Witness

_____
Witness

Subscribed, sworn to and acknowledged before me by _____, the Testator, and subscribed and sworn to before me by _____ and _____ , witnesses, this _____ day of _____ , 19 _____ .

_____
Notary Public
Seal   My Commission Expires _____

Source: The Judge Advocate General's School, U.S. Army, JA 262, Legal Assistance Wills Guide (pages 3–16 and 3–17) (May 1993)

2. Letter of Last Instructions

The letter of last instructions is not part of the will and has no legal effect. It may be incorporated by reference into the will. It is a letter to the personal representative and family that explains where important assets and records are located including all bank accounts, safe deposit boxes, and the will; lists current market values of assets or recommends appraisers; and makes management suggestions and investment recommendations to the personal representative. The letter should be updated each year.

3. Right to Die Laws and Related Advance Directive Documents

Over the past twenty years, state statutes and case law have established and recognized the right of a dying person to decline extraordinary treatment to prolong life or the right of a person's guardian or proxy to make such a request. The development of right to die laws began with the landmark case of *Matter of Quinlan,* 70 N.J. 10, 355 A.2d 647 (1976), which involved a young woman, Karen Ann Quinlan, who had lapsed into a coma. When it became clear their daughter would not recover, her parents went to court to request that the respirator supporting Karen's breathing be removed. After a long court battle, the New Jersey Supreme Court ordered the respirator removed. The case caused the legal and medical professions to resolve their differences concerning the legal and medical positions on a person's right to die and to acknowledge and eventually to agree to grant that all persons have the right to determine their quality of life, including the right to die.

In a later case, *Cruzan v. Director, Missouri Department of Health,* 497 U.S. 261, 110 S.Ct. 2841, 111 L.Ed.2d 224 (1990), the U.S. Supreme Court confirmed the constitutional "right to die." In this case the patient, Nancy Cruzan, was critically injured in a car accident leaving her in a coma with no hope of recovery. Her family knew she would not want to live in this condition and asked the hospital to stop her tube feeding. Because Nancy had not made her wishes known in a writing such as a living will, the Missouri Supreme Court rejected the family's request. The family appealed to the U.S. Supreme Court. The Court ruled that the tube could not be removed (thereby allowing the tube feeding to continue), but the Court confirmed a person's right to die and to refuse medical treatment so long as the wishes of the person are known and "clear and convincing evidence" of those wishes is established. The Court acknowledged that competent and incompetent persons have the same rights, but that a surrogate must be named to exercise the rights for the incompetent person, e.g., a patient such as Nancy Cruzan.

To alleviate an individual's concern and anxiety about becoming incompetent due to aging, illness, or accident, three different forms of Right to Die Advance Directives have been established by state legislatures. These directives allow a competent person to determine, in advance and in writing, the kind of future medical care and treatment he wishes to have in case he becomes incompetent or to appoint a surrogate, agent, or proxy to exercise his wishes to continue or discontinue future medical treatment. The three forms of advance directives used to make medical decisions for incompetent persons are (1) a living will, (2) a health care proxy, and (3) a durable power of attorney for health care. Each state has various forms of one or more of these documents.

The Patient Self-Determination Act enacted by Congress in 1991 was created to bring the existence of the directives to the attention of the public and promote their use. The new law requires health care providers who work with the Medicaid and Medicare programs to provide each patient or the patient's authorized surrogate, usually a family member, with written information about the patient's right to (1) make health care and medical treatment decisions including the use of life support systems, (2) be informed on admission by the health care facility, e.g., the hospital, hospice, or nursing home in which the patient resides or is being treated, of its policies concerning patient's rights, and (3) sign any of the previously mentioned advance directives for health and medical care decisions.

Living Will: Death with Dignity

Although it has been a long and hard-fought battle, it now is apparent that constitutional and common law assure any adult person the right to refuse medical treatment, including life-sustaining treatment; however, an incompetent person, e.g., a terminally ill patient, may be unable to communicate her wishes to exercise that right. The controversial decision to withhold or withdraw medical care and treatment must be made on the patient's behalf by someone else, e.g., a family member, doctor, or other medical care provider. Legislation has been passed and the U.S. Supreme Court has issued decisions that have established guidelines for the execution and implementation of a terminally ill patient's advance written health care directives including what is commonly known as a living will. Such a will states that in the event a person becomes incompetent due to a physical or mental disability with no reasonable expectation or hope for recovery, and because of the disability is unable to take part in decisions, the person can request that he not be kept alive by artificial means. Recent examples of famous public persons who have elected to make this request in their living wills are former First Lady Jacqueline Kennedy Onassis and former President Richard Nixon. The purpose of the request is to relieve family members from the responsibility of making the decision, to alleviate guilt feelings on their part, and to protect the physician and health care institution from personal liability if they refrain, as requested, from using certain medical treatment. The patient can revoke the living will at any time by spoken or written directions in the presence of witnesses. Because of their preference for another directive, three states, Massachusetts, Michigan, and New York, do not authorize living wills. Instead, they authorize only the appointment of a health care agent or proxy. On the other hand, two states, Alabama and Alaska, authorize *only* living wills.

Generally, the living will is not part of the will a testator makes to transfer property after death. It is a separate and distinct document. To be valid in most states, the living will must either be signed by the testator and two witnesses in the presence of one another or signed by the testator and notarized. Neither of the witnesses may be related to the testator, beneficiaries of the testator's estate, or employees of the attending physician. Copies of the living will should be placed in the testator's medical record file and given to family members and the testator's personal representative. A copy should also be placed in the same location as the testator's will. See the sample living will in Exhibit 7.4.

Health Care Proxy

All states, except Alabama and Alaska, have statutes that authorize an agent, also called a proxy or surrogate, to make medical care and treatment decisions for an

Exhibit 7.4   Declaration Pursuant to the Natural Death Act of California

DECLARATION

PURSUANT TO THE NATURAL DEATH ACT OF CALIFORNIA

(formerly referred to as "A Living Will")

If I should have an incurable and irreversible condition that has been diagnosed by two physicians and that will result in my death within a relatively short time without the administration of life-sustaining treatment or has produced an irreversible coma or persistent vegetative state, and I am no longer able to make decisions regarding my medical treatment, I direct my attending physician, pursuant to the Natural Death Act of California, to withhold or withdraw treatment, including artificially administered nutrition and hydration, that only prolongs the process of dying or the irreversible coma or persistent vegetative state and is not necessary for my comfort or to alleviate pain.

If I have been diagnosed as pregnant, and that diagnosis is known to my physician, this declaration shall have no force or effect during my pregnancy.

Other instructions:

Signed this _____ day of _____, _____.

Signature _____

Address _____

The declarant voluntarily signed this writing in my presence. I am not a health care provider, an employee of a health care provider, the operator of a community care facility, an employee of an operator of a community care facility, the operator of a residential care facility for the elderly, or an employee of an operator of a residential care facility for the elderly.

Witness _____

Witness _____

The declarant voluntarily signed this writing in my presence. I am not entitled to any portion of the estate of the declarant upon his or her death under any will or codicil thereto of the declarant now existing or by operation of law. I am not a health care provider, an employee of a health care provider, the operator of a community care facility, an employee of an operator of a community care facility, the operator of a residential care facility for the elderly, or an employee of an operator of a residential care facility for the elderly.

Witness _____

Witness _____

Please read informational questions and answers on the reverse side.

WOLCOTTS FORM 1672—DECLARATION PURSUANT TO THE NATURAL DEATH ACT OF CALIFORNIA—Rev. 8-92   (price class 3A)   ©1992 WOLCOTTS FORMS, INC.

7 67775 39672 0

Source: Wolcotts Forms, available at most stationary or office supply stores or by calling 1(800)421-2220.

Health care proxy
A document in which a patient designates a proxy or surrogate who has legal authority to make medical and health care decisions if the patient is too incapacitated to do so personally.

Attorney in fact
A person, not necessarily an attorney, who is given authority by another through a power of attorney for some particular purpose or to do a particular act not of a legal nature.

Durable power of attorney for health care
A document that gives an agent, as a substitute for the principal (the patient), the power and authority to make all medical and health care decisions when the patient is disabled and unable to make such decisions, including the authority to direct the withholding or withdrawal of life-sustaining treatment.

incompetent person. Alabama has no statute, while Alaska's statute specifically forbids an agent from requesting the withholding or withdrawal of life support for an incompetent person. The **health care proxy** document allows any competent adult person, after being fully informed by her physician of her medical condition, to select an agent to make future medical care decisions if the person becomes incompetent. To be valid, the document must be signed by the maker and attested by two witnesses or notarized. State statutes also protect physicians and other health care providers from personal liability for performing the agent's requests including the request to withhold or withdraw life support devices. Exhibit 7.5 shows a sample health care proxy.

Durable Power of Attorney for Health Care

A power of attorney is a written document that grants to another person, called the agent or **"attorney in fact,"** the power and right to act legally on behalf of the person, called the principal, who authorizes and grants the power. Notwithstanding the title of the document, the person (agent) authorized to act does not have to be an attorney. Spouses usually name the husband or wife to be the other spouse's agent. This general power of attorney is often granted for specific time periods, e.g., while the principal is out of the country or hospitalized; or for a specific purpose, e.g., to run a business or purchase a home; or for a specific circumstance, e.g., to manage property because of the principal's illness. A power of attorney granted during the principal's life terminates at the moment of the principal's death, however.

The **durable power of attorney for health care** is the third type of Right to Die Advance Directive. It is a written document that gives another person (agent), as a substitute for the patient (principal), the power and authority to make all decisions relating to the performance of medical and health care treatment by health care providers such as doctors, surgeons, and nurses. A person granted a durable power of attorney does more than simply act as an agent for another. Instead, the durable power of attorney allows the authorized designated agent not only to make health care and medical decisions in place of the patient (principal) when the patient is disabled and unable to make such decisions, but also to direct the withholding or withdrawal of such care and life-sustaining treatment. These decisions are based on current medically known facts and the wishes of the patient, even though he is incompetent. The durable power of attorney document also gives the designated agent the right to (1) employ and discharge health care personnel (doctors and nurses); (2) obtain and disclose the principal's medical records; and (3) select the health care facility, e.g., elder care, nursing home, or hospital, as the appropriate residence for the principal based on his level of need for medical care and assistance. Unlike the living will, which is limited to situations where the principal (patient) has a terminal condition due to illness or injury and death is imminent, the durable power of attorney has no such limitation, makes a broader grant of authority, and gives the patient a wider range to exercise self-determination. California's durable power of attorney for health care appears in Exhibit 7.6.

WHERE TO KEEP THE WILL

It is good practice to mark copies of the original will with the location of the original and to leave it in one of four places: (1) in the lawyer's office vault;

Exhibit 7.5 Sample Health Care Proxy

MASSACHUSETTS HEALTH CARE PROXY

(1) I, _____, hereby appoint

(name)

_____

_____

(name, home address and telephone number of agent)

as my health care agent to make any and all health care decisions for me, except to the extent that I state otherwise below.

This Health Care Proxy shall take effect in the event I become unable to make or communicate my own health care decisions.

(2) I direct my agent to make health care decisions in accord with my wishes and limitations as as may be stated below, or as he or she otherwise knows. If my wishes are unknown, I direct my agent to make health care decisions in accord with what he or she determines to be my best interests.

(3) Other directions (optional):

Exhibit 7.5   Sample Health Care Proxy—*continued*

PRINT THE
NAME, HOME
ADDRESS AND
TELEPHONE
NUMBER OF
YOUR
ALTERNATE
AGENT
(IF ANY)

(4) Name of alternate agent if the person I appoint above is unable, unwilling or unavailable to act as my health care agent (optional):

_____

_____

_____

(name, home address and telephone number of alternate agent)

SIGN AND DATE
THE DOCUMENT
AND PRINT
YOUR ADDRESS

(5) Signature: _____ Date: _____

Address: _____

WITNESSING
PROCEDURE
_____

Statement by Witnesses

I declare that the person who signed this document appears to be at least 18 years of age, of sound mind, and under no constraint or undue influence. He or she signed (or asked another to sign for him or her) this document in my presence. I am not the person appointed as agent or alternate agent by this document.

Witness 1: _____

Address: _____

_____

Date: _____

YOUR
WITNESSES
MUST SIGN AND
PRINT THEIR
ADDRESSES

Witness 2: _____

Address: _____

_____

Date: _____

PAGE 2

Exhibit 7.6 California's Durable Power of Attorney for Health Care

STATUTORY FORM DURABLE POWER OF ATTORNEY FOR HEALTH CARE

(California Probate Code Section 4771)

WARNING TO PERSON EXECUTING THIS DOCUMENT:

THIS IS AN IMPORTANT LEGAL DOCUMENT WHICH IS AUTHORIZED BY THE KEEN HEALTH CARE AGENT ACT. BEFORE EXECUTING THIS DOCUMENT, YOU SHOULD KNOW THESE IMPORTANT FACTS:

THIS DOCUMENT GIVES THE PERSON YOU DESIGNATE AS YOUR AGENT (THE ATTORNEY IN FACT) THE POWER TO MAKE HEALTH CARE DECISIONS FOR YOU. YOUR AGENT MUST ACT CONSISTENTLY WITH YOUR DESIRES AS STATED IN THIS DOCUMENT OR OTHERWISE MADE KNOWN.

EXCEPT AS YOU OTHERWISE SPECIFY IN THIS DOCUMENT, THIS DOCUMENT GIVES YOUR AGENT THE POWER TO CONSENT TO YOUR DOCTOR NOT GIVING TREATMENT OR STOPPING TREATMENT NECESSARY TO KEEP YOU ALIVE.

NOTWITHSTANDING THIS DOCUMENT, YOU HAVE THE RIGHT TO MAKE MEDICAL AND OTHER HEALTH CARE DECISIONS FOR YOURSELF SO LONG AS YOU CAN GIVE INFORMED CONSENT WITH RESPECT TO THE PARTICULAR DECISION. IN ADDITION, NO TREATMENT MAY BE GIVEN TO YOU OVER YOUR OBJECTION AT THE TIME, AND HEALTH CARE NECESSARY TO KEEP YOU ALIVE MAY NOT BE STOPPED OR WITHHELD IF YOU OBJECT AT THE TIME.

THIS DOCUMENT GIVES YOUR AGENT AUTHORITY TO CONSENT, TO REFUSE TO CONSENT, OR TO WITHDRAW CONSENT TO ANY CARE, TREATMENT, SERVICE, OR PROCEDURE TO MAINTAIN, DIAGNOSE, OR TREAT A PHYSICAL OR MENTAL CONDITION. THIS POWER IS SUBJECT TO ANY STATEMENT OF YOUR DESIRES AND ANY LIMITATIONS THAT YOU INCLUDE IN THIS DOCUMENT. YOU MAY STATE IN THIS DOCUMENT ANY TYPES OF TREATMENT THAT YOU DO NOT DESIRE. IN ADDITION, A COURT CAN TAKE AWAY THE POWER OF YOUR AGENT TO MAKE HEALTH CARE DECISIONS FOR YOU IF YOUR AGENT (1) AUTHORIZES ANYTHING THAT IS ILLEGAL, (2) ACTS CONTRARY TO YOUR KNOWN DESIRES, OR (3) WHERE YOUR DESIRES ARE NOT KNOWN, DOES ANYTHING THAT IS CLEARLY CONTRARY TO YOUR BEST INTERESTS.

THE POWERS GIVEN BY THIS DOCUMENT WILL EXIST FOR AN INDEFINITE PERIOD OF TIME UNLESS YOU LIMIT THEIR DURATION IN THIS DOCUMENT.

YOU HAVE THE RIGHT TO REVOKE THE AUTHORITY OF YOUR AGENT BY NOTIFYING YOUR AGENT OR YOUR TREATING DOCTOR, HOSPITAL, OR OTHER HEALTH CARE PROVIDER ORALLY OR IN WRITING OF THE REVOCATION.

YOUR AGENT HAS THE RIGHT TO EXAMINE YOUR MEDICAL RECORDS AND TO CONSENT TO THEIR DISCLOSURE UNLESS YOU LIMIT THIS RIGHT IN THIS DOCUMENT.

UNLESS YOU OTHERWISE SPECIFY IN THIS DOCUMENT, THIS DOCUMENT GIVES YOUR AGENT THE POWER AFTER YOU DIE TO (1) AUTHORIZE AN AUTOPSY, (2) DONATE YOUR BODY OR PARTS THEREOF FOR TRANSPLANT OR THERAPEUTIC OR EDUCATIONAL OR SCIENTIFIC PURPOSES, AND (3) DIRECT THE DISPOSITION OF YOUR REMAINS.

THIS DOCUMENT REVOKES ANY PRIOR DURABLE POWER OF ATTORNEY FOR HEALTH CARE.

YOU SHOULD CAREFULLY READ AND FOLLOW THE WITNESSING PROCEDURE DESCRIBED AT THE END OF THIS FORM. THIS DOCUMENT WILL NOT BE VALID UNLESS YOU COMPLY WITH THE WITNESSING PROCEDURE.

IF THERE IS ANYTHING IN THIS DOCUMENT THAT YOU DO NOT UNDERSTAND, YOU SHOULD ASK A LAWYER TO EXPLAIN IT TO YOU.

YOUR AGENT MAY NEED THIS DOCUMENT IMMEDIATELY IN CASE OF AN EMERGENCY THAT REQUIRES A DECISION CONCERNING YOUR HEALTH CARE. EITHER KEEP THIS DOCUMENT WHERE IT IS IMMEDIATELY AVAILABLE TO YOUR AGENT AND ALTERNATE AGENTS OR GIVE EACH OF THEM AN EXECUTED COPY OF THIS DOCUMENT. YOU MAY ALSO WANT TO GIVE YOUR DOCTOR AN EXECUTED COPY OF THIS DOCUMENT.

DO NOT USE THIS FORM IF YOU ARE A CONSERVATEE UNDER THE LANTERMAN-PETRIS-SHORT ACT AND YOU WANT TO APPOINT YOUR CONSERVATOR AS YOUR AGENT. YOU CAN DO THAT ONLY IF THE APPOINTMENT DOCUMENT INCLUDES A CERTIFICATE OF YOUR ATTORNEY.

1. DESIGNATION OF HEALTH CARE AGENT.

I, _____

_____

_____

_____

(Insert your name and address)

do hereby designate and appoint _____

_____

_____

(Insert name, address, and telephone number of one individual only as your agent to make health care decisions for you. None of the following may be designated as your agent: (1) your treating health care provider, (2) a nonrelative employee of your treating health care provider, (3) an operator of a community care facility, (4) a nonrelative employee of an operator of a community care facility, (5) an operator of a residential care facility for the elderly, or (6) a nonrelative employee of an operator of a residential care facility for the elderly.)

as my agent to make health care decisions for me as authorized in this document. For the purpose of this document, "health care decision" means consent, refusal of consent, or withdrawal of consent to any care, treatment, service, or procedure to maintain, diagnose, or treat an individual's physical or mental condition.

2. CREATION OF DURABLE POWER OF ATTORNEY FOR HEALTH CARE.

By this document I intend to create a durable power of attorney for health care under Sections 4600 to 4752, inclusive, of the California Probate Code. This power of attorney is authorized by the Keen Health Care Agent Act and shall be construed in accordance with the provisions of Sections 4770 to 4779, inclusive, of the Probate Code. This power of attorney shall not be affected by my subsequent incapacity.

3. GENERAL STATEMENT OF AUTHORITY GRANTED.

Subject to any limitations in this document, I hereby grant to my agent full power and authority to make health care decisions for me to the same extent that I could make those decisions for myself if I had the capacity to do so. In exercising this authority, my agent shall make health care decisions that are consistent with my desires as stated in this document or otherwise made known to my agent, including, but not limited to, my desires concerning obtaining or refusing or withdrawing life-prolonging care, treatment, services, and procedures.

(If you want to limit the authority of your agent to make health care decisions for you, you can state the limitations in paragraph 4 ("Statement of Desires, Special Provisions, and Limitations") below. You can indicate your desires by including a statement of your desires in the same paragraph.)

Exhibit 7.6   California's Durable Power of Attorney for Health Care—*continued*

4. STATEMENT OF DESIRES, SPECIAL PROVISIONS, AND LIMITATIONS.

(Your agent must make health care decisions that are consistent with your known desires. You can, but are not required to, state your desires in the space provided below. You should consider whether you want to include a statement of your desires concerning life-prolonging care, treatment, services, and procedures. You can also include a statement of your desires concerning other matters relating to your health care. You can also make your desires known to your agent by discussing your desires with your agent or by some other means. If there are any types of treatment that you do not want to be used, you should state them in the space below. If you want to limit in any other way the authority given your agent by this document, you should state the limits in the space below. If you do not state any limits, your agent will have broad powers to make health care decisions for you, except to the extent that there are limits provided by law.)

In exercising the authority under this durable power of attorney for health care, my agent shall act consistently with my desires as stated below and is subject to the special provisions and limitations stated below:

(a) Statement of desires concerning life-prolonging care, treatment, services, and procedures:

_____

_____

_____

_____

_____

_____

_____

_____

_____

(b) Additional statement of desires, special provisions, and limitations:

_____

_____

_____

_____

_____

_____

_____

_____

---

(2) in the bank named as corporate personal representative (executor) in the will; (3) with the client (if it can be stored in a fireproof metal box or family safe at the client's home or office); or (4) filed with the clerk of the appropriate probate court as is allowed in some states. If the choice for safekeeping a will is to file it in the proper county probate court, anyone holding the receipt issued for the filed will and signed by the testator may obtain the original will while the testator is living. After the testator's death, the probate court retains the original will and gives copies to the personal representative (see U.P.C. § 2–515).

Keeping a will in a personal safe deposit box in a bank is less desirable because it makes the will less accessible. If the will is in a safe deposit box, probate proceedings may be delayed. Ordinarily, a person must have permission from the state tax commission representative or a county treasurer to open the safe deposit box belonging to another. Generally, when the safe deposit box is rented in the decedent's name only, bank representatives will seal the box when they are notified of the person's death after first removing the will if it is known that the box contains the will. Once the box is sealed, a court order is often required to open the box to remove the will (see the Petition and Order to Open Safe Deposit Box in Exhibit 7.7). After the will is removed, the box is resealed. Depending on the state in which the testator resides, one of the following procedures is advisable:

(You may attach additional pages if you need more space to complete your statement. If you attach additional pages, you must date and sign EACH of the additional pages at the same time you date and sign this document.)

5. INSPECTION AND DISCLOSURE OF INFORMATION RELATING TO MY PHYSICAL OR MENTAL HEALTH.

Subject to any limitations in this document, my agent has the power and authority to do all of the following:

(a) Request, review, and receive any information, verbal or written, regarding my physical or mental health, including, but not limited to, medical and hospital records.

(b) Execute on my behalf any releases or other documents that may be required in order to obtain this information.

(c) Consent to the disclosure of this information.

(If you want to limit the authority of your agent to receive and disclose information relating to your health, you must state the limitations in paragraph 4 ("Statement of Desires, Special Provisions, and Limitations") above.)

6. SIGNING DOCUMENTS, WAIVERS, AND RELEASES.

Where necessary to implement the health care decisions that my agent is authorized by this document to make, my agent has the power and authority to execute on my behalf all of the following:

(a) Documents titled or purporting to be a "Refusal to Permit Treatment" and "Leaving Hospital Against Medical Advice".

(b) Any necessary waiver or release from liability required by a hospital or physician.

7. AUTOPSY; ANATOMICAL GIFTS; DISPOSITION OF REMAINS.

Subject to any limitations in this document, my agent has the power and authority to do all of the following: (a) Authorize an autopsy under Section 7113 of the Health and Safety Code, (b) Make a disposition of a part or parts of my body under the Uniform Anatomical Gift Act (Chapter 3.5(commencing with Section 7150) of Part 1 of Division 7 of the Health and Safety Code), (c) Direct the disposition of my remains under Section 7100 of the Health and Safety Code.

(If you want to limit the authority of your agent to consent to an autopsy, make an anatomical gift, or direct the disposition of your remains, you must state the limitations in paragraph 4 ("Statement of Desires, Special Provisions, and Limitations") above.)

8. DURATION:

(Unless you specify otherwise in the space below, this power of attorney will exist for an indefinite period of time.)

This durable power of attorney for health care expires on _____

(Fill in this space ONLY if you want to limit the duration of this power of attorney.)

9. DESIGNATION OF ALTERNATE AGENTS.

(You are not required to designate any alternate agents but you may do so. Any alternate agent you designate will be able to make the same health care decisions as the agent you designated in paragraph 1, above, in the event that agent is unable or ineligible to act as your agent. If the agent you designated is your spouse, he or she becomes ineligible to act as your agent if your marriage is dissolved.)

If the person designated as my agent in paragraph 1 is not available or becomes ineligible to act as my agent to make a health care decision for me or loses the mental capacity to make health care decisions for me, or if I revoke that person's appointment or authority to act as my agent to make health care decisions for me, then I designate and appoint the following persons to serve as my agent to make health care decisions for me as authorized in this document, these persons to serve in the order listed below:

A. First Alternate Agent _____

_____

_____

(Insert name, address, and telephone number of first alternate agent)

B. Second Alternate Agent _____

_____

_____

(Insert name, address, and telephone number of second alternate agent)

1. If the testator lives in a state in which the county treasurer or the state tax representative does not have to be present when the safe deposit box is opened, the box should be rented in the names of the testator and the testator's spouse or another person as joint tenants. Whenever either spouse dies, the other may open the box. Widows, widowers, or single parents may want to name themselves and an adult child as the joint tenants for the same reason.

2. If the testator lives in a state in which the county treasurer or the state tax representative must be present, the testator should put the will in a safe deposit box rented in the name of the testator's spouse. Upon the testator's death, the testator's will is readily accessible.

Leaving the will with the testator's lawyer with whom the testator is familiar and has had a long time working relationship based on confidence and trust makes for easy access and convenient periodic review of the will whenever the testator wishes. The request for the review must be initiated by the testator and *not be solicited by the attorney or paralegal.*

ETHICAL ISSUE

10. NOMINATION OF CONSERVATOR OF PERSON.

(A conservator of the person may be appointed for you if a court decides that one should be appointed. The conservator is responsible for your physical care, which under some circumstances includes making health care decisions for you. You are not required to nominate a conservator but you may do so. The court will appoint the person you nominate unless that would be contrary to your best interests. You may, but are not required to, nominate as your conservator the same person you named in paragraph 1 as your health care agent. You can nominate an individual as your conservator by completing the space below.)

If a conservator of the person is to be appointed for me, I nominate the following individual to serve as conservator of the person

_____

_____

_____

_____

(Insert name and address of person nominated as conservator of the person)

11. PRIOR DESIGNATIONS REVOKED.

I revoke any prior durable power of attorney for health care.

DATE AND SIGNATURE OF PRINCIPAL
(YOU MUST DATE AND SIGN THIS POWER OF ATTORNEY)

I sign my name to this Statutory Form Durable Power of Attorney for Health Care on _____

(Date)

at _____, _____
(City)   (State)

_____
(You sign here)

(THIS POWER OF ATTORNEY WILL NOT BE VALID UNLESS IT IS SIGNED BY TWO QUALIFIED WITNESSES WHO ARE PRESENT WHEN YOU SIGN OR ACKNOWLEDGE YOUR SIGNATURE. IF YOU HAVE ATTACHED ANY ADDITIONAL PAGES TO THIS FORM, YOU MUST DATE AND SIGN EACH OF THE ADDITIONAL PAGES AT THE SAME TIME YOU DATE AND SIGN THIS POWER OF ATTORNEY.)

STATEMENT OF WITNESSES

(This document must be witnessed by two qualified adult witnesses. None of the following may be used as a witness: (1) a person you designate as your agent or alternate agent, (2) a health care provider, (3) an employee of a health care provider, (4) the operator of a community care facility, (5) an employee of an operator of a community care facility, (6) the operator of a residential care facility for the elderly, or (7) an employee of an operator of a residential care facility for the elderly. At least one of the witnesses must make the additional declaration set out following the place where the witnesses sign.)

(**READ CAREFULLY BEFORE SIGNING.** You can sign as a witness only if you personally know the principal or the identity of the principal is proved to you by convincing evidence.)

(To have convincing evidence of the identity of the principal, you must be presented with and reasonably rely on any one or more of the following:

(1) An identification card or driver's license issued by the California Department of Motor Vehicles that is current or has been issued within five years.

(2) A passport issued by the Department of State of the United States that is current or has been issued within five years.

(3) Any of the following documents if the document is current or has been issued within five years and contains a photograph and description of the person named on it, is signed by the person, and bears a serial or other identifying number:

(a) A passport issued by a foreign government that has been stamped by the United States Immigration and Naturalization Service.

(b) A driver's license issued by a state other than California or by a Canadian or Mexican public agency authorized to issue driver's licenses.

(c) An identification card issued by a state other than California.

(d) An identification card issued by any branch of the armed forces of the United States.

(4) If the principal is a patient in a skilled nursing facility, a witness who is a patient advocate or ombudsman may rely upon the representations of the administrator or staff of the skilled nursing facility, or of family members, as convincing evidence of the identity of the principal if the patient advocate or ombudsman believes that the representations provide a reasonable basis for determining the identity of the principal.

(Other kinds of proof of identity are not allowed.)

I declare under penalty of perjury under the laws of California that the person who signed or acknowledged this document is personally known to me (or proved to me on the basis of convincing evidence) to be the principal, that the principal signed or acknowledged this durable power of attorney in my presence, that the principal appears to be of sound mind and under no duress, fraud, or undue influence, that I am not the person appointed as agent by this document, and that I am not a health care provider, an employee of a health care provider, the operator of a community care facility, an employee of an operator of a community care facility, the operator of a residential care facility for the elderly, nor an employee of an operator of a residential care facility for the elderly.

Signature: _____   Residence Address: _____

Print Name: _____   _____

Date: _____

Signature: _____   Residence Address: _____

Print Name: _____   _____

Date: _____

(AT LEAST ONE OF THE ABOVE WITNESSES MUST ALSO SIGN THE FOLLOWING DECLARATION.)

I further declare under penalty of perjury under the laws of California that I am not related to the principal by blood, marriage, or adoption, and, to the best of my knowledge, I am not entitled to any part of the principal's estate upon the principal's death under a will now existing or by operation of law.

_____   _____
(Signature)   (Signature)

STATEMENT OF PATIENT ADVOCATE OR OMBUDSMAN

(If you are a patient in a skilled nursing facility, one of the witnesses must be a patient advocate or ombudsman. The following statement is required only if you are a patient in a skilled nursing facility—a health care facility that provides the following basic services: skilled nursing care and supportive care to patients whose primary need is for availability of skilled nursing care on an extended basis. The patient advocate or ombudsman must sign both parts of the "Statement of Witnesses" above AND must also sign the following statement.)

I further declare under penalty of perjury under the laws of California that I am a patient advocate or ombudsman as designated by the State Department of Aging and that I am serving as a witness as required by subdivision (e) of Section 4701 of the Probate Code.

_____
(Signature)

Source: Wolcotts Forms, available at most stationery, or office supply stores or by calling 1(800)421-2220.

Exhibit 7.7 Petition and Order to Open Safe Deposit Box

Approved, SCAO   JDC CODE: DBP, DBO

STATE OF MICHIGAN PROBATE COURT COUNTY OF	PETITION AND ORDER TO OPEN SAFE DEPOSIT BOX TO LOCATE WILL OR BURIAL DEED	FILE NO.

Estate of _____

PETITION

1. I am an interested party as _____ of decedent, who died _____.
   Heir, devisee, etc.   Date

2. _____ , as lessor, leased to decedent alone safe deposit box
   Name of bank, trust company, or safe deposit company

   number_____ , located at _____ in _____ in this county,
                                                Branch   City or township

   and the safe deposit box may contain decedent's will or a deed to a burial plot in which the decedent is to be interred.

3. I REQUEST that this court issue an order directing the lessor to permit _____
                                                                                                          Name

   to open and examine the contents of the safe deposit box for the purpose of locating and removing a will or burial deed only.

I declare that this petition has been examined by me and that its contents are true to the best of my information, knowledge, and belief.

_____
Date

_____   _____
Attorney signature   Petitioner signature

_____   _____
Name (type or print)   Bar no.   Name (type or print)

_____   _____
Address   Address

_____   _____
City, state, zip   Telephone no.   City, state, zip   Telephone no.

ORDER

IT IS ORDERED:

4. The above petition is granted and the lessor is ordered to permit _____
   to open and examine the above described safe deposit box in the presence of an officer or other authorized employee of the lessor.

5. Only the will of the decedent and/or the deed to a burial plot shall be removed from the box and shall be delivered by the lessor to the probate register of this court.

6. The lessor shall file the required certificate with the probate register of this court as to whether or not a will or deed is found.

_____   _____
Date   Judge   Bar no.

Do not write below this line - For court use only

MCL 205.209g; MSA 7.570(7)

PC 02 (11/88) PETITION AND ORDER TO OPEN SAFE DEPOSIT BOX TO LOCATE WILL OR BURIAL DEED

⚏ ASSIGNMENT 7.16

1. Explain your position on a living will, health care proxy, and a durable power of attorney for health care. Are you in favor of any of them or not? Has your state passed any of these directives?

2. In your state, must a doctor or hospital follow the patient's requests that are written in a living will? If they are required to honor the requests, are there any exceptions? Discuss these questions with your family physician.

3. Are patients who execute a living will in your state allowed to designate a proxy? Who would you select as your proxy? Why?

4. Must a patient hire a lawyer to make a valid living will, a health care proxy, or a durable power of attorney? If not, why might the patient choose to have a lawyer draft these directives?

5. If you execute a valid living will in your home state and then move your domicile (home) to another state that has no living will statute, will your wishes in the living will be honored in your new domicile? Explain.

6. Draft a living will. Obtain your state's living will form and compare it to your draft. How do they differ? How are they similar? Also draft and execute forms for a health care proxy and a durable power of attorney for health care and compare them to your state's forms.

KEY TERMS

Exordium clause
Revocatory clause
Residuary clause
Simultaneous death
  clause

Rule Against
  Perpetuities
Testimonium clause
Attestation clause

Notary public
Health care proxy
Attorney in fact

Durable power of
  attorney for health
  care

REVIEW QUESTIONS

1. What is the purpose of the following clauses of a will? Exordium, Revocatory, Residuary, Simultaneous death, Testimonium, and Attestation.

2. If a testator uses more than one name or alias when signing written statements or documents, is it necessary to include all such names in the will? Explain.

3. How does any person who wishes to donate body organs accomplish that purpose both within a will and using other nontestamentary documents?

4. According to your state statute, if any, who may make an anatomical gift in addition to the testator-decedent?

5. When a testator has numerous items of tangible personal property that she wishes to leave to an equal number of beneficiaries, how can she list these items and ensure that

they are distributed to the desired recipients without writing them directly into the will?

6. Confusion exists in the law of wills concerning the use of the words *issue, child, heirs, descendants,* and *adopted, natural, nonmarital,* and *stepchildren*. How would you avoid this confusion when drafting a client's will?

7. If there is no residuary clause in a will and not all the testator's estate is distributed to named beneficiaries, how and to whom would such property be distributed?

8. How are personal representatives appointed (authorized to act)? In general, what are the powers granted to them?

9. What is the difference between a property guardian and a conservator?

10. Does your state have any requirements for the placement of the testator's signature on the

will? Are initials, a nickname, or simply an "X" valid signatures in your state?

11. What is the Rule Against Perpetuities and does it affect both private and public trusts?

12. Which of the statutory requirements of a will is eliminated by the self-proving affidavit or the self-proved will?

13. What are the purposes of the three kinds of advance medical directives, i.e., the living will, the health care proxy, and the durable power of attorney for health care? How do these directives differ?

14. Where is the best place to keep your will?

CASE PROBLEMS

Problem 1

Hans Heidelberger died testate. He owned a considerable amount of property and made many specific legacies and devises to numerous relatives and friends. However, his will had no residue clause. In the will, Hans specifically disinherited by name his only two children. A number of very valuable stock certificates and bonds that Hans owned were not included as gifts in the will. Answer and explain the following:

A. Through what process and to whom will the valuable stocks and bonds be distributed?

B. Since Hans specifically stated that his two children were not to receive any of his estate, does that provision of the will bar them from receiving an interest in the stocks and bonds? See *Ferguson v. Croom,* 73 N.C.App. 316, 326 S.E.2d 373 (1985).

Problem 2

While on a weekend trip, Steward and Patricia Kincaid and their two minor children die simultaneously in a plane crash. Two adult children, Frank and Ruth, living at home, are the surviving family members. The major asset Stewart owned was a life insurance policy worth over $500,000 that was payable to Patricia as the primary beneficiary and then to all four children as the secondary beneficiaries. The Kincaids live in a state that has adopted the Uniform Simultaneous Death Act. Under the Act, when the insured policyholder (Stewart) and the beneficiary (Patricia) die simultaneously, the life insurance proceeds are distributed as if the insured has survived the beneficiary.

A. To whom would the life insurance proceeds be paid? How is this decision determined?

B. If all six members of the Kincaid family had died in the crash, to whom would the life insurance proceeds be paid? Explain. See *Keegan v. Keegan's Estate,* 157 N.J.Super.279, 384 A.2d 913 (1978).

C. If Stewart and Patricia had owned property in joint tenancy, how does the Uniform Simultaneous Death Act resolve the problem of dividing the jointly owned property?

CHAPTER EIGHT

INTRODUCTION TO TRUSTS

OBJECTIVES

After completing this chapter, you should be able to:

- Understand the basic terminology of trusts.
- Identify and define the essential elements of trusts.
- Identify the participants in the creation and operation of a trust and be able to explain their functions and roles.
- Explain the ways in which a trust terminates.

SCOPE OF THE CHAPTER

To practice successfully in the field of trusts, you must learn the terminology of trust law. Once you have developed a basic vocabulary, you must learn to identify the various kinds of trusts and understand their functions; you will then learn how to draft trust agreements that meet the client's objectives. After considerable experience working under the supervision of a trust attorney, a trust officer, or a trust administrator of a bank, you will be able to handle these matters with confidence. The purpose of this and the following chapter on trusts is to begin training you toward obtaining that confidence.

Although all states have adopted or enacted some form of probate code by statute, only a few states have trust codes. When appropriate, statutes of the states that have developed trust codes will be cited in this chapter. Another major authority often cited is the Restatement of Trusts. But for the most part, the American law of trusts is found in a combination of state statutes, judicial decisions, and the Restatement.

This chapter begins with the terminology associated with trusts and presents an example of how a trust works. You will be asked to identify the terms in an actual trust instrument. The remaining units of the chapter discuss the purposes of trusts; the elements of a trust, including the participants, their interests, selection, duties, and liabilities; the trust property; and the ways in which a trust terminates.

TERMINOLOGY RELATING TO TRUSTS

Before you can prepare a preliminary draft of a trust agreement, you must master the terminology of trusts. The major terms are defined as follows:

- *Trust.* A trust is a property arrangement in which real or personal property is transferred from the settlor to one or more trustees who hold the legal title to the property for the benefit of one or more beneficiaries who hold the equitable title (see the definitions below).

Example: Barry gives Charles $30,000 to hold and invest in trust for the benefit of William.

- *Settlor.* The person who creates a trust is the settlor, also called the creator, donor, grantor, or trustor. In the above example, Barry is the settlor.

- *Trustee.* The trustee (or trustees) is the person who holds the legal title to property in trust for the benefit of one or more beneficiaries. A trustee is a fiduciary and, as such, is required to perform all trustee duties according to the terms of the trust instrument with loyalty, honesty, and in good faith for the sole benefit of the beneficiary. In the above example, Charles is the trustee; he holds legal title to the property and must invest it for William's benefit.

- *Legal title.* Legal title is a title, enforceable in a court of law, that is the complete and absolute right of ownership and possession. In the law of trusts, the trustee, who manages and administers the trust, holds the legal title but without the benefits of the trust, i.e., without the right to receive financial profit from it. The benefits of the trust go to the beneficiary who holds this beneficial interest, called the equitable title.

Example: By deed, John transfers a farm to Mary to hold in trust for the benefit of Shirley. Mary is the trustee and has legal title. Shirley is the beneficiary and holds the equitable title.

■ *Beneficiary or "cestui que trust."* The beneficiary (also called the cestui que trust) is the person (or persons) having the enjoyment and benefit of property (real or personal) of which a trustee has the legal title. The beneficiary is said to hold equitable title (see below) to the trust property; i.e., the beneficiary has the right to the benefits (profits) of the trust. In the first example, William is the beneficiary and holds the equitable title.

■ *Equitable title.* In the law of trusts, equitable title, or beneficial title, refers to the right of the beneficiary to receive the benefits of the trust. Another way to view equitable title is that the beneficiary of the trust is regarded as the real "owner"; i.e., the beneficiary is entitled to the beneficial interest (the right to profit or benefit from the trust property), although the legal title to the property is held by another, the trustee (see Exhibit 8.1).

■ *Trust property.* The trust property is the real or personal property that the trustee holds subject to the right of one or more beneficiaries. The trust property in the example above is the farm transferred by John. Other names for trust property are the trust corpus, trust res, trust fund, trust estate, or subject matter of the trust.

■ *Trust instrument.* A trust instrument is any writing under which a trust is created, such as a will, trust agreement, or declaration of trust. These terms are defined as follows:

■ *Will.* A trust included in a will is called a testamentary trust.

■ *Trust agreement.* A written agreement (contract) between the settlor and trustee(s) that creates the trust and is signed by them (see Exhibit 8.2 later in this chapter).

■ *Declaration of trust.* A document that creates a trust in which the settlor is also the trustee. The document declares the creation of a trust in which the settlor names herself as trustee and retains the legal title but transfers the equitable title to the trust property to another person, the beneficiary. When the property being transferred to a trust is real estate, the method of transfer is often a deed of trust or a trust transfer deed. (For further discussion, see Chapter 9 and Exhibits 9.3 and 9.5).

■ *Revocable trust.* A revocable trust is a trust that the creator (settlor) has a right or power to revoke (cancel) or change at any time prior to death. Such a power must be expressly stated or reserved by the settlor in the trust instrument; otherwise trusts are generally irrevocable. Property placed in revocable trusts becomes a nonprobate asset and is therefore not subject to probate or creditors'

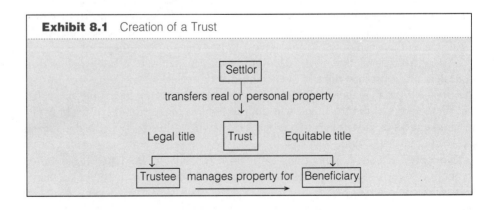

Exhibit 8.1 Creation of a Trust

claims. It is included in the decedent's gross estate, however, and is subject to federal estate tax.

■ *Irrevocable trust.* Once created, an irrevocable trust cannot be revoked or changed by the settlor. Property placed in an irrevocable trust is not only not subject to probate, but is also not subject to federal estate tax.

■ *Principal.* The principal is the capital or property of a trust as opposed to the income, which is the fruit of the capital, i.e., profits generated by the capital.

Example: The farm John transferred to Mary would be the principal, and the profits generated by the farm, say, $10,000, would be the income.

■ *Income.* Income is the gain measured in money that is generated from property (principal) and the appreciation and/or investment thereof.

■ *Income beneficiary.* The income beneficiary is the person or charity that is entitled to receive the income produced from trust property (principal).

■ *Restatement of Trusts.* In 1935, recognizing the need to simplify and clarify the American law of trusts, a group of trust experts working for the American Law Institute set forth the existing rules of law affecting trust creation and administration and included illustrations and comments. The completed work was called the Restatement of the American Law of Trusts. In 1959, the original Restatement was revised, and the revisions were incorporated into the Restatement (Second) of Trusts. In 1992, another revision was completed. Throughout the trust chapters of this book, relevant sections of the Restatement (Second) or (Third) of Trusts will be cited.

■ *Parol evidence rule.* The parol evidence rule is a general rule of contract law that oral or written evidence (testimony) is not allowed to vary, change, alter, or modify any of the terms or provisions of a written contract (agreement).

Example: After much deliberation and many changes by both parties, Lou and Bud write out and sign a contract. Later, Lou decides that the contract does not truly reflect what he and Bud had agreed. In court, neither Lou nor Bud could introduce oral or other written evidence (parol evidence) of the precontractual negotiations in hopes of changing the original written contract.

■ *Parol evidence.* Parol evidence is oral or written evidence.

■ **Statute of Frauds.** State laws that provide that no suit or civil action shall be maintained on certain classes of oral contracts unless the agreement is put in writing and signed by the party to be charged, i.e., the person being sued or an authorized agent of that person.

Statute of Frauds
State laws that provide that no suit or civil action shall be maintained on certain classes of oral contracts unless the agreement is put in writing and signed by the party to be charged, i.e., the person being sued or an authorized agent of that person.

Illustrating the Use of Trust Terminology

To better understand the meaning and use of trust terms, consider the following situation.

The Facts

Jack Alston Carter gives 600 shares of Successful Corp. stock to his financial adviser and best friend, Timothy Connor McEvoy, to hold in trust and to invest for the benefit of Jack's only child, Jill, and Jill's children, Mary and Joe. Named as successor trustee is Timothy's wife, Marilyn May McEvoy, who is also an accountant. This instrument (written agreement) provides that Timothy will pay Jill the income from the stock annually for the rest of her life and that after Jill's death the stock will be given to Jill's children (Jack Carter's grandchildren). Exhibit 8.2 presents the trust agreement establishing the Carter Trust.

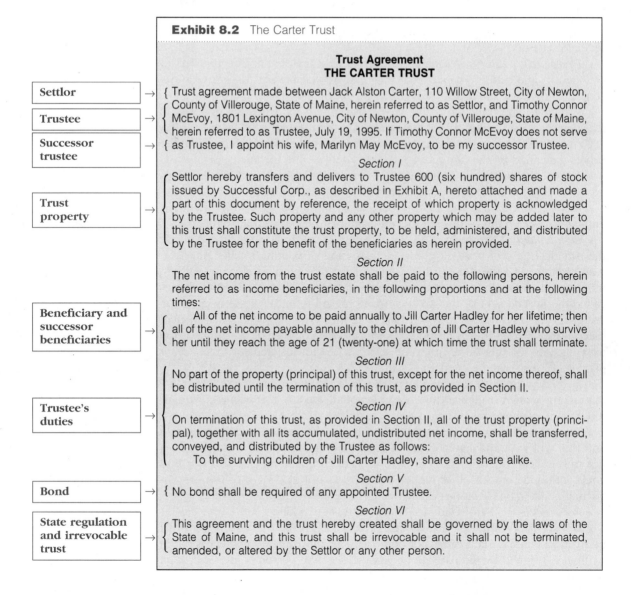

Exhibit 8.2 The Carter Trust

Trust Agreement
THE CARTER TRUST

Settlor →
Trustee →
Successor trustee →

Trust agreement made between Jack Alston Carter, 110 Willow Street, City of Newton, County of Villerouge, State of Maine, herein referred to as Settlor, and Timothy Connor McEvoy, 1801 Lexington Avenue, City of Newton, County of Villerouge, State of Maine, herein referred to as Trustee, July 19, 1995. If Timothy Connor McEvoy does not serve as Trustee, I appoint his wife, Marilyn May McEvoy, to be my successor Trustee.

Section I

Trust property →

Settlor hereby transfers and delivers to Trustee 600 (six hundred) shares of stock issued by Successful Corp., as described in Exhibit A, hereto attached and made a part of this document by reference, the receipt of which property is acknowledged by the Trustee. Such property and any other property which may be added later to this trust shall constitute the trust property, to be held, administered, and distributed by the Trustee for the benefit of the beneficiaries as herein provided.

Section II

The net income from the trust estate shall be paid to the following persons, herein referred to as income beneficiaries, in the following proportions and at the following times:

Beneficiary and successor beneficiaries →

    All of the net income to be paid annually to Jill Carter Hadley for her lifetime; then all of the net income payable annually to the children of Jill Carter Hadley who survive her until they reach the age of 21 (twenty-one) at which time the trust shall terminate.

Section III

No part of the property (principal) of this trust, except for the net income thereof, shall be distributed until the termination of this trust, as provided in Section II.

Section IV

Trustee's duties →

On termination of this trust, as provided in Section II, all of the trust property (principal), together with all its accumulated, undistributed net income, shall be transferred, conveyed, and distributed by the Trustee as follows:

    To the surviving children of Jill Carter Hadley, share and share alike.

Section V

Bond →

No bond shall be required of any appointed Trustee.

Section VI

State regulation and irrevocable trust →

This agreement and the trust hereby created shall be governed by the laws of the State of Maine, and this trust shall be irrevocable and it shall not be terminated, amended, or altered by the Settlor or any other person.

Review of Terminology

Jack Carter, the person who creates the trust, is the settlor, a word that comes from the old legal language of "settling the property in trust." He may also be called the trustor, donor, grantor, or creator. The trustee, the person to whom the property is transferred in trust for the benefit of another and who manages and administers the trust, is Timothy McEvoy. The legal title to the property is held by Timothy, the trustee, while the right to the use and benefit of the income from the property, i.e., the equitable title, is enjoyed (held) by the beneficiaries, Jill and Jill's children. Another name for the beneficiary is "cestui que trust," which means "he for whom certain property in trust is held." Property held in trust (in our case the 600 shares of stock) is called the trust property, trust fund, trust corpus, trust estate, trust res, or the subject matter of the trust. The trust instrument that created this contract or agreement between the settlor, Jack, and the trustee, Timothy, is the Carter Trust. The objectives of the Carter Trust are to vest in (transfer to) the trustee and the beneficiaries the property interests it

Exhibit 8.2 The Carter Trust—*continued*

In witness whereof, the Settlor, the Trustee, and the successor Trustee have executed this agreement on July 19, 1995, in the City of Newton, State of Maine.

Jack Alston Carter	Settlor
Timothy Connor McEvoy	Trustee
Marilyn May McEvoy	Successor Trustee

← **Signatures**

[Exhibit A omitted here]

STATE OF MAINE

COUNTY OF VILLEROUGE } SS.

On this 19th day of July, 1995, before me, a Notary Public within and for said County, personally appeared Jack Alston Carter, Timothy Connor McEvoy, and Marilyn May McEvoy, to me known to be the persons described in and who executed the foregoing instrument, and acknowledged that they executed the same as their free act and deed.

← **Notary**

Sally Madison	Notary Public

My commission expires June 1, 1998

Acceptance of the said Trust and Trust Property

I, Timothy Connor McEvoy, do hereby, as evidenced by my signature hereto, acknowledge the receipt of the trust property in said trust, to be held by me in escrow until the operation of the said trust as set forth, and I do accept said trust to be administered in my own name, for purposes therein set forth.

Dated this 19th day of July, 1995.

Timothy Connor McEvoy	Trustee

describes and to establish the parties' respective rights and duties. If the trustee fails to perform the terms of the trust or to act within the laws of the state (Maine), the beneficiaries are entitled to seek remedies from a court of equity.

A distinction is made between the principal, the property held in trust, and the income, which is earned by the principal and distributed by the trustee to the beneficiaries. In this case, the principal would be the shares of stock, and the income would be the profits in the form of dividends paid by the corporation to the shareholders. According to the trust instrument's provisions, Jill is entitled to the income (dividends) from the trust property (stock) for the duration of her life. Jill's children are entitled to a future interest called the **remainder** of the trust property, i.e., the principal (the stock) remaining after their mother dies. The children are called **remaindermen.** A trustee may also be given the power to distribute part of the trust property (the stock) to the beneficiaries on the basis of financial need or simply the wishes of the beneficiary. In this trust agreement, however, the trustee was not given this power. Powers are granted by the settlor when the trust is created (see Restatement [Second] of Trusts § 3 for definitions and § 37 for reservation and creation of powers).

Remainder
A future estate in real property that takes effect on the termination of a prior estate created by the same instrument at the same time.

Remainderman
A person entitled to the future fee simple estate after a particular smaller estate, e.g., a life estate, has expired.

⚖ ASSIGNMENT 8.1

Mary Schrader gives a four-unit apartment building to her only nephew, John Simmons, to hold in trust for the benefit of his children (Mary's grandnieces and grandnephews). The trust agreement provides that the monthly rents, less maintenance, insurance, taxes, and other expenses, are to be given to the children until John's death, when ownership of the property will pass to them.

1. Who is the cestui que trust in the above case? What other terms are used to identify such persons?
2. Explain the difference between income and principal in reference to this case.
3. Who is the settlor? What other terms are used to identify the settlor?
4. Who is the trustee? What is the trustee's function?

THE ESSENTIAL ELEMENTS OF A TRUST

Each trust has the following elements: (1) a settlor who must intend to create the trust; (2) one or more trustees who must be named to administer and manage the trust; (3) one or more beneficiaries who must be named to receive the benefits (income and/or principal) and enforce the trust; and (4) real or personal property that must be transferred to the trust. Since a trust differs from other legal transactions concerning property, such as a sale or gift of property, it is essential that all participants' interest in a trust be understood. After a sale or gift of property, the entire legal title to it passes from seller to buyer (sale) or from donor to donee (gift). But after the creation of a trust, title to property placed in the trust must pass to at least two persons. The title is "split" into legal title and equitable title. The trustee receives the legal title, and the beneficiary receives the equitable title. For this reason, the trustee and the beneficiary are indispensable to the existence of a trust. In fact, a trust does not begin until legal and equitable interests (title) in specific property are vested in different individuals or sets of individuals. The trust relationship commences when the separation of legal and equitable title takes place; see *In re Coutts' Will,* 260 N.Y.128, 183 N.E.200 (1931). Once a trust is created, the settlor is not so important. Beyond furnishing property for the trust, the settlor drops out of the picture during the life of the trust unless the same person is both the settlor and either the trustee or beneficiary of the trust. In certain circumstances, the settlor can also be both the sole trustee and one of several beneficiaries of the trust.

Another feature that distinguishes a trust from a sale is that consideration, i.e., payment to the settlor based on the trust property's reasonable value, is not a requirement for the creation of a trust. In other words, when property is placed in trust for the beneficiary, the settlor does not require the beneficiary to pay for the transfer. A trust is a gratuitous transfer of property; consideration is not necessary (Restatement [Second] of Trusts §§ 28, 29).

The Settlor: The Creator of the Trust

The settlor is the person who creates the trust. When a trust is created, it is common practice to execute a writing called a trust agreement or declaration of trust. Provided the settlor manifests a clear intent to establish a trust, i.e., the settlor expressly imposes a duty on the trustee with respect to specific property, no particular words are necessary to create the trust so long as the trust purpose, the property, and the beneficiaries are designated (Restatement [Second] of Trusts §§ 23, 24). A common trust provision is "to X, as trustee, to have and hold under the trust's provisions hereinafter set forth," but the settlor could establish a valid trust by giving property "to X for the benefit of Y." Use of the word "trust" or "trustee" is helpful but not mandatory, as illustrated by the case of *Mahoney v. Leddy,* 126 Vt. 98, 223 A.2d 456 (1966), in which Terese Egan signed a paper stating that "in the event of my death" certain stock held in her name "belongs to Miss Peck." This was held to be a trust. Also, as noted above, the settlor's creation of the trust is not invalidated by its gratuitous nature; i.e., the beneficiary is not required to give the settlor money, service, or any other consideration in return for the settlor's act of establishing the trust.

⚏ ASSIGNMENT 8.2

Shirley gives Joanna $30,000 cash to hold and invest for the benefit of Carl. A trust is created even though the words "trust" and "trustee" were not used in its creation. The trust property is transferred as a gift. Neither Joanna nor Carl has purchased the property, so neither of them pays for receiving it.

1. Name the settlor, beneficiary, trustee, and trust corpus.
2. How does this trust differ from a sale or a gift?

"Who may be a settlor?" What qualifications or limitations exist that allow courts to enforce the trust the settlor creates? To be a settlor, a person must own a transferable interest in property, have the right or power of disposing of a property interest, and have the ability to make a valid contract. Only those who have contractual capacity, i.e., who are not insane, intoxicated, or minors, can make an outright transfer of property into a trust (Restatement [Second] of Trusts §§ 18–22). Thus, the limitations placed on persons to make contracts, wills, and other legal transactions are also limitations on settlors. Unless a person meets the qualifications, he cannot create a trust, and any attempt to do so is voidable. In addition, even though a person is qualified to make a trust, if the property transfer is accomplished through duress, fraud, or undue influence, the settlor may avoid or cancel the trust.

Once the settlor intentionally creates a trust, assuming he does not appoint himself trustee or beneficiary, the settlor has no further rights, duties, or liabilities with respect to the trust administration.

Example: Harding owns a farm, Blackacre, which he conveys by deed to Barrett in trust for the benefit of Stewart. Harding is the settlor and retains no interest. He has no further powers, duties, rights, or liabilities concerning the trust administration. Barrett is the trustee and has legal title. Stewart is the beneficiary and has equitable title. Blackacre is the trust property.

At the termination of the trust, the settlor may have the right to the return of the trust property, i.e., the settlor's (grantor's) reversionary interest (see Chapter 2).

While alive, the settlor may expressly retain the power to revoke or cancel the trust and recover the trust property. When the settlor has such a power, the trust is called a **revocable trust** (Restatement [Second] of Trusts § 330). When the settlor does not expressly reserve this power, the trust is **irrevocable.**

At first, the settlor may want the trust to be revocable in order to have the opportunity to see how well it works and what changes, if any, are necessary before the trust is made irrevocable. Eventually, the settlor may wish to make

Revocable trust
A trust that the settlor has a right or power to cancel or revoke.
Irrevocable trust
A trust that may not be revoked by the settlor after its creation.

the trust irrevocable, since the retention of control over the trust arrangement, including the power to revoke, exposes the settlor to tax liability for the trust income and principal. Generally, the settlor must make the trust irrevocable and retain only limited powers over the trust before death; if these requirements are not met, the trust income and principal will be included in the settlor's gross estate and will be subject to estate and inheritance taxes.

The Settlor as Trustee or Beneficiary

Although customarily three parties participate in the creation of a trust, the law demands the involvement of at least two. The same person cannot be the settlor, trustee, and beneficiary, but the same person could be the settlor and trustee, or the settlor and beneficiary. Thus, a settlor may appoint herself sole trustee and legally transfer the trust property from herself personally to herself as trustee using a declaration of trust document.

Example: Harding owns 1,000 shares of IBC, Inc. stock and declares himself trustee of the stock for the benefit of Stewart. Harding is the settlor and trustee who retains legal title. Stewart is the beneficiary and has equitable title. The IBC, Inc. stock is the trust property.

A settlor may also convey property in trust to another for her own benefit, i.e., the settlor is the beneficiary.

Example: Harding owns a farm that he conveys by deed to Barrett in trust for the benefit of himself (Harding). Harding is the settlor and beneficiary with an equitable interest in the farm. Barrett is the trustee and has legal title. The farm is the trust property.

Notice, however, that the same person cannot be both the sole trustee and the sole beneficiary. The reason is that a trust exists when the trustee has a fiduciary obligation to administer the trust property for the benefit of another and when someone (the beneficiary) exists to enforce that obligation. Therefore, a sole trustee cannot also be a sole beneficiary because there would be no one to enforce the trust. If the sole trustee, who holds legal title to the trust property, acquires the equitable title of the sole beneficiary as well, the legal and equitable titles merge, and the trust ends. Where the sole trustee is also one of several beneficiaries, or the sole beneficiary is also one of several trustees, the legal and equitable titles do not merge, and the trust is valid (Restatement [Second] of Trusts § 99). Thus, the settlor can name himself sole trustee and co-beneficiary or co-trustee and sole beneficiary, but not sole trustee and sole beneficiary (see also the discussion under Co-Trustees below).

Example: A settlor, Ray Norton, signs a declaration of trust naming himself trustee of four stock certificates for the benefit of himself and his wife, Vera. Because he holds complete legal title but only partial equitable title to the trust property, Ray is allowed to fill all three of these roles (settlor, trustee, and co-beneficiary) while Vera is alive. When Vera dies, however, Ray holds the entire equitable as well as legal title. This merger of title in one person ends the trust.

The Trustee: The Fiduciary and Administrator of the Trust

The trustee is the participant in a trust who holds a legal title to the trust property for the benefit of the beneficiary. The trustee is a fiduciary and, as such, owes fiduciary duties to act honestly and loyally for the sole benefit of the beneficiary. This fiduciary relationship between the trustee and the beneficiary is identified and defined in the case of *Scotti's Drive In Restaurants, Inc. v. Mile High-Dart*

In Corp., 526 P.2d 1193 (Wyo. 1974). Normally, the settlor has the right or power to select the trustee, but this right may be given to the beneficiary or to another; failure of the settlor to name a trustee is not fatal to the trust, however, because in such cases the court will appoint a trustee.

Natural or Legal Person as Trustee

Generally, the trustee selected is a person, either natural (e.g., settlor, family member, attorney, or financial adviser) or legal (e.g., a private corporation authorized to act as a trustee by its charter and state statute, such as a trust company or bank). If a trust is created to last a considerable length of time, it may be best to select a corporate trustee (bank) to assure continued reliable management. (But see the discussion of the Rule Against Perpetuities.) As a matter of practicality, settlors often choose a bank as the trustee or co-trustee because of the experience and expertise of bank trust officers. The cost of using such trustees is always an important consideration. Corporate trustees make their published fee schedules available to attract prospective clients.

Any natural person having the legal capacity to hold, own, and administer property may receive trust property as a trustee. However, even though minors, intoxicated individuals, and mentally incompetent persons can take and own property, they lack the capacity to make a valid contract; therefore, they cannot properly administer a trust since their contracts are voidable (revocable). In other words, if such persons make contracts as part of their duties while administering a trust, they can avoid, disaffirm, or cancel their contracts because the contracts are voidable. Therefore, such trustees will ordinarily be removed and a new trustee appointed by the equity court on request of the beneficiary.

In most cases the settlor selects the trustee on the basis of the person's proven integrity, ability, experience, and, of course, capacity. If there is a question about the selected person's fitness or capacity, the equity court either ratifies (confirms) or denies the selection. Therefore, in some instances, the settlor is considered to have only nominated a trustee; selection is the court's prerogative (see Cal. Prob. Code § 17200). But the most important rule of trust law concerning the selection of a trustee is that the court will not allow a trust to fail (neither commence nor terminate) for lack of a trustee. Thus, the court has the power and authority to appoint or replace a trustee if any of the following events occurs:

1. No one is nominated as trustee.
2. The trustee dies.
3. The trustee is incompetent.
4. The named trustee declines the position.
5. No successor is named as a replacement in the provisions of the trust.

Example: Larry Parks, a natural person, has capacity (or ability in the legal sense) to take, hold, own, and administer property for himself; therefore he can do the same for the benefit of someone else in a trust. Before a trust is created, however, Larry becomes mentally ill (insane). Sally Parks, Larry's sister, transfers a substantial sum of money to Larry in trust to hold and invest for the benefit of their father, Samuel. If the beneficiary, Samuel, petitioned (filed an application to) the equity court and established that Larry was insane, the court would either decline to appoint Larry trustee or refuse to ratify his appointment, even though the settlor, Sally, named Larry the trustee. Here the court would do the former. In this case a trust is created, but the named trustee is incapable of administering the trust. As in this case and most other instances of the trustee's failure to qualify, fairness to the beneficiary demands that the trust be allowed to continue. Since Larry can and does hold legal title to the trust property but cannot be trustee, most states' statutes compel the transfer of the title from the incompetent (Larry) to the new trustee appointed by the court. This is accomplished by compelling Larry to transfer the trust property, i.e., the money, to the new trustee.

Example: The trust department of the Lincoln National Bank, a private corporation, is composed of persons who offer their services to the public as professional trustees. Since the bank's charter enables it to act as a trustee, it does so through these employees. Betty White transfers all her I.B.M. stock to the bank to hold and manage for the benefit of her son, Willard. The bank's trust employees would perform this service for an agreed-on fee.

Example: Ella Cunningham, age 80, transfers part of the assets of her estate in trust to her favorite niece, Paula, age 17. Ella is the beneficiary. Paula makes and signs a contract as trustee, but then she decides not to honor her obligation, as she may do, being a minor. Since minors make voidable contracts, they may choose to avoid or cancel them. If Paula's act of avoiding the contract dissatisfies Ella, Ella may request the court to remove Paula as trustee and appoint a successor trustee.

Example: Darnella Swanson, a single parent, appoints Newton Marshall, her attorney, trustee of a trust for the benefit of her son, Roy. Newton sells some of his own property to the trust, buys other trust property for his family, and adds the money to his own account instead of the trust account. Because of these serious breaches of his fiduciary duties, Darnella can have Newton replaced as trustee.

Co-Trustees

As noted earlier, the same person cannot be both sole trustee and sole beneficiary, thus holding both legal and equitable title, because that would defeat the separation-of-title mechanism inherent in every trust. A settlor may, however, be the sole trustee and one of several beneficiaries or a co-trustee and the sole beneficiary of the trust (Restatement [Second] of Trusts § 99). Exhibit 8.3 illustrates various combinations of single and multiple participants that result in the creation of valid or invalid trusts.

Ownership of trust property by co-trustees has always been construed as joint tenancy of that property. Under common law rules, a settlor could become one of the co-trustees only by transferring the property to another person (a straw man) who had agreed to receive and immediately retransfer legal title to the trust property to the group of co-trustees of which the settlor was a member. The straw man transaction was necessary because the owner of property could not confer joint tenancy on himself and another (because the tenancy so created would lack the unities of time and title; see Chapter 2). The straw man, being a third person, could create a valid joint tenancy. In many jurisdictions today, however, a settlor may convey directly to himself and the co-trustee(s) and create a joint tenancy (Restatement [Second] of Trusts § 100).

Example: Clive Yarborough plans to create a trust for the two Vietnamese war orphans adopted by his friends Laurence and Victoria Sutton, making Laurence and Victoria co-trustees with himself. The trust property is Clive's farm. In his state, Clive may make himself trustee and appoint Laurence and Victoria co-trustees at the same time without having to convey the farm to another person (the straw man) who would then reconvey it to the three as joint tenants.

Exhibit 8.3 Creation of Valid or Invalid Trusts

Valid Trust Combinations

Settlor	Trustee or Co-Trustees	Beneficiary or Co-Beneficiaries
Tom	Mary	Joe
Tom	Tom and Mary	Joe
Tom	Mary	Tom and Joe
Tom	Tom and Mary	Tom and Joe
Tom	Tom	Joe
Tom	Mary	Tom
Tom	Tom and Mary	Tom
Tom	Tom	Tom and Joe

Invalid Trust Combinations

Tom	Tom	Tom
Tom	Mary	Mary

These last two examples do not create a valid trust because the same individual cannot be the sole trustee and the sole beneficiary; that would cause the legal and equitable titles to be merged and would automatically terminate the trust.

The following rules generally apply when co-trustees have been appointed and decisions concerning the administration of the trust must be made:

- If there are two trustees, both must agree on any action concerning trust property.
- If there are more than two trustees, the general rule is that all must agree, but the trust document determines whether action can be taken only by unanimous vote, majority vote, or even by one trustee (usually the settlor-trustee) acting alone (Restatement [Second] of Trusts § 194). Some states allow a majority vote when more than two people are co-trustees.

Acceptance or Disclaimer of Trusteeship

Normally, the settlor will name a trustee, but if the settlor does not, a trustee can be appointed by a court (Restatement [Second] of Trusts § 108). Since the trust imposes fiduciary duties on the trustee, the trustee has the right to renounce or reject (disclaim) the trust. The person named as trustee is free to choose whether to accept or reject the appointment by words or conduct.

In the absence of a definite rejection or **disclaimer,** acceptance will be presumed, and any positive act such as taking possession of the trust property will confirm the trustee's acceptance. Likewise, the failure of a trustee to do or say anything to indicate acceptance within a reasonable length of time will be construed as a disclaimer.

Example: Lydia Metaxis creates a testamentary trust for her grandchildren, naming her friend, Isabel Leclerc, trustee. Isabel feels that she would be unable to carry out the task of administration. Therefore she executes a disclaimer of responsibility as trustee and files it with the probate court handling Lydia's will. The court would then appoint a different trustee. Isabel's disclaimer follows (Exhibit 8.4).

Once disclaimed, a trusteeship cannot thereafter be accepted. The disclaimer does not affect the validity of the trust, however, because a court will appoint a successor trustee if the settlor had not provided for one. The best way to eliminate

Disclaimer
The right a person has to refuse or reject appointment as trustee of a trust.

Exhibit 8.4   Sample Disclaimer

I, Isabel Andrewes Leclerc, named as trustee under the will of Lydia Metaxis, deceased, respectfully decline to act as said trustee.

In witness whereof, I have executed this instrument at the City of Puentavilla, Tarpon County, Florida.

_____

Isabel Andrewes Leclerc

January 16, 1995

---

any doubt of the trustee's acceptance or rejection is for the trustee to deliver to the proper person, e.g., the settlor, a signed document of the decision to accept or disclaim.

Removal or Resignation of Trustee

Trusteeship is a solemn undertaking. After accepting the duties outlined in a trust, a trustee can be relieved of the duties and office by the settlor, by death, by removal by the equity or probate court, or by resignation (Restatement [Second] of Trusts §§ 103, 104, 105, 106). Resignation is an exercise of the trustee's own discretion and must be accepted by the proper court (a court of equity or probate court). Removal of the trustee is an exercise of the court's discretion when it believes the continuation of acts by the trustee would be detrimental to the beneficiary's interests (Restatement [Second] of Trusts § 107). Grounds for the removal of a trustee include:

- Lack of capacity.
- Commission of a serious breach of trust.
- Refusal to give bond when bond is required.
- Refusal to account for expenditures, investments, and the like.
- Commission of a crime, particularly one involving dishonesty.
- Long or permanent absence from the state.
- Showing of favoritism to one or more beneficiaries.
- Unreasonable failure to cooperate with the co-trustee if one exists (Restatement [Second] of Trusts § 107).

Mere friction between the trustee and the beneficiary is not sufficient grounds for removal. Remember, too, that even if a trustee resigns or is appropriately removed, the court will appoint a new (successor) trustee as a replacement unless the trust document provides for a successor.

Unless required by a state statute, by terms of the trust, or by an order of a court of equity, a trustee is not required to take an oath that he will faithfully discharge the duties or to secure a certificate of authority from a court. Whether or not an oath is required, the trustee still has a fiduciary duty to the beneficiary. In some jurisdictions, becoming a trustee depends on performance of one or more of these acts, and failure to perform the act prevents the person from assuming the office. In other jurisdictions, failure of the trustee to perform a required qualifying act does not prevent assumption of the office, but is considered a breach of trust that will allow the court to remove the trustee at the request of a beneficiary and to appoint another trustee (Restatement [Second] of Trusts § 107).

Powers of the Trustee

The powers of the trustees are determined by the following:

- The express authority granted by the terms of the trust instrument.
- The statutes in the state in which the trust is established; for an example of the powers granted by a typical state statute, see N.Y. E.P.T.L. § 11–1.1.

The powers granted to the trustee by the trust document are often purposely broad to give the trustee the flexibility, like that of the owner-settlor, to manage and administer the trust property. It is common, in modern trusts, to give the trustee wide discretionary powers to determine and resolve problems that the settlor could not have foreseen.

Example: By the terms of the trust, Hannah, the trustee, is given discretionary power to "use and disburse principal as well as income if, in the opinion of the trustee, it is necessary for the education or medical care of the beneficiary."

Powers granted to a trustee in the trust instrument frequently include any or all of the following:

1. To sell assets, including real estate, and reinvest the proceeds.
2. To lease or rent trust property.
3. To carry on a business.
4. To vote stock and give proxies.
5. To lend or borrow money, including pledging or mortgaging trust property.
6. To hire attorneys, stockbrokers, accountants, and insurance agents.
7. To compromise, settle, contest, or arbitrate claims and disputes.
8. To subdivide, exchange, develop, or improve real property.
9. To do anything necessary to carry out any of the above.
10. To do whatever a legal owner of property can do subject to the required performance of the trustee to act as a fiduciary.

Duties of the Trustee

In general, a trust does not exist unless specific actions and enforceable duties are placed on the trustee, such as a duty to manage the property in some manner or to exercise discretion or judgment (Restatement [Second] of Trusts § 25). The settlor's mere order to the trustee to hold the property in trust without any direction as to its use or distribution does not suffice to create a valid trust; it creates, instead, a passive trust that the law declares void (see Chapter 9).

Example: In his will, George, the decedent, gives $100,000 to Howard expressing the hope that Howard will use the money "for religious and family purposes." Such phraseology does not indicate that George is "settling" or creating a trust. He has not indicated the duties Howard must perform as the trustee of an active trust. George might well have intended the $100,000 as a gift to Howard with "advice" on its use.

When a trust is created, it establishes a fiduciary relationship of trust and confidence between the trustee and beneficiary, in which the trustee, as the fiduciary, must faithfully follow the directions of the trust and be loyal to the beneficiary throughout its duration. Acting as a fiduciary, the trustee has the following duties:

1. *Duty of performance and due care (Restatement [Second] of Trusts § 169).*
- The trustee's main duty is to carry out the terms and purpose of the trust. The trustee is personally liable, i.e., must pay out of personal funds, for any loss

sustained by failure to perform the duties of the trust unless the failure can be justified. There is no personal liability for loss sustained if the trustee has exercised the degree of care that a reasonable person would exercise under the circumstances.

■ The trustee cannot delegate the performance of personal duties (Restatement [Third] of Trusts § 171). The case of *U.A. of Joliet v. First National Bank of Joliet,* 93 Ill.App.3d 890, 49 Ill.Dec. 250, 417 N.E.2d 1077 (1981), illustrates a trustee's inability to delegate duties.

■ The trustee has a fiduciary duty to use ordinary, reasonable skill, prudence, and diligence in the administration of the trust and in the performance of trust duties (Restatement [Second] of Trusts § 174). In other words, the trustee must use the care a reasonable, prudent person would exercise under the circumstances. In the case of *Costello v. Costello,* 209 N.Y. 252, 103 N.E. 148 (1913), the court defined a trustee's responsibility as follows: ". . . trustees are bound in the management of all matters of the trust to act in good faith and employ such vigilance, diligence, and prudence as in general, prudent men of discretion and intelligence in like matters employ in their affairs." The law does not hold a trustee who acts in accord with such a rule responsible for errors in judgment.

Example: Nathan Maxwell transfers 100 shares of stock to William Mann in trust to hold and invest for the benefit of Nathan's invalid mother, Marilyn.

Whether a trustee, such as William Mann in the example above, receives compensation for his services or not, he must use at least ordinary care, skill, prudence, and diligence in the execution (performance) of the trust. The degree of ability required may be increased if William actually has greater than normal abilities or if he, as trustee, represented to the settlor that he possessed unusual capabilities before the trust was created. Therefore, professional fiduciaries, such as banks and trust companies with specialists in various areas of trust work, may be held to a higher standard because they give a sense of security to a trust, because of their claims of special expertise and because of the rule that more is expected of a trustee who has a special skill or knowledge of the subject. At the very least, professional fiduciaries must measure up to the standard of skill and prudence of the average, ordinary corporate trustee located in the community where the trust is created.

The law would not hold William, as trustee, responsible for every error in judgment he might make, but he is obliged to use the care and skill of an ordinary capable person who is charged with conserving a trust. If William disregards this obligation, he cannot defend himself against liability on the grounds that he acted in good faith or did not intentionally misuse the trust property. In addition, William, as trustee, cannot disclaim any personal liability on the grounds that he was simply following the practices that the settlor had always followed when ordinary skill and prudence would dictate another course.

🏛 ASSIGNMENT 8.3

In performing the following acts, is William Mann violating his duty of reasonable care of the trust property? Why or why not?

1. William receives a dividend on one of the shares of stock in the amount of $90. He uses this to buy a birthday present for Marilyn.
2. One of the stocks William holds is performing poorly. On the advice of another executive in the corporation where William works, he sells this stock and invests in

Goldbrick, Inc., which subsequently falls in value below the level of the stock formerly owned.

....

2. *Duty of loyalty (Restatement [Third] of Trusts § 170).*

▪ The trustee is not permitted to profit personally from her position as trustee, other than to receive the compensation allowed by contract or by law. The loyalty duty applies to all persons in a fiduciary capacity.

Example: The will of Colin Wilcox appoints Judith Ames trustee of a $150,000 business, the Wilcox Bakery, for the benefit of Colin's minor sons, Reynold and Richard.

Loyalty to the beneficiaries of the trust is one of the most important duties of a trustee. The duty of loyalty means that the trustee is obliged to act solely in the best interests of the beneficiary. A disloyal act would include any transaction by Judith as trustee that creates a **conflict of interest** between herself and the beneficiaries of the trust, or between the beneficiaries and third persons. A conflict of interest is the creation of circumstances by the fiduciary (trustee) in the administration of the trust that benefits someone other than the beneficiary, thereby establishing the conflict of interest. The other party benefited is most often the trustee, but it could be any person. In the case above, a disloyal act by Judith is not automatically void. The beneficiaries may elect to disaffirm and avoid the transactions or to treat them as legal and binding. As trustee, Judith must avoid placing herself in a position where her personal interest or that of a third person might conflict with the interest of the beneficiaries.

> **Conflict of interest**
> Divided loyalties (it would be a conflict of interest for an attorney to represent both sides in a dispute).

The trustee must act in the sole and exclusive interests of the beneficiaries. For example, *buying or leasing trust property to herself, or profiting from the sale of her own property to the trust as an investment, would be acts of disloyalty* by Judith. It does not matter that Judith acted in good faith or with honest intentions, or that the beneficiaries suffered no loss because of her disloyal acts. It is also immaterial that the trustee has made no profit for herself from her disloyal transaction, even though in most cases she does benefit in some manner. When responsible for such disloyal acts, the trustee (Judith), may be held liable for the amount of gain to herself or a third person, and the court may even remove her from the trusteeship by decree. These quite strict standards are designed not only to prevent actual unfair dealing but also to keep trustees initially from getting into positions of conflict of interest.

> **ETHICAL ISSUE**
> ◄

⚏ ASSIGNMENT 8.4

Judith Ames performs the following acts in the course of trusteeship. Are they disloyal? Are they voidable? What additional facts, if any, would you need in order to answer these questions?

1. Judith buys a display case from the bakery, paying fair market value for it. Reynold was fully aware that she did this.
2. Colin's executor is preparing to sell some real estate as instructed by the will. Judith causes one piece of property to be withheld so that a friend may buy it. Her friend pays the amount of the property's appraised value.
3. As trustee, Judith persuades the bakery manager to sign a contract to buy flour from the Hanrahan Co. for the next year. Hanrahan does not offer the lowest contract price for flour, nor is there any evidence that its product is better than that of

other companies; however, the Ameses and the Hanrahans have been friends for many years.

....

3. *Duty to take possession of and preserve trust property (Restatement [Second] of Trusts § 176).*

- The trustee has a duty to take possession of and preserve the trust property from possible loss or damage, and if the property includes outstanding debts, the trustee has the duty to collect them, *but the trustee must not add the money collected to her own bank account.*

ETHICAL ISSUE
`............>`

Example: John Yeats creates an *inter vivos* trust consisting of stocks, bonds, and items of personal property for the benefit of his son, Roderick. He names as trustee his sister, Marcela, who is an attorney.

In accordance with the terms of the trust instrument, Marcela has the duty to take possession of the property. If the trust property consists of money or goods and chattels, she should take immediate possession of the chattels and open a separate fiduciary bank account for the cash. Such an account should be identified as a trust account, i.e., "Marcela Yeats, Trustee for Roderick Yeats." Since Marcela handles funds for the benefit of Roderick, she has a duty to keep the trust property separate from her own individual property and from property held for other trusts. Since the trust property includes such property as promissory notes, bonds, shares of stock, and deeds to real estate, Marcela should take possession of the documents representing title (ownership) to such property and place them in a safe deposit box registered in the name of the trust. If you are

ETHICAL ISSUE
`............>`

a paralegal working with Marcela, you should remind her that *all trust property should be clearly distinguished from Marcela's own property.* If it is not, Marcela will have the burden of proving which commingled property belongs to whom and might even lose her own property in the process if a court rules that the mixture of trust and personal property belongs to the trust. Possession is usually obtained from the settlor, or, if the trust was created in a will (a testamentary trust), from the named executor or personal representative. Failing to act promptly and reasonably in securing possession of the trust property makes the trustee personally liable for any loss caused by such negligence.

In brief, Marcela has the duty to perform whatever acts a reasonably prudent businesswoman would deem necessary in order to preserve and protect the trust property. Such acts would include placing cash in a trust account; filing legal documents such as deeds and mortgages; depositing important legal papers, documents, and valuable personal property in an appropriate place such as a safe deposit box; paying taxes on realty and maintaining that property in reasonable condition to avoid deterioration; transferring shares of stock to the appropriate person's name; maintaining adequate insurance coverage on all appropriate trust property; and the like.

⚖ ASSIGNMENT 8.5

Are the following acts examples of a violation of the trustee's duty to preserve and protect the trust property? What additional facts would you want to know to assist you in answering the questions?

1. Marcela withdraws a substantial part of the trust fund from its bank account and gives it to a friend to invest. Her friend is not a professional investor, and the advice proves shortsighted financially. All the investments end as losses.

2. Same facts as in question 1 above except the friend's advice is very lucky. The earnings on the investments suggested by Marcela's friend triple the trust account.
3. A building on which Marcela holds title for Roderick has a defective staircase. While visiting the premises, Flora Atkinson falls down the stairs and injures herself. Was Marcela's neglecting to repair the staircase a breach of her fiduciary duty.

....

4. Duty to invest the trust property (Restatement [Third] of Trusts §§ 181, 207, and 227).

▪ The trustee is required to invest the money or property in enterprises or transactions that will yield an income to the trust.

Example: Carmine diGrazia, a widower living in Maryland, created a trust of $100,000 and his interest in a building construction business in his will for the benefit of his two sons, Paola and Carlo. He appoints as trustee his cousin, Catarina, who is his accountant and a newly naturalized citizen. Carmine dies and Catarina assumes trusteeship.

Catarina must make the trust property productive by investing it in income-producing investments as soon as possible. Delay could constitute negligence and make her liable for any loss. Of course, Catarina's investment policies may be controlled by the authority granted her by Carmine, by the court, and by statute. Today some states establish by statute a list of specific types of investments that may or must be made by the trustee. The law of the state of Maryland gives examples of the statutory investments fiduciaries may make.

Md. Code Ann. § 15–106 Lawful Investments

(a) *List of lawful investments*—The following investments shall be lawful investments for any person:

(1) Debentures issued by federal intermediate credit banks or by banks for cooperatives;

(2) Bonds issued by federal land banks or by the Federal Home Loan Bank Board;

(3) Mortgages, bonds, or notes secured by a mortgage or deed of trust, or debentures issued by the Federal Housing Administration;

(4) Obligations of national mortgage associations;

(5) Shares, free-share accounts, certificates of deposit, or investment certificates of any insured financial institution, as defined in § 13–301(g) of this article;

(6) Bonds or other obligations issued by a housing authority pursuant to the provisions of Article 44A of the Code, or issued by any public housing authority or agency in the United States, when such bonds or other obligations are secured by a pledge of annual contributions to be paid by the United States or any agency of the United States;

(7) Obligations issued or guaranteed by the International Bank for Reconstruction and Development.

* * *

(e) *Liability for lack of reasonable care*—This section shall not be construed as relieving any person from the duty of exercising reasonable care in selecting securities.

* * *

(g) *Other investments*—This section shall not be construed to make unlawful any investment not listed in this section.

Catarina must periodically review her investment methods and policies. If she fails to examine or review at regular intervals the investments that she has made, she can be liable for the loss or lessening of the value of the trust property.

The case of *Witmer v. Blair,* 588 S.W.2d 222 (Mo.App. 1979), involved this duty. Because the trustee of the testamentary trust had kept no records and had not invested the money of the trust, the court ruled the trustee had violated the fiduciary duty to "make the trust property productive" by properly investing the trust funds.

▥ ASSIGNMENT 8.6

Catarina makes the following investments. Do they violate her duty to make the trust property productive? What additional facts must you know to assist you in answering the following?

1. Carmine had often complained that his building construction business was unprof-itable. At the time of his death, he was preparing to sell it to a business associate. Catarina, who was also named executrix of Carmine's estate, executes the sale in the name of the estate and adds the money to the trust fund.
2. Catarina buys bonds issued by the Vittore Emanuele Lodge, to which Carmine had belonged. The bonds pay 8 percent interest annually. Several of Catarina's neigh-bors and friends hold the same kind of bonds. Other kinds of debentures costing the same amount would have yielded higher rates of interest.
3. After Carmine's death, Catarina is preoccupied with details of the funeral and put-ting his affairs in order. She neglects to deposit part of the cash portion of the trust, i.e., $8,000, in a bank until it is too late to earn interest on the money for the quarter. Carmine kept the $8,000 in a small safe at home.

5. *Duty to make payments of income and principal to the named beneficiaries (Restatement [Second] of Trusts § 182).*

■ Most trusts establish two kinds of beneficiaries: income beneficiaries, who receive the net income from the trust property for a determined number of years or for the beneficiaries' lives, and remainder beneficiaries, who receive the prin-cipal of the trust after the rights of the income beneficiaries in the trust are sat-isfied. A person who receives the property after an income beneficiary is called the remainderman.

Example: Celia Brosniak, the oldest child in her family, is named trustee of a large sum of money in the will of her aunt. The trust is for the benefit of Celia's brothers and sisters, who are to receive income from the money until the young-est attains majority. Then, according to the will, Celia is to receive the balance (principal) of the trust fund. Celia's brothers and sisters are the income benefi-ciaries, and Celia is the remainder beneficiary and remainderman.

If the settlor provides for separate disposition of the trust income and trust principal, and if the trust property is cash, it is advisable that the trustee open two accounts, one for the principal and one for the interest. In the example above, this would be necessary. The aunt not only designated income-receiving beneficiaries but also chose Celia to receive the principal as a lump sum. Celia should open a separate principal account so that she may readily take her gift when the time comes. Also, when there are two or more beneficiaries, as in this case, the trustee, Celia, must deal with them impartially, i.e., treat them equally.

It may happen that during the course of the trust administration, Celia will obtain money or property other than what she was given in the trust. In such cases she must decide whether to credit the receipt of such property to the income or principal account of the trust. If a trust agreement does not specify how to allocate the trust funds, a statute, the Uniform (or Revised Uniform) Principal and Income Act adopted in most states, provides for the method of allocation. These acts define in detail the duties of the trustee in regard to the receipt of property and its disbursement into the income or principal account. Trustees are personally liable for any loss if they fail to comply with the trust agreement or the statute.

The general rule for disbursement is that money paid for the use of the trust property and any benefit received from the employment of that property are to be treated as trust income, while substitutes for the original trust property, such as the proceeds from the sale of the property, are to be considered trust principal. When allocating receipts or expenses between the income beneficiaries and remaindermen, the general rule is that ordinary or current receipts and expenses are allocated or assigned to the income beneficiary, whereas extraordinary receipts and expenses are allocated to the remaindermen (see Exhibit 8.5).

Example: Howard wills his property to a trust. The trustees are to pay the income from the property to his wife, Mary, during her life and to distribute the property to Howard and Mary's children when Mary dies. Howard can direct the trustees to allocate receipts and charge expenses between the income beneficiary (Mary) and the remaindermen (children).

ASSIGNMENT 8.7

If the trust agreement in the above example authorized Celia to distribute income "at best, quarterly, and at least, annually," would she be acting within her fiduciary obligations if she withheld certain amounts from the quarterly distributions for possible emergency expenses and thereby created a separate fund?

Exhibit 8.5 Allocation of Ordinary and Extraordinary Receipts and Expenses between Beneficiaries and Remaindermen

Ordinary—Income Beneficiary	Extraordinary—Remaindermen
Receipts	Receipts
Rents	Proceeds from sale or exchange of
Royalties	trust principal
Cash dividends	**Stock Dividends**
Interest	**Stock Splits***
	Settlement of claims for injury to
	principal
Expenses	Expenses
Insurance	Extraordinary repairs
Ordinary taxes	Principal amortization
Ordinary repairs	Costs incurred in the sale or
Depreciation	purchase of principal
Interest payments	Long-term improvements

*A stock split is the issuance by a corporation of a number of new shares in exchange for each old share held by a stockholder; the result is a proportional change in the number of shares owned by each stockholder. A common purpose of a stock split is to reduce the per share market price to encourage wider trading and ownership and eventually a higher per share value (i.e., price).

Stock dividend
A dividend of shares of stock distributed to stockholders.
Stock split
One share of stock is split into a larger number of shares resulting in a proportional change in the number of shares owned by each stockholder.

6. *Duty to account (Restatement [Second] of Trusts § 172).*

▪ The trustee must keep accurate records so that it can be determined whether the trust has been properly administered.

Example: Nicholas Walheimer creates an *inter vivos* trust for the benefit of his mentally handicapped son, David. He names Felix Basch trustee of the fund, which consists of $65,000 worth of stock. Felix is given the power to sell and invest the stock. Nicholas thereafter dies. Frederika Wolfram is appointed David's personal and property guardian.

Felix has the duty to render an account (complete and accurate information) of his administrative activities at reasonable intervals to those who are "interested" in the trust, namely, the settlor, Nicholas, while alive, and the beneficiary, David, acting through his personal and property guardian, Frederika. The trustee, Felix, alone has the right to manage and control the trust property. He must retain trust documents and records, secure and file vouchers for all expenditures and disbursements, and keep an accurate and complete set of books. He is obliged to show these to Nicholas and Frederika on request. Felix has a fiduciary duty to account voluntarily (e.g., quarterly) for changes in the trust property. If the trustee fails to perform these duties, the trustee may be removed by the court, denied compensation, or even charged with the cost to the beneficiary of an accounting proceeding.

▥ ASSIGNMENT 8.8

Felix has been a trustee for two years. He tries to make periodic reports on the trust, but this is not always feasible because he frequently travels while conducting business. In performing the following acts, did Felix violate his duty to account? (These are opinion questions, but you must give reasons for your answers).

1. Felix sells some stock from the trust and buys land in the Santo Affonso Valley. Frederika asks him to account for this, so he sends her copies of the contract of sale and the deed of title.
2. At the end of the calendar year, Felix sends a balance sheet indicating the financial status of the trust property but neglects to include a dividend paid one week before the issue date of the balance sheet. Later he discovers his error. He sends Frederika a receipt for payment of the dividend, informing her that he will rectify the error on the next annual statement.
3. Felix has the second annual statement prepared by an accountant. Having read it, Frederika complains that it is too technical for her to understand. Felix replies that the statement is correct to the best of his knowledge and that he has fulfilled the duty to account required of a trustee.

▥ ASSIGNMENT 8.9

1. John Williams, a customer's representative in a stock brokerage firm, is appointed sole trustee of the Carter Trust. If John uses the firm to buy and sell stock for the trust, is this a violation of John's fiduciary duty? If so, which duty?
2. Continuing with the John Williams case in question 1, if John temporarily put the money obtained from the sale of trust property, e.g., shares of stock owned by the trust, into his own bank account, would this violate his fiduciary duty? If so, which duty?
3. Sally Feldman is an attorney and sole trustee of a trust. An unhappy beneficiary of the trust demands that Sally transfer the trust property to an investment company,

which will manage and invest the property. Must Sally make the transfer? Would this violate her fiduciary duty? If so, which duty?

....

Liability of Trustee to Beneficiary

A breach of trust by the trustee may occur in a variety of ways, which in turn determine the remedies available and the party who is entitled to bring suit. To restore the damage committed by a trustee, the beneficiary has the right to judicial remedies at law or a suit in equity. An action at law is a civil lawsuit commenced by the person, called the plaintiff, who seeks the remedy at law called damages, i.e., to be compensated monetarily.

■ The beneficiary can maintain a civil lawsuit to compel the trustee to reimburse the trust for any loss or depreciation in value of the trust property caused by the trustee's breach of the trust instrument (Restatement [Second] of Trusts §§ 199, 205).

Example: Sharon has agreed to act as trustee for Joan's benefit. The trust property is a lake cottage. Sharon has obtained the deed but has not insured the property. Lightning strikes the cottage, and it is destroyed. Sharon would be personally responsible and liable for this loss.

■ The beneficiary can obtain an injunction, i.e., a court order, to compel the trustee to do, or refrain from doing, an act that would constitute a breach of trust. The beneficiary can bring a civil suit in equity against the trustee asking for the court order.

Example: Stephen Adams holds shares of stock in trust for Evelyn Sandberg. According to the terms of the trust agreement, he is not authorized to sell the stock. The value of the stock has recently increased substantially. Stephen intends to sell the stock. Evelyn, on learning of the pending sale, could obtain an injunction from the equity court forbidding the sale by Stephen.

■ The beneficiary can trace and recover the trust property that the trustee has wrongfully taken, unless the property has been acquired by a purchaser who, believing the trustee has a right to sell, pays an adequate price and purchases the property without having been informed of the breach of trust (Restatement [Second] of Trusts §§ 202, 284).

Example: In the preceding example, Stephen sells the stock to Jane Brown, who pays full market value for the stock unaware that Stephen has no right to sell the stock or that the stock is trust property. Jane becomes the owner of the stock. Evelyn would not have a right to sue Jane, a good-faith purchaser, but she would have a right to sue Stephen for damages because of his fraud.

■ The beneficiary can request the court of equity to remove the trustee for misconduct and to appoint a successor trustee (Restatement [Second] of Trusts §§ 107, 108, 109). The *Witmer v. Blair* case previously discussed illustrates the removal of a trustee for misconduct, i.e., failure to invest the trust property.

Example: Ronald Caster is the trustee, and Vincent Price is the beneficiary of a trust. The trust agreement gives Ronald the discretion of determining the amount of income from the trust property that Vincent shall receive each year. The amount actually given to Vincent by Ronald causes a great deal of friction between them. Vincent can petition the court to remove Ronald as trustee, but the court will not do so unless Vincent can prove that the hostility causes Ronald to mismanage his trusteeship. By itself, hostility between the trustee and beneficiary is not enough reason for the court to remove the trustee.

■ The beneficiary can sue for specific performance to compel the trustee to perform the duties created by the terms of a private trust (Restatement [Second] of Trusts §§ 198, 199).

Example: According to the trust agreement, the trustee, Monica Murphy, is to give the trust property to the beneficiary, Julie Anderson, on Julie's attaining age 21. Six months have passed since Julie's twenty-first birthday, and Monica has not transferred the property. Julie sues Monica in the court of equity for specific performance of the agreement. If Julie succeeds in proving Monica in violation of her duty, Monica must complete the transfer.

■ The beneficiary can sue for breach of the trustee's loyalty (Restatement [Second] of Trusts § 206). Breach of loyalty by the trustee includes many things. In general, breach of loyalty is any action by the trustee that upsets the trustee-beneficiary relationship. It results from the trustee's failure to administer the trust solely in the interest of the beneficiary.

Example: By will, Hollis Stately leaves his ranch, Bluelake, to Lavinia Turner in trust for his son, Francis, directing her to sell or exchange Bluelake for investment securities. Lavinia sells Bluelake for $200,000 and uses the money to buy bonds that she herself owns. Lavinia has breached the duty of loyalty by "self-dealing" with trust money (the proceeds of the sale).

Cost of a Trustee

Trustees perform work for the trust when they buy, sell, invest, receive income, and the like on behalf of the beneficiary, and they must be compensated. The settlor may provide a reasonable allowance for the trustee in the trust instrument; if the settlor does not, state statutes fix the amount, or in the absence of such statutes, the courts will fix a just annual compensation. There is a feeling (originating in common law principles) that the trustee should not make an unreasonable profit from the trust; therefore the actual amount of compensation is usually a small percentage of the trust's annual income and principal set by statute (see N.J. Stat. Ann. § 3B: 18–24, 18–25). In a testamentary trust, the probate court may set the annual fee for a corporate trustee, such as a bank, at three-fourths of 1 percent of the fair market value of the trust estate. In determining whether the fee charged is reasonable, the court considers the size of the estate, the services performed, the time spent, and the results achieved. In an *inter vivos* trust, fees are generally negotiated. State statutes may also set fees in some cases.

The Beneficiary: The Recipient of the Trust Property or Benefits

Every trust must have a beneficiary. In a private trust, the beneficiaries must either be identified by name, description, designation of the class to which the beneficiaries belong, or if no beneficiary is in existence at the time the trust is created (such as a trust for the benefit of unborn children), the trustee must be able to ascertain the identity of the beneficiary within the period of the Rule Against Perpetuities (Restatement [Second] of Trusts § 112). In a charitable trust, however, it is sufficient that the beneficiaries be members of the public at large or a general class of the public (Restatement [Second] of Trusts §§ 122, 123, 364, 375).

To create a private trust, the settlor must name or sufficiently describe a beneficiary or co-beneficiaries, of whom the settlor may herself be one, to receive the equitable interest in the trust property. If the trust instrument describes the beneficiary too vaguely, a court of equity cannot validate the trust. There must be someone to enforce the trust and to ensure that the trustee will faithfully perform the previously mentioned duties. That was the position in the case of *Scotti's Drive In Restaurants, Inc. v. Mile High–Dart In Corp.,* cited earlier, where the court stated: "A trust is an obligation imposed, either expressly or by implication of law, whereby the obligor [trustee] is bound to deal with property over which he has control for the benefit of certain persons [beneficiaries], of whom he may himself be one, and any one of whom may enforce the obligation." Consequently, the beneficiaries of a trust must be specifically identified.

Example: Howard establishes a trust and directs Mary, the trustee, to pay the trust income to "whomever Mary selects" without adequately describing the persons or class of persons from which the selection is to be made. Such a trust is too vague and is invalid.

Any person who is capable of owning property, including infants, insane persons in some states, and public or private corporations, may be a beneficiary in a trust, but incompetents and minors generally require guardians to act as beneficiaries for them. Trusts in which aliens, the United States, a state, a municipality, and a foreign country are beneficiaries have been upheld. In sum, the beneficiary may be any entity capable of taking title to property in the manner as a person, whether natural or created by law, e.g., a corporation, state, or nation. It is important to note that the beneficiary of the trust, however, need not have capacity to hold property or to make a contract, since the trustee has legal title to and control of the trust property. Many trusts are created specifically because the beneficiary lacks legal or actual capacity to manage property without assistance.

Example: Martha Kirk places $20,000 in trust for the benefit of the Red Cross. The Red Cross is a "corporate person." It is a definite beneficiary. This trust is as valid as if Martha had created it for the benefit of a natural person.

Example: Giovanna Bonetto belongs to a card club. The members meet once a month to play cards, amuse themselves, and perform works of charity. She dies, leaving a trust for the purpose of the club's continuing to meet and carry on its activities. This trust will fail because the card club, as such, is not a "person." The individual members are. Had Giovanna's trust named them individually as beneficiaries, the trust would have been valid.

Although it is required that the beneficiaries be definite, they need not be, and frequently are not, described by name but rather by class designation. Examples of such designation are "my grandchildren" or "my issue," in which cases the identification of the beneficiaries is ascertainable, i.e., capable of being determined (Restatement [Second] of Trusts § 120). Words such as "friends," "family," and "relatives," used to designate beneficiaries, have sometimes caused trusts to fail for lack of definite beneficiaries because such terms have broad and varied application. A trust to benefit "relatives," however, occasionally proves an exception to the rule. A court, construing "relatives" to mean those who would inherit the settlor's property according to the statutes of descent and distribution rather than those who are related to the settlor either closely or remotely by either blood or marriage, would in all likelihood uphold the trust (Restatement [Second] of Trusts § 121). Similarly, interpretation of the word "family" to mean "the settlor's spouse and issue" leads to the same result (Restatement [Second] of Trusts § 120b). Note that this requirement of definiteness of beneficiary for a private trust directly opposes the requirement of indefiniteness of beneficiary for a public (charitable) trust.

Beneficiaries need not always be persons or institutions. As the case *In re Searight's Estate,* 87 Ohio App. 417, 95 N.E.2d 779 (1950), illustrates, placing property "in trust for" the care and benefit of pets, such as dogs or cats, or for the maintenance of pet cemeteries has been declared valid and enforceable because of the social interests that are involved. But compare *In re Estate of Russell,* 69 Cal.2d 200, 70 Cal.Rptr. 561, 444 P.2d 353 (1968).

🏛 ASSIGNMENT 8.10

1. Harding Mulholland lived at the home of his niece, Cecelia, and her husband, Edwin. He provided in his will that a trust be set up for the benefit of his nieces and nephews, Cecelia being the only one of that class at the time. Subsequently, another niece, Teresa, was born, and Cecelia died in the same year. When Harding died, Edwin petitioned the court to set aside the trust, claiming that Harding neither knew nor could have known of the current beneficiary, Teresa. Should the trust fail for lack of a definite beneficiary?

2. Willis Rokeby lives in Bangor, Maine. For five months each year, he visits his daughter in Texarkana. He hires Jacques Santin, a citizen of Canada, to take care of his house in Maine. He pays Jacques a small salary and creates a testamentary trust of the house and surrounding land for Jacques's benefit. After Willis's death, his sister, named trustee in the trust instrument, claims that Jacques cannot be beneficiary because he is not subject to the laws of either Maine or the United States. Is she correct?

Nature of the Beneficiary's Interest
(Restatement [Second] of Trusts § 130)

The length of time the beneficiary holds the equitable interest in the trust property may be limited to a period of years, to the life of the beneficiary or that of someone else, to a condition precedent, to a condition subsequent, or to the nonoccurrence of a specified event.

Example: Patrice Avery sets aside stocks and bonds for three *inter vivos* trusts for each of her children: The first to be created for her son, Vinton, on the condition that he return to the family home in West Virginia. This trust is based on a condition precedent. The second for her daughter, Susanna, on the condition that she continue to support Patrice as she had been doing. This trust is created on a condition subsequent. The third for her daughter, Alberta, as long as she continues to study medicine at State University. This trust is created on the nonhappening of a specific event, e.g., Alberta's switching to another course of study or another school.

Note that both Susanna's and Alberta's trusts begin immediately but the possibility of the premature termination of the trusts exists, whereas Vinton's does not begin until he has complied with the condition precedent.

The beneficiary's equitable interest in realty (real property) usually passes on his or her death to the beneficiary's heirs or devisees; personal property passes to the beneficiary's personal representative, e.g., the administrator or executor. Another possible result is that the trust instrument itself may provide that the beneficiary's interest terminates on death, as in the case in which the beneficiary receives a life estate.

A single trust may have more than one beneficiary. Multiple beneficiaries usually hold the property as tenants in common unless the settlor expressly makes the beneficiaries joint tenants or tenants by the entireties. The doctrine of survivorship applies if the co-beneficiaries are joint tenants or tenants by the entireties (Restatement [Second] of Trusts § 113). For example, if Charles and Dennis are co-beneficiaries as joint tenants, and Charles dies, Dennis will then be the sole beneficiary and will own the entire equitable interest in the trust property, just as any joint owner with the right of survivorship succeeds to full ownership upon the death of the other joint owner.

The beneficiary of a trust is free to transfer the interest in trust property by mortgage or devise, in the absence of any restriction imposed by statute or by the terms of the trust, to the same extent that a person who holds both equitable and legal titles is free to do so (Restatement [Second] of Trusts § 132). In some states, all transfers of beneficial interests must be in writing and signed by the beneficiary; in other states, this requirement applies only to the transfer of real property (Restatement [Second] of Trusts § 139).

Unless prohibited by statute or the trust agreement, beneficiaries may ordinarily transfer their interest in a trust by an assignment. This legal transaction allows the beneficiary to transfer to another the benefits of the trust. This may be done to make a gift of the trust benefits or to pay the beneficiary's debts.

Example: Greg receives an income as a beneficiary of a trust. He assigns his interest (transfers his right to receive income) to June. Thereafter, June receives the income from the trust.

Creditors may attach the beneficiary's equitable interest in trust property unless statutes or trust provisions exempt the interest from creditors' claims (Restatement [Second] of Trusts § 147). If statutes exempt a legal interest from creditors' claims, a corresponding equitable interest of a beneficiary in trust property is also exempt, e.g., homestead exemptions (which apply to both legal and equitable interests). The method by which a creditor reaches an equitable interest varies from state to state. The only remedy in some states is a creditor's bill in chancery (equity) in which the creditor commences the lawsuit in an equity court. In other states, the equitable interest is subject to execution, attachment, and garnishment by the beneficiary's creditors just as if it were a legal interest. An exception occurs when the settlor has restricted the trust so that the beneficiary cannot assign nor creditors reach the equitable interest of the beneficiary; such a trust is commonly called a spendthrift trust (see the discussion in Chapter 9).

Trust Property

The trust property is the property interest that is transferred to the trustee to hold for the benefit of another. It is sometimes called the *res, corpus, principal,* or *subject matter* of the trust. Any transferable interest in an object of ownership may become trust property. This includes ownership of real or personal property. Thus, a fee simple estate in land, a co-owner's interest (joint tenants, tenants in common, and the like), a mortgage, a life estate in land, a right to remove coal, a business interest, promissory notes, bonds or shares of stock (securities), a trade secret, copyright, patent, or cash could serve as trust property. Examples of nontransferable property are government pensions, existing spendthrift trusts, or tort claims of wrongful injury, i.e., the victim's right to sue a negligent party for personal injury. Nontransferable property interests may not be the subject matter of a trust.

A trust involving the transfer of personal property only may be created orally, but a settlor transferring title to real property to a trust must comply with the state statute, i.e., the Statute of Frauds, requiring a written agreement establishing the details of the trust. The latter requirement is designed to prevent fraud and perjury(see further discussion below). The court in *State ex rel. Wirt v. Supreme Court for Spokane County,* 10 Wash.2d 362, 116 P.2d 752 (1941), expressed this principle when it ruled: "It has become the settled law of this state, in harmony with the general accepted rule in this country, that an express trust in real property cannot rest in parol [evidence], but must be evidenced in writing." See also the *Mahoney* case, cited earlier, where the court stated that a "trust involving only personal property may be instituted [commenced] without being reduced to writing." The terms of the written agreement (*trust instrument*) as designated by the settlor must include the purpose of the trust, the length of time the trust will last, and a description and conveyance of the trust property. It must also include the names of the trustee and beneficiary, and the powers, duties, and rights of such parties, including how much the beneficiaries are to receive, and when they will receive it. It is not necessary to use a particular form or particular language to frame the trust as long as the settlor makes these elements clear.

⚏ ASSIGNMENT 8.11

Read the trust instrument on page 242 and determine whether the requirements in the preceding two paragraphs have been met.

As noted above, the English Statute of Frauds was enacted in 1677 to prevent fraud and perjury between sellers and buyers by requiring certain kinds of contracts to be written. Its American counterparts, drawn chiefly from sections 4 and 17 of the original statute, demand that a written contract, signed by the parties, be used in certain transactions. When trusts involve the transfer of land, they must conform to the state Statute of Frauds and thereby be in writing if they are to be enforced. If the trust property transferred in an *inter vivos* (living) trust is an interest in land, the Statute of Frauds requires that the trust be written setting forth the details of the trust (Restatement [Second] of Trusts, § 40). If a trust is created by the will of the settlor, there must be a writing that meets the requirements of a will (see Chapter 9 and the example of a trust instrument on page 308). Many U.S. states have enacted requirements similar to those of the English Statute of Frauds. North Dakota is an example.

N.D. Cent. Code Ann. § 59–03–03   Requisites of Trust Relating to Real Property
No trust in relation to real property is valid unless created or declared:
  1. By a written instrument, subscribed by the trustee or by his agent thereto authorized in writing;
  2. By the instrument under which the trustee claims the estate affected; or
  3. By operation of law.

In addition to requiring a written agreement whenever land is transferred in trust, the method of transfer is also strictly regulated. Land must be transferred by specific legal documents, e.g., either a deed or a will. Personal property, on the other hand, may be simply delivered to the trustee.

Example: Sharon signed a trust agreement transferring title to Greenvale, a country home, to Susan in trust for the benefit of Thomas. Sharon executed and delivered the deed to Greenvale to Susan. Sharon and Susan are parties to a trust agreement (trust instrument). Sharon is the grantor. Susan is the trustee and holds the legal title that she received from Sharon. Thomas is the beneficiary (*cestui que trust*) of the agreement and holds equitable title.

The agreement satisfies the state Statute of Frauds because it is written. It also complies with requirements for trusts of this nature, i.e., trusts to which real property is transferred, and is therefore enforceable.

🏛 ASSIGNMENT 8.12

Simon Rothstein executes a trust instrument with the Third National Bank, placing his lakeshore property in trust for the benefit of his nephew, Norman. Norman, however, does not know of the trust. Simon dies one year later. His widow, Evelyn, contends that the trust is not valid because it was not signed by Norman. Norman contends that it is valid. Who is right?

As noted above, the trust instrument must either specifically describe the trust property or clearly define the manner to be followed in identifying it. The validity of a trust depends on its enforceability. If a court is to enforce a trust, the trust property must be *in existence* (i.e., definite and certain on the *date* the trust is created, or definitely ascertainable) and *owned* by the settlor.

Example: Mary Holland is an investor and collector of art. If Mary attempts to create a trust by declaring herself trustee of the next work of art she buys, no trust is created, because the trust property is neither specifically identifiable nor owned and in existence at the time of the trust creation.

Example: Today Mike Wilson declares himself trustee of the stocks he will own on the next December 1st. No trust is created. Likewise, a trust consisting of "securities which I may purchase in 1995" or "all gas and oil leases which I may possess by next August 1st" is too vague to be enforced (Restatement [Second] of Trusts § 74).

On the other hand, a testamentary trust created in the "residue of the decedent's estate" *is* valid, even though the exact amount of the residue cannot be determined until the decedent's assets and liabilities are known. In this case, the facts needed to specifically identify the amount of the residue do exist on the date the trust is created, i.e., the date of the testator's death.

Example: In an *inter vivos* trust instrument, Alicia Schell states, "I give to Joan Warfield, to hold and to manage, the amount of my savings and checking accounts for the benefit of Roberta Polenek." This instrument creates a valid trust. The trust corpus is not stated, but it is ascertainable. It is the amount of money in Alicia's checking and savings accounts on the date of the trust instrument's execution.

The fact that trust property may change from time to time during the trust period does not make the trust void.

Example: Alex Knight, trustee of real estate for the benefit of Letita Kruse, has the power of sale and reinvestment. He sells part of the land for cash and deposits this cash in the Citizens Bank. He buys bonds for the trust and pays for them by drawing a check on the Citizens Bank. He has effected three changes in the trust property—real estate into cash, cash into a claim on the bank (i.e., a right to withdraw the amount deposited), and the claim on the bank into bonds. The trust property has changed, but the trust is still valid.

TERMINATION OF TRUSTS

A trust may be terminated in the following ways:

- In accordance with its terms (Restatement [Second] of Trusts §§ 330, 334).

Example: Sarah gives Roberta $100,000 to hold and invest in trust for Katherine and to pay the income produced to Katherine annually for ten years. At the end of the ten years, the trust would terminate.

- By completely accomplishing the trust's valid purpose (Restatement [Second] of Trusts § 337).

Example: Sarah gives Roberta $100,000 to hold and invest and to pay the income produced to Sarah's mother annually for her lifetime and then return the trust property to Sarah. When Sarah's mother dies and the property is returned, the trust purpose is accomplished.

- By revocation by the settlor when allowed by the terms of the trust (Restatement [Second] of Trusts § 330).

Example: Sarah creates a trust that includes a provision that states, "This trust is revocable and the settlor reserves the right to amend or revoke the trust in whole or in part at any time." The trust will terminate if Sarah chooses to revoke it.

- By merger of all interests (legal and equitable) in the same person (Restatement [Second] of Trusts §§ 337, 341).

Example: Sarah creates a trust in which she names herself as trustee and names Roberta and herself as the beneficiaries. Roberta dies, and Sarah now holds both the legal and equitable titles to the trust property by herself. Since the titles have merged in one person, the trust terminates.

- On the request of all the beneficiaries when there is no express purpose that requires continuation of the trust (Restatement [Second] of Trusts § 337).

The majority of U.S. courts hold that if one or more of the settlor's purposes for creating the trust may still be achieved by the continuance of the trust, the court will not allow termination unless all the beneficiaries join in the request for termination along with the settlor. When a trust does terminate, the trustee must also account for all assets and obtain a receipt and release from the recipients. But remember that a trust does not terminate for want of a trustee.

KEY TERMS

Statute of Frauds	Revocable trust	Disclaimer	Stock dividend
Remainder	Irrevocable trust	Conflict of interest	Stock split
Remainderman			

REVIEW QUESTIONS

1. What is meant by the following statement: "The most unique feature of a trust is that a trust splits the title to property." Explain.
2. In trust law, what is the difference between legal and equitable title?
3. In what ways can a trust be created?
4. What are the essential elements of a valid trust?
5. What are the qualifications required for a person to become a settlor, the creator of a trust?
6. Why would a settlor create a revocable trust, and what are the advantages of making the trust irrevocable?
7. What are the standard powers and duties of a trustee who, like a personal representative, is a fiduciary?
8. What are the beneficiary's rights for breach of trust by a trustee? Explain.

9. Must a person have contractual capacity to be a beneficiary of a trust? Explain.
10. May a settlor be the sole trustee and sole beneficiary of a trust? Explain.
11. Does a trust always have to be in writing? Explain.

12. Are there any limits on the kind of property that can be placed in trust? Explain.
13. How are trusts terminated?

CASE PROBLEMS

Problem 1

Suki Nakajima, a widow in failing health, intends to leave her ample estate equally to her adult children, a daughter, Tomoko, and a son, Hito. Suki has two concerns. With good reason, she lacks confidence that Hito can manage property because of his irresponsible spending habits, and she does not want any property she gives to Tomoko to pass to Tomoko's husband. Suki writes, but does not sign, a letter to her best friend, Tomura, requesting that he manage money for the benefit of her two children, and asking him, if he agrees, to sign and return the letter. After receiving the letter back from Tomura with his signature and acceptance, Suki mails a cashier's check for $200,000 to Tomura. Answer and explain the following:

A. Is Suki's letter a valid holographic will?
B. Is the use of the words "trust" or "trustee" in a formal written document necessary to create a valid trust?
C. Does Suki's letter create an *inter vivos* (living) trust? See *Estate of Baker*, 82 Misc.2d 974, 370 N.Y.S.2d 404 (1975).
D. *If* a trust exists, must it be written and signed to be valid?

Problem 2

In a testamentary trust, Alanzo Lopez names his friend, Ricardo LaPalma, trustee of substantial property placed in trust for the benefit of Alanzo's wife, Maria, and his sister, Yolanda. Hostility had existed between Ricardo and Maria long before the trust was created, and it became worse soon after Alanzo's death when the trust became active. Alanzo had given Ricardo broad discretion in distributing trust income, and when Ricardo distributed a much greater percentage of the trust's annual income to Yolanda than to Maria, Maria became outraged. She demanded that Ricardo be removed as an unsuitable trustee because of his act of disloyalty by favoring one beneficiary over another.

A. Is hostility between a trustee and beneficiary a valid reason for the removal of a trustee?
B. If there were five beneficiaries in the trust and three were pleased with the trustee's actions and two were incensed and wanted the trustee removed, should the "majority rule" apply to this decision?
C. Read and compare the following cases: *Matter of Brecklein's Estate*, 6 Kan.App.2d 1001, 637 P.2d 444 (1981) and *Edinburg v. Cavers*, 22 Mass. App. Ct. 212, 492 N.E.2d 1171 (1986). What are the circumstances a court should consider before deciding a request for removal of a trustee based on hostility between the trustee and a beneficiary?

CHAPTER NINE

CLASSIFICATION OF TRUSTS, THE LIVING TRUST, AND OTHER SPECIAL TRUSTS

OBJECTIVES

After completing this chapter, you should be able to:

- Identify and define the classes of trusts.
- Explain the uses and functions of various kinds of trusts.
- Explain the formation, use, advantages, and disadvantages of living revocable and irrevocable trusts.
- Identify and explain the function of Totten, spendthrift, and sprinkling trusts and a pour-over will.
- Prepare preliminary drafts of private express trusts including living trusts.
- Avoid common errors in the initial drafts of such trusts.

SCOPE OF THE CHAPTER

This chapter identifies and discusses the various kinds of trusts including the increasingly popular living (*inter vivos*) trust. The chapter begins with the classification of trusts, followed by an examination of a private express trust including various examples that eventually lead to a detailed discussion of the living trust. The chapter outlines the steps necessary for drafting trusts including the accumulation of data through appropriate checklists. Actual drafts of these trusts and a pour-over will are also contained in the chapter.

CLASSIFICATION OF TRUSTS

All trusts may be divided into two major categories, express and implied. An express trust is established by intentional deliberate acts and is represented by a written document or an oral declaration. A simple statement that the settlor intends to hold property in trust for another creates a trust by declaration. No special words are necessary to create a trust, provided the intent of the settlor to establish the trust is clear. In most jurisdictions, as previously mentioned, an express trust of real property must be in writing to meet the requirements of the Statute of Frauds.

Depending on the purpose for which they are created, express trusts fall into the following subcategories: (1) private or public (charitable) trusts; (2) active or passive trusts; or (3) *inter vivos* (living) or testamentary trusts. The most common types of express trusts are the testamentary and *inter vivos* (living) trusts. The living trust is one of the major topics of this chapter.

Implied trusts are created not by deliberate acts but by the presumed intent of the settlor or by a decree (order) of the equity court. Implied trusts are categorized as either resulting trusts or constructive trusts (see Exhibit 9.1).

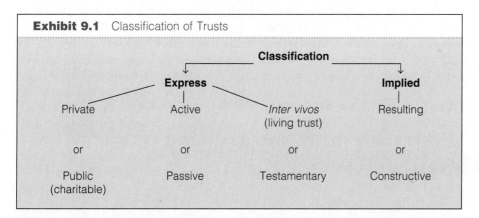

Exhibit 9.1 Classification of Trusts

Express Trusts—Private versus Public (Charitable)

Private Trust

A *private trust* is created expressly (orally or in writing) between a person who has the power to be a settlor and one or more trustees who hold legal title to trust property for the financial benefit of a certain named beneficiary or beneficiaries. It is one of the most common types of trusts. The essential elements of an express private trust are as follows:

- The settlor must intend to create a private trust.
- A trustee must be named to administer the trust.
- A beneficiary must be named to enforce the trust.
- The settlor must transfer sufficiently identified property to the trust.

The court in *City Bank Farmers' Trust Co. v. Charity Organization Society,* 238 App.Div. 720, 265 N.Y.S. 267 (1933), upheld these elements as being essential for a private trust.

Example: Loraine Katz owns a one-third interest in a boutique. In her will she gives the interest to her nephew, David, to hold and manage in trust for the benefit of her niece, Tracy. Loraine, the owner of the interest, is the settlor. David, to whom she conveys the legal title to the one-third interest, is the trustee. Tracy, who is to receive the benefit of the interest (i.e., one-third of the profits of the boutique), is the beneficiary. This is a private (for benefit of a person), express (written), and testamentary (established by will) trust.

▥ ASSIGNMENT 9.1

Sidney Benchman transfers (assigns) the royalties to his book, to which he holds the copyright, to his business adviser, Martin Lorenz, to hold and invest for the benefit of Martitia Hughes.
1. Does the settlor intend to create a trust?
2. Is there a trustee to administer the trust?
3. Is trust property included in the instrument?
4. Is there a beneficiary or *cestui que trust*?

Public Trust

A *public* or *charitable trust* is an express trust established for the purpose of accomplishing social benefit for the public or the community (Restatement [Second] of Trusts §§ 348, 349). Although charitable trusts are public trusts, the beneficiary of the trust need not always be the *general* public. The trust fund, however, must be designated either for the benefit of the general public, e.g., a charitable trust benefiting a hospital, *or* a reasonably large, indefinite class of persons within the public who may be personally unknown to the settlor, e.g., a charitable trust benefiting the deaf in a certain city (Restatement [Second] of Trusts §§ 362, 364, 368–374). If the terms of the trust limit the distribution of its fund to named individuals rather than to an indefinite class of persons, the trust will not be classified as public. Instead, it would be a private trust. In the majority of states, the true test for creation of a valid public trust is not the indefiniteness of the persons aided by the trust but rather the amount of social benefit that accrues to the public (Restatement [Second] of Trusts § 375). Also, the purpose of the charitable trust must not include profit-making by the settlor, trustee, or other persons (Restatement [Second] of Trusts § 376). Therefore, the essential elements of an express public (charitable) trust are as follows:

- The settlor must intend to create a public trust.
- A trustee must be named to administer the trust.
- Property must be transferred to the trust.
- A charitable purpose must be expressly designated.
- The general public must be benefited, or
- An indefinite class of persons must be named beneficiaries.

Examples of charitable trusts that advance the public welfare are trusts created to maintain or propagate religion, religious education, and missionary work (see *In re Dobbins' Will,* 206 Misc. 64, 132 N.Y.S.2d 236 [1953]); further health and relieve poverty and human suffering by establishing institutions, funding research into the causes of certain diseases, or providing direct aid of food, clothing, shelter, and medical care to the needy; found or maintain educational institutions, art galleries, museums, or libraries (see *In re Tiffany's Estate,* 157 Misc. 873, 285 N.Y.S. 971 [1935]), or aid students or teachers; care for and maintain public cemeteries; erect monuments to public figures or national heroes; construct and maintain public buildings or improvements, such as an irrigation system or a playground; further patriotism; conserve natural resources and scenery; or prevent cruelty to animals.

Example: Agnes Swanson died testate, providing in her will, "I give State University $100,000 to provide scholarships for mothers on welfare in the field of nurse's training." In the absence of other evidence, an express, testamentary, charitable trust is created.

Agnes is the settlor, State University is the trustee, and "mothers on welfare" are the beneficiaries. The $100,000 is the trust property. Agnes intended to create a public or charitable trust, which desire she expressed in her will. The class of persons to be benefited is smaller than "the general public" but sufficiently large and indefinite enough to enable the trust to be classified as public. For example, Verneta Baker, a mother, begins to receive welfare a year after Agnes dies; therefore, Agnes could not have named Verneta a beneficiary personally. Verneta was not a member of the class to be benefited when Agnes made her will, but now she qualifies. She and others in the same situation are indefinite beneficiaries.

The mere fact that the purpose of a trust is to give money to others does not make it a charitable trust. The settlor of a charitable trust must describe a purpose that is of substantial public benefit.

🏛 ASSIGNMENT 9.2

Mark Nelson gives $100,000 to Luke Mellows to be distributed as Luke feels is appropriate for the benefit of Vietnamese orphans formerly living in DaNang.
1. Did the settlor intend to create a trust?
2. Is there a trustee to administer the trust?
3. Is trust res (property) included?
4. Is a charitable purpose expressly designated?
5. Will the general public be benefited?
6. Are there indefinite beneficiaries within a definite class who are the persons who actually receive the benefit?
The presence of these characteristics indicates an express, public (charitable) trust.

Public Trust—*Cy-pres* Doctrine

Where it is clear that the donor intended a private trust to be performed exactly as indicated or not at all, the trust fails (terminates) when it is not possible to follow such direction. However, in the absence of this clear intent by the donor in the trust agreement, the law will *not* permit a public *charitable* trust to end (fail) even though the beneficiary no longer exists or the original purpose has been accomplished or can no longer be achieved. Here the courts will apply the doctrine of ***cy-pres*** (an abbreviation of the French words *cy pres comme possible*

Cy-pres
As near as possible.

or "as near as possible") (Restatement [Second] of Trusts § 399), which is applicable only to public (charitable) trusts, not private trusts. In practice, the *cy-pres* doctrine means that where a testator or settlor makes a gift to charity or for a charitable purpose and it subsequently becomes impossible or impractical to apply the gift to that particular charity, the equity court may order the gift applied to another charity "as near as possible" to the one designated by the settlor.

Example: In 1955, Etta Barranger established a trust fund to provide relief to victims suffering from a particular kidney disease. In 1975, an inventor created a kidney machine that cured the disease. In order to continue the trust, it will be necessary for the court to apply the *cy-pres* doctrine by finding a charity whose purposes correspond "as nearly as possible" to Etta's motives in setting up the trust. For example, the court might apply the trust principal to a charity that aids the victims of a liver ailment.

The court will direct that the trust fund be held for another purpose that will be "as near as possible" to that intended by the settlor. The rationale behind the application of *cy-pres* is that the law tries to continue the operation of charitable trusts so as not to terminate public benefits. If a charitable trust fails for lack of foresight on the part of its settlor or simply due to modern-day advances in science, a court will review the settlor's intent in creating the trust and, if possible, transfer the trust fund to a more viable charitable use approximating that intent. The courts are anxious for the public to receive the benefits. For the doctrine to be applied to a charitable trust, however, the settlor's intent must be broad and general, and it must not be restricted to one specific objective or to one particular method of accomplishing the purpose of the trust.

Example: Through his will, Elmer Wilson gives the National Polio Foundation $500,000. Dr. Salk invents a vaccine that cures and prevents polio. Elmer's heirs ask the court to distribute the money to them now that the disease is preventable. Instead, the court of equity would apply the *cy-pres* doctrine and transfer the balance of the funds to a charity as near as possible to the testator's (Elmer's) wishes, e.g., the court may give the money to the National Crippled Children's Foundation.

The case of *In re Bletsch's Estate,* 25 Wisc.2d 40, 130 N.W.2d 275 (1964), illustrates the use of the *cy-pres* doctrine. The testator, Jack Bletsch, left his entire estate to his wife and daughter if they survived him, but if they did not, he left his estate to the Masonic Home for Crippled Children in Illinois. Both his wife and daughter predeceased Jack, but there was no Masonic Home for Crippled Children in Illinois. However, there was a Shriner's Hospital for Crippled Children in Illinois. The Wisconsin court ruled the hospital was ". . . an identifiable beneficiary whose charitable or public program and goals are reasonably close to those expressed by the testator." The estate passed to the Shriner's Hospital, as the *cy-pres* doctrine was applied and upheld by the court.

☷ ASSIGNMENT 9.3

The will of Nehemiah Bridwell, dated 1925, created a trust for the benefit of widows of men who died while serving on whaling ships. In 1960, Jared Bridwell, Nehemiah's descendant, petitioned the court to terminate the trust without applying the *cy-pres* doctrine. Jared alleged that the trust's purpose had become unnecessary since statistics showed that deaths "while serving on whaling ships" were negligible because of improved safety standards and the diminished whaling industry. What action should the court take?

Express Trusts—Active versus Passive

The features that distinguish *active trusts* from *passive trusts* are the obligations of management and administration that active trusts impose on the trustee. An active trust is an express trust that can be either private or public (charitable). Implied trusts, such as resulting and constructive trusts, are passive trusts, as are some public trusts. A settlor who desires to create an express private active trust must give oral or written affirmative powers and duties to a trustee to perform discretionary acts of management or administration for the benefit of named beneficiaries.

In contrast, in a passive trust, the trustee does not have responsibilities or discretionary duties to perform; in fact, a passive trust often involves no administrative duties at all. The trustee's mere holding of the trust property for the beneficiary with no obligations or powers to administer the trust indicates that the trust is passive. Modern-day passive trusts stem from the failure of the settlor to create an active trust, either accidentally, e.g., through a poor choice of words in the trust instrument, or deliberately, e.g., an attempt to evade the law for the settlor's own fraudulent purposes. To avoid accidentally creating a passive trust, the drafter must properly designate the active functions or duties of the trustee. The following example illustrates a trust declared passive by the equity court.

Example: Silvia appoints Arnold trustee of securities for the benefit of Harriet but neglects to give him duties to perform. Silvia dies. Legal title to the securities should have passed to Arnold, but instead under these circumstances it passes directly to Harriet, who holds equitable title as well. Since the legal and equitable titles are held by one person, no trust is created.

Additional examples involving resulting and constructive trusts, which are also passive, are discussed below.

🏛 ASSIGNMENT 9.4

Neal Sanderson owns a farm, Springlake, which he conveys by deed to Rudolf Meyerling for the benefit of Barbara Jacoby. Neal directs Rudolf to rent the land to tenants and to use part of the income produced thereby to pay taxes and to apply the remainder for Barbara's benefit at his own discretion. Answer the following and compare your answers with the statements in the next paragraph:
1. Is the trust express or implied?
2. Is the trust private or public?
3. Are there administrative duties that the trustee must perform?
4. Is the trust active or passive?
This trust is a private express trust. Neal Sanderson, the settlor, conveyed his farm, the trust property, to Rudolf Meyerling, the trustee. Barbara Jacoby is the beneficiary. The trust is active because Rudolf has the duties of renting the farm, collecting income (rent), paying taxes, and paying the remainder of the income to Barbara.

Express Trusts—*Inter Vivos* versus Testamentary

Both *inter vivos (living) trusts* (Restatement [Second] of Trusts §§ 17, 31) and *testamentary trusts* (Restatement [Second] of Trusts §§ 33, 54) refer to express trusts either private or public in nature. As the generic names of these trusts imply, they are created at different times in the settlor's life: *inter vivos* (pertaining to a gift in trust made "between living persons") and testamentary (pertaining to a gift in trust made after death as a testament, i.e., as part of a last will). In the event of a question of whether a trust is living or testamentary, the criterion will be the time at which the trust became effective (for examples, see page 283, where the reasons for creating trusts, especially living trusts, are discussed). If a settlor wishes to see how well the trust operates while she is alive, then a living trust must be established. Otherwise the living trust differs little from the testamentary trust. Both types of trusts are widely employed as a means of conserving property for the benefit of a surviving spouse and children or for the child or children of a single parent.

 ASSIGNMENT 9.5

Carolyn is a single parent whose only child is her daughter, Charise. Carolyn's will dated May 1, 1995, reads, in part: "I give the residue of my property to the Fourth State Bank as trustee, pursuant to the trust agreement of October 19, 1990, for the benefit of my daughter, Charise, to be held and managed in accordance with the terms of said agreement."
1. Has Carolyn created a valid trust by this instrument? Is it testamentary or *inter vivos*? Why?
2. How might Carolyn have created a trust of the kind opposite to your answer in question 1?

ASSIGNMENT 9.6

Herb gives Janet $40,000 to be distributed as she sees fit for the benefit of poor Amish children in Kentucky between the ages of 6 and 12. Determine whether the essential elements of an express, active *inter vivos,* public trust are present:
1. Does the settlor intend to create a trust?
2. Is there a trustee to administer the trust?
3. Is trust res included?
4. Is a charitable purpose expressly designated?
5. Is the general public benefited?
6. Are there indefinite beneficiaries within a definite class who are the persons who actually receive the benefit?

Implied Trusts—Resulting and Constructive

The second major category in the classification of trusts is the *implied trust,* subdivided into *resulting trusts* and *constructive trusts.* Both types of implied trusts are also passive trusts. Implied trusts are trusts imposed on property by the equity courts when trust intent is lacking. Such trusts are said to be created by "operation of law." In these trusts there is no settlor in the sense in which an express trust has a settlor. The settlor who creates an express trust does so with intent, even though the details (i.e., the language of the trust instrument or identities of the trustee or beneficiaries) might be vague enough to require court interpretation. It is impossible, however, for any person in the capacity of settlor to create an implied trust since these, by definition, are mechanisms imposed by the equity court.

Resulting Trusts

A resulting trust is created because of inferred or presumed intent of a property owner (Restatement [Second] of Trusts §§ 404–460). There are basically three kinds of situations in the United States in which an implied, resulting trust may be created.

Situation One.   When one person's money has paid for land or personal property, but the legal title of the property is conveyed to another person, the law presumes that a resulting trust, called a **purchase-money resulting trust,** has been created for the benefit of the person who paid the money. That person receives equitable title to the property. The person to whom the property was conveyed, i.e., the holder of legal title to the property, is considered the trustee (Restatement [Second] of Trusts § 440).

Since a purchase-money resulting trust is created by implication and operation of law, it need not be in writing. However, if there is a conflict later, it may be difficult to prove whether the conveyor intended to make a gift to the alleged trustee instead of allowing a resulting trust to be created by implication.

Courts generally require very careful proof to establish a resulting trust. The evidence must be strong and unmistakable, and the burden of proof rests on the party seeking to establish the resulting trust. Because of the difficulty in establishing the proof, the court allows **parol evidence** to be used in these cases. The grounds for the court's presuming a purchase-money resulting trust are that a person who makes a gratuitous conveyance most likely intends to make a gift, but a person who furnishes consideration (pays for) a conveyance to another probably does so for reasons other than gift giving, e.g., to facilitate resale of the property, repay a debt, obtain services of management from the transferee, or seek to avoid creditors. Seven states (Indiana, Kansas, Kentucky, Michigan, Minnesota, New York, and Wisconsin) have abolished or modified purchase-money resulting trusts by statute.

Example: Aron Samuels, age 70, buys 200 shares of Honeywell, Inc., stock with money that he needs to live. He instructs the corporation's agent to issue the certificates in the name of Miriam Slater. Miriam is not related by blood or marriage to Aron. In the absence of further evidence, Miriam holds the shares as trustee in a *resulting trust* for Aron.

Situation Two.   When a settlor creates an express private trust gratuitously (without requiring payment of the beneficiary) and the trust fails or is declared void for any reason except that it has an illegal objective, a resulting trust arises for the benefit of the settlor or the settlor's successors (Restatement [Second] of Trusts § 411). In other words, the trust arrangement no longer exists, but the trust property does, and with it the problem of disposing of it. Should the settlor be allowed to recover the property? In general, the law considers such recovery to be the only fair solution. However, if the court rules that the private express trust was created for an illegal purpose, it generally does not decree (order) a resulting trust for the benefit of the settlor but instead declares the trust void. In such cases, the settlor of an illegal trust is generally not allowed to recover the trust property from the trustee since equity discourages such transactions and will not be a party to their enforcement.

A resulting trust also arises when a charitable trust fails in an instance where the court cannot apply the *cy-pres* doctrine. The trust property is held by the trustee for the benefit of the original settlor or the settlor's successors.

Example: Perrin Williams conveys his farm, Oakburne, by deed to Lee Hunter in trust for Stephen Grant. Unknown to Perrin, Stephen is dead at the time of the conveyance. The trust property now reverts to Perrin, but until Perrin takes possession of it, Lee holds Oakburne in a resulting trust for Perrin.

Purchase-money resulting trust
A resulting trust in which property is purchased and paid for by one person, and at his direction, the seller transfers possession and title to another person.

Parol evidence
Oral or written evidence.

Example: Harmon Course, wishing to keep his majority interest in the Burmingham Power Company in the family, inserts in his will a provision that the stock will be held by the Transylvania Trust Company in trust for his grandchildren. This attempted trust is declared void by the court for contravening the state Rule Against Perpetuities. The Trust Company does *not* hold the stock in a resulting trust for Harmon's successors. The stock returns instead to the estate, where it will be distributed according to the will's residuary clause or, if no such clause exists, according to the statutes of descent and distribution, i.e., intestacy statutes.

🏛 ASSIGNMENT 9.7

Allen Greenfield gratuitously transfers by deed his lakeshore cottage to Patricia Wiliams in trust for the benefit of Allen's son. Unknown to Patricia, Allen makes the transfer to avoid claims of his creditors. The creditors seek to have the trust set aside so that they can attach the property in payment of their claims. Patricia agrees that the trust should be declared void because of its illegal purpose, but she claims that, as an innocent party, she should be entitled to keep the property since equity should not return it to the fraudulent settlor. Who wins? Answer the question according to the laws of your own state.

Situation Three. When the corpus (property) of a private express trust exceeds what is needed for the purpose intended by the settlor, or some part of the trust property remains after the trust has accomplished what its settlor had intended, the court may establish a resulting trust for the benefit of the settlor or the settlor's successors (Restatement [Second] of Trusts § 430).

Example: Regina Andrews died testate providing in her will "I give my 200 shares of Highly Successful, Inc., stock to Harriet Backer in trust to pay the income to Timothy Collins for life." The will does not mention who will receive the remainder. After Timothy dies, there is a resulting trust for Regina's successors of the principal remaining in the trust fund.

🏛 ASSIGNMENT 9.8

In 1992, Eustacia devises (gives) by deed all the land she owns in Pike County to the Westside State Bank for the benefit of her grandchildren and their heirs. Her grandchildren, Daniel and Dorothy, die in 1995 without leaving heirs or wills. Two months later, Eustacia dies.
1. What kind of trust, if any, did Eustacia create in 1992?
2. What kind of trust, if any, is formed in 1995?
3. Dorothy's cousin, Laverne, claims the land because she is Dorothy's next-of-kin. Is she entitled to it?
4. Who receives the equitable and the legal titles, respectively?

Evidence of a Resulting Trust. The English Statute of Frauds, which serves as the model for U.S. statutes on the same subject, required written instruments for certain important transactions. In the spirit of section 7 of the English statute, the majority of U.S. jurisdictions require, either by enacted law or by legal tradition (case law), that trust agreements concerning real estate be "reduced to writing."

A notable exception to this is the *resulting trust*. Since its creation depends not on the act of any person, but on the working of the law, it does not fall within the category of ordinary express trusts and therefore does not have to follow the requirement of written evidence as to its existence. In most circumstances, the proof of the existence of a real estate trust requires written evidence. However, the law allows resulting trusts to be proved by oral (parol) evidence. Difficulties surrounding a purchase-money resulting trust illustrate the importance of this exception to the **Parol Evidence Rule** (Restatement [Second] of Trusts §§ 429, 439, 460). As previously stated, a purchase-money resulting trust involves two parties: one who pays for the property but does not receive legal title to it, and one who receives legal title but does not pay for the property. Does the person who paid (furnished) consideration hold equitable title to the property, or is the transaction a gift from the payor to the recipient? The transaction has the outward appearance of a gift: indeed, when the parties are related by blood or by marriage, there is a strong tendency, even a presumption, to regard it as a gift. A court may determine the true nature of the transaction in the following manner:

Parol Evidence Rule
A general rule of contract law that oral or written evidence (testimony) is not allowed to vary, change, alter, or modify any terms or provisions of a written contract (agreement).

▪ It may presume that the transaction was intended by the parties to be a purchase-money resulting trust instead of a gift. (A presumption is not an indication of how the court feels about the issue or what its ruling will be. It is simply a contention that must be proved or disproved.)

▪ If the party who contends that it was a gift can offer in support convincing evidence that overcomes the presumption that it was not a gift, the presumption will fail.

▪ But failure to represent enough evidence will allow the opposing party (whom the presumption supports) to win.

Since the resulting trust is not controlled by the parol evidence rule, either party may use oral or verbal evidence to prove the case, even when such evidence contradicts the terms of a written instrument (Restatement [Second] of Trusts §§ 440, 441, 458, and generally §§ 440–460).

Example: Harold Wilkerson buys a farm with his own money from James Mason and directs James to convey the farm by deed to Harold's wife, Maude. Maude receives legal title to the farm even though Harold supplied the purchase money. Because Harold and Maude are married, it appears that the farm is a gift from husband to wife. In fact, a presumption to that effect would be made. If anything should impair the marital relationship, e.g., the spouses are divorced, causing Harold to want the farm returned to him, he must prove that the transfer to Maude was not intended as a gift and request that the equity court declare the farm in a purchase-money resulting trust for his benefit.

In summary, payment for property to which the payor does not receive legal title raises the presumption of a resulting trust for the payor's benefit unless the parties involved are spouses or family members. Evidence that can be used to corroborate the presumption may include proof of an oral agreement between the parties; acts of the parties before, at the time of, and after the transfer; or other proof that indicates that a gift or loan was not intended. For instance, if Alma's parents furnish the consideration for a transfer of property to Alma, the parents' earning ability, financial status, age, health, and the like will be considered to determine whether the parents intended a gift to her or a resulting trust for their own benefit.

▥ ASSIGNMENT 9.9

Upon his insolvency, Oliver Sherwood was forced to sell the building in which he conducted business. His children agreed to contribute to a fund to buy back the building. Martha Sherwood, Oliver's eldest child, presented $100,000 to the owner of the building as the repurchase price. The owner of the property reconveyed the legal title to Oliver in return for the $100,000. According to the laws of your own state, what kind of trust is this? Why? Could Oliver again sell the building as he had previously? Could he devise (will) it to a friend or relative?

Constructive Trusts

A constructive trust is *not* created by the stated intent of a settlor. That is an express trust. Nor is a constructive trust created by the implied or presumed intent of a property owner whose acts cause the equity court to enforce a trust established by operation of law. That is a resulting trust. The point of similarity between a constructive trust and a resulting trust is that both are implied, passive trusts. Resulting trusts arise by implication of law or by an equity court decree that declares the property holder to be a trustee as a result of implied intent or because of presumed intent of the parties based on the consequences of their acts. Constructive trusts are not based on express or even implied or presumed intent. A constructive trust is exclusively a creation of the equity court and is established for the purpose of rectifying a serious wrong such as fraud, duress, or unconscionable conduct or preventing unjust enrichment of the wrongdoer. In the case of *Beatty v. Guggenheim Exploration Co.,* 225 N.Y. 380, 122 N.E. 378 (1919), Supreme Court Justice Cardozo identified a constructive trust as "the formula through which the conscience of equity finds expression. When property has been acquired in such circumstances that the holder of the legal title may not in good conscience retain the beneficial interest, equity converts him into a trustee" [of a constructive trust].

When a person has acquired title to property by unlawful or unfair means or by breach of duty as trustee, the court will construct a trust for the benefit of the person rightfully entitled to that property. In such cases, the court declares that the person who has acquired or retained property wrongfully holds the property as "constructive trustee" for the person who has been unjustly deprived of the property. A constructive trust is therefore imposed to remedy a wrong and to prevent unjust enrichment by the person who acquired title at the expense of another. The constructive trustee has no administrative duty other than the obligation to transfer the title and possession of the property to the proper person. The case of *Sharp v. Kosmalski,* 40 N.Y.2d 119, 386 N.Y.S.2d 72, 351 N.E.2d 721 (1976), illustrates the creation of a constructive trust. Rodney Sharp was a 56-year-old farmer whose education did not go beyond the eighth grade. Upon the death of his wife of 32 years, he developed a very close relationship with Jean Kosmalski, 16 years his junior. Sharp proposed marriage to her, but she refused. He continued to make substantial gifts to her including executing a deed naming her joint owner of the farm. Later Sharp transferred his remaining joint interest in the farm to Kosmalski. Kosmalski then ordered Sharp to move out of the house and vacate the farm. Sharp brought this action to impose a constructive trust on the property transferred to Kosmalski. The court ruled that a person may be determined to be unjustly enriched if that person has received a benefit, the retention of which would be unjust, as in this case; therefore, the court decided in favor of Sharp.

When there is a violation (breach) of an agreement between two persons on whom the law imposes a duty to exercise loyalty and good faith toward one another, such as partners in an enterprise or an agent acting for a principal, the court may impose a constructive trust.

Example: Ronald Landis and Anne Chapman agree to a formal written instrument to be business partners and to buy a motel to be operated under the partnership. They employ a real estate agent who finds a property that fits their specifications at a price of $225,000. Later Ronald learns that Anne has bought the property for her own personal use. If he so chooses, Ronald may bring a court action against Anne, charging that she used the knowledge she acquired by virtue of being a business partner to enrich herself unjustly and in violation of their agreement. If Ronald succeeds in convincing the court, it could decree Anne a constructive trustee of the property for the benefit of Ronald, thereby allowing the partnership to obtain the property at the listed price.

A court may also construct a trust when a settlor intends but fails to create an express trust.

Example: By will, Joseph Riccard devises his interest in land to Burton McKeever because Burton had promised orally, in the presence of Virginia Moore and Joseph, to hold the property in trust for Virginia. When the will is probated, the court refuses to recognize the trust because evidence of it was not written into the will. The Statute of Frauds makes orally created trusts of real estate invalid. If Burton is allowed to keep absolute title to the land because Joseph failed to create what he intended to be a testamentary trust, Burton would be unjustly enriched. Virginia's only recourse would be to petition the equity court to "construct" a trust of Joseph's land, placing equitable title in her and leaving Burton with legal title as constructive trustee. This is within the court's power because a constructive trust, like a resulting trust, is exempt from the parol evidence rule. The trust may be based on oral evidence, which, in this case, is Burton's promise as corroborated by Virginia. The burden of proving the oral allegation (promise) would fall on Virginia.

Note that in the last two examples the persons who are made constructive trustees have violated the fiduciary relationship between themselves and another, therefore requiring intervention by a court of equity. Legally, it may appear that neither Anne nor Burton has done anything wrong; however, from the viewpoint of equity they have proceeded improperly by acting unfairly in situations that demanded fairness. In each case the wronged party generally has a choice of remedies, e.g., a choice between an action at law for damages or a suit in equity for the creation of a constructive trust. Both types of relief will not be granted, however, so the wronged party must choose which remedy to pursue.

The court may also construct a trust for the benefit of the rightful owner when a person obtains property by fraud or willfully converts another's personal property for her own use.

Example: Clare Allison works for the Benedict Corporation. She embezzles $10,000 from the corporation and uses the money to buy a mink coat. Under these circumstances, the equity court could decree Clare to be a constructive trustee for the corporation with the duty to transfer possession and title of the coat to the company.

See Exhibit 9.2 for a summary of the types of trusts.

Exhibit 9.2   An Outline Summary of the Main Types of Trusts

A. Two main types of trusts
  1. **Express trust** A trust intentionally created or declared in express terms either by oral declaration or by a written instrument. Express trusts may be—
    a. Private or public (charitable) trusts.
    b. Active or passive trusts.
    c. *Inter vivos* (living) trusts or testamentary trusts.
  2. **Implied trust** A trust imposed on property by the court when trust intent is lacking but the acts of the parties make the imposition necessary. Implied trusts may be—
    a. Resulting trusts.
    b. Constructive trusts.
B. **Express trusts**
  1. Private or public (charitable) trusts
    a. **Private trust** An oral or written trust created for the financial benefit of a certain named individual or individuals.
    b. **Public trust** An express trust created for the social benefit of the public, or specific groups within the public; often called a charitable trust.
  2. Active or passive trusts
    a. **Active trust** A trust that gives the trustee the power and duty to perform discretionary acts of management or administration.
    b. **Passive trust** A trust in which the trustee is a mere holder of the legal title and has no duties of administration or only minor duties that are of a mechanical or formal nature.
  3. *Inter vivos* or testamentary trusts
    a. **Inter vivos (living) trust** An express active trust, either private or public, created during the settlor's lifetime.
    b. **Testamentary trust** An express active trust, either public or private, created in a decedent's will.
C. **Implied trusts**
  1. **Resulting trust** An implied trust created by the equity court to carry out the true intent of a property owner or settlor in cases where the intent of such person is inadequately expressed.
  2. **Constructive trust** An implied trust imposed by courts of equity as a means of accomplishing justice and preventing unjust enrichment. Such trusts are not based on either actual or presumed intent of the parties.

☰ ASSIGNMENT 9.10

1. Russell Haberman owned a tract of land that he believed was practically worthless. His brother-in-law, Francis Holgate, offered to buy the land for one dollar an acre, knowing that it contained valuable mineral deposits of which Russell was unaware. Russell sold the land and subsequently discovered its true value. Has Francis been unjustly enriched by the transaction? Would it be advisable for Russell to ask the court to create a constructive trust for his benefit?
2. In a will dated June 6, 1987, Michelle Walker named her nephew, Clarence Wilson, beneficiary of a substantial portion of her estate. In 1995, Michelle wrote a new will in which Clarence was left nothing; later that year Michelle died. Clarence discovered the second (1995) will but concealed its existence until the probate of the first (1987) will was completed. Then a beneficiary of the second will uncovered the truth. Some states hold that a constructive trust may be created in this case. How would your state decide this matter?

Miscellaneous Trusts

A number of special trust forms need to be discussed. These include the spendthrift, Totten, and sprinkling trusts.

Spendthrift Trusts

A spendthrift is a person who spends money improvidently and foolishly, wasting the funds. As defined in the *Matter of Estate of Sowers v. Southwest National Bank,* 1 Kan.App.2d 675, 574 P.2d 224 (1977), *spendthrift trusts* are trusts created to provide a fund for the maintenance of a beneficiary while safeguarding the fund against the beneficiary's own extravagance or inexperience in spending money. In such trusts, only a certain portion of the total amount of the funds is given to the spendthrift beneficiary at any one time. The settlor provides that the beneficiary cannot assign (transfer) to anyone the right to receive future payments of income or principal from the trust (which the settlor believes the beneficiary would do in times of financial difficulty). At the same time, the settlor declares that creditors of the spendthrift beneficiary cannot reach the trust benefits by obtaining a court order awarding them to the creditors. In this way, settlors seek to protect the beneficiary who cannot or will not handle money wisely. This protection ends once the beneficiary actually receives the distribution of the trust income from the trustee.

Spendthrift trusts do not place limitations on income once it is received by the beneficiary, who may spend it, give it away at will, or use it to satisfy creditors' claims. The trust only guarantees that the beneficiary will not lose the income before receiving it. The rule that principal or income is subject to creditors' claims only after it is received by the beneficiary, and not before, is illustrated by the case of *Sherrow v. Brookover,* 174 Ohio St. 310, 189 N.E.2d 90 (1963); see also N.H. Rev. Stats. Ann. § 498:8 and 9. A majority of states allow settlors to create spendthrift trusts and do not allow creditors to reach (invade the trust) and obtain a beneficiary's interest in the trust if it contains a spendthrift provision. However, if there is no spendthrift provision, the creditors can enforce their claims against the beneficiary's interest. State statutes and case law do allow creditors to reach the beneficiary's trust income despite a spendthrift clause if they have supplied **"necessaries"** to the beneficiary. See Ky. Rev. Stat. § 381.180(6)(b), and *Matter of Dodge's Estate,* 281 N.W.2d 447 (Iowa 1979). Necessaries include necessary services a creditor performs for a beneficiary or necessary supplies a creditor delivers to the beneficiary. See *In re Mayer's Will,* 59 N.Y.S.2d 561 (1945).

Necessaries
Necessary items that supply the personal needs of an individual or family, such as food, clothing, or shelter.

Example: Leo Demarest, a resident of Nevada, wishes to leave a considerable amount of property to his favorite son, Robert, although he knows Robert is irresponsible about handling money. He fears that Robert may go into debt and pledge the income to be received from the trust to pay his creditors. Leo could enable Robert to keep the right to the trust income by inserting the following "spendthrift trust" clause in his will: "It is the purpose of this trust to protect Robert Demarest from want or his own mismanagement and improvidence and to provide him with a reasonable means of support free from claims or interest of any other person. The beneficiary, Robert Demarest, of this trust shall not have the power to transfer, pledge, or assign his interest in the principal or the income of this trust in any manner, nor shall such interest be subject to the claims of his creditors, attachment, garnishment, execution, or other process of law. All payments from the trust shall be paid directly to Robert Demarest and to no other person or entity."

𝍩 ASSIGNMENT 9.11

Theodore Phelps wishes to make a gift of his utility company stocks to his daughter, Jana, who is about to be married. He knows that Jana, being inexperienced in handling securities, might very well sell them at a loss, and being headstrong, she would not listen to sound advice. Would a gift of the property be wise? Is it advisable for Theodore to establish a spendthrift trust for her?

Totten Trusts

A *Totten trust,* also called a P.O.D. (payable on death) account, is a savings account in a bank or savings and loan association in which money is deposited in the depositor's name as trustee for another person named as beneficiary. The name derives from the first case in which such trusts were upheld—*In re Totten,* 179 N.Y. 112, 71 N.E. 748 (1904). Commonly, the trust is created by A, the depositor, in the name of "A, in trust (or as trustee) for B," or in the name of "A, payable on death to B." Such deposits permit the depositor-trustee to withdraw the money while alive and allow any remaining balance of the funds to be transferred to the beneficiary after the depositor's death. If the named beneficiary dies before the depositor, the trust terminates, and the money passes into the depositor's estate on his death. In addition, some courts have held that the depositor in such cases may revoke the "trust" by withdrawing the entire fund or changing the form of the account. The requirements for the creation and distribution of funds in such trusts vary from state to state. Therefore, the individual state statutes must be checked to determine how Totten trusts will be administered. Sections 6–212 and 6–223 of the Uniform Probate Code states that a bank account, such as a Totten trust, belongs to the beneficiary when the trustee dies. In the case of *Hall's Estate v. Father Flanagan's Boys' Home,* 30 Colo.App. 296, 491 P.2d 614 (1971), the court ruled that a Totten trust was created, and the beneficiary, "Boys Town, Nebraska," actually known as Father Flanagan's Boys' Home, was entitled to the trust funds. The money in a Totten trust is a nonprobate asset and is, therefore, not part of the depositor's estate.

Example: Esther Brown changes a savings account in her own name to "Esther Brown, in trust for Jean Brown." Esther has converted her own account into a Totten trust, which is allowed in her state. She has the option of withdrawing any or all of the money as she wishes during her lifetime because the Totten trust is revocable until the settlor's death. Upon Esther's death, Jean, the beneficiary, will own the remaining funds in the savings account. If Jean dies before Esther, however, the Totten trust ends, and the money in the savings account belongs to Esther. If no change is made in this savings account and Esther dies after Jean, the money will be transferred to Esther's estate and will be subject to probate.

Sprinkling Trusts

A *sprinkling trust* gives the trustee the authority and power to accumulate or distribute the income of the trust, the principal, or both among the trust beneficiaries in varying amounts. The financial needs of family members named as beneficiaries constantly change, and a trustee with sprinkling powers has the opportunity to change distributions from the trust to meet the needs of the beneficiaries.

Example: Barbara is a single parent with three adult children. Barbara dies with a testamentary trust in her will that gives the trustee discretionary power to "sprinkle" income to the beneficiaries (the three children) in greatest need. Barbara's youngest child, Sara, is permanently injured in an accident and is obviously in greater financial need than Barbara's other two children, Susan and Elizabeth, both of whom are married and financially secure. The trustee accomplishes what Barbara herself would have wanted by giving the trust's income to Sara.

Example: Barbara's testamentary trust in the above example would also allow her trustee to save income tax dollars for the trust since any distribution to the daughters, Susan and Elizabeth, would be taxed at a higher rate because of their family income.

A sprinkling trust also offers two other advantages: the trust funds are more difficult for creditors of the beneficiaries to reach since the trustee alone decides how much to give each beneficiary; and such trusts may help to reduce estate taxes.

Example: Wanda sets up a sprinkling trust for Harold for life, then to their children. Harold uses up his own estate funds, and the trustee allows the trust funds to accumulate. The trust funds pass to the children on Harold's death free of estate tax.

A disadvantage of a sprinkling trust is that if the trust is intended to qualify for the marital deduction on the decedent's estate tax return, the surviving spouse must receive all the income during the spouse's lifetime.

Since the trustee is given the authority to make important family financial decisions, the settlor must select a trustee that the settlor knows is reliable, experienced, and reasonable. The following is an example of a sprinkling trust provision from West's McKinney's Forms, ESP, § 10:593:

> It is desired that, while the underlying principle of equality shall be followed in making distributions of net income or principal to or for the benefit of any beneficiary, the Trustee is to be entirely free to pay out either more or less to or for the benefit of any particular beneficiary as it deems advisable because of variations in health, character, education, or other requirements, and the Trustee may use both net income and principal in disproportionate amounts to provide security and opportunities for higher education for each beneficiary during the term of the trust. . . . The judgment of the Trustee shall be final and conclusive upon all persons. (Reprinted with permission from West's McKinney's Forms, Copyright ©, by West Publishing Company.)

THE PURPOSES OF TRUSTS

A trust can be created for any lawful purpose, but it must not contravene common or statutory law (Restatement [Second] of Trusts § 59). Most trusts are created to distribute the income from the trust property to family members, friends, or a charity and/or to preserve the trust property for later distribution to such persons on termination of the trust. This can be accomplished during the settlor's lifetime by an *inter vivos* (living) trust or at death by a testamentary trust.

A trust is a practical way to manage and transfer property in the best interests of a beneficiary. Upon the creation of a trust, the trustee assumes the duty of administering the trust, relieving, if desired, both the settlor (grantor) and the beneficiary from the responsibility of managing and conserving the property. Numerous advantages of trusts become obvious. By means of such a device, the settlor can provide:

- Funds for the support of dependent family members, e.g., parents, spouse, children.

Example: Clinton McBride supports his elderly mother, Martha. He realizes she is unable to handle her own financial affairs. Because of her age and frail health, Martha will most likely predecease Clinton. Transferring income-producing property by outright gift in order to have the income taxed in Martha's lower tax bracket would be illogical, since on her death the property will return to Clinton, reduced by his mother's estate and administration expenses. If Clinton places the property in trust for life for his mother, with the remainder to his only child, Jennifer, the income would be taxed to Martha without her receiving legal title to the property. When Martha dies, the property will pass to Jennifer, if she survives Martha.

- Funds for the college education of children.

Example: Kathleen Shannon, a widow, has been a homemaker and mother all her adult life. Her husband died two years ago, leaving her a substantial life insurance benefit. She wants to establish a fund for the college education of her two children. Because of inflation, she realizes that placing the money in a bank and collecting interest may not be the best way financially to achieve her purpose. Since she lacks business experience and the children are minors, the creation of a trust using an experienced trustee to invest the trust property, i.e., the money, may be a good alternative.

- Professional expert financial management for those inexperienced in handling large sums of money, relieving a spouse or children from this responsibility or sparing a settlor the burden of managing property.

Example: Kevin Perry, a single parent, age 55, has recovered from a series of mild heart attacks. He owns property that he wants to transfer by will to his children, Abby and Kent. Since Kevin is concerned about the way the property may be used or spent by his children, he would prefer to transfer it now, while he is alive, in order to determine how well the property is managed. A living trust with a spendthrift clause under experienced and expert corporate management could relieve the children of this administration responsibility, benefit them immediately, and continue after Kevin's death.

Example: Alfred Johnson, an 80-year-old bachelor, in failing health, transfers all his stock to Expert Management Corporation to hold, invest, and manage and to pay the income to him during the remaining years of his life. After his death, the trust property is to be returned to Alfred's estate to be distributed according to his will. This is an *inter vivos* express trust.

- That the trust property will ultimately go to the children of a first marriage on their surviving parent's death. Otherwise, if the surviving parent remarried, the second husband or wife might spend the trust property income that would otherwise be the subject matter of the trust or possibly exert influence on the surviving spouse to convey the property to him or her either during the spouse's lifetime or in the spouse's will to the exclusion of the children of the first marriage.

Example: Larry and Janet Rice are married and desire to have a substantial portion of their property transferred to their children after their respective deaths. If Larry were to die and Janet to remarry, her new husband might inherit Janet's entire estate in her will or convince Janet to transfer her estate to him during her lifetime. In addition, Larry and Janet might obtain a divorce and Janet might remarry, with the same property consequences just described. To avoid these possibilities, Janet and Larry could create a trust that would assure their children of that portion of their parents' estate that the parents intend the children to receive.

■ A method of avoiding probate (court administration of a will), thus cutting costs by acting as a substitute for a will.

Example: Marc Livingston wants to avoid the expense of probate, ancillary proceedings, and the publicity of probate. He may, therefore, choose to create, as a will substitute, a revocable *inter vivos* (living) trust to continue after his death.

■ The flexibility required for a family to meet changing conditions in the future. For instance, if a settlor spouse feels the trust income may exceed the needs of the beneficiary spouse in the future, the settlor may give the trustee the power to determine the needs, distribute such income to the beneficiary, and distribute any excess income to other family members. In another example of the flexibility possible, the trustee may be authorized to invade the principal and pay out portions of it to the beneficiary for special needs. In addition, the settlor may direct the trustee to pay portions of the trust property to the beneficiary on the beneficiary's written demand. In other words, the form and content of a trust can be tailored to fit the specific needs of the individuals involved.

Example: It is possible for the settlor to achieve more than one objective by establishing an *inter vivos* trust continuing after death. Randy Johnson creates a trust naming himself as the beneficiary. In addition, Randy states that he wants to give the subject matter of the trust, the stock, to his nephew, Charles, after his death. He will thus be creating successive enjoyment of (successive interests in) the trust property—in himself before death and in Charles afterward. The income from the stock will be paid to Randy while he lives, and then the property will be transferred to Charles. If Randy is concerned that once the stock belongs to Charles, Charles will foolishly sell the stock and spend the money, Randy could empower the trustee to pay only the income to Charles until he reaches a certain age (see the previous discussion of spendthrift trusts).

■ A preview of how well a trust works for a particular beneficiary while the settlor is still alive and able to alter or terminate the arrangement.

■ A public, charitable trust for a religious or educational institution.

Example: Anna wants to give a substantial amount of money to St. Mary's Hospital, but she wants to control the way the money will be used. She could establish an *inter vivos* trust and name herself as trustee with such powers (see the discussion of express trusts).

■ Savings on taxes (see Chapters 10 and 14).

⚏ ASSIGNMENT 9.12

Charlotte died testate, giving her farm, Longacre, "to Wallace in trust for my husband, Gerard, for his lifetime, and at his death, then in equal shares, as tenants in common, to our two children, Wilma and Richard." At the time of Charlotte's death, all other parties mentioned were living. Does this provision of the will create a trust? Classify it. Wilma and Richard are remaindermen. What does this mean?

⚏ ASSIGNMENT 9.13

Jean-Luc Bernadois, a naturalized citizen, wishes to set up a trust for the benefit of his sister, Claire, who has recently arrived from Martinique and has little knowledge of financial matters. He has government bonds valued at $25,000.

1. Assuming that Jean-Luc does set up a trust, identify the settlor, the beneficiary, and the trust property.

2. Whom might the settlor appoint trustee? Why?
3. Would it be advisable to make a gift of the bonds rather than a transfer of them in trust? Why or why not?

Legal Restrictions

Generally, a trust can be created for any purpose that is legal, but the law has imposed some restrictions on what constitutes legal purposes (Restatement [Second] of Trusts §§ 59, 60). Restrictions on purposes of trusts fall into several categories. There are restrictions on purposes contrary to public policy, such as imposing total restraint on marriage or attempting to encourage divorce (Restatement [Second] of Trusts § 62).

Example: Otto Lindberg tells his son, Scott, that he will transfer his ski resort, Arrowhead, to Daniel Maulkin in trust for Scott's benefit if Scott will divorce his wife, Elizabeth. Such a condition is against public policy and would invalidate the trust. In this case, Otto would retain the trust property. An actual case in which a trust to encourage a divorce was declared invalid is *Rapp v. Cansdale*, 29 Misc.2d 236, 214 N.Y.S.2d 522 (1960).

Some restrictions are imposed by statute. Statutes restricting trusts are usually framed in general language, e.g., N.Y. Estates Powers and Trusts Law § 7–1.4 (McKinney 1967) states: "An express trust may be created for any lawful purpose." The definition of what is "lawful" is then subject to interpretation by the New York courts. Some statutes contain further restrictions, usually in the area of real property trusts.

Example: Hermann Pfalz lives in South Dakota. As a gift to his daughter, Freida, he transfers to her in trust a part of his wheat acreage. Hermann's gift must be in writing to be valid, according to S.D. Comp. Laws Ann. § 55–1–1.

Some restrictions are imposed on private noncharitable trusts by the Rule Against Perpetuities, which prohibits indefinite accumulations of wealth or property. The perpetuation of a trust that effectively prohibits any but members of a certain class from possessing the trust property beyond an extended statutory period contravenes public policy and the Rule Against Perpetuities.

Example: In his will, Howard Engel gives $100,000 in trust to Investors, Inc., to hold and invest, to accumulate the income of the trust property for the next 100 years, and then to transfer the trust estate to the heirs of Howard equally. The trust is invalid because the rule against perpetual interests in trust property requires that the period be no greater than the continuance of lives in being at the time the trust instrument takes effect plus 21 years thereafter.

Another restriction is that a valid trust cannot be formed if it is based on an illegal contract or agreement. Where a trust is created and income is to be paid to the beneficiary on condition that the beneficiary aids in the suppression of criminal proceedings, the purpose is illegal and the trust is invalid. Any illegal purpose, such as inducing the beneficiary to live in adultery with the settlor or defrauding the settlor's creditors, will invalidate the trust. Any trust designed to induce criminal acts is invalid, e.g., a trust set up to reward a beneficiary for committing perjury or to pay legal costs and fines for a beneficiary who commits a crime (Restatement [Second] of Trusts §§ 62b, d, and 63). Any trust designed to induce tortious acts (see Tort in the Glossary) is also invalid, e.g., a trust established to finance one family's feud against another.

The court is faced with difficulties not only when the entire trust is motivated by an illegal purpose but also when a legal trust contains one or more illegal provisions (Restatement [Second] of Trusts § 65). Illegal provisions rarely appear in the trust instrument, and in many cases they are not in writing at all but expressed orally to avoid making the true purpose known. When the trust fails for being entirely motivated by an illegal purpose, every vestige of a "trust" disappears, and the court must decide whether the trust property should be returned to the settlor by means of a "resulting trust" or be disposed of in some other manner (Restatement [Second] of Trusts §§ 422, 444). On the other hand, if the trust has several purposes, some legal and some not, the question is whether the entire trust should fail.

The court's decision depends on whether the purposes are independent or dependent. If the purposes can be easily separated, and the valid purpose enforced without violating the settlor's objective for establishing the trust, then the valid sections can be enforced and the illegal sections voided (Restatement [Second] of Trusts § 65). If the purposes are so inextricably connected that the settlor's intent cannot be achieved without executing both the valid and invalid sections, then the entire trust must fail.

The facts surrounding each case play a major role in determining the result. They must be carefully reviewed by the court before it enforces or voids a multipurpose trust containing legal as well as illegal provisions.

Example: Martin Remek transfers to a trust real and personal property that he owns, naming his sister, Sarah, trustee and his brother, Melvin, beneficiary. The true intent of this trust is to avoid payment of Martin's creditors. If the creditors petition the equity court, the court will set aside the trust and issue a decree (court order) that the trust is void and the property still belongs to the settlor, Martin. The creditors would then be entitled to satisfy (collect) their claims out of the property.

Example: Warren Hammond establishes a trust of $100,000 for the benefit of his daughter, Leslie. Warren names himself trustee and adds that income from the trust property will be given to Leslie as soon as she divorces her husband, Charles. Most courts would hold this latter condition to be contrary to public policy and enforce the trust for the benefit of Leslie notwithstanding the fact that the divorce (condition) did not occur.

🏛 ASSIGNMENT 9.14

Sherman Aldrich, retired president of a paper products firm, creates the Northwest Environmental Trust to preserve valuable forest land in the Pacific Northwest. He endows the trust with $500,000 and, in the trust instrument, directs the trustees, to invest and reinvest the money for the purpose of reforesting certain tracts of land, cultivating them, and encouraging legislation favorable to the continuation of these aims.
1. Is this trust legal of illegal? Why? (Hint: See Restatement [Second] of Trusts § 65.)
2. Under what circumstances, if any, might this trust be declared invalid?
3. In the event that one of the purposes of the trust becomes or is declared to be illegal, could the remainder of the trust be enforced?

As noted in the Hammond example above, just as a trust may not violate statutory law, it may not violate public policy. A provision in a trust imposing total restraint of a marriage on a beneficiary is invalid (see *Young v. Kraeling,*

134 N.Y.S.2d 109 [1954], in which the court held the restraint to be invalid). For instance, if the trust provides that a beneficiary will be divested of an interest if the beneficiary should *ever* marry anyone, the provision is invalid since it is against public policy to prevent a person from marrying, having children, and a normal family life (Restatement [Second] of Trusts § 62h). A trust providing income payments to a person whose spouse has died until that person remarries does not, oppose public policy however, since it restrains not marriage but remarriage. Courts have generally upheld trusts that provide that the beneficiary will lose her interest if she:

- marries a particular person
- marries before reaching majority
- marries before reaching majority without the consent of the trustee (or someone else)
- marries a person of a particular religious faith
- marries a person of a faith different from that of the beneficiary

These restrictions are considered to not "unduly" restrain marriage and are referred to as "reasonable restraints." In determining the validity or invalidity of a partially illegal trust, if the court determines that the settlor's intent was not to restrain marriage but merely to provide support to the beneficiary as long as the beneficiary remains single, it will likely declare the trust valid. The facts, in particular the settlor's intent, are crucial to the court's decision.

If a testamentary trust provides that a beneficiary will be divested for marrying without the consent of executors and trustees, and, if under provisions of the will those persons will profit by refusing to consent to the beneficiary's marriage, the provision is invalid. Provisions that are designed to prevent hasty or imprudent marriages and that subject a minor to the restraint of parents or friends during minority are allowed. The reasoning is that the law should uphold such a provision because it protects the minor from unscupulous persons who could dissipate the proceeds established for the minor's benefit.

Likewise, a provision in a trust that divests beneficiaries of their interests if they communicate or have social relations with certain other family members is invalid as being against public policy and disruptive of family relations (Restatement [Second] of Trusts § 62g).

Another invalid provision is one that constitutes an inducement to change the religious faith of the beneficiary (Restatement [Second] of Trusts § 62i). For example, if a trust provides that Maureen Shannon is to receive her interest only if she changes her religious faith or that her interest ceases if she does not change her religious faith, the courts hold as a general rule that enforcement of such provisions restrains the religious freedom of the beneficiary by improperly inducing her to change her faith.

Normally, a beneficiary of a trust whose rights have been infringed by a trust may gain equitable relief from the court (Restatement [Second] of Trusts § 65d, e, f) except when the beneficiary has also been involved in the illegal bargain or arrangement, e.g., a trust created to defraud the settlor's creditors in which the beneficiary had knowledge of the fraud and agreed to the trust's formation. In such cases, courts will deny relief to the beneficiary by application of the "clean hands" doctrine (see the Glossary) (Restatement [Second] of Trusts §§ 60a(3), 63). The doctrine is useful to the court in dealing with the effect that a trust with an illegal purpose will have on the validity and enforceability of the trust. The doctrine holds that the equity court refuses to be a party to help achieve and enforce such a trust. Therefore, to discourage others from pursuing similar schemes, the equity court leaves the parties to the illegal transaction in their present status. Thus, if a settlor transfers property to a trustee to defraud the settlor's creditors with the understanding that the trustee is ultimately to return the property to the settlor who is also the beneficiary, and the trustee does not perform to the settlor's satisfaction, the court may refuse to direct the trustee to return the property. This result would depend on whether any creditor of the settlor attacked (challenged) the trust. Various resolutions are available to the equity court. If the settlor's creditors challenge the trust, the court will generally set aside the trust as previously discussed. If the defrauded creditors of the settlor are not actually damaged by the settlor's wrongful action or can satisfy their claims against the settlor in other ways, the court may not apply the "clean hands" doctrine but instead may nullify the illegal trust and hold that an implied resulting trust is created in its place.

FORMAL REQUIREMENTS FOR A PRIVATE TRUST

A settlor's declaration of trust and a trust agreement are simple methods of establishing a private trust. The owner of property, i.e., the settlor, simply declares herself trustee of the property for the benefit of another person or signs a trust agreement with a trustee and a successor trustee to create the trust. As mentioned previously, the settlor and the trustee or the settlor and the beneficiary may be the same person. No trust is created, however, until the declaration or the transfer of the trust property takes place. If the conveyance is a transfer of personal property to an *inter vivos* trust, no formalities are required for declaring the trust except that the settlor must manifest an intention to hold or place the property in trust. If the trust property is realty, the settlor must put the declaration in writing to satisfy the requirements of the Statute of Frauds (Restatement [Second] of Trusts § 40). Likewise, delivery requirements are simple. For example, if the conveyance is a gift of land, the settlor must deliver the deed to the trustee; if the gift is personal property, usually delivery of the gift itself is necessary.

Example: Carol Flexner, a widow with four children, received her father's resort, Edgewater, from his estate. If Carol wishes to create a trust using this property, she will have to put the trust agreement in writing. She will also have to deliver the deed to Edgewater to the trustee.

A manifestation of intention to create an *inter vivos* trust at some later time does not create a trust at the time the settlor manifests this intent (Restatement [Second] of Trusts § 26). If a settlor declares an intention to create a trust some time in the future or makes an unenforceable promise at a subsequent time to transfer property to another person in trust, a trust does not exist. Until the settlor actually makes the transfer, a trust is not created.

Example: Cliff Reid tells Enoch Mitchell that he intends to transfer securities to Enoch in trust for Mary Alexander Webb in the coming week. No trust arises until Cliff actually transfers the securities to Enoch in trust. Cliff has not created a trust until he does so; therefore, he may change his mind and create no trust at all, or appoint someone else trustee.

If Cliff had intended himself to be both settlor and beneficiary of the trust, but had not yet acquired the trust property, he could not have created a trust simply by informing Enoch of his intention. A trust depends on the separation of the settlor's absolute title into legal and equitable titles. This cannot be done until the settlor actually owns the absolute title.

Example: Bill Taylor promises Teresa Hall that when he purchases certain shares of stock, he will execute a declaration of trust declaring himself trustee of the shares for Teresa's benefit. A trust is not created until Bill has both acquired the shares and declared himself trustee.

If the settlor intends to create a trust at the time of the declaration, a trust may arise at that time even if it gives the beneficiary a future interest that will not take effect until some later time (Restatement [Second] of Trusts § 26g).

Example: Luisa Harper owns 75 shares of stock in IBM and declares herself trustee of the stock for ten years for Rose Maguire's benefit. After the expiration of ten years, the income will then be paid to Tony Harper. Even though Tony's beneficial interest does not take effect until the end of the ten-year period, the trust is created at the time of Luisa's declaration.

Example: Franklin Folger's will provided in part: "To my daughter Aileen, I leave in trust the proceeds of the sale of my interest in the Great West Company, of which I am presently a partner, if the sale of such interest shall be perfected within six months of my death. If it shall not have been perfected, I leave said interest to my wife, Gladys." This provides that a trust shall begin in the future and is valid even though the sale will probably not be perfected (completed) immediately upon Franklin's death. The trust property is currently owned by the settlor. The intended trust would not take effect if Franklin did not own an interest in the company at the time he signed and dated the will.

The creation of a present trust of a promise to be performed in the future must be distinguished from the case where a settlor promises to create a trust in the future (Restatement [Second] of Trusts §§ 26n and 17e).

Example: If John Rollings, intending to create an immediate trust, makes an enforceable promise to pay money or to convey property to Clare Barrett as trustee at some time in the future, a present trust is created. Clare holds the right to be a trustee provided that John manifests an intention to create an immediate trust based on that right. Had he promised to create the trust at the time when the money is paid or the property conveyed, no trust would have resulted.

The promisor is generally not bound if the promise is made at no cost to either party, gratuitously, i.e., no consideration is given the promisor. If the gratuitous promise, however, is solemnized (notarized, i.e., the promise is made under oath before a notary public), it is binding. The promisor has created a trust, and the promisee immediately becomes a trustee of the rights that the promise produces.

Example: George Hart promises orally to give Reginald Johnston $25,000 in trust for Michael Foreman. No money is exchanged (i.e., the promise is "without consideration"), and the promise has not been notarized. Therefore the promise does not bind George to create or Reginald to manage a trust.

INFORMAL AND INCOMPLETE CREATION OF A TRUST

When competent legal advice is not sought, a private express trust might be drafted improperly, and litigation could result. We will now take a look at some of the major mistakes made in an improperly drafted trust instrument:

Precatory word
Words such as hope, desire, request, ask, beseech, wish, or recommend.

■ A testator-settlor, in a hand-drawn will, indicates that he wants certain testamentary trust objectives accomplished but expresses this using **precatory**

words such as hope, desire, request, or wish rather than expressing it as a mandate.

■ The trust document does not sufficiently identify the beneficiary or fails to name a beneficiary.

■ The trust instrument fails to name a trustee or fails to name a successor when the named trustee does not want to serve.

■ The document names the trustee and describes the beneficiaries but does not specify the duties of the trustee.

■ Although the trust instrument purports to be transferring legal title, the trust terms are not specified, or they have only been implied in an informal oral agreement.

Failure to Make Intentions Clear

It is possible to create a trust without actually using the words "trustee" or "in trust." On the other hand, in a hand-drawn instrument the use of these words is not conclusive evidence of the intent to create a trust. In order to create an express trust, the court must be satisfied that the settlor manifested an intention to impose enforceable duties on the trustee to manage the property for the benefit of others. When a testator uses precatory words such as "hope," "wish," "desire," or "recommend" to devise the property of his estate, the court must determine whether he intended an absolute gift or a trust (Restatement [Second] of Trusts § 25). It will consider all relevant factors before reaching a conclusion.

Example: Desmond Cormac's will provides, in part: "I give to my wife in the event of my death all my interest in the farm we own as tenants in common and all the stock, farm implements, etc., after my debts are paid. To have and to hold the same in fee simple and to dispose of the same among the children as she may think best." An argument could be made that the will establishes a trust in the property for the benefit of the children, but another view is that the devisee (the wife) is given an estate in fee simple.

Example: John Vanderhaavn's will gives property to his wife "to be her absolute estate forever," then added the words, "it is my request that upon her death, my said wife shall give, devise, and bequeath the real property given her to persons named in the fourth clause of this will." An ambiguity is created because the testator cannot create a fee simple estate for his wife and then request that the same property be transferred on her death to others. That right belongs to the fee owner, i.e., the testator's wife. The court held that the wife took the property in fee simple and not in trust.

These examples illustrate the effects that unclear terms may have on an intended trust. In many cases, inclusion of these precatory words results in the undoing of the would-be settlor's intentions.

The early English view held that the use of such words as "request," "desire," "hope," and "wish" were a courteous means of creating duties enforceable by the courts. Today, both English and American courts hold that the use of such precatory words does *not* create a trust. The intent to create a trust containing such words must be proven by other sections of the trust instrument or by extrinsic circumstances (Restatement [Second] of Trusts § 25).

Example: Suppose a testator, Marvin Rothman, wills all his property to his wife, and then adds, "I recommend to her the care and protection of my mother and sister, and request her to make such provision for them as in her judgment will be best." Both mother and sister are invalids and in need, and the testator had supported them for some time before his death. A court could hold that the wife took the property in trust with the obligation to make a reasonable provision for the continual care of the testator's mother and sister. Such a testamentary trust is poorly drafted because it creates an ambiguity, i.e., a conveyance of the estate property to the testator's spouse but with a request that the spouse "care and protect" the testator's invalid mother and sister. A court's decision to call this will provision a testamentary trust could be based on the circumstances, i.e., the fact that the mother and sister were invalids, and the testator had previously cared for them. But consider and compare the case of *In re Estate of Lubenow,* 146 N.W.2d 166 (N.D. 1966), in which the testator left his estate to his nephew with directions, "to see to it that my brothers are provided for." The court held "these [precatory] words do no more than express a wish or desire on the part of the testator." Therefore no testamentary trust was created. The nephew received the entire estate.

When drafting wills and trusts, it is best to avoid these precatory words altogether.

Failure to Name or Identify the Beneficiary

When the trust instrument fails to name any beneficiary, a few cases give the trustee absolute ownership, but the general rule is that a "resulting trust" arises in favor of the decedent's estate if the trust instrument was testamentary (Restatement [Second] of Trusts §§ 44e and 45e). If the trust is *inter vivos* and the instrument fails to name a beneficiary, the attempt to create a trust fails.

Example: If Mel Bowles had set aside money for a trust, executed the instrument, and directed the trustee to distribute the income to persons that the trustee considered deserving, the trust would be void because Mel did not indicate clearly who were to be the beneficiaries. Had he augmented the description, e.g., "to be distributed to my nieces and nephews" or "to the descendants of my sister, Judith," the beneficiaries would at least be discoverable.

When the trust property is in excess of the trust purposes, e.g., the settlor directs payment of such part of the income as is necessary for the support of the named beneficiary and makes no provision for the excess, the excess takes the form of a resulting trust for the benefit of the settlor or her successors if the settlor has died (Restatement [Second] of Trusts §§ 430–439). When the trust fails or its purpose is accomplished and the settlor is dead, the law imposes a resulting trust for the settlor's successors.

Example: Cyrus Heymann is the chief stockholder of Silver City, Inc., a retirement community. Seeking tax savings, he transfers 2,500 shares, half his holdings, to his sister, Sybil, to hold in trust for him (Cyrus being both settlor and beneficiary). Cyrus dies suddenly. The trust is therefore, terminated for lack of a beneficiary. If she continues to be the trustee, Sybil holds the shares in a resulting trust for Cyrus's estate.

The presumption of a resulting trust can be rebutted if it can be shown that the settlor did not intend to create a resulting trust, e.g., where the settlor clearly intended the trustee to retain and fully own the property or the surplus.

Example: If it appeared doubtful whether Cyrus Heymann in the above example intended a gift or a trust in transferring the stock to Sybil, evidence clarifying his intent would have to be produced. It could not, however, be verbal, such as Cyrus's bookkeeper's oral testimony on Cyrus's conversations on the subject, but would have to be written, such as a letter written by Cyrus or his tax returns, in which Cyrus makes clear that he did or did not intend to make a gift of the property to Sybil.

Failure to Name a Trustee or a Successor Trustee

A valid trust will not fail for want of a trustee or successor trustee. Lack of a trustee to administer the trust may come about in any of the following ways:

- If the settlor does not name a trustee in the trust instrument or fails to name a successor trustee to resolve the problem of the original trustee's death, resignation, or nonacceptance, i.e., the trustee's unwillingness or inability to serve.
- If the named trustee does not qualify, e.g., refuses to accept the duty, dies before the effective date of the trust, or is refused confirmation of the office by the court because of incompetence.
- If the named trustee does not have legal capacity to hold property in trust, e.g., in some states an unincorporated association.
- If the named trustee is removed or resigns after the effective date of the trust.

Courts will preserve trusts. Normally, the court will not allow a trust to fail for any of the above reasons and will appoint a new trustee so long as the trust is otherwise valid. Where a trustee is needed to execute and manage a trust, state statutes authorize the court to appoint the following: (1) an original trustee where the trust document or will creating the trust has not nominated a trustee or the nominee is unable or unwilling to serve; and (2) a successor trustee, when the original trustee has ceased to act and a replacement is required to finish the administration of the trust. The trust will fail only if it can be shown that the settlor intended that only the named person and no one else could be the trustee.

Although the laws of a few states prohibit the creation of joint tenancy, this prohibition does not apply to property held in trust. Co-trustees generally hold title to trust property as joint tenants with the right of survivorship, so if one dies, disclaims, resigns, or is removed by a court, legal title passes to the remaining co-trustee(s) by operation of law (Restatement [Second] of Trusts § 103).

Example: Curt Baird places 500 shares of Behl, Inc., in trust for the benefit of his son, Kyle, naming Curt's three brothers trustees. Later one brother resigns due to ill health. The court decides that two trustees will suffice because the settlor did not specify that there be three at all times. Therefore, the court does not appoint a new trustee. At the annual stockholders' meeting of Behl, the two trustees vote in the name of the trust. Another major stockholder objects that the Baird trust votes were invalid because they were cast by two, not three, trustees. The votes are valid. The two trustees hold the entire legal title to the trust by the right of survivorship.

LIVING (*INTER VIVOS*) TRUSTS

An *inter vivos* trust, commonly known as a living trust today, is one of the two ways property can be placed in a trust; the other is a testamentary trust, a trust within a will. A living trust is created by a settlor and operates during the settlor's lifetime. The trust property is a nonprobate asset; therefore, it is not part of the decedent's probate estate and is not under the jurisdiction or supervision of the probate court.

A living trust can be created by either of the following:

1. A declaration of trust in which the settlor retains the legal title to the trust property and is therefore the trustee and then names another person or persons to be the beneficiaries. The declaration of trust must be signed by the settlor and at least two witnesses and notarized (see Exhibit 9.3 for a sample declaration of trust).

2. A trust agreement in which the settlor transfers legal title to another party, the trustee, who manages or administers the property in trust for the beneficiary who holds the equitable title and receives the benefits of the trust (see the Carter Trust in Exhibit 8.2).

Revocable Living Trusts

A living trust is either revocable or irrevocable. In a revocable trust, the settlor reserves the right to amend, revoke, or cancel the trust at any time while living. Upon the death of the settlor, the living trust becomes irrevocable and the trust property is disposed of or distributed according to the terms of the trust. Because revocable trusts avoid the need for and cost of probate or estate administration, they are commonly used in estate planning (see Chapter 10). A revocable living trust is not a device for saving estate taxes, however; only an irrevocable trust offers that tax benefit (see the discussion below). Many people today are using a revocable living trust as a substitute for a will. It allows them to transfer their entire estate to the trust, manage and control the trust, receive the income from the trust during their lifetime, distribute the trust property to the named beneficiaries (usually their children) after they die, and avoid the often substantial costs and delays of probate (see the discussion of advantages below).

When a revocable living trust is created a trustee must be named to manage and control the trust. Generally, the settlor will name himself trustee, or, if married, the settlor and the settlor's spouse will act as co-trustees or joint-trustees, which grants either spouse the legal authority to act as trustee. Then if one spouse becomes disabled or dies, the other spouse automatically has control of the trust without the delays and expense of the probate process or the intervention of the probate court. Even though a settlor no longer owns the trust property, the revocable living trust enables the settlor-trustee to retain complete control of the property and to avoid paying any management fees. As trustee, the settlor can invest, buy, and sell the trust property, distribute the income from the trust to himself or to whomever the settlor chooses, change the trust beneficiaries, or, because it is revocable, cancel the trust at any time. The former owner (settlor) of the trust property who is now the trustee is still obligated to perform duties concerning the trust property such as preserving, maintaining, and insuring the property and filing the annual income tax returns. If the settlor appoints someone else trustee, the trust agreement usually provides that the trustee is to manage and invest the trust property for the benefit of the settlor-beneficiary for life, and pay to the settlor-beneficiary all the income and as much of the principal of the trust as the settlor or the trustee determines to be required for the settlor's care. Problems that arise due to the disability, incompetence, or death of the settlor are discussed below.

In the past, the revocable living trust was most commonly used for the primary benefit of an elderly settlor who owned a substantial amount of income-producing property (assets) and desired to be relieved of the responsibility of managing the property. Today, many people of all income brackets are substituting revocable living trusts for wills.

Exhibit 9.3   Sample Declaration of Trust

DECLARATION OF TRUST
(A-B Revocable Trust)

[Trust Name (Number) _____]

This DECLARATION OF TRUST made and executed this _____ day of _____ ,

19_____ , in the _____ of _____ , State of _____ ,

by and between, the herein named Trustor(s) and Trustee(s):

Trustor		Trustor
Name: _____	(and)	Name: _____
Address: _____		Address: _____
_____		_____

Trustee		Trustee
Name: _____	(☐ and)(☐ or)	Name: _____
Address: _____		Address: _____
_____		_____

Successor Trustee		Successor Trustee
Name: _____	(☐ and)(☐ or)	Name: _____
Address: _____		Address: _____
_____		_____

BENEFICIARY (BENEFICIARIES)

Name of Beneficiaries	Name of Beneficiaries
_____	_____
_____	_____
_____	_____
_____	_____

WITNESSETH:

1. TRUST INTENT AND BENEFICIARY SURVIVORSHIP CLAUSE.

The Trustor(s) has(have) caused the transfer of all of his(her)(their) rights, title and interest in and to the property herein described in Clause No. 2 of this Declaration of Trust, to the above named Trustee(s) to be held In Trust for the use, benefit and enjoyment of the above named Beneficiary(Beneficiaries) in equal shares, except that if any such beneficiary named above does not survive me(us), then that Beneficiary's share of the Trust Property shall be distributed as follows:

_____

_____

_____

_____ .

FORM AABT-101-1   **Page 1 of 7 Pages**

Exhibit 9.3   Sample Declaration of Trust—*continued*

2. TRUST PROPERTY CLAUSE. (*When Page 1 is either Form AABT-101-1 or Form AABT-101-2*)

(a) The property being initially transferred by the Trustor(s) to establish this DECLARATION OF TRUST is situated and

described as follows: (Describe separately each item of property and its situate, i.e., City, County, State, etc.) _____

_____

_____

_____

_____

_____

_____

_____

_____

_____

_____

_____

_____

_____

_____

_____

_____

_____

_____

_____

_____

_____

_____

_____

_____

_____

_____

_____

_____

_____

_____

_____

_____

_____

including all other real and/or personal property of every kind and nature that the Trustee(s) may, pursuant to any of the provisions hereof, at any time hereafter acquire, hold or cause to be made payable to this Trust, and the investments and reinvestments (all such property being hereinafter referred to collectively as the Trust Property) for the benefit, purposes and uses, and upon the terms and conditions herein set forth.

FORM AABT-102-1   **Page 2 of 7 Pages**

Exhibit 9.3   Sample Declaration of Trust—*continued*

3. AUTHORITY, POWER AND RIGHTS OF TRUSTOR(S).

(a) The Trustor(s) reserves unto himself(herself)(themselves) the authority, power and right to amend, modify or revoke the TRUST hereby created. No prior notice to or consent of any Beneficiary or the Trustee(s) shall be required.

(b) The Trustor(s) may at any time appoint, substitute or otherwise change the person(s) designated to act as Trustee(s) or Successor Trustee under this TRUST hereby created. No prior notice to or consent of any such Trustee, Successor Trustee or Beneficiary shall be required.

(c) All amendments, notices or other documents and instruments affecting or furthering the purposes of this Declaration of Trust shall be in writing and upon proper form.

4. TRUSTOR'S(S') EXCLUSIVE RIGHT TO TRUST INCOME.

The Trustor(s) during his(her)(their) lifetime, shall be exclusively entitled to all income accruing from the Trust Property. No beneficiary named herein shall have any claim, or be authorized to make any claim upon the trust income, profits or property, except as herein provided below under Clause No. 7(c).

5. TRUSTOR'S(S') AUTHORITY TO ENCUMBER TRUST PROPERTY.

The Trustor(s), in his(her)(their) capacity as Trustee(s) shall be empowered with the discretionary authority to mortgage, pledge, hypothecate or otherwise encumber with a lien any or all of the Trust Property. Said lien(s) may be satisfied, settled or discharged from the income, rents or profits accruing from the Trust Property, or any other non-trust property owned by the Trustor(s), if he(she)(they) so elect.

6. POWERS OF TRUSTEE(S).

(a) The Trustee(s) under this Declaration of Trust has(have) all of the discretionary powers deemed necessary and appropriate to administer this Trust, including, but not limited to, the power to buy, sell trade, deal, encumber, mortgage, pledge, lease or improve the Trust Property of every kind and nature, whether real or personal, including every type and nature of both debt and equity instruments, including option contracts and limited partnership interest, when such action is deemed to be in the best interest and furtherance of the Trust purposes.

(b) In the event this Declaration of Trust provides for more than one Trustee (Co-Trustees), and unless the Co-Trustee designation on Page 1 of this Declaration Of Trust utilizes the conjunction "and", the exercise of any and all authorities, powers and rights accorded to said Trustees under this Trust shall not be construed as requiring the Trustees to act in unison in order to exercise the Trust Authorities and Powers, but that each such Trustee may severally exercise any of the enumerated Trust Authorities and Powers.

(c) In the event of a physical or mental incapacity or death of one of the Co-Trustees, the survivor shall continue as the Sole Trustee with full authority to exercise all of the powers accorded to a Trustee under this Trust, except as herein provided below under Paragraph 7, including the appointment of a new Co-Trustee or sole Trustee, if desired.

(d) The Trustee(s) shall be fully authorized to pay over or disburse to the Trustor(s), any amounts requested by said Trustor(s) from the income or principal of the Trust, from time to time, as herein provided.   All references hereinafter made regarding withdrawals by Trustor, mean and include, payments authorized and made by Trustee(s) under this Trust..

7. DEATH OF ONE CO-TRUSTOR.

Upon the death of one Co-Trustor, the surviving Trustor shall make an equitable division of this Trust into two separate and distinct Trust. One Trust shall be designated "Trust A" while the other shall be designated "Trust B".

(a) "Trust A" Allocation.   "Trust A" shall be allocated that portion of the Trust Corpus that exceeds in value the maximum amount allowable under the Unified Federal Estate Tax Credits, which said amounts shall accordingly take into account not only the property interest in the Trust Corpus, but any property interest that may exist under the provisions of Deceased Trustor's Last Will And Testament, if any, or otherwise than under this Trust, provided, however, that all amounts allocated to "Trust A" that are greater than the maximum amount allowable under the Unified Federal Estate Tax Credits, which represents that portion of the deceased trustor's joint community interest in excess of the maximum amount allowable under the Unified Federal Estate Tax Credits, shall be subject to the "Federal Estate Tax Marital Deduction."

"Trust A" shall thereafter be continued as a Revocable Living Trust incorporating all of the applicable authorities, powers, rights and provisions set forth in this Declaration of Trust.

(b) "Trust B" Allocation.   "Trust B" shall be allocated that portion of the Trust Corpus or any other property interest that may exist under Deceased Trustor's Last Will And Testament, if any, or otherwise than in this Trust that does not exceed in value the maximum amount allowable under the Unified Federal Estate Tax Credits.

"Trust B" shall thereafter be continued as an Irrevocable Trust, specifically, terminating those authorities, powers, rights and

FORM AABT-103   **Page 3 of 7 Pages**

Exhibit 9.3   Sample Declaration of Trust—*continued*

provisions granted to the Trustors to amend, modify or revoke any beneficiary designation and Trust Corpus distribution, except as may otherwise be provided in this Clause under subsections "d" and "e", respectively. Further enumeration of the authorities, powers, rights and provisions applicable to the Trustors, Trustees and Beneficiaries under both "Trust A' and "Trust B" are inclusive herein in said subsections "d" and "e", respectively.

(c) Recognizable Intent.   It being fully recognized that the purpose of this Trust division rest upon the advantages gained in applying the maximum allowable Unified Federal Estate Tax Credits under Section 2010(a) of the Internal Revenue Code, as amended. It shall therefore be considered that, at the time of the death of one Co-Trustor, each Co-Trustor owns a Joint Community interest in the total value of the Trust Corpus, with said value being subject to the trust divisions herein specified.

(d) Trust A.   The Trust designated "Trust A" shall continue to be a Revocable Living Trust which shall provide to the surviving Trustor, a frequent and convenient source of income. Such income shall be paid by the Trustee first from the net income produced by the Trust Corpus, provided, however, that if such income is insufficient to provide adequately for the surviving Trustor's health, support, education and/or accustomed manner of living and comfort, then, such income payments may be made from the principal of said "Trust A."

(e) Trust B.   The Trust designated "Trust B" shall be an Irrevocable Trust, designating as beneficiary or beneficiaries, the individuals or entities so named in this Declaration Of Trust or subsequently added to this Trust with a proper instrument after the initial establishment of the Trust, but prior to the death of one Trustor, unless any such beneficiary designation was previously revoked or such beneficiary(ies) did not survive the Trustor and his or her share was not per stirpes, but the survivors of them. In which case, said beneficiary, beneficiaries or beneficiary's estate shall not receive consideration of any kind or nature under either "Trust A" or "Trust B."

The surviving Trustor may be paid from said "Trust B," all or any portion of the income produced by the Trust Corpus, provided, however, that if such sums are not sufficient to provide for the support and maintenance of surviving Trustor's accustomed manner of living, including those amounts necessary to pay his or her medical expenses, then, such additional amounts in excess of the income produced by the Trust Corpus may be withdrawn from the principal of the Trust Corpus.

This right to invade the principal of the Trust Corpus is clothed within the meaning of an *ascertainable standard* relating to the support, maintenance and health care of the surviving Trustor as promulgated under the Internal Revenue Code.

The surviving Trustor may also withdraw annually from the principal of the Trust Corpus, an amount not exceeding $5,000 or 5 percent of the principal value of the Trust Corpus without regards to any other sums withdrawn for the support and maintenance of Trustor's accustomed manner of living as above provided. Said withdrawal shall be on a non-cumulative basis.

8. AUTHORITY OF SUCCESSOR TRUSTEE(S) TO ADMINISTER THE TRUST.

(a) The Successor Trustee(s) shall, upon either the death of the Trustor, if no Co-Trustor, the simultaneous deaths of the Co-Trustors, or the death of the surviving Co-Trustor, assume the active administration of this Trust and carry out those duties as herein provided, including, but not limited to, the forthwith transfer of all rights, title and interest in and to the Trust Property unto the Beneficiaries, subject, however, to the provisions of Clause No. 11 below.

(b) The Successor Trustee(s) shall assume the active administration of this Trust during the lifetime of the Trustor(s) when the Trustor or Trustors is(are) unable to actively and competently exercise any of the authorities, powers or rights so accorded under this Trust by reason of a sustaining Medical or Mental Impairment, as certified by a competent attending medical authority.

9. TERMINATION OF SUCCESSOR TRUSTEE'S AUTHORITY.

The Successor Trustee's authority and power as provided under Clause No. 8(b) may be subsequently terminated by the Trustor(s) without the consent of, or prior notice to, said Successor Trustee(s) when the Trustor or Trustor(s) is(are) sufficiently recovered from the medical or mental impairment as described under Clause No. 8(b) above, and thus, fully and competently capable of actively administering this Trust.

The termination of the Successor Trustee's authority to actively administer this Trust under Clause No. 8(b) shall be effective immediately upon the Successor Trustee's receipt of the Trustor's Notice terminating all such authorities and powers previously granted by the Trustor(s).

10. AUTHORITY OF SUCCESSOR TRUSTEE(S) TO DISBURSE FUNDS.

The Successor Trustee(s) shall be fully authorized to pay or disburse such sums from the income or principal as may be required, necessary or desirable to maintain the comfort and welfare of the Trustor(s) when the conditions described in Clause No. 8(b) of this Declaration of Trust prevail.

Exhibit 9.3 Sample Declaration of Trust—*continued*

11. AUTHORITY OF SUCCESSOR TRUSTEE(S) TO CONTINUE TRUST.

(a) The Successor Trustee(s) shall hold in Continuing Trust, upon the deaths of the Trustor or the surviving Trustor(s), that share of a Beneficiary's Trust Assets when such Beneficiary either shall not have attained majority age, or the distribution of the Trust Assets to any Beneficiary(ies) is limited by a proper document executed by Trustor(s) which effectively continues the Trust. During such period of Continuing Trust, the Successor Trustee, at his(her)(their) discretion, may retain, sell or invest and reinvest certain and specific Trust Property, if it is deemed to be in the best interest of the beneficiary and accomplished in a reasonably prudent manner.

If said specific Trust Property shall be productive of income, or if such property be sold or otherwise disposed of, the Successor Trustee may pay, disburse or otherwise expend any or all of the income or principal accruing from such property toward the maintenance, education or support of such beneficiary without the intervention of any parent or guardian, and without application to any Court.

Said payments may be made either to the parents, guardian or any other person or institution exercising the responsibility of maintaining, educating or supporting such beneficiary and without any liability upon the Successor Trustee as to the application thereof.

(b) In the event said beneficiary survives the Trustor(s), but dies before attaining the age of 21 years, the Successor Trustee shall transfer, pay over and deliver the Trust Property being held for such beneficiary to the Estate of said beneficiary, if said beneficiary is married or there are one or more issues of such beneficiary(ies), otherwise, said Trust Property shall be distributed to, divided between or among, whichever applicable, the surviving beneficiary or beneficiaries.

12. INALIENABILITY OF BENEFICIARY'S INTEREST IN TRUST.

The interest of the Beneficiary(ies) under the Trust shall be inalienable. Said Beneficiary(ies) can not assign, sell, pledge, encumber or otherwise transfer his(her)(their) inalienable interest in the Trust Property to a third party. Nor can such interest be attached, garnished, levied upon or otherwise subjected to any proceedings whether at law or in equity, including any such interest under both Trust A and Trust B when they become effective.

13. BENEFICIARY'S PROPORTIONATE LIABILITY FOR ESTATE TAXES.

Each Beneficiary hereunder shall be liable for his(her) proportionate share of any Estate Taxes that may be levied upon the total value of the Trust Property distributed to said Beneficiary(ies) upon the death of either the Trustor or the survivor of the Trustor(s).

14. REVOCATION OF DESIGNATION OF BENEFICIARY.

(a) The Trustor(s) is(are) reserved with the right to revoke, at any time, the designation of a herein named Beneficiary, without prior notice to or the consent of any other such Beneficiary.

(b) The Trustor(s) may, at any time, either designate a new beneficiary to replace a previously revoked beneficiary designation or designate an additional beneficiary, notwithstanding all previous beneficiary designations. No prior notice to or the consent of any other beneficiary is required.

(c) In the event any Beneficiary under this Trust shall not survive the Trustor(s), the Trustor(s) may designate a new beneficiary to replace such Beneficiary by amending this Declaration of Trust. If however, the Trustor(s) fails to so designate a new beneficiary as herein provided, then, upon the death of either the Trustor or the survivor of the Trustor(s), such beneficiary's share of the Trust Property shall be distributed in accordance with the survivor designation provided hereinbefore in Paragraph 1.

15. NON-LIABILITY OF THIRD PARTIES.

(a) This Trust is created with the express intent and understanding that any third parties, including their Agents, Employees or Vendors, who, upon the written request of the Trustor(s), or under the color of authority granted to the Trustee(s) in this Trust Instrument, perform any duties or render any services in the furtherance of the purposes and intents of this Trust, absent any showing of fraud, shall be under no liability for the proper administration of any assets or properties being the subject of the said third party's acts.

(b) This limitation of liability gives specific protection to any third party who acts, performs or renders any services pursuant to any Notice, Instrument or Document believed (and represented) to be genuine, and to have been signed and presented by the proper party(ies).

Exhibit 9.3   Sample Declaration of Trust—*continued*

(c) It is further the express intent of this Trust that the non-liability of all third parties be given broad and prospective application. In particular, a Depository, Custodial Agent or Financial Institution, including, but not limited thereby to: Banks, Brokerage Firms, Credit Unions, Savings and Loan Associations, Transfer Agents, Thrift Associations, or any other person or entity acting in a Fiduciary capacity with regards to any assets or property comprising the TRUST RES, shall suffer no liability, nor incur any express or implied obligations when acting in the capacity of a transferor, upon proper request, of any assets or property constructively sought to be transferred to the Trust, Trustee or Beneficiary(ies).

16. EXTENSION OF TRUST POWERS.

This Declaration of Trust shall extend to and be binding upon the Heirs, Executors, Administrators and Assigns of the undersigned Trustor(s) and upon the Successor(s) to the Trustee(s).

17. BOND AND EXPENSES.

(a) The Trustee(s) under this Declaration of Trust shall serve without Bond.

(b) The Successor Trustee(s) may also serve without bond, at the election of the Beneficiary(ies) or the parent or guardian of such Beneficiary(ies) not of majority age, except that bond *(check one)* ☐ shall (☐ may) be required when, upon the death(s) of the Trustor(s), whichever applicable, the Beneficiary(ies) either shall not have attained majority age, or the Trust will be continued as herein provided in Clause No. 11, or the distribution of the Trust Res to any beneficiary(ies) is limited by a proper document executed by Trustor(s) which effectively continues the Trust.

The requirement of Bond in this instance shall be in a nominal amount and chargeable to the Trust Res.

(c) The Successor Trustee shall be reimbursed out of the Trust Res before final distribution to the Beneficiary(ies) for all out-of-pocket expenses incurred in the discharge of duties as Successor Trustee.

(d) Upon the agreement of the Beneficiary(ies), including the parent or guardian of such Beneficiary(ies) not of majority age, the Successor Trustee may be reasonably compensated for extraordinary time and efforts employed to accomplish the discharge of duties as Successor Trustee.

18. COMMON DISASTER.

(a) In the event Trustors shall both die, in, or as a result of, a common accident or disaster, or under circumstances that the order of deaths cannot be established by proof, then Trustor's Wife shall be conclusively presumed to have survived him for the purposes of this Declaration Of Trust.

(b). In the event any beneficiary(ies) named in this Declaration Of Trust shall die with Trustors, in, or as a result of, a common accident or disaster, or under circumstances that the order of deaths cannot be established by proof, then such beneficiary(ies) shall be conclusively presumed to have predeceased Trustors.

19. APPLICABILITY OF STATE LAWS.

This Declaration of Trust shall be construed and enforced in accordance with the Laws of the State of _____

_____ .

20. SAVING CLAUSE.

If a State Court of competent jurisdiction shall at any time invalidate any of the separate provisions of this Declaration of Trust, such invalidation shall not be construed as invalidating the whole of the Declaration of Trust, but only that separate provision in controversy. All of the remaining provisions shall be undisturbed as to their legal force and effect.

IN WITNESS WHEREOF, the Trustors have hereunto set their hands and seals the day and year first above written.

_____
(Trustor)

_____
(Co-Trustor)

Exhibit 9.3 Sample Declaration of Trust—*continued*

ACKNOWLEDGMENT

State of _____)
) ss.
County of _____)

On this _____ day of _____ , 19 ____ , before me, the undersigned Notary

Public, personally appeared, _____

_____ ,

to me known to be the individual(s) described in and who executed the foregoing instrument and acknowledged that
he(she)(they) executed the same as his(her)(their) free act and deed.

My Commission Expires: _____   _____
                                                                    Notary Public

Source: The A-B Trust forms provided in this text are available from the publisher Alpha Publications of America, Inc., P.O. Box 12488, Tucson, AZ 85732-2488.

Transfer of Trust Property to a Living Trust

If a revocable living trust is to act as a will substitute, all assets (real and personal property) owned by the settlor or in which the settlor has or acquires an interest must be transferred to the living trust. No matter in which state it is located and whether or not it is income producing, all real estate including rental units such as apartment buildings, duplexes, rooming houses, and commercial buildings plus residential property including the settlor's house, vacation home, cottage, or condominium must be transferred to the trustee of the trust. When asked to assist the personal representative with these transfers, you will most likely use a quit-claim deed (Exhibit 9.4) or a deed of trust [trust transfer deed] (Exhibit 9.5) as the documents to correct or change title (ownership) of real property either from an individual or from spouses holding title as joint tenants to the trustee of the living trust. This is just a change of title, not a transfer of title.

Example: To change the title to his real property, Adam Jones, a single person, would sign the trust transfer deed from "Adam Jones, single" to "Adam Jones, Trustee under trust dated August 1, 1995" and record the deed.

Example: If Alex Brown and his wife, Janet Brown, own real property as joint tenants, they could change the title by both signing the deed from "Alex and Janet Brown, husband and wife as joint tenants" to "Alex and Janet Brown, Trustees under trust dated August, 1, 1995" and record the deed.

You must also change title to personal property such as checking and savings accounts, stocks, bonds, certificates of deposit, mutual funds, cars, boats, and any other titled property to the name of the trustee. Untitled property such as clothing, furs, jewelry, art objects, antiques, stamp and coin collections, and household furnishings can be transferred into the trust more easily by making a list of the items and stating that they are to be added to the trust. You must also have the

Exhibit 9.4   Sample Quitclaim Deed

RECORDING REQUESTED BY

AND WHEN RECORDED MAIL THIS DEED AND, UNLESS
OTHERWISE SHOWN BELOW, MAIL TAX STATEMENT TO:

NAME

STREET
ADDRESS

CITY, STATE &
ZIP CODE

TITLE ORDER NO. _____   ESCROW NO. _____

──── SPACE ABOVE THIS LINE FOR RECORDER'S USE ────

QUITCLAIM DEED

DOCUMENTARY TRANSFER TAX $ _____
☐ computed on full value of property conveyed, or
☐ computed on full value less liens and
    encumbrances remaining at time of sale.

Signature of Declarant or Agent Determining Tax   Firm Name

_____ ,
(NAME OF GRANTOR(S))
the undersigned grantor(s), for a valuable consideration, receipt of which is hereby acknowledged, do__ hereby remise,

release and forever quitclaim to _____
(NAME OF GRANTEE(S))
the following described real property in the City of _____ ,

County of _____ , State of _____ :

Assessor's parcel No. _____

Executed on _____ , _____ , at _____
(CITY AND STATE)

STATE OF _____

COUNTY OF _____

On _____ before me, _____
(NAME/TITLE, i.e. "JANE DOE, NOTARY PUBLIC")
personally appeared _____
personally known to me (or proved to me on the basis of satisfactory evidence) to be
the person(s) whose name(s) is/are subcribed to the within instrument and
acknowledged to me that he/she/they executed the same in his/her/their authorized
capacity(ies), and that by his/her/their
signature(s) on the instrument the person(s),
or the entity upon behalf of which the
person(s) acted, executed the instrument.

WITNESS my hand and official seal.

_____
(SIGNATURE OF NOTARY)

MAIL TAX   (Seal)
STATEMENTS TO: _____
_____

RIGHT THUMBRINT (Optional)

CAPACITY CLAIMED BY SIGNER(S)
☐ INDIVIDUAL(S)
☐ CORPORATE _____
   OFFICER(S)
             (TITLES)
☐ PARTNER(S) ☐ LIMITED
             ☐ GENERAL
☐ ATTORNEY IN FACT
☐ TRUSTEE(S)
☐ GUARDIAN/CONSERVATOR
☐ OTHER _____

SIGNER IS REPRESENTING:
(NAME OF PERSON(S) OR ENTITY(IES):

Before you use this form, fill in all blanks, and make whatever changes are appropriate and necessary to your
particular transaction. Consult a lawyer if you doubt the form's fitness for your purpose and use. Wolcotts
makes no representation or warranty, express or implied, with respect to the merchantability or fitness of this
form for an intended use or purpose.

WOLCOTTS FORM 790 - Rev. 3-94a (price class 3A)
QUITCLAIM DEED

7 67775 39790 1

©1994 WOLCOTTS FORMS, INC.

Source: Wolcotts Forms, available at most stationery or office supply stores or by calling 1(800)421–2220.

Exhibit 9.5 Sample Deed of Trust

WOLCOTTS FORM 822   **- DETACH STUB BEFORE RECORDING -**

RECORDING REQUESTED BY

AND WHEN RECORDED MAIL THIS DEED AND, UNLESS
OTHERWISE SHOWN BELOW, MAIL TAX STATEMENT TO:

NAME

STREET
ADDRESS

CITY, STATE &
ZIP CODE

TITLE ORDER NO._____ ESCROW NO._____

SPACE ABOVE THIS LINE FOR RECORDER'S USE

SHORT FORM DEED OF TRUST AND ASSIGNMENT OF RENTS (With Future Borrowing Clause)
incorporating by reference certain provisions of a fictitious deed of trust of record

This Deed of Trust, Made this   day of   ,between

herein called TRUSTOR,

whose address is

(Number and Street)   (City)   (State)   (Zip)

herein called TRUSTEE, and

herein called BENEFICIARY.

WITNESSETH: That Trustor IRREVOCABLY GRANTS, TRANSFERS AND ASSIGNS TO TRUSTEE IN TRUST, WITH POWER OF SALE, that

property in   County, California, described as:

TOGETHER WITH the rents, issues and profits thereof, SUBJECT, HOWEVER, to the right, power and authority given to and conferred upon Beneficiary by paragraph (10) of the provisions incorporated herein by reference to collect and apply such rents, issues and profits.
For the Purpose of Securing: 1. Performance of each agreement of Trustor incorporated by reference or contained herein. 2. Payment of the indebtedness evidenced by one promissory note of even date herewith, and any extension or renewal thereof, in the principal sum of $_____ executed by Trustor in favor of Beneficiary or order. 3. Payment of such further sums as the then record owner of said property hereafter may borrow from Beneficiary, when evidenced by another note (or notes) reciting it is so secured.
To protect the Security of This Deed of Trust, Trustor Agrees: By the execution and delivery of this Deed of Trust and the note secured hereby, that provisions (1) to (14), inclusive, of the fictitious deed of trust recorded June 1, 1953, in the book and at the page of Official Records in the office of the county recorder of the county where said property is located, noted below opposite the name of such county, viz.:

COUNTY	BOOK	PAGE	COUNTY	BOOK	PAGE	COUNTY	BOOK	PAGE	COUNTY	BOOK	PAGE
Alameda	7043	119	Kings	558	124	Placer	629	311	Sierra	6	1
Alpine	G	65	Lake	235	108	Plumas	64	277	Siskiyou	315	114
Amador	52	393	Lassen	90	305	Riverside	1477	255	Solano	670	214
Butte	675	4	Los Angeles	41866	80	Sacramento	2420	317	Sonoma	1210	616
Calaveras	81	369	Madera	582	315	San Benito	196	295	Stanislaus	1154	443
Colusa	198	142	Marin	808	420	San Bernardino	3179	87	Sutter	397	248
Contra Costa	2133	208	Mariposa	43	242	San Diego	4874	512	Tehama	244	379
Del Norte	37	241	Mendocino	345	92	San Francisco	6165	282	Trinity	52	167
El Dorado	325	506	Merced	1110	55	San Joaquin	1528	314	Tulare	1679	106
Fresno	3313	673	Modoc	109	221	San Luis Obispo	712	43	Tuolumne	62	47
Glenn	295	536	Mono	30	343	San Mateo	2425	243	Ventura	1137	136
Humboldt	252	449	Monterey	1458	561	Santa Barbara	1156	1	Yolo	395	302
Imperial	862	639	Napa	415	331	Santa Clara	2627	445	Yuba	179	259
Inyo	103	83	Nevada	186	337	Santa Cruz	916	153			
Kern	2070	417	Orange	2512	500	Shasta	402	1			

(which provisions, identical in all counties, are printed on pages 3 & 4 hereof) hereby are adopted and incorporated herein and made a part hereof as fully as though set forth herein at length; that he will observe and perform said provisions; and that the references to property, obligations, and parties in said provisions shall be construed to refer to the property, obligations, and parties set forth in this Deed of Trust.

The undersigned Trustor requests that a copy of any Notice of Default and of any Notice of Sale hereunder be mailed to him at his address hereinbefore set forth.

Signature of Trustor

MAIL TAX
STATEMENTS
TO:

WOLCOTTS FORM 822 - rev. 4-94 (price class 2C)
SHORT FORM DEED OF TRUST
©1994 WOLCOTTS FORMS, INC.
Before you use this form, fill in all blanks, and make whatever changes are appropriate and necessary to your particular transaction. Consult a lawyer if you doubt the form's fitness for your purpose and use. Wolcotts wakes no representation or sarranty, express or implied, with respect to the merchantability or fitness of this form for an intended use or purpose.

RECORD PAGES 1 & 2 ONLY, Page 1 of 4

Exhibit 9.5   Sample Deed of Trust—*continued*

RIGHT THUMBPRINT (Optional)

State of _____

County of _____

TOP OF THUMB HERE

RIGHT THUMBPRINT (Optional)

On _____ before me, _____
      (DATE)   (NAME/TITLE OF OFFICER-I.E."JANE DOE, NOTARY PUBLIC")
personally appeared _____
                              (NAME(S) OF SIGNER(S))

_____

TOP OF THUMB HERE

_____

☐ personally known to me -**OR**- ☐

CAPACITY CLAIMED BY SIGNER(S)

proved to me on the basis of satisfactory evidence to be the person(s) whose name(s) is/are subscribed to the within instrument and acknowl-edged to me that he/she/ they executed the same in his/her/their authorized capacity(ies), and that by his/her/their signature(s) on the instrument the person(s), or the entity upon behalf of which the person(s) acted, executed the instrument.

Witness my hand and official seal.

☐ INDIVIDUAL(S)
☐ CORPORATE _____
    OFFICERS
                    (TITLES)
☐ PARTNER(S)   ☐ LIMITED
                    ☐ GENERAL
☐ ATTORNEY IN FACT
☐ TRUSTEE(S)
☐ GUARDIAN/CONSERVATOR
☐ OTHER_____

_____

_____

_____

SIGNER IS REPRESENTING:
(NAME OF PERSON(S) OR ENTITY(IES)):

_____

_____

_____

_____

_____
           (SIGNATURE OF NOTARY)

RECORD PAGES 1 & 2 ONLY, Page 2 of 4

Source: Wolcotts Forms, available at most stationery or office supply stores or by calling 1(800)421–2220.

document in which the property is listed signed and notarized. In addition, all property that allows the settlor to name a beneficiary (such as life insurance policies, IRAs, 401(k) plans, pension plans, and Keogh plans) should be changed so that the beneficiary is the name of the revocable living trust. Although the above property items that name a beneficiary already avoid probate, it is necessary to change the beneficiary to the revocable living trust to consolidate these assets, resulting in more efficient and better coordinated administration, *and* to avoid the possible dilemma if the current owner and named beneficiary of the items die in a common accident.

A settlor may wish to continue to list her spouse as beneficiary instead of the living trust on the above items, but the living trust should be added as the successor beneficiary to the policy or plans.

Advantages of a Revocable Living Trust as a Substitute for a Will

The following are some of the advantages of a revocable living trust:

■ It avoids probate since trust property is a nonprobate asset, and it avoids probate expense—the costs of probating the estate of a decedent who dies with a will or intestate may include filing fees, court costs, publication and advertising expenses, appraisal and auction fees, bond expense, costs of will contests, expenses of challenges to creditors' claims, expenses of establishing guardianships for minor children, and, most expensive of all, the fees for attorneys and personal representatives. It is estimated that the average total probate expense ranges from 5 to 15 percent of an estate's gross value and that the smaller the gross estate, the higher the percentage cost. In comparison, the cost of establishing a living trust is generally a one-time expense averaging $1,500 to $1,800 depending on the complexity of the settlor's estate.

■ It avoids the lengthy delays often associated with estate administration—even if a testamentary trust is included in a decedent's will, it takes time to have a trustee appointed whenever beneficiaries of the will are minors, disabled, or incompetent persons.

Other routine problems of probating a will such as locating assets, finding beneficiaries, and simply waiting for the backlog of court cases that clogs the court calendar delay the estate administration of the deceased. It is not unusual for the final distribution of the estate property to beneficiaries and the closing of the probate process to take a year or more.

■ It can also diminish the cost and delays caused by will contests or invalid creditors' claims. *Note:* A living trust can be contested but not as easily as a will. Time is also a factor when a will is contested by disgruntled family members who are not included as named beneficiaries of the decedent or who are disappointed in the amount of property left to them. Since the settlor creates the trust while living, it is in operation while the settlor can personally alter it; thus, the trust clearly reflects the settlor's true wishes, and the probate court would be correspondingly reluctant to change it. On the other hand, where a will exists, all persons who would inherit from the decedent if the decedent died intestate must be notified of the petition to probate the will. This allows, even invites, the disinherited family members to challenge the will's validity. Even if this will contest is unfounded, delays and expense are the result. Creditors may also make unsubstantiated claims against the decedent's estate, which the personal representative must challenge in a court hearing. All of these concerns take time and cost money. If a living trust is already in operation, the delays and added costs described above are usually avoided.

■ It avoids publicity—the will, its contents, and the probate file and documents are public records (i.e., they are open to the public). This means anyone can examine these records to determine what property the decedent owned at the time of death and who the beneficiaries are. Vulnerable family members, especially spouses, may possibly be exploited by individuals who obtain information from these public records and offer to sell investments, unnecessary or expensive insurance, or their management services. Business competitors may attempt to take advantage of an owner-manager's death by offering to buy the business at unfavorable prices or other terms. The use of a revocable living trust can assure the settlor-decedent of complete privacy in the distribution of the trust property and enable family members to avoid the potential problem of dishonest opportunists.

■ It is not under the control or supervision of the probate court. Instead, it enables the settlor, while living, or the settlor's trustee, to continue to control and manage the property; after the settlor's death, the family members can retain control of the trust property. Whereas with a will, the family may find they must obtain court approval before any assets of the deceased can be sold or distributed to named beneficiaries. As noted above, this process is time-consuming and expensive.

■ It is established while the settlor is living, and if it is a revocable living trust, the settlor has an opportunity to view the operation of the trust, verify its performance, and make necessary and appropriate changes, such as granting more or less power to trustees, changing beneficiaries, or selling and giving away trust property. Settlors can even cancel the trust whenever they wish.

■ It provides lifetime or longer management of trust assets by experienced professional corporate trustees for the benefit of the settlor, the settlor's spouse and family (e.g., children or grandchildren), or other named beneficiaries. A will, on the other hand, obviously takes effect only after death.

■ It allows the settlor who owns real estate in other states to avoid the time and expense of the ancillary administration normally required to pass the title to such real estate to beneficiaries of the trust. The ancillary administration is required because only the state in which the real estate is located has jurisdiction to convey (transfer) title to the property. A will would necessitate the ancillary procedures; a living trust would avoid them.

■ It avoids the need, expense, and delay of appointing a guardian or conservator required under state law should the settlor become disabled or be declared incompetent. A living trust provides a convenient, reviewable, and private administration of the settlor's affairs by a trustee who can control all of the settlor's property, wherever located, with much more flexible powers of investment and property management than a court-appointed guardian or conservator who must report to the probate court and whose functions and duties can be restricted by both the court and state statutes. In addition, a trustee may continue to administer trust assets after the settlor's death, whereas a guardian or conservator's authority to act terminates at death.

■ It also eliminates the need, expense, and delay for court-appointed guardians for minors or conservators for dependents with special needs due to physical or mental incapacity. A living trust can provide for these individuals specifically and also reassure the settlor, while living, that they are properly cared for and will continue to be cared for after the settlor's death. A will cannot verify such matters for a testator who must die before the will takes effect.

■ It may allow the settlor to save on death taxes, e.g., the federal estate tax, the state inheritance tax, and the state estate tax, but only if it is an irrevocable living trust. However, wills containing testamentary trusts may also limit these taxes.

Disadvantages of a Revocable Living Trust

The following are some of the disadvantages of a revocable living trust:

■ It may be more costly to create the trust than to draft a will depending on the amount of assets the settlor-testator owns or the complexity of the estate, and the trustee's management and administration fees are a continual expense throughout the life of the trust. However, wills are frequently changed and re-drawn, often many times, and the final total cost of many wills plus the probate costs will most likely exceed the cost of a living trust.

■ It does not provide for or establish a time limit on the length of time cred-itors have to present their claims after the settlor has died. A will and the sub-sequent probate do establish this time limit. A few states, however, have passed statutes that allow a living trust to limit the time for creditors to make their claims; see Cal. Prob. Code §§ 19003, 19040, and 19050. The California statute allows a trustee of the living trust to file an affidavit of the settlor's death with the probate court and then file the "Notice to Creditors" in a newspaper (pub-lication of notice discussed earlier) to set the time for limiting and discharging creditor claims.

■ It requires that all of the settlor's assets be transferred into the living trust by changing titles to the property and beneficiary designations to the name of the trustee of the trust. If this is not done because the settlor forgets or pro-crastinates, the property whose title is unchanged must go through the probate process.

As an added protection and a recommendation to settlors of revocable living trusts, a "pour-over will" should be executed declaring that any property the settlor may have neglected to transfer into the trust shall pass into the trust at the settlor's death. This property will have to be probated, but it will eventually be transferred to the trust and then distributed according to the terms of the trust (see the examples of a revocable living trust and a pour-over will in Exhibits 9.6 and 9.7).

Pour-Over Wills

If a revocable living trust is substituted for a will as the legal document of choice to avoid the probate process and to transfer and distribute the settlor's property after death, a pour-over will should also be executed. The **pour-over will** as-sures that property acquired by the settlor after the revocable living trust was established or property that the settlor forget to transfer into the trust will be distributed according to the terms of the trust rather than pass by intestate suc-cession. The existence of the pour-over will helps to eliminate challenges to the living trust by dissatisfied family members who might otherwise be entitled to the settlor's property, and it resolves the probate problems of every decedent concerning the payments of his debts and settlement of any tax liabilities.

Pour-over will
A provision in a will that directs the residue of the estate into a trust.

Exhibit 9.6 Sample Revocable Living Trust

WILLIAM T. BROWN
TRUST AGREEMENT

This trust agreement is made on _____ , 19 _____ , between William T. Brown of _____ County, State of _____ , hereinafter called the "settlor," and William T. Brown of _____ County, State of _____ , Charles T. Brown of _____ County, State of _____ , and Sarah J. Brown of _____ County, State of _____ , hereinafter collectively called the "trustees."

Recitals

I have transferred certain property to the trustees contemporaneously with signing this trust agreement, the receipt of which they acknowledge and which is described on Exhibit "A" attached hereto; and the parties to this agreement acknowledge that all property transferred or devised to the trust now or in the future is to be administered and distributed according to the terms of this trust agreement.

Article I
Reservation of Rights

During my life I reserve the following rights, to be exercised without the consent or participation of any other person:

1. To amend, in whole or in part, or to revoke this agreement by a written declaration.

2. To add any other real or personal property to the trust by transferring such property to the trustees, and to add any other property by my will. The trustees shall administer and distribute such property as though it had been a part of the original trust property.

3. To make payable to the trustees death benefits from insurance on my life, annuities, retirement plans, or other sources. If I do so, I reserve all incidents of ownership, and I shall have the duties of safekeeping all documents, of giving any necessary notices, of obtaining proper beneficiary designations, of paying premiums, contributions, assessments or other charges, and of maintaining any litigation.

4. To receive annual written accounts from all trustees (or the personal representative of any deceased trustee). My approval of these accounts by writings delivered to another trustee shall cover all transactions disclosed in these accounts and shall be binding and conclusive as to all persons.

5. To direct the trustees as to the retention, acquisition, or disposition of any trust assets by a writing delivered to the trustees. Any assets retained or acquired pursuant to such directions shall be retained as a part of the trust assets unless I otherwise direct in writing. The trustees shall not be liable to anyone for any loss resulting from any action taken in accordance with any such direction of mine.

6. To examine at all reasonable times the books and records of the trustees insofar as they relate to the trust.

Article II
Disposition of Trust Assets

Unless I am disabled, the trustees, after paying the proper charges and expenses of the trust, shall pay to me during my lifetime the entire net income from the trust property in monthly installments, and the trustees shall also pay to me and any other person who is a financial dependent of mine, in accordance with my written instructions, such portions of the principal of the trust property as I direct. If I become disabled by reason of illness, accident, or other emergency, or I am adjudicated incompetent, the trustees, other than myself, are authorized and directed to pay to me or for my benefit such portions of the trust income or principal as the trustees deem necessary to provide for my care, comfort, support, and maintenance.

Upon my death, the trustees, if requested by the personal representative of my estate shall, or in their own discretion may, directly or through the personal representative of my estate, pay the expenses of my last illness and funeral, my valid debts, the expenses of administering my estate, including nonprobate assets; and pay all estate, inheritance, generation-skipping, or other death taxes that become due because of my death, including any interest and penalties.

Also, upon my death, I give all my tangible personal property to Charles T. Brown, my son, if he survives me, or if he does not survive me, to Sarah J. Brown, my daughter. (I request the recipient of any such tangible personal property to distribute the same as I may have indicated informally by memorandum or otherwise.) The trustees shall distribute all the trust property not effectively disposed of by the preceding provisions of this agreement in equal shares to the persons named below. If any person named below does not survive me, such person's share shall be distributed per stirpes to such person's descendants who survive me.

Charles T. Brown, my son
Sarah J. Brown, my daughter

Exhibit 9.6   Sample Revocable Living Trust—*continued*

Article III
Selection of Trustees

Trustees shall be appointed, removed, and replaced as follows: unless I am disabled, I reserve the right and power to remove any trustee and to appoint successor or additional trustees. If I become disabled, I shall cease to be a trustee. Upon my death or disability, my son, Charles T. Brown, may at any time appoint an individual or corporate trustee and may remove any individual or corporate trustee so appointed.

Article IV
Trustee Powers and Provisions

The powers granted to my trustees may be exercised during the term of this trust and after the termination of the trust as is reasonably necessary to distribute the trust assets. All of the powers are to be discharged without the authorization or approval of any court. I hereby give to my trustees the following powers: (specific administrative powers are listed).

Among the administrative provisions of this trust, I request no bond or other indemnity shall be required of any trustee nominated or appointed in this trust. I expressly waive any requirement that this trust be submitted to the jurisdiction of any court, or that the trustees be appointed or confirmed, that their actions be authorized, or that their accounts be allowed, by any court. This waiver shall not prevent any trustee or beneficiary from requesting any of these procedures.

(General governing provisions may also be added).

The settlor and the trustees have signed this agreement in duplicate on or as of the date appearing at the beginning of this agreement and the trustees accept their appointments as trustees by signing this agreement. IN THE PRESENCE OF:

_____ Witness	_____ William T. Brown—Settlor and Trustee
_____ Witness	
_____ Witness	_____ Charles T. Brown—Trustee
_____ Witness	
_____ Witness	_____ Sarah J. Brown—Trustee
_____ Witness	

STATE OF _____ ⎫
                ⎬ ss.
COUNTY OF _____ ⎭

On this _____ day of _____ , 19 _____ , before me, a Notary Public within and for said County, personally appeared William T. Brown, a single person, to me known to be the person described in and who executed the foregoing instrument as settlor and trustee, and acknowledged that he executed the same as his free act and deed.

_____
Notary Public

On this _____ day of _____ , 19_____ , before me, a Notary Public within and for said County, personally appeared Charles T. Brown and Sarah J. Brown, to me personally known, who being by me duly sworn, executed the foregoing instrument as trustees, and acknowledged that they executed the same as their free act and deed.

[*Notarial Seal*]

_____
Notary Public

Exhibit 9.7   Sample Pour-Over Will

WILL
OF
WILLIAM T. BROWN

I, William T. Brown, of _____ County, _____ State, revoke any prior wills and codicils and make this my last will.

Article I
Payment of Taxes and Expenses

I direct my personal representative to pay from the residue of my estate or to direct the trustee of the William T. Brown Trust under Agreement dated _____ , 19 _____ , (referred to hereafter as the "William T. Brown Trust") to pay, or both, as determined in the sole discretion of my personal representative all expenses of my last illness and funeral, my valid debts, the expenses of administering my estate, including nonprobate assets; and to pay all estate, inheritance, generation-skipping, or other death taxes that become due because of my death, including any interest and penalties.

Article II
Special Gifts

I give all my tangible personal property to Charles T. Brown, my son, if he survives me, or if he does not survive me, to Sarah J. Brown, my daughter. (I request the recipient of any such tangible personal property to distribute the same as I may have indicated informally by memorandum or otherwise.)

Article III
Residue

I give the residue of my estate consisting of all the real and personal property I can dispose of by will and not effectively disposed of by preceding articles of this will to the trustee or trustees of the William T. Brown Trust, executed by me on _____ , 19 _____ , at [city]_____ , [state] , as amended and existing at my death, to be added to the remaining assets of that trust and disposed of according to the terms and provisions of that trust.

Article IV
Personal Representative

I nominate and appoint Charles T. brown, my son, as my personal representative. If Charles T. Brown fails or ceases to act or is unable or unwilling to serve as personal representative; I nominate and appoint Sarah T. Brown, my daughter, as successor personal representative.

Article V
Personal Representative and Trustee Provisions

My personal representative, in addition to all other powers conferred by law that are not inconsistent with those contained in this will, shall have the power, exercisable without authorization of any court, to sell at private or public sale, to retain, to lease, and to mortgage or pledge any or all of the real or personal property of my estate; and to settle, contest, compromise, submit to arbitration or litigate claims in favor of or against my estate. I request that my estate be administered as an Informal Administration and that no bond or other indemnity shall be required of my personal representative. I expressly waive any requirement that the William T. Brown Trust be submitted to the jurisdiction of any court, or that the trustees be appointed or confirmed, or that their actions be authorized, or that their accounts be allowed, by any court. This waiver shall not prevent any trustee or beneficiary from requesting any of these procedures.

(Other Articles may be added.)

I have signed this Will consisting of _____ pages, including this page, on _____ , 19 _____ .

_____
William T. Brown—Testator

Irrevocable Living Trusts

An irrevocable living trust may not be amended, revoked, or canceled after its creation. Living trusts are generally irrevocable unless the trust instrument contains a provision stating it is revocable. To avoid any confusion concerning a

---

Exhibit 9.7 Sample Pour-Over Will—*continued*

We certify that in our presence on the date appearing above in the State of _____ , William T. Brown signed the foregoing instrument and acknowledged it to be his Will, that at his request and in his presence and in the presence of each other, we have signed our names below as witnesses, and that we believe him to be of sound mind and memory, over 18 years of age, and under no constraint or undue influence.

_____   residing at _____

Witness

_____   residing at _____

Witness

Self-Proved Affidavit

STATE OF _____
                        ⎫
                        ⎬ ss.
                        ⎭
COUNTY OF _____

We, _____ , _____ , and _____ , the Testator and the witnesses, respectively, whose names are signed to the attached or foregoing instrument, consisting of _____ typewritten pages, being first duly sworn, do hereby declare to the undersigned authority that the Testator signed and executed the instrument as his Last Will and Testament, that he signed willingly, and that he executed it as his free and voluntary act for the purposes therein expressed; and that each of the witnesses, in the presence and hearing of the Testator, signed the Will as witnesses, and that to the best of their knowledge the Testator was at the time 18 or more years of age, of sound mind and under no constraint or undue influence.

_____
                                        William T. Brown—Testator

_____
                                                        Witness

_____
                                                        Witness

Subscribed, sworn to and acknowledged before me by William T. Brown, the Testator, and subscribed and sworn to before me by _____ and _____ , witnesses, this _____ day of _____ 19_____ .

[*Notarial Seal*]

_____
                                                  Notary Public

---

settlor's intent, the trust should include a provision such as, "The settlor hereby declares that this trust agreement and all its provisions shall be irrevocable and not subject to any amendment or modification by the settlor or any other person." An irrevocable living trust not only has the advantages of avoiding probate and its expense, but also can be used as a tax saving device:

1. The trust can save on a family's federal income taxes by shifting the trust income from the settlor to the trust itself when it is in a lower tax bracket than the settlor.

2. It can save on federal estate tax by, in appropriate established trusts, excluding the trust property from the decedent-settlor's gross estate, thereby

reducing or avoiding the federal estate tax. This is commonly accomplished using an irrevocable life insurance trust.

Example: Pauline Hayes is a single parent with two teenage children. The total value of her gross estate including the face amount (proceeds) of her life insurance is over $600,000. If Pauline wishes to avoid probate, but completely control her property, she could create two trusts: a revocable trust, into which she would place all of her property except her life insurance, and an irrevocable life insurance trust, into which she would place her life insurance polices worth $300,000 and the ownership of them. By funding the irrevocable trust with an amount of money sufficient to pay the annual life insurance premiums, when Pauline dies, the amount of the life insurance will be paid to the trust, but it will not be added to Pauline's gross estate. This will keep the estate value under $600,000 and thereby avoid the U.S. (federal) estate tax (see the discussion and details in Chapter 10).

Example: Spouses such as Harold and Marilyn Sheppard, who have three children, can also take advantage of a revocable trust and an irrevocable life insurance trust to preserve an estate worth over $1,700,000. Assume, for example, that their life insurance is worth $500,000. Using a revocable trust, they can control their property during their lifetime and avoid probate at death. Using one or more irrevocable life insurance trusts as appropriate, they can eliminate the value of their life insurance from their gross estate(s) and thereby pass to their children the maximum amount of their estate by avoiding the federal estate tax (see the discussion of estate planning in Chapter 10).

DRAFTING A PRIVATE EXPRESS IRREVOCABLE LIVING TRUST

A trust is a convenient device to transfer assets out of a settlor's estate. Its greatest advantage is its flexibility, its adaptability to many purposes. It is important to delegate the drafting of a trust instrument only to counsel knowledgeable in this area. Often you will be asked to prepare a preliminary draft. The instrument must conform not only to the requirements of the Internal Revenue Code but to state law as well. Therefore, before preparing the preliminary draft of a trust under the attorney's supervision, you must have a clear understanding of the settlor's purposes and desires in creating the trust as well as the applicable federal and state tax consequences.

The hypothetical case below describes the settlor's purposes for establishing a trust and provides a sample checklist of information you need to prepare a preliminary draft. On the basis of the checklist data, a sample agreement is drawn, creating a private express irrevocable living active trust.

The Facts

Helen A. Flynn, age 60, lives at 1520 Holly Drive, Flowertown, Apple County, State A. Helen is a widow with two adult children, Jerry Flynn, residing at 1402 Oak Drive, Flowertown, and Janet Flynn, living at home with her mother. Helen has been a very successful businesswoman. She has also been a wise investor. Helen wants to transfer 10,000 shares of common stock of Golden Harvest, Inc., to an irrevocable trust for her son's benefit (to be designated Trust I). The annual income produced by the stock varies. Jerry has had serious business reverses, and his mother wants to help him overcome these problems. Helen wants the income produced from the stock paid to Jerry annually for the next five years. At the end of that time period, Helen instructs the trustee to transfer the trust property into two separate, equal trusts, Trust II and Trust III, for the benefit of her two children, as successor beneficiaries, for their respective lifetimes. Upon the death of Janet and Jerry, Helen wants the trusts to terminate and the principal of the trust (stock) to pass into their respective estates. Therefore Janet and Jerry will have the opportunity to determine through their individual wills to whom the stock will eventually be transferred.

Helen names her close friend and financial adviser, Betty R. White, trustee. Betty lives at 1040 Merry Lane, in Flowertown. Helen names Betty's husband, Bob, successor trustee. He would take over Betty's duties, e.g., pay trust income to the beneficiary, should Betty become legally unable to perform. Betty and Bob agree to serve without compensation. The powers and duties granted by Helen to her trustee include the trustee's right to vote the stock, to sell and reinvest in other stocks or bonds when in the best interests of the beneficiaries, and to distribute the income and principal as outlined in the trust agreement. Also, Helen wants to retain the right to remove any trustee she selects or to allow the beneficiaries to remove the trustee.

Using a Checklist

A checklist similar to the one in Exhibit 9.8 should be used to gather the information necessary for drafting the Flynn trust. This checklist is for illustrative purposes only. It reflects details to be included in the prospective trust instrument based on the situation previously outlined. Drafters of trust instruments would not and should not use this checklist in every situation. For example, the settlor might not want to name a successor beneficiary who would receive the benefit of the trust should the first-named beneficiary die.

ASSIGNMENT 9.15

From the completed checklist in Exhibit 9.8, draft a private, express, irrevocable living trust with the appropriate provisions based on the facts in the Flynn case. Compare your draft with the annotated sample trust below and point out the similarities and differences in the two drafts.

ANNOTATED SAMPLE PRIVATE EXPRESS IRREVOCABLE LIVING TRUST

This trust agreement is made June 1, 1995, between Helen A. Flynn of 1520 Holly Drive, City of Flowertown, County of Apple, State of A, hereinafter referred to as Settlor, Betty R. White of 1040 Merry Lane, City of Flowertown, County of Apple, State of A, hereinafter referred to as Trustee, and Robert C. White of 1040 Merry Lane, City of Flowertown, County of Apple, State of A, hereinafter referred to as Successor Trustee.

COMMENT: The major purpose of the introductory clause in a trust is to identify the parties involved. Always include addresses to assist in proper identification.

Settlor and trustees agree to the following:

Article I

Settlor hereby transfers to trustee 10,000 shares of common corporate stock of Golden Harvest, Inc., described in Schedule A, annexed hereto and made a part hereof by this reference, the receipt of which property is hereby acknowledged by trustee, to be held in trust upon the terms herein set forth.

COMMENT: This article identifies the property of the trust. It also establishes the willingness of the person nominated to act as trustee and to accept the responsibilities outlined in later articles. Incorporation by reference, i.e., use of the words, "Schedule A, annexed hereto," enables the drafter to define the trust estate without making the trust instrument unduly long.

Article II

Trustee is authorized to receive property added to the trust estate from any person, provided such property is acceptable to the trustee.

COMMENT: If the trustee is to care for property added to the trust throughout its duration, such as stock resulting from a split, this must be stipulated. Generally, property can be added to the trust throughout its existence.

Article III

Trustee shall hold, invest, and reinvest the trust property; collect the dividends, interest, and other income thereof; and, after deducting all necessary administration expenses, dispose and distribute the net income and principal as follows:

First: The net income from the trust estate shall be placed in a trust, Trust I, and shall be paid annually to Jerry Flynn, son of the settlor, of 1402 Oak Drive, Flowertown, Apple County, State A, for five (5) years commencing from the date of this agreement.

Second: At the end of the five-year period, the trustee shall divide the trust principal and income into equal amounts and place them into two separate trusts, Trust II and Trust III. Trust II shall be established for the benefit of Jerry Flynn and Trust III for Janet Flynn, daughter of settlor, currently residing at settlor's address. The net incomes of Trust II and Trust III shall be paid annually to the respective beneficiaries, Jerry and Janet, until their deaths. The death of each beneficiary named herein shall terminate the respective trust created for his or her benefit, and the principal and remaining income of the trust shall become part of the decedent beneficiary's estate and shall be distributed to the beneficiary's personal representative.

COMMENT: This article describes in detail the way income and principal of the trust estate shall be distributed. The settlor's directions for payment should be clear, specific, and complete. Ambiguities should be avoided. For example, the instrument should not recite. "The settlor wishes the trustee to manage and invest the trust estate and pay the income to Jerry Flynn for five years, and thereafter to Jerry Flynn and Janet Flynn in equal shares." Perhaps the settlor knows exactly what she intends the trust to accomplish, but the trust instrument does not convey this. The lack of definiteness leads to questions concerning the implementation of the trust, e.g.. Is the trustee obliged to reinvest the trust funds? May she deduct administrative expenses? Could the trust continue indefinitely? Spelling out the powers and duties of the trustee will lessen the risk of injured feelings and litigation.

Article IV

The trustee shall have the following powers and discretions in addition to those conferred by law:

(a) To retain the property described in "Schedule A," and any other property added to the trust estate;
(b) To invest and reinvest, to sell or exchange the principal of this trust in such stocks or bonds as trustee shall in its discretion deem to be reasonable, expedient or proper regardless of whether such stocks, bonds, or other property shall be legal investments for trusts under the laws of State A;
(c) To vote in person or by proxy all stocks or other securities held by trustee;
(d) To exchange the securities of any corporation or company for other securities issued by the same, or by any other corporation or company at such times and upon such terms, as trustee shall deem proper; and
(e) To exercise with respect to all stock, bonds, and other investments held by trustee, all rights, powers, and privileges as are lawfully exercised by any person owning similar property in his/her own right.

COMMENT: All powers that a settlor wishes to grant to the trustee should be included in the trust instrument and clearly defined. Limitations, if desired, should also be specifically enumerated. The settlor of this trust has definite ideas about what she wants the trustee to do. Section *b* above, for example, states that the trustee shall decide what investments shall be made on behalf of the trust, despite the statutes of State A, which declare and enumerate permissible trust investments. It is possible, and perfectly legal, for settlors to include such provisions in trust agreements. It is only when the settlor fails to mention the type of investments the trustee may make that such statutes go into effect. The intent of these statutes is benevolent rather than restrictive. They are designed to help inexperienced investors to invest prudently.

Article V

The settlor hereby declares that this agreement and the trusts hereby created shall be irrevocable and not subject to modification by the settlor or any other person and the settlor further declares that no trustee shall be required to furnish bond or other security to any court.

COMMENT: Placing property in trust saves income and estate tax only if the trust is irrevocable and not included in the settlor's estate. The settlor is taxed on the income and capital gains of the trust property if:

1. The settlor retains the right to revoke the trust (I.R.C. § 676).
2. The settlor or the settlor's spouse currently or at any time in the future receive or "may receive" the trust income (I.R.C. § 677 [a]).
3. The settlor retains certain dispositions or administrative powers (I.R.C. §§ 674 and 675).

Also, the trust must be irrevocable and the settlor must relinquish all interest in the trust property in order for the settlor to avoid federal estate tax. It is common today that trustees can serve without bond.

Article VI

Both trustee and successor trustee have agreed to waive compensation for their services.

COMMENT: The trust instrument should provide expressly for the trustee's compensation or its waiver. In the absence of such a provision, statutes in many states fix or limit the rates of the commission. Unless the settlor indicates whether the trustee shall receive or forgo compensation as agreed, the court may order the statutory amount paid from the trust income.

Article VII

The settlor hereby appoints as successor trustee, Robert C. White of 1040 Merry Lane, Flowertown, Apply County, State A. In the event that trustee or successor trustee shall die, resign, become incapacitated, or for any reason fail or refuse to act as trustee, settlor shall have the power to appoint a successor. Any successor trustee shall have all the powers and obligations of the trustee named herein.

COMMENT: It is important for the settlor to name a successor in case the original trustee is unable or unwilling to serve. Because of their fiduciary responsibilities, all trustees should be selected with care, keeping in mind the specific purposes for which the trust is created.

Article VIII

The validity of this trust and the construction of its provisions shall be governed solely by the laws of the State of A as they now exist or may exist in the future.

COMMENT: Each state may have certain restrictions on trusts that may affect the purpose of the trust. Such restrictions must be determined before a workable instrument can be drafted. A clause similar to this may prove more valuable than it would appear. For example, Helen Flynn, the settlor, lives in State A, as does Betty White, the trustee. At the inception of the trust, at least, it will be governed by the laws of A because that is the place where it is to be administered (carried out by the trustee), according to Article VIII. However, this situation can change. Suppose Betty moves to the State of N and transacts business there. The laws of N regarding trusts might be quite different from the laws of A, with the result that new limitations are placed on Betty and the trust does not achieve what Helen had intended. Or suppose that a year from now state A enacts a special tax on living trusts. Does the Flynn Trust have to pay the tax since such a law was not in existence at the time of the trusts's creation? A court could resolve such problems, but the process would be both time- and money-consuming (e.g., the question involving the laws of two states, A and N, might require a federal action). It is advisable to include a clause that prevents such questions from arising.

IN WITNESS WHEREOF, settlor and trustees have executed this agreement at Flowertown, the day and year written above.

IN PRESENCE OF:

_____	_____
(Witness)	(Settlor)
_____	_____
(Witness)	(Trustee
	_____
	(Successor Trustee)

STATE OF A ⎫
                  ⎬   ss.
County of Apple ⎭

The foregoing instrument was acknowledged before me this 1st day of June, 1995, by Helen A. Flynn as settlor and Betty R. White and Robert C. White, as trustees.

[*Notarial Seal*]

_____
Notary Public

Exhibit 9.8   Sample Checklist for Drafting a Private Express Irrevocable Living Trust

Names and Addresses of Necessary Parties

Settlor:	Helen A. Flynn	1520 Holly Drive,
		Flowertown
		Apple County, State A
Trustee:	Betty R. White	1040 Merry Lane
		Flowertown
		Apple County, State A
Successor trustee:	Robert C. White	1040 Merry Lane
		Flowertown
		Apple County, State A
Relationship of trustee(s) to settlor:	Financial adviser and friend	
Beneficiaries:		
Income beneficiary:	Jerry Flynn, son	1402 Oak Drive,
		Flowertown
		Apple County, State A
Successor beneficiary:	Jerry Flynn	Same as above
	and	
	Janet Flynn, daughter	Same as Helen
		(mother)
Remainderman:	Respective estates of Jerry and Janet Flynn	
Relationship of beneficiaries to settlor:	Beneficiaries (Janet and Jerry) are the children of settlor (Helen)	

Trust Property

Stocks:	10,000 shares of common stock, Golden Harvest, Inc.
Location:	Stock shares—transferred to trustee on acceptance

Revocability of Trust   Trust is irrevocable

Trustee's Powers and Duties

Payment of income (Trust I):	Annually to Jerry for five years
Payment to successor beneficiaries (Trusts II & III):	After five years, income to be paid equally to Janet and Jerry for life
Payment (transfer) of principal:	Principal transferred in equal shares to the respective estates of Janet and Jerry on their deaths
Investment powers:	Invest and reinvest the securities and other general powers

Exhibit 9.8   Sample Checklist for Drafting a Private Express Irrevocable Living Trust—*continued*

Term of Trustee	
Removal:	Removal may be by either settlor or both beneficiaries acting jointly
Successor in office:	Robert White, husband of proposed trustee
Trustee's Rights	
Acceptance or rejection (determine trustee's intention):	Trustees agree to serve
Compensation:	Trustees agree to serve without charge
Termination of Trust	
Duration of trust:	Settlor intends to transfer income to son for five years (Trust I); then in equal shares (Trusts II and III) to both children for life. Remainder to the children's estates
Distribution of principal of Trust I on termination of trust:	Transferred in equal shares to Trusts II and III
Distribution of principal and income of Trusts II and III on termination of said trusts:	Transferred in equal shares to respective estates of Janet and Jerry on their deaths

ASSIGNMENT 9.16

George Conover decides to create a living trust for his children, Melissa and Gary, with his wife, Grace, as trustee and trust property consisting of real estate in your state that he operates as a summer residence for tourists. Using this information, and supplying more, as necessary to indicate the settlor's intention, compile checklists similar to the one in Exhibit 9.8 and, using both checklists, draft an instrument for the Conover Trust.

The sample checklist in Exhibit 9.9 may be used for drafting a trust.

ASSIGNMENT 9.17

In Assignment 9.16, George Conover created a living trust. Draft a self-proved pour-over will to accompany the Conover living trust.

Exhibit 9.9 Sample Checklist for Drafting a Living Trust

Names and Addresses of Necessary Parties
Settlor(s): _____

Trustee(s): _____
  Relationship, if any, to
  settlor:
  Successor trustee: _____
  Corporate trustee: _____
Beneficiaries:
  Income beneficiary: _____
  Successor beneficiary: _____
  Remainderman: _____
  Relationship of
    beneficiary, if any, to
    settlor: _____

Trust Property*
Real estate: _____
Stocks, bonds: _____
Cash: _____
Insurance policy: _____
Other property: _____

Trust Purpose
Description: _____

Legality: _____

Revocability of Trust
Revocable by settlor: _____
Irrevocable: _____

Trustee's Duties
Payment or withholding of
  income: _____

"Sprinkling" of income
  among beneficiaries: _____

Accumulation of income: _____

Invasion of trust principal: _____
Payment of principal: _____
Bonding and accounting: _____

Trustee's Powers
Discretionary: _____
Restrictions: _____
Sale, lease, or mortgage
  trust property: _____

Allowance or limitation on
  investments: _____
Others: _____

_____

*An attached schedule describes the trust property in detail. Schedule not included here.

Exhibit 9.9   Sample Checklist for Drafting a Living Trust—*continued*

Term of Trustee
Resignation: _____

Removal: _____

**Trustee's Rights and
    Liabilities**
Rights: _____
Acceptance or rejection: _____
Compensation: _____
Liabilities: _____

Special Clauses in Trust
Spendthrift: _____
Others: _____

Termination of Trust
Death of settlor: _____
Death of beneficiary: _____
Trust duration: _____
Distribution of trust
    principal on termination
    of trust: _____

KEY TERMS

Cy-pres

Purchase-money
   resulting trust

Parol evidence

Parol Evidence Rule

Necessaries

Precatory word

Pour-over will

REVIEW QUESTIONS

1. What are the differences between the following kinds or classes of trusts: express versus implied; private versus public; active versus passive; *inter vivos* (living) versus testamentary; and resulting versus constructive?

2. What elements are necessary to create an express private trust? How do they differ from the elements needed to create an express public trust?

3. Does the cy-pres doctrine apply to all trusts? Explain.

4. What is meant by the phrase "the law allows resulting trusts to be proved by parol evidence"?

5. What are spendthrift and sprinkling trusts, and why would a settlor create them?

6. What is the proper way of creating a Totten trust, and can it be used to disinherit a surviving spouse? Explain.

7. What are some of the most common reasons or purposes for creating trusts?

8. Give three examples of trust restrictions that are "reasonable restraints" and do not violate public policy.

9. Why is a precatory trust generally declared invalid?

10. What is the court's position on a trust that has all its required elements but lacks a trustee? Explain.

11. Why are living trusts today often considered to be more desirable than wills? Which do you prefer? Why?

12. What are the major disadvantages of revocable living trusts?

13. How are real and personal property properly transferred into a living trust?
14. What is the purpose of a pour-over will? Do assets included in such a will have to be probated? Explain.

15. What are some of the uses of an irrevocable living trust?

CASE PROBLEMS

Problem 1

Duncan Bennett, a single parent, wants to leave his entire estate to his only child, Bonnie. He knows Bonnie is extravagant and often spends her money foolishly; therefore, he establishes a trust with a spendthrift provision, "to protect Bonnie from her own mismanagement and wasteful habits in spending money." The trust also provides that Bonnie cannot transfer, pledge, or assign her interest in the trust income or principal in any manner and that such interest is not to be subject to any of Bonnie's creditors' claims by attachment, garnishment, execution, or other process of law. Answer the following:

A. Are spendthrift trusts valid in all states?
B. Would this trust be valid in your state? If so, cite the statute.
C. If one of Bonnie's creditors supplies her with property items that are obviously "necessaries," can that creditor reach (obtain) Bonnie's trust income despite the spendthrift clause? See *Erickson v. Bank of California*, 97 Wash.2d 246, 643 P.2d 670 (1982).

Problem 2

Amy purchased twenty acres of land from Ben. Because Amy was immediately leaving the country to serve in the Peace Corps for two years and was unable to attend the closing, she asked Ben to deed the property to her close friend, Sally. Ben conveyed the property by deed to Sally in her name. When Amy returns, Sally refuses to turn over the property, claiming that the property was a gift to her from Amy. Amy denies the property was a gift and demands that Sally return the property. Answer and explain the following:

A. Since real property (land) is involved in this case, does the Statute of Frauds apply?
B. In this case, can parol evidence be used to determine whether or not a resulting trust is established?
C. If Amy and Sally go to court, what methods might a court use to decide whether Sally's claim is correct?
D. If it goes to court, in your opinion, which party would win this case? See *Rainey v. Rainey*, 795 S.W.2d 139 (Tenn.App. 1990).
E. If Amy died while in the Peace Corps, would the property belong to Sally?

CHAPTER TEN

ESTATE PLANNING

OBJECTIVES

After completing this chapter, you should be able to:

- Explain the need for and purpose of an estate plan and the procedures used in creating a plan.

- Understand the adverse factors that diminish an estate's value and how to minimize them.

- Utilize the knowledge acquired from earlier chapters to draft appropriate wills and trusts necessary for an estate plan.

- Identify and incorporate into an estate plan the tax-saving devices that increase the deductions from the gross estate or reduce the gross estate, thereby reducing or possibly eliminating federal and/or state death taxes.

OUTLINE

SCOPE OF THE CHAPTER

This chapter discusses the need for an estate plan and the process for creating such a plan. The legal documents, e.g., wills and trusts, required for an estate plan are discussed in detail as are devices that save estate tax either by reducing the decedent's gross estate or by increasing the deductions from the estate.

THE ESTATE PLAN

Estate planning is the determination and utilization of a method to accumulate, manage, and dispose of real and personal property by the owner of the property during life and after death and to minimize the income, gift, inheritance, and estate taxes due. The purpose of estate planning is to identify, preserve, and expand or increase the assets owned and to provide for distribution of these assets, with the least possible tax expense, to family members and institutions the owner wishes to benefit during life as well as after death. If estate planning is properly performed, the intent and desires of the owner will be accomplished, and the beneficiary-recipients (family primarily) will receive the maximum benefit and enjoyment of the property.

Unfortunately, most people have neither an estate plan nor a will or trust. They are so involved in their daily activities that they give little thought to the consequences of their deaths. Many do realize the importance of purchasing life insurance to protect their dependents, and as people grow older, they are likely to give some thought to their mortality. But people often die prematurely, leaving dependents unprotected, and all too many people die without having made provisions through a valid will or an appropriate trust for those for whom they care. The consequences of these acts of procrastination can be financially devastating.

Earlier chapters in this book explained in detail how you can assist in the creation and use of trusts and wills to resolve and avoid these unfortunate consequences. It is also important that you understand the need for estate planning and be prepared to assist parties who have the responsibility for estate planning and administration. These parties will include your supervising attorney and the personal representative of the decedent's estate.

In addition to the attorney, numerous other individuals are qualified to give estate planning advice. They include trust officers from banks and trust companies, accountants, investment advisers, financial planners, and life insurance agents. Acting as a team, many of these advisers will take an active role in developing an appropriate estate plan for each client. The attorney you assist will give advice on legal matters; the accountant will handle income, gift, inheritance, and estate tax concerns; the financial planner will advise on investments; and the life insurance agent may play a key role in developing an insurance policy to ensure financial security for the family of the insured decedent. While you assist these estate planners by gathering information, keeping records, communicating by phone or letters to keep the client and planners informed of the plan's pro-

ETHICAL ISSUE ▶ gress, and performing similar tasks, *you must be constantly on guard to neither divulge confidential information nor submit or propose unauthorized legal advice even in response to a specific request.*

Everyone who lives a normal life span accumulates assets that he wants to transfer after death. Real estate, cash, art, jewelry, securities, mineral rights, business ownership, boats, planes, antiques, profit sharing plans, pension plans, life insurance, IRAs, 401(k) plans, Social Security, and other employment and government benefit plans are a few examples of the wide variety of assets that are frequently acquired during one's life. The total value of the property items that form an individual's estate can be considerable and may be much larger than initially anticipated; e.g., the value of an appreciated home and other unencumbered real estate, sizable pension plans, and often the proceeds of life insurance policies alone may add substantially to the estate.

These assets and their value create a need to formulate a sound and appropriate financial plan—called an **estate plan.** The estate plan is an arrangement of a person's property and estate that takes into account the laws of wills, property, trusts, insurance, and taxes in order to gain maximum benefit of all these laws while accomplishing the major objective of the estate plan, i.e., carrying out the person's own wishes for the **disposition** (distribution) of the property upon death. If the plan is properly formed and executed, it should produce the best possible economic security for the individual and her family. The estate plan encompasses the creation of the estate, its maximum growth and conservation, and, ultimately, its distribution. It necessitates active planning strategies during the individual's life and important postmortem decisions after death. If designed appropriately, the estate plan should meet all the individual's objectives by providing her with (1) a comfortable retirement income; (2) financial protection for her family; (3) proper custodial care should incompetency or any serious physical or other mental health problem occur; and (4) expedient, efficient, and harmonious distribution of the estate according to her wishes after death. Minimizing taxes and expenses during the implementation of the plan is obviously an essential corollary objective.

Developing an estate plan for the client begins when the client reaches a "comfort level" with the supervising attorney and paralegal so that the paralegal can start accumulating the personal and financial data. In helping the client create an appropriate estate plan, you will use all of the same techniques (interviewing, negotiating, drafting, and counseling skills) and professional conduct that were described earlier in the discussion of drafting wills and trusts.

Estate plan
An arrangement using the laws of various disciplines, e.g., wills, trusts, taxes, insurance, and property, to gain maximum financial benefits for the disposition of a person's assets during life and at death.
Disposition
The parting with, transfer of, or conveyance of property.

𝕀 ASSIGNMENT 10.1

1. A new client is coming to your office to discuss the drafting of a will. You have not met the client, but your supervising attorney has told you that the client is shy, reserved, and reluctant to discuss private family and financial matters with "strangers." Explain some of the things you might do or say to begin to establish a "comfort level" between the client and yourself so that you can obtain the requisite information for drafting the will.
2. Review the checklists in Chapter 6 (Exhibits 6.1, 6.2, and 6.5 through 6.8), and determine if they are adequate to elicit the necessary information to develop and draft an estate plan. What is missing? What could you add?
3. Starting with your great-grandparents, draw a diagram of your family tree.

Before discussing the utilization of the data and information accumulated through the interview, checklists, worksheets, and questionnaire, it will be helpful to summarize the potential adverse factors that will diminish any estate. It is necessary to understand these factors so that measures can be included in the estate plan to minimize their effect. Five factors in particular require attention:

federal and state death taxes; administration expenses; losses resulting from the forced liquidation (sale) of assets to raise funds to pay debts of the deceased; and losses due to the termination of the decedent's management skills.

1. *Federal death (estate) tax.* This tax is imposed upon the privilege of transferring property at death whether to beneficiaries of a will or to heirs by the intestate succession statutes. Current federal law exempts from federal gift or estate tax transfers from the decedent of up to $600,000 in value. Thus, anyone can give while living or transfer after death assets worth $600,000 to donees, beneficiaries, or heirs without paying any federal gift or estate tax. Although the number of individuals dying with estates valued over $600,000 is increasing, the percentage of the population dying with such estates is still very small. Since the federal estate tax rates range from a low of 37 percent for estates over $600,000 to 55 percent on estates over $3,000,000, any procedure that can diminish the tax must be included in the estate plan. With proper planning, a married couple can use planning devices, such as trusts, to transfer $1,200,000 free of estate tax after the deaths of both spouses.

2. *State death taxes.* The taxes imposed by the states vary considerably. State taxes may include estate taxes, a "credit estate tax" that "picks up" or absorbs the amount of the federal estate tax credit allowed for taxes paid to the state, or an inheritance tax, a tax on the beneficiaries of property received from a decedent's estate. The inheritance tax is determined by the amount of property received and the relationship of the beneficiaries to the decedent. If the only state tax is the equivalent of the federal estate tax, the state estate tax does not present a tax planning problem for two reasons: (1) if no federal estate tax is due, no state estate tax is levied either, and (2) if federal estate tax is levied, the state tax offsets the federal tax so that the total tax remains the same. See Exhibit 14.2 in Chapter 14, which describes the taxes of each state.

3. *Administration expenses.* The commission (fee) of the personal representative, attorney's fee, court costs and filings, and costs of administering the estate including the decedent's funeral and burial expenses are all incurred during an estate administration. All of these expenses must be paid from the assets of the decedent's estate and may substantially lessen its value. If the decedent owned property in more than one state, ancillary administration expense will add to these costs. Obviously, then, any method that reduces the decedent's gross estate, e.g., by making lifetime gifts, also reduces the probate fees and administration expenses, which are commonly computed as a percentage of the probate estate itself. The personal representative may elect to take the administration expenses as a deduction on the decedent's federal estate tax return (I.R.C. § 2053) or as a deduction on the estate's fiduciary income tax return (I.R.C. § 642[g]).

4. *Forced liquidation.* The personal representative may be forced to sell (at a sacrifice) assets of the estate in order to obtain the cash needed to pay legitimate and approved creditors' claims, federal and state taxes, and administration expenses. After reviewing the potential property to be sold with the beneficiaries, the personal representative will select and sell, according to statutory guidelines, the assets that cause the least shrinkage from their fair market value and consequently from the estate.

5. *Loss of management.* This potential problem involves the loss of management skills of running a business such as a sole proprietorship or personally handling a large investment portfolio. The inability to find someone to take on

these responsibilities, especially in cases such as the sole proprietorship, may result in a substantial loss of profits (income) to the estate as a direct consequence of the "manager's" death. The adverse effects of some or all of these factors may not be entirely eliminated, but a well-designed estate plan can help to limit them.

After information has been accumulated from interviews and questionnaires and has been reviewed with the client, an estate plan is created using the following documents and devices that save estate tax either by increasing the deductions from the gross estate or by reducing the gross estate itself:

- Documents:
  - Wills and trusts.
- Estate tax–saving devices that increase the deductions from the gross estate:
  - The marital deduction.
  - The charitable deduction.
- Estate tax–saving devices that reduce the gross estate:
  - Gifts.
  - Powers of appointment.
  - Trusts.
  - Life insurance.

The next sections discuss the role these elements play in the development of an estate plan. Earlier chapters described in detail the planning, drafting, and uses of wills and trusts, so this chapter will emphasize the tax-saving devices.

Periodic Review

No matter how well an estate plan is designed to meet the objectives of a client, changes in tax laws, domicile, family relationships (including marital status), and accumulated assets necessitate periodic review of the plan. *Another ethical issue could result if the attorney or paralegal openly solicited clients to conduct this review.* Therefore, it must be made clear to the client that she is responsible for initiating a review when changes known only to her occur that mandate the modification of the estate plan.

ETHICAL ISSUE

DOCUMENTS

Wills

A will is one of the most common and most important estate planning documents. Unfortunately, as you have learned, most people die without one, thereby allowing state statutes (primarily those of the decedent's domicile, i.e., home state) to determine who will inherit the decedent's property. As part of an estate plan, a will allows the testator to:

- Leave the entire estate to a surviving spouse *or* limit the spouse's interest to the share required by state statute (see the discussions of elective or forced share of a surviving spouse and the method used in community property states in Chapters 1 and 2).
- Leave the estate to children, e.g., natural, adopted, or nonmarital (illegitimate), *or* disinherit one or more or all of them completely.
- Leave the estate to anyone, such as friends or faithful employees, whether they are family (relatives) or not. The one exception is the surviving spouse who cannot be completely disinherited.

- Leave the entire estate to charity or other public institutions, except for the surviving spouse's elective share.
- Identify the estate assets and the beneficiaries who are to receive them, thereby minimizing confusion and the possibility of costly will contests.
- Appoint both personal and property guardians for minor children. One person may serve as both types of guardian, or a financial institution, e.g., a bank, may be the property guardian, while a relative or friend is the personal guardian.
- Establish testamentary trusts within the will to reduce or even avoid estate taxes and select the trustee who will administer the trusts.
- Appoint an executor or executrix or, using the Uniform Probate Code term, a personal representative to carry out the terms of the will and administer the estate.
- Make financial arrangements to cover funeral and burial instructions.

A will can be changed throughout the testator's lifetime since the will takes effect only on death.

Trusts

Trusts are the other key planning documents. As previously discussed, a trust can be created *inter vivos,* the living trust, or placed in a will, the testamentary trust. A trust can be revocable or irrevocable. If it is irrevocable, the income produced by the trust property is taxable to the trust as a legal entity, or to the beneficiaries, if they receive the income, but in either case, the trust property is no longer part of the settlor's assets. Estate planners can use trusts to benefit family members in numerous other ways:

- Obtain professional management of the trust property.
- Provide lifetime income for a surviving spouse and then pass property to children and grandchildren.
- Preserve privacy, because, unlike a will, a trust is not a public document.
- Protect a spendthrift child.
- Spread or sprinkle trust income or principal to family members years after the testator's death when their needs are better known.
- Enable the trust property to be controlled by the settlor-trustee while living and then by the successor trustee for the benefit of the beneficiary.
- Avoid the lengthy delays and expense, including ancillary administration expense, of probate.
- Diminish problems such as will contests.
- Eliminate the need for the probate court to appoint a guardian or conservator for minors or for oneself due to declining health.
- Reduce federal and state death taxes by using trusts to increase the marital and charitable deductions and make maximum use of the $600,000 individual estate tax exemption to allow a married couple to pass a $1,200,000 estate after their deaths free of estate tax to their beneficiaries, usually their children (see the discussion of estate tax-saving devices in the next sections).

ESTATE TAX–SAVING DEVICES THAT INCREASE DEDUCTIONS FROM THE GROSS ESTATE

Two types of deductions are frequently used to produce a lower net estate subject to the federal estate tax. They are (1) the marital deduction and (2) the charitable deduction.

The Marital Deduction

Section 2056 of the Internal Revenue Code (I.R.C.) allows an unlimited **marital deduction** for lifetime gifts made between spouses as well as for property passing from the decedent spouse to the surviving spouse upon death. Thus, a lifetime gift to a spouse or a gift that passes from a decedent to a surviving spouse is free from federal gift or estate tax. This unlimited marital deduction is an essential consideration in estate tax planning for a married couple since spouses frequently leave their estates to the surviving spouse. Without an appropriate estate tax plan, however, considerable federal estate tax that could have been avoided may be owed on the death of the second spouse.

Example: William and Melva are married. William owns assets worth $200,000; Melva's assets are worth $1,000,000. If William dies first and leaves everything to Melva, his estate would pay no tax because of the unlimited marital deduction. (Note: Although William's estate pays no estate tax on his death, he has lost the opportunity to take advantage of every person's right to the $600,000 estate tax exemption.) When Melva dies (assuming she does not remarry), her $1,200,000 estate will pay approximately $235,000 in taxes (calculated as $427,800 tentative tax on the $1,200,000 estate minus $192,800 unified tax credit = $235,000; for more on the calculation of federal estate tax, see Chapter 14). To avoid this estate tax and enable more of their combined estates to pass to their children, Melva, while living, should transfer by gift $400,000 of her estate to William so that each would have assets of $600,000. (This suggestion assumes that Melva and William are not contemplating a legal separation or divorce and that they want to maximize the estate they pass to their children.)

This process of rearranging property ownership of total estate assets so that each spouse's estate has approximately the same value, enabling each spouse to take the maximum advantage of the unified credit amount, is called **estate equalization.** *The attorney and paralegal must be especially careful when acting for and advising both spouses about interspousal gifts because serious ethical problems can result when the attorney advises one spouse to make substantial gifts to the other spouse.* The ethical concern for the attorney is that the marriage might subsequently be dissolved. The solution is for the attorney and paralegal to explain the difficulty and make sure both spouses understand the situation, acknowledge their awareness of the potential problem, and indicate their consent to this estate plan, in writing. Then, when William dies first, he can create what is called a bypass trust in which a deceased spouse's estate passes to a trust (bypass trust) rather than to the surviving spouse. The bypass trust is established with William's $600,000 estate. The trust will pay the income to Melva for life but then pass to their children without being taxed when she dies. Melva can then pass her $600,000 estate, free of estate tax, to their children because she still has her individual $600,000 estate tax exemption available. See Exhibit 10.1 illustrating this tax planning example.

The bypass trust is funded with all of the first deceased spouse's (William's) $600,000 unused unified credit exemption without incurring any estate tax. Because the interests of the surviving spouse (Melva) as beneficiary of the bypass trust are sufficiently limited (to only a life estate), when she dies, the trust assets are not included in her gross estate for estate tax purposes. Thus, the trust "bypasses" Melva's taxable estate, and the assets pass tax-free to their children. Melva's own $600,000 unified credit exemption will apply to her separate property, which is valued at exactly $600,000.

Marital deduction
An unlimited amount of the decedent's gross estate, which may be given to the surviving spouse without becoming subject to the federal estate tax levied against the decedent's estate.

Estate equalization
Rearranging property ownership of total estate assets owned by the spouses so that each spouse's individual estate has approximately the same value.

ETHICAL ISSUE ◀

Exhibit 10.1   Tax Planning Illustration

Case One		**Case Two**
First estate: William dies, leaving $200,000 to Melva.	Compare after Melva gives William $400,000, which is not taxed because of the unlimited marital gift tax deduction.	First estate: William dies, leaving $600,000 in a life estate for Melva in a bypass trust.
First estate qualifies for marital deduction; **no** federal estate tax.	The success of this financial plan to pass the maximum estate to the couple's children depends solely on Melva's willingness to gift $400,000 of her property to her husband. Marital problems between them might make this impractical and disadvantageous to Melva with ethical consequences for any attorney or paralegal acting for both spouses.	First estate qualifies for $600,000 individual estate tax exemption; **no** federal estate tax. Bypass trust: Melva has no interest in this property when she dies, and it is not taxed to her estate; **no** federal estate tax.
Second estate: Melva dies, leaving $1,200,000 to children.		Second estate: Melva dies, leaving separate $600,000 to children.
Second estate qualifies for only $600,000 individual estate tax exemption.		Second estate qualifies for her $600,000 individual estate tax exemption.
Result: $235,000 federal estate tax		Result: **No** federal estate tax

---

Melva is giving up a lot. She has transferred $400,000 to William by gift, and in return, she receives only a life estate in his now combined $600,000 estate. If she is willing to make this arrangement, however, after both spouses die, $1,200,000 of their property will pass to their children free of estate tax, saving $235,000. Although Melva must forgo ownership of the assets used to fund the bypass trust, she still receives substantial benefits from the trust. She receives all trust income during her lifetime, and principal may be distributed to her at the discretion of the trustee; *she* may even act as trustee or co-trustee, but in such cases, the discretion to distribute principal to herself is limited to an "ascertainable standard," such as her need for health, education, support, or maintenance (see I.R.C. § 2041[b][1]). Melva may also have the right to appoint principal of the trust during her lifetime or at death, provided that she does not appoint the property to herself, her estate, her creditors, or creditors of her estate. Note, however, that she does not have a **general power of appointment** (see the discussion below) over the trust assets, which would cause them to be taxable to her estate when she died.

General power of appointment
The right to pass on an interest in property to whomever a donee (the one who is given a general power of appointment) chooses, including herself or her estate, creditors, or creditors of the estate.

Section 2056 of the I.R.C. establishes that a "qualifying" marital deduction is not limited to a bequest (gift) in a probate transfer (will) or to transfers made at the time of the decedent's death. The following transfers all qualify as part of the marital deduction from the estate of the decedent spouse for property that passes to the surviving spouse: property transferred by joint tenancy, *inter vivos* gifts, trust transfers, pension plan benefits, life insurance proceeds, and transfers made through the exercise of powers of appointment.

The Charitable Deduction

To be a charitable gift, a gift must be made for religious, scientific, charitable, literary, or educational purposes. Similarly, if a trust is to qualify and be approved as a charitable trust, it must be established for one of these purposes; see I.R.C. § 170(c). A charity cannot be an individual. There are various methods of establishing charitable gifts that reduce or avoid specific taxes.

Charitable gifts made during the donor's lifetime can be used to reduce both estate and income taxes. Also, the value of real or personal property given by a will or trust to certain kinds of qualified charities is deductible from the donor's gross estate for federal and state estate tax purposes; see I.R.C. § 2055. A lifetime donor or testator will most often make a direct, outright charitable gift of cash; alternatively, the donor may give highly appreciated securities and real estate because doing so can reduce both estate taxes and **capital gains taxes.** In addition, a donor can establish a trust that allows him to retain a lifetime interest in the property and receive income from it for life; after his death, the remainder passes to an appropriate charity. Such trusts are called Charitable Remainder Unitrusts or Charitable Remainder Annuity Trusts; see I.R.C. § 664(d).

Capital gains tax
An income tax on profits from the sale or exchange of a capital asset at a lower rate than the rates applied to ordinary income.

Charitable Remainder Trusts

A charitable remainder trust allows a settlor or the named beneficiary to retain the income from the trust, generally for life; then the trust property is given to a "qualified" charity. Two types of charitable remainder trusts are the Charitable Remainder Unitrusts and the Charitable Remainder Annuity Trusts.

In a Charitable Remainder Unitrust, cash or property is placed in the trust, which must provide a distribution of a fixed percentage of not less than 5 percent of the fair market value of the trust property (this value is determined annually) to a noncharitable income beneficiary for life (I.R.C. § 664[d][2] & [3]). When the life beneficiary dies, the trust property passes to the qualified charity. Therefore, if the value of the trust property increases, so does the beneficiary's income.

In a Charitable Remainder Annuity Trust, the settlor places property in the trust, which must pay a fixed amount (sum certain) annually to the noncharitable income beneficiary for life; after the beneficiary dies, the trust property passes to the qualified charity. Under Section 664(d)(1) of the I.R.C., the fixed annual income given to the noncharitable life beneficiary must be at least 5 percent of the initial net fair market value of all property placed in the trust. This amount can never change. The court in the case of *In re Danforth's Will,* 81 Misc.2d 452, 366 N.Y.S.2d 329 (1975) upheld this definition of a Charitable Remainder Annuity Trust. If the trust property's income diminishes for some reason such as a slump in the economy, the annual fixed payment must come from the principal of the trust. On the other hand, if the economy flourishes, the excess income, after the fixed payment is paid, remains in the trust. Unlike the unitrust, the annuity trust does not allow additional contributions to be made to the trust property.

If a client does not have enough property to set up one of these charitable remainder trusts by herself, she can contribute her property to a public "pooled income" fund such as the American Cancer Society or the March of Dimes. All individual gifts are placed in the larger "pooled" fund, and each donor receives annual income based on her contribution compared to the value of the entire fund. When the client dies, her property passes to the charity.

ESTATE TAX–SAVING DEVICES THAT REDUCE THE GROSS ESTATE

When preparing an estate plan, one of the most important goals is to identify and incorporate into the plan various ways to reduce or eliminate federal and state estate taxes. Among the most common methods used to reduce these death taxes are:

- Gifts made during the donor's lifetime.
- Powers of appointment.
- Trusts that qualify for the marital deduction or avoid multiple taxation.
- Life insurance.

Gifts Made During the Donor's Lifetime—The Gift Tax Annual Exclusion

Gift splitting
For gift tax purposes, an election by spouses to make a gift by one of them to a third party as being made one-half by each spouse.

According to tax law (I.R.C. § 2503[b]), any donor can make a gift of up to $10,000 to each of any number of recipients (donees) each year during the donor's life without being required to pay gift tax. In addition, spouses may join in the annual gift to any number of donees and combine their individual $10,000 gifts so as to give $20,000 to each donee free of gift tax. This practice is called **gift splitting,** and it is only available between spouses. In such cases a gift tax return must be filed with the Internal Revenue Service. In appropriate family situations, lifetime gifts are important tax-saving devices that are essential to a well-designed estate plan. Whenever donors are looking for a method to reduce their estates in order to diminish their potential federal estate tax liability, gift giving is an obvious solution.

Example: Bob and Mary have five children. To reduce their estate and the corresponding federal estate tax, they can give each of their five children $20,000 each year for a total of $100,000. If they make these same gifts for ten years, Bob and Mary will reduce their estate by $1,000,000.

Assuming that a donor has not made any previous gifts that year to the donees, he can give them each $10,000 on his deathbed to diminish his federal estate tax. Such gifts would qualify for the $10,000 exclusion.

The annual $10,000 gift tax exclusion is available only for **present interests,** i.e., unrestricted rights to the immediate possession, use, or enjoyment of property (or the income of property). A gift of a present interest results whenever the donor makes a direct transfer of property to a donee. Donors may be individuals during life or may act through wills, trusts, estates, or guardianships. An unrestricted right to receive trust income, a **legal life estate,** and a gift to a **custodian** under the Uniform Transfers to Minors Act are all examples of a present interest. This act allows any kind of real or personal property to be transferred to a custodian for the benefit of a minor. The **custodianship,** however, must end and all property must be transferred to the minor at age 21 (see the discussion of this act in Chapter 14).

MINI-GLOSSARY BOX

Present interest
An immediate and unrestricted interest in real or personal property including the privilege of possession or enjoyment of the property.

Legal life estate
A life estate created by operation of law and not directly by the parties themselves.

Custodian
A person who has charge or custody of property for the benefit of another, usually for a minor.

Custodianship
An alternative to a trust or guardianship that allows a person (called a custodian) to be appointed by the court to manage property for the benefit of a minor.

Future interest
Any fixed estate or interest, except a reversion, in which the privilege of possession or enjoyment is future and not present.

Gifts of **future interests,** such as gifts of remainder interests and gifts in trust subject to a preceding life estate, do *not* qualify for the annual gift tax exclusion. Sometimes clients must be cautioned not to become too eager to part with their property to reduce federal tax liability since the gifts, once executed, transfer title to the property and its control. Once clients have gifted away their property, unforeseen and disastrous financial circumstances could cause them to become dependent on others for support.

In addition to the $10,000 annual exclusion, no gift tax is owed for certain tuition and medical care payments to an individual donee regardless of the relationship of the donor to the donee. See I.R.C. § 2503(e).

All lifetime gifts made to a donee in a given year that exceed the $10,000 exclusion must be reported on Form 709 or Form 709A, if the gift is split between spouses. However, no tax is owed or paid for gifts over the $10,000 annual exclusion until the unified credit of $192,800, based on a gross estate of $600,000, is exceeded.

A donor who is planning to make gifts to his children should leave them highly appreciated property, such as real estate (e.g., a house, cottage, condominium, or apartment building) in his will or in a trust and give them other property during his lifetime. The problem with making a gift of highly appreciated property while living is that the advantage of the "stepped-up basis" of the property is lost. Property "basis" is the value that is used to determine loss or gain for income tax purposes. The difference (loss or gain) between what the donor paid for the property and the amount received when the property is sold is taxable. If the donor, while alive, gives the property to his children, the property retains the donor's basis. However, if the donor passes the property to his children through a will or trust when he dies, the property takes a new "stepped-up basis," which is the current value of the property on the date of the donor-testator's death.

Example: Debbie, the donor, purchased a lakeshore cottage in Minnesota in 1960 for $20,000. In her will, Debbie leaves the cottage to her two children. When Debbie dies in 1995, the property is worth $200,000. The children receive the property with the stepped-up basis of $200,000. If they sell the property for $200,000 in 1995, they will owe no federal income tax on the sale because there was no income gain. (*Note:* The stepped-up basis of $200,000 would be included in Debbie's gross estate for estate tax purposes and could result in an estate tax liability if her gross estate exceeds $600,000.) On the other hand, if the property had been given to the children while Debbie was alive, the basis for the property when it was sold would be Debbie's basis of $20,000. There is *no* stepped-up basis when property is passed by gift when the donor is alive. Therefore, if the basis is $20,000 and the children sell the cottage for $200,000 in 1995, the gain of $180,000 would be subject to income tax.

Powers of Appointment

Donor (of a power of appointment)
The testator or settlor who creates and confers a power or authority upon another (called the donee) to appoint, that is, to select the person(s) (called the appointee) to receive an estate or an income therefrom after the testator's or donee's death.

Donee (of a power of appointment)
The person to whom a power of appointment is given, also called the holder, who selects the appointee to receive an estate or an income therefrom.

Appointee
The person who is to receive the benefit of the power of appointment.

A power of appointment is created by will or in a trust when one person (a testator or settlor, now also called the **donor**) confers a power or authority upon another (called the **donee**) to appoint (i.e., to select and nominate) the person who is to receive and enjoy an estate, or an income therefrom, or receive a trust fund after the donee's death. The purpose of a power of appointment is to enable the persons (called the **appointees**) who will receive the estate or trust fund to be named later when their needs are better known.

Section 2041 of the I.R.C. identifies two types of powers:

1. A general power of appointment, which the Code defines as follows:

The term general power of appointment means a power which is exercisable in favor of the decedent, his estate, his creditors, or the creditors of his estate. . . .

Example: In her will, Margaret Brower, creates a testamentary trust naming her daughter, Elizabeth Brower, beneficiary of the trust and provides that all income of the trust will be distributed to Elizabeth during her lifetime. Upon Elizabeth's death, she will be given the power to "appoint" the principal of the trust to anyone she selects.

- Margaret Brower is the testatrix and donor who creates the power of appointment.
- Elizabeth is the beneficiary of the testamentary trust and donee who holds the power of appointment. She has the right to exercise the power during her life or after death in her own will by naming anyone, including herself or her estate, as the beneficiaries of the trust principal.
- The person appointed by Elizabeth is the appointee.
- Elizabeth has a general power of appointment.

It allows the donee to appoint the property to anybody, including herself, her estate, or her creditors. *Note:* Only a general power of appointment causes the value of the property appointed to be included in the gross estate of the person who possesses the power of appointment for federal estate tax purposes.

2. A **special or limited power of appointment** in which the donor limits the donee's right of appointment to an identified person or persons, other than the donee, to whom the property can be distributed.

Special power of appointment
A power of appointment that cannot be exercised in favor of the donee or his estate, but only in favor of identifiable person(s) other than the donee.

Example: In the above example, Margaret, in the testamentary trust, gives Elizabeth the power to "appoint" the principal only to Elizabeth's brother, Henry, or only to any siblings that survive Elizabeth.

- Margaret is still the testatrix and donor.
- Elizabeth is still the beneficiary and donee who holds the power of appointment.
- Henry, or Elizabeth's siblings, are the appointee(s).
- Elizabeth has a special power of appointment.

A common use of special powers of appointment occurs between spouses where one spouse, say, the husband in a trust or will names his wife as his beneficiary and gives her a power to appoint the principal only to their children. This special power of appointment does *not* cause the value of the property appointed to be included in the gross estate of the wife, who is the beneficiary (donee).

Trusts That Qualify for the Marital Deduction or Avoid Multiple Taxation

Transfers of property that qualify for the gift or estate tax marital deduction include the following: (1) outright transfers by gift or trust; (2) general power of appointment trusts; (3) qualified terminable interest property (QTIP) trusts; and (4) bypass trusts, which are also known as A-B trusts, credit shelter trusts, or exemption equivalent trusts.

Outright Transfers by Gift or through Trusts

Direct transfer of ownership from one spouse to the other spouse by a gift, will, or operation of law is the simplest and most common form of a marital deduction transfer. A transfer in trust may be more appropriate, however, if the recipient spouse is unable to manage the trust property properly or if the settlor wants to guarantee the ultimate beneficiaries of the property at the spouse's death instead of allowing the surviving spouse to make that decision. Consider the following trust examples.

Example: Maria establishes a trust that states that "upon Maria's death, the trustee shall distribute all principal and income directly to Maria's surviving spouse, Howard." This is an outright transfer by trust of property that qualifies for the marital deduction from Maria's gross estate.

The major tax problem created by an outright transfer to a spouse is that the entire trust property is now part of the surviving spouse's estate and may be liable for considerable estate taxes upon that spouse's death if the value of his estate is greater than $600,000.

General Power of Appointment Trusts

A common alternative to an outright transfer that also qualifies trust property for the marital deduction is the general power of appointment trust. This living or testamentary trust alternative established by the settlor spouse requires the trustee to distribute trust income to the surviving spouse for life and gives the spouse an unqualified general power to appoint the trust property to "anyone," including herself, her estate, or her creditors, that she names in her will. Since no limitations exist on the spouse's exercise of the power of appointment, this is a general power of appointment. When the general power is given to the surviving spouse, it causes the trust property to be included in the taxable estate of the "person who possesses the power," i.e., the surviving spouse. See I.R.C. § 2041(a)(2).

Example: In his will, Sherman creates a trust transferring property to his spouse, Roxanne, for life and giving Roxanne on her death the power to appoint the balance of the trust principal to "such beneficiaries as she may designate in her will." Since there are no limitations on the power of appointment, and Roxanne can appoint the remaining principal at her death to "her estate, her creditors, or the creditors of her estate," this is a general power of appointment, and the trust property will be added to Roxanne's estate and be subject to federal estate tax when she dies.

A general power of appointment also occurs, for example, when a decedent spouse in a testamentary trust gives property for life to the surviving spouse and gives that spouse an unrestricted right to withdraw all or any part of the principal at any time. This would give the surviving spouse the power to appoint the principal to herself at any time and thus becomes a general power of appointment.

To avoid the unfavorable estate tax consequences of the general power of appointment trust, a special power of appointment trust can be created instead, if appropriate. Such trusts limit the surviving spouse to appointing only an identifiable person or class of persons designated in the trust document creating the power. The appointee(s) cannot be the spouse or the spouse's estate or creditors. When special powers of appointment are created, the trust property is not included in the surviving spouse's estate on death.

Under a general power of appointment trust, the surviving spouse must receive all the trust income at least annually, and only the surviving spouse may have the power to appoint any part of the interest in the trust property. If the spouse fails to exercise the power of appointment in her own will, the trust assets pass as directed in the trust document. An advantage of this trust is that it may permit the surviving spouse to make gifts of trust property to children that may qualify for the gift tax annual exclusion ($10,000 per donee per year), which, in turn, reduces estate taxes at the surviving spouse's death.

QTIP Trusts

QTIP trust (qualified terminable interest property)
A type of trust that will qualify for the marital deduction in which the surviving spouse receives all the income for life but is not given a general power of appointment.

Since its creation in 1982, the **QTIP trust** has been a popular type of trust that qualifies for the marital deduction. This type of trust occurs when the settlor wants the surviving spouse to have all the income from the trust for life, but wants the principal of the trust to pass to someone other than the surviving spouse. Therefore, the surviving spouse is *not* given a general power of appointment. Property qualifies for the estate marital deduction only to the extent that the personal representative (executor), after the settlor's death, so elects (the QTIP election) on the federal estate tax return (I.R.C. § 2056[b][7]), and for the gift marital deduction, if the donor spouse makes the QTIP election (see the discussion below).

Generally, the marital deduction (for gift and estate tax purposes) is not available if the interest transferred will terminate upon the death of the transferee–surviving spouse and pass to someone else. For example, if a husband places property in trust for his wife for life, and the remainder to their children when his wife dies, this is a **terminable interest** that does not qualify as a marital deduction for the husband or for the husband's estate. If, however, the QTIP election is made so that the property transferred into the trust is treated as qualified terminable interest property, the terminable interest restriction is waived, and the marital deduction is allowed. In exchange for this deduction, the surviving spouse's (wife's) gross estate must include the value of the QTIP election assets, even though she has no control over the ultimate disposition of these assets, i.e., she has no general power of appointment. Terminable interest property qualifies for this election if the donee or heir (the wife in this example) is the only beneficiary of the asset during her lifetime, and she receives income distributions from the trust property at least annually. If the trust property is transferred as a gift, the donor spouse (the husband) is the one who makes the QTIP election. If the trust property is transferred by death, the personal representative (executor) of the estate of the deceased spouse (the husband) has the right to make the election on Schedule M of Form 706, the United States Estate Tax Return (see text Form 96*).

Thus, the QTIP trust offers two unique advantages. First, the testator of a testamentary trust or the settlor of an irrevocable living QTIP trust is allowed to

Terminable interest
An interest in property that terminates upon the death of the holder or upon the occurrence of some other specified event.

---

*See Appendix A.

direct the disposition (distribution) of the trust principal at the death of the surviving spouse. This assures that the testator's or settlor's children or other intended family members will be the ultimate beneficiaries of the trust. The second advantage is the trust's flexibility for purposes of the gift or estate tax marital deduction. The testator of a testamentary trust can direct the personal representative (executor) or the settlor can direct the trustee (who may be the settlor) in the irrevocable living trust to elect on the estate tax return to qualify all or any part of the trust principal for the marital deduction. The portion of the trust for which the election is made must be included in the surviving spouse's estate for federal estate tax purposes.

Example: Betty and Bob are married. Betty has two children by a previous marriage, and Bob has three children by a previous marriage. If Betty dies leaving all her property to Bob in her will, no federal estate tax will be owed on her death because of the marital deduction. When Bob dies, however, he may pass all the property he inherited from Betty to his own children only. Using a QTIP trust, Betty can create a testamentary trust that pays all the trust income annually to Bob for life; on his death, the trust principal passes to *her* children. In addition, Betty can direct her personal representative to elect on her estate tax return that all or part of the trust property be treated as QTIP property and therefore qualify for the marital deduction. Upon Bob's death, the value of the QTIP election assets, which qualified for the marital deduction on Betty's death and now pass to her children, must be included in Bob's gross estate.

To qualify for the QTIP election, the trust must pay all its net income to the surviving spouse at least annually for the spouse's lifetime. Neither the spouse nor any other person may have a power to appoint the trust property to any person other than the spouse during the spouse's lifetime. The trust document may permit the trustee to invade the trust principal for the spouse's benefit only. The major disadvantage of the QTIP trust is that the spouse is not permitted to make gifts to children from the trust principal.

Bypass Trusts

A bypass trust (also called an A-B trust, credit shelter trust, or exemption equivalent trust) is an estate planning device whereby a deceased spouse's estate passes to a trust rather than to the surviving spouse, thereby reducing the likelihood that the surviving spouse's subsequent estate will exceed the estate tax threshold. The surviving spouse is given a life estate in the bypass trust. This trust allows spouses with substantial estates to transfer their property, after both have died, to their children and avoid paying any federal estate tax by appropriately planning and using the marital deduction and their individual $600,000 estate tax exemptions. As long as a husband and wife each hold $600,000 in separately owned assets, and they do not use the marital deduction exclusively for those assets, the couple can use a bypass trust and a marital deduction trust to retain combined total assets worth up to $1,200,000 that will avoid federal tax liability.

As explained earlier, the process of rearranging the spouses' assets so that each spouse's estate takes maximum advantage of its unified credit is known as estate equalization. Harmony between the spouses is essential to this strategy. Marital friction and discord may make this sound estate planning device impossible.

Life Insurance

When designing an estate plan, one of the important planning devices available to conserve the value of the estate is life insurance. Life insurance is a contract between the policyholder, generally the owner of the policy and the person whose life is insured, and an insurance company whereby the company agrees, in return for annual premium payments, to pay a specific sum of money, i.e., the face value, to the designated beneficiary upon the death of the policyholder. The insurance company is called the insurer or carrier; the policyholder is also called the insured.

Example: Sarahana contracts with Metro Life Insurance Company to buy a $200,000 term life insurance policy. Sarahana pays an annual premium of $600 to the company. She has named her son, Joshua, as her primary beneficiary. When Sarahana dies, the insurance company must pay Joshua $200,000. Sarahana is the policyholder or insured. Metro Life Insurance Company is the insurer or carrier. Joshua is the beneficiary. The premium is $50 per month or $600 per year, and the face amount or value of the policy or contract is $200,000.

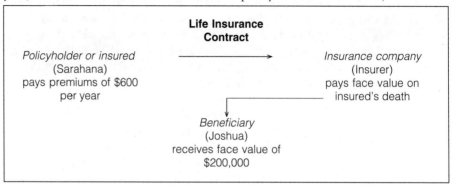

Types of Life Insurance

The three major types of life insurance are ordinary, straight, or whole life insurance; term life insurance; and universal life insurance.

1. *Ordinary, straight, or whole life insurance.* Whole or straight life insurance combines lifetime protection with a minimum savings feature called cash surrender value or, more commonly, cash value. Premium payments remain the same during the contract and are required throughout the policyholder's lifetime. After the first few years, the cash value slowly increases throughout the duration of the contract. The policyholder may surrender (cash in) the policy at any time and take out the cash value (money) for his own use or retain the policy until death for the benefit of the named beneficiary.

Example: Phyllis buys a $50,000 policy of straight life insurance, naming her daughter, Barbara, beneficiary. Each year Phyllis pays the premium for the policy. If Phyllis desires, she may at any point withdraw for her own use the cash value (savings) accumulated, but she must surrender (terminate) the policy to obtain the cash value. If Phyllis dies before the policy is terminated, Barbara will receive the proceeds ($50,000).

2. *Term life insurance.* Term insurance is life insurance that is pure protection without savings (cash surrender value). It is by far the least expensive insurance. It requires the insurance company to pay the face amount (value) of insurance, i.e., the proceeds, to the beneficiary if the policyholder dies within a given time

period (term). It is generally renewable from term to term. The cost of term insurance increases with the age of the insured.

Example: If, in the above example, Phyllis had bought a ten-year policy of term insurance in the amount of $50,000 and died within that period, Barbara would receive the proceeds.

3. *Universal life insurance.* Universal life insurance is life insurance that covers a specific period of time and builds a cash value for the policyholder over that time. This coverage emphasizes the separation of the portion of the premium that is used to cover the insurance protection from the portion of the premium allocated to an investment that is used to build the policy's cash value. Investments are usually flexible and selected with a view to maximizing the rate of return.

Tax Consequences of Life Insurance

Regardless of the type of life insurance, the entire proceeds, i.e., the face amount of the policy, are included in the decedent-policyholder's estate if (1) the proceeds are payable to the decedent's estate or (2) the proceeds are payable to other beneficiaries and the decedent possessed "incidents of ownership" in the life insurance policy. An **incident of ownership** is an element or right of ownership or degree of control over a life insurance contract. The following are examples of incidents or rights of ownership:

Incident of ownership
An element or right of ownership or degree of control over a life insurance contract.

- The right to change the named beneficiary of the policy.
- The right to cancel or surrender (cash in) the policy.
- The right to transfer or assign ownership of the policy to another person or to a trust.
- The right to pledge the policy as collateral for a loan.
- The right to obtain a loan against the cash value of the policy from the insurer (company).

The retention by the policyholder of any incident of ownership in a life insurance policy will cause the policy proceeds (face amount) to be included in the policyholder's gross estate upon death and be subject to federal estate tax; see I.R.C. § 2042(2). In the case of *Estate of Lumpkin v. Commissioner,* 474 F.2d 1092 (1973), the U.S. Court of Appeals ruled that the decedent taxpayer (Lumpkin), under the provisions of a group term life insurance policy, had the right to alter the time and manner of the benefits of the policy and thereby possessed an incident of ownership with respect to that policy. Therefore, the court decided that the value of the insurance proceeds must be included in Lumpkin's gross estate and be subject to federal estate tax. *Note:* The policyholder can avoid this detrimental tax consequence to his estate by doing either of the following:

1. Transferring the ownership of the policy to a trust or to another person (but not to a spouse since there is no tax advantage because of the unlimited marital deduction).

2. In a written statement given to the insurance company, formally relinquishing (giving up) all incidents of ownership.

In both cases, however, the Internal Revenue Code also requires that the policyholder live *three* more years after the date of the transfer or the date of the formal relinquishment in order for the proceeds of the policy *not* to be included in the decedent's gross estate and thus *not* to be subject to federal estate tax.

Since the proceeds of life insurance can be and often are worth more than $600,000, it is obvious how important this tax-saving procedure becomes.

Another important tax outcome associated with life insurance is the payment of the proceeds to the named beneficiary. Generally, when the proceeds are paid to the beneficiary upon the death of the policyholder, they are exempt from federal and state income tax (see I.R.C. § 101[a]).

Life insurance proceeds are distributed by various methods. If the policyholder's estate is the beneficiary, the proceeds are normally distributed as a lump sum since it provides immediate cash for the family and a source of funds to pay creditors' claims and administration expenses. As noted above, however, the proceeds are then subject to federal estate tax; since they enlarge the gross estate, they also increase the probate costs. When the beneficiary is an individual, several settlement options are available under most policies, including the following:

- The company holds the proceeds and interest accumulates.
- The company pays the beneficiaries the proceeds and interest in installments over a specific time period.
- The company uses the proceeds to purchase an annuity for lifetime payments to the beneficiary.
- The company pays the beneficiary a lump sum to be invested or used as the beneficiary wishes.

Life insurance proceeds can be used for many purposes besides the payment of the decedent's debts, taxes, and administration expenses. The proceeds can supply a source of funds to replace the lost income of the decedent wage earner, maintain a family's lifestyle, pay for the college education of children, help to cover the ongoing expenses of an elderly parent or handicapped child, and provide for the financial security of future generations of family members.

Life Insurance Trusts

Irrevocable life insurance trust
A living trust that cannot be revoked or amended that is established by a settlor who assigns the ownership of a new or existing life insurance policy on her life to the trust and contributes money annually to the trustee to pay the premiums.

One method often used by families to conserve wealth is the **irrevocable life insurance trust,** a common device used in estate planning. A settlor establishes one of these irrevocable living trusts by assigning the ownership of a new or existing policy to the trust and/or annually contributing money to the trust, which is used by the trustee to pay premiums for the purchase of life insurance on the settlor. Each year while alive, the settlor gives the trust a certain amount of money with which the trustee pays the policy premiums. The policy is owned by the trustee, and the proceeds of the policy are paid to the trust, which is the named beneficiary of the policy, on the death of the insured (settlor). This device enables the settlor to direct the trustee to pass the proceeds to the trust's named beneficiaries (usually children) and keeps the proceeds from being included in the settlor's taxable estate for federal estate tax purposes. *Note:* If the settlor transfers an existing policy to the trust, thereby relinquishing the incidents of ownership, the settlor must live for three years from the date of the establishment of the irrevocable life insurance trust for the proceeds to avoid the federal estate tax. In addition, depending on the replacement value of the existing policy, i.e., the amount of money it would cost to buy the policy at the present time, gift tax may be due, unless the cost was under the annual $10,000 gift tax exclusion.

If the life insurance trust is designed properly, it can take advantage of an important decision on tax law that allows the trust's income to be given to the settlor's surviving spouse for life and passes the principal to their children tax-free after the spouse's death. The decision came in the case of *Crummey v. Commissioner,* 397 F.2d 82 (9th Cir. 1968). The money the settlor contributes each year to pay the insurance premiums is not given to the beneficiaries (the children) directly, but goes instead to the trustee of the trust. The trustee must give each beneficiary (child) a written notice, called a Crummey letter, indicating that the gift from the settlor has been delivered and that each beneficiary may elect (demand) to receive the gift at this time. If the demand is not made, the trustee will invest the money by paying the premiums due on the policy. Because the settlor's annual gift to the trustee can be acquired by the beneficiaries each year, it constitutes a present interest and qualifies for the annual $10,000 gift tax exclusion. See Exhibit 10.2 for an illustration of an irrevocable life insurance trust.

🏛 ASSIGNMENT 10.2

1. In the chart below, fill in the missing Yes or No for each estate planning device (document).

This Document Can (be)	Documents		
	Will (without a testamentary trust)	Revocable Living Trust	Irrevocable Living Trust (if funded)
1. Private.	No	_____	Yes
2. Avoid probate.	_____	Yes	Yes
3. Avoid court appointment of fiduciaries.	_____	Yes	Yes
4. Use professional management.	Yes	_____	Yes
5. Protect a spendthrift child.	No	_____	Yes
6. Avoid ancillary administration.	No	_____	Yes
7. Allow maker to control assets while alive.	Yes	Yes	_____
8. Delay inheritance.	_____	Yes	Yes
9. Avoid federal estate tax.	No	No	_____
10. Diminish contests of the document.	No	Yes	_____
11. Revoked.	Yes	Yes	_____
12. Provide for the maker's disability.	_____	Yes	Yes

POSTMORTEM ESTATE PLANNING

Important estate planning opportunities are available even after the testator's death. This estate planning is called **postmortem** planning, and it is often used for tax-saving purposes.

Postmortem
After death; pertaining to matters occurring after death.

Example: At age 82, Barney dies, leaving half of his estate to his wife, Wilma, who is 86 and the other half to their only child, Doreen. Either Wilma or Doreen could reject the testamentary gifts from Barney by a disclaimer.

A disclaimer is a refusal to accept a bequest, inheritance, or gift acquired through a will, trust, or the law of intestate succession or to accept proceeds from

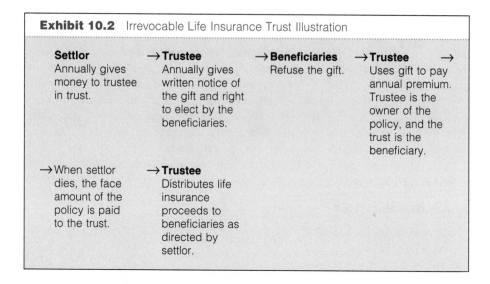

Exhibit 10.2   Irrevocable Life Insurance Trust Illustration

Settlor	**→ Trustee**	**→ Beneficiaries**	**→ Trustee** →
Annually gives money to trustee in trust.	Annually gives written notice of the gift and right to elect by the beneficiaries.	Refuse the gift.	Uses gift to pay annual premium. Trustee is the owner of the policy, and the trust is the beneficiary.
→ When settlor dies, the face amount of the policy is paid to the trust.	**→ Trustee** Distributes life insurance proceeds to beneficiaries as directed by settlor.		

life insurance or other gratuitous transfers. Named beneficiaries disclaim gifts primarily because of their age, health, and financial security and because disclaimers offer the opportunity to make sound tax-saving decisions. The following are some examples of how disclaimers and other strategies can be used to save on taxes after the testator's death:

- *Gift and estate tax savings.* When a beneficiary or donee disclaims a gift of an estate that results in a transfer of the property from the disclaimant to another person, the question arises whether the transfer is subject to gift or estate tax. The case of *Brown v. Routzahn,* 63 F.2d 914 (6th Cir. 1933), has settled the issue that a "valid" transfer or qualified disclaimer is not subject to either tax. In the *Brown* case, the court ruled that a donee's rejection of a testamentary gift before the distribution of the estate was not a taxable transfer and therefore was not subject to tax. The types of disclaimers that qualify to avoid gift and estate tax are found in state statutes and in Section 2518(c)(3) of the Internal Revenue Code, which provides that prior to acceptance of any benefit or gift:

1. The disclaimant must make an irrevocable, unqualified, and unequivocal refusal to accept an interest in property.

2. The refusal must be in writing.

3. The written instrument of disclaimer must be received by the personal representative (or trustee in a trust) no later than nine (9) months after the decedent's death. If the potential disclaimant is a minor, the time for the disclaimer may be the date the minor reaches age 21. See Exhibit 10.3 for a sample written disclaimer.

4. The refusal must be legally effective to pass the specific gift to another person without direction from the disclaimant.

As a result of the disclaimer, the interest does not pass to the disclaimant and therefore is not subject to gift or estate tax. Thus qualified, the property can pass directly to another person without following the directive for its disposition from the disclaimant.

Example: Tom's will leaves a majority of his estate to Jolene, his wife. Jolene is financially secure, so she executes a written disclaimer and gives it to the

---

Exhibit 10.3   Sample Disclaimer

STATE OF NEW YORK
SURROGATE'S COURT: COUNTY OF _____

In the Matter of the Administration
of the Estate of _____ ,   RENUNCIATION OF INTEREST IN ESTATE
                                 PURSUANT TO EPTL 2–1.11
              Deceased.   File No. _____

TO THE SURROGATE'S COURT OF THE COUNTY OF _____ :
    I, the undersigned, _____ , domiciled at _____ , New York, pursuant to Section 2–1.11 of the New York Estates, Powers and Trusts Law, irrevocably renounce wholly all of the right, title, and interest in and to any portion of the estate of _____ , deceased, to which I may be or become entitled under the laws of the State of New York.

                                          _____ [L.S.]

[Notary]

Source: Reprinted with permission from West's McKinney's Forms, ESP, § 7:418. Copyright ©, by West Publishing Company.

---

personal representative and files a copy with the probate court. The disclaimer keeps the property out of Jolene's estate and is not subject to gift or estate tax. It also allows the property to pass directly to Tom and Jolene's children, which, although not specified by Jolene, is actually what she wishes.

A disclaimer is accomplished by delivering the written disclaimer to the personal representative and filing a copy with the probate court. In the case of a trust, the disclaimer would be given to the trustee. Estate tax reduction after death can also be achieved by purposely allowing the personal representative to transfer the amount of the property disclaimed to a charity or spouse. This strategy can substantially increase the charitable and marital deductions and thereby lower the gross estate of the decedent and correspondingly the estate tax. A surviving spouse's elective rights against a will can also be used to increase the marital deduction if the elective share is greater than the amount the spouse receives through the will.

▪ *State inheritance tax savings.* Inheritance taxes levied by some states are based on the amount of the property given to the recipient and the relationship of that person to the testator. Assuming a bequest to a child in the testator's will would be taxed at a lower rate than a bequest to a surviving spouse, the testator–decedent's spouse, by a disclaimer, may cause the property to pass to the child and be taxed at a lower rate for inheritance tax purposes. See *Matter of Wisely's Estate,* 402 N.E.2d 14 (Ind.App. 1980), in which the court held that the beneficiary's renunciation of her interest in the decedent's estate under the will related back to the time of the decedent's death. Consequently, none of the estate had been transferred to her under the will, and therefore there was no basis for assessment of inheritance tax to her.

▪ *Federal and state income tax savings.* The decedent's estate as a taxable entity and the beneficiaries' income taxes may be affected by controlling the timing and amount of property distributed to the beneficiaries or prolonging the time period of the estate administration into a second taxable year if this procedure is economically sound.

■ *Deduction for administration expenses.* As a final postmortem tax-saving method, the personal representative can also elect to use estate administration expenses as a deduction for either estate tax or income tax purposes.

KEY TERMS

Estate plan	Gift splitting	Donee (of a power	Terminable interest
Disposition	Present interest	of appointment)	Incident of
Marital deduction	Legal life estate	Appointee	ownership
Estate equalization	Custodian	Special power of	Irrevocable life
General power of	Custodianship	appointment	insurance trust
appointment	Future interest	QTIP trust (qualified	Postmortem
Capital gains tax	Donor (of a power	terminable interest	
	of appointment)	property)	

REVIEW QUESTIONS

1. Who are the individuals you would choose to assist you in preparing an estate plan for a client?
2. What is the purpose of an estate plan? Methods for reducing or avoiding taxes are part of every estate plan. Such tax avoidance methods may be legal, but are they ethical?
3. How do potential adverse factors diminish the value of an estate? List at least three such factors.
4. What are the two key documents used to prepare an estate plan? How does each document benefit a decedent's surviving family members?
5. How is the marital deduction used to lower the net estate that is subject to federal estate tax?
6. Under what circumstances does estate equalization between spouses become important?
7. How does the charitable deduction reduce both federal estate and income taxes?
8. How does a charitable remainder unitrust differ from a charitable remainder annuity trust? What function does each charitable trust serve?
9. What are the most common methods used to reduce federal and state death taxes? List four methods and explain how each reduces these federal and state taxes.
10. According to current federal tax law, what are the gift tax annual exclusion, the marital deduction, and the unified transfer tax credit for gifts and estates? Explain how each is used to reduce federal taxes.
11. What is the distinction between a general and a special power of appointment? Why is a power of appointment used in a will or a trust?
12. What are four methods of transferring property that qualify for the gift or estate tax marital deduction? Explain each one.
13. What is a QTIP trust? Explain its function and advantages.
14. Why is life insurance such an important planning device for an estate plan? What is the function of an irrevocable life insurance trust?
15. What are the incidents of ownership of a life insurance policy? What effect do they have on a decedent-policyholder's potential federal estate tax?

CASE PROBLEMS

Problem 1

Marsha Thompson, age 34, is a single parent having divorced her husband, Ben Thompson, three years earlier. Marsha has custody of their two children, Andrea, age 12, and Jonas, age 8. Marsha is a marketing manager for a local retail store. She earns $35,000 per year. The company provides her and her dependents with a health insurance plan; a group term life insurance policy worth $20,000; and a 401(k) employee benefit plan to which the company annually contributes 3 percent of her salary. Marsha makes contributions of $200 per month to the 401(k) plan, and she has named her two children the beneficiaries of the plan and her life insurance. Marsha has a checking account of $1,200; owns a 1989 Ford; and after the divorce, has title to a house worth $85,000 with equity of $15,000. She has no other savings or investments.

Marsha's former husband, Ben, is a salesman who has difficulty keeping a job because of his dependency on alcohol. Currently, he is selling new and used cars. He has visitation rights with the children, but he frequently fails to show up. Ben has been ordered to pay monthly child support of $300, which he has paid sporadically depending on whether he had a job. He is now $4,500 behind in support payments, and Marsha has little hope of enforcing payment. According to your state statutes, answer and explain the following:

A. As part of an estate plan for Marsha, would you recommend a will, a will with a testamentary trust, or a revocable living trust?
B. Name the fiduciaries who would need to be appointed as part of Marsha's estate plan.
C. If Marsha were to die first, can she exclude her former husband, Ben, from becoming the guardian of the person of her minor children? What about the guardian of the property?
D. Are the children old enough to voice their preference for a guardian?
E. What other kinds of insurance, if any, would you recommend Marsha buy, e.g., homeowners, car, life, disability, or health?
F. What kinds of investments, if any, would you recommend e.g., stocks, bonds, certificates of deposit, and IRAs?

Problem 2

Jake Costello, a confirmed bachelor, has been a workaholic his entire life. Financially, he has been immensely successful. Jake's net worth is over $10 million. Now 86 years of age and in failing health, Jake has outlived his immediate family members and has no surviving relatives. Realizing "you can't take it with you," Jake decides that the one beneficiary he does not want to receive any death benefits, i.e., federal taxes, from his estate is the government. What options could you suggest to Jake to accomplish his wish or is it a fantasy?

CHAPTER ELEVEN

PERSONAL REPRESENTATIVES: TYPES, PRE-PROBATE DUTIES, AND APPOINTMENT

OBJECTIVES

After completing this chapter, you should be able to:

- Identify and define the various types of personal representatives involved in the administration of decedents' estates.

- Understand the procedures for appointing the personal representative in formal probate proceedings.

- Explain the basic functions performed by the personal representative in preparing for probate administration.

- Recognize your role in assisting the personal representative in performing the required duties of estate administration.

OUTLINE

SCOPE OF THE CHAPTER

This chapter provides a more in-depth review of the law governing personal representatives. It identifies and defines them and reviews their duties in preparation for the administration of a decedent's estate. The chapter discusses only those functions that must be performed soon after the decedent's death, i.e., duties the personal representative should be ready to perform even before the probate court confirms his appointment. Because you will often be asked to assist the personal representative, knowledge of these duties is essential.

The chapter begins by defining the types of personal representatives, describing the mechanics of their appointment, and citing sample statutes that outline appointment procedures. Then the basic powers and duties of the personal representative in preparing for formal proceedings are explained, along with your role in assisting with these duties. For an overview of the duties of the personal representative, see Chapter 3.

TYPES OF PERSONAL REPRESENTATIVES

The U.P.C. term *personal representative* refers to anyone empowered or authorized to administer the estate of the deceased, whether the deceased died testate or intestate. Minors, incompetent persons, convicted felons, and judges of a court are prohibited from being personal representatives. Personal representatives must be U.S. citizens.

The role of the personal representative may be performed by a private individual (usually a family member), an attorney, or a trust officer of a corporate business such as a bank or trust company. In intestacy cases, the personal representative is selected according to the order of preference for appointment set by statute. An example of a state statute illustrating the order of preference is 20 Pa. Stat. Ann. § 3155:

(a) *Letters testamentary*—Letters testamentary shall be granted by the register to the executor designated in the will, whether or not he has declined a trust under the will.

(b) *Letters of administration*—Letters of administration shall be granted by the register, in such form as the case shall require, to one or more of those hereinafter mentioned and, except for good cause, in the following order:

(1) Those entitled to the residuary estate under the will.

(2) The surviving spouse.

(3) Those entitled under the intestate law as the register, in his discretion, shall judge will best administer the estate, giving preference, however, according to the sizes of the shares of those in this class.

(4) The principal creditors of the decedent at the time of his death.

(5) Other fit persons.

(6) If anyone of the foregoing shall renounce his right to letters of administration, the register, in his discretion, may appoint a nominee of the person so renouncing in preference to the persons set forth in any succeeding clause.

. . . .

(c) *Time limitation*—Except with the consent of those enumerated in clauses (1), (2) and (3) no letters shall be issued to those enumerated in clauses (4) and (5) of subsection (b) until seven days after the decedent's death. [For comparison see U.P.C. § 3–203 in Appendix C.]

In some states, if no one appears who is entitled to act as administrator, the court or registrar may appoint an official, called the public administrator, to administer the estate of an intestate decedent. This and other terms relating to personal representatives are defined as follows:

- *Executor or executrix.* The executor (a man) or executrix (a woman) is the person designated by a will when the decedent dies testate to see that all of the will's provisions are fulfilled and to handle the affairs of the decedent's estate (see U.P.C. § 1–201[36]). The only time a personal representative can be named an executor or executrix is when the decedent has nominated that person in the will. Provided that person is legally competent, the person is entitled to be appointed as executor or executrix by state statute.

- *General administrator or administratrix.* The general administrator or administratrix is the personal representative, either man or woman, selected and appointed by a probate court to administer the entire estate of an intestate.

- *Special administrator or administratrix.* The special administrator or administratrix is the personal representative, either man or woman, appointed temporarily by a probate court to handle certain immediate needs of an estate, such as managing a business in the capacity of the decedent, until a general administrator or executor can be appointed. This representative usually handles Summary Proceedings when the amount of the decedent's property qualifies as a "small estate" (see Chapter 12).

- *Administrator or administratrix* cum testamento annexo. The administrator or administratrix *cum testamento annexo,* also called administrator C.T.A. (means administrator with the will annexed), is the personal representative appointed by the court in two situations: (1) where the maker of the will does not name an executor or executrix or (2) where the maker of the will does name an executor or executrix but the latter cannot serve because of a deficiency in qualifications or competency. The following state statutes identify the position of administrator C.T.A.

20 Pa. Stat. Ann. § 3325 Administrator C.T.A.
An administrator with the will annexed shall have all the powers given by the will to the executor, unless otherwise provided by the will. When he has been required to give bond, no proceeds of real estate shall be paid to him until the court has made an order excusing him from entering additional security or requiring additional security, and in the latter event, only after he has entered the additional security.

Cal. Prob. Code § 8441 Priority for Appointment
(a) Except as provided in subdivision (b), persons and their nominees are entitled to appointment as administrator with the will annexed in the same order of priority as for appointment of an administrator.

Cal. Prob. Code § 8442 Authority over Estate
(a) Subject to subdivision (b), an administrator with the will annexed has the same authority over the decedent's estate as an executor named in the will would have.
(b) If the will confers a discretionary power or authority on an executor that is not conferred by law and the will does not extend the power or authority to other personal representatives, the power or authority shall not be deemed to be conferred on an administrator with the will annexed, but the court in its discretion may authorize the exercise of the power or authority.

Example: Geraldine writes and executes a will, but she neglects to name an executor. On her death, the probate court will decide if the document is admissible to probate and if so will appoint an administrator C.T.A. for Geraldine's estate.

■ *Administrator or administratrix* de bonis non. The administrator or administratrix *de bonis non,* also called administrator D.B.N. (means administrator of goods not administered), is a court-appointed personal representative who replaces a previous personal representative who has begun but failed to complete the administration of a decedent's estate for any reason, including death. The following is a sample statute that creates the administrator D.B.N. position.

20 Pa. Stat. Ann. § 3326   Administrator D.B.N. and D.B.N.C.T.A.

An administrator de bonis non, with or without a will annexed, shall have the power to recover the assets of the estate from his predecessor in administration or from the personal representative of such predecessor and, except as the will shall provide otherwise, shall stand in his predecessor's stead for all purposes, except that he shall not be personally liable for the acts of his predecessor. When he has been required to give bond, no proceeds of real estate shall be paid to him until the court has made an order excusing him from entering additional security or requiring additional security, and in the latter event, only after he has entered the additional security.

Example: Frazier is the executor of Eleanor's will. While he is in the process of settling her estate, he dies suddenly. The probate court will appoint a replacement who will have the title of administrator D.B.N.

■ *Public administrator.* The public administrator is a public official appointed by the court to administer the property of an intestate who has left no kindred (blood relative) entitled to apply for appointment and Letters of Administration.

Example: Arnold dies intestate. He never married and has no blood relatives (kindred). Some states would appoint a public administrator to handle Arnold's estate.

■ *Ancillary (foreign) administrator or administratrix.* The ancillary administrator or administratrix is the personal representative appointed by the court overseeing the distribution of that part of a decedent's estate located in a jurisdiction (state, referred to as the "foreign" state) different from the one of the main administration, which is the decedent's domicile state at the time of death (see U.P.C. § 1–201[17]). For further discussion, see Chapter 12.

Example: Bernice, a legal resident of California, dies in Oregon at the summer cottage she owns. Her will is admitted to probate in Orange County, California, where she had been domiciled. The court will have to appoint an ancillary administrator in Oregon to see that Bernice's Oregon estate is distributed according to the will. Remember, if Bernice had died intestate, then her real property in Oregon, the summer cottage, would be distributed according to Oregon's intestate succession statute.

Exhibit 11.1 summarizes the different types of personal representatives.

🏛 ASSIGNMENT 11.1

Joshua Foley's will named his son, William, to be executor, but William refused to serve after Joshua's death and no contingent (successor) executor was named in the will.

1. If Joshua's wife, Ethel, was appointed as personal representative by the probate court, what title would she have?

Exhibit 11.1 Types of Personal Representatives: Summary Chart

- The personal representative of a testate decedent is called executor (if a man) or executrix (if a woman).
- The personal representative of an intestate decedent is called general administrator or simply the administrator (if a man) or administratrix (if a woman).
- A special administrator (-trix) is appointed by the probate court to handle problems and immediate needs of the estate administration that arise before the court appoints a personal representative.
- A public administrator is appointed by the probate court to administer the property of an intestate who has left no person entitled to appointment.
- In special cases the personal representative for either a testate decedent or an intestate decedent may be called:
  1. An administrator (-trix) C.T.A. is the person appointed by the court when the maker of the will either does not name an executor or does name one, but that person cannot serve.
  2. An administrator (-trix) D.B.N. is the person appointed by the court to replace a previous personal representative who has failed to complete the administration of a decedent's estate.
  3. An ancillary administrator (-trix) is the person appointed by the court to oversee the administration of a decedent's estate located in a foreign state.

---

2. If instead William had commenced probate proceedings but was unable to complete them due to illness, and Ethel was then appointed by the court as his replacement, what would her title be?
3. If Ethel was appointed by a probate court to handle the administration of the estate of her brother, George Clark, who lived and died in another state, what would her title be?
4. If Joshua had forgotten to name an executor, what would the court most likely do?
5. If Joshua had been in the process of completing a transfer of the majority interest in a corporation when he died and the court named a person to continue the transfer before a regular probate proceeding could be held, what would be the title of that person?

🏛 ASSIGNMENT 11.2

Harriet died intestate. Her only heirs were her son, Henry, and her mother, Maude. Harriet's only debt outstanding, which was valued at $2,000, was to her best friend, Sally. Explain who would have priority of appointment as personal representative in Pennsylvania and in your own state.

INTRODUCTION TO ESTATE ADMINISTRATION: A DIALOGUE

The following discussion describes the probate procedures involved in a typical case. The participants include the decedent's named personal representative (the executor), the attorney for the estate, and the paralegal. It is essential that the participants maintain continuous communication between and among themselves so that the administration of the decedent's estate will be timely and efficient. The participants and facts of the case are as follows:

Participants
- Decedent—John T. Smith
- Executor—William R. Smith

- Attorney—Ms. Brown
- Paralegal—Ms. Jones

Facts

John T. Smith, the decedent, died August 15, 1994, owning property in two states, State A and State B. He was domiciled at 1024 Pleasure Lane, Heavenly City, in Cotton County, State A, owning a house there. In addition to the homestead held in joint tenancy with his wife, John owned the following property: a car, licensed in State A and owned in his name only; stocks and bonds owned jointly with his wife; a savings account jointly owned; a checking account in his name only; a life insurance policy with his wife named beneficiary; some valuable paintings given to him by his grandfather; and a summer cottage in his name only, located in State B. John had only a few debts at the time of his death, and no one owed him any money. He was survived by his wife, Mary, and only child, William, age 22.

An attorney, Ms. Brown, had previously been retained to help with the drawing of John Smith's will. Ms. Jones, the paralegal, had collected all the pertinent information from John Smith and had written a preliminary draft of the will, which had then been finalized in a meeting between John Smith, Ms. Brown, and Ms. Jones on January 10, 1989 (see Exhibit 11.2). The final draft of the executed will had been placed in a vault in Ms. Brown's office.

The provisions of John's will left his wife all property not already transferred to her by joint ownership, gift, or other means. William R. Smith, son of the decedent, had been named executor of the will. He had made all the necessary funeral arrangements for his father's burial and, knowing he had been named executor, went to the office of Ms. Brown to discuss the handling of the administration of his father's estate.

In the presence of the paralegal (Ms. Jones), the attorney (Ms. Brown), and the executor (William Smith), the following dialogue takes place.

Attorney: Come in and sit down, William. Here is your father's will. As you know, you have been asked to be his executor.

Executor: (Reads the will) Before his death, my father and I discussed the handling of his estate. I knew he had named me executor, and I agreed to serve. But we also decided, and my mother agreed, to ask you, Ms. Brown, to act as my attorney and advise me in carrying out the duties of the executor since I have no experience in these matters and feel I should learn and understand completely the responsibilities.

Attorney: I will be happy to serve as your attorney. It has been the practice of this law firm when advising clients named as executors to work with our paralegal in the field of estate administration. As you know, William, Ms. Jones helped both to collect the necessary data for and to prepare the preliminary draft of your father's will. Now, under my supervision, she will handle many of the details necessary to help settle your father's estate. She will participate in all our conferences on administration, and she will keep you informed of all meetings, hearings, correspondence, and the current status of the administration of your father's estate. She will be available to answer some of the questions you might have about your executor's duties. Others she will discuss with me, and we shall then communicate the information to you. Please feel free to ask either of us any questions or contact us any time you have matters that you want to discuss.

Exhibit 11.2 John T. Smith's Will

LAST WILL AND TESTAMENT
OF
JOHN T. SMITH

I, John T. Smith, residing at 1024 Pleasure Lane, Heavenly City, Cotton County, State A, declare this instrument to be my Last Will and Testament, hereby revoking all former Wills and Codicils by me made.

Article I

I direct that my debts, funeral expenses and expenses of administration be paid out of my estate as soon as possible after my death.

Article II

I give all of my property, now owned or hereafter acquired by me, to my wife, Mary K. Smith, if she survives me.

Article III

In the event my said wife, Mary K. Smith, shall predecease me, or if we should die in a common accident, then I give all of my said property, now owned or hereafter acquired by me, to my son, William R. Smith, now residing at 1024 Pleasure Lane.

Article IV

I hereby nominate and appoint my son, William R. Smith, Executor of this, my Last Will and Testament. In the event he should predecease me or should be unwilling or unable to serve in that capacity, then I hereby nominate and appoint my brother, Joseph B. Smith, Executor of this, my Last Will and Testament. I hereby give and grant unto my said Executor full power to sell and convey, lease or mortgage any and all real estate that I may own at the time of my death or which may be acquired by my estate, without license or leave of court.

Article V

No bond shall be required of any individual named above as Executor of this Will.

IN WITNESS WHEREOF, I have hereunto signed this my last Will and Testament this 10th day of January, 1989.

John T. Smith
_____
John T. Smith—Testator

THIS INSTRUMENT, consisting of one (1) typewritten page, bearing the signature of the above named Testator, was on the date hereof signed, published and declared by him to be his Last Will and Testament in our presence, who, at his request and in his presence, and in the presence of each other, we believing him to be over 18 years of age, of sound mind and disposing memory, and under no constraint or undue influence hereunder do sign our names as attesting witnesses.

Francis A. Miller _____ residing at *1712 State Street*
Witness

Janet F. Strom _____ residing at *34 S. Seventh Street*
Witness

Executor: Yes, I have met Ms. Jones. My father told me how pleased he was with the help she had given him in drafting his will. I am very happy that Ms. Jones will be working with us.

Paralegal: Thank you. Before we begin our discussion about your father's will and the administration of his estate, let me review for you the things that have been done to this point. As you know, our firm assisted your father in planning for the distribution of his estate after his death. Ms. Brown discussed with your father the purpose of and need for a will. I compiled checklists of all the property that your father owned or in which he had any interest. After discussing the estate plan with Ms. Brown, I then drew up a preliminary draft of the will. Ms. Brown, utilizing methods that took advantage of all possible tax considerations, drew up the final draft of your father's will in its present form. The will ensures that the estate will be distributed according to your father's wishes.

Attorney: Let's get started. What we try to accomplish, William, when we assist executors, is to explain the basic procedure that must be followed in administering an estate from beginning to end.

Estate administration procedures

Executor: A few years ago my uncle died without a will. I recall my aunt talking about it. Are the same procedures followed whether a person dies with or without a will?

Attorney: I intend to discuss with you procedures that occur whether a decedent dies *testate,* meaning with a will, as in your father's case, or *intestate,* which means without a will, as in your uncle's case. In either case, a *personal representative* must be appointed to administer the decedent's estate. In the situation such as your father's, where someone has died leaving a will, the personal representative named in the will is generally called an *executor,* if a man, or an *executrix,* if a woman. When a person has died without a will, the personal representative is referred to as an *administrator,* if a man, or an *administratrix,* if a woman. An executor is named in the will and then confirmed by the court to handle the estate. An administrator, however, must be appointed by the court when there is no will. You, William, will perform the duties of an executor.

Executor: Well, how do we begin? What must I do?

Attorney: Any personal representative must perform three basic duties:

Personal representative's duties

1. All your father's assets must be collected.
2. His debts, claims against the estate, and taxes due must be paid.
3. The remainder of his estate or property must be distributed according to his will within guidelines set by the *statutes* or laws of this state.

When a person dies, the county and state in which the decedent resides at death, the *domicile,* is the proper *venue,* or place, for the *"domiciliary"* administration of the decedent's estate. In this state, as in most states, the court that handles the decedent's estate is called the *probate court.* Each county has its own probate court. The right, power, and authority a probate court has to hear and decide these matters is referred to as the court's *jurisdiction.* Jurisdiction of the probate court over the administration of a decedent's estate continues until the proceeding is finished. Since your father also owned *real property,* your summer cottage in State B, a second or *"ancillary"* administration must be commenced in that state. The county in which the property is located is the proper venue for the ancillary proceeding. Ms. Jones will give you additional information and assistance in handling such matters.

Executor: So far I believe I understand the basic functions that must be performed and how the probate court fits into the picture. Since my father named me executor, do I give the money and property to the people mentioned in his will?

Attorney: Not right away. Although you have been named executor, you have no authority to act as personal representative until you file a petition and are appointed by the probate court. This will be done once your father's will has been admitted, which means the will is validated and accepted by the probate court. Now that we are ready to discuss procedural steps and the checklists of information necessary to accomplish them, I am turning you over to Ms. Jones to have her go through the steps with you. As we previously mentioned, if you have any questions about your responsibilities, please call. We shall see that any problems are resolved.

Executor: Thank you for the information, Ms. Brown. If I have any problems, I'll be sure to ask you. Good-bye, and thanks again.

**Petition
to probate
will**

Paralegal: As Ms. Brown mentioned, in order for you to become authorized as executor, you must petition the court to admit and accept your father's will. This is done by filling out one of the numerous forms required for estate administration. We have in our law office all the necessary forms that you must complete

**Tickler
system**

as part of this administration. In addition, we will set up what is called a "tickler" system, which lists chronologically all the important steps and dates in the stages of the administration of the estate.

Here is an example of a "tickler" form (see Exhibit 11.3). Using both this system and a list of procedural steps will help reduce the possibility that some important detail or significant date might be forgotten, with resulting damage to the beneficiary's *(successor's)* interest and with potential liability to you, the executor.

Executor: In that case, let's set up this "tickler" system right away. If we each have a copy, then we can remind one another of the essential steps and important dates. Right?

Paralegal: Yes. This is exactly what we will do. But remember, you must first get your position as executor authorized as well as establish the necessary ancillary administration in State B where the summer cottage is located. You recall that administration in your father's county of residence is called the "domiciliary" administration. Administration necessary in any other state is "ancillary." Although your father left a will naming you as executor of his estate, a person must also be appointed in State B to handle the ancillary administration. Even though there is a will, that person, who is a resident of State B, is usually called the *ancillary administrator.*

Executor: Now I understand the term. But how is the ancillary administrator authorized, and what does he or she do?

Paralegal: You and your mother are given the opportunity to select the person to act in this representative, *fiduciary* capacity. As a representative of the estate, the ancillary administrator generally must submit a copy of your father's will, a certified copy of his death certificate, and a petition for appointment to the probate court of the county in which the *real property,* the cottage, is located, using a form similar to the one you will use for authorization in our state. Once authorized by the local county probate court in State B, the ancillary administrator will:

1. Collect the local assets.
2. Pay the local creditors and taxes, if any.
3. Transfer the balance of the estate to you, the domiciliary representative.

Some states allow the domiciliary representative to apply for appointment as ancillary administrator if there is no law to the contrary. We shall check this out

---

Exhibit 11.3 Sample "Tickler" Form

ESTATE OF JOHN T. SMITH
"Tickler"

ESTATE OF _____ deceased, _____ , 19 ___

Date of Death _____ Date of Birth _____ Domicile _____

Probate Court _____ County, File No. _____

Name, Mailing Address, and Telephone of Personal Representative and Date of Appointment: _____
_____

Ancillary Administration Necessary _____

Date of Last Will _____

Probate Court File No. _____ Tax Identification No. _____

Proceeding	Person Who Performed	Due or Dated	Filed or Paid
Original will filed with probate court			
Petition for probate, administration, etc.			
Mailing of notice of hearing			
Hearing on petition for probate or appointment with registrar			
Affidavit of mailing (family allowances, etc.)			
Bond			
Letters issued			
Notice to creditors and affidavit of mailing			
Inventory and appraisement			
Personal property tax		Feb.	
Real estate taxes: (First half		May 15	
Second half) if necessary		Oct. 15	
Last date for spouse's election			
Property set apart for surviving spouse and/or minor children			
Maintenance ordered			
State and other inheritance tax waivers obtained			
Last date for filing claims			
Claims hearing			
Decedent's final income and gift tax returns due			
Federal			
State			
Fiduciary's final income tax returns due			
Federal			
State			
Last date for filing claims with leave of court			
Optional alternative valuation date			
Federal estate tax return due			
State inheritance and/or estate tax due			
Closing letter (federal estate tax)			
Date maintenance ends			
Final account			
Closing statement			
Hearing on final account			
Decree or order of distribution issued			
Discharge of personal representative			

because, if it is allowed, your acting as ancillary as well as domiciliary representative might be desirable. If there are creditors of your father in State B, you will be faced with the choice of paying their claims out of ancillary assets or the domiciliary estate funds. If you want to protect the summer cottage against being sold to satisfy such debts, you must discuss this with Ms. Brown.

Executor: By all means, I will consult with Ms. Brown. We would not want to sell the summer cottage unless necessary, since both my mother and I enjoy it so much.

Paralegal: Once you petition the court for probating the will, and the court has proved and accepted it, you will be the authorized personal representative—the executor. The probate court signs an order admitting the will as valid and issuing to you *Letters Testamentary.* This particular legal form is the authorization given to executors to handle the administration of a decedent's estate. If your father had died intestate, without a will like your uncle, either your mother or you as *next-of-kin* would petition the probate court for general administration of your father's estate, requesting that the probate court appoint one or both of you as administrators. The form used to authorize an administrator is called *Letters of Administration.*

Letters testamentary

Letters of administration

Executor: Then, Letters Testamentary authorize an executor named in a will to handle the decedent's estate, and Letters of Administration authorize a general administrator to do the work when the decedent dies leaving no will. Are the duties of the executor and administrator the same?

Paralegal: Basically, yes. Administrators do much the same thing as executors, but they must rely on the state laws to guide their actions, whereas executors follow the provisions of the will within statutory limitations, of course.

Executor: I've heard that in some cases an estate can be probated in a simpler manner—informally, I believe it is called. Is this possible?

Paralegal: That is a good question. Many states, including our own, have adopted the *Uniform Probate Code*'s recommendations for administration of decedents' estates. Two forms of probate procedures are included in the Code: *formal* or *solemn* and *informal* or *common.* Some states use only the formal procedures; some follow the Uniform Probate Code and use both formal and informal procedures; others use a variation of these forms.

Estate administration

Basically, formal probate refers to proceedings or a hearing conducted before a *judge* with the requirement that *notice* be given to all *interested persons,* such as beneficiaries, devisees, or heirs, so they might be present to contest the will or, in *intestacy* cases, to contest the appointment of a general administrator. Informal probate, on the other hand, is also known as unsupervised probate since it is necessary only to present a will or petition for administration to an appropriate court representative, who may be a judge but likely will be a *registrar* or *clerk.* After the will has been admitted or the administrator appointed, no notice to interested parties is necessary. The administration of the decedent's estate can thus be rapidly completed. Another advantage of informal probate is that it may reduce the expenses of administration, including the elimination of the need for an attorney to assist in the procedures. Every personal representative should consider administering an estate informally.

After hearing of the person's death, interested parties such as beneficiaries, successors, or creditors of the decedent who want to contest the validity of the will or the appointment of the administrator must request a formal hearing. An original informal proceeding then becomes a formal one, with all associated procedures. Because of the size of your father's estate and the real property involved, you will have to discuss with Ms. Brown the type of proceeding to be followed.

Executor: So what exactly would be the advantages of formal as opposed to informal probate for an estate like my father's?

Paralegal: Basically, the choice of formal or informal probate depends on a number of variables, such as the nature of estate assets and the preferences of the personal representative. The probate court must supervise formal probate, whereas it does not have to supervise informal probate unless someone who has an interest in the estate requests it. The personal representative might feel that it would be better for the court rather than the registrar to oversee administration of the estate because of problems presented by certain assets. Since your father's estate hasn't been inventoried or valued yet, I can't give you facts or figures. However, Ms. Brown will advise you of the method that would better suit your case. One word of caution—informal probate sounds effortless, but I assure you it isn't. It leaves the personal representative to administer the estate with the help of the registrar. The court will step in only when requested, but knowing when to request the court's help isn't all that easy.

Executor: I can see that the procedures can be complicated. What information is needed to commence the formal probate?

Paralegal: First, we need a *petition to prove the will* (see Form 1*). It requests the following information:

- The name, age, and Social Security number of the decedent.
- His domicile.
- The place and date of his death.
- The name and address of the executor (personal representative) named in the will.
- The date and original copy of the will being probated.
- The estimated value of the decedent's estate, including both real and personal property.
- The names, ages, relationships, and addresses of the decedent's known heirs, devisees, and successors.
- The request by you as the petitioner that notice that the will be admitted to probate be given to all the decedent's creditors, and that you, the petitioner, be appointed executor and Letters Testamentary issued.

The petition, like so many of the forms we use, must be verified, that is, signed and sealed by a notary public.

Executor: What happens after the petition is completed?

Paralegal: We file the petition with the probate court, which establishes the court's jurisdiction over the estate, and the probate judge sets a date and time for the hearing on the petition. This order also limits the time for any of your father's creditors to file their claims and sets the date for hearing any disputed claim. Notice of the hearing is given to all interested parties either by direct mail to each heir, devisee, or successor, or by publication once a week for three weeks

---

*See Appendix A

in a legal newspaper within the county for the benefit of creditors. Copies of this notice are also given to the state's tax department.

Executor: What happens at the hearing?

Paralegal: Before the actual hearing, we correspond with the witnesses to your father's will and make arrangements to have them meet you and Ms. Brown at the judge's chambers on the hearing day. Ms. Brown will have with her at that time the necessary forms for presentation to the court. You and I shall prepare these forms with Ms. Brown's supervision and review. The forms include:

- A *proof of publication* of notice of the hearing (Form 5*).
- An *affidavit* stating when and where publication was made, obtained from the newspaper publishing the notice (Form 6*).
- An *order admitting the will to probate* (Form 10*), which states that this is the last will of the decedent, grants *Letters Testamentary* (Form 17*), and specifies the amount of *bond* (Form 76*), if required.
- The personal representative's *oath of office,* which is usually on the same form as the bond but in other states is sometimes on a separate form (Form 13*).
- The *certificate of probate* certifying that the will attached to it is the decedent's last will that the court allows, thus verifying its validity (Form 12*).

We shall also prepare Letters Testamentary for the signature of the probate judge. These authorize you to act as the executor of your father's estate. Remember, had your father died intestate like your uncle, we would prepare Letters of Administration instead.

Executor: Yes, I understand that clearly now.

Paralegal: The final forms we prepare and present to the court are:

- The *order appointing the appraisers,* which names the persons who will appraise or value the estate (Form 22*).
- The *notice to the surviving spouse,* your mother, of her *right to renounce* or waive what your father left to her in the will and take, instead, a percentage of his total probate estate, as she is allowed by statute (form 7*). Widows or widowers who receive little under their spouse's will find this *statutory election,* also known as the "forced share," advantageous, but since your father left your mother everything, she will obviously not pursue this right.

Executor: All right. We have the forms and the witnesses to my father's will at the courtroom. Are we ready for the hearing?

Hearing on petition to probate will

Paralegal: Yes. As petitioner, you will take the stand and be sworn in. Ms. Brown will elicit from you the information contained in the petition. Under oath, you will verify that it is correct and request appointment as executor of your father's estate. Then Ms. Brown will ask the witnesses who *attested* and *subscribed* to your father's will to take the stand and under oath testify that your father *acknowledged* the document as his last will and signed it in their presence and that they each signed in each other's presence as attesting witnesses. They will also testify that your father was of sound mind at the time he signed the will. Ms. Brown then asks the court to admit the will to probate and that you be authorized as executor.

———————————

*See Appendix A

Executor: What happens if my father's brother, Uncle Joe, objects to the will?

Paralegal: Good question. That's called a contest of the will. The probate court would then have to set up a separate hearing date for the will contest. Do you expect this to happen?

Executor: No, I was just wondering about the procedure.

Paralegal: In that case, I assume the probate judge will agree to the requests made by Ms. Brown. The execution of the will is thereby proved, and probate of the estate can begin.

Executor: What happens at the hearing?

Paralegal: The probate judge asks you to take the required oath and sign the executor's *bond* if the judge deems it necessary. Since your father's will specifically requested that his representative be exempted from this, the judge will try to comply with the request, unless our statute requires the personal representative to be bonded in estates like your father's. A bond guarantees to the court and to those parties with an interest in the decedent's estate (beneficiaries, devisees, creditors, and the like) that you, the executor, will act in a fiduciary manner and perform your duties faithfully. The amount of the bond is determined by the court, and if it is needed, we will seek the lowest amount possible to lessen the bond premium expense.

Bond

After you have signed the bond and it is approved by the court, Ms. Brown asks the court to appoint two persons, previously agreed on, as appraisers for your father's estate. Not all states require appraisers, but ours does. Before the hearing, we will contact and receive the consent of these persons to act as appraisers. They are paid for their work out of the assets of the estate by you, the executor.

Finally, Ms. Brown requests the clerk to issue *Letters Testamentary* to you. These become your official authorization from the court to act as executor of your father's will and estate. You will use the Letters to obtain the assets of your father's estate that are currently in the possession of others such as banks and corporations. A few of the forms I have mentioned are provided by the court, but it will be necessary for us to prepare most of the forms we previously discussed.

Executor: The procedures are just as complex as I imagined. What next?

Paralegal: Well, remember we discussed ancillary administration?

Executor: Yes, in connection with the summer cottage.

Paralegal: That's right. We petition the county probate court in State B, where the cottage is located, asking that you be appointed ancillary administrator. I shall check to make sure you qualify. If I remember correctly, State B does not require the personal representative to be a resident of that state. I will check on this and on all similar matters under instructions from Ms. Brown before we act. If you are appointed, you will follow procedures similar to those we have discussed. You should notify creditors, if any, collect other assets, and pay taxes and debts. Doing these things will prevent creditors from attaching the cottage to satisfy debts, so you will be able to transfer it to your mother according to your father's wishes.

Executor: I am sure my father had no debts in State B where the cottage is located.

Paralegal: We must still go through these procedures, but the ancillary administration should create no problems.

Executor: Good. Let's get back to our state procedures.

Inventory and appraisal

Paralegal: The next step is to prepare a complete inventory of your father's property with an estimate of the value of each asset. I prepare an *inventory and appraisal form* (Form 23*), which Ms. Brown reviews. The two appointed appraisers will value the inventory according to one of the methods allowed by Section 2032 of the Internal Revenue Code—assigning to each asset either the value it had at the time your father died or the value it had six months after his death. We will discuss the tax advantages of both methods and choose the one we think best once we have completed the inventory. The inventory and appraisal serve as a basis for the federal and state tax returns that must be filed and provide information to all interested parties concerning the value of the estate. You will also find them helpful when filing your *final account* (Form 39*) after completing all required procedures.

Executor: I was wondering about the taxes. What taxes must be paid and when are they due?

Paralegal: This area, resolving tax problems, is probably one of the most important functions Ms. Brown and I will help you perform in administering the estate. Death tax laws, both state and federal, are very complex. Ms. Brown determines whether any of the following tax returns must be filed and paid: *federal estate tax* (Form 96*), *State A and B inheritance tax* (Form 101*) *and/or estate tax* (Form 100*), *federal and state individual income tax* (Forms 82* and 86*), *federal and state fiduciary income tax* (Forms 91* and 93*), *federal and state gift tax* (Forms 94* and 95*).

Now you see why the "ticker" system and the checklists we previously discussed are so valuable. They help us avoid forgetting any important step or date in the administration of the estate. They are especially useful and timely when dealing with potential tax problems.

I prepare all the necessary tax returns, and then we review them thoroughly with Ms. Brown. She then files them, along with your check as executor for any tax payments due, with the appropriate federal or state tax department as well as the probate court.

Executor: I am glad we have the opportunity to review the tax consequences together because I know very little about this area, but I have been interested in it.

Paralegal: Now, let's discuss the major items of property that compromise your father's estate. As you know, your duties as executor are basically to collect the estate assets, to pay your father's creditors and necessary taxes, and to distribute the remaining assets according to the provisions of his will.

Some of your father's property was owned by him and your mother in *joint tenancy* and will automatically pass to her by *"operation of law."* This results from the *right of survivorship,* which means that the surviving joint tenant (your mother) gets the property without having to wait for a court order. The home, the stocks and bonds, and the savings account automatically belong to your mother because she is a joint tenant owner. These property items, along with the benefits from your father's life insurance policy, are called *"nonprobate"*

---

*See Appendix A

assets since they do not have to be disposed of by will nor do they *descend* to an heir as intestate property. Other items, which he owned, were in his name alone, such as the car, the checking account, the paintings, and the summer cottage. These are *probate assets,* and, I might add, anything he may have owned as a tenant in common with someone else would be a probate asset also. Tenancy in common is a form of ownership between two or more persons. It differs from joint tenancy in that each co-owner can transfer his property interest not only while alive as in joint tenancy but also, unlike joint tenancy, after death, for example, through a will.

As executor, you will collect and preserve only *probate assets* such as the car, paintings, and checking account. All probate and generally all nonprobate assets are included, however, in the decedent's estate for computing death taxes. There are additional procedural steps we must follow to clear the passage of the non-probate property to your mother.

Executor: What do we need to do now?

Paralegal: At this time, you must open an account at your father's bank in your name as executor of his estate. In order to do this, we must file for an employer identification number using Form SS–4 from the Internal Revenue Service and a Notice of Fiduciary Relationship. These forms must be executed and the employer identification number obtained before we can open the account. Here is an example of what the check imprint on your father's account should look like (see Exhibit 11.4). You can then submit to the bank Letters Testamentary authorizing you to withdraw your father's checking account and have it transferred to the estate account. All the estate funds you collect must be deposited into this account, and receipts for such funds and any disbursements you make must be retained. You will need the canceled checks and other receipts or vouchers you receive during the administration of the estate when you present your *final account* to the probate court. It is essential that you keep complete and accurate records of all transactions affecting the estate because the court will hold you personally responsible for any discrepancies or negligence.

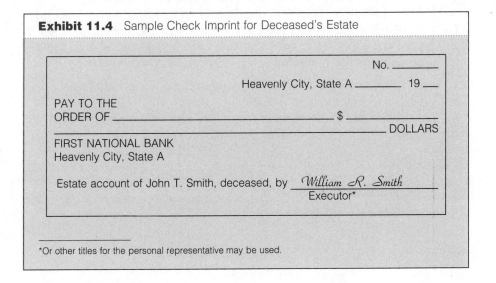

Exhibit 11.4 Sample Check Imprint for Deceased's Estate

No. _____
Heavenly City, State A _____ 19 ___

PAY TO THE
ORDER OF _____ $ _____
_____ DOLLARS

FIRST NATIONAL BANK
Heavenly City, State A

Estate account of John T. Smith, deceased, by *William R. Smith* _____
Executor*

*Or other titles for the personal representative may be used.

Executor: What about some of the other property that I can't deposit—the probate assets I believe you called them—like the car, the paintings, and Dad's life insurance?

Paralegal: Let's back up one moment and discuss again which are probate assets and which are nonprobate assets. Probate assets are those that can be passed by will or by intestate succession statutes. They include property owned solely in the decedent's name or, as previously mentioned, owned as a tenant in common. No other person takes them automatically when the owner dies. The car and the paintings that belonged to your father are probate assets because he alone owned them. The life insurance benefits are different. When the owner dies, the named beneficiary more-or-less automatically becomes the owner of the benefits—because life insurance benefits are derived from a contract between an insured person and an insurer (the insurance company) to pay a certain sum of money to a third person, the beneficiary, should the insured die. When your father died, your mother, whom he named beneficiary, became entitled to the insurance benefits directly, without having to wait for the probate court's approval.

Executor: Then the insurance benefits are nonprobate assets like the property my parents owned as joint tenants?

Paralegal: That's right. You must notify the insurance agent of your father's death and see that the agent receives the policy so that your mother can be given its proceeds without their passing through probate. Remember, however, that we still must report this insurance as part of your father's *gross (total) estate* for federal estate tax purposes, unless he had relinquished the *"incidents of ownership"* on the policy. If your father contacted his insurance agent three years before his death and gave up the incidents of ownership, which are certain contractual rights under the policy, such as the right to cancel the policy or change the beneficiary and the right to borrow on or assign the policy, then the amount of the policy will not be part of his gross estate for federal estate tax purposes. We must check this out.

Executor: It's getting complicated.

Paralegal: Right now I'm sure it seems complicated. But let me assure you that if we work on this together in a systematic manner, everything will go smoothly.

Let's see. We were discussing the car and the paintings. The title to the car must be transferred to your mother. This cannot be accomplished until you receive Letters Testamentary. The following, however, will be necessary:

- The *title registration card* (Exhibit 11.5) or certificate of title must be executed (filled in with any required information and signed by you as executor).
- A transfer fee must accompany the executed registration card or certificate and be mailed within 14 days of the date of transfer to the register to avoid penalties.
- A certified copy of Letters Testamentary—your authorization from the court to act as executor.
- A certified copy of the *Order Setting Apart Personal Property* (Form 25*). (We will discuss this in greater detail later.)

---

*See Appendix A

Exhibit 11.5 Registration Card or Certificate of Title

STATE OF MINNESOTA
CERTIFICATE OF TITLE
TO A MOTOR VEHICLE
THIS TITLE IS PRIMA FACIE PROOF OF OWNERSHIP
KEEP IN A SAFE PLACE — ANY ALTERATION OR ERASURE VOIDS THIS TITLE

VEHICLE IDENTIFICATION NUMBER | MAKE | YEAR | TYPE

TITLE NUMBER | DATE ISSUED | NEW OR USED | IF NEW, DATE OF FIRST SALE | FOR CENTRAL OFFICE USE ONLY

FIRST SECURED PARTY'S INTEREST RELEASED BY: | SECOND SECURED PARTY'S INTEREST RELEASED BY:

AUTHORIZED SIGNATURE **X** | AUTHORIZED SIGNATURE

ASSIGNMENT BY RECORDED OWNER(S): I (WE), CERTIFY THIS VEHICLE IS FREE FROM ALL SECURITY INTERESTS, WARRANT TITLE, AND ASSIGN THE VEHICLE TO:
PRINT BUYER'S NAME(S) | OWNER'S SIGNATURE(S) ALL OWNERS MUST SIGN | DATE OF SALE

X

APPLICATION FOR TITLE BY BUYER(S) | **COMPLETE FRONT AND BACK** | **PLEASE PRINT (DARK INK)**

PRINT BUYER'S NAME(S) LAST, FIRST, AND MIDDLE | DATE OF BIRTH

STREET ADDRESS | CITY | COUNTY | STATE | ZIP CODE

IS THIS VEHICLE SUBJECT TO SECURITY AGREEMENT(S)? YES ☐ NO ☐ **IF YES, COMPLETE SECTION BELOW**

FIRST SECURED PARTY (PRINT NAME) | DATE OF SECURITY AGREEMENT

STREET ADDRESS | CITY | STATE | ZIP CODE

SECOND SECURED PARTY (PRINT NAME) | DATE OF SECURITY AGREEMENT

STREET ADDRESS | CITY | STATE | ZIP CODE

IF THERE IS AN ADDITIONAL SECURITY AGREEMENT(S) COMPLETE AND ATTACH DPS2017. | NAME OF INSURANCE COMPANY | POLICY NUMBER

BUYER SUBSCRIBED AND SWORN TO BEFORE ME:
X | I (we), certify I (we) am (are) of legal age, have bought this vehicle subject to liens shown and no others, this vehicle is and will continue to be insured while operating upon the public streets and highways, and all of my (our) declarations are true and correct.

NOTARY SIGNATURE | DATE | **X**

COUNTY | DATE MY COMMISSION EXPIRES | BUYER'S SIGNATURE(S) ALL BUYERS SIGN.

DETACH THIS PORTION | **DO NOT SEPARATE UNTIL SOLD**

MINNESOTA MOTOR VEHICLE REGISTRATION CARD | **RECORDED OWNER(S) RECORD OF SALE**

PLATE NUMBER | TITLE NUMBER | PLATE NUMBER
PLATES EXPIRE | TAX | TAX BASE | TITLE NUMBER
MAKE | MODEL YEAR | TYPE | V.I.N.
V.I.N. | STICKER NUMBER

RECORDED OWNER(S)

BUYER'S SIGNATURE(S) | SALE DATE

STREET ADDRESS

CITY | STATE | ZIP CODE

The paintings, like the car, are part of the inventory, and title will be transferred to your mother after creditors' claims and taxes due are paid. Determination of your father's debts and payment of those claims are other topics we must discuss.

Executor: Suppose my mother wanted to obtain and use some of the probate property now. Could she?

Paralegal: Yes. Some states, including ours, allow a surviving spouse and/or minor child to petition the probate court for a *family maintenance allowance* and the receipt of certain *exempt personal property* reserved for them by law. Your mother can petition for these things as the surviving spouse. Because your father was solvent and left his entire estate to your mother, however, I do not believe this will be necessary. If some unknown creditors of your father with considerable claims appear, we will then review the situation.

Executor: If the creditors do appear and there isn't enough property in my father's estate to pay all of them, would my mother still receive these things?

Paralegal: Yes. This is true in our state. Such claims of the spouse are given priority even over funeral expenses as well as various other debts within statutory limitations. Now concerning creditors' claims, do you remember what was said during our previous discussion about creditors and the hearing on the petition to approve the will?

Executor: Yes. You mentioned that time limits are set for filing creditors' claims against my father's estate.

Paralegal: Right. When that time expires, we shall check to determine whether any filed claims should be contested. If you reasonably believe a particular claim is not legitimate, you will file an *Objections to Claim* form (Form 29*) with the probate court and serve a copy on the alleged creditor. Contested claims are not heard on the same date as uncontested claims. A separate hearing date is set, at which time the court will decide which contested claims are to be allowed. Since it appears that your father had only a few debts and you have already acknowledged their validity, a hearing for contested claims may not be necessary. If one is necessary, however, you must pay the claims the court allows.

Executor: How do I pay the claims?

Paralegal: By writing checks on the estate account. Remember to ask for receipts from each creditor so that the receipts and the canceled checks can be filed with the court as evidence of payment. Be cautioned that overpayment to a creditor, or payment of an invalid claim, makes you, the executor, personally liable. This means that you must be very careful not to pay any doubtful claim until the hearing is over.

Executor: What if debts occur during our handling of the estate?

Paralegal: These expenses, including the fee our law firm will charge for its assistance in handling the estate, are priority debts according to statute and are paid just before you make the final distribution of the assets of the estate. As executor, you also are entitled to reasonable compensation as the personal representative of the estate, which is another priority debt.

Executor: My father mentioned that to me, but I do not intend to charge a fee.

---

*See Appendix A

Paralegal: That, of course, is entirely up to you. After claims are paid and receipts filed, the *final account* can be prepared. Each state generally sets a time limit for settlement of an estate, which the court may extend for proper reasons. This state allows the personal representative, you as executor, one year from the date of the appointment to settle the estate. Again, a hearing is held for final settlement, and forms must be prepared.

Final account

Executor: What forms are required, and what is the procedure?

Paralegal: To close the estate after having distributed its assets—

- You must submit a *final account* containing a listing of all the assets you have collected, such as personal property and monies from sales, rents, and other sources.
- You must list the liabilities you claim as credits against the estate, including payments for expenses of administration, creditors' claims allowed by the court, funeral expenses, taxes due, and other necessary and proper expenses. Your account must show in detail these receipts and disbursements.
- You must prove that you have distributed the *remaining assets* of the estate, and this figure must correspond to the inventory actually remaining.
- You must sign and file a *petition for settlement and distribution* (Form 40*).

The court will then issue an *order* (Form 41*) setting a hearing on the final account so parties interested in the estate can have the opportunity to be present and make any objections to the accounting.

As with the hearing to prove the will, *notice* (Form 6*) must be published once a week for three consecutive weeks in a local newspaper for the probate court. Copies of the notice must be sent to all heirs, devisees, or successors as well as the state Department of Taxation within a specified statutory time period before the hearing. In our state, it is 14 days. *Proof* of this publication and mailing must be filed with the court (Forms 6* and 42*).

Executor: Then is the hearing held?

Paralegal: Yes. At the hearing, if satisfied that the final account is correct and that all the taxes due have been paid, the probate judge will sign an order allowing the final account. Proof of payment of necessary taxes is provided by a certificate of release of tax lien. All the tax returns I have previously mentioned must be filed and any tax due must be paid before the court will determine the persons entitled to the remaining assets of the estate. The court will then issue the *Decree of Distribution* (Form 45*) assigning these assets. The Decree of Distribution states that notice of the final account and settlement was given; that the decedent died testate; that the final account was approved and allowed; that all allowed claims were paid; that all other expenses, such as funeral and administration expenses have been paid; and that all beneficiaries or successors are named and the share of the decedent's property to which each is entitled is listed.

Decree of distribution

Executor: Is that it? Are my duties finished then?

Paralegal: No. You must record a certified copy of the Decree of Distribution with the county recorder's office, specifically the register of deeds, for the real estate that your father willed to your mother. Other documents might also have to be recorded in State B, depending on its own laws.

---

*See Appendix A

Finally, you can distribute the estate in compliance with the Decree of Distribution. Each distributee or recipient must sign a receipt for the property passed to him or her, and you must file the receipts with the court. The last act is *petitioning* the court for your discharge as personal representative (Form 47*). In this case, the court will sign an *order* discharging you, as executor (Form 48*). A certified copy of this order should be sent to the surety company that holds your executor's bond. With that, you have completed your responsibilities.

Executor: And there are quite a few! I very much appreciate your taking the time to explain the probate procedures to me. It gives me a much clearer picture of what happens in an administration and what duties I have to perform.

Paralegal: Well, I enjoy being able to assist you in these matters. I am sure we will work well together. I have some questionnaires and checklists for you to complete, and I will give you some written materials on the duties of a personal representative and procedures for probating a will that our office has prepared. I would like you to take these home and read them. Also, our local county probate court in the county courthouse offers a pamphlet on probate and estate administration that I will obtain for you. It explains the tasks you will perform and may clear up any confusion you may have about the things we have discussed today. We may need to cover some matters more fully, such as what happens if you decide to sell any of your father's real property, but we can wait to discuss those matters with Ms. Brown when they arise. Now let's go set up our "tickler" system.

PREPARATION FOR PROBATE AND ESTATE ADMINISTRATION—GENERAL OVERVIEW

The personal representative has a fiduciary obligation with respect to the assets of the estate, that is, a duty to utilize the highest degree of care and integrity in handling the decedent's property for the benefit of the estate beneficiaries and devisees. Once appointed by the court, the personal representative has the following general responsibilities:

1. To discover, collect, and preserve all probate assets of any value and manage the probate estate of the decedent if it includes real estate, securities, or an ongoing business until the estate is settled.
2. To notify the deceased's creditors of the death, giving them the opportunity to present their claims and then settle all just claims against the estate and see that the creditors are paid (money for this will come out of the estate assets).
3. To file all required federal and state income, gift, estate, or inheritance tax returns and pay all taxes due.
4. To distribute the remainder of the estate as required by the terms of the will or by law (the intestate succession statutes when there is no valid will).

The mechanics of administering an estate are complex and varied. The authority of the personal representative to administer the decedent's property is governed by the will or state statute. Statutes vary from state to state. Therefore, the list of duties presented here is intended only to provide a basis for under-

---

*See Appendix A

standing the major duties in any given administration; it is not meant to be all-inclusive or exhaustive.

Pre-Probate Duties of the Personal Representative and Paralegal

Both you and the personal representative will have numerous duties to perform in the days immediately after the decedent's death. If the decedent left a letter of instructions concerning her funeral and burial or had entered into a prepaid contract with a funeral director, the personal representative will help the family make the necessary arrangements according to the decedent's wishes or will defer to those of the surviving spouse and family members. Generally, your supervising attorney will be hired by the personal representative at this time, and your work as the paralegal in this case will also begin.

Preparations for probate should begin immediately after the death of the testator. The needs of the family take priority on the death of one of its members, especially when the decedent was the family breadwinner. As the paralegal acting for the law firm selected by the personal representative to assist in administering the estate, you must see that the family's needs are satisfied. The duties you may be asked to perform include the following: (1) search for and obtain the will and other personal and business records; (2) notify appropriate parties of the decedent's death; (3) obtain certified copies of the death certificate from the funeral director; and (4) after contacting the appropriate persons, set a date for the family conference.

Search for and Obtain the Will and Other Personal and Business Records

One of your first responsibilities while assisting the client, i.e., the personal representative, in testate proceedings is to obtain, review, and make copies of the will. As the paralegal performing this investigative function, you should check the letter of instructions, if one exists, for the will's location; if not, you should check your law firm's files. If your firm did not draft the will, you should contact the office of the decedent's attorney who drafted the will. At this point, if you have not discovered the will, check other locations such as the vault where the decedent banked, the decedent's safe deposit box, and places in the decedent's home considered secure. You should also determine if the will was filed with the court.

Example: Maxine has a will. Her husband, Malcolm, has seen the will and knows he has been named executor. Maxine dies, but her will cannot be found. Malcolm believes the will is located in Maxine's safe deposit box. Although a bank must seal the safe deposit box upon learning of the owner's death, generally an officer of the bank will be allowed to determine whether the owner's (decedent's) will is in the box. If it is, before sealing the safe deposit box, the bank will forward the will directly to the probate court, thereby avoiding unnecessary delays in locating the will and enabling the decedent's estate administration to begin.

You must interview family, friends, business advisers, and associates (such as partners, accountants, brokers, agents, and the employer of the decedent), or contact them by phone or mail for information about the will's existence and location and about other personal or business records that may help you locate all assets belonging to the decedent. If the search is successful and the will is found, copies of the will are prepared for the beneficiaries, devisees, and the court, and a summary of the contents of the will is made. The original will must be given to the probate court in the county of the state that is the decedent's legal home (domicile) within a specific time period, usually thirty days after death. Any person in possession of a will who neglects or refuses to deliver the will to the court may, by law, be civilly liable for damages caused by such neglect or possibly criminally prosecuted. Some states have established a "procedure to compel production of a will" when there is reason to believe that a will or codicil exists but the written document cannot be located. The petition requests that the judge issue an order requiring the person who allegedly has knowledge of the location or existence of the document to appear and be examined in court. A case that illustrates the use of this procedure to compel production to determine the existence of a will is *In re Vieillard's Will*, 17 Misc.2d 703, 182 N.Y.S.2d 558 (1959).

☷ ASSIGNMENT 11.3

To test your investigatory abilities, make a list of as many places as possible where a will might be kept. Then select members of your family, e.g., spouse, parents, brothers, or sisters, who have made wills and determine if your list would help you find their wills. If your list does not locate their wills, what additional steps would you follow to discover whether a will exists and its location?

Notify Appropriate Parties of the Decedent's Death

After finding the will, you may be asked to summarize it and send copies to persons named in the will. You also will notify by phone or mail the witnesses and other appropriate parties, such as banks or depositories, e.g., savings and loan associations or credit unions, of the decedent's death so these financial institutions may meet certain legal obligations including the following:

- Prevent persons (holders of accounts with the decedent) from withdrawing money from the decedent's accounts in an attempt to avoid death taxes levied on the transfer of assets at the time of death.
- Provide for the safekeeping of any safe deposit box contents.
- Close all demand accounts (checking accounts) of the decedent.

Obtain Certified Copies of the Death Certificate

Your attorney will seldom be contacted to assist in sorting out a decedent's estate before the funeral arrangements are complete. The funeral director obtains the necessary burial permits and the death certificate, which is the document executed by a physician listing the name of the decedent and the place, time, date, and cause of death. Once your attorney is employed, you will obtain certified copies of the death certificate from the funeral director. If additional copies are needed, you may obtain them from the City Health Department, the Bureau of Vital Statistics, the Clerk of District Court, or a state Registrar. You must include a certified copy when you apply to file claims, obtain insurance benefits, transfer stocks, collect benefits from Social Security or the Veterans Administration, and file deeds transferring title to real estate with the county recorder's office or the Registrar of Deeds office (see the sample death certificate in Exhibit 11.6).

Exhibit 11.6 Death Certificate

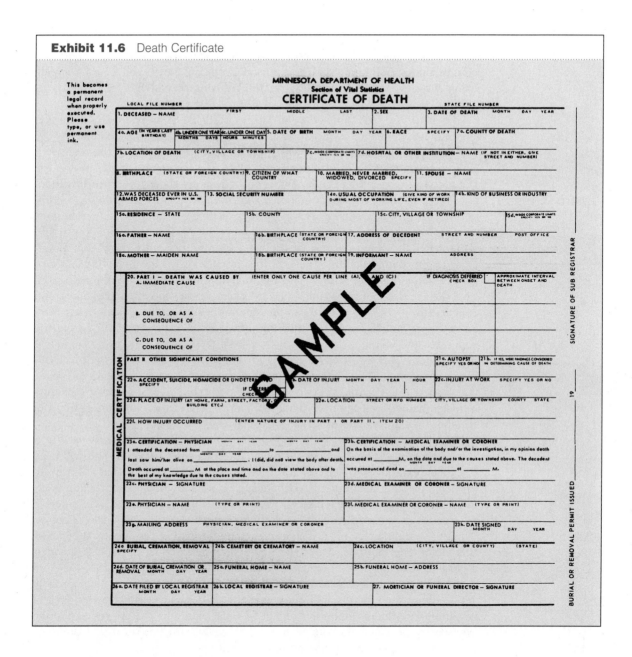

Set a Date for the Family Conference

Shortly after the decedent's death, you may also be asked to schedule a family conference in the immediate future. All persons named in the will should be asked to attend this conference. If the decedent died intestate, you must give notice of the death to all heirs (blood relatives of the decedent) and request that they—and, of course, the surviving spouse—attend the family conference. In some states, a convenient time for this meeting may be on the day of the opening of the safe deposit box, if the decedent had one.

The Family Conference

At the family conference, you must obtain information pertinent to future administrative duties. While assisting the personal representative, you or your supervising attorney should openly discuss the following points with the family:

1. *Explain the provisions of the will* if it is available. If no will exists, then you must explain in detail how the intestate-decedent's property will be inherited, by whom, and which state statute will apply to specific property of the deceased. Only a paralegal who has mastered the intestate succession statutes and is experienced in responding accurately to any questions should perform this function, *but remember that legal advice about family concerns must come from the attorney.* If property such as real property is located in another state, you must also explain the need for an ancillary administrator. The attorney and you should also explain the general nature of probate administration, including the appointment of the personal representative, the preparation of the inventory and appraisal, the various tax returns, and the final account and decree of distribution. You should also point out the dates by which these steps must be taken and explain how a "tickler" system can prevent important deadlines from being overlooked (see No. 17 below). If possible, provide an estimate of how long the administration will take.

> **ETHICAL ISSUE** ▶

2. *Discuss with the family the need for appointing fiduciaries,* e.g., guardians for minors or conservators for incompetent persons, if the decedent died intestate. If there is a will, and the persons selected to act in these capacities, including a trustee named in a testamentary trust, are present at the conference, find out whether they are willing to serve.

3. *Obtain information from the family about the general size and nature of the decedent's estate* using checklists similar to those in Chapter 6. You will need to explain that only probate assets will be subject to probate and that nonprobate property passes directly to the beneficiary or joint owners. Nonprobate assets include property in joint tenancy, property in living trusts, and assets where a named beneficiary is to receive the property, as in life insurance policies, pension or profit-sharing plans, or IRAs. Based on the information obtained in the checklists, determine the type of probate proceeding to be used, or for U.P.C. states, determine whether formal or informal probate proceedings should be followed or whether it is possible to settle the estate by a method other than probate proceedings. (See the discussion on administering "small estates" by affidavit or by Summary Administration in Chapter 12.) Also note that if all beneficiaries and devisees oppose the probate of the will, the Uniform Probate Code does not allow the personal representative to probate it.

4. *Take measures to ensure that the personal representative protects all personal assets of the decedent* (including cars, jewelry, and the like) and make sure all real or personal property is sufficiently insured and protected and that any premiums due are paid. You may be asked to assist the personal representative in obtaining written verification of coverage from insurance agents. You should also advise the personal representative to safeguard expensive personal property such as jewelry, coin collections, and other valuables by placing them in a newly opened safe deposit box.

5. *Inquire about and obtain a list of known debts and obligations,* both personal and those relating to any business interest of the decedent that family members are aware of, so that you can give these known creditors actual notice

of the death and the need to file their claims. Other creditors will be given notice by publication, which is discussed in detail in Chapter 12.

6. *Obtain the facts necessary to prepare the Petition to Prove the Will,* if the decedent died testate, or Petition for General Administration, if the decedent died intestate. Be sure you use the appropriate state or county forms for these petitions.

7. *If the deceased owed any members of the family a debt,* explain to that creditor the need to file a claim. The time limits for procedures to approve such claims will be discussed in subsequent chapters.

8. *To alleviate the family's anxiety and concern about immediate financial matters,* you should discuss the various forms of protection given a surviving spouse and children by some state statutes, such as the homestead exemption or allowance; exempt property; family allowances and maintenance (see No. 10 below); dower, curtesy, or election rights of a surviving spouse; and children's rights, including rights of pretermitted (omitted) children, adopted children, and nonmarital (illegitimate) children.

Explain that if the decedent has made a provision in the will for the surviving spouse, the spouse has the right to elect to take the property provided in the will or a minimum statutory amount of the decedent's estate (as determined by the state in which the estate is probated) instead of the amount in the will. *The*   **ETHICAL ISSUE** ⬅
surviving spouse should be advised of the right to obtain his or her own attorney and elect against the will. The only exception to this elective right is when the spouse has previously waived the right to take the forced or elective share by an antenuptial agreement. If the surviving spouse requests that your supervising attorney handle the election to reject the will and to take the statutory share, you will prepare a "Notice of Election" renouncing the provisions of the will for the spouse's signature, and arrange to have it witnessed according to the statute. Note on the "tickler" form (Exhibit 11.3) that a Notice of Election must be filed with the probate court within a statutory time period, e.g., usually six to nine months after the will has been accepted by the court. For each state, the time limit and the possibility of an extension must be determined.

9. *Explain what a disclaimer is,* the procedures, and the effects. Some state statutes provide that a beneficiary or devisee may disclaim in whole or in part any interest that he would receive from the will by filing a disclaimer in probate court (see Exhibit 10.3). If a beneficiary or devisee determines that a disclaimer is in the best interests of both the family and himself, you will obtain and prepare the disclaimer form to be executed and then file it with the probate court. Disclaimers can also be executed and filed by an executor or administrator on behalf of the estate of a deceased devisee or beneficiary or by a guardian on behalf of a minor. If the statutory requirements are satisfied, a beneficiary or devisee who waives an interest by disclaimer may have the right to transfer or assign the interest to anyone. Otherwise, the interest disclaimed will be distributed according to the directives of the will or by intestate succession, and it will be disposed of just as if the disclaimant had died immediately before the decedent (compare U.P.C. § 2–801).

Example: Mathilda dies leaving her summer home to her brother, Jeremiah, age 70. Jeremiah has no need of the home and does not wish to pay inheritance tax on the gift. He knows that if he rejects this gift, the summer home will pass to Mathilda's daughter according to other terms of the will. Since this is what he wants, he executes and files a disclaimer of the home.

10. *Determine the wishes of the beneficiaries or devisees* of your decedent client's will and prepare the necessary documents and forms to implement their wishes. Explain that whether the decedent died with or without a will, the surviving spouse and minor children are entitled to reasonable maintenance during administration of the decedent's estate for a statutory time period, e.g., twelve to eighteen months, as determined by the probate court. A typical state statute on maintenance is *Md. Estates and Trusts Code § 3–201,* Family Allowance:

(a) *Surviving spouse*—The surviving spouse is entitled to receive an allowance of $5,000 for personal use.

(b) *Children*—An allowance of $2,500 for the use of each unmarried child of the decedent who has not attained the age of 18 years at the time of the death of the decedent shall be paid by the personal representative as provided in § 13–501 of this article.

When maintenance is necessary, forms known as *petitions for maintenance* (Form 26*) are completed and presented to the probate court. Property belonging to the surviving spouse, the income of the family, the size of the decedent's estate, and the socioeconomic status of the family are considered in determining the amount of maintenance. State statutes setting the amount of maintenance are worded vaguely enough to give the court and the personal representative leeway to accommodate these factors (e.g., the personal representative is to allow a "reasonable" amount, which the court may modify at its discretion). Find the statutory requirements of your state and plan accordingly. Have family members decide the amount necessary to support themselves adequately for the time period allowed. If the estate is insolvent, an effort should be made to obtain the largest family maintenance possible so that the decedent's limited assets are used primarily for the family.

In some states, a surviving spouse (or if there is none, then minor children) is entitled, in addition to maintenance, to all the decedent's wearing apparel plus household goods and furniture not exceeding in value a statutory dollar amount, e.g., $5,000 (compare U.P.C. § 2–403 on exempt property). In many states, the spouse may receive this property before the estate is liable for debts, including the decedent's funeral costs. The form employed is usually called "Petition to Set Apart Personal Property" (see Form 24*).

If a spouse survives, she is the petitioner, and if not, the guardian of the minor children signs the petition. No notice need be given within the petition and order. The spouse, under certain circumstances, is also allowed the decedent's automobile.

11. *Determine whether assets will need to be sold during probate administration* to pay debts, taxes, and expenses of the decedent's estate; then, if assets must be sold, ask the family whether they wish to retain any particular items. If the personal representative has been given the power of sale by the will, he might sell an item of property, e.g., a painting, that the family would prefer to keep for sentimental reasons. If property must be sold to pay debts, you must explain the abatement process, previously discussed in Chapter 4.

12. *If authorized by state statute or the decedent's will,* you must discuss the arrangements that will be necessary for the continuation or sale of the decedent's business, e.g., a sole proprietorship, partnership, or limited partnership.

---

*See Appendix A

13. *Check the estate plans of the surviving spouse* and, if requested, make arrangements to amend his will. *Be careful about improper solicitation for this will.* If there is no surviving spouse and the decedent was the last occupant in a home, you may be asked to notify the post office to forward mail to the personal representative of the estate and stop newspapers and all other deliveries.

ETHICAL ISSUE

14. *In intestacy cases, you must determine if the decedent-intestate made any advancements* to any of the heirs.

15. *Discuss or inquire about any other documents that may have a direct or indirect bearing on the status or transfer of the decedent's estate,* such as marital agreements, a legal separation or divorce, or transactions such as living trust agreements.

16. *Obtain names and addresses of the decedent's advisers,* including tax advisers, accountant, banker, trust officer, insurance agent or broker, and stockbroker.

17. *In preparation for the probate procedure,* you must prepare a calendar checklist (tickler) of important tax dates and deadlines (Exhibit 11.3) and a checklist of probate procedures (Chapter 3). After obtaining the necessary information, explaining the probate process, and answering the questions of the family members, the conference is concluded. Your duties and the duties of the personal representative, however, are just beginning.

Appointment Procedure—The Beginning

To begin the probate process and obtain appointment, the personal representative must complete the following steps. You will assist the personal representative in performing some of these tasks.

- File the original will or codicil if there is one.
- File a petition either for (1) a will and appointment of the personal representative (executor) or for (2) administration and appointment of the personal representative (administrator). These petitions are usually two separate forms that request, basically, the same information.
- Contact the witnesses to the will who, if needed, must be present to testify at the hearing for probate of the will and appointment of the personal representative (executor). Witnesses will not be needed if the will is self-proved or is a valid holographic will.
- File a death certificate, if needed.
- Pay filing fees, which you will verify.
- Arrange for bond, if necessary (see the discussions of bond and surety in the next sections).

In some states, e.g., Minnesota, the mechanics for beginning the probate procedures when a decedent dies testate or intestate require the use of one of two legal forms. When the decedent dies with a will, the form that commences probate is called the Petition to Probate (Prove) a Will and for Appointment of the Personal Representative (Executor). If the decedent dies without a will, the form is called the Petition for General Administration in which the personal representative appointed is also known as the administrator. Both petitions contain the facts establishing that a specific probate court has jurisdiction. Notice that whether the decedent died testate or intestate, these petitions must list all heirs, i.e., persons who would have inherited under the laws of intestate succession.

These heirs must be given notice of the court hearing and also the opportunity to be present to contest the will or challenge the personal representative's appointment. In most states, the petitions include the name and domicile (address) of the decedent; the date and place of death; the names, ages, relationship to the decedent, and addresses of heirs or successors; the value and the nature of the decedent's real and personal property; the decedent's debts; and the name and address of the petitioner. As you would expect, the forms used for this petition vary from state to state. Some states, e.g., Michigan, use the same form for commencing probate for all decedents, whether they die with or without a will, by simply having the petitioner check the appropriate box on the form or cross out the incorrect words concerning the choice of probate on the one common form. The following state forms reflect this diversity:

- Exhibit 11.7 Michigan Petition for Commencement of Proceedings
- Exhibit 11.8 Delaware Petition for Authority to Act as Personal Representative

In both testate and intestate cases, the probate court sets a time and place for a hearing on the petition. At the hearing, after the witnesses testify, if the probate court allows the will or grants administration, the court appoints the personal representative (executor or administrator), who must file an oath of office and in some cases post a bond, which constitutes an expense of the estate and may be deducted on the death tax forms. These procedural matters will be discussed in greater detail in subsequent chapters.

Bond

A bond or surety bond is a certificate in which a "surety," an individual or surety company, promises to pay the amount of the bond to the probate court if the personal representative fails to faithfully perform the duties of administering the decedent's estate (see Form 76*). A "surety or bonding" company is an incorporated insurance company licensed to offer bonds to fiduciaries, such as personal representatives (executors or administrators) and trustees. The purpose of the bond is to protect and insure the estate beneficiaries, heirs, creditors, and government tax collectors against losses due to the personal representative's improper, negligent, or fraudulent administration of the decedent's estate. It is also the best protection a personal representative can have against lawsuits by beneficiaries or creditors for allegations of negligence or malfeasance. If required, a bond must be filed at the time of the personal representative's appointment or shortly thereafter. Often an employee of a bonding company will be present at court on hearing days with the appropriate bond forms, and arrangements can then be made to complete and file the bond with the court immediately after the hearing.

The requirement that a personal representative file a bond is generally set by state statute. Typical statutes are Sections 8480(a) and 8481(a)(1) of the California Probate Code:

Cal. Prob. Code § 8480

(a) Except as otherwise provided by statute, every person appointed as personal representative shall, before letters are issued, give a bond approved by the court. If two or

---

*See Appendix A

Exhibit 11.7   Michigan Petition for Commencement of Proceedings

JDC CODE: COP

STATE OF MICHIGAN PROBATE COURT COUNTY OF	PETITION FOR COMMENCEMENT OF PROCEEDINGS ☐ Supervised ☐ Independent ☐ Small estate	FILE NO.

Estate of _____

1. I, _____ , am interested in the estate and make this petition as
   _____Name_____

   _____ of the deceased.
   Relationship

2. Decedent information: _____ _____m.   _____   _____
                         Date of death   Time (if known)   Age   Social Security Number

   ☐ did

3. Decedent ☐ did not leave a will, dated _____ . Subscribing witnesses are: _____

   _____

4. At date of death, decedent was an inhabitant and resident of _____ , in this County
                                                                City/Township/Village

   and/or left an estate to be administered in this County with the estimated value: Real estate $ _____

                                                                         Personal estate $ _____

5. The names, ages relationships and residences of the heirs-at-law, devisees and other interested persons are:
   (Identify children of the deceased who are not issue of the surviving spouse)

NAME	AGE	RELATIONSHIP Also indicate if devisee	RESIDENCE

PLEASE SEE OTHER SIDE

Do not write below this line - For court use only

PC 04 (8/87) **PETITION FOR COMMENCEMENT OF PROCEEDINGS**   MCR 5.113, MCR 5.702
                                                                MCL 700.115 -.145; MSA 27.5115 -.5145

Exhibit 11.7   Michigan Petition for Commencement of Proceedings—*continued*

---

5. (continued)

NAME	AGE	RELATIONSHIP Also indicate if devisee	RESIDENCE

6. Of the above interested persons, the following are under legal disability or otherwise represented and presently have or will require representations as follows:

NAME	LEGAL DISABILITY	REPRESENTED BY Name, address, and capacity

7. I further represent:

8. I request:
   ☐ the will be admitted to probate and administration be granted to _____ ,
   Name

   personal representative named in the will, who resides at _____
   Complete address

   ☐ administration of the estate be granted to _____ ,
   Name

   who resides at _____
   Complete address

   or to some other suitable person.

9. I further request that this be a   ☐ supervised
                                      ☐ independent   administration.
                                      ☐ small estate (MCL 700.101)

10. I further request:

I declare that this petition has been examined by me and that its contents are true to the best of my information, knowledge, and belief.

Date _____

Attorney signature	Petitioner signature
Attorney name (type or print) Bar no.	Petitioner name (type or print)
Attorney address	Petitioner address
City, state, zip Telephone no.	City, state, zip Telephone no.

more persons are appointed, the court may require either a separate bond from each or a joint and several bond.

Cal. Prob. Code § 8481

(a) A bond is not required in either of the following cases:

   (1) The will waives the requirement of a bond.

. . . .

Another example of a statute requiring a bond is:

20 Pa. Stat. Ann. § 3175 Requiring or Changing Amount of Bond

The court, upon cause shown and after such notice, if any, as it shall direct, may require a surety bond, or increase or decrease the amount of an existing bond, or require more or less security therefor. (See also U.P.C. §§ 3–603 and 3–604 for examples of when a bond is required and the amount of the bond.)

The requirements for a bond and surety vary from state to state:

▪ In some states, both a bond and a surety are required of all personal representatives.

▪ A bond is generally required if the testator requests it in the will, but the court could decide it was "unnecessary."

▪ In most states, a bond is not required if the testator states in the will that the personal representative may serve without bond. A sample clause would read:

I direct that no bond or other indemnity shall be required of any personal representative including successor personal representatives nominated or appointed pursuant to this will. The term personal representative shall include any person appointed to administer this will.

▪ Even if the will waives the bond, a probate court may agree to require one at the request (sometimes a demand) and for the protection of interested parties, e.g., beneficiaries and creditors (see Md. Estates and Trusts Code § 6–102[b]); Ohio Rev. Code § 2109.04; and Cal. Prob. Code § 8481(b). But compare the comment in U.P.C. § 3–603 that rejects the idea that a bond should always be required, or required unless the will waives the bond.)

▪ If a will does not mention the bond, and the personal representative is a family member or close friend and a resident of the state in which the estate is administered, the court can agree to exclude a bond if all the beneficiaries agree and waive the filing of a bond.

▪ If an attorney is named the personal representative in a will, the court usually requires the attorney to obtain a bond and to be supervised by the court.

▪ No bond is required if a corporation, e.g., a bank or trust company, is appointed personal representative.

▪ If there is no will, generally the personal representative must post a bond, especially if one or more minor children survive the intestate.

▪ A few states, among them Massachusetts, allow the personal representative to serve with a pledge rather than a bond and without using a surety, thereby avoiding the expense.

Today the majority of financial planners believe a bond is unnecessary. When a bond is required, the amount of the bond is determined by the order of the court based on the value of the estate, the type of assets, the relationship of the personal representative to the decedent, and other relevant facts including the demands of beneficiaries and creditors. The amount varies from state to state and ranges from the same as the estimated value of the decedent's personal property

FORM NO. 1 - PETITION FOR AUTHORITY TO ACT AS PERSONAL REPRESENTATIVE

TO: The Register of Wills for the County of New Castle in the State of Delaware

In the matter of the estate of:

....   } **PETITION**
                                                                    Decedent

I.   ...., the "Petitioner(s):
     represent(s) that:

     (1) The decedent died on .... a resident of ....

     ....

     (2) The decedent had a/had no will dated ....

     (3) Since the execution of the will (if referred to above), the decedent has/has not married, and ....child(ren) were born
         to the decedent.

     (4) Petitioner(s) basis for qualification to act or other explanation:...

     ....

     ....

II. Petitioner(s) request(s) the grant of: (check one)
     ...... Letters Testamentary.   ...... Letters of Ancillary Administration with Will Annexed.
     ...... Letters of Administration.   ...... Letters for Appointment of a Successor Administrator/rix.
     ...... Letters of Administration with Will Annexed.   ...... Letters for Appointment of a Successor Administrator/rix
     ...... Letters of Ancillary Administration.   with Will Annexed.

III. The decedent was survived by the following persons:

NAME	RELATIONSHIP	ADDRESS
SPOUSE:		
NEXT OF KIN: **(BLOOD RELATIVE)**		

IV. The decedent owned personal property valued at $ .... and/or real estate to the value of $ ....

     located in.................... County, State of Delaware, as follows: (describe real estate)..................

     ....

     ....

V.   A bond is/is not required.

     STATE OF DELAWARE   }
     NEW CASTLE COUNTY   } SS.

     ....named in this application, being duly

     sworn according to law say(s) that the matters alleged in this petition are true and correct to the best of .... knowledge
     and belief.

     Attorney of Record..........................   ....

     Address...................................   ....

     ....

     SWORN TO AND SUBSCRIBED before me, at Wilmington, Delaware this..........day of.....................;

     A.D.........

                                          .... REGISTER OF WILLS ....

to twice that amount. Generally, the value of real property, unless sold at the direction of the testator's will to pay for estate debts, is not included in determining the value of the bond. In some states, the annual premium for a bond of $100,000 (the value of the decedent's personal property) is approximately $500 for each year until the estate administration ends.

If a bond is required, you must remind the personal representative to purchase the bond and file it promptly and, after the estate is finally settled, to cancel the bond as soon as the estate is closed by sending the surety company a copy of the Order Discharging the Personal Representative (see Form 48*) and request a refund of the unearned premium. Since the testator can waive the requirement of a bond in the will, this expense can be avoided. In any event, the cost of the personal representative's bond is charged to the estate and paid with estate funds.

Surety

Surety is a guarantee of an individual or company that, at the request of another, usually a fiduciary, e.g., a personal representative (executor or administrator), trustee, or guardian, it will pay a specified sum of money to the court if the personal representative, trustee, or guardian fails to perform the fiduciary's duties. An example would be the surety of a personal representative's bond.

Example: Marilyn Williams is the personal representative named in Hugh Howard's will. Hugh did not include a clause in his will excluding a bond. The court orders that a bond be posted. Marilyn obtains a bond from the Allstate United Surety Insurance Company. If Marilyn, through negligence or fraud, fails to perform her duties as personal representative, the company as surety of her bond must pay to the court a specific amount up to the maximum of the bond.

⚖ ASSIGNMENT 11.4

Determine whether your state has bond requirements. If so, state briefly what they are. Cite all relevant statutes.

Probating (Proving) the Will or Granting Administration

Depending on the state, a will is proved in a variety of ways. The court may require the subscribing witnesses to testify to the following in court:

- That in attendance in the lawyer's office were the testator, her attorney, and the two witnesses.
- That the testator declared to the witnesses that a document she held in her hand was her will and requested them to act as witnesses to the execution of her will.
- That the witnesses then saw the testator sign the will and also sign her initials in the margin of each page of the will.
- That the testator handed the will to each witness and asked that the witness read aloud the attestation clause that precedes the place for the witnesses' signatures.
- That both witnesses knew the testator and that she was over the age of majority (18), of sound mind, and not acting under any constraint or undue influence.

---

*See Appendix A

▪ That each witness then signed the will and added his address while the testator and the other witness watched.

Note: If a notary public had been present at the execution of the will, had heard the oaths and observed the acknowledgments and signatures, and had officially notarized the will, the will would have been "self-proved," and the witnesses' testimony would not have been necessary.

Another method used to prove a will is to have an affidavit signed by one or more of the witnesses attesting to the facts and the proper execution of the will (see Exhibit 11.9).

Once the probate court, in testate cases, has approved the will and the appointment of the personal representative (executor) or, in intestate cases, has granted administration and the appointment of the personal representative (administrator), the court issues **Letters of Authority.** These are certificates of appointment that are often called Letters Testamentary or Letters of Administration.

Letters Testamentary and Letters of Administration

When the probate court grants Letters Testamentary, an executor or executrix is appointed; when it grants Letters of Administration, and administrator or administratrix is appointed (see Form 17* and 77*). Both Letters Testamentary and Letters of Administration are conclusive proof and evidence that the person named therein is the duly appointed, qualified, and acting personal representative of the decedent's estate with the powers, rights, duties, and obligations conferred by law. Certified copies of the letters issued to the personal representative by the probate court or registrar will be required for specific estate administration procedures including the following:

Letters of Authority
Certificates of appointment called either Letters Testamentary, when there is a will, or Letters of Administration, when there is no will.

Exhibit 11.9 Affidavit of Attesting Witnesses

The undersigned, being severally duly sworn on their respective oaths, depose and say that on the _____ day of _____ , 19 ___ . _____ , the Testator of the attached Will, in their presence, subscribed said Will at the end thereof and at the time of making such subscription declared the instrument so subscribed by him [her] to be his [her] Last Will and Testament; that they, at the request of said Testator and in his [her] presence and in the presence of each other, thereupon witnessed the execution of said Will by said Testator by subscribing their names as witnesses thereto; that in their opinion said Testator at the time of the execution of said Will was in all respects competent to make a Will and not under any restraint; and that they make this affidavit at the request of said Testator.

Witness

_____

Witness

_____

[Notary]

_____

Source: Reprinted with permission from West's McKinney's Forms, ESP, § 7:85. Copyright ©, by West Publishing Company.

---

*See Appendix A

- Opening the decedent's safe deposit box.
- Opening an estate safe deposit box to safeguard certain valuable assets, such as expensive jewelry, coins, and other valuables, and documents, such as deeds, birth and marriage certificates, passports, insurance policies, stock certificates, record of military service, automobile and boat titles and registrations, mortgages, savings certificates, promissory notes, bills of sale, and other contracts.
- Withdrawing money from existing bank accounts of the decedent.
- Opening a bank account for the estate to hold all cash from the decedent's accounts and from all property sold by the personal representative, debts collected, dividends from securities, salary checks, and other funds owed to the decedent.
- Transferring all assets (e.g., sale of real estate, sale or gift of stock, life insurance proceeds when the estate is the beneficiary, and so on).
- Forwarding the decedent's mail to the personal representative.

The person who applies for either Letters Testamentary or Letters of Administration must be competent, i.e., suitable in the opinion of the court, to discharge the personal representative's obligations. A person who has a felony record, is not a resident of the domicile state, or has a history of mental illness may be rejected as "unsuitable." The decision on competency is an exercise in discretion by the court. An executor is named by the will, so the court cannot arbitrarily appoint someone else to fill the position. This does not mean, however, that the court is compelled to appoint the named executor or that the appointee must be the most suitable and competent of all possibilities. For example, the court would not name a minor as executor even though he was selected by the testator. The minor lacks competency since a minor cannot make binding contracts for the estate. If the minor, however, had attained majority age at the time of the testator's death or subsequently at the time for admission or proof of the will, he could be competent to act as personal representative and could be appointed by the court.

The appointment of an administrator calls for greater discretion on the part of the court. Where the decedent has left no indication of who is to supervise the distribution of the estate, the court must decide who, of all the applicants, would be appropriate. In most states the order of preference is set by statute. Again, the court cannot overrule a preference with or without cause unless the state statutes grant the court this power, but the court may use its discretion to appoint one who occupies a lower position in the statutory order.

Example: Ridgely names his wife, Yvonne, executrix. Following his death, she will become the executrix of his estate unless the court finds her mentally incompetent or otherwise subject to disqualification. Ridgely's sister, Loretta, is an accountant and more experienced in business than Yvonne, but the court will not replace Yvonne with Loretta or anyone else unless it finds Yvonne unqualified to act as executrix. Similarly, if Ridgely had died intestate, Yvonne, being his wife, would be the first in most states to be considered by the court when it names the administrator or administratrix.

If, in intestacy, an administrator or administratrix has been appointed, but then a will naming a personal representative is discovered and admitted by petition to probate, the court will terminate the powers of the intestate personal representative (administrator) and approve the appointment of the executor or executrix, who will continue the probate of the estate. The following statute illustrates the basis for the termination of an intestate appointment and the appointment of a new personal representative.

> *20 Pa. Stat. Ann. § 3181*   Revocation of Letters
>
> (a) When no will—the register may revoke letters of administration granted by him whenever it appears that the person to whom the letters were granted is not entitled thereto.
>
> (b) When a will—The register may amend or revoke letters testamentary or of administration granted by him not in conformity with the provisions of a will admitted to probate. [Compare U.P.C. § 3–612.]

Example: Roxanne Bridges dies. According to state law, her husband, Neil, is appointed administrator since no will can be found. After he is appointed administrator and Letters of Administration are issued, Neil discovers a will drawn by Roxanne in an old shoe box in the family home. Roxanne names her father, Harold Jensen, executor in the will. On the basis of this discovery, Neil's administration terminates, and Harold will be appointed executor in order to continue the probate administration.

The specific procedures of administration and the personal representative's duties after appointment are discussed in succeeding chapters.

🏛 ASSIGNMENT 11.5

Juliana was in her last illness when she made a will naming her brother, Roland, executor. Unknown to her, Roland had been declared legally insane the previous year. A month after Juliana's death, Roland is declared sane and applies for Letters Testamentary. Juliana's sister, Clarissa, contests Roland's application, stating that his insanity disqualifies him from acting as executor. In your state, is she correct?

KEY TERMS

Letters of Authority

REVIEW QUESTIONS

1. Who is prohibited from being a personal representative?
2. What is the difference between the following: an executor v. an executrix; a general administrator v. a special administrator; an administratrix *cum testamento annexo* v. an administratrix *de bonis non;* and a public administrator v. an ancillary administrator?
3. The personal representative is one type of a fiduciary. What does that mean? List other fiduciaries.
4. What are the primary or general duties of a personal representative when administering a decedent's estate?
5. How is a "tickler" system used for an estate administration?
6. Is there a time limit for commencing probate in your state? How long does your state allow for the completion of an estate administration? Cite your state statute for each time period.
7. In general, what are a paralegal's duties in organizing, preparing, and executing a family conference after a testator's death?
8. When does the probate court require a personal representative to post a bond? What is a surety bond? Draft a bond using your state's form.
9. How do Letters Testamentary and Letters of Administration differ?
10. Using the attesting and subscribing witnesses, what procedures are required to prove a will's validity?

CASE PROBLEMS

Problem 1

Assume some married member of your family has died. Perform the following tasks. (To preserve confidentiality, you should change the names of all parties concerned.)

A. Determine whether the decedent left a will.

B. If a will exists, locate it.

C. Using the sample from this text, prepare a "tickler" system.

D. Using the text's checklists or your own, determine the assets and liabilities of the "decedent's" estate. Fill in the checklists.

E. Obtain the facts necessary for the Petition to Prove the Will or, if no will exists, the Petition for General Administration. Then fill out the appropriate form.

F. Assume the decedent owed you a $5,000 debt based on a promissory note and you are willing to cancel the debt. How might this be done?

G. Determine whether your state grants an election right to a surviving spouse. Cite the statute and determine whether the decedent's spouse would receive a greater share under the will or under the statute.

H. Assume you are named as a beneficiary or devisee in the will. Fill out the disclaimer form. Can you assign your interest to your best friend?

I. Cite your state statute, if any, on maintenance, family allowance, and exempt property. Fill out the forms that pass these property items to family members.

J. Check to see if the "decedent's" spouse has a will. Ethically, could your supervising attorney be hired by the spouse to prepare the will? Explain.

Problem 2

Carmella Lamas is a wealthy widow. She has prepared a preliminary draft of her will but has not decided who she will name as her personal representative. Answer and explain the following questions according to your state's statutes:

A. Carmella's favorite relative is her nephew, Ferdinand, age 19. If she names him to be her personal representative, is he qualified to serve in your state? See and compare U.P.C. § 3–203(f).

B. Would Ferdinand be eligible to serve if he had been convicted of the felony of possessing and using drugs? See *Smith v. Christley*, 684 S.W.2d 158 (Tex.App. 1984).

Unless the person is unsuitable, courts routinely appoint the personal representative the testator names in her will.

A. If Carmella appoints her brother, Carlos, her personal representative, can Carlos be removed after his appointment because he is insolvent? See *In re Quinlan's Estate*, 441 Pa. 266, 273 A.2d 340 (1971).

B. Once appointed, can Carlos be removed for any of the following acts of misconduct?

   1. Carlos fails to file a final account.

   2. Carlos omits items from the inventory he files with the court. See *Aaberg's Estate*, 25 Wash.App. 336, 607 P.2d 1227 (1980).

   3. Carlos makes payments to himself for work he performs while administering Carmella's estate.

Since all states provide for the choice of a personal representative for an intestate's estate, answer the following if Carmella dies intestate:

A. Since Carmella is a widow and never remarried, who has priority in your state to be appointed her personal representative?

B. Some states do not allow persons who live in another state to become personal representatives. If Carlos lived in a different state than Carmella's domicile (your state), could he be appointed her personal representative?

CHAPTER TWELVE

PROBATE AND ESTATE ADMINISTRATION

OBJECTIVES

After completing this chapter, you should be able to:

- Explain the distinction between probate proceedings and estate administration.
- Identify and explain alternative procedures to probate and estate administration when administering "small estates."
- Recognize and define the traditional forms of probate and estate administration and compare the Uniform Probate Code alternative.
- List the circumstances under which solemn or formal probate proceedings are appropriate.
- Identify and explain the use of formal probate procedures and forms for administering a decedent's estate whether death occurred testate or intestate.
- Explain the potential liability of the personal representative.
- Apply the procedures and prepare the legal forms used in formal probate administration for a set of facts involving a decedent's estate.

OUTLINE

SCOPE OF THE CHAPTER

The probate and estate administration procedures involved in administering a testator's or an intestate's estate are the concerns of this and the next chapter. The distinction between probate and estate administration is explained, and alternative methods for administering "small estates" are listed and discussed. The two traditional methods of probate and estate administration, solemn and common, are explained, and the Uniform Probate Code alternatives, formal and informal probate, are introduced. The chapter then discusses the procedures and forms used in administering a typical estate using the formal probate method. The chapter ends with illustrated case problems, one with accompanying executed forms (found in Appendix A), and one with an assignment asking you to complete a similar case problem.

PROBATE OR ESTATE ADMINISTRATION

In previous chapters of the text, you have learned the identity, role, and duties of the participants (e.g., personal representative, attorney, paralegal, probate judge, registrar, clerk) in preparing for the administration of a decedent's estate. You have traveled through the procedures that begin soon after the time of death, whether the decedent died testate or intestate: possibly helping with arrangements for the funeral and burial; finding the will, if one exists; holding the family conference; locating witnesses, if necessary; and petitioning the court for "probating the will" (see below) and appointment of the personal representative or applying for appointment of the personal representative when there is no will.

The remaining steps of the probate procedures involved in administering an intestate's or testator's estate are the concerns of this and the following chapter. The word *estate,* also called the gross estate, includes the interest in every type of property, real and personal, owned by the decedent at the time of death. When death occurs, everything the decedent owns becomes part of the estate. The decedent's personal representative holds and manages only the probate assets of the estate until those who are entitled to them (beneficiaries and devisees, if the decedent left a will; heirs, if the decedent died without a will) can assume ownership. In either instance, the personal representative's work is termed estate administration or the probating of the estate of the deceased. The decedent's estate, or gross estate, includes probate as well as nonprobate property, and it is subject to taxes, both federal and state, when the owner dies. Only the probate property, however, is subject to the payment of creditors' claims as well as to federal and state taxes. These assets are the ones handled by the probate court whether a will exists or not. A decedent's will gives the court specific instructions as to what is to be done with the decedent's probate property, i.e., the solely owned property and any property owned in tenancy in common. It has no effect on nonprobate assets. Estate administration is not an issue and is not needed if the decedent's entire estate consists of nonprobate property. If there is no will, the court follows the probate procedures under the laws of intestate succession.

This chapter deals with the actual probate procedures for handling an estate when the decedent dies either testate or intestate. Included in the discussion are samples of the various forms that must be completed. It is the personal representative's duty to see that these procedures and forms are properly and timely executed. The attorney, retained by the personal representative, and you, acting as the paralegal, will help the representative perform this duty. The "tickler system" (Exhibit 11.3) will play an important role in keeping the estate administration on schedule.

The term *probate* initially meant "the act or process of proving the validity of a will." Over the years, the term has evolved so that today, in many states, probate generally refers to all matters over which the court, usually called the probate court, has jurisdiction. Thus the probate court has the power and authority to:

- Establish the validity of a will and appoint the personal representative (executor) or appoint the personal representative (administrator) of an estate when there is no will.
- Supervise the personal representative's actions in paying creditors' claims and distributing and settling the decedent's estate.
- Supervise the guardianship of minors or incompetent persons.
- Determine the statutory rights of a spouse and children.
- Supervise all other matters pertaining to these subjects.

Sometimes the terms *probate administration* (or probate proceedings) and *estate administration* are used synonymously to refer to the actual administration of the decedent's estate from appointment of the personal representative to the final distribution of the property and the personal representative's discharge. Therefore, to avoid confusion, this chapter and Chapter 13 will use the term probate to refer to the process and procedures involved in establishing the validity of a will and the appointment of the personal representative in testate or intestate cases. The term estate administration will be used for the remaining procedures and duties of the personal representative, including the collection and inventory of assets, the payment of approved claims against the estate, the payment of all state or federal taxes due, and the final distribution of the remaining assets to the beneficiaries, devisees, or heirs entitled to them.

Before discussing the various methods and procedures individual states use to administer a decedent's estate, it is important to identify those cases in which estate administration may not be needed. In some states, estate administration may be avoided if the decedent:

1. Has no property in registered form, e.g., recorded deeds for real property and certificates for securities (stocks and bonds).

2. Has no individually owned property in the possession of third parties, e.g., savings and checking accounts, employee benefit plans, and the like, which cannot be transferred to a personal representative without the authorization of Letters Testamentary or Letters of Administration.

3. Has no outstanding creditors' claims, e.g., the decedent has no debts or all creditors have been paid.

4. Has an estate that is classified as a "small estate" where all assets consist entirely of exempt property with a limited monetary value such as family allowances or a homestead and no other real property (see Tex. Prob. Code §§ 137 and 138; Cal. Prob. Code § 13100; and compare U.P.C. §§ 3–1203 and 3–1204).

As an alternative to probate and estate administration, some states allow the heirs and devisees to collect, divide, and distribute the decedent's assets in "small estates" subject to their personal liability for paying all valid creditors' claims and all taxes (see Cal. Prob. Code §§ 13650–13655; and compare U.P.C §§ 3–312 to 3–322). In addition, as previously discussed, there is no need for estate administration if all of the decedent's assets consist of nonprobate property.

Small Estate Settlement and Administration

All states allow decedents with "small estates" to avoid the more common, but also more expensive, methods of probate or estate administration. Most states set a certain monetary limit for the total value of an estate's assets that can qualify as a **small estate.** The amount varies from state to state. If the value of a decedent's estate is below the statutory amount, the estate can be administered as a "small estate." Lengthier, more expensive probate procedures are unnecessary. Small estate procedures are simple: for example, collection of assets is quick and easy; court fees are greatly reduced; debts are generally minimal and promptly paid; death taxes are usually not owed; and assets can be distributed almost immediately, typically to a spouse and children. State statutes commonly identify **"qualified small estates"** as those where the estate assets are within a certain limited monetary amount and/or consist entirely of exempt property, homestead allowance or exemption, family allowances, and where the estate has limited debts such as costs and expenses of administration, reasonable funeral and burial expenses, and reasonable and necessary hospital and medical expenses of the last illness of the decedent.

The procedures adopted by state legislatures for expediting the distribution of small estates vary widely. You must review your state statutes and these procedures and familiarize yourself with the required forms, some of which will be available from your local county probate court. The county clerks or Registrars will give you the forms they can distribute. In addition, they often have developed an outline, pamphlet, or booklet for personal representatives that lists the required forms and procedures for handling small estates. Other necessary forms will generally be available from local or state publishers of legal documents.

Although specific procedures vary from state to state, in general three traditional methods are used: Collection by Affidavit, Summary Probate Administration, and Family Settlement Agreements.

Collection by Affidavit

Many states allow an affidavit procedure to collect and transfer personal property to a beneficiary or heir; to collect debts owed the decedent; or to take possession of the decedent's property held by third parties, e.g., banks and credit unions (see U.P.C. § 3–1201 and Exhibit 12.1). This collection method eliminates the need for the appointment of a personal representative, for supervision by the probate court, or for notice to creditors. To collect the property, the beneficiary or heir must present a certified copy of the decedent's death certificate to the debtor or possessor of the property with an affidavit stating:

- That the value of the entire estate, less liens and encumbrances, does not exceed the state's maximum limit (ranging from $500 to $70,000 depending on the state).
- That a minimum number of days, usually thirty (30) to forty-five (45), have elapsed since the death of the decedent.
- That no application or petition for the appointment of a personal representative (executor) is pending or has been granted in any state court.
- That the claiming beneficiary or heir is legally entitled to inherit the decedent's estate including the right to the payment or delivery of the property.

The affidavit procedure can be used to transfer insurance proceeds, accounts in banks or credit unions, promissory notes, and the property kept in a safe

Small estate
A decedent's estate with few assets and a limited monetary value.

Qualified small estate
A decedent's estate that consists entirely of statutory exempt property or allowances and funeral and administration expenses, and is within a certain limited monetary value.

Exhibit 12.1   Affidavit for Collection of Personal Property

MD **Form No. 4476** Miller-Davis Legal Forms (Rev. 8-1-91) 524.3 1201

**AFFIDAVIT FOR COLLECTION
OF PERSONAL PROPERTY**

STATE OF MINNESOTA)
) ss.
COUNTY OF _____)

Affiant, _____ , being first duly sworn,
deposes and states:

1. Affiant resides at _____ ;

2. _____ died at the age of _____ on _____ ,
   19 ____ , and at the time of death, resided at _____ ,
   City of _____ , County of _____ State of _____ ,
   having Social Security Number _____ ;

3. Affiant as _____ is the successor of the above identified
   decedent;

4. The value of the entire estate, wherever located, less liens and encumbrances, does not exceed
   $10,000.00;

5. Thirty (30) days have elapsed since the death of the decedent;

6. No application or petition for the appointment of a personal representative is pending or has been
   granted in any jurisdiction;

7. Affiant, the claiming successor, is entitled to payment or delivery of the following described
   property, to-wit: _____
   _____
   _____

FURTHER AFFIANT SAYETH NOT.

Dated: _____

_____

Subscribed and sworn to before me this
_____day of _____ , 19____

_____
SIGNATURE OF NOTARY PUBLIC OR OTHER OFFICIAL

NOTARIAL STAMP OR SEAL (OR OTHER TITLE OR RANK)

Source: Miller/Davis Company, Minneapolis, Minnesota.
Currently in Minnesota, the value of the entire estate, wherever located, less liens and encumbrances, cannot exceed $20,000.

deposit box so long as their combined value does not exceed the maximum limit set by statute. Generally, real property cannot be transferred by affidavit. If the decedent died with a will, some possessors, e.g., banks, may require a copy of the will before they will transfer the property. In Illinois, the affidavit method allows the holder of the property, e.g., a debtor who pays the beneficiary or heir, to be discharged of the debt (see S.H.A. 755 ILCS 5/25–1). If the **affiant** was not legally entitled to the collected property, the affiant is responsible to the person who had the legal right to possession of the property, and the former possessor (such as the debtor above) who acted in good faith on the affidavit is released from any further liability based on the transfer.

Affiant
The person who makes, subscribes, and files an affidavit.

Example: Tom's will left his entire estate to his daughter, Carol, his only heir. When he died, Tom had $1,500 in a savings account; a fishing boat in joint tenancy with his best friend, Fred; a $75,000 life insurance policy naming Carol the beneficiary; and an unpaid debt of $15,000 owed to Tom by Mark for a car Tom sold to Mark. The boat and the proceeds of the life insurance are nonprobate assets and do not apply toward the state maximum for collection by affidavit, which is $25,000 in Illinois, Tom's domiciliary state. After thirty days, Carol can execute an affidavit stating that she is Tom's only heir and entitled to his estate under his will and that the total value of Tom's probate assets (i.e., $16,500) is below the state's $25,000 limit. Carol would be entitled to collect the $16,500 (the savings account plus the debt) from the bank and from Mark by affidavit. Carol may also have to present a copy of Tom's will with the affidavit.

Other individual state restrictions on the use of an affidavit for collection include the following: allowing only spouses and children to collect by affidavit; allowing only certain personal property (e.g., bank accounts) to be collected by affidavit; and requiring some minimal court involvement such as filing the affidavit with the probate court.

Summary Probate Administration

After appointment, a personal representative may apply for a special form of administration called Summary Administration for certain small estates. This form of administration, which is shorter than the regular estate administration, can be utilized when the sum of the decedent's probate assets does not exceed the maximum limit set by statute or when the assets do not include any real property. Exhibit 12.2 lists the maximum amounts allowed for settling small estates by Affidavit or Summary Administration in each of the fifty states. Summary Administration is generally limited to small estates that have insufficient assets to pay all creditors and to distribute to heirs of the decedent-intestate or to named beneficiaries or devisees of a will, and also have survivors that include a spouse and minor children. In other words, if the value of the entire estate, less liens and encumbrances, does not surpass the amount payable for exempt property, family allowances, administration expenses, reasonable funeral and burial costs, the homestead exemption or allowance, and reasonable hospital and medical expenses of the last illness of the decedent, then Summary Administration may be permitted (see U.P.C. § 3–1203). When this method is allowed, the personal representative immediately distributes the estate assets according to the will or in the order of priority set by an intestate statute and files a final account or a closing sworn statement with the probate court (see U.P.C. § 3–1204 and Exhibit 12.3). Accordingly, the intermediate procedures required under the solemn or formal probate process may be eliminated including notice to creditors, presentation of their claims, the formal inventory and appraisal, and the court's decree of distribution.

Exhibit 12.2 Monetary Limits That Allow the Transfer of Small Estates by Affidavit or Summary Administration by State

State	Amount	State	Amount
Alabama	$30,000	Montana	7,500
Alaska	15,000	Nebraska	10,000
Arizona	30,000	Nevada	100,000
Arkansas	50,000	New Hampshire	500–5,000
California	60,000	New Jersey	10,000
Colorado	27,000	New Mexico	20,000
Connecticut	20,000	New York	10,000
Delaware	12,500	North Carolina	10,000
Florida	25,000	North Dakota	15,000
Georgia	No ceiling	Ohio	25,000
Hawaii	5,000/20,000	Oklahoma	60,000
Idaho	5,000	Oregon	25,000/60,000
Illinois	25,000	Pennsylvania	10,000
Indiana	15,000	Rhode Island	10,000
Iowa	50,000	South Carolina	10,000
Kansas	10,000/21,000	South Dakota	10,000/60,000
Kentucky	7,500	Tennessee	10,000
Louisiana	50,000	Texas	50,000
Maine	10,000	Utah	25,000
Maryland	20,000	Vermont	10,000
Massachusetts	15,000	Virginia	5,000
Michigan	5,000	Washington	30,000
Minnesota	20,000	West Virginia	50,000
Mississippi	20,000	Wisconsin	10,000/30,000
Missouri	15,000	Wyoming	70,000

Example: May is appointed the personal representative of the estate of Richard who dies intestate and is survived by his spouse and a minor child. A preliminary inventory of the estate's probate property shows that the estate assets will not be sufficient to pay Richard's unsecured creditors' claims and that the total value of his estate is below his state's maximum limit and qualifies for Summary Administration as a "small estate." Therefore, May immediately distributes Richard's assets according to the order of priority set by his state's statute and files a closing sworn statement with the court. Copies are sent to all heirs, beneficiaries, and known creditors.

In the states of New Hampshire and New York, the person who performs duties similar to those involved in Summary Administration is called a "voluntary administrator."

Family Settlement Agreements

A Family Settlement Agreement is a private agreement among heirs of an intestate or beneficiaries of a will by which these parties unanimously agree on the distribution of the decedent's estate without supervision by the court having jurisdiction over the estate. In either testate or intestate cases, the settlement must be agreed to by all interested parties, and once it is executed, the settlement agreement supersedes and replaces the intestate succession statute or the will (see U.P.C. § 3–912). The Uniform Probate Code requires the settlement agreement to be in writing. Although the Family Settlement Agreement speeds the distribution

Exhibit 12.3 Statement Closing Small Estate by Sworn Statement of Personal Representative

Form No. 4477 BUSINESS RECORDS CORPORATION, MINNESOTA   524.3-1204   UPC --

STATE OF MINNESOTA

COUNTY OF _____   **DISTRICT COURT**

In Re: **Estate of**   Court File No. _____

**STATEMENT CLOSING SMALL
ESTATE BY SWORN STATEMENT OF
PERSONAL REPRESENTATIVE**

_____
                Deceased

TO THE HONORABLE JUDGE OF THE ABOVE NAMED COURT:

The undersigned, _____, respectfully states:

1. The undersigned resides at _____ ;

2. The undersigned is the personal representative in the above named estate.

3. That disbursement and distribution of the entire estate of the above named estate has been made.

4. That to the best of the knowledge of the undersigned personal representative, the entire estate, less leins and encumbrances, did not exceed an exempt homestead as provided for in Section 525.145, the allowances provided for in Section 525.15, costs and expenses of administration, reasonable funeral expenses, and reasonable, necessary medical and hospital expenses of the last illness of the decedent.

5. That the undersigned personal representative has fully administered the estate by disbursing and distributing it to the persons entitled thereto.

6. That the undersigned personal representative has sent a copy of the closing statement to all distributees of the estate and to all creditors or other claimants of whom ___he is aware whose claims are neither paid nor barred and has furnished a full account in writing of h___ administration to the distributees whose interests are affected.

FURTHER, under penalties for perjury for deliberate falsification therein, I declare or affirm that I have read the foregoing statement and to the best of my knowledge or information, its representations are true, correct and complete.

Dated: _____

_____
Personal Representative

_____
Attorney for Personal Representative

_____
Address/Phone

_____

Source: Miller/Davis Company, Minneapolis, Minnesota.

of estate assets, a court order is still required to protect the estate from creditors and to clear title to the assets involved (see U.P.C. § 3–1102).

FORMS OF PROBATE OR ESTATE ADMINISTRATION

Before the creation and subsequent adoption of the Uniform Probate Code, traditionally two forms of probate or estate administration, *solemn* and *common* probate, were used. Many states continue to use these two methods today. With solemn probate, also called probate in solemn form, formal court supervision is required throughout the administration of the estate, and notice must be given to all interested parties, e.g., beneficiaries and heirs of the decedent, so that they may be present at an initial hearing to contest the validity of the will or the appointment of a personal representative and may also request continued solemn probate proceedings. Solemn probate procedures are followed in intestate as well as testate estates. Solemn probate results in a final order by the court determining the existence and validity of a will, and it may be used to set aside an earlier common probate proceeding or prevent a pending petition for common probate.

Common probate, which is primarily used for smaller estates and is usually uncontested, is less formal, and involves less supervision or none. It is a simpler procedure that does not require notice to all interested parties such as heirs, beneficiaries, and creditors. In company with the witnesses to the will, the executor or administrator delivers the will to an officer of the court, usually a Registrar or Surrogate. This officer has the power and authority to do what the probate judge would normally do, i.e., appoint the executor or administrator and make findings of fact in relation to the will or the intestacy statutes when there is no will. Under oath, the witnesses attest that the testator asked them to sign the will, that they saw the testator sign it, and that their own signatures are also on the will. Once this is done, the will is considered proven (admitted to probate). If others contest the will, they must petition the Registrar or Surrogate to hold a formal hearing to determine the will's validity. The burden of proof is on the contestant. Common probate may be superseded and set aside by a request of an interested party for implementation of solemn probate. Common probate provides a faster and less expensive statutory method of administering an estate than solemn probate (see and compare Cal. Prob. Code §§ 10500 and 10501; Tex. Prob. Code §§ 145 et seq.; and Wash. Rev. Code Ann. § 11.68.010).

The Uniform Probate Code has added another method for administering an estate. The options are similar to the traditional forms of probate except that they are called *formal* and *informal* probate rather than *solemn* and *common* probate. Under the Code, formal probate (proceedings) is conducted under the supervision of the judge with notice to interested persons; informal probate (proceedings) is conducted, without notice to interested persons, by an officer of the court acting as a Registrar for probate of a will or appointment of a personal representative; see U.P.C. §§ 1–201(18) and (23). "Interested persons" are heirs, devisees, children, spouses, creditors, beneficiaries, and any others having a property right or claim against a trust estate or the estate of a decedent; see U.P.C. § 1–201(24). Formal probate can be either supervised or unsupervised. With formal (supervised) probate, the probate court has supervision over the entire duration of the estate administration. With formal (unsupervised) probate, the estate administration commences formally until the appointment of the personal representative, but the supervision lessens after the appointment unless an interested party requests that formal (supervised) probate continue.

The purpose of the Uniform Probate Code is primarily to:

- Simplify and clarify the law, terms, and procedures in estate administration.
- Lessen the expense and time for the administration.
- Provide an alternative system, which, if adopted by the states, establishes uniform law.

The states are not required to adopt the Code, although they are free to adopt it individually through their legislatures. As noted earlier, many states have continued to use the more traditional methods of estate administration, sometimes in revised form. Exhibit 12.4 identifies the states that have used the traditional forms of estate administration and those that have adopted the Uniform Probate Code. As the exhibit shows, fifteen states have adopted the Uniform Probate Code, and ten have followed the solemn-common form. The remainder either follow a hybrid mixture that possibly combines some features of the Code with their own statutes or have adopted an independent method. Whatever the method, all states require some form of notice prior to the admission of a will to probate and afford an opportunity to interested parties to object to the probate of the will or to the appointment of the personal representative or executor.

In the majority of cases, formal or solemn probate is used for the administration of decedents' estates. Formal probate is unnecessary when the value of the estate is low (see the earlier discussion of small estates), when it is not complex, or when the estate assets consist solely of nonprobate property. Formal probate would normally be the choice in any of the following situations: some beneficiaries are minors whose rights must be protected; real estate problems exist; a beneficiary or creditor intends to challenge the proceedings; the estate presents

---

Exhibit 12.4 Method of Estate Administration by State

States that have followed the English system of common and solemn form probate:

Delaware	Mississippi
Georgia	New Hampshire
Indiana	Tennessee
Kentucky	Virginia
Louisiana	West Virginia

States that have adopted the Uniform Probate Code with some modifications:

Alaska	Idaho	Nebraska
Arizona	Maine	New Mexico
Colorado	Michigan	North Dakota
Florida	Minnesota	South Carolina
Hawaii	Montana	Utah

States that require some form of notice prior to the admission of a will to probate and afford an opportunity to interested persons to object to the probate of the will:

Alabama	Missouri	Pennsylvania
Arkansas	Nevada	Rhode Island
California	New Jersey	South Dakota
Connecticut	New York	Texas
Illinois	North Carolina	Vermont
Iowa	Ohio	Washington
Kansas	Oklahoma	Wisconsin
Maryland	Oregon	Wyoming
Massachusetts		

tax law difficulties; in an intestate case, the number of the decedent's heirs is uncertain; in a testate case, the beneficiaries cannot be located; or family members disagree about their respective inheritances or the continuation or sale of a family business.

COMMENCING PROBATE AND ESTATE ADMINISTRATION PROCEEDINGS

Assuming all the preliminary work and correspondence have been completed by the personal representative with the attorney's assistance and your help (e.g., finding the will, if one exists, and holding the family conference), probate and estate administration can begin.

As probate and estate administration begin, you will play a major role by helping the personal representative with the following procedures:

1. Petition for probate of will or petition to prove a will.
2. Petition for administration when no will exists.
3. Obtain an Order for Hearing the Petition to Prove a Will or for Administration.
4. Arrange for publication of the Notice of Order for Hearing and Affidavit of Publication.
5. Mail the Notice of Order for Hearing and Affidavit of Mailing Notice to all interested persons including creditors.
6. Mail notice of rights to the spouse and minor children and prepare an Affidavit of Mailing.
7. Pay funeral bills.
8. Identify and review objections and arrange for the appearance of witnesses.
9. Miscellaneous duties before the hearing.

As the paralegal who is working directly with the personal representative, you must be familiar with these procedures, the contents of the related documents, and the time limits for filing them. You should also be aware that the forms and procedures vary from state to state. The following discussion includes a series of **"What You Do"** lists, which identify tasks you may be asked to perform while assisting the personal representative. Although not mentioned in each "What You Do" list, you should always be in contact with the clerk of the probate court to verify that you have completed the required forms and procedures accurately and to obtain helpful advice and guidance concerning these procedures, but the clerk is forbidden by law to give you legal advice.

1. *Petition for probate of will or petition to prove a will.* The form used to commence probate proceedings with a will is the Petition for Probate of Will or Petition to Prove a Will (Form 1* and Exhibit 12.5). Any person, called the petitioner, having an interest in the estate, such as a spouse, child, beneficiary, heir, devisee, successor, the named executor, or creditor of the decedent, may file the will and a petition with the court to have the will proved (admitted to probate). Some states have a statute of limitations that limits the time allowed for offering a will for probate by filing the petition for probating a will, e.g., Arizona, Kansas, and Montana (see *Matter of the Estate of Taylor,* 207 Mont. 400, 675 P.2d 944

---

*See Appendix A.

Exhibit 12.5   Petition for Probate of Will

ATTORNEY OR PARTY WITHOUT ATTORNEY *(Name and Address)*:   TELEPHONE NO.:   *FOR COURT USE ONLY*

ATTORNEY FOR *(Name)*:

SUPERIOR COURT OF CALIFORNIA, COUNTY OF

STREET ADDRESS:

MAILING ADDRESS:

CITY AND ZIP CODE:

BRANCH NAME:

ESTATE OF (NAME):

                                                                      DECEDENT

PETITION FOR

☐ Probate of Will and for Letters Testamentary

☐ Probate of Will and for Letters of Administration
   with Will Annexed

☐ Letters of Administration

(For deaths after December 31, 1984)

☐ Letters of Special Administration

☐ Authorization to Administer Under the Independent
   Administration of Estates Act ☐ with limited authority

CASE NUMBER:

HEARING DATE:

DEPT.:   TIME:

1. Publication will be in *(specify name of newspaper)*:
   a. ☐ Publication requested.
   b. ☐ Publication to be arranged.

▶ _____
   (Signature of attorney or party without attorney)

2. Petitioner *(name of each)*:

   requests

   a. ☐ decedent's will and codicils, if any, be admitted to probate.
   b. ☐ *(name)*:
      be appointed (1) ☐ executor   (3) ☐ administrator
                    (2) ☐ administrator with will annexed   (4) ☐ special administrator
      and Letters issue upon qualification.
   c. ☐ that ☐ full ☐ limited authority be granted to administer under the Independent Administration of Estates Act.
   d. ☐ bond not be required for the reasons stated in item 3d.
      ☐ $ bond be fixed. It will be furnished by an admitted surety insurer or as otherwise provided
         by law. *(Specify reasons in Attachment 2d if the amount is different from the maximum required by Probate Code, § 8482.)*
      ☐ $ in deposits in a blocked account be allowed. Receipts will be filed. *(Specify institution and
         location)*:

3. a. Decedent died on *(date)*:   at *(place)*:
      ☐ a resident of the county named above.
      ☐ a nonresident of California and left an estate in the county named above located at *(specify location permitting publication
         in the newspaper named in item 1)*:
   b. Street address, city, and county of decedent's residence at time of death:

   c. Character and estimated value of the property of the estate
      (1) Personal property . . . . $
      (2) Annual gross income from
          (i) ☐ real property . . . . $
          (ii) ☐ personal property . . . . . $
                        Total . . . . . . $
      (3) Real property: $ *(If full authority under the Independent Administration of Estates Act is requested,
                                     state the fair market value of the real property less encumbrances.)*
   d. ☐ Will waives bond. ☐ Special administrator is the named executor and the will waives bond.
      ☐ All beneficiaries are adults and have waived bond, and the will does not require a bond. *(Affix waiver as Attachment 3d.)*
      ☐ All heirs at law are adults and have waived bond. *(Affix waiver as Attachment 3d.)*
      ☐ Sole personal representative is a corporate fiduciary.

                        (Continued on reverse)

Form Approved by the
Judicial Council of California
DE-111 [Rev. July 1, 1989]   **PETITION FOR PROBATE**   Probate Code, §§ 8002, 10450

Exhibit 12.5 Petition for Probate of Will—*continued*

ESTATE OF (NAME):

DECEDENT

CASE NUMBER:

3. e. ☐ Decedent died intestate.
    ☐ Copy of decedent's will dated: ☐ codicils dated: are affixed as Attachment 3e.
    ☐ The will and all codicils are self-proving *(Probate Code, § 8220).*

   f. **Appointment of personal representative** *(check all applicable boxes)*

> *Attach a typed copy of a holographic will and a translation of a foreign language will.*

    (1) Appointment of executor or administrator with will annexed
        ☐ Proposed executor is named as executor in the will and consents to act.
        ☐ No executor is named in the will.
        ☐ Proposed personal representative is a nominee of a person entitled to Letters. *(Affix nomination as Attachment 3f(1).)*
        ☐ Other named executors will not act because of ☐ death ☐ declination ☐ other reasons *(specify in Attachment 3f(1).)*
    (2) Appointment of administrator
        ☐ Petitioner is a person entitled to Letters. *(If necessary, explain priority in Attachment 3f(2).)*
        ☐ Petitioner is a nominee of a person entitled to Letters. *(Affix nomination as Attachment 3f(2).)*
        ☐ Petitioner is related to the decedent as *(specify):*
    (3) ☐ Appointment of special administrator requested. *(Specify grounds and requested powers in Attachment 3f(3).)*

   g. Proposed personal representative is a ☐ resident of California ☐ nonresident of California *(affix statement of permanent address as Attachment 3g)* ☐ resident of the United States ☐ nonresident of the United States.

4. ☐ Decedent's will does not preclude administration of this estate under the Independent Administration of Estates Act.

5. a. The decedent is survived by
    (1) ☐ spouse ☐ no spouse as follows: ☐ divorced or never married ☐ spouse deceased
    (2) ☐ child as follows: ☐ natural or adopted ☐ natural adopted by a third party ☐ step ☐ foster
        ☐ no child
    (3) ☐ issue of a predeceased child ☐ no issue of a predeceased child
   b. Petitioner ☐ has no actual knowledge of facts ☐ has actual knowledge of facts reasonably giving rise to a parent-child relationship under Probate Code section 6408(b).
   c. ☐ All surviving children and issue of predeceased children have been listed in item 8.

6. *(Complete if decedent was survived by (1) a spouse but no issue (only a or b apply); or (2) no spouse or issue. Check the **first** box that applies):*
   a. ☐ The decedent is survived by a parent or parents who are listed in item 8.
   b. ☐ The decedent is survived by issue of deceased parents, all of whom are listed in item 8.
   c. ☐ The decedent is survived by a grandparent or grandparents who are listed in item 8.
   d. ☐ The decedent is survived by issue of grandparents, all of whom are listed in item 8.
   e. ☐ The decedent is survived by issue of a predeceased spouse, all of whom are listed in item 8.
   f. ☐ The decedent is survived by next of kin, all of whom are listed in item 8.
   g. ☐ The decedent is survived by parents of a predeceased spouse or issue of those parents, if both are predeceased, all of whom are listed in item 8.

7. *(Complete only if no spouse or issue survived the decedent)* Decedent ☐ had no predeceased spouse ☐ had a predeceased spouse who (1) ☐ died not more than 15 years before decedent owning an interest in **real property** that passed to decedent,
   (2) ☐ died not more than five years before decedent owning **personal property** valued at $10,000 or more that passed to decedent,
   (3) ☐ neither (1) nor (2) apply. *(If you checked (1) or (2), check only the **first** box that applies):*
   a. ☐ The decedent is survived by issue of a predeceased spouse, all of whom are listed in item 8.
   b. ☐ The decedent is survived by a parent or parents of the predeceased spouse who are listed in item 8.
   c. ☐ The decedent is survived by issue of a parent of the predeceased spouse, all of whom are listed in item 8.
   d. ☐ The decedent is survived by next of kin of the decedent, all of whom are listed in item 8.
   e. ☐ The decedent is survived by next of kin of the predeceased spouse, all of whom are listed in item 8.

8. **Listed in Attachment 8** are the names, relationships, ages, and addresses of all persons named in decedent's will and codicils, whether living or deceased, and all persons checked in items 5, 6, and 7, so far as known to or reasonably ascertainable by petitioner, **including** stepchild and foster child heirs and devisees to whom notice is to be given under Probate Code section 1207.

9. ☐ Number of pages attached:

Date:

▶   ▶

_____   _____
  (SIGNATURE OF PETITIONER*)   (SIGNATURE OF PETITIONER*)

I declare under penalty of perjury under the laws of the State of California that the foregoing is true and correct.
Date:
....   ▶
  (TYPE OR PRINT NAME)   (SIGNATURE OF PETITIONER*)

* All petitioners must sign the petition. Only one need sign the declaration.

DE-111 [Rev. July 1, 1989]   **PETITION FOR PROBATE**   Page two

Source: Wolcotts Forms, available at most stationery or office supply stores or by calling 1(800)421-2220.

[1984], which allowed a limit of three years after the decedent's death, and compare U.P.C. § 3–108). Other states have no limits on the time for allowing probate, e.g., Oklahoma.

A petition is a written document addressed to a court or judicial official requesting that the court order certain legal actions. The petition is essential for determining that the court has jurisdiction over the decedent's estate. The original will is filed with the petition. To establish jurisdiction in a state probate court, the petition to prove a will generally must allege the following:

- The name, date of death, age, Social Security number, and place of death of the decedent.
- The domicile of the decedent.
- The existence of the will and, in some cases, the names of its witnesses. Unless it has previously been forwarded to the court, the will usually accompanies and is filed with the petition.
- The name and address of the person (petitioner) seeking appointment as personal representative, e.g., the executor or executrix, named in the will.
- Names, addresses, ages, relationship to the decedent, and identity of any persons under legal disability (e.g., incompetents), of any devisees, and also of those persons (heirs) who would be entitled to distribution of the decedent's estate in the absence of the will. For all estates, whether testate or intestate, the heirs must be listed in the court petition for probate of a will or for administration of an estate.
- The estimated value of the real and personal property that are probate assets.
- The amount and general character of decedent's debts, if known.
- In some states, if the decedent was survived by children and a spouse, a statement that "the children of the decedent are/are not also children or issue of the decedent's surviving spouse."
- In some states, if the decedent was over sixty-five years of age, an affidavit of Medical Assistance must be filed and sent to the Department of Welfare along with a copy of the Petition for Probate of Will if the decedent received any health benefits from the state's Medical Assistance program.

What You Do:

- Contact the county clerk of the probate court and obtain the forms and information provided for commencing probate. Obtain all other forms needed from local (state) legal form publishers.
- Collect all necessary information needed to complete and execute the Petition for Probate of Will.
- Make sure you or the personal representative files the will and petition.
- Obtain and file an affidavit of Medical Assistance (if needed).
- Whenever any document is filed, see that the personal representative pays the filing fee. *Note:* Filing fees will be required on many occasions, so this statement will not be repeated on the ensuing pages.

2. *Petition for administration when no will exists.* When there is no will, a form called the Petition for Administration (Form 2*) sets forth facts similar to the Petition for Probate of Will. It should contain the following:

- The name, date of death, age, Social Security number, and place of death of the decedent.

---

*See Appendix A.

- The domicile of the decedent.
- The name and address of the person (petitioner) requesting appointment as personal representative (administrator[trix]) and Letters of Administration.
- The name and address of the surviving spouse of the decedent, if any.
- The names, ages, relationship to the decedent, and addresses of all heirs or heirs at law of the decedent so far as they are known to the petitioner.
- The estimated value of the real and personal property that are probate assets.
- The amount and general character of the decedent's debts, if known.

As a general rule, the surviving spouse has first priority to be appointed as general administrator, then the next-of-kin, or both, at the discretion of the court. If the surviving spouse or next-of-kin so choose, they may nominate another person to serve as administrator. If all of the possible administrators are incompetent, unsuitable, or unwilling to serve, or if no petition has been filed within a statutory number of days, e.g., forty-five days after the decedent's death, administration may be granted to one or more creditors of the decedent or to the creditors' nominee. In that case, the petition must be accompanied by an itemized and verified statement of the creditor's claim. Generally, minors, mentally incompetent persons (as determined by a court), and often nonresidents of the state cannot act as personal representatives. Additional probate proceedings are necessary whenever a decedent-intestate owns real property or, in some cases, tangible personal property in more than one state.

What You Do:

- Obtain the information needed to execute the required forms and obtain the forms from the county clerk or local publishers of legal forms.
- Check your state statutes on priority of appointment of a personal representative (administrator) and ask the person who has first priority, i.e., the surviving spouse, whether he is willing to serve (see U.P.C. § 3–203[a]).
- Make sure you or the personal representative files the petition.

3. *Obtain an Order for Hearing the Petition to Prove a Will or for Administration.* As soon as possible after the filing of the petition either to have the will admitted to probate or for administration of the intestate estate, the court will make and enter its order (also called a **citation**) fixing a date, time, and place for hearing the petition. In some states the date of the order generally signals the beginning of the statutory period for creditors of the estate to file their claims against the estate (see the discussion of claims later in this chapter). A court officer, such as the clerk, may prepare the order, but you should check to make sure this is done (Forms 3* and 4*). In most states the statutory period for creditors to file their claims against the estate with the personal representative is between two and six months from the appointment and issuance of the Letters of Authority.

4. *Arrange for publication of the Notice of Order for Hearing and Affidavit of Publication.* The next task you must perform for the attorney and client is to contact a legal newspaper (one that specializes in printing legal notices), or at least a newspaper that is generally circulated in the county in which the proceedings are pending, and arrange for publication of the Notice of the Order for Hearing (Form 5*).

Citation
The legal form, used in some states, that is the court's order fixing a date, time, and place for hearing the petition to prove a will or for administration; the petitioner is required to give notice of the hearing to all interested persons.

---

*See Appendix A.

What You Do:

▪ Call the county clerk for information about procedures for publication. The clerk may tell you which newspapers are available for this purpose. Then contact a local "legal notice" newspaper publisher and arrange for publication of the executed Notice of the Order for Hearing. Make sure the order is published within the statutory time required before the hearing is held.

▪ Make sure the Affidavit (Proof) of Publication is filed. This affidavit will include an attached cut-out copy of the notice as it appeared in the newspaper. For an example of such a publication, see Form 6*.

Publication requirements vary from state to state. In some states, the order must be published once a week for two or three consecutive weeks. The first publication must occur within a statutory time period, e.g., two weeks after the date of the court order fixing the time and place for the hearing. The Affidavit (Proof) of Publication must be filed with the probate court within a statutory number of days prior to the hearing. Sometimes the county clerk of the probate court makes the arrangements for publication, but you must check to be sure it is done within the time allotted by court rules. In some counties, the newspaper publisher sends the Affidavit of Publication directly to the court; in others the publisher fills out the affidavit, which is filed with the probate court by the personal representative, the attorney, or you.

5. *Mail the Notice of Order for Hearing and Affidavit of Mailing Notice to all interested persons including creditors.* The Order for Hearing requires the petitioner to serve the order personally or, after having the order published in a local legal newspaper, to mail the publication attached to the Notice of Order for Hearing the Petition to all interested persons named in the petition whose names and addresses are known, informing them that the petition has been filed and the order given listing the date, time, and place for the hearing (Form 7*). In states using the citation, it contains the notice that all interested persons must receive and, in some states, the affidavit of service as well.

"Interested persons" who must receive formal legal notice include all those who have a property right or claim against the decedent's estate; they include creditors as well as all heirs, devisees, beneficiaries, spouses, and children (see U.P.C. § 1–201[24]). Therefore, you must identify all known individuals or businesses to whom the decedent owed money (e.g., family, friends, business associates, credit card companies, loans from banks, utilities, hospitals, doctors, financial advisers) and see that they receive actual notice. Other creditors will be given notice by publication in a local newspaper as required by state statutes. Notice is required to set the starting date for the statutory time period, usually two to six months from the date of the order or the appointment of the personal representative, that creditors have to file their claims with the court stating the amount and basis of their claim. Once a creditor files a claim, the creditor is known as the claimant. Notice also serves the purpose of allowing the interested person to file an objection to the appointment of the personal representative and propose another candidate or to contest the will. In addition, notice allows the surviving spouse to choose the elective share rather than the will's provisions and enables the family to claim the statutory allowance available in many states (see Item 6).

---

*See Appendix A.

This notice is necessary to establish the court's jurisdiction over the decedent's estate, and the proceedings will be invalid if it is not delivered and/or mailed. If there are no heirs, beneficiaries, or devisees, i.e., persons entitled to the estate, the property will escheat (pass) to the state, and the notice should then be sent to the state attorney general. If an heir does not receive notice, the heir may later contest the will (see the *Tobin* case in Chapter 5). If the decedent was born in a foreign country, notice must also be mailed to the consul or other representative of that country if a consul resides in the state and has filed a copy of her appointment with the state's secretary of state. The personal representative must submit the affidavit, attesting to the mailing of the notices, to be filed with the court.

What You Do:

- Mail a copy of the Notice of Order for Hearing to all interested persons listed in the petition, e.g., heirs, beneficiaries, devisees, and all known creditors.

- Make sure personal (actual) service or service through the local paper is accomplished. Then prepare the Affidavit of Mailing notice and make sure the personal representative sends the Affidavit of Mailing of these notices and that it is filed with the court.

Any person (called the **demandant**) having financial property interests in the decedent's estate may file with the court a demand for notice of any order of filing pertaining to the estate. The **demand** must state the person's name, address, and the nature of her interest in the estate (see Form 9*). The clerk mails a copy of the demand to the personal representative who must, in turn, mail the Notice of the Order for Hearing the Petition to the demandant (see also Chapter 13).

6. *Mail notice of rights to the spouse and minor children and prepare an Affidavit of Mailing.* In most states, if a decedent has left a spouse or minor children, a notice of right to the family allowances must be mailed to each such person within a period of time set by statute, e.g., fourteen days prior to the date set for hearing on the petition (see the reverse side of Form 7*). Also, if the spouse has not already contested the will, notice of rights dealing with renunciation and election must be mailed to the spouse. You will prepare these notices and the affidavit the personal representative must file with the court showing the mailing of both notices. An explanatory letter accompanying these notices can help avoid confusion. A child of the testator does not have the right to elect against the will. Only the surviving spouse has the right of election.

7. *Pay funeral bills.* The funeral bill is a debt for which a claim can be filed by the funeral director. The personal representative cannot pay the bill until appointed and need not pay it until the claim period expires; however, it may be possible to obtain a discount by paying the bill promptly. Sometimes there is a limit on the amount that can be spent for funerals, or by statute, the funeral bill is limited to a stipulated amount. In addition, the funeral bill is generally a preferred claim (see the discussion of priority of debts later in the chapter). Timely payment is important when an estate has few assets since failure to pay this bill and other priority debts before distributing the assets can lead to individual liability for the personal representative.

Demandant
Any person who has a financial or property interest in a decedent's estate and who files with the court a demand for notice of any order or filing pertaining to the estate.

Demand
To assert and file a claim for payment based on a legal right.

*See Appendix A.

What You Do:

■ You must contact the decedent's spouse and family or the funeral director to determine how payment is to be made. Sometimes the decedent prepaid the expenses by arrangement with the funeral director. In other cases, the spouse and family make separate arrangements for the funeral, burial, and reception with the funeral director and pay the bill themselves with the understanding that the decedent's estate will reimburse them. You must remind the personal representative that the funeral expenses must be "reasonable" considering the amount of assets and liabilities of the estate and that these expenses must be discussed with the family. You must also obtain the receipts for all funeral and related expenses from family members.

8. *Identify and review objections and arrange for the appearance of witnesses.* If anyone with an interest in the estate raises objections to the will, he must file them with the court before the hearing and the witnesses to the will must be contacted. Objections are most commonly filed by the following:

■ A spouse dissatisfied with the amount received in the will.

■ A child who has been omitted or disinherited.

■ A devisee who claims that the will was signed under fraud or undue influence.

■ A devisee who claims that the testator was incompetent.

What You Do:

■ If there are any objections to the will, you must arrange for the witnesses to the will to appear in court to testify that the testator knew and declared the document to be a will and freely signed it in accordance with state statutes. If a witness lives more than a hundred miles away from the place of the hearing, a written statement that the witness affirms to be true (a **deposition**) may serve in lieu of testimony in open court (see Exhibit 12.6 and Form 8*). Usually, the testimony of one witness is sufficient to establish the will's validity. If neither witness can be found, then others familiar with the testator's signature, such as a banker or business associate, may acknowledge the validity of the signature. Many states provide for the self-proved will, which makes the testimony of subscribing witnesses unnecessary. For an example of such a statute, see U.P.C. § 2–504. Also, holographic wills do not have to be witnessed, but they are not legal in all states.

9. *Miscellaneous duties before the hearing.* Before the hearing, you may be asked to perform various other tasks under the supervision of an attorney.

What You Do:

■ Send copies of the will and a preliminary estimate of the estate to the appropriate beneficiaries, devisees, and/or heirs.

■ Collect all available pertinent information for final income tax returns and prepare a "tickler" form (Exhibit 11.3), a list of the probate and estate administration procedures with all deadline dates and the person who performs the tasks.

■ Assemble data on nonprobate property (see the discussion later in the chapter).

■ If the decedent owned real property in joint tenancy with another, contact the state department of taxation and determine whether an affidavit of survivorship will be necessary to resolve tax concerns (Exhibit 12.7). Since the title to the property

Deposition
A written statement signed under oath by a witness that may serve to validate a will in place of testimony given in open court.

*See Appendix A.

Exhibit 12.6 Deposition of Witness

Form No. 4373 MILLER-DAVIS CO., MPLS.   Form 524.3-405 #3   UPC — —

STATE OF MINNESOTA **COUNTY OF** _____ **In Re: Estate of**	**PROBATE COURT** **COUNTY COURT-PROBATE DIVISION** Court File No. _____

_____
Deceased

COMMISSION TO TAKE DEPOSITION
OF WITNESS TO WILL
AND DEPOSITION

TO _____ , Greeting:

You are hereby appointed commissioner to take the deposition of _____
_____ , a subscribing witness to the last will of the above named
decedent, which will is transmitted herewith. You will cause the said witness to come before you at a time and
place designated by you and examine ___h___, on oath or affirmation, respecting the due execution of said will,
and immediately thereafter return such deposition signed by such witness and certified by you, together with this
commission and such will, by registered mail in a sealed envelope addressed to the County Court,
_____ , Minnesota.

Dated: _____   _____
Judge

(COURT SEAL)

DEPOSITION

_____ , residing at _____ being
duly sworn deposes and says that ___he is of legal age; that ___he is one of the subscribing witnesses to the
instrument now shown, bearing date of_____day of _____ , A.D. 19___,
and purporting to be the Last Will and Testament of _____ ,
of the County of _____ and State of_____ _____ ,
now here presented for probate; that ___he knew and was well acquainted with the said Decedent, in _____
lifetime, that on the day and date of said instrument, to-wit, the_____ day of _____ ,
A.D. 19___, the said instrument was published and declared by the said decedent, to be_____
Last Will and Testament, in the presence of deponent, and that deponent did then and there in the presence of the
said decedent, and at decedent's request, sign said instrument as witness thereto.

Deponent further says that at the time of the execution of said instrument as aforesaid, the said Decedent was of
sound and disposing mind, memory and understanding, of lawful age and under no restraint to the best of
deponent's knowledge, and as ___he verily believes.

_____

COMMISSIONER'S CERTIFICATE

STATE OF MINNESOTA
COUNTY OF _____
BE IT KNOWN that I took the annexed deposition pursuant to the annexed commission; that I was then and
there_____ (state title and office); that I exercised
the power of that office in taking such deposition; that by virtue thereof I was then and there authorized to
administer an oath; that said witness, before testifying, was duly sworn to testify the whole truth and nothing but
the truth relative to the cause specified in the annexed commission; that the testimony of said witness was
carefully read over to h____ by me before ___he signed the same; that the examination was conducted by me
personally.

Witness my hand and seal this_____day of _____ , 19___.

_____
Commissioner

(SEAL)

Source: Miller/Davis Company, Minneapolis, Minnesota.

Exhibit 12.7 Affidavit of Survivorship

MD Form No. 3816-Affidavit of Survivorship-Joint Tenancy or Remainderman and Certified Copy of Death.
Department of Taxation, Form IG-10 (Revised 1986)

Miller Davis Legal Forms

State of Minnesota,

County of _____

Affidavit of Survivorship-

Joint Tenancy or Remainderman

Estate of _____, deceased.

_____, of _____,
Minnesota, being duly sworn, on oath says that __he is the surviving joint tenant-remainderman of the
decedent named herein.

That _____ died on the _____day of
          (Decedent)

_____, 19 ____, at the age of_____years at _____

State of_____, with residence at _____, County
          (Address)

of _____, State of_____. That a duly certified copy of

the record of h____ death as contained herein or attached hereto is made a part hereof.

That said decedent at and prior to death was the owner of an interest as joint tenant-life tenant in the
hereinafter described property in which the following named person(s) is-are-surviving joint tenant or
remainderman.

| | | Relationship | |
Name	Age	to Decedent	Residence

That the respective interests of decedent and survivor(s) as joint tenants-life tenant and remainderman-

were created by an instrument of conveyance dated _____, 19____,

*and filed for record _____, 19____, and recorded in the office of the County

Recorder of _____ County, Minnesota, in Book_____of_____,

page_____, *in the following described property, to-wit:

That no part of the above property was the homestead of decedent unless so specified in the description.
That affiant has disclosed to the Commissioner of Revenue all transfers of property from the decedent to
any beneficiary of which affiant has knowledge or information, which transfers may be subject to Minnesota
inheritance tax.
That affiant makes this affidavit and files said certified copy of record of death as evidence of the
death of said joint tenant-life tenant-and the termination of said joint tenancy and all such estate, title
interest and lien as was or is limited upon the life of said decedent.

| NOTARIAL STAMP OR SEAL(OR OTHER TITLE OR RANK) | Subscribed and sworn to before me this |
| | _____day of _____, 19____. |

*Statement between asterisks applies if property is an interest in land.

_____
SIGNATURE OF NOTARY PUBLIC OR OTHER OFFICIAL

_____
THIS INSTRUMENT WAS DRAFTED BY

Exhibit 12.7   Affidavit of Survivorship—*continued*

COURT ADMINISTRATOR'S CERTIFIED COPY OF DEATH RECORD

In cities of the first class where the Court Administrator does not have on file the death record, the death certificate may be obtained from the Local Registrar or the Registrar of Vital Statistics and be attached hereto.

NAME OF DECEASED	DATE OF DEATH	SEX
PLACE OF DEATH		COLOR OR RACE
USUAL RESIDENCE		MARITAL STATUS
DATE OF BIRTH	PLACE OF BIRTH	NAME OF SPOUSE	SOCIAL SECURITY NUMBER
NAME OF FATHER	MAIDEN NAME OF MOTHER	DATE OF FILING

State of Minnesota,   **DISTRICT COURT**

County of_____ _____ Judicial District

I, _____, Court Administrator in and for the County and State aforesaid, do hereby certify that the above is a complete and correct copy of the death record as appears in Death Record_____, page_____, section_____, of the records of this office.

IN TESTIMONY WHEREOF, I have hereunto set my hand and affixed the seal of said court at _____, Minnesota, this _____day of _____, 19____

_____ Court Administrator

By _____Deputy

INSTRUCTIONS (For Instruction Only: Not To Be Recorded)

1. (a) To complete the record title in all cases where an interest in land terminates at death a record of death must be filed with the County Recorder, and "When a certified copy of such death certificate is attached to an affidavit of survivorship ... the same shall, prior to recordation ... be presented to the county auditor ..., and such auditor shall note the transfer on his/her books and shall inscribe upon the instrument over his/her official signature, the words " Transfer" entered ... "(Minn. Statutes, Sec. 600.21). This instrument may also be used for corporate securities where transfer agent requires a record of death and waiver of inheritance tax.

(b) In heritance tax liability to the State of Minnesota, the state's lien for such tax and the duty of the Commissioner of Revenue to give certificates in respect to such liens, are created by Minn. Statues, Secs. 291.01. Subd. 4.291.11.270.08.

(c) Where there is more than one property, the taxpayer at his/her convenience may use any combination of one or several affidavits. All such properties will be shown in an inheritance tax return for computation of tax.

2. This affidavit with attached death certificate should be executed by the surviving joint tenant or remainderman and submitted together with a copy of the affidavit to the Department of Revenue, Inheritance and Gift Tax Division. Centennial Office Building, St. Paul, Minnesota 55101. The original will be endorsed and returned for recording. The copy will remain in the files of the Department.

3. All transfers from decedent must be disclosed in an inheritance tax return when any tax waiver is requested. If there are probate proceedings copies of the petition for probate, will, if any, inventory and final account must be filed. In estates closed in probate court by summary proceedings or by decrees of descent, copies of the petition, will, if any, and inheritance tax return must be filed.

COMMISSIONER OF REVENUE

CERTIFICATE OF NO INHERITANCE TAX

Date_____

Upon the facts stated in the within affidavit and upon facts disclosed in the files and records of the Department of Taxation. I find that no inheritance tax is due under the laws of the State of Minnesota upon the the transfers herein described. Any lien for inheritance taxes that the State of Minnesota may have had upon the property herein described is hereby waived.

COMMISSIONER OF REVENUE STATE OF MINNESOTA

By_____

Inheritance and Gift Tax Division

(SEAL)

CERTIFICATE OF PAYMENT OF INHERITANCE TAX

Date_____

Upon the within affidavit and upon the facts disclosed in the files and records of the Department of Taxation, I find that an inheritance tax was due the State of Minnesota upon the transfer(s) described herein and that such tax has been assessed and paid. The lien for inheritance taxes of the State of Minnesota upon the property described in the within affidavit is hereby satisfied.

COMMISSIONER OF REVENUE STATE OF MINNESOTA

BY_____

Inheritance and Gift Tax Division

(SEAL)

Doc. No. _____

Estate of _____ (Deceased)

Affidavit and Certificate of Death of Joint Tenant or Life Tenant

Office of County Recorder
State of Minnesota,
County of _____
I hereby certify that the within Affidavit and Certificate of Death was filed in this office for record on the _____ day of _____ 19____, at _____ o'clock ____M., and was duly recorded in Book _____ of _____ page _____

County Recorder.
By _____, Deputy.

Transfer entered this _____ day of _____ 19____.

County Auditor.
By _____, Deputy.

Source: Miller/Davis Company, Minneapolis, Minnesota.

will now be in the name of the survivor, check the state public records division to verify the documents required to transfer the title. Frequently, the survivorship affidavit must be cleared with the proper county tax official and filed with the county real estate recorder. Your own state procedure must be followed.

■ Inquire into all substantial gifts made by the decedent and all transfers made in trust. Such items have special tax considerations and are discussed further in Chapter 14.

PROBATE COURT PROCEDURE

The next steps in probate and estate administration include the following:

10. Hearing to prove the will or for administration.
11. Selection of the personal representative.
12. Order admitting the will or granting administration.
13. Issuance of Letters Testamentary or Letters of Administration.
14. File for a federal employer identification number.
15. Open a checking account for the estate.
16. Notice to creditors.
17. Appointment of trustees and guardians.
18. Order admitting a foreign will to probate.

10. *Hearing to prove the will or for administration.* On the date set for the hearing to prove the will or for general administration, the personal representative, either the executor named in the will or the petitioner seeking appointment, and at least one subscribing witness, if necessary, should accompany the attorney to the court. No testimony from a subscribing witness is necessary if the will is self-proved. Any person who has an interest in the estate and who wishes to contest the validity of the will or the appointment of the petitioner as administrator must file the objection with the court and should appear at the hearing. For the purpose of hearing the will contest, the court will then set a different hearing date and time. If no interested person raises an objection, the petitioner, i.e., either the person who petitions to have the will admitted to probate or the person seeking appointment as administrator, testifies to the facts of the will or intestacy. Usually, this testimony will suffice to prove the will or to appoint the administrator (but compare U.P.C. § 3–405). If the petitioner is unable to testify to the facts, another person who can give such evidence must be present at the hearing. This person testifies under oath and answers questions that elicit such information as the date of the decedent's birth, death, and will, the domicile of the decedent, the probable value of the decedent's estate and debts, and the names of devisees, executors, and other interested parties (any person entitled to receive a share of the decedent's assets). Then, if necessary when the hearing is to prove a will, one or both of the subscribing witnesses are also sworn and testify as to the execution of the will and the capacity (age and sanity) of the testator. In addition, they verify the testimony of the first witness, the petitioner, insofar as possible. Exhibit 12.8 is an example of a typical transcript at a hearing to prove a will. Note that the questions are asked from the information requested on the petition itself in a manner that requires a simple yes or no answer (see Form 1*). Proof of publication and mailing of notice of the hearing to all interested parties should also be offered in evidence at this hearing. Finally, after the

---

*See Appendix A.

hearing, the testimony of the subscribing witness(es) should be signed and delivered to the judge unless the signature(s) may be waived.

If the will is contested and a date is set for the contest hearing, all witnesses to the will's execution should be present to testify at the hearing. A witness living more than a hundred miles away or an ill or disabled witness may testify by deposition, as mentioned above. If the party contesting the will is successful, the probate court may set aside part or all of the will and declare it invalid. The decedent's estate will then pass by the state's intestate succession statute.

11. *Selection of the personal representative.* As discussed in Chapter 11, the kind of personal representative the court appoints at the hearing depends on the action, or lack of action, taken by the decedent. If the decedent names a personal representative in the will, the court usually confirms and appoints that individual executor (or executrix) to carry out the directions and requests of the testator. If

---

Exhibit 12.8   Transcript of Hearing to Prove a Will

1. Are you the petitioner _____ as named in the petition for the probate of the estate of _____ , the deceased?
2. And you reside at _____ ?
3. And have an interest in the proceeding as _____ ?
4. And to your knowledge decedent was born _____ at _____ ?
5. And that the decedent died on _____ at _____ ?
6. And the decedent at the time of his death resided at _____ in the city of _____ , county of _____ , state of _____ ?
7. And that the names and addresses of decedent's spouse, children, heirs, and devisees and other persons interested in this proceeding and the ages of any who are minors so far known or ascertainable with reasonable diligence by you are: _____ ? Is that correct?
8. And that no personal representative of the decedent has been appointed in this state or elsewhere whose appointment has not been terminated?
9. And that the original of decedent's last will duly executed on _____ , 19___ , is in the possession of the court, and there is no codicil or codicils to the will?
10. And that to the best of your knowledge, you believe the will has been validly executed. Is that correct?
11. And that you are unaware of any instrument revoking the will?
12. And that you are entitled to priority and appointment as personal representative because you are nominated in the last will of the decedent as personal representative with no bond required. Correct?

Finally, that you request the court enter a judicial order formally:

1. Finding that the testator is dead
2. Finding that venue is proper
3. Finding that the proceeding was commenced within the time limitations prescribed by the laws of this state
4. Determining decedent's domicile at death
5. Determining decedent's heirs
6. Determining decedent's state of testacy
7. Probating the valid and unrevoked last will of decedent including any valid and unrevoked codicil thereto
8. Determining that petitioner is entitled to appointment as personal representative under the laws of this state
9. Appointing petitioner as the executor of the estate of decedent with no bond in a(n) (formal) (informal) administration
10. Authorizing issuance of letters testamentary to petitioner upon qualification and acceptance
11. Granting such other and further relief as may be proper

the decedent dies intestate, the court appoints a general administrator (or general administratrix) to handle the estate. Review the priority of appointment of the administrator in Chapter 11 and compare U.P.C. § 3–203(a).

12. *Order admitting the will or granting administration.* At testate proceedings, after the witness(es) testify and the will has been proved, the court makes its order admitting the will to probate (Form 10* and Exhibit 12.9). In intestate proceedings, the court issues an order granting administration of the estate (Form 11*). A copy of the Certificate of Probate also appears in Appendix A (Form 12*). In both cases, the court appoints a personal representative (i.e., executor or administrator) and fixes the personal representative's bond, if one is needed, based on the value of the estate, the type of assets, the relationship of the personal representative to the decedent, and other relevant facts.

Before a bond is purchased from a bonding company, you may be asked to shop around for the best price and then make arrangements with the bonding agent. Although the bond may be prepared by a surety (bonding) company or others, the personal representative or the attorney is responsible for it. Therefore, it may become your task to prepare the form(s) of both bond and oath (Form 14*). To facilitate this process, an employee of a bonding company may be present in court on hearing days with appropriate bond forms. In that case, the bond and oath can be completed and filed with the court immediately after the hearing. In the case of a corporate representative or bank, the order will require the filing of an acceptance of the position of personal representative of the estate (Form 13*). No bond is required, however, in the case of a corporate representative, and bond may not be required of a personal representative. The court will consider, and usually grants, a request for a minimum bond or no bond when the request is made in a decedent's will or is signed by all persons interested in the estate and submitted at or before the time of the hearing (Form 15*). The personal representative will normally make this request for the benefit of interested parties.

13. *Issuance of Letters Testamentary or Letters of Administration.* After the court has signed an order appointing the personal representative and approved the bond, if one is required, the personal representative will file an oath of office, and the court issues the appropriate documents conferring authority on the personal representative. In most states, these documents, for an executor or executrix, are called Letters Testamentary; for an administrator or administratrix, they are called Letters of Administration.

The authority conferred by these letters is the same. The letters are certified (accompanied by a certificate from the clerk of the probate court stating they are in full force). The personal representative is then authorized and qualified to act for the decedent's estate (Forms 17*, 77*, Exhibit 12.10, and Exhibit 12.11).

14. *File for a federal employer identification number.* After the appointment, one of the first duties of the personal representative is to file Form SS–4 to obtain a federal employer identification number, which is required on fiduciary income tax returns and is needed before a Notice Concerning Fiduciary Relationship can be filed as required by the I.R.C. § 6903(1954) (Forms 89* and 90*). Because the decedent's estate is an entity in itself and will be taxed as such on income produced by the estate after the decedent's death, these forms must be filed to establish that a fiduciary relationship exists. The employer number identifies the fiduciary responsible for preparing the fiduciary income tax return and for paying any tax due. This filing enables the Internal Revenue Service to mail the notices

---

*See Appendix A.

Exhibit 12.9 Order for Probate

ATTORNEY OR PARTY WITHOUT ATTORNEY *(Name and Address):*   TELEPHONE NO.:   *FOR COURT USE ONLY*

ATTORNEY FOR *(Name):*

SUPERIOR COURT OF CALIFORNIA, COUNTY OF

STREET ADDRESS:

MAILING ADDRESS:

CITY AND ZIP CODE:

BRANCH NAME:

ESTATE OF (NAME):

DECEDENT

ORDER FOR PROBATE

ORDER
APPOINTING
- ☐ Executor
- ☐ Administrator with Will Annexed
- ☐ Administrator   ☐ Special Administrator
- ☐ Order Authorizing Independent Administration of Estate
  - ☐ with full authority   ☐ with limited authority

CASE NUMBER:

1. Date of hearing: Time: Dept/Rm: Judge:

THE COURT FINDS

2. a. All notices required by law have been given.
   b. Decedent died on *(date):*
      (1) ☐ a resident of the California county named above
      (2) ☐ a nonresident of California and left an estate in the county named above
   c. Decedent died
      (1) ☐ intestate
      (2) ☐ testate   and decedent's will dated:
           and each codicil dated:
           was admitted to probate by Minute Order on *(date):*

THE COURT ORDERS

3. *(Name):*
   is appointed **personal representative:**
   a. ☐ Executor of the decedent's will   d. ☐ Special Administrator
   b. ☐ Administrator with will annexed   (1) ☐ with general powers
   c. ☐ Administrator   (2) ☐ with special powers as specified in Attachment 3d
                                                (3) ☐ without notice of hearing
   and letters shall issue on qualification.

4. a. ☐ **Full authority** is granted to administer the estate under the Independent Administration of Estates Act.
   b. ☐ **Limited authority** is granted to administer the estate under the Independent Administration of Estates Act (there is no authority, without court supervision, to (1) sell or exchange real property or (2) grant an option to purchase real property or (3) borrow money with the loan secured by an encumbrance upon real property).

5. a. ☐ Bond is not required.
   b. ☐ Bond is fixed at: $ to be furnished by an authorized surety company or as otherwise provided by law.
   c. ☐ Deposits of: $ are ordered to be placed in a blocked account at *(specify institution and location):*
        and receipts shall be filed. No withdrawals shall be made without a court order.

6. ☐ *(Name):*   is appointed probate referee.

Date:

JUDGE OF THE SUPERIOR COURT

7. ☐ Number of pages attached: ☐ Signature follows last attachment.

Form Approved by the
Judicial Council of California
DE-140 [Rev. July 1, 1988]
WOLCOTTS FORM DE-140 (price class 6-1)

ORDER FOR PROBATE

Probate Code, § 329

Source: Wolcotts Forms, available at most stationery or office supply stores or by calling 1(800)421-2220.

Exhibit 12.10 Letters of Authority

ATTORNEY OR PARTY WITHOUT ATTORNEY *(Name and Address)*:

TELEPHONE NO.:

FOR COURT USE ONLY

ATTORNEY FOR *(Name)*:

SUPERIOR COURT OF CALIFORNIA, COUNTY OF

STREET ADDRESS:

MAILING ADDRESS:

CITY AND ZIP CODE:

BRANCH NAME:

ESTATE OF (NAME):

DECEDENT

LETTERS

☐ TESTAMENTARY   ☐ OF ADMINISTRATION

☐ OF ADMINISTRATION WITH WILL ANNEXED   ☐ SPECIAL ADMINISTRATION

CASE NUMBER:

LETTERS

1. ☐ The last will of the decedent named above having been proved, the court appoints *(name)*:

    a. ☐ Executor

    b. ☐ Administrator with will annexed

2. ☐ The court appoints *(name)*:

    a. ☐ Administrator of the decedent's estate

    b. ☐ Special administrator of decedent's estate

      (1) ☐ with the special powers specified in the Order for Probate

      (2) ☐ with the powers of a general administrator

3. ☐ The personal representative is authorized to administer the estate under the Independent Administration of Estates Act ☐ **with full authority** ☐ **with limited authority** (no authority, without court supervision, to (1) sell or exchange real property or (2) grant an option to purchase real property or (3) borrow money with the loan secured by an encumbrance upon real property).

WITNESS, clerk of the court, with seal of the court affixed.

Date:

Clerk, by _____ , Deputy

(SEAL)

AFFIRMATION

1. ☐ PUBLIC ADMINISTRATOR: No affirmation required (Prob. Code, § 1140(b)).

2. ☐ INDIVIDUAL: **I solemnly affirm** that I will perform the duties of personal representative according to law.

3. ☐ INSTITUTIONAL FIDUCIARY *(name)*:

    I solemnly affirm that the institution will perform the duties of personal representative according to law.

    I make this affirmation for myself as an individual and on behalf of the institution as an officer. *(Name and title)*:

4. Executed on *(date)*:

    at *(place)*: , California.

▶ _____

(SIGNATURE)

CERTIFICATION

I certify that this document is a correct copy of the original on file in my office and the letters issued the personal representative appointed above have not been revoked, annulled, or set aside, and are still in full force and effect.

(SEAL) | Date:

Clerk, by

_____

(DEPUTY)

Form Approved by the Judicial Council of California
DE-150 [Rev. July 1, 1988]
WOLCOTTS FORM DE-150 (price class 6-1)

LETTERS
(Probate)

Probate Code, §§ 463, 465, 501, 502, 540
Code of Civil Procedure, § 2015.6

Source: Wollcotts Forms, available at most stationery or office supply stores or by calling 1(800)421-2220.

Exhibit 12.11   Domiciliary Letters

STATE OF WISCONSIN, CIRCUIT COURT,_____**COUNTY**   **-PROBATE-**

IN THE MATTER OF THE ESTATE OF

_____ }   **DOMICILIARY
LETTERS**

_____

File No. _____

To: _____
                                                    Name(s)

The above named person died, domiciled in_____County, Wisconsin, on

_____ .
                Date

You have been appointed personal representative and have fully qualifed.

THEREFORE, these Letters are issued to you, and you are ordered to administer this estate according to law.

                                            BY THE COURT:

   Seal

                                            _____
                                                                Circuit Judge

                                            _____
                                                                Date

PR-1403, 6/85 - (16A) DOMICILIARY LETTERS
s.856.21, Wisconsin Statutes   Wisconsin Legal Blank Co., Inc
                                                                Milwaukee. WI

Source: Wisconsin Legal Blank Co., Inc., Milwaukee, Wisconsin.

and tax forms to the new person (fiduciary) who is now responsible for the tax liability of the decedent's estate. As mentioned in Chapter 9 on trusts, the trustee must also apply for an employer identification number when trust income is subject to federal tax.

15. *Open a checking account for the estate.* To help the personal representative keep complete and accurate records of all financial transactions throughout the administration of the decedent's estate, a bank checking account for the estate must be opened. Once the federal employer identification number is obtained, the account is opened in the name of the estate of the decedent with the personal representative authorized to make deposits or withdrawals. The estate checking

account allows the personal representative to consolidate and deposit into this one account all current and future liquid probate assets, e.g., all existing cash and funds obtained from the sale of estate assets; payments of debts owed to the decedent; dividends from stock; checking and savings deposits located in other banks, credit unions, or savings and loan associations; proceeds from life insurance, pension or profit sharing plans, and other retirement plans *if* the estate was named the beneficiary; and all other funds that belong to the decedent's estate as they mature during the estate administration.

All cash transactions of the estate will be handled through the estate checking account. Therefore, using the estate checks, the personal representative pays the decedent's debts, taxes due, and all of the expenses throughout the estate administration including funeral expenses, court costs and filing fees, costs of insuring and maintaining estate property, and fees of the personal representative and attorney. Then the remaining property is distributed to the estate beneficiaries or heirs.

The estate checking account allows the personal representative and you to keep an accurate and complete accounting of all receipts and disbursements. The final account that is filed with the probate court to settle and close the estate and the death tax returns that must be prepared are absolutely dependent upon the accuracy and completeness of the checkbook records. The checks accomplish three essential record-keeping functions:

- They establish a total record of all payments and disbursements.
- Once the check is endorsed, they act as creditors' admissions of the payment of their debts.
- When canceled, they serve as evidence and verification of payment of taxes and the personal representative's final account.

The personal representative should select a competitive interest-bearing checking account that is insured by the FDIC (Federal Deposit Insurance Corporation). See Exhibit 11.4 for a sample check imprint for a deceased's estate.

What You Do:

- If the personal representative asks you to open a checking account for the estate and cannot come with you to the bank, you should bring to the bank a signature card signed by the personal representative, a check for the initial deposit, and a certified copy of the Letters Testamentary or Letters of Administration.

16. *Notice to creditors.* Many states give notice to creditors either by formal (actual) notice or by publication *after* the "Letters" have been issued. The procedure covered previously in Item 5 would be performed at this time. The United States Supreme Court has held that actual notice, i.e., delivery of notice directly to a creditor or by mail, must be given to all known or readily identified creditors of the deadline to file a claim against a decedent's estate.

17. *Appointment of trustees and guardians.* Other fiduciaries besides the personal representative can be selected and appointed by the testator. While alive, the testator can establish testamentary trusts in the will to take effect upon death. This allows the testator to appoint a trustee who will administer the trust created in the will. Since the will and therefore the trust become effective only upon the death of the testator, technically, the trustee is appointed at that time. The trustee's powers must conform to statutory guidelines whether the testator incorporated them into the testamentary trust or not.

Other fiduciaries appointed by the probate court include guardians for children of the deceased who are minors. The guardian of the person of a minor is responsible for the custody and care, specifically, the education, health, and welfare of the minor. The guardian or conservator of the property is responsible for managing and safeguarding the minor's property, prudently investing the assets when appropriate, and making disbursements in accordance with the will and the laws of the state until the minor reaches adulthood. Both guardians should be named in the will and may be the same person, but like the personal representative, they must be approved and appointed by the probate court. Once appointed, the guardians are accountable to the court (Form 18*). The guardian's duties and powers are set by statute or the will's provisions. When acting in the name of the minor, the guardian should always sign legal documents listing the minor's name followed by the words "by _____ , guardian."

If the decedent-testator has included a clause naming and appointing a surviving spouse as guardian of the person and property of minor children, the court generally appoints that spouse. If the decedent fails to name either type of guardian or dies intestate, the court will appoint a suitable guardian(s) for the benefit of the minor children. Guardians or conservators may also be appointed for persons who may or may not be minors but are physically or mentally handicapped. In choosing a trustee to administer a testamentary trust or a guardian of a minor's property, the testator should select a person who is responsible, competent, experienced in the management of property and investments, and capable of maintaining well-organized checkbooks and records.

What You Do:

- Contact the local county clerk and identify and/or obtain the proper forms used by the county for the appointment of fiduciaries and review procedures with the clerk.

- If the deceased died intestate, your work will be more complex and time-consuming since substantial legal research may be necessary to convince the probate judge your client's nominee for guardian is "in the best interests of the minor children," the criterion used by the court when considering the application for guardianship. For example, your research would discover that in cases involving a minor child age 14 or older, some states allow the child to request that a person other than the natural parent be appointed guardian (see Tex. Prob. Code § 118[b] or U.P.C. § 5–203).

Parents are considered, by law, to be the natural guardians of their children, but are not necessarily considered natural guardians over the children's property. Usually, a parent will act as guardian of both the child's person and the child's property, but in all states, the court has the final word in the appointment of guardians. State laws that allow a parent to act as guardian of the child's property or to act as guardian of both the child's person and property are permissive rather than mandatory. The following example illustrates a typical problem of guardianship.

Example: In his will, John Casey leaves his estate to his wife, Sharon, and their two minor children, Kimberly, age 16, and James, age 13, equally as tenants in common. John dies. Sharon is appointed guardian of the children. If Sharon wants or needs to use inherited family funds, sell family property, or move to another state, she must get permission from the court. This is both time-consuming and expensive. Using similar facts, except John dies intestate, the state intestate succession statute also passes John's estate to Sharon and the two children. Sharon is

---

*See Appendix A.

again appointed guardian, and once again, she will need court approval for decisions involving the property. John could have avoided these problems if he had left all his estate to Sharon and relied on her to care properly for their children or if he had established a living or testamentary trust, naming Sharon the trustee or co-trustee with another responsible and suitable person.

18. *Order admitting a foreign will to probate.* The decedent may die leaving real property or, in some cases, tangible personal property in another state (foreign state) as well as in the state of domicile. All property must be distributed to interested parties, e.g., beneficiaries, devisees, heirs, or creditors. Disposing of property in the state of residence is comparatively easy; disposing of property in the foreign (nondomiciliary) state requires a separate procedure.

If a will has been admitted to probate by a proper court in the state where the decedent was domiciled, this will may thereafter be admitted to probate as a foreign will in another state (Form 21*). In many states, the personal representative appointed to administer this property in the other (foreign) state is called the ancillary administrator, and the form used is the Petition for Probate of Foreign Will (Form 19*).

If the decedent was born in or has left heirs in another country and no petition has been filed within a statutory number of days, e.g., thirty days after the decedent's death, administration may be granted to the consul or other representative of that country or his nominee, but only if the person appointed resides in the state and files a copy of the appointment with the state's secretary of state. Finally, administration may be granted to any suitable and competent person, whether interested in the estate or not, provided the court considers the appointment to be in the best interest of the estate and heirs.

According to provisions in the will or the statutes, the ancillary administrator collects assets and pays debts and taxes due in the state where the property is located and remits the residue and final documents to the personal representative of the principal (domicile) state for final settlement. The estate cannot be closed until the ancillary administration is completed since the determination of estate tax cannot be settled until the property, debts, and claims in all states are known.

The ancillary procedures in the foreign state generally include the following:

■ The Petition for Probate of a Foreign Will must be filed. Generally, along with the petition, the personal representative may be asked to send the following documents: an authenticated copy of the will; a certificate from the clerk of the court in the domiciliary state affirming the will's correctness; a certificate from the probate judge reinforcing the clerk's certificate; a certificate affirming the court's authority to admit the will; and a copy of the order admitting the will to probate in the domiciliary state. Note, however, that requirements vary from state to state.

■ The Order for Hearing on the Petition must be published, and notice of the Order for Hearing must be sent to all interested persons including creditors (see Form 20*).

■ After the hearing on the petition, the court will execute an order accepting and admitting the will admitted to probate in the testator's domiciliary state and appointing the ancillary administrator. In a few states, a person appointed ancillary administrator must meet the same qualifications as a domiciliary

---

*See Appendix A.

administrator. Most states, however, do have specific qualifications for a person to be appointed an ancillary administrator (see Exhibit 3.3 in Chapter 3).

- The court will issue Letters of Authority, e.g., Letters Ancillary Testamentary, to the ancillary administrator. The Letters permit the real property located in the foreign state to be transferred to the designated devisee named in the will if all creditors of the testator in the foreign state have been paid.

- If the foreign state imposes any inheritance or estate tax, these taxes must be paid to that state before the property can be transferred back to the domiciliary state.

What You Do:

- Identify the property that must be administered and its location (county) in the foreign state.

- Check the foreign state's statutes to determine the qualifications and residency requirements for the ancillary administrator, and see if your client, the domiciliary personal representative, qualifies.

- Contact the county court personnel in the foreign state and obtain the forms and written procedures they make available for ancillary administration as well as their advice and guidance regarding any local requirements.

- Execute all required forms and documents (see the listed examples above) and file them with the foreign state's court.

- Verify that all foreign state creditors, if any, are paid and retain receipts.

- Verify that legal title to property in the foreign state has been cleared and is submitted to the domiciliary state court for distribution to the beneficiaries or devisees of the decedent's will or to the heirs of the decedent according to the foreign state's intestate succession statute for appropriate assets, e.g., real property located in the foreign state.

What You Do (if the ancillary administrator is a resident of the foreign state rather than the personal representative)

- Obtain the name and address of the person selected by the testator's will or by the personal representative to be the ancillary administrator in the other state.

- Obtain all required documents listed above, or others required by the local county court, execute them with appropriate signatures, and mail them to the ancillary administrator for filing.

- Keep in contact to help with any other data or documents the ancillary administrator may need.

- Once the foreign state's court accepts the approved will from the domiciliary state, the court issues the Letters Ancillary Testamentary to the ancillary administrator to authorize that person to administer the property of the decedent located in the foreign state. If there is no will, Letters of Ancillary Administration are issued.

- Once the court in the foreign state acts, obtain the final documents and personal property from the foreign state and add it to the inventory. If the property consists of real estate, the personal representative generally does not include it in the inventory, but may elect to include it in a memorandum at the end of the inventory.

Exhibit 12.12 is a summary comparison of the procedures to follow in formal probate administration for testate and intestate cases. Note that there are some differences between the two procedures (testate and intestate) up to the point of appointment and acceptance. Thereafter, for all practical purposes, the testate

Exhibit 12.12 Comparison of Formal Testate and Intestate Procedures

Testate Procedures	Intestate Procedures
1. File will (and codicils if any) and petition to prove (admit) will and for appointment of the personal representative (executor).	1. File petition for administration and appointment of the personal representative (administrator).
2. Order for hearing on petition.	2. Order for hearing on petition.
3. See to publication of order for hearing (in some counties the clerk does this).	3. See to publication of order for hearing (in some counties the clerk does this).
4. File affidavit of publication (in some counties the publisher does this).*	4. File affidavit of publication (in some counties the publisher does this).*
5. Mail notices to interested parties entitled to them.	5. Mail notices to interested parties entitled to them.
6. Mail notice of rights of spouse and minor children, if required.	6. Mail notice of rights of spouse and minor children, if required.
7. File affidavit of mailing notices.	7. File affidavit of mailing notices.
8. Ensure appearance of petitioner and witness(es) to will at hearing.	8. Ensure appearance of petitioner at hearing.
9. File request for reduced bond, if appropriate. Will can waive bond.	9. File request for reduced bond, if appropriate.
10. Hearing to prove will.	10. Hearing for administration.
11. Order admitting will to probate and appointing personal representative (in some counties this is prepared by the clerk), certificate of probate.	11. Order granting administration and appointing administrator (in some counties this is prepared by the clerk).
12. Prepare and file bond and oath (if personal representative is an individual).	12. Prepare and file bond and oath (if personal representative is an individual).
13. Prepare and file acceptance (if personal representative is a corporation).	13. Prepare and file acceptance (if personal representative is a corporation).
14. Issuance of Letters Testamentary.	14. Issuance of Letters of Administration.
15. Apply for federal employer identification number.	15. Apply for federal employer identification number.
16. Send notice of fiduciary relationship to IRS.	16. Send notice of fiduciary relationship to IRS.
17. Establish checking account for estate.	17. Establish checking account for estate.
18. Notice to creditors.	18. Notice to creditors.
19. Appointment of guardians or trustees, if any.	19. Appointment of guardians or trustees, if any.
20. Review ancillary administration matters, file petition for probate of foreign will, and obtain order admitting foreign will.	20. Review ancillary administration matters.

*Some publishers send the affidavit directly to the probate court; others fill out the affidavit form, but the personal representative must file it with the court.

and intestate procedures are similar until it is time to distribute the assets of the estate. Then, either the will directs the personal representative, or the intestate succession statute does.

PROCEDURES BEFORE ESTATE DISTRIBUTION

We have covered probate procedures up to and including the order appointing the personal representative and the establishment of the personal representative's authority by issuance of Letters. In both testacy and intestacy, before the estate is distributed, the personal representative must be concerned with the following:

19. Open the safe deposit box.
20. Collect and preserve the decedent's assets.

21. Prepare the inventory.
22. Prepare an appraisal (same form as for inventory).
23. Prepare a schedule of nonprobate assets.
24. File the inventory and appraisal.

It is essential that the personal representative, assisted by you and an attorney, accomplish these tasks carefully and expeditiously since complete information as to the value of the decedent's gross estate, including the probate and nonprobate assets, is necessary for the determination of death taxes. Thus the personal representative must not only take possession of all property when required to do so, but must also inventory (list) all probate assets accurately and report all nonprobate assets, making certain that these assets are properly valued in preparation for executing and filing the necessary federal and state tax returns.

19. *Open the safe deposit box.* Most states require that once a bank learns of a decedent's death, it must freeze all savings and checking accounts and seal any safe deposit box leased by the decedent (whenever the decedent held the box solely) until the contents of the box have been examined by the county treasurer's office or a representative thereof. In some states the statutory requirements for opening the box may cause serious problems because of the delay in obtaining the will. In many states, if the decedent's will is in the safe deposit box, the bank usually is allowed to take it out and forward it to the probate court before sealing the box. It is the responsibility of the bank to prevent anyone from removing any other contents of the box. The box should be unsealed only when the personal representative, the county treasurer or deputy, a representative of the bank, and you (the paralegal) or the estate's attorney are all present. After the box is unsealed, the bank's representative is permitted to distribute the contents to the personal representative. You must make a complete inventory of the contents of the box.

Proper disposition of the contents may present problems. In some states, if the box had been owned jointly, the surviving owner could be entitled to its contents. If the contents were not also jointly owned, however, the survivor is not entitled to them and may have to relinquish possession if the will or intestacy statute gives them to others.

Often life insurance policies are kept in safe deposit boxes. When the named beneficiary is someone other than the estate of the decedent, the policies may be handed over to the appropriate beneficiary, but only after you make photocopies so that they can be used in the calculation of possible state and/or federal death taxes. If a federal estate tax return must be filed, U.S. Treasury Form 712 must be completed for each policy and filed with the return (Form 97*). This form lists the names of the beneficiary, the decedent, and the insurance company, the face amount of the policy, the premium cost, and the like.

20. *Collect and preserve the decedent's assets.* One of your vital duties and major responsibilities is to help the personal representative to find, collect, preserve, value, and either liquidate or distribute all of the decedent's probate personal property. The personal representative does not take title to the decedent's real property unless it must be used to satisfy creditor claims. Your job concerning the real property is to locate it and keep records for future tax concerns or distribution. Apart from personal property set aside as family allowances for the

---

*See Appendix A.

surviving spouse and minor children, all personal property owned solely by the decedent comes under the care of the personal representative. The court holds the personal representative personally responsible for collecting and preserving existing probate assets. Upon request, you will help the personal representative perform the following duties:

a. To locate the decedent's real and personal property. It will be necessary for the personal representative and you, by phone, by letter, or in person, to contact many people: relatives, friends, business associates, tax adviser, banking officials, stockbrokers, accountant, attorneys, trust officers, insurance agent or broker, employers, and persons handling the decedent's claims within the Social Security Administration and the Veterans Administration. With the help of the family or these advisers, examine financial records to find all bank accounts, stock and bond holdings, insurance policies (including credit life insurance on any credit cards, loans, or savings accounts), outstanding loans or other debts owed to the decedent, and any stock options or deferred compensation.

b. To take possession of all the decedent's probate personal property. Non-probate assets, including jointly owned property, life insurance benefits, and the like, are not subject to the marshaling (collection) authority of the personal representative. You will prepare a separate list of nonprobate assets that must be maintained (see the later discussion). Title to the decedent's personal property passes to (vests in) the personal representative when appointed by the probate court. This passage of title is retroactive to the decedent's death. In other words, title vests in the personal representative as if the personal representative had assumed title as soon as the decedent died. Title to the decedent's real property, however, passes to (vests in) the devisees or heirs immediately upon death, but it is subject to the payment of debts of the estate (see the discussion below).

What You Do:

At the direction and with the consent of the personal representative:

▪ You must identify all nonprobate assets and list them for future required documents, e.g., a schedule of nonprobate assets required for filing death tax returns.

▪ As previously noted, you will make phone calls and prepare all correspondence, e.g., letters to banks (for checking and savings accounts), insurance companies (for policies and named beneficiaries), stockbrokers (for all investments), and business associates, for the personal representative's signature to identify, locate, and collect, when appropriate, all personal property of the decedent to which the personal representative is entitled and required to possess. You will verify that all checking and savings accounts wherever located are closed and that the cash and money obtained from the sale of all personal property is transferred into the estate account. You will also verify that proceeds collected from life insurance and retirement plans naming the estate the beneficiary are deposited in the account. If the will specifically states that securities (stocks and bonds), certificates of deposits, and mutual funds are to be given to named persons, these will pass through the will; otherwise the personal representative may have to sell them. The money from this sale must also be transferred to the estate account. The collected assets, wherever located, are to be used to pay all creditors' claims. After payment of all debts, the personal representative will eventually transfer title to the remaining personal property to those who are entitled to it.

Title to the decedent's real property, however, vests immediately, upon the decedent's death, in the devisees of a testate estate or the heirs of an intestate estate, but it is subject to divestiture (to be taken away) to pay creditors of the estate. In appropriate instances, therefore, the personal representative may obtain possession of real property (by entering onto the land with a court order) and convey (sell) it in order to satisfy creditors' claims. A typical state statute on this matter is Pennsylvania's:

20 Pa. Stat. Ann. § 3311   Possession of Real and Personal Estate; Exception
A personal representative shall have the right to and shall take possession of, maintain and administer all the real and personal estate of the decedent, except real estate occupied at the time of death by an heir or devisee with the consent of the decedent. He shall collect the rents and income from each asset in his possession until it is sold or distributed, and, during the administration of the estate, shall have the right to maintain any action with respect to it and shall make all reasonable expenditures necessary to preserve it. The court may direct the personal representative to take possession of, administer and maintain real estate so occupied by an heir or a devisee if this is necessary to protect the rights of claimants or other parties. Nothing in this section shall affect the personal representative's power to sell real estate occupied by an heir or devisee. [Compare U.P.C. § 3–709.]

c. To keep all real property (e.g., houses and other buildings) protected and in reasonably good repair.

What You Do:

▪ You must contact an insurance company and obtain information so that the personal representative can maintain reasonable coverage for all real property. This must include both property and liability insurance usually in the form of a "homeowner's policy." If such a policy already exists, you will determine the expiration date. If necessary, a policy must be purchased until the home is sold or transferred to the devisee. If the property needs repair, you must inform the personal representative so that the property is properly maintained until it is distributed or sold. You must also make sure no property taxes become delinquent. The transfer or distribution of real estate is discussed in detail later in this chapter. You must immediately notify all tenants in possession of any real property owned by the decedent that rent is to be paid to the personal representative and give them his name and address. You must verify that all such rent payments are then included in the estate account.

d. To search for important documents, records, and papers that might contain information on the location of unknown assets.

What You Do:

▪ You may be asked to help in finding checkbooks, saving account statements, insurance policies, charge account cards, credit cards, canceled or uncashed checks, income tax returns for the last three years and any gift tax returns, deeds, contracts for deed, trust documents, bills of sale for personal property, title cards or certificates for automobile, boat, and mobile home ownership transfer, and cards for membership in various agencies and fraternal organizations. You must review records filed with various county and city departments for additional clues to unknown or missing property.

e. To protect certain items of value in the estate, once they are collected, including stocks, bonds, insurance policies, promissory notes, mortgages, jewelry, and stamp or coin collections. You must contact a bank and, with the personal representative, rent a safe deposit box for their safekeeping.

f. To check other insurance policies (life, hospitalization, disability, and automobile liability) for coverage and expiration dates. Although the personal representative decides these matters, you will prepare all the correspondence to terminate, continue, or transfer the benefits under the policies to the appropriate parties or to transfer ownership to the "Estate of John Doe" account. You must verify these transfers.

g. Miscellaneous. Inheritance coming from others (family and friends not yet collected).

Procedures for Collecting Specific Estate Assets

Collecting estate assets can be complex work, depending on the number and diversity of the assets. The personal representative of a typical estate will be dealing with such assets as bank accounts, securities, debts owed the decedent, causes of action, jointly owned property, insurance benefits, sale of a business, death benefits, and automobiles. Complete, accurate, and detailed records of each asset must be kept, including a record of all cash receipts and expenditures on a check register (see the previous discussion of opening a checking account.)

■ *Bank accounts.* Accounts solely in the name of the decedent will be released only to the personal representative of the estate. After determining the location of the decedent's bank accounts (savings, checking, and credit union), the personal representative must withdraw the funds using the decedent's bank statement and certified copies of the Letters Testamentary or Letters of Administration. The personal representative may wait to withdraw these funds until after the interest earning period, e.g., monthly or quarterly. The withdrawn funds are to be placed in the "Estate of John Doe" account.

What You Do:

If asked by the personal representative:

■ You must prepare a letter for the signature of the personal representative with an order directing that the account be closed and a check for the balance including interest payable to the estate of the decedent be sent to the personal representative's address. Other required documents, e.g., Letters Testamentary or Letters of Administration, must accompany your letter.

Joint accounts must also be located, although these accounts go to the surviving joint tenant, e.g., a spouse. The date on which the joint account was established, the source from which the account was created, and the amounts must be obtained and reported on the death tax forms. For further discussion on tax consequences of joint ownership, see Chapter 14.

"Totten trusts" or P.O.D. (payable on death) accounts (savings account trusts in the decedent's name for the benefit of another) are payable directly to the named beneficiary in many but not all states. For tax purposes, you must obtain information on Totten trusts and the date the account was opened.

■ *Securities.* Securities are often found either among the decedent's possessions or in a safe deposit box.

What You Do:

■ You must search for all the decedent's securities (stocks, bonds) including accounts with brokers or stocks held in the broker's name. Generally, securities remain registered in the decedent's name and are transferred to the proper beneficiaries or devisees named in the will or to heirs through intestate succession after administration of the estate is completed. Determination must be made as to whether the decedent, before death, effectively transferred ownership of the stock to another. Transfer of securities is discussed in detail later in the chapter. In other situations, the personal representative must decide whether to liquidate (sell) the securities immediately or wait until a later time when their value may increase. When the securities are sold, you must verify that the proceeds are placed in the estate checking account.

- *Debts owed the decedent.* Inquiries should be made into all outstanding debts owed to the decedent.

What You Do:

- You must review county and city records and filings to determine whether the decedent held any mortgages, contracts for deed, promissory notes, or similar evidences of indebtedness to the decedent.

- You must interview family to determine if such debtors may include friends, relatives, devisees, or heirs. Because they must repay the estate, their debts might cancel out the benefits they receive from it unless their debts are forgiven in the will.

- You must arrange by letter, phone, or personally for the continued collection of loans, rents from tenants, interest from financial institutions, alimony (maintenance) from a divorced spouse, dividends, royalties from publishers, unemployment compensation, worker's compensation, and federal or state income tax refunds and attempt to collect delinquent obligations. These monies must be transferred into the estate account. At the request of the personal representative, you may have to contact and hire a collection agency to collect delinquent debts. The probate court will approve a reasonable compromise settlement of a disputed debt owed to the decedent so long as it appears to be in the best interest of the estate. *Because legal advice may be involved in the settlement, this must be done by the attorney and personal representative.*

- *Causes of action.* A legal wrong for which a civil lawsuit for **damages** can be brought creates for the wronged or injured party a **cause of action,** i.e., a right to sue. If the person suing dies while in the process of litigation, the claim or "cause of action" may also die (end). When by statute, the personal representative is allowed to pursue the "cause of action" for the benefit of the decedent's estate or heirs, any recovery in damages becomes an asset of the estate. State statutes on the subject of "causes of action" as assets of the estate allow or bar such lawsuits depending on the circumstances surrounding death, the nature of the action, and many other factors.

What You Do:

- You must carefully read the state statutes and commentaries on them and perform any necessary legal research to determine if a particular decedent's "cause of action" survives the decedent's death and should be continued. *The findings must be discussed with the supervising attorney for final resolution.*

Example: Sally Simmons negligently backs her car into her neighbor's yard striking a supporting beam of the neighbor's porch, which causes the porch roof to collapse. Considerable property damage results. Susan Swan-

---

▶ **ETHICAL ISSUE**

Damages
The monetary remedy from a court of law that can be recovered by the person who has suffered loss or injury to her person, property, or rights by the unlawful act, omission, or negligence of another.

Cause of action
The right of a person to commence a lawsuit.

▶ **ETHICAL ISSUE**

son, the neighbor, sues Sally in civil court, but after commencing the lawsuit, Susan dies. The personal representative of Susan's estate must continue the suit if no settlement is reached. Any recovery becomes an asset of Susan's estate and is paid into the estate's checking account.

Example: Tom Jensen is struck by a car driven negligently by Michael Howard. Although Tom is seriously injured, causing him to be hospitalized, his doctors assure him that he will completely recover in time. While convalescing two months after the accident and after commencing a lawsuit against Michael, Tom has a heart attack and dies. Medical experts establish that the heart attack is totally unrelated to the previous accident. Under these circumstances in some states, Tom's "cause of action" dies with him. The personal representative of Tom's estate would not be allowed to continue Tom's lawsuit except to recover "special damages," i.e., the medical and hospital expenses and loss of wages incurred by Tom because of the automobile accident. "Pain and suffering" damages are not recoverable.

■ *Jointly owned property.* Property of any kind, real or personal, held in the form of ownership known as joint tenancy does not become a probate asset of the decedent's estate. If the decedent held such property with another person as joint tenants, the property would automatically become the surviving joint tenant's upon the decedent's death.

What You Do:

To clear title to real property held in joint tenancy by the decedent, you must help the personal representative to take the following steps:

■ Execute in duplicate an Affidavit of Survivorship if the property is the homestead and the surviving joint tenant is the decedent's spouse (see Exhibit 12.7).

■ File a certified copy of the death certificate of the decedent and one copy of the Affidavit of Survivorship with the proper section of the county land office, i.e., the county recorder or registrar (see Exhibit 11.6).

■ Send one copy of the Affidavit of Survivorship to the office of the commissioner of taxation or the appropriate state tax officer.

■ If the real property is Torrens (registered) property, the surviving joint tenant must also file an Affidavit of Purchaser of Registered Land and the owner's duplicate Certificate of Title.

In some states, when the value of the homestead does not exceed a statutory amount, e.g., $75,000, and the homestead goes to the surviving joint tenant, i.e., the spouse, the above procedures may cancel the state inheritance tax lien (claim) on the homestead that would otherwise exist. To cancel an inheritance tax lien on all other jointly held real property, the surviving joint tenant must file the following with the county land office:

■ An Affidavit of Survivorship on which the appropriate state tax official, e.g., commissioner of taxation, has certified that no inheritance tax is due or that the tax has been paid.

■ A certified copy of the decedent's death certificate.

■ *Insurance benefits.* A life insurance policy is a written contract between the buyer (our decedent) and an insurance company in which the buyer pays annually a specified amount of money called a premium to the company and it, in turn, agrees to pay a designated beneficiary named by the buyer an agreed-on amount of money, usually at the time of the buyer's death. If the decedent held life insurance policies payable to named beneficiaries (e.g., a spouse or children) and did not retain any incidents of ownership (see below), then the proceeds of the policy are paid directly to the beneficiaries, are not part of the estate and, therefore, are not subject to federal estate tax, and are also exempt from federal income tax. For each policy to be listed on the federal estate tax return, the personal representative should obtain U.S. Treasury Form 712 Life Insurance Statement (Form 97*). These forms must be filed with the return and contain information needed in order to prepare the death tax returns (see Chapter 14).

If the decedent retained the incidents of ownership (e.g., the right to change the beneficiary, to convert the policy to another form of insurance, or to cancel it altogether), the Internal Revenue Service considers that the decedent held enough control over the policy for it to be considered an asset of the estate. As such, it is subject to both state and federal death taxes. Death benefits will go directly to the named beneficiary without being subject to tax, only if the insurance company was informed that the insured person was giving up these rights (incidents of ownership) at least three years before death (see I.R.C. § 2042 and Chapter 14). No death taxes are due on an insurance policy taken out on the decedent's life by another person so long as the beneficiary is not the decedent's estate.

What You Do:

- At the request of the personal representative, obtain and partially complete Form 712 for every insurance policy on the life of the decedent. Mail the forms to each insurance company for final completion and signature.

- When the decedent's estate is the beneficiary of the policy, assist the personal representative in executing the proper forms for filing the claim to receive the proceeds from the policy. Notice of the date of the decedent's death should be given to the insurance company, and all other documents required by the company should be prepared. These generally include a certified copy of the death certificate, the return of the original life insurance policy, and, if required, a certified copy of the Letters Testamentary or Letters of Administration. Make sure you keep a copy of the life insurance policy.

- Hospitalization, medical (doctor), and disability insurance companies must be notified, especially where the decedent was hospitalized for any length of time due to a last illness before death. Payments from these policies may be made directly to those who provided care during the last illness; otherwise, they are paid directly into the decedent's estate. Any uncollected claims owed and unpaid by an insurance company due to incidents prior to the decedent's death must be paid into the estate checking account. Cancellation of life, disability, auto, home, and other types of insurance premiums, when appropriate, must be made, and refunds received should be paid into the estate checking account. As needed, you will perform the above tasks.

- *Sale of or continuation of a business—sole proprietorship, partnership, or limited partnership.* If the decedent was the sole owner and manager of a business, the personal representative may have to run the business until it can be liquidated. A personal representative has no authority to continue a decedent's business, and most states hold that the business must be liquidated. However, if the testator-decedent named a devisee to inherit the business and/

---

*See Appendix A.

or manage it, or a state statute authorizes it, the personal representative may select a long-time employee willing to continue to manage the business until the devisee or heir takes over or the business is liquidated. Complete and accurate records of all business activities must be kept and reviewed by the personal representative during this transition.

If the decedent was a partner in a partnership or limited partnership, the personal representative must obtain a copy of the partnership or limited partnership agreement to determine the procedures and partner's rights when a partner dies. If the agreement contains a clause that allows a buyout of the decedent partner's interest, the personal representative must see that a fair price is obtained for the estate.

Sample Clause [Will]: (West's McKinney's Forms ESP, § 7:393)
I authorize my Personal Representative(s) for the time being to carry on the whole or any part of the [name of business] now operated and managed by me at [address] until such time as they shall deem it expedient to sell the same or to wind up the said business, as the case may be. (Reprinted with permission from West's McKinney's Forms, Copyright ©, by West Publishing Company.)

■ *Death benefits.* Other death benefits, payable to the decedent's estate, must be collected.

What You Do:

■ You must contact federal and state government benefit plans, such as Medicare, Medicaid, Social Security, and, if appropriate, farm subsidy benefits, Railroad Retirement Fund benefits, and the Veterans Administration for benefits.

■ You must contact the decedent's employer to determine if the decedent was entitled to accrued earned pay, accrued vacation pay, commissions, sick leave, terminal pay, pension or profit-sharing plans, 401(k) plans, deferred compensation plans, employee stock-ownership plans, group insurance plans, stock options, year-end bonus, or back pay uncollected, and labor union benefit plans. Such compensation should go into the estate checking account.

If the benefits are a form of employee compensation such as pension or profiting-sharing plans, the personal representative must identify them and determine to whom these benefits are to be paid.

If the decedent was a veteran of any war, including the Korean, Vietnam, and Persian Gulf Wars, the decedent's beneficiaries or heirs may be entitled to benefits such as insurance, pensions, and burial expenses, according to the rules of the Veterans Administration or state law. Death benefits under Social Security and veterans benefits are generally either paid directly to the surviving spouse or applied to the payment of funeral and burial expenses. A Social Security lump sum death benefit, a maximum of $255, may be available to the decedent's estate. The form used to apply for this benefit is Social Security Form SSA–8. Funeral directors have the forms, which authorize applying such benefits toward the settlement of the funeral bill.

A union or fraternal lodge to which the decedent may have belonged should be checked to see if any benefits are due the decedent or the successors. In addition, the surviving spouse and minor children of a decedent covered under Social Security benefits may have the right to a claim for monthly income benefits given to survivors of the decedent. The local Social Security office must be contacted.

■ *Automobiles.* As owner of the decedent's automobile(s), the estate or the personal representative could become legally liable for injuries or damage caused by improper and negligent use. Therefore, the automobile(s) should be transferred to the persons entitled to them as soon as possible after the death of the decedent or, if a state statute demands, within a certain number of days. The ways of transferring title to the decedent's car to the appropriate person vary from state to state. State statutes or regulations control the transfer of title to the car. The appropriate person to whom title is transferred could be a surviving spouse who elects to take the car (see Minn. Stat. Ann. § 524.2–403 for a typical state statute), a surviving joint tenant owner, a devisee in the decedent's will, or a purchaser who pays the market value to the personal representative. The statutory requirements or regulations for title transfer must be checked.

21. *Prepare the inventory.* An inventory is a complete physical check of all the probate assets owned by the decedent and a detailed listing of these assets and their estimated fair market value at the time of the decedent's death on the forms provided for the inventory (Form 23*, Exhibit 12.13, and Exhibit 12.14). The inventory should be made jointly by the personal representative and either the attorney or you. In practice, this becomes one of your more important paralegal tasks. Nonprobate assets are not included in the inventory but are listed separately for death tax purposes. The organization of the inventory and the degree of particularity with which items should be listed are matters of judgment, but the inventory should include serial numbers of certificates for stocks, automobiles, or deposits; account numbers for savings or checking; and legal descriptions of real property. The inventory should be well organized, complete, and accurate. The appraisers hired by the personal representative and appointed by the court (if required by state law or on demand by an interested party) can then expeditiously appraise and value the assets. You must complete and file this inventory so all data will be available as necessary for the preparation of the federal estate tax return, and you must mail or deliver copies of the inventory to the surviving spouse, beneficiaries, devisees, heirs, creditors, and all interested parties who requested a copy. Some states do not require an inventory to be filed and use their state death tax return instead. Often both of these documents are filed together at the same time for those states that use an inventory. The time limit for filing the inventory is determined by state statute, but is usually between sixty and ninety days. As previously mentioned, the value of securities for purposes of the inventory is generally computed as of the date of the decedent's death or the alternate valuation date, as are all the other assets, and must include the following often forgotten items: (1) interest and rent accrued at the date of death and (2) any dividends declared before death. A preliminary or partial inventory can be made if it is necessary to sell assets before the inventory and appraisal can be completed; if additional property is found, an amended inventory may be required.

22. *Prepare an appraisal.* An appraisal or appraisement is a true and just valuation placed on real or personal property by a recognized expert. The appraisal is generally filed with the inventory. All estate property must be appraised, but if the value of the property can be easily determined, the personal representative is allowed to do it. When the estate property is real estate or expensive personal property such as art, jewelry, antiques, collections of coins or stamps, furs, boats,

---

*See Appendix A.

Exhibit 12.13 Inventory and Appraisal

ATTORNEY OR PARTY WITHOUT ATTORNEY *(Name and Address)*:	TELEPHONE NO.:	*FOR COURT USE ONLY*

ATTORNEY FOR *(Name)*:

SUPERIOR COURT OF CALIFORNIA, COUNTY OF

STREET ADDRESS:

MAILING ADDRESS:

CITY AND ZIP CODE:

BRANCH NAME:

ESTATE OF (NAME):

☐ DECEDENT ☐ CONSERVATEE ☐ MINOR

INVENTORY AND APPRAISEMENT ☐ Complete ☐ Final ☐ Partial No.: ☐ Supplemental ☐ Reappraisal for Sale	CASE NUMBER: Date of Death of Decedent or of Appointment of Guardian or Conservator:

APPRAISALS

1. Total appraisal by representative (attachment 1) $
2. Total appraisal by referee (attachment 2) $

TOTAL: $

DECLARATION OF REPRESENTATIVE

3. Attachments 1 and 2 together with all prior inventories filed contain a true statement of
   ☐ all ☐ a portion of the estate that has come to my knowledge or possession, including particularly all money and all just claims the estate has against me. I have truly, honestly, and impartially appraised to the best of my ability each item set forth in attachment 1.

4. ☐ No probate referee is required ☐ by order of the court dated *(specify)*:

I declare under penalty of perjury under the laws of the State of California that the foregoing is true and correct.

Date:

▶

. . . .
(TYPE OR PRINT NAME) (Include title if corporate officer)   (SIGNATURE OF PERSONAL REPRESENTATIVE)

STATEMENT REGARDING BOND
(Complete if required by local court rule)

5. ☐ Bond is waived.
6. ☐ Sole personal representative is a corporate fiduciary.
7. ☐ Bond filed in the amount of: $ ☐ Sufficient ☐ Insufficient
8. ☐ Receipts for: $ have been filed with the court for deposits in a blocked account
   at *(specify institution and location)*:

▶

Date: (SIGNATURE OF ATTORNEY OR PARTY WITHOUT ATTORNEY)

DECLARATION OF PROBATE REFEREE

9. I have truly, honestly, and impartially appraised to the best of my ability each item set forth in attachment 2.
10. A true account of my commission and expenses actually and necessarily incurred pursuant to my appointment is
    Statutory commission: $
    Expenses *(specify)*: $
         TOTAL: $

I declare under penalty of perjury under the laws of the State of California that the foregoing is true and correct.

Date:

▶

. . . .
(TYPE OR PRINT NAME)   (SIGNATURE OF REFEREE)

(Instructions on reverse)

Form Approved by the Judicial Council of California DE-160, GC-040 [Rev. January 1, 1985] WOLCOTTS FORM DE-160 · or WOLCOTTS FORM GC-040 ∴ (price class 6-2)	**INVENTORY AND APPRAISEMENT** **(Probate)**	Prob C 600-611, 2610-2616

Exhibit 12.13   Inventory and Appraisal—*continued*

INSTRUCTIONS

See Probate Code, §§ 604, 608, 609, 611, 2610-2616 for additional instructions.

If required in a decedent's estate proceeding by local court rule, furnish an extra copy for the clerk to transmit to the assessor (Probate Code, § 600).

See Probate Code, §§ 600-602 for items to be included.

If the minor or conservatee is or has been during the guardianship or conservatorship confined in a state hospital under the jurisdiction of the State Department of Mental Health or the State Department of Developmental Services, mail a copy to the director of the appropriate department in Sacramento (Probate Code, § 2611).

The representative shall list on attachment 1 and appraise as of the date of death of the decedent or date of appointment of the guardian or conservator at fair market value moneys, currency, cash items, bank accounts and amounts on deposit with any financial institution (as defined in Probate Code, § 605), and the proceeds of life and accident insurance policies and retirement plans payable upon death in lump sum amounts to the estate, except items whose fair market value is, in the opinion of the representative, an amount different from the ostensible value or specified amount.

The representative shall list on attachment 2 all other assets of the estate which shall be appraised by the referee.

If joint tenancy and other assets are listed for appraisal purposes only and not as part of the probate estate, they must be separately listed on additional attachments and their value excluded from the total valuation of attachments 1 and 2.

Each attachment should conform to the format approved by the Judicial Council (see form Inventory and Appraisement (Attachment) (DE-161, GC-041) and Cal. Rules of Court, rule 201).

DE-160, GC-040 (Rev. January 1, 1985)

INVENTORY AND APPRAISEMENT
(Probate)

Page two

Source: Wolcotts Forms, available at most stationery or office supply stores or by calling 1(800)421-2220.

---

or aircraft, you will need to employ professional appraisers, or the court will appoint them (usually two are selected). Ask the clerk which type of appraiser you will need and, if a court-appointed appraiser is necessary, how to obtain one. Once the inventory is completed and the personal representative has signed an oath stating that all known property of the decedent has been inventoried, you must contact the court-appointed or independently hired appraisers, if needed. Generally, if real property is involved, the appraisers are real estate agents or brokers selected from the local real estate association. An appraiser must not have any interest in the estate or property.

In states that require appointment of appraisers, the probate judge generally appoints qualified persons to determine the value of the particular type of property of the estate (see Form 22*). Often the appointment is made at the original hearing without the necessity of filing a petition. Even in those states in which appointment of appraisers is not required, the personal representative, the court, or any interested party may request a professional appraisal.

Before the appraisers begin their work, they should sign the oath of appraisers (see Form 35*). Then, accompanied by the attorney or more often by you, they should complete their work. Appraisers are often used to resolve disagreements between heirs or devisees about the value of the decedent's property. They are

---

*See Appendix A.

Exhibit 12.14 Inventory

STATE OF WISCONSIN, CIRCUIT COURT, _____ COUNTY   -PROBATE-

IN THE MATTER OF THE ESTATE OF

_____

_____   }   **INVENTORY**

File No. _____

I, the undersigned personal representative, certify that to the best of my knowledge this Inventory (with attached schedules) includes all property, encumbrances, liens or charges of the decedent required to be shown and identifies marital property, if any.

Subscribed and sworn to before me

on _____

_____
Notary Public, Wisconsin

_____
Signature

My commission expires: _____

_____
Signature

SUMMARY OF PROPERTY (Value of Decedent's Interest at Date of Death)	Date of Death	TOTAL VALUES
1. PROPERTY SUBJECT TO ADMINISTRATION		
(a) Net Value of Property Other Than Marital Property (Individual and Predetermination Date Property)	$ _____ *	
(b) Net Value of Decedent's Interest in Marital Property	$ _____ *	
NET VALUE OF PROPERTY SUBJECT TO ADMINISTRATION		$ _____
2. PROPERTY NOT SUBJECT TO ADMINISTRATION		
(a) Net Value of Decedent's Interest in Joint Property	$ _____ *	
(b) Net Value of Decedent's Interest in Survivorship Marital Property	$ _____ *	
(c) Other (s. 814.66, Wis. Stats.)	$ _____ *	
NET VALUE OF PROPERTY NOT SUBJECT TO ADMINISTRATION		$ _____
TOTAL VALUE OF PROPERTY		$

*ATTACH SCHEDULES SHOWING DETAILS.

PR-1422, 3/86-(19A) INVENTORY
s. 858.01 and 858.07, Wisconsin Statutes

Wisconsin Legal Blank Co., Inc.
Milwaukee, WI

Source: Wisconsin Legal Blank Co., Inc., Milwaukee, Wisconsin.

also used when the beneficiaries are uncertain about the property's true market value.

After a written appraisal is obtained, you will assign the appraised fair market value to each property item as of the date of the decedent's death or the alternate valuation date and ensure that the personal representative files this inventory and appraisal with the probate court and pays the appraisers' fees. The normal fee for each appraiser is generally set by statute (either a percentage of the estate or whatever the court determines to be fair and reasonable). Some states set minimum and/or maximum appraisal fees depending on the size of the estate. Other states no longer permit percentage fees. Fees charged by the appraisers can be deducted as a proper administration expense on both federal and state, if any, estate tax returns.

23. *Prepare a schedule of nonprobate assets.* Previously, we have discussed probate and nonprobate assets (property). In summary, property that passes by will is probate property and is the only property subject to estate administration. After the decedent's assets have been collected and the inventory and appraisal have been completed, assets that are not part of the probate estate but are included in the decedent's gross estate for estate tax purposes must be identified. All such assets are exempt from creditors' claims since only probate assets are subject to the debts of the decedent. Exhibit 12.15 contains examples of nonprobate and probate assets.

24. *File the inventory and appraisal.* When completed, the original Inventory and Appraisal form with appraisal reports from any independent appraisers attached is filed with the probate court. You will also mail copies to the surviving

---

Exhibit 12.15   Nonprobate and Probate Assets

Nonprobate Assets Not Subject to Creditors' Claims but are Subject to Federal Estate Tax	Probate Assets Subject to Creditors' Claims and Federal Estate Tax
1. Real property (house, cottage, business building) owned and held in joint tenancy.	1. Real property owned in severalty (single) ownership or in tenancy in common.
2. Personal property owned in joint tenancy (automobile, stocks and bonds, mutual funds, jewelry, stamp collection, art, savings and checking accounts, etc.).	2. Personal property owned in severalty or as tenants in common (jewelry, art, automobile, boat, coin collection, stocks and bonds, bank accounts, etc.).
3. Life insurance proceeds with a named beneficiary and not payable to the estate so long as the policyholder retains incidents of ownership.	3. Life insurance proceeds payable to the estate.
4. Annuity contracts with named beneficiary (not the estate).	4. Debts owed the decedent (mortgage, promissory notes, contracts for deed, loans, rents, dividends, income tax refunds, interest, royalties, copyrights, etc.).
5. Employment contract benefits that contain named beneficiary (pension, profit sharing, 401[k], group life insurance, etc.) and not payable to the estate.	5. Sale of business.
6. Individual retirement accounts (IRAs) with named beneficiary (not the estate).	6. Social Security benefits, Railroad Retirement benefits, Veterans Administration benefits.
7. Trusts (Totten trust and living *(inter vivos)* trust).	7. Lawsuit for damages.
8. U.S. savings bonds payable on death to a named beneficiary.	8. Trusts (testamentary trust and trusts not registered as owned by the decedent).

spouse and interested persons, i.e., heirs, beneficiaries, devisees, and creditors who have requested it.

DISTRIBUTION OF THE ESTATE AND PAYMENT OF CLAIMS

The following procedures are essential for the distribution of a decedent's estate:

25. Distribution of family allowances and/or exempt property to surviving spouse and/or minor children.
26. Filing and hearing of creditors' claims and payment of allowed claims.
27. Transfer of assets—real and personal property.

25. *Distribution of family allowances and/or exempt property to surviving spouse and/or minor children.* After the property is appraised, and the Inventory and Appraisal filed, the surviving spouse or minor children, or the guardian of minor children, may submit a petition to set apart the personal property of the decedent allowed by statute whether the decedent died testate or intestate (see Form 24*). You will prepare the petition. Most states grant this family allowance and/or exempt property to a surviving spouse and/or minor children, and some states also grant a homestead allowance or exemption prior to the payment of any creditor claims. Some states, e.g., Pennsylvania, include the family allowance or exemption in their priority of payment of debts (see the later discussion). After approving the petition, the court will issue an order "setting apart" said property (see Form 25*). In some states, separate petitions and orders are used, one for the homestead, another for the personal property.

We have already discussed the types and value of the property that can be set aside according to one state's law (see Chapter 4). If the homestead passes directly by state statute to the surviving spouse and/or to the minor children, the state will often exempt the homestead (up to a statutory amount) from inheritance taxation. If the spouse receives ownership greater than a life estate in the homestead, federal tax law will allow the homestead to be part of the marital deduction. A homestead may qualify as part of the marital deduction for federal estate tax purposes if it passes directly to the surviving spouse. It would not qualify for the marital deduction if the spouse receives only a life estate in the homestead (I.R.C. § 2056). It should also be noted (1) that in most states any of the decedent's personal property set apart as a family allowance is not subject to state inheritance tax but instead is allowed as a deduction on the inheritance tax return and (2) that no federal estate tax deduction is granted for such property (see I.R.C. §§ 2056 and, generally, 2053–2057, 2106).

Until final settlement of the estate, the surviving spouse and/or minor children may receive reasonable maintenance from the assets of the estate. The amount is determined by the value of the estate and the socioeconomic status of the decedent, but compare Tex. Prob. Code § 288, where no allowance is granted if the surviving spouse has adequate separate property. State statutes determine the length of time that the family may receive maintenance (e.g., usually twelve to eighteen months). The court, at its discretion, may lengthen this period. In most states, maintenance and the statutory family allowances are exempt from the claims of all creditors, including claims for administration of the estate and funeral

---

*See Appendix A.

expenses, but compare 20 Pa. Stat. Ann. § 3392, where a family allowance (exemption) is granted after administration expenses. The Petition for an Order Allowing Maintenance and the order from the court granting it to the decedent's family are found on Forms 26* and 27*. For state inheritance tax purposes, the amount of maintenance established and allowed by the court for one year is a proper deduction and therefore is not taxed by the state on the inheritance tax return. State statutes should be consulted to determine the monetary limit allowed as a tax deduction.

26. *Filing and hearing of creditors' claims and payment of allowed claims.* After the family allowances and maintenance have been set apart, the decedent's valid and approved debts must be paid before any of the decedent's assets can be distributed to the beneficiaries, devisees, or heirs of the estate. Those to whom the decedent owed money are given actual notice or notice through publication (see the previous discussion) that their debtor has died and that they must file their claims with the probate court or with the decedent's personal representative within the time period set by each state.

What You Do:

- You will collect and keep complete records of all claims sent to the personal representative and those filed with the probate court.
- You will determine that all claims have been filed within the required time period.
- You will refer the personal representative to the attorney for legal advice on contesting any claim. The clerk of court should be contacted to help explain the procedures for denying claims.

Statutes have established a definite procedure for the filing and hearing of creditors' claims. In most states, the time limits for creditors to file their claims are established by either (1) the court's order setting the date for the hearing of the Petition to Prove the Will or the Petition for Administration or (2) the official appointment of the personal representative. For this purpose, creditors should use the Proof of Claim form containing the claimant's address and signature and the affirmation of a notary public (see Form 28*, Exhibit 12.16, and Exhibit 12.17). Section 3–804 of the Uniform Probate Code allows a claimant to file the claim with the probate court or "deliver or mail to the personal representative a written statement of claim." If the claim is based on any written instrument, such as a contract, promissory note, or bank draft, the claimant must attach a copy of the instrument to the Proof of Claim.

In many states, creditors have from two to six months from the date of the first publication of notice to creditors to file their claims; alternatively, the time period commences after the "Letters" are issued by the court and the personal representative is officially appointed. An estate cannot be closed before this time period has expired. If the claimant does not act within the time allowed, the right to present the claim at any other time is lost, and even a valid claim will not be paid. You must remind the personal representative that payment of late claims will create personal liability for him. If, however, the claimant can demonstrate a good reason for requesting an extension, the court may extend the period by giving notice to the personal representative of the estate.

During and after the time period for filing claims, it is necessary to check with the personal representative to determine whether any of the claims should be contested. If the decision is made to contest a claim, the personal representative

---

*See Appendix A.

Exhibit 12.16 Creditor's Claim

ATTORNEY OR CREDITOR WITHOUT ATTORNEY *(Name and Address)*:

TELEPHONE NO.:

FOR COURT USE ONLY

ATTORNEY FOR *(Name)*:

SUPERIOR COURT OF CALIFORNIA, COUNTY OF

STREET ADDRESS:

MAILING ADDRESS:

CITY AND ZIP CODE:

BRANCH NAME:

ESTATE OF (NAME):

DECEDENT

CREDITOR'S CLAIM*
(for estate administration proceedings filed after June 30, 1988)

CASE NUMBER:

You must file this claim with the court clerk at the court address above before the LATER of (a) four months after the date letters (authority to act for the estate) were first issued to the personal representative, or (b) thirty days after the date Notice of Administration was given to the creditor, if notice was given as provided in Probate Code section 9051. Mail or deliver a copy of this claim to the personal representative. A proof of service is on the reverse.

---

1. Total amount of the claim: $
2. Claimant *(name)*:
   a. ☐ an individual.
   b. ☐ an individual or entity doing business under the fictitious name of *(specify)*:

   c. ☐ a partnership. The person signing has authority to sign on behalf of the partnership.
   d. ☐ a corporation. The person signing has authority to sign on behalf of the corporation.
   e. ☐ other *(specify)*:
3. Address of claimant *(specify)*:

4. Claimant is ☐ the creditor ☐ a person acting on behalf of creditor *(state reason)*:

5. ☐ Claimant is ☐ the personal representative ☐ the attorney for the personal representative.
   (Claims against the estate by the personal representative and the attorney for the personal representative must be filed within the claim period allowed in Probate Code section 9100. See the notice box above.)
6. I am authorized to make this claim which is just and due or may become due. All payments on or offsets to the claim have been credited. Facts supporting the claim are ☐ on reverse ☐ attached.

I declare under penalty of perjury under the laws of the State of California that this creditor's claim is true and correct.
Date:

▶

. . . .
(TYPE OR PRINT NAME AND TITLE)

_____
(SIGNATURE OF CLAIMANT)

INSTRUCTIONS TO CLAIMANT

A. On the reverse, itemize the claim and show the date the service was rendered or the debt incurred. Describe the item or service in detail, and indicate the amount claimed for each item. Do not include debts incurred after the date of death, except funeral claims.
B. If the claim is not due or contingent, or the amount is not yet ascertainable, state the facts supporting the claim.
C. If the claim is secured by a note or other written instrument, the original or a copy must be attached (state why original is unavailable). If secured by mortgage, deed of trust, or other lien on property that is of record, it is sufficient to describe the security and refer to the date or volume and page, and county where recorded. (See Probate Code section 9152.)
D. Mail or take this original claim to the court clerk's office for filing. If mailed, use certified mail, with return receipt requested.
E. Mail or deliver a copy to the personal representative. Complete the Proof of Mailing or Personal Delivery on the reverse.
F. The personal representative will notify you when your claim is allowed or rejected.

(Continued on reverse)

---

* See instructions before completing. Use Creditor's Claim form No. DE-170 for estates filed before July 1, 1988.

Form Approved by the
Judicial Council of California
DE-172 [New July 1, 1988]
WOLCOTTS FORM DE-172 (PRICE CLASS 6-2)

CREDITOR'S CLAIM
(Probate)

Probate Code, §§ 9000 et seq., 9153

Exhibit 12.16   Creditor's Claim—*continued*

ESTATE OF (NAME):	CASE NUMBER:
DECEDENT	

FACTS SUPPORTING THE CREDITOR'S CLAIM
☐ **See attachment** *(if space is insufficient)*

Date of Item	Item and Supporting Facts	Amount Claimed
	TOTAL	$

PROOF OF ☐ MAILING ☐ PERSONAL DELIVERY   TO PERSONAL REPRESENTATIVE
(Be sure to mail or take the original to the court clerk's office for filing)

1. I am the creditor or a person acting on behalf of the creditor. At the time of mailing or delivery I was at least 18 years of age.
2. My residence or business address is *(specify)*:

3. I mailed or delivered a copy of this Creditor's Claim to the personal representative as follows *(check either a or b below)*:
   a. ☐ **First-class mail.** I deposited a copy of the claim with the United States Postal Service, in a sealed envelope with postage fully prepaid. I used first-class mail. I am a resident of or employed in the county where the mailing occurred. The envelope was addressed and mailed as follows:
   (1) Name of personal representative served:
   (2) Address on envelope:

   (3) Date of mailing:
   (4) Place of mailing *(city and state)*:

   b. ☐ **Personal delivery.** I personally delivered a copy of the claim to the personal representative as follows:
   (1) Name of personal representative served:
   (2) Address where delivered:

   (3) Date delivered:
   (4) Time delivered:

   I declare under penalty of perjury under the laws of the State of California that the foregoing is true and correct.
   Date:

▶

....
(TYPE OR PRINT NAME OF CLAIMANT)   (SIGNATURE OF CLAIMANT)

DE-172 [New July 1, 1988]   **CREDITOR'S CLAIM**   Page two
                                            (Probate)

Source: Wolcotts Forms, available at most stationery or office supply stores or by calling 1(800)421-2220.

Exhibit 12.17 Claim Against Estate

STATE OF WISCONSIN, CIRCUIT COURT, _____ COUNTY   -PROBATE-

IN THE MATTER OF THE ESTATE OF

_____

_____   } **CLAIM AGAINST ESTATE**

File No. _____

Name of claimant: _____

STATEMENT OF CLAIM: *(If a claim is founded on a written instrument, a copy with all endorsements must be attached.)*

If the decedent was survived by a spouse, the classification of the obligation is as follows:

☐ Support obligation owed spouse or child [s. 766.55(2)(a), Wis. Stats.].
☐ Obligation incurred in the interest of the marriage [s. 766.55(2)(b), Wis. Stats.].
☐ Obligation incurred prior to marriage or prior to January 1, 1986 [s. 766.55(2)(c), Wis. Stats.].
☐ Tort [s. 766.55(2)(cm), Wis. Stats.].
☐ Other [s. 766.55(2)(d), Wis. Stats.].

I swear that this statement is correct and there is due to claimant from this estate

$ _____

No payments have been made which are not credited, and there are no offsets except as stated above.

Subscribed and sworn to before me

on _____   _____
                                                Signature of Claimant

_____   _____
Notary Public, Wisconsin   Address

My commission expires: _____   _____

_____
Attorney for Claimant

_____
Address

_____

NOTE: A statutory filing fee of $3.00 shall accompany each claim.

PR-1421, 3/86-(25A) CLAIM AGAINST ESTATE   s. 859.13, Wisconsin Statutes   Wisconsin Legal Blank Co., Inc.
                                                                                  Milwaukee. WI

Source: Wisconsin Legal Blank Co., Inc., Milwaukee, Wisconsin.

must, before or on the date of the hearing, file all objections to the claim or file a claim against the claimant (a counterclaim) asserting that the decedent was actually entitled to the property. The document you prepare to file an objection or counterclaim is called the Objection to Claim and is served on the claimant and filed with the probate court (see Form 29*). Contested claims are not heard on the date set for hearing allowed claims, but on another hearing date, for which arrangements must be made. Notice of this second date for contested claims must be given to the creditors.

The personal representative of the estate can admit, in writing, the claims that are valid and proper debts of the decedent. All other contested claims must be proven legitimate at this hearing in order to be allowed (approved) by the court. Also, claims of the personal representative or claims in which the personal representative has an interest are allowed only if proven by evidence satisfactory to the court. Once the claims are allowed, it is the duty of the personal representative to pay them and to file receipts or vouchers (canceled checks). You will keep records of all payments for the Final Account (Form 39* and Exhibit 12.18) when it is presented to the probate court. Payments to creditors should be made from the estate checking account. Creditors' debts are generally payable only from probate assets, but taxes due are payable from *both* probate and nonprobate assets.

The laws that regulate probate procedures have given certain kinds of debts priority. In the event that assets of the decedent's estate are insufficient to pay all valid creditors' claims in full, all states have statutes that set the priority of payment of debts. In most states, any or all of the following may be paid before the debts: the support or family allowances, homestead allowance or exemption, and the exempt property. The priority of debts in the following Pennsylvania statute is typical:

> *20 Pa. Stat. Ann. 3392* Classification and Order of Payment
> If the applicable assets of the estate are insufficient to pay all proper charges and claims in full, the personal representative, subject to any preference given by law to claims due the United States, shall pay them in the following order, without priority as between claims of the same class:
> (1) The costs of administration.
> (2) The family exemption.
> (3) The costs of the decedent's funeral and burial, and the costs of medicines furnished to him within six months of his death, of medical or nursing services performed for him within that time, of hospital services including maintenance provided him within that time, and of services performed for him by any of his employees within that time.
> (4) The cost of a gravemarker.
> (5) Rents for the occupancy of the decedent's residence for six months immediately prior to his death.
> (6) All other claims, including claims by the Commonwealth [compare U.P.C. § 3–805].

Notice that, unlike many states, the Pennsylvania statute lists the costs of administration before the amount of the family exemption granted in Pennsylvania.

Example: In Pennsylvania, Rashanna's estate has assets worth $40,500. The approved claims against her estate are as follows:

a. $2,500 in administration expense.
b. $6,000 for family exemption.

---

*See Appendix A.

Exhibit 12.18 Final Account and Petition

STATE OF WISCONSIN, CIRCUIT COURT, _____ COUNTY   -PROBATE-

IN THE MATTER OF THE ESTATE OF

_____

_____

} **FINAL ACCOUNT AND PETITION**

File No. _____

I, the personal representative of this estate, certify that this Final Account is true and correct, and this estate is ready for final settlement.

The following is my account of the administration of this estate from

_____ to _____

ATTACH SCHEDULES SHOWING DETAILS AND A LIST OF INTERESTED PERSONS (Include Addresses).

RECEIPTS		ITEMS	DISBURSEMENTS		ITEMS
Inventoried Assets		$	Funeral Expenses	(Schedule F)	$
Added Property	(Schedule A)		Debts	(G)	
Dividends	(B)		Claims by Judgment	(H)	
Interest	(C)		Taxes Paid	(I)	
Capital Gains (Losses)	(D)		Interest Paid	(J)	
Other Receipts	(E)		Administration Expenses		
			Other Than Fees	(K)	
			Other Payments	(L)	
			Distributions Paid to Date	(M)	
			TOTAL DISBURSEMENTS		$
			Assets on Hand	(N)	$
BALANCING TOTALS		$			$

Assets on Hand (Schedule N) $ _____

Less Requested Fees:

   Attorney $ _____

   Personal Representative   _____

   Guardian Ad Litem   _____   - $ _____

BALANCE AVAILABLE FOR DISTRIBUTION $ _____

Schedule O, showing the proposed distribution of the balance is attached.

The personal representative requests that the Court schedule a hearing to approve this account, the classification of assets, and the allocation of expenses; to certify that the decedent's interest in life estates and joint tenancies has terminated and that survivorship marital property has vested in the surviving spouse; and to assign the assets of the estate.

Subscribed and sworn to before me

_____
Signature of Personal Representative

on _____

_____
Name (Typed)

_____
Notary Public, Wisconsin

_____
Address

My commission expires: _____

PR-1423, 3/86-(27A) FINAL ACCOUNT AND PETITION   s. 862.07, Wisconsin Statutes

   c. $4,000 for funeral and burial.

   d. $50,000 for medical, hospital, and nursing expenses.

   e. $2,000 in credit card expenses.

The $2,500 in administration expenses is paid first; then the $6,000 family exemption is granted; then since the funeral/burial expenses ($4,000) and the expenses for medical, hospital, and nursing services ($50,000) are on the same priority level (3) and their sum exceeds the remaining assets of the estate, each creditor on that level gets a prorated share of the remaining assets calculated as follows:

Total estate assets	$40,500
Less administration expenses and family exemption	8,500
Remaining estate assets	$32,000
Combined level 3 claims	$54,000
Percentage of remaining assets to level 3 claims	59.259%

There are ten creditors in priority level 3 with claims of varying amounts making up the combined total of $54,000. Each creditor will receive 59.259 percent of his total claim using up the remaining $32,000 of estate assets. The credit card company would receive nothing for its $2,000 claim.

For the priority of creditors' claims as set out in Section 3–805 of the Uniform Probate Code, see Exhibit 12.19.

One of the personal representative's primary functions is to pay all approved creditors' claims from the estate assets according to the domicile state's statutory list of priorities. You will assist by identifying, locating, and giving notice to all creditors and then reviewing their claims. Classifying these approved claims and categorizing them by priority are among your tasks. *The accuracy of your classification must, of course, be confirmed by your supervising attorney.* All such creditors must be paid according to their priority rights before the personal representative can distribute the balance of the estate assets according to the decedent's will or by intestacy when the decedent died without a will.

ETHICAL ISSUE
➤

Remember that only probate assets of the decedent's estate are subject to creditors' claims. Nonprobate and statutory allowances or exemptions are not.

Since creditors have a prior claim to the assets of the decedent's estate, the named devisees of the testator or the heirs may receive nothing from the estate through the will or the intestate statute. It is quite possible that no assets will be left after all the creditors have been paid. An estate that has more debts than assets is called an insolvent estate. Unless they are co-signers with the decedent on any of the debts, the spouse and family have no personal liability to pay all or any part of the debts. The decedent's estate is solely responsible, and furthermore, as noted earlier, creditors have no claim against the nonprobate assets of the deceased.

🏛 ASSIGNMENT 12.1

Erma Gledig, recently deceased, left the bills listed below. According to your own state law, in what order are the following to be paid, if at all, by her executor, Sherwin Gledig, her husband?

1. Salary payable to Erma's nurse-companion for a week prior to Erma's death.
2. State inheritance tax due on a devise to Erma from her brother, who predeceased her.
3. Attorney's fee payable to a lawyer who advised Erma during a real estate transaction.

Exhibit 12.19   Priority of Debts according to Section 3–805 of the Uniform Probate Code

1. **Costs and expenses of administration.** Expenses of the estate administration such as mailing and filing fees; court costs; publication and advertising expenses; renting an estate safe deposit box; opening an estate checking account; bond fees; costs for protecting, preserving, and selling estate property; appraisers' and auctioneers' costs; and attorney and personal representative fees are examples of debts within this priority.

2. **Reasonable funeral expenses.** As determined by the probate court, reasonable expenses include transporting the body to the funeral home; the funeral director's fees; burial or cremation costs; and payment for religious services, reception expenses, and other necessary funeral costs.

3. **Debts and taxes with preference under federal law.** Any financial obligations the decedent owed the federal government while alive, including debts and taxes, are the next priority. The federal estate tax is not included in this priority category, however, because it is a death tax, i.e., payable after death. The following are examples of federal debts and federal taxes included in this priority category:

Federal Debts

- Student loans
- Tax court judgments
- Fines for criminal convictions
- Overpayments for:
  - Medicare
  - Welfare benefits
  - Social Security benefits for survivors or disability
  - Veterans' benefits

Federal Taxes

- Individual income tax
- Gift tax
- Tax lien levied against the decedent for prior years

4. **Expenses of the last illness.** This category includes unpaid debts that were incurred during the decedent's last illness such as the following:
   - Reasonable and necessary medical (doctor), nurse, and hospital services
   - Hospice care
   - Outpatient and home health care by professional personnel
   - All prescription drugs
   - Physical, occupational, and speech therapy
   - Necessary medical equipment, e.g., walker, wheelchair, hospital beds, and the like
   - Drug and alcohol treatment
   - Personal live-in attendant, e.g., nurse or companion who cared for the decedent in the last months before death and may qualify for this category

5. **Debts and taxes with preference under state law.** Included are debts due the individual state government and state agencies and those due local, county, and city governmental agencies, which may be a state specific priority, e.g., a creditor priority for only the domicile state, not for other states where the decedent had debts or taxes that were due. State taxes are also part of this priority; however, state death taxes such as the inheritance tax, estate tax, and credit estate tax, i.e., for estates that have gross assets of over $600,000 and owe federal estate tax, are excluded. The following are examples of items in this category:

State Debts

- Recyclables and waste disposal
- Water and sewer charges
- Overpayments for:
  - Medicaid
  - Unemployment compensation
  - Worker's compensation

State Taxes

- Individual income tax
- Property tax
- Sales tax
- Gift tax
- Tax lien

Some states combine federal and state debts and taxes into one priority category.

6. **All other claims.** The remaining creditors of the decedent constitute the last category of priority creditors. Although a contract for personal services, e.g., a singer to perform a concert, a tailor to make a suit of clothes, a surgeon to perform an organ transplant, or a professional athlete to play a game, may obviously be terminated by injury or death, most other creditor claims are binding and can be collected from the decedent's estate.

Example: If Karl negligently causes bodily harm to Leonard or damages Leonard's property, or if Leonard sells a car to Karl or lends Karl money, and Karl dies before paying Leonard in each of these cases, Leonard is the creditor, and Karl's estate is responsible for these creditor's claims.

4. Claim for services rendered by the Cahill Funeral Home.
5. Claim from the U.S. Commissioner of Internal Revenue for income tax unpaid in the previous year.
6. Sherwin's executor's bond.
7. Unpaid installment on an automobile owned jointly by Erma and Sherwin.

27. Transfer of assets—real estate. If the decedent's personal property is sufficient to pay the allowances, expenses, taxes, and the rest of the debts, all real estate will pass free and clear to the named devisees in the will or to heirs by intestate succession. In such cases, the personal representative is usually not obliged to take possession of the real estate but must manage it (e.g., pay monthly mortgage payments, insurance premiums, state property taxes, utility bills, and maintenance expenses) until it is distributed to the beneficiaries or devisees or sold. In addition, if the decedent's personal property assets are insufficient to pay the debts, the personal representative is obligated to take possession of the real estate and sell it to satisfy these obligations. Also, the court may decide that the sale of the real estate is in the best interest of the persons with an interest in the realty and order such a sale. The homestead, however, may not be sold without written consent of the surviving spouse, which must be filed with the court.

The sale of real estate can be accomplished in two ways: (1) if the decedent's will gives the personal representative (executor) the power to sell the estate's real estate, the personal representative needs no court order to proceed; (2) if the decedent had no will or failed to include in the will a power of sale, the personal representative may not proceed without a court order, which may authorize either a private or public sale of the real property. In either instance, the personal representative must execute numerous legal forms. It will be your obligation to prepare all the necessary documents for execution by the personal representative and the purchasers. Caution: The personal representative may *not* sell, encumber, lease, or distribute real estate for thirty days from the date the Letters are issued.

If the personal representative (executor) is granted power of sale by the decedent's will, it is possible to sell real estate without a court order, but it is still advisable to obtain such an order. The assistance of a real estate broker is usually obtained when real estate is to be sold. The personal representative will also need, and you will obtain or prepare, a certified copy of the will, a certified copy of the Order Admitting Will to Probate, a certified copy of the Letters Testamentary, and a Probate Deed (see Form 38*).

If the decedent's will does not contain a power of sale or if the decedent dies intestate and the personal representative of the estate deems it wise to sell, mortgage, or lease real estate owned by the decedent, the probate court may authorize a *private sale* as requested. To accomplish this, the following steps are necessary:

■ You will assist the personal representative in preparing and filing a Petition to Sell-Mortgage-Lease Real Estate to be presented to the court after the Inventory and Appraisal has been filed. This document is necessary only if the will does *not* give the power of sale to the personal representative (executor) or if there is no will (see Form 31*).

---

*See Appendix A.

■ The probate judge then signs the Order for Hearing Petition to Sell-Mortgage-Lease Real Estate requested by the personal representative (see Form 32*). The order sets the date, place, and time for the hearing and must be published and printed in the same manner as the hearing to prove the will. You will see to it that notice of this hearing in the form of the publication or a copy of the Order for Hearing is sent to the devisees or heirs in order to comply with the general probate notice requirements.

■ At the Hearing on the Petition to Sell-Mortgage-Lease, the personal representative of the estate presents certified copies of the will, the order admitting a will to probate, the Letters Testamentary, and a Probate Deed, along with the probate judge's order. Oral testimony of the personal representative as to the facts set forth in the petition is presented. If satisfied as to the need to sell the real estate, the judge signs the Order for Sale-Mortgage-Lease of Real Estate at Private Sale (see Form 33*).

■ If required by the court, the real estate must be reappraised by two or more disinterested persons where a considerable period of time has elapsed since issuance of the order. This is necessary because of the possible substantial increase or decrease in the property's value. The form used is the Warrant to Appraisers at Private Sale (see Form 34*). Generally, you will contact the appraisers who are usually the same persons who made the original appraisal for the estate. Once the market value of the realty has been determined, the property cannot be sold at private sale for less than that price. The appraisers sign the Oath of Appraisers and Appraisal of Lands Under Order for Sale (see Form 35*).

■ The court may require, at its discretion, that the personal representative post an additional bond (see Form 76*).

■ Once the private sale is completed, you will prepare and the personal representative will file the Report of Sale of Land at Private Sale Under Order for Sale with the court (see Form 36*). (You will delete those parts of the form applicable only to a public sale.)

■ After the personal representative has filed the report of sale and complied with the terms of the order for sale, the court will approve the sale and enter its Order Confirming Private Sale of Real Estate. With only a few modifications, it can be used to confirm a public sale as well (see Form 37*). Next, the court authorizes the personal representative to execute and deliver the proper deed (see Form 38*).

■ To complete the sale and to ensure that the buyer will have clear and marketable title to the land, you must verify that the personal representative has filed the following in the county recorder's office: certified copies of the Letters of Administration or Letters Testamentary, the Order for Sale of Real Estate at Private Sale, the Order Confirming Private Sale of Real Estate, and the Probate Deed issued by the personal representative, called either the administrator's deed or the executor's deed.

Public sale of real estate may also be authorized by the court. The personal representative executes the same documents as those used in a private sale, including the Petition and Order for Hearing to Sell Real Estate; the Order for Sale of Real Estate at Public Auction; the Report of Sale of Land at Public Auction; and the Order Confirming Sale of Real Estate at Public Auction. You will prepare

---

*See Appendix A.

or assist the personal representative in gathering these documents; you will also help the personal representative file an additional bond if necessary and obtain and file certified copies of the same instruments used in the private sale covered previously. The only additional requirement for the public auction is that if such a sale is authorized by the court, published notice of the time and place of the sale are often required for a specific statutory notice period. Proof of such publication must be filed with the court before the court will formally confirm the sale. You will perform these tasks (see the procedures previously discussed).

27A. *Transfer of assets—securities (corporate stock).* As a general rule, stocks need not be transferred to the name of the personal representative of the estate. They may be left in the name of the decedent and sold or transferred to the persons entitled to them at the conclusion of the administration of the estate. If the securities are sold, the proceeds must be placed in the estate checking account and not, even temporarily, in the personal representative's account. Whenever stock is transferred from one person to another, whether by sale, gift, devise, or inheritance, the transfer is handled by a transfer agent or corporation. A transfer agent (often a bank) is the party designated by the corporation as the one to be contacted whenever a stock transfer, e.g., a sale or gift of stock, is performed. When the decedent's stock is to be transferred to a devisee under the will or an heir under intestacy proceedings, you must give the transfer agent the following:

- The stock certificate representing the number of shares to be transferred, endorsed (signed) by the personal representative, and the signature guaranteed by a bank or a member firm of the New York Stock Exchange
- A certified copy of the Letters Testamentary or Letters of Administration
- A certified copy of the Decree of Distribution (see Form 45*)
- The name, address, and Social Security number of the devisee or heir receiving the stock

If the securities are registered in the name of the decedent and another person as joint tenants, a transfer from joint tenancy to sole ownership requires, in addition to the documents and data mentioned above, that you send to the transfer agent a death certificate of the decedent, an Affidavit of Survivorship (see Exhibit 12.7), and a state inheritance tax waiver for those states that require a stock transfer tax to be paid, if applicable. After obtaining the required materials, the transfer agent changes the registry on the corporate books by writing in the new owner's name and address and issues new stock certificates to the new owner. Questions about transferring corporate stock can best be answered by contacting the appropriate stock transfer agent.

If the decedent lived in a rural area, you should make inquiries concerning the decedent's ownership of stock in a grain elevator, creamery, or other farmer cooperatives. It is possible that the decedent kept no records of such stock ownership in obvious locations such as the safe deposit box or at home; consequently, a thorough check of outside sources (e.g., the associations themselves) is necessary.

If the decedent owned any U.S. savings bonds of Series A, B, C, D, F, or G that were not redeemed before death, they should be presented immediately for payment if they have matured and no longer bear interest. Most banks are able to assist the personal representative in reissuing bonds in the name of the

---

*See Appendix A.

distributee, if that is the person's preference. The personal representative will be required to endorse the existing bonds in the presence of the appropriate bank official.

THE FINAL ACCOUNT AND CLOSING THE ESTATE

Before the probate court can discharge the personal representative from obligations to the decedent's estate, devisees, or heirs at law, the following final steps must be taken:

28. File the Final Account and Petition for Settlement and Distribution.
29. Request Order for Hearing on Final Account and Petition for Distribution.
30. Give notice of the hearing to interested parties.
31. Prepare and file copies of federal and state estate and income tax returns with the Final Account.
32. Hearing on the Final Account and Petition for Distribution.
33. Request Order Allowing Final Account.
34. Compute and file state inheritance tax return or waiver.
35. Receive Order for Settlement and Decree of Distribution.
36. Collect receipts for assets by distributee.
37. File Petition for Discharge of Personal Representative.
38. Request Order Discharging Personal Representative.
39. Cancellation of personal representative's bond.

28. *File the Final Account and Petition for Settlement and Distribution.* Once all just claims have been paid and receipts for such payments collected, you must prepare and the personal representative must file a verified (notarized) final account (see Form 39* and Exhibit 12.18) and petition the court for settlement of the estate (see Form 40*). Beginning with the original inventory, the personal representative's final account must show all changes in the assets of the estate, including debits and credits of cash and any interest that may have accrued during administration of the estate. This accounting should fully disclose the balance of property available for distribution to named devisees under the will or heirs after the payment of creditors.

You must identify property remaining on hand for distribution in such a way that the personal representative may readily determine the persons entitled to receive such property. The personal representative should keep vouchers in the form of canceled checks or receipts to substantiate the payments for any and all disbursements or for assets distributed during administration of the estate including the personal representative's own fees and claims against the estate, and you must keep records of all these matters.

You must verify that the final account is filed within the time allotted by statute for settlement of the estate, which in some states is one year from the date of the personal representative's appointment. For good cause, the probate court may grant an extended time for settlement.

The form for the final account lists the steps and information that must be included for the court's review. Incidental expenses (for miscellaneous items such as copies of the final decree and filing fees) necessarily occur after the final decree has been granted and can only be estimated.

---

*See Appendix A.

29. *Request Order for Hearing on Final Account and Petition for Distribution.* The probate court issues an order for a hearing on the final account, setting the time and place for the hearing (see Form 41*). Notice of the hearing must be published in conformity with the state's statutory requirements, e.g., publication of the notice once a week for three weeks in a legal newspaper in the county of the court's jurisdiction. As before, you will handle this notice requirement. The newspaper publishing the notice may be required to file an affidavit with the probate court proving that the notice was published and to send a copy of this proof to the personal representative (see Form 6*).

30. *Give notice of the hearing to interested parties.* On request of the personal representative, you will give notice of the hearing to interested parties by mailing a copy of the court's order for a hearing to each devisee or heir within a statutory time period, e.g., at least fourteen days before the hearing. You also prepare an affidavit, which the personal representative submits to the court verifying that notice has been mailed to these persons and also the state's tax official, e.g., the state officer of taxation (see Form 42*).

31. *Prepare and file copies of federal and state estate and income tax returns with the Final Account.* Before the final account is allowed and the Decree of Distribution is issued, you must complete all federal and state death and income tax returns and file them with the final account (see Chapter 14).

32. *Hearing on the Final Account and Petition for Distribution.* The hearing on the Final Account and Petition for Distribution gives all parties with an interest in the estate of the decedent the opportunity to appear and examine the personal representative's accounting. Explanations and corrections of the account and intended distribution should be discussed and resolved at this time. Then the personal representative requests that the court accept the final account.

33. *Request Order Allowing Final Account.* After all taxes have been paid and the final account has been accepted, the court signs an Order Allowing Final Account (see Form 43*).

34. *Compute and file state inheritance tax return or waiver.* In states that have an inheritance tax, a copy of the order Allowing the Final Account generally must be filed with the state's official tax collector. You prepare a tax return if an inheritance tax is due, and the personal representative must pay the tax after the final account has been allowed. In such cases, the personal representative does not make the tax payment or prepare the tax waiver (if no tax is due) until this time (see Form 44*). Within a specified time after the filing of the tax return, objections to the amount of tax may be made. After this time period expires, the state inheritance tax return becomes final.

35. *Receive Order for Settlement and Decree of Distribution.* After the final account has been allowed, the court enters an Order of Complete Settlement of the Estate and Decree of Distribution (see Form 45*). In its decree, the court determines the persons entitled to the estate, names the heirs, beneficiaries, or devisees, states their relationship to the decedent, describes the property, and determines the property to which each person is entitled. This decree also states (1) that notice for the final hearing was duly given; (2) that the deceased died testate or intestate, including the date of death and the residency of the decedent; (3) that the estate has been fully administered, including the payment of all allowed claims, and administration, funeral, and last illness expenses; (4) that the

---

*See Appendix A.

final account has been approved and settled; and (5) that all inheritance, estate, and income taxes have been paid.

Once the final decree is entered, the assets of the decedent's estate can be transferred. Title to personal property passes immediately to the appropriate heirs, beneficiaries, or devisees. In some states, real property passes differently. The right to possess the decedent's real property may vest in the heirs or devisees immediately after the Decree of Distribution, but legal title may remain with the personal representative until a certified copy of the decree has been filed with the county recorder or other official in the county where the land is located. The statutes of the individual state must be checked to determine the exact procedure.

To transfer legal title to real property held in joint tenancy by the decedent to the surviving joint tenant or tenants, the following must be filed with the county recorder: an Affidavit of Survivorship that has been certified by the state department of taxation, a certified copy of the death certificate, and a certified copy of the Decree of Distribution.

36. *Collect receipts for assets by distributee.* After all distributions have been made, the personal representative must collect receipts for all property distributed, real or personal, from each person to whom property has been distributed. You will add these receipts to your records. The personal representative must file these receipts in order to account for all the assets transferred (see Form 46*).

37. *File Petition for Discharge of Personal Representative.* When the distributions have been made and the receipts obtained from the heirs, beneficiaries, or devisees, the personal representative (executor or administrator) files a form you prepare called the Petition for Discharge of Personal Representative (see Form 47*).

38. *Request Order Discharging Personal Representative.* After presenting the Petition for Discharge, the personal representative will request an Order for Discharge from the probate court. This order or, in some states, the form called the Order for Final Distribution terminates the potential personal liability of the personal representative. Local custom determines whether the attorney for the estate or the probate court prepares this order allowing the personal representative to close the estate (see Form 48*). You may have to prepare this form.

39. *Cancellation of personal representative's bond.* A copy of the Order Discharging Personal Representative is sent to the bonding company (surety) to cancel the personal representative's bond. Usually, the personal representative requests the return of any unused premium for the bond. This act terminates the administration of a decedent's estate.

SPECIAL PROBATE PROCEEDINGS

In certain circumstances, special probate proceedings may be required. They include special administration, administration of omitted property, and decree of descent.

Special Administration

In some states, special administration is a procedure used by the probate court to administer the estate of a decedent under specific circumstances. It has limited

---

*See Appendix A.

purposes and is commenced only when a good reason for it exists. Reasons for appointing a special administrator include the following: (1) to preserve the decedent's estate until an executor or general administrator is appointed, e.g., in cases where a will or the appointment of an executor or general administrator is being contested; and (2) to give immediate attention, when necessary, to the management of a business left by the decedent.

Special administration is accomplished in the following manner:

1. A person having an interest in the estate files a Petition for Appointment of a Special Administrator (see Form 49*). This includes an itemized listing of the estate's real and personal property and a valid reason why it is necessary and expedient to have a special administrator appointed.

2. The judge signs the Order Granting Special Administration and appoints the special administrator (see Form 50*).

3. The special administrator files the *oath and bond* (see Form 14*). The amount of the bond is fixed by the court. You must check individual state statutes to see if a bond is required.

4. The court issues Letters of Special Administration conferring appropriate powers on the special administrator (see Form 51*).

5. The special administrator files an Inventory and Appraisal of the personal property of the decedent (see Form 23*). As a rule, if another person is to act as general administrator, the special administrator does not take possession or control of real property. If there is to be a summary distribution without general administration, then the special administrator must include real estate in the inventory and may take possession of it.

6. The powers of the special administrator officially cease when the personal representative (executor or general administrator) is appointed and the Letters Testamentary or Letters of General Administration are issued. Before being discharged, the special administrator must file a Final Account and Report of the Special Administrator, including vouchers and receipts for all disbursements (see Form 52*). This final account will also provide for all remaining assets of the estate to be delivered into the hands of the new personal representative (executor or general administrator).

7. The probate judge then signs the Order Approving the Final Account and Report of the Special Administrator (see Form 53*). The order allows the final account and discharges the special administrator and the sureties. When the special administrator and the executor or general administrator are the same person, only one inventory and one final account need be filed.

Administration of Omitted Property

After the estate has been closed and the personal representative discharged, someone may discover additional property belonging to the decedent that has not been administered (e.g., rare books, to which the will referred but which could not be located during administration). Proper disposition of the assets will necessitate reopening the estate. A petition may be filed by any person claiming an interest in the omitted property (see Form 54*). The court that has jurisdiction of the recently discovered assets will, upon petition by the interested person,

---

*See Appendix A.

appoint a personal representative, the same person as previously appointed, if possible (see U.P.C. § 3–1008). Reopening the estate and subsequent administration are both court-supervised proceedings. At the hearing on the petition, the court will determine to whom the omitted property will be distributed. The court can then, without notice, summarily decree the distribution of the property once all tax liability has been paid (see Form 55*).

Decree of Descent

When more than three years have passed since the date of the decedent's death and no probate proceedings have been commenced, an interested party may petition the court to determine the descent of the decedent's property. The petition requires that a formal proceeding be held with notice and a hearing (see Form 56*).

LIMITATIONS ON AND LIABILITY OF THE PERSONAL REPRESENTATIVE

In collecting and managing the assets of an estate, the personal representative cannot personally profit because profit taking would violate the fiduciary duty to the estate. The personal representative is also not allowed to purchase claims against the estate or to sell property to the estate while retaining a personal interest in the estate (compare U.P.C. § 3–713).

Example: Paulina Neven, the administratrix of Charlotte Neven's estate, obtained an order from the probate court allowing her to rent out land belonging to Charlotte while the estate was being settled. Paulina rents it to herself. If one of Charlotte's heirs objects to this apparent self-dealing, Paulina would have to prove that she had paid as much or more rent than anyone else renting the land would have been charged.

The personal representative who acts reasonably and in good faith faces no personal liability for decreases in the value of estate assets during administration. If decreases occur because of a breach of fiduciary duties due to negligence or delay, however, the court will impose damages on the personal representative to compensate the estate for the loss. The compensation, often called a **"surcharge,"** is paid by the personal representative out of her personal funds (compare U.P.C. § 3–808).

Surcharge
An overcharge beyond what is just and right, e.g., an amount the fiduciary is required by court order to make good because of negligence or other failure of duty.

Example: If in the above example the court had found Paulina guilty of self-dealing with the estate's assets, it would require her to compensate the estate, e.g., by paying, from her own funds, the amount of loss she had caused the estate.

When total assets of an estate are not sufficient to pay all approved debts and other charges against it, the law provides an order of priority for payments, as described earlier. The personal representative is individually liable for placing a less preferred creditor in a more favorable position than is appropriate and thus causing improper payment.

Example: Charlotte died leaving bills for her last illness, federal taxes payable for the previous year, and a bill from a local grocery. Paulina pays the grocer's bill before the federal tax lien. Because the grocer is a "less preferred creditor,"

---

*See Appendix A.

Paulina must pay the amount due the federal government from her own funds if the estate cannot pay it.

If the decedent's estate owes any federal taxes, the personal representative is held personally liable for any taxes that are not paid; see I.R.C. § 2002.

KEY TERMS

Small estate	Affiant	Demand	Cause of action
Qualified small	Citation	Deposition	Surcharge
estate	Demandant	Damages	

REVIEW QUESTIONS

1. What are the steps in the probate or estate administration of a decedent's estate? List each step and explain your function in the performance of each procedure.
2. What is the distinction, if any, in your state between the words *probate* and *estate administration?*
3. How are "small estates" administered in your state? What is the monetary limit in your state that allows an estate to be classified as a "small estate"?
4. How do the following differ: solemn v. common probate; formal v. informal probate; and solemn v. formal probate (under the U.P.C.)?
5. When would you choose to follow formal (solemn) probate instead of informal (common) probate when administering a decedent's estate?
6. In what ways can a county clerk or registrar assist you in your estate administration tasks? What are some things they cannot do?
7. What information must you obtain to complete the form used to petition to probate a will? Are this information and the form the same when a person dies intestate?
8. In your state, what are the statutory requirements for giving notice to creditors? When and how is the notice given in your state, and what is the time limit creditors have to file their claims?
9. How is a personal representative appointed? What document authorizes a personal representative to manage a decedent's estate? How

is a fiduciary employer identification number obtained, and for what purposes does a personal representative use it?
10. What are the various assets that you will help the personal representative collect and preserve in an estate administration, and what procedures do you use for the collection? List ten assets.
11. What are the inventory and appraisal, and how are they prepared?
12. How does a creditor present a claim against the decedent's estate, and how does the personal representative contest a claim?
13. What is your state's priority for payment of creditors' claims? Cite the statute and give examples of items within each category.
14. How is the final account prepared, and what does it contain?
15. At what point can the personal representative transfer the decedent's assets (both real and personal property) to the appropriate parties? When does legal title pass to them?
16. Can a decedent have more than one domicile? How would you resolve this problem so that ancillary proceedings can be finalized?
17. What happens to property of the decedent that is discovered after the estate administration has been completed?
18. Who is responsible for paying a surcharge, and under what circumstances would this occur?
19. Should all states adopt the Uniform Probate Code? Explain.

CASE PROBLEMS

Problem 1

Jane M. Doe of 1005 Elm Street, St. Paul, Minnesota, died testate (with a will) on September 20, 1994. She was married to John C. Doe, age 83, and had one child, Sandy R. Doe, age 45. Mrs. Doe was born on November 6, 1912, in the state of

Michigan. Her parents moved to Minnesota that year. On September 4, 1936, she married John C. Doe in St. Paul, Minnesota. Mrs. Doe was a retired real estate broker, and her legal residence (domicile) at the time of her death was St. Paul, Minnesota. Mrs. Doe died in the Porta Veta Hospital in St. Paul after suffering from cancer for approximately nine months. Her attending physician was Dr. Norma J. Dennison, 2067 Doctor's Exchange Building, St. Paul, Minnesota. Her attorneys were Cranwall and Schuster, 999 St. Paul First Trust Company Building, St. Paul, Minnesota.

Beneficiaries under Mrs. Doe's will are her husband, John C. Doe, who is also the personal representative of the estate; daughter Sandy R. Doe; the American Cancer Society; Girls' Clubs of America; and the Newark Institute of Higher Learning. Beneficiaries under insurance contracts (not taking under the will) are her brother, Jay A. Daw; husband, John C. Doe; and the estate.

Exhibit 12.20 shows the assets that Mrs. Doe individually owned or in which she owned an interest as specified at her death. Exhibit 12.21 shows liabilities and debts owed by Mrs. Doe at her death. Exhibit 12.22 shows costs incurred after Mrs. Doe's death. Exhibit 12.23 shows the beneficiaries of Mrs. Doe's estate and the maintenance of the family during administration.

Forms must be completed (executed) for the formal probate of the Jane M. Doe estate. From the information given in the above exhibits, the following sample forms (found in Appendix A) have been executed.

1. Petition for Formal Probate of Will and for Formal Appointment of the Personal Representative (Executor) (Form 1*).
2. Order and Notice of Formal Appointment of Personal Representative, Notice of Hearing for Formal Probate of Will, and Notice to Creditors (Form 3*).
3. Proof of Placing Order for Publication (Form 5*).
4. Affidavit of Publication (Form 6*).
5. Affidavit of Mailing Order or Notice of Hearing (Form 7*).
6. Statutory Notice of Rights of Surviving Spouse and/or Minor Children (reverse side of Form 7*).

7. Testimony of Subscribing Witness to Will (Form 8*).
8. Order of Formal Probate of Will and Formal Appointment of Executor (Form 10*).
9. Acceptance of Appointment and Oath by Individual (Form 13*).
10. Bond, if required, or Request for Waiver of Bond (Form 16*).
11. Letters Testamentary (Form 17*).
12. Application for Employer Identification Number (Form 89*).
13. Notice Concerning Fiduciary Relationship (Form 90*).
14. Inventory and Appraisement (Form 23*).
15. Petition for Allowance of Selection of Personal Property (Form 24*).
16. Order Allowing Selection of Personal Property (Form 25*).
17. Petition for Family Maintenance (Form 26*).
18. Order for Family Maintenance (Form 27*).
19. Final Account (Form 39*).
20. Petition for Order of Complete Settlement of the Estate and Decree of Distribution (Form 40*).
21. Order for Hearing on Final Account and Petition for Distribution and for Mailed Notice (Form 41*).
22. Affidavit of Mailing Order or Notice of Hearing on Final Account (Form 42*).
23. Federal and state death and income tax returns (see Chapter 14).
24. Order Allowing Final Account (Form 43*).
25. Order of Complete Settlement of the Estate and Decree of Distribution (Form 45*).
26. Receipt for Assets by Distributee (Form 46*).
27. Petition for Discharge of Personal Representative (Form 47*).
28. Order Discharging Personal Representative (Form 48*).
A. Review the checklists shown in Exhibits 12.20 through 12.23 and the executed forms in Appendix A in the Jane M. Doe case. Develop checklists and add to your checklists the data necessary to fill in the required forms for formal (solemn) probate of a testator's estate in your state. Use and follow the probate procedures in your state to execute (complete) the necessary forms.

---

*See Appendix A.

Exhibit 12.20   Assets of Jane M. Doe

Cash*
Traveler's checks (not cashed)	$ 1,000
Checking account—First National City Bank of St. Paul no. 55–5555	50,000
Savings deposit—American National Bank of St. Paul no. 44—4444	15,000

Stocks and Bonds
Tenneco, Inc., 100 shares (6 months after Mrs. Doe's death decreased in value to $4,800)	$ 5,000
Minnesota Co-op, 1,000 shares	4,500
American National Slide Rule, 1,000 shares (joint tenancy with husband)	75,000
Minnesota Company, 100 shares (joint tenancy with daughter)	5,000

U.S. Government Bonds
Bond No. R4502363E	$ 574
Bond No. R4502364E	574

Personal Property
Clothing—personal effects	$ 4,500
Furs—mink coat	11,500
Automobile—1992 Mazda	12,000
Furniture and household goods	22,000

Real Property
Residential (homestead) 1005 Elm Street St. Paul, MN Legal description: Lot 615, Block 42, Reiser's Addition to St. Paul Mortgage $130,000 at St. Paul Bank and Trust Company	$350,000

Rental Property
Duplex 776 Cliff Road St. Paul, MN Legal description: Lots 16 & 17, Block 20, Lovey's Addition to St. Paul $91,000: ¼ interest = $22,750 Mortgage $10,000 at St. Paul Bank and Trust Company $40,000: ¼ interest = $10,000	$ 22,750

Receivables
Johnson Furriers—Promissory Note (accrued interest = $350)	$ 10,350
Judgment against Forrest R. Redding	20,000

Interests in Trusts and Other Estates
St. Paul Trust Co.—Annual income to Mrs. Doe until her death, then to her daughter, Sandy R. Doe until her death. Established by Mrs. Doe's uncle.	$ 6,000 annual
Power of Appointment (general; unexercised)—To distribute income or corpus (500 shares Green Giant). Established by Mrs. Doe's father.	50,000

Insurance and Annuities
Prudential Life Insurance Company—No dividends. Beneficiary: Jay A. Daw (brother).	$ 50,000
Minnesota Life Insurance Company—Dividends. Beneficiary: Estate	120,000
Accumulated dividends.	100
Ecko Life Insurance Company (premiums of $50 per month paid by Order of the Doves). $100 per month to Mrs. Doe for life; then $100 per month to her husband for his life.	100 per month
Life expectancy of 4 years.	4,800 ($100 per month times 48 months)

*Note: Five months prior to her death, Mrs. Doe transferred funds from her checking account to her husband ($30,000) and to her daughter ($20,000). Mrs. Doe obtained this cash by selling Airco Corporation stock that she owned, and she then placed the cash in her checking account.

Exhibit 12.21 Liabilities and Debts of Jane M. Doe

Liabilities

Mortgage on homestead, 1005 Elm Street, St. Paul Bank and Trust Company	$130,000
Mortgage on duplex, 776 Cliff Rd., St. Paul Bank and Trust Company ($40,000; 1/4 interest = $10,000).	10,000
Total	$140,000

Debts

Approved claims against the estate

Ace's Plumbing Co. (company claims *$480* is owed; Mrs. Doe's personal representative claims *$230* is owed) (contested claim)	$ 480
St. Paul Telephone Company	50
St. Paul Electric Company	100
Harvey's Garbage Pickup	50
Dr. Norma J. Dennison	600
St. Paul Rents (rental of wheelchair)	50
Total	$ 1,330

Exhibit 12.22 Costs Incurred after Jane Doe's Death

Funeral Expenses

Newark and Newark Funeral Home	$ 9,500
Morningside Florists	100
Riverside Cemetery	1,000
Brown Monument Company—gravestone	500
Rev. B. Stone	25
Total	$11,125

Administration Expenses

Philip Masterson Co., Inc., appraisals	$ 500
Smith & Smith, Inc., preparation of tax returns	250
Attorney's fees	15,000
Compensation of personal representative	10,000
Publication of orders	50
Certified copies	5
Bond premiums (none)	0
Miscellaneous expenses	450
Expenses of last illness unpaid at death (Porta Veta Hospital)	850
Total	$27,105

Problem 2

Harvey R. Horwell of 999 Okinawa Street, St. Paul, Minnesota, 55101, died intestate on June 3, 1995. He was married to Harriet O. Horwell and had seven children, all minors, named Larry H., Harry O., Gary R., Sherrie E., Mary A., Terry R., and Jerry I. Horwell. Mr. Horwell was born on September 9, 1945, in the state of Hawaii. His parents moved to Minnesota in 1952. On December 12, 1975, Mr. Horwell married Harriet O. Narriet in Watertown, South Dakota. Mr. Horwell was a funeral director, and his legal residence at the time of his death was Ramsey County, St. Paul, Minnesota. Mr. Horwell died in St. Paul Ramsey Hospital in St. Paul, Minnesota. His attending physician was Dr. May B. Borg, 2113 Medical Center, St. Paul, Minnesota, 55104. His attorneys were Peterson, Peterson, Wojtowicz and Peteroni, 906 First State Bank Building, St. Paul, Minnesota 55101.

A. Obtain and complete the forms for the formal probate of Mr. Horwell's intestate estate as though he is a resident of your state.

Exhibit 12.23   Those Who Receive Benefits from the Estate of Jane M. Doe

Individuals

John C. Doe (husband)

Under will—Any interest in real property, and residue after specific gifts (bequests)	$502,378
Joint tenancy—Stock	75,000
Gift—Cash	30,000

Sandy R. Doe (daughter)

Joint tenancy—Stock	$ 5,000
Gift—Cash	20,000

Jay A. Daw (brother)

Life insurance policy	$ 50,000

Charitable Devises

American Cancer Society

Under will	$ 10,000

Girls' Clubs of America

Under will	$ 5,000

Newark Institute for Higher Learning

Under will	$ 1,000

Estate

Life insurance policy (part of residue, see above)	$120,100

Family Maintenance during Administration

$400 per month for 12 months	$ 4,800

CHAPTER THIRTEEN

INFORMAL PROBATE ADMINISTRATION

OBJECTIVES

After completing this chapter, you should be able to:

- Identify and explain the informal probate method of administering decedents' estates under the Uniform Probate Code.
- Recognize the circumstances under which informal probate procedures are appropriate.
- Explain the steps in informal probate administration of a decedent's estate.
- Apply the procedures and prepare the legal forms used in informal probate administration for a set of facts involving a decedent's estate.

SCOPE OF THE CHAPTER

This chapter outlines the method of selection and the proceedings involved in informal probate according to the Uniform Probate Code (U.P.C.). The procedures are listed, the relevant U.P.C. sections are cited, and sample forms that are available in Appendix A are identified. Next a case study of an estate that would appropriately be administered by informal probate procedures is presented. You are taken step by step through the informal proceedings so you can become familiar with the procedures. Then case problems involving both testate and intestate situations illustrate estate administration using informal probate procedures. Executed forms required for informal probate administration are available in Appendix A for your review.

THE CHOICE OF FORMAL OR INFORMAL PROBATE

The administration of a decedent's estate may be initiated by any of several procedures under the Uniform Probate Code.

- Formal appointment of the personal representative and formal proceedings thereafter, in testacy and intestacy (U.P.C. §§ 3–401 through 3–414) (see the discussion in Chapter 12).
- Informal appointment of the personal representative and informal proceedings thereafter, in testacy and intestacy (U.P.C. §§ 3–301 through 3–311).
- Collection of the decedent's personal property by affidavit and summary proceedings thereafter for small or moderate-sized estates (U.P.C. §§ 3–1201 through 3–1204) (see the discussion in Chapter 12).

Some states require the personal representative to follow a formal (solemn) procedure in the course of administration. Others combine the U.P.C. procedures, noted above, with local practices such as elimination or lowering of the requirement for a personal representative's bond. The states that have adopted all or part of the U.P.C. are able to offer all the above-mentioned procedures. Noteworthy contributions of the U.P.C. include the introduction of (1) procedures that are unsupervised or only partially supervised by the court (informal or common probate) and (2) simplified summary procedures that reduce the expenses of administration and make the transfer of small estates to the heirs or devisees much easier. In view of the great diversity among state practices, even among those that have enacted the U.P.C., your wisest course is to become familiar with the laws of the state in which you live and work.

When one applies for the position of personal representative of an estate that exceeds the limits for summary proceedings (see Exhibit 12.2), the applicant may select a formal or informal method of settling the estate. The U.P.C. defines formal proceedings as "those conducted before a judge with notice to interested persons" (U.P.C. § 1–201[18]) and informal proceedings as "those conducted without notice to interested persons by an officer of the court acting as a registrar for probate of a will or appointment of a personal representative" (U.P.C. § 1–201[23]). A court-appointed officer (registrar or surrogate) skilled in overseeing decedents' estates takes the place of the judge in informal probate. That officer has the power to do whatever the judge normally would do (e.g., appoint the personal representative and make findings of fact in relation to the will).

The U.P.C. allows a unique "in and out" method of settling estates—partly "in" the probate court (formally) even though most of the administration takes place "out" of it (informally). In informal proceedings, the personal representative or any person interested in the estate, as defined by U.P.C. § 1–201(24), may petition the court to adjudicate a disputed issue (e.g., the amount of a creditor's claim). After settlement of the dispute, the personal representative may resume informal procedures. This flexible use of formal proceedings within informal probate proves advantageous to the personal representative who prefers the freedom of informal probate but who may encounter a complexity that the court is better suited to handle.

Example: Reginald Canby died testate leaving all his property to his son, Damon. Reginald's wife predeceased him. Vanessa, Reginald's daughter, contends that Damon unduly influenced their father during his last illness to persuade him to write this will. Although the executor of Reginald's estate had elected to follow informal probate procedures, Vanessa may petition the probate court to settle this question using formal probate procedures. After the court has made its decision, it may allow the estate to resume informal probate or order it to continue formal, supervised probate (U.P.C. §§ 3–501, 3–502).

Informal probate generally reduces the amount of time between the beginning and end of administration. It involves fewer steps and less complicated procedures (e.g., the filing of fewer papers) than formal probate. The estate can be more easily distributed since the personal representative does not have to give notice of hearings, or obtain court approval for every item distributed, and may not be required to obtain a bond or submit an account at the end, depending on the circumstances.

The personal representative may request court supervision at any time; however, informal probate does not demand that the court supervise even the personal representative's closing of the estate after administering it. Because the purpose of informal probate is in part to help relieve congestion in the probate court, the greater part of informal probate transactions are carried out without the court's direct involvement. Not infrequently a hearing to prove the will and to appoint a personal representative is the only in-court proceeding. Of course, this is not always the case since any person interested in the estate (e.g., a creditor or devisee) may petition the court to determine a matter using formal proceedings.

Example: Fred McManus dies intestate, survived by a son, Bruce, and a brother, Paul. The registrar of probate court, who is empowered to conduct informal probate proceedings, appoints Paul personal representative of Fred's estate. Bruce challenges the informal appointment of his uncle, Paul, to administer the estate. The court will then appoint a personal representative in a formal proceeding, according to the order of priority (see the next section).

Although the U.P.C. does away with the required appraisal of estate assets unless demanded by the personal representative, another interested party, or the court, the value of real estate and closely held businesses should be appraised by an independent expert. The personal representative is entitled to hire and pay the appraiser(s) out of estate assets (U.P.C. § 3–707).

Example: Tillie's (decedent) estate, according to her will, is to be divided equally among her two sisters, Sherie and Noreen, and one brother, Waldo. Included in her estate are valuable paintings. Waldo, who was informally appointed to administer the estate, set the value of the paintings at $5,000. The other property in the estate was sold at public auction for $10,000 cash. Waldo decided to keep the paintings for himself and give Sherie and Noreen $5,000 in cash each. The two sisters, who believe the art collection is worth much more, can demand that it be appraised by an art expert.

The availability of informal proceedings for probating a will and settling the estate is one of the chief advantages of the Uniform Probate Code. Now that the U.P.C. has been either wholly or partially adopted by many state legislatures, informal probate is available to a great number of persons.

PRIORITY OF PERSONS SEEKING APPOINTMENT AS PERSONAL REPRESENTATIVES

In both formal and informal proceedings, persons who could qualify as personal representatives of the estate are considered in the following order of priority:

1. The person named as personal representative (executor) by the will, if there is one.

2. The surviving spouse of the decedent who is a named devisee (or beneficiary) in the will of the decedent.

3. Other named devisees (or beneficiaries) of the decedent.

4. The surviving spouse of the decedent when not a named devisee (or beneficiary).

5. Other heirs of the decedent.

6. Any creditor of the decedent, provided that no one with a higher priority standing has applied for appointment within forty-five days of the death of the decedent (U.P.C. § 3–203[a]). Compare a non–Uniform Probate Code state statute, Mass. Gen. Laws ch. 193 § 1.

The person who has the highest standing in this order and who is willing to serve does not always become the personal representative. The court or the registrar must appoint the personal representative and will not appoint a person who is under the age of eighteen or otherwise unsuitable for the position. This decision must be made by the court on the petition of an interested person.

In some instances, persons having priority fail to apply or are in some way disqualified. If that happens, the court, in a formal proceeding, will consider the nominees or persons having priority and try to arrive at a solution beneficial to the estate and satisfactory to those interested in it (U.P.C. § 3–203[b]). Any objection to the appointment of a personal representative must be made in a formal proceeding.

APPLICATION FOR INFORMAL PROBATE AND APPOINTMENT OF PERSONAL REPRESENTATIVE

Informal probate commences when an applicant seeking to be appointed personal representative submits a completed application for informal probate and informal appointment to the registrar for screening and acceptance. If your firm has been hired to assist the personal representative, you will be asked to perform the following tasks to help with these procedures:

- Gather the information necessary to complete the forms.
- Prepare the forms and file them or verify the filing.
- Communicate with the personal representative and registrar to ensure all procedures and forms are properly executed.

The applicant must verify (i.e., swear under oath) that the application is accurate and complete to the best of the applicant's knowledge. It is filed with the registrar or clerk of the probate court (U.P.C. § 3–301 and Form 57*).

1. The following general information is required on all applications for informal probate of a will or for informal appointment:

- The interest of the applicant in the decedent's estate (e.g., named personal representative–executor).
- Name, age, date of death of decedent, county and state of decedent's domicile at time of death; names and addresses of spouse, children, heirs, devisees, and ages of those who are minors.
- A statement indicating the county or city where the proceedings are to take place, if decedent was not domiciled at the date of death in the state where the application for informal probate has been filed.
- The name and address of any personal representative of the decedent who has been appointed in this state or elsewhere whose appointment has not been terminated.
- A statement that the applicant has not received nor is aware of any "demand for notice of any probate or appointment proceeding concerning the decedent that may have been filed in this state or elsewhere."
- A statement that the time limit for informal probate or appointment has not expired either because three years or less have passed since the decedent's death or, if more than three years from death have passed, circumstances as described by § 3–108 authorizing late probate or appointment have occurred.

2. If the application is for informal probate of a will, it must, in addition to giving the information and statements listed under 1 above, affirm:

- That the court has possession of the original last will, or that the original will or an authenticated copy probated in another jurisdiction is included with the application.
- That the applicant believes the will to have been validly executed.
- That the applicant is unaware of any instrument revoking the will and believes the submitted instrument is the decedent's last will.

3. An application for informal appointment of a personal representative (e.g., an executor) to administer an estate under a will sets forth the following in addition to the general information referred to in 1 above:

- A description of the will by date and place of execution.
- The time and place of probate or the pending application or petition for probate.
- An adaptation of the statements in the application or petition for probate and the name, address, and standing of the applicant among those who are entitled to be personal representative under U.P.C. § 3–203.

4. In addition to the statements listed in 1 above, an application for informal appointment of an administrator when the decedent died intestate states the following:

- That the applicant is not aware of any unrevoked testamentary instrument relating to property located in the state, or if the applicant is aware of any such instrument, the reason for its not being probated (U.P.C. § 3–301[4]).
- The priority of the applicant, and the names of any other persons who have a prior or equal right to the appointment under U.P.C. § 3–203 (see Form 71*).

---

*See Appendix A.

Example: Martha Engle, whose mother died testate, naming Martha executrix, desires to be appointed informally and to have the will probated informally. She must complete the data listed in 1, 2, and 3 above.

Example: Corey Davis desires to be named personal representative to the estate of his father who died intestate. Corey's mother predeceased his father. Corey must complete the data listed in 1 and 4 above.

In the example of Martha Engle, suppose that when Martha's mother died, no will could be found, and Maria Engle, Martha's sister, was informally appointed personal representative in intestacy. Subsequently, the will was discovered and Martha sought the appointment. Martha would then have to complete, in addition to the data listed in 1, 2, and 3, a "change of testacy status" form, requesting that she replace Maria (U.P.C. § 3–301[5]) (see Form 58*).

In the example of Corey Davis, suppose that when Corey's father died, Corey's brother, Alton, produced an instrument resembling a will under which Alton was named executor and that he was appointed personal representative (executor) by the court. Subsequently, the document was proved not to be a will, and Corey sought appointment as personal representative. Corey would also have to complete a "change of testacy status" form because the decedent, formerly considered testate, is now intestate.

By definition, informal probate of a will and informal appointment are proceedings conducted "without notice to interested persons" (U.P.C. § 1–201[23]). A person applying for informal appointment and/or informal probate of a will does not have to notify persons interested in the estate unless those persons have filed a written demand to be notified in accordance with U.P.C. § 3–204 (see also U.P.C. § 3–306). The applicant must, however, notify anyone having a superior right to be personal representative, e.g., a person who has been previously appointed personal representative or a person who stands higher in the order of priority for appointment.

Example: Ernest Falcott wants to be informally appointed personal representative to his father's estate and have the will informally probated. No personal representative has been previously appointed. His cousin, Julia, files a demand to be notified. Ernest must therefore notify Julia of his applications for informal probate of a will and informal appointment. He must also notify his mother, Letitia, who has a superior right to be personal representative.

Persons applying for informal proceedings must verify under oath the statements of their applications (e.g., Form 59*). The registrar is required to make "proofs and findings" for informal probate and informal appointment applications to check the truth and accuracy of statements therein and has the power to disqualify or decline applications if not satisfied (U.P.C. §§ 3–303, 3–305, 3–308, 3–309). Unintentional mistakes made by the applicant are correctable, but deliberate falsification that injures someone interested in the estate will give the injured person a cause of action against the applicant (U.P.C. §§ 1–106 and 3–301[b]).

ACCEPTANCE BY THE REGISTRAR

Having completed the forms necessary for informal proceedings, the applicant submits them to the registrar, who scrutinizes them for errors or omissions that might invalidate the application. The registrar must be satisfied of the following:

---

*See Appendix A.

- That the applicant has carried out the requirements of the Uniform Probate Code.
- That the applicant has solemnly affirmed the statements made in the application to be true to the best of the applicant's knowledge.
- That the applicant is an interested person as defined by U.P.C. § 1–201(24) (see Appendix C).
- That the applicant has chosen the proper venue (location) for having the will probated or for being appointed personal representative.
- That persons who have demanded notice of proceedings (U.P.C. § 3–204) have been notified of this proceeding.
- That 120 hours have elapsed since the decedent's death—U.P.C. § 2–104 requires that a person must survive the decedent for 120 hours to be an heir.

In addition, the registrar will check each application for particular requirements. For example, for informal probate, the registrar must possess the original of a properly executed will that has not been revoked, the statutory time limit for probate must not have expired, and the will must be the kind that may be probated informally. Informal probate of certain wills may not be advisable. The registrar has a duty to decline informal probate of alleged copies of lost or destroyed wills, wills consisting of a series of testamentary instruments (rather than a single one), and other irregular instruments. For informal appointment, the person seeking appointment must be entitled to do so by the order of priority (U.P.C. § 3–203).

It may be that the registrar will not be satisfied with the contents of the application for any of several reasons. Some of these are illustrated below.

Example: The registrar denies Joceyln Galbreth's application for informal probate of her brother's will because another sister, Elin Galbreth, had applied for probate earlier.

Example: The registrar denies Gilbert Havlicek's application for informal probate of his mother's will because the will is written on two apparently unconnected papers and it is not clear if one revokes the other.

Example: The registrar denies Conrad Marquart's application for informal appointment as personal representative of his sister's estate because another personal representative had been appointed and has not died or resigned.

Example: The registrar denies Marina Yladak's application for informal appointment as personal representative of her father's estate because she indicated on her application that her father might have had another will that is still in existence (U.P.C. §§ 3–305, 3–309).

Informal probate is available only for uncomplicated wills or estates. The registrar's denial of an application usually results in the commencement of formal probate proceedings. When the registrar accepts an application, it does not constitute a recommendation of informal over formal probate for a particular estate. The responsibility for that choice belongs to the applicant. The acceptance of an application by the registrar means only that the application meets the statutory requirements for filing.

If satisfied with the information contained in the application for informal proceedings, and if 120 hours have elapsed since the decedent's death, the registrar signifies acceptance of the application by issuing a Written Statement of Informal Probate (Form 60*) and/or appoints the applicant the personal representative of

---

*See Appendix A.

the estate by issuing Letters Testamentary or Letters of Administration (see Forms 65* and 77*). The Letters empower the applicant to assume the powers and duties of the office of personal representative but do not take effect until the applicant has filed a statement of acceptance of these powers and duties and has paid the necessary fees (Form 64*). At this time, the personal representative's bond, if required, must be filed with the court (Form 76*). Any person who has an interest in the estate worth more than $1,000, including creditors with claims greater than $1,000, may demand that the personal representative be required to post a bond, or the court may require it (U.P.C. §§ 3–603 and 3–605).

⚖ ASSIGNMENT 13.1

Laurel Shepard, the granddaughter of Maryanna Means, who died intestate, has applied to be informally appointed personal representative (administratrix) of her grandmother's estate. Before submitting the application, she brings it to you, the legal assistant of the attorney who is representing the estate, to be checked. Comment on the following queries that you must bring to the attention of the attorney:

1. Laurel is not sure that she qualifies as an "interested person" because she had seen her grandmother only two or three times before her death.
2. Laurel believes that her priority may be inferior to that of Florence Kingsley, Maryanna's nurse for seventeen years, who had lived with and cared for Maryanna.
3. Laurel has not given notice to Georgina Means, Maryanna's daughter, because she does not know Georgina's address and has not been in contact with her for a long time.
4. Maryanna had resided and died in Lafayette County, Indiana, but left a farm and a bank account in Orange County, California. Laurel does not know if Lafayette County, where she is applying, is the proper place for administration.
5. Laurel thinks her uncle, Jason Means, who lives in Orange County, may have been appointed personal representative. If so, this might present a challenge to her own application.
6. Laurel does not believe that she can affirm the truth of her statements in the application because of the uncertainties stated above.

NOTICE REQUIREMENTS

Informal probate is not supervised by the probate court and does not require that notice be given to interested parties. However, persons having an interest in the estate may file a demand to be notified (Demand for Notice, Form 9*) of the petitioner's application for informal probate or informal appointment (U.P.C. § 3–204). (See the discussion of notice requirements and methods below.) An interested person might be one who has a financial interest in the estate, a previously appointed personal representative who is still acting in that capacity, or someone who occupies a place in the order of priority for appointment (U.P.C. §§ 1–201[24] and 3–203).

Once a demand has been filed, the registrar will notify the personal representative to keep the demandant informed of proceedings related to the estate. If the demandant believes that the applicant is not qualified to be the personal representative, is using a revoked will, or otherwise objects to informal proceed-

*See Appendix A.

ings, the demand for notice ensures an opportunity to request formal or supervised administration when necessary. If the demandant is not given notice of a subsequent order or proceeding, it remains effective. However, the personal representative will be liable for any damages the demandant suffers as a result of the omission of notice (U.P.C. § 3–204).

Notice of Application for Informal Probate

After the registrar accepts the application and grants informal probate and appointment of the personal representative, the petitioner seeking informal probate must give notice as required by U.P.C. § 1–401 of the application for informal probate to any person demanding it pursuant to U.P.C. § 3–204 and Form 61*. No other notice of informal probate is required.

Notice of Application for Informal Appointment

The petitioner seeking informal appointment as personal representative must give notice as required by U.P.C. § 1–401 of the intention to seek an informal appointment to any person who has a financial or property interest and is demanding notice pursuant to U.P.C. § 3–204 and to any person having a prior or equal right to appointment not waived in writing and filed with the court (U.P.C. § 3–310 and Form 61*). No other notice of an informal appointment proceeding is required.

Demand for Notice of Order or Filing

At any time after the death of the decedent any person who has a financial or property interest in a decedent's estate may file a demand with the court for notice of any order or filing relating to that estate (see U.P.C. §§ 3–204, 3–306). The demand for notice must state the name of the decedent, the nature of the demandant's (person making the demand) interest in the estate, and the person's address or that of the attorney representing the person (see Form 9*). The clerk will mail a copy of such demand to the personal representative, if any. After such a demand is filed, no order or filing to which the demand relates can be made or accepted without notice to the demandant or his attorney, as required in U.P.C. § 1–401. If such notice is not given, the order or filing is still valid, but the person receiving the order or making the filing may be liable for any damage caused by the omission of notice.

The notice requirement arising from a demand may be waived in writing by the demandant and will cease when the demandant's interest in the estate terminates. Interested persons are protected by their right to demand prior notice of informal proceedings (see U.P.C. § 3–204) or to contest a requested appointment by use of a formal testacy proceeding, or by use of a formal proceeding seeking the appointment of another person. Interested persons also have available to them the remedies provided in U.P.C. § 3–605 (demand for bond by interested persons) and § 3–607 (order restraining personal representative).

Although not obligated to do so unless a demand has been filed, since publication under U.P.C. § 3–801 is sufficient, the personal representative should give

*See Appendix A.

personal notice to creditors. The Uniform Probate Code allows creditors four months from the date of the first publication of notice to file claims (see U.P.C. §§ 3–801, 3–802, and 3–803). If the estate is still open, the court has the discretion to allow late claims, but can refuse them unless good cause is shown. Once the account of the personal representative is settled, the court cannot allow the claim (see Forms 30*, 61*, and 67*).

Method and Time for Giving Notice

If notice of a hearing on any petition, application, order, or filing is required (except for specific notice requirements as otherwise provided in the U.P.C.), the petitioner or applicant must give notice of the time and place of hearing of any petition, application, order, or filing to any interested person or to her attorney (U.P.C. § 1–401). Again, if requested, the petitioner must give notice in one of three ways:

- By mailing a copy of the notice at least fourteen days *before the time set* for the hearing by certified, registered, or ordinary first class mail addressed to the person being notified at the post office address given in the demand for notice, or at the person's office or place of residence.
- By delivering a copy of the notice to the person being notified personally at least fourteen days before the time set for the hearing.
- If the address, or identity of any person is not known and cannot be ascertained with reasonable diligence, by publishing at least once a week for three consecutive weeks a copy of the notice in a newspaper having general circulation in the county where the hearing is to be held, the last publication of which is to be at least ten days before the time set for the hearing.

For good cause, the court may provide a different method or time of giving notice for any hearing. Prior to or at the hearing, proof of giving the notice and the Affidavit of Mailing Notice must be made and filed (see U.P.C. § 1–401 and Forms 62* and 63*). Any person, including a *guardian ad litem,* conservator, or other fiduciary (see the Glossary), may waive notice by a writing signed by the person or her attorney and filed in the proceeding (see U.P.C. § 1–402).

Notice must be given to every interested person or to one who can bind an interested person, as described in U.P.C. § 1–403. U.P.C. § 1–403 also describes pleading and notice requirements when parties are bound by others.

DUTIES AND POWERS OF THE PERSONAL REPRESENTATIVE IN INFORMAL PROBATE

The greatest responsibility of the personal representative is the proper distribution of the decedent's estate. In a testate administration, the personal representative distributes according to the will and within the bounds of law (e.g., the personal representative pays priority family allowances and debts first). In an intestate administration, the personal representative distributes according to the state statutes of descent and distribution.

The duties and powers of the personal representative in informal probate are outlined generally in U.P.C. §§ 3–701 to 3–721.

---

*See Appendix A.

As a fiduciary, the personal representative must observe the standards of care applicable to fiduciaries (see Chapter 1). Since it is necessary for the personal representative to hold temporary title to assets that belong to others (the devisees or heirs), the personal representative is liable to successors for damage resulting from improper use of power or mishandling estate assets, e.g., selling an asset when there was no need to do so (U.P.C. §§ 3–703, 3–712).

An informally appointed personal representative possessing Letters Testamentary or Letters of Administration needs no further approval before beginning distribution (see Forms 65* and 77*). Only when the personal representative or another interested person requests court supervision of heretofore unsupervised proceedings (the "in and out" feature) does the personal representative have to obtain the court's order to proceed (U.P.C. § 3–704).

Notification to Devisees or Heirs and Creditors

Not later than thirty days following appointment, the personal representative must notify the decedent's devisees or heirs of the appointment (U.P.C. § 3–705). The notice is sent by ordinary mail and must include the name and address of the personal representative, indicate that it is being sent to all persons who have or may have some interest in the estate, indicate whether bond has been filed, and describe the court where papers relating to the estate are on file. This notice is part of the fiduciary obligation, but the personal representative's neglect to give notice will not invalidate the appointment or powers of the office. If it causes loss or damage to a devisee or heir, however, that person has a cause of action for damages against the personal representative for breach of the fiduciary duty (U.P.C. §§ 3–204 and 3–712).

Example: Eula Gribben died intestate in Virginia leaving a small estate. All of her heirs live in Virginia except her son, Lewis, who lives in Delaware. Her brother, Lloyd Adcock, was informally appointed administrator and gave notice to all of the heirs except Lewis. Should Lloyd omit Lewis in the distribution of the estate, Lewis would have a cause of action against Lloyd for the omitted share and possibly for damages if Lloyd's mistake caused him harm (e.g., needless expense of court fees).

The personal representative must also notify creditors of the estate of the appointment by publishing in a general-circulation county newspaper the announcement of the personal representative's appointment. The notice must appear once a week for three successive weeks. Creditors have four months after the date of the first publication to present their claims; otherwise the claims are barred (U.P.C. § 3–801 and Form 67*).

Payment of Creditors' Claims

After the four-month period, the personal representative must pay creditors' claims that are determined to be valid (i.e., are approved). The order in which valid claims are to be paid is found in U.P.C. §§ 3–805 and 3–807. The personal representative has the power to disallow or disqualify claims that creditors have made fraudulently or otherwise unjustly against the estate (U.P.C. § 3–803). The creditors can appeal the personal representative's decision in court.

---

*See Appendix A.

Example: Bertrand Dorn had a credit account with the National Oil Company. Before his death, the company sent him a bill for $48.79. Bertrand disputed this, claiming that he owed only $18.79 according to service station receipts. His personal representative may refuse to pay the $48.79 claim by following U.P.C. procedures for "allowance of claims" (U.P.C. § 3–806).

Inventory Property

Within the time set by state statute, e.g., three to six months after appointment or nine months after the date of the decedent's death, the personal representative must prepare an inventory of all real or personal property owned by the decedent at the time of death and mail it to the surviving spouse and all other interested persons who request it. The personal representative may also file the original copy of the inventory with the court (U.P.C. § 3–706). The inventory must list the assets of the estate with sufficient description for accurate identification, value the assets at fair market value, and include the kind of mortgage or other encumbrance on each item and the amount of that encumbrance (see Form 66*).

The estate assets may be of such a kind that the personal representative is unfamiliar with their fair market value, or the court may order that a third person who has no interest in the estate appraise the estate assets. In either case, the personal representative has permission to hire independent appraisers to assist in valuation, but if they do perform appraisals, the personal representative must list on the inventory their names, their addresses, and the items they valued (U.P.C. § 3–707).

Hold and Manage the Estate

Until discharged or released from the appointment, the personal representative has the same power over the title to the decedent's property as the decedent. The personal representative holds title in a manner similar to that of a trustee in an express trust (see Chapter 9). Both a trustee and the personal representative are given powers and duties that require the exercise of the prudence and restraint expected of a fiduciary for the benefit of others: the trustee for beneficiaries; the personal representative for devisees, heirs, or creditors. The personal representative is liable for loss or damage caused to such persons by improper exercise of these powers. In other words, the personal representative is liable as is a trustee who misuses the power given by the settlor and causes harm to those whom the power was intended to benefit (U.P.C. § 3–712).

Example: Merle Hendricks, the informally appointed personal representative for his father's estate, was given the power of sale by the will. He sells an antique lamp from the estate to his wife at a lower price than he would have asked of a stranger. Merle has violated his fiduciary duty by self-dealing with estate assets (U.P.C. § 3–713).

Final Account and Closing the Estate

After the minimum time period for closing an estate has passed and all approved creditor claims have been paid, the personal representative must prepare and file

---

*See Appendix A.

the final account. It consists of a listing of the decedent's probate assets, showing any increases or decreases in the assets; the payment of creditors' claims; administration expenses; funeral and last illness expenses; taxes; and the balance of assets on hand for distribution. Only after a copy of the final account has been given to every distributee of the estate can the personal representative distribute the remaining assets to the persons entitled to receive them and seek a discharge (termination) from office.

An informally appointed personal representative may choose to close the estate informally and be discharged by signing a sworn **closing statement** (affidavit) to the effect that he believes the estate's assets have been distributed correctly and its business transacted (see Form 70*). The personal representative may use this method if the administration has not been continuously supervised by the court. In the case of continuous supervision, the U.P.C. demands a final account and formal closing, as described in detail in Chapter 12, by either of the methods described in U.P.C. §§ 3–1001, 3–1003, and 3–505 or 3–1002 (see Forms 39* and 48*).

Closing statement
An affidavit signed by the personal representative at the end of informal probate proceedings to close the estate and to be discharged.

The personal representative's sworn closing statement informally closing the estate must verify the following:

- That a notice to creditors was published more than six months before the date of the present statement.
- That the personal representative has fully administered the estate, paying all federal and state taxes due on it and claims against it (including creditors' and successors' claims), and that the assets of the estate have been distributed to the persons entitled. If the personal representative has not completed distribution, the reasons for partial distribution must be explained in the closing statement.
- That the personal representative has mailed a copy of this closing statement to all of the claimants (creditors) who have made themselves known and to all distributees of the estate (see U.P.C. § 3–1003). Once copies have been mailed, the original "Statement to Close" is filed with the probate court.

The time periods creditors have to assert and present claims include the following:

- Under U.P.C. § 3–803, all claims against a decedent's estate that arose before the decedent's death are barred against the estate, the personal representative, and the heirs and devisees of the decedent unless presented within four months after the date of the first publication of notice to creditors if notice is given in compliance with U.P.C. § 3–801, or within three years after the decedent's death, if notice to creditors has not been published.
- Under U.P.C. § 3–1005, the rights of all creditors whose claims have not been previously barred against the personal representative for breach of fiduciary duty (see U.P.C. § 3–803 above) are barred unless a proceeding to assert the claim is commenced within six months after the filing of the personal representative's *closing statement*. Creditors do, however, have the right to recover from a personal representative for fraud or inadequate disclosure related to the settlement of the decedent's estate.
- Under U.P.C. § 3–1006, the claim of a creditor, heir, or devisee of a decedent for recovery of property or the property's value from a distributee of improperly

---

*See Appendix A.

distributed property is forever barred at the later of three years after the decedent's death or one year after the time of distribution of the property. This section does not bar an action to recover property or its value due to fraud.

If a personal representative has distributed the assets of the estate to other claimants, e.g., devisees, heirs, or other creditors, a creditor with a valid but undischarged claim must press the claim in a judicial proceeding against one or more of those who received the assets (U.P.C. § 3–1004).

Example: Annelise Frechette closes her mother's estate informally by filing a sworn statement with the probate court. Two months afterward, the owner of a gift shop who had not been given notice presents a bill for some items that Annelise's mother had bought on credit. Annelise is personally liable to the creditor for not having given him notice as she had given the other creditors. The creditor can obtain payment of the bill by initiating a judicial proceeding against Annelise or any distributee, but the creditor cannot collect from both. If the creditor obtains a judgment and payment from Corinee Mays, one of the five distributees, then Corinee may demand of the other four distributees, who were given notice of the creditor's claim and pending litigation, four fifths of the amount that she had to pay so that all will bear the burden equally.

If no proceedings involving the personal representative are pending in the court one year after the closing statement is filed, the personal representative's authority is terminated (U.P.C. § 3–1003). Termination does not automatically accompany closing. The authority of the personal representative remains active for one year. Once the authority is terminated, the personal representative has no power to conduct affairs in the name of the estate. The U.P.C. provides the one-year grace period between closing and termination for the resolution of unforeseen business, such as that in the preceding example.

It is important that the personal representative obtain receipts or evidence of payment for everything distributed from the estate whether or not he has decided to close the estate under one of the methods described in U.P.C. § 3–1001 through § 3–1003. (*Note:* it is legitimate but impractical not to close the estate at all but simply to rely on the receipts collected to show that the estate has been fully distributed. Relying on receipts affords no protection to the personal representative should complications arise.) Collecting and retaining receipts enables the personal representative to reinforce the closing statement or the request that the court formally close the estate. Alternatively, the personal representative may obtain from each distributee an affidavit reciting that each received the correct amount.

After the estate has been closed and the personal representative discharged, someone may discover additional omitted property belonging to the decedent that has not been administered (e.g., rare books, to which the will referred but which could not be located during administration). Proper disposition of those assets will necessitate reopening the estate.

STEP-BY-STEP PROCEDURES IN INFORMAL PROBATE

The following case study describes a small estate that could conveniently be administered through the use of the U.P.C. informal probate procedures by an informally appointed personal representative. Follow the personal representative step by step through the informal procedures. As a further review of informal probate procedures, three Case Problems, with appropriate forms and/or questions, are included.

Case Study

Elvira Krueger died testate on February 4, 1995, in a state that has adopted the Uniform Probate Code. Elvira left a son, Ralph, a daughter, Sara, and a daughter, Christa, none of whom are minors. Elvira's husband predeceased her. Elvira owned property valued at $16,500 at the time of her death: household furniture and goods valued at $12,500, a few pieces of antique furniture valued at $2,000, an automobile valued at $1,400, and a tent trailer for camping valued at $600. In her will, Elvira appointed her daughter, Sara, personal representative (executrix) of her estate and directed that the estate assets be distributed as follows: "the automobile and tent trailer to my son, Ralph; the antique furniture to my daughter, Sara; and the household furniture and goods to be sold and the proceeds to be distributed to my three children, Ralph, Sara, and Christa so that each of them will receive an amount of my property equal to that of the others." Sara later sells the household furniture and goods for $12,500.

Under the terms of the will, Sara must distribute the antique furniture (valued at $2,000) and $3,500 cash to herself (total—$5,500), $5,500 cash to Christa, and the automobile (valued at $1,400), the tent trailer (valued at $600), and $3,500 cash to Ralph. These devises, however, will be reduced by expenses and debts that must first be paid out of the estate assets.

Informal Procedures to Be Utilized by Sara

Sara will file an application with the registrar requesting both informal probate of her mother's will and informal appointment of herself as personal representative (executrix). She must verify that the application is accurate and complete to the best of her knowledge and belief. The application must set forth information regarding Sara's interest in the estate and identifying the decedent (U.P.C. § 3–301). Since Elvira resided in the state in which Sara is applying for informal appointment, Sara must wait 120 hours (five days) after Elvira's death before the registrar will finalize her appointment.

| File application |

Sara must give notice of the application for informal probate and appointment by one of the methods specified by U.P.C. § 1–401 to (1) any interested person who has filed a written demand with the clerk pursuant to U.P.C. § 3–204; (2) any personal representative of the decedent whose appointment has not been terminated; and (3) any interested person who has a prior or equal right to appointment that has not been waived in writing and filed with the court (U.P.C. §§ 3–306 and 3–310).

| Notice |

Both Ralph and Christa have filed demands for notice with the court. Therefore, Sara must give notice of the application to her sister and brother. The validity of an order that is issued or a filing that is accepted without notice to Ralph or Christa will not be affected by the lack of notice, but Sara may be liable for any damage caused to either of them by the absence of notice (U.P.C. § 3–204).

Example: Christa filed with the court a demand for notice according to U.P.C. § 3–204, stating her interest in Elvira's estate (devisee) and her own name and address. Sara, the personal representative, finds it necessary to use the money from the sale of Elvira's household goods to pay creditors and obtains a court order permitting her to do this. Christa's share in the proceeds of the sale is therefore reduced, but in anticipation of the share of cash she was to receive originally, she had negotiated a bank loan. If Sara fails to notify her of the order permitting payment of creditors so that Christa is damaged by not being able to repay the loan, Christa will have a cause of action against Sara.

Application for appointment

On receiving Sara's application and making the findings required by U.P.C. § 3–303, the registrar will issue a Written Statement of Informal Probate. The informal probate will be conclusive on all persons unless the probate court, upon petition of an interested party, issues a superseding order changing the estate administration to a formal testacy proceeding. Defects in Sara's application or in procedures followed in informally probating her mother's will do not by themselves render the probate void (U.P.C. § 3–302).

Appointment of personal representative

When the registrar approves Sara's application for informal probate and appointment as personal representative, she must qualify and file her acceptance pursuant to U.P.C. §§ 3–307, 3–601 and 3–602. Once the registrar issues the Letters of Appointment (Letters Testamentary or Letters of Administration) (U.P.C. § 1–305), Sara will have all the powers and be entitled to perform all the duties pertaining to her office pursuant to U.P.C. Article 3, Part 7.

Bond

As an informally appointed general personal representative, Sara will not have to file a bond. She would be required to post a bond if it is demanded by any interested party, e.g., a creditor or devisee, having an interest in the estate exceeding $1,000, or if the will had required her to file a bond, or if she had been appointed special administratrix (see Chapter 11) (U.P.C. §§ 3–603, 3–605). The person who demands a bond must file a written request with the court (U.P.C. §§ 3–603, 3–604, 3–605, and 3–606). For example, if Ralph files a written demand for a bond with the court, the registrar will mail a copy of the demand for a bond to Sara. Sara must then obtain a bond and file it with the court unless the court determines in formal proceedings that a bond is unnecessary or that Sara had deposited cash or collateral with an agency of the state to secure performance of her duties (U.P.C. §§ 3–603, 3–605).

If the registrar is satisfied that Elvira had complied with the requirements for executing a will pursuant to U.P.C. § 2–502, e.g., that the will contains the required signatures of two witnesses and attestation clause, the registrar will allow the proceedings to continue without further proof. The registrar may assume execution if the will appears to have been properly executed or may accept an affidavit (sworn statement) of any person having knowledge of the circumstances of execution, whether or not that person actually witnessed the will (U.P.C. § 3–303[c]).

Acceptance of application

Elvira's will contained signatures of two competent witnesses (her brother and aunt) and a proper attestation clause. The registrar approved Sara's application for informal probate and appointment. If for any reason the registrar had decided that the will should not be admitted to probate or that the informal appointment should be denied, the application would have been denied. In that case, if the estate is to be administered, Sara would be required to initiate formal probate proceedings (U.P.C. §§ 3–305 and 3–309).

Sara is now officially Elvira's personal representative, possessing the powers (e.g., to distribute the assets according to the will) and duties (e.g., to pay creditors before devisees) of a general representative (U.P.C. § 3–307[b]). Her appointment can be terminated, either voluntarily or by court order, at any time during administration of the estate. Sara's death, disability (such as being declared legally insane), or resignation would terminate her office. She might be removed by court order after a hearing initiated by a person interested in the estate (U.P.C. §§ 3–608 through 3–612).

Example: Marston Keefe, a creditor of Elvira, believes that Sara should be removed from office for failing to pay his claim against the estate. Pursuant to U.P.C. § 3–611, he files with the court a petition for a hearing seeking her removal. The court arranges a hearing at which Sara must appear to defend her action. If the court decides that she has abused the power of a personal representative, it may direct that Sara be removed and someone else appointed to the position. If it so decides, the court may also regulate the disposition of assets remaining in the estate until the successor in office takes charge.

Sara must inform the heirs and devisees, Ralph and Christa, of her appointment by personal delivery or first class mail not later than thirty days after the appointment. Her failure to do this constitutes a breach of her fiduciary duty but does not render invalid her acts as personal representative (U.P.C. § 3–705).

Within three months after her appointment, Sara must prepare and file with the court either by mail or in person an inventory of all property owned by Elvira at the time of her death. The inventory must list all assets with reasonable detail and indicate, for each listed item, its fair market value at the date of her mother's death and the type and amount of all encumbrances against any item (U.P.C. § 3–706). Sara herself is allowed to appoint appraisers without the approval of the court, but that appointment may be challenged by an interested party as provided by U.P.C. § 3–607. Sara must send a copy of the inventory to interested persons who have requested it (U.P.C. § 3–706). She must also file the original with the court.

> **Inventory**

A personal representative owes a fiduciary duty to the devisees comparable to that of a trustee and is not permitted to engage in "self-dealing," i.e., dealing for one's own benefit (U.P.C. § 3–713).

Example: Sara appraised the fair market value of a grand piano at $1,500 and decided that she would purchase it from the estate. Ralph and Christa objected, asserting the fair market value of the piano was at least $5,000. Ralph petitioned the probate court to issue an order restraining Sara from purchasing the piano and ordering an independent appraisal, pursuant to U.P.C. § 3–607. The court issued an order temporarily prohibiting Sara from proceeding with the purchase and notified both of them of a hearing on the matter to take place within ten days. At the hearing, the court will decide if Sara's course of action is unfair to the interests of the petitioner or the estate, as it might be if, for example, the independent appraiser had valued the piano substantially above $1,500. If so, the court will then issue an order permanently restraining Sara's action.

Sara would be liable to Ralph and Christa for any damage or loss resulting from any breach of her fiduciary duty to the same extent as a trustee of an express trust.

If Sara had bought the piano from the estate for $1,500 instead of its fair market value, i.e., $5,000, the estate would suffer because less money would result from the sale of the household goods and furnishings and therefore less would be available to pay Elvira's creditors or to be distributed to her devisees. According to law, creditors are the first to be paid from nonspecific or general devises, e.g., the sale proceeds (money). If Elvira left many expenses, these expenses might consume much of the general devise, leaving little for Ralph or Christa (U.P.C. § 3–712).

Example: Suppose the sale of household goods brings $7,500 to the estate. If Elvira's bills total $7,600, all of which must be paid from the estate's assets, the

$7,500 will have to be apportioned among the creditors. They will receive a percentage of what Elvira had owed them. Any of the creditors would have a cause of action against Sara, who caused the total to be smaller by undervaluing the piano.

Elvira specified in her will that Sara would not receive any compensation for her services as personal representative, but nothing was mentioned about payment of creditors' claims, funeral expenses, and the like. Elvira had hospitalization and medical insurance that paid all the expenses of her last illness except for $300 to her doctor and $735 to the hospital. She also owed $90 to a local department store for clothing she had purchased. There was no provision in the will for payment of these obligations or for payment of funeral expenses ($1,800) or expenses of administration, such as filing fees ($75). Since the funeral and administration expenses have priority, Sara must pay these bills before the other debts (U.P.C. § 3–805).

Since none of Elvira's three children are minors or dependent children, U.P.C. § 2–402 (homestead allowance) and U.P.C. § 2–404 (family allowance) are not applicable to her estate. The three children, however, are entitled to share the $10,000 exempt property allowance (U.P.C. § 2–403). Together they are entitled to a sum not exceeding $10,000 in the form of household furniture, automobiles, furnishings, appliances, and personal effects, except for the portion of these chattels owned by creditors with security interests, e.g., an unpaid car dealer who sold the decedent a car on an installment payment plan.

Example: Two months prior to her death, Elvira had bought a $900 stove from an appliance dealer. She agreed to make a down payment and pay $25 per month plus interest. The dealer was to retain title to the stove as a security interest until Elvira had finished paying for it. At the time of her death, she had paid $150 toward the purchase price. Under the terms of the contract, the dealer could repossess the stove if Elvira died before completing the payments. Therefore, the stove is not available as part of the exempt property. The children's rights to the exempt property have priority over all claims against the estate. Homestead and family allowances, however, are not applicable in this case because there is no surviving spouse or minor children. Elvira's estate has sufficient assets, after distributing the exempt property ($10,000) to Sara, Ralph, and Christa, to pay debts, expenses of a last illness, and expenses of administration. Therefore, Sara will distribute the assets of her mother's estate as follows:

Exempt property (to be shared by Sara, Ralph, and Christa)	$10,000
Funeral expenses	1,800
Administration expenses	75
Doctor	300
Hospital	735
Department store	90
Total prior obligations	$13,000
Value of all estate assets	16,500
Less prior obligations	13,000
	$3,500

After prior obligations are accounted for, $3,500 in estate assets remain. Sara will add that amount to the $10,000 exempt property to determine the shares of the three children.

$$\begin{array}{r} \$10,000 \\ +3,500 \\ \hline \$13,500 \end{array} \div\ 3\ =\ \$4,500$$

Each child is entitled to estate assets valued at $4,500. The children will receive less than Sara had determined prior to consideration of debts and expenses. Originally, each child would have received estate assets and/or cash valued at $5,500. After payment of debts and expenses, each child is entitled to receive estate assets and/or cash valued at $4,500.

Therefore, Sara may distribute the assets of Elvira's estate to Ralph, Christa, and herself as follows:

Sara		Ralph		Christa	
Antique furniture	$2,000	Automobile	$1,400	Cash	$4,500
Cash	2,500	Tent trailer	600		
Total	$4,500	Cash	2,500	*Total*	$4,500
		Total	$4,500		

Asset distribution

Sara must make the distribution expeditiously and may do so without order by the court (U.P.C. § 3–704). Ralph, Christa, Sara (the distributees of the estate), and Elvira's creditors take the property subject to the proviso that they return it to the personal representative should some unexpected event occur (U.P.C. § 3–909). This section of the U.P.C. protects the personal representative from unjustified litigation by distributees. The personal representative is liable, however, for improper distribution or payment of claims (U.P.C. §§ 3–703, 3–712, and 3–808).

Example: If Sara had overlooked the hospital bill ($735) and therefore paid $245 more to each devisee, each devisee (including herself) would be responsible for returning his or her share of the money improperly paid plus one-third of the interest that would have accrued on $735 from the date of distribution to the present date. The reason for the payment of interest is that the creditor does not have the use of the money until later (when it would be supposedly less valuable than earlier), so interest is added.

Persons who purchase from the distributees are also protected (U.P.C. § 3–910). Sara will execute instruments or deeds of distribution transferring or releasing the antique furniture, automobile, and the tent trailer to Ralph and herself as evidence of their respective titles to these assets (U.P.C. § 3–907).

Having completed the distribution of estate assets, Sara's last duty is to close the estate (wind up its affairs) in one of two ways:

Closing the estate

- Formally, by petitioning the court to declare that the estate has been settled fully in regard to all persons interested in it. This method protects the estate against potential danger from details overlooked by the personal representative, e.g., the payment of inheritance taxes, because it avails the estate of the court's experience (U.P.C. § 3–1001).
- Informally, by filing a sworn closing statement with the court in which Sara gives her word that she has completed every detail of the administration.

If Sara chooses to close her administration by filing a closing statement with the court, she need not file a formal accounting with the court. She must, however, furnish Ralph and Christa and other interested parties with a full account in writing, together with a copy of the closing statement filed with the court (U.P.C. §§ 3–1001, 3–1002, and 3–1003).

Sara chose to close the estate by filing a closing statement with the court pursuant to U.P.C. § 3–1003. No earlier than six months after the date of her original appointment, she must file a verified statement asserting that she has (1) published notice to creditors and that the first publication occurred more than six months prior to the date of the present statement; (2) fully administered her mother's estate by making payment, settlement, or other disposition of all claims presented, paying expenses of administration and estate, inheritance, and other death taxes, except as specified in the statement, and distributing the assets of the estate to the persons entitled; and (3) sent a copy of the closing statement to all the distributees of the estate and to all creditors or other claimants of whom she is aware whose claims are neither paid nor barred, and has furnished a full account in writing of her administration to the distributees (U.P.C. § 3–1003).

If no proceedings involving Sara are pending in court one year after the closing statement is filed, her authority (appointment) terminates. An order closing an estate under U.P.C. § 3–1001 or 3–1002 would terminate Sara's appointment. Her closing statement under U.P.C. § 3–1003 would not terminate the appointment, however, because the statement is an affirmation by Sara that she believes the affairs of the estate are completed. Any creditor not paid whose claim has not been barred by the time limit can assert that claim against the distributees, i.e., Sara, Ralph, and Christa (U.P.C. § 3–1004).

Example: When Sara was appointed, she published a notice to creditors in accordance with U.P.C. § 3–801. Several creditors presented claims within the period allowed for presentation, and Sara paid all except the $90 clothing bill from a local store. The store may obtain payment, even though Sara has filed a closing statement, by demanding $90 from one of the three distributees. That distributee is then entitled to demand $30 from each of the other distributees so that each will have contributed an equal amount. Sara can also be sued pursuant to U.P.C. § 3–608 for actions that she performed before the termination of her appointment. Under U.P.C. § 3–610(a), her authority ends one year after she has filed the closing statement. Even after termination, Sara remains liable to a lawsuit unless the applicable statute of limitations has run or unless her administration has been terminated by an adjudication settling her accounts (U.P.C. § 3–1005).

Example: Before giving the automobile to Ralph as Elvira had directed in her will, Sara used it for her personal convenience. She was involved in a collision resulting in $1,000 damage to the automobile. Because this occurred while Sara was the personal representative of the estate, Ralph may sue her for having failed to exercise due care with respect to one of the estate's assets during or within six months after the termination of her administration.

Suits against Sara by successors of the will and creditors for breach of her fiduciary duty are barred unless begun within six months after Sara filed the closing statement. Rights of successors and creditors to recover for fraud, misrepresentation, or inadequate disclosure are not barred by the six-month limitation (U.P.C. §§ 3–1005, 3–807, and 3–808).

Using a closing statement offers Sara more protection than if she had relied merely on the receipts collected to show that the estate has been fully distributed.

Sections 3–1001, 3–1002, and 3–1003 of the Uniform Probate Code provide for judicial proceedings for closing by which Sara could gain protection from all interested persons or from Ralph and Christa, the other devisees (successors), only. Section 3–703 of the U.P.C. provides very limited protection for a personal representative who relies only on receipts. These sections afford protection to the personal representative for acts or distributions that were authorized when done but that became doubtful because of a later change in testacy status. There is no protection against later claims of breach of fiduciary obligation except for those arising from consent or waiver of individual distributees who may have bound themselves by receipts given to the personal representative. In addition, the closing statement method provides notice to third persons that Sara's authority has terminated, whereas reliance on receipts alone does not. The closing statement method provides a useful means of closing small, uncomplicated estates where the distributees are all members of the family and disputes are unlikely.

🏛 ASSIGNMENT 13.2

1. Make a list of and obtain all the forms Sara would use in administering her mother's estate according to the Uniform Probate Code. Fill in the forms after reviewing Case Problem 2 (see page 471).

2. Suppose that six months before Sara filed the closing statement Christa found a will that devised all Elvira's property to Christa. The will was executed by Elvira at a date later than the probated will. What should Christa do?

3. Would distribution of the assets of Elvira's estate have been different if Christa had been a minor at the time of her mother's death? If so, how? Suppose Elvira in her will had appointed neither a personal guardian nor a property guardian for Christa. How would the guardianship be determined?

4. Ralph claims that he, not Sara, should be appointed personal representative because he is the oldest of the children and thus has a higher priority. Should he petition the court to remove Sara and appoint himself on these grounds?

5. In her inventory, Sara omits a living-room chair valued at $50. If she discovers the error but neglects to file an amended inventory, what might be the consequence?

6. Before her death, Elvira had begun to negotiate the sale of the automobile to Moira Byrne, but they had not agreed on a purchase price. Sara completes the sale at a price of $1,350 intending to give the money, instead of the automobile, to Ralph. Has Sara breached her fiduciary duty?

7. Sara discovers a policy of insurance on Elvira's life that Elvira had taken out twenty-five years ago and that was not mentioned in the will. Should Sara record the value of this policy in her inventory of estate assets? May she use the proceeds to pay Elvira's creditors? The beneficiary of the policy is Elvira's estate.

8. Elvira had opened a charge account at a local department store. Prior to her death she had charged but had not yet paid for $50 worth of merchandise. The credit manager of the store wants to be sure that Sara will not overlook or disallow the claim. Could he demand that Sara be bonded to ensure against loss to the store?

9. The registrar declines to issue an order of informal probate because the registrar doubts that Elvira's signature on the will is genuine. One of the witnesses to the will is deceased, and the other cannot be located. How could Sara have the will admitted to probate? Could she still follow informal procedures as planned?

KEY TERM

Closing statement

REVIEW QUESTIONS

1. According to your state statute, who has top priority to be appointed the personal representative of a testator's estate? Of an intestate's estate?

2. What function does a registrar or surrogate perform in an informal or common probate administration?

3. How do informal probate procedures differ in testate versus intestate cases?

4. Under what circumstances can a registrar reject an application for informal probate proceedings? If the registrar denies an application, what results?

5. Since informal probate procedures are not supervised by the court and do not require that notice be given, what rights and procedural steps are available to creditors?

6. Explain what is meant by the Uniform Probate Code's "in and out" feature available for those using informal probate proceedings.

7. Must an inventory be prepared in informal probate? If required, to whom must the inventory be given?

8. Using informal probate, how is an estate administration closed?

9. In informal probate, what time limits are placed upon creditors for claims against the decedent's estate and the personal representative for breach of fiduciary duty?

10. In informal probate, when does the personal representative's authority officially terminate?

CASE PROBLEMS

Problem 1

Carl Bergmeister dies intestate on September 19, 1995, leaving outstanding assets valued at $322,800:

Homestead	$ 88,000
Furniture and household items	16,000
Shares of stock in Alcoa Aluminum	62,000
One-half interest in an apartment building held in tenancy in common (building valued at $250,000)	125,000
Two Miro paintings	28,000
1986 automobile	3,800
Total	$322,800

Several relatives survive Carl: Jenneille Bergmeister, wife; Naomi Bergmeister, daughter; Scott Bergmeister, son, who is a minor; David Bergmeister, son from a previous marriage; Carolyn Bergmeister, mother; Gustaf Bergmeister, father; Nora Stark, sister; Robin Stark, niece (daughter of Nora); Jarod Harrison, brother-in-law (wife's brother); and Verlayne Sather, first cousin.

Suppose that Naomi Bergmeister, Carl's daughter, makes an application for informal appointment of herself in intestacy pursuant to U.P.C. § 3–301.

A. Who has priority for such an appointment?

B. If someone else having priority over Naomi is an invalid and does not feel capable of assuming the duties of administering Carl's estate, could that person decline the appointment? How can the priority be waived?

C. What steps must Naomi take to assure her own informal appointment? What forms would she use?

Assume that Naomi is appointed personal representative.

A. Describe the steps she will take in administering, distributing, and closing her father's estate. Use the informal methods you think most appropriate.

B. Make a list of and fill in all forms Naomi will use. Assume that prior to his death on September 19, 1995, Carl earned $30,000 from his employment and $8,000 from dividends on his stock and that accrued but unpaid dividends amounted to $1,000. Assume also that a $10,000 mortgage exists on the homestead; funeral expenses were $3,500; expenses for Carl's last illness were $270 to his doctor and $420 to the hospital; and Carl owed $4,200 to a contractor for repairs on the homestead.

C. It must also be determined whether federal or state estate and/or inheritance taxes must be paid. Read Chapter 14 and obtain and complete the necessary tax forms for the Bergmeister estate, including the decedent's final income tax return and the fiduciary income tax return for income earned by the estate

With regard to handling the real property owned by Carl at his death, Naomi should consider U.P.C. § 3–715, especially subparagraphs 3, 6, 7, 8, 9, 10, 11, 15, 18, and 23, which discuss the transactions authorized for a personal representative, especially those relating to land transactions. She must also consult the probate court of the county where Carl's land is located (if different from the county of his domicile) to see if there are local laws pertaining to real estate transactions (e.g., that the personal representative must obtain the court's permission to sell, mortgage, or lease real estate, and that the personal representative must wait a certain number of days before finalizing such transactions).

How will Naomi convey real property to heirs entitled to it—by deed or otherwise?

Assume that David Bergmeister, Carl's son by a previous marriage, files a petition with the probate court for *formal* appointment of a personal representative because he is dissatisfied with Naomi's appointment. What will be the result? Could Naomi still exercise her powers while the formal proceeding is pending (see U.P.C. § 3–401)?

What documents, if any, should Naomi file in order to convey a clear marketable title to the successors?

Problem 2

Cheryl Ann Kennedy died testate on August 1, 1994, at 1010 Willow Street in Hennepin County, Minneapolis, Minnesota 55409. She was born January 13, 1960, in Minneapolis, Minnesota.

Cheryl's successors include her husband, Charles; two twin daughters, Cherry and Cindy; three sons, Carl, Corey, and Christopher; her mother, Catherine Kelly; and one sister, Karen Kelly. The ages of the family members are Charles, 34, Cherry and Cindy, the twins, age 3, Carl is 5, Corey is 9, Christopher is 10, Catherine Kelly is 60, and Karen Kelly is 38. All members of the family live at 1010 Willow Street.

Cheryl's estate included the following assets:

- A home, the family residence, owned by Cheryl before her marriage and still recorded in her name only, valued at $95,000.
- A summer cottage in joint tenancy with Charles, given to Cheryl and Charles by Cheryl's father, valued at $35,000.
- A savings and a checking account in joint tenancy with Charles with a total value of $10,000.
- One thousand shares of Execo stock in joint tenancy with Charles worth $12,000.
- Fifty shares of Users, Inc., stock left to Cheryl by her father, worth $2,000 in her name only.

- A car (1990 Ford) worth $5,500 in her name.
- A life insurance burial policy payable to Charles with a face value of $5,000.
- A diamond ring worth $1,500.
- A mink coat worth $4,000.
- Household goods worth $5,000.
- Other personal property worth $300.
- Clothing worth $200.

The only debt Cheryl owed was $110 for two wigs purchased from Beauty Products, Inc.

Except for the diamond ring, which was left to her sister, Karen, Cheryl's will stated that all of her estate should go to her husband, Charles, if he survived her, and if not, to her children in equal shares. The will names Charles personal representative–executor and was executed on November 21, 1988. Charles hires an attorney, Susan Brown, 1400 Main Street, Minneapolis, Minnesota 55455, to help with the estate administration.

For the informal, unsupervised probate administration of Cheryl's will, the following forms must be executed. Review them in Appendix A.

1. Application for Informal Probate of Will and for Informal Appointment of Personal Representative (Executor) (Form 57*).
2. Testimony of Subscribing Witness to Will (not executed; see Form 8*).
3. Statement of Informal Probate of Will and Order of Informal Appointment of Personal Representative–Executor (Form 60*).
4. Notice of Informal Probate of Will and Appointment of Personal Representative and Notice to Creditors (Form 61*).
5. Proof of Placing Order for Publication (Form 62*).
6. Proof (Affidavit) of Publication, often provided to registrar by publisher (not executed; see Form 6*).
7. Affidavit of Mailing Notice of Informal Probate of Will (Form 63*).
8. Statutory Notice of Rights of Surviving Spouse and/or Minor Children (reverse side of Form 63*).
9. Acceptance of Appointment and Oath by Individual (Form 64*).
10. Bond, if required (not executed; see Form 76*).
11. Letters Testamentary (Form 65*).
12. Inventory and Appraisal (Form 66*).
13. Written Statement of Claim (Form 67*).
14. Final Account (not executed; see Form 39*).

---

*See Appendix A.

15. Informal Deed of Distribution by Personal Representative (Form 68*).
16. Receipt for Assets by Distributee (Form 69*).
17. Informal Administration: Personal Representative's Statement to Close Estate (Closing Statement) (Form 70*).

Problem 3

All the facts in the Cheryl Kennedy case, including the assets and liabilities listed, are the same, except in this instance Cheryl died intestate. The forms that must be executed for the informal probate administration of Cheryl's estate in Minnesota are the following:

1. Application for Informal Appointment of Administrator (Form 71*).
2. Order and Notice of Informal Appointment of Personal Representative and Notice to Creditors (Form 72*).
3. Proof of Placing Order for Publication (Form 73*).
4. Proof (Affidavit) of Publication, often provided to registrar by publisher (not executed, see Form 6*).
5. Affidavit of Mailing Notice of Informal Appointment (Form 74*).
6. Statutory Notice of Rights of Surviving Spouse and/or Minor Children (reverse side of Form 74*).

7. Acceptance of Appointment and Oath by Individual (Form 75*).
8. Bond, if required (Form 76*).
9. Letters of General Administration (Form 77*).
10. Inventory and Appraisal (Form 66*).
11. Written Statement of Claim (Form 67*).
12. Final Account (not executed; see Form 39*).
13. Informal Deed of Distribution by Personal Representative (Form 78*).
14. Receipt for Assets by Distributee (Form 79*).
15. Informal Administration: Personal Representative's Statement to Close Estate (closing statement) (Form 70*).
16. Application for Certificate from Registrar—Application for Release of Bond (Form 80*).
17. Certificate of Registrar—Release of Bond (Form 81*).
A. Review the forms that must be executed in Case Problem 3, the Cheryl Ann Kennedy intestate case. Identify and complete the forms required for the probate administration of her estate if Cheryl had died intestate in your state. Compare your executed forms with those in Appendix A.

---

*See Appendix A.

CHAPTER FOURTEEN

TAX CONSIDERATIONS IN THE ADMINISTRATION OF ESTATES

OBJECTIVES

After completing this chapter, you should be able to:

- Distinguish and identify the different kinds of income and death taxes that must be paid.
- Understand and explain various ways to transfer assets while alive in order to lessen the amount of taxes owed to the state and federal governments by a decedent's estate.
- Understand the tax consequences for gifts and estates created by the 1976 Tax Reform Act and substantially amended by the 1981 Economic Recovery Tax Act and the 1986 Tax Reform Act.
- Prepare the tax returns of a decedent's estate.

OUTLINE

SCOPE OF THE CHAPTER

Although the personal representative and the attorney have the ultimate responsibility for probating an estate properly and promptly, as the paralegal assisting the attorney, you must also be knowledgeable about legal and procedural matters applicable to estate administration, including the tax consequences to the estate of the decedent. If you intend to specialize in estate administration, you will need to acquire an extensive knowledge of tax laws and procedures. Appropriate steps must be taken to ensure familiarity with all currently applicable federal and state tax laws. Federal and state statutes must be checked to see if they have been repealed or amended, or if new statutes have been enacted. Good sources for current federal tax laws are the Prentice-Hall and the Commerce Clearing House (CCH) loose-leaf tax services as well as the updated IRS Publication 448, *Federal Estate and Gift Taxes*, and state publications. *You will need to consult with other professionals, i.e., the attorney and an accountant, who are current on tax laws and the preparation of tax returns.*

> **ETHICAL ISSUE**

This chapter provides a foundation for understanding tax considerations in the administration of estates. For purposes of illustration, it incorporates the basic materials used in the preparation of federal tax returns and some state death tax returns. State tax forms vary substantially. You must familiarize yourself with your own state's forms and tax law. The forms mentioned appear in Appendix A.

The first part of this chapter provides an introduction to tax concerns; an overview of the tax changes brought about by the 1976 Tax Reform Act, the 1981 Economic Recovery Tax Act, and the 1986 Tax Reform Act; and a discussion of such tax considerations as the unified credit, the unified transfer gift and estate tax, the marital deduction, trusts, lifetime gifts, and generation-skipping transfers. Next, the tax returns themselves are discussed, including the decedent's final income tax returns, federal and state; the fiduciary's income tax returns, federal and state; the gift tax returns, federal and state; the estate tax returns, federal and state; and the state inheritance tax return.

INTRODUCTION TO TAX CONCERNS

The federal government and many state governments levy and collect taxes on income. The income subject to such tax includes personal income, corporate income, and trust income, which is a form of personal income. It is the duty of the personal representative of the decedent's estate to file the decedent's personal income tax returns for the decedent's year of death and to see that any income tax owed the federal and state governments is paid out of estate assets. In addition, the personal representative must file federal and state income tax returns for any income that accrues or is earned after the decedent's death until the close of the taxable year or until the date of final distribution of the estate. These tax returns are called U.S. or state fiduciary income tax returns.

Successor
An all-inclusive U.P.C. term meaning any person, other than a creditor, who is entitled to real or personal property of a decedent either under the will or through intestate succession.

Death taxes are measured by the amount of property transferred at death. There are two kinds of death taxes: estate taxes and inheritance taxes.

The estate tax is a tax levied on the privilege of transferring property at death. This tax is levied on the estate itself, not on the **successors.** The rate and amount of the estate tax are determined by the size of the estate; like the income tax, the estate tax is progressive, i.e., the larger the estate, the higher the tax rate. At the present time, the federal estate tax rate ranges from 18 percent to 55 percent.

Generally, state estate taxes are imposed in an amount equal to the credit allowable under the federal estate tax law. Currently, five states have both a credit estate tax and an estate tax (see Exhibit 14.1).

A state inheritance or succession tax is levied on the privilege of receiving property from a decedent at death. The rate or amount of this tax is determined by state law and depends on the amount of the share of the decedent's estate received by a particular successor and on the relationship of the successor to the decedent. It is also a progressive tax. Seventeen states impose an inheritance tax on successors (see Exhibit 14.1). Individual state statutes must be checked.

A gift tax is a tax levied on the privilege of transferring property during life. This is a tax on the donor, not on the donee. The federal gift tax rate is the same schedule used for the federal estate tax. The state gift taxes generally follow the rates and exemptions prescribed under the state inheritance statutes.

The federal government imposes an estate tax and gift tax but no inheritance tax. States usually have either an estate tax, an inheritance tax, a gift tax, or some combination of the three. The federal and state estate, gift, and inheritance tax statutes require the personal representative to file the appropriate tax returns by a prescribed time, unless he has filed an Application for Extension of Time to File with the appropriate agencies. These statutes also require the personal representative to pay the tax due within the prescribed time. Generally, extensions of time to file do not extend the time to pay taxes, which are due by the regular due date. Extensions may be allowed in certain cases where reasonable cause can be shown. *A personal representative who fails to make timely payment is personally liable for any interest charged or penalties resulting from this neglect. You must remind him of such deadlines.*

ETHICAL ISSUE ◄

The personal representative is responsible for paying all taxes out of the estate assets. These include income, fiduciary, gift, estate, and inheritance taxes, unless the will specifies that the devisees pay the inheritance tax out of their legacies or devises. If prior to distribution of the estate the personal representative proves that the estate does not have enough cash (or assets to be sold) to pay the taxes and that this shortfall is not due to any fault on her part, she is free from individual liability to pay the taxes. If the personal representative distributes the estate, however, and then does not have enough assets left to pay the taxes, she must pay the taxes out of her own pocket (see I.R.C. § 2002). Therefore, it is imperative that the personal representative make sure that sufficient assets remain for the payment of all taxes and debts before distributing any of the estate assets. Certain preferred claims have priority for payment before taxes are paid, e.g., administrative expenses, funeral expenses, and expenses of the last illness (see Chapter 12 for an example of a priority of debts statute, but compare U.P.C. § 3–805).

AN OVERVIEW OF THE TAX CHANGES OF 1976, 1981, AND 1986

In 1976, 1981, and 1986, Congress extensively overhauled the federal estate and gift tax laws; with the exception of a law providing for a marital deduction in 1948, these were the first major changes in these laws since 1942. The three acts—the 1976 Tax Reform Act (TRA), the 1981 Economic Recovery Tax Act (ERTA), and the 1986 Tax Reform Act (TRA)—contain more than a thousand separate provisions. Both individuals and businesses are affected by these complex tax laws.

Exhibit 14.1 Income, Gift, Estate, Inheritance, and Generation-Skipping Transfer Taxes Imposed by States

State	Income Tax	Gift Tax	Estate Tax	Credit Estate Tax	Inheritance Tax	Generation-Skipping Transfer Tax
Alabama	X			X		X
Alaska				X		
Arizona	X			X		X
Arkansas	X			X		
California	X			X		X
Colorado	X			X		
Connecticut	X	X		X	X	
Delaware	X	X		X	X	
Florida				X		X
Georgia	X			X		
Hawaii	X			X		X
Idaho	X			X		X
Illinois	X			X		X
Indiana	X			X	X	X
Iowa	X			X	X	X
Kansas	X			X	X	X
Kentucky	X			X	X	
Louisiana	X	X		X	X	
Maine	X			X		
Maryland	X			X	X	X
Massachusetts	X		X	X		X
Michigan	X			X		X
Minnesota	X			X		
Mississippi	X		X	X		
Missouri	X			X		X
Montana	X			X	X	X
Nebraska	X			X	X	X
Nevada				X		X
New Hampshire	X			X	X	
New Jersey	X			X	X	
New Mexico	X			X		
New York	X	X	X	X		X
North Carolina	X	X		X	X	X
North Dakota	X			X		
Ohio	X		X	X		X
Oklahoma	X		X	X		
Oregon	X			X		
Pennsylvania	X			X	X	
Rhode Island	X			X		X
South Carolina	X			X		X
South Dakota				X	X	
Tennessee	X	X		X	X	X
Texas					X	X
Utah	X			X		
Vermont	X			X		
Virginia	X			X		X
Washington				X		X
West Virginia	X			X		
Wisconsin	X			X		
Wyoming				X		

The three tax acts have had a tremendous impact on estate planning and administration as well as on income tax considerations for grantors, testators, and beneficiaries. Many of the provisions are complex and require numerous qualifying regulations and rulings. Attorneys, paralegals, and others who specialize in estate planning and administration must be well versed on these comprehensive changes and their effects. Under the laws, death tax payments are assessed only against the wealthy and the moderately wealthy. Smaller estates benefited from the changes; the vast majority of estates that were previously required to file federal estate tax returns and pay estate taxes are now required to do neither.

The following is a brief summary of some of the major changes in federal estate and gift tax laws included in the three acts:

▪ The 1976 TRA combined the previously separate gift and estate tax rate schedules into one unified transfer tax system (see Exhibit 14.2).

▪ The 1976 TRA eliminated the previous estate tax and gift tax exemptions and replaced them with a flat-rate unified transfer tax credit. This credit amounts to $192,800 (effective since 1987) and is equivalent to an exemption of $600,000 in estate property.

▪ The 1981 ERTA increased the annual gift tax exclusion from $3,000 to $10,000 per donee per year beginning in 1982.

▪ Under the 1981 ERTA, all taxable gifts made after December 31, 1976 (called adjusted taxable gifts), are included in the decedent's gross estate and are subject to the federal estate tax. Note, however, that the double taxation effect of including these gifts (i.e., taxed first as a gift and second as part of the decedent's estate) is mitigated by allowing a credit against the federal estate tax for the gift taxes previously paid.

As another exception, gifts of life insurance in which the insured policyholder does not retain the "incidents or rights of ownership" in the policy are still included in the gross estate if they are made within three years of death. In addition, certain incomplete transfers, e.g., retained life estates or revocable transfers, will continue to be included in the decedent's gross estate regardless of when made.

▪ The 1981 ERTA completely changed the marital deduction for both gift and estate tax purposes. Under the ERTA, the gift and estate tax marital deduction for transfers between spouses is unlimited.

▪ The 1986 TRA changed the law concerning the generation-skipping tax. Under the 1986 TRA, direct skips (transfers), i.e., a gift or bequest made directly to a grandchild or great-grandchild, are taxed. See the discussion later in this chapter.

▪ The 1981 ERTA changed and simplified the rules relating to jointly held property by providing that when spouses jointly own property with the right of survivorship, the gross estate of the first spouse to die includes half the property's value regardless of which spouse furnished the funds to purchase the property and also regardless of how the joint tenancy was created.

GENERAL TAX CONSIDERATIONS

Before turning to the various tax returns that usually must be completed as part of the administration of a decedent's estate, certain general tax considerations

Exhibit 14.2   Unified Transfer Tax Rate Schedule for Gift and Estate Taxes: For Gifts Made and for Deaths after 1983

If the Amount with Respect to Which the Tentative Tax to Be Computed Is:	The Tentative Tax Is:
Not over $10,000	18 percent of such amount.
Over $10,000 but not over $20,000	$1,800, plus 20 percent of the excess of such amount over $10,000.
Over $20,000 but not over $40,000	$3,800, plus 22 percent of the excess of such amount over $20,000.
Over $40,000 but not over $60,000	$8,200, plus 24 percent of the excess of such amount over $40,000.
Over $60,000 but not over $80,000	$13,000, plus 26 percent of the excess of such amount over $60,000.
Over $80,000 but not over $100,000	$18,200 plus 28 percent of the excess of such amount over $80,000.
Over $100,000 but not over $150,000	$23,800 plus 30 percent of the excess of such amount over $100,000.
Over $150,000 but not over $250,000	$38,800 plus 32 percent of the excess of such amount over $150,000.
Over $250,000 but not over $500,000	$70,800, plus 34 percent of the excess of such amount over $250,000.
Over $500,000 but not over $750,000	$155,800, plus 37 percent of the excess of such amount over $500,000.
Over $750,000 but not over $1,000,000	$248,300, plus 39 percent of the excess of such amount over $750,000.
Over $1,000,000 but not over $1,250,000	$345,800, plus 41 percent of the excess of such amount over $1,000,000.
Over $1,250,000 but not over $1,500,000	$448,300 plus 43 percent of the excess of such amount over $1,250,000.
Over $1,500,000 but not over $2,000,000	$555,800, plus 45 percent of the excess of such amount over $1,500,000.
Over $2,000,000 but not over $2,500,000	$780,800 plus 49 percent of the excess of such amount over $2,000,000.
Over $2,500,000 but not over $3,000,000	$1,025,800, plus 53 percent of the excess of such amount over $2,500,000.
Over $3,000,000*	$1,290,800, plus 55 percent of the excess of such amount over $3,000,000.

*For large taxable transfers (generally in excess of $10 million) there is a phase-out of the benefits of the graduated rates and the unified tax credit.

need to be mentioned. One should remember that after the decedent's death, the estate is a new legal being; the legal existence of the decedent has terminated. The estate has rights and obligations, and it is a taxpayer.

Everybody wants to reduce the death taxes owed the government or to avoid them entirely whenever legally possible. There are numerous ways to accomplish tax savings on a decedent's estate. The most frequently used methods include (1) making use of the unified credit and the Unified Transfer Tax Rate Schedule for federal estate and gift taxes; (2) making use of the marital deduction; (3) creating trusts; and (4) making gifts during the decedent's lifetime.

Unified Transfer Tax Credit and Unified Transfer Gift and Estate Tax Rates

The 1976 TRA not only created a unified transfer tax credit for gifts and estates, but also unified federal gift and estate tax rates into a single schedule. The unified rate is applied to all transfers of assets subject to tax, whether the transfers occur during life by *inter vivos* gift or after death by will or intestate succession.

Unified Transfer Tax Credit

The 1976 TRA, which took effect on January 1, 1977, replaced previous estate and gift tax exemptions with the unified credit, which is subtracted from the tax due. The unified credit was phased in over a five-year period (1976 TRA) and extended under the 1981 ERTA (see Exhibit 14.3). In 1987 and thereafter, the credit amounts to $192,800.

Unified Transfer Gift and Estate Tax Rates

In the 1976 TRA, the tax rates for estate and gift taxes were unified into a single schedule. The rates are progressive and are based on cumulative lifetime and deathtime transfers (see Exhibit 14.2).

Since 1987, the unified credit has been fully phased in, so that today the lowest applicable rate is 37 percent, with a unified credit of $192,800 and an **exemption equivalent** of $600,000.

Example: Jody Carter died in November 1994, leaving a taxable estate of $600,000. The formula for computing the federal estate tax was $155,800 plus 37 percent of the excess of such amount over $500,000, equaling a tentative tax of $192,800. In 1994 the unified credit of $192,800 was allowed, which canceled out the $192,800 tentative tax. Therefore Jody Carter's estate owed no federal estate tax (see Exhibit 14.4).

Any taxpayer who dies leaving a taxable estate of the value of the exemption equivalent (i.e., $600,000) or less would not be liable for any federal estate tax.

Exemption equivalent
Immunity from paying estate tax for a decedent's estate currently valued to a maximum of $600,000.

Exhibit 14.3 Unified Transfer Tax Credit

Year	Unified Credit	Exemption Equivalent
1977	$ 30,000	$120,667
1978	34,000	134,000
1979	38,000	147,333
1980	42,500	161,563
1981	47,000	175,625
1982	62,800	225,000
1983	79,300	275,000
1984	96,300	325,000
1985	121,800	400,000
1986	155,800	500,000
1987 and after	192,800	600,000

Congress estimated that after 1987 only 0.5% of all decedents' estates would be subject to federal estate tax. As the exhibit illustrates, a single person dying in 1987 or thereafter would have to have an estate valued at more than $600,000 in order for federal estate taxes to be owed the government.

Exhibit 14.4   Calculating the 1994 Federal Estate Tax on Jody Carter's Estate

Taxable estate (value) $600,000
Tax computation from Unified Rate Schedule ($155,800, plus 37% of the excess
  over $500,000 from the tax schedule)
Calculation:

Taxable estate over $500,000 times 37%	$100,000	
	× .37	
	$ 37,000	
	$155,800	
	+ 37,000	
	$192,800	
Tentative tax		$192,800
Less unified credit for 1994		− 192,800
Tax owed		$ 0

Under the law, gift taxes are computed by applying the Unified Transfer Tax Rate Schedule to cumulative lifetime taxable transfers and subtracting the taxes paid for prior taxable periods. Federal estate taxes are computed by applying the Unified Transfer Tax Rate Schedule to cumulative lifetime and deathtime transfers, then subtracting the gift taxes paid. Thus, if you give away $200,000 of property during your lifetime, over and above the $10,000 per donee per year exclusion, you have only $400,000 of property available to pass tax-free at death. In some circumstances, adjustments must be made for taxes in lifetime transfers in the decedent's estate (see the discussion under Lifetime Gifts below). (Caveat: In general, any portion of the unified credit that is used against gift taxes will reduce the credit available to be used against the federal estate tax.) The amount of the unified credit allowed cannot be greater than the amount of the computed transfer tax.

Calculating the Federal Estate Tax

Under current law, the amount of the federal estate tax is computed by applying the unified rates to the decedent's cumulative lifetime transfers and transfers made at death, then subtracting the taxes paid on the lifetime transfers (the gift tax, as computed by applying the unified rate, would have been paid previously at the time assets were transferred during the decedent's life). The computation of the federal estate tax is outlined in Exhibit 14.5. Review the outline carefully for future computation examples. See also the discussion and examples under The Marital Deduction below.

The tax credits listed in Exhibit 14.5 include the previously discussed unified credit; the credit for state death taxes, i.e., the decedent's estate is allowed a federal credit for the state death taxes actually paid up to specific limits; the credit for foreign death taxes, i.e., credit allowed for death taxes actually paid to a foreign country by the decedent's estate; and for estate taxes paid by the estates of other decedents for assets included in the current decedent's estate. This is called the "credit for tax on prior transfers" and is allowed only if the two deaths occur within a short time of each other, e.g., within ten years before or two years after the current decedent's death. The purpose of this credit is to prevent the same property from being taxed too often. The credit is limited to the smaller of the following amounts:

Exhibit 14.5 Method for Computing Federal Estate Tax

Gross Estate (all property owned at decedent's death)		$ _____
Less:		
Funeral expenses	_____	
Administration expenses	_____	
Debts	_____	
Losses	_____	
Taxes	_____	
Total deductions	_____	_____
Equals:		
Adjusted Gross Estate		_____
Less:		
Marital deduction	_____	
Charitable deduction	_____	
Total deductions	_____	_____
Equals:		
Taxable Estate		_____
Plus:		
Adjusted taxable gifts (post-1976 lifetime taxable transfers not included in gross estate)		_____
Equals:		
Tentative Tax base (Taxable Amount)		_____
Compute:		
Tentative tax (using the Unified Rate Schedule in Exhibit 14.2)	_____	
Less:		
Gift taxes paid or payable on post-1976 taxable gifts	_____	
Equals:		
Tax Payable before Credits		_____
Less:		
Tax credits:		
Unified credit	_____	
Credit for state death taxes	_____	
Credit for foreign death taxes	_____	
Credit for estate taxes on prior transfers	_____	
Total Credit Reduction	_____	_____
Equals:		
Federal Estate Tax Due		_____
Plus:		
Generation-skipping transfer taxes		_____
Increased estate tax on excess retirement accumulations	_____	
Equals:		
Total Transfer Taxes Due		$ _____

Note: When a decedent leaves everything to his or her spouse, there would be no estate tax because of the unlimited marital deduction.

1. The amount of the federal estate tax attributable to the transferred property in the transferor's estate.

2. The amount of the federal estate tax attributable to the transferred property in the current decedent's estate.

The credit is allowed in a declining percentage of the smaller of these amounts (see Exhibit 14.6).

Example: Mary Perkins dies, leaving her daughter, Molly, property worth $400,000. Mary's estate paid $80,000 in federal estate taxes on the property transferred to Molly. Now Molly dies. Assuming the $80,000 of federal estate tax is the same or the smaller under the two limitations above, the amount of the credit available to Molly's estate would be as follows:

Year of Molly's Death after Mary's Death	Credit to Molly's Estate
1 or 2 years	$80,000 (100%)
3 or 4 years	$64,000 (80%)
5 or 6 years	$48,000 (60%)
7 or 8 years	$32,000 (40%)
9 or 10 years	$16,000 (20%)
Over 10 years	No credit

The Marital Deduction

The marital deduction can be a substantial tax-saving device for an estate (see the discussion under Determining the Taxable Estate below). The 1981 ERTA provided for an unlimited federal estate tax marital deduction for transfers between spouses. A testator's estate is entitled to the marital deduction if there is a surviving spouse and if the decedent leaves all or a portion of his or her estate to the surviving spouse. If the decedent spouse dies intestate, the surviving spouse is entitled to a statutory share of the decedent's estate. The amount of the surviving spouse's statutory share is the amount of the marital deduction in such cases.

The 1981 ERTA also added language to I.R.C. § 2056, pertaining to the estate tax marital deduction, and to I.R.C. § 2523, pertaining to the gift marital deduction (see Gifts and the Marital Deduction below). The 1981 law contains a "terminable interest rule," which allows certain property to qualify for the estate and gift tax

---

Exhibit 14.6 The Credit for Tax on Prior Transfers

Transferee's Death Occurring before or after Transferor's Death	Credit (Percentage of Tax Attributed to Transferred Property)
1 to 2 years before	100%
1 to 2 years after	100%
3 to 4 years after	80%
5 to 6 years after	60%
7 to 8 years after	40%
9 to 10 years after	20%
Over 10 years after	No credit

marital deduction that previously did not qualify. The eligible property is called "qualified terminable interest property" (QTIP), i.e., property that passes from the decedent spouse in which the surviving spouse has a qualified income interest for life. Examples of QTIP property that qualify for marital deduction treatment are (1) trusts with a life interest to the surviving spouse, the remainder to the children; and (2) a legal life estate to the surviving spouse and the remainder to others, e.g., their children.

As Chapter 10 observed, the qualifying of QTIP property for the marital deduction can be an important estate-planning tool that also permits the testator to direct the disposition of the trust principal at the death of the surviving spouse (e.g., providing for children of a previous marriage and the like).

In order for property to qualify as QTIP property for marital deduction treatment, the following are necessary:

- The surviving spouse life tenant must have a "qualifying income interest for life" in the property. The surviving spouse has a qualified income interest for life if (1) the surviving spouse is entitled to all the income for life from the property, payable at least annually or at more frequent intervals, and (2) no person during the surviving spouse's lifetime has the power to appoint any part of the property to any person other than the surviving spouse.

- The personal representative or executor of the decedent spouse's estate must *elect* to treat the property as QTIP property on the decedent's federal estate tax return (Form 706 and Form 96 in Appendix A). If the executor makes the election, the property will qualify for the marital deduction. In the case of a lifetime transfer, however, the donor-spouse makes the QTIP election (see definition in the Glossary).

The use of a testamentary trust with a life interest to a surviving spouse is one method of substantially reducing the tax consequences to a decedent's estate. An example of such a trust is included in Appendix B.

Gifts and the Marital Deduction

The marital deduction can also be used when there is a transfer by gift of any property between spouses. Since 1982, the annual gift tax exclusion is $10,000 per donee per year (previously $3,000), and the marital deduction on gift taxes for lifetime transfers (gifts) of any property between spouses is unlimited. Therefore, whether John gives his spouse, Mary, $10,000, $100,000, or $1,000,000, none of the property or cash is subject to gift tax. There is no upper limit on how much John can give his spouse. Regardless of the amount of the gift transferred between spouses that is offset by the unlimited marital deduction, such gifts do not require the filing of the gift tax return Form 709 (see Form 94*). Computation of the federal gift tax is outlined in Exhibit 14.7.

Creation of Trusts

Another method used to diminish death taxes is the creation of trusts (see Chapters 8 and 9). It is possible to leave property in a testamentary trust for

---

*See Appendix A.

beneficiaries named by the testator-settlor so that additional estate taxes are not due at the death of the beneficiary. If properly planned and executed, one such trust, combined with the marital deduction, can result in substantial savings to the estate of a decedent over the course of two generations (see the discussion under Determining the Taxable Estate). Taxes can also be diminished using *inter vivos* or lifetime trusts.

Lifetime Gifts

A person who makes a gift is called a donor, and a person who receives a gift is called a donee. A federal gift tax is levied on the right to transfer property from a donor to a donee for less than full or adequate consideration. The donor is responsible for the payment of the tax. Gifts made during the lifetime *(inter vivos)* of the decedent can in some cases result in tax advantages. The current tax laws (the 1976 TRA and the 1981 ERTA) have unified the gift and estate tax rates into a single rate schedule with progressive rates that are computed on the basis of cumulative transfers made both during lifetime and at death. All taxable gifts made after December 31, 1976 (called adjusted taxable gifts), are included in the decedent's gross estate and are subject to the federal estate tax. A credit against the tax for gift taxes previously paid is then deducted.

Exhibit 14.7　Method for Computing Federal Gift Tax

Total taxable gifts made during current calendar　　　　$ _____
　　year (I.R.C. §§ 2511–2519)
Less:
　Exclusions and deductions
　Annual exclusion (I.R.C. § 2503) ($10,000 per
　　donee)
　Unlimited marital deduction (I.R.C. § 2523)　　_____
　Charitable deduction (I.R.C. § 2522)　　　　　_____
　Total deductions and exclusions　　　　　　　_____　_____
Equals:
　Taxable gifts for calendar year (I.R.C. § 2503[a])　　　　_____
Add:
　Taxable gifts from prior years (I.R.C. § 2504)　　　　　_____
Equals:
　Total of current and prior taxable gifts　　　　　　　_____
Compute:
Tentative gift tax on total taxable gifts (using the　　　　_____
　　Unified Rate Schedule)
Less:
　Tentative gift tax on prior taxable gifts　　　　　　　_____
Equals:
　Gift tax before unified tax credit　　　　　　　　　_____
Less:
　Allowable unified tax credit (I.R.C. § 2505)　　　　　_____
Equals:
　Federal Gift Tax Due (for current period)　　　　　$ _____

But some incentives for *inter vivos* gift giving remain under the laws. The $3,000 per donee annual exclusion was increased by the ERTA to $10,000 per donee to allow larger gifts to be exempt from the federal gift tax. The increase reflects the economy's inflationary trend and encourages compliance with the tax law by taxpayers. Any appreciation in value of a lifetime gift that may accrue between the date the gift is made and the date of the donor's death is not subject to a transfer tax. Also, income taxes may be reduced when the gift property produces income and the property is transferred during life to a donee who is in a lower income tax bracket than the donor. Finally, lifetime gifts can reduce the value of the decedent's estate and thereby also reduce the federal estate tax, especially in the estate of the surviving spouse.

The laws governing gifts and taxes on such gifts provide as follows:

- A gift must be intended and delivered by the donor.
- Any person can give a gift of up to $10,000 per year tax-free to each donee, and, if the donor's spouse joins in the gift, the exclusions of both spouses may be used, resulting in an exclusion of $20,000. This is called *gift splitting*. These joint gifts are tax-free to both the donor and the donee.
- The federal unified gift and estate tax rate is a progressive and cumulative tax.
- When the gift is to the donor's spouse, there is an unlimited gift tax marital deduction.
- When a gift is made to a charitable organization, some limits are placed on the amount of the charitable deduction from the gift tax, depending on the type of gift and the charity to which it is given.

Before becoming too enthusiastic about transferring property by gift, it is well to remember that, once transferred, the property can no longer be controlled by the donor. The property passes to the new owner, the donee, and that person alone has title to it. Also, one must guard against giving gifts with strings attached. In most cases, when the donor retains control over the gift, income from the gift property will be taxed to the donor, and the property will be included in the donor's gross estate for federal estate tax purposes upon the donor's death (I.R.C. §§ 2036–2038).

Example: In 1980, Janet Brown made a gift to her niece, Sue, of property valued at $173,625. Janet had made no previous taxable gifts. The unified credit for 1980 is $42,500. Janet computes her gift tax for 1980 as follows:

Total taxable gifts for 1980	$173,625	Tentative gift tax on	
Annual exclusion	− 3,000	total taxable gifts[1]	$45,400
Taxable gifts for 1980	$170,625	Tentative gift tax on prior	
Taxable gifts from prior years	+ 0	taxable gifts	− 0
Total Taxable Gifts	$170,625	Gift tax before unified tax credit	$45,400
		Allowable unified tax credit	− 42,500
		Federal Gift Tax Due	$ 2,900

In 1983, Janet makes another gift to Sue of $100,000. The gift tax annual exclusion is now $10,000 instead of $3,000, and the unified credit for 1983 is $79,300. Janet computes her gift tax for 1983 as follows:

---

1. This figure is obtained from the Unified Rate Schedule using the over $150,000 but not over $250,000 line. The tentative tax is $38,800 plus 32 percent of the excess over $150,000. This becomes $38,800 plus $6,600, which equals $45,400.

Total taxable gifts for 1983	$100,000	Tentative gift tax on total		
Annual exclusion	− 10,000	taxable gifts (rounded)[2]		$74,413
Taxable gifts for 1983	$ 90,000	Tentative gift tax on prior		
Taxable gifts from prior years		taxable gifts		− 45,400
(1980 gift)	+ 170,625	Gift tax before unified tax credit		$29,013
Total Taxable Gifts	$260,625	Allowable unified tax credit		
		($79,300 − $42,500)		− 36,800
		Federal Gift Tax Due		$ 0

In order to avoid any gift tax for 1983, Janet would use only $29,013 of the $36,800 remaining credit for that year and would thereby have no gift tax liability. *Note:* If Janet died in 1983 and had made no other taxable gifts that year, her estate would have, from the unified gift and estate tax schedule, $7,787 ($36,800 − $29,013) remaining as her unified credit that could be subtracted from any estate tax liability she might have at the time of her death.

Finally, in 1990, Janet makes a third gift to Sue of $200,000. The gift tax annual exclusion is still $10,000, and the unified credit for 1990 is $192,800. Janet computes her gift tax for 1990 as follows:

Total taxable gifts for 1990		$200,000	Tentative gift tax on total		
Annual exclusion		− 10,000	taxable gifts (rounded)[3]		$139,013
Taxable gifts for 1990		$190,000	Tentative gift tax on prior		
Taxable gifts from			taxable gifts		− 74,413
prior years:	1980 $170,625		Gift tax before unified tax credit		$ 64,600
	1983 90,000		Allowable unified tax credit		
	$260,625	+ 260,625	($192,800 − $71,513)[4]		− 121,287
Total Taxable Gifts		$450,625	Federal Gift Tax Due		$ 0

In order to avoid any gift tax for 1990, Janet would use only $64,600 of the $121,287 remaining credit for that year and would therefore have no gift tax liability. *Note:* If Janet died in 1990 and had made no other taxable gifts that year, her *estate* would have $56,687 ($121,287 − $64,600) remaining as her unified credit that could be subtracted from any estate tax liability she might have at the time of her death.

Gift making, gift splitting between spouses, and the unified credit are all means of reducing tax liability. But remember that the unified credit is allowed against lifetime gift taxes, or estate taxes, or both. Unlike the $10,000 per donee annual exclusion, however, which is available to the donor each year, once the unified credit is used, it is terminated. It can be used to diminish or eliminate the tax on lifetime gifts or to diminish or eliminate the estate tax.

The Gift-Splitting Provision

Gift splitting by spouses has been retained under the current law. When married, the donor, with the other spouse's consent, may split the lifetime gift to the donee. The gift will then be treated as though half was given by the donor and the other half by the spouse. Thus, the spouses may give $20,000 annually to each donee tax-free if each spouse consents to having the gift treated as being given half by each spouse. As a result, a married donor can put more property

---

2.   From the Unified Rate Schedule (Exhibit 14.2), the tentative tax is $70,800 plus 34 percent of the excess over $250,000. This becomes $70,800 plus $3,613, which equals $74,413.

3.   From the Unified Rate Schedule (Exhibit 14.2), the tentative tax is $70,800 plus 34 percent of the excess over $250,000. This becomes $70,800 plus $68,213, which equals $139,013.

4.   The figure $71,513 is obtained by adding $42,500 to $29,013, the amounts of the credit previously used.

into a trust while paying less gift tax than a single person would pay (I.R.C. § 2513).

Example: Using the $10,000 annual exclusion, a gift may be given free of gift tax as in the following examples:

If You Are	Married	Single
and giving to one person	two $10,000 annual exclusions = $20,000	one $10,000 annual exclusion = $10,000
and giving to two persons	four $10,000 annual exclusions = $40,000	two $10,000 annual exclusions = $20,000
and giving to three persons	six $10,000 annual exclusions = $60,000	three $10,000 annual exclusions = $30,000

ASSIGNMENT 14.1

Michele and Bruce, husband and wife, decided to give a gift of $625,000 to their niece, Trudy, in December 1995. Assuming the couple has not used either of their $10,000 exclusions for Trudy for 1995 nor the $192,800 unified credit, compute the aggregate gift tax the couple would have to pay on the gift (before the unified credit is subtracted), using the Unified Rate Schedule. Now, assume that the couple chooses to reduce the gift tax as much as possible. (Remember that a *credit* is deducted *after* the tax has been computed.) How much gift tax would the couple pay?

Do the same computations, except that the amount of the gift is $1,000,000.

Uniform Gifts (Transfers) to Minors Act

Most states have adopted the Uniform Gifts (Transfers) to Minors Act or a variation thereof. This act (revised in 1983) provides a means of transferring any kind of property, e.g., money, securities, or land, to a minor by creating a custodianship to manage the property for the benefit of the minor.

A custodianship is an alternative to a trust or guardianship. It is easily created by registering the property transferred in the name of the custodian "as custodian for the donee (minor) under the Uniform Gifts (Transfers) to Minors Act" for the appropriate state, which can be the residence of the custodian, minor, or donor, or the location of the property. This procedure incorporates by reference all provisions of the state's act.

A gift (transfer of property) under this act is irrevocable (cannot be returned to the donor). It belongs to the donee (minor), and both the property and its income may be used for the benefit of the minor. Income earned on the property is taxable to the minor, and the custodianship ends when the beneficiary (minor) reaches age 21 (18 in some states), at which time the property and any undisposed income must be given to the minor. If the minor dies before age 21, the property passes to the minor's estate or to whomever the minor may appoint under a general power of appointment.

For the donor, the creation of a custodianship under the Uniform Gifts (Transfers) to Minors Act is a present interest and as such is a gift that qualifies for the $10,000 annual gift tax exclusion.

Generation-Skipping Transfers and Their Tax Consequences

The stated purpose of the federal estate and gift taxes is not only to raise revenue but also to tax death transfers consistently generation by generation. Congress

Generation-skipping transfer trust
A trust that partially avoids federal gift and estate taxes on transfers of large sums of money or other valuable assets between generations of family members.

Generation-skipping transfer tax
A federal tax on the transfer of property valued at more than $1,000,000 to a person who is two or more generations below the generation of the transferor (grantor), e.g., a grandparent transferring property to a grandchild thereby skipping a child.

Transferor (grantor)
The decedent or donor who creates a generation-skipping trust.

realized a tax loophole existed by which family members could create a **generation-skipping transfer trust** that partially avoided federal gift and estate taxes on large transfers of money or other valuable assets between generations of family members. Therefore, Congress closed the tax loophole by creating the **generation-skipping transfer tax.** Caveat: The definitions and rules concerning generation-skipping transfers and their tax computations are complicated. You must review the Code provisions carefully and work closely with your supervising attorney when preparing the appropriate tax returns.

This tax is levied when a younger generation is bypassed in favor of a later generation: it is applied in addition to other death taxes. The tax law was initially enacted in 1976 to impose the tax on transfers that shifted wealth (assets) from a generation (i.e., children) below the generation of the grantor or **transferor** (i.e., parent) to another lower generation (i.e., grandchildren). The tax was levied upon the death of the grantor's children, when the property passed to the grandchildren.

The 1986 TRA repealed the generation-skipping transfer tax that had been enacted in the 1976 TRA, retroactive to January 1, 1977, and replaced it with a new Chapter 13 of the Internal Revenue Code §§ 2601–2663. The current generation-skipping transfer tax applies to lifetime *(inter vivos)* transfers by gift made after September 25, 1985, and to transfers by will or revocable trust where the decedent or grantor dies after October 22, 1986. A controversial provision in the 1976 statute, which used a concept called a "deemed transferor" to establish the method of calculating the amount of the generation-skipping tax due, was abolished by the 1986 TRA. Under the 1976 TRA, the "deemed transferor's" taxable estate at death formed the basis for the generation-skipping transfer tax. The 1986 TRA eliminated the "deemed transferor" concept as the basis for determining the generation-skipping transfer tax and replaced it with a flat rate—the maximum rate allowed under the unified gift and estate tax schedule, which is 55 percent.

The 1986 generation-skipping tax is similar to the original 1976 tax in the following respects:

1. The generation-skipping tax is imposed on transfers that are **"taxable terminations"** and **"taxable distributions."** (The 1986 tax also added **direct skips.**) The tax is imposed based on the value of the property transferred.

2. The concept of what constitutes a person's "interest" in a trust is basically the same (i.e., a present interest is included in the gross estate and is subject to the generation-skipping tax, but a future interest is not).

3. The method of assigning individuals to specific generations is generally the same as under the 1976 statute.

MINI-GLOSSARY BOX

Taxable termination
Any termination of an interest in property held in trust; however, a termination is not a taxable termination if (1) immediately afterward any nonskip person has an interest in the trust property or

(2) distribution can never thereafter be made to a skip person.

Skip person
An individual (such as a grandchild) who receives the property in a generation-skipping transfer and

is two or more generations below the generation of the transferor (grantor).

Taxable distribution
Any distribution of income or principal from a trust to a skip person.

Direct skip
A generation-skipping transfer of an interest in property that is transferred to a skip person; a direct skip is subject to the federal estate tax.

4. The generation-skipping transfer tax does not apply to an *inter vivos* (lifetime) gift that is exempt from gift tax because of the annual exclusion ($10,000 per donee per year). Spouses can elect to "split" such gifts, thereby increasing the annual exclusion to $20,000 per donee per year.

The generation-skipping transfer tax is reported on Schedule R of the U.S. Treasury Form 706, United States Estate (and Generation-Skipping Transfer) Tax Return.

The 1986 generation-skipping tax differs from the original 1976 tax in the following ways:

1. The 1986 tax adds direct skips (e.g., from grandparent to grandchild) to the types of generation-skipping transfers that are taxed. (See point 1 above.)

2. The 1986 tax applies to income *and* principal distributions from trusts.

3. As noted above, the concept of a "deemed transferor" for determining the amount of the generation-skipping tax due is eliminated and replaced with a flat rate at the maximum rate allowed under the unified gift and estate tax schedule.

4. An exemption of $1,000,000 ($2,000,000 for a husband and wife) before the tax applies that can be used for any generation-skipping transfer replaces the 1976 $250,000 grandchildren's exclusion. This exemption applies at the time of transfer, and any future appreciation of the value of the property transferred is not subject to the generation-skipping transfer tax.

5. The amount of generation-skipping transfer tax due is determined by multiplying the tax base ("taxable amount") by the tax rate. The "taxable amount" is the value of property (in excess of deductions and exclusions) that passes pursuant to a generation-skipping transfer (i.e., either a taxable termination, taxable distribution, or direct skip). The tax rate is the maximum federal estate tax rate (55 percent) times the inclusion ratio, which is a new feature of the 1986 TRA.

6. The 1986 TRA also added special rules for allocation of the generation-skipping tax exemption (see I.R.C. §§ 2631 and 2632).

TAX RETURNS

It is the responsibility of the personal representative (the fiduciary) of the decedent's estate to file income tax returns for the estate and to pay any taxes owed out of the estate assets. Depending on the situation, the representative may have to file some or all of the following returns:

- U.S. Individual Income Tax Return
- State Individual Income Tax Return
- U.S. Fiduciary Income Tax Return
- State Fiduciary Income Tax Return
- U.S. Gift Tax Return
- State Gift Tax Return
- U.S. Estate Tax Return
- State Estate Tax Return
- State Inheritance Tax Return

Decedent's Final Income Tax Returns, Federal and State

The personal representative, also called the fiduciary, of the decedent's estate has the obligation to file the required federal and state income tax returns for the decedent (I.R.C. § 6012[b], and Minn. Stat. Ann. § 289A.08. The filing and payment of the income tax due must be completed within the time period determined by law, e.g., on or before the fifteenth day of the fourth month following the close of the taxable year in which the decedent died. Failure to do this may make the personal representative personally liable for any interest and penalties assessed.

The Internal Revenue Code § 6109 requires that an identification number be included on tax returns and other documents. On the decedent's final federal income tax return, this number is usually the decedent's Social Security number.

Federal Individual Income Tax Return

A few of the instructions for a 1994 final Form 1040, U.S. Individual Income Tax Return, are summarized below. With some exceptions, a federal income tax return for 1994 must be filed for persons who fall into the following categories (the list is not all-inclusive):

- Single and under age 65, earning at least $6,250.
- Single and 65 or older, earning at least $7,200.
- Married, filing jointly, both under 65, and earning at least $11,250.
- Married, filing jointly, and one spouse is 65 or older, earning at least $12,000.
- Married, filing jointly, both 65 or older, earning at least $12,750.
- A widow or widower, under 65, earning at least $6,250, or if 65 or older, earning at least $7,200.
- Self-employed, with net earnings of at least $400.

Examples of income that must be reported include income from self-employment, rents, pensions, annuities, royalties, alimony, dividends, profits from partnerships, income from trusts or estates, bartering income, and interest on deposits, bonds, or notes. Examples of income that need not be reported are gifts and inheritances, compensation for injuries or sickness, child support, life insurance proceeds received due to a person's death, interest on most state or local bonds, welfare benefits, and the one-time $125,000 exclusion of gain from the sale of a home by an individual age 55 or over. Whenever the decedent during the year of his death earned income exceeding the amounts and under the circumstances described above, the decedent's personal representative must file the federal income tax return (see Form 82*).

If a refund is due for income withheld for taxes during the year of the decedent's death, the personal representative can file a Statement of Person Claiming Refund Due a Deceased Taxpayer along with the federal income tax return (see Form 83*). Alternatively, the personal representative can attach to the return a copy of the court certificate showing her appointment as personal representative.

When preparing the decedent's final federal income tax return, there are a number of special tax considerations. First, if the decedent is survived by a spouse, a joint return can be filed if the surviving spouse agrees and if the surviving spouse has not remarried before the close of the taxable year. A joint federal return includes the income of the decedent to the date of death and the income of the surviving spouse for the entire year. For the client's benefit, both federal and state tax returns should be computed separately and jointly to determine which method results in the lesser tax and whether prompt filing or requesting an extension would be more advantageous. If the decedent's final

---

*See Appendix A.

federal income tax return is filed as a separate return, it may be advantageous to file the return as soon as possible and to request early audits by the Internal Revenue Service. This prevents the discovery of a large unplanned tax deficiency at some later date. With a joint federal return, the proportion of the total tax due to be paid by each spouse is determined by the percentage of the total income each earned during the year.

Second, I.R.C. § 213(c) permits the personal representative to treat the decedent's medical expenses (including prescription drug expenses) that are paid from the estate within one year after death, as deductions on the income tax return for the year. If the personal representative makes this election, a Medical Expenses Deduction Waiver must be filed, waiving the right to claim the medical expenses as an estate tax deduction (see I.R.C. § 2053) (see Form 1040, Schedule A, Itemized Deductions, in Appendix A as Form 84). The personal representative has the option of using the medical expenses either as a deduction for the final income tax return or as an expense of the decedent's last illness on the estate tax return. Generally, the choice should be made on the basis of which offers the greater tax saving, e.g., if the decedent's income was small for that year but he dies leaving a large estate, it would be more advantageous to use medical costs as an expense for estate tax purposes because this deduction will reduce the taxable estate. This election may not be available on a state return. *Note:* Only medical and dental expenses that exceed 7.5 percent of the taxpayer's adjusted gross income may be deducted.

Third, on the decedent's final federal income tax return, a personal exemption is allowed for each taxpayer ($2,450 for 1994). An additional exemption is allowed for a spouse and for each dependent who qualifies under the tax law.

Finally, income "in respect of the decedent" is the gross income that the decedent had a right to receive or could have received had he continued to live. This income should properly be included in the decedent's final return. The interest on stocks, bonds, income from sales of assets on an installment basis, and the like are examples of continuing income that should be included in the decedent's final return. For various reasons, certain income may be omitted from the decedent's final return, e.g., where the decedent's final return is filed before such income is received by the executor. Income "in respect of the decedent" that has been omitted from the decedent's final income tax return would then be included in the fiduciary's income tax return for the year in which the income is received. For example, if the decedent died in December 1994, interest on bonds received in May 1995 (which would have been omitted from the decedent's final income tax return filed by April 15, 1995) would be included in the fiduciary's income tax return. Tax may be saved on certain bonds, e.g., U.S. Series E and EE savings bonds, by electing not to pay the tax on the interest earned until they are cashed (I.R.C. § 454).

State Individual Income Tax Return

On the state level, a final individual income tax return is also required. The following states do *not* have a state income tax: Alaska, Florida, Nevada, South Dakota, Texas, Washington, and Wyoming. As an example, in Minnesota, the personal representative of the estate of a decedent who was a resident, a nonresident, or a person who moved into or out of Minnesota during the year must file a return if the decedent earned enough income in Minnesota to require a filing (Minn. Stat. Ann. § 289A.08). A form called the Minnesota Individual Income

Tax Return (Form M–1) is used for this purpose (see Form 86*). The personal representative may also file a claim for a state refund on behalf of the decedent's estate if a refund is due (see Form 87*).

Both the federal Form 1040 and Minnesota's M–1 form are due on or before the fifteenth day of April following the close of the decedent's tax year, unless that day falls on a weekend. These returns must include all the decedent's income from the first day of the taxable year until the date of death.[5] The opportunity to request an extension of time to file these final returns is allowed at both the federal and state levels.

Extensions for Federal and State Returns

An Application for Automatic Extension of Time to File U.S. Individual Income Tax Return (U.S. Treasury Form 4868; see Form 85*) may be filed, *except* in cases where the Internal Revenue Service is requested to compute the tax, there is a court order to file the return by the original due date, or a six-month extension while traveling abroad has been given previously. This application must be filed on or before April 15 or the normal due date of the return.

The extension of time for filing usually does *not* extend the time for payment of the tax due. With a payment equal to the estimated tax, the form is completed in duplicate, signed by the personal representative, and sent to the District Director of Internal Revenue. If the tax is not paid at this time, interest accrues from the regular due date of the return until the tax is paid. In addition, for each month the return is late, the law provides a 5 percent penalty of the tax due, not to exceed a maximum of 25 percent. If the taxpayer intends to request an extension to file both federal and state income tax returns, a copy of the federal automatic extension form must accompany the state return when that return is filed.

States may or may not require that the taxpayer file a form requesting an extension to file, but as with the federal extension, all tax must be paid on or before the original due date, i.e., April 15, even if the return is not filed. For example, Minnesota residents file Form M–13, Payment of Income Tax (see Form 88*). Like the federal form, it must be submitted on or before the due date for filing the return. The form is sent to the Department of Revenue with payment. Interest and penalties apply to any unpaid tax.

⛫ ASSIGNMENT 14.2

Find out how a taxpayer in your state obtains an extension of time to file the state income tax return. Is there a form? If so, what is it called and what is its number? Check your state statutory code and/or your state tax regulations on this. If an extension is permitted in your state, for how long and under what conditions can it be obtained? Is there an interest assessment? Any penalty?

Fiduciary's Income Tax Returns, Federal and State

Federal Fiduciary Income Tax Return

In addition to filing the decedent's final federal individual income tax return, the personal representative of the estate must also file the federal Fiduciary Income

---

5.   The federal Individual Income Tax Return must be filed with the Internal Revenue Service Center for the district in which the decedent was domiciled at the date of death.
*See Appendix A.

Tax Return (I.R.C. § 6012). This return includes accrued income and income earned after the decedent's death that is not included on the decedent's final individual income tax return. The personal representative is obligated to prepare and file such an income tax return for the estate for the period from the date of the decedent's death to the date of final distribution. Any tax due the federal government for that time period must be paid by the personal representative out of estate assets.

Within a statutory number of days of appointment (e.g., thirty days), the personal representative must file a Notice Concerning Fiduciary Relationship with the Internal Revenue Service (I.R.C. § 6903) (see Form 90*). Accompanying the form must be satisfactory evidence that the personal representative has the authority to act as a fiduciary, such as a certified copy of the Letters appointing the personal representative.

The identification number used on the fiduciary income tax return is not the decedent's Social Security number. Instead, the personal representative or trustee uses the Employer Identification Number obtained from the Internal Revenue Service Center for the district where the decedent lived (see Form 89*).

Form 1041, U.S. Income Tax Return for Estates and Trusts (see Form 91*), must be filed for all domestic decedent estates with gross income for the taxable year of $600 or more; for estates that have a beneficiary who is a nonresident alien; and for some domestic trusts (I.R.C. § 6012). The return must be filed on or before the fifteenth day of the fourth month following the close of the taxable year of the estate or trust. When filing the first return, a personal representative may choose the same accounting period as the decedent, e.g., a calendar year or any fiscal year. If the decedent's accounting year (most likely a calendar year) is chosen, the first return will cover that part of the year from the decedent's date of death to the end of the tax year. For consistency in filing returns, the personal representative should choose a taxable year that coincides with the state estate filing requirements. The return is sent to the Internal Revenue Service Center for the state where the fiduciary resides.

If an extension of time is needed, the personal representative can file an Application for Extension of Time to File Fiduciary and Certain Other Returns (see Form 92*). Once the tax payment is due, interest will accrue on the tax due from the due date until total payment is made. Prior to distribution of the estate assets, the fiduciary pays the tax on income earned; after distribution, the successors (heirs or devisees) pay tax on income earned from assets that were distributed to them.

Example: Jean Carlton died on February 3, 1994. Stocks that Jean owned earned dividends of $5,000 between the date of Jean's death and October 19, 1994, the date of distribution of estate assets to heirs and devisees. The $5,000 will be included in the federal fiduciary income tax return. All dividends earned by the stock after October 19, 1994, will be income of the heirs or devisees to whom the stocks were distributed. For instance, if the stock was distributed to Karen and earned $2,000 in dividends from October 19, 1994, through December 31, 1994, Karen would report the $2,000 on her own individual income tax return for the year 1994, which she will file on or before April 15, 1995.

When the federal fiduciary return is filed, a copy of the will, if any, must be filed with it only if the IRS requests it. When a copy of the will is required, the personal representative must attach to the copy a written declaration that it is a

---

*See Appendix A.

true and complete copy; the personal representative should also include a statement saying that the will, in her opinion, determines the extent to which the income of the estate is taxable to the estate and the beneficiaries, respectively (Reg. § 1.6012–3[a][2]).

State Fiduciary Income Tax Return

On the state level, using Minnesota as an example, the personal representative of every estate must obtain a Minnesota identification number and file a Form M–2, Minnesota Fiduciary Income Tax Return (see Form 93*) if the income of the decedent's estate for the year is more than $600. The first fiduciary return covers the period from the date of the decedent's death to the close of the taxable year, and subsequent returns cover a full twelve-month period.

Important considerations for fiduciary income taxes are the determination of the state's share of distributable net income, distribution deductions, the character of distributed income, simple or complex trusts, and the like. Ancillary administration in another state could entail the filing of more than one state's fiduciary return.

Like the federal form, the state fiduciary income tax return is due on or before the fifteenth day of the fourth month following the close of the taxable year of the estate or trust. The return is submitted to the state fiduciary income tax division at the state Revenue Department. States may require that a copy of the federal fiduciary income tax return be attached to the state return as well as a copy of the will and a statement similar to that required by the federal government.

🏛 ASSIGNMENT 14.3

1. Whose obligation is it to complete and file income tax returns for a decedent's estate in your state?
2. How much interest, if any, is charged in your state for filing a late income tax return? Are there any penalties? Who is liable for interest and penalties in your state?
3. What constitutes sufficient income to require filing of a decedent's final income tax and fiduciary income tax returns—state and federal?
4. What are the conditions under which a joint tax return can be filed by the surviving spouse?
5. Describe the content and purposes of the federal Fiduciary Income Tax Return. Where is this explained in the Internal Revenue Code?

🏛 ASSIGNMENT 14.4

John Jones died in June. Following his death, his personal representative received checks from the A & M Mining Co. ($350), Bester Power & Light ($50), Social Security ($400), and Pronot Can Co. ($100). Will the personal representative have to file a federal Fiduciary Income Tax Return? Assume that the estate earned no other income after John's death.

---

*See Appendix A.

Decedent's Gift Tax Returns, Federal and State

Federal Gift Tax Return

U.S. Treasury Form 709, the U.S. Gift Tax Return (see Form 94*), must be executed and returned whenever a donor makes a gift in excess of $10,000 in any calendar year to any person (donee). The method of calculating the gift tax was discussed previously under Gifts and the Marital Deduction. The return is due on or before the fifteenth day of April following the close of the calendar year the donor made the gifts. If the donor dies, the personal representative must file the return no later than the earlier of the due date for the donor's estate tax return or April 15. The identification number used on this return is the donor's Social Security number. Payment of the tax is due when the tax return is filed. An extension of time for filing the return and paying the tax may be granted upon proper application. U.S. Treasury Form 709 is also used to report generation-skipping tax due the federal government on *inter vivos* direct skips. The instructions that accompany Form 709 (the U.S. Gift Tax Return) should be reviewed carefully.

State Gift Tax Return

In addition to the federal gift tax, the following states impose a state gift tax: Connecticut, Delaware, Louisiana, New York, North Carolina, and Tennessee. When applicable, refer to the individual state's forms and instructions for filing. Form 95 in Appendix A is an example of the Delaware Gift Tax Return.

Decedent's Estate Tax Returns, Federal and State

Federal Estate Tax Return

U. S. Treasury Form 706, U.S. Estate Tax Return (see Form 96*), must be filed within nine months of the decedent's death for the estate of every citizen or resident of the United States whose gross estate on the date of the person's death is greater than $600,000. The same Form 706 is also used to report any generation-skipping transfer tax owed the federal government on direct skips occurring at death. The identification number used on this return is the decedent's Social Security number. An extension of time to file Form 706 and to pay the tax may be obtained by completing the application on Form 4768, Application for Extension of Time to File a Return and/or Pay U.S. Estate Tax (see Form 99*).

The federal government imposes a tax on the total value of a decedent's estate, i.e., the value of all property, real or personal, tangible or intangible, wherever situated, to the extent of the decedent's interest therein at the time of death (I.R.C. §§ 2031, 2033). However, any personalty (household furnishings, stocks and bonds, an automobile, and the like) that a surviving spouse claims belongs to said spouse is not included in the deceased person's total estate for estate tax purposes if such a claim can be reasonably supported. The value of the decedent's property transferred under circumstances subject to the tax is called the gross estate (I.R.C. § 2033).

Determining the Gross Estate

The gross estate includes all assets owned by the decedent at death and the value of any interest the decedent held in any property, e.g., the entire interest in a

---

*See Appendix A.

home less the mortgage balance. The gross estate will also include lifetime gifts of property in which the decedent retained "incidents of ownership" and all taxable gifts made after December 31, 1976, which are given the technical name of *adjusted taxable gifts.*

For estate tax purposes, the property owned by a decedent that is included in the gross estate is valued in one of two ways. The assets may be valued on the basis of their fair market value on the date of the decedent's death. This date-of-death rule is established by statute (I.R.C. § 2031). Or the personal representative of the decedent's estate may elect an *alternate valuation date* for determining the fair market value of decedent's property (I.R.C. § 2032). (But note that although the alternate valuation date is allowed for federal estate tax purposes, it is usually not allowed for a state's inheritance tax calculations, and if the election is to be allowed, the alternate valuation date must decrease both the value of the gross estate and the federal estate tax liability.) The purpose of the alternate valuation date is to prevent an unreasonable tax liability on the decedent's estate whenever the value of this property takes a drastic plunge shortly after the decedent's death. For example, if the decedent owned a large number of shares of stock and the stock's value on the market decreased substantially shortly after her death, the estate could have an enormous tax burden if the property was valued at the date of death for estate tax purposes. Therefore the I.R.C. provides that property included in the gross estate that has not been distributed, disposed of, sold, or exchanged as of the alternate valuation date, a date six months after the decedent's death, may be valued as of that date if the personal representative so elects instead of assigning the value that prevailed at the date of death (I.R.C. § 2032). The personal representative must elect the alternate valuation date on the decedent's estate tax return during the statutory time period allotted for filing such a return, e.g., nine months after the date of the decedent's death unless an extension of time has been properly requested and granted; otherwise the right to the election is lost. Once the alternate date is elected, it cannot be changed.

Example: Ben died on July 2, 1994. On that date, 100 shares of stock that he owned in Benville Mining Company were valued at $10,000. Six months later, the value of the stock had dropped to $7,500 (a $2,500 loss). In determining the value of Ben's gross estate, the personal representative has the option of assigning the value to the stock (and all other estate assets) that prevailed on July 2, 1994, i.e., the stock would be valued at $10,000, or assigning the value to the stock (and all other estate assets) that prevailed on January 2, 1995, six months after Ben's death, i.e., the stock would be valued at $7,500.

In the example above, assuming the value of other estate assets had not increased sufficiently to offset the $2,500 loss on the stock, it would be advantageous to the estate to choose the alternate valuation date. Because the gross estate would therefore be reduced by $2,500, no estate tax would be paid on that amount.

The problem of taxing the proceeds from life insurance policies is also resolved by the I.R.C. Obviously, if the decedent's estate or personal representative (executor) is the named beneficiary of the life insurance policy, the proceeds of the policy are part of the decedent's gross estate for tax purposes. Under I.R.C. § 2042, the gross estate will also include the proceeds of all life insurance policies payable to all other beneficiaries in which the decedent at her death possessed any of the "incidents of ownership," or, within three years of her death, had assigned all the "incidents of ownership," as defined by the I.R.C. "Incidents of ownership" refer to the right of the insured (decedent) or the estate to the economic benefits of the policy. Therefore, they include the right to change the beneficiary or to cancel the policy.

The assets comprising the decedent's gross estate must be listed in separate sections, called schedules, and identified as Schedules A through I in the U.S. Estate Tax Return. Exhibit 14.8 describes some of the basic data to be included on each schedule. For more complete information on the individual schedules, see the updated instructions for Form 706, U.S. Estate Tax Return, published by the Internal Revenue Service.

Exhibit 14.9 shows a gross estate as an example of some of the kinds of property found in Schedules A through I.

According to common law dower or curtesy rights or their statutory substitutes, a surviving spouse is entitled to receive a percentage (forced or elective share) of the value of the gross estate. By will, the decedent may leave a greater portion of the estate to the surviving spouse, but the decedent cannot defeat the common law or statutory share to which the spouse is entitled.

Determining the Taxable Estate

After all the decedent's property subject to the federal estate tax, i.e., the gross estate, has been determined, the various exemptions, deductions, and claims allowed by statute are subtracted from the gross estate to determine the *taxable estate,* which is the estate on which the tax is imposed (see I.R.C. § 2051). The estate tax is computed using the Unified Rate Schedule (Exhibit 14.2). Any credits allowed against the tax are then subtracted from the gross tax, and the difference is the final *net tax due.*

In determining the taxable estate and computing the tax, the deductions, claims, and credits allowed by statute include the following:

- Specific deductible items (expenses, liens, encumbrances, debts, and taxes).
- Losses during the handling of the estate.
- Marital deduction.
- Charitable deductions.
- Unified credit (and other allowable credits, e.g., foreign death taxes).

These deductions, excluding the marital deduction and unified credit, generally average from 5 to 10 percent of the gross estate. Deductions, credits, and special taxes are reported on Schedules J through S of the U.S. Estate Tax Return. Exhibit 14.10 shows the basic data to be included in Schedules J through S.

Deductible Items.   I.R.C. § 2053 identifies deductible expenses and liabilities. The expenses that are deductible from the gross estate include funeral and estate administration expenses, e.g., the fees for the personal representative and the attorney (if used) for the estate. As such, these fees are deductible either for federal estate tax purposes (I.R.C. § 2053) or for purposes of figuring the federal fiduciary income tax of the estate (I.R.C. § 212). If administration expenses are taken as a deduction on the federal estate tax return, they cannot be used again as a deduction on the federal fiduciary income tax return. The same is true of medical expenses for the last illness, which cannot be used again on the decedent's final individual income tax return. Proper administration expenses besides the personal representative's compensation and attorney's fees include such miscellaneous items as court costs, surrogate's (judge's) fees, accountant's fees,

Exhibit 14.8   Basic Data for Schedules A–I of the U.S. Estate Tax Return

Schedule A—Real Estate

Regardless of the property's location, all interests in real property (except joint tenancy and tenancy by the entirety) owned by the decedent at the time of death must be listed in Schedule A. This includes all land, buildings, fixtures attached to the real estate, growing crops, and mineral rights. An interest in real property that terminates on the decedent's death, such as a life estate, is not included. Property owned in joint tenancy and tenancy by the entirety is not included in Schedule A, but is listed in Schedule E.

Schedule A–1—Section 2032A Valuation

The personal representative may elect to value certain real property in the decedent's estate that is devoted to farming or used in a closely held business on the basis of the property's actual use for these purposes, as opposed to its fair market value based on its potential or best use. Property passing in trust and property owned indirectly through a corporation or partnership qualify for this valuation. *This is a complex schedule that will require the expertise of other professionals (i.e., an attorney and tax accountant) to prepare.*

Schedule B—Stocks and Bonds

All stocks and bonds owned by the decedent are listed in Schedule B at their fair market value. The exact name of the corporation, the number of shares, the class of shares (common or preferred), the price per share, the CUSIP (Committee on Uniform Securities Identification Procedures) number, and the par value, if any, are some of the data listed for stocks. The principal stock exchange on which the stock is listed and traded should be given. For unlisted stock, the state and date of incorporation and the location of the principal place of business must be given.

   The data on bonds must include the number held, the principal amount, the name of the obligor, the date of maturity, the rate of interest, the dates on which interest is payable, the series number if there is more than one issue, and the principal exchange on which the bonds are listed. Also, interest accrued on bonds to the date of the decedent's death must be shown. For unlisted bonds, the business office of the obligor must be given.

Schedule C—Mortgages, Notes, and Cash

Information on Schedule C should include the following:

- Mortgages owned by the decedent (original face value and unpaid balance of principal, date of mortgage, date of maturity, name of maker, property mortgaged, interest dates, and rate of interest).
- Promissory notes owned by the decedent (the maker's name, date given, date of maturity, principal amount, rate of interest, and amount of unpaid principal and interest).
- Contracts to sell land (description of interest owned by the decedent, name of buyer, date of contract, description of property, sale price, initial payment, amounts of installment payments, unpaid balance of principal and accrued interest, interest rate, last date to which interest has been paid, and termination date of the contract).
- Cash and its location, whether in possession of the decedent, bank, other person, or safe deposit box.
- All bank accounts except accounts in joint tenancy (name and address of depositor, amount on deposit, whether checking, savings, or time deposit account, rate of interest, amount of interest accrued and payable as of date of death, and account or serial number).

Schedule D—Insurance on the Decedent's Life

Included in Schedule D are proceeds of insurance on the decedent's life received or receivable by or for the benefit of the decedent's estate or personal representative; insurance on the decedent's life receivable by any other beneficiary if the decedent at death possessed any incidents of ownership in the policy or within three years of death had assigned all the incidents of ownership; benefits received from fraternal benefit societies operating under a lodge system, group insurance, accidental death benefits, double indemnity, accumulated dividends on life insurance, and war risk insurance, but not annuities (annuities are included in Schedule I).

Schedule E—Jointly Owned Property

Schedule E includes the value of any interest in property held by the decedent and any other person in joint tenancy or tenancy by the entirety. The full value of jointly owned property must be included in the decedent's gross estate, except where a surviving joint tenant can prove he provided all or a portion of the consideration for

Exhibit 14.8 Basic Data for Schedules A–I of the U.S. Estate Tax Return—*continued*

the property or that the property or a fractional share therein was acquired by gift, bequest, devise, or inheritance. However, if the property is owned in a joint tenancy by a husband and wife, regardless of who paid for the property, only one-half of the value of the property is included in the estate of the first spouse to die.

Schedule F—Other Miscellaneous Property Not Reportable Under Any Other Schedule

Schedule F is a catchall schedule for probate assets owned by the decedent but not reportable in other schedules. It includes debts due the decedent; interest in business (sole proprietorship or partnership); patents, copyrights, and royalties; judgments; insurance on the life of another; household goods, clothing, and personal effects; automobiles; farm machinery; livestock; farm products and growing crops that have been severed from the land; reversionary or remainder interests; interests in other trusts and estates; uncashed checks payable to the decedent; and numerous other items.

Schedule G—Transfers During Decedent's Life

Transfers made by the decedent during life where the decedent retained the benefits of the property (except life Insurance included in Schedule D) or transferred the benefits within three years of death, by trust or otherwise, except for bona fide sales for an adequate and full consideration in money or money's worth, are subject to tax and are included in Schedule G.

Schedule H—Powers of Appointment

Included in the gross estate under Schedule H is the value of certain property with respect to which the decedent possessed a general power of appointment at the time of death or once possessed a general power of appointment and exercised or released that power prior to death.

Schedule I—Annuities

Annuities (periodic payments for a specified period of time) are included in Schedule I. These include annuities or other payments receivable by any beneficiary by reason of surviving the decedent under any form of contract or agreement (other than life insurance) entered into after March 3, 1931. The amount to be included is only that portion of the value of the annuity receivable by the surviving beneficiary that the decedent's contribution to the purchase price of the annuity or agreement bears to the total purchase price. Such benefits as pension, retirement, and profit-sharing plans and IRAs are included in this schedule.

appraiser's fees, storing costs, and other expenses necessary for preserving and distributing the assets of the estate. The rule regarding funeral expenses is that "a reasonable amount may be spent." What is reasonable must be considered in light of the size of the estate and the amount of indebtedness. Objections usually come from other successors, not from the Internal Revenue Service. If one successor spends too much out of the residuary estate for funeral or other expenses, other successors can object. If the court determines that such expenditure was unreasonable, it may order the spender to reimburse the estate. When the estate is small after obligations are paid, the court is concerned that enough will be left to support the family and will not allow excessive funeral expenses.

Expenses incurred by the decedent for estate planning, including fees paid to the estate planner (attorney or other adviser) regarding tax matters, investment, and setting up a revocable funded living trust, are deductible. Fees incurred for planning for disposition of property by will or *inter vivos* gift are among the expenses that are not deductible.

The lifetime debts of the decedent are proper deductions. Debts incurred after death as part of the administration of the estate are not deductible as debts of the decedent, but they may be deductible as administration expenses. All allowed debts, including unpaid mortgages, are proper deductions.

Exhibit 14.9 Sample Gross Estate

1. Home	$ 40,000
Household furniture	10,000
IT&T Stocks	50,000
2. Joint tenancy in an apartment building, which, when established, was not subject to a gift tax. One-half of the value is included in decedent's gross estate.	$150,000
3. 100 shares of Nelson Manufacturing Co. stock. Decedent devised the income (dividends) from the stock to his son for life, the stock itself to be transferred to the decedent's daughter upon his son's death.	$ 25,000
4. *Office building* Decedent had placed the building in a trust for his niece—the income to be paid to himself for 10 years, then the building to be transferred to the niece. The decedent, however, had retained the right to change the beneficiary of the trust and to revoke it.	$100,000
5. *Annuity* Decedent made deductible payments of $1,500 each for five years to an Individual Retirement Account. In addition, nondeductible payments of $1,000 each were made for five years. The surviving spouse is eligible to receive the benefits of this account as an annuity having a value of $18,000. The amount of the annuity to be included is arrived at as follows:	$ 7,200

$$\frac{\text{Nondeductible payments}}{\text{Total payments}} \quad \frac{1{,}000 \times 5}{2{,}500 \times 5} = \frac{5{,}000}{12{,}500} = 40\% \text{ of } 18{,}000 = 7{,}200$$

6. The decedent's uncle established a trust in which he placed $100,000 worth of various stocks. The trust named the decedent the trustee and gave the decedent a general power of appointment over the trust income and the trust property.	$100,000
7 Accumulated, undistributed income from trust.	$ 10,000
8. Life insurance policy naming the executor as beneficiary.	$ 10,000
9. Life insurance policy naming the estate as beneficiary.	$ 5,000
TOTAL ASSETS (gross estate)	$507,200

The deduction for taxes is limited to taxes that accrued against the decedent while alive. It does not extend to taxes accruing after death. Thus, the final federal income tax paid by the personal representative for the decedent's own income is deductible, but the income tax on the estate's income is not. Federal estate and state inheritance taxes paid for the privilege of transferring the estate are not deductible. Certain credits, however, are allowed for state and foreign death taxes that must be paid (see below).

Note: Although double deductions (Form 706 and 1041) are disallowed, deductions for taxes, interest, and business expenses accrued at the date of the decedent's death are allowed both as (1) claims against the estate (Schedule K, Form 706), see I.R.C. § 2053(a); and (2) deductions of the decedent (Form 1041), see I.R.C. § 691(b).

Losses. The next deduction subtracted from the gross estate is for losses sustained during the administration of the decedent's estate (see I.R.C. § 2054). Such losses do not include the lessening of the value of assets of the estate, e.g., a drop in the value of stock or the loss in the sale of some property. Losses that are deductible are theft and casualty losses that occur during the administration of the estate. Casualty losses include losses due to fires, storms, shipwrecks, and the like. When such losses are recovered from insurance policies or from a suit for damages, they are not deductible. In addition, if the casualty or theft loss has already been deducted from the decedent's or the estate's income tax, such losses cannot be deducted from the gross estate for tax purposes.

Exhibit 14.10 Basic Data for Schedules J–S of the U.S. Estate Tax Return

Schedule J—Funeral Expenses and Expenses Incurred in Administering Property Subject to Claims

All deductible funeral expenses, including burial, headstone, mausoleum, cost of transporting the body to the funeral home, and payment of clergy, are included in Schedule J. Funeral expenses must be reasonable, as judged by the size of the decedent's estate. Other deductible expenses are the administration expenses, including the personal representative's commission, attorney's fees, court filing fees, accountant's fees, expenses of selling assets if the sale is necessary to pay decedent's debts, and so on.

Schedule K—Debts of the Decedent, and Mortgages and Liens

Only valid debts owed by the decedent at the time of death can be included on Schedule K. Any debt that is disputed or the subject of litigation cannot be deducted unless the estate concedes it is a valid claim. Property tax deductions are limited to taxes that accrued prior to the date of the decedent's death. Federal taxes on income during the decedent's lifetime are deductible, but taxes on income received after death are not deductible. Notes unsecured by a mortgage or another lien are also included in this schedule. "Mortgages and liens" are those obligations secured on property that are included in the gross estate at the full values and are deductible only to the extent that the liability was contracted for an adequate and full consideration in money or money's worth.

Schedule L—Net Losses During Administration and Expenses Incurred in Administering Property Not Subject to Claims

Included in Schedule L are losses limited strictly to those that occur during the settlement of the estate from fire, storm, shipwreck, or other casualty, or from theft to the extent that such losses are not compensated for by insurance or otherwise. Expenses incurred in administering property not subject to claims are usually expenses resulting from the administration of trusts established by the decedent before death or the collection of other assets or the clearance of title to other property included in the decedent's gross estate for estate tax purposes but not included in the decedent's probate estate.

Schedule M—Bequests, etc., to Surviving Spouse (Marital Deduction)

Schedule M lists any property that passes to the surviving spouse. The marital deduction is authorized for certain property interests passing from the decedent to the surviving spouse. It includes property interests that are part of the decedent's gross estate. The QTIP marital deduction election is made on this schedule.

Schedule N—Qualified ESOP Sales (Under Section 2057)

This deduction has been repealed, and this schedule is no longer used.

Schedule O—Charitable, Public, and Similar Gifts and Bequests

Included in Schedule O are charitable gifts or transfers made by will or other written instruments. A gift is charitable if it is for a public purpose, such as the furtherance of religion, science, literature, education, art, and the prevention of cruelty to children and animals.

Schedule P—Credit for Foreign Death Taxes

Schedule P includes credit for foreign death taxes, which is allowable only when the decedent was a citizen or resident of the United States. In some cases, noncitizens who are residents may claim credit if the president has issued a proclamation granting the credit to citizens of a foreign country of which the resident was a citizen and if that country allows a similar credit to decedents who were citizens of the United States residing in that country.

Schedule Q—Credit for Tax on Prior Transfers

Included in Schedule Q is property received by the transferee (the decedent) from a transferor who died within 10 years before or 2 years after the decedent (see the earlier discussion). Credit is allowable for all or a part of the federal estate tax paid by the transferor's estate with respect to the transfer as long as the specified period of time has not elapsed. Where the transferee was the transferor's surviving spouse, no credit is given to the extent that a marital deduction was allowed the transferor's estate. Also, no credit is authorized for federal gift taxes paid in connection with the transfer of the property to the transferee.

Schedules R and R–1—Generation-Skipping Transfer Tax

Included in Schedules R and R–1 are the reporting and computation of the generation-skipping transfer tax imposed only on "direct skips."

Schedule S—Increased Estate Tax on Excess Retirement Accumulations

Included in Schedule S are the reporting and computation of the increased estate tax imposed on excess accumulations in qualified employer plans (pensions) and IRAs.

When the above expenses, losses, and debts have been subtracted from the gross estate, what remains is called the *adjusted gross estate* (I.R.C. § 2056[c]2).

Marital Deduction. The next and potentially most valuable deduction, the marital deduction, is then calculated (see I.R.C. §§ 2056 and 2523). The current statute gives each spouse the right to leave to the surviving spouse an unlimited amount of the decedent spouse's estate free from estate tax.

For example, suppose a decedent's gross estate is $1,000,000. The total amount of deductions allowed for expenses, liens, debts, taxes, and losses is $300,000. The decedent has left $100,000 to various charitable organizations, with the balance of the estate going to the decedent's surviving spouse. The *adjusted gross estate* is the gross estate minus the deductions for expenses, encumbrances, indebtedness, taxes, estate-planning expenses, and losses previously mentioned. Therefore, the adjusted gross estate in our example is $1,000,000 less the $300,000—or $700,000. Note that the charitable deduction is not involved in determining the adjusted gross estate. It is a proper deduction in determining the *taxable estate,* but it is deducted only after the amount of the marital deduction has been determined and deducted.

The marital deduction allowed in this illustration would then be $600,000 since the decedent has left the entire estate (less the $100,000 to various charities) to her spouse. If a decedent had left the surviving spouse less than $600,000, e.g., had given the spouse $400,000, the amount of the marital deduction would be limited to the amount passing to the spouse outright, the $400,000.

Note that in every state a surviving spouse is entitled to common law dower or curtesy rights, or statutory rights in lieu thereof. If a decedent devises less to the surviving spouse than the amount to which he or she is entitled under applicable state law, the spouse may elect to receive the amount to which he or she is entitled under the above rights (usually the larger amount). The amount received by the spouse pursuant to such election then becomes the amount of the marital deduction up to the statutory maximum.

The marital deduction applies to either the husband's estate or the wife's estate when one dies and the other spouse survives. Because of its tax-saving advantages, the marital deduction is an important tax consideration in estate planning. However, indiscriminate use of the marital deduction without regard for other methods of disposition, such as successive estates to avoid a second tax upon the death of the surviving spouse, may actually increase rather than decrease the tax liability of the two estates. Such overuse of the marital deduction may needlessly subject too much property to taxation when the surviving spouse dies.

Example: Suppose a husband has an adjusted gross estate valued at $1,200,000. Assuming he dies in 1995 without having made any taxable lifetime gifts, he could leave his entire estate to his wife outright, and with the unlimited marital deduction, no tax would be due from his estate upon his death. However, his wife now has the entire estate, and assuming her adjusted gross estate totals the same $1,200,000 at her death, her estate is taxed on the entire $1,200,000. The tax is $427,800 less the $192,800 unified credit, or $235,000.

From a tax-saving viewpoint, it is more economical for the husband to leave $600,000 of his estate to his wife outright or in a so-called "marital trust." This trust could provide for investment advice or management protection, but it makes the property available to the spouse (wife) on her request. The other $600,000 is placed in a "family" or "bypass trust", with all income from the trust payable to the spouse (wife) for her lifetime; the remainder goes to their children at the death of the wife. Using this method, there is no tax on the husband's estate at his death because of the marital deduction and the unified credit. There is also no estate tax on the wife's estate at her death because the $600,000 in the bypass trust in which she has only a life estate is not taxable to her estate on her death. It passes free of tax to the remaindermen (the children). Her taxable estate, therefore, is only the $600,000 from the marital deduction trust on which the tax is $192,800; the $192,800 unified credit will be subtracted from this, leaving a tax payable of zero. The tax saving (to the wife's estate) that results from using the second method rather than the first is $235,000.

Therefore, a principal means of reducing the tax impact when there is a surviving spouse is the creation of two testamentary trusts. It is very important in this case to follow the requirements laid out in the Internal Revenue Code. For example, assuming the *wife* is the decedent, her estate may be divided into two testamentary trusts. One trust is called the "marital deduction trust" (Trust A), representing an amount equal to half the adjusted gross estate, which the husband receives tax-free, as previously discussed. The husband has the right to use the income from this trust (and as much of the principal as he desires, if this provision is included in the trust instrument), and he can dispose of Trust A property at his death according to his own wishes. Only the property the husband disposes of at his death is taxable against his estate, i.e., the value of his adjusted gross estate. The husband's estate will be entitled to subtract the available unified credit from the tax payable. None of the property in Trust A is taxable against his deceased wife's estate.

The second half of the decedent wife's estate is put into a second trust, the bypass trust, (Trust B). Trustees will pay to the surviving spouse, the husband in this case, the income from this trust for his life and as much of the principal as they in their discretion deem necessary. Upon the death of the widower, the balance of the property remaining in Trust B goes to the children or other named beneficiaries. Therefore, the property in Trust B is not subject to estate tax when the widower dies (I.R.C. § 2033). However, Trust B property may be subject to the estate tax upon the death of the decedent wife. The wife's estate is entitled to subtract the available unified credit for the year of her death from the tax payable.

To avoid subjecting Trust A property to estate tax upon the death of the decedent wife, the surviving husband, in addition to being entitled to all the income from the trust, must be given a general power of appointment over the assets of this trust, including the right to direct how and to whom the property in Trust A is to be distributed during his lifetime and after his death through his will. The income from Trust A is distributed at least annually to the widower. Trust B is responsible for all debts, taxes, and expenses of the decedent wife's estate. All the income and as much of the principal of the bypass trust (Trust B) as the trustees deem necessary go to the widower during his life, the remainder to their children upon his death.

In this way, only the portion of the decedent wife's estate that is placed in Trust B (i.e., one-half) is subject to tax at her death, and only the amount still remaining of the portion of her estate that is placed in Trust A is taxed at the subsequent death of the widower, her husband. A substantial tax saving is therefore possible. Other factors, such as the value of the surviving husband's property prior to the wife's death, may limit the tax advantages of the "marital deduction trust" (see the sample trust provisions and explanations in Chapter 9).

Many spouses were reluctant to take advantage of the marital deduction because they did not want to give their spouses the general power of appointment that allowed the surviving spouse to determine to whom the trust property would be given on that spouse's death. They wanted to be sure, for example, that the assets acquired during a first marriage eventually went to the children of that marriage. Granting a general power of appointment made property eligible for the marital deduction tax advantages, but it also created the problem of the children's inheritance if, for example, the surviving spouse remarried or chose to leave the property to someone other than the children. The ERTA resolved this problem with the creation of the "qualified terminable interest property" (QTIP) and its QTIP trust. This trust allows property to qualify for the marital deduction *and* ensures the right of the children to receive the assets when the second spouse dies. The requirements for property with its "qualifying income interest" to be used in a QTIP trust were discussed previously and must be reviewed. The essential difference between the standard marital deduction trust with the general power of appointment and the QTIP trust is the executor's election on the decedent spouse's estate tax return to specifically elect QTIP status for that trust. In other words, in our example above, the QTIP trust, like Trust B, would give income to the husband for life, then the remainder to the children, but the husband has no power to dispose of the principal at his death. The executor would elect to have this trust become a QTIP trust, and the property would then be transferred to the children when the husband dies. The one disadvantage is that the executor's election causes the QTIP trust property to be taxed in the second spouse's (the husband's in our case) estate when he dies even though he does not get the property or have the right to determine to whom it will go. The I.R.C. provides that any additional taxes generated by the QTIP trust will be paid from assets of the QTIP trust unless the surviving spouse (the husband in our example) directs otherwise. In other words, those who inherit the QTIP property must pay these additional taxes.

Charitable Deductions. Another federal estate tax deduction allowed by statute is the charitable deduction (see I.R.C. §§ 2055 and 2522). After the adjusted gross estate has been computed, the marital deduction and charitable deductions are subtracted to arrive at the net taxable estate. The charitable deduction includes any transfer of estate assets for public, charitable, educational, and religious purposes. The amount of the charitable deduction allowed under I.R.C. § 2055 is the value of property in the decedent's estate that was transferred by the decedent during life or by will to a charitable institution. The deduction is limited to the amount actually available for charitable uses. Therefore, if under the terms of a will the federal estate tax, the federal generation-skipping tax, or any other estate or inheritance tax is payable in whole or in part out of any bequest, legacy or devise that would otherwise be allowed as a charitable deduction, the amount that can be deducted is the amount of the bequest, legacy, or devise reduced by the total amount of these taxes. The kinds of transfers that qualify for the charitable deduction are described in I.R.C. § 2055 and include the following:

(a) *In general*—For purposes of the tax imposed by section 2001, the value of the taxable estate shall be determined by deducting from the value of the gross estate the amount of all bequests, legacies, devises, or transfers.—

(1) to or for the use of the United States, any State, any political subdivision thereof, or the District of Columbia, for exclusively public purposes;

(2) to or for the use of any corporation organized and operated exclusively for religious, charitable, scientific, literary, or educational purposes, including the encouragement of art, or to foster national or international amateur sports competition (but only if no part of its activities involve the provision of athletic facilities or equipment), and the prevention of cruelty to children or animals, no part of the net earnings of which inures to the benefit of any private stockholder or individual, which is not disqualified for tax exemption under section 501(c)(3) by reason of attempting to influence legislation, and which does not participate in, or intervene in (including the publishing or distributing of statements), any political campaign on behalf of any candidate for public office;

(3) to a trustee or trustees, or a fraternal society, order, or association operating under the lodge system, but only if such contributions or gifts are to be used by such trustee or trustees, or by such fraternal society, order, or association, exclusively for religious, charitable, scientific, literary, or educational purposes, or for the prevention of cruelty to children or animals, such trust, fraternal society, order, or association would not be disqualified for tax exemption under section 501(c)(3) by reason of attempting to influence legislation, and such trustee or trustees, or such fraternal society, order, or association, does not participate in, or intervene in (including the publishing or distributing of statements), any political campaign on behalf of any candidate for public office; or

(4) to or for the use of any veterans' organization incorporated by Act of Congress, or of its departments or local chapters or posts, no part of the net earnings of which inures to the benefit of any private shareholder or individual. For purposes of this subsection, the complete termination before the date prescribed for the filing of the estate tax return of a power to consume, invade, or appropriate property for the benefit of an individual before such power has been exercised by reason of the death of such individual or for any other reason shall be considered and deemed to be a qualified disclaimer with the same full force and effect as though he had filed such qualified disclaimer.

Since charities may have similar names, it is important that the charity be designated in the will or trust by its full and correct name. It is also possible that another charity may have the same name. It is wise to consider this possibility and make sure the charity is properly identified to prevent later conflicts. The testator may limit the use of the gift if he wishes. Gifts made to individuals are not deductible under the charitable deduction provision. Two tax advantages may be obtained by making charitable gifts: (1) by decreasing the value of the donor's estate and (2) by claiming an income tax deduction for the amount of the gift on the donor's federal income tax return.

Gross Estate Tax. After the taxable estate (total gross estate less allowable deductions) is determined, the adjusted taxable gifts made by the decedent after 1976 (lifetime taxable gifts from all the decedent's gift tax returns, Form 709, not included in the gross estate [see Schedule G]) are added to the taxable estate. A tentative estate tax is calculated on this sum using the Unified Rate Schedule. The *gift* tax payable on the post-1976 adjusted taxable gifts is then subtracted from the tentative tax to arrive at the gross estate tax, which is subject to the allowable credits.

Credits.   The following credits against the gross estate tax are included under I.R.C. §§ 2010–2015:

- The unified estate and gift tax credit.
- The credit for state death taxes that have actually been paid to the decedent's state. The credit allowed is limited to the lesser of the amount of tax actually paid or the amount provided for in Exhibit 14.11. The adjusted taxable estate is the federal taxable estate less $60,000. If the adjusted taxable estate is $40,000 or less, no credit for state death taxes is allowed.
- The credit for federal gift taxes on certain transfers the decedent made before January 1, 1977, that are included in the gross estate. Obtain Form 4808, Computation of Credit for Gift Tax, to calculate this credit.
- The credit for foreign death taxes (to help alleviate the burden of double taxation on the decedent's estate from two or more nations).
- The credit for tax on prior transfers, e.g., a credit for estate taxes paid on the estate of the spouse of the decedent when the spouse died ten years or less prior to or two years after the decedent (see the previous discussion).

Net Estate Tax.   Once the allowable credits are determined and subtracted from the gross estate tax, the remaining figure, called the net estate tax, is the tax due the federal government.

Exhibit 14.11   Computation of Maximum Credit for State Death Taxes

(A) Adjusted Taxable Estate* Equal to or More Than:	(B) Adjusted Taxable Estate* Less Than:	(C) Credit on Amount in Column (A)	(D) Rates of Credit on Excess over Amount in Column (A)
$ 0	$ 40,000	$ 0	None
40,000	90,000	0	0.8%
90,000	140,000	400	1.6
140,000	240,000	1,200	2.4
240,000	440,000	3,600	3.2
440,000	640,000	10,000	4.0
640,000	840,000	18,000	4.8
840,000	1,040,000	27,600	5.6
1,040,000	1,540,000	38,800	6.4
1,540,000	2,040,000	70,800	7.2
2,040,000	2,540,000	106,800	8.0
2,540,000	3,040,000	146,800	8.8
3,040,000	3,540,000	190,800	9.6
3,540,000	4,040,000	238,800	10.4
4,040,000	5,040,000	290,800	11.2
5,040,000	6,040,000	402,800	12.0
6,040,000	7,040,000	522,800	12.8
7,040,000	8,040,000	650,800	13.6
8,040,000	9,040,000	786,800	14.4
9,040,000	10,040,000	930,800	15.2
10,040,000		1,082,800	16.0

*Adjusted Taxable Estate = Taxable Estate − $60,000.

Additional Taxes. The following additional taxes are added to the net estate tax to arrive at the total transfer taxes to be paid when the federal estate tax return is filed:

- The generation-skipping transfer tax imposed on direct skips.
- The increased estate tax on excess retirement accumulations.

Federal estate, state estate, and state inheritance taxes must be paid either out of the estate assets or by the persons to whom the estate assets are distributed. The will may contain a provision that requires such persons to pay estate and/ or inheritance taxes due on a devise; otherwise, these taxes are generally paid out of the residue of the estate. Sometime after the personal representative files the estate tax return, the IRS sends an "estate tax closing letter" or notifies the personal representative that the return is not acceptable. If it is not acceptable, the IRS will determine the proper tax and request prompt payment. Because an estate tax return is routinely audited, the personal representative should file Form 2848, Power of Attorney and Declaration of Representative (see Form 98 in Appendix A), with the federal estate tax return, authorizing the attorney for the personal representative to represent the estate.

ASSIGNMENT 14.5

1. Review the section in the Internal Revenue Code dealing with alternate valuation. How does it work? What is its purpose?
2. Define "incidents of ownership." On what tax form does this phrase appear?
3. List examples of property subject to federal estate tax. Give imaginary figures for your examples (e.g., $10,000 to Mary Doe as provided in paragraph 3 of decedent's will). Using the examples, create a fact situation from which a sample federal estate tax return can be completed.
4. Explain the marital deduction and its use. Review the section of the Internal Revenue Code where it is discussed.
5. List the expenses, claims (debts), deductions, and credits allowed by the federal government when computing the federal estate tax.
6. Describe the marital deduction trust and its tax-saving function.
7. List examples of charitable deductions.

State Estate Tax Return

State estate taxes are imposed on the decedent's privilege of transferring property and are measured by the value of the property transferred. Only the state of the decedent's domicile has power to impose an estate tax on the decedent's estate. The exception to this general rule is that property located in a state other than the decedent's domicile is taxable in that state.

Most states levy an estate tax equal to the credit for state death taxes allowed on the federal estate tax return (see Exhibit 14.11). Form 100 in Appendix A is an example of the Minnesota Estate Tax Return. Individual state statutes must be checked for any estate taxes imposed in addition to the credit estate tax and for applicable deductions, exemptions, and credits.

The due date for the state estate tax return is usually the same as for the federal return, and any extension of time granted for the federal return automatically

Exhibit 14.12   Inheritance Tax Rates for Individual States

State	Surviving Spouse	Other Beneficiaries
Connecticut	0	3–14%
Delaware	2–4%	1–16%
Indiana	0	1–20%
Iowa	0	1–15%
Kansas	0	1–15%
Kentucky	0	2–16%
Louisiana	0	2–10%
Maryland	1%	1 & 10%
Montana	0	2–32%
Nebraska	0	1 & 6–18%
New Hampshire	0	0 & 18%
New Jersey	0	0 & 11–16%
North Carolina	0	1–17%
Pennsylvania	3% 7/1/94	6 & 15%
	2% 1/1/96	
	1% 1/1/97	
	0 1/1/98	
South Dakota	0	3.75–30%
Tennessee	0	5.5–9.5%
Texas	Federal credit	Federal credit

Rates are generally graduated for different classes of beneficiaries grouped according to relationship to the decedent; lower rates apply to closer relationships.

Check individual states for classification of beneficiaries, exemptions, and applicable rates of tax.

extends the filing deadline for the state return. State statutes vary, however, and should be reviewed.

State Inheritance Tax Return

A number of states impose an inheritance tax on the recipients of both real and personal property transferred to them from the estate of a decedent resident of the state. It is a tax on inherited property, i.e., a tax on the beneficiaries' right to receive the decedent's property, and the rate of tax (usually graduated) varies with the relationship of the heir or devisee to the decedent and the value of the property received (see Exhibit 14.12 for the inheritance tax rates of individual states). As with the estate tax, state statutes must be checked for deductions, exemptions, and credits that apply to the inheritance tax, as well as due dates and extensions of time to file and pay the tax. Form 101 in Appendix A is an example of the Iowa Inheritance Tax Return.

KEY TERMS

Successor
Exemption
   equivalent

Generation-skipping
   transfer trust
Generation-skipping
   transfer tax

Transferor (grantor)
Taxable termination
Skip person

Taxable distribution
Direct skip

REVIEW QUESTIONS

1. What is the difference between estate and inheritance taxes? Are they levied by both the state and federal governments?
2. What types of taxes, e.g., income, gift, or death taxes, are imposed or levied by your state?
3. Who is responsible for paying taxes of the estate, and what funds are used to pay them?
4. Although Congress changes the tax code every year, explain the major changes it passed in the years 1976, 1981, and 1986.
5. Explain the unified transfer tax credit and the unified transfer gift and estate tax rates. What is the current unified transfer tax credit or, simply, unified credit for 1995? What is meant by the "exemption equivalent"?
6. How does the use of the marital deduction save estate taxes?
7. What is QTIP property and how does it qualify for the marital deduction?
8. How are gifts made between spouses taxed before and after death? Also explain gift splitting.
9. Briefly explain the Uniform Gifts (Transfers) to Minors Act.
10. Who is responsible for filing the decedent's tax returns? What liability exists? How is a tax refund obtained?
11. Which states have no state income tax? Which states have a state gift tax?
12. When preparing the federal estate tax return, how are the decedent's gross estate and taxable estate determined?
13. Briefly explain the generation-skipping transfer tax.
14. Does your state have an inheritance tax? How is this tax determined? Who pays the tax?

CASE PROBLEMS

Problem 1
Return to the Jane Doe case in Chapter 12. After reading the case, review the executed federal estate tax form found in Appendix A (Form 96). Assume you have been appointed personal representative of your own estate (even though that would be impossible), and now you must file estate tax returns for the federal government and, if required, for your state government.
A. Develop appropriate checklists for your own set of circumstances, e.g., assets, liabilities, forms of ownership, and beneficiaries.
B. Execute the required federal and state estate tax returns using the forms in the Jane Doe case as a guide.

Problem 2
A. Describe the types of property that are included on an inheritance tax return, if any, in your state. Give imaginary monetary figures for each item of property. Describe and list the deductions, exemptions, and credits allowed by your state's inheritance tax return. Cite the authority and give figures for each item on your list.
B. Using this information, create your own fact situation and complete the following forms according to the laws of your state: Inventory and Appraisal, Schedule of Nonprobate Assets, and Inheritance Tax Return.

CHAPTER FIFTEEN

ETHICAL PRINCIPLES RELEVANT TO PRACTICING LEGAL ASSISTANTS

OBJECTIVES

After completing this chapter, you should be able to:

- Identify, understand, and explain the ethical employment responsibilities of practicing legal assistants in the field of wills, trusts, and estate administration.

- Understand the types of legal tasks that a paralegal may perform and be able to identify and therefore avoid those that would constitute the "unauthorized practice of law."

- Identify the codes and rules, specifically the 1969 Model Code of Professional Responsibility and the 1983 Model Rules of Professional Conduct written by the American Bar Association, that establish the ethical guidelines for the practice of law and provide the basis for disciplining attorneys and paralegals.

- Identify the specific rules and opinions adopted and enforced by the bar association of the specific state in which you live and intend to practice law.

SCOPE OF THE CHAPTER

The final chapter of this text discusses the standards of legal ethics that apply to individuals who practice law, e.g., lawyers and nonlawyers (including paralegals). To understand your employment responsibilities as a practicing paralegal, the legal and ethical principles that affect your work must be examined. This chapter discusses the various ethical standards and guidelines that apply to typical legal assistant employment tasks. These ethical standards, which are established by the American Bar Association, the National Association of Legal Assistants, and the National Federation of Paralegal Associations, set the guidelines that help to identify and direct the ethical conduct required for practicing paralegals.

PARALEGALS AND CANONS OF ETHICS

Ethical standards and guidelines that apply to the legal profession are written by the **American Bar Association (ABA)** and published in codes and rules that, although not binding on individual state bar associations, have by and large been enacted by these organizations. The 1969 **Model Code of Professional Responsibility** and the 1983 **Model Rules of Professional Conduct** are the regulatory cornerstones of the legal profession. Both were enacted to establish ethical guidelines for the practice of law as well as to provide a basis for disciplining attorneys whose professional conduct violates the guidelines. A violation of either the Model Code or the Model Rules could result in a disciplinary action that costs the offending attorney his license to practice law. Courses on legal ethics are usually required in law school, and state bar examinations include ethics questions. Both the ABA and state bar associations issue **opinions** interpreting and applying these standards to everyday legal practices and issues.

It is important for you as a practicing paralegal to know the ethical standards and guidelines directing attorneys in their legal practice so that you can avoid violating the directives. Additionally, *ABA guidelines require attorneys to educate the legal assistants they employ on the various ethical issues that affect the practice of law.*

◄ ETHICAL ISSUE

The 1969 Model Code, forerunner of the 1983 Model Rules, is made up of **Canons of Ethics** (general rules or statements regarding behavior and professional responsibilities that apply to lawyers in their practice of law), **Ethical Considerations (EC)** (ideals of professional conduct that attorneys should strive

MINI-GLOSSARY BOX

American Bar Association (ABA)
A national association of attorneys in the United States that sets the ethical standards and guidelines that apply to the legal profession.

Model Code of Professional Responsibility
Rules of conduct governing the legal profession written by the ABA and adopted by many states.

Model Rules of Professional Conduct
Standards of conduct written by the ABA to establish ethical guidelines for the practice of law.

Opinions
Statements issued by the ABA and state bar associations interpreting and applying their codes and rules that establish ethical guidelines for the practice of law.

MINI-GLOSSARY BOX

Canons of Ethics
General rules or principles regarding behavior and professional responsibilities that apply to attorneys in their practice of law.

Ethical Considerations (EC)
Ideals of professional conduct that attorneys should strive to achieve.

Disciplinary Rules (DR)
Statements of minimum professional conduct that, if violated, lead to sanctions against the offending attorney.

to achieve), and **Disciplinary Rules (DR)** (statements of minimum professional conduct that if violated lead to sanctions against the offending lawyer). The following statements briefly summarize the Canons:

- Lawyers should help preserve the competence and integrity of the legal profession.
- Lawyers should facilitate the broad availability of legal counsel.
- Lawyers should seek to prevent the unauthorized practice of law.
- Lawyers should preserve client confidences and secrets.
- Lawyers should provide clients with independent professional judgment.
- Lawyers should represent clients zealously without violating the law.
- Lawyers should represent clients competently.
- Lawyers should promote progress and improvement of the legal system.
- Lawyers should refrain from engaging in conduct that creates the appearance of professional impropriety.

The 1983 Model Rules consolidate the Canons, Ethical Considerations, and Disciplinary Rules of the Code into a *single* set of rules governing the following areas of the legal profession: attorney-client relationship; lawyer as counselor; lawyer as advocate; lawyers dealings with nonclients; law firms and associations; community service; legal services information; and the preservation and the promotion of the integrity of the legal profession.

Since legal assistants are prevented from becoming full bar association members, neither the Model Code nor the Model Rules directly apply to their employment activities. *Paralegals are therefore not subject to disciplinary action (reprimand, private and public censure, suspension, or disbarment) as are attorneys for violations of these ethical guidelines. Instead, attorneys are disciplined for the unethical conduct of legal assistants under their control and supervision.* This fact is reflected to the following excerpt from the Model Code:

> Obviously the Canons, Ethical Considerations, and Disciplinary Rules cannot apply to nonlawyers; however, they do define the type of ethical conduct that the public has a right to expect not only of lawyers but also of their nonprofessional employees and associates in all matters pertaining to professional employment. A lawyer should ultimately be responsible for the conduct of employees and associates in the course of the professional representation of the client.

The Model Rules also address this issue in the Comment that follows Rule 5.3:

> A lawyer should give [legal] assistants appropriate instruction and supervision concerning the ethical aspects of their employment . . . and should be responsible for their work product. The measures employed in supervising nonlawyers should take account of the fact that they do not have legal training and are not subject to professional discipline.

Thus, the attorney-paralegal relationship is governed by the Model Code and the Model Rules. It is the supervisory function of attorneys working with legal assistants that forms the basis of authority for allowing law office use of legal assistants. In this capacity, attorneys are directly responsible for ensuring that paralegals do not engage in the unauthorized practice of law. Likewise, paralegals must not engage in obviously unethical practices that are requested or directed by the supervising attorney, and paralegals must insist that any unethical activities they become aware of are brought to the attorney's attention and immediately discontinued. It is therefore essential for you as a paralegal to know the ethical guidelines governing the practice of law, especially the Model Code and the Model Rules provisions that are relevant to the attorney-paralegal business relationship.

Model Code Provisions Relating to the Attorney-Paralegal Relationship

Although legal assistants, under the supervision of an attorney, may perform a considerable amount of the work normally undertaken by a lawyer, care must be taken in delegating responsibility to the paralegal since Canon 3 of the Code prohibits nonlawyers from performing tasks reserved exclusively for attorneys. For example, legal assistants may not "act in matters involving professional judgment. Where this professional judgment is not involved, nonlawyers . . . may engage in occupations that require a special knowledge of law in certain areas" (EC 3–5). "A lawyer often delegates tasks to . . . lay persons. Such delegation is proper if the lawyer maintains a direct relationship with a client, supervises the delegated work, and has complete professional responsibility for the work product" (EC 3–6).

Issues and problems relating to confidential and privileged communications are covered under Canon 4. "It is a matter of common knowledge that the normal operation of a law office exposes confidential professional information to nonlawyer employees. . . . [T]his obligates a lawyer to exercise care in selecting and training employees so that the sanctity of all confidences and secrets of clients may be preserved" (EC 4–2). "A lawyer should endeavor to act in a manner which preserves this evidentiary privilege. . . . [A lawyer] should avoid professional discussions in the presence of persons to whom the privilege does not extend" (EC 4–4). The disciplinary rule that accompanies Canon 4 warns lawyers to use care in preventing employees from revealing or using confidential information (DR 4–101D). This duty applies to legal assistants as well.

Issues involving conflicts of interest are covered by Canon 5. Situations in which lawyers are cautioned against accepting clients or cases because of potential conflicts of interest may also apply to legal assistants. When such problems arise, you must inform your supervising attorney.

Model Rules of Professional Conduct and the Attorney-Paralegal Relationship

Practicing attorneys employ extensive support staffs, including clerks, interns, secretaries, and investigators, to help maintain daily law office operations. Over the past three decades, the emergence and growth of paralegals as a distinct profession have led to the creation of a specific provision in the Model Rules concerning law office employment of nonlawyer assistants. Rule 5.3, Responsibilities Regarding Nonlawyer Assistants, states:

With respect to a nonlawyer employed or retained by or associated with a lawyer:

(a) A partner in a law firm shall make reasonable efforts to ensure that the firm has in effect measures giving reasonable assurance that the person's conduct is compatible with the professional obligations of the lawyer;

(b) A lawyer having direct supervisory authority over the nonlawyer shall make reasonable efforts to ensure that the person's conduct is compatible with the professional obligations of the lawyer; and

(c) A lawyer shall be responsible for conduct of such a person that would be a violation of the Rules of Professional Conduct if engaged in by a lawyer if:

(1) the lawyer orders or, with the knowledge of the specific conduct, ratifies the conduct involved; or

(2) the lawyer is a partner in the law firm in which the person is employed, or has direct supervisory authority over the person, and knows of the conduct at a time when its consequences can be avoided or mitigated but fails to take reasonable remedial action. [Also, see Model Rule 8.4.]

The Model Rules also contains guidelines that direct the manner in which lawyers may delegate work to nonlawyer office personnel. Under Rule 5.5(b), attorneys are cautioned not to "assist a person who is not a member of the bar in the performance of activity that constitutes the unauthorized practice of law." The Comment following this Rule goes on to say that the Rule "does not prohibit a lawyer from employing the services of paraprofessionals and delegating functions to them, so long as the lawyer supervises the delegated work and retains responsibility for their work."

American Bar Association Committees Dealing with Legal Assistants

The ABA Standing Committee on Legal Assistants has taken a leading role in identifying the rights and duties of paralegals as practicing professionals. The following definition of paralegals reflects this effort:

Persons who, although not members of the legal profession, are qualified through education, training, or work experience, are employed or retained by a lawyer, law office, governmental agency, or other entity in a capacity or function which involves the performance, under the direction and supervision of an attorney, of specifically-delegated substantive legal work, which work, for the most part, requires a sufficient knowledge of legal concepts such that, absent that legal assistant, the attorney would perform the task.

Other activities of this committee include accrediting legal assistant education programs, issuing reports on various issues related to the profession (an example is whether legal assistants should be certified to practice), and publishing articles on how paralegals can be effectively used in law offices. In 1991 this committee provided and the American Bar Association published the ABA Model Guidelines for the Utilization of Legal Assistant Services (see Exhibit 15.1).

The ABA Committee on Ethics and Professional Responsibility has produced several advisory opinions on the proper role of legal assistants in law office settings. Committee action includes approving the use of paralegals' names on law office letterheads and business cards so long as the paralegals are conspicuously identified as "Legal Assistants." Bar associations in some states, e.g., Colorado, do not allow paralegals' names to appear on the letterhead of a law firm. However, such states generally do allow paralegals to author and sign

Exhibit 15.1 ABA Model Guidelines for the Utilization of Legal Assistant Services

Preamble

State courts, bar associations, or bar committees in at least seventeen states have prepared recommendations for the utilization of legal assistant services. While their content varies, their purpose appears uniform: to provide lawyers with a reliable basis for delegating responsibility for performing a portion of the lawyer's tasks to legal assistants. The purpose of preparing model guidelines is not to contradict the guidelines already adopted or to suggest that other guidelines may be more appropriate in a particular jurisdiction. It is the view of the Standing Committee on Legal Assistants of the American Bar Association, however, that a model set of guidelines for the utilization of legal assistant services may assist many states in adopting or revising such guidelines. The Standing Committee is of the view that guidelines will encourage lawyers to utilize legal assistant services effectively and promote the growth of the legal assistant profession. In undertaking this project, the Standing Committee has attempted to state guidelines that conform with the American Bar Association's Model Rules of Professional Conduct, decided authority, and contemporary practice. Lawyers, of course, are to be first directed by Rule 5.3 of the Model Rules in the utilization of legal assistant services, and nothing contained in these guidelines is intended to be inconsistent with that rule. Specific ethical considerations in particular states, however, may require modification of these guidelines before their adoption. In the commentary after each guideline, we have attempted to identify the basis for the guideline and any issues of which we are aware that the guideline may present; those drafting such guidelines may wish to take them into account.

Guideline 1: A lawyer is responsible for all of the professional actions of a legal assistant performing legal assistant services at the lawyer's direction and should take reasonable measures to ensure that the legal assistant's conduct is consistent with the lawyer's obligations under the ABA Model Rules of Professional Conduct.

Guideline 2: Provided the lawyer maintains responsibility for the work product, a lawyer may delegate to a legal assistant any task normally performed by the lawyer except those tasks proscribed to one not licensed as a lawyer by statute, court rule, administrative rule or regulation, controlling authority, the ABA Model Rules of Professional Conduct, or these Guidelines.

Guideline 3: A lawyer may not delegate to a legal assistant:

(a) Responsibility for establishing an attorney-client relationship.
(b) Responsibility for establishing the amount of a fee to be charged for a legal service.
(c) Responsibility for a legal opinion rendered to a client.

Guideline 4: It is the lawyer's responsibility to take reasonable measures to ensure that clients, courts, and other lawyers are aware that a legal assistant, whose services are utilized by the lawyer in performing legal services, is not licensed to practice law.

Guideline 5: A lawyer may identify legal assistants by name and title on the lawyer's letterhead and on business cards identifying the lawyer's firm.

Guideline 6: It is the responsibility of a lawyer to take reasonable measures to ensure that all client confidences are preserved by a legal assistant.

Guideline 7: A lawyer should take reasonable measures to prevent conflicts of interest resulting from a legal assistant's other employment or interests insofar as such other employment or interests would present a conflict of interest if it were that of the lawyer.

Guideline 8: A lawyer may include a charge for the work performed by a legal assistant in setting a charge for legal services.

Guideline 9: A lawyer may not split legal fees with a legal assistant nor pay a legal assistant for the referral of legal business. A lawyer may compensate a legal assistant based on the quantity and quality of the legal assistant's work and the value of that work to a law practice, but the legal assistant's compensation may not be contingent, by advance agreement, upon the profitability of the lawyer's practice.

Guideline 10: A lawyer who employs a legal assistant should facilitate the legal assistant's participation in appropriate continuing education and pro bono publico activities.

THE STANDING COMMITTEE ON
LEGAL ASSISTANTS OF THE
AMERICAN BAR ASSOCIATION
May 1991

correspondence on the firm's letterhead so long as the paralegal's status is disclosed and no legal advice or opinions are given in the correspondence.

Ethical Guidelines and State Action

Various state bar associations have issued guidelines concerning the proper role of legal assistants in law offices. An example is the New York State Bar Association guidelines, which address the EC 6 requirement that lawyers preserve "direct relationships" with clients in delegating work to paralegals. New York guidelines determine that "direct relationships" does not mean attorneys must contact clients with a "specified degree of regularity or frequency." Instead, the guidelines instruct attorneys to be available "at all reasonable times" for client consultation and to promote the interest of the client when supervising a paralegal's work. However, today's legal assistants are faced with an ongoing dilemma concerning their professional conduct. At this time, although the states have discussed and proposed various kinds of regulation including certification and licensing legislation, they have not established a uniform position on the statutory regulation of the work performed by practicing legal assistants. In the absence of a single nationally authorized regulatory agency to govern legal assistant conduct, the two existing legal assistant associations have sought to address the dilemma, as discussed in the next section.

Professional Standards and Paralegal Associations

The **National Federation of Paralegal Associations (NFPA)** in Kansas City, Missouri, and the **National Association of Legal Assistants (NALA)** in Tulsa, Oklahoma, have both issued ethical guidelines regarding the attorney-paralegal relationship. The NFPA, consisting of state and local legal assistant groups and individual paralegals from across the nation, first published an "Affirmation of Professional Responsibility." Then, in 1993 the NFPA adopted the Model Code of Ethics and Professional Responsibility. This document is presented as Exhibit 15.2.

The NALA, an organization of individual paralegals, has published a "Code of Ethics and Professional Responsibility" as well as "Model Standards and Guidelines for Utilization of Legal Assistants." The Code consists of twelve canons and is presented in Exhibit 15.3.

The Model Standards and Guidelines published by the NALA present minimum qualifications for paralegals and list employment responsibilities appropriate for them. Establishing minimum competency standards for paralegals, gained either

---

MINI-GLOSSARY BOX

National Federation of Paralegal Associations (NFPA)
One of the two national professional associations of paralegals that issues recommended ethical guidelines regarding the attorney-paralegal relationship. The other is the NALA.

National Association of Legal Assistants (NALA)
One of the two national professional associations of paralegals that issues recommended ethical guidelines regarding the attorney-paralegal relationship. The other is the NFPA.

Exhibit 15.2   NFPA Model Code of Ethics and Professional Responsibility

Preamble

The National Federation of Paralegal Associations, Inc. ("NFPA") is a professional organization comprised of paralegal associations and individual paralegals throughout the United States. Members of NFPA have varying types of backgrounds, experience, education, and job responsibilities which reflect the diversity of the paralegal profession. NFPA promotes the growth, development and recognition of the paralegal profession as an integral partner in the delivery of legal services.

NFPA recognizes that the creation of guidelines and standards for professional conduct are important for the development and expansion of the paralegal profession. In May 1993, NFPA adopted this Model Code of Ethics and Professional Responsibility ("Model Code") to delineate the principles for ethics and conduct to which every paralegal should aspire. The Model Code expresses NFPA's commitment to increasing the quality and efficiency of legal services and recognizes the profession's responsibilities to the public, the legal community, and colleagues.

Paralegals perform many different functions, and these functions differ greatly among practice areas. In addition, each jurisdiction has its own unique legal authority and practices governing ethical conduct and professional responsibilities.

It is essential that each paralegal strive for personal and professional excellence and encourage the professional development of other paralegals as well as those entering the profession. Participation in professional associations intended to advance the quality and standards of the legal profession is of particular importance. Paralegals should possess integrity, professional skill and dedication to the improvement of the legal system and should strive to expand the paralegal role in the delivery of legal services.

Canon 1.

A PARALEGAL[1] SHALL ACHIEVE AND MAINTAIN A HIGH LEVEL OF COMPETENCE.
EC-1.1   A paralegal shall achieve competency through education, training, and work experience.
EC-1.2   A paralegal shall participate in continuing education to keep informed of current legal, technical and general developments.
EC-1.3   A paralegal shall perform all assignments promptly and efficiently.

Canon 2.

A PARALEGAL SHALL MAINTAIN A HIGH LEVEL OF PERSONAL AND PROFESSIONAL INTEGRITY.
EC-2.1   A paralegal shall not engage in any ex parte[2] communications involving the courts or any other adjudicatory body in an attempt to exert undue influence or to obtain advantage for the benefit of only one party.
EC-2.2   A paralegal shall not communicate, or cause another to communicate, with a party the paralegal knows to be represented by a lawyer in a pending matter without the prior consent of the lawyer representing such other party.
EC-2.3   A paralegal shall ensure that all timekeeping and billing records prepared by the paralegal are thorough, accurate, and honest.
EC-2.4   A paralegal shall be scrupulous, thorough and honest in the identification and maintenance of all funds, securities, and other assets of a client and shall provide accurate accountings as appropriate.
EC-2.5   A paralegal shall advise the proper authority of any dishonest or fraudulent acts by any person pertaining to the handling of the funds, securities or other assets of a client.

Canon 3.

A PARALEGAL SHALL MAINTAIN A HIGH STANDARD OF PROFESSIONAL CONDUCT.
EC-3.1   A paralegal shall refrain from engaging in any conduct that offends the dignity and decorum of proceedings before a court or other adjudicatory body and shall be respectful of all rules and procedures.

---

1. "Paralegal" is synonymous with **"Legal Assistant"** and is defined as a person qualified through education, training, or work experience to perform substantive legal work that requires knowledge of legal concepts and is customarily, but not exclusively, performed by a lawyer. This person may be retained or employed by a lawyer, law office, governmental agency or other entity or may be authorized by administrative, statutory or court authority to perform this work.
2. **"Ex Parte"** denotes actions or communications conducted at the instance and for the benefit of one party only, and without notice to, or contestation by, any person adversely interested.

Exhibit 15.2   NFPA Model Code of Ethics and Professional Responsibility—*continued*

EC-3.2   A paralegal shall advise the proper authority of any action of another legal professional which clearly demonstrates fraud, deceit, dishonesty, or misrepresentation.

EC-3.3   A paralegal shall avoid impropriety and the appearance of impropriety.

Canon 4.

A PARALEGAL SHALL SERVE THE PUBLIC INTEREST BY CONTRIBUTING TO THE DELIVERY OF QUALITY LEGAL SERVICES AND THE IMPROVEMENT OF THE LEGAL SYSTEM.

EC-4.1   A paralegal shall be sensitive to the legal needs of the public and shall promote the development and implementation of programs that address those needs.

EC-4.2   A paralegal shall support bona fide efforts to meet the need for legal services by those unable to pay reasonable or customary fees; for example, participation in pro bono projects and volunteer work.

EC-4.3   A paralegal shall support efforts to improve the legal system and shall assist in making changes.

Canon 5.

A PARALEGAL SHALL PRESERVE ALL CONFIDENTIAL INFORMATION[3] PROVIDED BY THE CLIENT OR AC-QUIRED FROM OTHER SOURCES BEFORE, DURING, AND AFTER THE COURSE OF THE PROFESSIONAL RELATIONSHIP.

EC-5.1   A paralegal shall be aware of and abide by all legal authority governing confidential information.

EC-5.2   A paralegal shall not use confidential information to the disadvantage of the client.

EC-5.3   A paralegal shall not use confidential information to the advantage of the paralegal or of a third person.

EC-5.4   A paralegal may reveal confidential information only after full disclosure and with the client's written consent; or, when required by law or court order; or, when necessary to prevent the client from committing an act which could result in death or serious bodily harm.

EC-5.5   A paralegal shall keep those individuals responsible for the legal representation of a client fully informed of any confidential information the paralegal may have pertaining to that client.

EC-5.6   A paralegal shall not engage in any indiscreet communications concerning clients.

Canon 6.

A PARALEGAL'S TITLE SHALL BE FULLY DISCLOSED.[4]

EC-6.1   A paralegal's title shall clearly indicate the individual's status and shall be disclosed in all business and professional communications to avoid misunderstandings and misconceptions about the paralegal's role and responsibilities.

EC-6.2   A paralegal's title shall be included if the paralegal's name appears on business cards, letterhead, brochures, directories, and advertisements.

Canon 7.

A PARALEGAL SHALL NOT ENGAGE IN THE UNAUTHORIZED PRACTICE OF LAW.

EC-7.1   A paralegal shall comply with the applicable legal authority governing the unauthorized practice of law.

Canon 8.

A PARALEGAL SHALL AVOID CONFLICTS OF INTEREST AND SHALL DISCLOSE ANY POSSIBLE CONFLICT TO THE EMPLOYER OR CLIENT, AS WELL AS TO THE PROSPECTIVE EMPLOYERS OR CLIENTS.

EC-8.1   A paralegal shall act within the bounds of the law, solely for the benefit of the client, and shall be free of compromising influences and loyalties. Neither the paralegal's personal or business interest, nor those of other clients or third persons, should compromise the paralegal's professional judgment and loyalty to the client.

EC-8.2   A paralegal shall avoid conflicts of interest which may arise from previous assignments whether for a present or past employer or client.

EC-8.3   A paralegal shall avoid conflicts of interest which may arise from family relationships and from personal and business interests.

---

3. **"Confidential Information"** denotes information relating to a client, whatever its source, which is not public knowledge nor available to the public. (*"Nonconfidential Information"* would generally include the name of the client and the identity of the matter for which the paralegal provided services.)

4. **"Disclose"** denotes communication of information reasonably sufficient to permit identification of the significance of the matter in question.

Exhibit 15.2 NFPA Model Code of Ethics and Professional Responsibility—*continued*

EC-8.4 A paralegal shall create and maintain an effective recordkeeping system that identifies clients, matters, and parties with which the paralegal has worked, to be able to determine whether an actual or potential conflict of interest exists.

EC-8.5 A paralegal shall reveal sufficient nonconfidential information about a client or former client to reasonably ascertain if an actual or potential conflict of interest exists.

EC-8.6 A paralegal shall not participate in or conduct work on any matter where a conflict of interest has been identified.

EC-8.7 In matters where a conflict of interest has been identified and the client consents to continued representation, a paralegal shall comply fully with the implementation and maintenance of an Ethical Wall.[5]

---

5. **"Ethical Wall"** refers to the screening method implemented in order to protect a client from a conflict of interest. An Ethical Wall generally includes, but is not limited to, the following elements: (1) prohibit the paralegal from having any connection with the matter; (2) ban discussions with or the transfer of documents to or from the paralegal; (3) restrict access to files; and (4) educate all members of the firm, corporation or entity as to the separation of the paralegal (both organizationally and physically) from the pending matter. For more information regarding the Ethical Wall, see the NFPA publication entitled "The Ethical Wall—Its Application to Paralegals." *Source: National Federation of Paralegal Associations, Inc., Model Code of Ethics and Professional Responsibility* (1993). Reprinted with permission.

---

through formal educational programs or on-the-job training, is a concept strongly endorsed by the NALA. This organization also supports the concept of certifying paralegal professional competence, and it administers the only national certification program through an examination it has developed and gives to applicants on a voluntary basis. Applicants must pass a two-day exam on topics that include analytical ability, communications, ethics, human relations, legal research, legal terminology, and four topics selected from administration law, bankruptcy, civil litigation, contracts, corporations, criminal law, estate planning and probate, and real estate. Applicants who pass the test are entitled to use the designation C.L.A. (the abbreviation for Certified Legal Assistant) after their names, on their offices, and on their communications and advertisements. A C.L.A. who passes a second exam from one of several specialty topics can use the designation C.L.A.S. (the abbreviation for Certified Legal Assistant Specialists) as well.

In the fall of 1994, the National Federation of Paralegal Associations changed its position on the use of standardized tests for experienced paralegals and now joins the NALA in advocating the use of a competency exam for paralegals. NFPA's proficiency exam, called the Paralegal Advanced Competency Exam (PACE), differs in several ways from the CLA exam. The PACE will be developed by a professional testing company supported by an independent committee of lawyers, paralegals, educators, and members of the general public, and it will be administered by an independent agency. Before a paralegal is eligible to take the two-tiered exam, specific educational and experience requirements must be satisfied. The first tier of the test, which includes general questions, ethics, and state specific sections, will require the paralegal to have finished the necessary educational background plus two years of work experience. Paralegals taking the second tier must have four years of work experience. The PACE will be voluntary unless a state adopts the test and its legislature makes it mandatory.

The Model Standards and Guidelines the NALA has written are intended to guide paralegals and to assist attorneys in effectively utilizing and supervising legal assistants. The complete document appears in Exhibit 15.4.

Exhibit 15.3   Code of Ethics and Professional Responsibility of National Association of Legal Assistants, Inc.

Preamble

It is the responsibility of every legal assistant to adhere strictly to the accepted standards of legal ethics and to live by general principles of proper conduct. The performance of the duties of the legal assistant shall be governed by specific canons as defined herein in order that justice will be served and the goals of the profession attained.

The canons of ethics set forth hereafter are adopted by the National Association of Legal Assistants, Inc., as a general guide, and the enumeration of these rules does not mean there are not others of equal importance although not specifically mentioned.

Canon 1. A legal assistant shall not perform any of the duties that lawyers only may perform nor do things that lawyers themselves may not do.

Canon 2. A legal assistant may perform any task delegated and supervised by a lawyer so long as the lawyer is responsible to the client, maintains a direct relationship with the client, and assumes full professional responsibility for the work product.

Canon 3. A legal assistant shall not engage in the practice of law by accepting cases, setting fees, giving legal advice, or appearing in court (unless otherwise authorized by court or agency rules).

Canon 4. A legal assistant shall not act in matters involving professional legal judgment as the services of a lawyer are essential in the public interest whenever the exercise of such judgment is required.

Canon 5. A legal assistant must act prudently in determining the extent to which a client may be assisted without the presence of a lawyer.

Canon 6. A legal assistant shall not engage in the unauthorized practice of law and shall assist in preventing the unauthorized practice of law.

Canon 7. A legal assistant must protect the confidences of a client, and it shall be unethical for a legal assistant to violate any statute now in effect or hereafter to be enacted controlling privileged communications.

Canon 8. It is the obligation of the legal assistant to avoid conduct which would cause the lawyer to be unethical or even appear to be unethical, and loyalty to the employer is incumbent upon the legal assistant.

Canon 9. A legal assistant shall work continually to maintain integrity and a high degree of competency throughout the legal profession.

Canon 10. A legal assistant shall strive for perfection through education in order to better assist the legal profession in fulfilling its duty of making legal services available to clients and the public.

Canon 11. A legal assistant shall do all other things incidental, necessary, or expedient for the attainment of the ethics and responsibilities imposed by statute or rule of court.

Canon 12. A legal assistant is governed by the American Bar Association Code of Professional Responsibility and the American Bar Association Model Rules of Professional Conduct.

Source: Copyright 1975, revised 1979, 1988. National Association of Legal Assistants, 1516 S. Boston, Ste. 200, Tulsa, OK 74119. Reprinted with permission.

ATTORNEY-CLIENT-PARALEGAL ISSUES

Two major areas of concern relating to the attorney-paralegal professional relationship are the issues of the unauthorized practice of law and privileged/confidential communications. What is the proper role of practicing legal assistants regarding these concerns? What problems might arise? How should they be resolved? These topics occupy the balance of our discussion.

Unauthorized Practice of Law

As previously discussed, regulations governing the practice of law allow attorneys to delegate various responsibilities to legal assistants and other nonlawyer staff. Typical tasks assigned to legal assistants include interviewing clients and

Exhibit 15.4 NALA Model Standards and Guidelines for Utilization of Legal Assistants

Preamble

Proper utilization of the services of legal assistants affects the efficient delivery of legal services. Legal assistants and the legal profession should be assured that some measures exist for identifying legal assistants and their role in assisting attorneys in the delivery of legal services. Therefore, the National Association of Legal Assistants, Inc., hereby adopts these Model Standards and Guidelines as an educational document for the benefit of legal assistants and the legal profession.

Definition

Legal assistants are a distinguishable group of persons who assist attorneys in the delivery of legal services. Through formal education, training, and experience, legal assistants have knowledge and expertise regarding the legal system and substantive and procedural law which qualify them to do work of a legal nature under the supervision of an attorney.

Standards

A legal assistant should meet certain minimum qualifications. The following standards may be used to determine an individual's qualifications as a legal assistant:

1. Successful completion of the Certified Legal Assistant (CLA) examination of the National Association of Legal Assistants, Inc.;
2. Graduation from an ABA approved program of study for legal assistants;
3. Graduation from a course of study for legal assistants which is institutionally accredited but not ABA approved, and which requires not less than the equivalent of 60 semester hours of classroom study;
4. Graduation from a course of study for legal assistants, other than those set forth in (2) and (3) above, plus not less than six months of in-house training as a legal assistant;
5. A baccalaureate degree in any field, plus not less than six months of in-house training as a legal assistant;
6. A minimum of three years of law-related experience under the supervision of an attorney, including at least six months of in-house training as a legal assistant; or
7. Two years of in-house training as a legal assistant.

For purposes of these standards, "in-house training as a legal assistant" means attorney education of the employee concerning legal assistant duties and these guidelines. In addition to review and analysis of assignments, the legal assistant should receive a reasonable amount of instruction directly related to the duties and obligations of the legal assistant.

Guidelines

These guidelines relating to standards of performance and professional responsibility are intended to aid legal assistants and attorneys. The responsibility rests with an attorney who employs legal assistants to educate them with respect to the duties they are assigned and to supervise the manner in which such duties are accomplished.

Legal assistants should:

1. Disclose their status as legal assistants at the outset of any professional relationship with a client, other attorneys, a court or administrative agency or personnel thereof, or members of the general public.
2. Preserve the confidences and secrets of all clients; and
3. Understand the attorney's Code of Professional Responsibility and these guidelines in order to avoid any action which would involve the attorney in a violation of that Code, or give the appearance of professional impropriety.

Legal assistants should not:

1. Establish attorney-client relationships; set legal fees; give legal opinions or advice; or represent a client before a court; nor
2. Engage in, encourage, or contribute to any act which could constitute the unauthorized practice of law.

Legal assistants may perform services for an attorney in the representation of a client, provided:

1. The services performed by the legal assistant do not require the exercise of independent professional legal judgment;
2. The attorney maintains a direct relationship with the client and maintains control of all client matters;
3. The attorney supervises the legal assistant;

Exhibit 15.4   NALA Model Standards and Guidelines for Utilization of Legal Assistants—*continued*

4. The attorney remains professionally responsible for all work on behalf of the client, including any actions taken or not taken by the legal assistant in connection therewith; and
5. The services performed supplement, merge with, and become the attorney's work product.

In the supervision of a legal assistant, consideration should be given to:

1. Designating work assignments that correspond to the legal assistant's abilities, knowledge, training, and experience;
2. Educating and training the legal assistant with respect to professional responsibility, local rules and practices, and firm policies;
3. Monitoring the work and professional conduct of the legal assistant to ensure that the work is substantively correct and timely performed;
4. Providing continuing education for the legal assistant in substantive matters through courses, institutes, workshops, seminars, and in-house training; and
5. Encouraging and supporting membership and active participation in professional organizations.

Except as otherwise provided by statute, court rule or decision, administrative rule or regulation, or the attorney's Code of Professional Responsibility; and within the preceding parameters and proscriptions, a legal assistant may perform any function delegated by an attorney, including, but not limited to the following:

1. Conduct client interviews and maintain general contact with the client after the establishment of the attorney-client relationship, so long as the client is aware of the status and function of the legal assistant, and the client contact is under the supervision of the attorney.
2. Locate and interview witnesses, so long as the witnesses are aware of the status and function of the legal assistant.
3. Conduct investigations and statistical and documentary research for review by the attorney.
4. Conduct legal research for review by the attorney.
5. Draft legal documents for review by the attorney.
6. Draft correspondence and pleadings for review by and signature of the attorney.
7. Summarize depositions, interrogatories, and testimony for review by the attorney.
8. Attend executions of wills, real estate closings, depositions, court or administrative hearings and trials with the attorney.
9. Author and sign letters provided the legal assistant's status is clearly indicated and the correspondence does not contain independent legal opinions or legal advice.

Source: Copyright 1984, revised 1991. National Association of Legal Assistants, 1516 S. Boston, Ste. 200, Tulsa, OK 74119. Reprinted with permission.

Unauthorized practice of law
Engaging in any legal work that involves exercising professional judgment or advice usually reserved for an attorney.

witnesses, drafting documents, conducting case investigations, and performing legal research. Usually, such work does not breach the prohibition against the **unauthorized practice of law** so long as a lawyer actively oversees the legal assistant's work and maintains an active, direct relationship with the client for whom the tasks are performed. Generally, paralegals are prohibited from engaging in any work that involves exercising professional judgment usually reserved for an attorney. Accordingly, legal assistants may not offer legal advice or counsel to a client, nor may they make a court appearance in a formal judicial proceeding. Various states, however, permit nonlawyers (including legal assistants) to make appearances before certain administrative proceedings, e.g., a nonlawyer may act on behalf of clients at Social Security disability hearings. The regulations dealing with nonattorney appearances before administrative proceedings vary from state to state. Your own state laws must be reviewed carefully before any such activity is undertaken.

Usually, so long as legal assistants are working under an attorney's supervision, no difficulties involving the unauthorized practice of law arise. Such problems will occur when legal assistants offer professional advice and counsel to persons encountering routine legal matters. Various state associations have prosecuted nonlawyers for establishing services that help people obtain default divorces, assist in drafting wills and contracts, or guide people through bankruptcy proceedings. Courts have generally ruled that nonattorneys may sell sample forms and informational publications but are prohibited from advising clients regarding legal remedies, informing clients on the proper form of documents, helping clients fill out forms, or preparing pleadings for clients. Certain exceptions to these limitations are recognized in some states. For example, real estate brokers or agents are allowed to use standard legal forms in real estate transactions without risking unauthorized practice of law charges.

It has been proposed that paralegals working in the area of public interest law could provide standardized, routine legal advice if the following conditions are met:

- The legal assistants advise the client of their nonlawyer status.
- The legal assistants work under the close supervision of an attorney.
- The supervising attorney maintains ready access to the client to check the competence of the paralegal's work and to make changes necessary to correct mistakes.
- The client is cautioned not to rely on nor take any action based on the paralegal's advice without first consulting with the supervising attorney.

In conclusion, to effectively avoid any unauthorized practice of law problems when working with clients, *you should always inform the client of your nonlawyer status during the first meeting* with the client. This can help prevent any misunderstandings from arising regarding your role or responsibilities. Additionally, *before talking to or meeting with a client, you should inform and obtain approval from your supervising lawyer.*

Rules Protecting Client Confidences

Under present-day rules of civil and criminal procedure, the court can usually order evidence that is pertinent to pending litigation or other legal proceedings to be disclosed to an opponent. At the investigation and pretrial discovery stages, or during a trial, civil and criminal courts allow few exceptions to the duties of witnesses to offer testimony, or of parties and their counsel to produce material documents or other relevant evidence vital to a case. Exceptions that are recognized to this general policy favoring parties sharing evidence are called "privileges," which allow witnesses to refuse to give testimony and allow attorneys to refuse to turn over documents or otherwise cooperate in providing requested evidence. Such evidentiary privileges in a criminal prosecution include protection against self-incrimination and the privilege that prevents married persons from testifying against one another. Most relevant to the work of paralegals, whether engaged in civil or criminal legal matters, are the **attorney-client privilege** and the attorney's **work product privilege.** Therefore, understanding the meaning of these privileges and their application to the legal assistant profession is crucial.

The attorney-client privilege protects confidential statements, e.g., secrets of the client, exchanged between attorney and client from being disclosed in an open court hearing or other judicial proceeding. The purpose of this doctrine is

MINI-GLOSSARY BOX

Attorney-client privilege
A rule that confidential communications in the course of professional employment between attorney and client may not be divulged by the attorney without the client's consent.

Work product privilege
Work of an attorney for a client that includes private memoranda prepared in anticipation of litigation or
for trials that does not have to be disclosed (given to the opposing party).

to encourage open, unrestrained communication between an attorney and client based on the total confidence that these communications will not be conveyed to others. This enables the attorney to obtain the fullest range of information from a client necessary to prepare the strongest case on the client's behalf. The scope, meaning, and application of the privilege are complicated and are not consistent among the states. In general terms, the doctrine prevents compulsory disclosure of spoken or written statements from a client to an attorney that are intended to be confidential. Similarly, statements from an attorney to a client are protected against disclosure although in some cases, usually involving no intended client confidentiality, courts lift the protection of the privilege to compel disclosure of relevant, material information. The protection under this privilege is also lifted when statements between attorney and client are made with other persons present or are later disclosed to another person. The complex elements of the attorney-client privilege, seen in the context of the attorney-client-legal assistant relationship, pose such difficult legal issues that a detailed examination is beyond the scope of this discussion.

Another exception to the policy favoring mandatory disclosure of information relates to the work of an attorney associated with pending litigation, called "work product." Referred to as the "work product" privilege, this disclosure shield applies to "documents . . . prepared in anticipation of litigation or for trials" from being disclosed to aid adversaries (Fed.R.Civ.P. 26[b][3]). The purpose of the doctrine is to facilitate the lawyer's preparation and presentation of a client's case without fear of outside interference that might threaten confidentiality or disrupt the smooth, orderly flow of office operations. The work product rule is not, however, an absolute privilege. Its protection is lifted and disclosure is required upon a showing that the party seeking discovery has substantial need of the materials in the preparation of the case and that the party is unable to obtain the substantial equivalent of the materials by other means without undue hardship. Work consisting of "mental impressions, conclusions, opinions or legal theories of an attorney or other representatives of a party concerning the litigation," however, is usually given complete protection in most cases by most courts.

As mentioned, ABA ethical standards require confidentiality. The Model Code of Professional Responsibility states that "[a] lawyer should preserve the confidences and secrets of a client" (Canon 4). This Canon is enforced through DR 4–101, which requires lawyers to preserve client confidences regarding information subject to the attorney-client privilege as well as information "gained in the professional relationship that the client has requested to be held inviolate or the disclosure of which would be embarrassing or would be likely to be detrimental to the client." Further elaboration of the lawyer's duty of confidentiality under EC 4–4 requires attorneys to meet this responsibility "without regard to the nature or source of the information or the fact that others share the knowledge." Under the Model Rules of Professional Conduct, the lawyer's duty of confidentiality is defined as follows, subject to certain exceptions: "[a] lawyer shall not reveal information relating to representation of a client unless the client consents after consultation" (Model Rule 1.6[a]). Comments accompanying this rule state that it should be interpreted broadly to include information obtained prior or subsequent to the existence of an attorney-client relationship. This policy is intended to eliminate the potentially disruptive and burdensome tasks of clients having to specify which statements are intended to be confidential and attorneys having to decide which statements contain potentially embarrassing or confidential information.

The Model Code and the Model Rules both require that lawyers act to prevent disclosing information falling within the attorney-client privilege and the work product doctrine as well as information arising out of and related to representing a client. Only when a client consents to disclosure, or disclosure is otherwise required by law, may an attorney disclose information. Lawyers who violate these rules are subject to significant disciplinary action.

It is important for legal assistants to be familiar with the doctrines relating to client confidences and the attorney-client privilege. You need to be aware of the risks of disclosing otherwise protected information that could result in weakening a client's case and possibly exposing the supervising attorney to malpractice liability. You will face this problem in many different aspects of your employment responsibilities, especially in document discovery settings. Although the supervising attorney has the final word regarding what information may, may not, or must be disclosed, you can perform the crucial task of recognizing potential confidential information, especially while examining and preparing documents for delivery to an opposing party. Caution must be exercised since turning over just one privileged document could trigger wholesale waiver of the protection granted under the privilege, in turn possibly undermining the strength of a client's case.

Paralegals should recognize that a considerable amount of their work falls within the scope of the work product disclosure restrictions. Although a few states limit the work product doctrine to lawyers only, most states apply the protection under this doctrine not only to direct work undertaken by attorneys, but to "other representative[s] of a party concerning litigation" as well.

For attorneys to represent their client effectively, they must be able to carry out their professional responsibilities efficiently. Efficiency is enhanced by careful delegation of duties to responsible, competent staff. To help lawyers accomplish these goals, courts have acknowledged the need to extend the protection of the work product doctrine to various classes of employees who usually assist attorneys in handling cases. Such subordinates as messengers, accountants, law clerks, secretaries, and special agents, working under the direct supervision of an attorney, have been accorded the protection of the work product doctrine in various court rulings. In *Dabney v. Investment Corp. of America,* 82 F.R.D. 464, 465 (E.D.Pa. 1979), the court stated that "protected subordinates would include any law student, paralegal, investigator or other person acting as the agent of a duly qualified attorney." As a general proposition, paralegals employed directly under an attorney's supervision should have their work protected by the work product doctrine under circumstances where their efforts as subordinates to the attorney are reasonably related to professional services carried out on their client's behalf.

Ethical standards governing the practice of law contain provisions for protecting client confidences against disclosure by nonlawyers. DR 4–101(D) implementing Canon 4 states: "A lawyer shall exercise reasonable care to prevent employees, associates, and others whose services are utilized from disclosing or using confidences or secrets of a client, except that a lawyer may reveal the information allowed [to be disclosed] through an employee."

Regarding a lawyer's duty of confidentiality, the Model Rules state that "a lawyer having direct supervisory authority over [a] nonlawyer shall make reasonable efforts to ensure that the person's conduct is compatible with the professional obligations of the lawyer" (Model Rule 5.3[b]). The comment accompanying the Rule states "a lawyer should give assistants appropriate instruction and supervision concerning the ethical aspects of their employment, particularly regarding the obligation not to disclose information relating to representation of the client."

The ABA's Annotated Rules of Professional Conduct 66 (1984) speak to this issue by providing that "a lawyer's duty to maintain client confidences extends to nonlawyer assistants of the lawyer, and a supervisory lawyer has a duty to ensure that employees understand the obligation not to disclose and are reliable."

It is clear that paralegals are covered by both the protections and duties of these disclosure rules. You need to be aware of these doctrines and exercise sound judgment to safeguard client confidences. You must refrain from sharing information or experiences with others, including family, friends, and colleagues, to ensure that client confidences are not compromised. Merely revealing that a client has retained an attorney could be potentially embarrassing for a client and might possibly jeopardize the client's position. Additionally, you should avoid any relations with the news media and should leave that task for the attorney or client to handle.

KEY TERMS

American Bar Association (ABA)

Model Code of Professional Responsibility

Model Rules of Professional Conduct

Opinions

Canons of Ethics

Ethical Considerations (EC)

Disciplinary Rules (DR)

National Federation of Paralegal Associations (NFPA)

National Association of Legal Assistants (NALA)

Unauthorized practice of law

Attorney-client privilege

Work product privilege

REVIEW QUESTIONS

1. Identify, explain, and distinguish the two major ethical standards (codes) established by the American Bar Association that have been adopted in the majority of states.

2. Explain the functions of the Ethical Considerations (EC) and Disciplinary Rules (DR) within the 1969 Model Code.

3. Determine if one of the national paralegal (legal assistant) organizations is located in your county or state. If you joined the organization, what kind of resources would be available to

you, e.g., job searches, job listings, job placement, and so on?

4. What are the ethical responsibilities of a supervising attorney toward nonlawyer assistants (including paralegals)?

5. In your opinion, should a nationally authorized regulatory agency or association be established to certify and govern the conduct of all paralegals? Explain.

6. Review the Codes of Ethics from the ABA, the NFPA, and the NALA and prepare a single

consolidated list of their rules of ethical conduct, i.e., a "do and do not do" list, for paralegals. What, if anything, would you add to this list?

7. What is meant by the "unauthorized practice of law"? List some examples.

8. Are standardized tests given to experienced paralegals the best way to determine competency? Should such tests be mandatory?

9. Explain the differences between the NALA's CLA exam and the NFPA's PACE. What qualifications are required of paralegals before they can take each exam?

10. Explain the attorney's "work product privilege" and list some examples.

CASE PROBLEMS

Problem 1

Jerome Thompson hires an attorney, Sahandra Adams, to advise him about the need for and, if necessary, the filing of a petition for bankruptcy. After the initial interview, Sahandra asks her certified legal assistant (CLA), Kathryn Clark, to obtain the necessary data to complete the required forms for filing. Jerome gave Kathryn information about his assets and liabilities for purposes of preparing the bankruptcy petition and other forms, e.g., bankruptcy schedules. Some of Jerome's assets were omitted from the bankruptcy schedules. After Jerome stated in his deposition that "all information regarding assets had been given to and discussed with the CLA," a motion was made to the U.S. Bankruptcy Court to compel discovery in the form of a deposition of the CLA, Kathryn, with regard to Jerome's communications concerning those assets. At the deposition, Sahandra, the attorney, instructed Kathryn not to answer questions relating to the initial "data-gathering" interview, and Kathryn, therefore, refused to answer several questions on the topic she considered protected by the attorney-client privilege. The issue before the court is whether Kathryn should be compelled to provide those answers. Answer the following:

A. Explain what is meant by the attorney-client privilege.

B. Could Kathryn disobey her attorney's instructions not to answer the deposition questions? Ethically, should she?

C. The information sought by the questions was factual data about a debtor's assets to prepare the forms for bankruptcy. In your opinion, should that information be privileged? Explain. (See *In re French,* 162 B.R. 541 [Bkrtcy. D.S.D. 1994]).

Problem 2

Margerita Clark, a paralegal, discovered that her supervising attorney, Edgar Carmella, billed their client for the billable hours Margerita had worked on the client's case at his hourly rate rather than her lower hourly rate. In addition, no notice was given to the client that much of the work done on the case was done by a nonlawyer (Margerita). She brought this information to Edgar's attention, but nothing was done. Later, her supervisors directed Margerita at times to bill her work directly as attorney's time instead of at her hourly rate despite her protests that the practice was improper. When she continued to protest, the firm responded by imposing new work rules and hours, and subsequently, she was terminated. Margerita brought a lawsuit for wrongful discharge from her employment. Her former employers moved to dismiss the case. Answer the following:

A. After Margerita told her attorney about the improper billing and the firm directed her to bill her time as attorney's time, what would you recommend that she do?

B. If Margerita had informed the clients and authorities of the firm's fraudulent billing practices, what would be her purpose in "blowing the whistle" on the firm? What would you expect the court's decision to be?

C. Should the court allow the case to go to court? Explain your answer. (See *Brown v. Hammond,* 810 F.Supp. 644 [E.D. Pa. 1993]).

APPENDIX A

SAMPLE FORMS

Form*

1. Petition for Formal Probate of Will and for Formal Appointment of Personal Representative (Executor)
2. Petition for Formal Appointment of Administrator
3. Order and Notice of Formal Appointment of Personal Representative, Notice of Hearing for Formal Probate of Will and Notice to Creditors
4. Order and Notice of Hearing Petition for Administration
5. Proof of Placing Order for Publication
6. Proof (Affidavit) of Publication
7. Affidavit of Mailing Order or Notice of Hearing for Formal Probate of Will; and Statutory Notice of Rights of Surviving Spouse and/or Minor Children (Reverse Side of Form)
8. Testimony of Subscribing Witness to Will
9. Demand for Notice
10. Order of Formal Probate of Will and Formal Appointment of Personal Representative (Executor)
11. Order of Formal Appointment of Administrator
12. Certificate of Probate
13. Acceptance of Appointment and Oath by Individual
14. Bond and Oath
15. Request for Minimum Bond
16. Request for Waiver of Bond
17. Letters Testamentary
18. Order Appointing Guardian
19. Petition for Probate of Foreign Will
20. Order and Notice of Hearing for Foreign Will
21. Order Admitting Foreign Will to Probate
22. Order Appointing Appraisers
23. Inventory and Appraisal
24. Petition for Allowance of Selection of Personal Property
25. Order Setting Apart (Allowing Selection of) Personal Property
26. Petition for Family Maintenance
27. Order for Family Maintenance
28. Proof of Claim
29. Petition for Disallowance of Claim (Objections to Claim)
30. Order for Disallowance of Claim
31. Petition to Sell-Mortgage-Lease Real Estate (Land)
32. Order for Hearing Petition to Sell-Mortgage-Lease Real Estate
33. Order for Sale, Mortgage, or Lease of Real Estate at Private Sale
34. Warrant to Appraisers at Private Sale
35. Oath of Appraisers and Appraisal of Real Estate Under Order for Sale
36. Report of Sale of Real Estate at Private Sale Under Order for Sale
37. Order Confirming Private Sale of Real Estate
38. Probate Deed
39. Final Account
40. Petition for Order of Complete Settlement of the Estate and Decree of Distribution
41. Order for Hearing on Final Account and Petition for Distribution and for Mailed Notice
42. Affidavit of Mailing Order or Notice of Hearing on Final Account and Petition for Distribution
43. Order Allowing Final Account
44. State Inheritance Tax Waiver
45. Order of Complete Settlement of the Estate and Decree of Distribution
46. Receipt for Assets by Distributee
47. Petition for Discharge of Personal Representative
48. Order Discharging Personal Representative
49. Petition for Appointment of Special Administrator

---

*These forms are for purposes of illustration only. They represent the types of documents that might be used in particular situations and jurisdictions.

50. Order Granting Special Administration
51. Letters of Special Administration
52. Final Account and Report of Special Administrator
53. Order Approving Final Account and Report of Special Administrator
54. Petition Claiming Interest in Omitted Property (Petition for Determination of Descent)
55. Decree of Distribution (Descent) of Omitted Property
56. Decree of Descent
57. Application for Informal Probate of Will and for Informal Appointment of Personal Representative (Executor)
58. Change of Testacy Status—Application for Informal Appointment of Successor Personal Representative
59. Verification
60. Statement of Informal Probate of Will and Order of Informal Appointment of Personal Representative (Executor)
61. Notice of Informal Probate of Will and Appointment of Personal Representative and Notice to Creditors
62. Proof of Placing Order for Publication
63. Affidavit of Mailing Notice of Informal Probate of Will; and Statutory Notice of Rights of Surviving Spouse and/or Minor Children (Reverse Side of Form)
64. Acceptance of Appointment and Oath by Individual
65. Letters Testamentary
66. Inventory and Appraisal
67. Written Statement of Claim
68. Informal Deed of Distribution by Personal Representative
69. Receipt for Assets by Distributee
70. Informal Administration: Personal Representative's Statement to Close Estate
71. Application for Informal Appointment of Administrator
72. Order and Notice of Informal Appointment of Personal Representative and Notice to Creditors
73. Proof of Placing Order for Publication
74. Affidavit of Mailing Notice of Informal Appointment of Personal Representative; and Statutory Notice of Rights of Surviving Spouse and/or Minor Children (Reverse Side of Form)

75. Acceptance of Appointment and Oath by Individual
76. Bond
77. Letters of General Administration
78. Informal Deed of Distribution by Personal Representative
79. Receipt for Assets by Distributee
80. Application for Certificate from Registrar—Release of Bond
81. Certificate of Registrar—Release of Bond
82. U.S. Individual Income Tax Return (Form 1040)
83. Statement of Person Claiming Refund Due a Deceased Taxpayer (Form 1310)
84. Schedule A—Itemized Deductions (Form 1040)
85. Application for Automatic Extension of Time to File U.S. Individual Income Tax Return (Form 4868)
86. State (Minnesota as Example) Individual Income Tax Return
87. Claim for a Refund Due a Deceased Taxpayer (Minnesota)
88. Payment of Income Tax (if you are filing your return later than the due date—Minnesota)
89. Application for Employer Identification Number (Form SS-4)
90. Notice Concerning Fiduciary Relationship (Form 56)
91. U.S. (Fiduciary) Income Tax Return for Estates and Trusts (Form 1041)
92. Application for Extension of Time to File Fiduciary and Certain Other Returns (Form 2758)
93. State (Minnesota as Example) Fiduciary Income Tax Return
94. United States Gift Tax Return (Form 709)
95. State (Delaware as Example) Gift Tax Return
96. United States Estate Tax Return (Form 706)
97. Life Insurance Statement (Form 712)
98. Power of Attorney and Declaration of Representative (Form 2848)
99. Application for Extension of Time to File a Return and/or Pay U.S. Estate Taxes (Form 4768)
100. State (Minnesota as Example) Estate Tax Return
101. State (Iowa as Example) Inheritance Tax Return

Form 1   Petition for Formal Probate of Will and for Formal Appointment of Personal Representative (Executor)

M/D Form No. 4353 Miller-Davis Legal Forms (Rev. 1969)   Form 524.3-401 #3   Form 524.3-502 #2   UPC 33

STATE OF MINNESOTA

COUNTY OF ___Ramsey___

In Re: Estate of

       ___Jane M. Doe___
              Deceased

**PROBATE COURT
DISTRICT-COUNTY COURT
PROBATE DIVISION**

Court File No. ___999999___

**PETITION FOR FORMAL PROBATE
OF WILL AND FOR FORMAL
APPOINTMENT OF EXECUTOR**

TO THE HONORABLE JUDGE OF THE ABOVE NAMED COURT:

Petitioner, ___John C. Doe___, respectfully states:

1. Petitioner resides at ___1005 Elm Street, St. Paul, MN 55102___ ;

2. Petitioner has an interest herein as ___heir, devisee, and nominated personal representative___ and is, therefore, an interested person as defined by the laws of this State;

3. Decedent was born ___November 6___, 19 _12_ , at ___Detroit, Michigan___ ;

4. Decedent died on ___September 20___, 19 _94_ , at ___St. Paul, Minnesota 55102___ ;

5. Decedent at the time of h_er_ death resided at ___1005 Elm Street___ ,
City of ___St. Paul___ , County of ___Ramsey___ , State of ___Minnesota___ ;

6. That the names and addresses of decedent's spouse, children, heirs and devisees and other persons interested in this proceeding and the ages of any who are minors so far as known or ascertainable with reasonable deligence by the petitioner are:

> NOTE — Classify the heirs and others entitled to take per stirpes and give the name, date of death, relationship/interest and address, if known, of their predeceased ancestor. Give the birthdate of any heir or devisee taking a life interest. Remember to include a "Negative Allegation Statement".

Name	Age	Relationship/Interest	Address
John C. Doe	83	Spouse/heir/devisee/ nominated personal rep.	1005 Elm Street St. Paul, MN 55102
Sandy R. Doe	45	Daughter/heir/devisee	1005 Elm Street St. Paul, MN 55102
American Cancer Society		Devisee	222 Glen Acre Drive St. Paul, MN 55102
Girls' Clubs of America		Devisee	111 Aspen Lane St. Paul, MN 55102
Newark Institute of Higher Learning		Devisee	444 Wirth Drive St. Paul, MN 55102

Negative Allegation Statement (see Probate Court Rule 7 (1)): ___Decedent left surviving no spouse,___ ___children, or parents, other than herein named, and no issue of deceased children.___

7. That all persons identified as heirs have survived the decedent by at least 120 hours.

8. That all issue of decedent are also issue of decedent's surviving spouse ~~except that~~ _____

9. That venue for this proceeding is in the above named County of the State of Minnesota, because the decedent was domiciled in such County at the time of h_er_ death, and was the owner of property located in the State of Minnesota, ~~or because, though not domiciled in the State of Minnesota, the decedent was the owner of property located in the~~ ~~above named County at the time of his XXXXX death (Gen back)~~

Form 1   Petition for Formal Probate of Will and for Formal Appointment of Personal Representative
(Executor)—*continued*

10. That no personal representative of the decedent has been appointed in this state or elsewhere ̶X̶X̶X̶X̶X̶X̶ ̶X̶X̶X̶X̶X̶X̶X̶X̶X̶X̶X̶X̶X̶X̶X̶ ̶X̶X̶X̶ ̶X̶X̶X̶ ̶X̶X̶X̶X̶ ̶X̶X̶X̶X̶X̶X̶X̶X̶X̶

11. That petitioner has not received a demand for notice and is not aware of any demand for notice of any probate or appointment proceeding concerning the decedent that may have been filed in this state or elsewhere or proper notice has been given.

12. That the original of decedent's last will duly executed on _____June 2_____ , 19 _85_ , ̶X̶X̶X̶ ̶X̶X̶X̶X̶X̶X̶X̶X̶X̶X̶X̶X̶X̶X̶X̶X̶X̶X̶X̶X̶X̶X̶X̶X̶xxxxxxxxxxxxxxxxxxxxxxxxxxxxxxxxxxxxxxx̶X̶X̶X̶X̶X̶X̶X̶X̶ ̶X̶X̶X̶X̶ ̶X̶X̶X̶X̶X̶X̶X̶X̶X̶X̶X̶ ̶X̶X̶X̶X̶X̶X̶ ̶X̶X̶X̶X̶X̶X̶X̶X̶X̶X̶X̶X̶X̶X̶ ̶X̶X̶X̶X̶ ̶X̶X̶X̶X̶X̶X̶X̶X̶X̶X̶X̶X̶X̶X̶X̶ ̶X̶X̶ ̶X̶X̶X̶ ̶X̶X̶X̶X̶ ̶X̶X̶X̶X̶X̶X̶X̶X̶X̶X̶X̶X̶X̶ ̶X̶X̶ ̶X̶X̶X̶ ̶X̶X̶X̶X̶X̶X̶X̶ accompanies this petition.

13. That the petitioner, to the best of h _is_ knowledge, believes the will and any codicil or codicils thereto has or have been validly executed.

14. That after the exercise of reasonable diligence, the petitioner is unaware of any instrument revoking the will, and the petitioner believes that the instrument which is the subject of this petition is the decedent's last will.

15. That the time limit for formal probate and appointment as provided by the laws of this state has not expired because three years or less have passed since the decedent's death.

16. That the petitioner ̶X̶X̶ ____John C. Doe_____ is entitled to priority and appointment as personal representative because petitioner ̶X̶X̶ xxxxxxxxxxxxxxxxxxxxxxxxxxxxxxxxx is nominated in the last will of the decedent as personal representative, with (no) ̶X̶X̶X̶X̶X̶X̶X̶X̶X̶X̶X̶X̶ xxxxxxxxxxxxxxxxxxxxxxxxxxxxxxxxxxx bond, in an (̶X̶X̶X̶X̶X̶X̶X̶X̶X̶X̶X̶ (undesignated) administration ̶X̶X̶X̶X̶X̶X̶X̶X̶X̶ xxxxxxxxxxxxxxxxxxxxxxxxxxxxxxxxxxxxxxxx xxxxxxxxxxxxxxxxxxxxxxxxxxxxxxxxxxxxxxxxxxxxxxxxxxxxxxxxxxxxxxxxxxxxxx xxxxxxxxxxxxxxxxxxxxxxxxxxxxxxxxxxxxxxxxxxxxxxxxxxxx and is not disqualified to serve as a personal representative of the decedent.

WHEREFORE, your petitioner request the order of this Court fixing a time and place for hearing on this petition, and that after the time for any notice has expired, upon proof of notice, and hearing, the Court enter a judicial order formally:

1. Finding that the Testator is dead;
2. Finding that venue is proper;
3. Finding that the proceeding was commenced within the time limitations prescribed by the laws of this state;
4. Determining decedent's domicile at death;
5. Determining decedent's heirs;
6. Determining decedent's state of testacy;
7. Probating the valid and unrevoked last will of decedent including any valid and unrevoked codicil thereto;
8. Determining that petitioner ̶X̶X̶ ____John C. Doe_____ is entitled to appointment as personal representative under the laws of this state;
9. Appointing petitioner ̶X̶X̶ ____John C. Doe_____ as the executor of the estate of decedent with no ̶X̶X̶ xxxxxxxxxxxxxxxxxxxxxxxxxxxxxxxxx bond, in an ̶X̶X̶X̶X̶X̶X̶X̶X̶X̶X̶ (supervised) administration;
10. Authorizing issuance of letters testamentary to petitioner ̶X̶X̶ ____John C. Doe_____ upon qualification and acceptance.
11. Granting such other and further relief as may be proper.

FURTHER, under penalties for perjury for deliberate falsification therein; I declare or affirm that I have read the foregoing petition and to the best of my knowledge or information, its representations are true, correct and complete.

Dated: _____September 26, 1994_____   _____/S/ John C. Doe_____
                                                                        Petitioner
                                                                        First Trust Co. Bldg.
_____/S/ John W. Cranwall, License_____   St. Paul, MN 55101 (612) 555-5555
Attorney for Petitioner   #1234567   Attorney's Address/Phone

*ASSETS

Probate Assets			Non-Probate Assets		
Homestead	$	220,000.00 (net)	Joint Tenancy	$	80,000.00
Other Real Estate	$	12,750.00 (net)	Insurance	$	50,000.00
Cash	$	76,350.00	Other	$	0
Securities	$	10,648.00	Approximate		
Other	$	240,100.00	Indebtedness	$	2,180.00

Form 2 Petition for Formal Appointment of Administrator

....

MD Form No. 4359 Miller-Davis Legal Forms (Rev. 1989)   Form 524.3-401 #9   Form 524.3-502 #4   UPC — —

STATE OF MINNESOTA

COUNTY OF _____

In Re: Estate of

_____
                    Deceased

PROBATE COURT
DISTRICT-COUNTY COURT
PROBATE DIVISION

Court File No. _____

**PETITION FOR
FORMAL APPOINTMENT
OF ADMINISTRATOR**

TO THE HONORABLE JUDGE OF THE ABOVE NAMED COURT:

Petitioner, _____, respectfully states:

1. Petitioner resides at _____ ;

2. Petitioner has an interest herein as_____
   and is, therefore, an interested person as defined by the laws of this State;

3. Decedent was born _____ , 19 ____ , at _____ ;

4. Decedent died on _____ , 19 ____ , at _____ ;

5. Decedent at the time of h____ death resided at _____ ,
   City of _____ , County of _____ , State of _____ ;

6. That the names and addresses of decedent's spouse, children, heirs and devisees and other persons interested
   in this proceeding and the ages of any who are minors so far as known or ascertainable with reasonable
   deligence by the petitioner are:
   NOTE — Classify the heirs and others entitled to take per stirpes and give the name, date of death,
   relationship/interest and address, if known, of their predeceased ancestor. Give the birthdate of
   any heir or devisee taking a life interest. Remember to include a "Negative Allegation Statement".

Name	Age	Relationship/Interest	Address

Negative Allegation Statement (see Probate Court Rule 7 (1)): _____

7. That all persons identified as heirs have survived the decedent by at least 120 hours.

8. That all issue of decedent are also issue of decedent's surviving spouse except for: _____

9. That venue for this proceeding is in the above named County of the State of Minnesota, because the decedent was
   domiciled in such County at the time of h____ death, and was the owner of property located in the State of Minnesota,
   or because, though not domiciled in the State of Minnesota, the decedent was the owner of property located in the
   above named County at the time of h____ death. (See back*)

Form 2 Petition for Formal Appointment of Administrator—*continued*

10. That no personal representative of the decedent has been appointed in this State or elsewhere whose appointment has not been terminated.

11. That petitioner has not received a demand for notice and is not aware of any demand for notice of any probate or appointment proceeding concerning the decedent that may have been filed in this State or elsewhere or proper notice has been given.

12. That the time limit for formal appointment proceeding as provided by the laws of this state has not expired because three years or less have passed since the decedent's death.

13. That after the exercise of reasonable diligence, petitioner is unaware of any unrevoked testamentary instrument relating to property having a situs in this state under the laws of this state.

14. That petitioner or _____ is entitled to priority for appointment as administrator of the estate of decedent because petitioner or _____
    is _____ and is not disqualified to serve as a personal representative of the decedent.

15. That the names of any other persons having a prior or equal right to appointment as administrator of the estate of decedent are: _____
    _____

WHEREFORE, your petitioner requests that after the time required for any notice has expired, upon proof of notice, and hearing, the court enter a judicial order formally:

1. Finding that the decedent is dead;
2. Finding that venue is proper;
3. Finding that the proceeding was commenced within the time limitation prescribed by the laws of this state;
4. Determining decedent's domicile at death;
5. Determining decedent's state of testacy;
6. Determining decedent's heirs;
7. Appointing petitioner or _____ as the administrator of the estate of decedent with _____ bond, in an (unsupervised) (supervised) administration;
8. Authorizing issuance of letters of administration to petitioner or _____ upon qualification and acceptance;
9. Granting such other and further relief as may be proper.

FURTHER, under penalties for perjury for deliberate falsification therein; I declare or affirm that I have read the foregoing petition and to the best of my knowledge or information, its representations are true, correct and complete.

Dated: _____

_____
Petitioner

_____
Attorney for Petitioner

_____
Address/Phone

NOTE: If notice to creditors has been previously given, delete the notice to creditors herein.

*ASSETS

Probate Assets		Non-Probate Assets	
Homestead	$ _____	Joint Tenancy	$ _____
Other Real Estate	$ _____	Insurance	$ _____
Cash	$ _____	Other	$ _____
Securities	$ _____	Approximate	
Other	$ _____	Indebtedness	$ _____

Form 3 Order and Notice of Formal Appointment of Personal Representative, Notice of Hearing for Formal Probate of Will and Notice to Creditors

Form No. 4350 GOVERNMENT BUSINESS SYSTEMS, MPLS. (Rev. 1986) Forms 524.3-310#3, 524.3-403 #8, 524.3-801 #4 UPC — —

STATE OF MINNESOTA

COUNTY OF ___Ramsey___

In Re: Estate of

_____Jane M. Doe_____
Deceased

**PROBATE COURT
DISTRICT—COUNTY COURT
PROBATE DIVISION**

Court File No. ___999999___

ORDER AND
**NOTICE OF INFORMAL
APPOINTMENT OF PERSONAL
REPRESENTATIVE, NOTICE OF
HEARING FOR FORMAL PROBATE
OF WILL AND NOTICE TO CREDITORS**

ORDERED AND
NOTICE TO ALL INTERESTED PERSONS AND CREDITORS:
It is ordered and
Notice is hereby given that informal appointment of___John C. Doe___

_____, whose address is___1005 Elm Street, St. Paul, MN 55102___

as personal representative of the estate of the above decedent, has been made. Any heir, devisee or other interested person may be entitled to appointment as personal representative or may object to the appointment of the personal representative and the personal representative is empowered to fully administer the estate including, after 30 days from the date of issuance of his letters, the power to sell, encumber, lease or distribute real estate, unless objections thereto are filed with the Court (pursuant to Section 524.3-607) and the Court otherwise orders.

Notice is hereby given that on the___31st___day of___October___, 19_94_, at _10:00_ o'clock _A._ .m., a hearing will be held in this Court at___St. Paul___, Minnesota, for the formal probate of an instrument purporting to be the Will of the above named decedent, dated___June 2___, 19_85_, _____

and that any objections thereto must be filed with the Court.

Notice is further given that ALL CREDITORS having claims against said estate are required to present the same to said personal representative or to the Court Administrator within four months after the date of this notice or said claims will be barred.

Dated: ___September 30, 1994___

___/S/ Richard B. Evans___
~~Registrar~~ Judge

___/S/ Thomas Malone___
Court Administrator

___/S/ John W. Cranwall___
Attorney
First Trust Co. Bldg.
St. Paul, MN 55101
Address   (612) 555-5555

NOTE: If notice to creditors has been previously given, delete the notice to creditors herein.

Form 4   Order and Notice of Hearing Petition for Administration

W/D Form No. 4562 MILLER-DAVIS CO. MPLS., MN   524.3-105 #4   UPC

STATE OF MINNESOTA

COUNTY OF _____   **DISTRICT COURT**

In Re: Estate of   Court File No. _____

**ORDER AND NOTICE OF HEARING
PETITION FOR ~~INFORMAL~~
~~PROCEEDINGS FOR~~** ADMINISTRATION

_____
          Deceased

     NOTICE IS HEREBY GIVEN that a petition dated _____,19_____, has been filed herein for a judicial order formally _____

and any objections thereto must be filed with the Court.

     IT IS ORDERED and notice is hereby given that the petition will be heard on the _____ day of _____, 19 _____, at _____ o'clock _____.M. by the above named Court at _____, Minnesota. That, if proper, and no objections are filed, the petition will be granted.

     IT IS FURTHER ORDERED That the petitioner give notice of said hearing by _____ _____ .

Dated: _____

_____
                 Judge

_____
        Court Administrator

_____
Attorney for Petitioner

_____
Address/Phone

Form 5 Proof of Placing Order for Publication

STATE OF MINNESOTA

COUNTY OF RAMSEY

PROBATE COURT

COURT FILE NO. <u>999999</u>

In Re: Estate of

PROOF OF PLACING ORDER

FOR PUBLICATION

Jane M. Doe

Deceased

TO THE CLERK OF PROBATE COURT:

This is to verify that <u>John C. Doe, whose address is 1005 Elm St., St. Paul,</u> <u>MN 55102</u>, applicant(s)

has XXXXX made arrangements for the publication of:

☐ NOTICE OF INFORMAL APPOINTMENT OF PERSONAL REPRESENTATIVE(S) AND NOTICE TO CREDITORS

☒ NOTICE OF FORMAL PROBATE OF WILL AND APPOINTMENT OF PERSONAL REPRESENTATIVE(S) AND NOTICE TO CREDITORS

☐

once a week for two consecutive weeks in the <u>FINANCE AND COMMERCE</u>

Daily Newspaper

and this is to confirm that the same will be published accordingly commencing in the next available issue, and that arrangements for payment of the cost of said publication have been made.

Dated: <u>September 30, 1994</u>

FINANCE AND COMMERCE Daily Newspaper

Publisher

By: <u>/S/ Dorothy L. Wolf</u>

Form 6 Proof (Affidavit) of Publication

AFFIDAVIT OF PUBLICATION

State of Minnesota,

County of ..Ramsey...............................   }ss.

COURT FILE NO. 999999
———

ORDER AND NOTICE OF
HEARING ON PETITION FOR
PROBATE OF WILL
, AND
APPOINTMENT OF
PERSONAL REPRESENTATIVES
IN SUPERVISED
ADMINISTRATION AND NOTICE
TO CREDITORS
———

STATE OF MINNESOTA
COUNTY OF Ramsey

PROBATE COURT
———

In Re: Estate of
Jane M. Doe,
Deceased.
———

TO ALL INTERESTED PERSONS
AND CREDITORS:

It is ordered and notice is hereby given
that on Monday, the 31st day of October, 1994, at ten o'clock A.M., a hearing
will be held in the above named Court at
C-4 Ramsey County Court House, St.
Paul, Minnesota, for the probate of an
instrument purporting to be the Will of
the above decedent and for the appointment of John C. Doe, whose address is
1005 Elm St., St. Paul, Minnesota
55102.

, as personal representative of the
estate of the above named decedent in
supervised administration. That, if
proper, and no objections are filed, said
personal representatives will be appointed to administer the estate, to collect all assets, pay all legal debts, claims,
taxes, and expenses, and sell real and
personal property, and do all necessary
acts for the estate. Upon completion of
the administration, the representatives
shall file a final account for allowance
and shall distribute the estate to the
persons thereunto entitled as ordered by
the Court, and close the estate.

Notice is further given that ALL
CREDITORS having claims against said
estate are required to present the same to
said personal representatives or to the
Clerk of Probate Court within four
months after the date of this notice or
said claims will be barred.

Dated: September 30th, 1994.
HON. Richard B. Evans,
Judge of Probate Court.
Thomas Malone,
Clerk of Probate Court.

(COURT SEAL)

By: John Cranwall,
Attorney,
First Trust Bldg.
St. Paul, MN 55101

..........Warren E. Maul..., *being duly sworn, on oath says:*
That ...*he now is, and during all the times herein stated has been the editor and*
publisher of the newspaper known as .Finance and Commerce......................, *and*
has full knowledge of the facts hereinafter stated.

(1) *That said newspaper is printed in the English language in newspaper format and in*
column and sheet form equivalent in printed space to at least 1200 square inches;

(2) *That said newspaper, if a weekly, be distributed at least once each week for 50 weeks*
each year, or if a daily, at least five days each week; but in any week in which a legal
holiday is included, not more than four issues of a daily paper are necessary;

(3) *That said newspaper has 25 percent, if published more often than weekly, or 50*
percent, if a weekly, of its news columns devoted to news of local interest to the
community which it purports to serve, and it may contain general news, comment,
and miscellany, but not wholly duplicate any other publication, or be made up
entirely of patents, plate matter, and advertisements;

(4) *That said newspaper is circulated in and near the municipality which it purports to*
serve, has at least 500 copies regularly delivered to paying subscribers, has an
average of at least 75% of its total circulation currently paid or no more than three
months in arrears, and has entry as second-class matter in its local postoffice;

(5) *That said newspaper has its known office of issue in the County of*
.......Ramsey............................. *in which lies, in whole or in part, the*
municipality which the newspaper purports to serve;

(6) *That said newspaper files a copy of each issue immediately with the State His-*
torical Society;

(6a) *Be made available at single or subscription prices to any person, corporation,*
partnership or other unincorporated association requesting the newspaper and
making the applicable payment;

(7) *That said newspaper has complied with all the foregoing conditions of this sub-*
division for at least one year last past.

(8) *That said newspaper has filed with the Secretary of State of Minnesota prior to*
January 1, of each year, an affidavit in the form prescribed by the Secretary of State
and signed by the publisher or managing officer and sworn to before a Notary
Public stating that the newspaper is a legal newspaper.

Probate Notice
That the printed ~~Notice of Mortgage Foreclosure Sale~~ *hereto attached as a part*
hereof was cut from the columns of said newspaper; was published therein in the English
Language once each week for___2___successive weeks; that it was first so published on

the ..30th...*day of* ...September............................., *19*..94. *and thereafter*

on ..Wednesday............... *of each week to and including the* ..19.th................. *day*

of ...October............., *19*.94..; *and that the following is a copy of the lower*
case alphabet which is acknowledged as the size and kind of type used in the printed
publication of said notice.

abcdefghijklmnopqrstuvwxyz

............/S/..Warren E. Maul.......................................

Subscribed and sworn to before me this ..30th.*day of* ..September..........., *19*..94..,

.............../S/..Dorothy L. Wolf....................................

Notary Public. Ramsey .... *County, Minnesota*

My Commission Expires. ..September 23................... . *19*.99....

Form 7 Affidavit of Mailing Order or Notice of Hearing for Formal Probate of Will

---

***MD* Form No. 4307** Miller Davis Legal Forms (Rev. 1988)   Form 524.1-401 #2   UPC - -

STATE OF MINNESOTA
COUNTY OF ___Ramsey___   **DISTRICT COURT**

IN RE: (ESTATE)   Court File No. ___999999___

OF _____Jane M. Doe_____   **AFFIDAVIT OF MAILING ORDER**
                                      OR NOTICE OF HEARING Formal
                                      Appointment of Personal Representative,
          Deceased   Notice of Hearing for Formal Probate of
                                      Will and Notice to Creditors.
                                        STATE OF MINNESOTA
                                        COUNTY OF ___Ramsey___ ss.

ATTACH COPY OF ORDER   J. M. Golden
OR NOTICE HERE   being first duly sworn on oath deposes and
                                        says that on the ___5th___ day of ___October___,
                                        19_94_, at ___St. Paul, MN___ in said
                                        County and State ___ he mailed a copy of the
                                        Order or Notice hereto attached to each ___heir,___
                                        __devisee, and personal representative__

whose name and address are known to affiant, after exercising due diligence in ascertaining the correctness of said name and address, by placing a true and correct copy thereof in a sealed envelope, postage prepaid and depositing the same in the U.S. Mails at ___St. Paul, Minnesota___

and addressed to the following named persons:
NOTE: (Instructions at bottom of page)

NAME	STREET or POST OFFICE	CITY	STATE
John C. Doe	1005 Elm Street	St. Paul	MN 55102
Sandy R. Doe	1005 Elm Street	St. Paul	MN 55102
American Cancer Society	222 Glen Acre Drive	St. Paul	MN 55102
Girls' Clubs of America	111 Aspen Lane	St. Paul	MN 55102
Newark Institute of Higher Learning	444 Wirth Drive	St. Paul	MN 55102

/S/ J. M. Golden

NOTARIAL STAMP OF SEAL (OR OTHER TITLE OR RANK)

Subscribed and sworn to before me this day of
___5th___ day of ___October___, 19_94_.

/S/ Judith Harris
SIGNATURE OF NOTARY PUBLIC OR OTHER OFFICIAL

NOTED INSTRUCTIONS: In Estates To each heir, devisee, personal representative, the foreign consul pursuant to M.S. 524.3-306 and M.S. 524.3-403, and the Minnesota Attorney General, if a devisee is the trustee of a charitable trust or if the decedent left no devisees or heirs.

Form 7 Statutory Notice of Rights of Surviving Spouse and/or Minor Children (Reverse Side of Form)

AFFIDAVIT OF MAILING
ALLOWANCES TO SPOUSE AND/OR CHILDREN

When a decedent dies with or without a will the allowances to the spouse or children are as follows:

525 15 ALLOWANCES TO SPOUSE. When any person dies testate or intestate

(1) The surviving spouse shall be allowed from the personal property of which the decedent was possessed or to which _____she was entitled at the time of h er death, the wearing apparel, and as selected by h im , furniture and household goods not exceeding $6,000 in value, and other personal property not exceeding $3,000 in value, subject to an award of property with sentimental value to the decedent's children under section 3;

(2) When, except for one automobile, all of the personal estate of the decedent is allowed to the surviving spouse by clause (1), the surviving spouse shall also be allowed the automobile.

(3) If there be no surviving spouse, the minor children shall receive the property specified in clause (1) as selected in their behalf;

(4) During administration, but not exceeding 18 months, unless an extension shall have been granted by the court, or, if the estate be insolvent, not exceeding 12 months, the spouse or children, or both, constituting the family of the decedent shall be allowed reasonable maintenance.

(5) In the administration of an estate of a nonresident decedent, the allowances received in the domiciliary administration shall be deducted from the allowances under this section.

_____

In all estates where there is a will the following rule applies to the spouse who has not consented to the will:

524.2-205 PROCEEDING FOR ELECTIVE SHARE; TIME LIMIT.

(a) The surviving spouse may elect to take an elective share in the augmented estate by filing in the court and mailing or delivering to the personal representative, if any, a petition for the elective share within nine months after the date of death, or within six months after the probate of the decedent's will, whichever limitation last expires. However, nonprobate transfers, described in section 524.2-202, clauses (l) and (3), shall not be included within the augmented estate for the purpose of computing the elective share, if the petition is filed ;later than nine months after death The court may extend the time for election as it sees fit for cause shown by the surviving spouse before the time for election has expired.

(b) The surviving spouse shall give notice of the time and place set for hearing to persons interested in the estate and to the distributees and recipients of portions of the augmented net estate whose interests will be affected by the taking of the elective share.

(c) The surviving spouse may withdraw a demand for an elective share at any time before entry of any order by the court determining the elective share.

(d) After notice and hearing, the court shall determine the amount of the elective share and shall order its payment from the assets of the augmented net estate or by contribution as appears appropriate under section 524.2-207. If it appears that a fund or property included in the augmented net estate has not come into the possession of the personal representative, or has been distributed by the personal representative, the court nevertheless shall fix the liability of any person who has any interest in the fund or property or who has possession thereof, whether as trustee or otherwise. The proceeding may be maintained against fewer than all persons against whom relief could be sought, but no person is subject to contribution in any greater amount than he would have been if relief had been secured against all persons subject to contribution.

(e) The order or judgment of the court may be enforced as necessary in suit for contribution or payment in other courts of this state or other jurisdictions.

(f) Whether or not an election has been made under subsection (a), the surviving spouse may elect statutory rights in the homestead by filing in the manner provided in this section a petition in which the spouse asserts the rights provided in section 525.145, provided that:

(1) when the homestead is subject to a testamentary disposition, the filing must be within nine months after the date of death, or within six months after the probate of the decedent's will, whichever limitation last expires; or

(2) where the homestead is subject to other disposition, the filing must he within nine months after the date of death.

The court may extend the time for election for cause shown by the surviving spouse before the time for filing has expired.

STATE OF MINNESOTA

COUNTY OF __Ramsey_____ ss.

_____J. M. Golden_____ being first duly sworn on oath deposes and says that on the 5th day of_____October_____, 19 94 , at___St. Paul_____ in said County and State, ____he mailed a copy of Sections 525.15 and 524.2-205 of Minnesota Statutes as hereinbefore set out to decedent's spouse and children constituting the family of the decedent at their last known address after exercising due diligence and ascertaining the correctness of said addresses by placing a true and correct copy thereof in a sealed envelope, postage pre-paid and depositing the same in the U.S. mails at _____St. Paul_____ , Minnesota, and addressed to the following:

NAME	STREET or POST OFFICE	CITY	STATE
John C. Doe	1005 Elm Street	St. Paul	MN 55102

Subscribed and sworn to before me this

_5th__ day of ____October_____ , 1994

/S/ Judith Harris
SIGNATURE OF NOTARY PUBLIC OR OTHER OFFICIAL

/S/ J. M. Golden

NOTARIAL STAMP OR SEAL (OR OTHER TITLE OR RANK)

Form 8 Testimony of Subscribing Witness to Will

524.3-303
MD **Form No. 4340** Miller-Davis Legal Forms (Rev. 6-88) 524.3-405 #1

UPC—

STATE OF MINNESOTA

COUNTY OF _____Ramsey_____

In Re: Estate of

DISTRICT COURT

Court File No. _____999999_____

**TESTIMONY OF
SUBSCRIBING WITNESS TO WILL**

_____Jane M. Doe_____
Deceased

STATE OF MINNESOTA

COUNTY OF _____Ramsey_____) *ss.*

TESTIMONY

_____Harvey R. Horwell_____ residing at _____999 Okinawa St., St. Paul, MN 55101_____ being first duly sworn on behalf of the proponent of decedent's will states that I am one of the subscribing witnesses to the instrument now shown me dated the_____2nd_____ day of _____June_____, 19 _85_ , and purporting to be XXXXXXXXXXXXXXXXXXXXXXX the Last Will and Testament of _____Jane M. Doe_____ now here petitioned for probate; that on the day of the date thereof, said instrument was to me published by said decedent and declared by h _er_ that _____she had signed the same as (XXXXXXXXXXXXXXXXXXXXXXXXXXXXX XXXXXXXXh _er_ Last Will and Testament; that at decedent's request, I did then and there sign my name as a subscribing witness there to in the presence of decedent.

That to the best of my knowledge and belief, decedent at the time of the execution of said instrument as aforesaid was of sound and disposing mind, memory and understanding, of lawful age and under no constraint or undue influence.

_____/S/ Harvey R. Horwell_____
Subscribing Witness

Subscribed and sworn to before me this
_7th_ day of _____October_____, 19 _94_

_____/S/ Richard B. Evans_____
XXXXXXXXXXXXXX Judge/XXXXXXXX

(NOTARIAL SEAL)

Form 9 Demand for Notice

Form No. 4329 Miller-Davis Legal Forms   Form 524.3-204 #1   UPC——

STATE OF MINNESOTA   **PROBATE COURT**
                                              DISTRICT—COUNTY COURT
COUNTY OF _____   **PROBATE DIVISION**

In Re: Estate of   Court File No. _____

_____   **DEMAND FOR NOTICE**
                Deceased

TO THE COURT ADMINISTRATOR:

Demandant. _____ , respectfully states:

1. The Demandant resides at _____ ;

2. The Demandant has financial or property interest in the estate of the above named decedent, and is, therefore, an interested person as defined by the laws of this state by reason of the following facts: _____
_____

WHEREFORE, the undersigned hereby demands notice of all orders and filings pertaining to decedent's estate. Notice may be served upon the undersigned at h___ above stated address, or upon h___ attorney, _____ .

FURTHER, under penalties for perjury for deliberate falsification therein, I declare or affirm that I have read the foregoing demand and to the best of my knowledge or information, its representations are true, correct and complete.

Dated: _____

                                              _____
                                              Demandant

_____
Attorney for Demandant

_____
Address/Phone

Form 10 Order of Formal Probate of Will and Formal Appointment of Personal Representative (Executor)

Form No. 4376 - Miller-Davis Legal Forms (Rev. 8-87)   Form 524.3-409 #2,   524.3-414 #4,   524.3-502 #11   UPC 34

STATE OF MINNESOTA

COUNTY OF _Ramsey_

In Re: Estate of

_____ Jane M. Doe _____
Deceased

**PROBATE COURT
DISTRICT-COUNTY COURT
PROBATE DIVISION**

Court File No. _999999_

**ORDER OF FORMAL PROBATE
OF WILL AND FORMAL
APPOINTMENT OF EXECUTOR**

The petition of _____ John C. Doe _____ dated_ September 26 _, 19_94_ for the formal probate of the last will and for formal appointment of executor of the above named decedent having duly come on for hearing before the Judge of the above named court, the undersigned Judge having heard and considered such petition, being fully advised in the premises, makes the following findings and determination:

1. That the petition for formal probate of will and for formal appointment of a personal representative is complete.

2. That the time for any notice has expired and any notice as required by the laws of this state has been given and proved.

3. That the petitioner has declared or affirmed that the representations contained in the petition are true, correct and complete to the best of h_is_ knowledge or information.

4. That the petitioner appears from the petition to be an interested person as defined by the laws of this state.

5. That the above named decedent testator herein is dead having died on _ September 20 _, 19_94_, at_ St. Paul, Minnesota 55102 _.

6. That, on the basis of the statements in the petition, this court has jurisdiction of this estate, proceeding and subject matter.

7. That venue for this proceeding is in the above named County of the State of Minnesota, because the decedent was domiciled in such county at the time of h_er_ death, and was the owner of property located in the State of Minnesota, ~~or because, though not domiciled in the State of Minnesota, the decedent was the owner of property located in the above named county at the time of his death~~.

8. That decedent's heirs are as identified in the petition commencing this proceeding.

9. That all persons identified as heirs have survived the decedent by at least 120 hours.

10. That all issue of decedent are issue of decedent's surviving spouse~~except for~~ _____
_____
_____.

11. That decedent died testate.

12. That the original, duly executed and apparently unrevoked last will of the decedent~~or if previously probated elsewhere, an authenticated copy thereof and a separate probating the same~~ is in the court's possession, and therefore, that any will to which the requested appointment relates has been or will be formally probated upon the entry of this order.

13. That the petition does not indicate the existence of a possible unrevoked testamentary instrument which may relate to property subject to the laws of this state, and which is not filed for probate in this court.

14. That it appears from the petition that the time limit for original probate and appointment proceedings has not expired.

Form 10   Order of Formal Probate of Will and Formal Appointment of Personal Representative (Executor)—*continued*

15. That from the statements in the petition, petitioner xx xxxxxxxxxxxxxxxxxxxxxxxxxxxxxxxxxxxxxxxxxx has priority entitling appointment because petitioner xx xxxxxxxxxxxxxxxxxxxxxxxxxxxxxxxxxxxxxxxxxx is nominated in the last will of the decedent as executor, with (no) xxxxxxxxxxxxxxxxxxxxxxxxxx bond, in an xxxxxxxxxxxxxxxxxxxxxxx (undesignated) administration, xxxxxxxx xxxxxxxxxxxxxxxxxxxxxxxxxxxxxxxxxxxxxxx xxxxxxxxxxxxxxxxxxxxxxxxxxxxxxxxxxxxxxxxxxxxxxxxxxxxxxxxxxxxxxxxxxxxxxxxxxxxxxxxxxxxxx and is not disqualified to serve as a personal representative of the decedent;

16. That the petition does not indicate that a personal representative has been appointed in this or another county of this state whose appointment has not been terminated.

17. That this proceeding is uncontested, the petition being unopposed, no objections having been filed.

Now, therefore, it is ORDERED, ADJUDGED and DECREED by the court as follows:

1. That the petition is hereby granted.

2. That the last will duly executed _____ June 2 _____ , 19 85 , and codicil or codicils thereto, if any, of the decedent is hereby formally probated.

3. That _____ John C. Doe _____ is hereby formally appointed as the executor of the estate of _____ Jane M. Doe _____ , deceased, with _____ no _____ bond, in an xxxxxxxxxxxxx (supervised) administration.

4. That upon qualification and acceptance, letters testamentary be issued to _____ John C. Doe _____
_____ .

Dated: _____ October 31, 1994 _____

_____ /S/ Richard B. Evans _____
                                          Judge

(COURT SEAL)

Form 11 Order of Formal Appointment of Administrator

MD FORM NO. 4392   MILLER DAVIS CO., MPLS, MN

STATE OF MINNESOTA	DISTRICT COURT

COUNTY OF_____

In Re: **Estate of**   Court File No. _____

_____
                Deceased

**ORDER OF FORMAL APPOINTMENT
OF ADMINISTRATOR**

The petition of _____ , dated _____ , 19____
for the formal appointment of administrator of the above named decedent having duly come on for
hearing before the above named court, the undersigned Judge having heard and considered such
petition, being fully advised in the premises, makes the following findings and determinations:

1. That the petition for formal appointment of a personal representative is complete.

2. That the time for any notice has expired and any notice as required by the laws of this state
   has been given and proved.

3. That the petitioner has declared or affirmed that the representations contained in the
   petition are true, correct and complete to the best of h__ knowledge or information.

4. That the petitioner appears from the petition to be an interested person as defined by the
   laws of this state.

5. That the above named decedent is dead having died on _____ , 19____
   at_____

6. That, on the basis of the statements in the petition, this court has jurisdiction of this estate,
   proceeding and subject matter.

7. That venue for this proceeding is in the above named County of the State of Minnesota,
   because the decedent was domiciled in such county at the time of h__ death, and was the
   owner of property located in the State of Minnesota, or because, though not domiciled in the
   State of Minnesota, the decedent was the owner of property located in the above named
   county at the time of h__ death.

8. That the petition states after the exercise of reasonable diligence, petitioner is unaware of
   any unrevoked testamentary instrument relating to property having a situs in this state
   under the laws of this state.

9. That decedent's heirs are as identified in the petition commencing this proceeding.

10. That all persons identified as heirs have survived the decedent by at least 120 hours.

11. That all issue of decedent are issue of decedent's surviving spouse except for_____
    _____
    _____.

12. That decedent left no valid will, and therefore, died intestate.

13. That it appears from the petition that the time limit for original appointment proceedings
    has not expired.

Form 11   Order of Formal Appointment of Administrator—*continued*

14. That from the statements in the petition, the petitioner or _____ is entitled to priority and appointment as administrator because petitioner or _____ is the _____ of the decedent and is not disqualified to serve as a personal representative of the decedent.

15. That the petition does not indicate that a personal representative has been appointed in this or another county of this state whose appointment has not been terminated.

16. That this proceeding is uncontested, the petition being unopposed, no objections having been filed.

Now, therefore, it is ORDERED, ADJUDGED, and DECREED by the court as follows:

1. That the petition is hereby granted.

2. That _____ is hereby formally appointed as the administrator of the estate of _____, deceased, with_____ bond, in an (unsupervised) (supervised) administration.

3. That upon qualification and acceptance, letters of administration be issued to _____ _____

Dated: _____

_____
Judge

(COURT SEAL)

Form 12 Certificate of Probate

No. 3554—Certificate of Probate of Will.

State of Minnesota,

County of _____

IN COUNTY COURT
PROBATE DIVISION
CERTIFICATE OF PROBATE

In the Matter of the Estate of _____, Decedent

Be it Remembered. That on the day of the date hereof at a _____ Term of said County Court, pursuant to the notice duly given, the last will and testament of _____, Decedent, late of said County of _____ bearing date the _____ day of _____, 19_____, and being the annexed written instrument, was duly proved before the County Court, in and for the County of _____ aforesaid; and was duly allowed and admitted to probate by said Court according to law; as and for the last Will and Testament of said _____ deceased, which said last Will and Testament is recorded and the examination taken thereon filed in this office.

In Testimony Whereof. The Judge of the County Court of said County has hereunto set his hand and affixed the seal of said Court at _____ in said County, this _____ day of _____, 19_____

_____
Judge

(Court Seal)

Form 13   Acceptance of Appointment and Oath by Individual

MD Form No. 4401   Miller-Davis Legal Forms   524.3-601#1   UPC 43

STATE OF MINNESOTA

COUNTY OF ___Ramsey___

In Re: Estate of

_____ Jane M. Doe _____
Deceased

PROBATE COURT
DISTRICT-COUNTY COURT
PROBATE DIVISION

Court File No. ___999999___

ACCEPTANCE OF APPOINTMENT
AND OATH BY INDIVIDUAL

TO THE ABOVE NAMED COURT:

STATE OF MINNESOTA

COUNTY OF ___Ramsey___   } *ss.*

I, _____ John C. Doe _____ , residing at _1005 Elm Street_
in the City of ___St. Paul___ , County of ___Ramsey___ , State of ___Minnesota___
as a condition to receiving letters as ___Personal Representative___
in the above entitled matter, hereby accept the duties of the office, agree to be bound by the provisions
of the statutes relating thereto and hereby submit to the jurisdiction of the Court in any proceeding
relating to the said matter that may be instituted by any person interested therein; and swear that I
will faithfully and justly perform all duties of the office and trust that I now assume as _____
___Personal Representative___
in the above entitled matter to the best of my ability.

/S/ John C. Doe
Personal Representative

Subscribed and sworn to before me this
__31st__ day of __October__ , 19 __94__ .
__/S/ Judith Harris__
SIGNATURE OF NOTARY PUBLIC OR OTHER OFFICIAL

NOTARIAL STAMP OR SEAL (OR OTHER TITLE OR RANK)

Form 14 Bond and Oath

HC 4777

Bond and Oath of Executor; Special Administrator; Administrator; Administrator C.T.A.; D.B.N.; D.B. N.C.T.A.; Guardian

STATE OF MINNESOTA
COUNTY OF HENNEPIN } ss.

IN THE MATTER OF THE { GUARDIANSHIP
ESTATE   OF

IN PROBATE COURT

File No. _____

BOND

KNOW ALL MEN BY THESE PRESENTS, That _____
_____ of _____
in the County of Hennepin, State of Minnesota, as principal and _____
_____ of said County and State, as surety _____, are
held and firmly bound to HON. MELVIN J. PETERSON, Judge of Probate of the County of Hennepin, Minnesota, in the
sum of _____ DOLLARS,
lawful money of the United States, to be paid to the said Judge of Probate or his successors in office; for which payment
well and truly to be made, we bind ourselves, our and each of our heirs, executors and administrators, jointly and severally
firmly by these presents.

The condition of this obligation is such that if the above bounden _____
_____ who has been appointed _____
of the estate of the above named _____ shall
well and faithfully discharge all the duties of _____ trust as such representative of said estate according to law
then this obligation shall be void otherwise it shall be and remain in full force and virtue.

WITNESS, Our hands and seals this _____ day of _____ , 19_____

_____ (Seal)
_____ (Seal)
_____ (Seal)

STATE OF MINNESOTA
COUNTY OF HENNEPIN } ss.

ACKNOWLEDGMENT

BE IT KNOWN, That on this _____ day of _____ , 19_____ , personally appeared before me
_____ , to me well known
to be the person who executed the foregoing bond, and _____ acknowledged the same to be _____
own free act and deed, and that _____ executed the same for the uses and purposes therein expressed.

SEAL
_____
Notary Public, Hennepin County, Minn.
My Commission expires _____ , 19_____

STATE OF MINNESOTA
COUNTY OF HENNEPIN } ss.

ACKNOWLEDGMENT OF SURETY

On this _____ day of _____ , 19_____ , before me appeared _____
_____ , to me personally known, who
being duly sworn did say that he is the Attorney-in-Fact of _____
_____ that the seal affixed to the foregoing instrument is the corporate
seal of that corporation and that said instrument was executed in behalf of the corporation by authority of its Board of
Directors; he acknowledged said instrument to be the free act and deed of said corporation.

SEAL
_____
Notary Public, Hennepin County, Minn.
My Commission expires _____ , 19_____

APPROVAL

I do hereby approve the within Bond, this _____ day of _____ , A. D. 19_____

_____
Judge.

STATE OF MINNESOTA
COUNTY OF HENNEPIN } ss.

OATH

I _____
of _____
     (Number), (Street or Avenue)   (City or Town)
in the County of _____ State of _____
do swear that I will faithfully and justly perform all duties of the office and trust which I now assume as
_____ of the person and estate of _____
(Guardian; Executor; Special Administrator; Administrator; Administrator C.T.A.; D.B. N.; D.B.N. C.T.A.)

_____
(Deceased, Minor, Mentally Ill, Incompetent, or Mentally Deficient)
late of _____ to the best of my ability. So help me God.
          (County and State)

Subscribed and sworn to before

me this _____ day of _____ , 19_____

_____
Notary Public, Hennepin County, Minn.   _____
My Commission expires _____
SEAL

Form 15   Request for Minimum Bond

HC 4796

STATE OF MINNESOTA
COUNTY OF HENNEPIN

RE ESTATE OF

_____
Decedent.

IN PROBATE COURT

File No. ....

REQUEST FOR
MINIMUM BOND

The undersigned, being all of the persons interested in said estate as heirs, devisees or legatees, do hereby request the Court to fix the bond of the representative in an amount not to exceed $ _____.

Dated _____, 19____.

_____

_____

_____

_____

_____

_____

Form 16 Request for Waiver of Bond

MD Form No. 4405   MILLER DAVIS CO., MPLS

STATE OF MINNESOTA

COUNTY OF ___Ramsey___

In Re: Estate of

___Jane M. Doe___
Deceased

PROBATE COURT
DISTRICT-COUNTY COURT
PROBATE DIVISION

Court File No.___999999___

REQUEST FOR WAIVER OF BOND

The undersigned, being all interested persons with an apparent interest in excess of $1,000.00, other than creditors, hereby request that no bond be required of___John C. Doe___, The nominated or appointed personal representative in the above estate.

Dated:___October 31, 1994___

___/S/ John C. Doe___
Personal Representative

Form 17 Letters Testamentary

MD Form No. 4403 Rev. 1-88 Miller-Davis Legal Forms 524.3-601 #3   UPC 43

STATE OF MINNESOTA

COUNTY OF Ramsey

DISTRICT COURT

In Re: Estate of

Court File No. ___999999___

LETTERS TESTAMENTARY

_____ Jane M. Doe _____
                Deceased

The above named decedent having died on _____ September 20 _____, 19 94 , and

_____ John C. Doe _____

having been appointed and qualified, (is) (are) hereby authorized to act as personal representative(s) according to law.

Dated: _____ October 31, 1994 _____

_____ /S/ Richard B. Evans _____
                Judge/Registrar

(COURT SEAL)

Form 18 Order Appointing Guardian

....

MD Form No. GC-14 MILLER-DAVIS CO., MPLS. MN (7-87)   Form 525.551 #1

STATE OF MINNESOTA

COUNTY OF _____

In Re: Guardianship of

_____
                                    Ward

PROBATE COURT
DISTRICT-COUNTY COURT

Court File No. _____
ORDER APPOINTING
GENERAL GUARDIAN OF THE
PERSON AND ESTATE

This matter came duly on for hearing on _____, 19____, on the petition of
_____ seeking appointment
of a guardian for _____.
Petitioner appeared personally and by and through his/her attorney, _____
_____, Esq. The above named ward appeared personally and by and through
his/her attorney, _____, Esq.
The Court having considered the evidence and being fully advised in the premises now makes the following:

FINDINGS OF FACT

1.   (In a meeting with a Court appointed visitor the ward waived his/her right to be present personally and to be represented by an attorney.) (The ward was unable to attend the hearing by reason of medical condition as evidenced by a written statement from a licensed physician.)

2.   The ward lacks sufficient understanding or capacity to make or communicate responsible decisions concerning his/her person.

3.   The ward has demonstrated behavioral deficits evidencing inability to meet his/her needs for medical care, nutrition, clothing, shelter, or safety.

4.   The ward lacks sufficient understanding or capacity to make or communicate responsible decisions concerning his/her estate or financial decisions.

5.   The ward has demonstrated behavioral deficits evidencing inability to manage his/her estate.

6.   The ward has property which will be dissipated without proper management. (Funds are needed for the care, support, and welfare of the ward and/or those entitled to the support of the ward.)

7.   No appropriate alternative to guardianship exists which is less restrictive of civil rights and liberties, including any protective arrangement under M.S. 525.54 Subd. 7.

8.   The ward is incapable of exercising the following rights and powers:

    a.   To establish his/her place of abode.

    b.   To determine his/her food, clothing, shelter, health care, social and recreational requirements, and training, educational and rehabilitation requirements.

M.S. 525.551 #1   (Over)   Order Appoint. Gen. Gdn. of Person & Estate

Form 18   Order Appointing Guardian—*continued*

  c. To dispose of his/her clothing, personal effects, vehicles, furniture or other property.

  d. To consent to necessary medical or other professional care, counseling, treatment, or service.

  e. To approve or withhold approval of any contract, except for necessities which the ward may make or wish to make.

  f. To pay reasonable charges for the support, maintenance and education of the ward.

  g. To pay any debts of the ward and the reasonable charges for the support, maintenance and education of the ward's spouse and dependent children.

  h. To possess and manage his/her estate, collect all debts and claims in his/her favor or compromise them, to invest all funds not needed for current debts and charges, and to represent himself/herself in court proceedings or institute suit.

  i. To vote.

9. The ward is not a patient of a State Hospital for the mentally ill or a mentally retarded or dependent or neglected ward of the Commissioner of Human Services, or under the temporary custody of the Commissioner of Human Services.

10. The ward is in need of a guardian to supervise and to protect his/her person and estate.

11. The guardian___ is_____the most suitable and best qualified among those available and willing to discharge the trust. (The guardian has been duly nominated by the ward.)

CONCLUSIONS OF LAW

1. _____ is an incapacitated person.

2. A guardian of the person and estate of _____ _____ should be appointed.

Now therefore IT IS ORDERED:

1. That _____ be and hereby is ____ appointed guardian ____ of the person and estate of _____ _____ with all the powers enumerated in M.S. 525.56 Subds. 3 (and 4).

2. That letters of guardianship issue to _____ _____ upon filing an oath and a bond in the amount of $_____.

Dated _____   BY THE COURT:

   (COURT SEAL)   _____
                 Judge

Filed

Court Administrator

Form 19 Petition for Probate of Foreign Will

No. 3665 — Petition for Probate of Foreign Will.

State of Minnesota, }
County of.................................

IN THE MATTER OF THE ESTATE OF

....

**COUNTY COURT
PROBATE DIVISION**

PETITION FOR PROBATE OF

FOREIGN WILL.

Your petitioner respectfully represents and states to the Court:

First—That he is a resident of the............................of...

in the County of..................................State of..........................and has

an interest in the estate of the above named decedent, in this to-wit:

..

Second—That the above named decedent then being a citizen of the Country of...............

died on the..................................day of.............................19........,

at..................................in the County of..........................

State of..................................., leaving a last will and testament; and that in and by said

will..................................was named and appointed to be the

executor.....thereof, ...(1)

Third—That said last will and testament of said decedent was duly proved, allowed and admitted to

probate in and by the..................................court in and for the County of

..................................State of.........................., on the.........................

day of..................................19........, and that letters..........................

..................................thereon were duly issued to..........................

..................................on the..................................day of..........................19........

..................................(1)

Fourth—That said decedent died seized and possessed of certain..................................property

and estate lying and being in the County of..................................State of Minnesota, de-

scribed and of the estimated value as follows, to-wit:..

Fifth—That your petitioner herewith presents duly authenticated copies of said will and of the pro-
bate thereof in the court above named, and represents that said court above named was a court having
jurisdiction to admit said will to probate, and that its order and decree admitting said will to probate is
still in force.

Form 20   Order and Notice of Hearing for Foreign Will

No. 3669

State of Minnesota, } ss.

County of ....

IN RE ESTATE OF

....

.... Decedent.

IN COUNTY COURT
PROBATE DIVISION

Order for Hearing on Petition for Probate of Foreign Will, Limiting Time to File Claims and for Hearing Thereon

Authenticated copies of the last Will of said decedent and of the instrument admitting it to probate in the .... Court in the County of .... and the State of .... having been filed with the Petition of .... praying for the allowance of said Will in this Court and for the appointment of .... as ....

It is Ordered, That the hearing thereof be had on ...., 19........, at .... o'clock .... M., before this Court in the probate court room in the court house in ...., Minnesota; that the time within which creditors of said decedent may file their claims be limited to 60 days from the date hereof, and that the claims so filed be heard on ...., 19........, at .... o'clock .... M., before this Court in the probate court room in the court house in ...., Minnesota, and that notice hereof be given by publication of this order in the .... and by mailed notice as provided by law.

Dated ...., 19........

....
Judge.

(Court Seal)

....
Attorney   for Petitioner.

Form 21 Order Admitting Foreign Will to Probate

No. 3664—Order Admitting Foreign Will to Probate.

State of Minnesota, }ss.   IN COUNTY COURT
County of................................   PROBATE DIVISION

In the Matter of the Estate of   **Order Admitting Foreign Will**
.... }   **to Probate**
                                    Decedent

The above entitled matter came on to be heard by the Court, on the .... day of

...., 19 ...., upon the petition of ....

....praying for the admittance and allowance of the

will of said decedent to probate; and the Court, having heard the said petition and the evidence in support

thereof, and examined the said will and the authentication thereof and the files and records in said

matter, finds the following facts:

First—That notice of said hearing has been given by the publication in................................

....

of the order of this court for said hearing issued on the................ day of ...., 19........,

as required by law..

....

....

Second—That said decedent died on the .... day of ...., 19........, at

....in the County of..

State of ....leaving a last will and testament, in which

....

named and appointed to be executor.... thereof.. (1)

....

....

Third—That said will of said decedent was duly proved, allowed and admitted to probate in and by

the ....Court in and for the County of........................

State of........................ on the................ day of........................, 19........,

and letters..thereon

issued to..on the

.... day of........................, 19........, ... (2)

....

Fourth—That the..Court above named, in which the

said will was proved, allowed and admitted to probate, was a court of competent jurisdiction to allow said

will and admit it to probate, and that it appears that the order and decree of said Court allowing said

will and admitting the same to probate is still in force.

Form 22 Order Appointing Appraisers

525.51 #8   UPC --

STATE OF MINNESOTA

COUNTY OF _____

PROBATE COURT
COUNTY COURT-PROBATE DIVISION

In Re: Estate of ·

Court File No. _____

ORDER APPOINTING APPRAISERS

_____
            Deceased

The petition of _____ dated _____, 19 ___,
for an order appointing appraisers in the estate of the above named decedent having duly come on for
hearing before the above named court, the undersigned Judge having heard and considered such
petition, being fully advised in the premises, makes the following findings and determinations:

1. That the petition for an order appointing appraisers is complete.

2. That the time for any notice has expired and any notice as required by the laws of this state has
been given and proved.

3. That the petitioner has declared or affirmed that the representations contained in the petition are
true, correct and complete to the best of his knowledge or information.

4. That the petitioner appears from the petition to be an interested person as defined by the laws of
this state.

5. That appraisers should be appointed in the estate of the above named decedent because:
_____
_____

6. The following named persons are qualified to be appraisers herein: _____
_____

Now, therefore, it is ORDERED, ADJUDGED, and DECREED by the court as follows:

1. That the petition is hereby granted.

2. That the above named persons are hereby appointed appraisers.

Dated: _____

_____
(COURT SEAL)   Judge

Form 23 Inventory and Appraisal

Form No. 4428—Miller-Davis Legal Forms (Rev. 1-88)   Form 524.3-706   UPC 54

STATE OF MINNESOTA   **DISTRICT COURT**

COUNTY OF Ramsey

In Re: Estate of   Court File No. ___999999___

_____   **INVENTORY AND APPRAISEMENT**
         Jane M. Doe
            Deceased   Date of Death ___September 20___, 19 94
                                          Social Security No. _321-54-9876_

TO THE HONORABLE JUDGE AND/OR REGISTRAR OF THE ABOVE NAMED COURT:

___John C. Doe_____, the undersigned personal representative, respectfully
states:

1. That the following is a true and correct inventory and appraisement, at date of death values,
   of all the property of the above named estate, both real and personal, which has come into
   the.possession of said representative and of which said representative has knowledge after
   diligent search and inquiry concerning the same, classified as follows, to-wit: (See instructions at end of last page.)

SCHEDULE A — Real Estate

Item number	Legal Description (Specify street address of city realty; acreage of rural land; and liens, if any)	Assessor's Estimated Market Value (Do not use "Green Acres" Value or Assessor's Limited Market Value)	GROSS APPRAISED VALUE
1	Homestead, being in the County of ___Ramsey___, State of Minnesota: 1005 Elm St., St. Paul, MN. Legally described as follows, to wit: Lot 615, Block 42, Reiser's Addition to St. Paul (Plat #22760 Parcel #7600)	$337,500.00	$350,000.00
2	Other Real Estate, being in the County of ___Ramsey___ State of Minnesota: an undivided 1/4 interest in duplex located at 776 Cliff Road, St. Paul, MN. Legally described as follows, to wit: Lots 16 & 17, Block 20, Lovey's Addition to St. Paul (Plat #32689 Parcel #5562) Liens:	68,250.00 Total 17,062.50 (1/4)	91,000.00 Total 22,750.00 (1/4)
1	Mortgage balance at St. Paul Bank and Trust Company - $130,000.00		
2	Mortgage balance at St. Paul Bank and Trust Company - $ 40,000.00 1/4 interest - $ 10,000.00		

Form 23 Inventory and Appraisal—*continued*

Real Estate SCHEDULE A — TOTAL $ 372,750.00

SCHEDULE B — Stocks and Bonds

Item number	Description (Specify face amount of bonds or number of shares and par value where needed for identification; and liens, if any)	GROSS APPRAISED VALUE
	Stocks:	
1	100 Shares Tenneco, Inc., Common Stock, CUSIP 674322189, Cert. C068297 dated 12/31/72, N.Y.S.E., at $50.00/share.	$ 5,000.00
2	1000 Shares Minnesota Co-op, Common Stock, Cert. D2289663 dated 12/31/74, at $4.50/share.	4,500.00
	United States Savings Bonds:	
3	$500 U.S. Savings Bond, Series E, Bond R4502363E, 04/85.	574.00
4	$500 U.S. Savings Bond, Series E, Bond R4502364E, 04/85.	574.00

Personal Property SCHEDULE B — TOTAL $ 10,648.00

SCHEDULE C — Mortgages, Notes, and Cash

Item number	Description (Specify recording data; bank and account numbers; accrued interest; location of actual cash; and liens, if any)	GROSS APPRAISED
1	American Express Traveler's Checks #10008-10017, $100/ea.	$ 1,000.00
2	First National City Bank of St. Paul – Checking Account No. 55-5555.	50,000.00
3	American National Bank of St. Paul – Savings Certificate No. 44-4444, at 5.5% per annum.	15,000.00
4	Johnson Furriers, Promissory Note dated 03/20/89, payable 03/20/95 with interest at 7% per annum.	10,000.00
5	Accrued interest on Item 4 from 03/20/94 to 09/20/94.	350.00

Personal Property SCHEDULE C — TOTAL $ 76,350.00

Form 23 Inventory and Appraisal—*continued*

* Trust created under agreement dated 12/02/65 by father of decedent for decedent's benefit under which decedent had a general power of appoint-ment (to distribute income and/or principal) which power had not been exercised during decedent's lifetime, but which decedent exercised under her will. The assets remaining in this trust and subject to this power are 500 shares of Green Giant common stock and undistributed earnings (dividends) thereon. Unit value $100.00 per share.

SCHEDULE D — Other Miscellaneous Property

Item number	Description (Specify location of property and liens, if any)	GROSS APPRAISED VALUE
1	Furniture and Household goods:	$ 22,000.00
2	Wearing apparel and Ornaments: Furs - Mink coat.	11,500.00
3	Clothing and personal effects.	4,500.00
	All other personal property (including partnership and business interests, insurance and annuities payable to estate, other receivables, farm crops, machinery, etc.):	
4	1992 Mazda, Vehicle Identification Number 6778899926, Title Number 03618957.	12,000.00
5	Judgment dated February 19, 1991 for personal injuries in auto accident against Forrest R. Redding collected in full on December 20, 1994.	20,000.00
6	Minnesota Life Insurance Company Policy J666221, face amount $120,000, accumulated dividends $100. Beneficiary: Estate of Jane M. Doe.	120,100.00
7	Power of Appointment. See above.*	50,000.00

Personal Property SCHEDULE D — TOTAL $ 240,100.00

SUMMARY

Total Gross Value of Real Estate	$	372,750.00	
Less Liens	$	140,000.00	
Net Value of Real Estate			$ 232,750.00
Total Gross Value of Personal Property	$	327,098.00	
Less Liens	$	0	
Net Value of Personal Property			$ 327,098.00
TOTAL NET APPRAISEMENT			$ 559,848.00

2. That a copy hereof has been mailed to the surviving spouse if there be one, and to all residuary distributees of the above named decedent and to interested persons or creditors who have requested the same.

Form 23   Inventory and Appraisal—*continued*

FURTHER, under penalties for perjury for deliberate falsification therein, I declare or affirm that I have read the foregoing and to the best of my knowledge or information, its representations are true, correct and complete.

Dated: December 21, 1994

                                                    /S/ John C. Doe
                                                    Personal Representative

      /S/ John W. Cranwall
Attorney   John W. Cranwall
           First Trust Co. Bldg.
           St. Paul, MN 55101
Address/Phone (612) 555-5555

INSTRUCTIONS:

(1) The classification of assets herein is intended for them to be comparable to the Federal Estate Tax Return Form 706 with the exception of Schedule D herein which includes insurance and annuities payable to the estate and which are otherwise includable under separate Schedules of said Form 706.

(2) It is to be noted that the GROSS APPRAISED VALUE is requested of each asset without reduction by any lien requested to be specified as a part of its description. The reduction for liens is later taken under the Summary of Assets.

(3) It is also to be noted that each asset of a Schedule is to be given its "Item number" to facilitate a ready reference similar to the Estate Tax Form 706.

(4) Finally, it is to be noted that the Assessor's Estimated Market Value is requested. This information is always available to the Department of Revenue upon its request. The accurate furnishing of the information can result in better servicing of the inheritance tax returns.

(5) It is recommended that the appraisal report of any independent appraiser should be properly referenced and attached as an Exhibit including the name and address of any such appraisers.

Form 24 Petition for Allowance of Selection of Personal Property

MD Form No. 4481 Miller Davis Co., Mpls   525.151 #1   UPC—

STATE OF MINNESOTA

COUNTY OF ___Ramsey___

**PROBATE COURT
DISTRICT-COUNTY COURT
PROBATE DIVISION**

In Re: Estate of

Court File No. ___999999___

**PETITION FOR ALLOWANCE OF
SELECTION OF PERSONAL
PROPERTY**

___Jane M. Doe___
Deceased

TO THE HONORABLE JUDGE OF THE ABOVE NAMED COURT:

Petitioner, ___John C. Doe___, respectfully states:

1. Petitioner resides at ___1005 Elm Street, St. Paul, MN 55102___;

2. Petitioner has an interest herein as ___personal representative, heir, and devisee___ and is, therefore, an interested person as defined by the laws of this state;

3. The above named decedent was survived by ___John C. Doe___, her spouse and the following minor children whose names and ages are:
   ___none___

4. Petitioner hereby selects the following items of personal property listed and described in the inventory of decedent's estate, to-wit:

Description	Value	Description	Value
1992 Mazda	$ 12,000.00		$
		TOTAL VALUE	$ 12,000.00

WHEREFORE, your petitioner requests the Order of this Court fixing a time and place for hearing on this petition, and that after the time for any notice has expired, upon proof of notice, and hearing, and/or the Court enter a judicial order allowing the selection of said property to ___John C. Doe___ according to law, and granting such other and further relief as may be proper.

FURTHER, under penalties for perjury for deliberate falsification therein, I declare or affirm that I have read the foregoing petition and to the best of my knowledge or information, its representations are true, correct and complete.

Dated: ___December 21, 1994___

___/S/ John C. Doe___
Petitioner

___/S/ John W. Cranwall___
Attorney for Petitioner
First Trust Co. Bldg.
St. Paul, MN 55101
Address/Phone (612) 555-5555

Form 25   Order Setting Apart (Allowing Selection of) Personal Property

MD Form No. 4482 Miller Davis Co., Mpls, MN   525.151 #2   UPC

STATE OF MINNESOTA

COUNTY OF _____Ramsey_____

In Re: Estate of

_____Jane M. Doe_____
Deceased

**PROBATE COURT
DISTRICT—COUNTY COURT
PROBATE DIVISION**

Court File No. _____999999_____

**ORDER ALLOWING SELECTION OF
PERSONAL PROPERTY**

The petition of _____John C. Doe_____ dated _____December 21_____, 19_94_, for allowance of selection of personal property in the estate of the above named decedent having duly come on for hearing before the above named court, the undersigned Judge having heard and considered such petition, being fully advised in the premises, makes the following findings and determinations:

1. That the petition for allowance of selection of personal property is complete.
2. That the time for any notice has expired and any notice as required by the laws of this state has been given and proved.
3. That the petitioner has declared or affirmed that the representations contained in the petition are true, correct and complete to the best of h_is_ knowledge or information.
4. That the petitioner appears from the petition to be an interested person as defined by the laws of this state.
5. That the above named decedent was survived by _____John C. Doe_____, her spouse and the following minor children whose names and ages are:
   _____none_____

6. That the petitioner has selected certain items of personal property listed and described in the inventory of decedent's estate.

   Now, therefore, it is ORDERED, ADJUDGED, and DECREED by the court as follows:

1. That the petition is hereby granted.
2. That the selection of the following personal property to-wit:

Description	Value	Description	Value
1992 Mazda	$ 12,000.00		$
		Total Value	$ 12,000.00

Form 25 Order Setting Apart (Allowing Selection of) Personal Property—*continued*

be, and the same is hereby allowed and that the personal representative of said estate immediately transfer and make delivery of said personal property to _____ John C. Doe _____

_____

IT IS FURTHER ORDERED that the lien of Minnesota inheritance taxes on said described property is hereby waived.

Dated: _____ January 20, 1995 _____

(COURT SEAL)

_____ /S/ Richard B. Evans _____
                                Judge

Form 26   Petition for Family Maintenance

MD Form No. 4483   525.151 #3   UPC 7

STATE OF MINNESOTA   **PROBATE COURT**
                                           DISTRICT-COUNTY COURT
COUNTY OF___Ramsey_____   **PROBATE DIVISION**

In Re: Estate of   Court File No.___999999_____

                                           PETITION FOR
                                           FAMILY MAINTENANCE

_____Jane M. Doe_____
              Deceased

TO THE HONORABLE JUDGE OF THE ABOVE NAMED COURT:

Petitioner, _____John C. Doe_____ , respectfully states:

1. Petitioner resides at ____1005 Elm Street, St. Paul, MN 55102_____ ;

2. Petitioner has an interest herein as__personal representative, heir, and devisee._____
_____and is, therefore, an interested person
as defined by the laws of this state;_____

3. The above named decedent was survived by____John C. Doe_____, h er
   spouse and the following minor and/or dependent children whose names and ages are:
   ____none_____
   _____
   _____

4. That decedent's estate is (solvent) ~~insolvent~~.

5. That a reasonable and necessary family allowance of $ ___4,800.00_____ should be paid
to and for the use and benefit of decedent's surviving spouse and minor and/or dependent children constituting the
family of decedent.

    WHEREFORE, your petitioner requests the Order of this Court fixing a time and place for hearing on this petition,
and that after the time for any notice has expired, upon proof of notice, and hearing, and/or the Court enter a judicial
order directing the payment of a family allowance in the amount of $___4,800.00_____ to be paid in
periodic installments of $____400.00_____ per month, and granting such other and further relief as may
be proper.

FURTHER, under penalties for perjury for deliberate falsification therein, I declare or affirm that I have read the
foregoing petition and to the best of my knowledge or information, its representations are true, correct and complete.

Dated: ____December 21, 1994_____

                                           ____/S/ John C. Doe_____
                                           Petitioner

____/S/ John W. Cranwall_____
Attorney for Petitioner
    First Trust Co. Bldg.
    St. Paul, MN 55101
Address/Phone

Form No. 4484 GOVERNMENT BUSINESS SYSTEMS, MPLS.   525.151 #4   UPC 8

STATE OF MINNESOTA

COUNTY OF _____Ramsey_____

**PROBATE COURT
DISTRICT - COUNTY COURT
PROBATE DIVISION**

In Re: Estate of

Court File No. _____999999_____

ORDER FOR FAMILY MAINTENANCE

_____Jane M. Doe_____
Deceased

The petition of _____John C. Doe_____ dated _____December 21_____, 19 94, for an order for family maintenance in the estate of the above named decedent having duly come on for hearing before the above named court, the undersigned Judge having heard and considered such petition, being fully advised in the premises, makes the following findings and determinations:

1. That the petition for an order for family maintenance is complete.

2. That the time for any notice has expired and any notice as required by the laws of this state has been given and proved.

3. That the petitioner has declared or affirmed that the representations contained in the petition are true, correct and complete to the best of his knowledge or information.

4. That the petitioner appears from the petition to be an interested person as defined by the laws of this state.

5. That the above named decedent was survived by _____John C. Doe_____, her spouse and the following minor and/or dependent children whose names and ages are:
_____none_____
_____

6. That decedent's estate is (solvent) ~~insolvent~~.

7. That a family allowance of $ _____4,800.00_____ is reasonable and necessary for the use and benefit of decedent's surviving spouse and minor and/or dependent children constituting the family of decedent to be paid in periodic installments of $ ___400.00___ per month.

Now, therefore, it is ORDERED, ADJUDGED, and DECREED by the court as follows:

1. That the petition is hereby granted.

2. That the personal representative be and is hereby directed to pay as family allowance the sum of $ ___4,800.00___ in installments of $ _____400.00_____ per month to _____John C. Doe_____, surviving spouse of _____Jane M. Doe_____ _____, deceased, for the use and benefit of said spouse and minor and/or dependent children constituting the family of decedent.

Dated: _____January 20, 1995_____

_____/S/ Richard B. Evans_____
Judge

(COURT SEAL)

Form 28 Proof of Claim

MD Form No. 3817 -Proof of Claim (Rev. 5-28-80)

Miller-Davis Legal Forms

State of Minnesota,

County of _____

In the Matter of the Estate of

_____
                              Decedent

State of Minnesota,

County of _____

IN _____ COURT

PROBATE DIVISION
PROOF OF CLAIM

ss.

_____

being duly sworn says that _____ he is _____
the claimant herein; that at the time of h _____ death the above named decedent was justly indebted to
_____ in the sum of
_____ Dollars.
   That said indebtedness arose and was incurred on account of _____
_____
_____

   That hereto annexed, herewith filed and hereby made a part hereof is a true and correct statement of the
items of such account, and that there is now due and owing to said _____
on account thereof from the estate of said decedent the sum of _____
Dollars, with interest from the _____ day of _____, 19 _____.
   That no credits, payments, offsets or counterclaims exist against such indebtedness, except as stated in
said account or herein stated _____
_____

   That said claimant has no security for said debt except _____
_____

   That the address of the claimant is _____
   Subscribed and sworn to before me this ____
day of _____, 19 _____   *(Signed) _____*

_____

Notary Public _____ County, Minn.
My commission expires _____

Itemized statement of account must be attached and claim signed and notarized

Form 29 Petition for Disallowance of Claim (Objections to Claims)

Form No. 4445 MILLER-DAVIS CO., MPLS.   524.3-806(b) #5   UPC --

STATE OF MINNESOTA

COUNTY OF _____

PROBATE COURT
COUNTY COURT-PROBATE DIVISION

In Re: Estate of

Court File No. _____

PETITION FOR DISALLOWANCE
OF CLAIM

_____
              Deceased

TO THE HONORABLE JUDGE OF THE ABOVE NAMED COURT:

Petitioner, _____, respectfully states:

1. Petitioner resides at _____ ;

2. Petitioner has an interest herein as _____,
   and is, therefore, an interested person as defined by the laws of this state;

3. _____, Claimant, presented a claim on _____
   _____ in the amount of $ _____ .

4. That the claim should be disallowed for the reason that _____
   _____

5. That no notice of disallowance was mailed to claimant within two months of the presentment of
   said claim.

6. That payment of said claim has not been made.

WHEREFORE, your petitioner requests the Order of this Court fixing a time and place for hearing
of this petition, and that after the time for any notice has expired, upon proof of notice, and hearing,
the Court enter a judicial order formally permitting the disallowance of said claim and granting such
other and further relief as may be proper.

FURTHER, under penalties for perjury for deliberate falsification therein, I declare or affirm that I
have read the foregoing petition and to the best of my knowledge or information, its representations
are true, correct and complete.

Dated: _____

_____
Petitioner

_____
Attorney for Petitioner

_____
Address/Phone

Form 30 Order for Disallowance of Claim

Form No. 4446 MILLER-DAVIS CO., MPLS.   524.3-806(b) #6   UPC --

STATE OF MINNESOTA

COUNTY OF _____

In Re: Estate of

_____
                    Deceased

PROBATE COURT
COUNTY COURT-PROBATE DIVISION

Court File No. _____

ORDER FOR DISALLOWANCE
OF CLAIM

The petition of _____ dated _____, 19___, for an order for disallowance of claim in the estate of the above named decedent having duly come on for hearing before the above named court, the undersigned Judge having heard and considered such petition, being fully advised in the premises, makes the following findings and determinations:

1. That the petition for an order for disallowance of claim is complete.

2. That the time for any notice has expired and any notice as required by the laws of this state has been given and proved.

3. That the petitioner has declared or affirmed that the representations contained in the petition are true, correct and complete to the best of h___ knowledge or information.

4. That the petitioner appears from the petition to be an interested person as defined by the laws of this state.

5. That _____ , Claimant, presented a claim on _____ _____ in the amount of $_____.

6. That the claim should be disallowed for the reason that _____ _____ .

7. That no notice of disallowance was mailed to claimant within two months of the presentment of said claim.

8. That payment of said claim has not been made.

Now, therefore, it is ORDERED, ADJUDGED, and DECREED by the court as follows:

1. That the petition is hereby granted.

2. That the claim of_____ , presented on _____, 19___, in the amount of $_____, is hereby formally disallowed.

Dated: _____

_____
                                    Judge

(COURT SEAL)

Form 31   Petition to Sell-Mortgage-Lease Real Estate (Land)

No. 3882 — Petition of Representative to Sell-Mortgage-Lease Land.

State of Minnesota,

County of.. } ss

In the Matter of the Estate of:

Ward   Decedent

IN PROBATE COURT

File No.............................

Petition of Representative
to Sell-Mortgage-Lease Land

YOUR PETITIONER respectfully represents and shows to the Court:

That he is the duly appointed representative in the above entitled matter, with LETTERS in full force and effect.

That it is expedient to sell-mortgage-lease the land hereinafter described for the best interest of the estate and for the benefit of the heirs thereof, viz: (state reasons)

*(A) HOMESTEAD: That tract of land lying and being in the County of...,
State of Minnesota described as follows, viz:*

(1) The terms and conditions of the mortgage, or the lease, proposed herein on the above homestead, are as follows:

Form 32 Order for Hearing Petition to Sell-Mortgage-Lease Real Estate

No. 3847

State of Minnesota, } ss.

County of ....

IN RE ESTATE OF

....
.... Decedent - Ward

IN PROBATE COURT

Order for Hearing on Petition

to .... Sell .... Real Estate

The representative of said estate having filed herein a petition to ....

certain real estate described in said petition;

It is Ordered, That the hearing thereof be had on ....

19 ...., at .... o'clock .... M., before this Court in the probate court room in the court house in

.............................., Minnesota, and that notice hereof be given by mail as

provided by law.

Dated ...., 19 ....

(Probate Court Seal)

.... Probate Judge.

.... Attorney for Petitioner.

Form 33 Order for Sale, Mortgage, or Lease of Real Estate at Private Sale

No. 3875—Order for Sale of Real Estate at Private Sale.

State of Minnesota, } ss.

County of...

In the Matter of the Estate of

....

IN PROBATE COURT

File No.................................

**Order For Sale of Real Estate
at Private Sale**

The above entitled matter came on to be heard by the Court on the... day of..., 19........., upon the petition of... ....as representative in the above entitled matter, praying for an order to sell certain real estate described in said petition; and the Court having heard the said petition and all the evidence adduced in support thereof, and having duly considered the same and examined the files and records in said matter, finds the following facts:

FIRST—That notice of said hearing has been given and served as required by law and the order of this Court for said hearing.

SECOND—That the said representative appeared at said hearing in person and by attorney ....and was duly examined relative to said matter by the Court and that ....appeared in opposition to said petition.

THIRD—That it would be for the best interest of said estate and the persons interested therein that the property hereinafter described, be sold.

It is Therefore Ordered, FIRST—That the said representative of said estate be, and hereby is, authorized and directed to sell at private sale the real estate hereinafter described, situate and being in the County of..., State of Minnesota, to-wit:

Form 34　Warrant to Appraisers at Private Sale

No. 3605—Warrant to Appraisers at Private Sale and Oath of Appraisers

State of Minnesota, ⎱ss.
County of .... ⎰

IN PROBATE COURT

IN THE MATTER OF

.... ⎱
.... ⎰

The STATE OF MINNESOTA To ....

.... of said County, GREETING:

Whereas, *License to sell real estate at private sale was issued and granted to*..............................

....

on the...*day of*...19..........

And Whereas, *We are desirous that the said real estate be duly appraised, pursuant to the statute in such case made and provided;*

Therefore, *Trusting in your integrity and disinterestedness, we have appointed and do by these presents, appoint you appraisers of the following described real estate, situate and being in the County of*

....*and State of Minnesota, to-wit:*

and being severally duly sworn, to the faithful execution of said trust, you are hereby required faithfully and honestly to appraise the same, at its full cash value, as by you determined; and the said appraisal so made, you will certify and subscribe, and together with this Warrant deliver without delay to the said

....*Hereof fail not.*

In Testimony Whereof, *We have caused the seal of the Probate Court of said County to be hereunto affixed.*

WITNESS: The Honorable ....

(L. S.)　　　　*Judge of Probate, at*...*in said County,*

this .... *day of* ....19..........

....
Judge of Probate.

Form 35 Oath of Appraisers and Appraisal of Real Estate Under Order for Sale

No. 3606—Oath of Appraisers of Lands Under Order for Sale.

State of Minnesota, } ss.

County of........................

IN PROBATE COURT

In the Matter of the Estate of

....
Decedent—Ward

Oath of Appraisers and Appraisal
of Lands Under Order for Sale

OATH OF APPRAISERS

State of Minnesota, }

County of........................ I, ...

and I, ..., *do swear that I will faithfully and*

justly perform all the duties of the office and trust which I now assume as appraiser of the lands of the

above named ....*under and pursuant*

to that certain order for sale of said lands at private sale, made by the above named Court on the

........................*day of*..., 19........, *and that I will appraise*

the said land described in said order for sale at its true and full value, So Help Me God.

   Subscribed and sworn to before me this

........................*day of*........................., 19........   ....

....

Notary Public

....*County, Minn.*

My commission expires........................, 19........

APPRAISAL

   We, the undersigned appraisers appointed by the above named Court in and by its certain order for

sale to ....*to sell certain lands*

belonging to the above named..., *dated*

the........................*day of*..., 19........, *do hereby certify and report:*

   That we did first and before making said appraisal take and subscribe the foregoing oath as by law

required and thereafter did appraise at their true and full value in cash those certain tracts or parcels of

land lying and being in the County of..., *State of Minnesota, described*

in said order for sale, as follows, to-wit:

Form 36 Report of Sale of Real Estate at Private Sale Under Order for Sale

No. 3641—Report of Sale of Land at Private Sale Under Order For Sale.

State of Minnesota,

County of_____

In the Matter of the Estate of

_____
Decedent—Ward

IN PROBATE COURT

REPORT OF SALE OF LAND AT PRIVATE SALE UNDER ORDER FOR SALE

Your petitioner respectfully reports to the court his proceedings under that certain order for sale granted to him in the above entitled matter on the_____day of_____, 19____, to sell at private sale the lands of said_____

hereinafter described, as follows, to-wit:

First—That before making sale of the real estate hereinafter described under said order for sale, he executed and filed in this court his bond required by the said order for sale.

Second—That before making sale of said real estate under said order for sale, he caused the same to be re-appraised by_____

the appraisers appointed in said order for sale to appraise the same, and the appraisement thereof to be filed in this court_____(1)

Third—That on the_____day of_____, 19____, he, pursuant to said order for sale, sold to_____

_____of_____

th____tract____ or parcel____ of land, described in said order for sale, and lying and being in the County of_____, State of Minnesota, described as follows, to-wit:_____

for the sum of_____Dollars,

Form 37 Order Confirming Private Sale of Real Estate

No. 3876—Order Confirming Private Sale of Real Estate

State of Minnesota, $\bigg\}$ ss.

County of...

In the Matter of the Estate of

....

IN PROBATE COURT

File No...

**Order Confirming Private Sale
of Real Estate**

The above entitled matter came on to be heard on the...day of
...., 19........., upon the report of..
....as representative in the above entitled matter of the sale of certain
real estate pursuant to the order of this court for sale thereof granted therefor, and on petition for the
confirmation of said sale; and the court having considered the said report, and having been advised relative to the same, and having examined the files and records in said matter, finds herein the following
facts, to-wit:

FIRST—That pursuant to a petition duly made and filed in this court, and the order of this court
duly issued for hearing on said petition, and notice of said hearing duly given as provided by law, and a
hearing duly had by this court on said petition, an order for sale in said above entitled matter was duly
made and filed in this court whereby the said representative of said estate was authorized and directed
to sell at private sale the real estate hereinafter described.

SECOND—That pursuant to said order for sale, the said representative before making the sale of
real estate specified in said report and hereinafter referred to, complied with all the conditions and provisions in said order contained.

THIRD—That the said representative, before making said sale, did cause the real estate hereinafter and in said order for sale described to be re-appraised by the persons appointed for that purpose in

said order for sale, and their re-appraisal thereof to be filed in this court..

FOURTH—That on the...day of.., 19.........,
the said representative, pursuant to said order for sale, did sell, at private sale, to..
....
for the sum of...DOLLARS,
the tract...... of land, described in said order for sale, lying and being in the County of................................
...., State of Minnesota, described as follows, to-wit:

Form 38　Probate Deed

Form 4570

PROBATE DEED OF SALE INDIVIDUAL PERSONAL REPRESENTATIVE TO INDIVIDUAL

THIS INDENTURE, Made this _____ day of _____ , 19 _____ ,
between _____ ,
as Personal Representative ____ of the Estate of _____ , deceased,

part ____ of the first part, and _____
_____
of the County of _____ and State of _____ ,
part ____ of the second part,

WITNESSETH, that whereas _____ a (single) (married) person of
the County of _____ and State of _____ died on
_____ , 19 _____ , and the _____ Court of _____ County,
Minnesota did appoint _____
_____ Personal Representative ____
of the estate, and whereas by the laws of the State of Minnesota, said Personal Representative ____
(is) (are) empowered to make and execute a conveyance of real estate.

NOW, THEREFORE, the said part ____ of the first part, in consideration of the sum
of _____ DOLLARS,
to _____ in hand paid by the said part ____ of the second part, the
receipt whereof is hereby acknowledged, do _____ hereby Grant, Bargain, Sell, and Convey
unto the said part ____ of the second part, _____ heirs and assigns, Forever, all
the tract _____ or parcel _____ of land lying and being in the County of
_____ and State of Minnesota, described as follows, to-wit:

TO HAVE AND TO HOLD AND SAME, Together with all the hereditaments and appurtenances
thereunto belonging or in anywise appertaining, to the said part ____ of the second part, _____
heirs and assigns, Forever.

IN TESTIMONY WHEREOF, The said part ____ of the first part ha____ hereunto set _____
hand _____ the day and year first above written.

_____

_____

_____
as personal representative _____ of the Estate of
_____
Deceased.

I, _____ , spouse of the above named
decedent, do hereby consent to the within conveyance.

_____

Form 39 Final Account

Form No. 4462 Rev. 6-76 Miller-Davis Legal Forms   524.3-1001 #1   524.3-1002 #1   524.3-1003 #2   UPC 82

STATE OF MINNESOTA

COUNTY OF _____Ramsey_____   **DISTRICT COURT**

In Re: Estate of   Court File No. ___999999___

                                      FINAL ACCOUNT

          _____Jane M. Doe_____
               Deceased

READ INSTRUCTIONS AT END OF FORM

		DEBITS	CREDITS
DEBITS			
Personal Estate described in Inventory ...... $ 327,098.00			
Increase on same:			
Interest .... $ 23,230.00			
Dividends .... $ 2,460.00			
Refunds .... $ 0.00			
Other _____ $ 0.00			
_____ $			
Personal Estate Omitted in Inventory ____ $ 0.00			
_____ $			
Received from Sale of Real Estate:			
Cash .... $ 0.00			
Contract for Deed . $ 0.00 $ 0.00			
Received Rent of Real Estate .... $ 1,100.00			
Gain on Sale of Personal Property .... $ 0.00			
Advanced to Estate .... $ 0.00			
TOTAL DEBITS		$ 353,888 00	
CREDITS-DISBURSEMENTS			
Decrease in Personal Estate:			
Loss on Sale of			
Personal Property $ 0.00			
Other _____ $ 0.00			
TOTAL Decrease			$ 0 00
EXPENSES OF ADMINISTRATION			
Fees Probate Court .... $ 2.00			
Certified Copies .... $ 5.00			
Appraisers Fees .... $ 500.00			
Printing Fees .... $ 50.00			
Compensation of Representative .... $ 10,000.00			
Attorneys Fees to date hereof .... $ 15,000.00			
Estimated future fees to be charged ..... $ 0.00			
Maintenance of Family .... $ 4,800.00			
Statutory Selection .... $ 10,000.00			
Bond Premiums .... $ 0.00			
Mortgage Principal & Interest $ 13,850.00			
Miscellaneous _____ $ 698.00			
TOTAL Expenses of Administration			$ 54,905 00

Form 39 Final Account—*continued*

	DEBITS		CREDITS	
FUNERAL EXPENSES				
Mortician ....$ 9,500.00				
Marker ....$ 500.00				
Flowers ....$ 100.00				
Cemetery ....$ 1,000.00				
Rev. B. Stone $ 25.00				
$				
TOTAL Funeral Expenses			$ 11,125	00
EXPENSES OF LAST ILLNESS				
Medical Attendance ....$ 0.00				
Medicine, etc. ....$ 0.00				
Nursing ....$ 0.00				
Hospital ....$ 850.00				
$				
$				
TOTAL Expenses of Last Illness			$ 850	00
TAXES				
Real Estate Taxes:				
Homestead ....$ 3,650.00				
Other Real Estate ....$ 250.00 $ 3,900.00				
Income Taxes of Decedent:				
Minnesota ....$				
Federal ....$ $ 0.00				
Fiduciary Income Taxes				
Minnesota ....$				
Federal ....$ $ 0.00				
Personal Property Tax ....$ 0.00				
$				
$				
TOTAL Taxes			$ 3,900	00
* Assume Tax Clause in will				
OTHER CLAIMS ALLOWED AND PAID (SEE INSTRUCTIONS J.)				
Ace's Plumbing Co. $ 230.00				
St. Paul Telephone Co. $ 50.00				
St. Paul Electric Co. $ 100.00				
Harvey's Garbage Pickup $ 50.00				
Dr. Norma J. Dennison $ 600.00				
St. Paul Rents $ 50.00				
$				
$				
$				
$				
$				
TOTAL Claims Paid			$ 1,080	00
DEVISES PAID AND DISTRIBUTED (SEE INSTRUCTION H.)				
$				
$				
$				
$				
$				
$				
$				
TOTAL DEVISES Paid and Distributed			$	
TOTAL DEBITS AND CREDITS	$ 353,888	00	$ 71,860	00
*BALANCE OF PERSONAL PROPERTY ON HAND FOR DISTRIBUTION	$ 282,028	00		

Form 39   Final Account—*continued*

PERSONAL PROPERTY ON HAND FOR DISTRIBUTION
(Attach Schedules Where Necessary)

Household Goods and Wearing Apparel	$ 26,500.00
Corporation Stock	
100 Shares Tenneco, Inc., Common Stock, Certificate C068297	5,000.00
1000 Shares Minnesota Co-op, Common Stock, Certificate D2289663	4,500.00
$500 U.S. Savings Bond R4502363E	574.00
$500 U.S. Savings Bond R4502364E	574.00
Mortgages, Bonds, Notes, Contracts for Deed, Etc.	
Johnson Furriers, Promissory Note dated 03/20/89 due 09/20/95	10,350.00
(Due date extended)	
Cash on Hand	161,030.00
All Other Personal Property (Describe):	
1992 Mazda	12,000.00
Fur-Mink Coat	11,500.00
Power of Appointment Trust	50,000.00
TOTAL (Must agree with *Balance shown above)	$ 282,028.00

REAL ESTATE ON HAND FOR DISTRIBUTION

Homestead:
Homestead being in the County of Ramsey, State of Minnesota:
   Legally described as follows, to wit:
   Lot 615, Block 42, Reiser's Addition to St. Paul
   (Plat #22760 Parcel #7600)

   Lien:
   Mortgage balance at St. Paul Bank and Trust Company - $ 130,000.00
   Less Principal payments included in Administration Exp.   3,000.00
   Balance as of this Final Account $ 127,000.00
Other Real Estate in the County of ____Ramsey____, State of Minnesota:
An undivided 1/4 interest in duplex located in the following described property:
   Lots 16 & 17, Block 20, Lovey's Addition to St. Paul
   (Plat #32689 Parcel #5562)
   Lien:
   Mortgage balance at St. Paul Bank and Trust Company - $ 40,000.00
                         1/4 interest - $ 10,000.00
   Less Principal payments included in Administration Exp.   600.00
   Balance as of this Final Account $ 9,400.00

Under penalties for perjury for deliberate falsification therein, I declare or affirm that I have read the foregoing account and to the best of my knowledge or information, its representations are true, correct and complete.

Dated: ____August 03, 1995____

                                /S/ John C. Doe

____/S/ John W. Cranwall____
Attorney   John W. Cranwall
       First Trust Co. Bldg.
       St. Paul, MN 55101
Address/Phone   (612) 555-5555

Form 40 Petition for Order of Complete Settlement of the Estate and Decree of Distribution

MD Form No. 4463– Miller Davis Legal Forms (Rev. 8-87) 524.3-1001 #2 UPC 82

STATE OF MINNESOTA

COUNTY OF_____Ramsey_____

In Re: Estate of

_____Jane M. Doe_____
      Deceased

PROBATE COURT
DISTRICT—COUNTY COURT
PROBATE DIVISION

Court File No. _____999999_____

PETITION FOR ORDER OF COMPLETE
SETTLEMENT OF THE ESTATE AND
DECREE OF DISTRIBUTION

TO THE HONORABLE JUDGE OF THE ABOVE NAMED COURT:

Petitioner, _____John C. Doe_____ , respectfully states:

1. Petitioner resides at _____1005 Elm Street, St. Paul, MN 55102_____ ;

2. Petitioner has an interest herein as__personal representative, heir, and devisee_____ ,
   and is, therefore, an interested person as defined by the laws of this state;

3. Decedent was born_____November 6_____ 19_12_ at _____Detroit, Michigan_____ ;

4. Decedent died_____testate at the age of__81__years on_____September 20_____ , 19_94_,
   at_____St. Paul, Minnesota 55102_____ .

5. Decedent at the time of h_er_ death resided at _____1005 Elm Street_____ ,
   City of_____St. Paul_____ , County of __Ramsey_____ , State of __Minnesota_____

6. That the names and addresses of decedent's spouse, children, heirs and devisees and other persons interested in this proceeding and the ages of any who are minor so far known or ascertainable with reasonable diligence by the petitioner are:

Note: Classify the heirs and others entitled to take per stirpes and give the name, date of death, relationship/interest and address, if known, of their predeceased ancestors. Give the birth date of any heir or devisee taking a life interest.

Name	Age	Relationship/Interest	Address
John C. Doe	83	Spouse/heir/devisee/ personal representative	1005 Elm Street St. Paul, MN 55102
Sandy R. Doe	45	Daughter/heir/devisee	1005 Elm Street St. Paul, MN 55102
American Cancer Society		Devisee	222 Glen Acre Drive St. Paul, MN 55102
Girls' Clubs of America		Devisee	111 Aspen Lane St. Paul, MN 55102
Newark Institute of Higher Learning		Devisee	444 Wirth Drive St. Paul, MN 55102

7. That all persons identified as heirs have survived the decedent by at least 120 hours.

8. That all issue of decedent are issue of decedent's surviving spouse ~~xxxxxxxxx~~ _____

Form 40 Petition for Order of Complete Settlement of the Estate and Decree of Distribution—
continued

....

9. The venue for this proceeding is in the above named County of the State of Minnesota, because the decedent was domiciled in such county at the time of her death, and was the owner of property located in the State of Minnesota, ▓▓ ▓▓▓▓▓▓▓▓▓▓▓▓▓▓▓▓▓▓▓▓▓▓▓▓▓▓▓▓▓▓▓▓▓▓▓▓▓▓▓

10. That petitioner has not received a demand for notice and is not aware of any demand for notice of any probate or appointment proceeding concerning the decedent that may have been filed in this state or elsewhere or proper notice has been given.

11. That the estate of the above named decedent has been fully administered and all expenses, debts, valid charges and claims allowed have been fully paid.

12. That a final account has been or herewith is duly filed and presented for consideration and approval or should be completed.

13. That the original of decedent's will, if any, duly executed on _____June 2_____ , 19_85_, and any codicil or codicils thereto was formally probated by this court's order dated _____October 31_____ , 19_94_

14. That the time for presenting claims which arose prior to the death of the decedent has expired.

WHEREFORE, your petitioner requests the order of this Court fixing a time and place for hearing on this petition, and that after the time for any notice has expired, upon proof of notice, and hearing, the Court enter a judicial order formally:

1. Determining decedent's state of testacy if not previously determined.
2. Considering the final account herein or compelling an accounting and distribution or approving the accounting and distribution made herein.
3. Construing decedent's will, if any, duly executed on _____June 2_____ , 19_85_, and any codicil or codicils thereto probated by this court's order dated _____October 31_____ , 19_94_
4. Determining decedent's heirs.
5. Adjudicating the final settlement and distribution of the estate.
6. Determining the persons entitled to distribution of the estate.
7. As circumstances require, approving settlement and directing or approving distribution of the estate and/or issuing a decree of distribution determining the persons entitled to the estate and assigning the same to them in lieu of ordering the assignment.
8. Waiving the lien of inheritance taxes or finding that taxes have been satisfied by payment or decree the property subject to lien.
9. Determining testacy as it affects any previously omitted or unnotified persons and other interested parties and confirming any previous order of testacy as it affects all interested persons.
10. Granting such other and further relief as may be proper.

FURTHER, under penalties for perjury for deliberate falsification therein, I declare or affirm that I have read the foregoing petition and to the best of my knowledge or information, its representations are true, correct and complete.

Dated: _____August 03, 1995_____   _____/S/ John C. Doe_____
                                           Petitioner
                                           First Trust Co. Bldg.
                                           St. Paul, MN 55101   (612) 555-5555
/S/ John W. Cranwall, License
Attorney for Petitioner   #1234567   Attorney Address/Phone

*ASSETS

Probate Assets		Non-Probate Assets	
Homestead	$ 223,000.00 (net)	Joint Tenancy	$ 80,000.00
Other Real Estate	$ 13,350.00 (net)	Insurance	$ 50,000.00
Cash	$ 161,030.00	Other	$ 0
Securities	$ 10,648.00		
Other	$ 110,350.00		

Form 41   Order for Hearing on Final Account and Petition for Distribution and for Mailed Notice

MD Form No. 4465 Miller-Davis Legal Forms (Rev. 9-85)   524.3-1001 #4   UPC--

STATE OF MINNESOTA

COUNTY OF _____ Ramsey _____

In Re: Estate of

_____ Jane M. Doe _____
Deceased

**PROBATE COURT
DISTRICT — COUNTY COURT
PROBATE DIVISION**

Court File No. _____ 999999 _____

**ORDER FOR HEARING ON FINAL
ACCOUNT AND PETITION FOR
DISTRIBUTION AND FOR
MAILED NOTICE**

The personal representative of the above named estate having filed h _is_ final account and petition for order of settlement of estate and distribution and allowance thereof and for decree or order of distribution to the persons thereunto entitled;

IT IS ORDERED, That the hearing thereof be had on _____ September 18 _____ , 19 95 , at _10_ o'clock _A_ .M., before the above named Court at _____ St. Paul _____ _____ , Minnesota, and that all persons having an interest in said estate present objection, if any they have, why said petition should not be granted.

This Order shall be served at least 14 days prior to such date of hearing by mailing copies hereof to all distributees according to law.

Dated: _____ August 10, 1995 _____

(COURT SEAL)

_____ /S/ Richard B. Evans _____
Judge

By _/S/ Thomas Malone_
Court Administrator

_____ /S/ John W. Cranwall _____
Attorney for Personal Representative
    First Trust Co. Bldg.

_____ St. Paul, MN 55101 _____
Address/Phone   (612) 555-5555

Form 42 Affidavit of Mailing Order or Notice of Hearing on Final Account and Petition for Distribution

MD Form No. 4307 Miller Davis Legal Forms (Rev. 1988)   Form 524.1-401 #2   UPC - -

STATE OF MINNESOTA

COUNTY OF _____Ramsey_____

IN RE: (ESTATE)

DISTRICT COURT

Court File No. _____999999_____

OF _____Jane M. Doe_____

_____

Deceased

**ATTACH COPY OF ORDER
OR NOTICE HERE**

**AFFIDAVIT OF MAILING ORDER
OR NOTICE OF HEARING** on
Final Account and Petition for
Distribution and for Mailed Notice

STATE OF MINNESOTA
COUNTY OF __Ramsey__   ss.
__J. M. Golden__
being first duly sworn on oath deposes and says that on the ___11th___ day of ___August___, 19 _95_, at ___St. Paul___ in said County and State _____ he mailed a copy of the Order or Notice hereto attached to each _heir,_ _devisee, beneficiary of trust, and_ _the personal representative_

whose name and address are known to affiant, after exercising due diligence in ascertaining the correctness of said name and address, by placing a true and correct copy thereof in a sealed envelope, postage prepaid and depositing the same in the U.S. Mails at _St. Paul, Minnesota_

and addressed to the following named persons:
NOTE: (Instructions at bottom of page)

NAME	STREET or POST OFFICE	CITY	STATE
John C. Doe	1005 Elm Street	St. Paul	MN 55102
Sandy R. Doe	1005 Elm Street	St. Paul	MN 55102
American Cancer Society	222 Glen Acre Drive	St. Paul	MN 55102
Girls' Clubs of America	111 Aspen Lane	St. Paul	MN 55102
Newark Institute of Higher Learning	444 Wirth Drive	St. Paul	MN 55102

_____/S/ J. M. Golden_____

NOTARIAL STAMP OF SEAL (OR OTHER TITLE OR RANK)

Subscribed and sworn to before me this day of
__11th__ day of ___August___ , 19 _95_ .

_____/S/ Judith Harris_____
SIGNATURE OF NOTARY PUBLIC OR OTHER OFFICIAL

NOTED INSTRUCTIONS: In Estates To each heir, devisee, personal representative, the foreign consul pursuant to M.S. 524.3-306 and M.S. 524.3-403, and the Minnesota Attorney General, if a devisee is the trustee of a charitable trust or if the decedent left no devisees or heirs.

Form 42   Affidavit of Mailing Order or Notice of Hearing on Final Account and Petition for Distribution—*continued*

AFFIDAVIT OF MAILING
ALLOWANCES TO SPOUSE AND/OR CHILDREN

When a decedent dies with or without a will the allowances to the spouse or children are as follows:

525 15 ALLOWANCES TO SPOUSE. When any person dies testate or intestate

(1)   The surviving spouse shall be allowed from the personal property of which the decedent was possessed or to which __s_he was entitled at the time of h_er_ death, the wearing apparel, and as selected by h_im_ , furniture and household goods not exceeding $6,000 in value, and other personal property not exceeding $3,000 in value, subject to an award of property with sentimental value to the decedent's children under section 3;

(2)   When, except for one automobile, all of the personal estate of the decedent is allowed to the surviving spouse by clause (1), the surviving spouse shall also be allowed the automobile.

(3)   If there be no surviving spouse, the minor children shall receive the property specified in clause (1) as selected in their behalf;

(4)   During administration, but not exceeding 18 months, unless an extension shall have been granted by the court, or, if the estate be insolvent, not exceeding 12 months, the spouse or children, or both, constituting the family of the decedent shall be allowed reasonable maintenance.

(5)   In the administration of an estate of a nonresident decedent, the allowances received in the domiciliary administration shall be deducted from the allowances under this section.

In all estates where there is a will the following rule applies to the spouse who has not consented to the will:

524.2-205 PROCEEDING FOR ELECTIVE SHARE; TIME LIMIT.

(a)   The surviving spouse may elect to take an elective share in the augmented estate by filing in the court and mailing or delivering to the personal representative, if any, a petition for the elective share within nine months after the date of death, or within six months after the probate of the decedent's will, whichever limitation last expires. However, nonprobate transfers, described in section 524.2-202, clauses (1) and (3), shall not be included within the augmented estate for the purpose of computing the elective share, if the petition is filed ;later than nine months after death The court may extend the time for election as it sees fit for cause shown by the surviving spouse before the time for election has expired.

(b)   The surviving spouse shall give notice of the time and place set for hearing to persons interested in the estate and to the distributees and recipients of portions of the augmented net estate whose interests will be affected by the taking of the elective share.

(c)   The surviving spouse may withdraw a demand for an elective share at any time before entry of any order by the court determining the elective share.

(d)   After notice and hearing, the court shall determine the amount of the elective share and shall order its payment from the assets of the augmented net estate or by contribution as appears appropriate under section 524.2-207. If it appears that a fund or property included in the augmented net estate has not come into the possession of the personal representative, or has been distributed by the personal representative, the court nevertheless shall fix the liability of any person who has any interest in the fund or property or who has possession thereof, whether as trustee or otherwise. The proceeding may be maintained against fewer than all persons against whom relief could be sought, but no person is subject to contribution in any greater amount than he would have been if relief had been secured against all persons subject to contribution.

(e)   The order or judgment of the court may be enforced as necessary in suit for contribution or payment in other courts of this state or other jurisdictions.

(f)   Whether or not an election has been made under subsection (a), the surviving spouse may elect statutory rights in the homestead by filing in the manner provided in this section a petition in which the spouse asserts the rights provided in section 525.145, provided that:

(1)   when the homestead is subject to a testamentary disposition, the filing must be within nine months after the date of death, or within six months after the probate of the decedent's will, whichever limitation last expires; or

(2)   where the homestead is subject to other disposition, the filing must he within nine months after the date of death.

The court may extend the time for election for cause shown by the surviving spouse before the time for filing has expired.

STATE OF MINNESOTA
COUNTY OF __Ramsey__   ss.

_____J. M. Golden_____ being first duly sworn on oath deposes and says that on the_11th_ day of___August_____, 19_95_ , at ____St. Paul_____ in said County and State, ___he mailed a copy of Sections 525.15 and 524.2-205 of Minnesota Statutes as hereinbefore set out to decedent's spouse and children constituting the family of the decedent at their last known address after exercising due diligence and ascertaining the correctness of said addresses by placing a true and correct copy thereof in a sealed envelope, postage pre-paid and depositing the same in the U.S. mails at _____St. Paul_____ , Minnesota, and addressed to the following:

NAME	STREET or POST OFFICE	CITY	STATE
John C. Doe	1005 Elm Street	St. Paul	MN 55102

Subscribed and sworn to before me this
_11th_ day of ____August_____ , 19_95_

/S/ Judith Harris
SIGNATURE OF NOTARY PUBLIC OR OTHER OFFICIAL

/S/ J. M. Golden

NOTARIAL STAMP OR SEAL (OR OTHER TITLE OR RANK)

Form 43 Order Allowing Final Account

MD Form No. 4467 Miller-Davis Legal Forms   524.3-1001 #6   524.3-1002 #5   525.51 #12   UPC 85

STATE OF MINNESOTA

DISTRICT COURT

COUNTY OF __Ramsey__

In Re: Estate of

Court File No. ___999999___

FINAL

ORDER ALLOWING ACCOUNT

_____Jane M. Doe_____
Deceased

The_____personal_____ representative having accounted for every part of the estate of decedent according to law, and a summary statement of the accounts being as follows:

Debits . . . . $ _353,888.00_

Credits . . . . $ _71,860.00_

Balance . . . . $ _282,028.00_

IT IS ORDERED, that said accounts are hereby finally settled and allowed.

Dated: _____September 18, 1995_____

_____/S/ Richard B. Evans_____
(COURT SEAL)   **Judge**

Form 44 State Inheritance Tax Waiver

Form No. 4300—BUSINESS RECORDS CORPORATION. MINNESOTA (Rev. 4-1-87)   Form 291.09 #1   UPC — —

STATE OF MINNESOTA

COUNTY OF _____

In Re: Estate of

_____
                    Deceased

Died _____, 19____

Residing at _____
            _____

PROBATE COURT
DISTRICT-COUNTY COURT
PROBATE DIVISION

Court File No. _____

PETITION FOR
INHERITANCE TAX RETURN WAIVER
        (Decree of descent)
        (Summary distribution)
        (Administration)

TO THE HONORABLE JUDGE OF THE ABOVE NAMED COURT:

   Petitioner, _____, respectfully states:
1. Petitioner resides at _____ ;
2. Petitioner has an interest herein as _____ ;
   and is therefore, an interested person as defined by the laws of this state;
3. That petitioner knows of no omission from h____ petition and/or inventory and appraisal and schedule of non-probate assets;
4. That there is no inheritance tax due the State of Minnesota by reason of any transfer of property caused by decedent's death;
5. That the required filing of any self assessed inheritance tax return should be waived by the Court pursuant to Minnesota Statutes Section 291.09 Subdivision 1. (e).

                    SUMMARY OF ASSETS
Probate:

   Homestead............. $_____
   Other real estate .... _____
   Personal property .... _____

Heirs or devisees thereof	Relationship	Age	Share

Form 44   State Inheritance Tax Waiver—*continued*

Non-probate:		Survivor-Beneficiary	Relation
Joint homestead	$		
Joint other real estate			
Joint personal property			
Insurance			
Annuities and Deposits			
Transfers by decedent			
Miscellaneous			

WHEREFORE, petitioner requests that the Court issue a waiver of the filing of any self assessed inheritance tax return herein.

FURTHER, under penalties for perjury for deliberate falsification therein, I declare or affirm that I have read the foregoing petition and to the best of my knowledge or information, its representations are true, correct and complete.

Dated: _____

_____
Petitioner

_____
Attorney for Petitioner

_____
Address/Phone

NOTE: Make proper deletions within the parentheses so that the Commissioner of Taxation can know the type of Court proceedings.

Form 45   Order of Complete Settlement of the Estate and Decree of Distribution

Order of Complete Settlement
of the Estate and Decree
of Distribution

Form No. 101—M
524.3-1001 #7, 524.1002 #6

Miller/Davis Co., Minneapolis (Rev. 12-85)
Minnesota Uniform Conveyancing Blanks
UPC 85

STATE OF MINNESOTA

COUNTY OF _____Ramsey_____

PROBATE COURT
DISTRICT— COUNTY COURT
PROBATE DIVISION

In Re: Estate of

Court File No. _____999999_____

ORDER OF COMPLETE SETTLEMENT
OF THE ESTATE AND DECREE
OF DISTRIBUTION

_____Jane M. Doe_____
Deceased

The petition of _____John C. Doe_____,
dated _____August 3_____, 19_95_, for an order of complete settlement of the estate and decree of distribution in the estate of the above named decedent having duly come on for hearing before the above named Court on _____September 18_____, 19_95_, the undersigned Judge having heard and considered such petition, being fully advised in the premises, makes the following findings and determinations:

1. That the petition for order of complete settlement of the estate and decree of distribution is complete.

2. That the time for any notice has expired and any notice as required by the laws of this State has been given and proved.

3. That the petitioner(s) (has) (have) declared or affirmed that the representations contained in the petition are true, correct and complete to the best knowledge or information of petitioner(s).

4. That the petitioner(s) appear(s) from the petition to be (an) interested person(s) as defined by the laws of this State.

5. That the decedent died _____ testate at the age of _____81_____ years on _September 20_, 19_94_, at _St. Paul, Minnesota 55102_.

6. That venue for this proceeding is in the above named County of the State of Minnesota, because the decedent was domiciled in such County at the time of death, and was the owner of property located in the State of Minnesota, ~~or because, though not domiciled in the State of Minnesota, the decedent was the owner of property located in the above named County at the time of death~~.

7. That this Court has jurisdiction of this estate, proceedings and subject matter.

8. That the said estate has been in all respects fully administered, and all expenses, debts, valid charges and all claims allowed against said estate have been paid.

9. That a final account has been filed herein by the personal representative(s) for consideration and approval.

10. That decedent's last will duly executed on _____June 2_____, 19_85_, ~~and codicils~~ ~~thereto duly executed xxxxxxxxxxxxxxxxxxxxxxxxxxxxxxx19xxx~~, (was) (were) probated by the order of this Court dated _____October 31_____, 19_94_, or (is) (are) formally probated by this order, and should be construed to provide that under the provisions thereof, the estate of decedent is devised as follows:

(State actual legal relationship of each devisee to decedent)

Form 45 Order of Complete Settlement of the Estate and Decree of Distribution—*continued*

American Cancer Society	Charitable Devisee	$ 10,000.00
Girls' Clubs of America	Charitable Devisee	5,000.00
Newark Institute of Higher Learning	Charitable Devisee	1,000.00

John C. Doe, Husband, all the rest, residue, and remainder of the real and personal property of the decedent's estate.

Personal Property	$ 266,028.00	266,028.00
		282,028.00
Real Property	236,350.00	236,350.00
John C. Doe Total	$ 502,378.00	
Total Devises of Jane M. Doe Estate		$518,378.00

11. **That the following named persons are all the heirs of the decedent and their actual relationship to decedent is as stated (If decedent died testate, do not list heirs unless all heirs are ascertained):**

John C. Doe   husband,

Sandy R. Doe   daughter.

12. **That the property of the decedent on hand for distribution.consists of the following:**

(A) Personal property of the value of $ 282,028.00   **described as follows:**

Household Goods and Wearing Apparel	$ 26,500.00
Stocks and Bonds	
100 Shares Tenneco, Inc.	5,000.00
1000 Shares Minnesota Co-op.	4,500.00
U. S. Savings Bonds	1,148.00
Mortgages and Notes	
Johnson Furrier's Promissory Note dated 3/20/89	
due 9/20/95	10,350.00
Cash	161,030.00
All Other Personal Property	
1992 Mazda	12,000.00
Fur-Mink Coat	11,500.00
Power of Appointment Trust	50,000.00
Total	$282,028.00

Form 45   Order of Complete Settlement of the Estate and Decree of Distribution—*continued*

(B) Real property described as follows:

    (1) The homestead of the decedent situated in the County of   <u>Ramsey</u> ,
        State of Minnesota, described as follows:

        Lot 615, Block 42, Reiser's Addition to St. Paul $350,000.00

        <u>Lien:</u>
        Mortgage balance at St. Paul Bank and Trust Co.   <u>127,000.00</u>

                                        Net $223,000.00

    (2) Other real property situated in the County of   <u>Ramsey</u> ,
        State of Minnesota, described as follows:

        Lots 16 & 17, Block 20, Lovey's Addition to $ 22,750.00
           St. Paul

        <u>Lien:</u>
        Mortgage balance at St. Paul Bank and Trust Co.   <u>9,400.00</u>

                                          Net $ 13,350.00

Form 45 Order of Complete Settlement of the Estate and Decree of Distribution—*continued*

....

13. That the inheritance taxes on the herein described property have been paid or waived.

14. That any previous order determining testacy should be confirmed as it affects any previously omitted or un-notified persons and other interested persons.

NOW, THEREFORE, it is ORDERED, ADJUDGED, and DECREED by the Court as follows:

1. That the petition is hereby granted.

2. That the final account of the personal representative(s) herein is approved.

3. That decedent's last will duly executed on _____ June 2 _____ , 19 85 , ~~and codicil thereto duly executed on xxxxxxxxxxxxxxxxxxxxxxxxxxxxxxxxxxxxxxxxxxxxxxxxx 19 xxxxx~~ (is) (~~are~~) (hereby) (~~has or have been~~) formally probated and (is) (~~are~~) construed as above stated.

4. That the heirs of the decedent are determined to be as set forth above.

5. That the property of the decedent on hand for distribution is as above stated.

6. That title to the personal and real property described herein, subject to any lawful disposition heretofore made, is hereby assigned to and vested in the following named persons in the following proportions or parts:

   The whole thereof to decedent's husband, John C. Doe.

7. That the lien of inheritance taxes, if any, on the above described property is hereby waived.

8. That any previous order determining testacy is hereby confirmed as it affects any previously omitted or unnotified persons and other interested persons.

Dated: _____ September 18, 1995 _____   _____ /S/ Richard B. Evans _____
                                                                                              Judge

(COURT SEAL)

FILED:

Form 46 Receipt for Assets by Distributee

MD Form No. 4564   524.3-1001 (4) 524.3-1003 (2)   MILLER-DAVIS LEGAL FORMS

STATE OF MINNESOTA

COUNTY OF ____Ramsey____   **DISTRICT COURT**

In Re: Estate of   Court File No.____999999____

_____Jane M. Doe_____   **RECEIPT FOR ASSETS BY**
              Deceased   **DISTRIBUTEE**

I, __Phyllis L. Taylor for the American Cancer Society__ , the undersigned distributee, hereby acknowledge receipt from the personal representative(s) of the above entitled estate, of the following assets, to-wit:

    Charitable Devise $ 10,000.00

in full satisfaction of the complete and final settlement of my distributive share of the above entitled estate.

Dated:____September 20, 1995____   AMERICAN CANCER SOCIETY

          BY: /S/ Phyllis L. Taylor_____
          Distributee

INSTRUCTIONS:

1. To be executed after Order or Decree of Distribution under 524.3-1001 (4) and furnished with petition for discharge Form 524.3-1001 #9.

2. To be executed under 524.3-1003 (2) prior to personal representative's closing statement Form 524.1003 #1.

Form 47 Petition for Discharge of Personal Representative

MD Form No. 4470 Miller- Davis Legal Forms   524.3-1001 #9   524.3-1002 #8   UPC—

STATE OF MINNESOTA

COUNTY OF _____Ramsey_____   DISTRICT COURT

In Re:Estate of   Court File No. __999999__

_____Jane M. Doe_____   **PETITION FOR DISCHARGE OF**

Deceased   **PERSONAL REPRESENTATIVE**

TO THE HONORABLE JUDGE OF THE ABOVE NAMED COURT:

Petitioner, _____John C. Doe_____, respectfully states:

1. Petitioner resides at _____1005 Elm Street, St. Paul, MN 55102_____ ;
2. Petitioner has an interest herein as __personal representative, heir, and devisee__, and is, therefore, an interested person as defined by the laws of this state;
3. That petitioner has fully administered upon the estate of said decedent, and has paid all expenses, debts and charges chargeable upon the same;
4. That petitioner's final account as such personal representative has been heretofore presented to and allowed by said Court, and the decree or order of distribution made therein, and that petitioner has paid all taxes required to be paid by the personal representative and filed proper receipts therefor.
5. That the balance of the said estate remaining in petitioner's hands for distribution as per said order allowing said final account, has been paid out and distributed in accordance with said decree or order of distribution, as follows, to-wit:

LEGACIES AND/OR DISTRIBUTIVE SHARES	SHARE VALUE
1. American Cancer Society, 222 Glen Acre Dr., St. Paul, MN	$ 10,000.00
2. Girls' Clubs of America, 111 Aspen Lane, St. Paul, MN	$ 5,000.00
3. Newark Institute of Higher Learning, 444 Wirth Drive, St. Paul, MN	$ 1,000.00
4. John C. Doe, Surviving Spouse, 1005 Elm St., St. Paul, MN	$ 502,378.00
5.	$
6.	$
7.	$
8.	$
9.	$
10.	$
11.	$
12.	$

and has filed in said Court proper receipts from all parties above named for their respective legacies and/or distributive shares.

WHEREFORE, your petitioner requests the Order of this court fixing a time and place for hearing on this petition, and that after the time for any notice has expired, upon proof of notice, and hearing, the Court enter a judicial order formally discharging the personal representative and releasing and discharging the sureties upon the personal representative's bond and granting such other and further relief as may be proper.

FURTHER, under penalties for perjury for deliberate falsification therein, I declare or affirm that I have read the foregoing petition and to the best of my knowledge or information, its representations are true, correct and complete.

Dated: _____September 29, 1995_____

_____/S/ John W. Cranwall_____   _____/S/ John C. Doe_____

Attorney for Petitioner   Petitioner
    First Trust Co. Bldg.
    St. Paul, MN 55101

Address/Phone (612) 555-5555

Form 48   Order Discharging Personal Representative

Form No. 4471 — Miller-Davis Legal Forms   524.3-1001 #10   524.3-1002 #9   525.51 #15   UPC—

STATE OF MINNESOTA

COUNTY OF _Ramsey_

In Re: Estate of

Jane M. Doe
Deceased

DISTRICT COURT

Court File No. _999999_

**ORDER DISCHARGING
PERSONAL REPRESENTATIVE**

The petition of _John C. Doe_, dated _September 29_, 19_95_, for an order discharging personal representative in the estate of the above named decedent having duly come on for hearing before the above named court, the undersigned Judge having heard and considered such petition, being fully advised in the premises, makes the following findings and determinations:

1. That the petition for an order discharging personal representative is complete.

2. That the time for any notice has expired and any notice as required by the laws of this state has been given and proved.

3. That the petitioner has declared or affirmed that the representations contained in the petition are true, correct and complete to the best of his knowledge or information.

4. That the petitioner appears from the petition to be an interested person as defined by the laws of this state.

5. That the personal representative herein, having paid or transferred all of the property of the estate of decedent to the persons entitled thereto, paid all taxes required to be paid by said representative and filed proof thereof, complied with all the orders and decree of the Court and with the provisions of law, and fully discharged the personal representative's trust,

Now, therefore, it is ORDERED, ADJUDGED, and DECREED by the court as follows:

1. That the petition is hereby granted.

2. That the personal representative and the sureties on said representative's bond, if any, are hereby finally discharged.

Dated: _October 20, 1995_

(COURT SEAL)

/S/ Richard B. Evans
Judge

Form 49 Petition for Appointment of Special Administrator

MD Form No. 4424 Miller-Davis Legal Forms (Rev. 1989)   Form 524.3-614 #3   UPC—

STATE OF MINNESOTA   PROBATE COURT
                                            DISTRICT-COUNTY COURT
COUNTY OF _____   PROBATE DIVISION

In Re: Estate of   Court File No. _____

                                            PETITION FOR
                                            FORMAL APPOINTMENT
                                            OF SPECIAL ADMINISTRATOR

_____
                    Deceased

TO THE HONORABLE JUDGE OF THE ABOVE NAMED COURT:

Petitioner, _____, respectfully states:

1. Petitioner resides at _____ ;

2. Petitioner has an interest herein as_____
   and is, therefore, an interested person as defined by the laws of this State;

3. Decedent was born _____ , 19 _____ , at _____ ;

4. Decedent died on _____ , 19 _____ , at _____ ;

5. Decedent at the time of h_____ death resided at _____ ,
   City of _____ , County of _____ , State of _____ ;

6. That the names and addresses of decedent's spouse, children, heirs and devisees and other persons interested
   in this proceeding and the ages of any who are minors so far as known or ascertainable with reasonable
   deligence by the petitioner are:
   NOTE — Classify the heirs and others entitled to take per stirpes and give the name, date of death,
          relationship/interest and address, if known, of their predeceased ancestor. Give the birthdate of
          any heir or devisee taking a life interest. Remember to include a "Negative Allegation Statement".

Name	Age	Relationship/Interest	Address

Negative Allegation Statement (see Probate Court Rule 7 (1)): _____
_____

7. That all persons identified as heirs have survived the decedent by at least 120 hours.

8. That all issue of decedent are also issue of decedent's surviving spouse except for: _____
_____

Form 49   Petition for Appointment of Special Administrator—*continued*

9. That the decedent died (in)testate.

10. That there is - is not - pending an application or petition for probate of the Will of the decedent in the _____ Court of the State of _____ , and that _____ is named as executor in the Will and is (un) available and qualified.

11. That venue for this proceeding is in the above named County of the State of Minnesota, because the decedent was domiciled in such county at the time of h_____ death, and/or was the owner of property located in the State of Minnesota.

12. That no personal representative has been appointed, except _____ whose appointment has been terminated by death or disability.

13. That it is necessary to protect the estate of the decedent prior to the appointment of a personal representative because

_____
_____
_____
_____
_____
_____
_____

14. That a personal representative has been appointed but cannot or should not act because _____
_____

or that no personal representative has been appointed.

15. That it is necessary to protect the estate of the decedent because _____
_____
_____
_____
_____

16. That an emergency exists to the extent that appointment should be made without notice because _____
_____ .

WHEREFORE, your petitioner requests the order of this Court fixing a time and place for hearing of this petiton, and that after the time for any notice has expired upon proof of notice, and hearing, the Court enter a judicial order formally appointing _____ as special administrator of the above estate and granting such other and further relief as may be proper.

FURTHER, under penalties for perjury for deliberate falsification therein, I declare or affirm that I have read the foregoing petition and to the best of my knowledge or information, its representations are true, correct and complete.

Dated: _____

_____
Petitioner

_____
Attorney for Petitioner

_____
Attorney Address/Phone

*ASSETS

Probate Assets		Non-Probate Assets	
Homestead	$ _____	Joint Tenancy	$ _____
Other Real Estate	$ _____	Insurance	$ _____
Cash	$ _____	Other	$ _____
Securities	$ _____	Approximate	
Other	$ _____	Indebtedness	$ _____

Form 50 Order Granting Special Administration

MD Form No. 4425 — Miller-Davis Co. (REV. 8-87)   Form 524.3-614 #4   UPC–

STATE OF MINNESOTA

COUNTY OF _____

In Re: Estate of

_____
                    Deceased

PROBATE COURT
DISTRICT—COUNTY COURT
PROBATE DIVISION

Court File No. _____

ORDER OF
FORMAL APPOINTMENT
OF SPECIAL ADMINISTRATOR

The petition of _____ , dated_____, 19____
for an order of formal appointment of special administrator of the above named decedent having duly
come on for hearing before the above named court, the undersigned Judge having heard and considered
such petition, being fully advised in the premises, makes the following findings and determinations:

1. That the petition for an order of formal appointment of special administrator is complete.

2. That the time for any notice has expired and any notice as required by the laws of this state has been given and proved.

3. That the petitioner has declared or affirmed that the representations contained in the petition are true, correct and complete to the best of h__ knowledge or information.

4. That the petitioner appears from the petition to be an interested person as defined by the laws of this state.

5. That the above named decedent is dead having died on_____ , 19____,
   at_____ .

6. That, on the basis of the statements in the petition, this court has jurisdiction of this estate, proceeding and subject matter.

7. That, on the basis of the statements in the petition, venue is proper because the decedent's domicile at the time of h___ death was in the above named County of the State of Minnesota and/or decedent was the owner of property located in the State of Minnesota.

8. That decedent's heirs are as identified in the petition commencing this proceeding.

9. That all persons identified as heirs have survived the decedent by at least 120 hours.

10. That all issue of decedent are issue of decedent's surviving spouse except for _____
    _____ .

11. That the decedent died (in) testate.

12. That there is — is not —pending an application or petition for probate of the Will of the
    decedent in the_____ Court of the State of _____,
    and that _____ is named as executor in the Will and is (un)available
    and qualified.

13. That no personal representative has been appointed, except _____
    whose appointment has been terminated by death or disability.

Form 50 Order Granting Special Administration—*continued*

14. That it is necessary to protect the estate of the decedent prior to the appointment of a personal representative because _____
_____
_____
_____
_____
_____

15. That a personal representative has been appointed but cannot or should not act because _____
_____

    or that no personal representative has been appointed.

16. That it is necessary to protect the estate of the decedent because _____
_____
_____
_____
_____

17. That an emergency exists to the extent that appointment should be made without notice because_____
_____

    Now, therefore, it is ORDERED, ADJUDGED, and DECREED by the court as follows:

    1. That for good causes shown, the petition is hereby granted.

    2. That _____ is hereby formally appointed as the special administrator of the estate of _____ , deceased, with _____ bond, in an (unsupervised) (supervised) administration to preserve the estate and to secure its proper administration until such time as a general personal representative is appointed by the Registrar or by the Court, and until further order of this Court.

    3. That upon qualification and acceptance, letters of special administration be issued to _____ , subject to the following limitations, if any:
_____
_____
_____

Dated:_____

                                            _____
                                                        Judge

Form 51 Letters of Special Administration

MD Form No. 4555   MILLER-DAVIS LEGAL FORMS, MPLS., MN   524.3-614 #7   UPC

STATE OF MINNESOTA   **DISTRICT COURT**

COUNTY OF _____

                                                                Court File No. _____

In Re: Estate of

                                                                LETTERS OF
_____   **SPECIAL ADMINISTRATION**
            Deceased

The above named decedent having died on _____, 19 _____, and

_____

_____

having been appointed and qualified, (is) (are) hereby authorized to act as special administrator(s) according to law.

Dated: _____

        (COURT SEAL)   Judge/Registrar

Form 52   Final Account and Report of Special Administrator

State of Minnesota,

County of..

IN PROBATE COURT

IN THE MATTER OF THE ESTATE OF

....

.... *Decedent.*

Final Account and Report of Special Administrator

Your petitioner..*respectfully represents and shows to the court:*

FIRST—That letters of special administration of the above named estate were to him issued on the..*day of*..*, 19........*

SECOND—That he has collected all the personal property of said decedent,..

....

and preserved all the property of said decedent for the general representative of said estate; and made and filed in this court on the..*day of*..*, 19........ a true inventory of all the goods, chattels, rights, credits and effects of said decedent.*

THIRD—..*(1)*

....

....

FOURTH—That under and by leave of the court, he has sold the following described personal property of said decedent and collected and received therefor the following sums, to-wit:

.... $..

.... $..

.... $..

.... $..

.... $..

.... $..

.... $..

         Total receipts from sales $..

FIFTH—That he has collected and received other sums due said decedent from other sources as follows:

.... $..

.... $..

.... $..

.... $..

.... $..

Total amount collected other than from sales $..

Total of all receipts - - - - - - $..

SIXTH — That he has necessarily paid out and expended in administrating said estate and caring for the same, the following amounts for the following purposes:

Form 53 Order Approving Final Account and Report of Special
Administrator

No. 3652.—Order Approving Account of Special Administrator.

State of Minnesota,

County of_____

IN PROBATE COURT

IN THE MATTER OF THE ESTATE OF

_____
                                    Decedent.

**Order Approving Account and Report of
Special Administrator.**

The report and final account of_____*as special*
administrator of the estate of the above named decedent having been made and filed in this court on
the_____day of_____19____, and the court having read and considered the
same, and having heard and considered the evidence adduced in support thereof, and examined the
files and records in said matter, finds as follows:

FIRST—That the said special administrator has collected all the personal property of said dece-
dent, cared for, gathered and secured all the crops belonging to his said estate, preserved all the pro-
perty of said decedent and cared for the same, has sold all the personal property of said decedent he
was authorized to sell by leave of this court and accounted for the proceeds of the same, has taken
charge of the real property of said decedent as he was authorized to do by leave of this court, and cared
for the same and reported his doings thereon to this court, has made and filed in this court a true in-
ventory of all said property of said decedent, has in all things obeyed the orders of this court in said
matter, and is ready to turn over and deliver to the general representative of said estate all the property
of said decedent.

SECOND—That said special administrator has made and filed in this court a full account of all
his receipts and disbursements in said special administration of said estate, a summary statement of
which is as follows, to-wit:

Total receipts from sales of personal property
        under leave of court,   -   -   -   - $_____
Total collections from other sources;   -   - $_____
Total expenditures and expenses,   -   -   _____ $_____
Balance,   -   -   -   -   -   - $_____ $_____

THIRD—That_____has been appointed general re-
presentative of said decedent, and that letters_____
have been to him issued

Therefore it is Hereby Ordered, That the report and account of said special administrator,
as adjusted and settled by the court herein, be, and the same hereby is, approved and allowed; and
that said special administrator be, and he hereby is, authorized and directed, to forthwith turn over
and deliver to said general representative of said estate all of the property of said decedent in his
possession and under his control, and that upon the filing in this court of the receipt of said general
representative therefor, the said special administrator, together with the sureties on his bond, be dis-
charged from all further liabilities and duties in said matter.

Dated_____19____

_____
                                    Judge of Probate.

Form 54 Petition Claiming Interest in Omitted Property (Petition for Determination of Descent)

M/D Form No. 4573 Miller-Davis Legal Forms (Rev. 8-87) **524.413 #5**   UPC

STATE OF MINNESOTA

COUNTY OF _____

In Re: Estate of

_____
Deceased

PROBATE COURT
DISTRICT-COUNTY COURT
PROBATE DIVISION

Court File No. _____

PETITION FOR
DETERMINATION OF DESCENT
(Omitted property)
(Incorrectly described property)

TO THE HONORABLE JUDGE OF THE ABOVE NAMED COURT:

Petitioner, _____ , respectfully states:
1. Petitioner resides at _____ ;

2. Petitioner has an interest herein as _____ ;
   and is, therefore, an interested person as defined by the laws of this State;

3. Decedent was born _____ , 19 ____ , at _____ ;

4. Decedent died ____testate at the age of _____ on _____ , 19 ____ , at _____
   _____ ;

5. Decedent at the time of h_ death resided at _____ ,
   City of _____ County of _____ , State of _____ ;

6. That the names and addresses of decedent's spouse, children, heirs and devisees and other persons
   interested in this proceeding and the ages of any who are minors so far as known or ascertainable
   with reasonable diligence by the applicant are:
   NOTE — Classify the heirs and others entitled to take per stirpes and give the name, date of
   death, relationship/interest and address, if known, of their predeceased ancestor.
   Give the birthdate of any heir or devisee taking a life interest.

Name	Age	Relationship/Interest	Address

7. That all persons identified as heirs have survived the decedent by at least 120 hours.

8. That all issue of decedent are issue of decedent's surviving spouse except for_____

_____ .

Form 55 Decree of Distribution (Descent) of Omitted Property

Decree of Descent

Form No. 104—M.
524.3-413 #6

Miller-Davis Co., Minneapolis (Rev. 12-85)
Minnesota Uniform Conveyancing Blanks
UPC

STATE OF MINNESOTA

COUNTY OF _____

In Re: Estate of

_____
Deceased

**PROBATE COURT
DISTRICT—COUNTY COURT
PROBATE DIVISION**

Court File No. _____

**DECREE OF DESCENT
(Omitted property)
(Incorrectly described property)**

The petition of _____ ,
dated _____ , 19_____ , for decree of descent (omitted property) (incorrectly described property) in the estate of the above named decedent having duly come on for hearing before the above named Court on _____ , 19_____ , the undersigned Judge having heard and considered such petition, being fully advised in the premises, makes the following findings and determinations:

1. That the petition for decree of descent (omitted property) (incorrectly described property) is complete.

2. That the time for any notice has expired and any notice as required by the laws of this State has been given and proved.

3. That the petitioner(s) (has) (have) declared or affirmed that the representations contained in the petition are true, correct and complete to the best knowledge or information of petitioner(s).

4. That the petitioner(s) appear(s) from the petition to be (an) interested person(s) as defined by the laws of this State.

5. That the decedent died _____testate at the age of _____ years on _____ , 19_____ , at _____ .

6. That venue for this proceeding is in the above named County of the State of Minnesota, because the decedent was domiciled in such County at the time of death, and was the owner of property located in the State of Minnesota, or because, though not domiciled in the State of Minnesota, the decedent was the owner of property located in the above named County at the time of death.

7. That this Court has jurisdiction of this estate, proceeding and subject matter.

8. That no will or authenticated copy of a will of decedent probated outside of this State in accordance with the laws in force in the place where probated has been admitted to probate nor administration had in this State except in the _____ Court of _____ County under file number _____ in which proceedings the (Order) (Decree) of (Distribution) (Descent) was entered on _____ , 19_____ , wherein the hereinafter described real and/or personal property was (omitted) (incorrectly described). The (Order) (Decree) in which the real property hereinafter described was (omitted) (incorrectly described) was (filed) (recorded) in the Office of the (County Recorder) (Registrar of Titles), _____ County, Minnesota, on the _____ day of _____ , 19_____ , and was duly recorded in Book _____ of _____ , page _____ , or was duly filed as Document No. _____ .

9. That the said (Order) (Decree) contained the following incorrect description(s):

    (A) Personal property:

Form 56   Decree of Descent

MD Form No. 103-M   525.312 #8

Miller Davis Legal Forms (Rev. 1978)
Minnesota Uniform Conveyancing Blank
UPC -

STATE OF MINNESOTA

COUNTY OF _____

In Re: Estate of

_____
                    Deceased

**PROBATE COURT
DISTRICT COURT-PROBATE DIVISION**

Court File No. _____

DECREE OF DESCENT
(Testate) (Intestate)

The petition of _____ ,
dated _____, 19_____, for determination of descent in the estate of the above named decedent having duly come on for hearing before the above Court, on _____,
19_____, the undersigned Judge having heard and considered such petition, being fully advised in the premises, makes the following finding and determinations:

1.   That the petition for determination of descent is complete.

2.   That the time for any notice has expired and any notice as required by the laws of this State has been given and proved.

3.   That the petitioner(s) (has) (have) declared or affirmed that the representations contained in the petition are true, correct and complete to the best knowledge or information of petitioner(s).

4.   That the petitioner(s) appear(s) from the petition to be (an) interested person(s) as defined by the laws of this State.

5.   That the decedent died _____testate at the age of _____ years on _____ ,19____,
at _____
and that more than three years have elapsed since the death of said decedent and it appears from the petition that the time limit for original appointment proceedings has expired.

6.   That venue for this proceeding is in the above named County of the State of Minnesota, because the decedent was domiciled in such County at the time of death, was the owner of property located in the State of Minnesota, or because, though not domiciled in the State of Minnesota, the decedent was the owner of property located in the above named County at the time of death.

7.   That this Court has jurisdiction of this estate, proceeding and subject matter.

8.   That no will or authenticated copy of a will of decedent probated outside of this State in accordance with the laws in force in the place where probated has been probated nor adminstration had in this State.

9.   That the petition does not indicate the existence of a possible unrevoked testamentary instrument which may relate to property subject to the laws of this State, and which is not filed for probate in this Court.

10.   That decedents last will duly executed on_____, 19_____, and codicil or codicils thereto duly executed on _____ , 19____,
(is) (are) formally probated by this order and should be construed to provide that under the provisions thereof, the estate of decedent is devised as follows:
(State actual legal relationship of each devise to decedent)

Form 57 Application for Informal Probate of Will and for Informal Appointment of Personal Representative (Executor)

M/D Form No. 4334 Miller-Davis Legal Forms (Rev. 1989)   Form 524.3-301 #3   UPC 21

STATE OF MINNESOTA

COUNTY OF _____Hennepin_____

In Re: Estate of

_____Cheryl Ann Kennedy_____
Deceased

PROBATE COURT
DISTRICT-COUNTY COURT
PROBATE DIVISION

Court File No. ____198540____

APPLICATION FOR INFORMAL
PROBATE OF WILL AND FOR
INFORMAL APPOINTMENT
OF EXECUTOR

TO THE HONORABLE JUDGE OF THE ABOVE NAMED COURT:

Applicant, ____Charles Kennedy____, respectfully states:

1. Applicant resides at ____1010 Willow Street, Minneapolis, MN 55409____;

2. Applicant has an interest herein as__spouse, heir, devisee, and nominated executor__
   and is, therefore, an interested person as defined by the laws of this State;

3. Decedent was born ____January 13____, 19_60_, at ____Minneapolis, Minnesota____;

4. Decedent died on ____August 1____, 19_94_, at ____Minneapolis, Minnesota____;

5. Decedent at the time of h er death resided at ____1010 Willow Street____,
   City of ____Minneapolis____, County of ____Hennepin____, State of ____Minnesota____;

6. That the names and addresses of decedent's spouse, children, heirs and devisees and other persons interested
   in this proceeding and the ages of any who are minors so far as known or ascertainable with reasonable
   deligence by the petitioner are:
   NOTE — Classify the heirs and others entitled to take per stirpes and give the name, date of death,
   relationship/interest and address, if known, of their predeceased ancestor. Give the birthdate of
   any heir or devisee taking a life interest. Remember to include a "Negative Allegation Statement".

Name	Age	Relationship/Interest	Address
Charles Kennedy	34	Spouse/heir/devisee/ nominated executor	1010 Willow Street Minneapolis, MN 55409
Cherry Kennedy	3	Daughter/heir/devisee	same
Cindy Kennedy	3	Daughter/heir/devisee	same
Carl Kennedy	5	Son/heir/devisee	same
Corey Kennedy	9	Son/heir/devisee	same
Christopher Kennedy	10	Son/heir/devisee	same
Catherine Kelly	60	Mother/heir	same
Karen Kelly	38	Sister/heir/devisee	same

Negative Allegation Statement (see Probate Court Rule 6 (1)): __Decedent left surviving no spouse,__
__children, parents, or brothers or sisters, other than herein named, and no issue__
__of deceased children.__

7. That all persons identified as heirs have survived the decedent by at least 120 hours.

8. That all issue of decedent are also issue of decedent's surviving spouse except for _____
   _____
   _____

Form 57   Application for Informal Probate of Will and for Informal Appointment of Personal Representative (Executor)—*continued*

9. That venue for this proceeding is in the above named County of the State of Minnesota, because the decedent was domiciled in such county at the time of her ____ death, and was the owner of property located in the State of Minnesota, xxxxxxxxx, xxxxxx xxxx xxx xxxxxxxxx xxxxx xxxxxx xxxxxxx xxx xxxxxxxx xxx xxx xxxxxx xx xxxxxxxx xxxxxxx xxxxxxx xxxxxxxx xxxxxxx xx xxx xxxx xx xxxxxxx xxxxx

10. That no personal representative of the decedent has been appointed in this state or elsewhere whose appointment has not been terminated.

11. That applicant has not received a demand for notice and is not aware of any demand for notice of any probate or appointment proceeding concerning the decedent that may have been filed in this state or elsewhere xx xxxxxx xxxxxx xxx xxxx xxxxx.

12. That the original of decedent's last will duly executed on _____November 21_____, 19 88 xxxx xxxxxx xxx xxxxxx xxxxxx xxx xxxxxx xxx xxxxxxxxxxxxxxxxxxxxxxxxxxxxxxxx, xx xxxxxx xxxx xxxxxxxx xxxxxxxx xxxx xxxxx xx xxx xxxxxxxx xxx xx xxxxxxxxx xxxxxxxx xx xxx xxxx, xx xx xxx xxxxxxxx xx xxx xxxxx xx accompanies this application.

13. That the applicant, to the best of his ____ knowledge, believes the will and codicil or codicils thereto, if any, has or have been validly executed.

14. That after the exercise of reasonable diligence, the applicant is unaware of any instrument revoking the will and codicil or codicils thereto, and the applicant believes that the instrument which is the subject of this application is the decedent's last will.

15. That the time limit for informal probate and appointment as provided by the laws of this state has not expired because three years or less have passed since the decedent's death.

16. That the applicant, xx _____Charles Kennedy_____ is entitled to priority and appointment as executor because applicant xx xxxxxxxxxxxxxxxxxxxxxxxxxxxxxxxxxxxxxxxx is nominated in the last will of the decedent as executor, with (no) (xxxxxxxxx) xxx xxxxxxxxxxxxxxxxxxxxxxxxxxxxxxxxxxx) bond, in an (xxxxxxxxxx) (undesignated) administration; xx xxxxxxx xxxxxxxxxxxxxxxxxxxxxxxxxxxxxxxxxxxxxxxxxxxxxxxxxxxxxxxxxxxxxxxxxxxxxxxxxx xxxxxxxxxxxxxxxxxxxxxxxxxxxxxxand is not disqualified to serve as a personal representative of the decedent.

17. That at least 120 hours have elapsed since decedent's death.

WHEREFORE, your applicant requests that said will, xxxxxxx xxx xxxxx xxx xxxxxxxx xxxxxxx xxxxxx xxxxxx be informally probated; that applicant xx _____Charles Kennedy_____ be informally appointed as executor, with no xxx xxxxxxxxxxxxxxxxxxxxxxxxxxxxxxxxx bond, in an unsupervised adminstration, that upon qualification and acceptance, letters testamentary be issued to applicant xx _____Charles Kennedy_____; and granting such other and further relief as may be proper.

FURTHER, under penalties for perjury for deliberate falsification therein, I declare or affirm that I have read the foregoing application and to the best of my knowledge or information, its representations are true, correct and complete.

Dated: _____August 30, 1994_____

_____/S/ Charles Kennedy_____
Applicant

__/S/ Susan G. Brown, License #9876543__
Attorney for Applicant
   1400 Main Street
   __Minneapolis, MN 55455__
Address/Phone (612) 773-3777

*ASSETS

Probate Assets			Non-Probate Assets		
Homestead	$	95,000.00	Joint Tenancy	$	57,000.00
Other Real Estate	$	0.00	Insurance	$	5,000.00
Cash	$	0.00	Other	$	0.00
Securities	$	2,000.00	Approximate		
Other	$	16,610.00	Indebtedness	$	110.00
		(personal property)			

Form 58 Change of Testacy Status—Application for Informal Appointment of Successor Personal Representative

---

Form No. 4336 MILLER-DAVIS CO., MPLS.   Form 524.3-301 (5)   UPC — —

STATE OF MINNESOTA   **PROBATE COURT**
                                        COUNTY COURT-PROBATE DIVISION
COUNTY OF_____

In Re: Estate of   Court File No. _____

                                        APPLICATION FOR INFORMAL
                                        APPOINTMENT OF SUCCESSOR
_____   **PERSONAL REPRESENTATIVE**
              Deceased   **APPOINTED UNDER DIFFERENT**
                                        TESTACY STATUS

TO THE HONORABLE REGISTRAR OF THE ABOVE NAMED COURT:

Applicant, _____, respectfully states:

1. Applicant resides at _____;

2. Applicant has an interest herein as _____,
   and is, therefore, an interested person as defined by the laws of this state.

3. That on _____, 19___, _____ was
   appointed the personal representative of the above named decedent under a different testacy
   status by order of the above named court upon the application or petition filed in said matter
   by _____, dated _____, 19___.

4. That the applicant or _____ has priority for appointment as personal representative of the estate of the decedent because: _____
   _____
   _____

   WHEREFORE, your applicant requests that applicant or _____ be informally
appointed as successor personal representative, with no or _____ bond, in an unsupervised administration; that letters testamentary be issued to applicant or _____;
and such other and further relief as may be proper.

   FURTHER, under penalties for perjury for deliberate falsification therein, I declare or affirm
that I have read the foregoing application and to the best of my knowledge or information, its
representations are true, correct and complete.

Dated: _____

                                        _____
                                        Applicant

_____
Attorney for Applicant

_____
Address/Phone

Form 59   Verification

MD Form No. 4305 MILLER-DAVIS CO., MPLS   Form 524. 1-310   UPC – –

STATE OF MINNESOTA   **PROBATE COURT**
                                                    DISTRICT COURT-PROBATE DIVISION
COUNTY OF_____

In Re: Estate of   Court File No._____

                                                         VERIFICATION

_____
               Deceased

_____

STATE OF MINNESOTA

COUNTY OF_____ *ss.*

   I, _____, being duly sworn state that I am the_____
herein; that I have read the foregoing_____ and know the contents thereof; that the
same is true of my own knowledge, except as to those matters therein stated on information and
belief, and as to those matters I believe them to be true, and I know and am informed that the
penalties for perjury may follow from deliberate falsification therein.

Dated:_____

          Subscribed and sworn to before me this   _____
_____day of_____, 19___.

_____
     SIGNATURE OF NOTARY PUBLIC OR OTHER OFFICIAL

┌──────────────────────────────────────┐
│ NOTARIAL STAMP OR SEAL (OR OTHER TITLE OR RANK) │
│   │
│   │
│   │
│   │
│   │
└──────────────────────────────────────┘

_____
Attorney

_____
Address/Phone

Form 60 Statement of Informal Probate of Will and Order of Informal Appointment of Personal Representative (Executor)

Form No. 4339—MILLER-DAVIS CO., MPLS. (Rev. 1979)

Form 524.3-302 #2   UPC 22

STATE OF MINNESOTA

COUNTY OF ____Hennepin____

In Re: Estate of

_____Cheryl Ann Kennedy_____
Deceased

**PROBATE COURT
DISTRICT-COUNTY COURT
PROBATE DIVISION**

Court File No. ____198540____

**STATEMENT OF INFORMAL PROBATE
OF WILL AND ORDER OF INFORMAL
APPOINTMENT OF EXECUTOR**

The application of ____Charles Kennedy____ dated ____August 30____ , 19_94_, for the informal probate of the last will and for informal appointment of executor of the above named decedent having come before the undersigned Registrar of the above named court, the undersigned Registrar having considered such application makes the following determinations:

1. That the application for informal probate of will and for informal appointment of a personal representative is complete.
2. That the applicant has declared or affirmed that the representations contained in the application are true, correct and complete to the best of h_is_ knowledge or information.
3. That the applicant appears from the application to be an interested person as defined by the laws of this state.
4. That, on the basis of the statement in the application, jurisdiction of this estate, proceeding and subject matter is proper.
5. That, on the basis of the statements in the application, venue is proper because the decedent's domicile at the time of h_er_ death was in the above named County of the State of Minnesota and was the owner of property located in the State of Minnesota, ~~xxxxxxxxxxxxxxxxxxxxxxxxxxxxxxxxxxxxxxxxxxxxxxxxxxxxxxxxxxxxxxxxxxxxx~~ ~~xxxxxxxxxxxxxxxxxxxxxxxxxxxxxxxxxxxxxxxxxxxxxxxxxxxxxxxxxxxxxxxx~~.
6. That the original, duly executed and apparently unrevoked last will of the decedent ~~xxxxxxxxxxxxxxxxxxxxx~~ ~~xxxxxxxxxxxxxxxxxxxxxxxxxxxxxxxxxxxxxxxxxxxxxxxxxxxxxxxxx~~ is in the Registrar's possession, and therefore, that any will to which the requested appointment relates has been or will be informally probated upon the entry of this order.
7. That any notice as required by the laws of this state has been given.
8. That the application does not indicate the existence of a possible unrevoked testamentary instrument which may relate to property subject to the laws of this state, and which is not filed for probate in this court.
9. That it appears from the application that the time limit for original probate and appointment proceedings has not expired.
10. That from the statements in the application, the person whose appointment is sought has priority entitling appointment because _____he is nominated in the last will of the decedent as executor, with no ~~xxx~~ ~~xxxxxxxxxxxxxxxxxxxxxxxxxxxxxxxxx~~ bond, in an ~~xxxxxxxxxxxxxx~~ (undesignated) administration, ~~xxxxxxxxx~~ ~~xxxxxxxxxxxxxxxxxxxxxxxxxxxxxxxxxxxxxxxxxxxxxxxxxxxxxxxxxxxxxxxxxxxxxxxxxxxxxxxxxxxxxxxxx~~ ~~xxxxxxxxxxxxxxxxxxxxxxxxxxx~~ and is not disqualified to serve as a personal representative of the decedent.
11. That the application does not indicate that a personal representative has been appointed in this or another county of this state whose appointment has not been terminated.
12. That at least 120 hours have elapsed since the decedent's death.

Now, therefore, it is ORDERED by the Registrar as follows:

1. That the last will last executed ____November 21____ , 19_88_, of the decedent, including any codicil or codicils thereto is hereby informally probated.
2. That ____Charles Kennedy____ is hereby informally appointed as the executor of the estate of ____Cheryl Ann Kennedy____ , deceased, with ____no____ bond, in an unsupervised administration.
3. That upon qualification and acceptance letters testamentary be issued to ____Charles Kennedy____ .
_____.

Dated: ____September 7, 1994____   ____/S/ Lorina B. Arneson____
                                          Registrar

Form 61   Notice of Informal Probate of Will and Appointment of Personal Representative and Notice to Creditors

MD **Form No. 4343** —Miller-Davis Legal Forms (Rev. 6-85)   524.3-306 #2   524.3-310 #2   524.3-801 #2   UPC– –

STATE OF MINNESOTA

COUNTY OF _____Hennepin_____

In Re: Estate of

_____Cheryl Ann Kennedy_____
Deceased

**PROBATE COURT
DISTRICT—COUNTY COURT
PROBATE DIVISION**

Court File No. _____198540_____

**NOTICE OF INFORMAL PROBATE OF
WILL AND APPOINTMENT OF
PERSONAL REPRESENTATIVE AND
NOTICE TO CREDITORS**

TO ALL INTERESTED PERSONS AND CREDITORS:

Notice is hereby given, that an application for informal probate of the above named decedent's last will, dated _____November 21_____, 19 88 , _____,

has been filed with the Registrar herein, and the application has been granted informally probating such will. Any objections may be filed in the above named court and the same will be heard by the Court upon notice of hearing fixed for such purpose.

Notice is hereby further given that informal appointment of _____Charles Kennedy_____

whose address is _____1010 Willow Street, Minneapolis, MN 55409_____,

as personal representative of the estate of the above named decedent, has been made. Any heir, devisee or other interested person may be entitled to appointment as personal representative or may object to the appointment of the personal representative and the personal representative is empowered to fully administer the estate including, after 30 days from the date of issuance of h is letters, the power to sell, encumber, lease or distribute real estate, unless objections thereto are filed with the Court (pursuant to Section 524.3-607) and the Court otherwise orders.

Notice is further given that ALL CREDITORS having claims against said estate are required to present the same to said personal representative or to the Court Administrator within four months after the date of this notice or said claims will be barred.

Dated: _____September 7, 1994_____

_____/S/ Lorina B. Arneson_____
Registrar

_____/S/ Susan G. Brown, License_____
Attorney   #9876543

1400 Main Street
__Minneapolis, MN 55455__
Address   (612) 773-3777

_____/S/ Bradford R. Mitlar_____
Court Administrator

NOTE: If notice to creditors has been previously given, delete the Notice to Creditors herein.

Form 62 Proof of Placing Order for Publication

STATE OF MINNESOTA

COUNTY OF HENNEPIN

PROBATE COURT—UNSUPERVISED

COURT FILE NO. 198540

In Re: Estate of

PROOF OF PLACING ORDER
FOR PUBLICATION

_____ Cheryl Ann Kennedy _____
Deceased

_____

_____

TO THE CLERK OF PROBATE COURT:

This is to verify that Susan G. Brown _____

_____

Attorney for , applicant(s)

has X(have)X made arrangements for the publication of:

☐ NOTICE OF INFORMAL APPOINTMENT OF PERSONAL
REPRESENTATIVE(S) AND NOTICE TO CREDITORS

☒ NOTICE OF INFORMAL PROBATE OF WILL AND APPOINTMENT OF
PERSONAL REPRESENTATIVE(S) AND NOTICE TO CREDITORS

☐

once a week for two consecutive weeks in the _____ FINANCE AND COMMERCE _____
Daily Newspaper

and this is to confirm that the same will be published accordingly commencing in the next available issue, and that arrangements for payment of the cost of said publication have been made.

Dated: _____ September 8, 1994 _____

/S/ D. C. Morrison _____
Publisher

Form 63 Affidavit of Mailing Notice of Informal Probate of Will

MD **Form No. 4307** Miller Davis Legal Forms (Rev. 1988)   Form 524.1-401 #2   UPC --

STATE OF MINNESOTA   **DISTRICT COURT**
COUNTY OF _____Hennepin_____
IN RE: (ESTATE)   Court File No. _____198540_____

OF _____Cheryl Ann Kennedy_____   **AFFIDAVIT OF MAILING** ~~ORDER~~
                                          ~~OR~~ **NOTICE OF** ~~HEARING~~ Informal
_____   Probate of Will and Informal Appoint-
            Deceased   ment of Personal Representative and
                                          Notice to Creditors.
                                          STATE OF MINNESOTA
                                          COUNTY OF_____Hennepin_____ ss.
                                          _Susan G. Brown_____
       ATTACH COPY OF ORDER   being first duly sworn on oath deposes and
          OR NOTICE HERE   says that on the _____8th_____ day of _September_ ,
                                          19_94_____ , at ___Minneapolis___ in said
                                          County and State _____s_ he mailed a copy of the
                                          Order or Notice hereto attached to each _heir and_
                                          devisee of said decedent, Cheryl Ann
                                          Kennedy, and the personal
                                          representative
                                          whose name and address are known to affiant,
                                          after exercising due diligence in ascertaining the
                                          correctness of said name and address, by placing a
                                          true and correct copy thereof in a sealed envelope,
                                          postage prepaid and depositing the same in the
                                          U.S. Mails at _Minneapolis, Minnesota_____

                                          and addressed to the following named persons:
                                          NOTE: (Instructions at bottom of page)

NAME	STREET or POST OFFICE	CITY	STATE
Charles Kennedy	1010 Willow Street	Minneapolis	MN 55409
Cherry Kennedy	1010 Willow Street	Minneapolis	MN 55409
Cindy Kennedy	1010 Willow Street	Minneapolis	MN 55409
Carl Kennedy	1010 Willow Street	Minneapolis	MN 55409
Corey Kennedy	1010 Willow Street	Minneapolis	MN 55409
Christopher Kennedy	1010 Willow Street	Minneapolis	MN 55409
Karen Kelly	1010 Willow Street	Minneapolis	MN 55409
Catherine Kelly	1010 Willow Street	Minneapolis	MN 55409

                              _/S/ Susan G. Brown_____

NOTARIAL STAMP OF SEAL (OR OTHER TITLE OR RANK)

                                          Subscribed and sworn to before me this day of
                                          ___8th___ day of _September_____ ,19_94_ .

                                          _/S/ Astrid M. Martensen_____
                                          SIGNATURE OF NOTARY PUBLIC OR OTHER OFFICIAL

NOTED INSTRUCTIONS: In Estates To each heir, devisee, personal representative, the foreign consul pursuant to M.S. 524.3-306 and M.S. 524.3-403, and the Minnesota Attorney General, if a devisee is the trustee of a charitable trust or if the decedent left no devisees or heirs.

Form 63 Statutory Notice of Rights of Surviving Spouse and/or Minor Children (Reverse Side of Form)

AFFIDAVIT OF MAILING
ALLOWANCES TO SPOUSE AND/OR CHILDREN

When a decedent dies with or without a will the allowances to the spouse or children are as follows:

525 15 ALLOWANCES TO SPOUSE. When any person dies testate or intestate

(1) The surviving spouse shall be allowed from the personal property of which the decedent was possessed or to which __S__he was entitled at the time of __her__ death, the wearing apparel, and as selected by h __im__ , furniture and household goods not exceeding $6,000 in value, and other personal property not exceeding $3,000 in value, subject to an award of property with sentimental value to the decedent's children under section 3;

(2) When, except for one automobile, all of the personal estate of the decedent is allowed to the surviving spouse by clause (1), the surviving spouse shall also be allowed the automobile.

(3) If there be no surviving spouse, the minor children shall receive the property specified in clause (1) as selected in their behalf;

(4) During administration, but not exceeding 18 months, unless an extension shall have been granted by the court, or, if the estate be insolvent, not exceeding 12 months, the spouse or children, or both, constituting the family of the decedent shall be allowed reasonable maintenance.

(5) In the administration of an estate of a nonresident decedent, the allowances received in the domiciliary administration shall be deducted from the allowances under this section.

_____

In all estates where there is a will the following rule applies to the spouse who has not consented to the will:

524.2-205 PROCEEDING FOR ELECTIVE SHARE; TIME LIMIT.

(a) The surviving spouse may elect to take an elective share in the augmented estate by filing in the court and mailing or delivering to the personal representative, if any, a petition for the elective share within nine months after the date of death, or within six months after the probate of the decedent's will, whichever limitation last expires. However, nonprobate transfers, described in section 524.2-202, clauses (l) and (3), shall not be included within the augmented estate for the purpose of computing the elective share, if the petition is filed ;later than nine months after death The court may extend the time for election as it sees fit for cause shown by the surviving spouse before the time for election has expired.

(b) The surviving spouse shall give notice of the time and place set for hearing to persons interested in the estate and to the distributees and recipients of portions of the augmented net estate whose interests will be affected by the taking of the elective share.

(c) The surviving spouse may withdraw a demand for an elective share at any time before entry of any order by the court determining the elective share.

(d) After notice and hearing, the court shall determine the amount of the elective share and shall order its payment from the assets of the augmented net estate or by contribution as appears appropriate under section 524.2-207. If it appears that a fund or property included in the augmented net estate has not come into the possession of the personal representative, or has been distributed by the personal representative, the court nevertheless shall fix the liability of any person who has any interest in the fund or property or who has possession thereof, whether as trustee or otherwise. The proceeding may be maintained against fewer than all persons against whom relief could be sought, but no person is subject to contribution in any greater amount than he would have been if relief had been secured against all persons subject to contribution.

(e) The order or judgment of the court may be enforced as necessary in suit for contribution or payment in other courts of this state or other jurisdictions.

(f) Whether or not an election has been made under subsection (a), the surviving spouse may elect statutory rights in the homestead by filing in the manner provided in this section a petition in which the spouse asserts the rights provided in section 525.145, provided that:

(1) when the homestead is subject to a testamentary disposition, the filing must be within nine months after the date of death, or within six months after the probate of the decedent's will, whichever limitation last expires; or

(2) where the homestead is subject to other disposition, the filing must he within nine months after the date of death.

The court may extend the time for election for cause shown by the surviving spouse before the time for filing has expired.

STATE OF MINNESOTA
COUNTY OF __Hennepin__   ss.

_____Susan G. Brown_____ being first duly sworn on oath deposes and says that on the __8th__ day of ____September____ , 19 __94__ , at ___Minneapolis_____ in said County and State, __s__he mailed a copy of Sections 525.15 and 524.2-205 of Minnesota Statutes as hereinbefore set out to decedent's spouse and children constituting the family of the decedent at their last known address after exercising due diligence and ascertaining the correctness of said addresses by placing a true and correct copy thereof in a sealed envelope, postage pre-paid and depositing the same in the U.S. mails at _____Minneapolis_____ , Minnesota, and addressed to the following:

NAME	STREET or POST OFFICE	CITY	STATE
Charles Kennedy and children	1010 Willow Street	Minneapolis	MN 55409

Subscribed and sworn to before me this

__8th__ day of ____September____ , 19__94__

/S/ Astrid M. Martensen
SIGNATURE OF NOTARY PUBLIC OR OTHER OFFICIAL

NOTARIAL STAMP OR SEAL (OR OTHER TITLE OR RANK)

_____/S/ Susan G. Brown_____

Form 64   Acceptance of Appointment and Oath by Individual

MD Form No. 4401   Miller-Davis Legal Forms   524.3-601#1   UPC 43

STATE OF MINNESOTA   PROBATE COURT
                                               DISTRICT-COUNTY COURT
COUNTY OF _____Hennepin_____   PROBATE DIVISION

In Re: Estate of   Court File No. _____198540_____

_____Cheryl Ann Kennedy_____   **ACCEPTANCE OF APPOINTMENT
             Deceased   AND OATH BY INDIVIDUAL**

TO THE ABOVE NAMED COURT:

STATE OF MINNESOTA   ⎫
                                          ⎬ ss.
COUNTY OF __Hennepin_____   ⎭

I, _____Charles Kennedy_____ , residing at _1010 Willow St._

in the City of __Minneapolis__ , County of __Hennepin__ , State of __Minnesota__
as a condition to receiving letters as __personal representative__
in the above entitled matter, hereby accept the duties of the office, agree to be bound by the provisions
of the statutes relating thereto and hereby submit to the jurisdiction of the Court in any proceeding
relating to the said matter that may be instituted by any person interested therein; and swear that I
will faithfully and justly perform all duties of the office and trust that I now assume as _____
_____personal representative_____
in the above entitled matter to the best of my ability.

                                        ____/S/ Charles Kennedy_____

                                        ┌─────────────────────────────────────┐
                                        │ NOTARIAL STAMP OR SEAL (OR OTHER TITLE OR RANK) │
     Subscribed and sworn to before me this │   │
__7th__ day of __September__ , 19 __94__ . │   │
__/S/ Mariana S. Halsted_____   │   │
SIGNATURE OF NOTARY PUBLIC OR OTHER OFFICIAL └─────────────────────────────────┘

Form 65 Letters Testamentary

MD Form No. 4403 Rev. 1-88 Miller-Davis Legal Forms 524.3-601 #3   UPC 43

STATE OF MINNESOTA

COUNTY OF ___Hennepin___   **DISTRICT COURT**

In Re: Estate of   Court File No.___198540___

                                             LETTERS TESTAMENTARY

_____Cheryl Ann Kennedy_____
                 Deceased

The above named decedent having died on _____August 1_____, 19_94_, and

_____Charles Kennedy_____

having been appointed and qualified, (is) ~~(are)~~ hereby authorized to act as personal representative~~(s)~~ according to law.

Dated: ____September 7, 1994____

                              ____/S/ Lorina B. Arneson____
                                   ~~Judge~~/Registrar

          (COURT SEAL)

Form 66   Inventory and Appraisal

Form No. 4428— Miller-Davis Legal Forms (Rev. 1-88)   Form 524.3-706   UPC 54

STATE OF MINNESOTA

COUNTY OF __Hennepin__   **DISTRICT COURT**

In Re: Estate of   Court File No. ___198540___

_____Cheryl Ann Kennedy_____   **INVENTORY AND APPRAISEMENT**
                    Deceased
                                             Date of Death __August 1_____, 19_94_
                                             Social Security No. ____217-48-4307_____

TO THE HONORABLE JUDGE AND/OR REGISTRAR OF THE ABOVE NAMED COURT:

___Charles Kennedy_____, the undersigned personal representative, respectfully states:

1. That the following is a true and correct inventory and appraisement, at date of death values, of all the property of the above named estate, both real and personal, which has come into the possession of said representative and of which said representative has knowledge after diligent search and inquiry concerning the same, classified as follows, to-wit: (See instructions at end of last page.)

SCHEDULE A — Real Estate

Item number	Legal Description (Specify street address of city realty; acreage of rural land; and liens, if any)	Assessor's Estimated Market Value (Do not use "Green Acres" Value or Assessor's Limited Market Value)	GROSS APPRAISED VALUE
1	Homestead, being in the County of ____Hennepin_____, State of Minnesota: 1010 Willow Street, Minneapolis, MN. Legally described as follows, to wit: Lot 3, Block 1,Loring Park Addition to Minneapolis (Plat #17068 Parcel #3196) Other Real Estate, being in the County of _____ State of Minnesota: N/A		$ 95,000.00

Form 66 Inventory and Appraisal—*continued*

	Real Estate SCHEDULE A — TOTAL $	95,000.00

SCHEDULE B — Stocks and Bonds

Item number	Description (Specify face amount of bonds or number of shares and par value where needed for identification; and liens, if any)	GROSS APPRAISED VALUE
1	Stock: 50 Shares Users, Inc., Common Stock, Certificate No. U0556484 dated 01/13/78, at $40.00/share.	$ 2,000.00
	Personal Property SCHEDULE B — TOTAL $	2,000.00

SCHEDULE C — Mortgages, Notes, and Cash

Item number	Description (Specify recording data; bank and account numbers; accrued interest; location of actual cash; and liens, if any)	GROSS APPRAISED
	N/A	
	Personal Property SCHEDULE C — TOTAL $	0.00

Form 66 Inventory and Appraisal—*continued*

SCHEDULE D — Other Miscellaneous Property

Item number	Description (Specify location of property and liens, if any)	GROSS APPRAISED VALUE
1	Furniture and Household goods:	$ 5,000.00
	Wearing apparel and Ornaments:	
2	Fur – Mink coat	4,000.00
3	Diamond ring	1,500.00
4	Clothing	200.00
5	Wigs (2)	110.00
	All other personal property (including partnership and business interests, insurance and annuities payable to estate, other receivables, farm crops, machinery, etc.):	
6	1990 Ford, Vehicle Identification Number 5342718653, Title Number 04142313.	5,500.00
7	Miscellaneous	300.00

Personal Property SCHEDULE D — TOTAL $ 16,610.00

SUMMARY

Total Gross Value of Real Estate	$ 95,000.00		
Less Liens	$ 0.00		
Net Value of Real Estate		$	95,000.00
Total Gross Value of Personal Property	$ 18,610.00		
Less Liens	$ 110.00		
Net Value of Personal Property		$	18,500.00
TOTAL NET APPRAISEMENT		$	113,500.00

2. That a copy hereof has been mailed to the surviving spouse if there be one, and to all residuary distributees of the above named decedent and to interested persons or creditors who have requested the same.

Form 66 Inventory and Appraisal—*continued*

FURTHER, under penalties for perjury for deliberate falsification therein, I declare or affirm that I have read the foregoing and to the best of my knowledge or information, its representations are true, correct and complete.

Dated: ____September 17, 1994____

____/S/ Charles Kennedy____
Personal Representative

____/S/ Susan G. Brown____
Attorney
1400 Main Street
Minneapolis, MN 55455
Address/Phone (612) 773-3777

INSTRUCTIONS:

(1) The classification of assets herein is intended for them to be comparable to the Federal Estate Tax Return Form 706 with the exception of Schedule D herein which includes insurance and annuities payable to the estate and which are otherwise includable under separate Schedules of said Form 706.

(2) It is to be noted that the GROSS APPRAISED VALUE is requested of each asset without reduction by any lien requested to be specified as a part of its description. The reduction for liens is later taken under the Summary of Assets.

(3) It is also to be noted that each asset of a Schedule is to be given its "Item number" to facilitate a ready reference similar to the Estate Tax Form 706.

(4) Finally, it is to be noted that the Assessor's Estimated Market Value is requested. This information is always available to the Department of Revenue upon its request. The accurate furnishing of the information can result in better servicing of the inheritance tax returns.

(5) It is recommended that the appraisal report of any independent appraiser should be properly referenced and attached as an Exhibit including the name and address of any such appraisers.

Form 67 Written Statement of Claim

MD Form No. 4434 Miller-Davis Legal Forms   Form 524.3-804#1   UPC 59

STATE OF MINNESOTA

COUNTY OF Hennepin

DISTRICT COURT

In Re: Estate of

Court File No. ___198540___

WRITTEN STATEMENT OF CLAIM

_____Cheryl Ann Kennedy_____
                  Deceased

TO THE PERSONAL REPRESENTATIVE OF THE ABOVE NAMED ESTATE:

Claimant ___Beauty Products, Inc.___, states:

1. Claimant's address ___230 Dunkirk Lane, Minnetonka, MN 55606___;

2. Claimant claims that the estate is indebted or will become indebted in the amount of
$___110.00___;

3. That the nature of the claim is merchandise (wigs) bought by decedent:

    Primavera (#7743) $ 64.00
    Carefree (#7739)   46.00
    Total $110.00

4. That the claim arose prior to the death of the decedent on or about ___July 27___,
19_94_, xxxxxxxxxxxxxxxxxxxxxxxxxxxxxxxxxxxxxxxxxxxxxxxxxxxxxxxxxxxxxxxxxxx,
xxxxx;

5. That the claim is secured by ___no security___;

6. That the claim was xxxxxxxxx due and payable on ___August 27___, 19_94_;

7. That if the claim is contingent or unliquidated, the nature of the uncertainty is as
   follows: _____
   _____.

Dated: ___September 18, 1994___

___/S/ Rafael Y. Santelo, License___
Attorney for Claimant   #5347194
     1341 Stevens Avenue
___Minneapolis, MN 55410___
Address/Phone   (612) 841-7662

BEAUTY PRODUCTS, INC.

___/S/ Martin R. Kromstad___
Claimant

Note: Claim may be presented to Personal
     Representative or filed with
     Court Administrator.
     Presentation of claim does **not**
     commence proceedings.
     See 3-806

Form 68 Informal Deed of Distribution by Personal Representative

MD Form No. 4452 Miller-Davis Legal Forms (Rev 4-88)   524.3-907 #1   UPC--

STATE OF MINNESOTA

DISTRICT COURT

COUNTY OF ___Hennepin___

In Re: Estate of

Court File No. ___198540___

**INFORMAL DEED OF DISTRIBUTION
BY PERSONAL REPRESENTATIVE**

_____Cheryl Ann Kennedy_____
Deceased

This instrument dated this ___8th___ day of ___January___ 19_95_, by and between ___Charles Kennedy___, personal representative of the estate of ___Cheryl Ann Kennedy___, decedent, first party, and ___Karen Kelly___ _____, of the County of___Hennepin___ and State of Minnesota, second party;

WHEREAS, ___Cheryl Ann Kennedy___ died on the ___1st___ day of ___August___, 19_94_, and;

WHEREAS, thereafter, on the ___7th___ day of ___September___, 19_94_, first party was duly appointed and qualified as personal representative of the above entitled estate in an informal probate administration, and:

WHEREAS, the second party as a~~n heir~~ (devisee) of the estate of ___Cheryl Ann Kennedy___, deceased, is entitled to the property hereby distributed;

NOW, THEREFORE, in accordance with the laws of the State of ___Minnesota___, first party hereby assigns, transfers, conveys, and releases to ___Karen Kelly___

all the estate, right, title, interest, claims, and demand whatsoever, which the said decedent had at the time of death in the following described ___personal___ property located in the County of ___Hennepin___ and State of Minnesota, legally described as follows:

One blue-white marquise cut diamond ring, silver setting, valued at $1,500.00.

Dated: ___January 8, 1995___

___/S/ Charles Kennedy___
Personal Representative

I, ___Charles Kennedy___, spouse of the above named decedent, do hereby consent to the within conveyance.

___/S/ Charles Kennedy___

Form 68 Informal Deed of Distribution by Personal Representative—*continued*

(Individual Acknowledgment)

STATE OF MINNESOTA

COUNTY OF ___Hennepin_____

  The foregoing instrument was acknowledged before me this ___8th___ day of ___January___, 19_95_ ;
by _____Charles Kennedy_____
as_____ personal representative of the estate of _____Cheryl Ann Kennedy_____
_____, deceased.

NOTARIAL STAMP OR SEAL (OR OTHER TITLE OR RANK)

___/S/ Georgeann Holtzer_____
SIGNATURE OF NOTARY PUBLIC OR OTHER OFFICIAL

THIS INSTRUMENT WAS DRAFTED BY

___Susan G. Brown_____
(Name)

___1400 Main Street_____
(Address)

___Minneapolis, MN 55455_____

Tax statements for the real property described in this instrument should be sent to: N/A

_____   _____
(Name)   (Address)

STATE DEED TAX
TRANSFER STAMPS DUE

_____

Form 69 Receipt for Assets by Distributee

MD Form No. 4564   524.3-1001 (4)   524.3-1003 (2)   MILLER-DAVIS LEGAL FORMS

STATE OF MINNESOTA

COUNTY OF Hennepin   **DISTRICT COURT**

In Re: Estate of   Court File No. 198540

                                            RECEIPT FOR ASSETS BY
                                            DISTRIBUTEE

          Cheryl Ann Kennedy
                  Deceased

I, Karen Kelly , the undersigned distributee, hereby acknowledge receipt from the personal representative(s) of the above entitled estate, of the following assets, to-wit:

One blue-white marquise cut diamond ring, silver setting, valued at $1,500.00

in full satisfaction of the complete and final settlement of my distributive share of the above entitled estate.

Dated: January 8, 1995

                              /S/ Karen Kelly
                              Distributee

INSTRUCTIONS:

1. To be executed after Order or Decree of Distribution under 524.3-1001 (4) and furnished with petition for discharge Form 524.3-1001 #9.

2. To be executed under 524.3-1003 (2) prior to personal representative's closing statement Form 524.1003 #1.

Form 70   Informal Administration: Personal Representative's Statement to Close Estate

MID Form No. 4475 – Miller-Davis Legal Forms (Rev. 1-7-86)   524.3 –1003 #1   UPC --

STATE OF MINNESOTA

COUNTY OF __Hennepin__

In Re: Estate of

_____
              Cheryl Ann Kennedy
                     Deceased

PROBATE COURT
DISTRICT COURT– COUNTY COURT
PROBATE DIVISION

Court File No. ____198540_____

INFORMAL ADMINISTRATION:
PERSONAL REPRESENTATIVE'S
STATEMENT TO CLOSE ESTATE

TO THE HONORABLE REGISTRAR OF THE ABOVE NAMED COURT:

_____Charles Kennedy_____ the undersigned personal representative herein respectfully states that ____he ~~the prior personal representative whom xxx he has succeeded~~ has:

1. Published notice to creditors and that the date of the notice was more than four months prior to the date of this statement;

2. Fully administered the estate of the decedent by making payment, settlement or other disposition of all claims which were presented, expenses of administration and estate, inheritance and other taxes, except as specified in this statement, and that the assets of the estate have been inventoried and distributed to the persons entitled thereto. Listed below are unpaid claims, expenses or taxes which remain undischarged together with the detailed arrangements which have been made to accommodate all outstanding liabilities: (If none, so state)

   NONE

3. Sent a copy of this statement to all distributees of the estate and to all creditors or other claimants of whom ____he is aware whose claims are neither paid or barred and has furnished a full account in writing of this administration to the distributees whose interests are affected thereby.

   This statement is filed for the purpose of closing this estate and terminating the appointment of the undersigned.

DATED: _____March 1, 1995_____   ____/S/ Charles Kennedy_____
                                                 Personal Representative

STATE OF MINNESOTA   ⎫
                                                ⎬ SS.
COUNTY OF __Hennepin_____   ⎭

I, _____Charles Kennedy_____, being duly sworn state that I am the personal representative herein; that I have read the foregoing statement and know the contents thereof; that the same is true of my own knowledge, except as to those matters therein stated on information and belief, and as to those matters I believe it to be true.

Subscribed and sworn to before me this   ____/S/ Charles Kennedy_____
__1st_____ day of ____March_____, 19 _95_.   Personal Representative

__/S/ Georgeann Holtzer_____
   SIGNATURE OF NOTARY PUBLIC OR OTHER OFFICIAL

```
   NOTARIAL STAMP OR SEAL (OR OTHER TITLE OR RANK)
```

____/S/ Susan G. Brown_____
Attorney for Personal Representative
    1400 Main Street
    Minneapolis, MN 55455
Address/ Phone   (612) 773-3777

Form 71 Application for Informal Appointment of Administrator

M/D Form No. 4335 Miller-Davis Legal Forms (Rev. 1989)   Form 524.3-301 #4   UPC 23

STATE OF MINNESOTA

COUNTY OF _____ Hennepin _____

In Re: Estate of

_____ Cheryl Ann Kennedy _____
Deceased

PROBATE COURT
DISTRICT-COUNTY COURT
PROBATE DIVISION

Court File No. _____ 198541 _____

**APPLICATION FOR
INFORMAL APPOINTMENT
OF ADMINISTRATOR**

TO THE HONORABLE JUDGE OF THE ABOVE NAMED COURT:

Applicant, _____ Charles Kennedy _____, respectfully states:

1. Applicant resides at _____ 1010 Willow Street, Minneapolis, MN 55409 _____;

2. Applicant has an interest herein as _____ spouse and heir _____
and is, therefore, an interested person as defined by the laws of this State;

3. Decedent was born _____ January 13 _____, 19 60, at _____ Minneapolis, Minnesota _____;

4. Decedent died on _____ August 1 _____, 19 94, at _____ Minneapolis, Minnesota _____;

5. Decedent at the time of h er death resided at _____ 1010 Willow Street' _____,
City of _____ Minneapolis _____, County of _____ Hennepin _____, State of _____ Minnesota _____;

6. That the names and addresses of decedent's spouse, children, heirs and devisees and other persons interested in this proceeding and the ages of any who are minors so far as known or ascertainable with reasonable deligence by the petitioner are:

   NOTE — Classify the heirs and others entitled to take per stirpes and give the name, date of death, relationship/interest and address, if known, of their predeceased ancestor. Give the birthdate of any heir or devisee taking a life interest. Remember to include a "Negative Allegation Statement".

Name	Age	Relationship/Interest	Address
Charles Kennedy	34	Born 02/03/60 Spouse/heir	1010 Willow Street, Minneapolis, MN 55409
Cherry Kennedy	3	Daughter/heir	same
Cindy Kennedy	3	Daughter/heir	same
Carl Kennedy	5	Son/heir	same
Corey Kennedy	9	Son/heir	same
Christopher Kennedy	10	Son/heir	same
Catherine Kelly	60	Mother/heir	same
Karen Kelly	38	Sister/heir	same

Negative Allegation Statement (see Probate Court Rule 6 (1)): _____ Decedent left surviving no spouse, _____

children, parents, or brothers or sisters, other than herein named, and no issue

of deceased children.

7. That all persons identified as heirs have survived the decedent by at least 120 hours.

8. That all issue of decedent are also issue of decedent's surviving spouse except for: _____

Form 71   Application for Informal Appointment of Administrator—*continued*

9. That venue for this proceeding is in the above named County of the State of Minnesota, because the decedent was domiciled in such County at the time of h̲_er̲_ death, and was the owner of property located in the State of Minnesota, ~~xx because though not domiciled in the State of Minnesota, the decedent was the owner of property located in the above named County at the time of his xxxxx death xx~~

10. That no personal representative of the decedent has been appointed in this State or elsewhere whose appointment has not been terminated.

11. That applicant has not received a demand for notice and is not aware of any demand for notice of any probate or appointment proceeding concerning the decedent that may have been filed in this State or elsewhere ~~xx xxxxxx xxxxxx xxx xxxxx xxxxx~~

12. That the time limit for informal appointment proceeding as provided by the laws of this State has not expired because three years or less have passed since the decedent's death.

13. That after the exercise of reasonable diligence, applicant is unaware of any unrevoked testamentary instrument relating to property having a situs in this State under the laws of this State.

14. That applicant ~~xxxxxxxxxxxxxxxxxxxxxxxxxxxxxxxxxxxxxxxxxxxxxxxx~~ is entitled to priority and appointment as the administrator because applicant ~~xxxxxxxxxxxxxxxxxxxxxxxxxxxxxxxxxxxxxxxxxxxxxxxxxxxxx~~ (i) is the ___spouse_____ _____ of the decedent, (ii) is not disqualified to serve as a personal representative of the decedent, and (iii) there are no persons having a prior or equal right to the appointment under the laws of this State ~~xxxxx~~ xxxxxxxxxxxxxxxxxxxxxxxxxxxxxxxxxxxxxxxxxxxxxxxxxxxxxxxxxxxxxxxxxxxxxxxxxxxx

15. That at least 120 hours have elapsed since decedent's death.

    WHEREFORE, your applicant requests that applicant ~~xxx~~ xxxxxxxxxxxxxxxxxxxxxxxxxxxxxxxxxxxxxxxxxxx be informally appointed as the administrator of said estate, with ~~xxxxx~~ $10,000.00 _____ bond, in an unsupervised administration; that, upon qualification and acceptance, letters of administration be issued to applicant ~~xxxxxxxxxxxxxxxxxxxxxxxxxxxxxxxxxxxxxxxxxxxxxxxxxx~~ and grantings such other and further relief as may be proper.

    FURTHER, under penalties for perjury for deliberate falsification therein, I declare or affirm that I have read the foregoing application and to the best of my knowledge or information, its representations are true, correct and complete.

Dated: ___August 30, 1994_____

                       ___/S/ Charles Kennedy_____
                       Applicant

___/S/ Susan G. Brown, License #9876543___
Attorney for Applicant
 1400 Main Street
_Minneapolis, MN 55455_____
Address/Phone (612) 773-3777

*ASSETS

Probate Assets			**Non-Probate Assets**		
Homestead	$	95,000.00	Joint Tenancy	$	57,000.00
Other Real Estate	$	0.00	Insurance	$	5,000.00
Cash	$	0.00	Other	$	0.00
Securities	$	2,000.00	Approximate		
Other	$	16,610.00	Indebtedness	$	110.00
		(personal property)			

Form 72 Order and Notice of Informal Appointment of Personal Representative and Notice to Creditors

Form No. 4350 GOVERNMENT BUSINESS SYSTEMS, MPLS. (Rev. 1986) Forms 524.3-310#3, 524.3-403 #8, 524.3-801 #4   UPC — —

STATE OF MINNESOTA	PROBATE COURT
	DISTRICT—COUNTY COURT
COUNTY OF __Hennepin__	PROBATE DIVISION

In Re: Estate of

Court File No. ____198541____

ORDER AND
**NOTICE OF INFORMAL
APPOINTMENT OF PERSONAL
REPRESENTATIVE, XXXXXXXXX**

____Cheryl Ann Kennedy____
Deceased

**XXXXXXXXXXXXXXXXXXXXXXXX
XXXXXXX AND NOTICE TO CREDITORS**

ORDER AND
NOTICE TO ALL INTERESTED PERSONS AND CREDITORS:
   It is ordered and
   Notice is hereby given that informal appointment of____Charles Kennedy____

_____, whose address is____1010 Willow Street, Minneapolis, MN 55409____

as personal representative of the estate of the above decedent, has been made. Any heir, devisee or other interested person may be entitled to appointment as personal representative or may object to the appointment of the personal representative and the personal representative is empowered to fully administer the estate including, after 30 days from the date of issuance of his letters, the power to sell, encumber, lease or distribute real estate, unless objections thereto are filed with the Court (pursuant to Section 524.3-607) and the Court otherwise orders.

Notice is hereby given that on the xxxxxxxxxxxxxxxxxxxxxxxx day of xxxxxxxxxxxxxxxxxxxxxxxxxxxxxxxxx, xxxxxxxxxxx o'clock xxxxxx xx xx hearing will be held in this Court at xxxxxxxxxxxxxxxxxxxxxxxxxxxxxxxxxxxxx, Minnesota for the formal probate of the instrument purporting to be the Will of the above named decedent, dated xxxxxxxxxxxxxxxxxxxxxxxxxxxxxxx xx xxxxxxxxxxxxxxxxxxxxxxxxxxxxxxxxxxxxxxxxxxxxxxxxxxxxx xxxxxxxxxxxxxxxxxxxxxxxxxxxxxxxxxxxxxxxxxxxxxxxxxxxxxxxxxxxxxxxxxxxxxxxxxxxxxxxxxxxxxxx and that any objections thereto must be filed with the Court.

   Notice is further given that ALL CREDITORS having claims against said estate are required to present the same to said personal representative or to the Court Administrator within four months after the date of this notice or said claims will be barred.

Dated: ____September 8, 1994____

____/S/ Lorina B. Arneson____
Registrar

____/S/ Bradford R. Mitlar____
Court Administrator

____/S/ Susan G. Brown, License____
Attorney   #9876543
      1400 Main Street
      Minneapolis, MN 55455
Address   (612) 773-3777

NOTE: If notice to creditors has been previously given, delete the notice to creditors herein.

Form 73   Proof of Placing Order for Publication

STATE OF MINNESOTA

COUNTY OF HENNEPIN

PROBATE COURT—UNSUPERVISED

COURT FILE NO. <u>198541</u>

In Re: Estate of

PROOF OF PLACING ORDER
FOR PUBLICATION

<u>   Cheryl Ann Kennedy   </u>
Deceased

_____

_____

TO THE CLERK OF PROBATE COURT:

This is to verify that <u>Susan G. Brown   </u>

_____

<u>   </u> <u>Attorney for </u>, applicant(s)

has X(have)X made arrangements for the publication of:

[X] **NOTICE OF INFORMAL APPOINTMENT OF PERSONAL
     REPRESENTATIVE(S) AND NOTICE TO CREDITORS**

[ ] **NOTICE OF INFORMAL PROBATE OF WILL AND APPOINTMENT OF
     PERSONAL REPRESENTATIVE(S) AND NOTICE TO CREDITORS**

[ ]

once a week for two consecutive weeks in the <u>   FINANCE AND COMMERCE   </u>
Daily Newspaper

and this is to confirm that the same will be published accordingly commencing in the next available
issue, and that arrangements for payment of the cost of said publication have been made.

Dated: <u>   September 8, 1994   </u>

<u>/S/ D. C. Morrison   </u>
Publisher

Form 74 Affidavit of Mailing Notice of Informal Appointment of Personal Representative

MD Form No. 4307 Miller Davis Legal Forms (Rev. 1988)   Form 524.1-401 #2   UPC - -

STATE OF MINNESOTA
COUNTY OF _____Hennepin_____   **DISTRICT COURT**

IN RE: (ESTATE)   Court File No. _____198541_____

OF _____Cheryl Ann Kennedy_____   **AFFIDAVIT OF MAILING ~~ORDER~~**
~~OR NOTICE OF HEARING~~ Informal
Appointment of Personal Representative
and Notice to Creditors

_____
Deceased

STATE OF MINNESOTA
COUNTY OF_____Hennepin_____ ss.
_____Susan G. Brown_____

ATTACH COPY OF ORDER
OR NOTICE HERE

being first duly sworn on oath deposes and
says that on the_____8th_____ day of _____September_____,
19_94_____, at _____Minneapolis_____ in said
County and State _____s he mailed a copy of the
Order or Notice hereto attached to each_____heir and_____
_____personal representative_____

_____

_____

whose name and address are known to affiant,
after exercising due diligence in ascertaining the
correctness of said name and address, by placing a
true and correct copy thereof in a sealed envelope,
postage prepaid and depositing the same in the
U.S. Mails at_____Minneapolis, Minnesota_____

_____

and addressed to the following named persons:
NOTE: (Instructions at bottom of page)

NAME	STREET or POST OFFICE	CITY	STATE
Charles Kennedy	1010 Willow Street	Minneapolis	MN 55409
Cherry Kennedy	1010 Willow Street	Minneapolis	MN 55409
Cindy Kennedy	1010 Willow Street	Minneapolis	MN 55409
Carl Kennedy	1010 Willow Street	Minneapolis	MN 55409
Corey Kennedy	1010 Willow Street	Minneapolis	MN 55409
Christopher Kennedy	1010 Willow Street	Minneapolis	MN 55409
Catherine Kelly	1010 Willow Street	Minneapolis	MN 55409
Karen Kelly	1010 Willow Street	Minneapolis	MN 55409

/S/ Susan G. Brown

NOTARIAL STAMP OF SEAL (OR OTHER TITLE OR RANK)

Subscribed and sworn to before me this day of
8th _____ day of _____September_____ ,19_94_.

/S/ Astrid M. Martensen
SIGNATURE OF NOTARY PUBLIC OR OTHER OFFICIAL

NOTED INSTRUCTIONS: In Estates To each heir, devisee, personal representative, the foreign consul
pursuant to M.S. 524.3-306 and M.S. 524.3-403, and the Minnesota Attorney General, if a devisee is the
trustee of a charitable trust or if the decedent left no devisees or heirs.

Form 74 Statutory Notice of Rights of Surviving Spouse and/or Minor Children (Reverse Side of Form)

AFFIDAVIT OF MAILING
ALLOWANCES TO SPOUSE AND/OR CHILDREN

When a decedent dies with or without a will the allowances to the spouse or children are as follows:

525 15 ALLOWANCES TO SPOUSE. When any person dies testate or intestate

(1) The surviving spouse shall be allowed from the personal property of which the decedent was possessed or to which __S__ he was entitled at the time of h _er_ death, the wearing apparel, and as selected by h_im_ , furniture and household goods not exceeding $6,000 in value, and other personal property not exceeding $3,000 in value, subject to an award of property with sentimental value to the decedent's children under section 3;

(2) When, except for one automobile, all of the personal estate of the decedent is allowed to the surviving spouse by clause (1), the surviving spouse shall also be allowed the automobile.

(3) If there be no surviving spouse, the minor children shall receive the property specified in clause (1) as selected in their behalf;

(4) During administration, but not exceeding 18 months, unless an extension shall have been granted by the court, or, if the estate be insolvent, not exceeding 12 months, the spouse or children, or both, constituting the family of the decedent shall be allowed reasonable maintenance.

(5) In the administration of an estate of a nonresident decedent, the allowances received in the domiciliary administration shall be deducted from the allowances under this section.

In all estates where there is a will the following rule applies to the spouse who has not consented to the will:

524.2-205 PROCEEDING FOR ELECTIVE SHARE; TIME LIMIT.

(a) The surviving spouse may elect to take an elective share in the augmented estate by filing in the court and mailing or delivering to the personal representative, if any, a petition for the elective share within nine months after the date of death, or within six months after the probate of the decedent's will, whichever limitation last expires. However, nonprobate transfers, described in section 524.2-202, clauses (1) and (3), shall not be included within the augmented estate for the purpose of computing the elective share, if the petition is filed ;later than nine months after death The court may extend the time for election as it sees fit for cause shown by the surviving spouse before the time for election has expired.

(b) The surviving spouse shall give notice of the time and place set for hearing to persons interested in the estate and to the distributees and recipients of portions of the augmented net estate whose interests will be affected by the taking of the elective share.

(c) The surviving spouse may withdraw a demand for an elective share at any time before entry of any order by the court determining the elective share.

(d) After notice and hearing, the court shall determine the amount of the elective share and shall order its payment from the assets of the augmented net estate or by contribution as appears appropriate under section 524.2-207. If it appears that a fund or property included in the augmented net estate has not come into the possession of the personal representative, or has been distributed by the personal representative, the court nevertheless shall fix the liability of any person who has any interest in the fund or property or who has possession thereof, whether as trustee or otherwise. The proceeding may be maintained against fewer than all persons against whom relief could be sought, but no person is subject to contribution in any greater amount than he would have been if relief had been secured against all persons subject to contribution.

(e) The order or judgment of the court may be enforced as necessary in suit for contribution or payment in other courts of this state or other jurisdictions.

(f) Whether or not an election has been made under subsection (a), the surviving spouse may elect statutory rights in the homestead by filing in the manner provided in this section a petition in which the spouse asserts the rights provided in section 525.145, provided that:

(1) when the homestead is subject to a testamentary disposition, the filing must be within nine months after the date of death, or within six months after the probate of the decedent's will, whichever limitation last expires; or

(2) where the homestead is subject to other disposition, the filing must be within nine months after the date of death.

The court may extend the time for election for cause shown by the surviving spouse before the time for filing has expired.

STATE OF MINNESOTA

COUNTY OF __Hennepin__   ss.

__Susan G. Brown_____ being first duly sworn on oath deposes and says that on the__8th__day of____September_____ , 19_94_ , at__Minneapolis_____ in said County and State, __she mailed a copy of Sections 525.15 and 524.2-205 of Minnesota Statutes as hereinbefore set out to decedent's spouse and children constituting the family of the decedent at their last known address after exercising due diligence and ascertaining the correctness of said addresses by placing a true and correct copy thereof in a sealed envelope, postage pre-paid and depositing the same in the U.S. mails at _____Minneapolis_____ , Minnesota, and addressed to the following:

NAME	STREET or POST OFFICE	CITY	STATE
Charles Kennedy and children	1010 Willow Street	Minneapolis	MN 55409

Subscribed and sworn to before me this

__8th__ day of __September_____ , 19_94_

__/S/ Susan G. Brown_____

__/S/ Astrid M. Martensen_____
SIGNATURE OF NOTARY PUBLIC OR OTHER OFFICIAL

NOTARIAL STAMP OR SEAL (OR OTHER TITLE OR RANK)

Form 75 Acceptance of Appointment and Oath by Individual

....

MD Form No. 4401   Miller-Davis Legal Forms   524.3-601#1   UPC 43

STATE OF MINNESOTA	**PROBATE COURT**
	DISTRICT-COUNTY COURT
COUNTY OF ___Hennepin___	**PROBATE DIVISION**
In Re: Estate of	Court File No. ___198541___

**ACCEPTANCE OF APPOINTMENT
AND OATH BY INDIVIDUAL**

_____Cheryl Ann Kennedy_____
Deceased

TO THE ABOVE NAMED COURT:

STATE OF MINNESOTA

COUNTY OF _Hennepin_____ } _ss._

     I, _____Charles Kennedy_____ , residing at _1010 Willow St._

in the City of _Minneapolis_____ , County of _Hennepin___ , State of ___Minnesota_____
as a condition to receiving letters as ___personal representative_____
in the above entitled matter, hereby accept the duties of the office, agree to be bound by the provisions
of the statutes relating thereto and hereby submit to the jurisdiction of the Court in any proceeding
relating to the said matter that may be instituted by any person interested therein; and swear that I
will faithfully and justly perform all duties of the office and trust that I now assume as _____
_____personal representative_____
in the above entitled matter to the best of my ability.

_____/S/ Charles Kennedy_____

NOTARIAL STAMP OR SEAL (OR OTHER TITLE OR RANK)

    Subscribed and sworn to before me this
__8th__ day of _September___ , 19 _94_ .
_/S/ Mariana S. Halsted_____
SIGNATURE OF NOTARY PUBLIC OR OTHER OFFICIAL

Form 76 Bond

Form No. 4411—MILLER-DAVIS CO., MPLS., (Rev. 2-13-81)   Form 524.3-606 #2,   525.551 #5,   525.591 #9   UPC 49

STATE OF MINNESOTA   **PROBATE COURT**
                                                     COUNTY COURT-PROBATE DIVISION
COUNTY OF ___Hennepin_____
                    (ESTATE
IN THE MATTER OF THE (XXXXXXXXXXXXXX   Court File No. _____198541_____
                     (XXXXXXXXXXXX OF
                                                          BOND
                                                   (PERSONAL SURETIES)
_____Cheryl Ann Kennedy_____
     Deceased — XXXXXXXXXxxXXXXX

KNOW ALL BY THESE PRESENTS, That __`Charles Kennedy_____
of ___Minneapolis_____in the County of___Hennepin_____,
State of ____Minnesota_____as principal(s) and ____Midwest Surety Company_____

of said County and State as sureties, are held and firmly bound to the State of Minnesota for the benefit of the
person interested in the above named estate in the sum of ($_10,000.00__) _____
___Ten Thousand and 00/100---------------- DOLLARS lawful money of the United States, to be paid
to the said State of Minnesota; for which payment well and truly to be made, we bind ourselves, our and each of our
heirs, executors and administrators, jointly and severally firmly by these presents.
     The condition of this obligation is such that if the above bounden principal(X) who has (XXXX) accepted his
(XXXXXXXX appointment is ____personal representative_____
of the above named _____decedent_____ shall well and faithfully discharge
all the duties of his (XXXXXXXX) trust as such representative of said estate according to law then this obligation
shall be void; otherwise it shall be and remain in full force and virtue.

     WITNESS, Our hands and seal this__8th___day of_____September_____, 19_94.

                              _____/S/ Charles Kennedy_____
                              Principal(X)

                              _____/S/ Ira G. Benson_____
                              Attorney-in-Fact

                              ____Midwest Surety Company_____
                              Sureties

STATE OF MINNESOTA   )
) ss.
COUNTY OF ___Hennepin_____)   ACKNOWLEDGEMENT

     BE IT KNOWN, That on this__8th___day of____September_____, 19_94_, personally
appeared before me____Charles Kennedy and Ira G. Benson_____
_____

to me well known to be the same persons who executed the foregoing bond, and they severally acknowledged the
same to be their free act and deed, and that they executed the same for the purposes therein expressed.

                                         ┌─────────────────────────────────────┐
                                         │ NOTARIAL STAMP OR SEAL (OR OTHER TITLE OR RANK) │
     Subscribed and sworn to before me this   │   │
__8th___day of ___September____, 19_94   │   │
                                         │   │
___/S/ Mariana S. Halsted_____   │   │
SIGNATURE OF NOTARY PUBLIC OR OTHER OFFICIAL   └─────────────────────────────────────┘

Form 77 Letters of General Administration

M/D Form No. 4404 — Miller-Davis Legal Forms (REV. 6-76)   524.3-601 #4   UPC 43

STATE OF MINNESOTA

COUNTY OF _Hennepin_   **DISTRICT COURT**

In Re: Estate of   Court File No. __198541__

_____   **LETTERS OF**
    Cheryl Ann Kennedy   **GENERAL ADMINISTRATION**
         Deceased

The above named decedent having died on _____August 1_____ , 19_94_ , and

_____Charles Kennedy_____

_____

having been appointed and qualified, (is) ~~(are)~~ hereby authorized to act as personal representative~~(s)~~ according to law.

Dated: ____September 8, 1994____

                                          ____/S/ Lorina B. Arneson____
(COURT SEAL)   ~~Judge~~Registrar

Form 78   Informal Deed of Distribution by Personal Representative

MD Form No. 4452 Miller-Davis Legal Forms (Rev 4-88)   524.3-907 #1   UPC--

STATE OF MINNESOTA

DISTRICT COURT

COUNTY OF _____Hennepin_____

In Re: Estate of

Court File No. _____198541_____

INFORMAL DEED OF DISTRIBUTION
BY PERSONAL REPRESENTATIVE

_____Cheryl Ann Kennedy_____
Deceased

This instrument dated this ___8th___ day of _____January_____ 19_95_, by and between ___Charles Kennedy___, personal representative of the estate of ___Cheryl Ann Kennedy___, decedent, first party, and ___Charles Kennedy for___ ___Christopher Kennedy, a minor___, of the County of_____Hennepin_____ and State of Minnesota, second party;

WHEREAS, ___Cheryl Ann Kennedy___ died on the___1st___ day of ___August___, 19_94_, and;

WHEREAS, thereafter, on the_____8th_____ day of _September_, 19_94_, first party was duly appointed and qualified as personal representative of the above entitled estate in an informal probate administration, and:

WHEREAS, the second party as an (heir) (~~devisee~~) of the estate of ___Cheryl Ann Kennedy___, deceased, is entitled to the property hereby distributed;

NOW, THEREFORE, in accordance with the laws of the State of ___Minnesota___, first party hereby assigns, transfers, conveys, and releases to ___Charles Kennedy for Christopher___ ___Kennedy (a minor)___

all the estate, right, title, interest, claims, and demand whatsoever, which the said decedent had at the time of death in the following described _____real_____ property located in the County of _____Hennepin_____ and State of Minnesota, legally described as follows:

    Lot 3, Block 1, Loring Park Addition to Minneapolis (Plat #17068 Parcel #3196):
    To Charles Kennedy for Christopher Kennedy, a minor, son of the decedent,
    an undivided one-fifth (1/5) of said homestead real estate, subject to the
    life estate of Charles Kennedy.

Dated: _January 8, 1995_

_____/S/ Charles Kennedy_____
Personal Representative

I,___Charles Kennedy___, spouse of the above named decedent, do hereby consent to the within conveyance.

_____/S/ Charles Kennedy_____

Form 78 Informal Deed of Distribution by Personal Representative—*continued*

(Individual Acknowledgment)

STATE OF MINNESOTA

COUNTY OF ___Hennepin___

The foregoing instrument was acknowledged before me this __8th__ day of __January__, 19_95_;
by _____Charles Kennedy_____
as_____ personal representative of the estate of _____Cheryl Ann Kennedy_____
_____, deceased.

NOTARIAL STAMP OR SEAL (OR OTHER TITLE OR RANK)

_____/S/ Georgeann Holtzer_____
SIGNATURE OF NOTARY PUBLIC OR OTHER OFFICIAL

THIS INSTRUMENT WAS DRAFTED BY

___Susan G. Brown_____
(Name)

___1400 Main Street_____
(Address)

___Minneapolis, MN 55455_____

Tax statements for the real property described in this instrument should be sent to:

___Charles Kennedy_____
(Name)

___1010 Willow Street, Minneapolis, MN 55409___
(Address)

STATE DEED TAX
TRANSFER STAMPS DUE

_____

Form 79 Receipt for Assets by Distributee

MD Form No. 4564   524.3-1001 (4) 524.3-1003 (2)   MILLER-DAVIS LEGAL FORMS

STATE OF MINNESOTA

COUNTY OF Hennepin   **DISTRICT COURT**

In Re: Estate of   Court File No.   198541

                                                     RECEIPT FOR ASSETS BY
         Cheryl Ann Kennedy   **DISTRIBUTEE**
              Deceased

I,   Charles Kennedy, for Christopher Kennedy, a minor   , the undersigned
distributee, hereby acknowledge receipt from the personal representative(s) of the above entitled estate,
of the following assets, to-wit:

    Lot 3, Block 1, Loring Park Addition to Minneapolis (Plat #17068 Parcel #3196):
    an undivided one-fifth (1/5) of said homestead real estate, subject to the
    life estate of Charles Kennedy.

in full satisfaction of the complete and final settlement of my distributive share of the above entitled estate.

Dated: January 8, 1995

                                         /S/ Charles Kennedy for Christopher
                                    Distributee   Kennedy (a minor)

INSTRUCTIONS:

1. To be executed after Order or Decree of Distribution under 524.3-1001 (4) and furnished with petition for
discharge Form 524.3-1001 #9.

2. To be executed under 524.3-1003 (2) prior to personal representative's closing statement Form 524.1003 #1.

Form 80 Application for Certificate from Registrar—Release of Bond

MD Form No. 4565 Miller-Davis Legal Forms · 524.3-1007 #1 · UPC

STATE OF MINNESOTA

COUNTY OF ___Hennepin___

In Re: **Estate of**

___Cheryl Ann Kennedy___
Deceased

DISTRICT COURT

Court File No. ____198541____

APPLICATION FOR CERTIFICATE FROM REGISTRAR THAT THE PERSONAL REPRESENTATIVE APPEARS TO HAVE FULLY ADMINISTERED THE ESTATE OF DECEDENT
APPLICATION FOR RELEASE OF BOND

TO THE HONORABLE REGISTRAR OF THE ABOVE NAMED COURT:

Applicant, ____Charles Kennedy____ , respectfully states:
1. Applicant resides at ____1010 Willow Street, Minneapolis, MN 55409____ ;
2. Applicant has an interest herein as ___personal representative, spouse, and heir___ ,
   and is, therefore, a proper applicant as defined by the laws of this State;
3. That ____Charles Kennedy (applicant)____
   (was) (ⓍⓍⓍⓍ) the duly appointed personal representative(s) of the estate of decedent;
4. That the appointment of said personal representative(s) has terminated;
5. So far as known to applicant, no action concerning the estate of decedent is pending in any court.

   WHEREFORE, Your applicant requests the certificate from the Registrar that the personal representative(s) appear(s) to have fully administered the estate of decedent as evidence to discharge any lien on any property given to secure the obligation of the personal representative(s) in lieu of bond or any surety.

Dated: ____March 8, 1995____   ____/S/ Charles Kennedy____
                                          Applicant

VERIFICATION

STATE OF MINNESOTA)
) ss.
COUNTY OF ___Hennepin___)

   I, ____Charles Kennedy____ , being duly sworn state that I am the applicant herein; that I have read the foregoing application and know the contents thereof; that the same is true of my own knowledge, except as to those matters therein stated on information and belief, and as to those matters I believe them to be true, and I know and am informed that the penalties for perjury may follow from deliberate falsification therein.

Dated: ____March 8, 1995____   ____/S/ Charles Kennedy____
                                          Applicant

____/S/ Susan G. Brown, License #9876543____
Attorney

1400 Main Street
Minneapolis, MN 55455
Address/Phone (612) 773-3777

Subscribed and sworn to before me this
__8th__ day of __March__ , 19 _95_ .

____/S/ Georgeann Holtzer____
SIGNATURE OF NOTARY PUBLIC OR OTHER OFFICIAL

NOTARIAL STAMP OR SEAL (OR OTHER TITLE OR RANK)

Form 81   Certificate of Registrar—Release of Bond

Form No. 4566 MILLER-DAVIS CO., MPLS.   524.3-1007 #2   UPC

STATE OF MINNESOTA

COUNTY OF ___Hennepin___

In Re: Estate of

PROBATE COURT
COUNTY COURT-PROBATE DIVISION

Court File No. ___198541___

CERTIFICATE OF REGISTRAR THAT PERSONAL REPRESENTATIVE APPEARS TO HAVE FULLY ADMINISTERED THE ESTATE OF DECEDENT
RELEASE OF BOND

___Cheryl Ann Kennedy___
Deceased

The application of ___Charles Kennedy___ dated ___March 8___ , 19 __95__ , for the certificate from the Registrar that the personal representative appears to have fully administered the estate of the above named decedent having come before the undersigned Registrar of the above named Court, the undersigned Registrar having considered such application makes the following determinations:

1. That the said application is complete.

2. That the applicant has declared that the representations contained in the application are true, correct and complete to the best of his knowledge or information.

3. That the applicant appears from the application to be an interested person as defined by the laws of this State.

4. That, on the basis of the statements in the application and from the records on file herein, the application is proper.

Now, Therefore, it is CERTIFIED by the Registrar as follows:

1. That the application is hereby granted.

2. That ___Charles Kennedy___ , personal representative(s) of the estate of decedent appear(s) to have fully administered the estate of decedent.

3. That this Certificate evidences discharge of any lien on any property given to secure the obligation of the personal representative(s) in lieu of bond or any surety, but does not preclude action against the personal representative(s) or the surety.

Dated: ___March 10, 1995___

___/S/ Lorina B. Arneson___
Registrar

Form 82 U.S. Individual Income Tax Return (Form 1040)

Department of the Treasury—Internal Revenue Service

Form 1040

U.S. Individual Income Tax Return (O) **1994**

IRS Use Only—Do not write or staple in this space.

For the year Jan. 1–Dec. 31, 1994, or other tax year beginning , 1994, ending , 19   OMB No. 1545-0074

Label

(See instructions on page 12.)

Use the IRS label. Otherwise, please print or type.

L A B E L   H E R E

Your first name and initial   Last name

Your social security number

If a joint return, spouse's first name and initial   Last name

Spouse's social security number

Home address (number and street). If you have a P.O. box, see page 12.   Apt. no.

City, town or post office, state, and ZIP code. If you have a foreign address, see page 12.

For Privacy Act and Paperwork Reduction Act Notice, see page 4.

Presidential Election Campaign
(See page 12.)

Do you want $3 to go to this fund? . . . .

If a joint return, does your spouse want $3 to go to this fund? . . . .

Yes | No | Note: Checking "Yes" will not change your tax or reduce your refund.

Filing Status

(See page 12.)

Check only one box.

1 Single

2 Married filing joint return (even if only one had income)

3 Married filing separate return. Enter spouse's social security no. above and full name here. ▶ _____

4 Head of household (with qualifying person). (See page 13.) If the qualifying person is a child but not your dependent, enter this child's name here. ▶ _____

5 Qualifying widow(er) with dependent child (year spouse died ▶ 19   ). (See page 13.)

Exemptions

(See page 13.)

If more than six dependents, see page 14.

6a ☐ **Yourself.** If your parent (or someone else) can claim you as a dependent on his or her tax return, **do not** check box 6a. But be sure to check the box on line 33b on page 2 .

b ☐ **Spouse** . . . .

c **Dependents:**

(1) Name (first, initial, and last name)	(2) Check if under age 1	(3) If age 1 or older, dependent's social security number	(4) Dependent's relationship to you	(5) No. of months lived in your home in 1994

No. of boxes checked on 6a and 6b

No. of your children on 6c who:
● lived with you
● didn't live with you due to divorce or separation (see page 14)

Dependents on 6c not entered above

d If your child didn't live with you but is claimed as your dependent under a pre-1985 agreement, check here ▶ ☐

e Total number of exemptions claimed . . . .

Add numbers entered on lines above ▶

Income

Attach Copy B of your Forms W-2, W-2G, and 1099-R here.

If you did not get a W-2, see page 15.

Enclose, but do not attach, any payment with your return.

7	Wages, salaries, tips, etc. Attach Form(s) W-2	7
8a	**Taxable** interest income (see page 15). Attach Schedule B if over $400	8a
b	**Tax-exempt** interest (see page 16). DON'T include on line 8a 8b	
9	Dividend income. Attach Schedule B if over $400	9
10	Taxable refunds, credits, or offsets of state and local income taxes (see page 16) . .	10
11	Alimony received	11
12	Business income or (loss). Attach Schedule C or C-EZ	12
13	Capital gain or (loss). If required, attach Schedule D (see page 16)	13
14	Other gains or (losses). Attach Form 4797	14
15a	Total IRA distributions . 15a b Taxable amount (see page 17)	15b
16a	Total pensions and annuities 16a b Taxable amount (see page 17)	16b
17	Rental real estate, royalties, partnerships, S corporations, trusts, etc. Attach Schedule E	17
18	Farm income or (loss). Attach Schedule F	18
19	Unemployment compensation (see page 18)	19
20a	Social security benefits 20a b Taxable amount (see page 18)	20b
21	Other income. List type and amount—see page 18	21
22	Add the amounts in the far right column for lines 7 through 21. This is your **total income** ▶	22

Adjustments to Income

Caution: See instructions . . ▶

23a	Your IRA deduction (see page 19)	23a
b	Spouse's IRA deduction (see page 19)	23b
24	Moving expenses. Attach Form 3903 or 3903-F . . .	24
25	One-half of self-employment tax	25
26	Self-employed health insurance deduction (see page 21)	26
27	Keogh retirement plan and self-employed SEP deduction	27
28	Penalty on early withdrawal of savings	28
29	Alimony paid. Recipient's SSN ▶ _____	29
30	Add lines 23a through 29. These are your **total adjustments** . . . . ▶	30

Adjusted Gross Income

31 Subtract line 30 from line 22. This is your **adjusted gross income.** If less than $25,296 and a child lived with you (less than $9,000 if a child didn't live with you), see "Earned Income Credit" on page 27 ▶ | 31

Cat. No. 11320B   Form **1040** (1994)

Form 82 U.S. Individual Income Tax Return (Form 1040)—*continued*

Form 1040 (1994)   Page **2**

Tax Compu-tation (See page 23.)	32	Amount from line 31 (adjusted gross income)	32	
	33a	Check if: ☐ **You** were 65 or older, ☐ Blind; ☐ **Spouse** was 65 or older, ☐ Blind. Add the number of boxes checked above and enter the total here . . ▶ 33a ☐		
	b	If your parent (or someone else) can claim you as a dependent, check here . ▶ 33b ☐		
	c	If you are married filing separately and your spouse itemizes deductions or you are a dual-status alien, see page 23 and check here . . . . ▶ 33c ☐		
	34	Enter the larger of your: { **Itemized deductions** from Schedule A, line 29, **OR Standard deduction** shown below for your filing status. **But if you checked any box on line 33a or b,** go to page 23 to find your standard deduction. If you checked **box 33c,** your standard deduction is zero. • Single—$3,800 • Head of household—$5,600 • Married filing jointly or Qualifying widow(er)—$6,350 • Married filing separately—$3,175 }	34	
	35	Subtract line 34 from line 32	35	
	36	If line 32 is $83,850 or less, multiply $2,450 by the total number of exemptions claimed on line 6e. If line 32 is over $83,850, see the worksheet on page 24 for the amount to enter .	36	
If you want the IRS to figure your tax, see page 24.	37	**Taxable income.** Subtract line 36 from line 35. If line 36 is more than line 35, enter -0-	37	
	38	Tax. Check if from **a** ☐ Tax Table, **b** ☐ Tax Rate Schedules, **c** ☐ Capital Gain Tax Worksheet, or **d** ☐ Form 8615 (see page 24). Amount from Form(s) 8814 ▶ **e** ☐	38	
	39	Additional taxes. Check if from **a** ☐ Form 4970 **b** ☐ Form 4972	39	
	40	Add lines 38 and 39. . . . . ▶	40	
Credits (See page 24.)	41	Credit for child and dependent care expenses. Attach Form 2441	41	
	42	Credit for the elderly or the disabled. Attach Schedule R . .	42	
	43	Foreign tax credit. Attach Form 1116	43	
	44	Other credits (see page 25). Check if from **a** ☐ Form 3800 **b** ☐ Form 8396 **c** ☐ Form 8801 **d** ☐ Form (specify) _____	44	
	45	Add lines 41 through 44	45	
	46	Subtract line 45 from line 40. If line 45 is more than line 40, enter -0- . . . . . . ▶	46	
Other Taxes (See page 25.)	47	Self-employment tax. Attach Schedule SE	47	
	48	Alternative minimum tax. Attach Form 6251	48	
	49	Recapture taxes. Check if from **a** ☐ Form 4255 **b** ☐ Form 8611 **c** ☐ Form 8828	49	
	50	Social security and Medicare tax on tip income not reported to employer. Attach Form 4137	50	
	51	Tax on qualified retirement plans, including IRAs. If required, attach Form 5329 . .	51	
	52	Advance earned income credit payments from Form W-2	52	
	53	Add lines 46 through 52. This is your **total tax** . . . . ▶	53	
Payments Attach Forms W-2, W-2G, and 1099-R on the front.	54	Federal income tax withheld. If any is from Form(s) 1099, check ▶ ☐	54	
	55	1994 estimated tax payments and amount applied from 1993 return .	55	
	56	**Earned income credit.** If required, attach Schedule EIC (see page 27). Nontaxable earned income: amount ▶ [ ] and type ▶ _____	56	
	57	Amount paid with Form 4868 (extension request)	57	
	58	Excess social security and RRTA tax withheld (see page 32) . .	58	
	59	Other payments. Check if from **a** ☐ Form 2439 **b** ☐ Form 4136	59	
	60	Add lines 54 through 59. These are your **total payments** . . . . ▶	60	
Refund or Amount You Owe	61	If line 60 is more than line 53, subtract line 53 from line 60. This is the amount you **OVERPAID.** ▶	61	
	62	Amount of line 61 you want **REFUNDED TO YOU** . . . . . . ▶	62	
	63	Amount of line 61 you want APPLIED TO YOUR 1995 ESTIMATED TAX ▶	63	
	64	If line 53 is more than line 60, subtract line 60 from line 53. This is the **AMOUNT YOU OWE.** For details on how to pay, including what to write on your payment, see page 32.	64	
	65	Estimated tax penalty (see page 33). Also include on line 64	65	

Sign Here Keep a copy of this return for your records.	Under penalties of perjury, I declare that I have examined this return and accompanying schedules and statements, and to the best of my knowledge and belief, they are true, correct, and complete. Declaration of preparer (other than taxpayer) is based on all information of which preparer has any knowledge.

Your signature ▶	Date	Your occupation
Spouse's signature. If a joint return, BOTH must sign.	Date	Spouse's occupation

Paid Preparer's Use Only	Preparer's signature ▶	Date	Check if self-employed ☐	Preparer's social security no.
	Firm's name (or yours if self-employed) and address ▶		E.I. No.	
			ZIP code	

✿ Printed on recycled paper   ☆U.S. Government Printing Office: 1994--375-190

Form 83 Statement of Person Claiming Refund Due a Deceased Taxpayer (Form 1310)

Form **1310** (Rev. June 1992) Department of the Treasury Internal Revenue Service	**Statement of Person Claiming Refund Due a Deceased Taxpayer** ▶ See instructions below.	OMB No. 1545-0073 Expires 5-31-95 Attachment Sequence No. **87**

Tax year decedent was due a refund:

Calendar year _____ , or other tax year beginning _____ , 19 _____ , and ending _____ , 19 _____

Please type or print	Name of decedent		Date of death	Decedent's social security number
	Name of person claiming refund			
	Home address (number and street). If you have a P.O. box, see instructions			Apt. no.
	City, town or post office, state, and ZIP code. If you have a foreign address, see instructions			

Part I Check the box that applies to you. Check only one box. **Be sure to complete Part III below.**

A ☐ Surviving spouse, requesting reissuance of a refund check (see instructions).

B ☐ Court-appointed or certified personal representative. You may have to attach a court certificate showing your appointment (see instructions).

C ☐ Person, **other** than A or B, claiming refund for the decedent's estate (see instructions). Complete Part II and attach a copy of the death certificate or proof of death.

Part II Complete this part only if you checked the box on line C above.

		Yes	No
1	Did the decedent leave a will?		
2a	Has a court appointed a personal representative for the estate of the decedent?		
b	If you answered "No" to 2a, will one be appointed?		
	If you answered "Yes" to 2a or 2b, the personal representative must file for the refund.		
3	As the person claiming the refund for the decedent's estate, will you pay out the refund according to the laws of the state where the decedent was a legal resident?		
	If you answered "No" to 3, a refund cannot be made until you submit a court certificate showing your appointment as personal representative or other evidence that you are entitled under state law to receive the refund.		

Part III Signature and verification. All filers must complete this part.

I request a refund of taxes overpaid by or on behalf of the decedent. Under penalties of perjury, I declare that I have examined this claim, and to the best of my knowledge and belief, it is true, correct, and complete.

Signature of person claiming refund ▶ _____ Date ▶ _____

General Instructions

Paperwork Reduction Act Notice

We ask for the information on this form to carry out the Internal Revenue laws of the United States. You are required to give us the information. We need it to ensure that you are complying with these laws and to allow us to figure and collect the right amount of tax.

The time needed to complete and file this form will vary depending on individual circumstances. The estimated average time is:

Recordkeeping	7 min.
Learning about the law or the form	3 min.
Preparing the form	14 min.
Copying, assembling, and sending the form to the IRS	17 min.

If you have comments concerning the accuracy of these time estimates or suggestions for making this form more simple, we would be happy to hear from you. You can write to both the **Internal Revenue Service,** Washington, DC

20224, Attention: IRS Reports Clearance Officer, T:FP; and the **Office of Management and Budget,** Paperwork Reduction Project (1545-0073), Washington, DC 20503. **DO NOT** send this form to either of these offices.

Purpose of Form

Use Form 1310 to claim a refund on behalf of a deceased taxpayer.

Who Must File

If you are claiming a refund on behalf of a deceased taxpayer, you must file Form 1310 unless **either** of the following applies:

● You are a surviving spouse filing an original joint return with the decedent, OR

● You are a personal representative (see back of form) filing an original Form 1040, Form 1040A, Form 1040EZ, or Form 1040NR for the decedent and a court certificate showing your appointment is attached to the return.

Example. Assume Mr. Green died on January 4 before filing his tax return. On April 3 of the same year, you were appointed by the court as the personal representative for Mr. Green's estate and you file Form 1040 for Mr. Green.

Cat. No. 11566B   Form **1310** (Rev. 6-92)

Form 84 Schedule A—Itemized Deductions (Form 1040)

SCHEDULES A&B	**Schedule A—Itemized Deductions**	OMB No. 1545-0074
(Form 1040)	(Schedule B is on back)	19**94**
Department of the Treasury Internal Revenue Service (O)	▶ **Attach to Form 1040.** ▶ **See Instructions for Schedules A and B (Form 1040).**	Attachment Sequence No. **07**

Name(s) shown on Form 1040 | Your social security number

Medical and Dental Expenses		Caution: *Do not include expenses reimbursed or paid by others.*		
	1	Medical and dental expenses (see page A-1)	1	
	2	Enter amount from Form 1040, line 32 .	2		
	3	Multiply line 2 above by 7.5% (.075)	3	
	4	Subtract line 3 from line 1. If line 3 is more than line 1, enter -0-		4
Taxes You Paid (See page A-1.)	5	State and local income taxes	5	
	6	Real estate taxes (see page A-2)	6	
	7	Personal property taxes	7	
	8	Other taxes. List type and amount ▶ _____		
		_____	8	
	9	Add lines 5 through 8		9
Interest You Paid (See page A-2.)	10	Home mortgage interest and points reported to you on Form 1098	10	
	11	Home mortgage interest not reported to you on Form 1098. If paid to the person from whom you bought the home, see page A-3 and show that person's name, identifying no., and address ▶		
Note: Personal interest is not deductible.		_____		
		_____	11	
	12	Points not reported to you on Form 1098. See page A-3 for special rules	12	
	13	Investment interest. If required, attach Form 4952. (See page A-3.)	13	
	14	Add lines 10 through 13		14
Gifts to Charity	15	Gifts by cash or check. If any gift of $250 or more, see page A-3	15	
If you made a gift and got a benefit for it, see page A-3.	16	Other than by cash or check. If any gift of $250 or more, see page A-3. If over $500, you **MUST** attach Form 8283	16	
	17	Carryover from prior year	17	
	18	Add lines 15 through 17		18
Casualty and Theft Losses	19	Casualty or theft loss(es). Attach Form 4684. (See page A-4.)		19
Job Expenses and Most Other Miscellaneous Deductions	20	Unreimbursed employee expenses—job travel, union dues, job education, etc. If required, you **MUST** attach Form 2106 or 2106-EZ. (See page A-5.) ▶ _____		
		_____	20	
	21	Tax preparation fees	21	
(See page A-5 for expenses to deduct here.)	22	Other expenses—investment, safe deposit box, etc. List type and amount ▶ _____		
		_____	22	
	23	Add lines 20 through 22	23	
	24	Enter amount from Form 1040, line 32 .	24		
	25	Multiply line 24 above by 2% (.02)	25	
	26	Subtract line 25 from line 23. If line 25 is more than line 23, enter -0-		26
Other Miscellaneous Deductions	27	Moving expenses incurred before 1994. Attach Form 3903 or 3903-F. (See page A-5.) .	27	
	28	Other—from list on page A-5. List type and amount ▶ _____		28
Total Itemized Deductions	29	Is Form 1040, line 32, over $111,800 (over $55,900 if married filing separately)?		
		NO. Your deduction is not limited. Add the amounts in the far right column for lines 4 through 28. Also, enter on Form 1040, line 34, the **larger** of this amount or your standard deduction. ▶	29	
		YES. Your deduction may be limited. See page A-5 for the amount to enter.		

For Paperwork Reduction Act Notice, see Form 1040 instructions. Cat. No. 11330X Schedule A (Form 1040) 1994

Form 85 Application for Automatic Extension of Time to File U.S. Individual Income Tax Return (Form 4868)

Form **4868** Department of the Treasury Internal Revenue Service	**Application for Automatic Extension of Time To File U.S. Individual Income Tax Return**	OMB No. 1545-0188 1994

Please Type or Print	Your first name and initial	Last name	Your social security number
	If a joint return, spouse's first name and initial	Last name	Spouse's social security number
	Home address (number, street, and apt. no. or rural route). If you have a P.O. box, see the instructions.		
	City, town or post office, state, and ZIP code		

I request an automatic 4-month extension of time to August 15, 1995, to file Form 1040EZ, Form 1040A, or Form 1040 for the calendar year 1994 or to _____ , 19 ___ , for the fiscal tax year ending _____ , 19 ___ .

Part I Individual Income Tax—You must complete this part.

1 **Total tax liability for 1994.** This is the amount you expect to enter on Form 1040EZ, line 9; Form 1040A, line 27; or Form 1040, line 53. If you expect this amount to be zero, enter -0-. . . . | **1**

  Caution: You MUST enter an amount on line 1 or your extension will be denied. You can estimate this amount, but be as exact as you can with the information you have. If we later find that your estimate was not reasonable, the extension will be null and void.

2 **Total payments for 1994.** This is the amount you expect to enter on Form 1040EZ, line 8; Form 1040A, line 28d; or Form 1040, line 60 (excluding line 57) . . . . | **2**

3 **BALANCE DUE.** Subtract line 2 from line 1. If line 2 is more than line 1, enter -0-. If you are making a payment, you must use the Form 4868-V at the bottom of page 3. For details on how to pay, including what to write on your payment, see the instructions . . . . ▶ | **3**

Part II Gift or Generation-Skipping Transfer (GST) Tax—Complete this part if you expect to owe either tax.

Caution: Do not include income tax on lines 5a and 5b. See the instructions.

4 If you or your spouse plan to file a gift tax return (Form 709 or 709-A) for 1994, generally due by April 17, 1995, see the instructions and check here . . . } Yourself ▶ ☐ Spouse ▶ ☐

5a Enter the amount of gift or GST tax **you** are paying with this form. Also, you must use the Form 4868-V at the bottom of page 3 . . . . | **5a**

  b Enter the amount of gift or GST tax **your spouse** is paying with this form. Also, you must use the Form 4868-V at the bottom of page 3 . . . . | **5b**

Signature and Verification

Under penalties of perjury, I declare that I have examined this form, including accompanying schedules and statements, and to the best of my knowledge and belief, it is true, correct, and complete; and, if prepared by someone other than the taxpayer, that I am authorized to prepare this form.

▶ _____ Your signature   Date   ▶ _____ Spouse's signature, if filing jointly   Date

▶ _____ Preparer's signature (other than taxpayer)   Date

If you want correspondence regarding this extension to be sent to you at an address other than that shown above or to an agent acting for you, please enter the name of the agent and/or the address where it should be sent.

Please Type or Print	Name
	Number and street (include suite, room, or apt. no.) or P.O. box number if mail is not delivered to street address
	City, town or post office, state, and ZIP code

For Paperwork Reduction Act Notice, see page 3.   Cat. No. 13141W   Form **4868** (1994)

Form 86 State (Minnesota as Example) Individual Income Tax Return

MINNESOTA Department of Revenue

Individual Income Tax 1994

M-1

Your first name and initial	Last name	Social Security number

State Elections Campaign Fund
If you want $5 to go to help candidates for state offices pay campaign expenses, you may each check one box. This will not increase your tax or reduce your refund.

Spouse's first name and initial	Last name	Social Security number

Present home address (street, apartment number, route)

City or town	State	Zip code

	Democratic Farmer-Labor	Independent Republican	General Campaign Fund
You:	☐	☐	☐
Spouse:	☐	☐	☐

Check your 1994 federal filing status:
☐ Single ☐ Married filing joint ☐ Married filing separate ☐ Head of household ☐ Qualifying widow(er)

1 Federal taxable income *(from line 37 of your federal Form 1040 or line 22 of Form 1040A or line 5 of Form 1040EZ)* .... **1** _____ .

2 State income tax addition. If you itemized deductions on federal Form 1040, fill out the worksheet on page 8 of the Form M-1 instructions to determine the amount to fill in here .... **2** _____ .

3 Other additions to your income *(see instructions on page 9)* .... **3** _____ .

4 Add lines 1, 2, and 3 .... **4** _____ .

5 State income tax refund *(from line 10 of your federal Form 1040)* .... **5** _____ .

6 Other subtractions from your income *(see instructions on page 9)* ..... **6** _____ .

7 Add lines 5 and 6 .... **7** _____ .

8 Subtract line 7 from line 4. This is your Minnesota taxable income .... **8** _____ .

9 Tax: from the table on pages 15 through 19 of the instructions, or from Schedule *(check boxes)*: M-1MT ☐, M-1NR ☐, M-1LS ☐, M-1CR ☐ .... **9** _____ .

10 If you wish to donate to the Nongame Wildlife Fund, fill in the amount here. This will reduce your refund or increase your tax .... **10** _____ .

11 Add lines 9 and 10 .... **11** _____ .

12 Minnesota income tax withheld *(from your 1994 W-2 forms)* .... **12** _____ .

13 Minnesota estimated tax and Form M-13 payments you made for 1994, if any .... **13** _____ .

14 Child and dependent care credit *(attach Schedule M-1CD)* .... **14** _____ .

15 Minnesota working family credit *(see instructions on page 13)* ...... **15** _____ .

16 Add lines 12, 13, 14, and 15 .... **16** _____ .

17 If line 16 is more than line 11, subtract line 11 from line 16 and fill in the amount of your **REFUND** .... **17** _____ .

18 If line 11 is more than line 16, subtract line 16 from line 11 and fill in the **AMOUNT YOU OWE** .... Make check payable to: MN Department of Revenue **18** _____ .

19 If you are paying estimated tax for 1995, fill in the amount from line 17 you want applied to it, if any .... **19** _____ .

20 If you underpaid your estimated tax for 1994, fill in your penalty, if any *(from line 16 of Schedule M-15)* .... **20** _____ .

I declare that this form is correct and complete to the best of my knowledge and belief. I admit I owe the tax listed above, and confess judgment to the commissioner for the tax shown on the return to the extent not timely paid.

Your signature	Spouse's signature	Date	Daytime phone ( )
Paid preparer's signature **ONLY**	MN tax ID or Social Security number	Date	Daytime phone ( )

Stock No. 1094010

You must attach a copy of your 1994 federal income tax return and schedules
Mail this form to: Minnesota Individual Income Tax, St. Paul, MN 55145-0010

(Side margin text:) Use label or print or type · Figure your Minnesota income · Your tax and credits · Refund or amount due · Sign your return · Please staple your W-2 forms here. Place check or money order here but do not staple.

Form 87 Claim for a Refund Due a Deceased Taxpayer (Minnesota)

MINNESOTA Department of Revenue

Claim for a Refund Due a Deceased Taxpayer   M-23

You must attach a copy of the decedent's death certificate to this form.

Print or type

| Name of decedent | Social Security number |

| Name of person claiming refund | Social Security number |

| Claimant's address (street, apartment, number, route) | City or town   State   Zip code |

| Day, month, and year of decedent's death | Year for which refund is due |

Property tax refund

If you are claiming the decedent's Minnesota property tax refund:

Check the one box that applies to you, skip the rest of this form, and sign at the bottom

☐ I am the decedent's surviving spouse

☐ I am the decedent's dependent *(Read "Who is eligible to claim the property tax refund?" in the instructions on the back to determine if you are a dependent.)*

Income tax refund

If you are claiming the decedent's Minnesota income tax refund:

If a personal representative has been appointed by the court to represent the decedent's estate, only the personal representative is entitled to claim the decedent's refund. If you have been appointed as personal representative, you do NOT have to file this form. Instead, when you file the decedent's final income tax form, attach a copy of the court document showing your appointment as personal representative.

If no personal representative has been appointed, you can obtain the decedent's refund if you are the decedent's surviving spouse. You can obtain the decedent's refund without filing this form if you file a joint income tax form for the decedent. If you file a separate final income tax form for the decedent, you must file this form to obtain the decedent's refund.

If no personal representative has been appointed, there is no surviving spouse, and the value of the estate is less than $10,000, you are entitled to claim the decedent's refund only if you are the first living person on the list below. If there is more than one person in your category below, you must have all the other persons in your category sign the waiver on the back of this form to obtain the refund.

Check the one box that applies to you:

☐ I am the decedent's surviving spouse and I am filing a separate final income tax return for the decedent

☐ I am the decedent's child

☐ I am a grandchild of the decedent

☐ I am the decedent's mother or father

☐ I am the decedent's brother or sister

☐ I am the child of the decedent's brother or sister

Sign here

I request that the refund of the decedent named above be made to me.
I declare the information I have filled in on this form is correct and complete to the best of my knowledge and belief.

| Signature of person claiming refund | Date | Daytime phone number |
| | | ( ) |

Mail this form to: Minnesota Decedent Refund, Minnesota Department of Revenue, St. Paul MN 55146-4431

Be sure to attach a copy of the decedent's death certificate

Stock No. 1000230
(Rev. 11/93)

Printed on recycled paper with 10% post-consumer waste using soy-based ink.

Form 88 Payment of Income Tax (if you are filing your return later than the due date—Minnesota)

MINNESOTA Department of Revenue   **1994**

Payment of Income Tax

Use this form to pay your 1994 income tax if you are filing
your return later than April 17, 1995.

Your Social Security number		Spouse's Social Security number
Your first name	Spouse's first name	Last name
Address (street, apartment, route)		
City or town	State	Zip code

Amount of payment

.00

Stock No.
1094130

Make your check out to: **Minnesota Department of Revenue**
Mail form and check to: Minnesota Individual Income Tax, St. Paul, MN 55145-0025

Due April 17, 1995

006 999999999999993 999999999999993 1294

Instructions for 1994 Form M-13

There are no extensions to pay your individual income
tax return. All of your tax must be paid by April 17,
1995, even if you have an extension to file your federal
returns. If you fail to pay by April 17, you will be
charged a penalty on the unpaid balance of 3 percent
per month or fraction of a month (up to a maximum of
24 percent). You will also have to pay interest of 7
percent per year on the unpaid tax and penalties.

Fill in the information required on Form M-13:

- your Social Security number. Please check your
  Social Security number to be sure it is written
  correctly. If your Social Security number is not
  correct, we cannot properly credit your account.

- you must list your spouse's Social Security number
  if you will be filing a joint return. If you will be
  filing a separate return, list only your Social Security
  number.

- estimate the amount of tax you owe and fill in the
  amount.

Attach a check or money order to this form and send it to:

  Minnesota Individual Income Tax
  St. Paul, MN 55145-0025

This payment will be deposited as a payment in your
1994 estimated tax account. When you do file your
Minnesota income tax return, you must use Form M-1.
Be sure to fill in the amount of this payment on line 13
of Form M-1.

Form 89 Application for Employer Identification Number (Form SS-4)

Form **SS-4** (Rev. December 1993) Department of the Treasury Internal Revenue Service	**Application for Employer Identification Number** (For use by employers, corporations, partnerships, trusts, estates, churches, government agencies, certain individuals, and others. See instructions.)	EIN OMB No. 1545-0003 Expires 12-31-96

Please type or print clearly.

1 Name of applicant (Legal name) (See instructions.)
Estate of Jane M. Doe

2 Trade name of business, if different from name in line 1
N/A

3 Executor, trustee, "care of" name
John C. Doe, Personal Representative

4a Mailing address (street address) (room, apt., or suite no.)
1005 Elm Street

5a Business address, if different from address in lines 4a and 4b

4b City, state, and ZIP code
St. Paul, MN 55102

5b City, state, and ZIP code

6 County and state where principal business is located
Ramsey County, Minnesota

7 Name of principal officer, general partner, grantor, owner, or trustor—SSN required (See instructions.) ▶
N/A

8a Type of entity (Check only one box.) (See instructions.)
☐ Sole Proprietor (SSN) _____
☐ REMIC   ☐ Personal service corp.
☐ State/local government   ☐ National guard
☐ Other nonprofit organization (specify) _____
☐ Other (specify) ▶ _____
☒ Estate (SSN of decedent) 321 54 9876
☐ Plan administrator-SSN _____
☐ Other corporation (specify) _____
☐ Federal government/military   ☐ Church or church controlled organization
(enter GEN if applicable) _____
☐ Trust
☐ Partnership
☐ Farmers' cooperative

8b If a corporation, name the state or foreign country (if applicable) where incorporated ▶
State N/A
Foreign country N/A

9 Reason for applying (Check only one box.)
☐ Started new business (specify) ▶ _____
☐ Hired employees
☐ Created a pension plan (specify type) ▶ _____
☐ Banking purpose (specify) ▶
☐ Changed type of organization (specify) ▶ _____
☐ Purchased going business
☐ Created a trust (specify) ▶ _____
☒ Other (specify) ▶ Fiduciary-Death

10 Date business started or acquired (Mo., day, year) (See instructions.)
September 20, 1994

11 Enter closing month of accounting year. (See instructions.)
September

12 First date wages or annuities were paid or will be paid (Mo., day, year). **Note:** If applicant is a withholding agent, enter date income will first be paid to nonresident alien. (Mo., day, year) . . . . ▶ N/A

13 Enter highest number of employees expected in the next 12 months. **Note:** If the applicant does not expect to have any employees during the period, enter "0." . . . . ▶

Nonagricultural	Agricultural	Household
N/A	N/A	N/A

14 Principal activity (See instructions.) ▶ N/A

15 Is the principal business activity manufacturing? . . . . ☐ Yes ☒ No
If "Yes," principal product and raw material used ▶

16 To whom are most of the products or services sold? Please check the appropriate box. ☐ Business (wholesale)
☐ Public (retail)   ☐ Other (specify) ▶   ☒ N/A

17a Has the applicant ever applied for an identification number for this or any other business? . . . . ☐ Yes ☒ No
Note: If "Yes," please complete lines 17b and 17c.

17b If you checked the "Yes" box in line 17a, give applicant's legal name and trade name, if different than name shown on prior application.
Legal name ▶ N/A   Trade name ▶ N/A

17c Enter approximate date, city, and state where the application was filed and the previous employer identification number if known.
Approximate date when filed (Mo., day, year) | City and state where filed | Previous EIN
N/A   N/A   N/A

Under penalties of perjury, I declare that I have examined this application, and to the best of my knowledge and belief, it is true, correct, and complete.

Business telephone number (include area code)

Name and title (Please type or print clearly.) ▶ John C. Doe, Personal Representative

(612) 345-5000

Signature ▶ /S/ John C. Doe   Date ▶ 10/31/94

Note: *Do not write below this line.*   For official use only.

Please leave blank ▶	Geo.	Ind.	Class	Size	Reason for applying

For Paperwork Reduction Act Notice, see attached instructions.   Cat. No. 16055N   Form **SS-4** (Rev. 12-93)

Form 90 Notice Concerning Fiduciary Relationship (Form 56)

Form **56**
(Rev. July 1994)

Department of the Treasury
Internal Revenue Service

Notice Concerning Fiduciary Relationship

(Internal Revenue Code sections 6036 and 6903)

OMB No. 1545-0013

Part I   Identification

Name of person for whom you are acting (as shown on the tax return)	Identifying number	Decedent's social security no.
Estate of Jane M. Doe	41-6246975	

Address of person for whom you are acting (number, street, and room or suite no.)
1005 Elm Street

City or town, state, and ZIP code (If a foreign address, enter city, province or state, postal code, and country.)
St. Paul, MN 55102

Fiduciary's name
John C. Doe

Address of fiduciary (number, street, and room or suite no.)
1005 Elm Street

City or town, state, and ZIP code	Telephone number (optional)
St. Paul, MN 55102	(612) 345-5000

Part II   Authority

1   Authority for fiduciary relationship. Check applicable box:

a(1) ☒ Will and codicils or court order appointing fiduciary. Attach certified copy . . **(2)** Date of death ....09/20/94......

b(1) ☐ Court order appointing fiduciary. Attach certified copy . . . . **(2)** Date (see instructions) ....

c ☐ Valid trust instrument and amendments. Attach copy

d ☐ Other. Describe ▶ ....

Part III   Tax Notices

Send to the fiduciary listed in Part I all notices and other written communications involving the following tax matters:

2   Type of tax (estate, gift, generation-skipping transfer, income, excise, etc.) ▶ Estate, gift, income...............

3   Federal tax form number (706, 1040, 1041, 1120, etc.) ▶ ...706, 709, 1041.................

4   Year(s) or period(s) (if estate tax, date of death) ▶ September 20, 1994

Part IV   Revocation or Termination of Notice

Section A—Total Revocation or Termination

5   Check this box if you are revoking or terminating all prior notices concerning fiduciary relationships on file with the Internal Revenue Service for the same tax matters and years or periods covered by this notice concerning fiduciary relationship . ▶ ☐

Reason for termination of fiduciary relationship. Check applicable box:

a ☐ Court order revoking fiduciary authority. Attach certified copy.

b ☐ Certificate of dissolution or termination of a business entity. Attach copy.

c ☐ Other. Describe ▶

Section B—Partial Revocation

6a   Check this box if you are revoking earlier notices concerning fiduciary relationships on file with the Internal Revenue Service for the same tax matters and years or periods covered by this notice concerning fiduciary relationship · · · · · · · · · ▶ ☐

b   Specify to whom granted, date, and address, including ZIP code, or refer to attached copies of earlier notices and authorizations
▶ ....

Section C—Substitute Fiduciary

7   Check this box if a new fiduciary or fiduciaries have been or will be substituted for the revoking or terminating fiduciary(ies) and specify the name(s) and address(es), including ZIP code(s), of the new fiduciary(ies) · · · · · · · · · · · · · · ▶ ☐

Part V   Court and Administrative Proceedings

Name of court (if other than a court proceeding, identify the type of proceeding and name of agency)	Date proceeding initiated
Ramsey County Probate Court	September 26, 1994

Address of court	Docket number of proceeding
65 West Kellogg Blvd.	12

City or town, state, and ZIP code	Date	Time	a.m.	Place of other proceedings
St. Paul, MN 55102	10/31/94	10:00	~~p.m.~~	

I certify that I have the authority to execute this notice concerning fiduciary relationship on behalf of the taxpayer.

Please Sign Here

▶ /S/ John C. Doe

Fiduciary's signature

Personal Representative   11/30/94

Title, if applicable   Date

▶

Fiduciary's signature   Title, if applicable   Date

For Paperwork Reduction Act and Privacy Act Notice, see back page.   Cat. No. 16375I   Form **56** (Rev. 7-94)

Form 91 U.S. (Fiduciary) Income Tax Return for Estates and Trusts (Form 1041)

Form 1041

Department of the Treasury—Internal Revenue Service

U.S. Income Tax Return for Estates and Trusts **1994**

For the calendar year 1994 or fiscal year beginning October 1 , 1994, and ending September 30 , 1995 | OMB No. 1545-0092

A Type of entity:	Name of estate or trust (if a grantor type trust, see page 7 of the instructions)	C Employer identification number
[X] Decedent's estate	Estate of Jane M. Doe	41 : 6246975
[ ] Simple trust		**D** Date entity created
[ ] Complex trust		09/20/94
[ ] Grantor type trust	Name and title of fiduciary	**E** Nonexempt charitable and split-interest trusts, check applicable boxes (see page 8 of the instructions):
[ ] Bankruptcy estate–Ch. 7	John C. Doe, Personal Representative	
[ ] Bankruptcy estate–Ch. 11	Number, street, and room or suite no. (If a P.O. box, see instructions.)	
[ ] Pooled income fund	1005 Elm Street	[ ] Described in section 4947(a)(1)
B Number of Schedules K-1 attached (see instructions) . ▶ 0	City or town, state, and ZIP code	[ ] Not a private foundation
	St. Paul, MN 55102	[ ] Described in section 4947(a)(2)

F Check applicable boxes:	[ ] Initial return [X] Final return [ ] Amended return	G Pooled mortgage account (see instructions):
	[ ] Change in fiduciary's name [ ] Change in fiduciary's address	[ ] Bought [ ] Sold Date:

Income

1	Interest income	1	23,230
2	Dividends	2	2,460
3	Business income or (loss) (attach Schedule C or C-EZ (Form 1040))	3	
4	Capital gain or (loss) (attach Schedule D (Form 1041))	4	
5	Rents, royalties, partnerships, other estates and trusts, etc. (attach Schedule E (Form 1040))	5	1,100
6	Farm income or (loss) (attach Schedule F (Form 1040))	6	
7	Ordinary gain or (loss) (attach Form 4797)	7	
8	Other income. List type and amount	8	
9	**Total income.** Combine lines 1 through 8 . . . . ▶	9	26,790

Deductions

10	Interest. Check if Form 4952 is attached ▶ [ ]	10	10,250
11	Taxes	11	3,900
12	Fiduciary fees	12	10,000
13	Charitable deduction (from Schedule A, line 7)	13	
14	Attorney, accountant, and return preparer fees	14	2,040
15a	Other deductions NOT subject to the 2% floor (attach schedule)	15a	
b	Allowable miscellaneous itemized deductions subject to the 2% floor. . . .	15b	
16	**Total.** Add lines 10 through 15b	16	26,190
17	Adjusted total income or (loss). Subtract line 16 from line 9. Enter here and on Schedule B, line 1 ▶	17	600
18	Income distribution deduction (from Schedule B, line 17) (attach Schedules K-1 (Form 1041))	18	
19	Estate tax deduction (including certain generation-skipping taxes) (attach computation).	19	
20	Exemption	20	600
21	**Total deductions.** Add lines 18 through 20 . . . . ▶	21	600

Tax and Payments

22	Taxable income. Subtract line 21 from line 17. If a loss, see instructions	22	0
23	**Total tax** (from Schedule G, line 7)	23	0
24	**Payments: a** 1994 estimated tax payments and amount applied from 1993 return . . . ▶	24a	
b	Estimated tax payments allocated to beneficiaries (from Form 1041-T)	24b	
c	Subtract line 24b from line 24a	24c	
d	Tax paid with extension of time to file: [ ] Form 2758 [ ] Form 8736 [ ] Form 8800	24d	
e	Federal income tax withheld. If any is from Form(s) 1099, check ▶ [ ]	24e	
	Other payments: **f** Form 2439 .... ; **g** Form 4136 .... ; Total ▶	24h	
25	**Total payments.** Add lines 24c through 24e, and 24h . . . . ▶	25	
26	Estimated tax penalty (see instructions)	26	
27	**Tax due.** If line 25 is smaller than the total of lines 23 and 26, enter amount owed . . .	27	0
28	**Overpayment.** If line 25 is larger than the total of lines 23 and 26, enter amount overpaid	28	
29	Amount of line 28 to be: **a Credited to 1995 estimated tax** ▶ ; **b Refunded** ▶	29	

Please Sign Here

Under penalties of perjury, I declare that I have examined this return, including accompanying schedules and statements, and to the best of my knowledge and belief, it is true, correct, and complete. Declaration of preparer (other than fiduciary) is based on all information of which preparer has any knowledge.

▶ /S/ John C. Doe | 10/02/95 | ▶
Signature of fiduciary or officer representing fiduciary | Date | EIN of fiduciary if a financial institution (see page 3 of the instructions)

Paid Preparer's Use Only

Preparer's signature ▶	Date	Check if self-employed ▶ [ ]	Preparer's social security no.
Firm's name (or yours if self-employed) and address ▶		E.I. No. ▶	
		ZIP code ▶	

For Paperwork Reduction Act Notice, see page 1 of the separate instructions. Cat. No. 11370H Form **1041** (1994)

Form 91   U.S. (Fiduciary) Income Tax Return for Estates and Trusts (Form 1041)—*continued*

Form 1041 (1994)   Page **2**

Schedule A	**Charitable Deduction.** Do not complete for a simple trust or a pooled income fund.			
1	Amounts paid for charitable purposes from gross income	1		
2	Amounts permanently set aside for charitable purposes from gross income	2		
3	Add lines 1 and 2	3		
4	Tax-exempt income allocable to charitable contributions (see instructions).	4		
5	Subtract line 4 from line 3	5		
6	Capital gains for the tax year allocated to corpus and paid or permanently set aside for charitable purposes.	6		
7	**Charitable deduction.** Add lines 5 and 6. Enter here and on page 1, line 13.	7		

Schedule B	**Income Distribution Deduction** (see instructions)			
1	Adjusted total income (from page 1, line 17) (see instructions).	1		
2	Adjusted tax-exempt interest.	2		
3	Total net gain from Schedule D (Form 1041), line 17, column (a) (see instructions)	3		
4	Enter amount from Schedule A, line 6.	4		
5	Long-term capital gain for the tax year included on Schedule A, line 3.	5		
6	Short-term capital gain for the tax year included on Schedule A, line 3.	6		
7	If the amount on page 1, line 4, is a capital loss, enter here as a positive figure.	7		
8	If the amount on page 1, line 4, is a capital gain, enter here as a negative figure	8		
9	**Distributable net income (DNI).** Combine lines 1 through 8	9		
10	If a complex trust, enter accounting income for the tax year as determined under the governing instrument and applicable local law 10			
11	Income required to be distributed currently	11		
12	Other amounts paid, credited, or otherwise required to be distributed	12		
13	Total distributions. Add lines 11 and 12. If greater than line 10, see instructions	13		
14	Enter the amount of tax-exempt income included on line 13	14		
15	Tentative income distribution deduction. Subtract line 14 from line 13	15		
16	Tentative income distribution deduction. Subtract line 2 from line 9	16		
17	**Income distribution deduction.** Enter the smaller of line 15 or line 16 here and on page 1, line 18	17		

Schedule G	**Tax Computation** (see instructions)			
1	**Tax: a** ☐ Tax rate schedule or ☐ Schedule D (Form 1041)	1a		
	b Other taxes	1b		
	c Total. Add lines 1a and 1b. ▶	1c		
2a	Foreign tax credit (attach Form 1116)	2a		
b	Check: ☐ Nonconventional source fuel credit ☐ Form 8834	2b		
c	General business credit. Enter here and check which forms are attached: ☐ Form 3800 or ☐ Forms (specify) ▶	2c		
d	Credit for prior year minimum tax (attach Form 8801)	2d		
3	**Total credits.** Add lines 2a through 2d ▶	3		
4	Subtract line 3 from line 1c	4		
5	Recapture taxes. Check if from: ☐ Form 4255 ☐ Form 8611.	5		
6	Alternative minimum tax (from Schedule H, line 39)	6		
7	**Total tax.** Add lines 4 through 6. Enter here and on page 1, line 23 ▶	7		

Other Information (see instructions)

		Yes	No
1	Did the estate or trust receive tax-exempt income? If "Yes," attach a computation of the allocation of expenses. Enter the amount of tax-exempt interest income and exempt-interest dividends ▶ $		
2	Did the estate or trust receive all or any part of the earnings (salary, wages, and other compensation) of any individual by reason of a contract assignment or similar arrangement?		
3	At any time during calendar year 1994, did the estate or trust have an interest in or a signature or other authority over a bank, securities, or other financial account in a foreign country? See the instructions for exceptions and filing requirements for Form TD F 90-22.1. If "Yes," enter the name of the foreign country ▶		
4	Was the estate or trust the grantor of, or transferor to, a foreign trust which existed during the current tax year, whether or not the estate or trust has any beneficial interest in it? If "Yes," you may have to file Form 3520, 3520-A, or 926.		
5	Did the estate or trust receive, or pay, any seller-financed mortgage interest? If "Yes," see instructions for required attachment		
6	If this is a complex trust making the section 663(b) election, check here ▶ ☐		
7	To make a section 643(e)(3) election, attach Schedule D (Form 1041), and check here ▶ ☐		
8	If the decedent's estate has been open for more than 2 years, check here ▶ ☐		

Form 92 Application for Extension of Time to File Fiduciary and Certain Other Returns (Form 2758)

Form **2758** (Rev. July 1993) Department of the Treasury Internal Revenue Service	**Application for Extension of Time To File** **Certain Excise, Income, Information, and Other Returns** ▶ **File a separate application for each return.**	OMB No. 1545-0148 Expires 5-31-95

Please type or print. File the **original and one copy** by the due date for filing your return. See instructions on back.	Name	Employer identification number
	Number and street (or P.O. box no. if mail is not delivered to street address)	Apt. or suite no.
	City, town or post office, state, and ZIP code. For a foreign address, see instructions.	

Note: *Corporate income tax return filers must use* **Form 7004** *to request an extension of time to file. Partnerships, REMICs, and trusts (except those filing Form 990-T) must use* **Form 8736** *to request an extension of time to file.*

1 An extension of time until .... , 19 .... , is requested to file (check only one):

☐ Form 706GS(D)   ☐ Form 990-T (401(a) or 408(a) trust)   ☐ Form 1042-S   ☐ Form 6069   ☐ Form 8831
☐ Form 706GS(T)   ☐ Form 990-T (trust other than above)   ☐ Form 1120-ND (4951 taxes)   ☐ Form 8612
☐ Form 990 or 990-EZ   ☐ Form 1041 (estate) (see instructions)   ☐ Form 3520-A   ☐ Form 8613
☐ Form 990-BL   ☐ Form 1041-A   ☐ Form 4720   ☐ Form 8725
☐ Form 990-PF   ☐ Form 1042   ☐ Form 5227   ☐ Form 8804

    If the organization does not have an office or place of business in the United States, check this box . . . . . . ▶ ☐

2a For calendar year 19 ..... , or other tax year beginning .... and ending ....
 b If this tax year is for less than 12 months, check reason: ☐ Initial return ☐ Final return ☐ Change in accounting period
3 Has an extension of time to file been previously granted for this tax year? . . . . ☐ Yes ☐ No
4 State in detail why you need the extension. ....
....
....

5a If this form is for Form 706GS(D), 706GS(T), 990-BL, 990-PF, 990-T, 1041 (estate), 1042, 1120-ND, 4720, 6069, 8612, 8613, 8725, 8804, or 8831, enter the tentative tax, less any nonrefundable credits. See instructions. $ _____
 b If this form is for Form 990-PF, 990-T, 1041 (estate), 1042, or 8804, enter any refundable credits and estimated tax payments made. Include any prior year overpayment allowed as a credit . . . . . $ _____
 c **Balance due.** Subtract line 5b from line 5a. Include your payment with this form, or deposit with FTD coupon if required. See instructions. . . . . $ _____

Signature and Verification

Under penalties of perjury, I declare that I have examined this form, including accompanying schedules and statements, and to the best of my knowledge and belief, it is true, correct, and complete; and that I am authorized to prepare this form.

Signature ▶ _____ Title ▶ _____ Date ▶ _____

FILE ORIGINAL AND ONE COPY. The IRS will show below whether or not your application is approved and will return the copy.

Notice to Applicant—To Be Completed by the IRS

☐ We **HAVE** approved your application. Please attach this form to your return.

☐ We **HAVE NOT** approved your application. However, we have granted a 10-day grace period from the later of the date shown below or the due date of your return (including any prior extensions). This grace period is considered to be a valid extension of time for elections otherwise required to be made on a timely return. Please attach this form to your return.

☐ We **HAVE NOT** approved your application. After considering the reasons stated in item 4, we cannot grant your request for an extension of time to file. We are not granting the 10-day grace period.

☐ We cannot consider your application because it was filed after the due date of the return for which an extension was requested.

☐ Other: _____

_____ By: _____ _____
Director   Date

If you want a copy of this form to be returned to an address other than that shown above, please enter the address to which the copy should be sent.

Please Type or Print	Name	
	Number and street (or P.O. box no. if mail is not delivered to street address)	Apt. or suite no.
	City, town or post office, state, and ZIP code. For a foreign address, see instructions.	

For Paperwork Reduction Act Notice, see back of form.   Cat. No. 11976B   Form **2758** (Rev. 7-93)

Form 93   State (Minnesota as Example) Fiduciary Income Tax Return

MINNESOTA Department of Revenue

Fiduciary Income Tax Return 1994   M-2

For calendar year 1994 or fiscal year beginning __10/01__, 1994, ending __09/30__, 19 _95_
Check box if this is an amended return ☐

Use label or print or type		
Name of estate or trust Estate of Jane M. Doe	Federal ID number 41-6246975	Minnesota ID number MN 41-6246975
Name and title of fiduciary John C. Doe, Personal Representative	Decedent's Social Security number 321-54-9876	Date of death 09/20/94
Address of fiduciary 1005 Elm Street	If return is for an estate, fill in decedent's last address 1005 Elm Street, St. Paul, MN	
City or town State Zip code St. Paul, MN 55102	Check all boxes that apply: ☒ Estate ☐ Trust ☒ Final return	

Income

1 Federal taxable income (from line 22 of federal Form 1041) . . . .**1**   0.

2 Fiduciary's deductions not allowed by Minnesota *(read instructions)* . . . .**2**   0.

3 Fiduciary's losses not allowed by Minnesota *(read instructions)* . . . .**3**   .

4 Capital gain amount of lump-sum distribution *(attach federal Form 4972)* . . . .**4**   .

5 Additions (from line 37, column E, on the back of this form) . . . .**5**   .

6 Add lines 1 through 5 . . . .**6**   0.

7 Subtractions (from line 37, column E, on the back of this form) . . . . **7** _____ .

8 Fiduciary's income from non-Minnesota sources *(read instructions)* . . . **8** _____ .

9 Add lines 7 and 8 . . . .**9**

10 Subtract line 9 from line 6. This is your Minnesota taxable net income . . . .**10**   0.

Figuring the tax

11 Fill in the tax from table on income shown on line 10 . . . .**11**   0.

12 Tax on a lump-sum distribution *(attach Schedule M-1LS)* . . . .**12**   .

13 Alternative minimum tax *(attach Schedule M-2MT)* . . . .**13**   .

14 Add lines 11 through 13. This is your total 1994 income tax . . . .**14**   0.

15 Tax previously paid **15**

Refund or tax owed

16 If line 15 is greater than line 14, subtract line 14
from line 15 and fill in the amount of the **REFUND** . . . .**16**   .

17 If line 14 is greater than line 15, subtract line 15
from line 14 and fill in the amount of **AMOUNT OWED** . . . .**17**   0.

                                                                    Make the check out to:
                                                                    MN Department of Revenue

18 If you are paying estimated tax for 1995, fill
in the amount from line 16 you want applied to it, if any . . . . **18** _____ .

19 Additional charge for underpayment of
estimated tax (trusts only) . . . . **19** _____ .

I declare that this form is correct and complete to the best of my knowledge and belief. I admit that I owe the tax listed above, and confess judgment to the commissioner for the tax shown on the return to the extent not timely paid.

Signature of fiduciary or officer representing fiduciary	Minn. ID or Soc. Sec. number	Date	Daytime phone
/S/ John C. Doe	374-29-4665	10/02/95	(612)345-5000
Paid preparer's signature	Minn. ID or Soc. Sec. number	Date	Daytime phone ( )

You must attach a copy of federal Form 1041, Schedules K-1, and other federal schedules
Mail to: Minnesota Fiduciary Income Tax, Mail Station 1310, St. Paul, Minnesota 55146-1310

Stock No. 3094200

Form 94 United States Gift Tax Return (Form 709)

Form **709** (Rev. November 1993) Department of the Treasury Internal Revenue Service	**United States Gift (and Generation-Skipping Transfer) Tax Return** (Section 6019 of the Internal Revenue Code) (For gifts made after December 31, 1991) Calendar year 19 _94_ ▶ See separate instructions. For Privacy Act Notice, see the Instructions for Form 1040.	OMB No. 1545-0020 Expires 5-31-96

Part 1—General Information

1 Donor's first name and middle initial	2 Donor's last name	3 Donor's social security number
Jane M.	Doe	321 ¦ 54 ¦ 9876

4 Address (number, street, and apartment number)	5 Legal residence (Domicile) (county and state)
1005 Elm Street	Ramsey County, Minnesota

6 City, state, and ZIP code	7 Citizenship
St. Paul, MN 55102	United States

		Yes	No
8	If the donor died during the year, check here ▶ ⊠ and enter date of death September 20, 19 94		
9	If you received an extension of time to file this Form 709, check here ▶ ☐ and attach the Form 4868, 2688, 2350, or extension letter		
10	Enter the total number of separate donees listed on Schedule A—count each person only once . . . . ☐ 1		
11a	Have you (the donor) previously filed a Form 709 (or 709-A) for any other year? If the answer is "No," do not complete line 11b .		X
11b	If the answer to line 11a is "Yes," has your address changed since you last filed Form 709 (or 709-A)?		
12	Gifts by husband or wife to third parties.—Do you consent to have the gifts (including generation-skipping transfers) made by you and by your spouse to third parties during the calendar year considered as made one-half by each of you? (See instructions.) (If the answer is "Yes," the following information must be furnished and your spouse must sign the consent shown below. **If the answer is "No," skip lines 13–18 and go to Schedule A.**)	X	
13	Name of consenting spouse John C. Doe **14** SSN 374-29-4665		
15	Were you married to one another during the entire calendar year? (see instructions)		X
16	If the answer to 15 is "No," check whether ☐ married ☐ divorced or ☒ widowed, and give date (see instructions) ▶ 9/20		
17	Will a gift tax return for this calendar year be filed by your spouse?		X
18	**Consent of Spouse—**I consent to have the gifts (and generation-skipping transfers) made by me and by my spouse to third parties during the calendar year considered as made one-half by each of us. We are both aware of the joint and several liability for tax created by the execution of this consent.		

Consenting spouse's signature ▶ /S/ John C. Doe   Date ▶ February 15, 1995

Part 2—Tax Computation

1	Enter the amount from Schedule A, Part 3, line 15	**1**	0
2	Enter the amount from Schedule B, line 3	**2**	
3	Total taxable gifts (add lines 1 and 2)	**3**	0
4	Tax computed on amount on line 3 (see Table for Computing Tax in separate instructions) . .	**4**	0
5	Tax computed on amount on line 2 (see Table for Computing Tax in separate instructions) . .	**5**	
6	Balance (subtract line 5 from line 4)	**6**	0
7	Maximum unified credit (nonresident aliens, see instructions)	**7**	192,800 ¦ 00
8	Enter the unified credit against tax allowable for all prior periods (from Sch. B, line 1, col. C) . .	**8**	
9	Balance (subtract line 8 from line 7)	**9**	192,800
10	Enter 20% (.20) of the amount allowed as a specific exemption for gifts made after September 8, 1976, and before January 1, 1977 (see instructions)	**10**	
11	Balance (subtract line 10 from line 9)	**11**	192,800
12	Unified credit (enter the smaller of line 6 or line 11)	**12**	0
13	Credit for foreign gift taxes (see instructions)	**13**	
14	Total credits (add lines 12 and 13)	**14**	0
15	Balance (subtract line 14 from line 6) (do not enter less than zero)	**15**	0
16	Generation-skipping transfer taxes (from Schedule C, Part 3, col. H, total)	**16**	
17	Total tax (add lines 15 and 16)	**17**	0
18	Gift and generation-skipping transfer taxes prepaid with extension of time to file	**18**	
19	If line 18 is less than line 17, enter BALANCE DUE (see instructions)	**19**	0
20	If line 18 is greater than line 17, enter AMOUNT TO BE REFUNDED	**20**	

Under penalties of perjury, I declare that I have examined this return, including any accompanying schedules and statements, and to the best of my knowledge and belief it is true, correct, and complete. Declaration of preparer (other than donor) is based on all information of which preparer has any knowledge.

Donor's signature ▶ _____ Date ▶ _____

Preparer's signature (other than donor) ▶ /S/ John C. Doe, Personal Representative   Date ▶ February 15, 1995

Preparer's address (other than donor) ▶ 1005 Elm Street, St. Paul, MN 55102

Attach check or money order here.

For Paperwork Reduction Act Notice, see page 1 of the separate instructions for this form.   Cat. No. 16783M   Form **709** (Rev. 11-93)

Form 94   United States Gift Tax Return (Form 709)—*continued*

Form 709 (Rev. 11-93)   Page **2**

SCHEDULE A   Computation of Taxable Gifts

Part 1—Gifts Subject Only to Gift Tax. *Gifts less political organization, medical, and educational exclusions—see instructions*

A Item number	B • Donee's name and address • Relationship to donor (if any) • Description of gift • If the gift was made by means of a trust, enter trust's identifying number and attach a copy of the trust instrument • If the gift was of securities, give CUSIP number	C Donor's adjusted basis of gift	D Date of gift	E Value at date of gift	
1	Sandy R. Doe, daughter, cash gift 1005 Elm Street St. Paul, MN 55102 (Gift to be split with spouse)	20,000	04/20/94	20,000	00

Note: Not required to list gift of $30,000 to spouse, John C. Doe. The only circumstances that require listing gifts to a spouse are: (1) it is a gift of a terminable interest; (2) it is a gift of a future interest; or (3) the spouse was not a citizen of the United States at the time of the gift.

Part 2—Gifts That are Direct Skips and are Subject to Both Gift Tax and Generation-Skipping Transfer Tax. You must list the gifts in chronological order. *Gifts less political organization, medical, and educational exclusions—see instructions. (Also list here direct skips that are subject only to the GST tax at this time as the result of the termination of an "estate tax inclusion period." See instructions.)*

A Item number	B • Donee's name and address • Relationship to donor (if any) • Description of gift • If the gift was made by means of a trust, enter trust's identifying number and attach a copy of the trust instrument • If the gift was of securities, give CUSIP number	C Donor's adjusted basis of gift	D Date of gift	E Value at date of gift
1				

Part 3—Taxable Gift Reconciliation

1	Total value of gifts of donor (add column E of Parts 1 and 2)	1	20,000	00
2	One-half of items __1__ .... attributable to spouse (see instructions)	2	10,000	00
3	Balance (subtract line 2 from line 1)	3	10,000	00
4	Gifts of spouse to be included (from Schedule A, Part 3, line 2 of spouse's return—see instructions) . .	4	0	00
	If any of the gifts included on this line are also subject to the generation-skipping transfer tax, check here ▶ ☐ and enter those gifts also on Schedule C, Part 1.			
5	Total gifts (add lines 3 and 4)	5	10,000	00
6	Total annual exclusions for gifts listed on Schedule A (including line 4, above) (see instructions) . . .	6	10,000	00
7	Total included amount of gifts (subtract line 6 from line 5)	7	0	00

Deductions (see instructions)

8	Gifts of interests to spouse for which a marital deduction will be claimed, based on items .... of Schedule A	8			
9	Exclusions attributable to gifts on line 8	9			
10	Marital deduction—subtract line 9 from line 8	10			
11	Charitable deduction, based on items .... to .... less exclusions	11			
12	Total deductions—add lines 10 and 11	12		
13	Subtract line 12 from line 7	13	0	00
14	Generation-skipping transfer taxes payable with this Form 709 (from Schedule C, Part 3, col. H, Total) .	14		
15	Taxable gifts (add lines 13 and 14). Enter here and on line 1 of the Tax Computation on page 1 . . .	15	0	00

(If more space is needed, attach additional sheets of same size.)

Form 94 United States Gift Tax Return (Form 709)—*continued*

Form 709 (Rev. 11-93)

Page **3**

SCHEDULE A **Computation of Taxable Gifts** *(continued)*

16 Terminable Interest (QTIP) Marital Deduction. (See instructions for line 8 of Schedule A.)

If a trust (or other property) meets the requirements of qualified terminable interest property under section 2523(f), and

a. The trust (or other property) is listed on Schedule A, and

b. The value of the trust (or other property) is entered in whole or in part as a deduction on line 8, Part 3 of Schedule A,

then the donor shall be deemed to have made an election to have such trust (or other property) treated as qualified terminable interest property under section 2523(f).

If less than the entire value of the trust (or other property) that the donor has included in Part 1 of Schedule A is entered as a deduction on line 8, the donor shall be considered to have made an election only as to a fraction of the trust (or other property). The numerator of this fraction is equal to the amount of the trust (or other property) deducted on line 10 of Part 3. The denominator is equal to the total value of the trust (or other property) listed in Part 1 of Schedule A.

If you make the QTIP election (see instructions for line 8 of Schedule A), the terminable interest property involved will be included in your spouse's gross estate upon his or her death (section 2044). If your spouse disposes (by gift or otherwise) of all or part of the qualifying life income interest, he or she will be considered to have made a transfer of the entire property that is subject to the gift tax (see Transfer of Certain Life Estates on page 3 of the instructions).

17 Election out of QTIP Treatment of Annuities

☐ ◄ Check here if you elect under section 2523(f)(6) **NOT** to treat as qualified terminable interest property any joint and survivor annuities that are reported on Schedule A and would otherwise be treated as qualified terminable interest property under section 2523(f). (See instructions.) Enter the item numbers (from Schedule A) for the annuities for which you are making this election ► _____

SCHEDULE B **Gifts From Prior Periods**

If you answered "Yes" on line 11a of page 1, Part 1, see the instructions for completing Schedule B. If you answered "No," skip to the Tax Computation on page 1 (or Schedule C, if applicable).

A Calendar year or calendar quarter (see instructions)	B Internal Revenue office where prior return was filed	C Amount of unified credit against gift tax for periods after December 31, 1976	D Amount of specific exemption for prior periods ending before January 1, 1977	E Amount of taxable gifts

1	Totals for prior periods (without adjustment for reduced specific exemption)	**1**			
2	Amount, if any, by which total specific exemption, line 1, column C, is more than $30,000		**2**		
3	Total amount of taxable gifts for prior periods (add amount, column E, line 1, and amount, if any, on line 2). (Enter here and on line 2 of the Tax Computation on page 1.)		**3**		

(If more space is needed, attach additional sheets of same size.)

Form 94 United States Gift Tax Return (Form 709)—*continued*

Form 709 (Rev. 11-93)   Page **4**

SCHEDULE C   Computation of Generation-Skipping Transfer Tax

Note: *Inter vivos direct skips that are completely excluded by the GST exemption must still be fully reported (including value and exemptions claimed) on Schedule C.*

Part 1—Generation-Skipping Transfers

A Item No. (from Schedule A, Part 2, col. A)	B Value (from Schedule A, Part 2, col. E)	C Split Gifts (enter ½ of col. B) (see instructions)	D Subtract col. C from col. B	E Nontaxable portion of transfer	F Net Transfer (subtract col. E from col. D)
1					
2					
3					
4					
5					
6					

If you elected gift splitting and your spouse was required to file a separate Form 709 (see the instructions for "Split Gifts"), you must enter all of the gifts shown on Schedule A, Part 2, of your spouse's Form 709 here.	Split gifts from spouse's Form 709 (enter item number)	Value included from spouse's Form 709	Nontaxable portion of transfer	Net transfer (subtract col. E from col. D)
In column C, enter the item number of each gift in the order it appears in column A of your spouse's Schedule A, Part 2. We have preprinted the prefix "S-" to distinguish your spouse's item numbers from your own when you complete column A of Schedule C, Part 3.	S-			
	S-			
	S-			
	S-			
	S-			
In column D, for each gift, enter the amount reported in column C, Schedule C, Part 1, of your spouse's Form 709.	S-			
	S-			
	S-			

Part 2—GST Exemption Reconciliation (Code section 2631) and Section 2652(a)(3) Election

Check box ▶ ☐ if you are making a section 2652(a)(3) (special QTIP) election (see instructions)

Enter the item numbers (from Schedule A) of the gifts for which you are making this election ▶ ....

1	Maximum allowable exemption	1	$1,000,000
2	Total exemption used for periods before filing this return	2	
3	Exemption available for this return (subtract line 2 from line 1)	3	
4	Exemption claimed on this return (from Part 3, col. C total, below)	4	
5	Exemption allocated to transfers not shown on Part 3, below. You must attach a Notice of Allocation. (See instructions.)	5	
6	Add lines 4 and 5	6	
7	Exemption available for future transfers (subtract line 6 from line 3)	7	

Part 3—Tax Computation

A Item No. (from Schedule C, Part 1)	B Net transfer (from Schedule C, Part 1, col. F)	C GST Exemption Allocated	D Divide col. C by col. B	E Inclusion Ratio (subtract col. D from 1.000)	F Maximum Estate Tax Rate	G Applicable Rate (multiply col. E by col. F)	H Generation-Skipping Transfer Tax (multiply col. B by col. G)
1					55% (.55)		
2					55% (.55)		
3					55% (.55)		
4					55% (.55)		
5					55% (.55)		
6					55% (.55)		
					55% (.55)		
					55% (.55)		
					55% (.55)		

Total exemption claimed. Enter here and on line 4, Part 2, above. May not exceed line 3, Part 2, above		**Total generation-skipping transfer tax.** Enter here, on line 14 of Schedule A, Part 3, and on line 16 of the Tax Computation on page 1	

(If more space is needed, attach additional sheets of same size.)

*U.S. Government Printing Office: 1993 — 301-628/80256

Form 95 State (Delaware as Example) Gift Tax Return

FORM 500
DIVISION OF REVENUE

052

DELAWARE GIFT TAX RETURN

(For gifts made after December 31. 1982)   Calendar year 19_____.

DONOR'S FIRST NAME AND MIDDLE INITIAL	DONOR'S LAST NAME	SOCIAL SECURITY NUMBER

ADDRESS [NUMBER AND STREET]

CITY. STATE. AND ZIP CODE	YES	NO
If you (the donor) filed a previous Form 500, has your address changed since the last Form 500 was filed?...		

1. Gifts by husband or wife to third parties-Do you consent to have the gifts by you & by your spouse to third parties during the calendar year considered as made one-half by each of you? (See Instructions)............
    If the answer is "Yes." the following information must be furnished and the consent shown below signed by your spouse.

1(a) Name of Spouse:	1(b) Social Security Number:

2. Were you married during the entire calendar year?...

3. If the answer to '2' is "NO." check whether ☐ married ☐ divorced or ☐ widowed and give date: ►

4. Will a gift tax return for this calendar year be filed by your spouse?.................................

CONSENT OF SPOUSE - I consent to have the gifts made by me and my spouse to third parties during the calendar year considered as made one-half by each of us. We are both aware of the joint and several liabilities for tax credited by the execution of this consent.

Spouses's Signature ►_____   Date ► _____

COMPUTATION OF TAX

1. Enter the amount from Schedule A. Line 13..	1	------------------
2. Enter the amount from Schedule B. Line 1..	2	
3. Total (add amounts on Lines 1 and 2)..	3	
4. Tax computed on amount on Line 3 (See Table A on Page 2)........................	4	------------------
5. Tax computed on amount on Line 2 (See Table A on Page 2)........................	5	
6. Tax Due - (subtract amount on Line 5 from amount on Line 4).....................	6	

6a. Penalty ► [_____]   Interest ► [_____]

6b. Total - add Lines 6 and 6a and...PAY IN FULL...► | 6b |

Under penalties of perjury. I declare that I have examined this return. including any accompanying schedules and statements and to the best of my knowledge and belief it is true. correct. and complete. Declaration of preparer (other than spouse) is based on the on all information of which preparer has any knowledge.

Donor's Signature _____   Date ►_____

Paid Preparer's Signature (other than donor's) _____   Date ►_____

Paid Preparer's Address _____   Date ►_____

MAKE CHECK PAYABLE AND MAIL TO: DELAWARE DIVISION OF REVENUE. 820 N. FRENCH STREET WILMINGTON. DELAWARE 19899

FORM 500 (Revised 11/93)

Form 95   State (Delaware as Example) Gift Tax Return—*continued*

SCHEDULE A - COMPUTATION OF TAXABLE GIFTS

ITEM NUMBER	DONEE'S NAME AND ADDRESS AND DESCRIPTION OF GIFT. IF THE GIFT WAS MADE BY MEANS OF A TRUST, ENTER A TRUST'S IDENTIFYING NUMBER BELOW AND ATTACH A COPY OF THE TRUST INSTRUMENT.	DONOR'S ADJUSTED BASIS OF GIFT	DATE OF GIFT	VALUE AT DATE OF GIFT
1				$

1. Total gifts of donor (see instructions).. **1**

2. One-half of items _____ attributable to spouse (see instructions)........................... **2**

3. Balance (subtract Line 2 from Line 1)... **3**

4. Gifts of spouse to be included (from Line 2 of spouse's return - see instructions)..................... **4**

5. Total gifts (add Lines 3 and 4).. **5**

6. Total annual exclusions for gifts listed on Schedule A (see instructions)........................... **6**

7. Total included amount of gifts, subtract Line 6 from Line 5.................................... **7**

DEDUCTIONS (SEE INSTRUCTIONS)

8. Gifts of interest to spouse for which a martial deduction will be claimed, based on items _____ of Schedule A............................. **8**

9. Exclusions attributable to gifts on Line 8.. **9**

10. Martial deduction - Subtract Line 9 from Line 8................................. **10**

11. Charitable deduction, based on items _____ to _____ less exclusions........ **11**

12. Total deductions - Add Lines 10 and 11...................................... **12**

13. Taxable gifts (subtract Line 12 from Line 7)................................... **13**

TERMINABLE INTEREST MARTIAL DEDUCTION (SEE INSTRUCTIONS)

☐   Check here if you elect under the rules of Section 2523(f) of the Internal Revenue Code, to include gifts of terminable interest property on Line 8, above.
Enter the item numbers (from Schedule A, above) of the gifts for which you made this election _____

SCHEDULE B - Did you (the donor) file gift tax returns for prior periods? (If "Yes," complete Schedule B below) ☐ Yes ☐ No

CALENDAR QUARTERS (1971-1981) OR CALENDAR YEARS	DATE PRIOR RETURN WAS FILED	AMOUNT OF TAXABLE GIFTS

1. Total amount of taxable gifts for prior periods...

TABLE A - TABLE FOR COMPUTING GIFT TAX

(A) Amount of Taxable Gifts Equaling-	(B) Amount of Taxable Gifts Not Exceeding-	Tax on Amount in Column A	Rate of Tax on Excess Over Amount in Col. (A)
$ 25,000	$ 25,000		1%
50,000	50,000	$ 250.00	2%
75,000	75,000	750.00	3%
100,000	100,000	1500.00	4%
200,000	200,000	2500.00	5%
		7500.00	6%

FORM 500 p.2 (REVISED 11/93)

Form 96 United States Estate Tax Return (Form 706)

Form **706** (Rev. August 1993) Department of the Treasury Internal Revenue Service	**United States Estate (and Generation-Skipping Transfer) Tax Return** Estate of a citizen or resident of the United States (see separate instructions). To be filed for decedents dying after October 8, 1990. For Paperwork Reduction Act Notice, see page 1 of the instructions.	OMB No. 1545-0015 Expires 12-31-95

Part 1.—Decedent and Executor

1a Decedent's first name and middle initial (and maiden name, if any) Jane M.	**1b** Decedent's last name Doe	**2** Decedent's social security no. 321 : 54 : 9876

3a Domicile at time of death (county and state, or foreign country) Ramsey County, Minnesota	**3b** Year domicile established 1960	**4** Date of birth 11/06/12	**5** Date of death 09/20/94

6a Name of executor (see instructions) John C. Doe	**6b** Executor's address (number and street including apartment or suite no. or rural route; city, town, or post office; state; and ZIP code) 1005 Elm Street St. Paul, MN 55102

6c Executor's social security number (see instructions) 374 : 29 : 4665	

7a Name and location of court where will was probated or estate administered Ramsey County Probate Court	**7b** Case number 999999

8 If decedent died testate, check here ▶ ☒ and attach a certified copy of the will. **9** If Form 4768 is attached, check here ▶ ☐

10 If Schedule R-1 is attached, check here ▶ ☐

Part 2.—Tax Computation

1	Total gross estate (from Part 5, Recapitulation, page 3, item 10)	**1**	797,148
2	Total allowable deductions (from Part 5, Recapitulation, page 3, item 20)	**2**	737,348
3	Taxable estate (subtract line 2 from line 1)	**3**	59,800
4	Adjusted taxable gifts (total taxable gifts (within the meaning of section 2503) made by the decedent after December 31, 1976, other than gifts that are includible in decedent's gross estate (section 2001(b))	**4**	0
5	Add lines 3 and 4	**5**	59,800
6	Tentative tax on the amount on line 5 from Table A in the instructions	**6**	12,952
7a	If line 5 exceeds $10,000,000, enter the lesser of line 5 or $21,040,000. If line 5 is $10,000,000 or less, skip lines 7a and 7b and enter -0- on line 7c. **7a**		
b	Subtract $10,000,000 from line 7a **7b**		
c	Enter 5% (.05) of line 7b	**7c**	0
8	Total tentative tax (add lines 6 and 7c)	**8**	12,952
9	Total gift tax payable with respect to gifts made by the decedent after December 31, 1976. Include gift taxes by the decedent's spouse for such spouse's share of split gifts (section 2513) only if the decedent was the donor of these gifts and they are includible in the decedent's gross estate (see instructions)	**9**	0
10	Gross estate tax (subtract line 9 from line 8)	**10**	12,952
11	Maximum unified credit against estate tax **11** 192,800 00		
12	Adjustment to unified credit. (This adjustment may not exceed $6,000. See page 6 of the instructions.) **12**		
13	Allowable unified credit (subtract line 12 from line 11)	**13**	192,800
14	Subtract line 13 from line 10 (but do not enter less than zero)	**14**	0
15	Credit for state death taxes. Do not enter more than line 14. Compute the credit by using the amount on line 3 less $60,000. See Table B in the instructions and **attach credit evidence** (see instructions)	**15**	0
16	Subtract line 15 from line 14	**16**	0
17	Credit for Federal gift taxes on pre-1977 gifts (section 2012) (attach computation) **17**		
18	Credit for foreign death taxes (from Schedule(s) P). (Attach Form(s) 706CE) **18**		
19	Credit for tax on prior transfers (from Schedule Q) **19**		
20	Total (add lines 17, 18, and 19)	**20**	0
21	Net estate tax (subtract line 20 from line 16)	**21**	0
22	Generation-skipping transfer taxes (from Schedule R, Part 2, line 10)	**22**	0
23	Section 4980A increased estate tax (from Schedule S, Part I, line 17) (see instructions)	**23**	0
24	Total transfer taxes (add lines 21, 22, and 23)	**24**	0
25	Prior payments. Explain in an attached statement **25**		
26	United States Treasury bonds redeemed in payment of estate tax **26**		
27	Total (add lines 25 and 26)	**27**	0
28	Balance due (or overpayment) (subtract line 27 from line 24)	**28**	0

Under penalties of perjury, I declare that I have examined this return, including accompanying schedules and statements, and to the best of my knowledge and belief, it is true, correct, and complete. Declaration of preparer other than the executor is based on all information of which preparer has any knowledge.

/S/ John C. Doe Signature(s) of executor(s)	August 3, 1995 Date

/S/ John W. Cranwall Signature of preparer other than executor	First Trust Co. Bldg. St. Paul, MN 55101 Address (and ZIP code)	August 3, 1995 Date

Cat. No. 20548R

Form 96 United States Estate Tax Return (Form 706)—*continued*

Form 706 (Rev. 8-93)

Estate of: Jane M. Doe

Part 3.—Elections by the Executor

Please check the "Yes" or "No" box for each question.

		Yes	No
1	Do you elect alternate valuation?		x
2	Do you elect special use valuation? . . . . If "Yes," you must complete and attach Schedule A–1		x
3	Do you elect to pay the taxes in installments as described in section 6166? . . . . If "Yes," you must attach the additional information described in the instructions.		x
4	Do you elect to postpone the part of the taxes attributable to a reversionary or remainder interest as described in section 6163?		x

Part 4.—General Information (Note: *Please attach the necessary supplemental documents.* **You must attach the death certificate.**)

Authorization to receive confidential tax information under Regulations section 601.504(b)(2)(i), to act as the estate's representative before the Internal Revenue Service, and to make written or oral presentations on behalf of the estate if return prepared by an attorney, accountant, or enrolled agent for the executor:

Name of representative (print or type) John W. Cranwall	State MN	Address (number, street, and room or suite no., city, state, and ZIP code) First Trust Co. Bldg., St. Paul, MN 55101

I declare that I am the ☒ attorney/ ☐ certified public accountant/ ☐ enrolled agent (you must check the applicable box) for the executor and prepared this return for the executor. I am not under suspension or disbarment from practice before the Internal Revenue Service and am qualified to practice in the state shown above.

Signature /S/ John W. Cranwall	CAF number 111111119	Date 08/03/95	Telephone number (612) 555-5555

1 Death certificate number and issuing authority (attach a copy of the death certificate to this return).
#876543, Minnesota Department of Health

2 Decedent's business or occupation. If retired, check here ▶ ☒ and state decedent's former business or occupation.
Real Estate Broker

3 Marital status of the decedent at time of death:
☒ Married
☐ Widow or widower—Name, SSN, and date of death of deceased spouse ▶ -----------------------------

☐ Single
☐ Legally separated
☐ Divorced—Date divorce decree became final ▶

4a Surviving spouse's name John C. Doe	4b Social security number 374 29 4665	4c Amount received (see instructions) $554,078

5 Individuals (other than the surviving spouse), trusts, or other estates who receive benefits from the estate (do not include charitable beneficiaries shown in Schedule O) (see instructions). For Privacy Act Notice (applicable to individual beneficiaries only), see the Instructions for Form 1040.

Name of individual, trust, or estate receiving $5,000 or more	Identifying number	Relationship to decedent	Amount (see instructions)
Jay A. Daw	321-29-8106	Brother	50,000
Sandy R. Doe	373-16-2693	Daughter	5,000

All unascertainable beneficiaries and those who receive less than $5,000 . . . . ▶

Total	55,000

(Continued on next page)   **Page 2**

Form 96 United States Estate Tax Return (Form 706)—*continued*

Form 706 (Rev. 8-93)

Part 4.—General Information *(continued)*

Please check the "Yes" or "No" box for each question.	Yes	No
6 Does the gross estate contain any section 2044 property (qualified terminable interest property (QTIP) from a prior gift or estate) (see page 5 of the instructions)?		x
7a Have Federal gift tax returns ever been filed? . . . . If "Yes," please attach copies of the returns, if available, and furnish the following information:	x	

7b Period(s) covered 1994	**7c** Internal Revenue office(s) where filed Kansas City, MO 64999-0002		

If you answer "Yes" to any of questions 8–16, you must attach additional information as described in the instructions.		
8a Was there any insurance on the decedent's life that is not included on the return as part of the gross estate?		x
b Did the decedent own any insurance on the life of another that is not included in the gross estate?		x
9 Did the decedent at the time of death own any property as a joint tenant with right of survivorship in which (a) one or more of the other joint tenants was someone other than the decedent's spouse, and (b) less than the full value of the property is included on the return as part of the gross estate? If "Yes," you must complete and attach Schedule E		x
10 Did the decedent, at the time of death, own any interest in a partnership or unincorporated business or any stock in an inactive or closely held corporation?		x
11 Did the decedent make any transfer described in section 2035, 2036, 2037, or 2038 (see the instructions for Schedule G)? If "Yes," you must complete and attach Schedule G	x	
12 Were there in existence at the time of the decedent's death:		
a Any trusts created by the decedent during his or her lifetime?		x
b Any trusts not created by the decedent under which the decedent possessed any power, beneficial interest, or trusteeship?	x	
13 Did the decedent ever possess, exercise, or release any general power of appointment? If "Yes," you must complete and attach Schedule H	x	
14 Was the marital deduction computed under the transitional rule of Public Law 97-34, section 403(e)(3) (Economic Recovery Tax Act of 1981)? If "Yes," attach a separate computation of the marital deduction, enter the amount on item 18 of the Recapitulation, and note on item 18 "computation attached."		x
15 Was the decedent, immediately before death, receiving an annuity described in the "General" paragraph of the instructions for Schedule I? If "Yes," you must complete and attach Schedule I	x	
16 Did the decedent have a total "excess retirement accumulation" (as defined in section 4980A(d)) in qualified employer plans and individual retirement plans? If "Yes," you must complete and attach Schedule S		x

Part 5.—Recapitulation

Item number	Gross estate	Alternate value	Value at date of death
1	Schedule A—Real Estate		372,750
2	Schedule B—Stocks and Bonds		10,648
3	Schedule C—Mortgages, Notes, and Cash		76,350
4	Schedule D—Insurance on the Decedent's Life (attach Form(s) 712)		170,100
5	Schedule E—Jointly Owned Property (attach Form(s) 712 for life insurance) . . .		42,500
6	Schedule F—Other Miscellaneous Property (attach Form(s) 712 for life insurance) .		70,000
7	Schedule G—Transfers During Decedent's Life (attach Form(s) 712 for life insurance)		0
8	Schedule H—Powers of Appointment		50,000
9	Schedule I—Annuities		4,800
10	Total gross estate (add items 1 through 9). Enter here and on line 1 of the Tax Computation		797,148

Item number	Deductions	Amount
11	Schedule J—Funeral Expenses and Expenses Incurred in Administering Property Subject to Claims . . .	25,340
12	Schedule K—Debts of the Decedent	1,930
13	Schedule K—Mortgages and Liens	140,000
14	Total of items 11 through 13	167,270
15	Allowable amount of deductions from item 14 (see the instructions for item 15 of the Recapitulation) . . .	167,270
16	Schedule L—Net Losses During Administration	0
17	Schedule L—Expenses Incurred in Administering Property Not Subject to Claims	0
18	Schedule M—Bequests, etc., to Surviving Spouse	554,078
19	Schedule O—Charitable, Public, and Similar Gifts and Bequests	16,000
20	Total allowable deductions (add items 15 through 19). Enter here and on line 2 of the Tax Computation . .	737,348

Page 3

Form 96 United States Estate Tax Return (Form 706)—*continued*

Form 706 (Rev. 8-93)

Estate of: Jane M. Doe

SCHEDULE A—Real Estate

(For jointly owned property that must be disclosed on Schedule E, see the instructions for Schedule E.)

(Real estate that is part of a sole proprietorship should be shown on Schedule F. Real estate that is included in the gross estate under section 2035, 2036, 2037, or 2038 should be shown on Schedule G. Real estate that is included in the gross estate under section 2041 should be shown on Schedule H.)

(If you elect section 2032A valuation, you must complete Schedule A and Schedule A-1.)

Item number	Description	Alternate valuation date	Alternate value	Value at date of death
1	House and lot, 1005 Elm St., St. Paul, MN, Lot 615, Block 42, Reiser's Addition to St. Paul, Ramsey County (Plat #22760 Parcel #7600), in name of decedent. Copy of Appraisal attached as Exhibit_____. Mortgage balance at St. Paul Bank and Trust Company - $130,000			350,000
2	An undivided one-fourth (1/4) interest in duplex and lots, 776 Cliff Rd., St. Paul, MN, Lots 16 & 17, Block 20, Lovey's Addition to St. Paul, Ramsey County (Plat #32689 Parcel #5562), in name of decedent. (1/4 x $91,000) Copy of Appraisal attached as Exhibit_____. (Assume all rent due and collected prior to death.) Mortgage balance at St. Paul Bank and Trust Company - $10,000 (1/4 x $40,000)			22,750
	Total from continuation schedule(s) (or additional sheet(s)) attached to this schedule . .			
	TOTAL. (Also enter on Part 5, Recapitulation, page 3, at item 1.)			372,750

(If more space is needed, attach the continuation schedule from the end of this package or additional sheets of the same size.)

(See the instructions on the reverse side.)

Schedule A—Page 4

Form 96 United States Estate Tax Return (Form 706)—*continued*

Form 706 (Rev. 8-93)

Estate of: Jane M. Doe

Decedent's Social Security Number

SCHEDULE A-1—Section 2032A Valuation

Part 1.—Type of Election (Before making an election, see the checklist on page 7.):

☐ **Protective election (Regulations section 20.2032A-8(b)).**—Complete Part 2, line 1, and column A of lines 3 and 4. (See instructions.)

☐ **Regular election.**—Complete all of Part 2 (including line 11, if applicable) and Part 3. (See instructions.)

Before completing Schedule A-1, see the checklist on page 7 for the information and documents that must be included to make a valid election.

The election is not valid unless the agreement (i.e., Part 3-Agreement to Special Valuation Under Section 2032A)—

● Is signed by each and every qualified heir with an interest in the specially valued property, and

● Is attached to this return when it is filed.

Part 2.—Notice of Election (Regulations section 20.2032A-8(a)(3))

Note: *All real property entered on lines 2 and 3 must also be entered on Schedules A, E, F, G, or H, as applicable.*

1 Qualified use—check one ▶ ☐ Farm used for farming, or

                      ▶ ☐ Trade or business other than farming

2 Real property used in a qualified use, passing to qualified heirs, and to be specially valued on this Form 706.

A Schedule and item number from Form 706	B Full value (without section 2032A(b)(3)(B) adjustment)	C Adjusted value (with section 2032A(b)(3)(B) adjustment)	D Value based on qualified use (without section 2032A(b)(3)(B) adjustment)
Totals			

Attach a legal description of all property listed on line 2.

Attach copies of appraisals showing the column B values for all property listed on line 2.

3 Real property used in a qualified use, passing to qualified heirs, but not specially valued on this Form 706.

A Schedule and item number from Form 706	B Full value (without section 2032A(b)(3)(B) adjustment)	C Adjusted value (with section 2032A(b)(3)(B) adjustment)	D Value based on qualified use (without section 2032A(b)(3)(B) adjustment)
Totals			

If you checked "Regular election," you must attach copies of appraisals showing the column B values for all property listed on line 3.

(Continued on next page)

Schedule A-1—Page 8

Form 96 United States Estate Tax Return (Form 706)—*continued*

Form 706 (Rev. 8-93)

4 Personal property used in a qualified use and passing to qualified heirs.

A Schedule and item number from Form 706	B Adjusted value (with section 2032A(b)(3)(B) adjustment)	A (continued) Schedule and item number from Form 706	B (continued) Adjusted value (with section 2032A(b)(3)(B) adjustment)
		"Subtotal" from Col. B, below left	

Subtotal . . . .   **Total adjusted value** . . .

5 Enter the value of the total gross estate as adjusted under section 2032A(b)(3)(A). ▶

6 Attach a description of the method used to determine the special value based on qualified use.

7 Did the decedent and/or a member of his or her family own all property listed on line 2 for at least 5 of the 8 years immediately preceding the date of the decedent's death? . . . . ☐ **Yes** ☐ **No**

8 Were there any periods during the 8-year period preceding the date of the decedent's death during which the decedent or a member of his or her family:

	Yes	No
a Did not own the property listed on line 2 above?		
b Did not use the property listed on line 2 above in a qualified use?		
c Did not materially participate in the operation of the farm or other business within the meaning of section 2032A(e)(6)?. . . .		

If "Yes" to any of the above, you must attach a statement listing the periods. If applicable, describe whether the exceptions of sections 2032A(b)(4) or (5) are met.

9 Attach affidavits describing the activities constituting material participation and the identity and relationship to the decedent of the material participants.

10 Persons holding interests. Enter the requested information for each party who received any interest in the specially valued property. **(Each of the qualified heirs receiving an interest in the property must sign the agreement, and the agreement must be filed with this return.)**

	Name	Address
A		
B		
C		
D		
E		
F		
G		
H		

	Identifying number	Relationship to decedent	Fair market value	Special use value
A				
B				
C				
D				
E				
F				
G				
H				

You must attach a computation of the GST tax savings attributable to direct skips for each person listed above who is a skip person. (See instructions.)

11 Woodlands election.—Check here ▶ ☐ if you wish to make a woodlands election as described in section 2032A(e)(13). Enter the Schedule and item numbers from Form 706 of the property for which you are making this election ▶
You must attach a statement explaining why you are entitled to make this election. The IRS may issue regulations that require more information to substantiate this election. You will be notified by the IRS if you must supply further information.

Schedule A-1—Page 9

Form 96   United States Estate Tax Return (Form 706)—*continued*

Form 706 (Rev. 8-93)

Part 3.—Agreement to Special Valuation Under Section 2032A

Estate of:	Date of Death	Decedent's Social Security Number

There cannot be a valid election unless:

- The agreement is executed by each and every one of the qualified heirs, and
- The agreement is included with the estate tax return when the estate tax return is filed.

We (list all qualified heirs and other persons having an interest in the property required to sign this agreement)

_____

_____ ,

being all the qualified heirs and _____

_____ ,

being all other parties having interests in the property which is qualified real property and which is valued under section 2032A of the Internal Revenue Code, do hereby approve of the election made by _____ ,

Executor/Administrator of the estate of _____ ,

pursuant to section 2032A to value said property on the basis of the qualified use to which the property is devoted and do hereby enter into this agreement pursuant to section 2032A(d).

The undersigned agree and consent to the application of subsection (c) of section 2032A of the Code with respect to all the property described on line 2 of Part 2 of Schedule A-1 of Form 706, attached to this agreement. More specifically, the undersigned heirs expressly agree and consent to personal liability under subsection (c) of 2032A for the additional estate and GST taxes imposed by that subsection with respect to their respective interests in the above-described property in the event of certain early dispositions of the property or early cessation of the qualified use of the property. It is understood that if a qualified heir disposes of any interest in qualified real property to any member of his or her family, such member may thereafter be treated as the qualified heir with respect to such interest upon filing a Form 706-A and a new agreement.

The undersigned interested parties who are not qualified heirs consent to the collection of any additional estate and GST taxes imposed under section 2032A(c) of the Code from the specially valued property.

If there is a disposition of any interest which passes or has passed to him or her or if there is a cessation of the qualified use of any specially valued property which passes or passed to him or her, each of the undersigned heirs agrees to file a **Form 706-A**, United States Additional Estate Tax Return, and pay any additional estate and GST taxes due within 6 months of the disposition or cessation.

It is understood by all interested parties that this agreement is a condition precedent to the election of special use valuation under section 2032A of the Code and must be executed by every interested party even though that person may not have received the estate (or GST) tax benefits or be in possession of such property.

Each of the undersigned understands that by making this election, a lien will be created and recorded pursuant to section 6324B of the Code on the property referred to in this agreement for the adjusted tax differences with respect to the estate as defined in section 2032A(c)(2)(C).

As the interested parties, the undersigned designate the following individual as their agent for all dealings with the Internal Revenue Service concerning the continued qualification of the specially valued property under section 2032A of the Code and on all issues regarding the special lien under section 6324B. The agent is authorized to act for the parties with respect to all dealings with the Service on matters affecting the qualified real property described earlier. This authority includes the following:

- To receive confidential information on all matters relating to continued qualification under section 2032A of the specially valued real property and on all matters relating to the special lien arising under section 6324B.
- To furnish the Service with any requested information concerning the property.
- To notify the Service of any disposition or cessation of qualified use of any part of the property.
- To receive, but not to endorse and collect, checks in payment of any refund of Internal Revenue taxes, penalties, or interest.
- To execute waivers (including offers of waivers) of restrictions on assessment or collection of deficiencies in tax and waivers of notice of disallowance of a claim for credit or refund.
- To execute closing agreements under section 7121.

(continued on next page)

Schedule A-1—Page 10

Form 96   United States Estate Tax Return (Form 706)—*continued*

Form 706 (Rev. 8-93)

Part 3.—Agreement to Special Valuation Under Section 2032A *(Continued)*

Estate of:	Date of Death	Decedent's Social Security Number

● Other acts (specify) ▶ _____

By signing this agreement, the agent agrees to provide the Service with any requested information concerning this property and to notify the Service of any disposition or cessation of the qualified use of any part of this property.

Name of Agent	Signature	Address

The property to which this agreement relates is listed in Form 706, United States Estate (and Generation-Skipping Transfer) Tax Return, and in the Notice of Election, along with its fair market value according to section 2031 of the Code and its special use value according to section 2032A. The name, address, social security number, and interest (including the value) of each of the undersigned in this property are as set forth in the attached Notice of Election.

IN WITNESS WHEREOF, the undersigned have hereunto set their hands at _____,

this _____ day of _____ .

SIGNATURES OF EACH OF THE QUALIFIED HEIRS:

Signature of qualified heir	Signature of qualified heir
Signature of qualified heir	Signature of qualified heir
Signature of qualified heir	Signature of qualified heir
Signature of qualified heir	Signature of qualified heir
Signature of qualified heir	Signature of qualified heir
Signature of qualified heir	Signature of qualified heir

Signatures of other interested parties

Signatures of other interested parties

Schedule A-1—Page 11

Form 96 United States Estate Tax Return (Form 706)—*continued*

Form 706 (Rev. 8-93)

Estate of: Jane M. Doe

SCHEDULE B—Stocks and Bonds

(For jointly owned property that must be disclosed on Schedule E, see the instructions for Schedule E.)

Item number	Description including face amount of bonds or number of shares and par value where needed for identification. Give CUSIP number if available.	Unit value	Alternate valuation date	Alternate value	Value at date of death
1	100 shares Tenneco, Inc., Common, NYSE, CUSIP 674322189	50.00			5,000
2	1000 shares Minnesota Co-op, Common, OTC	4.50			4,500
3	$500 U.S. Savings Bond, Series E, #R4502363E, dated April 1985				574
4	$500 U.S. Savings Bond, Series E, #R4502364E, dated April 1985				574
	(Assume no accrued dividends on Items 1 and 2.)				

Total from continuation schedule(s) (or additional sheet(s)) attached to this schedule . .			
TOTAL. (Also enter on Part 5, Recapitulation, page 3, at item 2.)	·		10,648

(If more space is needed, attach the continuation schedule from the end of this package or additional sheets of the same size.)
(The instructions to Schedule B are in the separate instructions.)

Schedule B—Page 12

Form 96   United States Estate Tax Return (Form 706)—*continued*

Form 706 (Rev. 8-93)

Estate of: Jane M. Doe

SCHEDULE C—Mortgages, Notes, and Cash

(For jointly owned property that must be disclosed on Schedule E, see the instructions for Schedule E.)

Item number	Description	Alternate valuation date	Alternate value	Value at date of death
1	Promissory Note of $10,000 from Johnson Furriers dated 03/20/89 payable 03/20/95 (extended to 09/20/95) with interest at 7% per annum payable 09/20.			10,000
	Interest accrued on Item 1 from 03/20/94 to 09/20/94.			350
2	Traveler's checks, American Express Nos. 10008-10017, in the amount of $100 each in name of decedent, uncashed at date of death.			1,000
3	Checking Account No. 55-5555, First National City Bank of St. Paul, in name of decedent, reconciled balance as of date of death.			50,000
4	Savings Certificate No. 44-4444, American National Bank of St. Paul, in name of decedent, dated 01/20/94 with interest at 5.5% per annum payable monthly. (Assume interest check in the amount of $68.75 payable 09/20/94 was received and deposited in checking account on 09/20/94.)			15,000

Total from continuation schedule(s) (or additional sheet(s)) attached to this schedule .

TOTAL. (Also enter on Part 5, Recapitulation, page 3, at item 3.). . . . . . . | 76,350

(If more space is needed, attach the continuation schedule from the end of this package or additional sheets of the same size.)
(See the instructions on the reverse side.)

Schedule C—Page 13

Form 96 United States Estate Tax Return (Form 706)—*continued*

Form 706 (Rev. 8-93)

Estate of: Jane M. Doe

SCHEDULE D—Insurance on the Decedent's Life

You must list **all** policies on the life of the decedent and attach a Form 712 for each policy.

Item number	Description	Alternate valuation date	Alternate value	Value at date of death
1	Minnesota Life Insurance Company Policy J 666221 Estate of Jane M. Doe, Beneficiary Face Amount $120,000 Accumulated Dividends 100 $120,100			120,100
2	Prudential Life Insurance Company Policy 11-1111-123 Jay A. Daw, Beneficiary Face Amount $ 50,000 Forms 712 attached			50,000
	Total from continuation schedule(s) (or additional sheet(s)) attached to this schedule .			
	TOTAL. (Also enter on Part 5, Recapitulation, page 3, at item 4.).			170,100

(If more space is needed, attach the continuation schedule from the end of this package or additional sheets of the same size.)

(See the instructions on the reverse side.)

Schedule D—Page 15

357-328 O - 93 - 2

Form 96 United States Estate Tax Return (Form 706)—*continued*

Form 706 (Rev. 8-93)

Estate of: Jane M. Doe

SCHEDULE E—Jointly Owned Property

(If you elect section 2032A valuation, you must complete Schedule E and Schedule A-1.)

PART 1.—Qualified Joint Interests—Interests Held by the Decedent and His or Her Spouse as the Only Joint Tenants (Section 2040(b)(2))

Item number	Description For securities, give CUSIP number, if available.	Alternate valuation date	Alternate value	Value at date of death
1	1000 shares American National Slide Rule Company, Common, NYSE, CUSIP 911384275, at $75.00 per share (Assume no accrued dividends.)			75,000
	Total from continuation schedule(s) (or additional sheet(s)) attached to this schedule			
1a	Totals			75,000
1b	Amounts included in gross estate (one-half of line 1a)			37,500

PART 2.—All Other Joint Interests

2a State the name and address of each surviving co-tenant. If there are more than three surviving co-tenants, list the additional co-tenants on an attached sheet.

	Name	Address (number and street, city, state, and ZIP code)
A.	Sandy R. Doe	1005 Elm Street, St. Paul, MN 55102
B.		
C.		

Item number	Enter letter for co-tenant	Description (including alternate valuation date if any) For securities, give CUSIP number, if available.	Percentage includible	Includible alternate value	Includible value at date of death
1	A	100 shares Minnesota Company, Common, NYSE, CUSIP 812456213, at $50.00 per share (Assume no accrued dividends.) (Assume surviving joint tenant provided no consideration.)	100%		5,000
		Total from continuation schedule(s) (or additional sheet(s)) attached to this schedule			
2b		Total other joint interests			5,000
3		**Total includible joint interests** (add lines 1b and 2b). Also enter on Part 5, Recapitulation, page 3, at item 5			42,500

(If more space is needed, attach the continuation schedule from the end of this package or additional sheets of the same size.)
(See the instructions on the reverse side.)

Schedule E—Page 17

Form 96 United States Estate Tax Return (Form 706)—*continued*

Form 706 (Rev. 8-93)

Estate of: Jane M. Doe

SCHEDULE F—Other Miscellaneous Property Not Reportable Under Any Other Schedule
(For jointly owned property that must be disclosed on Schedule E, see the instructions for Schedule E.)
(If you elect section 2032A valuation, you must complete Schedule F and Schedule A-1.)

		Yes	No
1	Did the decedent at the time of death own any articles of artistic or collectible value in excess of $3,000 or any collections whose artistic or collectible value combined at date of death exceeded $10,000? . . . . If "Yes," submit full details on this schedule and attach appraisals.	x	
2	Has the decedent's estate, spouse, or any other person, received (or will receive) any bonus or award as a result of the decedent's employment or death? . . . . If "Yes," submit full details on this schedule.		x
3	Did the decedent at the time of death have, or have access to, a safe deposit box? . . . . If "Yes," state location, and if held in joint names of decedent and another, state name and relationship of joint depositor.		x

If any of the contents of the safe deposit box are omitted from the schedules in this return, explain fully why omitted.

Item number	Description For securities, give CUSIP number, if available.	Alternate valuation date	Alternate value	Value at date of death
1	Furniture and household goods located at homestead.			22,000
2	Fur - Mink coat. Copy of Appraisal attached as Exhibit_____ .			11,500
3	Clothing and personal effects.			4,500
4	1992 Mazda, Vehicle Identification Number 6778899926, Title Number 03618957, Bluebook market value.			12,000
5	Judgment dated February 19, 1991 against Forrest R. Redding, collected in full on December 20, 1994.			20,000
6	Trust created by decedent's uncle with income distributable to decedent for her lifetime and thereafter to her daughter; St. Paul Trust Co., Trustee; decedent had no power of appointment nor other incidents of ownership, therefore trust assets are not taxable to decedent's estate. (Assume all income distributable to decedent's date of death had been received by 09/20/94.)			0
	Total from continuation schedule(s) (or additional sheet(s)) attached to this schedule. .			
	TOTAL. (Also enter on Part 5, Recapitulation, page 3, at item 6.)			70,000

(If more space is needed, attach the continuation schedule from the end of this package or additional sheets of the same size.)
(See the instructions on the reverse side.)

Schedule F—Page 19

Form 96　United States Estate Tax Return (Form 706)—*continued*

Form 706 (Rev. 8-93)

Estate of:　Jane M. Doe

SCHEDULE G—Transfers During Decedent's Life

(If you elect section 2032A valuation, you must complete Schedule G and Schedule A-1.)

Item number	Description For securities, give CUSIP number, if available.	Alternate valuation date	Alternate value	Value at date of death
A.	Gift tax paid by the decedent or the estate for all gifts made by the decedent or his or her spouse within 3 years before the decedent's death (section 2035(c))	X X X X X		0
B.	Transfers includible under section 2035(a), 2036, 2037, or 2038:			
1				
	(Refer to gift tax return filed 02/15/95)			
	Total from continuation schedule(s) (or additional sheet(s)) attached to this schedule .			
	TOTAL. (Also enter on Part 5, Recapitulation, page 3, at item 7.).			0

SCHEDULE H—Powers of Appointment

(Include "5 and 5 lapsing" powers (section 2041(b)(2)) held by the decedent.)

(If you elect section 2032A valuation, you must complete Schedule H and Schedule A-1.)

Item number	Description	Alternate valuation date	Alternate value	Value at date of death
1	Trust created under agreement dated 12/02/65 by father of decedent for decedent's benefit under which decedent had a general power of appointment (to distribute income and/or principal) which power had not been exercised during decedent's lifetime, but which decedent exercised under her will. The assets remaining in this trust and subject to this power are 500 shares of Green Giant common stock and undistributed earnings (dividends) thereon. Unit value $100.00 per share.			50,000
	Total from continuation schedule(s) (or additional sheet(s)) attached to this schedule .			
	TOTAL. (Also enter on Part 5, Recapitulation, page 3, at item 8.).			50,000

(If more space is needed, attach the continuation schedule from the end of this package or additional sheets of the same size.)
(The instructions to Schedules G and H are in the separate instructions.)

Schedules G and H—Page 21

Form 96 United States Estate Tax Return (Form 706)—*continued*

Form 706 (Rev. 8-93)

Estate of: Jane M. Doe

SCHEDULE I—Annuities

Note: *Generally, no exclusion is allowed for the estates of decedents dying after December 31, 1984 (see instructions).*

		Yes	No
A Are you excluding from the decedent's gross estate the value of a lump-sum distribution described in section 2039(f)(2)? . . . . If "Yes," you must attach the information required by the instructions.			x

Item number	Description Show the entire value of the annuity before any exclusions.	Alternate valuation date	Includible alternate value	Includible value at date of death
1	Ecko Life Insurance Company Policy 99-9999. Annuity of $100.00 per month payable to decedent for life, thereafter to John C. Doe, husband of decedent (value of annuity based upon life expectancy of male, age 83, is approximately 4.000 x $1,200.00)			4,800
	Total from continuation schedule(s) (or additional sheet(s)) attached to this schedule .			
	TOTAL. (Also enter on Part 5, Recapitulation, page 3, at item 9.).			4,800

(If more space is needed, attach the continuation schedule from the end of this package or additional sheets of the same size.)

(The instructions to Schedule I are in the separate instructions.)

Schedule I—Page 22

Form 96　United States Estate Tax Return (Form 706)—*continued*

Form 706 (Rev. 8-93)

Estate of:　Jane M. Doe

SCHEDULE J—Funeral Expenses and Expenses Incurred in Administering Property Subject to Claims

Note: *Do not list on this schedule expenses of administering property not subject to claims. For those expenses, see the instructions for Schedule L.*

　If executors' commissions, attorney fees, etc., are claimed and allowed as a deduction for estate tax purposes, they are not allowable as a deduction in computing the taxable income of the estate for Federal income tax purposes. They are allowable as an income tax deduction on Form 1041 if a waiver is filed to waive the deduction on Form 706 (see the Form 1041 instructions).

Item number	Description	Expense amount	Total Amount
	A. Funeral expenses:		
1	Newark & Newark Funeral Home - funeral.	9,500	
2	Morningside Florists - funeral flowers.	100	
3	Riverside Cemetery - burial.	1,000	
4	Brown Monument Company - gravestone.	500	
5	Rev. B. Stone - funeral services.	25	
	Total funeral expenses		11,125
	B. Administration expenses:		
1	Executors' commissions—amount estimated/agreed upon/paid. (Strike out the words that do not apply.) (Claimed on estate's fiduciary income tax return)		0
2	Attorney fees—amount estimated/agreed upon/paid. (Strike out the words that do not apply.) . . (Claimed $2,040 on estate's fiduciary income tax return)		12,960
3	Accountant fees—amount estimated/agreed upon/paid. (Strike out the words that do not apply.) . .		250

		Expense amount
4	Miscellaneous expenses:	
	Fees Probate Court	2
	Certified copies	5
	Printing fees	50
	Miscellaneous expenses	448
	Philip Masterson Co., Inc., appraisals	500

Total miscellaneous expenses from continuation schedule(s) (or additional sheet(s)) attached to this schedule		
Total miscellaneous expenses		1,005
TOTAL. (Also enter on Part 5, Recapitulation, page 3, at item 11.)		25,340

(If more space is needed, attach the continuation schedule from the end of this package or additional sheets of the same size.)
(See the instructions on the reverse side.)

Schedule J—Page 23

APPENDIX A SAMPLE FORMS

Form 96 United States Estate Tax Return (Form 706)—*continued*

Form 706 (Rev. 8-93)

Estate of: Jane M. Doe

SCHEDULE K—Debts of the Decedent, and Mortgages and Liens

Item number	Debts of the Decedent—Creditor and nature of claim, and allowable death taxes	Amount unpaid to date	Amount in contest	Amount claimed as a deduction
1	Porta Veta Hospital - last illness expense.			850
2	Ace's Plumbing Co. - plumbing debt contracted by decedent, company claims $480 is owed, personal representative claims $230 is owed.		250	230
3	St. Paul Telephone Co. - telephone.			50
4	St. Paul Electric Co. - electricity.			100
5	Harvey's Garbage Pickup - rubbish removal.			50
6	Dr. Norma J. Dennison - medical.			600
7	St. Paul Rents - medical (wheelchair).			50

Total from continuation schedule(s) (or additional sheet(s)) attached to this schedule . . . .

TOTAL. (Also enter on Part 5, Recapitulation, page 3, at item 12.) **1,930**

Item number	Mortgages and Liens—Description	Amount
1	Mortgage on house and lot at St. Paul Bank and Trust Company, including accrued interest to date of death. (Schedule A, Item 1)	130,000
2	Mortgage on duplex and lots at St. Paul Bank and Trust Company, including accrued interest to date of death (1/4 x $40,000). (Schedule A, Item 2)	10,000

Total from continuation schedule(s) (or additional sheet(s)) attached to this schedule . . . .

TOTAL. (Also enter on Part 5, Recapitulation, page 3, at item 13.) **140,000**

(If more space is needed, attach the continuation schedule from the end of this package or additional sheets of the same size.)
(The instructions to Schedule K are in the separate instructions.) **Schedule K —Page 25**

Form 96   United States Estate Tax Return (Form 706)—*continued*

Form 706 (Rev. 8-93)

Estate of: Jane M. Doe

SCHEDULE L—Net Losses During Administration and Expenses Incurred in Administering Property Not Subject to Claims

Item number	Net losses during administration (**Note:** *Do not deduct losses claimed on a Federal income tax return.*)	Amount
1		
	Total from continuation schedule(s) (or additional sheet(s)) attached to this schedule	
	TOTAL. (Also enter on Part 5, Recapitulation, page 3, at item 16.)	0

Item number	Expenses incurred in administering property not subject to claims (Indicate whether estimated, agreed upon, or paid.)	Amount
1		
	Total from continuation schedule(s) (or additional sheet(s)) attached to this schedule	
	TOTAL. (Also enter on Part 5, Recapitulation, page 3, at item 17.)	0

(If more space is needed, attach the continuation schedule from the end of this package or additional sheets of the same size.)

Schedule L —Page 26   (The instructions to Schedule L are in the separate instructions.)

Form 96 United States Estate Tax Return (Form 706)—*continued*

Form 706 (Rev. 8-93)

Estate of: Jane M. Doe

SCHEDULE M—Bequests, etc., to Surviving Spouse

Election To Deduct Qualified Terminable Interest Property Under Section 2056(b)(7).—If a trust (or other property) meets the requirements of qualified terminable interest property under section 2056(b)(7), and

a. The trust or other property is listed on Schedule M, and

b. The value of the trust (or other property) is entered in whole or in part as a deduction on Schedule M,

then unless the executor specifically identifies the trust (all or a fractional portion or percentage) or other property to be excluded from the election the executor shall be deemed to have made an election to have such trust (or other property) treated as qualified terminable interest property under section 2056(b)(7).

If less than the entire value of the trust (or other property) that the executor has included in the gross estate is entered as a deduction on Schedule M, the executor shall be considered to have made an election only as to a fraction of the trust (or other property). The numerator of this fraction is equal to the amount of the trust (or other property) deducted on Schedule M. The denominator is equal to the total value of the trust (or other property).

Election To Deduct Qualified Domestic Trust Property Under Section 2056A.—If a trust meets the requirements of a qualified domestic trust under section 2056A(a) and this return is filed no later than 1 year after the time prescribed by law (including extensions) for filing the return, and

a. The entire value of a trust or trust property is listed on Schedule M, and

b. The entire value of the trust or trust property is entered as a deduction on Schedule M,

then unless the executor specifically identifies the trust to be excluded from the election, the executor shall be deemed to have made an election to have the entire trust treated as qualified domestic trust property.

		Yes	No
1	Did any property pass to the surviving spouse as a result of a qualified disclaimer?		x
	If "Yes," attach a copy of the written disclaimer required by section 2518(b).		
2a	In what country was the surviving spouse born? __United States__		
b	What is the surviving spouse's date of birth? __06/14/11__		
c	Is the surviving spouse a U.S. citizen?	x	
d	If the surviving spouse is a naturalized citizen, when did the surviving spouse acquire citizenship?_____		
e	If the surviving spouse is not a U.S. citizen, of what country is the surviving spouse a citizen? _____		
3	**Election out of QTIP Treatment of Annuities.**—Do you elect under section 2056(b)(7)(C)(ii) **not** to treat as qualified terminable interest property any joint and survivor annuities that are included in the gross estate and would otherwise be treated as qualified terminable interest property under section 2056(b)(7)(C)? (see instructions)		x

Item number	Description of property interests passing to surviving spouse		Amount
1	Jointly owned property, Schedule E, Item 1		37,500
2	Property passing under will to spouse:		
	Real Estate, Schedule A, Items 1-2	372,750	
	Stock & Bonds, Schedule B, Items 1-4	10,648	
	Mortgages, Notes & Cash, Schedule C, Items 1-4	76,350	
	Insurance payable to estate, Schedule D, Item 1	120,100	
	Miscellaneous property, Schedule F, Items 1-5	70,000	
	Powers of Appointment, Schedule H, Item 1	50,000	
		699,848	
	Less:		
	Deductions, Schedules J & K	167,270	
	Charitable devises, Schedule O	16,000 183,270	516,578

	Total from continuation schedule(s) (or additional sheet(s)) attached to this schedule			
4	**Total** amount of property interests listed on Schedule M	**4**	554,078
5a	Federal estate taxes (including section 4980A taxes) payable out of property interests listed on Schedule M	**5a**	
b	Other death taxes payable out of property interests listed on Schedule M . . .	**5b**	
c	Federal and state GST taxes payable out of property interests listed on Schedule M	**5c**	
d	Add items a, b, and c	**5d**	0
6	Net amount of property interests listed on Schedule M (subtract 5d from 4). Also enter on Part 5, Recapitulation, page 3, at item 18	**6**	554,078

(If more space is needed, attach the continuation schedule from the end of this package or additional sheets of the same size.)

(See the instructions on the reverse side.)

Schedule M—Page 27

Note: Annuity payable to spouse does not qualify for marital deduction (terminable interest).

Form 96 United States Estate Tax Return (Form 706)—*continued*

Form 706 (Rev. 8-93)

Estate of: Jane M. Doe

SCHEDULE O—Charitable, Public, and Similar Gifts and Bequests

	Yes	No
1a If the transfer was made by will, has any action been instituted to have interpreted or to contest the will or any of its provisions affecting the charitable deductions claimed in this schedule? . . . . If "Yes," full details must be submitted with this schedule.		x
b According to the information and belief of the person or persons filing this return, is any such action planned? If "Yes," full details must be submitted with this schedule.		x
2 Did any property pass to charity as the result of a qualified disclaimer? . . . . If "Yes," attach a copy of the written disclaimer required by section 2518(b).		x

Item number	Name and address of beneficiary	Character of institution	Amount
1	American Cancer Society	Medical Research	10,000
2	Girls' Clubs of America	Charitable	5,000
3	Newark Institute of Higher Learning	Educational Research	1,000

Total from continuation schedule(s) (or additional sheet(s)) attached to this schedule		
3 Total	**3**	16,000
4a Federal estate tax (including section 4980A taxes) payable out of property interests listed above	**4a**	
b Other death taxes payable out of property interests listed above	**4b**	
c Federal and state GST taxes payable out of property interests listed above	**4c**	
d Add items a, b, and c	**4d**	0
5 Net value of property interests listed above (subtract 4d from 3). Also enter on Part 5, Recapitulation, page 3, at item 19	**5**	16,000

(If more space is needed, attach the continuation schedule from the end of this package or additional sheets of the same size.)
(The instructions to Schedule O are in the separate instructions.)

Schedule O—Page 31

Form 96 United States Estate Tax Return (Form 706)—*continued*

Form 706 (Rev. 8-93)

Estate of: Jane M. Doe

SCHEDULE P—Credit for Foreign Death Taxes

List all foreign countries to which death taxes have been paid and for which a credit is claimed on this return.

If a credit is claimed for death taxes paid to more than one foreign country, compute the credit for taxes paid to one country on this sheet and attach a separate copy of Schedule P for each of the other countries.

The credit computed on this sheet is for the ....
(Name of death tax or taxes)

.... imposed in ....
(Name of country)

Credit is computed under the ....
(Insert title of treaty or "statute")

Citizenship (nationality) of decedent at time of death

(All amounts and values must be entered in United States money)

1 Total of estate, inheritance, legacy, and succession taxes imposed in the country named above attributable to property situated in that country, subjected to these taxes, and included in the gross estate (as defined by statute)	
2 Value of the gross estate (adjusted, if necessary, according to the instructions for item 2)	
3 Value of property situated in that country, subjected to death taxes imposed in that country, and included in the gross estate (adjusted, if necessary, according to the instructions for item 3)	
4 Tax imposed by section 2001 reduced by the total credits claimed under sections 2010, 2011, and 2012 (see instructions)	
5 Amount of Federal estate tax attributable to property specified at item 3. (Divide item 3 by item 2 and multiply the result by item 4.)	
6 Credit for death taxes imposed in the country named above (the smaller of item 1 or item 5). Also enter on line 18 of Part 2, Tax Computation	

SCHEDULE Q—Credit for Tax on Prior Transfers

Part 1.—Transferor Information

	Name of transferor	Social security number	IRS office where estate tax return was filed	Date of death
A				
B				
C				

Check here ▶ ☐ if section 2013(f) (special valuation of farm, etc., real property) adjustments to the computation of the credit were made (see instructions).

Part 2.—Computation of Credit (see instructions)

Item	Transferor			Total A, B, & C
	A	B	C	
1 Transferee's tax as apportioned (from worksheet, (line 7 ÷ line 8) × line 35 for each column) . .				
2 Transferor's tax (from each column of worksheet, line 20)				
3 Maximum amount before percentage requirement (for each column, enter amount from line 1 or 2, whichever is smaller)				
4 Percentage allowed (each column) (see instructions)	%	%	%	
5 Credit allowable (line 3 × line 4 for each column)				
6 TOTAL credit allowable (add columns A, B, and C of line 5). Enter here and on line 19 of Part 2, Tax Computation				

Schedules P and Q—Page 32   (The instructions to Schedules P and Q are in the separate instructions.)

Form 96 United States Estate Tax Return (Form 706)—*continued*

Form 706 (Rev. 8-93)

SCHEDULE R—Generation-Skipping Transfer Tax

Note: *To avoid application of the deemed allocation rules, Form 706 and Schedule R should be filed to allocate the GST exemption to trusts that may later have taxable terminations or distributions under section 2612 even if the form is not required to be filed to report estate or GST tax.*

*The GST tax is imposed on taxable transfers of interests in property located **outside the United States** as well as property located inside the United States.*

Part 1.—GST Exemption Reconciliation (Section 2631) and Section 2652(a)(3) (Special QTIP) Election

Check box ▶ ☐ if you are making a section 2652(a)(3) (special QTIP) election (see instructions)

1 Maximum allowable GST exemption	1	$1,000,000
2 Total GST exemption allocated by the decedent against decedent's lifetime transfers	2	
3 Total GST exemption allocated by the executor, using Form 709, against decedent's lifetime transfers	3	
4 GST exemption allocated on line 6 of Schedule R, Part 2	4	
5 GST exemption allocated on line 6 of Schedule R, Part 3	5	
6 Total GST exemption allocated on line 4 of Schedule(s) R-1	6	
7 Total GST exemption allocated to intervivos transfers and direct skips (add lines 2–6)	7	
8 GST exemption available to allocate to trusts and section 2032A interests (subtract line 7 from line 1)	8	

9 Allocation of GST exemption to trusts (as defined for GST tax purposes):

A Name of trust	B Trust's EIN (if any)	C GST exemption allocated on lines 2–6, above (see instructions)	D Additional GST exemption allocated (see instructions)	E Trust's inclusion ratio (optional—see instructions)

9D Total. May not exceed line 8, above	9D	
10 GST exemption available to allocate to section 2032A interests received by individual beneficiaries (subtract line 9D from line 8). You must attach special use allocation schedule (see instructions)	10	

(The instructions to Schedule R are in the separate instructions.)

Schedule R—Page 33

Form 96 United States Estate Tax Return (Form 706)—*continued*

Form 706 (Rev. 8-93)

Estate of: Jane M. Doe

Part 2.—Direct Skips Where the Property Interests Transferred Bear the GST Tax on the Direct Skips

Name of skip person	Description of property interest transferred	Estate tax value

1 Total estate tax values of all property interests listed above	**1**	
2 Estate taxes, state death taxes, and other charges borne by the property interests listed above .	**2**	
3 GST taxes borne by the property interests listed above but imposed on direct skips other than those shown on this Part 2. (See instructions.)	**3**	
4 Total fixed taxes and other charges. (Add lines 2 and 3.)	**4**	
5 Total tentative maximum direct skips. (Subtract line 4 from line 1.)	**5**	
6 GST exemption allocated	**6**	
7 Subtract line 6 from line 5	**7**	
8 GST tax due. (Divide line 7 by 2.818182)	**8**	
9 Enter the amount from line 8 of Schedule R, Part 3	**9**	
10 **Total GST taxes payable by the estate.** (Add lines 8 and 9.) Enter here and on line 22 of the Tax Computation on page 1	**10**	

Schedule R—Page 34

Form 96   United States Estate Tax Return (Form 706)—*continued*

Form 706 (Rev. 8-93)

Estate of: Jane M. Doe

Part 3.—Direct Skips Where the Property Interests Transferred Do Not Bear the GST
Tax on the Direct Skips

Name of skip person	Description of property interest transferred	Estate tax value

1	Total estate tax values of all property interests listed above	1	
2	Estate taxes, state death taxes, and other charges borne by the property interests listed above .	2	
3	GST taxes borne by the property interests listed above but imposed on direct skips other than those shown on this Part 3. (See instructions.)	3	
4	Total fixed taxes and other charges. (Add lines 2 and 3.)	4	
5	Total tentative maximum direct skips. (Subtract line 4 from line 1.)	5	
6	GST exemption allocated	6	
7	Subtract line 6 from line 5	7	
8	GST tax due (multiply line 7 by .55). Enter here and on Schedule R, Part 2, line 9	8	

Schedule R—Page 35

Form 96 United States Estate Tax Return (Form 706)—*continued*

SCHEDULE R-1
(Form 706)
(August 1993)
Department of the Treasury
Internal Revenue Service

Generation-Skipping Transfer Tax
Direct Skips From a Trust
Payment Voucher

OMB No. 1545-0015
Expires 12-31-95

Executor: File one copy with Form 706 and send two copies to the fiduciary. Do not pay the tax shown. See the separate instructions.
Fiduciary: See instructions on following page. Pay the tax shown on line 6.

Name of trust	Trust's EIN
Name and title of fiduciary	Name of decedent
Address of fiduciary (number and street)	Decedent's SSN	Service Center where Form 706 was filed
City, state, and ZIP code	Name of executor
Address of executor (number and street)	City, state, and ZIP code
Date of decedent's death	Filing due date of Schedule R, Form 706 (with extensions)

Part 1.—Computation of the GST Tax on the Direct Skip

Description of property interests subject to the direct skip	Estate tax value

1 Total estate tax value of all property interests listed above **1**
2 Estate taxes, state death taxes, and other charges borne by the property interests listed above . **2**
3 Tentative maximum direct skip from trust. (Subtract line 2 from line 1.) **3**
4 GST exemption allocated **4**
5 Subtract line 4 from line 3 . . . . **5**
6 **GST tax due from fiduciary.** (Divide line 5 by 2.818182) **(See instructions if property will not bear the GST tax.)** **6**

Under penalties of perjury, I declare that I have examined this return, including accompanying schedules and statements, and to the best of my knowledge and belief, it is true, correct, and complete.

Signature(s) of executor(s)   Date

                                                                      Date

Signature of fiduciary or officer representing fiduciary   Date

Schedule R-1 (Form 706)—Page 36

Form 96   United States Estate Tax Return (Form 706)—*continued*

Form 706 (Rev. 8-93)

Estate of: Jane M. Doe

SCHEDULE S—Increased Estate Tax on Excess Retirement Accumulations
(Under section 4980A(d) of the Internal Revenue Code)

Part I   Tax Computation

1   Check this box if a section 4980A(d)(5) spousal election is being made. ▶ ☐
    You must attach the statement described in the instructions.

2   Enter the name and employer identification number (EIN) of each qualified employer plan and individual retirement account in which the decedent had an interest at the time of death:

	Name	EIN
Plan #1		
Plan #2		
Plan #3		
IRA #1		
IRA #2		
IRA #3		

		A Plan #1	B Plan #2	C Plan #3	D All IRAs
3	Value of decedent's interest				
4	Amounts rolled over after death	▨	▨	▨	
5	Total value (add lines 3 and 4)				
6	Amounts payable to certain alternate payees (see instructions)				▨
7	Decedent's investment in the contract under section 72(f)				
8	Excess life insurance amount				▨
9	Decedent's interest as a beneficiary				
10	Total reductions in value (add lines 6, 7, 8, and 9) . . .				
11	Net value of decedent's interest (subtract line 10 from line 5)				

12   Decedent's aggregate interest in all plans and IRAs (add columns A–D of line 11) . . . . . . ▶ | **12** |

13   Present value of hypothetical life annuity (from Part III, line 4) . . . . . | **13** | |

14   Remaining unused grandfather amount (from Part II, line 4) . . . . . | **14** | |

15   Enter the greater of line 13 or line 14 . . . . | **15** |

16   Excess retirement accumulation (subtract line 15 from line 12) . . . . | **16** |

17   Increased estate tax (multiply line 16 by 15%). Enter here and on line 23 of the Tax Computation on page 1 . . . . | **17** |

(The instructions to Schedule S are in the separate instructions.)

Schedule S —Page 38

Form 96 United States Estate Tax Return (Form 706)—*continued*

Form 706 (Rev. 8-93)

Part II	Grandfather Election

1 Was a grandfather election made on a previously filed Form 5329? . . . . ▶ ☐ Yes ☐ No
If "Yes," complete lines 2–4 below. **You may not make or revoke the grandfather election after the due date (with extensions) for filing the decedent's 1988 income tax return.** If "No," enter -0- on line 4 and skip to Part III.

2 Initial grandfather amount . . . . | **2** |

3 Total amount previously recovered . . . . | **3** |

4 Remaining unused grandfather amount (subtract line 3 from line 2). Enter here and on Part I, line 14, on page 38 . . . . | **4** |

Part III	Computation of Hypothetical Life Annuity

1 Decedent's attained age at date of death (in whole years, rounded down) . . . . | **1** |

2 Applicable annual annuity amount (see instructions) . . . . | **2** |

3 Present value multiplier (see instructions) . . . . | **3** |

4 Present value of hypothetical life annuity (multiply line 2 by line 3). Enter here and on Part I, line 13, on page 38 . . . . | **4** |

Schedule S—Page 39

Form 96   United States Estate Tax Return (Form 706)—*continued*

Form 706 (Rev. 8-93)   (Make copies of this schedule before completing it if you will need more than one schedule.)

Estate of: Jane M. Doe

CONTINUATION SCHEDULE

Continuation of Schedule _____
(Enter letter of schedule you are continuing.)

Item number	Description For securities, give CUSIP number, if available.	Unit value (Sch B, E, or G only)	Alternate valuation date	Alternate value	Value at date of death or amount deductible

TOTAL. (Carry forward to main schedule.) . . . .

See the instructions on the reverse side.

Continuation Schedule—Page 40

Form 97 Life Insurance Statement (Form 712)

Form **712**
(Rev. August 1994)
Department of the Treasury
Internal Revenue Service

Life Insurance Statement

OMB No. 1545-0022

Part I **Decedent—Insured** (To Be Filed by the Executor With United States Estate Tax Return, Form 706 or Form 706-NA)

1 Decedent's first name and middle initial	2 Decedent's last name	3 Decedent's social security number (if known)	4 Date of death
Jane M.	Doe	321–54–9876	9/20/94

5 Name and address of insurance company

Minnesota Life Insurance Company, 15121 Oak Street, Minneapolis, MN 55101

6 Type of policy	7 Policy number
Ordinary Life	J 666221

8 Owner's name. If decedent is not owner, attach copy of application.	9 Date issued	10 Assignor's name. Attach copy of assignment.	11 Date assigned
	11/06/68		

12 Value of the policy at the time of assignment	13 Amount of premium (see instructions)	14 Name of beneficiaries
		Estate of Jane M. Doe

15	Face amount of policy	$ 120,000.00
16	Indemnity benefits	$
17	Additional insurance	$
18	Other benefits.	$
19	Principal of any indebtedness to the company that is deductible in determining net proceeds . . .	$
20	Interest on indebtedness (line 19) accrued to date of death	$
21	Amount of accumulated dividends	$ 100.00
22	Amount of post-mortem dividends	$
23	Amount of returned premium	$
24	Amount of proceeds if payable in one sum	$ 120,100.00
25	Value of proceeds as of date of death (if not payable in one sum)	$

26 Policy provisions concerning deferred payments or installments.
Note: *If other than lump-sum settlement is authorized for a surviving spouse, attach a copy of the insurance policy.*

27 Amount of installments . . . . $

28 Date of birth, sex, and name of any person the duration of whose life may measure the number of payments.

29 Amount applied by the insurance company as a single premium representing the purchase of installment benefits . . . . $

30 Basis (mortality table and rate of interest) used by insurer in valuing installment benefits.

31 Was the insured the annuitant or beneficiary of any annuity contract issued by the company? . . . . ☐ **Yes** ☒ **No**

32 Names of companies with which decedent carried other policies and amount of such policies if this information is disclosed by your records.

The undersigned officer of the above-named insurance company hereby certifies that this statement sets forth true and correct information.

Signature ▶ /S/ Charles S. McDonald   Title ▶ Vice President   Date of Certification ▶ 1/05/95

Instructions

Paperwork Reduction Act Notice.—We ask for the information on this form to carry out the Internal Revenue laws of the United States. You are required to give us the information. We need it to ensure that you are complying with these laws and to allow us to figure and collect the right amount of tax.

The time needed to complete and file this form will vary depending on individual circumstances. The estimated average time is:

Form	Recordkeeping	Preparing the form
712	18 hrs., 25 min.	18 min.

If you have comments concerning the accuracy of these time estimates or suggestions for making this form more simple, we would be happy to hear from you. You can write to both the IRS and the Office of Management and Budget at the addresses listed in the instructions of the tax return with which this form is filed. **DO NOT** send the tax form to either of these offices. Instead, return it to the executor or representative who requested it.

Statement of insurer.—This statement must be made, on behalf of the insurance company that issued the policy, by an officer of the company having access to the records of the company. For purposes of this statement, a facsimile signature may be used in lieu of a manual signature and if used, shall be binding as a manual signature.

Separate statements.—File a separate Form 712 for each policy.

Line 13.—Report on line 13 the annual premium, not the cumulative premium to date of death. If death occurred after the end of the premium period, report the last annual premium.

Cat. No. 10170V   Form **712** (Rev. 8-94)

Form 98 Power of Attorney and Declaration of Representative (Form 2848)

| Form **2848**
(Rev. February 1993)
Department of the Treasury
Internal Revenue Service | **Power of Attorney**
and Declaration of Representative
▶ For Paperwork Reduction and Privacy Act Notice, see the instructions. | OMB No. 1545-0150
Expires 2-29-96 |

Part I **Power of Attorney** (Please type or print.)

1   Taxpayer Information (Taxpayer(s) must sign and date this form on page 2, line 9.)

| Taxpayer name(s) and address

John C. Doe, Personal Representative
1005 Elm Street
St. Paul, MN 55102

Estate of Jane M. Doe | Social security number(s)
374 : 29 :4665

321 : 54 :9876
Daytime telephone number
(612) 345-5000 | Employer identification number
41 : 6246975
Plan number (if applicable) |

hereby appoint(s) the following representative(s) as attorney(s)-in-fact:

2   Representative(s) (Representative(s) must sign and date this form on page 2, Part II.)

Name and address John W. Cranwall First Trust Co. Bldg. St. Paul, MN 55101	CAF No. .....111111119................ Telephone No. (612) 555-5555........ Fax No. (612) 777-7777............... Check if new: Address ☐ Telephone No. ☐
Name and address	CAF No. .... Telephone No. ( ) .... Fax No. ( ) ---------------------- Check if new: Address ☐ Telephone No. ☐
Name and address	CAF No. .... Telephone No. ( ) .... Fax No. ( ) ---------------------- Check if new: Address ☐ Telephone No. ☐

to represent the taxpayer(s) before the Internal Revenue Service for the following tax matters:

3   Tax Matters

Type of Tax (Income, Employment, Excise, etc.)	Tax Form Number (1040, 941, 720, etc.)	Year(s) or Period(s)
Estate Tax	706	Death 09/20/94
Gift Tax	709	1994
Fiduciary Income Tax	1041	10/01/94 – 09/30/95

4   Specific Use Not Recorded on Centralized Authorization File (CAF).— If the power of attorney is for a specific use not recorded on CAF, please check this box. (See **Line 4—Specific Uses Not Recorded on CAF** on page 3.). . . . . ▶ ☐

5   Acts Authorized.—The representatives are authorized to receive and inspect confidential tax information and to perform any and all acts that I (we) can perform with respect to the tax matters described in line 3, for example, the authority to sign any agreements, consents, or other documents. The authority does not include the power to receive refund checks (see line 6 below) or the power to sign certain returns (see **Line 5—Acts Authorized** on page 4).
List any specific additions or deletions to the acts otherwise authorized in this power of attorney: ....

Note: *In general, an unenrolled preparer of tax returns cannot sign any document for a taxpayer. See Revenue Procedure 81-38, printed as Pub. 470, for more information.*
Note: *The tax matters partner/person of a partnership or S corporation is not permitted to authorize representatives to perform certain acts. See the instructions for more information.*

6   Receipt of Refund Checks.—If you want to authorize a representative named in line 2 to receive, **BUT NOT TO ENDORSE OR CASH**, refund checks, initial here _____ and list the name of that representative below.

    Name of representative to receive refund check(s) ▶

Cat. No. 11980J   Form **2848** (Rev. 2-93)

Form 98 Power of Attorney and Declaration of Representative (Form 2848)—*continued*

Form 2848 (Rev. 2-93)   Page **2**

7   **Notices and Communications.**—Notices and other written communications will be sent to the first representative listed in line 2.

   a If you also want the second representative listed to receive such notices and communications, check this box . . . ▶ ☐

   b If you do not want any notices or communications sent to your representative, check this box . . . . ▶ ☐

8   **Retention/Revocation of Prior Power(s) of Attorney.**—The filing of this power of attorney automatically revokes all earlier power(s) of attorney on file with the Internal Revenue Service for the same tax matters and years or periods covered by this document. If you do not want to revoke a prior power of attorney, check here . . . . ▶ ☐

   YOU MUST ATTACH A COPY OF ANY POWER OF ATTORNEY YOU WANT TO REMAIN IN EFFECT.

9   **Signature of Taxpayer(s).**—If a tax matter concerns a joint return, **both** husband and wife must sign if joint representation is requested, otherwise, see the instructions. If signed by a corporate officer, partner, guardian, tax matters partner/person, executor, receiver, administrator, or trustee on behalf of the taxpayer, I certify that I have the authority to execute this form on behalf of the taxpayer.

   ▶ **IF THIS POWER OF ATTORNEY IS NOT SIGNED AND DATED, IT WILL BE RETURNED.**

		Personal
/S/ John C. Doe	08/03/95	Representative
Signature	Date	Title (if applicable)
John C. Doe		
Print Name		
Signature	Date	Title (if applicable)
Print Name		

Part II   **Declaration of Representative**

Under penalties of perjury, I declare that:

- I am not currently under suspension or disbarment from practice before the Internal Revenue Service;
- I am aware of regulations contained in Treasury Department Circular No. 230 (31 CFR, Part 10), as amended, concerning the practice of attorneys, certified public accountants, enrolled agents, enrolled actuaries, and others;
- I am authorized to represent the taxpayer(s) identified in Part I for the tax matter(s) specified there; and
- I am one of the following:
  - **a** Attorney—a member in good standing of the bar of the highest court of the jurisdiction shown below.
  - **b** Certified Public Accountant—duly qualified to practice as a certified public accountant in the jurisdiction shown below.
  - **c** Enrolled Agent—enrolled as an agent under the requirements of Treasury Department Circular No. 230.
  - **d** Officer—a bona fide officer of the taxpayer organization.
  - **e** Full-Time Employee—a full-time employee of the taxpayer.
  - **f** Family Member—a member of the taxpayer's immediate family (i.e., spouse, parent, child, brother, or sister).
  - **g** Enrolled Actuary—enrolled as an actuary by the Joint Board for the Enrollment of Actuaries under 29 U.S.C. 1242 (the authority to practice before the Service is limited by section 10.3(d)(1) of Treasury Department Circular No. 230).
  - **h** Unenrolled Return Preparer—an unenrolled return preparer under section 10.7(a)(7) of Treasury Department Circular No. 230.

▶ **If this declaration of representative is not signed and dated, the power of attorney will be returned.**

Designation —Insert above letter **(a–h)**	Jurisdiction (state) or Enrollment Card No.	Signature	Date
a	MN	/S/ John W. Cranwall	08/03/95

Form 99 Application for Extension of Time to File a Return and/or Pay U.S. Estate Taxes (Form 4768)

Form **4768**	**Application for Extension of Time To File a Return and/or Pay U.S. Estate (and Generation-Skipping Transfer) Taxes**	OMB No. 1545-0181

(Rev. May 1993)

Department of the Treasury
Internal Revenue Service

OMB No. 1545-0181
Expires 5-31-96

(For filers of Forms 706, 706-A, and 706-NA)

Note: *Use Form 2758 to request an extension for Forms 706GS(D) and 706GS(T).*

Part I   Identification

Decedent's first name and middle initial	Decedent's last name	Date of death
Name of executor	Name of application filer (if other than the executor)	**Decedent's social security number**
Address of executor (Number, street, and room or suite no.)		Estate tax return due date
City, state, and ZIP code		

Part II   Extension of Time To File (Sec. 6081)

You must attach your written statement to explain in detail why it is impossible or impractical to file a reasonably complete return within 9 months after the date of the decedent's death.

Extension date requested

Part III   Extension of Time To Pay (Sec. 6161)

You must attach your written statement to explain in detail why it is impossible or impractical to pay the full amount of the estate (or GST) tax by the return due date. If the taxes cannot be determined because the size of the gross estate is unascertainable, check here ▶ ☐ and enter "-0-" or other appropriate amount on Part IV, line 3. You must attach an explanation.

Extension date requested

Part IV   Payment To Accompany Extension Request

1	Amount of estate and GST taxes estimated to be due	**1**
2	Amount of cash shortage (complete Part III)	**2**
3	**Balance due (subtract line 2 from line 1) (Pay with this application.)**	**3**

Signature and Verification

If filed by executor—Under penalties of perjury, I declare that I am an executor of the estate of the above-named decedent and that to the best of my knowledge and belief, the statements made herein and attached are true and correct.

Executor's signature	Title	Date

If filed by someone other than the executor—Under penalties of perjury, I declare that to the best of my knowledge and belief, the statements made herein and attached are true and correct, that I am authorized by the executor to file this application, and that I am (check box(es) that applies):

☐ A member in good standing of the bar of the highest court of (specify jurisdiction) ▶ ....
☐ A certified public accountant duly qualified to practice in (specify jurisdiction) ▶ ....
☐ A person enrolled to practice before the Internal Revenue Service.
☐ A duly authorized agent holding a power of attorney. (The power of attorney need not be submitted unless requested.)

Filer's signature (other than the executor)	Date

Part V   Notice to Applicant—To be completed by the Internal Revenue Service

1 The application for extension of time to file (Part II) is:	2 The application for extension of time to pay (Part III) is:
☐ Approved	☐ Approved
☐ Not approved because	☐ Not approved because ....
☐ Other	☐ Other ....

Internal Revenue Service official	Date	Internal Revenue Service official	Date

For Paperwork Reduction Act Notice, see instructions on the back of this form.   Cat. No. 41984P   Form **4768** (Rev. 5-93)

Form 100 State (Minnesota as Example) Estate Tax Return

MINNESOTA Department of Revenue

Estate Tax Return

MN-706

For estates of Minnesota residents and Nonresidents who died after December 31, 1985

Check if this is an amended return ☐

Decedent's first name, middle initial	Last name	Social Security number
Jane M.	Doe	321-54-9876
Last home address (street, apartment, route)	City or town	County and state of residence
1005 Elm Street	St. Paul	Ramsey, Minnesota
Date of death	Check if decedent was married at time of death ☒	Minnesota probate county and file number, if any: Ramsey County 999999
September 20, 1994		
Personal Representative's first name, middle initial	Last name	Social Security number
John C	Doe	374-29-4665
Address (street, apartment, route)	City or town	State	Zip Code
1005 Elm Street	St. Paul	Minnesota	55102

Estates of Minnesota residents

1 Credit for state death taxes from line 15 of federal Form 706 .1 _____ 0
2 Estate or inheritance tax actually paid to other states . . . . .2 _____
3 Gross value of all tangible personal and real property in other states . . . . .3 _____
4 Fill in the total gross estate from line 1 of federal Form 706. . . . . .4 _____
5 Divide line 3 by line 4. The result is a percentage. .5 _____ %
6 Multiply line 1 by line 5 . . . . .6 _____
7 Fill in the amount from line 2 or line 6, whichever is smaller . . . . .7 _____
8 Subtract line 7 from line 1. The result is the Minnesota estate tax . . . . .8 _____ 0

Estates of Nonresidents

9 Fill in the credit for state death taxes from line 15 of federal Form 706 . . . . .9 _____
10 Gross value of all tangible personal and real property in Minnesota. *Attach itemized list* . . .10 _____
11 Fill in the total gross estate from line 1 of federal Form 706 . . . . .11 _____
12 Divide line 10 by line 11. The result is a percentage . . . . .12 _____ %
13 Multiply line 9 by line 12. The result is the Minnesota estate tax . . . . .13 _____

All estates

14 Penalty, if any, for late payment of tax and/or late filing of this return . . . . .14 _____
15 Interest, if any, from:_____ to: _____ . . . . .15 _____
16 Add line 8 or line 13 to the amounts on lines 14 and 15, if any . . . . .16 _____ 0
17 Total of any payments you have made on the amount on line 16 prior to filing this return . . .17 _____
18 If line 17 is more than line 16, subtract 16 from 17 and fill in the amount of **REFUND** . . . .18 _____
19 If line 16 is more than line 17, subtract 17 from 16 and fill in the **TOTAL DUE** . . . . .19 _____ 0
20 If paying federal estate tax in installments, attach copy of IRS approval and check box ☐

I declare that I have examined this return and all accompanying schedules and statements, and that they are true and complete to the best of my knowledge and belief

Sign here

Signature of personal representative	Date	Phone
/S/ John C. Doe	August 3, 1995	(612) 345-5000

You must attach a copy of the estate's federal Form 706 and all attachments

Mail this return and all attachments to:
Minnesota Estate Tax
St. Paul, MN 55146-1315

Please turn to the back to appoint an Attorney-in-Fact . . .

Stock No. 6000706
(Rev. 4/92)

Form 100   State (Minnesota as Example) Estate Tax Return—*continued*

Powers of Attorney

I, the Personal Representative of the decedent's estate, appoint the person named below as Attorney-in-Fact for the decedent's estate to hold the powers listed below. This power of attorney will remain in effect until the date on which the Minnesota Department of Revenue receives a written notice of revocation signed by me. I hereby revoke all powers of attorney previously filed by me in connection with the estate of this decedent.

(Cross out any powers you do not wish to grant)

I grant the Attorney-in-Fact the power to:

- receive written and oral communications from the Minnesota Department of Revenue concerning the involvement of the decedent's estate with any Minnesota and federal tax matters, and to discuss these matters with employees of the Department of Revenue;

- examine the contents of all types of Minnesota and federal tax returns of the decedent concerning matters of Minnesota and federal tax liability;

- conclude agreements to extend the period of time in which redeterminations can be made of information used in determining the amount of the estate's Minnesota estate or gift tax;

- notify the Department of Revenue of the estate's intention to make installment payments of estate tax, and to provide the schedule of payments;

- request a reduction in the amount of any penalty;

- receive Minnesota estate tax refunds; and

- hold the following additional powers:

Powers

Sign here

Signature of personal representative			Date
/S/ John C. Doe			August 3, 1995
Attorney-in-Fact's first name, middle initial	Last name		Daytime phone number
John W. Cranwall			(612) 555-5555
Address (street, apartment, route)	City or town	State	Zip code
First Trust Co. Bldg.	St. Paul	MN	55101

You must attach a copy of the estate's federal Form 706 and all attachments

Mail this return and all attachments to:
Minnesota Estate Tax
St. Paul, MN 55146-1315

Form 101 State (Iowa as Example) Inheritance Tax Return

IA 706
60-008 (12/94)
625-0603

IOWA INHERITANCE TAX RETURN
(For Deaths After December 31, 1987, Please See Instuctions)

Decedent's first name and middle initial	Decedent's Last Name	Age at Death	Date of Death
Domicile at time of death	Federal Identification Number	Decedent's Social Security Number	
Name of Executor		Executor's Social Security Number	

Executor's Address (Number and Street including apt. no. or rural route, city, town or post office, state and zip code)

Indicate county and state where will was probated or estate administered		Probate Number
County	State	

The inheritance tax clearance is to be mailed to:

Name	Address	Telephone Number

COMPUTATION OF SHARES AND TAX ON NET ESTATE

1. Real Estate (from Schedules A, E and G) 1

2. All Other Property..2

3. Total Gross Estate (must equal line 36, page 2)..........................3

4. Total Allowable Deductions (from line 40, page 2)......................4

5. Net Estate (subtract line 4 from line 3) 5

6. **Computation of Shares and Tax**

Name and Address of Beneficiary	Age	Social Security No.	Relationship	Share	Inheritance Tax

7. Total of Shares (attach any additional computation sheets) 7

8. **TOTAL INHERITANCE TAX** 8

9. **IOWA ESTATE TAX.** Federal credit for state death taxes (line 15 of Federal 706) 9

10. **TAX DUE** (line 8 or 9, whichever is GREATER) 10

11. **PENALTY** (see instructions - IA Form 60-066) 11

12. **INTEREST**...12

13. **REFUND PER AMENDED** 13

14. **TOTAL DUE** - Make checks payable to: **TREASURER, STATE OF IOWA**..........14

MAIL RETURN TO: Iowa Department of Revenue and Finance, Hoover State Office Bldg., P.O. Box 10467, Des Moines, Iowa 50306

Under penalties of perjury, I declare that I have examined this return, including accompanying schedules and statements, and to the best of my knowledge and belief, it is true, correct and complete. Declaration of preparer other than the executor is based on all information of which preparer has any knowledge. I/We grant power of attorney to the person designated on page 2 for the purpose indicated

Signature	Capacity or Title	Date
Signature of Preparer	Address (and ZIP Code)	Date Page 1

Form 101   State (Iowa as Example) Inheritance Tax Return—*continued*

POWER OF ATTORNEY AUTHORIZATION (Optional)

Authorization is granted to the attorney listed below to receive confidential tax information under Iowa Code Section 450.68 to act as the estate's representative before the Iowa Department of Revenue and Finance and to make written or oral presentation on behalf of the estate.

Name of Attorney   Address (Number and Street, City, State and ZIP Code)   Telephone No.

15. Marital status of decedent at death: Married ☐   Widow(er) ☐   Single ☐   Divorced ☐
(the relationship of decedent's children to surviving spouse must be furnished if decedent died intestate)

16. Were any children born to or adopted by decedent after execution of Last Will?   Yes ☐   No ☐
    In all cases of adoption, furnish copy of decree.

17. Decedent's occupation before death:

18. Decedent died: Testate ☐   Intestate ☐   If testate submit copy of the will.

19. Election of spouse: (Submit copy of election)   Under Will ☐   Distributive Share ☐

20. Was a disclaimer filed? (If yes, submit copy of disclaimer)   Yes ☐   No ☐

21. Do you elect the special use valuation? (If yes, complete and attach Schedule N)   Yes ☐   No ☐

22. Was a federal estate tax return filed? (If yes, submit copy)   Yes ☐   No ☐

23. Do you elect to claim qualified terminal interest property (QTIP) under Iowa Code 450.3(7) Section 2056(b)
    (7) (B) (IRC)?.If yes, attach copy of Schedule M of Federal Estate Tax Return.   Yes ☐   No ☐

24. Do you elect to pay the federal estate tax in installments as described in Section 6166?   Yes ☐   No ☐

25. Do you elect the alternate valuations under Iowa Code Section 450.37 (Section 2032 IRC)?   Yes ☐   No ☐

26. Were any of the contents of any safety deposit box which the decedent either owned or has access to omitted from the return as
    part of the gross estate? (If yes, attach explanation)   Yes ☐   No ☐

SUMMARY OF GROSS ESTATE
(Attach Applicable Schedules Only)
(Federal Schedules may be used in place of Iowa schedules)

Schedule	Alternate Value	Value at Date of Death
27. A—Real Estate	$	$
28. B—Stocks and Bonds		
29. C—Mortgages, Notes, and Cash		
30. D—Insurance on the Decendent's Life (attach Form(s) 712)		
31. E—Jointly Owned Property		
32. F—Other Miscellaneous Property		
33. G—Transfers During Decedent's Life		
34. H—Powers of Appointment		
35. I—Annuities		
36. **TOTAL GROSS ESTATE** (Add items 27 through 35) Total must equal line 3, page 1		

SUMMARY OF DEDUCTIONS
(Attach Schedules J and K)

Schedule	Amount
37. J—Funeral Expenses and Expenses Incurred in Administering Property in the gross estate	$
38. K—Debts of Decedent	
39. K—Mortgages and Liens	
40. **TOTAL DEDUCTIONS** (Add items 37 through 39) Enter here and on page 1, line 4	

SUMMARY OF REAL AND PERSONAL PROPERTY LOCATED OUTSIDE OF IOWA
(NOT INCLUDED IN LINES 27-35)

ITEM — Description	REAL	PERSONAL
	$	$
Include taxable intangible property in schedules B through I.	**TOTAL**	

CPL-44504

SAMPLE MARITAL DEDUCTION TESTAMENTARY TRUST

LAST WILL AND TESTAMENT OF JOHN P. DOE

I, John P. Doe, a/k/a _____ , of _____ , City of
(alias)   (address)
_____ , County of _____ , State of _____ , being of sound and disposing mind and memory, and not
acting under undue influence of any person, do make,
publish, and declare this document to be my last will
and testament, and do hereby expressly revoke all wills
and codicils previously made by me.

Article I

I hereby direct my personal representative, hereinafter named, to pay all my just debts, administrative expenses, and expenses for my last illness, funeral, and
burial out of my estate.

Article II

I give my homestead legally described as _____ ,
which I own in _____ County, State of _____ , to
my wife _____ , in fee simple, if she survives me.

Article III

I give my diamond ring to my son, _____ ,
(name and address)
and my collection of guns and rifles to my son,
_____ .
(name and address)

Article IV

I give all my other personal property including my
automobiles, household furnishings, clothing, jewelry,
ornaments, books, and personal effects of every kind
used about my home or person to my wife, _____ ,
to do with as she sees fit, if she survives me.

Article V

If my wife, _____ , survives me, I
give to the _____ of
(name of individual or corporate trustee, e.g., a bank)
_____ as trustee of a trust to be known as
(address), (city), and (state)
"TRUST A," assets of my estate to be selected by my
personal representative and having a value which, when
added to the value of all interests in property that pass
or have passed to my wife, either by this will or by other
means, in a manner which qualifies for and will be equal

to the maximum marital deduction allowable in my estate under the provisions of the United States Internal
Revenue Code in effect at the time of my death. Only
assets qualifying for the marital deduction shall be allocated to Trust A. My personal representative shall satisfy the foregoing transfer (devise) with such assets as
will qualify for said marital deduction and shall compute
all values of assets for these purposes in accordance
with the Federal Estate Tax values finally computed in
my estate except the assets allocated to "TRUST A" shall
have an aggregate market value which fairly represents
the net appreciation or depreciation of the available
property on the date or dates of distribution.

TRUST A shall be administered and distributed by my
trustee as follows:

1. Beginning on the date of my death, the net income
from TRUST A shall be paid to my wife, _____ ,
in convenient installments to be determined by my
trustee, but at least annually, during her life.

2. My trustee shall pay to my wife or apply for her
benefit such amounts from the principal of TRUST
A as she shall request at any time in writing. In
addition, my trustee may pay to my wife or apply
for her benefit amounts of the principal of TRUST
A as it determines is necessary or advisable for her
care, comfort, support, maintenance and welfare,
including reasonable luxuries.

3. Upon the death of my wife, my trustee shall distribute the entire assets in TRUST A, including income,
to appointee or appointees in the manner and proportions as my wife my designate by her last will
which shall expressly refer to this general power of
appointment; included in the power shall be her
right to appoint free of any other trust provisions
hereunder. This general power of appointment conferred upon my wife shall exist immediately upon
my death and shall be exercisable by my wife exclusively and in all events.

4. If, under the above provisions, any portion of TRUST A is not disposed of, it shall be added to TRUST B of ARTICLE VII and administered and distributed as a part of TRUST B.

5. It is my intention that TRUST A shall qualify for the marital deduction which is allowed under the Federal Estate Tax provisions of the Internal Revenue Code in effect at the time of my death. Any provisions of this will which relate to TRUST A shall be so construed and questions pertaining to TRUST A shall be resolved accordingly.

6. If my wife pre-deceases me or the creation of TRUST A does not effectively reduce the Federal Estate Tax payable by reason of my death, the devise and bequest of this ARTICLE V shall lapse and no TRUST A shall be established.

Article VI

I hereby direct my personal representative to pay out of my residuary estate (and not from TRUST A) all estate, income, and inheritance taxes assessed against my taxable estate or the recipients thereof, whether passing by this will or by other means, without contribution or reimbursement from any person.

Article VII

I give the residue of my estate to _____ of _____ , as trustee
(name of individual or corporate trustee)   (address, city, state)
of a separate trust which shall be known as "TRUST B", the bypass trust, and which shall be administered and distributed by my trustee as follows:

1. During the life of my wife, _____ .
   (a). Beginning on the date of my death, the net income form TRUST B shall be paid to my wife, _____ , in convenient installments to be determined by my trustee, but at least annually, during her life.

   (b). If there are not sufficient principal funds readily available in TRUST A, then in addition to the net income from TRUST B, my trustee may pay to my wife or apply for her benefit sums from the principal of TRUST B as my trustee determines to be necessary or advisable to provide for her proper care, support, and maintenance.

   (c). My trustee may also pay to or apply for the benefit of any child or other issue of mine sums from the principal of TRUST B as my trustee determines to be necessary in order to

provide for their proper care, support, maintenance and education. It is not required that such payments be for the equal benefit of my children and other issue.

2. After the death of my wife, _____ , or in the event she does not survive me, then upon my death, my trustee shall administer and distribute TRUST B as follows:
   (a). Until my youngest living child reaches the age of twenty-five (25) years, my trustee may pay to or apply directly for the benefit of my children and other issue sums from the net income and principal of TRUST B as my trustee determines necessary to provide for their proper care, support, maintenance and education. It is not required that such payments be for the equal benefit of my children and other issue.

   (b). When my youngest living child has reached the age of twenty-five (25) years, my trustee shall divide TRUST B into equal shares and shall provide one share for each of my then living children, and one share to be divided equally among the living issue, collectively, of each deceased child of mine. In making such division, my trustee shall take into account all advances of principal to a child made after such child reached the age of twenty-five (25) years. It shall be within the discretion of my trustee to take into account some, none or all advances of principal to a child made before such child had reached the age of twenty-five (25) years. After such division has been made, said shares shall be distributed outright to such children and to the issue of deceased children by right of representation.

Article VIII

If at any time before final distribution of my estate or trust estate, it happens that there not be in existence anyone who is or might become entitled to receive benefits therefrom as hereinabove provided, then upon the occurrence of such event, all of my estate and trust estate then remaining shall be paid over and distributed outright to my heirs-at-law, in such proportions as though I had at that time died without a will, a resident of the State of _____ , in accordance with the intestate succession laws of personal property of the State of _____ now/then in effect.

Article IX

It is an express condition of this will, which shall control over all other provisions, that in no event shall the duration of any trust created herein continue for a period longer than the lives of all of my wife, _____ , and of any of my issue who may be living at the time of my death, and the survivor of all of them and twenty-one (21) years thereafter, and at the end of such time the trustee shall distribute the entire trust estate, principal and any undistributed income outright to the persons then entitled to receive the income therefrom or to have it accumulated for their benefit, in shares which shall be the same as those in which such income is then being distributed to, or accumulated for, them.

Article X

My trustee shall have all powers and authority necessary or advisable to ensure the proper administration and distribution of each trust created by my will. Except as I may otherwise expressly direct or require in my will and in extension but not in limitation of the powers provided by applicable ___(state)___ law, I hereby grant to my trustee as to any properties, real, personal, or mixed, at any time constituting a part of any trust hereunder and without the necessity of notice to or license or approval of any court or person, full power and authority during the term of such and in the continuing sole discretion of my trustee:

1. To retain any assets, including cash, for so long as it deems advisable, whether or not such assets are hereinafter authorized for investment; to sell, exchange, mortgage, lease, or otherwise dispose of any assets of my trust estate for terms within and extending beyond the term of such trust; and to receive any additional properties acceptable to the trustee, from whatever source.

2. Within the trustee's discretion, to invest, reinvest, or exchange assets for, any securities and properties, including but not limited to common and preferred stocks, and no statutes, rules of law, custom or usage shall limit the selection of investments; and to commingle for the purpose of investment all or any part of the funds of said trust in any common trust fund or funds now or hereafter maintained by the trustee.

3. To collect, receive, and obtain receipts for any principal or income; to enforce, defend against, compromise or settle any claim by or against the trust; and to vote or issue proxies to vote, oppose or join in any plans for reorganization, and to exercise any other rights incident to the ownership of any stocks, bonds or other properties which constitute all or a part of the trust estate.

4. To hold assets in bearer form, in the name of the trustee, or in the name of the trustee's nominee or nominees without being required to disclose any fiduciary relationship; and to deposit cash assets as a general deposit in a special bank account without liability for interest thereon; provided that, at all times, such cash and assets shall be shown to be a part of the trust on the books of the trustee.

5. To charge premiums on bonds and other similar investments against principal. The trustee shall not be required to charge any depreciation or depletion against income from any real estate or personal property.

6. To make, without the necessity of intervention or consent of any legal guardian, any payments by the terms of this will payable to or for the benefit of any minor person in any or all of the following ways: (1) Directly for the maintenance, education and welfare of any such minor beneficiary; (2) To the parent or natural guardian of such minor beneficiary; or (3) To any person at that time having custody and care of the person of said minor beneficiary. The receipt of such person shall be full acquittance of the trustee and the trustee shall have no responsibility to oversee the application of the funds so paid.

7. To hold or make division or distribution whenever herein required in whole or in part in money, securities or other property, and in undivided interests therein, and to continue to hold any such undivided interest in any trust hereunder, and in such division or distribution the judgment of the trustee concerning the propriety thereof and the valuation of the properties and securities concerned shall be binding and conclusive on all persons in interest.

8. To charge against the trust principal and to receive on behalf of the trustee reasonable compensation for services hereunder and payment for all reasonable expenses and charges of the trust.

Article XI

In the event that my said wife, _____ , predeceases me or should we both die in some common accident, even though she should survive me by an appreciable length of time, such as one-hundred twenty (120) days, then my wife shall be deemed to have survived me with regard to all dispositive provisions for her benefit in this, my last will and testament. In the event that one or more of my children does not survive me, then I hereby give, devise, and bequeath the share of my property which that child would normally have taken under this will, to the living issue, collectively, of each deceased child of mine.

Article XII

If assets of my estate are to become a part of any trust by the terms of this will, and if such assets will immediately distribute upon receipt thereof by the trustee, the trustee may distribute such assets in exactly the same manner as provided in such trust without requiring such trust to be established.

Article XIII

Except for the income and general testamentary power of appointment reserved to my wife in TRUST A or ARTICLE V, no title in the trusts created by this will, or in the income from said trusts shall vest in any beneficiary and neither the principal nor the income of said trusts shall be liable for the debts of any beneficiary, and none of the beneficiaries herein shall have any power to sell, assign, transfer, encumber, or in any other manner to dispose of his or her interest in any such trust, or the income produced by such trust, prior to the actual distribution in fact, by the trustee to said beneficiary.

Article XIV

As used in this will, the singular includes the plural and the masculine includes the feminine, and the terms "issue" and "child" are defined as follows:

> **"issue"**   means all persons who are descended from the persons referred to , either by legitimate birth to or legally adopted by him or any of his legitimately born or legally adopted descendants.

> **"child"**   means an issue of the first generation.

Article XV

I hereby waive any and all requirements that any trust herein created be submitted to the jurisdiction of any court, that the trustee by appointed or confirmed by any court, that evidence of such appointment or confirmation be filed in any court, and that the trustee's accounts be examined, heard, filed with or allowed by any court. This provision shall be overridden by a request by any trust beneficiaries, trustees or executors to require the procedures waived in this article.

Article XVI

Any trusts herein created shall terminate if the trustee shall determine that the continued administration of such trusts could be unduly expensive or burdensome to the beneficiaries, and if such event should occur the assets of any such trusts shall be distributed to the beneficiaries then entitled to receive the net income of said trusts in such proportions as they are entitled to receive said net income.

Article XVII

If my estate includes any business, I hereby expressly authorize my personal representative and trustee to retain and carry on any such business regardless of the fact that such business may constitute a large or major portion of my estate or trust estate. My personal representative and trustee shall have all necessary powers to enable them to do any and all things deemed appropriate by them for the carrying on of such business, including the power to incorporate and reorganize the business, to put in additional capital, and to hire a business manager or other such employees as they shall deem necessary. My estate and trust estate shall bear the sole risk of any business interest so retained, and my personal representative and trustee shall not be liable for any loss incurred thereby except when such loss is caused by their own negligence. Because the desirability of retaining any such business interests may be affected by many factors, any powers given in this Article to my personal representative and trustee shall not be mandatory. My personal representative and trustee shall have the power to close out and liquidate or sell such business interests upon such terms as they in their sole discretion shall deem best.

Article XVIII

In the event that my trustee under this will is the beneficiary of proceeds of any pension, profit sharing or stock bonus plans which qualify under applicable provisions of the Internal Revenue Code, said trustee shall not use any of such proceeds to pay any taxes, debts or other obligations enforceable against my estate, including both probate and non-probate assets. Any such proceeds received from pension, profit sharing or stock bonus plans which qualify under applicable provisions of the Internal Revenue Code shall not be includable in my gross estate for Federal Estate Tax purposes nor shall they be subject to _____ Inheritance ₍state₎ Tax to such extent that said proceeds are attributable to contributions by my employer to any such qualified pension, profit sharing or stock bonus plans. All such funds shall be allocated to "TRUST B" and none to "TRUST A" s created in this will.

Article XIX

The payment by an insurance company of the proceeds of any policy of insurance to my trustee under this will as beneficiary, shall fully discharge all obligation of such insurance company on account of such policy and such insurance company shall bear no responsibility for the proper discharge of my trust or any part thereof. I direct my trustee to administer and distribute such insurance proceeds as follows:

1. If my wife survives me, my trustee shall allocate said insurance proceeds between "TRUST A", and "TRUST B", according to provisions in this will and as directed by my personal representative.

2. When acting under this will with respect to insurance proceeds as insurance beneficiary, rather than as distributee of my probate estate, my trustee shall have all duties, powers, rights, privileges and discretions given to my personal representative, and I direct that my trustee shall cooperate with my personal representative to ensure the most efficient and economical administration of my total gross estate.

Article XX

In the event my wife, _____ , does not survive me, I hereby nominate and appoint _____ as (name and address) guardian of the person for my minor child or children. The guardian may use the income from "TRUST B" for the support, education and well being of said child or children. In the event _____ is unable or unwilling to act as personal guardian, I hereby appoint _____ to serve in his place as personal guardian. (name and address)

Article XXI

I hereby nominate _____ of _____ as the per- (address) sonal representative of this my last will and testament, and I give and grant unto my personal representative with respect to my estate and to each and every portion thereof, real, personal, or mixed, all such duties, powers, and discretions herein given and granted to my trustee hereof with respect to my trust estate, all of which duties, powers, and discretions shall be in addition to and not in limitation of those which normally my personal representative would possess.

If at any time after my death, my wife shall file a request in writing with the herein named personal representative and trustee that she wishes to become a co-personal representative and/or co-trustee hereunder, I hereby nominate her as co-personal representative and/or co-trustee. Until such request if filed, the personal representative herein named shall be the sole personal representative and trustee.

Any trustee herein named may at any time after my death, resign by giving notice in writing to the then income beneficiary. The date of delivery shall be specified in such instrument of resignation, and such resignation shall take effect no earlier than thirty (30) days after delivery of such written resignation. Upon such effective resignation the resigning trustee shall be relieved of all further duties and responsibilities and shall bear no liability or responsibility for the acts of any successor trustee.

I hereby direct that my personal representative or trustee shall have custody and possession of all assets, shall bear the responsibility for all receipts and disbursements, and all accounting. I direct that bond shall not be required of my personal representative and trustee.

In witness whereof, I have hereunto set my hand to this my last will and testament, consisting of _____ typewritten pages, including this page and each bearing my signature, on this _____ day of _____ , 199__ at _____ , _____ , in the presence of each and all the (city) (state) subscribing witnesses, each of whom I have requested in the presence of the others to subscribe his/her name, with his/her address written opposite thereto, as an attesting witness, in my presence and in the presence of all the others.

_____

The above and foregoing instrument was on the date thereof, signed, published, sealed, and declared by the testator, _____ , to be his last will and testament in our presence, and we at his request and in his presence and in the presence of each other, have hereunto subscribed our names as witnesses thereto.

_____ Residing at _____
_____ Residing at _____

[Notary]

APPENDIX C

UNIFORM PROBATE CODE

PART 1

SHORT TITLE, CONSTRUCTION, GENERAL PROVISIONS

§1–101. [Short Title.]
This Act shall be known and may be cited as the Uniform Probate Code.

§1–102. [Purposes; Rule of Construction.]
(a) This Code shall be liberally construed and applied to promote its underlying purposes and policies.
(b) The underlying purposes and policies of this Code are:

(1) to simplify and clarify the law concerning the affairs of decedents, missing persons, protected persons, minors and incapacitated persons;

(2) to discover and make effective the intent of a decedent in distribution of his property;

(3) to promote a speedy and efficient system for liquidating the estate of the decedent and making distribution to his successors;

(4) to facilitate use and enforcement of certain trusts;

(5) to make uniform the law among the various jurisdictions.

§1–103. [Supplementary General Principles of Law Applicable.]
Unless displaced by the particular provisions of this Code, the principles of law and equity supplement its provisions.

§1–104. [Severability.]
If any provision of this Code or the application thereof to any person or circumstances is held invalid, the invalidity shall not affect other provisions or applications of the Code which can be given effect without the invalid provision or application, and to this end the provisions of this Code are declared to be severable.

§1–105. [Construction Against Implied Repeal.]
This Code is a general act intended as a unified coverage

of its subject matter and no part of it shall be deemed impliedly repealed by subsequent legislation if it can reasonably be avoided.

§1–106. [Effect of Fraud and Evasion.]

Whenever fraud has been perpetrated in connection with any proceeding or in any statement filed under this Code or if fraud is used to avoid or circumvent the provisions or purposes of this Code, any person injured thereby may obtain appropriate relief against the perpetrator of the fraud or restitution from any person (other than a bona fide purchaser) benefitting from the fraud, whether innocent or not. Any proceeding must be commenced within 2 years after the discovery of the fraud, but no proceeding may be brought against one not a perpetrator of the fraud later than 5 years after the time of commission of the fraud. This section has no bearing on remedies relating to fraud practiced on a decedent during his lifetime which affects the succession of his estate.

§1–107. [Evidence of Death or Status.]

In addition to the rules of evidence in courts of general jurisdiction, the following rules relating to a determination of death and status apply:

(1) Death occurs when an individual [is determined to be dead under the Uniform Determination of Death Act] [has sustained either (i) irreversible cessation of circulatory and respiratory functions or (ii) irreversible cessation of all functions of the entire brain, including the brain stem. A determination of death must be made in accordance with accepted medical standards].

(2) A certified or authenticated copy of a death certificate purporting to be issued by an official or agency of the place where the death purportedly occurred is prima facie evidence of the fact, place, date, and time of death and the identity of the decedent.

(3) A certified or authenticated copy of any record or report of a governmental agency, domestic or foreign, that an individual is missing, detained, dead, or alive is prima facie evidence of the status and of the dates, circumstances, and places disclosed by the record or report.

(4) In the absence of prima facie evidence of death under paragraph (2) or (3), the fact of death may be established by clear and convincing evidence, including circumstantial evidence.

(5) An individual whose death is not established under the preceding paragraphs who is absent for a continuous period of 5 years, during which he [or she] has not been heard from, and whose absence is not satisfactorily explained after diligent search or inquiry, is presumed to be dead. His [or her] death is presumed to have occurred at the end of the period unless there is sufficient evidence for determining that death occurred earlier.

(6) In the absence of evidence disputing the time of death stated on a document described in paragraph (2) or (3), a document described in paragraph (2) or (3) that states a time of death 120 hours or more after the time of death of another individual, however the time of death of the other individual is determined, establishes by clear and convincing evidence that the individual survived the other individual by 120 hours.

As amended in 1987 and 1991.

§1–108. [Acts by Holder of General Power.]

For the purpose of granting consent or approval with regard to the acts or accounts of a personal representative or trustee, including relief from liability or penalty for failure to post bond, to register a trust, or to perform other duties, and for purposes of consenting to modification or termination of a trust or to deviation from its terms, the sole holder or all co-holders of a presently exercisable general power of appointment, including one in the form of a power of amendment or revocation, are deemed to act for beneficiaries to the extent their interests (as objects, takers in default, or otherwise) are subject to the power.

PART 2
DEFINITIONS

§1–201. General Definitions.

Subject to additional definitions contained in the subsequent Articles that are applicable to specific Articles, parts, or sections, and unless the context otherwise requires, in this Code:

(1) "Agent" includes an attorney-in-fact under a durable or nondurable power of attorney, an individual authorized to make decisions concerning another's health care, and an individual authorized to make decisions for another under a natural death act.

(2) "Application" means a written request to the Registrar for an order of informal probate or appointment under Part 3 of Article III.

(3) "Beneficiary," as it relates to a trust beneficiary, includes a person who has any present or future interest, vested or contingent, and also includes the owner of an interest by assignment or other transfer; as it relates to a charitable trust, includes any person entitled to enforce the trust; as it relates to a "beneficiary of a beneficiary designation," refers to a beneficiary of an insurance or annuity policy, of an account with POD designation, of a security registered in beneficiary form (TOD), or of a pension, profit-sharing, retirement, or similar benefit plan, or other nonprobate transfer at death; and, as it relates to a "beneficiary designated in a governing instrument," includes a grantee of a deed, a devisee, a trust beneficiary, a beneficiary of a beneficiary designation, a donee, appointee, or taker in default of a

power of appointment, or a person in whose favor a power of attorney or a power held in any individual, fiduciary, or representative capacity is exercised.

(4) "Beneficiary designation" refers to a governing instrument naming a beneficiary of an insurance or annuity policy, of an account with POD designation, of a security registered in beneficiary form (TOD), or of a pension, profit-sharing, retirement, or similar benefit plan, or other nonprobate transfer at death.

(5) "Child" includes an individual entitled to take as a child under this Code by intestate succession from the parent whose relationship is involved and excludes a person who is only a stepchild, a foster child, a grandchild, or any more remote descendant.

(6) "Claims," in respect to estates of decedents and protected persons, includes liabilities of the decedent or protected person, whether arising in contract, in tort, or otherwise, and liabilities of the estate which arise at or after the death of the decedent or after the appointment of a conservator, including funeral expenses and expenses of administration. The term does not include estate or inheritance taxes, or demands or disputes regarding title of a decedent or protected person to specific assets alleged to be included in the estate.

(7) "Court" means the [. . . . . Court] or branch in this State having jurisdiction in matters relating to the affairs of decedents.

(8) "Conservator" means a person who is appointed by a Court to manage the estate of a protected person.

(9) "Descendant" of an individual means all of his [or her] descendants of all generations, with the relationship of parent and child at each generation being determined by the definition of child and parent contained in this Code.

(10) "Devise," when used as a noun, means a testamentary disposition of real or personal property and, when used as a verb, means to dispose of real or personal property by will.

(11) "Devisee" means a person designated in a will to receive a devise. For the purposes of Article II, in the case of a devise to an existing trust or trustee, or to a trustee on trust described by will, the trust or trustee is the devisee and the beneficiaries are not devisees.

(12) "Disability" means cause for a protective order as described in Section 5–401.

(13) "Distributee" means any person who has received property of a decedent from his [or her] personal representative other than as a creditor or purchaser. A testamentary trustee is a distributee only to the extent of distributed assets or increment thereto remaining in his [or her] hands. A beneficiary of a testamentary trust to whom the trustee has distributed property received from a personal representative is a distributee of the personal representative. For the purposes of this provision, "testamentary trustee" includes a trustee to whom assets are transferred by will, to the extent of the devised assets.

(14) "Estate" includes the property of the decedent, trust, or other person whose affairs are subject to this Code as originally constituted and as it exists from time to time during administration.

(15) "Exempt property" means that property of a decedent's estate which is described in Section 2–403.

(16) "Fiduciary" includes a personal representative, guardian, conservator, and trustee.

(17) "Foreign personal representative" means a personal representative appointed by another jurisdiction.

(18) "Formal proceedings" means proceedings conducted before a judge with notice to interested persons.

(19) "Governing instrument" means a deed, will, trust, insurance or annuity policy, account with POD designation, security registered in beneficiary form (TOD), pension, profit-sharing, retirement, or similar benefit plan, instrument creating or exercising a power of appointment or a power of attorney, or a dispositive, appointive, or nominative instrument of any similar type.

(20) "Guardian" means a person who has qualified as a guardian of a minor or incapacitated person pursuant to testamentary or court appointment, but excludes one who is merely a guardian ad litem.

(21) "Heirs," except as controlled by Section 2–711, means persons, including the surviving spouse and the state, who are entitled under the statutes of intestate succession to the property of a decedent.

(22) "Incapacitated person" means an individual described in Section 5–103.

(23) "Informal proceedings" means those conducted without notice to interested persons by an officer of the Court acting as a registrar for probate of a will or appointment of a personal representative.

(24) "Interested person" includes heirs, devisees, children, spouses, creditors, beneficiaries, and any others having a property right in or claim against a trust estate or the estate of a decedent, ward, or protected person. It also includes persons having priority for appointment as personal representative, and other fiduciaries representing interested persons. The meaning as it relates to particular persons may vary from time to time and must be determined according to the particular purposes of, and matter involved in, any proceeding.

(25) "Issue" of a person means descendant as defined in subsection (9).

(26) "Joint tenants with the right of survivorship" and "community property with the right of survivorship" includes co-owners of property held under circumstances that entitle one or more to the whole of the property on the death of the other or others, but excludes forms of co-ownership registration in which the underlying ownership of each party is in proportion to that party's contribution.

(27) "Lease" includes an oil, gas, or other mineral lease.

(28) "Letters" includes letters testamentary, letters of guardianship, letters of administration, and letters of conservatorship.

(29) "Minor" means a person who is under [21] years of age.

(30) "Mortgage" means any conveyance, agreement, or arrangement in which property is encumbered or used as security.

(31) "Nonresident decedent" means a decedent who was domiciled in another jurisdiction at the time of his [or her] death.

(32) "Organization" means a corporation, business trust, estate, trust, partnership, joint venture, association, government or governmental subdivision or agency, or any other legal or commercial entity.

(33) "Parent" includes any person entitled to take, or who would be entitled to take if the child died without a will, as a parent under this Code by intestate succession from the child whose relationship is in question and excludes any person who is only a stepparent, foster parent, or grandparent.

(34) "Payor" means a trustee, insurer, business entity, employer, government, governmental agency or subdivision, or any other person authorized or obligated by law or a governing instrument to make payments.

(35) "Person" means an individual or an organization.

(36) "Personal representative" includes executor, administrator, successor personal representative, special administrator, and persons who perform substantially the same function under the law governing their status. "General personal representative" excludes special administrator.

(37) "Petition" means a written request to the Court for an order after notice.

(38) "Proceeding" includes action at law and suit in equity.

(39) "Property" includes both real and personal property or any interest therein and means anything that may be the subject of ownership.

(40) "Protected person" is as defined in Section 5–103.

(41) "Protective proceeding" means a proceeding described in Section 5–103.

(42) "Registrar" refers to the official of the Court designated to perform the functions of Registrar as provided in Section 1–307.

(43) "Security" includes any note, stock, treasury stock, bond, debenture, evidence of indebtedness, certificate of interest or participation in an oil, gas, or mining title or lease or in payments out of production under such a title or lease, collateral trust certificate, transferable share, voting trust certificate or, in general, any interest or instrument commonly known as a security, or any certificate of interest or participation, any temporary or interim certificate, receipt, or certificate of deposit for, or any warrant or right to subscribe to or purchase, any of the foregoing.

(44) "Settlement," in reference to a decedent's estate, includes the full process of administration, distribution, and closing.

(45) "Special administrator" means a personal representative as described by Sections 3–614 through 3–618.

(46) "State" means a state of the United States, the District of Columbia, the Commonwealth of Puerto Rico, or any territory or insular possession subject to the jurisdiction of the United States.

(47) "Successor personal representative" means a personal representative, other than a special administrator, who is appointed to succeed a previously appointed personal representative.

(48) "Successors" means persons, other than creditors, who are entitled to property of a decedent under his [or her] will or this Code.

(49) "Supervised administration" refers to the proceedings described in Article III, Part 5.

(50) "Survive" means that an individual has neither predeceased an event, including the death of another individual, nor is deemed to have predeceased an event under Section 2–104 or 2–702. The term includes its derivatives, such as "survives," "survived," "survivor," "surviving."

(51) "Testacy proceeding" means a proceeding to establish a will or determine intestacy.

(52) "Testator" includes an individual of either sex.

(53) "Trust" includes an express trust, private or charitable, with additions thereto, wherever and however created. The term also includes a trust created or determined by judgment or decree under which the trust is to be administered in the manner of an express trust. The term excludes other constructive trusts and excludes resulting trusts, conservatorships, personal representatives, trust accounts as defined in Article VI, custodial arrangements pursuant to [each state should list its legislation, including that relating to [gifts] [transfers] to minors, dealing with special custodial situations], business trusts providing for certificates to be issued to beneficiaries, common trust funds, voting trusts, security arrangements, liquidation trusts, and trusts for the primary purpose of paying debts, dividends, interest, salaries, wages, profits, pensions, or employee benefits of any kind, and any arrangement under which a person is nominee or escrowee for another.

(54) "Trustee" includes an original, additional, or successor trustee, whether or not appointed or confirmed by court.

(55) "Ward" means an individual described in Section 5–103.

(56) "Will" includes codicil and any testamentary

instrument that merely appoints an executor, revokes or revises another will, nominates a guardian, or expressly excludes or limits the right of an individual or class to succeed to property of the decedent passing by intestate succession.

[FOR ADOPTION IN COMMUNITY PROPERTY STATES]

[(57) "Separate property" (if necessary, to be defined locally in accordance with existing concept in adopting state).

(58) "Community property" (if necessary, to be defined locally in accordance with existing concept in adopting state).]

As revised in 1990 and amended in 1991 and 1993.

PART 3
SCOPE, JURISDICTION AND COURTS

§1–301. [Territorial Application.]

Except as otherwise provided in this Code, this Code applies to (1) the affairs and estates of decedents, missing persons, and persons to be protected, domiciled in this state, (2) the property of nonresidents located in this state or property coming into the control of a fiduciary who is subject to the laws of this state, (3) incapacitated persons and minors in this state, (4) survivorship and related accounts in this state, and (5) trusts subject to administration in this state.

§1–302. [Subject Matter Jurisdiction.]

(a) To the full extent permitted by the constitution, the Court has jurisdiction over all subject matter relating to (1) estates of decedents, including construction of wills and determination of heirs and successors of decedents, and estates of protected persons; (2) protection of minors and incapacitated persons; and (3) trusts.

(b) The Court has full power to make orders, judgments and decrees and take all other action necessary and proper to administer justice in the matters which come before it.

(c) The Court has jurisdiction over protective proceedings and guardianship proceedings.

(d) If both guardianship and protective proceedings as to the same person are commenced or pending in the same court, the proceedings may be consolidated.

§1–303. [Venue; Multiple Proceedings; Transfer.]

(a) Where a proceeding under this Code could be maintained in more than one place in this state, the Court in which the proceeding is first commenced has the exclusive right to proceed.

(b) If proceedings concerning the same estate, protected person, ward, or trust are commenced in more than one Court of this state, the Court in which the proceeding was first commenced shall continue to hear the matter, and the other courts shall hold the matter in

abeyance until the question of venue is decided, and if the ruling Court determines that venue is properly in another Court, it shall transfer the proceeding to the other Court.

(c) If a Court finds that in the interest of justice a proceeding or a file should be located in another Court of this state, the Court making the finding may transfer the proceeding or file to the other Court.

§1–304. [Practice in Court.]

Unless specifically provided to the contrary in this Code or unless inconsistent with its provisions, the rules of civil procedure including the rules concerning vacation of orders and appellate review govern formal proceedings under this Code.

§1–305. [Records and Certified Copies.]

The [Clerk of Court] shall keep a record for each decedent, ward, protected person or trust involved in any document which may be filed with the Court under this Code, including petitions and applications, demands for notices or bonds, trust registrations, and of any orders or responses relating thereto by the Registrar or Court, and establish and maintain a system for indexing, filing or recording which is sufficient to enable users of the records to obtain adequate information. Upon payment of the fees required by law the clerk must issue certified copies of any probated wills, letters issued to personal representatives, or any other record or paper filed or recorded. Certificates relating to probated wills must indicate whether the decedent was domiciled in this state and whether the probate was formal or informal. Certificates relating to letters must show the date of appointment.

§1–306. [Jury Trial.]

(a) If duly demanded, a party is entitled to trial by jury in [a formal testacy proceeding and] any proceeding in which any controverted question of fact arises as to which any party has a constitutional right to trial by jury.

(b) If there is no right to trial by jury under subsection (a) or the right is waived, the Court in its discretion may call a jury to decide any issue of fact, in which case the verdict is advisory only.

§1–307. [Registrar; Powers.]

The acts and orders which this Code specifies as performable by the Registrar may be performed either by a judge of the Court or by a person, including the clerk, designated by the Court by a written order filed and recorded in the office of the Court.

§1–308. [Appeals.]

Appellate review, including the right to appellate review, interlocutory appeal, provisions as to time, manner, notice, appeal bond, stays, scope of review, record on appeal, briefs, arguments and power of the appellate court, is governed by the rules applicable to the appeals to the [Supreme Court] in equity cases from the [court of general jurisdiction], except that in proceedings where jury trial has been had as a matter of right, the rules applicable to the scope of review in jury cases apply.

§1–309. [Qualifications of Judge.]

A judge of the Court must have the same qualifications as a judge of the [court of general jurisdiction.]

§1–310. [Oath or Affirmation on Filed Documents.]

Except as otherwise specifically provided in this Code or by rule, every document filed with the Court under this Code including applications, petitions, and demands for notice, shall be deemed to include an oath, affirmation, or statement to the effect that its representations are true as far as the person executing or filing it knows or is informed, and penalties for perjury may follow deliberate falsification therein.

PART 4
NOTICE, PARTIES AND REPRESENTATION IN ESTATE LITIGATION AND OTHER MATTERS

§1–401. [Notice; Method and Time of Giving.]

(a) If notice of a hearing on any petition is required and except for specific notice requirements as otherwise provided, the petitioner shall cause notice of the time and place of hearing of any petition to be given to any interested person or his attorney if he has appeared by attorney or requested that notice be sent to his attorney. Notice shall be given:

(1) by mailing a copy thereof at least 14 days before the time set for the hearing by certified, registered or ordinary first class mail addressed to the person being notified at the post office address given in his demand for notice, if any, or at his office or place of residence, if known;

(2) by delivering a copy thereof to the person being notified personally at least 14 days before the time set for the hearing; or

(3) if the address, or identity of any person is not known and cannot be ascertained with reasonable diligence, by publishing at least once a week for 3 consecutive weeks, a copy thereof in a newspaper having general circulation in the county where the hearing is to be held, the last publication of which is to be at least 10 days before the time set for the hearing.

(b) The Court for good cause shown may provide for a different method or time of giving notice for any hearing.

(c) Proof of the giving of notice shall be made on or before the hearing and filed in the proceeding.

§1–402. [Notice; Waiver.]

A person, including a guardian ad litem, conservator, or other fiduciary, may waive notice by a writing signed by him or his attorney and filed in the proceeding. A person for whom a guardianship or other protective order is sought, a ward, or a protected person may not waive notice.

§1–403. [Pleadings; When Parties Bound by Others; Notice.]

In formal proceedings involving trusts or estates of decedents, minors, protected persons, or incapacitated persons, and in judicially supervised settlements, the following apply:

(1) Interests to be affected shall be described in pleadings which give reasonable information to owners by name or class, by reference to the instrument creating the interests, or in other appropriate manner.

(2) Persons are bound by orders binding others in the following cases:

(i) Orders binding the sole holder or all co-holders of a power of revocation or a presently exercisable general power of appointment, including one in the form of a power of amendment, bind other persons to the extent their interests (as objects, takers in default, or otherwise) are subject to the power.

(ii) To the extent there is no conflict of interest between them or among persons represented, orders binding a conservator bind the person whose estate he controls; orders binding a guardian bind the ward if no conservator of his estate has been appointed; orders binding a trustee bind beneficiaries of the trust in proceedings to probate a will establishing or adding to a trust, to review the acts or accounts of a prior fiduciary and in proceedings involving creditors or other third parties; and orders binding a personal representative bind persons interested in the undistributed assets of a decedent's estate in actions or proceedings by or against the estate. If there is no conflict of interest and no conservator or guardian has been appointed, a parent may represent his minor child.

(iii) An unborn or unascertained person who is not otherwise represented is bound by an order to the extent his interest is adequately represented by another party having a substantially identical interest in the proceeding.

(3) Notice is required as follows:

(i) Notice as prescribed by Section 1–401 shall be given to every interested person or to one who can bind an interested person as described in (2)(i) or (2)(ii) above. Notice may be given both to a person and to another who may bind him.

(ii) Notice is given to unborn or unascertained

persons, who are not represented under (2)(i) or (2)(ii) above, by giving notice to all known persons whose interests in the proceedings are substantially identical to those of the unborn or unascertained persons.

(4) At any point in a proceeding, a court may appoint a guardian ad litem to represent the interest of a minor, an incapacitated, unborn, or unascertained person, or a person whose identity or address is unknown, if the Court determines that representation of the interest otherwise would be inadequate. If not precluded by conflict of interests, a guardian ad litem may be appointed to represent several persons or interests. The Court shall set out its reasons for appointing a guardian ad litem as a part of the record of the proceeding.

ARTICLE II
INTESTACY, WILLS, AND DONATIVE TRANSFERS (1990)

PART 1
INTESTATE SUCCESSION

PART 2
ELECTIVE SHARE OF SURVIVING SPOUSE

PART 3
SPOUSE AND CHILDREN UNPROVIDED FOR IN WILLS

PART 4
EXEMPT PROPERTY AND ALLOWANCES

PART 5
WILLS, WILL CONTRACTS, AND CUSTODY AND DEPOSIT OF WILLS

PART 6
RULES OF CONSTRUCTION APPLICABLE ONLY TO WILLS

PART 7
RULES OF CONSTRUCTION APPLICABLE TO WILLS AND OTHER GOVERNING INSTRUMENTS

PART 8
GENERAL PROVISIONS CONCERNING PROBATE AND NONPROBATE TRANSFERS

PART 9
STATUTORY RULE AGAINST PERPETUITIES; HONORARY TRUSTS

SUBPART 1.
STATUTORY RULE AGAINST PERPETUITIES

SUBPART 2.
[HONORARY TRUSTS]

PART 10
UNIFORM INTERNATIONAL WILLS ACT [INTERNATIONAL WILL; INFORMATION REGISTRATION]

PART 1
INTESTATE SUCCESSION

§2–101. Intestate Estate.

(a) Any part of a decedent's estate not effectively disposed of by will passes by intestate succession to the decedent's heirs as prescribed in this Code, except as modified by the decedent's will.

(b) A decedent by will may expressly exclude or limit the right of an individual or class to succeed to property of the decedent passing by intestate succession. If that individual or a member of that class survives the decedent, the share of the decedent's intestate estate to which that individual or class would have succeeded passes as if that individual or each member of that class had disclaimed his [or her] intestate share.

§2–102. Share of Spouse.

The intestate share of a decedent's surviving spouse is:

(1) the entire intestate estate if:

(i) no descendant or parent of the decedent survives the decedent; or

(ii) all of the decedent's surviving descendants are also descendants of the surviving spouse and there is no other descendant of the surviving spouse who survives the decedent;

(2) the first [$200,000], plus three-fourths of any balance of the intestate estate, if no descendant of the decedent survives the decedent, but a parent of the decedent survives the decedent;

(3) the first [$150,000], plus one-half of any balance of the intestate estate, if all of the decedent's surviving descendants are also descendants of the surviving spouse and the surviving spouse has one or more surviving descendants who are not descendants of the decedent;

(4) the first [$100,000], plus one-half of any balance of the intestate estate, if one or more of the decedent's surviving descendants are not descendants of the surviving spouse.

[ALTERNATIVE PROVISION FOR COMMUNITY PROPERTY STATES]

[§2–102A. Share of Spouse.

2–102A. Share of Spouse.

(a) The intestate share of a surviving spouse in separate property is:

(1) the entire intestate estate if:

(i) no descendant or parent of the decedent survives the decedent; or

(ii) all of the decedent's surviving descendants are also descendants of the surviving spouse and there is no other descendant of the surviving spouse who survives the decedent;

(2) the first [$200,000], plus three-fourths of any balance of the intestate estate, if no descendant of the decedent survives the decedent, but a parent of the decedent survives the decedent;

(3) the first [$150,000], plus one-half of any balance of the intestate estate, if all of the decedent's surviving descendants are also descendants of the surviving spouse and the surviving spouse has one or more surviving descendants who are not descendants of the decedent;

(4) the first [$100,000], plus one-half of any balance of the intestate estate, if one or more of the decedent's surviving descendants are not descendants of the surviving spouse.

(b) The one-half of community property belonging to the decedent passes to the [surviving spouse] as the intestate share.]

§2–103. Share of Heirs other than Surviving Spouse.

Any part of the intestate estate not passing to the decedent's surviving spouse under Section 2–102, or the entire intestate estate if there is no surviving spouse, passes in the following order to the individuals designated below who survive the decedent:

(1) to the decedent's descendants by representation;

(2) if there is no surviving descendant, to the decedent's parents equally if both survive, or to the surviving parent;

(3) if there is no surviving descendant or parent, to the descendants of the decedent's parents or either of them by representation;

(4) if there is no surviving descendant, parent, or descendant of a parent, but the decedent is survived by one or more grandparents or descendants of grandparents, half of the estate passes to the decedent's paternal grandparents equally if both survive, or to the surviving paternal grandparent, or to the descendants of the decedent's paternal grandparents or either of them if both are deceased, the descendants taking by representation; and the other half passes to the decedent's maternal relatives in the same manner; but if there is no surviving grandparent or descendant of a grandparent on either the paternal or the maternal side, the entire estate passes to the decedent's relatives on the other side in the same manner as the half.

§2–104. Requirement that Heir Survive Decedent for 120 Hours.

An individual who fails to survive the decedent by 120 hours is deemed to have predeceased the decedent for purposes of homestead allowance, exempt property, and intestate succession, and the decedent's heirs are determined accordingly. If it is not established by clear and convincing evidence that an individual who would otherwise be an heir survived the decedent by 120 hours, it is deemed that the individual failed to survive for the required period. This section is not to be applied if its application would result in a taking of intestate estate by the state under Section 2–105.

§2–105. No Taker.

If there is no taker under the provisions of this Article, the intestate estate passes to the [state].

§2–106. Representation.

(a) **[Definitions.]** In this section:

(1) "Deceased descendant," "deceased parent," or "deceased grandparent" means a descendant, parent, or grandparent who either predeceased the decedent or is deemed to have predeceased the decedent under Section 2–104.

(2) "Surviving descendant" means a descendant who neither predeceased the decedent nor is deemed to have predeceased the decedent under Section 2–104.

(b) **[Decedent's Descendants.]** If, under Section 2–103(1), a decedent's intestate estate or a part thereof passes "by representation" to the decedent's descendants, the estate or part thereof is divided into as many equal shares as there are (i) surviving descendants in the generation nearest to the decedent which contains one or more surviving descendants and (ii) deceased descendants in the same generation who left surviving descendants, if any. Each surviving descendant in the nearest generation is allocated one share. The remaining shares, if any, are combined and then divided in the same manner among the surviving descendants of the deceased descendants as if the surviving descendants who were allocated a share and their surviving descendants had predeceased the decedent.

(c) [Descendants of Parents or Grandparents.] If, under Section 2–103(3) or (4), a decedent's intestate estate or a part thereof passes "by representation" to the descendants of the decedent's deceased parents or either of them or to the descendants of the decedent's deceased paternal or maternal grandparents or either of them, the estate or part thereof is divided into as many equal shares as there are (i) surviving descendants in the generation nearest the deceased parents or either of them, or the deceased grandparents or either of them, that contains one or more surviving descendants and (ii) deceased descendants in the same generation who left surviving descendants, if any. Each surviving descendant in the nearest generation is allocated one share. The remaining shares, if any, are combined and then divided in the same manner among the surviving descendants of the deceased descendants as if the surviving descendants who were allocated a share and their surviving descendants had predeceased the decedent.

§2–107. Kindred of Half Blood.
Relatives of the half blood inherit the same share they would inherit if they were of the whole blood.

§2–108. Afterborn Heirs.
An individual in gestation at a particular time is treated as living at that time if the individual lives 120 hours or more after birth.

§2–109. Advancements.
(a) If an individual dies intestate as to all or a portion of his [or her] estate, property the decedent gave during the decedent's lifetime to an individual who, at the decedent's death, is an heir is treated as an advancement against the heir's intestate share only if (i) the decedent declared in a contemporaneous writing or the heir acknowledged in writing that the gift is an advancement or (ii) the decedent's contemporaneous writing or the heir's written acknowledgment otherwise indicates that the gift is to be taken into account in computing the division and distribution of the decedent's intestate estate.

(b) For purposes of subsection (a), property advanced is valued as of the time the heir came into possession or enjoyment of the property or as of the time of the decedent's death, whichever first occurs.

(c) If the recipient of the property fails to survive the decedent, the property is not taken into account in computing the division and distribution of the decedent's intestate estate, unless the decedent's contemporaneous writing provides otherwise.

§2–110. Debts to Decedent.
A debt owed to a decedent is not charged against the intestate share of any individual except the debtor. If the debtor fails to survive the decedent, the debt is not taken into account in computing the intestate share of the debtor's descendants.

§2–111. Alienage.
No individual is disqualified to take as an heir because the individual or an individual through whom he [or she] claims is or has been an alien.

[§2–112. Dower and Curtesy Abolished.
The estates of dower and curtesy are abolished.]

§2–113. Individuals Related to Decedent Through Two Lines.
An individual who is related to the decedent through two lines of relationship is entitled to only a single share based on the relationship that would entitle the individual to the larger share.

§2–114. Parent and Child Relationship.
(a) Except as provided in subsections (b) and (c), for purposes of intestate succession by, through, or from a person, an individual is the child of his [or her] natural parents, regardless of their marital status. The parent and child relationship may be established under [the Uniform Parentage Act] [applicable state law] [insert appropriate statutory reference].

(b) An adopted individual is the child of his [or her] adopting parent or parents and not of his [or her] natural parents, but adoption of a child by the spouse of either natural parent has no effect on (i) the relationship between the child and that natural parent or (ii) the right of the child or a descendant of the child to inherit from or through the other natural parent.

(c) Inheritance from or through a child by either natural parent or his [or her] kindred is precluded unless that natural parent has openly treated the child as his [or hers], and has not refused to support the child.

PART 2
ELECTIVE SHARE OF SURVIVING SPOUSE

§2–201. Definitions.
In this Part:

(1) As used in sections other than Section 2–205, "decedent's nonprobate transfers to others" means the amounts that are included in the augmented estate under Section 2–205.

(2) "Fractional interest in property held in joint tenancy with the right of survivorship," whether the fractional interest is unilaterally severable or not, means the fraction, the numerator of which is one and the denominator of which, if the decedent was a joint tenant, is one plus the number of joint tenants who survive the decedent and which, if the decedent was not a joint tenant, is the number of joint tenants.

(3) "Marriage," as it relates to a transfer by the decedent during marriage, means any marriage of the decedent to the decedent's surviving spouse.

(4) 'Nonadverse party" means a person who does not have a substantial beneficial interest in the trust or other property arrangement that would be adversely affected by the exercise or nonexercise of the power that he [or she] possesses respecting the trust or other property arrangement. A person having a general power of appointment over property is deemed to have a beneficial interest in the property.

(5) "Power" or "power of appointment" includes a power to designate the beneficiary of a beneficiary designation.

(6) "Presently exercisable general power of appointment" means a power of appointment under which, at the time in question, the decedent, whether or not he [or she] then had the capacity to exercise the power, held a power to create a present or future interest in himself [or herself], his [or her] creditors, his [or her] estate, or creditors of his [or her] estate, and includes a power to revoke or invade the principal of a trust or other property arrangement.

(7) "Probate estate" means property that would pass by intestate succession if the decedent died without a valid will.

(8) "Property" includes values subject to a beneficiary designation.

(9) "Right to income" includes a right to payments under a commercial or private annuity, an annuity trust, a unitrust, or a similar arrangement.

(10) "Transfer," as it relates to a transfer by or of the decedent, includes (A) an exercise or release of a presently exercisable general power of appointment held by the decedent, (B) a lapse at death of a presently exercisable general power of appointment held by the decedent, and (C) an exercise, release, or lapse of a general power of appointment that the decedent created in himself [or herself] and of a power described in Section 2–205(2)(ii) that the decedent conferred on a nonadverse party.

§2–202. Elective Share.

(a) [Elective-Share Amount.] The surviving spouse of a decedent who dies domiciled in this State has a right of election, under the limitations and conditions stated in this Part, to take an elective-share amount equal to the value of the elective-share percentage of the augmented estate, determined by the length of time the spouse and the decedent were married to each other, in accordance with the following schedule:

If the decedent and the spouse were married to each other:	The elective-share percentage is:
Less than 1 year	Supplemental Amount Only.
1 year but less than 2 years	3% of the augmented estate.
2 years but less than 3 years	6% of the augmented estate.
3 years but less than 4 years	9% of the augmented estate.
4 years but less than 5 years	12% of the augmented estate.
5 years but less than 6 years	15% of the augmented estate.
6 years but less than 7 years	18% of the augmented estate.
7 years but less than 8 years	21% of the augmented estate.
8 years but less than 9 years	24% of the augmented estate.
9 years but less than 10 years	27% of the augmented estate.
10 years but less than 11 years	30% of the augmented estate.
11 years but less than 12 years	34% of the augmented estate.
12 years but less than 13 years	38% of the augmented estate.
13 years but less than 14 years	42% of the augmented estate.
14 years but less than 15 years	46% of the augmented estate.
15 years or more	50% of the augmented estate.

(b) [Supplemental Elective-Share Amount.] If the sum of the amounts described in Sections 2–207, 2–209(a)(1), and that part of the elective-share amount payable from the decedent's probate estate and nonprobate transfers to others under Section 2–209(b) and (c) is less than [$50,000], the surviving spouse is entitled to a supplemental elective-share amount equal to [$50,000], minus the sum of the amounts described in those sections. The supplemental elective-share amount is payable from the decedent's probate estate and from recipients of the decedent's nonprobate transfers to others in the order of priority set forth in Section 2–209(b) and (c).

(c) [Effect of Election on Statutory Benefits.] If the right of election is exercised by or on behalf of the surviving spouse, the surviving spouse's homestead allowance, exempt property, and family allowance, if any, are not charged against but are in addition to the elective-share and supplemental elective-share amounts.

(d) [Non-Domiciliary.] The right, if any, of the surviving spouse of a decedent who dies domiciled outside this State to take an elective share in property in this State is governed by the law of the decedent's domicile at death.

§2–203. Composition of the Augmented Estate.

Subject to Section 2–208, the value of the augmented estate, to the extent provided in Sections 2–204, 2–205, 2–206, and 2–207, consists of the sum of the values of all property, whether real or personal; movable or immovable, tangible or intangible, wherever situated, that constitute the decedent's net probate estate, the decedent's nonprobate transfers to others, the decedent's nonprobate transfers to the surviving spouse, and the surviving spouse's property and nonprobate transfers to others.

§2–204. Decedent's Net Probate Estate.

The value of the augmented estate includes the value of the decedent's probate estate, reduced by funeral and administration expenses, homestead allowance, family allowances, exempt property, and enforceable claims.

§2–205. Decedent's Nonprobate Transfers to Others.

The value of the augmented estate includes the value of the decedent's nonprobate transfers to others, not included under Section 2–204, of any of the following types, in the amount provided respectively for each type of transfer:

(1) Property owned or owned in substance by the decedent immediately before death that passed outside probate at the decedent's death. Property included under this category consists of:

(i) Property over which the decedent alone, immediately before death, held a presently exercisable general power of appointment. The amount included is the value of the property subject to the power, to the extent the property passed at the decedent's death, by exercise, release, lapse, in default, or otherwise, to or for the benefit of any person other than the decedent's estate or surviving spouse.

(ii) The decedent's fractional interest in property held by the decedent in joint tenancy with the right of survivorship. The amount included is the value of the decedent's fractional interest, to the extent the fractional interest passed by right of survivorship at the decedent's death to a surviving joint tenant other than the decedent's surviving spouse.

(iii) The decedent's ownership interest in property or accounts held in POD, TOD, or co-ownership registration with the right of survivorship. The amount included is the value of the decedent's ownership interest, to the extent the decedent's ownership interest passed at the decedent's death to or for the benefit of any person other than the decedent's estate or surviving spouse.

(iv) Proceeds of insurance, including accidental death benefits, on the life of the decedent, if the decedent owned the insurance policy immediately before death or if and to the extent the decedent alone and immediately before death held a presently exercisable general power of appointment over the policy or its proceeds. The amount included is the value of the proceeds, to the extent they were payable at the decedent's death to or for the benefit of any person other than the decedent's estate or surviving spouse.

(2) Property transferred in any of the following forms by the decedent during marriage:

(i) Any irrevocable transfer in which the decedent retained the right to the possession or enjoyment of, or to the income from, the property if and to the extent the decedent's right terminated at or continued beyond the decedent's death. The amount included is the value of the fraction of the property to which the decedent's right related, to the extent the fraction of the property passed outside probate to or for the benefit of any person other than the decedent's estate or surviving spouse.

(ii) Any transfer in which the decedent created a power over income or property, exercisable by the decedent alone or in conjunction with any other person, or exercisable by a nonadverse party, to or for the benefit of the decedent, creditors of the decedent, the decedent's estate, or creditors of the decedent's estate. The amount included with respect to a power over property is the value of the property subject to the power, and the amount included with respect to a power over income is the value of the property that produces or produced the income, to the extent the power in either case was exercisable at the decedent's death to or for the benefit of any person other than the decedent's surviving spouse or to the extent the property passed at the decedent's death, by exercise, release, lapse, in default, or otherwise, to or for the benefit of any person other than the decedent's estate or surviving spouse. If the power is a power over both income and property and the preceding sentence produces different amounts, the amount included is the greater amount.

(3) Property that passed during marriage and during the two-year period next preceding the decedent's death as a result of a transfer by the decedent if the transfer was of any of the following types:

(i) Any property that passed as a result of the termination of a right or interest in, or power over, property that would have been included in the augmented estate under paragraph (1)(i), (ii), or (iii), or under paragraph (2), if the right, interest, or power had not terminated until the decedent's death. The amount included is the value of the property that would have been included under those paragraphs if the property were valued at the time the right, interest, or power terminated, and is included only to the extent the property passed upon termination to or for the benefit of any person other than the decedent or the decedent's estate, spouse, or surviving spouse. As used in this subparagraph, "termination," with respect to a right or interest in property, occurs when the right or interest terminated by the terms of the governing instrument or the decedent transferred or relinquished the right or interest, and, with respect to a power over property, occurs when the power terminated by exercise, release, lapse, default, or otherwise, but, with respect to a power described in paragraph (1)(i), "termination" occurs when the power terminated by exercise or release, but not otherwise.

(ii) Any transfer of or relating to an insurance policy on the life of the decedent if the proceeds would have been included in the augmented estate under paragraph (1)(iv) had the transfer not occurred. The amount included is the value of the insurance proceeds to the extent the proceeds were payable at the decedent's death to or for the benefit of any person other than the decedent's estate or surviving spouse. (iii) Any transfer of property, to the extent not otherwise included in the augmented estate, made to or for the benefit of a person other than the decedent's surviving spouse. The amount included is the value of the transferred property to the extent the aggregate transfers to any one donee in either of the two years exceeded $10,000.

§2–206. Decedent's Nonprobate Transfers to the Surviving Spouse.

Excluding property passing to the surviving spouse under the federal Social Security system, the value of the augmented estate includes the value of the decedent's nonprobate transfers to the decedent's surviving spouse, which consist of all property that passed outside probate at the decedent's death from the decedent to the surviving spouse by reason of the decedent's death, including:
(1) the decedent's fractional interest in property held as a joint tenant with the right of survivorship, to the extent that the decedent's fractional interest passed to the surviving spouse as surviving joint tenant,
(2) the decedent's ownership interest in property or accounts held in co-ownership registration with the right of survivorship, to the extent the decedent's ownership interest passed to the surviving spouse as surviving co-owner, and
(3) all other property that would have been included in the augmented estate under Section 2–205(1) or (2) had it passed to or for the benefit of a person other than the decedent's spouse, surviving spouse, the decedent, or the decedent's creditors, estate, or estate creditors.

§2–207. Surviving Spouse's Property and Nonprobate Transfers to Others.

(a) [Included Property.] Except to the extent included in the augmented estate under Section 2–204 or 2–206, the value of the augmented estate includes the value of:
(1) property that was owned by the decedent's surviving spouse at the decedent's death, including:
(i) the surviving spouse's fractional interest in property held in joint tenancy with the right of survivorship,
(ii) the surviving spouse's ownership interest in property or accounts held in co-ownership registration with the right of survivorship, and
(iii) property that passed to the surviving spouse by reason of the decedent's death, but not including the spouse's right to homestead allowance, family allowance, exempt property, or payments under the federal Social Security system; and

(2) property that would have been included in the surviving spouse's nonprobate transfers to others, other than the spouse's fractional and ownership interests included under subsection (a)(1)(i) or (ii), had the spouse been the decedent.

(b) [Time of Valuation.] Property included under this section is valued at the decedent's death, taking the fact that the decedent predeceased the spouse into account, but, for purposes of subsection (a)(1)(i) and (ii), the values of the spouse's fractional and ownership interests are determined immediately before the decedent's death if the decedent was then a joint tenant or a co-owner of the property or accounts. For purposes of subsection (a)(2), proceeds of insurance that would have been included in the spouse's nonprobate transfers to others under Section 2–205(1)(iv) are not valued as if he [or she] were deceased.

(c) [Reduction for Enforceable Claims.] The value of property included under this section is reduced by enforceable claims against the surviving spouse.

§2–208. Exclusions, Valuation, and Overlapping Application.

(a) [Exclusions.] The value of any property is excluded from the decedent's nonprobate transfers to others (i) to the extent the decedent received adequate and full consideration in money or money's worth for a transfer of the property or (ii) if the property was transferred with the written joinder of, or if the transfer was consented to in writing by, the surviving spouse.

(b) [Valuation.] The value of property:
(1) included in the augmented estate under Section 2–205, 2–206, or 2–207 is reduced in each category by enforceable claims against the included property; and
(2) includes the commuted value of any present or future interest and the commuted value of amounts payable under any trust, life insurance settlement option, annuity contract, public or private pension, disability compensation, death benefit or retirement plan, or any similar arrangement, exclusive of the federal Social Security system.

(c) [Overlapping Application; No Double Inclusion.] In case of overlapping application to the same property of the paragraphs or subparagraphs of Section 2–205, 2–206, or 2–207, the property is included in the augmented estate under the provision yielding the greatest value, and under only one overlapping provision if they all yield the same value.

§2–209. Sources from Which Elective-Share Payable.

(a) [Elective-Share Amount Only.] In a proceeding for an elective share, the following are applied first to satisfy the elective-share amount and to reduce or eliminate any contributions due from the decedent's probate estate and recipients of the decedent's nonprobate transfers to others:

(1) amounts included in the augmented estate under Section 2–204 which pass or have passed to the surviving spouse by testate or intestate succession and amounts included in the augmented estate under Section 2–206; and

(2) amounts included in the augmented estate under Section 2–207 up to the applicable percentage thereof. For the purposes of this subsection, the "applicable percentage" is twice the elective-share percentage set forth in the schedule in Section 2–202(a) appropriate to the length of time the spouse and the decedent were married to each other.

(b) [Unsatisfied Balance of Elective-Share Amount; Supplemental Elective-Share Amount.] If, after the application of subsection (a), the elective-share amount is not fully satisfied or the surviving spouse is entitled to a supplemental elective-share amount, amounts included in the decedent's probate estate and in the decedent's nonprobate transfers to others, other than amounts included under Section 2–205(3)(i) or (iii), are applied first to satisfy the unsatisfied balance of the elective-share amount or the supplemental elective-share amount. The decedent's probate estate and that portion of the decedent's nonprobate transfers to others are so applied that liability for the unsatisfied balance of the elective-share amount or for the supplemental elective-share amount is equitably apportioned among the recipients of the decedent's probate estate and of that portion of the decedent's nonprobate transfers to others in proportion to the value of their interests therein.

(c) [Unsatisfied Balance of Elective-Share and Supplemental Elective-Share Amounts.] If, after the application of subsections (a) and (b), the elective-share or supplemental elective-share amount is not fully satisfied, the remaining portion of the decedent's nonprobate transfers to others is so applied that liability for the unsatisfied balance of the elective-share or supplemental elective-share amount is equitably apportioned among the recipients of the remaining portion of the decedent's nonprobate transfers to others in proportion to the value of their interests therein.

§2–210. Personal Liability of Recipients.
(a) Only original recipients of the decedent's nonprobate transfers to others, and the donees of the recipients of the decedent's nonprobate transfers to others, to the extent the donees have the property or its proceeds, are liable to make a proportional contribution toward satisfaction of the surviving spouse's elective-share or supplemental elective-share amount. A person liable to make contribution may choose to give up the proportional part of the decedent's nonprobate transfers to him [or her] or to pay the value of the amount for which he [or she] is liable.

(b) If any section or part of any section of this Part is preempted by federal law with respect to a payment, an item of property, or any other benefit included in the decedent's nonprobate transfers to others, a person who, not for value, receives the payment, item of property, or any other benefit is obligated to return the payment, item of property, or benefit, or is personally liable for the amount of the payment or the value of that item of property or benefit, as provided in Section 2–209, to the person who would have been entitled to it were that section or part of that section not preempted.

§2–211. Proceeding for Elective-Share; Time Limit.
(a) Except as provided in subsection (b), the election must be made by filing in the court and mailing or delivering to the personal representative, if any, a petition for the elective-share within nine months after the date of the decedent's death, or within six months after the probate of the decedent's will, whichever limitation later expires. The surviving spouse must give notice of the time and place set for hearing to persons interested in the estate and to the distributees and recipients of portions of the augmented estate whose interests will be adversely affected by the taking of the elective-share. Except as provided in subsection (b), the decedent's nonprobate transfers to others are not included within the augmented estate for the purpose of computing the elective-share, if the petition is filed more than nine months after the decedent's death.

(b) Within nine months after the decedent's death, the surviving spouse may petition the court for an extension of time for making an election. If, within nine months after the decedent's death, the spouse gives notice of the petition to all persons interested in the decedent's nonprobate transfers to others, the court for cause shown by the surviving spouse may extend the time for election. If the court grants the spouse's petition for an extension, the decedent's nonprobate transfers to others are not excluded from the augmented estate for the purpose of computing the elective-share and supplemental elective-share amounts, if the spouse makes an election by filing in the court and mailing or delivering to the personal representative, if any, a petition for the elective share within the time allowed by the extension.

(c) The surviving spouse may withdraw his [or her] demand for an elective share at any time before entry of a final determination by the court.

(d) After notice and hearing, the court shall determine the elective-share and supplemental elective-share amounts, and shall order its payment from the assets of the augmented estate or by contribution as appears appropriate under Sections 2–209 and 2–210. If it appears that a fund or property included in the augmented estate has not come into the possession of the personal representative, or has been distributed by the personal representative, the court nevertheless shall fix the liability of any person who has any interest in the fund or property or who has possession thereof, whether as trustee or otherwise. The proceeding may be maintained against fewer than all persons against whom relief could be sought, but no person is subject to contribution in any greater amount than he [or she] would have been under Sections 2–209 and 2–210 had relief been secured against all persons subject to contribution.

(e) An order or judgment of the court may be enforced as necessary in suit for contribution or payment in other courts of this State or other jurisdictions.

§2–212.   Right of Election Personal to Surviving Spouse; Incapacitated Surviving Spouse.

(a) [Surviving Spouse Must Be Living at Time of Election.] The right of election may be exercised only by a surviving spouse who is living when the petition for the elective-share is filed in the court under Section 2–211(a). If the election is not exercised by the surviving spouse personally, it may be exercised on the surviving spouse's behalf by his [or her] conservator, guardian, or agent under the authority of a power of attorney.

(b) [Incapacitated Surviving Spouse.] If the election is exercised on behalf of a surviving spouse who is an incapacitated person, that portion of the elective-share and supplemental elective-share amounts due from the decedent's probate estate and recipients of the decedent's nonprobate transfers to others under Section 2–209(b) and (c) must be placed in a custodial trust for the benefit of the surviving spouse under the provisions of the [Enacting state] Uniform Custodial Trust Act, except as modified below. For the purposes of this subsection, an election on behalf of a surviving spouse by an agent under a durable power of attorney is presumed to be on behalf of a surviving spouse who is an incapacitated person. For purposes of the custodial trust established by this subsection, (i) the electing guardian, conservator, or agent is the custodial trustee, (ii) the surviving spouse is the beneficiary, and (iii) the custodial trust is deemed to have been created by the decedent spouse by written transfer that takes effect at the decedent spouse's death and that directs the custodial trustee to administer the custodial trust as for an incapacitated beneficiary.

(c)   [Custodial Trust.] For the purposes of subsection (b), the [Enacting state] Uniform Custodial Trust Act must be applied as if Section 6(b) thereof were repealed and Sections 2(e), 9(b), and 17(a) were amended to read as follows:

(1) Neither an incapacitated beneficiary nor anyone acting on behalf of an incapacitated beneficiary has a power to terminate the custodial trust; but if the beneficiary regains capacity, the beneficiary then acquires the power to terminate the custodial trust by delivering to the custodial trustee a writing signed by the beneficiary declaring the termination. If not pre-

viously terminated, the custodial trust terminates on the death of the beneficiary.

(2) If the beneficiary is incapacitated, the custodial trustee shall expend so much or all of the custodial trust property as the custodial trustee considers advisable for the use and benefit of the beneficiary and individuals who were supported by the beneficiary when the beneficiary became incapacitated, or who are legally entitled to support by the beneficiary. Expenditures may be made in the manner, when, and to the extent that the custodial trustee determines suitable and proper, without court order but with regard to other support, income, and property of the beneficiary [exclusive of] [and] benefits of medical or other forms of assistance from any state or federal government or governmental agency for which the beneficiary must qualify on the basis of need.

(3) Upon the beneficiary's death, the custodial trustee shall transfer the unexpended custodial trust property in the following order: (i) under the residuary clause, if any, of the will of the beneficiary's predeceased spouse against whom the elective share was taken, as if that predeceased spouse died immediately after the beneficiary; or (ii) to that predeceased spouse's heirs under Section 2–711 of [this State's] Uniform Probate Code.

[STATES THAT HAVE NOT ADOPTED THE UNIFORM CUSTODIAL TRUST ACT SHOULD ADOPT THE FOLLOWING ALTERNATIVE SUBSECTION (b) AND NOT ADOPT SUBSECTION (b) OR (c) ABOVE]

[(b) [Incapacitated Surviving Spouse.] If the election is exercised on behalf of a surviving spouse who is an incapacitated person, the court must set aside that portion of the elective-share and supplemental elective-share amounts due from the decedent's probate estate and recipients of the decedent's nonprobate transfers to others under Section 2–209(b) and (c) and must appoint a trustee to administer that property for the support of the surviving spouse. For the purposes of this subsection, an election on behalf of a surviving spouse by an agent under a durable power of attorney is presumed to be on behalf of a surviving spouse who is an incapacitated person. The trustee must administer the trust in accordance with the following terms and such additional terms as the court determines appropriate:

(1) Expenditures of income and principal may be made in the manner, when, and to the extent that the trustee determines suitable and proper for the surviving spouse's support, without court order but with regard to other support, income, and property of the surviving spouse [exclusive of] [and] benefits of medical or other forms of assistance from any state or

federal government or governmental agency for which the surviving spouse must qualify on the basis of need.

(2) During the surviving spouse's incapacity, neither the surviving spouse nor anyone acting on behalf of the surviving spouse has a power to terminate the trust; but if the surviving spouse regains capacity, the surviving spouse then acquires the power to terminate the trust and acquire full ownership of the trust property free of trust, by delivering to the trustee a writing signed by the surviving spouse declaring the termination.

(3) Upon the surviving spouse's death, the trustee shall transfer the unexpended trust property in the following order: (i) under the residuary clause, if any, of the will of the predeceased spouse against whom the elective share was taken, as if that predeceased spouse died immediately after the surviving spouse; or (ii) to the predeceased spouse's heirs under Section 2–711.]

§2–213. Waiver of Right to Elect and of Other Rights.

(a) The right of election of a surviving spouse and the rights of the surviving spouse to homestead allowance, exempt property, and family allowance, or any of them, may be waived, wholly or partially, before or after marriage, by a written contract, agreement, or waiver signed by the surviving spouse.

(b) A surviving spouse's waiver is not enforceable if the surviving spouse proves that:

(1) he [or she] did not execute the waiver voluntarily; or

(2) the waiver was unconscionable when it was executed and, before execution of the waiver, he [or she]:

(i) was not provided a fair and reasonable disclosure of the property or financial obligations of the decedent;

(ii) did not voluntarily and expressly waive, in writing, any right to disclosure of the property or financial obligations of the decedent beyond the disclosure provided; and

(iii) did not have, or reasonably could not have had, an adequate knowledge of the property or financial obligations of the decedent.

(c) An issue of unconscionability of a waiver is for decision by the court as a matter of law.

(d) Unless it provides to the contrary, a waiver of "all rights," or equivalent language, in the property or estate of a present or prospective spouse or a complete property settlement entered into after or in anticipation of separation or divorce is a waiver of all rights of elective-share, homestead allowance, exempt property, and family allowance by each spouse in the property of the other and a renunciation by each of all benefits that would otherwise pass to him [or her] from the other by intestate succession or by virtue of any will executed before the waiver or property settlement.

§2–214. Protection of Payors and Other Third Parties.

(a) Although under Section 2–205 a payment, item of property, or other benefit is included in the decedent's nonprobate transfers to others, a payor or other third party is not liable for having made a payment or transferred an item of property or other benefit to a beneficiary designated in a governing instrument, or for having taken any other action in good faith reliance on the validity of a governing instrument, upon request and satisfactory proof of the decedent's death, before the payor or other third party received written notice from the surviving spouse or spouse's representative of an intention to file a petition for the elective share or that a petition for the elective-share has been filed. A payor or other third party is liable for payments made or other actions taken after the payor or other third party received written notice of an intention to file a petition for the elective-share or that a petition for the elective share has been filed.

(b) A written notice of intention to file a petition for the elective-share or that a petition for the elective-share has been filed must be mailed to the payor's or other third party's main office or home by registered or certified mail, return receipt requested, or served upon the payor or other third party in the same manner as a summons in a civil action. Upon receipt of written notice of intention to file a petition for the elective-share or that a petition for the elective-share has been filed, a payor or other third party may pay any amount owed or transfer or deposit any item of property held by it to or with the court having jurisdiction of the probate proceedings relating to the decedent's estate, or if no proceedings have been commenced, to or with the court having jurisdiction of probate proceedings relating to decedents' estates located in the county of the decedent's residence. The court shall hold the funds or item of property, and, upon its determination under Section 2–211(d), shall order disbursement in accordance with the determination. If no petition is filed in the court within the specified time under Section 2–211(a) or, if filed, the demand for an elective share is withdrawn under Section 2–211(c), the court shall order disbursement to the designated beneficiary. Payments or transfers to the court or deposits made into court discharge the payor or other third party from all claims for amounts so paid or the value of property so transferred or deposited.

(c) Upon petition to the probate court by the beneficiary designated in a governing instrument, the court may order that all or part of the property be paid to the beneficiary in an amount and subject to conditions consistent with this Part.

PART 3
SPOUSE AND CHILDREN UNPROVIDED FOR IN WILLS

§2–301. Entitlement of Spouse; Premarital Will.

(a) If a testator's surviving spouse married the testator after the testator executed his [or her] will, the surviving spouse is entitled to receive, as an intestate share, no less than the value of the share of the estate he [or she] would have received if the testator had died intestate as to that portion of the testator's estate, if any, that neither is devised to a child of the testator who was born before the testator married the surviving spouse and who is not a child of the surviving spouse nor is devised to a descendant of such a child or passes under Sections 2–603 or 2–604 to such a child or to a descendant of such a child, unless:

(1) it appears from the will or other evidence that the will was made in contemplation of the testator's marriage to the surviving spouse;

(2) the will expresses the intention that it is to be effective notwithstanding any subsequent marriage; or

(3) the testator provided for the spouse by transfer outside the will and the intent that the transfer be in lieu of a testamentary provision is shown by the testator's statements or is reasonably inferred from the amount of the transfer or other evidence.

(b) In satisfying the share provided by this section, devises made by the will to the testator's surviving spouse, if any, are applied first, and other devises, other than a devise to a child of the testator who was born before the testator married the surviving spouse and who is not a child of the surviving spouse or a devise or substitute gift under Section 2–603 or 2–604 to a descendant of such a child, abate as provided in Section 3–902.
As amended in 1993.

§2–302. Omitted Children.

(a) Except as provided in subsection (b), if a testator fails to provide in his [or her] will for any of his [or her] children born or adopted after the execution of the will, the omitted after-born or after-adopted child receives a share in the estate as follows:

(1) If the testator had no child living when he [or she] executed the will, an omitted after-born or after-adopted child receives a share in the estate equal in value to that which the child would have received had the testator died intestate, unless the will devised all or substantially all of the estate to the other parent of the omitted child and that other parent survives the testator and is entitled to take under the will.

(2) If the testator had one or more children living when he [or she] executed the will, and the will devised property or an interest in property to one or more of the then-living children, an omitted after-born or after-adopted child is entitled to share in the testator's estate as follows:

(i) The portion of the testator's estate in which the omitted after-born or after-adopted child is entitled to share is limited to devises made to the testator's then-living children under the will.

(ii) The omitted after-born or after-adopted child is entitled to receive the share of the testator's estate, as limited in subparagraph (i), that the child would have received had the testator included all omitted after-born and after-adopted children with the children to whom devises were made under the will and had given an equal share of the estate to each child.

(iii) To the extent feasible, the interest granted an omitted after-born or after-adopted child under this section must be of the same character, whether equitable or legal, present or future, as that devised to the testator's then-living children under the will.

(iv) In satisfying a share provided by this paragraph, devises to the testator's children who were living when the will was executed abate ratably. In abating the devises of the then-living children, the court shall preserve to the maximum extent possible the character of the testamentary plan adopted by the testator.

(b) Neither subsection (a)(1) nor subsection (a)(2) applies if:

(1) it appears from the will that the omission was intentional; or

(2) the testator provided for the omitted after-born or after-adopted child by transfer outside the will and the intent that the transfer be in lieu of a testamentary provision is shown by the testator's statements or is reasonably inferred from the amount of the transfer or other evidence.

(c) If at the time of execution of the will the testator fails to provide in his [or her] will for a living child solely because he [or she] believes the child to be dead, the child is entitled to share in the estate as if the child were an omitted after-born or after-adopted child.

(d) In satisfying a share provided by subsection (a)(1), devises made by the will abate under Section 3–902.
As amended in 1991 and 1993.

PART 4
EXEMPT PROPERTY AND ALLOWANCES

§2–401. Applicable Law.

This Part applies to the estate of a decedent who dies domiciled in this State. Rights to homestead allowance, exempt property, and family allowance for a decedent who dies not domiciled in this State are governed by the law of the decedent's domicile at death.

§2–402. Homestead Allowance.

A decedent's surviving spouse is entitled to a homestead allowance of [$15,000]. If there is no surviving spouse, each minor child and each dependent child of the decedent is entitled to a homestead allowance amounting to [$15,000] divided by the number of minor and dependent children of the decedent. The homestead allowance is exempt from and has priority over all claims against the estate. Homestead allowance is in addition to any share passing to the surviving spouse or minor or dependent child by the will of the decedent, unless otherwise provided, by intestate succession, or by way of elective share.

[§2–402A. Constitutional Homestead.

The value of any constitutional right of homestead in the family home received by a surviving spouse or child must be charged against the spouse or child's homestead allowance to the extent the family home is part of the decedent's estate or would have been but for the homestead provision of the constitution.]

§2–403. Exempt Property.

In addition to the homestead allowance, the decedent's surviving spouse is entitled from the estate to a value, not exceeding $10,000 in excess of any security interests therein, in household furniture, automobiles, furnishings, appliances, and personal effects. If there is no surviving spouse, the decedent's children are entitled jointly to the same value. If encumbered chattels are selected and the value in excess of security interests, plus that of other exempt property, is less than $10,000, or if there is not $10,000 worth of exempt property in the estate, the spouse or children are entitled to other assets of the estate, if any, to the extent necessary to make up the $10,000 value. Rights to exempt property and assets needed to make up a deficiency of exempt property have priority over all claims against the estate, but the right to any assets to make up a deficiency of exempt property abates as necessary to permit earlier payment of homestead allowance and family allowance. These rights are in addition to any benefit or share passing to the surviving spouse or children by the decedent's will, unless otherwise provided, by intestate succession, or by way of elective share.

§2–404. Family Allowance.

(a) In addition to the right to homestead allowance and exempt property, the decedent's surviving spouse and minor children whom the decedent was obligated to support and children who were in fact being supported by the decedent are entitled to a reasonable allowance in money out of the estate for their maintenance during the period of administration, which allowance may not

continue for longer than one year if the estate is inadequate to discharge allowed claims. The allowance may be paid as a lump sum or in periodic installments. It is payable to the surviving spouse, if living, for the use of the surviving spouse and minor and dependent children; otherwise to the children, or persons having their care and custody. If a minor child or dependent child is not living with the surviving spouse, the allowance may be made partially to the child or his [or her] guardian or other person having the child's care and custody, and partially to the spouse, as their needs may appear. The family allowance is exempt from and has priority over all claims except the homestead allowance.

(b) The family allowance is not chargeable against any benefit or share passing to the surviving spouse or children by the will of the decedent, unless otherwise provided, by intestate succession or by way of elective share. The death of any person entitled to family allowance terminates the right to allowances not yet paid.

§2–405. Source, Determination, and Documentation.

(a) If the estate is otherwise sufficient, property specifically devised may not be used to satisfy rights to homestead allowance or exempt property. Subject to this restriction, the surviving spouse, guardians of minor children, or children who are adults may select property of the estate as homestead allowance and exempt property. The personal representative may make those selections if the surviving spouse, the children, or the guardians of the minor children are unable or fail to do so within a reasonable time or there is no guardian of a minor child. The personal representative may execute an instrument or deed of distribution to establish the ownership of property taken as homestead allowance or exempt property. The personal representative may determine the family allowance in a lump sum not exceeding $18,000 or periodic installments not exceeding $1,500 per month for one year, and may disburse funds of the estate in payment of the family allowance and any part of the homestead allowance payable in cash. The personal representative or an interested person aggrieved by any selection, determination, payment, proposed payment, or failure to act under this section may petition the court for appropriate relief, which may include a family allowance other than that which the personal representative determined or could have determined.

(b) If the right to an elective share is exercised on behalf of a surviving spouse who is an incapacitated person, the personal representative may add any unexpended portions payable under the homestead allowance, exempt property, and family allowance to the trust established under Section 2–212(b).

As amended in 1993.

PART 5
WILLS, WILL CONTRACTS, AND CUSTODY AND DEPOSIT OF WILLS

§2–501. Who May Make Will.

An individual 18 or more years of age who is of sound mind may make a will.

§2–502. Execution; Witnessed Wills; Holographic Wills.

(a) Except as provided in subsection (b) and in Sections 2–503, 2–506, and 2–513, a will must be:

(1) in writing;

(2) signed by the testator or in the testator's name by some other individual in the testator's conscious presence and by the testator's direction; and

(3) signed by at least two individuals, each of whom signed within a reasonable time after he [or she] witnessed either the signing of the will as described in paragraph (2) or the testator's acknowledgment of that signature or acknowledgment of the will.

(b) A will that does not comply with subsection (a) is valid as a holographic will, whether or not witnessed, if the signature and material portions of the document are in the testator's handwriting.

(c) Intent that the document constitute the testator's will can be established by extrinsic evidence, including, for holographic wills, portions of the document that are not in the testator's handwriting.

§2–503. Writings Intended as Wills, etc.

Although a document or writing added upon a document was not executed in compliance with Section 2–502, the document or writing is treated as if it had been executed in compliance with that section if the proponent of the document or writing establishes by clear and convincing evidence that the decedent intended the document or writing to constitute (i) the decedent's will, (ii) a partial or complete revocation of the will, (iii) an addition to or an alteration of the will, or (iv) a partial or complete revival of his [or her] formerly revoked will or of a formerly revoked portion of the will.

§2–504. Self-Proved Will.

(a) A will may be simultaneously executed, attested, and made self-proved, by acknowledgment thereof by the testator and affidavits of the witnesses, each made before an officer authorized to administer oaths under the laws of the state in which execution occurs and evidenced by the officer's certificate, under official seal, in substantially the following form:

I, _____ , the testator, sign my name to this instrument this _____ day of _____ , and being first duly sworn, do hereby declare to the undersigned authority that I sign and execute this instrument as my will and that I sign it willingly (or willingly direct another to

sign for me), that I execute it as my free and voluntary act for the purposes therein expressed, and that I am eighteen years of age or older, of sound mind, and under no constraint or undue influence.

_____
Testator

We, _____ , _____ , the witnesses, sign our names to this instrument, being first duly sworn, and do hereby declare to the undersigned authority that the testator signs and executes this instrument as [his] [her] will and that [he] [she] signs it willingly (or willingly directs another to sign for [him] [her]), and that each of us, in the presence and hearing of the testator, hereby signs this will as witness to the testator's signing, and that to the best of our knowledge the testator is eighteen years of age or older, of sound mind, and under no constraint or undue influence.

_____
Witness

_____
Witness

The State of _____
County of _____

Subscribed, sworn to and acknowledged before me by _____ , the testator, and subscribed and sworn to before me by _____ , and _____ , witness, this ___ day of _____ .

(Seal)

(Signed) _____

_____
(Official capacity of officer)

(b) An attested will may be made self-proved at any time after its execution by the acknowledgment thereof by the testator and the affidavits of the witnesses, each made before an officer authorized to administer oaths under the laws of the state in which the acknowledgment occurs and evidenced by the officer's certificate, under the official seal, attached or annexed to the will in substantially the following form:

The State of _____
County of _____

We, _____ , _____ , and _____ , the testator and the witnesses, respectively, whose names are signed to the attached or foregoing instrument, being first duly sworn, do hereby declare to the undersigned authority that the testator signed and executed the instrument as the testator's will and that [he] [she] had signed willingly (or willingly directed another to sign for [him] [her]), and that [he] [she] executed it as [his] [her] free and voluntary act for the purposes therein expressed, and that each of the witnesses, in the presence and hearing of the testator, signed the will as witness and that to the best of [his] [her] knowledge the testator was at that time eighteen years or age or older, of sound mind, and under no constraint or undue influence.

_____
Testator

_____
Witness

_____
Witness

Subscribed, sworn to and acknowledged before me by _____ , the testator, and subscribed and sworn to before me by _____ , and _____ , witnesses, this _____ of _____ .

(Seal)

(Signed) _____

_____
(Official capacity of officer)

(c) A signature affixed to a self-proving affidavit attached to a will is considered a signature affixed to the will, if necessary to prove the will's due execution.

§2–505. Who May Witness.

(a) An individual generally competent to be a witness may act as a witness to a will.

(b) The signing of a will by an interested witness does not invalidate the will or any provision of it.

§2–506. Choice of Law as to Execution.

A written will is valid if executed in compliance with Section 2–502 or 2–503 or if its execution complies with the law at the time of execution of the place where the will is executed, or of the law of the place where at the time of execution or at the time of death the testator is domiciled, has a place of abode, or is a national.

§2–507. Revocation by Writing or by Act.

(a) A will or any part thereof is revoked:

(1) by executing a subsequent will that revokes the previous will or part expressly or by inconsistency; or

(2) by performing a revocatory act on the will, if the testator performed the act with the intent and for the purpose of revoking the will or part or if another individual performed the act in the testator's conscious presence and by the testator's direction. For purposes of this paragraph, "revocatory act on the will" includes burning , tearing, canceling, obliterating, or destroying the will or any part of it. A burning, tearing, or canceling is a "revocatory act on the will," whether or not the burn, tear, or cancellation touched any of the words on the will.

(b) If a subsequent will does not expressly revoke a previous will, the execution of the subsequent will wholly revokes the previous will by inconsistency if the testator intended the subsequent will to replace rather than supplement the previous will.

(c) The testator is presumed to have intended a subsequent will to replace rather than supplement a previous will if the subsequent will makes a complete disposition of the testator's estate. If this presumption arises and is not rebutted by clear and convincing evidence, the previous will is revoked; only the subsequent will is operative on the testator's death.

(d) The testator is presumed to have intended a subsequent will to supplement rather than replace a previous will if the subsequent will does not make a complete disposition of the testator's estate. If this presumption arises and is not rebutted by clear and convincing evidence, the subsequent will revokes the previous will only to the extent the subsequent will is inconsistent with the previous will; each will is fully operative on the testator's death to the extent they are not inconsistent.

§2–508. Revocation by Change of Circumstances.

Except as provided in Sections 2–803 and 2–804, a change of circumstances does not revoke a will or any part of it.

§2–509. Revival of Revoked Will.

(a) If a subsequent will that wholly revoked a previous will is thereafter revoked by a revocatory act under Section 2–507(a)(2), the previous will remains revoked unless it is revived. The previous will is revived if it is evident from the circumstances of the revocation of the subsequent will or from the testator's contemporary or subsequent declarations that the testator intended the previous will to take effect as executed.

(b) If a subsequent will that partly revoked a previous will is thereafter revoked by a revocatory act under Section 2–507(a)(2), a revoked part of the previous will is revived unless it is evident from the circumstances of the revocation of the subsequent will or from the testator's contemporary or subsequent declarations that the testator did not intend the revoked part to take effect as executed.

(c) If a subsequent will that revoked a previous will in whole or in part is thereafter revoked by another, later, will, the previous will remains revoked in whole or in part, unless it or its revoked part is revived. The previous will or its revoked part is revived to the extent it appears from the terms of the later will that the testator intended the previous will to take effect.

§2–510. Incorporation by Reference.

A writing in existence when a will is executed may be incorporated by reference if the language of the will manifests this intent and describes the writing sufficiently to permit its identification.

§2–511. Testamentary Additions to Trusts.

(a) A will may validly devise property to the trustee of a trust established or to be established (i) during the testator's lifetime by the testator, by the testator and some other person, or by some other person, including a funded or unfunded life insurance trust, although the settlor has reserved any or all rights of ownership of the insurance contracts, or (ii) at the testator's death by the testator's devise to the trustee, if the trust is identified in the testator's will and its terms are set forth in a written instrument, other than a will, executed before, concurrently with, or after the execution of the testator's will or in another individual's will if that other individual has predeceased the testator, regardless of the existence, size, or character of the corpus of the trust. The devise is not invalid because the trust is amendable or revocable, or because the trust was amended after the execution of the will or the testator's death.

(b) Unless the testator's will provides otherwise, property devised to a trust described in subsection (a) is not held under a testamentary trust of the testator, but it becomes a part of the trust to which it is devised, and must be administered and disposed of in accordance with the provisions of the governing instrument setting forth the terms of the trust, including any amendments thereto made before or after the testator's death.

(c) Unless the testator's will provides otherwise, a revocation or termination of the trust before the testator's death causes the devise to lapse.

§2–512. Events of Independent Significance.

A will may dispose of property by reference to acts and events that have significance apart from their effect upon the dispositions made by the will, whether they occur before or after the execution of the will or before or after the testator's death. The execution or revocation of another individual's will is such an event.

§2–513. Separate Writing Identifying Devise of Certain Types of Tangible Personal Property.

Whether or not the provisions relating to holographic wills apply, a will may refer to a written statement or list to dispose of items of tangible personal property not otherwise specifically disposed of by the will, other than money. To be admissible under this section as evidence of the intended disposition, the writing must be signed by the testator and must describe the items and the devisees with reasonable certainty. The writing may be referred to as one to be in existence at the time of the testator's death; it may be prepared before or after the execution of the will; it may be altered by the testator after its preparation; and it may be a writing that has no significance apart from its effect on the dispositions made by the will.

§2–514. Contracts Concerning Succession.

A contract to make a will or devise, or not to revoke a will or devise, or to die intestate, if executed after the effective date of this Article, may be established only by (i) provisions of a will stating material provisions of the contract, (ii) an express reference in a will to a contract and extrinsic evidence proving the terms of the contract, or (iii) a writing signed by the decedent evidencing the contract. The execution of a joint will or mutual wills does not create a presumption of a contract not to revoke the will or wills.

§2–515. Deposit of Will with Court in Testator's Lifetime.

A will may be deposited by the testator or the testator's agent with any court for safekeeping, under rules of the court. The will must be sealed and kept confidential. During the testator's lifetime, a deposited will must be delivered only to the testator or to a person authorized in writing signed by the testator to receive the will. A conservator may be allowed to examine a deposited will of a protected testator under procedures designed to maintain the confidential character of the document to the extent possible, and to ensure that it will be resealed and kept on deposit after the examination. Upon being informed of the testator's death, the court shall notify any person designated to receive the will and deliver it to that person on request; or the court may deliver the will to the appropriate court.

§2–516. Duty of Custodian of Will; Liability.

After the death of a testator and on request of an interested person, a person having custody of a will of the testator shall deliver it with reasonable promptness to a person able to secure its probate and if none is known, to an appropriate court. A person who wilfully fails to deliver a will is liable to any person aggrieved for any damages that may be sustained by the failure. A person who wilfully refuses or fails to deliver a will after being ordered by the court in a proceeding brought for the purpose of compelling delivery is subject to penalty for contempt of court.

§2–517. Penalty Clause for Contest.

A provision in a will purporting to penalize an interested person for contesting the will or instituting other proceedings relating to the estate is unenforceable if probable cause exists for instituting proceedings.

PART 6

RULES OF CONSTRUCTION APPLICABLE ONLY TO WILLS

§2–601. Scope.

In the absence of a finding of a contrary intention, the rules of construction in this Part control the construction of a will.

§2–602. Will May Pass All Property and After-Acquired Property.

A will may provide for the passage of all property the testator owns at death and all property acquired by the estate after the testator's death.

§2–603. Antilapse; Deceased Devisee; Class Gifts.

(a) [Definitions.] In this section:

(1) "Alternative devise" means a devise that is expressly created by the will and, under the terms of the will, can take effect instead of another devise on the happening of one or more events, including survival of the testator or failure to survive the testator, whether an event is expressed in condition-precedent, condition-subsequent, or any other form. A residuary clause constitutes an alternative devise with respect to a nonresiduary devise only if the will specifically provides that, upon lapse or failure, the nonresiduary devise, or nonresiduary devises in general, pass under the residuary clause.

(2) "Class member" includes an individual who fails to survive the testator but who would have taken under a devise in the form of a class gift had he [or she] survived the testator.

(3) "Devise" includes an alternative devise, a devise in the form of a class gift, and an exercise of a power of appointment.

(4) "Devisee" includes (i) a class member if the devise is in the form of a class gift, (ii) an individual or class member who was deceased at the time the testator executed his [or her] will as well as an individual or class member who was then living but who failed to survive the testator, and (iii) an appointee under a power of appointment exercised by the testator's will.

(5) "Stepchild" means a child of the surviving, deceased, or former spouse of the testator or of the donor of a power of appointment, and not of the testator or donor.

(6) "Surviving devisee" or "surviving descendant" means a devisee or a descendant who neither predeceased the testator nor is deemed to have predeceased the testator under Section 2–702.

(7) "Testator" includes the donee of a power of appointment if the power is exercised in the testator's will.

(b) [Substitute Gift.] If a devisee fails to survive the testator and is a grandparent, a descendant of a grandparent, or a stepchild of either the testator or the donor of a power of appointment exercised by the testator's will, the following apply:

(1) Except as provided in paragraph (4), if the devise is not in the form of a class gift and the deceased devisee leaves surviving descendants, a substitute gift is created in the devisee's surviving descendants. They take by representation the property to which the devisee would have been entitled had the devisee survived the testator.

(2) Except as provided in paragraph (4), if the devise is in the form of a class gift, other than a devise to "issue," "descendants," "heirs of the body," "heirs," "next of kin," "relatives," or "family," or a class described by language of similar import, a substitute gift is created in the surviving descendant's of any deceased devisee. The property to which the devisees would have been entitled had all of them survived the testator passes to the surviving devisees and the surviving descendants of the deceased devisees. Each surviving devisee takes the share to which he [or she] would have been entitled had the deceased devisees survived the testator. Each deceased devisee's surviving descendants who are substituted for the deceased devisee take by representation the share to which the deceased devisee would have been entitled had the deceased devisee survived the testator. For the purposes of this paragraph, "deceased devisee" means a class member who failed to survive the testator and left one or more surviving descendants.

(3) For the purposes of Section 2–601, words of survivorship, such as in a devise to an individual "if he survives me," or in a devise to "my surviving children," are not, in the absence of additional evidence, a sufficient indication of an intent contrary to the application of this section.

(4) If the will creates an alternative devise with respect to a devise for which a substitute gift is created by paragraph (1) or (2), the substitute gift is superseded by the alternative devise only if an expressly designated devisee of the alternative devise is entitled to take under the will.

(5) Unless the language creating a power of appointment expressly excludes the substitution of the descendants of an appointee for the appointee, a surviving descendant of a deceased appointee of a power of appointment can be substituted for the appointee under this section, whether or not the descendant is an object of the power.

(c) [More Than One Substitute Gift; Which One Takes.] If, under subsection (b), substitute gifts are created and not superseded with respect to more than one devise and the devises are alternative devises, one to the other, the determination of which of the substitute gifts takes effect is resolved as follows:

(1) Except as provided in paragraph (2), the devised property passes under the primary substitute gift.

(2) If there is a younger-generation devise, the devised property passes under the younger-generation substitute gift and not under the primary substitute gift.

(3) In this subsection:

(i) "Primary devise" means the devise that would have taken effect had all the deceased devisees of the alternative devises who left surviving descendants survived the testator.

(ii) "Primary substitute gift" means the substitute gift created with respect to the primary devise.

(iii) "Younger-generation devise" means a devise that (A) is to a descendant of a devisee of the primary devise, (B) is an alternative devise with respect to the primary devise, (C) is a devise for which a substitute gift is created, and (D) would have taken effect had all the deceased devisees who left surviving descendants survived the testator except the deceased devisee or devisees of the primary devise.

(iv) "Younger-generation substitute gift" means the substitute gift created with respect to the younger-generation devise.

As amended in 1991 and 1993.

§2–604. Failure of Testamentary Provision.

(a) Except as provided in Section 2–603, a devise, other than a residuary devise, that fails for any reason becomes a part of the residue.

(b) Except as provided in Section 2–603, if the residue is devised to two or more persons, the share of a residuary devisee that fails for any reason passes to the other residuary devisee, or to other residuary devisees in proportion to the interest of each in the remaining part of the residue.

§2–605. Increase in Securities; Accessions.

(a) If a testator executes a will that devises securities and the testator then owned securities that meet the description in the will, the devise includes additional securities owned by the testator at death to the extent the additional securities were acquired by the testator after the will was executed as a result of the testator's ownership of the described securities and are securities of any of the following types:

(1) securities of the same organization acquired by reason of action initiated by the organization or any successor, related, or acquiring organization, excluding any acquired by exercise of purchase options;

(2) securities of another organization acquired as a result of a merger, consolidation, reorganization, or other distribution by the organization or any successor, related, or acquiring organization; or

(3) securities of the same organization acquired as a result of a plan of reinvestment.

(b) Distributions in cash before death with respect to a described security are not part of the devise.

§2–606. Nonademption of Specific Devises; Unpaid Proceeds of Sale, Condemnation, or Insurance; Sale by Conservator or Agent.

(a) A specific devisee has a right to the specifically devised property in the testator's estate at death and:

(1) any balance of the purchase price, together with any security agreement, owing from a purchaser to the testator at death by reason of sale of the property;

(2) any amount of a condemnation award for the taking of the property unpaid at death;

(3) any proceeds unpaid at death on fire or casualty insurance on or other recovery for injury to the property;

(4) property owned by the testator at death and acquired as a result of foreclosure, or obtained in lieu of foreclosure, of the security interest for a specifically devised obligation;

(5) real or tangible personal property owned by the testator at death which the testator acquired as a replacement for specifically devised real or tangible personal property; and

(6) unless the facts and circumstances indicate that ademption of the devise was intended by the testator or ademption of the devise is consistent with the testator's manifested plan of distribution, the value of the specifically devised property to the extent the specifically devised property is not in the testator's estate at death and its value or its replacement is not covered by paragraphs (1) through (5).

(b) If specifically devised property is sold or mortgaged by a conservator or by an agent acting within the authority of a durable power of attorney for an incapacitated principal, or if a condemnation award, insurance proceeds, or recovery for injury to the property are paid to a conservator or to an agent acting within the authority of a durable power of attorney for an incapacitated principal, the specific devisee has the right to a general pecuniary devise equal to the net sale price, the amount of the unpaid loan, the condemnation award, the insurance proceeds, or the recovery.

(c) The right of a specific devisee under subsection (b) is reduced by any right the devisee has under subsection (a).

(d) For the purposes of the references in subsection (b) to a conservator, subsection (b) does not apply if after the sale, mortgage, condemnation, casualty, or recovery, it was adjudicated that the testator's incapacity ceased and the testator survived the adjudication by one year.

(e) For the purposes of the references in subsection (b) to an agent acting within the authority of a durable power of attorney for an incapacitated principal, (i) "incapacitated principal" means a principal who is an incapacitated person, (ii) no adjudication of incapacity before death is necessary, and (iii) the acts of an agent within the authority of a durable power of attorney are presumed to be for an incapacitated principal.

§2–607. Nonexoneration.

A specific devise passes subject to any mortgage interest existing at the date of death, without right of exoneration, regardless of a general directive in the will to pay debts.

§2–608. Exercise of Power of Appointment.

In the absence of a requirement that a power of appointment be exercised by a reference, or by an express or specific reference, to the power, a general residuary clause in a will, or a will making general disposition of all of the testator's property, expresses an intention to exercise a power of appointment held by the testator only if (i) the power is a general power and the creating instrument does not contain a gift if the power is not exercised or (ii) the testator's will manifests an intention to include the property subject to the power.

§2–609. Ademption by Satisfaction.

(a) Property a testator gave in his [or her] lifetime to a person is treated as a satisfaction of a devise in whole or in part, only if (i) the will provides for deduction of the gift, (ii) the testator declared in a contemporaneous writing that the gift is in satisfaction of the devise or that its value is to be deducted from the value of the devise, or (iii) the devisee acknowledged in writing that the gift is in satisfaction of the devise or that its value is to be deducted from the value of the devise.

(b) For purposes of partial satisfaction, property given during lifetime is valued as of the time the devisee came into possession or enjoyment of the property or at the testator's death, whichever occurs first.

(c) If the devisee fails to survive the testator, the gift is treated as a full or partial satisfaction of the devise, as appropriate, in applying Sections 2–603 and 2–604, unless the testator's contemporaneous writing provides otherwise.

PART 7
RULES OF CONSTRUCTION APPLICABLE TO WILLS AND OTHER GOVERNING INSTRUMENTS

§2–701. Scope.

In the absence of a finding of a contrary intention, the rules of construction in this Part control the construction of a governing instrument. The rules of construction in this Part apply to a governing instrument of any type, except as the application of a particular section is limited by its terms to a specific type or types of provision or governing instrument.

As amended in 1991.

§2–702. Requirement of Survival by 120 Hours.

(a) [Requirement of Survival by 120 Hours Under Probate Code.] For the purposes of this Code, except as provided in subsection (d), an individual who is not established by clear and convincing evidence to have survived an event, including the death of another individual, by 120 hours is deemed to have predeceased the event.

(b) [Requirement of Survival by 120 Hours under Governing Instrument.] Except as provided in subsection (d), for purposes of a provision of a governing instrument that relates to an individual surviving an event, including the death of another individual, an individual who is not established by clear and convincing evidence to have survived the event by 120 hours is deemed to have predeceased the event.

(c) [Co-owners With Right of Survivorship; Requirement of Survival by 120 Hours.] Except as provided in subsection (d), if (i) it is not established by clear and convincing evidence that one of two co-owners with right of survivorship survived the other co-owner by 120 hours, one-half of the property passes as if one had survived by 120 hours and one-half as if the other had survived by 120 hours and (ii) there are more than two co-owners and it is not established by clear and convincing evidence that at least one of them survived the others by 120 hours, the property passes in the proportion that one bears to the whole number of co-owners. For the purposes of this subsection, "co-owners with right of survivorship" includes joint tenants, tenants by the entireties, and other co-owners of property or accounts held under circumstances that entitles one or more to the whole of the property or account on the death of the other or others.

(d) [Exceptions.] Survival by 120 hours is not required if:

(1) the governing instrument contains language dealing explicitly with simultaneous deaths or deaths in a common disaster and that language is operable under the facts of the case;

(2) the governing instrument expressly indicates that an individual is not required to survive an event, including the death of another individual, by any specified period or expressly requires the individual to survive the event by a specified period; but survival of the event or the specified period must be established by clear and convincing evidence;

(3) the imposition of a 120-hour requirement of survival would cause a nonvested property interest or a power of appointment to fail to qualify for validity under Section 2–901(a)(1), (b)(1), or (c)(1) or to become invalid under Section 2–901(a)(2), (b)(2), or (c)(2); but survival must be established by clear and convincing evidence; or

(4) the application of a 120-hour requirement of survival to multiple governing instruments would result in an unintended failure or duplication of a disposition; but survival must be established by clear and convincing evidence.

(e) [Protection of Payors and Other Third Parties.]

(1) A payor or other third party is not liable for having made a payment or transferred an item of property or any other benefit to a beneficiary designated in a governing instrument who, under this section, is not entitled to the payment or item of property, or for having taken any other action in good faith reliance on the beneficiary's apparent entitlement under the terms of the governing instrument, before the payor or other third party received written notice of a claimed lack of entitlement under this section. A payor or other third party is liable for a payment made or other action taken after the payor or other third party received written notice of a claimed lack of entitlement under this section.

(2) Written notice of a claimed lack of entitlement under paragraph (1) must be mailed to the payor's or other third party's main office or home by registered or certified mail, return receipt requested, or served upon the payor or other third party in the same manner as a summons in a civil action. Upon receipt of written notice of a claimed lack of entitlement under this section, a payor or other third party may pay any amount owed or transfer or deposit any item of property held by it to or with the court having jurisdiction of the probate proceedings relating to the decedent's estate, or if no proceedings have been commenced, to or with the court having jurisdiction of probate proceedings relating to decedents' estates located in the county of the decedent's residence. The court shall hold the funds or item of property and, upon its determination under this section, shall order disbursement in accordance with the determination. Payments, transfers, or deposits made to or with the court discharge the payor or other third party from all claims for the value of amounts paid to or items of property transferred to or deposited with the court.

(f) [Protection of Bona Fide Purchasers; Personal Liability of Recipient.]

(1) A person who purchases property for value and without notice, or who receives a payment or other item of property in partial or full satisfaction of a legally enforceable obligation, is neither obligated under this section to return the payment, item of property, or benefit nor is liable under this section for the amount of the payment or the value of the item of property or benefit. But a person who, not for value, receives a payment, item of property, or any other benefit to which the person is not entitled under this section is obligated to return the payment, item of property, or benefit, or is personally liable for the amount of the payment or the value of the item of property or benefit, to the person who is entitled to it under this section.

(2) If this section or any part of this section is preempted by federal law with respect to a payment, an item of property, or any other benefit covered by this section, a person who, not for value, receives the payment, item of property, or any other benefit to which the person is not entitled under this section is obligated to return the payment, item of property, or benefit, or is personally liable for the amount of the payment or the value of the item of property or benefit, to the person who would have been entitled to it were this section or part of this section not preempted.

As amended in 1991 and 1993.

§2–703. Choice of Law as to Meaning and Effect of Governing Instrument.

The meaning and legal effect of a governing instrument is determined by the local law of the state selected in the governing instrument, unless the application of that law is contrary to the provisions relating to the elective share described in Part 2, the provisions relating to exempt property and allowances described in Part 4, or any other public policy of this State otherwise applicable to the disposition.

As amended in 1991 and 1993.

§2–704. Power of Appointment; Meaning of Specific Reference Requirement.

If a governing instrument creating a power of appointment expressly requires that the power be exercised by a reference, an express reference, or a specific reference, to the power or its source, it is presumed that the donor's intention, in requiring that the donee exercise the power by making reference to the particular power or to the creating instrument, was to prevent an inadvertent exercise of the power.

§2–705. Class Gifts Construed to Accord With Intestate Succession.

(a) Adopted individuals and individuals born out of wedlock, and their respective descendants if appropriate to the class, are included in class gifts and other terms of relationship in accordance with the rules for intestate succession. Terms of relationship that do not differentiate relationships by blood from those by affinity, such as "uncles," "aunts," "nieces," or "nephews", are construed to exclude relatives by affinity. Terms of relationship that do not differentiate relationships by the half blood from those by the whole blood, such as "brothers," "sisters," "nieces," or "nephews", are construed to include both types of relationships.

(b) In addition to the requirements of subsection (a), in construing a dispositive provision of a transferor who is not the natural parent, an individual born to the natural parent is not considered the child of that parent unless the individual lived while a minor as a regular member of the household of that natural parent or of that parent's parent, brother, sister, spouse, or surviving spouse.

(c) In addition to the requirements of subsection (a), in construing a dispositive provision of a transferor who is not the adopting parent, an adopted individual is not considered the child of the adopting parent unless the adopted individual lived while a minor, either before or after the adoption, as a regular member of the household of the adopting parent.

As amended in 1991.

§2–706. Life Insurance; Retirement Plan; Account With POD Designation; Transfer-on-Death Registration; Deceased Beneficiary.

(a) [Definitions.] In this section:

(1) "Alternative beneficiary designation" means a beneficiary designation that is expressly created by the governing instrument and, under the terms of the governing instrument, can take effect instead of another beneficiary designation on the happening of one or more events, including survival of the decedent or failure to survive the decedent, whether an event is expressed in condition-precedent, condition-subsequent, or any other form.

(2) "Beneficiary" means the beneficiary of a beneficiary designation under which the beneficiary must survive the decedent and includes (i) a class member if the beneficiary designation is in the form of a class gift and (ii) an individual or class member who was deceased at the time the beneficiary designation was executed as well as an individual or class member who was then living but who failed to survive the decedent, but excludes a joint tenant of a joint tenancy with the right of survivorship and a party to a joint and survivorship account.

(3) "Beneficiary designation" includes an alternative beneficiary designation and a beneficiary designation in the form of a class gift.

(4) "Class member" includes an individual who fails to survive the decedent but who would have taken under a beneficiary designation in the form of a class gift had he [or she] survived the decedent.

(5) "Stepchild" means a child of the decedent's surviving, deceased, or former spouse, and not of the decedent.

(6) "Surviving beneficiary" or "surviving descendant" means a beneficiary or a descendant who neither predeceased the decedent nor is deemed to have predeceased the decedent under Section 2–702.

(b) [Substitute Gift.] If a beneficiary fails to survive the decedent and is a grandparent, a descendant of a grandparent, or a stepchild of the decedent, the following apply:

(1) Except as provided in paragraph (4), if the beneficiary designation is not in the form of a class gift and the deceased beneficiary leaves surviving descendants, a substitute gift is created in the beneficiary's surviving descendants. They take by representation the property to which the beneficiary would have been entitled had the beneficiary survived the decedent.

(2) Except as provided in paragraph (4), if the beneficiary designation is in the form of a class gift, other than a beneficiary designation to "issue," "descendants," "heirs of the body," "heirs," "next of kin," "relatives," or "family," or a class described by language of similar import, a substitute gift is created in the surviving descendants of any deceased beneficiary. The property to which the beneficiaries would have been entitled had all of them survived the decedent passes to the surviving beneficiaries and the surviving descendants of the deceased beneficiaries. Each surviving beneficiary takes the share to which he [or she] would have been entitled had the deceased beneficiaries survived the decedent. Each deceased beneficiary's surviving descendants who are substituted for the deceased beneficiary take by representation the share to which the deceased beneficiary would have been entitled had the deceased beneficiary survived the decedent. For the purposes of this paragraph, "deceased beneficiary" means a class member who failed to survive the decedent and left one or more surviving descendants.

(3) For the purposes of Section 2–701, words of survivorship, such as in a beneficiary designation to an individual "if he survives me," or in a beneficiary designation to "my surviving children," are not, in the absence of additional evidence, a sufficient indication of an intent contrary to the application of this section.

(4) If a governing instrument creates an alternative beneficiary designation with respect to a beneficiary designation for which a substitute gift is created by paragraph (1) or (2), the substitute gift is superseded by the alternative beneficiary designation only if an expressly designated beneficiary of the alternative beneficiary designation is entitled to take.

(c) [More Than One Substitute Gift; Which One Takes.] If, under subsection (b), substitute gifts are created and not superseded with respect to more than one beneficiary designation and the beneficiary designations are alternative beneficiary designations, one to the other, the determination of which of the substitute gifts takes effect is resolved as follows:

(1) Except as provided in paragraph (2), the property passes under the primary substitute gift.

(2) If there is a younger-generation beneficiary designation, the property passes under the younger-

generation substitute gift and not under the primary substitute gift.

(3) In this subsection:

(i) "Primary beneficiary designation" means the beneficiary designation that would have taken effect had all the deceased beneficiaries of the alternative beneficiary designations who left surviving descendants survived the decedent.

(ii) "Primary substitute gift" means the substitute gift created with respect to the primary beneficiary designation.

(iii) "Younger-generation beneficiary designation" means a beneficiary designation that (A) is to a descendant of a beneficiary of the primary beneficiary designation, (B) is an alternative beneficiary designation with respect to the primary beneficiary designation, (C) is a beneficiary designation for which a substitute gift is created, and (D) would have taken effect had all the deceased beneficiaries who left surviving descendants survived the decedent except the deceased beneficiary or beneficiaries of the primary beneficiary designation.

(iv) "Younger-generation substitute gift" means the substitute gift created with respect to the younger-generation beneficiary designation.

(d) [Protection of Payors.]

(1) A payor is protected from liability in making payments under the terms of the beneficiary designation until the payor has received written notice of a claim to a substitute gift under this section. Payment made before the receipt of written notice of a claim to a substitute gift under this section discharges the payor, but not the recipient, from all claims for the amounts paid. A payor is liable for a payment made after the payor has received written notice of the claim. A recipient is liable for a payment received, whether or not written notice of the claim is given.

(2) The written notice of the claim must be mailed to the payor's main office or home by registered or certified mail, return receipt requested, or served upon the payor in the same manner as a summons in a civil action. Upon receipt of written notice of the claim, a payor may pay any amount owed by it to the court having jurisdiction of the probate proceedings relating to the decedent's estate or, if no proceedings have been commenced, to the court having jurisdiction of probate proceedings relating to decedents' estates located in the county of the decedent's residence. The court shall hold the funds and, upon its determination under this section, shall order disbursement in accordance with the determination. Payment made to the court discharges the payor from all claims for the amounts paid.

(e) [Protection of Bona Fide Purchasers; Personal Liability of Recipient.]

(1) A person who purchases property for value and without notice, or who receives a payment or other item of property in partial or full satisfaction of a legally enforceable obligation, is neither obligated under this section to return the payment, item of property, or benefit nor is liable under this section for the amount of the payment or the value of the item of property or benefit. But a person who, not for value, receives a payment, item of property, or any other benefit to which the person is not entitled under this section is obligated to return the payment, item of property, or benefit, or is personally liable for the amount of the payment or the value of the item of property or benefit, to the person who is entitled to it under this section.

(2) If this section or any part of this section is preempted by federal law with respect to a payment, an item of property, or any other benefit covered by this section, a person who, not for value, receives the payment, item of property, or any other benefit to which the person is not entitled under this section is obligated to return the payment, item of property, or benefit, or is personally liable for the amount of the payment or the value of the item of property or benefit, to the person who would have been entitled to it were this section or part of this section not preempted.

As amended in 1993.

§2–707. Survivorship with Respect to Future Interests under Terms of Trust; Substitute Takers.

(a) [Definitions.] In this section:

(1) "Alternative future interest" means an expressly created future interest that can take effect in possession or enjoyment instead of another future interest on the happening of one or more events, including survival of an event or failure to survive an event, whether an event is expressed in condition-precedent, condition-subsequent, or any other form. A residuary clause in a will does not create an alternative future interest with respect to a future interest created in a nonresiduary devise in the will, whether or not the will specifically provides that lapsed or failed devises are to pass under the residuary clause.

(2) "Beneficiary" means the beneficiary of a future interest and includes a class member if the future interest is in the form of a class gift.

(3) "Class member" includes an individual who fails to survive the distribution date but who would have taken under a future interest in the form of a class gift had he [or she] survived the distribution date.

(4) "Distribution date," with respect to a future interest, means the time when the future interest is to take effect in possession or enjoyment. The distribution date need not occur at the beginning or end of a calendar day, but can occur at a time during the course of a day.

(5) "Future interest" includes an alternative future interest and a future interest in the form of a class gift.

(6) "Future interest under the terms of a trust" means a future interest that was created by a transfer creating a trust or to an existing trust or by an exercise of a power of appointment to an existing trust, directing the continuance of an existing trust, designating a beneficiary of an existing trust, or creating a trust.

(7) "Surviving beneficiary" or "surviving descendant" means a beneficiary or a descendant who neither predeceased the distribution date nor is deemed to have predeceased the distribution date under Section 2–702.

(b) [Survivorship Required; Substitute Gift.] A future interest under the terms of a trust is contingent on the beneficiary's surviving the distribution date. If a beneficiary of a future interest under the terms of a trust fails to survive the distribution date, the following apply:

(1) Except as provided in paragraph (4), if the future interest is not in the form of a class gift and the deceased beneficiary leaves surviving descendants, a substitute gift is created in the beneficiary's surviving descendants. They take by representation the property to which the beneficiary would have been entitled had the beneficiary survived the distribution date.

(2) Except as provided in paragraph (4), if the future interest is in the form of a class gift, other than a future interest to "issue," "descendants," "heirs of the body," "heirs," "next of kin," "relatives," or "family," or a class described by language of similar import, a substitute gift is created in the surviving descendants of any deceased beneficiary. The property to which the beneficiaries would have been entitled had all of them survived the distribution date passes to the surviving beneficiaries and the surviving descendants of the deceased beneficiaries. Each surviving beneficiary takes the share to which he [or she] would have been entitled had the deceased beneficiaries survived the distribution date. Each deceased beneficiary's surviving descendants who are substituted for the deceased beneficiary take by representation the share to which the deceased beneficiary would have been entitled had the deceased beneficiary survived the distribution date. For the purposes of this paragraph, "deceased beneficiary" means a class member who failed to survive the distribution date and left one or more surviving descendants.

(3) For the purposes of Section 2–701, words of survivorship attached to a future interest are not, in the absence of additional evidence, a sufficient indication of an intent contrary to the application of this section. Words of survivorship include words of survivorship that relate to the distribution date or to an earlier or an unspecified time, whether those words of survivorship are expressed in condition-precedent, condition-subsequent, or any other form.

(4) If a governing instrument creates an alternative future interest with respect to a future interest for which a substitute gift is created by paragraph (1) or (2), the substitute gift is superseded by the alternative future interest only if an expressly designated beneficiary of the alternative future interest is entitled to take in possession or enjoyment.

(c) [More Than One Substitute Gift; Which One Takes.] If, under subsection (b), substitute gifts are created and not superseded with respect to more than one future interest and the future interests are alternative future interests, one to the other, the determination of which of the substitute gifts takes effect is resolved as follows:

(1) Except as provided in paragraph (2), the property passes under the primary substitute gift.

(2) If there is a younger-generation future interest, the property passes under the younger-generation substitute gift and not under the primary substitute gift.

(3) In this subsection:

(i) "Primary future interest" means the future interest that would have taken effect had all the deceased beneficiaries of the alternative future interests who left surviving descendants survived the distribution date.

(ii) "Primary substitute gift" means the substitute gift created with respect to the primary future interest.

(iii) "Younger-generation future interest" means a future interest that (A) is to a descendant of a beneficiary of the primary future interest, (B) is an alternative future interest with respect to the primary future interest, (C) is a future interest for which a substitute gift is created, and (D) would have taken effect had all the deceased beneficiaries who left surviving descendants survived the distribution date except the deceased beneficiary or beneficiaries of the primary future interest.

(iv) "Younger-generation substitute gift" means the substitute gift created with respect to the younger-generation future interest.

(d) [If No Other Takers, Property Passes Under Residuary Clause or to Transferor's Heirs.] Except as provided in subsection (e), if, after the application of subsections (b) and (c), there is no surviving taker, the property passes in the following order:

(1) if the trust was created in a nonresiduary devise in the transferor's will or in a codicil to the transferor's will, the property passes under the residuary clause in the transferor's will; for purposes of this section, the residuary clause is treated as creating a future interest under the terms of a trust.

(2) if no taker is produced by the application of paragraph (1), the property passes to the transferor's heirs under Section 2–711.

(e) [If No Other Takers and If Future Interest Created by Exercise of Power of Appointment.] If, after the application of subsections (b) and (c), there is no surviving taker and if the future interest was created by the exercise of a power of appointment:

(1) the property passes under the donor's gift-in-default clause, if any, which clause is treated as creating a future interest under the terms of a trust; and

(2) if no taker is produced by the application of paragraph (1), the property passes as provided in subsection (d). For purposes of subsection (d), "transferor" means the donor if the power was a nongeneral power and means the donee if the power was a general power.

As amended in 1993.

§2–708. Class Gifts to "Descendants," "Issue," or "Heirs of the Body"; Form of Distribution if None Specified.

If a class gift in favor of "descendants," "issue," or "heirs of the body" does not specify the manner in which the property is to be distributed among the class members, the property is distributed among the class members who are living when the interest is to take effect in possession or enjoyment, in such shares as they would receive, under the applicable law of intestate succession, if the designated ancestor had then died intestate owning the subject matter of the class gift.

§2–709. Representation; Per Capita at Each Generation; Per Stirpes.

(a) [Definitions.] In this section:

(1) "Deceased child" or "deceased descendant" means a child or a descendant who either predeceased the distribution date or is deemed to have predeceased the distribution date under Section 2–702.

(2) "Distribution date," with respect to an interest, means the time when the interest is to take effect in possession or enjoyment. The distribution date need not occur at the beginning or end of a calendar day, but can occur at a time during the course of a day.

(3) "Surviving ancestor," "surviving child," or "surviving descendant" means an ancestor, a child, or a

descendant who neither predeceased the distribution date nor is deemed to have predeceased the distribution date under Section 2–702.

(b) [Representation; Per Capita at Each Generation.] If an applicable statute or a governing instrument calls for property to be distributed "by representation" or "per capita at each generation," the property is divided into as many equal shares as there are (i) surviving descendants in the generation nearest to the designated ancestor which contains one or more surviving descendants (ii) and deceased descendants in the same generation who left surviving descendants, if any. Each surviving descendant in the nearest generation is allocated one share. The remaining shares, if any, are combined and then divided in the same manner among the surviving descendants of the deceased descendants as if the surviving descendants who were allocated a share and their surviving descendants had predeceased the distribution date.

(c) [Per Stirpes.] If a governing instrument calls for property to be distributed "per stirpes," the property is divided into as many equal shares as there are (i) surviving children of the designated ancestor and (ii) deceased children who left surviving descendants. Each surviving child, if any, is allocated one share. The share of each deceased child with surviving descendants is divided in the same manner, with subdivision repeating at each succeeding generation until the property is fully allocated among surviving descendants.

(d) [Deceased Descendant With No Surviving Descendant Disregarded.] For the purposes of subsections (b) and (c), an individual who is deceased and left no surviving descendant is disregarded, and an individual who leaves a surviving ancestor who is a descendant of the designated ancestor is not entitled to a share.

As amended in 1993.

§2–710. Worthier-Title Doctrine Abolished.

The doctrine of worthier-title is abolished as a rule of law and as a rule of construction. Language in a governing instrument describing the beneficiaries of a disposition as the transferor's "heirs," "heirs at law," "next of kin," "distributees," "relatives," or "family," or language of similar import, does not create or presumptively create a reversionary interest in the transferor.

As amended in 1991.

§2–711. Interests in "Heirs" and Like.

If an applicable statute or a governing instrument calls for a present or future distribution to or creates a present or future interest in a designated individual's "heirs," "heirs at law," "next of kin," "relatives," or "family," or language of similar import, the property passes to those persons, including the state, and in such shares as would succeed to the designated individual's intestate estate under the intestate succession law of the designated individual's domicile if the designated individual died when the disposition is to take effect in possession or enjoyment. If the designated individual's surviving spouse is living but is remarried at the time the disposition is to take effect in possession or enjoyment, the surviving spouse is not an heir of the designated individual.

As amended in 1991 and 1993.

PART 8
GENERAL PROVISIONS CONCERNING PROBATE AND NONPROBATE TRANSFERS

§2–801. Disclaimer of Property Interests.

(a) [Right to Disclaim Interest in Property.] A person, or the representative of a person, to whom an interest in or with respect to property or an interest therein devolves by whatever means may disclaim it in whole or in part by delivering or filing a written disclaimer under this section. The right to disclaim exists notwithstanding (i) any limitation on the interest of the disclaimant in the nature of a spendthrift provision or similar restriction or (ii) any restriction or limitation on the right to disclaim contained in the governing instrument. For purposes of this subsection, the "representative of a person" includes a personal representative of a decedent, a conservator of a disabled person, a guardian of a minor or incapacitated person, and an agent acting on behalf of the person within the authority of a power of attorney.

(b) [Time of Disclaimer.] The following rules govern the time when a disclaimer must be filed or delivered:

(1) If the property or interest has devolved to the disclaimant under a testamentary instrument or by the laws of intestacy, the disclaimer must be filed, if of a present interest, not later than [nine] months after the death of the deceased owner or deceased donee of a power of appointment and, if of a future interest, not later than [nine] months after the event determining that the taker of the property or interest is finally ascertained and his [or her] interest is indefeasibly vested. The disclaimer must be filed in the [probate] court of the county in which proceedings for the administration of the estate of the deceased owner or deceased donee of the power have been commenced. A copy of the disclaimer must be delivered in person or mailed by registered or certified mail, return receipt requested, to any personal representative or other fiduciary of the decedent or donee of the power.

(2) If a property or interest has devolved to the disclaimant under a nontestamentary instrument or contract, the disclaimer must be delivered or filed, if of a present interest, not later than [nine] months after the effective date of the nontestamentary instrument or contract and, if of a future interest, not later than [nine] months after the event determining that the taker of the property or interest is finally ascertained and his [or her] interest is indefeasibly vested. If the person entitled to disclaim does not know of the existence of the interest, the disclaimer must be delivered or filed not later than [nine] months after the person learns of the existence of the interest. The effective date of a revocable instrument or contract is the date on which the maker no longer has power to revoke it or to transfer to himself [or herself] or another the entire legal and equitable ownership of the interest. The disclaimer or a copy thereof must be delivered in person or mailed by registered or certified mail, return receipt requested, to the person who has legal title to or possession of the interest disclaimed.

(3) A surviving joint tenant [or tenant by the entireties] may disclaim as a separate interest any property or interest therein devolving to him [or her] by right of survivorship. A surviving joint tenant [or tenant by the entireties] may disclaim the entire interest in any property or interest therein that is the subject of a joint tenancy [or tenancy by the entireties] devolving to him [or her], if the joint tenancy [or tenancy by the entireties] was created by act of a deceased joint tenant [or tenant by the entireties], the survivor did not join in creating the joint tenancy [or tenancy by the entireties], and has not accepted a benefit under it.

(4) If real property or an interest therein is disclaimed, a copy of the disclaimer may be recorded in the office of the [Recorder of Deeds] of the county in which the property or interest disclaimed is located.*

* If Torrens system is in effect, add provisions to comply with local law.

(c) [Form of Disclaimer.] The disclaimer must (i) describe the property or interest disclaimed, (ii) declare the disclaimer and extent thereof, and (iii) be signed by the disclaimant.

(d) [Effect of Disclaimer.] The effects of a disclaimer are:

(1) If property or an interest therein devolves to a disclaimant under a testamentary instrument, under a power of appointment exercised by a testamentary instrument, or under the laws of intestacy, and the decedent has not provided for another disposition of that interest, should it be disclaimed, or of disclaimed, or failed interests in general, the disclaimed interest devolves as if the disclaimant had predeceased the decedent, but if by law or under the testamentary instrument the descendants of the

disclaimant would share in the disclaimed interest by representation or otherwise were the disclaimant to predecease the decedent, then the disclaimed interest passes by representation, or passes as directed by the governing instrument, to the descendants of the disclaimant who survive the decedent. A future interest that takes effect in possession or enjoyment after the termination of the estate or interest disclaimed takes effect as if the disclaimant had predeceased the decedent. A disclaimer relates back for all purposes to the date of death of the decedent.

(2) If property or an interest therein devolves to a disclaimant under a nontestamentary instrument or contract and the instrument or contract does not provide for another disposition of that interest, should it be disclaimed, or of disclaimed or failed interests in general, the disclaimed interest devolves as if the disclaimant has predeceased the effective date of the instrument or contract, but if by law or under the nontestamentary instrument or contract the descendants of the disclaimant would share in the disclaimed interest by representation or otherwise were the disclaimant to predecease the effective date of the instrument, then the disclaimed interest passes by representation, or passes as directed by the governing instrument, to the descendants of the disclaimant who survive the effective date of the instrument. A disclaimer relates back for all purposes to that date. A future interest that takes effect in possession or enjoyment at or after the termination of the disclaimed interest takes effect as if the disclaimant had died before the effective date of the instrument or contract that transferred the disclaimed interest.

(3) The disclaimer or the written waiver of the right to disclaim is binding upon the disclaimant or person waiving and all persons claiming through or under either of them.

(e) [Waiver and Bar.] The right to disclaim property or an interest therein is barred by (i) an assignment, conveyance, encumbrance, pledge, or transfer of the property or interest, or a contract therefor, (ii) a written waiver of the right to disclaim, (iii) an acceptance of the property or interest or a benefit under it or (iv) a sale of the property or interest under judicial sale made before the disclaimer is made.

(f) [Remedy Not Exclusive.] This section does not abridge the right of a person to waive, release, disclaim, or renounce property or an interest therein under any other statute.

(g) [Application.] An interest in property that exists on the effective date of this section as to which, if a present interest, the time for filing a disclaimer under this section has not expired or, if a future interest, the interest has not become indefeasibly vested or the taker finally as-

certained, may be disclaimed within [nine] months after the effective date of this section.

As amended in 1993.

§2–802.   Effect of Divorce, Annulment, and Decree of Separation.

(a) An individual who is divorced from the decedent or whose marriage to the decedent has been annulled is not a surviving spouse unless, by virtue of a subsequent marriage, he [or she] is married to the decedent at the time of death. A decree of separation that does not terminate the status of husband and wife is not a divorce for purposes of this section.

(b) For purposes of Parts 1, 2, 3, and 4 of this Article, and of Section 3–203, a surviving spouse does not include:

(1) an individual who obtains or consents to a final decree or judgment of divorce from the decedent or an annulment of their marriage, which decree or judgment is not recognized as valid in this State, unless subsequently they participate in a marriage ceremony purporting to marry each to the other or live together as husband and wife;

(2) an individual who, following an invalid decree or judgment of divorce or annulment obtained by the decedent, participates in a marriage ceremony with a third individual; or

(3) an individual who was a party to a valid proceeding concluded by an order purporting to terminate all marital property rights.

§2–803.   Effect of Homicide on Intestate Succession, Wills, Trusts, Joint Assets, Life Insurance, and Beneficiary Designations.

(a) [Definitions.] In this section:

(1) "Disposition or appointment of property" includes a transfer of an item of property or any other benefit to a beneficiary designated in a governing instrument.

(2) "Governing instrument" means a governing instrument executed by the decedent.

(3) "Revocable," with respect to a disposition, appointment, provision, or nomination, means one under which the decedent, at the time of or immediately before death, was alone empowered, by law or under the governing instrument, to cancel the designation, in favor of the killer, whether or not the decedent was then empowered to designate himself [or herself] in place of his [or her] killer and whether or not the decedent then had capacity to exercise the power.

(b) [Forfeiture of Statutory Benefits.] An individual who feloniously and intentionally kills the decedent forfeits all benefits under this Article with respect to the decedent's estate, including an intestate share, an elective share, an omitted spouse's or child's share, a homestead allowance, exempt property, and a family allowance. If the decedent died intestate, the decedent's intestate estate passes as if the killer disclaimed his [or her] intestate share.

(c) [Revocation of Benefits Under Governing Instruments.] The felonious and intentional killing of the decedent:

(1) revokes any revocable (i) disposition or appointment of property made by the decedent to the killer in a governing instrument, (ii) provision in a governing instrument conferring a general or nongeneral power of appointment on the killer, and (iii) nomination of the killer in a governing instrument, nominating or appointing the killer to serve in any fiduciary or representative capacity, including a personal representative, executor, trustee, or agent; and

(2) severs the interests of the decedent and killer in property held by them at the time of the killing as joint tenants with the right of survivorship [or as community property with the right of survivorship], transforming the interests of the decedent and killer into tenancies in common.

(d) [Effect of Severance.] A severance under subsection (c)(2) does not affect any third-party interest in property acquired for value and in good faith reliance on an apparent title by survivorship in the killer unless a writing declaring the severance has been noted, registered, filed, or recorded in records appropriate to the kind and location of the property which are relied upon, in the ordinary course of transactions involving such property, as evidence of ownership.

(e) [Effect of Revocation.] Provisions of a governing instrument are given effect as if the killer disclaimed all provisions revoked by this section or, in the case of a revoked nomination in a fiduciary or representative capacity, as if the killer predeceased the decedent.

(f) [Wrongful Acquisition of Property.] A wrongful acquisition of property or interest by a killer not covered by this section must be treated in accordance with the principle that a killer cannot profit from his [or her] wrong.

(g) [Felonious and Intentional Killing; How Determined.] After all right to appeal has been exhausted, a judgment of conviction establishing criminal accountability for the felonious and intentional killing of the decedent conclusively establishes the convicted individual as the decedent's killer for purposes of this section. In the absence of a conviction, the court, upon the petition of an interested person, must determine whether, under the preponderance of evidence standard, the individual would be found criminally accountable for the felonious and intentional killing of the decedent. If the court determines that, under that standard, the individual would be found criminally accountable for the felonious and intentional killing of the decedent, the determination conclusively establishes that individual as the decedent's killer for purposes of this section.

(h) [Protection of Payors and Other Third Parties.]

(1) A payor or other third party is not liable for having made a payment or transferred an item of property or any other benefit to a beneficiary designated in a governing instrument affected by an intentional and felonious killing, or for having taken any other action in good faith reliance on the validity of the governing instrument, upon request and satisfactory proof of the decedent's death, before the payor or other third party received written notice of a claimed forfeiture or revocation under this section. A payor or other third party is liable for a payment made or other action taken after the payor or other third party received written notice of a claimed forfeiture or revocation under this section.

(2) Written notice of a claimed forfeiture or revocation under paragraph (1) must be mailed to the payor's or other third party's main office or home by registered or certified mail, return receipt requested, or served upon the payor or other third party in the same manner as a summons in a civil action. Upon receipt of written notice of a claimed forfeiture or revocation under this section, a payor or other third party may pay any amount owed or transfer or deposit any item of property held by it to or with the court having jurisdiction of the probate proceedings relating to the decedent's estate, or if no proceedings have been commenced, to or with the court having jurisdiction of probate proceedings relating to decedents' estates located in the county of the decedent's residence. The court shall hold the funds or item of property and, upon its determination under this section, shall order disbursement in accordance with the determination. Payments, transfers, or deposits made to or with the court discharge the payor or other third party from all claims for the value of amounts paid to or items of property transferred to or deposited with the court.

(i) [Protection of Bona Fide Purchasers; Personal Liability of Recipient.]

(1) A person who purchases property for value and without notice, or who receives a payment or other item of property in partial or full satisfaction of a legally enforceable obligation, is neither obligated under this section to return the payment, item of property, or benefit nor is liable under this section for the amount of the payment or the value of the item of property or benefit. But a person who, not for value, receives a payment, item of property, or any other benefit to which the person is not entitled

under this section is obligated to return the payment, item of property, or benefit, or is personally liable for the amount of the payment or the value of the item of property or benefit, to the person who is entitled to it under this section.

(2) If this section or any part of this section is pre-empted by federal law with respect to a payment, an item of property, or any other benefit covered by this section, a person who, not for value, receives the payment, item of property, or any other benefit to which the person is not entitled under this section is obligated to return the payment, item of property, or benefit, or is personally liable for the amount of the payment or the value of the item of property or ben-efit, to the person who would have been entitled to it were this section or part of this section not preempted.

As amended in 1993.

§2–804. Revocation of Probate and Nonprobate Transfers by Divorce; No Revocation by other Changes of Circumstances.

(a) [Definitions.] In this section:

(1) "Disposition or appointment of property" in-cludes a transfer of an item of property or any other benefit to a beneficiary designated in a governing instrument.

(2) "Divorce or annulment" means any divorce or annulment, or any dissolution or declaration of in-validity of a marriage, that would exclude the spouse as a surviving spouse within the meaning of Section 2–802. A decree of separation that does not terminate the status of husband and wife is not a divorce for purposes of this section.

(3) "Divorced individual" includes an individual whose marriage has been annulled.

(4) "Governing instrument" means a governing in-strument executed by the divorced individual before the divorce or annulment of his [or her] marriage to his [or her] former spouse.

(5) "Relative of the divorced individual's former spouse" means an individual who is related to the divorced individual's former spouse by blood, adop-tion, or affinity and who, after the divorce or annul-ment, is not related to the divorced individual by blood, adoption, or affinity.

(6) "Revocable," with respect to a disposition, ap-pointment, provision, or nomination, means one un-der which the divorced individual, at the time of the divorce or annulment, was alone empowered, by law or under the governing instrument, to cancel the des-ignation in favor of his [or her] former spouse or for-mer spouse's relative, whether or not the divorced individual was then empowered to designate himself [or herself] in place of his [or her] former spouse or

in place of his [or her] former spouse's relative and whether or not the divorced individual then had the capacity to exercise the power.

(b) [Revocation Upon Divorce.] Except as provided by the express terms of a governing instrument, a court order, or a contract relating to the division of the marital estate made between the divorced individuals before or after the marriage, divorce, or annulment, the divorce or annulment of a marriage:

(1) revokes any revocable (i) disposition or appoint-ment of property made by a divorced individual to his [or her] former spouse in a governing instrument and any disposition or appointment created by law or in a governing instrument to a relative of the di-vorced individual's former spouse, (ii) provision in a governing instrument conferring a general or non-general power of appointment on the divorced in-dividual's former spouse or on a relative of the divorced individual's former spouse, and (iii) nomi-nation in a governing instrument, nominating a di-vorced individual's former spouse or a relative of the divorced individual's former spouse to serve in any fiduciary or representative capacity, including a per-sonal representative, executor, trustee, conservator, agent, or guardian; and

(2) severs the interests of the former spouses in property held by them at the time of the divorce or annulment as joint tenants with the right of survivor-ship [or as community property with the right of sur-vivorship], transforming the interests of the former spouses into tenancies in common.

(c) [Effect of Severance.] A severance under subsec-tion (b)(2) does not affect any third-party interest in property acquired for value and in good faith reliance on an apparent title by survivorship in the survivor of the former spouses unless a writing declaring the sev-erance has been noted, registered, filed, or recorded in records appropriate to the kind and location of the prop-erty which are relied upon, in the ordinary course of transactions involving such property, as evidence of ownership.

(d) [Effect of Revocation.] Provisions of a governing instrument are given effect as if the former spouse and relatives of the former spouse disclaimed all provisions revoked by this section or, in the case of a revoked nom-ination in a fiduciary or representative capacity, as if the former spouse and relatives of the former spouse died immediately before the divorce or annulment.

(e) [Revival if Divorce Nullified.] Provisions revoked solely by this section are revived by the divorced indi-vidual's remarriage to the former spouse or by a nulli-fication of the divorce or annulment.

(f) [No Revocation for Other Change of Circum-stances.] No change of circumstances other than as described in this section and in Section 2–803 effects a revocation.

(g) [Protection of Payors and Other Third Parties.]

(1) A payor or other third party is not liable for having made a payment or transferred an item of property or any other benefit to a beneficiary designated in a governing instrument affected by a divorce, annulment, or remarriage, or for having taken any other action in good faith reliance on the validity of the governing instrument, before the payor or other third party received written notice of the divorce, annulment, or remarriage. A payor or other third party is liable for a payment made or other action taken after the payor or other third party received written notice of a claimed forfeiture or revocation under this section.

(2) Written notice of the divorce, annulment, or remarriage under subsection (g)(2) must be mailed to the payor's or other third party's main office or home by registered or certified mail, return receipt requested, or served upon the payor or other third party in the same manner as a summons in a civil action. Upon receipt of written notice of the divorce, annulment, or remarriage, a payor or other third party may pay any amount owed or transfer or deposit any item of property held by it to or with the court having jurisdiction of the probate proceedings relating to the decedent's estate or, if no proceedings have been commenced, to or with the court having jurisdiction of probate proceedings relating to decedents' estates located in the county of the decedent's residence. The court shall hold the funds or item of property and, upon its determination under this section, shall order disbursement or transfer in accordance with the determination. Payments, transfers, or deposits made to or with the court discharge the payor or other third party from all claims for the value of amounts paid to or items of property transferred to or deposited with the court.

(h) [Protection of Bona Fide Purchasers; Personal Liability of Recipient.]

(1) A person who purchases property from a former spouse, relative of a former spouse, or any other person for value and without notice, or who receives from a former spouse, relative of a former spouse, or any other person a payment or other item of property in partial or full satisfaction of a legally enforceable obligation, is neither obligated under this section to return the payment, item of property, or benefit nor is liable under this section for the amount of the payment or the value of the item of property or benefit. But a former spouse, relative of a former spouse, or other person who, not for value, received a payment, item of property, or any other benefit to which that

person is not entitled under this section is obligated to return the payment, item of property, or benefit, or is personally liable for the amount of the payment or the value of the item of property or benefit, to the person who is entitled to it under this section.

(2) If this section or any part of this section is preempted by federal law with respect to a payment, an item of property, or any other benefit covered by this section, a former spouse, relative of the former spouse, or any other person who, not for value, received a payment, item of property, or any other benefit to which that person is not entitled under this section is obligated to return that payment, item of property, or benefit, or is personally liable for the amount of the payment or the value of the item of property or benefit, to the person who would have been entitled to it were this section or part of this section not preempted.

As amended in 1993.

PART 9

STATUTORY RULE AGAINST PERPETUITIES; HONORARY TRUSTS

SUBPART 1.

[STATUTORY RULE AGAINST PERPETUITIES]

§2–901. Statutory Rule Against Perpetuities.

(a) [Validity of Nonvested Property Interest.] A nonvested property interest is invalid unless:

(1) when the interest is created, it is certain to vest or terminate no later than 21 years after the death of an individual then alive; or

(2) the interest either vests or terminates within 90 years after its creation.

(b) [Validity of General Power of Appointment Subject to a Condition Precedent.] A general power of appointment not presently exercisable because of a condition precedent is invalid unless:

(1) when the power is created, the condition precedent is certain to be satisfied or becomes impossible to satisfy no later than 21 years after the death of an individual then alive; or

(2) the condition precedent either is satisfied or becomes impossible to satisfy within 90 years after its creation.

(c) [Validity of Nongeneral or Testamentary Power of Appointment.] A nongeneral power of appointment or a general testamentary power of appointment is invalid unless:

(1) when the power is created, it is certain to be irrevocably exercised or otherwise to terminate no later than 21 years after the death of an individual then alive; or

(2) the power is irrevocably exercised or otherwise terminates within 90 years after its creation.

(d) [Possibility of Post-death Child Disregarded.] In determining whether a nonvested property interest or a power of appointment is valid under subsection (a)(1), (b)(1), or (c)(1), the possibility that a child will be born to an individual after the individual's death is disregarded.

(e) [Effect of Certain "Later-of" Type Language.] If, in measuring a period from the creation of a trust or other property arrangement, language in a governing instrument (i) seeks to disallow the vesting or termination of any interest or trust beyond, (ii) seeks to postpone the vesting or termination of any interest or trust until, or (iii) seeks to operate in effect in any similar fashion upon, the later of (A) the expiration of a period of time not exceeding 21 years after the death of the survivor of specified lives in being at the creation of the trust or other property arrangement or (B) the expiration of a period of time that exceeds or might exceed 21 years after the death of the survivor of lives in being at the creation of the trust or other property arrangement, that language is inoperative to the extent it produces a period of time that exceeds 21 years after the death of the survivor of the specified lives.

§2–902. When Nonvested Property Interest or Power of Appointment Created.

(a) Except as provided in subsections (b) and (c) and in Section 2–905(a), the time of creation of a nonvested property interest or a power of appointment is determined under general principles of property law.

(b) For purposes of Subpart 1 of this Part, if there is a person who alone can exercise a power created by a governing instrument to become the unqualified beneficial owner of (i) a nonvested property interest or (ii) a property interest subject to a power of appointment described in Section 2–901(b) or (c), the nonvested property interest or power of appointment is created when the power to become the unqualified beneficial owner terminates. [For purposes of Subpart 1 of this Part, a joint power with respect to community property or to marital property under the Uniform Marital Property Act held by individuals married to each other is a power exercisable by one person alone.]

(c) For purposes of Subpart 1 of this Part, a nonvested property interest or a power of appointment arising from a transfer of property to a previously funded trust or other existing property arrangement is created when the nonvested property interest or power of appointment in the original contribution was created.

§2–903. Reformation.

Upon the petition of an interested person, a court shall reform a disposition in the manner that most closely ap-

proximates the transferor's manifested plan of distribution and is within the 90 years allowed by Section 2–901(a)(2), 2–901(b)(2), or 2–901(c)(2) if:

(1) a nonvested property interest or a power of appointment becomes invalid under Section 2–901 (statutory rule against perpetuities);

(2) a class gift is not but might become invalid under Section 2–901 (statutory rule against perpetuities) and the time has arrived when the share of any class member is to take effect in possession or enjoyment; or

(3) a nonvested property interest that is not validated by Section 2–901(a)(1) can vest but not within 90 years after its creation.

§2–904. Exclusions from Statutory Rule Against Perpetuities.

Section 2–901 (statutory rule against perpetuities) does not apply to:

(1) a nonvested property interest or a power of appointment arising out of a nondonative transfer, except a nonvested property interest or a power of appointment arising out of (i) a premarital or postmarital agreement, (ii) a separation or divorce settlement, (iii) a spouse's election, (iv) a similar arrangement arising out of a prospective, existing, or previous marital relationship between the parties, (v) a contract to make or not to revoke a will or trust, (vi) a contract to exercise or not to exercise a power of appointment, (vii) a transfer in satisfaction of a duty of support, or (viii) a reciprocal transfer;

(2) a fiduciary's power relating to the administration or management of assets, including the power of a fiduciary to sell, lease, or mortgage property, and the power of a fiduciary to determine principal and income;

(3) a power to appoint a fiduciary;

(4) a discretionary power of a trustee to distribute principal before termination of a trust to a beneficiary having an indefeasibly vested interest in the income and principal;

(5) a nonvested property interest held by a charity, government, or governmental agency or subdivision, if the nonvested property interest is preceded by an interest held by another charity, government, or governmental agency or subdivision;

(6) a nonvested property interest in or a power of appointment with respect to a trust or other property arrangement forming part of a pension, profit-sharing, stock bonus, health, disability, death benefit, income deferral, or other current or deferred benefit plan for one or more employees, independent contractors, or their beneficiaries or spouses, to which contributions are made for the purpose of distributing to or for the benefit of the participants or their beneficiaries or spouses the property, income, or principal in the trust or other prop-

erty arrangement, except a nonvested property interest or a power of appointment that is created by an election of a participant or a beneficiary or spouse; or

(7) a property interest, power of appointment, or arrangement that was not subject to the common-law rule against perpetuities or is excluded by another statute of this State.

§2–905.   Prospective Application.

(a) Except as extended by subsection (b), Subpart 1 of this Part applies to a nonvested property interest or a power of appointment that is created on or after the effective date of Subpart 1 of this Part. For purposes of this section, a nonvested property interest or a power of appointment created by the exercise of a power of appointment is created when the power is irrevocably exercised or when a revocable exercise becomes irrevocable.

(b) If a nonvested property interest or a power of appointment was created before the effective date of Subpart 1 of this Part and is determined in a judicial proceeding, commenced on or after the effective date of Subpart 1 of this Part, to violate this State's rule against perpetuities as that rule existed before the effective date of Subpart 1 of this Part, a court upon the petition of an interested person may reform the disposition in the manner that most closely approximates the transferor's manifested plan of distribution and is within the limits of the rule against perpetuities applicable when the nonvested property interest or power of appointment was created.

§2–906.   [Supersession][Repeal].

Subpart 1 of this Part [supersedes the rule of the common law known as the rule against perpetuities][repeals (list statutes to be repealed)].

SUBPART 2.
[HONORARY TRUSTS]

§2–907.   Honorary Trusts; Trusts for Pets.

(a) [Honorary Trust.] Subject to subsection (c), if (i) a trust is for a specific lawful noncharitable purpose or for lawful noncharitable purposes to be selected by the trustee and (ii) there is no definite or definitely ascertainable beneficiary designated, the trust may be performed by the trustee for [21] years but no longer, whether or not the terms of the trust contemplate a longer duration.

(b) [Trust for Pets.] Subject to this subsection and subsection (c), a trust for the care of a designated domestic or pet animal is valid. The trust terminates when no living animal is covered by the trust. A governing instrument must be liberally construed to bring the transfer within this subsection, to presume against the merely precatory or honorary nature of the disposition, and to carry out the general intent of the transferor. Extrinsic evidence is admissible in determining the transferor's intent.

(c) [Additional Provisions Applicable to Honorary Trusts and Trusts for Pets.] In addition to the provisions of subsection (a) or (b), a trust covered by either of those subsections is subject to the following provisions:

(1) Except as expressly provided otherwise in the trust instrument, no portion of the principal or income may be converted to the use of the trustee or to any use other than for the trust's purposes or for the benefit of a covered animal.

(2) Upon termination, the trustee shall transfer the unexpended trust property in the following order:

(i) as directed in the trust instrument;

(ii) if the trust was created in a nonresiduary clause in the transferor's will or in a codicil to the transferor's will, under the residuary clause in the transferor's will; and

(iii) if no taker is produced by the application of subparagraph (i) or (ii), to the transferor's heirs under Section 2–711.

(3) For the purposes of Section 2–707, the residuary clause is treated as creating a future interest under the terms of a trust.

(4) The intended use of the principal or income can be enforced by an individual designated for that purpose in the trust instrument or, if none, by an individual appointed by a court upon application to it by an individual.

(5) Except as ordered by the court or required by the trust instrument, no filing, report, registration, periodic accounting, separate maintenance of funds, appointment, or fee is required by reason of the existence of the fiduciary relationship of the trustee.

(6) A court may reduce the amount of the property transferred, if it determines that that amount substantially exceeds the amount required for the intended use. The amount of the reduction, if any, passes as unexpended trust property under subsection (c)(2).

(7) If no trustee is designated or no designated trustee is willing or able to serve, a court shall name a trustee. A court may order the transfer of the property to another trustee, if required to assure that the intended use is carried out and if no successor trustee is designated in the trust instrument or if no designated successor trustee agrees to serve or is able to serve. A court may also make such other orders and determinations as shall be advisable to carry out the intent of the transferor and the purpose of this section.]

As amended in 1993.

PART 10
UNIFORM INTERNATIONAL WILLS ACT
[INTERNATIONAL WILL; INFORMATION REGISTRATION]

NUMBERING SECTIONS OF ACT

§1. [2–1001.] [Definitions.]

In this Act: [Part:]

(1) "International will" means a will executed in conformity with sections 2 [2–1002] through 5 [2–1005].

(2) "Authorized person" and "person authorized to act in connection with international wills" mean a person who by section 9 [2–1009], or by the laws of the United States including members of the diplomatic and consular service of the United States designated by Foreign Service Regulations, is empowered to supervise the execution of international wills.

§2. [2–1002.] [International Will; Validity.]

(a) A will shall be valid as regards form, irrespective particularly of the place where it is made, of the location of the assets and of the nationality, domicile, or residence of the testator, if it is made in the form of an international will complying with the requirements of this Act. [Part.]

(b) The invalidity of the will as an international will shall not affect its formal validity as a will of another kind.

(c) This Act [Part] shall not apply to the form of testamentary dispositions made by two or more persons in one instrument.

§3. [2–1003.] [International Will; Requirements.]

(a) The will shall be made in writing. It need not be written by the testator himself. It may be written in any language, by hand or by any other means.

(b) The testator shall declare in the presence of two witnesses and of a person authorized to act in connection with international wills that the document is his will and that he knows the contents thereof. The testator need not inform the witnesses, or the authorized person, of the contents of the will.

(c) In the presence of the witnesses, and of the authorized person, the testator shall sign the will or, if he has previously signed it, shall acknowledge his signature.

(d) When the testator is unable to sign, the absence of his signature does not affect the validity of the international will if the testator indicates the reason for his inability to sign and the authorized person makes note thereof on the will. In these cases, it is permissible for any other person present, including the authorized person or one of the witnesses, at the direction of the testator to sign the testator's name for him, if the authorized person makes note of this also on the will, but it is not required that any person sign the testator's name for him.

(e) The witnesses and the authorized person shall there and then attest the will by signing in the presence of the testator.

§4. [2–1004.] [International Will; Other Points of Form.]

(a) The signatures shall be placed at the end of the will. If the will consists of several sheets, each sheet will be signed by the testator or, if he is unable to sign, by the person signing on his behalf or, if there is no such person, by the authorized person. In addition, each sheet shall be numbered.

(b) The date of the will shall be the date of its signature by the authorized person. That date shall be noted at the end of the will by the authorized person.

(c) The authorized person shall ask the testator whether he wishes to make a declaration concerning the safekeeping of his will. If so and at the express request of the testator the place where he intends to have his will kept shall be mentioned in the certificate provided for in Section 5.

(d) A will executed in compliance with Section 3 shall not be invalid merely because it does not comply with this section.

§5. [2–1005.] [International Will; Certificate.]

The authorized person shall attach to the will a certificate to be signed by him establishing that the requirements of this Act [Part] for valid execution of an international will have been complied with. The authorized person shall keep a copy of the certificate and deliver another to the testator. The certificate shall be substantially in the following form:

CERTIFICATE

(Convention of October 26, 1973)

1. I, _____ (name, address and capacity), a person authorized to act in connection with international wills

2. Certify that on _____ (date) at _____ (place)

3. (testator) _____ (name, address, date and place of birth) in my presence and that of the witnesses

4. (a) _____ (name, address, date and place of birth)

(b) _____ (name, address, date and place of birth) has declared that the attached document is his will and that he knows the contents thereof.

5. I furthermore certify that:

6. (a) in my presence and in that of the witnesses

(1) the testator has signed the will or has acknowledged his signature previously affixed.

*(2) following a declaration of the testator stating that he was unable to sign his will for the following reason _____ , I have mentioned this declaration on the will * and the signature has been affixed by ____ (name and address)

7. (b) the witnesses and I have signed the will;

8. *(c) each page of the will has been signed by ____ and numbered;

9. (d) I have satisfied myself as to the identity of the testator and of the witnesses as designated above;

10. (e) the witnesses met the conditions requisite to act as such according to the law under which I am acting;

11. * (f) the testator has requested me to include the following statement concerning the safekeeping of his will:

12. PLACE OF EXECUTION

13. DATE

14. SIGNATURE and, if necessary, SEAL

* to be completed if appropriate

§6. [2–1006.] [International Will; Effect of Certificate.]

In the absence of evidence to the contrary, the certificate of the authorized person shall be conclusive of the formal validity of the instrument as a will under this Act. [Part.] The absence or irregularity of a certificate shall not affect the formal validity of a will under this Act. [Part.]

§7. [2–1007.] [International Will; Revocation.]

The international will shall be subject to the ordinary rules of revocation of wills.

§8. [2–1008.] [Source and Construction.]

Sections 1 [2–1001] through 7 [2–1007] derive from Annex to Convention of October 26, 1973, Providing a Uniform Law on the Form of an International Will. In interpreting and applying this Act [Part], regard shall be had to its international origin and to the need for uniformity in its interpretation.

§9. [2–1009.] [Persons Authorized to Act in Relation to International Will; Eligibility; Recognition by Authorizing Agency.]

Individuals who have been admitted to practice law before the courts of this state and who are in good standing as active law practitioners in this state, are hereby declared to be authorized persons in relation to international wills.

§10. [2–1010.] [International Will Information Registration.]

The [Secretary of State] shall establish a registry system by which authorized persons may register in a central information center, information regarding the execution of international wills, keeping that information in strictest confidence until the death of the maker and then making it available to any person desiring information about any will who presents a death certificate or other satisfactory evidence of the testator's death to the center. Information that may be received, preserved in confidence until death, and reported as indicated is limited to the name, social-security or any other individual-identifying number established by law, address, and date and place of birth of the testator, and the intended place of deposit or safekeeping of the instrument pending the death of the maker. The [Secretary of State], at the request of the authorized person, may cause the information it receives about execution of any international will to be transmitted to the registry system of another jurisdiction as identified by the testator, if that other system adheres to rules protecting the confidentiality of the information similar to those established in this state.]

ARTICLE III
PROBATE OF WILLS AND ADMINISTRATION

PART 1
GENERAL PROVISIONS

Section

3–101. [Devolution of Estate at Death; Restrictions.]

[3–101A. [Devolution of Estate at Death; Restrictions.]]

3–102. [Necessity of Order of Probate For Will.]

3–103. [Necessity of Appointment For Administration.]

3–104. [Claims Against Decedent; Necessity of Administration.]

3–105. [Proceedings Affecting Devolution and Administration; Jurisdiction of Subject Matter.]

3–106. [Proceedings Within the Exclusive Jurisdiction of Court; Service; Jurisdiction Over Persons.]

3–107. [Scope of Proceedings; Proceedings Independent; Exception.]

3–108. [Probate, Testacy and Appointment Proceedings; Ultimate Time Limit.]

3–109. [Statutes of Limitation on Decedent's Cause of Action.]

PART 2
VENUE FOR PROBATE AND ADMINISTRATION; PRIORITY TO ADMINISTER; DEMAND FOR NOTICE

3–201. [Venue for First and Subsequent Estate Proceedings; Location of Property.]

3–202. [Appointment or Testacy Proceedings; Conflicting Claim of Domicile in Another State.]

3–203. [Priority Among Persons Seeking Appointment as Personal Representative.]

PART 1
GENERAL PROVISIONS

§3–101. [Devolution of Estate at Death; Restrictions.]

The power of a person to leave property by will, and the rights of creditors, devisees, and heirs to his property are subject to the restrictions and limitations contained in this Code to facilitate the prompt settlement of estates. Upon the death of a person, his real and personal property devolves to the persons to whom it is devised by his last will or to those indicated as substitutes for them in cases involving lapse, renunciation, or other circumstances affecting the devolution of testate estate, or in the absence of testamentary disposition, to his heirs, or to those indicated as substitutes for them in cases involving renunciation or other circumstances affecting devolution of intestate estates, subject to homestead allowance, exempt property and family allowance, to rights of creditors, elective share of the surviving spouse, and to administration.

ALTERNATIVE SECTION FOR COMMUNITY PROPERTY STATES

[§3–101A. [Devolution of Estate at Death; Restrictions.]

The power of a person to leave property by will, and the rights of creditors, devisees, and heirs to his property are subject to the restrictions and limitations contained in this Code to facilitate the prompt settlement of estates. Upon the death of a person, his separate property devolves to the persons to whom it is devised by his last will, or to those indicated as substitutes for them in cases involving lapse, renunciation or other circumstances affecting the devolution of testate estates, or in the absence of testamentary disposition to his heirs, or to those indicated as substitutes for them in cases involving renunciation or other circumstances affecting the devolution of intestate estates, and upon the death of a husband or wife, the decedent's share of their community property devolves to the persons to whom it is devised by his last will, or in the absence of testamentary disposition, to his heirs, but all of their community property which is under the management and control of the decedent is subject to his debts and administration, and that portion of their community property which is not under the management and control of the decedent but which is necessary to carry out the provisions of his will is subject to administration; but the devolution of all the above described property is subject to rights to homestead allowance, exempt property and family allowances, to renunciation, to rights of creditors, [elective share of the surviving spouse] and to administration.]

§3–102. [Necessity of Order of Probate For Will.]

Except as provided in Section 3–1201, to be effective to prove the transfer of any property or to nominate an executor, a will must be declared to be valid by an order of informal probate by the Registrar, or an adjudication of probate by the Court.

As amended in 1993.

§3–103. [Necessity of Appointment For Administration.]

Except as otherwise provided in Article IV, to acquire the powers and undertake the duties and liabilities of a personal representative of a decedent, a person must be appointed by order of the Court or Registrar, qualify and be issued letters. Administration of an estate is commenced by the issuance of letters.

§3–104. [Claims Against Decedent; Necessity of Administration.]

No proceeding to enforce a claim against the estate of a decedent or his successors may be revived or commenced before the appointment of a personal representative. After the appointment and until distribution, all proceedings and actions to enforce a claim against the estate are governed by the procedure prescribed by this Article. After distribution a creditor whose claim has not been barred may recover from the distributees as provided in Section 3–1004 or from a former personal representative individually liable as provided in Section 3–1005. This section has no application to a proceeding by a secured creditor of the decedent to enforce his right to his security except as to any deficiency judgment which might be sought therein.

§3–105. [Proceedings Affecting Devolution and Administration; Jurisdiction of Subject Matter.]

Persons interested in decedents' estates may apply to the Registrar for determination in the informal proceedings provided in this Article, and may petition the Court for orders in formal proceedings within the Court's jurisdiction including but not limited to those described in this Article. The Court has exclusive jurisdiction of formal proceedings to determine how decedents' estates subject to the laws of this state are to be administered, expended and distributed. The Court has concurrent jurisdiction of any other action or proceeding concerning a succession or to which an estate, through a personal representative, may be a party, including actions to determine title to property alleged to belong to the estate, and of any action or proceeding in which property distributed by a personal representative or its value is sought to be subjected to rights of creditors or successors of the decedent.

§3–106. [Proceedings Within the Exclusive Jurisdiction of Court; Service; Jurisdiction Over Persons.]

In proceedings within the exclusive jurisdiction of the Court where notice is required by this Code or by rule, and in proceedings to construe probated wills or determine heirs which concern estates that have not been and cannot now be open for administration, interested persons may be bound by the orders of the Court in respect to property in or subject to the laws of this state by notice in conformity with Section 1–401. An order is binding as to all who are given notice of the proceeding though less than all interested persons are notified.

§3–107. [Scope of Proceedings; Proceedings Independent; Exception.]

Unless supervised administration as described in Part 5 is involved, (1) each proceeding before the Court or Registrar is independent of any other proceeding involving the same estate; (2) petitions for formal orders of the Court may combine various requests for relief in a single proceeding if the orders sought may be finally granted without delay. Except as required for proceedings which are particularly described by other sections of this Article, no petition is defective because it fails to embrace all matters which might then be the subject of a final order; (3) proceedings for probate of wills or adjudications of no will may be combined with proceedings for appointment of personal representatives; and (4) a proceeding for appointment of a personal representative is concluded by an order making or declining the appointment.

§3–108. [Probate, Testacy and Appointment Proceedings; Ultimate Time Limit.]

(a) No informal probate or appointment proceeding or formal testacy or appointment proceeding, other than a proceeding to probate a will previously probated at the testator's domicile and appointment proceedings relating to an estate in which there has been a prior appointment, may be commenced more than three years after the decedent's death, except:

(1) if a previous proceeding was dismissed because of doubt about the fact of the decedent's death, appropriate probate, appointment, or testacy proceedings may be maintained at any time thereafter upon a finding that the decedent's death occurred before the initiation of the previous proceeding and the applicant or petitioner has not delayed unduly in initiating the subsequent proceeding;

(2) appropriate probate, appointment, or testacy proceedings may be maintained in relation to the estate of an absent, disappeared or missing person for whose estate a conservator has been appointed, at any time within three years after the conservator becomes able to establish the death of the protected person;

(3) a proceeding to contest an informally probated will and to secure appointment of the person with legal priority for appointment in the event the contest is successful, may be commenced within the later of twelve months from the informal probate or three years from the decedent's death;

(4) an informal appointment or a formal testacy or appointment proceeding may be commenced

thereafter if no proceedings concerning the succession or estate administration has occurred within the three year period after the decedent's death, but the personal representative has no right to possess estate assets as provided in Section 3–709 beyond that necessary to confirm title thereto in the successors to the estate and claims other than expenses of administration may not be presented against the estate; and

(5) a formal testacy proceeding may be commenced at any time after three years from the decedent's death for the purpose of establishing an instrument to direct or control the ownership of property passing or distributable after the decedent's death from one other than the decedent when the property is to be appointed by the terms of the decedent's will or is to pass or be distributed as a part of the decedent's estate or its transfer is otherwise to be controlled by the terms of the decedent's will.

(b) These limitations do not apply to proceedings to construe probated wills or determine heirs of an intestate.

(c) In cases under subsection (a)(1) or (2), the date on which a testacy or appointment proceeding is properly commenced shall be deemed to be the date of the decedent's death for purposes of other limitations provisions of this Code which relate to the date of death.
As amended in 1987 and 1993.

§3–109. [Statutes of Limitation on Decedent's Cause of Action.]

No statute of limitation running on a cause of action belonging to a decedent which had not been barred as of the date of his death, shall apply to bar a cause of action surviving the decedent's death sooner than four months after death. A cause of action which, but for this section, would have been barred less than four months after death, is barred after four months unless tolled.

PART 2
VENUE FOR PROBATE AND ADMINISTRATION; PRIORITY TO ADMINISTER; DEMAND FOR NOTICE

§3–201. [Venue for First and Subsequent Estate Proceedings; Location of Property.]

(a) Venue for the first informal or formal testacy or appointment proceedings after a decedent's death is:

(1) in the [county] where the decedent had his domicile at the time of his death; or

(2) if the decedent was not domiciled in this state, in any [county] where property of the decedent was located at the time of his death.

(b) Venue for all subsequent proceedings within the exclusive jurisdiction of the Court is in the place where the initial proceeding occurred, unless the initial proceeding

has been transferred as provided in Section 1–303 or (c) of this section.

(c) If the first proceeding was informal, on application of an interested person and after notice to the proponent in the first proceeding, the Court, upon finding that venue is elsewhere, may transfer the proceeding and the file to the other court.

(d) For the purpose of aiding determinations concerning location of assets which may be relevant in cases involving non-domiciliaries, a debt, other than one evidenced by investment or commercial paper or other instrument in favor of a non-domiciliary is located where the debtor resides or, if the debtor is a person other than an individual, at the place where it has its principal office. Commercial paper, investment paper and other instruments are located where the instrument is. An interest in property held in trust is located where the trustee may be sued.

§3–202. [Appointment or Testacy Proceedings; Conflicting Claim of Domicile in Another State.]

If conflicting claims as to the domicile of a decedent are made in a formal testacy or appointment proceeding commenced in this state, and in a testacy or appointment proceeding after notice pending at the same time in another state, the Court of this state must stay, dismiss, or permit suitable amendment in, the proceeding here unless it is determined that the local proceeding was commenced before the proceeding elsewhere. The determination of domicile in the proceeding first commenced must be accepted as determinative in the proceeding in this state.

§3–203. [Priority Among Persons Seeking Appointment as Personal Representative.]

(a) Whether the proceedings are formal or informal, persons who are not disqualified have priority for appointment in the following order:

(1) the person with priority as determined by a probated will including a person nominated by a power conferred in a will;

(2) the surviving spouse of the decedent who is a devisee of the decedent;

(3) other devisees of the decedent;

(4) the surviving spouse of the decedent;

(5) other heirs of the decedent;

(6) 45 days after the death of the decedent, any creditor.

(b) An objection to an appointment can be made only in formal proceedings. In case of objection the priorities stated in (a) apply except that

(1) if the estate appears to be more than adequate to meet exemptions and costs of administration but

inadequate to discharge anticipated unsecured claims, the Court, on petition of creditors, may appoint any qualified person;

(2) in case of objection to appointment of a person other than one whose priority is determined by will by an heir or devisee appearing to have a substantial interest in the estate, the Court may appoint a person who is acceptable to heirs and devisees whose interests in the estate appear to be worth in total more than half of the probable distributable value, or, in default of this accord any suitable person.

(c) A person entitled to letters under (2) through (5) of (a) above, and a person aged [18] and over who would be entitled to letters but for his age, may nominate a qualified person to act as personal representative. Any person aged [18] and over may renounce his right to nominate or to an appointment by appropriate writing filed with the Court. When two or more persons share a priority, those of them who do not renounce must concur in nominating another to act for them, or in applying for appointment.

(d) Conservators of the estates of protected persons, or if there is no conservator, any guardian except a guardian ad litem of a minor or incapacitated person, may exercise the same right to nominate, to object to another's appointment, or to participate in determining the preference of a majority in interest of the heirs and devisees that the protected person or ward would have if qualified for appointment.

(e) Appointment of one who does not have priority, including priority resulting from renunciation or nomination determined pursuant to this section, may be made only in formal proceedings. Before appointing one without priority, the Court must determine that those having priority, although given notice of the proceedings, have failed to request appointment or to nominate another for appointment, and that administration is necessary.

(f) No person is qualified to serve as a personal representative who is:

(1) under the age of [21];

(2) a person whom the Court finds unsuitable in formal proceedings.

(g) A personal representative appointed by a court of the decedent's domicile has priority over all other persons except where the decedent's will nominates different persons to be personal representative in this state and in the state of domicile. The domiciliary personal representative may nominate another, who shall have the same priority as the domiciliary personal representative.

(h) This section governs priority for appointment of a nuccessor personal representative but does not apply to the selection of a special administrator.

§3–204. [Demand for Notice of Order or Filing Concerning Decedent's Estate.]

Any person desiring notice of any order or filing pertaining to a decedent's estate in which he has a financial or property interest, may file a demand for notice with the Court at any time after the death of the decedent stating the name of the decedent, the nature of his interest in the estate, and the demandant's address or that of his attorney. The clerk shall mail a copy of the demand to the personal representative if one has been appointed. After filing of a demand, no order or filing to which the demand relates shall be made or accepted without notice as prescribed in Section 1–401 to the demandant or his attorney. The validity of an order which is issued or filing which is accepted without compliance with this requirement shall not be affected by the error, but the petitioner receiving the order or the person making the filing may be liable for any damage caused by the absence of notice. The requirement of notice arising from a demand under this provision may be waived in writing by the demandant and shall cease upon the termination of his interest in the estate.

PART 3
INFORMAL PROBATE AND APPOINTMENT PROCEEDINGS; SUCCESSION WITHOUT ADMINISTRATION

§3–301. [Informal Probate or Appointment Proceedings; Application; Contents.]

(a) Applications for informal probate or informal appointment shall be directed to the Registrar, and verified by the applicant to be accurate and complete to the best of his knowledge and belief as to the following information:

(1) Every application for informal probate of a will or for informal appointment of a personal representative, other than a special or successor representative, shall contain the following:

(i) a statement of the interest of the applicant;

(ii) the name, and date of death of the decedent, his age, and the county and state of his domicile at the time of death, and the names and addresses of the spouse, children, heirs and devisees and the ages of any who are minors so far as known or ascertainable with reasonable diligence by the applicant;

(iii) if the decedent was not domiciled in the state at the time of his death, a statement showing venue;

(iv) a statement identifying and indicating the address of any personal representative of the decedent appointed in this state or elsewhere whose appointment has not been terminated;

(v) a statement indicating whether the applicant has received a demand for notice, or is aware of any demand for notice of any probate or appointment proceeding concerning the decedent that may have been filed in this state or elsewhere; and

(vi) that the time limit for informal probate or appointment as provided in this Article has not expired either because 3 years or less have passed since the decedent's death, or, if more than 3 years from death have passed, circumstances as described by Section 3–108 authorizing tardy probate or appointment have occurred.

(2) An application for informal probate of a will shall state the following in addition to the statements required by (1):

(i) that the original of the decedent's last will is in the possession of the court, or accompanies the application, or that an authenticated copy of a will probated in another jurisdiction accompanies the application;

(ii) that the applicant, to the best of his knowledge, believes the will to have been validly executed;

(iii) that after the exercise of reasonable diligence, the applicant is unaware of any instrument revoking the will, and that the applicant believes that the instrument which is the subject of the application is the decedent's last will.

(3) An application for informal appointment of a personal representative to administer an estate under a will shall describe the will by date of execution and state the time and place of probate or the pending application or petition for probate. The application for appointment shall adopt the statements in the application or petition for probate and state the name, address and priority for appointment of the person whose appointment is sought.

(4) An application for informal appointment of an administrator in intestacy shall state in addition to the statements required by (1):

(i) that after the exercise of reasonable diligence, the applicant is unaware of any unrevoked testamentary instrument relating to property having a situs in this state under Section 1–301, or, a statement why any such instrument of which he may be aware is not being probated;

(ii) the priority of the person whose appointment is sought and the names of any other persons having a prior or equal right to the appointment under Section 3–203.

(5) An application for appointment of a personal representative to succeed a personal representative appointed under a different testacy status shall refer to the order in the most recent testacy proceeding, state the name and address of the person whose appointment is sought and of the person whose appointment will be terminated if the application is granted, and describe the priority of the applicant.

(6) An application for appointment of a personal representative to succeed a personal representative who has tendered a resignation as provided in 3–610(c), or whose appointment has been terminated by death or removal, shall adopt the statements in the application or petition which led to the appointment of the person being succeeded except as specifically changed or corrected, state the name and address of the person who seeks appointment as successor, and describe the priority of the applicant.

(b) By verifying an application for informal probate, or informal appointment, the applicant submits personally to the jurisdiction of the court in any proceeding for relief from fraud relating to the application, or for perjury, that may be instituted against him.

§3–302. [Informal Probate; Duty of Registrar; Effect of Informal Probate.]

Upon receipt of an application requesting informal probate of a will, the Registrar, upon making the findings required by Section 3–303 shall issue a written statement of informal probate if at least 120 hours have elapsed since the decedent's death. Informal probate is conclusive as to all persons until superseded by an order in a formal testacy proceeding. No defect in the application or procedure relating thereto which leads to informal probate of a will renders the probate void.

§3–303. [Informal Probate; Proof and Findings Required.]

(a) In an informal proceeding for original probate of a will, the Registrar shall determine whether:

(1) the application is complete;

(2) the applicant has made oath or affirmation that the statements contained in the application are true to the best of his knowledge and belief;

(3) the applicant appears from the application to be an interested person as defined in Section 1–201(24);

(4) on the basis of the statements in the application, venue is proper;

(5) an original, duly executed and apparently unrevoked will is in the Registrar's possession;

(6) any notice required by Section 3–204 has been given and that the application is not within Section 3–304; and

(7) it appears from the application that the time limit for original probate has not expired.

(b) The application shall be denied if it indicates that a personal representative has been appointed in another [county] of this state or except as provided in subsec-

tion (d) below, if it appears that this or another will of the decedent has been the subject of a previous probate order.
(c) A will which appears to have the required signatures and which contains an attestation clause showing that requirements of execution under Section 2–502, 2–503 or 2–506 have been met shall be probated without further proof. In other cases, the Registrar may assume execution if the will appears to have been properly executed, or he may accept a sworn statement or affidavit of any person having knowledge of the circumstances of execution, whether or not the person was a witness to the will.
(d) Informal probate of a will which has been previously probated elsewhere may be granted at any time upon written application by any interested person, together with deposit of an authenticated copy of the will and of the statement probating it from the office or court where it was first probated.
(e) A will from a place which does not provide for probate of a will after death and which is not eligible for probate under subsection (a) above, may be probated in this state upon receipt by the Registrar of a duly authenticated copy of the will and a duly authenticated certificate of its legal custodian that the copy filed is a true copy and that the will has become operative under the law of the other place.

§3–304. [Informal Probate; Unavailable in Certain Cases.]

Applications for informal probate which relate to one or more of a known series of testamentary instruments (other than a will and one or more codicils thereto), the latest of which does not expressly revoke the earlier, shall be declined.
As amended in 1987.

§3–305. [Informal Probate; Registrar Not Satisfied.]

If the Registrar is not satisfied that a will is entitled to be probated in informal proceedings because of failure to meet the requirements of Sections 3–303 and 3–304 or any other reason, he may decline the application. A declination of informal probate is not an adjudication and does not preclude formal probate proceedings.

§3–306. [Informal Probate; Notice Requirements.]

[*] The moving party must give notice as described by Section 1–401 of his application for informal probate to any person demanding it pursuant to Section 3–204, and to any personal representative of the decedent whose appointment has not been terminated. No other notice of informal probate is required.
[(b) If an informal probate is granted, within 30 days thereafter the applicant shall give written information of the probate to the heirs and devisees. The information shall include the name and address of the applicant, the name and location of the court granting the informal probate, and the date of the probate. The information shall be delivered or sent by ordinary mail to each of the heirs and devisees whose address is reasonably available to the applicant. No duty to give information is incurred if a personal representative is appointed who is required to give the written information required by Section 3–705. An applicant's failure to give information as required by this section is a breach of his duty to the heirs and devisees but does not affect the validity of the probate.]
*This paragraph becomes (a) if optional subsection (b) is accepted.

§3–307. [Informal Appointment Proceedings; Delay in Order; Duty of Registrar; Effect of Appointment.]

(a) Upon receipt of an application for informal appointment of a personal representative other than a special administrator as provided in Section 3–614, if at least 120 hours have elapsed since the decedent's death, the Registrar, after making the findings required by Section 3–308, shall appoint the applicant subject to qualification and acceptance; provided, that if the decedent was a non-resident, the Registrar shall delay the order of appointment until 30 days have elapsed since death unless the personal representative appointed at the decedent's domicile is the applicant, or unless the decedent's will directs that his estate be subject to the laws of this state.
(b) The status of personal representative and the powers and duties pertaining to the office are fully established by informal appointment. An appointment, and the office of personal representative created thereby, is subject to termination as provided in Sections 3–608 through 3–612, but is not subject to retroactive vacation.

§3–308. [Informal Appointment Proceedings; Proof and Findings Required.]

(a) In informal appointment proceedings, the Registrar must determine whether:
 (1) the application for informal appointment of a personal representative is complete;
 (2) the applicant has made oath or affirmation that the statements contained in the application are true to the best of his knowledge and belief;
 (3) the applicant appears from the application to be an interested person as defined in Section 1–201(24);
 (4) on the basis of the statements in the application, venue is proper;
 (5) any will to which the requested appointment relates has been formally or informally probated; but this requirement does not apply to the appointment of a special administrator;

(6) any notice required by Section 3–204 has been given;

(7) from the statements in the application, the person whose appointment is sought has priority entitling him to the appointment.

(b) Unless Section 3–612 controls, the application must be denied if it indicates that a personal representative who has not filed a written statement of resignation as provided in Section 3–610(c) has been appointed in this or another [county] of this state, that (unless the applicant is the domiciliary personal representative or his nominee) the decedent was not domiciled in this state and that a personal representative whose appointment has not been terminated has been appointed by a Court in the state of domicile, or that other requirements of this section have not been met.

§3–309. [Informal Appointment Proceedings; Registrar Not Satisfied.]

If the Registrar is not satisfied that a requested informal appointment of a personal representative should be made because of failure to meet the requirements of Sections 3–307 and 3–308, or for any other reason, he may decline the application. A declination of informal appointment is not an adjudication and does not preclude appointment in formal proceedings.

§3–310. [Informal Appointment Proceedings; Notice Requirements.]

The moving party must give notice as described by Section 1–401 of his intention to seek an appointment informally: (1) to any person demanding it pursuant to Section 3–204; and (2) to any person having a prior or equal right to appointment not waived in writing and filed with the Court. No other notice of an informal appointment proceeding is required.

§3–311. [Informal Appointment Unavailable in Certain Cases.]

If an application for informal appointment indicates the existence of a possible unrevoked testamentary instrument which may relate to property subject to the laws of this state, and which is not filed for probate in this court, the Registrar shall decline the application.

§3–312. [Universal Succession; In General.]

The heirs of an intestate or the residuary devisees under a will, excluding minors and incapacitated, protected, or unascertained persons, may become universal successors to the decedent's estate by assuming personal liability for (1) taxes, (2) debts of the decedent, (3) claims against the decedent or the estate, and (4) distributions due other heirs, devisees, and persons entitled to property of the decedent as provided in Sections 3–313 through 3–322.

§3–313. [Universal Succession; Application; Contents.]

(a) An application to become universal successors by the heirs of an intestate or the residuary devisees under a will must be directed to the [Registrar], signed by each applicant, and verified to be accurate and complete to the best of the applicant's knowledge and belief as follows:

(1) An application by heirs of an intestate must contain the statements required by Section 3–301(a)(1) and (4)(i) and state that the applicants constitute all the heirs other than minors and incapacitated, protected, or unascertained persons.

(2) An application by residuary devisees under a will must be combined with a petition for informal probate if the will has not been admitted to probate in this State and must contain the statements required by Section 3–301(a)(1) and (2). If the will has been probated in this State, an application by residuary devisees must contain the statements required by Section 3–301(a)(2)(iii). An application by residuary devisees must state that the applicants constitute the residuary devisees of the decedent other than any minors and incapacitated, protected, or unascertained persons. If the estate is partially intestate, all of the heirs other than minors and incapacitated, protected, or unascertained persons must join as applicants.

(b) The application must state whether letters of administration are outstanding, whether a petition for appointment of a personal representative of the decedent is pending in any court of this State, and that the applicants waive their right to seek appointment of a personal representative.

(c) The application may describe in general terms the assets of the estate and must state that the applicants accept responsibility for the estate and assume personal liability for (1) taxes, (2) debts of the decedent, (3) claims against the decedent or the estate and (4) distributions due other heirs, devisees, and persons entitled to property of the decedent as provided in Sections 3–316 through 3–322.

§3–314. [Universal Succession; Proof and Findings Required.]

(a) The [Registrar] shall grant the application if:

(1) the application is complete in accordance with Section 3–313;

(2) all necessary persons have joined and have verified that the statements contained therein are true, to the best knowledge and belief of each;

(3) venue is proper;

(4) any notice required by Section 3–204 has been given or waived;

(5) the time limit for original probate or appointment proceedings has not expired and the applicants claim under a will;

(6) the application requests informal probate of a will, the application and findings conform with Sections 3–301(a)(2) and 3–303(a)(c)(d) and (e) so the will is admitted to probate; and

(7) none of the applicants is a minor or an incapacitated or protected person.

(b) The [Registrar] shall deny the application if letters of administration are outstanding.

(c) Except as provided in Section 3–322, the [Registrar] shall deny the application if any creditor, heir, or devisee who is qualified by Section 3–605 to demand bond files an objection.

§3–315. [Universal Succession; Duty of Registrar; Effect of Statement of Universal Succession.]

Upon receipt of an application under Section 3–313, if at least 120 hours have elapsed since the decedent's death, the [Registrar], upon granting the application, shall issue a written statement of universal succession describing the estate as set forth in the application and stating that the applicants (i) are the universal successors to the assets of the estate as provided in Section 3–312, (ii) have assumed liability for the obligations of the decedent, and (iii) have acquired the powers and liabilities of universal successors. The statement of universal succession is evidence of the universal successors' title to the assets of the estate. Upon its issuance, the powers and liabilities of universal successors provided in Sections 3–316 through 3–322 attach and are assumed by the applicants.

§3–316. [Universal Succession; Universal Successors' Powers.]

Upon the [Registrar's] issuance of a statement of universal succession:

(1) Universal successors have full power of ownership to deal with the assets of the estate subject to the limitations and liabilities in this [Act]. The universal successors shall proceed expeditiously to settle and distribute the estate without adjudication but if necessary may invoke the jurisdiction of the court to resolve questions concerning the estate.

(2) Universal successors have the same powers as distributees from a personal representative under Sections 3–908 and 3–909 and third persons with whom they deal are protected as provided in Section 3–910.

(3) For purposes of collecting assets in another state whose law does not provide for universal succession, universal successors have the same standing and power as personal representatives or distributees in this State.

§3–317. [Universal Succession; Universal Successors' Liability to Creditors, Other Heirs, Devisees and Persons Entitled to Decedent's Property; Liability of Other Persons Entitled to Property.]

(a) In the proportions and subject to limits expressed in Section 3–321, universal successors assume all liabilities of the decedent that were not discharged by reason of death and liability for all taxes, claims against the decedent or the estate, and charges properly incurred after death for the preservation of the estate, to the extent those items, if duly presented, would be valid claims against the decedent's estate.

(b) In the proportions and subject to the limits expressed in Section 3–321, universal successors are personally liable to other heirs, devisees, and persons entitled to property of the decedent for the assets or amounts that would be due those heirs, were the estate administered, but no allowance having priority over devisees may be claimed for attorney's fees or charges for preservation of the estate in excess of reasonable amounts properly incurred.

(c) Universal successors are entitled to their interests in the estate as heirs or devisees subject to priority and abatement pursuant to Section 3–902 and to agreement pursuant to Section 3–912.

(d) Other heirs, devisees, and persons to whom assets have been distributed have the same powers and liabilities as distributees under Sections 3–908, 3–909, and 3–910.

(e) Absent breach of fiduciary obligations or express undertaking, a fiduciary's liability is limited to the assets received by the fiduciary.

§3–318. [Universal Succession; Universal Successors' Submission to Jurisdiction; When Heirs or Devisees May Not Seek Administration.]

(a) Upon issuance of the statement of universal succession, the universal successors become subject to the personal jurisdiction of the courts of this state in any proceeding that may be instituted relating to the estate or to any liability assumed by them.

(b) Any heir or devisee who voluntarily joins in an application under Section 3–313 may not subsequently seek appointment of a personal representative.

§3–319. [Universal Succession; Duty of Universal Successors; Information to Heirs and Devisees.]

Not later than thirty days after issuance of the statement of universal succession, each universal successor shall inform the heirs and devisees who did not join in the application of the succession without administration. The information must be delivered or be sent by ordinary mail to each of the heirs and devisees whose address is reasonably available to the universal successors. The information must include the names and addresses of the universal successors, indicate that it is being sent to persons who have or may have some interest in the estate, and describe the court where the application and statement of universal succession has been filed. The failure of a universal successor to give this information is a breach of duty to the persons concerned but does not affect the validity of the approval of succession without administration or the powers or liabilities of the universal successors. A universal successor may inform other persons of the succession without administration by delivery or by ordinary first class mail.

§3–320. [Universal Succession; Universal Successors' Liability For Restitution to Estate.]

If a personal representative is subsequently appointed, universal successors are personally liable for restitution of any property of the estate to which they are not entitled as heirs or devisees of the decedent and their liability is the same as a distributee under Section 3–909, subject to the provisions of Sections 3–317 and 3–321 and the limitations of Section 3–1006.

§3–321. [Universal Succession; Liability of Universal Successors for Claims, Expenses, Intestate Shares and Devises.]

The liability of universal successors is subject to any defenses that would have been available to the decedent. Other than liability arising from fraud, conversion, or other wrongful conduct of a universal successor, the personal liability of each universal successor to any creditor, claimant, other heir, devisee, or person entitled to decedent's property may not exceed the proportion of the claim that the universal successor's share bears to the share of all heirs and residuary devisees.

§3–322. [Universal Succession; Remedies of Creditors, Other Heirs, Devisees or Persons Entitled to Decedent's Property.]

In addition to remedies otherwise provided by law, any creditor, heir, devisee, or person entitled to decedent's property qualified under Section 3–605, may demand bond of universal successors. If the demand for bond precedes the granting of an application for universal succession, it must be treated as an objection under Section 3–314(c) unless it is withdrawn, the claim satisfied, or the applicants post bond in an amount sufficient to protect the demandant. If the demand for bond follows the granting of an application for universal succession, the universal successors, within 10 days after notice of

the demand, upon satisfying the claim or posting bond sufficient to protect the demandant, may disqualify the demandant from seeking administration of the estate.

PART 4
FORMAL TESTACY AND APPOINTMENT PROCEEDINGS

§3–401. [Formal Testacy Proceedings; Nature; When Commenced.]

A formal testacy proceeding is litigation to determine whether a decedent left a valid will. A formal testacy proceeding may be commenced by an interested person filing a petition as described in Section 3–402(a) in which he requests that the Court, after notice and hearing, enter an order probating a will, or a petition to set aside an informal probate of a will or to prevent informal probate of a will which is the subject of a pending application, or a petition in accordance with Section 3–402(b) for an order that the decedent died intestate.

A petition may seek formal probate of a will without regard to whether the same or a conflicting will has been informally probated. A formal testacy proceeding may, but need not, involve a request for appointment of a personal representative.

During the pendency of a formal testacy proceeding, the Registrar shall not act upon any application for informal probate of any will of the decedent or any application for informal appointment of a personal representative of the decedent.

Unless a petition in a formal testacy proceeding also requests confirmation of the previous informal appointment, a previously appointed personal representative, after receipt of notice of the commencement of a formal probate proceeding, must refrain from exercising his power to make any further distribution of the estate during the pendency of the formal proceeding. A petitioner who seeks the appointment of a different personal representative in a formal proceeding also may request an order restraining the acting personal representative from exercising any of the powers of his office and requesting the appointment of a special administrator. In the absence of a request, or if the request is denied, the commencement of a formal proceeding has no effect on the powers and duties of a previously appointed personal representative other than those relating to distribution.

§3–402. [Formal Testacy or Appointment Proceedings; Petition; Contents.]

(a) Petitions for formal probate of a will, or for adjudication of intestacy with or without request for appointment of a personal representative, must be directed to the Court, request a judicial order after notice and hearing and contain further statements as indicated in this section. A petition for formal probate of a will

(1) requests an order as to the testacy of the decedent in relation to a particular instrument which may or may not have been informally probated and determining the heirs,

(2) contains the statements required for informal applications as stated in the six subparagraphs under Section 3–301(a)(1), the statements required by subparagraphs (ii) and (iii) of Section 3–301(a)(2), and

(3) states whether the original of the last will of the decedent is in the possession of the Court or accompanies the petition.

If the original will is neither in the possession of the Court nor accompanies the petition and no authenticated copy of a will probated in another jurisdiction accompanies the petition, the petition also must state the contents of the will, and indicate that it is lost, destroyed, or otherwise unavailable.

(b) A petition for adjudication of intestacy and appointment of an administrator in intestacy must request a judicial finding and order that the decedent left no will and determining the heirs, contain the statements required by (1) and (4) of Section 3–301(a) and indicate whether supervised administration is sought. A petition may request an order determining intestacy and heirs without requesting the appointment of an administrator, in which case, the statements required by subparagraph (ii) of Section 3–301(a)(4) above may be omitted.

§3–403. [Formal Testacy Proceedings; Notice of Hearing on Petition.]

(a) Upon commencement of a formal testacy proceeding, the Court shall fix a time and place of hearing. Notice shall be given in the manner prescribed by Section 1–401 by the petitioner to the persons herein enumerated and to any additional person who has filed a demand for notice under Section 3–204 of this Code.

Notice shall be given to the following persons: the surviving spouse, children, and other heirs of the decedent, the devisees and executors named in any will that is being, or has been, probated, or offered for informal or formal probate in the [county,] or that is known by the petitioner to have been probated, or offered for informal or formal probate elsewhere, and any personal representative of the decedent whose appointment has not been terminated. Notice may be given to other persons. In addition, the petitioner shall give notice by publication to all unknown persons and to all known persons whose addresses are unknown who have any interest in the matters being litigated.

(b) If it appears by the petition or otherwise that the fact of the death of the alleged decedent may be in doubt, or on the written demand of any interested person, a copy of the notice of the hearing on said petition shall be sent by registered mail to the alleged decedent at his last known address. The Court shall direct the petitioner to report the results of, or make and report back concerning, a reasonably diligent search for the alleged decedent in any manner that may seem advisable, including any or all of the following methods:

(1) by inserting in one or more suitable periodicals a notice requesting information from any person having knowledge of the whereabouts of the alleged decedent;

(2) by notifying law enforcement officials and public welfare agencies in appropriate locations of the disappearance of the alleged decedent;

(3) by engaging the services of an investigator.

The costs of any search so directed shall be paid by the petitioner if there is no administration or by the estate of the decedent in case there is administration.

§3–404. [Formal Testacy Proceedings; Written Objections to Probate.]

Any party to a formal proceeding who opposes the probate of a will for any reason shall state in his pleadings his objections to probate of the will.

§3–405. [Formal Testacy Proceedings; Uncontested Cases; Hearings and Proof.]

If a petition in a testacy proceeding is unopposed, the Court may order probate or intestacy on the strength of the pleadings if satisfied that the conditions of Section 3–409 have been met, or conduct a hearing in open court and require proof of the matters necessary to support the order sought. If evidence concerning execution of the will is necessary, the affidavit or testimony of one of any attesting witnesses to the instrument is sufficient. If the affidavit or testimony of an attesting witness is not available, execution of the will may be proved by other evidence or affidavit.

§3–406. [Formal Testacy Proceedings; Contested Cases; Testimony of Attesting Witnesses.]

(a) If evidence concerning execution of an attested will which is not self-proved is necessary in contested cases, the testimony of at least one of the attesting witnesses, if within the state, competent and able to testify, is required. Due execution of an attested or unattested will may be proved by other evidence.

(b) If the will is self-proved, compliance with signature requirements for execution is conclusively presumed and other requirements of execution are presumed subject to rebuttal without the testimony of any witness upon filing the will and the acknowledgment and affidavits annexed or attached thereto, unless there is proof of fraud or forgery affecting the acknowledgment or affidavit.

§3–407. [Formal Testacy Proceedings; Burdens in Contested Cases.]

In contested cases, petitioners who seek to establish intestacy have the burden of establishing prima facie proof of death, venue, and heirship. Proponents of a will have the burden of establishing prima facie proof of due execution in all cases, and, if they are also petitioners, prima facie proof of death and venue. Contestants of a will have the burden of establishing lack of testamentary intent or capacity, undue influence, fraud, duress, mistake or revocation. Parties have the ultimate burden of persuasion as to matters with respect to which they have the initial burden of proof. If a will is opposed by the petition for probate of a later will revoking the former, it shall be determined first whether the later will is entitled to probate, and if a will is opposed by a petition for a declaration of intestacy, it shall be determined first whether the will is entitled to probate.

§3–408. [Formal Testacy Proceedings; Will Construction; Effect of Final Order in Another Jurisdiction.]

A final order of a court of another state determining testacy, the validity or construction of a will, made in a proceeding involving notice to and an opportunity for contest by all interested persons must be accepted as determinative by the courts of this state if it includes, or is based upon, a finding that the decedent was domiciled at his death in the state where the order was made.

§3–409. [Formal Testacy Proceedings; Order; Foreign Will.]

After the time required for any notice has expired, upon proof of notice, and after any hearing that may be necessary, if the Court finds that the testator is dead, venue is proper and that the proceeding was commenced within the limitation prescribed by Section 3–108, it shall determine the decedent's domicile at death, his heirs and his state of testacy. Any will found to be valid and unrevoked shall be formally probated. Termination of any previous informal appointment of a personal representative, which may be appropriate in view of the relief requested and findings, is governed by Section 3–612. The petition shall be dismissed or appropriate amendment allowed if the court is not satisfied that the alleged decedent is dead. A will from a place which does not provide for probate of a will after death, may be proved for probate in this state by a duly authenticated certificate of its legal custodian that the copy introduced is a true copy and that the will has become effective under the law of the other place.

§3–410. [Formal Testacy Proceedings; Probate of More Than One Instrument.]

If two or more instruments are offered for probate before a final order is entered in a formal testacy proceeding, more than one instrument may be probated if neither expressly revokes the other or contains provisions which work a total revocation by implication. If more than one instrument is probated, the order shall indicate what provisions control in respect to the nomination of an executor, if any. The order may, but need not, indicate how any provisions of a particular instrument are affected by the other instrument. After a final order in a testacy proceeding has been entered, no petition for probate of any other instrument of the decedent may be entertained, except incident to a petition to vacate or modify a previous probate order and subject to the time limits of Section 3–412.

§3–411. [Formal Testacy Proceedings; Partial Intestacy.]

If it becomes evident in the course of a formal testacy proceeding that, though one or more instruments are entitled to be probated, the decedent's estate is or may be partially intestate, the Court shall enter an order to that effect.

§3–412. [Formal Testacy Proceedings; Effect of Order; Vacation.]

Subject to appeal and subject to vacation as provided in this section and in Section 3–413, a formal testacy order under Sections 3–409 to 3–411, including an order that the decedent left no valid will and determining heirs, is final as to all persons with respect to all issues concerning the decedent's estate that the court considered or might have considered incident to its rendition relevant to the question of whether the decedent left a valid will, and to the determination of heirs, except that:

(1) The court shall entertain a petition for modification or vacation of its order and probate of another will of the decedent if it is shown that the proponents of the later-offered will: (i) were unaware of its existence at the time of the earlier proceeding: or (ii) were unaware of the earlier proceeding and were given no notice thereof, except by publication.

(2) If intestacy of all or part of the estate has been ordered, the determination of heirs of the decedent may be reconsidered if it is shown that one or more persons were omitted from the determination and it is also shown that the persons were unaware of their relationship to the decedent, were unaware of his death or were given no notice of any proceeding concerning his estate, except by publication.

(3) A petition for vacation under paragraph (1) or (2) must be filed prior to the earlier of the following time limits:

    (i) if a personal representative has been appointed for the estate, the time of entry of any order approving final distribution of the estate, or, if the estate is closed by statement, six months after the filing of the closing statement;

(ii) whether or not a personal representative has been appointed for the estate of the decedent, the time prescribed by Section 3–108 when it is no longer possible to initiate an original proceeding to probate a will of the decedent; or

(iii) twelve months after the entry of the order sought to be vacated.

(4) The order originally rendered in the testacy proceeding may be modified or vacated, if appropriate under the circumstances, by the order of probate of the later-offered will or the order redetermining heirs.

(5) The finding of the fact of death is conclusive as to the alleged decedent only if notice of the hearing on the petition in the formal testacy proceeding was sent by registered or certified mail addressed to the alleged decedent at his last known address and the court finds that a search under Section 3–403(b) was made.

If the alleged decedent is not dead, even if notice was sent and search was made, he may recover estate assets in the hands of the personal representative. In addition to any remedies available to the alleged decedent by reason of any fraud or intentional wrongdoing, the alleged decedent may recover any estate or its proceeds from distributees that is in their hands, or the value of distributions received by them, to the extent that any recovery from distributees is equitable in view of all of the circumstances.

As amended in 1993.

§3–413. [Formal Testacy Proceedings; Vacation of Order For Other Cause.]

For good cause shown, an order in a formal testacy proceeding may be modified or vacated within the time allowed for appeal.

§3–414. [Formal Proceedings Concerning Appointment of Personal Representative.]

(a) A formal proceeding for adjudication regarding the priority or qualification of one who is an applicant for appointment as personal representative, or of one who previously has been appointed personal representative in informal proceedings, if an issue concerning the testacy of the decedent is or may be involved, is governed by Section 3–402, as well as by this section. In other cases, the petition shall contain or adopt the statements required by Section 3–301(1) and describe the question relating to priority or qualification of the personal representative which is to be resolved. If the proceeding precedes any appointment of a personal representative, it shall stay any pending informal appointment proceedings as well as any commenced thereafter. If the proceeding is commenced after appointment, the previously appointed personal representative, after re-

ceipt of notice thereof, shall refrain from exercising any power of administration except as necessary to preserve the estate or unless the Court orders otherwise.

(b) After notice to interested persons, including all persons interested in the administration of the estate as successors under the applicable assumption concerning testacy, any previously appointed personal representative and any person having or claiming priority for appointment as personal representative, the Court shall determine who is entitled to appointment under Section 3–203, make a proper appointment and, if appropriate, terminate any prior appointment found to have been improper as provided in cases of removal under Section 3–611.

PART 5
SUPERVISED ADMINISTRATION

§3–501. [Supervised Administration; Nature of Proceeding.]

Supervised administration is a single in rem proceeding to secure complete administration and settlement of a decedent's estate under the continuing authority of the Court which extends until entry of an order approving distribution of the estate and discharging the personal representative or other order terminating the proceeding. A supervised personal representative is responsible to the Court, as well as to the interested parties, and is subject to directions concerning the estate made by the Court on its own motion or on the motion of any interested party. Except as otherwise provided in this Part, or as otherwise ordered by the Court, a supervised personal representative has the same duties and powers as a personal representative who is not supervised.

§3–502. [Supervised Administration; Petition; Order.]

A petition for supervised administration may be filed by any interested person or by a personal representative at any time or the prayer for supervised administration may be joined with a petition in a testacy or appointment proceeding. If the testacy of the decedent and the priority and qualification of any personal representative have not been adjudicated previously, the petition for supervised administration shall include the matters required of a petition in a formal testacy proceeding and the notice requirements and procedures applicable to a formal testacy proceeding apply. If not previously adjudicated, the Court shall adjudicate the testacy of the decedent and questions relating to the priority and qualifications of the personal representative in any case involving a request for supervised administration, even though the request for supervised administration may be denied. After notice to interested persons, the Court shall order supervised administration of a decedent's estate: (1) if the decedent's will directs supervised administration, it shall be ordered unless the Court finds that circumstances bearing on the need for supervised administration have changed since the execution of the will and that there is no necessity for supervised administration; (2) if the decedent's will directs unsupervised administration, supervised administration shall be ordered only upon a finding that it is necessary for protection of persons interested in the estate; or (3) in other cases if the Court finds that supervised administration is necessary under the circumstances.

§3–503. [Supervised Administration; Effect on Other Proceedings.]

(a) The pendency of a proceeding for supervised administration of a decedent's estate stays action on any informal application then pending or thereafter filed.

(b) If a will has been previously probated in informal proceedings, the effect of the filing of a petition for supervised administration is as provided for formal testacy proceedings by Section 3–401.

(c) After he has received notice of the filing of a petition for supervised administration, a personal representative who has been appointed previously shall not exercise his power to distribute any estate. The filing of the petition does not affect his other powers and duties unless the Court restricts the exercise of any of them pending full hearing on the petition.

§3–504. [Supervised Administration; Powers of Personal Representative.]

Unless restricted by the Court, a supervised personal representative has, without interim orders approving exercise of a power, all powers of personal representatives under this Code, but he shall not exercise his power to make any distribution of the estate without prior order of the Court. Any other restriction on the power of a personal representative which may be ordered by the Court must be endorsed on his letters of appointment and, unless so endorsed, is ineffective as to persons dealing in good faith with the personal representative.

§3–505. [Supervised Administration; Interim Orders; Distribution and Closing Orders.]

Unless otherwise ordered by the Court, supervised administration is terminated by order in accordance with time restrictions, notices and contents of orders prescribed for proceedings under Section 3–1001. Interim orders approving or directing partial distributions or granting other relief may be issued by the Court at any time during the pendency of a supervised administration on the application of the personal representative or any interested person.

PART 6
PERSONAL REPRESENTATIVE; APPOINTMENT, CONTROL AND TERMINATION OF AUTHORITY

§3–601. [Qualification.]

Prior to receiving letters, a personal representative shall qualify by filing with the appointing Court any required bond and a statement of acceptance of the duties of the office.

§3–602. [Acceptance of Appointment; Consent to Jurisdiction.]

By accepting appointment, a personal representative submits personally to the jurisdiction of the Court in any proceeding relating to the estate that may be instituted by any interested person. Notice of any proceeding shall be delivered to the personal representative, or mailed to him by ordinary first class mail at his address as listed in the application or petition for appointment or as thereafter reported to the Court and to his address as then known to the petitioner.

§3–603. [Bond Not Required Without Court Order, Exceptions.]

No bond is required of a personal representative appointed in informal proceedings, except (1) upon the appointment of a special administrator; (2) when an executor or other personal representative is appointed to administer an estate under a will containing an express requirement of bond or (3) when bond is required under Section 3–605. Bond may be required by court order at the time of appointment of a personal representative appointed in any formal proceeding except that bond is not required of a personal representative appointed in formal proceedings if the will relieves the personal representative of bond, unless bond has been requested by an interested party and the Court is satisfied that it is desirable. Bond required by any will may be dispensed with in formal proceedings upon determination by the Court that it is not necessary. No bond is required of any personal representative who, pursuant to statute, has deposited cash or collateral with an agency of this state to secure performance of his duties.

§3–604. [Bond Amount; Security; Procedure; Reduction.]

If bond is required and the provisions of the will or order do not specify the amount, unless stated in his application or petition, the person qualifying shall file a statement under oath with the Registrar indicating his best estimate of the value of the personal estate of the decedent and of the income expected from the personal and real estate during the next year, and he shall execute and file a bond with the Registrar, or give other suitable security, in an amount not less than the estimate. The Registrar shall determine that the bond is duly executed by a corporate surety, or one or more individual sureties whose performance is secured by pledge of personal property, mortgage on real property or other adequate security. The Registrar may permit the amount of the bond to be reduced by the value of assets of the estate deposited with a domestic financial institution (as defined in Section 6–101) in a manner that prevents their unauthorized disposition. On petition of the personal representative or another interested person the Court may excuse a requirement of bond, increase or reduce the amount of the bond, release sureties, or permit the substitution of another bond with the same or different sureties.

§3–605. [Demand For Bond by Interested Person.]

Any person apparently having an interest in the estate worth in excess of [$1000], or any creditor having a claim in excess of [$1000], may make a written demand that a personal representative give bond. The demand must be filed with the Registrar and a copy mailed to the personal representative, if appointment and qualification have occurred. Thereupon, bond is required, but the requirement ceases if the person demanding bond ceases to be interested in the estate, or if bond is excused as provided in Section 3–603 or 3–604. After he has received notice and until the filing of the bond or cessation of the requirement of bond, the personal representative shall refrain from exercising any powers of his office except as necessary to preserve the estate. Failure of the personal representative to meet a requirement of bond by giving suitable bond within 30 days after receipt of notice is cause for his removal and appointment of a successor personal representative.

§3–606. [Terms and Conditions of Bonds.]

(a) The following requirements and provisions apply to any bond required by this Part:

(1) Bonds shall name the [state] as obligee for the benefit of the persons interested in the estate and shall be conditioned upon the faithful discharge by the fiduciary of all duties according to law.

(2) Unless otherwise provided by the terms of the approved bond, sureties are jointly and severally liable with the personal representative and with each other. The address of sureties shall be stated in the bond.

(3) By executing an approved bond of a personal representative, the surety consents to the jurisdiction of the probate court which issued letters to the primary obligor in any proceedings pertaining to the fiduciary duties of the personal representative and naming the surety as a party. Notice of any proceeding shall be delivered to the surety or mailed to him by registered or certified mail at his address as listed with the court where the bond is filed and to his address as then known to the petitioner.

(4) On petition of a successor personal representative, any other personal representative of the same decedent, or any interested person, a proceeding in the Court may be initiated against a surety for breach of the obligation of the bond of the personal representative.

(5) The bond of the personal representative is not void after the first recovery but may be proceeded against from time to time until the whole penalty is exhausted.

(b) No action or proceeding may be commenced against the surety on any matter as to which an action or proceeding against the primary obligor is barred by adjudication or limitation.

§3–607. [Order Restraining Personal Representative.]

(a) On petition of any person who appears to have an interest in the estate, the Court by temporary order may restrain a personal representative from performing specified acts of administration, disbursement, or distribution, or exercise of any powers or discharge of any duties of his office, or make any other order to secure proper performance of his duty, if it appears to the Court that the personal representative otherwise may take some action which would jeopardize unreasonably the interest of the applicant or of some other interested person. Persons with whom the personal representative may transact business may be made parties.

(b) The matter shall be set for hearing within 10 days unless the parties otherwise agree. Notice as the Court directs shall be given to the personal representative and his attorney of record, if any, and to any other parties named defendant in the petition.

§3–608. [Termination of Appointment; General.]

Termination of appointment of a personal representative occurs as indicated in Sections 3–609 to 3–612, inclusive. Termination ends the right and power pertaining to the office of personal representative as conferred by this Code or any will, except that a personal representative, at any time prior to distribution or until restrained or enjoined by court order, may perform acts necessary to protect the estate and may deliver the assets to a successor representative. Termination does not discharge a personal representative from liability for transactions or omissions occurring before termination, or relieve him of the duty to preserve assets subject to his control, to account therefor and to deliver the assets. Termination does not affect the jurisdiction of the Court over the personal representative, but terminates his authority to represent the estate in any pending or future proceeding.

§3–609. **[Termination of Appointment; Death or Disability.]**

The death of a personal representative or the appointment of a conservator for the estate of a personal representative, terminates his appointment. Until appointment and qualification of a successor or special representative to replace the deceased or protected representative, the representative of the estate of the deceased or protected personal representative, if any, has the duty to protect the estate possessed and being administered by his decedent or ward at the time his appointment terminates, has the power to perform acts necessary for protection and shall account for and deliver the estate assets to a successor or special personal representative upon his appointment and qualification.

§3–610. **[Termination of Appointment; Voluntary.]**

(a) An appointment of a personal representative terminates as provided in Section 3–1003, one year after the filing of a closing statement.

(b) An order closing an estate as provided in Section 3–1001 or 3–1002 terminates an appointment of a personal representative.

(c) A personal representative may resign his position by filing a written statement of resignation with the Registrar after he has given at least 15 days written notice to the persons known to be interested in the estate. If no one applies or petitions for appointment of a successor representative within the time indicated in the notice, the filed statement of resignation is ineffective as a termination of appointment and in any event is effective only upon the appointment and qualification of a successor representative and delivery of the assets to him.

§3–611. **[Termination of Appointment by Removal; Cause; Procedure.]**

(a) A person interested in the estate may petition for removal of a personal representative for cause at any time. Upon filing of the petition, the Court shall fix a time and place for hearing. Notice shall be given by the petitioner to the personal representative, and to other persons as the Court may order. Except as otherwise ordered as provided in Section 3–607, after receipt of notice of removal proceedings, the personal representative shall not act except to account, to correct maladministration or preserve the estate. If removal is ordered, the Court also shall direct by order the disposition of the assets remaining in the name of, or under the control of, the personal representative being removed.

(b) Cause for removal exists when removal would be in the best interests of the estate, or if it is shown that a personal representative or the person seeking his appointment intentionally misrepresented material facts in the proceedings leading to his appointment, or that the personal representative has disregarded an order of the Court, has become incapable of discharging the duties of his office, or has mismanaged the estate or failed to perform any duty pertaining to the office. Unless the decedent's will directs otherwise, a personal representative appointed at the decedent's domicile, incident to securing appointment of himself or his nominee as ancillary personal representative, may obtain removal of another who was appointed personal representative in this state to administer local assets.

§3–612. **[Termination of Appointment; Change of Testacy Status.]**

Except as otherwise ordered in formal proceedings, the probate of a will subsequent to the appointment of a personal representative in intestacy or under a will which is superseded by formal probate of another will, or the vacation of an informal probate of a will subsequent to the appointment of the personal representative thereunder, does not terminate the appointment of the personal representative although his powers may be reduced as provided in Section 3–401. Termination occurs upon appointment in informal or formal appointment proceedings of a person entitled to appointment under the later assumption concerning testacy. If no request for new appointment is made within 30 days after expiration of time for appeal from the order in formal testacy proceedings, or from the informal probate, changing the assumption concerning testacy, the previously appointed personal representative upon request may be appointed personal representative under the subsequently probated will, or as in intestacy as the case may be.

§3–613. **[Successor Personal Representative.]**

Parts 3 and 4 of this Article govern proceedings for appointment of a personal representative to succeed one whose appointment has been terminated. After appointment and qualification, a successor personal representative may be substituted in all actions and proceedings to which the former personal representative was a party, and no notice, process or claim which was given or served upon the former personal representative need be given to or served upon the successor in order to preserve any position or right the person giving the notice or filing the claim may thereby have obtained or preserved with reference to the former personal representative. Except as otherwise ordered by the Court, the successor personal representative has the powers and duties in respect to the continued administration which the former personal representative would have had if his appointment had not been terminated.

§3–614. **[Special Administrator; Appointment.]**

A special administrator may be appointed:

(1) informally by the Registrar on the application of any interested person when necessary to protect the estate of a decedent prior to the appointment of a general personal representative or if a prior appointment has been terminated as provided in Section 3–609;

(2) in a formal proceeding by order of the Court on the petition of any interested person and finding, after notice and hearing, that appointment is necessary to preserve the estate or to secure its proper administration including its administration in circumstances where a general personal representative cannot or should not act. If it appears to the Court that an emergency exists, appointment may be ordered without notice.

§3–615. [Special Administrator; Who May Be Appointed.]

(a) If a special administrator is to be appointed pending the probate of a will which is the subject of a pending application or petition for probate, the person named executor in the will shall be appointed if available, and qualified.

(b) In other cases, any proper person may be appointed special administrator.

§3–616. [Special Administrator; Appointed Informally; Powers and Duties.]

A special administrator appointed by the Registrar in informal proceedings pursuant to Section 3–614(1) has the duty to collect and manage the assets of the estate, to preserve them, to account therefor and to deliver them to the general personal representative upon his qualification. The special administrator has the power of a personal representative under the Code necessary to perform his duties.

§3–617. [Special Administrator; Formal Proceedings; Power and Duties.]

A special administrator appointed by order of the Court in any formal proceeding has the power of a general personal representative except as limited in the appointment and duties as prescribed in the order. The appointment may be for a specified time, to perform particular acts or on other terms as the Court may direct.

§3–618. [Termination of Appointment; Special Administrator.]

The appointment of a special administrator terminates in accordance with the provisions of the order of appointment or on the appointment of a general personal representative. In other cases, the appointment of a special administrator is subject to termination as provided in Sections 3–608 through 3–611.

PART 7
DUTIES AND POWERS OF PERSONAL REPRESENTATIVES

§3–701. [Time of Accrual of Duties and Powers.]

The duties and powers of a personal representative commence upon his appointment. The powers of a personal representative relate back in time to give acts by the person appointed which are beneficial to the estate occurring prior to appointment the same effect as those occurring thereafter. Prior to appointment, a person named executor in a will may carry out written instructions of the decedent relating to his body, funeral and burial arrangements. A personal representative may ratify and accept acts on behalf of the estate done by others where the acts would have been proper for a personal representative.

§3–702. [Priority Among Different Letters.]

A person to whom general letters are issued first has exclusive authority under the letters until his appointment is terminated or modified. If, through error, general letters are afterwards issued to another, the first appointed representative may recover any property of the estate in the hands of the representative subsequently appointed, but the acts of the latter done in good faith before notice of the first letters are not void for want of validity of appointment.

§3–703. [General Duties; Relation and Liability to Persons Interested in Estate; Standing to Sue.]

(a) A personal representative is a fiduciary who shall observe the standards of care applicable to trustees as described by Section 7–302. A personal representative is under a duty to settle and distribute the estate of the decedent in accordance with the terms of any probated and effective will and this Code, and as expeditiously and efficiently as is consistent with the best interests of the estate. He shall use the authority conferred upon him by this Code, the terms of the will, if any, and any order in proceedings to which he is party for the best interests of successors to the estate.

(b) A personal representative shall not be surcharged for acts of administration or distribution if the conduct in question was authorized at the time. Subject to other obligations of administration, an informally probated will is authority to administer and distribute the estate according to its terms. An order of appointment of a personal representative, whether issued in informal or formal proceedings, is authority to distribute apparently intestate assets to the heirs of the decedent if, at the time of distribution, the personal representative is not aware of a pending testacy proceeding, a proceeding to vacate an order entered in an earlier testacy proceeding, a formal proceeding questioning his appointment or fitness to continue, or a supervised administration proceeding. Nothing in this section affects the duty of the personal representative to administer and distribute the estate in accordance with the rights of claimants, the surviving spouse, any minor and dependent children and any pretermitted child of the decedent as described elsewhere in this Code.

(c) Except as to proceedings which do not survive the death of the decedent, a personal representative of a decedent domiciled in this state at his death has the same standing to sue and be sued in the courts of this state and the courts of any other jurisdiction as his decedent had immediately prior to death.

§3–704. [Personal Representative to Proceed Without Court Order; Exception.]

A personal representative shall proceed expeditiously with the settlement and distribution of a decedent's estate and, except as otherwise specified or ordered in regard to a supervised personal representative, do so without adjudication, order, or direction of the Court, but he may invoke the jurisdiction of the Court, in proceedings authorized by this Code, to resolve questions concerning the estate or its administration.

§3–705. [Duty of Personal Representative; Information to Heirs and Devisees.]

Not later than 30 days after his appointment every personal representative, except any special administrator, shall give information of his appointment to the heirs and devisees, including, if there has been no formal testacy proceeding and if the personal representative was appointed on the assumption that the decedent died intestate, the devisees in any will mentioned in the application for appointment of a personal representative. The information shall be delivered or sent by ordinary mail to each of the heirs and devisees whose address is reasonably available to the personal representative. The duty does not extend to require information to persons who have been adjudicated in a prior formal testacy proceeding to have no interest in the estate. The information shall include the name and address of the personal representative, indicate that it is being sent to persons who have or may have some interest in the estate being administered, indicate whether bond has been filed, and describe the court where papers relating to the estate are on file. The information shall state that the estate is being administered by the personal representative under the [State] Probate Code without supervision by the Court but that recipients are entitled to information regarding the administration from the personal representative and can petition the Court in any matter relating to the estate, including distribution of assets and expenses of administration. The personal representative's

failure to give this information is a breach of his duty to the persons concerned but does not affect the validity of his appointment, his powers or other duties. A personal representative may inform other persons of his appointment by delivery or ordinary first class mail.

As amended in 1987.

§3–706. [Duty of Personal Representative; Inventory and Appraisement.]

Within 3 months after his appointment, a personal representative, who is not a special administrator or a successor to another representative who has previously discharged this duty, shall prepare and file or mail an inventory of property owned by the decedent at the time of his death, listing it with reasonable detail, and indicating as to each listed item, its fair market value as of the date of the decedent's death, and the type and amount of any encumbrance that may exist with reference to any item.

The personal representative shall send a copy of the inventory to interested persons who request it. He may also file the original of the inventory with the court.

§3–707. [Employment of Appraisers.]

The personal representative may employ a qualified and disinterested appraiser to assist him in ascertaining the fair market value as of the date of the decedent's death of any asset the value of which may be subject to reasonable doubt. Different persons may be employed to appraise different kinds of assets included in the estate. The names and addresses of any appraiser shall be indicated on the inventory with the item or items he appraised.

§3–708. [Duty of Personal Representative; Supplementary Inventory.]

If any property not included in the original inventory comes to the knowledge of a personal representative or if the personal representative learns that the value or description indicated in the original inventory for any item is erroneous or misleading, he shall make a supplementary inventory or appraisement showing the market value as of the date of the decedent's death of the new item or the revised market value or descriptions, and the appraisers or other data relied upon, if any, and file it with the Court if the original inventory was filed, or furnish copies thereof or information thereof to persons interested in the new information.

§3–709. [Duty of Personal Representative; Possession of Estate.]

Except as otherwise provided by a decedent's will, every personal representative has a right to, and shall take possession or control of, the decedent's property, except that any real property or tangible personal property may be left with or surrendered to the person presumptively entitled thereto unless or until, in the judgment of the personal representative, possession of the property by him will be necessary for purposes of administration. The request by a personal representative for delivery of any property possessed by an heir or devisee is conclusive evidence, in any action against the heir or devisee for possession thereof, that the possession of the property by the personal representative is necessary for purposes of administration. The personal representative shall pay taxes on, and take all steps reasonably necessary for the management, protection and preservation of, the estate in his possession. He may maintain an action to recover possession of property or to determine the title thereto.

§3–710. [Power to Avoid Transfers.]

The property liable for the payment of unsecured debts of a decedent includes all property transferred by him by any means which is in law void or voidable as against his creditors, and subject to prior liens, the right to recover this property, so far as necessary for the payment of unsecured debts of the decedent, is exclusively in the personal representative.

§3–711. [Powers of Personal Representatives; In General.]

Until termination of his appointment a personal representative has the same power over the title to property of the estate that an absolute owner would have, in trust however, for the benefit of the creditors and others interested in the estate. This power may be exercised without notice, hearing, or order of court.

§3–712. [Improper Exercise of Power; Breach of Fiduciary Duty.]

If the exercise of power concerning the estate is improper, the personal representative is liable to interested persons for damage or loss resulting from breach of his fiduciary duty to the same extent as a trustee of an express trust. The rights of purchasers and others dealing with a personal representative shall be determined as provided in Sections 3–713 and 3–714.

§3–713. [Sale, Encumbrance or Transaction Involving Conflict of Interest; Voidable; Exceptions.]

Any sale or encumbrance to the personal representative, his spouse, agent or attorney, or any corporation or trust in which he has a substantial beneficial interest, or any transaction which is affected by a substantial conflict of interest on the part of the personal representative, is voidable by any person interested in the estate except one who has consented after fair disclosure, unless

(1) the will or a contract entered into by the decedent expressly authorized the transaction; or

(2) the transaction is approved by the Court after notice to interested persons.

§3–714. [Persons Dealing with Personal Representative; Protection.]

A person who in good faith either assists a personal representative or deals with him for value is protected as if the personal representative properly exercised his power. The fact that a person knowingly deals with a personal representative does not alone require the person to inquire into the existence of a power or the propriety of its exercise. Except for restrictions on powers of supervised personal representatives which are endorsed on letters as provided in Section 3–504, no provision in any will or order of court purporting to limit the power of a personal representative is effective except as to persons with actual knowledge thereof. A person is not bound to see to the proper application of estate assets paid or delivered to a personal representative. The protection here expressed extends to instances in which some procedural irregularity or jurisdictional defect occurred in proceedings leading to the issuance of letters, including a case in which the alleged decedent is found to be alive. The protection here expressed is not by substitution for that provided by comparable provisions of the laws relating to commercial transactions and laws simplifying transfers of securities by fiduciaries.

§3–715. [Transactions Authorized for Personal Representatives; Exceptions.]

Except as restricted or otherwise provided by the will or by an order in a formal proceeding and subject to the priorities stated in Section 3–902, a personal representative, acting reasonably for the benefit of the interested persons, may properly:

(1) retain assets owned by the decedent pending distribution or liquidation including those in which the representative is personally interested or which are otherwise improper for trust investment;

(2) receive assets from fiduciaries, or other sources;

(3) perform, compromise or refuse performance of the decedent's contracts that continue as obligations of the estate, as he may determine under the circumstances. In performing enforceable contracts by the decedent to convey or lease land, the personal representative, among other possible courses of action, may:

(i) execute and deliver a deed of conveyance for cash payment of all sums remaining due or the purchaser's note for the sum remaining due secured by a mortgage or deed of trust on the land; or

(ii) deliver a deed in escrow with directions that the proceeds, when paid in accordance with the escrow agreement, be paid to the successors of the decedent, as designated in the escrow agreement;

(4) satisfy written charitable pledges of the decedent irrespective of whether the pledges constituted binding

obligations of the decedent or were properly presented as claims, if in the judgment of the personal representative the decedent would have wanted the pledges completed under the circumstances;

(5) if funds are not needed to meet debts and expenses currently payable and are not immediately distributable, deposit or invest liquid assets of the estate, including moneys received from the sale of other assets, in federally insured interest-bearing accounts, readily marketable secured loan arrangements or other prudent investments which would be reasonable for use by trustees generally;

(6) acquire or dispose of an asset, including land in this or another state, for cash or on credit, at public or private sale; and manage, develop, improve, exchange, partition, change the character of, or abandon an estate asset;

(7) make ordinary or extraordinary repairs or alterations in buildings or other structures, demolish any improvements, raze existing or erect new party walls or buildings;

(8) subdivide, develop or dedicate land to public use; make or obtain the vacation of plats and adjust boundaries; or adjust differences in valuation on exchange or partition by giving or receiving considerations; or dedicate easements to public use without consideration;

(9) enter for any purpose into a lease as lessor or lessee, with or without option to purchase or renew, for a term within or extending beyond the period of administration;

(10) enter into a lease or arrangement for exploration and removal of minerals or other natural resources or enter into a pooling or unitization agreement;

(11) abandon property when, in the opinion of the personal representative, it is valueless, or is so encumbered, or is in condition that it is of no benefit to the state;

(12) vote stocks or other securities in person or by general or limited proxy;

(13) pay calls, assessments, and other sums chargeable or accruing against or on account of securities, unless barred by the provisions relating to claims;

(14) hold a security in the name of a nominee or in other form without disclosure of the interest of the estate but the personal representative is liable for any act of the nominee in connection with the security so held;

(15) insure the assets of the estate against damage, loss and liability and himself against liability as to third persons;

(16) borrow money with or without security to be repaid from the estate assets or otherwise; and advance money for the protection of the estate;

(17) effect a fair and reasonable compromise with any debtor or obligor, or extend, renew or in any manner modify the terms of any obligation owing to the estate.

If the personal representative holds a mortgage, pledge or other lien upon property of another person, he may, in lieu of foreclosure, accept a conveyance or transfer of encumbered assets from the owner thereof in satisfaction of the indebtedness secured by lien;

(18) pay taxes, assessments, compensation of the personal representative, and other expenses incident to the administration of the estate;

(19) sell or exercise stock subscription or conversion rights; consent, directly or through a committee or other agent, to the reorganization, consolidation, merger, dissolution, or liquidation of a corporation or other business enterprise;

(20) allocate items of income or expense to either estate income or principal, as permitted or provided by law;

(21) employ persons, including attorneys, auditors, investment advisors, or agents, even if they are associated with the personal representative, to advise or assist the personal representative in the performance of his administrative duties; act without independent investigation upon their recommendations; and instead of acting personally, employ one or more agents to perform any act of administration, whether or not discretionary;

(22) prosecute or defend claims, or proceedings in any jurisdiction for the protection of the estate and of the personal representative in the performance of his duties;

(23) sell, mortgage, or lease any real or personal property of the estate or any interest therein for cash, credit, or for part cash and part credit, and with or without security for unpaid balances;

(24) continue any unincorporated business or venture in which the decedent was engaged at the time of his death (i) in the same business form for a period of not more than 4 months from the date of appointment of a general personal representative if continuation is a reasonable means of preserving the value of the business including good will, (ii) in the same business form for any additional period of time that may be approved by order of the Court in a formal proceeding to which the persons interested in the estate are parties; or (iii) throughout the period of administration if the business is incorporated by the personal representative and if none of the probable distributees of the business who are competent adults object to its incorporation and retention in the estate;

(25) incorporate any business or venture in which the decedent was engaged at the time of his death;

(26) provide for exoneration of the personal representative from personal liability in any contract entered into on behalf of the estate;

(27) satisfy and settle claims and distribute the estate as provided in this Code.

§3–716. [Powers and Duties of Successor Personal Representative.]

A successor personal representative has the same power and duty as the original personal representative to complete the administration and distribution of the estate, as expeditiously as possible, but he shall not exercise any power expressly made personal to the executor named in the will.

§3–717. [Co-representatives; When Joint Action Required.]

If two or more persons are appointed co-representatives and unless the will provides otherwise, the concurrence of all is required on all acts connected with the administration and distribution of the estate. This restriction does not apply when any co-representative receives and receipts for property due the estate, when the concurrence of all cannot readily be obtained in the time reasonably available for emergency action necessary to preserve the estate, or when a co-representative has been delegated to act for the others. Persons dealing with a co-representative if actually unaware that another has been appointed to serve with him or if advised by the personal representative with whom they deal that he has authority to act alone for any of the reasons mentioned herein, are as fully protected as if the person with whom they dealt had been the sole personal representative.

§3–718. [Powers of Surviving Personal Representative.]

Unless the terms of the will otherwise provide, every power exercisable by personal co-representatives may be exercised by the one or more remaining after the appointment of one or more is terminated, and if one of 2 or more nominated as co-executors is not appointed, those appointed may exercise all the powers incident to the office.

§3–719. [Compensation of Personal Representative.]

A personal representative is entitled to reasonable compensation for his services. If a will provides for compensation of the personal representative and there is no contract with the decedent regarding compensation, he may renounce the provision before qualifying and be entitled to reasonable compensation. A personal representative also may renounce his right to all or any part of the compensation. A written renunciation of fee may be filed with the Court.

§3–720. [Expenses in Estate Litigation.]

If any personal representative or person nominated as personal representative defends or prosecutes any proceeding in good faith, whether successful or not he is entitled to receive from the estate his necessary expenses and disbursements including reasonable attorneys' fees incurred.

§3–721. [Proceedings for Review of Employment of Agents and Compensation of Personal Representatives and Employees of Estate.]

After notice to all interested persons or on petition of an interested person or on appropriate motion if administration is supervised, the propriety of employment of any person by a personal representative including any attorney, auditor, investment advisor or other specialized agent or assistant, the reasonableness of the compensation of any person so employed, or the reasonableness of the compensation determined by the personal representative for his own services, may be reviewed by the Court. Any person who has received excessive compensation from an estate for services rendered may be ordered to make appropriate refunds.

PART 8
CREDITORS' CLAIMS

§3–801. [Notice to Creditors.]

(a) Unless notice has already been given under this section, a personal representative upon appointment [may] [shall] publish a notice to creditors once a week for three successive weeks in a newspaper of general circulation in the [county] announcing the appointment and the personal representative's address and notifying creditors of the estate to present their claims within four months after the date of the first publication of the notice or be forever barred.

(b) A personal representative may give written notice by mail or other delivery to a creditor, notifying the creditor to present his [or her] claim within four months after the published notice, if given as provided in subsection (a), or within 60 days after the mailing or other delivery of the notice, whichever is later, or be forever barred. Written notice must be the notice described in subsection (a) above or a similar notice.

(c) The personal representative is not liable to a creditor or to a successor of the decedent for giving or failing to give notice under this section.
As amended in 1989.

§3–802. [Statutes of Limitations.]

(a) Unless an estate is insolvent, the personal representative, with the consent of all successors whose interests would be affected, may waive any defense of limitations available to the estate. If the defense is not waived, no claim barred by a statute of limitations at the time of the decedent's death may be allowed or paid.

(b) The running of a statute of limitations measured from an event other than death or the giving of notice to creditors is suspended for four months after the decedent's death, but resumes thereafter as to claims not barred by other sections.

(c) For purposes of a statute of limitations, the presentation of a claim pursuant to Section 3–804 is equivalent to commencement of a proceeding on the claim.

As amended in 1989.

§3–803. [Limitations on Presentation of Claims.]

(a) All claims against a decedent's estate which arose before the death of the decedent, including claims of the state and any subdivision thereof, whether due or to become due, absolute or contingent, liquidated or unliquidated, founded on contract, tort, or other legal basis, if not barred earlier by another statute of limitations or non-claim statute, are barred against the estate, the personal representative, and the heirs and devisees of the decedent, unless presented within the earlier of the following:

    (1) one year after the decedent's death; or

    (2) the time provided by Section 3–801(b) for creditors who are given actual notice, and within the time provided in 3–801(a) for all creditors barred by publication.

(b) A claim described in subsection (a) which is barred by the non-claim statute of the decedent's domicile before the giving of notice to creditors in this State is barred in this State.

(c) All claims against a decedent's estate which arise at or after the death of the decedent, including claims of the state and any subdivision thereof, whether due or to become due, absolute or contingent, liquidated or unliquidated, founded on contract, tort, or other legal basis, are barred against the estate, the personal representative, and the heirs and devisees of the decedent, unless presented as follows:

    (1) a claim based on a contract with the personal representative, within four months after performance by the personal representative is due; or

    (2) any other claim, within the later of four months after it arises, or the time specified in subsection (a)(1).

(d) Nothing in this section affects or prevents:

    (1) any proceeding to enforce any mortgage, pledge, or other lien upon property of the estate;

    (2) to the limits of the insurance protection only, any proceeding to establish liability of the decedent or the personal representative for which he is protected by liability insurance; or

    (3) collection of compensation for services rendered and reimbursement for expenses advanced by the personal representative or by the attorney or accountant for the personal representative of the estate.

As amended in 1989.

§3–804. [Manner of Presentation of Claims.]

Claims against a decedent's estate may be presented as follows:

(1) The claimant may deliver or mail to the personal representative a written statement of the claim indicating its basis, the name and address of the claimant, and the amount claimed, or may file a written statement of the claim, in the form prescribed by rule, with the clerk of the Court. The claim is deemed presented on the first to occur of receipt of the written statement of claim by the personal representative, or the filing of the claim with the Court. If a claim is not yet due, the date when it will become due shall be stated. If the claim is contingent or unliquidated, the nature of the uncertainty shall be stated. If the claim is secured, the security shall be described. Failure to describe correctly the security, the nature of any uncertainty, and the due date of a claim not yet due does not invalidate the presentation made.

(2) The claimant may commence a proceeding against the personal representative in any Court where the personal representative may be subjected to jurisdiction, to obtain payment of his claim against the estate, but the commencement of the proceeding must occur within the time limited for presenting the claim. No presentation of claim is required in regard to matters claimed in proceedings against the decedent which were pending at the time of his death.

(3) If a claim is presented under subsection (1), no proceeding thereon may be commenced more than 60 days after the personal representative has failed a notice of disallowance; but, in the case of a claim which is not presently due or which is contingent or unliquidated, the personal representative may consent to an extension of the 60-day period, or to avoid injustice the Court, on petition, may order an extension of the 60-day period, but in no event shall the extension run beyond the applicable statute of limitations.

§3–805. [Classification of Claims.]

(a) If the applicable assets of the estate are insufficient to pay all claims in full, the personal representative shall make payment in the following order:

    (1) costs and expenses of administration;

    (2) reasonable funeral expenses;

    (3) debts and taxes with preference under federal law;

    (4) reasonable and necessary medical and hospital expenses of the last illness of the decedent, including compensation of persons attending him;

    (5) debts and taxes with preference under other laws of this state;

    (6) all other claims.

(b) No preference shall be given in the payment of any claim over any other claim of the same class, and a claim due and payable shall not be entitled to a preference over claims not due.

§3–806. [Allowance of Claims.]

(a) As to claims presented in the manner described in Section 3–804 within the time limit prescribed in 3–803, the personal representative may mail a notice to any claimant stating that the claim has been disallowed. If, after allowing or disallowing a claim, the personal representative changes his decision concerning the claim, he shall notify the claimant. The personal representative may not change a disallowance of a claim after the time for the claimant to file a petition for allowance or to commence a proceeding on the claim has run and the claim has been barred. Every claim which is disallowed in whole or in part by the personal representative is barred so far as not allowed unless the claimant files a petition for allowance in the Court or commences a proceeding against the personal representative not later than 60 days after the mailing of the notice of disallowance or partial allowance if the notice warns the claimant of the impending bar. Failure of the personal representative to mail notice to a claimant of action on his claim for 60 days after the time for original presentation of the claim has expired has the effect of a notice of allowance.

(b) After allowing or disallowing a claim the personal representative may change the allowance or disallowance as hereafter provided. The personal representative may prior to payment change the allowance to a disallowance in whole or in part, but not after allowance by a court order or judgment or an order directing payment of the claim. He shall notify the claimant of the change to disallowance, and the disallowed claim is then subject to bar as provided in subsection (a). The personal representative may change a disallowance to an allowance, in whole or in part, until it is barred under subsection (a); after it is barred, it may be allowed and paid only if the estate is solvent and all successors whose interests would be affected consent.

(c) Upon the petition of the personal representative or of a claimant in a proceeding for the purpose, the Court may allow in whole or in part any claim or claims presented to the personal representative or filed with the clerk of the Court in due time and not barred by subsection (a) of this section. Notice in this proceeding shall be given to the claimant, the personal representative and those other persons interested in the estate as the Court may direct by order entered at the time the proceeding is commenced.

(d) A judgment in a proceeding in another court against a personal representative to enforce a claim against a decedent's estate is an allowance of the claim.

(e) Unless otherwise provided in any judgment in another court entered against the personal representative, allowed claims bear interest at the legal rate for the period commencing 60 days after the time for original presentation of the claim has expired unless based on a contract making a provision for interest, in which case they bear interest in accordance with that provision.
As amended in 1987.

§3–807. [Payment of Claims.]

(a) Upon the expiration of the earlier of the time limitations provided in Section 3–803 for the presentation of claims, the personal representative shall proceed to pay the claims allowed against the estate in the order of priority prescribed, after making provision for homestead, family and support allowances, for claims already presented that have not yet been allowed or whose allowance has been appealed, and for unbarred claims that may yet be presented, including costs and expenses of administration. By petition to the Court in a proceeding for the purpose, or by appropriate motion if the administration is supervised, a claimant whose claim has been allowed but not paid may secure an order directing the personal representative to pay the claim to the extent funds of the estate are available to pay it.

(b) The personal representative at any time may pay any just claim that has not been barred, with or without formal presentation, but is personally liable to any other claimant whose claim is allowed and who is injured by its payment if:

(1) payment was made before the expiration of the time limit stated in subsection (a) and the personal representative failed to require the payee to give adequate security for the refund of any of the payment necessary to pay other claimants; or

(2) payment was made, due to negligence or willful fault of the personal representative, in such manner as to deprive the injured claimant of priority.
As amended in 1989.

§3–808. [Individual Liability of Personal Representative.]

(a) Unless otherwise provided in the contract, a personal representative is not individually liable on a contract properly entered into in his fiduciary capacity in the course of administration of the estate unless he fails to reveal his representative capacity and identify the estate in the contract.

(b) A personal representative is individually liable for obligations arising from ownership or control of the estate or for torts committed in the course of administration of the estate only if he is personally at fault.

(c) Claims based on contracts entered into by a personal representative in his fiduciary capacity, on obligations arising from ownership or control of the estate or on torts committed in the course of estate administration may be asserted against the estate by proceeding against the personal representative in his fiduciary capacity, whether or not the personal representative is individually liable therefor.

(d) Issues of liability as between the estate and the personal representative individually may be determined in a proceeding for accounting, surcharge or indemnification or other appropriate proceeding.

§3–809. [Secured Claims.]

Payment of a secured claim is upon the basis of the amount allowed if the creditor surrenders his security; otherwise payment is upon the basis of one of the following:

(1) if the creditor exhausts his security before receiving payment, [unless precluded by other law] upon the amount of the claim allowed less the fair value of the security; or

(2) if the creditor does not have the right to exhaust his security or has not done so, upon the amount of the claim allowed less the value of the security determined by converting it into money according to the terms of the agreement pursuant to which the security was delivered to the creditor, or by the creditor and personal representative by agreement, arbitration, compromise or litigation.

§3–810. [Claims Not Due and Contingent or Unliquidated Claims.]

(a) If a claim which will become due at a future time or a contingent or unliquidated claim becomes due or certain before the distribution of the estate, and if the claim has been allowed or established by a proceeding, it is paid in the same manner as presently due and absolute claims of the same class.

(b) In other cases the personal representative or, on petition of the personal representative or the claimant in a special proceeding for the purpose, the Court may provide for payment as follows:

(1) if the claimant consents, he may be paid the present or agreed value of the claim, taking any uncertainty into account;

(2) arrangement for future payment, or possible payment, on the happening of the contingency or on liquidation may be made by creating a trust, giving a mortgage, obtaining a bond or security from a distributee, or otherwise.

§3–811. [Counterclaims.]

In allowing a claim the personal representative may deduct any counterclaim which the estate has against the claimant. In determining a claim against an estate a Court shall reduce the amount allowed by the amount of any counterclaims and, if the counterclaims exceed the claim, render a judgment against the claimant in the amount of the excess. A counterclaim, liquidated or unliquidated, may arise from a transaction other than that upon which the claim is based. A counterclaim may give rise to relief exceeding in amount or different in kind from that sought in the claim.

§3–812. [Execution and Levies Prohibited.]

No execution may issue upon nor may any levy be made against any property of the estate under any judgment against a decedent or a personal representative, but this section shall not be construed to prevent the enforcement of mortgages, pledges or liens upon real or personal property in an appropriate proceeding.

§3–813. [Compromise of Claims.]

When a claim against the estate has been presented in any manner, the personal representative may, if it appears for the best interest of the estate, compromise the claim, whether due or not due, absolute or contingent, liquidated or unliquidated.

§3–814. [Encumbered Assets.]

If any assets of the estate are encumbered by mortgage, pledge, lien, or other security interest, the personal representative may pay the encumbrance or any part thereof, renew or extend any obligation secured by the encumbrance or convey or transfer the assets to the creditor in satisfaction of his lien, in whole or in part, whether or not the holder of the encumbrance has presented a claim, if it appears to be for the best interest of the estate. Payment of an encumbrance does not increase the share of the distributee entitled to the encumbered assets unless the distributee is entitled to exoneration.

§3–815. [Administration in More Than One State; Duty of Personal Representative.]

(a) All assets of estates being administered in this state are subject to all claims, allowances and charges existing or established against the personal representative wherever appointed.

(b) If the estate either in this state or as a whole is insufficient to cover all family exemptions and allowances determined by the law of the decedent's domicile, prior charges and claims, after satisfaction of the exemptions, allowances and charges, each claimant whose claim has been allowed either in this state or elsewhere in administrations of which the personal representative is aware, is entitled to receive payment of an equal proportion of his claim. If a preference or security in regard to a claim is allowed in another jurisdiction but not in this state, the creditor so benefited is to receive dividends from local assets only upon the balance of his claim after deducting the amount of the benefit.

(c) In case the family exemptions and allowances, prior charges and claims of the entire estate exceed the total value of the portions of the estate being administered separately and this state is not the state of the decedent's last domicile, the claims allowed in this state shall be paid their proportion if local assets are adequate for the purpose, and the balance of local assets shall be transferred to the domiciliary personal representative. If local assets are not sufficient to pay all claims allowed in this state the amount to which they are entitled, local assets shall be marshalled so that each claim allowed in this state is paid its proportion as far as possible, after taking into account all dividends on claims allowed in this state from assets in other jurisdictions.

§3–816. [Final Distribution to Domiciliary Representative.]

The estate of a non-resident decedent being administered by a personal representative appointed in this state shall, if there is a personal representative of the decedent's domicile willing to receive it, be distributed to the domiciliary personal representative for the benefit of the successors of the decedent unless (1) by virtue of the decedent's will, if any, and applicable choice of law rules, the successors are identified pursuant to the local law of this state without reference to the local law of the decedent's domicile; (2) the personal representative of this state, after reasonable inquiry, is unaware of the existence or identity of a domiciliary personal representative; or (3) the Court orders otherwise in a proceeding for a closing order under Section 3–1001 or incident to the closing of a supervised administration. In other cases, distribution of the estate of a decedent shall be made in accordance with the other Parts of this Article.

PART 9
SPECIAL PROVISIONS RELATING TO DISTRIBUTION

§3–901. [Successors' Rights if No Administration.]

In the absence of administration, the heirs and devisees are entitled to the estate in accordance with the terms of a probated will or the laws of intestate succession. Devisees may establish title by the probated will to devised property. Persons entitled to property by homestead allowance, exemption or intestacy may establish title thereto by proof of the decedent's ownership, his death, and their relationship to the decedent. Successors take subject to all charges incident to administration, including the claims of creditors and allowances of surviving spouse and dependent children, and subject to the rights of others resulting from abatement, retainer, advancement, and ademption.

§3–902. [Distribution; Order in Which Assets Appropriated; Abatement.]

(a) Except as provided in subsection (b) and except as provided in connection with the share of the surviving spouse who elects to take an elective share, shares of distributees abate, without any preference or priority as between real and personal property, in the following order: (1) property not disposed of by the will; (2) residuary devises; (3) general devises; (4) specific devises. For purposes of abatement, a general devise charged on any specific property or fund is a specific devise to the extent of the value of the property on which it is charged, and upon the failure or insufficiency of the property on which it is charged, a general devise to the extent of the failure or insufficiency. Abatement within each classification is in proportion to the amounts of property each of the beneficiaries would have received if full distribution of the property had been made in accordance with the terms of the will.

(b) If the will expresses an order of abatement, or if the testamentary plan or the express or implied purpose of the devise would be defeated by the order of abatement stated in subsection (a), the shares of the distributees abate as may be found necessary to give effect to the intention of the testator.

(c) If the subject of a preferred devise is sold or used incident to administration, abatement shall be achieved by appropriate adjustments in, or contribution from, other interests in the remaining assets.

[§3–902A. [Distribution; Order in Which Assets Appropriated; Abatement.]

(addendum for adoption in community property states)
[(a) and (b) as above.]
(c) If an estate of a decedent consists partly of separate property and partly of community property, the debts and expenses of administration shall be apportioned and charged against the different kinds of property in proportion to the relative value thereof.
[(d) same as (c) in common law state.]]

§3–903. [Right of Retainer.]

The amount of a non-contingent indebtedness of a successor to the estate if due, or its present value if not due, shall be offset against the successor's interest; but the successor has the benefit of any defense which would be available to him in a direct proceeding for recovery of the debt.

§3–904. [Interest on General Pecuniary Devise.]

General pecuniary devises bear interest at the legal rate beginning one year after the first appointment of a personal representative until payment, unless a contrary intent is indicated by the will.

§3–905.   [Penalty Clause for Contest.]

A provision in a will purporting to penalize any interested person for contesting the will or instituting other proceedings relating to the estate is unenforceable if probable cause exists for instituting proceedings.

§3–906.   [Distribution in Kind; Valuation; Method.]

(a) Unless a contrary intention is indicated by the will, the distributable assets of a decedent's estate shall be distributed in kind to the extent possible through application of the following provisions:

(1) A specific devisee is entitled to distribution of the thing devised to him, and a spouse or child who has selected particular assets of an estate as provided in Section 2–403 shall receive the items selected.

(2) Any homestead or family allowance or devise of a stated sum of money may be satisfied in kind provided

(i) the person entitled to the payment has not demanded payment in cash;

(ii) the property distributed in kind is valued at fair market value as of the date of its distribution, and

(iii) no residuary devisee has requested that the asset in question remain a part of the residue of the estate.

(3) For the purpose of valuation under paragraph (2) securities regularly traded on recognized exchanges, if distributed in kind, are valued at the price for the last sale of like securities traded on the business day prior to distribution, or if there was no sale on that day, at the median between amounts bid and offered at the close of that day. Assets consisting of sums owed the decedent or the estate by solvent debtors as to which there is no known dispute or defense are valued at the sum due with accrued interest or discounted to the date of distribution. For assets which do not have readily ascertainable values, a valuation as of a date not more than 30 days prior to the date of distribution, if otherwise reasonable, controls. For purposes of facilitating distribution, the personal representative may ascertain the value of the assets as of the time of the proposed distribution in any reasonable way, including the employment of qualified appraisers, even if the assets may have been previously appraised.

(4) The residuary estate shall be distributed in any equitable manner.

(b) After the probable charges against the estate are known, the personal representative may mail or deliver a proposal for distribution to all persons who have a right to object to the proposed distribution. The right of any distributee to object to the proposed distribution on the basis of the kind or value of asset he is to receive, if not waived earlier in writing, terminates if he fails to object in writing received by the personal representative within 30 days after mailing or delivery of the proposal. As amended in 1987.

§3–907.   [Distribution in Kind; Evidence.]

If distribution in kind is made, the personal representative shall execute an instrument or deed of distribution assigning, transferring or releasing the assets to the distributee as evidence of the distributee's title to the property.

§3–908.   [Distribution; Right or Title of Distributee.]

Proof that a distributee has received an instrument or deed of distribution of assets in kind, or payment in distribution, from a personal representative, is conclusive evidence that the distributee has succeeded to the interest of the estate in the distributed assets, as against all persons interested in the estate, except that the personal representative may recover the assets or their value if the distribution was improper.

§3–909.   [Improper Distribution; Liability of Distributee.]

Unless the distribution or payment no longer can be questioned because of adjudication, estoppel, or limitation, a distributee of property improperly distributed or paid, or a claimant who was improperly paid, is liable to return the property improperly received and its income since distribution if he has the property. If he does not have the property, then he is liable to return the value as of the date of disposition of the property improperly received and its income and gain received by him.

§3–910.   [Purchasers from Distributees Protected.]

If property distributed in kind or a security interest therein is acquired for value by a purchaser from or lender to a distributee who has received an instrument or deed of distribution from the personal representative, or is so acquired by a purchaser from or lender to a transferee from such distributee, the purchaser or lender takes title free of rights of any interested person in the estate and incurs no personal liability to the estate, or to any interested person, whether or not the distribution was proper or supported by court order or the authority of the personal representative was terminated before execution of the instrument or deed. This section protects a purchaser from or lender to a distributee who, as personal representative, has executed a deed of distribution to himself, as well as a purchaser from or lender to any other distributee or his transferee. To be protected under this provision, a purchaser or lender need not inquire whether a personal representative acted properly in making the distribution in kind, even if the personal representative and the distributee are the same person, or whether the authority of the personal representative had terminated before the distribution. Any recorded instrument described in this section on which a state documentary fee is noted pursuant to [insert appropriate reference] shall be prima facie evidence that such transfer was made for value.

§3–911. [Partition for Purpose of Distribution.]

When two or more heirs or devisees are entitled to distribution of undivided interests in any real or personal property of the estate, the personal representative or one or more of the heirs or devisees may petition the Court prior to the formal or informal closing of the estate, to make partition. After notice to the interested heirs or devisees, the Court shall partition the property in the same manner as provided by the law for civil actions of partition. The Court may direct the personal representative to sell any property which cannot be partitioned without prejudice to the owners and which cannot conveniently be allotted to any one party.

§3–912. [Private Agreements Among Successors to Decedent Binding on Personal Representative.]

Subject to the rights of creditors and taxing authorities, competent successors may agree among themselves to alter the interests, shares, or amounts to which they are entitled under the will of the decedent, or under the laws of intestacy, in any way that they provide in a written contract executed by all who are affected by its provisions. The personal representative shall abide by the terms of the agreement subject to his obligation to administer the estate for the benefit of creditors, to pay all taxes and costs of administration, and to carry out the responsibilities of his office for the benefit of any successors of the decedent who are not parties. Personal representatives of decedents' estates are not required to see to the performance of trusts if the trustee thereof is another person who is willing to accept the trust. Accordingly, trustees of a testamentary trust are successors for the purposes of this section. Nothing herein relieves trustees of any duties owed to beneficiaries of trusts.

§3–913. [Distributions to Trustee.]

(a) Before distributing to a trustee, the personal representative may require that the trust be registered if the state in which it is to be administered provides for registration and that the trustee inform the beneficiaries as provided in Section 7–303.

(b) If the trust instrument does not excuse the trustee from giving bond, the personal representative may petition the appropriate Court to require that the trustee post bond if he apprehends that distribution might jeopardize the interests of persons who are not able to protect themselves, and he may withhold distribution until the Court has acted.

(c) No inference of negligence on the part of the personal representative shall be drawn from his failure to exercise the authority conferred by subsections (a) and (b).

§[§3–914. [Disposition of Unclaimed Assets.]

(a) If an heir, devisee or claimant cannot be found, the personal representative shall distribute the share of the missing person to his conservator, if any, otherwise to the [state treasurer] to become a part of the [state escheat fund].

(b) The money received by [state treasurer] shall be paid to the person entitled on proof of his right thereto or, if the [state treasurer] refuses or fails to pay, the person may petition the Court which appointed the personal representative, whereupon the Court upon notice to the [state treasurer] may determine the person entitled to the money and order the [treasurer] to pay it to him. No interest is allowed thereon and the heir, devisee or claimant shall pay all costs and expenses incident to the proceeding. If no petition is made to the [court] within 8 years after payment to the [state treasurer], the right of recovery is barred.]

§3–915. [Distribution to Person Under Disability.]

(a) A personal representative may discharge his obligation to distribute to any person under legal disability by distributing in a manner expressly provided in the will.

(b) Unless contrary to an express provision in the will, the personal representative may discharge his obligation to distribute to a minor or person under other disability as authorized by Section 5–101 or any other statute. If the personal representative knows that a conservator has been appointed or that a proceeding for appointment of a conservator is pending, the personal representative is authorized to distribute only to the conservator.

(c) If the heir or devisee is under disability other than minority, the personal representative is authorized to distribute to:

(1) an attorney in fact who has authority under a power of attorney to receive property for that person; or

(2) the spouse, parent or other close relative with whom the person under disability resides if the distribution is of amounts not exceeding [$10,000] a year, or property not exceeding [$10,000] in value, unless the court authorizes a larger amount or greater value.

Persons receiving money or property for the disabled person are obligated to apply the money or property to the support of that person, but may not pay themselves except by way of reimbursement for out-of-pocket expenses for goods and services necessary for the support of the disabled person. Excess sums must be preserved for future support of the disabled person. The personal representative is not responsible for the proper application of money or property distributed pursuant to this subsection.

As amended in 1987.

§3–916. [Apportionment of Estate Taxes.]

(a) For purposes of this section:

(1) "estate" means the gross estate of a decedent as determined for the purpose of federal estate tax and the estate tax payable to this state;

(2) "person" means any individual, partnership, association, joint stock company, corporation, government, political subdivision, governmental agency, or local governmental agency;

(3) "person interested in the estate" means any person entitled to receive, or who has received, from a decedent or by reason of the death of a decedent any property or interest therein included in the decedent's estate. It includes a personal representative, conservator, and trustee;

(4) "state" means any state, territory, or possession of the United States, the District of Columbia, and the Commonwealth of Puerto Rico;

(5) "tax" means the federal estate tax and the additional inheritance tax imposed by _____ and interest and penalties imposed in addition to the tax;

(6) "fiduciary" means personal representative or trustee.

(b) Except as provided in subsection (i) and, unless the will otherwise provides, the tax shall be apportioned among all persons interested in the estate. The apportionment is to be made in the proportion that the value of the interest of each person interested in the estate bears to the total value of the interests of all persons interested in the estate. The values used in determining the tax are to be used for that purpose. If the decedent's will directs a method of apportionment of tax different from the method described in this Code, the method described in the will controls.

(c)(1) The Court in which venue lies for the administration of the estate of a decedent, on petition for the purpose may determine the apportionment of the tax.

(2) If the Court finds that it is inequitable to apportion interest and penalties in the manner provided in subsection (b), because of special circumstances, it may direct apportionment thereof in the manner it finds equitable.

(3) If the Court finds that the assessment of penalties and interest assessed in relation to the tax is due to delay caused by the negligence of the fiduciary, the Court may charge him with the amount of the assessed penalties and interest.

(4) In any action to recover from any person interested in the estate the amount of the tax apportioned to the person in accordance with this Code the determination of the Court in respect thereto shall be prima facie correct.

(d)(1) The personal representative or other person in possession of the property of the decedent required to pay the tax may withhold from any property distributable to any person interested in the estate, upon its distribution to him, the amount of tax attributable to his interest. If the property in possession of the personal representative or other person required to pay the tax and distributable to any person interested in the estate is insufficient to satisfy the proportionate amount of the tax determined to be due from the person, the personal representative or other person required to pay the tax may recover the deficiency from the person interested in the estate. If the property is not in the possession of the personal representative or the other person required to pay the tax, the personal representative or the other person required to pay the tax may recover from any person interested in the estate the amount of the tax apportioned to the person in accordance with this Act.

(2) If property held by the personal representative is distributed prior to final apportionment of the tax, the distributee shall provide a bond or other security for the apportionment liability in the form and amount prescribed by the personal representative.

(e)(1) In making an apportionment, allowances shall be made for any exemptions granted, any classification made of persons interested in the estate and for any deductions and credits allowed by the law imposing the tax.

(2) Any exemption or deduction allowed by reason of the relationship of any person to the decedent or by reason of the purposes of the gift inures to the benefit of the person bearing such relationship or receiving the gift; but if an interest is subject to a prior present interest which is not allowable as a deduction, the tax apportionable against the present interest shall be paid from principal.

(3) Any deduction for property previously taxed and any credit for gift taxes or death taxes of a foreign country paid by the decedent or his estate inures to the proportionate benefit of all persons liable to apportionment.

(4) Any credit for inheritance, succession or estate taxes or taxes in the nature thereof applicable to property or interests includable in the estate, inures to the benefit of the persons or interests chargeable with the payment thereof to the extent proportionately that the credit reduces the tax.

(5) To the extent that property passing to or in trust for a surviving spouse or any charitable, public or similar purpose is not an allowable deduction for purposes of the tax solely by reason of an inheritance tax or other death tax imposed upon and deductible from the property, the property is not included in the computation provided for in subsection (b) hereof, and to that extent no apportionment is made against the property. The sentence immediately preceding does not apply to any case if the result would be to deprive the estate of a deduction otherwise allowable under Section 2053(d) of the Internal Revenue Code of 1954, as amended, of the United States, relating to deduction for state death taxes on transfers for public, charitable, or religious uses.

(f) No interest in income and no estate for years or for life or other temporary interest in any property or fund is subject to apportionment as between the temporary interest and the remainder. The tax on the temporary interest and the tax, if any, on the remainder is chargeable against the corpus of the property or funds subject to the temporary interest and remainder.

(g) Neither the personal representative nor other person required to pay the tax is under any duty to institute any action to recover from any person interested in the estate the amount of the tax apportioned to the person until the expiration of the 3 months next following final determination of the tax. A personal representative or other person required to pay the tax who institutes the action within a reasonable time after the 3 months' period is not subject to any liability or surcharge because any portion of the tax apportioned to any person interested in the estate was collectible at a time following the death of the decedent but thereafter became uncollectible. If the personal representative or other person required to pay the tax cannot collect from any person interested in the estate the amount of the tax apportioned to the person, the amount not recoverable shall be equitably apportioned among the other persons interested in the estate who are subject to apportionment.

(h) A personal representative acting in another state or a person required to pay the tax domiciled in another state may institute an action in the courts of this state and may recover a proportionate amount of the federal estate tax, of an estate tax payable to another state or of a death duty due by a decedent's estate to another state, from a person interested in the estate who is either domiciled in this state or who owns property in this state subject to attachment or execution. For the purposes of the action the determination of apportionment by the Court having jurisdiction of the administration of the decedent's estate in the other state is prima facie correct.

(i) If the liabilities of persons interested in the estate as prescribed by this act differ from those which result under the Federal Estate tax law, the liabilities imposed by the federal law will control and the balance of this Section shall apply as if the resulting liabilities had been prescribed herein.

As amended in 1982.

PART 10
CLOSING ESTATES

§3–1001. [Formal Proceedings Terminating Administration; Testate or Intestate; Order of General Protection.]

(a) A personal representative or any interested person may petition for an order of complete settlement of the estate. The personal representative may petition at any time, and any other interested person may petition after one year from the appointment of the original personal representative except that no petition under this section may be entertained until the time for presenting claims which arose prior to the death of the decedent has expired. The petition may request the Court to determine testacy, if not previously determined, to consider the final account or compel or approve an accounting and distribution, to construe any will or determine heirs and adjudicate the final settlement and distribution of the estate. After notice to all interested persons and hearing the Court may enter an order or orders, on appropriate conditions, determining the persons entitled to distribution of the estate, and, as circumstances require, approving settlement and directing or approving distribution of the estate and discharging the personal representative from further claim or demand of any interested person.

(b) If one or more heirs or devisees were omitted as parties in, or were not given notice of, a previous formal testacy proceeding, the Court, on proper petition for an order of complete settlement of the estate under this section, and after notice to the omitted or unnotified persons and other interested parties determined to be interested on the assumption that the previous order concerning testacy is conclusive as to those given notice of the earlier proceeding, may determine testacy as it affects the omitted persons and confirm or alter the previous order of testacy as it affects all interested persons as appropriate in the light of the new proofs. In the absence of objection by an omitted or unnotified person, evidence received in the original testacy proceeding shall constitute prima facie proof of due execution of any will previously admitted to probate, or of the fact that the decedent left no valid will if the prior proceedings determined this fact.

§3–1002. [Formal Proceedings Terminating Testate Administration; Order Construing Will Without Adjudicating Testacy.]

A personal representative administering an estate under an informally probated will or any devisee under an informally probated will may petition for an order of settlement of the estate which will not adjudicate the testacy status of the decedent. The personal representative may petition at any time, and a devisee may petition after one year, from the appointment of the original personal representative, except that no petition under this section may be entertained until the time for presenting claims which arose prior to the death of the decedent has expired. The petition may request the Court to consider the final account or compel or approve an accounting and distribution, to construe the will and adjudicate final settlement and distribution of the estate. After notice to all devisees and the personal representative and hearing, the Court may enter an order or orders, on appropriate conditions, determining the persons entitled to distribution of the estate under the will, and, as circumstances require, approving settlement and directing or approving distribution of the estate and discharging the personal representative from further claim or demand of any devisee who is a party to the proceeding and those he represents. If it appears that a part of the estate is intestate, the proceedings shall be dismissed or amendments made to meet the provisions of Section 3–1001.

§3–1003. [Closing Estates; By Sworn Statement of Personal Representative.]

(a) Unless prohibited by order of the Court and except for estates being administered in supervised administration proceedings, a personal representative may close an estate by filing with the court no earlier than six months after the date of original appointment of a general personal representative for the estate, a verified statement stating that the personal representatives or a previous personal representative, has:

(1) determined that the time limited for presentation of creditors' claims has expired.

(2) fully administered the estate of the decedent by making payment, settlement, or other disposition of all claims that were presented, expenses of administration and estate, inheritance and other death taxes, except as specified in the statement, and that the assets of the estate have been distributed to the persons entitled. If any claims remain undischarged, the statement must state whether the personal representative has distributed the estate subject to possible liability with the agreement of the distributees or state in detail other arrangements that have been made to accommodate outstanding liabilities; and

(3) sent a copy of the statement to all distributees of the estate and to all creditors or other claimants of whom the personal representative is aware whose claims are neither paid nor barred and has furnished a full account in writing of the personal representative's administration to the distributees whose interests are affected thereby.

(b) If no proceedings involving the personal representative are pending in the Court one year after the closing statement is filed, the appointment of the personal representative terminates.

As amended in 1989.

§3–1004. [Liability of Distributees to Claimants.]

After assets of an estate have been distributed and subject to Section 3–1006, an undischarged claim not barred may be prosecuted in a proceeding against one or more distributees. No distributee shall be liable to claimants for amounts received as exempt property, homestead or family allowances, or for amounts in excess of the value of his distribution as of the time of distribution. As between distributees, each shall bear the cost of satisfaction of unbarred claims as if the claim had been satisfied in the course of administration. Any distributee who shall have failed to notify other distributees of the demand made upon him by the claimant in sufficient time to permit them to join in any proceeding in which the claim was asserted against him loses his right of contribution against other distributees.

§3–1005. [Limitations on Proceedings Against Personal Representative.]

Unless previously barred by adjudication and except as provided in the closing statement, the rights of successors and of creditors whose claims have not otherwise been barred against the personal representative for breach of fiduciary duty are barred unless a proceeding to assert the same is commenced within 6 months after the filing of the closing statement. The rights thus barred do not include rights to recover from a personal representative for fraud, misrepresentation, or inadequate disclosure related to the settlement of the decedent's estate.

§3–1006. [Limitations on Actions and Proceedings Against Distributees.]

Unless previously adjudicated in a formal testacy proceeding or in a proceeding settling the accounts of a personal representative or otherwise barred, the claim of a claimant to recover from a distributee who is liable to pay the claim, and the right of an heir or devisee, or of a successor personal representative acting in their behalf, to recover property improperly distributed or its value from any distributee is forever barred at the later of three years after the decedent's death or one year after the time of its distribution thereof, but all claims of creditors of the decedent, are barred one year after the decedent's death. This section does not bar an action to recover property or value received as a result of fraud. Amended in 1989.

§3–1007. [Certificate Discharging Liens Securing Fiduciary Performance.]

After his appointment has terminated, the personal representative, his sureties, or any successor of either, upon the filing of a verified application showing, so far as is known by the applicant, that no action concerning the estate is pending in any court, is entitled to receive a certificate from the Registrar that the personal representative appears to have fully administered the estate in question. The certificate evidences discharge of any lien on any property given to secure the obligation of the personal representative in lieu of bond or any surety, but does not preclude action against the personal representative or the surety.

§3–1008. [Subsequent Administration.]

If other property of the estate is discovered after an estate has been settled and the personal representative discharged or after one year after a closing statement has been filed, the Court upon petition of any interested person and upon notice as it directs may appoint the same or a successor personal representative to administer the subsequently discovered estate. If a new appointment is made, unless the Court orders otherwise, the provisions of this Code apply as appropriate; but no claim previously barred may be asserted in the subsequent administration.

PART 11
COMPROMISE OF CONTROVERSIES

§3–1101. [Effect of Approval of Agreements Involving Trusts, Inalienable Interests, or Interests of Third Persons.]

A compromise of any controversy as to admission to probate of any instrument offered for formal probate as the will of a decedent, the construction, validity, or effect of any governing instrument, the rights or interests in the estate of the decedent, of any successor, or the administration of the estate, if approved in a formal proceeding in the Court for that purpose, is binding on all the parties thereto including those unborn, unascertained or who could not be located. An approved compromise is binding even though it may affect a trust or an inalienable interest. A compromise does not impair the rights of creditors or of taxing authorities who are not parties to it.
As amended in 1993.

§3–1102. [Procedure for Securing Court Approval of Compromise.]

The procedure for securing court approval of a compromise is as follows:

(1) The terms of the compromise shall be set forth in an agreement in writing which shall be executed by all competent persons and parents acting for any minor child having beneficial interests or having claims which will or may be affected by the compromise. Execution is not required by any person whose identity cannot be ascertained or whose whereabouts is unknown and cannot reasonably be ascertained.

(2) Any interested person, including the personal representative, if any, or a trustee, then may submit the agreement to the Court for its approval and for execution by the personal representative, the trustee of every affected testamentary trust, and other fiduciaries and representatives.

(3) After notice to all interested persons or their representatives, including the personal representative of any estate and all affected trustees of trusts, the Court, if it finds that the contest or controversy is in good faith and that the effect of the agreement upon the interests of persons represented by fiduciaries or other representatives is just and reasonable, shall make an order approving the agreement and directing all fiduciaries subject to its jurisdiction to execute the agreement. Minor children represented only by their parents may be bound only if their parents join with other competent persons in execution of the compromise. Upon the making of the order and the execution of the agreement, all further disposition of the estate is in accordance with the terms of the agreement.
As amended in 1993.

PART 12
COLLECTION OF PERSONAL PROPERTY BY AFFIDAVIT AND SUMMARY ADMINISTRATION PROCEDURE FOR SMALL ESTATES

§3–1201. [Collection of Personal Property by Affidavit.]

(a) Thirty days after the death of a decedent, any person indebted to the decedent or having possession of tangible personal property or an instrument evidencing a debt, obligation, stock or chose in action belonging to the decedent shall make payment of the indebtedness or deliver the tangible personal property or an instrument evidencing a debt, obligation, stock or chose in action to a person claiming to be the successor of the decedent upon being presented an affidavit made by or on behalf of the successor stating that:

(1) the value of the entire estate, wherever located, less liens and encumbrances, does not exceed $5,000;

(2) 30 days have elapsed since the death of the decedent;

(3) no application or petition for the appointment of a personal representative is pending or has been granted in any jurisdiction; and

(4) the claiming successor is entitled to payment or delivery of the property.

(b) A transfer agent of any security shall change the registered ownership on the books of a corporation from the decedent to the successor or successors upon the presentation of an affidavit as provided in subsection (a).

§3–1202. [Effect of Affidavit.]

The person paying, delivering, transferring, or issuing personal property or the evidence thereof pursuant to affidavit is discharged and released to the same extent as if he dealt with a personal representative of the decedent. He is not required to see to the application of the personal property or evidence thereof or to inquire into the truth of any statement in the affidavit. If any person to whom an affidavit is delivered refuses to pay, deliver, transfer, or issue any personal property or evidence thereof, it may be recovered or its payment, delivery, transfer, or issuance compelled upon proof of their right in a proceeding brought for the purpose by or on behalf of the persons entitled thereto. Any person to whom payment, delivery, transfer or issuance is made is answerable and accountable therefor to any personal representative of the estate or to any other person having a superior right.

§3–1203. [Small Estates; Summary Administration Procedure.]

If it appears from the inventory and appraisal that the value of the entire estate, less liens and encumbrances, does not exceed homestead allowance, exempt property, family allowance, costs and expenses of administration, reasonable funeral expenses, and reasonable and necessary medical and hospital expenses of the last illness of the decedent, the personal representative, without giving notice to creditors, may immediately disburse and distribute the estate to the persons entitled thereto and file a closing statement as provided in Section 3–1204.

§3–1204. [Small Estates; Closing by Sworn Statement of Personal Representative.]

(a) Unless prohibited by order of the Court and except for estates being administered by supervised personal representatives, a personal representative may close an estate administered under the summary procedures of Section 3–1203 by filing with the Court, at any time after disbursement and distribution of the estate, a verified statement stating that:

(1) to the best knowledge of the personal representative, the value of the entire estate, less liens and encumbrances, did not exceed homestead allowance, exempt property, family allowance, costs and expenses of administration, reasonable funeral expenses, and reasonable, necessary medical and hospital expenses of the last illness of the decedent;

(2) the personal representative has fully administered the estate by disbursing and distributing it to the persons entitled thereto; and

(3) the personal representative has sent a copy of the closing statement to all distributees of the estate and to all creditors or other claimants of whom he is aware whose claims are neither paid nor barred and has furnished a full account in writing of his administration to the distributees whose interests are affected.

(b) If no actions or proceedings involving the personal representative are pending in the Court one year after the closing statement is filed, the appointment of the personal representative terminates.

(c) A closing statement filed under this section has the same effect as one filed under Section 3–1003.

ARTICLE IV
**FOREIGN PERSONAL REPRESENTATIVES;
ANCILLARY ADMINISTRATION**

PART 1
DEFINITIONS

Section

PART 2
**POWERS OF FOREIGN PERSONAL
REPRESENTATIVES**

PART 3
JURISDICTION OVER FOREIGN REPRESENTATIVES

PART 4
JUDGMENTS AND PERSONAL REPRESENTATIVE

PART 1
DEFINITIONS

§4–101. [Definitions.]

In this Article

(1) "local administration" means administration by a personal representative appointed in this state pursuant to appointment proceedings described in Article III.

(2) "local personal representative" includes any personal representative appointed in this state pursuant to appointment proceedings described in Article III and excludes foreign personal representatives who acquire the power of a local personal representative pursuant to Section 4–205.

(3) "resident creditor" means a person domiciled in, or doing business in this state, who is, or could be, a claimant against an estate of a non-resident decedent.

PART 2
POWERS OF FOREIGN PERSONAL REPRESENTATIVES

§4–201. [Payment of Debt and Delivery of Property to Domiciliary Foreign Personal Representative Without Local Administration.]

At any time after the expiration of sixty days from the death of a nonresident decedent, any person indebted to the estate of the nonresident decedent or having possession or control of personal property, or of an instrument evidencing a debt, obligation, stock or chose in action belonging to the estate of the nonresident decedent may pay the debt, deliver the personal property, or the instrument evidencing the debt, obligation, stock or chose in action, to the domiciliary foreign personal representative of the nonresident decedent upon being presented with proof of his appointment and an affidavit made by or on behalf of the representative stating:

(1) the date of the death of the nonresident decedent,

(2) that no local administration, or application or petition therefor, is pending in this state,

(3) that the domiciliary foreign personal representative is entitled to payment or delivery.

§4–202. [Payment or Delivery Discharges.]

Payment or delivery made in good faith on the basis of the proof of authority and affidavit releases the debtor or person having possession of the personal property to the same extent as if payment or delivery had been made to a local personal representative.

§4–203. [Resident Creditor Notice.]

Payment or delivery under Section 4–201 may not be made if a resident creditor of the nonresident decedent has notified the debtor of the nonresident decedent or the person having possession of the personal property belonging to the nonresident decedent that the debt should not be paid nor the property delivered to the domiciliary foreign personal representative.

§4–204. [Proof of Authority—Bond.]

If no local administration or application or petition therefor is pending in this state, a domiciliary foreign personal representative may file with a Court in this State in a [county] in which property belonging to the decedent is located, authenticated copies of his appointment and of any official bond he has given.

§4–205. [Powers.]

A domiciliary foreign personal representative who has complied with Section 4–204 may exercise as to assets in this state all powers of a local personal representative and may maintain actions and proceedings in this state subject to any conditions imposed upon nonresident parties generally.

§4–206. [Power of Representatives in Transition.]

The power of a domiciliary foreign personal representative under Section 4–201 or 4–205 shall be exercised only if there is no administration or application therefor pending in this state. An application or petition for local administration of the estate terminates the power of the foreign personal representative to act under Section 4–205, but the local Court may allow the foreign personal representative to exercise limited powers to preserve the estate. No person who, before receiving actual notice of a pending local administration, has changed his position in reliance upon the powers of a foreign personal representative shall be prejudiced by reason of the application or petition for, or grant of, local administration. The local personal representative is subject to all duties and obligations which have accrued by virtue of the exercise of the powers by the foreign personal representative and may be substituted for him in any action or proceedings in this state.

§4–207. [Ancillary and Other Local Administrations; Provisions Governing.]

In respect to a nonresident decedent, the provisions of Article III of this Code govern (1) proceedings, if any, in a Court of this state for probate of the will, appointment, removal, supervision, and discharge of the local personal representative, and any other order concerning the estate; and (2) the status, powers, duties and liabilities of any local personal representative and the rights of claimants, purchasers, distributees and others in regard to a local administration.

PART 3
JURISDICTION OVER FOREIGN REPRESENTATIVES

§4–301. [Jurisdiction by Act of Foreign Personal Representative.]

A foreign personal representative submits personally to the jurisdiction of the Courts of this state in any proceeding relating to the estate by (1) filing authenticated copies of his appointment as provided in Section 4–204, (2) receiving payment of money or taking delivery of personal property under Section 4–201, or (3) doing any act as a personal representative in this state which would have given the state jurisdiction over him as an individual. Jurisdiction under (2) is limited to the money or value of personal property collected.

§4–302.   [Jurisdiction by Act of Decedent.]
In addition to jurisdiction conferred by Section 4–301, a foreign personal representative is subject to the jurisdiction of the courts of this state to the same extent that his decedent was subject to jurisdiction immediately prior to death.

§4–303.   [Service on Foreign Personal Representative.]
(a) Service of process may be made upon the foreign personal representative by registered or certified mail, addressed to his last reasonably ascertainable address, requesting a return receipt signed by addressee only. Notice by ordinary first class mail is sufficient if registered or certified mail service to the addressee is unavailable. Service may be made upon a foreign personal representative in the manner in which service could have been made under other laws of this state on either the foreign personal representative or his decedent immediately prior to death.

(b) If service is made upon a foreign personal representative as provided in subsection (a), he shall be allowed at least [30] days within which to appear or respond.

PART 4
JUDGMENTS AND PERSONAL REPRESENTATIVE

§4–401.   [Effect of Adjudication For or Against Personal Representative.]
An adjudication rendered in any jurisdiction in favor of or against any personal representative of the estate is as binding on the local personal representative as if he were a party to the adjudication.

ARTICLE V
PROTECTION OF PERSONS UNDER DISABILITY AND THEIR PROPERTY

PART 1
GENERAL PROVISIONS AND DEFINITIONS

PART 2
GUARDIANS OF MINORS

PART 3
GUARDIANS OF INCAPACITATED PERSONS

PART 4
PROTECTION OF PROPERTY OF PERSONS UNDER DISABILITY AND MINORS

PART 5
DURABLE POWER OF ATTORNEY

PART 1
GENERAL PROVISIONS AND DEFINITIONS

§5–101. [Facility of Payment or Delivery.]

(a) Any person under a duty to pay or deliver money or personal property to a minor may perform the duty, in amounts not exceeding $5,000 a year, by paying or delivering the money or property to:

(1) the minor if 18 or more years of age or married;

(2) any person having the care and custody of the minor with whom the minor resides;

(3) a guardian of the minor; or

(4) a financial institution incident to a deposit in a state or federally insured savings account or certificate in the sole name of the minor with notice of the deposit to the minor.

(b) This section does not apply if the person making payment or delivery knows that a conservator has been appointed or proceedings for appointment of a conservator of the estate of the minor are pending.

(c) Persons, other than the minor or any financial institution, receiving money or property for a minor, are obligated to apply the money to the support and education of the minor, but may not pay themselves except by way of reimbursement for out-of-pocket expenses for goods and services necessary for the minor's support. Any excess sums must be preserved for future support and education of the minor and any balance not so used and any property received for the minor must be turned over to the minor when majority is attained. A person who pays or delivers money or property in accordance with provisions of this section is not responsible for the proper application thereof.

§5–102. [Delegation of Powers by Parent or Guardian.]

A parent or guardian of a minor or incapacitated person, by a properly executed power of attorney, may delegate to another person, for a period not exceeding 6 months, any power regarding care, custody or property of the minor child or ward, except the power to consent to marriage or adoption of a minor ward.

§5–103. [General Definitions.]

As used in Parts 1, 2, 3 and 4 of this Article:

(1) "Claims," in respect to a protected person, includes liabilities of the protected person, whether arising in contract, tort, or otherwise, and liabilities of the estate which arise at or after the appointment of a conservator, including expenses of administration.

(2) "Court" means the [_____] court.

(3) "Conservator" means a person who is appointed by a Court to manage the estate of a protected person and includes a limited conservator described in Section 5–419(a).

(4) "Disability" means cause for a protective order as described in Section 5–401.

(5) "Estate" includes the property of the person whose affairs are subject to this Article.

(6) "Guardian" means a person who has qualified as a guardian of a minor or incapacitated person pursuant to parental or spousal nomination or court appointment and includes a limited guardian as described in Sections 5–209(e) and 5–306(c), but excludes one who is merely a guardian ad litem.

(7) "Incapacitated person" means any person who is impaired by reason of mental illness, mental deficiency, physical illness or disability, chronic use of drugs, chronic intoxication, or other cause (except minority) to the extent of lacking sufficient understanding or capacity to make or communicate responsible decisions.

(8) "Lease" includes an oil, gas, or other mineral lease.

(9) "Letters" includes letters of guardianship and letters of conservatorship.

(10) "Minor" means a person who is under [21] years of age.

(11) "Mortgage" means any conveyance, agreement, or arrangement in which property is used as collateral.

(12) "Organization" includes a corporation, business trust, estate, trust, partnership, association, 2 or more persons having a joint or common interest, government, governmental subdivision or agency, or any other legal entity.

(13) "Parent" includes any person entitled to take, or who would be entitled to take if the child died without a will, as a parent by intestate succession from the child whose relationship is in question and excludes any person who is only a stepparent, foster parent, or grandparent.

(14) "Person" means an individual or an organization.

(15) "Petition" means a written request to the Court for an order after notice.

(16) "Proceeding" includes action at law and suit in equity.

(17) "Property" includes both real and personal property or any interest therein and means anything that may be the subject of ownership.

(18) "Protected person" means a minor or other person for whom a conservator has been appointed or other protective order has been made as provided in Sections 5–407 and 5–408.

(19) "Protective proceeding" means a proceeding under the provisions of Part 4 of this Article.

(20) "Security" includes any note, stock, treasury stock, bond, debenture, evidence of indebtedness, certificate of interest or participation in an oil, gas, or mining title or lease or in payments out of production under such a title or lease, collateral trust certificate, transferable share, voting trust certificate or, in general, any interest or instrument commonly known as a security, or any certificate of interest or participation, any temporary or interim certificate, receipt or certificate of deposit for, or any warrant or right to subscribe to or purchase any of the foregoing.

(21) "Visitor" means a person appointed in a guardianship or protective proceeding who is trained in law, nursing, or social work, is an officer, employee, or special appointee of the Court, and has no personal interest in the proceeding.

(22) "Ward" means a person for whom a guardian has been appointed. A "minor ward" is a minor for whom a guardian has been appointed solely because of minority.

As amended in 1989.

§5–104. [Request for Notice; Interested Person.]

Upon payment of any required fee, an interested person who desires to be notified before any order is made in a guardianship proceeding, including any proceeding subsequent to the appointment of a guardian under Section 5–312, or in a protective proceeding under Section 5–401, may file a request for notice with the clerk of the court in which the proceeding is pending. The clerk shall mail a copy of the request to the guardian and to the conservator if one has been appointed. A request is not effective unless it contains a statement showing the interest of the person making it and the address of that person or an attorney to whom notice is to be given. The request is effective only as to proceedings occurring after the filing. Any governmental agency paying or planning to pay benefits to the person to be protected is an interested person in protective proceedings.

PART 2
GUARDIANS OF MINORS

§5–201. [Appointment and Status of Guardian of Minor.]

A person may become a guardian of a minor by parental appointment or upon appointment by the Court. The guardianship status continues until terminated, without regard to the location from time to time of the guardian or minor ward.

§5–202. [Parental Appointment of Guardian for Minor.]

(a) The parent of an unmarried minor may appoint a guardian for the minor by will, or other writing signed by the parent and attested by at least 2 witnesses.

(b) Subject to the right of the minor under Section 5–203, if both parents are dead or incapacitated or the surviving parent has no parental rights or has been adjudged to be incapacitated, a parental appointment becomes effective when the guardian's acceptance is filed in the Court in which a nominating instrument is probated, or, in the case of a non-testamentary nominating instrument, in the Court at the place where the minor resides or is present. If both parents are dead, an effective appointment by the parent who died later has priority.

(c) A parental appointment effected by filing the guardian's acceptance under a will probated in the state of the testator's domicile is effective in this State.

(d) Upon acceptance of appointment, the guardian shall give written notice of acceptance to the minor and to the person having the minor's care or the minor's nearest adult relative.

§5–203. [Objection by Minor of Fourteen or Older to Parental Appointment.]

A minor 14 or more years of age who is the subject of a parental appointment may prevent the appointment or cause it to terminate by filing in the Court in which the nominating instrument is filed a written objection to the appointment before it is accepted or within 30 days after receiving notice of its acceptance. An objection may be withdrawn. An objection does not preclude appointment by the Court in a proper proceeding of the parental nominee or any other suitable person.

§5–204. [Court Appointment of Guardian of Minor; Conditions for Appointment.]

(a) The Court may appoint a guardian for an unmarried minor if all parental rights have been terminated or suspended by circumstances or prior Court order. A guardian appointed pursuant to Section 5–202 whose appointment has not been prevented or nullified under Section 5–203 has priority over any guardian who may be appointed by the Court, but the Court may proceed with another appointment upon a finding that the parental nominee has failed to accept the appointment within 30 days after notice of the guardianship proceeding.

(b) If necessary, and on appropriate petition or application, the Court may appoint a temporary guardian who shall have the full authority of a general guardian of a minor, but the authority of a temporary guardian may not last longer than 6 months. The appointment of a temporary guardian for a minor may occur even though the conditions described in subsection (a) have not been established.

§5–205. [Venue.]

The venue for guardianship proceedings for a minor is in the court at the place where the minor resides or is present at the time the proceedings are commenced.

§5–206. [Procedure for Court Appointment of Guardian of Minor.]

(a) A minor or any person interested in the welfare of the minor may petition for appointment of a guardian.

(b) After the filing of a petition, the Court shall set a date for hearing, and the petitioner shall give notice of the time and place of hearing the petition in the manner prescribed by Section 1–401 to:

(1) the minor, if 14 or more years of age and not the petitioner;

(2) any person alleged to have had the principal care and custody of the minor during the 60 days preceding the filing of the petition; and

(3) any living parent of the minor.

(c) Upon hearing, if the Court finds that a qualified person seeks appointment, venue is proper, the required notices have been given, the conditions of Section 5–204(a) have been met, and the welfare and best interest of the minor will be served by the requested appointment, it shall make the appointment and issue letters. In other cases, the Court may dismiss the proceedings or make any other disposition of the matter that will serve the best interest of the minor.

(d) If the Court determines at any time in the proceeding that the interests of the minor are or may be inadequately represented, it may appoint an attorney to represent the minor, giving consideration to the preference of the minor if the minor is 14 or more years of age.

§5–207. [Court Appointment of Guardian of Minor; Qualifications; Priority of Minor's Nominee.]

The Court may appoint as guardian any person whose appointment would be in the best interest of the minor. The Court shall appoint a person nominated by the minor, if the minor is 14 or more years of age, unless the Court finds the appointment contrary to the best interest of the minor.

§5–208. [Consent to Service by Acceptance of Appointment; Notice.]

By accepting a parental or court appointment as guardian, a guardian submits personally to the jurisdiction of the Court in any proceeding relating to the guardianship that may be instituted by any interested person. The petitioner shall cause notice of any proceeding to be delivered or mailed to the guardian at the guardian's address listed in the Court records and to the address then known to the petitioner. Letters of guardianship must indicate whether the guardian was appointed by court order or parental nomination.

§5–209. [Powers and Duties of Guardian of Minor.]

(a) A guardian of a minor ward has the powers and responsibilities of a parent regarding the ward's support, care, and education, but a guardian is not personally liable for the ward's expenses and is not liable to third persons by reason of the relationship for acts of the ward.

(b) In particular and without qualifying the foregoing, a guardian shall:

(1) become or remain personally acquainted with the ward and maintain sufficient contact with the ward to know of the ward's capacities, limitations, needs, opportunities, and physical and mental health;

(2) take reasonable care of the ward's personal effects and commence protective proceedings if necessary to protect other property of the ward;

(3) apply any available money of the ward to the ward's current needs for support, care, and education;

(4) conserve any excess money of the ward for the ward's future needs, but if a conservator has been appointed for the estate of the ward, the guardian, at least quarterly, shall pay to the conservator money of the ward to be conserved for the ward's future needs; and

(5) report the condition of the ward and of the ward's estate that has been subject to the guardian's possession or control, as ordered by the Court on petition of any person interested in the ward's welfare or as required by Court rule.

(c) A guardian may:

(1) receive money payable for the support of the ward to the ward's parent, guardian, or custodian under the terms of any statutory benefit or insurance system or any private contract, devise, trust, conservatorship, or custodianship, and money or property of the ward paid or delivered pursuant to Section 5–101;

(2) if consistent with the terms of any order by a court of competent jurisdiction relating to detention or commitment of the ward, take custody of the person of the ward and establish the ward's place of abode within or without this State;

(3) if no conservator for the estate of the ward has been appointed, institute proceedings, including administrative proceedings, or take other appropriate action to compel the performance by any person of a duty to support the ward or to pay sums for the welfare of the ward;

(4) consent to medical or other professional care, treatment, or advice for the ward without liability by reason of the consent for injury to the ward resulting from the negligence or acts of third persons unless a parent would have been liable in the circumstances;

(5) consent to the marriage or adoption of the ward; and

(6) if reasonable under all of the circumstances, delegate to the ward certain responsibilities for decisions affecting the ward's well-being.

(d) A guardian is entitled to reasonable compensation for services as guardian and to reimbursement for room, board and clothing personally provided to the ward, but only as approved by order of the Court. If a conservator, other than the guardian or one who is affiliated with the guardian, has been appointed for the estate of the ward, reasonable compensation and reimbursement to the guardian may be approved and paid by the conservator without order of the Court controlling the guardian.

(e) In the interest of developing self-reliance on the part of a ward or for other good cause, the Court, at the time of appointment or later, on its own motion or on appropriate petition or motion of the minor or other interested person, may limit the powers of a guardian otherwise conferred by this section and thereby create a limited guardianship. Any limitation on the statutory power of a guardian of a minor must be endorsed on the guardian's letters or, in the case of a guardian by parental appointment, must be reflected in letters that are issued at the time any limitation is imposed. Following the same procedure, a limitation may be removed and appropriate letters issued.

§5–210. [Termination of Appointment of Guardian; General.]

A guardian's authority and responsibility terminates upon the death, resignation, or removal of the guardian or upon the minor's death, adoption, marriage, or attainment of majority, but termination does not affect the guardian's liability for prior acts or the obligation to account for funds and assets of the ward. Resignation of a guardian does not terminate the guardianship until it has been approved by the Court. A parental appointment under an informally probated will terminates if the will is later denied probate in a formal proceeding.

§5–211. [Proceedings Subsequent to Appointment; Venue.]

(a) The Court at the place where the ward resides has concurrent jurisdiction with the Court that appointed the guardian or in which acceptance of a parental appointment was filed over resignation, removal, accounting, and other proceedings relating to the guardianship.

(b) If the Court at the place where the ward resides is neither the appointing court nor the court in which acceptance of appointment is filed, the court in which proceedings subsequent to appointment are commenced in all appropriate cases shall notify the other court, in this or another state, and after consultation with that court determine whether to retain jurisdiction or transfer the proceedings to the other court, whichever is in the best interest of the ward. A copy of any order accepting a resignation or removing a guardian must be sent to the appointing court or the court in which acceptance of appointment is filed.

§5–212. [Resignation, Removal, and Other Post-appointment Proceedings.]

(a) Any person interested in the welfare of a ward or the ward, if 14 or more years of age, may petition for removal of a guardian on the ground that removal would be in the best interest of the ward or for any other order that is in the best interest of the ward. A guardian may petition for permission to resign. A petition for removal or for permission to resign may, but need not, include a request for appointment of a successor guardian.

(b) Notice of hearing on a petition for an order subsequent to appointment of a guardian must be given to the ward, the guardian, and any other person as ordered by the court.

(c) After notice and hearing on a petition for removal or for permission to resign, the Court may terminate the guardianship and make any further order that may be appropriate.

(d) If the Court determines at any time in the proceeding that the interest of the ward is or may be inadequately represented, it may appoint an attorney to represent the minor, giving consideration to the preference of the minor if the minor is 14 or more years of age.

PART 3
GUARDIANS OF INCAPACITATED PERSONS

§5–301. [Appointment of Guardian for Incapacitated Person by Will or Other Writing.]

(a) The parent of an unmarried incapacitated person may appoint by will, or other writing signed by the parent and attested by at least 2 witnesses, a guardian of the incapacitated person. If both parents are dead or the surviving parent is adjudged incapacitated, a parental appointment becomes effective when, after having given 7 days prior written notice of intention to do so to the incapacitated person and to the person having the care of the person or to the nearest adult relative, the guardian files acceptance of appointment in the court in which the will is [informally or formally] probated, or in the case of a non-testamentary nominating instrument, in the Court at the place where the incapacitated person resides or is present. The notice shall state that the appointment may be terminated by filing a written objection in the Court, as provided by subsection (d). If both parents are dead, an effective appointment by the parent who died later has priority.

(b) The spouse of a married incapacitated person may appoint by will, or other writing signed by the spouse and attested by at least 2 witnesses, a guardian of the incapacitated person. The appointment becomes effective when, after having given 7 days prior written notice of intention to do so to the incapacitated person and to the person having care of the incapacitated person or to the nearest adult relative, the guardian files acceptance of appointment in the Court in which the will is informally or formally probated or, in the case of non-testamentary nominating instrument, in the Court at the place where the incapacitated person resides or is present. The notice shall state that the appointment may be terminated by filing a written objection in the Court, as provided by subsection (d). An effective appointment by a spouse has priority over an appointment by a parent.

(c) An appointment effected by filing the guardian's acceptance under a will probated in the state of the decedent's domicile is effective in this State.

(d) Upon the filing in the Court in which the will was probated or, in the case of a non-testamentary nominating instrument, in the Court at the place where the incapacitated person resides or is present, of written objection to the appointment by the incapacitated person for whom a parental or spousal appointment of guardian has been made, the appointment is terminated. An objection does not prevent appointment by the Court in a proper proceeding of the parental or spousal nominee or any other suitable person upon an adjudication of incapacity in proceedings under the succeeding sections of this Part.

As amended in 1987.

§5–302. [Venue.]

The venue for guardianship proceedings for an incapacitated person is in the place where the incapacitated person resides or is present at the time the proceedings are commenced. If the incapacitated person is admitted to an institution pursuant to order of a court of competent jurisdiction, venue is also in the [county] in which that court is located.

§5–303. [Procedure for Court Appointment of a Guardian of an Incapacitated Person.]

(a) An incapacitated person or any person interested in the welfare of the incapacitated person may petition for appointment of a guardian, limited or general.

(b) After the filing of a petition, the Court shall set a date for hearing on the issue of incapacity so that notices may be given as required by Section 5–304, and, unless the allegedly incapacitated person is represented by counsel, appoint an attorney to represent the person in the proceeding. The person so appointed may be granted the powers and duties of a guardian ad litem. The person alleged to be incapacitated must be examined by a physician or other qualified person appointed by the Court who shall submit a report in writing to the Court. The person alleged to be incapacitated also must be interviewed by a visitor sent by the Court. The visitor also shall interview the person who appears to have caused the petition to be filed and any person who is nominated to serve as guardian and visit the present place of abode of the person alleged to be incapacitated and the place it is proposed that the person will be detained or reside if the appointment is made and submit a report in writing to the Court. The Court may utilize the service of any public or charitable agency as an additional visitor to evaluate the condition of the allegedly incapacitated person and to make appropriate recommendations to the Court.

(c) A person alleged to be incapacitated is entitled to be present at the hearing in person. The person is entitled to be represented by counsel, to present evidence, to cross-examine witnesses, including the Court-appointed physician or other qualified person and any visitor [, and to trial by jury]. The issue may be determined at a closed hearing [or without a jury] if the person alleged to be incapacitated or counsel for the person so requests.

(d) Any person may apply for permission to participate in the proceeding, and the Court may grant the request, with or without hearing, upon determining that the best interest of the alleged incapacitated person will be served thereby. The Court may attach appropriate conditions to the permission.

§5–304. [Notice in Guardianship Proceeding.]

(a) In a proceeding for the appointment of a guardian of an incapacitated person, and, if notice is required in a proceeding for appointment of a temporary guardian, notice of hearing must be given to each of the following:

> (1) the person alleged to be incapacitated and spouse, or, if none, adult children, or if none, parents;
>
> (2) any person who is serving as guardian, conservator, or who has the care and custody of the person alleged to be incapacitated;
>
> (3) in case no other person is notified under paragraph (1), at least one of the nearest adult relatives, if any can be found; and
>
> (4) any other person as directed by the Court.

(b) Notice of hearing on a petition for an order subsequent to appointment of a guardian must be given to the ward, the guardian and any other person as ordered by the Court.

(c) Notice must be served personally on the alleged incapacitated person. Notices to other persons as required by subsection (a)(1) must be served personally if the person to be notified can be found within the state. In all other cases, required notices must be given as provided in Section 1–401.

(d) The person alleged to be incapacitated may not waive notice.

§5–305. [Who May Be Guardian; Priorities.]

(a) Any qualified person may be appointed guardian of an incapacitated person.

(b) Unless lack of qualification or other good cause dictates the contrary, the Court shall appoint a guardian in accordance with the incapacitated person's most recent nomination in a durable power of attorney.

(c) Except as provided in subsection (b), the following are entitled to consideration for appointment in the order listed:

> (1) the spouse of the incapacitated person or a person nominated by will of a deceased spouse or by other writing signed by the spouse and attested by at least 2 witnesses;
>
> (2) an adult child of the incapacitated person;
>
> (3) a parent of the incapacitated person, or a person nominated by will of a deceased parent or by other writing signed by a parent and attested by at least two witnesses;
>
> (4) any relative of the incapacitated person with whom the person has resided for more than 6 months prior to the filing of the petition; and
>
> (5) a person nominated by the person who is caring for or paying for the care of the incapacitated person.

(d) With respect to persons having equal priority, the Court shall select the one it deems best qualified to serve. The Court, acting in the best interest of the incapacitated person, may pass over a person having priority and appoint a person having a lower priority or no priority.

§5–306. [Findings; Order of Appointment.]

(a) The Court shall exercise the authority conferred in this Part so as to encourage the development of maximum self-reliance and independence of the incapacitated person and make appointive and other orders only to the extent necessitated by the incapacitated person's mental and adaptive limitations or other conditions warranting the procedure.

(b) The Court may appoint a guardian as requested if it is satisfied that the person for whom a guardian is sought is incapacitated and that the appointment is necessary or desirable as a means of providing continuing care and supervision of the person of the incapacitated person. The Court, on appropriate findings, may (i) treat the petition as one for a protective order under Section 5–401 and proceed accordingly, (ii) enter any other appropriate order, or (iii) dismiss the proceedings.

(c) The Court, at the time of appointment or later, on its own motion or on appropriate petition or motion of the incapacitated person or other interested person, may limit the powers of a guardian otherwise conferred by Parts 1, 2, 3 and 4 of this Article and thereby create a limited guardianship. Any limitation on the statutory power of a guardian of an incapacitated person must be endorsed on the guardian's letters or, in the case of a guardian by parental or spousal appointment, must be reflected in letters issued at the time any limitation is imposed. Following the same procedure, a limitation may be removed or modified and appropriate letters issued.

§5–307. [Acceptance of Appointment; Consent to Jurisdiction.]

By accepting appointment, a guardian submits personally to the jurisdiction of the Court in any proceeding relating to the guardianship that may be instituted by any interested person. Notice of any proceeding must be delivered or mailed to the guardian at the address listed in the Court records and at the address as then known to the petitioner.

§5–308. [Emergency Orders; Temporary Guardians.]

(a) If an incapacitated person has no guardian, an emergency exists, and no other person appears to have authority to act in the circumstances, on appropriate petition the Court may appoint a temporary guardian whose authority may not extend beyond [15 days] [the period of effectiveness of ex parte restraining orders], and who may exercise those powers granted in the order.

(b) If an appointed guardian is not effectively performing duties and the Court further finds that the welfare of the incapacitated person requires immediate action, it may appoint, with or without notice, a temporary guardian for the incapacitated person having the powers of a general guardian for a specified period not to exceed 6 months. The authority of any permanent guardian previously appointed by the Court is suspended as long as a temporary guardian has authority.

(c) The Court may remove a temporary guardian at any time. A temporary guardian shall make any report the Court requires. In other respects the provisions of Parts 1, 2, 3 and 4 of this Article concerning guardians apply to temporary guardians.

§5–309. [General Powers and Duties of Guardian.]

Except as limited pursuant to Section 5–306(c), a guardian of an incapacitated person is responsible for care, custody, and control of the ward, but is not liable to third persons by reason of that responsibility for acts of the ward. In particular and without qualifying the foregoing, a guardian has the same duties, powers and responsibilities as a guardian for a minor as described in Section 5–209(b), (c) and (d).

§5–310. [Termination of Guardianship for Incapacitated Person.]

The authority and responsibility of a guardian of an incapacitated person terminates upon the death of the guardian or ward, the determination of incapacity of the guardian, or upon removal or resignation as provided in Section 5–311. Testamentary appointment under an informally probated will terminates if the will is later denied probate in a formal proceeding. Termination does not affect a guardian's liability for prior acts or the obligation to account for funds and assets of the ward.

§5–311. [Removal or Resignation of Guardian; Termination of Incapacity.]

(a) On petition of the ward or any person interested in the ward's welfare, the Court, after hearing, may remove a guardian if in the best interest of the ward. On petition of the guardian, the Court, after hearing, may accept a resignation.

(b) An order adjudicating incapacity may specify a minimum period, not exceeding six months, during which a petition for an adjudication that the ward is no longer incapacitated may not be filed without special leave. Subject to that restriction, the ward or any person interested in the welfare of the ward may petition for an order that the ward is no longer incapacitated and for termination of the guardianship. A request for an order may also be made informally to the Court and any person who knowingly interferes with transmission of the request may be adjudged guilty of contempt of court.

(c) Upon removal, resignation, or death of the guardian, or if the guardian is determined to be incapacitated, the Court may appoint a successor guardian and make any other appropriate order. Before appointing a successor guardian, or ordering that a ward's incapacity has terminated, the Court shall follow the same procedures to safeguard the rights of the ward that apply to a petition for appointment of a guardian.

As amended in 1987.

§5–312. [Proceedings Subsequent to Appointment; Venue.]

(a) The Court at the place where the ward resides has concurrent jurisdiction with the Court that appointed the guardian or in which acceptance of a parental or spousal appointment was filed over resignation, removal, accounting, and other proceedings relating to the guardianship, including proceedings to limit the authority previously conferred on a guardian or to remove limitations previously imposed.

(b) If the Court at the place where the ward resides is not the Court in which acceptance of appointment is filed, the Court in which proceedings subsequent to appointment are commenced, in all appropriate cases, shall notify the other Court, in this or another state, and after consultation with that Court determine whether to retain jurisdiction or transfer the proceedings to the other Court, whichever may be in the best interest of the ward. A copy of any order accepting a resignation, removing a guardian, or altering authority must be sent to the Court in which acceptance of appointment is filed.

PART 4
PROTECTION OF PROPERTY OF PERSONS UNDER DISABILITY AND MINORS

§5–401. [Protective Proceedings.]

(a) Upon petition and after notice and hearing in accordance with the provisions of this Part, the Court may appoint a conservator or make any other protective order for cause as provided in this section.

(b) Appointment of a conservator or other protective order may be made in relation to the estate and affairs of a minor if the Court determines that a minor owns money or property requiring management or protection that cannot otherwise be provided or has or may have business affairs that may be jeopardized or prevented by minority, or that funds are needed for support and education and that protection is necessary or desirable to obtain or provide funds.

(c) Appointment of a conservator or other protective order may be made in relation to the estate and affairs of a person if the Court determines that (i) the person is unable to manage property and business affairs effectively for such reasons as mental illness, mental deficiency, physical illness or disability, chronic use of drugs, chronic intoxication, confinement, detention by a foreign power, or disappearance; and (ii) the person has property that will be wasted or dissipated unless property management is provided or money is needed for the support, care, and welfare of the person or those entitled to the person's support and that protection is necessary or desirable to obtain or provide money. As amended in 1989.

§5–402. [Protective Proceedings; Jurisdiction of Business Affairs of Protected Persons.]

After the service of notice in a proceeding seeking the appointment of a conservator or other protective order and until termination of the proceeding, the Court in which the petition is filed has:

(1) exclusive jurisdiction to determine the need for a conservator or other protective order until the proceedings are terminated;

(2) exclusive jurisdiction to determine how the estate of the protected person which is subject to the laws of this State must be managed, expended, or distributed to or for the use of the protected person, the protected person's dependents, or other claimants; and

(3) concurrent jurisdiction to determine the validity of claims against the person or estate of the protected person and questions of title concerning any estate asset.

§5–403. [Venue.]

Venue for proceedings under this Part is:

(1) in the Court at the place in this State where the person to be protected resides whether or not a guardian has been appointed in another place; or

(2) if the person to be protected does not reside in this State, in the Court at any place where property of the person is located.

§5–404. [Original Petition for Appointment or Protective Order.]

(a) The person to be protected or any person who is interested in the estate, affairs, or welfare of the person, including a parent, guardian, custodian, or any person who would be adversely affected by lack of effective management of the person's property and business affairs may petition for the appointment of a conservator or for other appropriate protective order.

(b) The petition must set forth to the extent known the interest of the petitioner; the name, age, residence, and address of the person to be protected; the name and address of the guardian, if any; the name and address of the nearest relative known to the petitioner; a general statement of the person's property with an estimate of the value thereof, including any compensation, insurance, pension, or allowance to which the person is entitled; and the reason why appointment of a conservator or other protective order is necessary. If the appointment of a conservator is requested, the petition must also set forth the name and address of the person whose appointment is sought and the basis of the claim to priority for appointment.

§5–405. [Notice.]

(a) On a petition for appointment of a conservator or other protective order, the requirements for notice described in Section 5–304 apply, but (i) if the person to be protected has disappeared or is otherwise situated so as to make personal service of notice impracticable, notice to the person must be given by publication as provided in Section 1–401, and (ii) if the person to be protected is a minor, the provisions of Section 5–206 also apply.

(b) Notice of hearing on a petition for an order subsequent to appointment of a conservator or other protective order must be given to the protected person, any conservator of the protected person's estate, and any other person as ordered by the Court.

§5–406. [Procedure Concerning Hearing and Order on Original Petition.]

(a) Upon receipt of a petition for appointment of a conservator or other protective order because of minority, the Court shall set a date for hearing. If the Court determines at any time in the proceeding that the interests of the minor are or may be inadequately represented, it may appoint an attorney to represent the minor, giving consideration to the choice of the minor if 14 or more years of age. An attorney appointed by the Court to represent a minor may be granted the powers and duties of a guardian ad litem.

(b) Upon receipt of a petition for appointment of a conservator or other protective order for reasons other than minority, the Court shall set a date for hearing. Unless the person to be protected has chosen counsel, the Court shall appoint an attorney to represent the person who may be granted the powers and duties of a guardian ad litem. If the alleged disability is mental illness, mental deficiency, physical illness or disability, chronic use of drugs, or chronic intoxication, the Court may direct that the person to be protected be examined by a physician designated by the Court, preferably a physician who is not connected with any institution in which the person is a patient or is detained. The Court may send a visitor to interview the person to be protected. The visitor may be a guardian ad litem or an officer or employee of the Court.

(c) The Court may utilize, as an additional visitor, the service of any public or charitable agency to evaluate the condition of the person to be protected and make appropriate recommendations to the Court.

(d) The person to be protected is entitled to be present at the hearing in person. The person is entitled to be represented by counsel, to present evidence, to cross-examine witnesses, including any Court-appointed physician or other qualified person and any visitor [, and to trial by jury]. The issue may be determined at a closed hearing [or without a jury] if the person to be protected or counsel for the person so requests.

(e) Any person may apply for permission to participate in the proceeding and the Court may grant the request, with or without hearing, upon determining that the best interest of the person to be protected will be served thereby. The Court may attach appropriate conditions to the permission.

(f) After hearing, upon finding that a basis for the appointment of a conservator or other protective order has been established, the Court shall make an appointment or other appropriate protective order.

As amended in 1989.

§5–407. [Permissible Court Orders.]

(a) The Court shall exercise the authority conferred in this Part to encourage the development of maximum self-reliance and independence of a protected person and make protective orders only to the extent necessitated by the protected person's mental and adaptive limitations and other conditions warranting the procedure.

(b) The Court has the following powers that may be exercised directly or through a conservator in respect to the estate and business affairs of a protected person:

(1) While a petition for appointment of a conservator or other protective order is pending and after preliminary hearing and without notice to others, the Court may preserve and apply the property of the person to be protected as may be required for the support of the person or dependents of the person.

(2) After hearing and upon determining that a basis for an appointment or other protective order exists with respect to a minor without other disability, the Court has all those powers over the estate and business affairs of the minor which are or may be necessary for the best interest of the minor and members of the minor's immediate family.

(3) After hearing and upon determining that a basis for an appointment or other protective order exists with respect to a person for reasons other than minority, the Court, for the benefit of the person and members of the person's immediate family, has all the powers over the estate and business affairs which the person could exercise if present and not under disability, except the power to make a will. Those powers include, but are not limited to, power to make gifts; to convey or release contingent and expectant interests in property, including marital property rights and any right of survivorship incident to joint tenancy or tenancy by the entirety; to exercise or release powers held by the protected person as trustee, personal representative, custodian for minors, conservator, or donee of a power of appointment; to enter into contracts; to create revocable or irrevocable trusts of property of the estate which may extend beyond the disability or life of the protected person; to exercise options of the protected person to purchase securities or other property; to exercise rights to elect options and change beneficiaries under insurance and annuity policies and to surrender the policies for their cash value; to exercise any right to an elective share in the estate of the person's deceased spouse and to renounce or disclaim any interest by testate or intestate succession or by inter vivos transfer.

(c) The Court may exercise or direct the exercise of the following powers only if satisfied, after notice and hearing, that it is in the best interest of the protected person, and that the person either is incapable of consenting or has consented to the proposed exercise of power:

(1) to exercise or release powers of appointment of which the protected person is donee;

(2) to renounce or disclaim interests;

(3) to make gifts in trust or otherwise exceeding 20 percent of any year's income of the estate; and

(4) to change beneficiaries under insurance and annuity policies.

(d) A determination that a basis for appointment of a conservator or other protective order exists has no effect on the capacity of the protected person.

§5–408. [Protective Arrangements and Single Transactions Authorized.]

(a) If it is established in a proper proceeding that a basis exists as described in Section 5–401 for affecting the property and business affairs of a person, the Court, without appointing a conservator, may authorize, direct or ratify any transaction necessary or desirable to achieve any security, service, or care arrangement meeting the foreseeable needs of the protected person. Protective arrangements include payment, delivery, deposit, or retention of funds or property; sale, mortgage, lease, or other transfer of property; entry into an annuity contract, a contract for life care, a deposit contract, or a contract for training and education; or addition to or establishment of a suitable trust.

(b) If it is established in a proper proceeding that a basis exists as described in Section 5–401 for affecting the property and business affairs of a person, the Court, without appointing a conservator, may authorize, direct, or ratify any contract, trust, or other transaction relating to the protected person's property and business affairs if the Court determines that the transaction is in the best interest of the protected person.

(c) Before approving a protective arrangement or other transaction under this section, the Court shall consider the interests of creditors and dependents of the protected person and, in view of the disability, whether the protected person needs the continuing protection of a conservator. The Court may appoint a special conservator to assist in the accomplishment of any protective arrangement or other transaction authorized under this section who shall have the authority conferred by the order and serve until discharged by order after report to the Court of all matters done pursuant to the order of appointment.

§5–409. [Who May Be Appointed Conservator; Priorities.]

(a) The Court may appoint an individual or a corporation with general power to serve as trustee or conservator of the estate of a protected person. The following are entitled to consideration for appointment in the order listed:

(1) a conservator, guardian of property, or other like fiduciary appointed or recognized by an appropriate court of any other jurisdiction in which the protected person resides;

(2) an individual or corporation nominated by the protected person 14 or more years of age and of sufficient mental capacity to make an intelligent choice;

(3) the spouse of the protected person;

(4) an adult child of the protected person;

(5) a parent of the protected person, or a person nominated by the will of a deceased parent;

(6) any relative of the protected person who has resided with the protected person for more than 6 months before the filing of the petition; and

(7) a person nominated by one who is caring for or paying benefits to the protected person.

(b) A person in priorities (1), (3), (4), (5), or (6) may designate in writing a substitute to serve instead and thereby transfer the priority to the substitute. With respect to persons having equal priority, the Court shall select the one it deems best qualified to serve. The Court, acting in the best interest of the protected person, may pass over a person having priority and appoint a person having a lower priority or no priority.

§5–410. [Bond.]

The Court may require a conservator to furnish a bond conditioned upon faithful discharge of all duties of the trust according to law, with sureties as it shall specify. Unless otherwise directed, the bond must be in the amount of the aggregate capital value of the property of the estate in the conservator's control, plus one year's estimated income, and minus the value of securities deposited under arrangements requiring an order of the Court for their removal and the value of any land which the fiduciary, by express limitation of power, lacks power to sell or convey without Court authorization. The Court, in lieu of sureties on a bond, may accept other collateral for the performance of the bond, including a pledge of securities or a mortgage of land.

§5–411. [Terms and Requirements of Bonds.]

(a) The following requirements and provisions apply to any bond required under Section 5–410.

(1) Unless otherwise provided by the terms of the approved bond, sureties are jointly and severally liable with the conservator and with each other.

(2) By executing an approved bond of a conservator, the surety consents to the jurisdiction of the Court that issued letters to the primary obligor in any proceeding pertaining to the fiduciary duties of the conservator and naming the surety as a party respondent. Notice of any proceeding must be delivered to the surety or mailed by registered or certified mail to the address listed with the Court at the place where the bond is filed and to the address as then known to the petitioner.

(3) On petition of a successor conservator or any interested person, a proceeding may be initiated against a surety for breach of the obligation of the bond of the conservator.

(4) The bond of the conservator is not void after the first recovery but may be proceeded against from time to time until the whole penalty is exhausted.

(b) No proceeding may be commenced against the surety on any matter as to which an action or proceeding against the primary obligor is barred by adjudication or limitation.

§5–412. [Effect of Acceptance of Appointment.]

By accepting appointment, a conservator submits personally to the jurisdiction of the Court in any proceeding relating to the estate which may be instituted by any interested person. Notice of any proceeding must be delivered to the conservator or mailed by registered or certified mail to the address as listed in the petition for appointment or as thereafter reported to the Court and to the address as then known to the petitioner.

§5–413. [Compensation and Expenses.]

If not otherwise compensated for services rendered, any visitor, attorney, physician, conservator, or special conservator appointed in a protective proceeding and any attorney whose services resulted in a protective order or in an order that was beneficial to a protected person's estate is entitled to reasonable compensation from the estate.

§5–414. [Death, Resignation, or Removal of Conservator.]

The Court may remove a conservator for good cause, upon notice and hearing, or accept the resignation of a conservator. Upon the conservator's death, resignation, or removal, the Court may appoint another conservator. A conservator so appointed succeeds to the title and powers of the predecessor.

§5–415. [Petitions for Orders Subsequent to Appointment.]

(a) Any person interested in the welfare of a person for whom a conservator has been appointed may file a petition in the appointing court for an order:

(1) requiring bond or collateral or additional bond or collateral, or reducing bond;

(2) requiring an accounting for the administration of the trust;

(3) directing distribution;

(4) removing the conservator and appointing a temporary or successor conservator; or

(5) granting other appropriate relief.

(b) A conservator may petition the appointing court for instructions concerning fiduciary responsibility.

(c) Upon notice and hearing, the Court may give appropriate instructions or make any appropriate order.

§5–416. [General Duty of Conservator.]

A conservator, in relation to powers conferred by this Part, or implicit in the title acquired by virtue of the proceeding, shall act as a fiduciary and observe the standards of care applicable to trustees.

§5–417. [Inventory and Records.]

(a) Within 90 days after appointment, each conservator shall prepare and file with the appointing Court a complete inventory of the estate subject to the conservatorship together with an oath or affirmation that the inventory is believed to be complete and accurate as far as information permits. The conservator shall provide a copy thereof to the protected person if practicable and the person has attained the age of 14 years and has sufficient mental capacity to understand the arrangement. A copy also shall be provided to any guardian or parent with whom the protected person resides.

(b) The conservator shall keep suitable records of the administration and exhibit the same on request of any interested person.

§5–418. [Accounts.]

Each conservator shall account to the Court for administration of the trust not less than annually unless the Court directs otherwise, upon resignation or removal and at other times as the Court may direct. On termination of the protected person's minority or disability, a conservator shall account to the Court or to the formerly protected person or the successors of that person. Subject to appeal or vacation within the time permitted, an order after notice and hearing allowing an intermediate account of a conservator adjudicates as to liabilities concerning the matters considered in connection therewith; and an order, following notice and hearing, allowing a final account adjudicates as to all previously unsettled liabilities of the conservator to the protected person or the protected person's successors relating to the conservatorship. In connection with any account, the Court may require a conservator to submit to a physical check of the estate, to be made in any manner the Court specifies.

As amended in 1987.

§5–419. [Conservators; Title By Appointment.]

(a) The appointment of a conservator vests in the conservator title as trustee to all property, or to the part thereof specified in the order, of the protected person, presently held or thereafter acquired, including title to any property theretofore held for the protected person by custodians or attorneys-in-fact. An order specifying that only a part of the property of the protected person vests in the conservator creates a limited conservatorship.

(b) Except as otherwise provided herein, the interest of the protected person in property vested in a conservator by this section is not transferrable or assignable by the protected person. An attempted transfer or assignment by the protected person, though ineffective to affect property rights, may generate a claim for restitution or damages which, subject to presentation and allowance, may be satisfied as provided in Section 5–427.

(c) Neither property vested in a conservator by this section nor the interest of the protected person in that property is subject to levy, garnishment, or similar process other than an order issued in the protective proceeding made as provided in Section 5–427.

§5–420. [Recording of Conservator's Letters.]

(a) Letters of conservatorship are evidence of transfer of all assets, or the part thereof specified in the letters, of a protected person to the conservator. An order terminating a conservatorship is evidence of transfer of all assets subjected to the conservatorship from the conservator to the protected person, or to successors of the person.

(b) Subject to the requirements of general statutes governing the filing or recordation of documents of title to land or other property, letters of conservatorship and orders terminating conservatorships, may be filed or recorded to give record notice of title as between the conservator and the protected person.

§5–421. [Sale, Encumbrance, or Transaction Involving Conflict of Interest; Voidable; Exceptions.]

Any sale or encumbrance to a conservator, the spouse, agent, attorney of a conservator, or any corporation, trust, or other organization in which the conservator has a substantial beneficial interest, or any other transaction involving the estate being administered by the conservator which is affected by a substantial conflict between fiduciary and personal interests is voidable unless the transaction is approved by the Court after notice as directed by the Court.

§5–422. [Persons Dealing With Conservators; Protection.]

(a) A person who in good faith either assists or deals with a conservator for value in any transaction other than those requiring a Court order as provided in Section 5–407 is protected as if the conservator properly exercised the power. The fact that a person knowingly deals with a conservator does not alone require the person to inquire into the existence of a power or the propriety of its exercise, but restrictions on powers of conservators which are endorsed on letters as provided in Section 5–425 are effective as to third persons. A person is not bound to see to the proper application of estate assets paid or delivered to a conservator.

(b) The protection expressed in this section extends to any procedural irregularity or jurisdictional defect occurred in proceedings leading to the issuance of letters and is not a substitution for protection provided by comparable provisions of the law relating to commercial transactions or to simplifying transfers of securities by fiduciaries.

§5–423. [Powers of Conservator in Administration.]

(a) Subject to limitation provided in Section 5–425, a conservator has all of the powers conferred in this section and any additional powers conferred by law on trustees in this State. In addition, a conservator of the estate of an unmarried minor [under the age of 18 years], as to whom no one has parental rights, has the duties and powers of a guardian of a minor described in Section 5–209 until the minor attains [the age of 18 years] or marries, but the parental rights so conferred on a conservator do not preclude appointment of a guardian as provided in Part 2.

(b) A conservator without Court authorization or confirmation, may invest and reinvest funds of the estate as would a trustee.

(c) A conservator, acting reasonably in efforts to accomplish the purpose of the appointment, may act without Court authorization or confirmation, to

(1) collect, hold, and retain assets of the estate including land in another state, until judging that disposition of the assets should be made, and the assets may be retained even though they include an asset in which the conservator is personally interested;

(2) receive additions to the estate;

(3) continue or participate in the operation of any business or other enterprise;

(4) acquire an undivided interest in an estate asset in which the conservator, in any fiduciary capacity, holds an undivided interest;

(5) invest and reinvest estate assets in accordance with subsection (b);

(6) deposit estate funds in a state or federally insured financial institution, including one operated by the conservator;

(7) acquire or dispose of an estate asset, including land in another state, for cash or on credit, at public or private sale, and manage, develop, improve, exchange, partition, change the character of, or abandon an estate asset;

(8) make ordinary or extraordinary repairs or alterations in buildings or other structures; demolish any improvements; and raze existing or erect new party walls or buildings;

(9) subdivide, develop, or dedicate land to public use; make or obtain the vacation of plats and adjust boundaries; adjust differences in valuation or exchange or partition by giving or receiving considerations; and dedicate easements to public use without consideration;

(10) enter for any purpose into a lease as lessor or lessee with or without option to purchase or renew for a term within or extending beyond the term of the conservatorship;

(11) enter into a lease or arrangement for exploration and removal of minerals or other natural resources or enter into a pooling or unitization agreement;

(12) grant an option involving disposition of an estate asset and take an option for the acquisition of any asset;

(13) vote a security, in person or by general or limited proxy;

(14) pay calls, assessments, and any other sums chargeable or accruing against or on account of securities;

(15) sell or exercise stock-subscription or conversion rights;

(16) consent, directly or through a committee or other agent, to the reorganization, consolidation, merger, dissolution, or liquidation of a corporation or other business enterprise;

(17) hold a security in the name of a nominee or in other form without disclosure of the conservatorship so that title to the security may pass by delivery, but the conservator is liable for any act of the nominee in connection with the stock so held;

(18) insure the assets of the estate against damage or loss and the conservator against liability with respect to third persons;

(19) borrow money to be repaid from estate assets or otherwise; advance money for the protection of the estate or the protected person and for all expenses, losses, and liability sustained in the administration of the estate or because of the holding or ownership of any estate assets, for which the conservator has a lien on the estate as against the protected person for advances so made;

(20) pay or contest any claim; settle a claim by or against the estate or the protected person by compromise, arbitration, or otherwise; and release, in whole or in part, any claim belonging to the estate to the extent the claim is uncollectible;

(21) pay taxes, assessments, compensation of the conservator, and other expenses incurred in the collection, care, administration, and protection of the estate;

(22) allocate items of income or expense to either estate income or principal, as provided by law, including creation of reserves out of income for depreciation, obsolescence, or amortization, or for depletion in mineral or timber properties;

(23) pay any sum distributable to a protected person or dependent of the protected person by paying the sum to the distributee or by paying the sum for the use of the distributee to the guardian of the distributee, or, if none, to a relative or other person having custody of the distributee;

(24) employ persons, including attorneys, auditors, investment advisors, or agents, even though they are associated with the conservator, to advise or assist in the performance of administrative duties; act upon their recommendation without independent investigation; and instead of acting personally, employ one or more agents to perform any act of administration, whether or not discretionary;

(25) prosecute or defend actions, claims, or proceedings in any jurisdiction for the protection of estate assets and of the conservator in the performance of fiduciary duties; and

(26) execute and deliver all instruments that will accomplish or facilitate the exercise of the powers vested in the conservator.

§5–424. [Distributive Duties and Powers of Conservator.]

(a) A conservator may expend or distribute income or principal of the estate without Court authorization or confirmation for the support, education, care, or benefit of the protected person and dependents in accordance with the following principles:

(1) The conservator shall consider recommendations relating to the appropriate standard of support, education, and benefit for the protected person or dependent made by a parent or guardian, if any. The conservator may not be surcharged for sums paid to persons or organizations furnishing support, education, or care to the protected person or a dependent pursuant to the recommendations of a parent or guardian of the protected person unless the conservator knows that the parent or guardian derives personal financial benefit therefrom, including relief from any personal duty of support or the recommendations are clearly not in the best interest of the protected person.

(2) The conservator shall expend or distribute sums reasonably necessary for the support, education, care, or benefit of the protected person and dependents with due regard to (i) the size of the estate, the probable duration of the conservatorship, and the likelihood that the protected person, at some future time, may be fully able to be wholly self-sufficient and able to manage business affairs and the estate; (ii) the accustomed standard of living of the protected person and dependents; and (iii) other funds or sources used for the support of the protected person.

(3) The conservator may expend funds of the estate for the support of persons legally dependent on the

protected person and others who are members of the protected person's household who are unable to support themselves, and who are in need of support.

(4) Funds expended under this subsection may be paid by the conservator to any person, including the protected person, to reimburse for expenditures that the conservator might have made, or in advance for services to be rendered to the protected person if it is reasonable to expect the services will be performed and advance payments are customary or reasonably necessary under the circumstances.

(5) A conservator, in discharging the responsibilities conferred by Court order and this Part, shall implement the principles described in Section 5–407(a), to the extent possible.

(b) If the estate is ample to provide for the purposes implicit in the distributions authorized by the preceding subsections, a conservator for a protected person other than a minor has power to make gifts to charity and other objects as the protected person might have been expected to make, in amounts that do not exceed in total for any year 20 percent of the income from the estate.

(c) When a minor who has not been adjudged disabled under Section 5–401(c) attains majority, the conservator, after meeting all claims and expenses of administration, shall pay over and distribute all funds and properties to the formerly protected person as soon as possible.

(d) If satisfied that a protected person's disability, other than minority, has ceased, the conservator, after meeting all claims and expenses of administration, shall pay over and distribute all funds and properties to the formerly protected person as soon as possible.

(e) If a protected person dies, the conservator shall deliver to the Court for safekeeping any will of the deceased protected person which may have come into the conservator's possession, inform the executor or beneficiary named therein of the delivery, and retain the estate for delivery to a duly appointed personal representative of the decedent or other persons entitled thereto. If, 40 days after the death of the protected person, no other person has been appointed personal representative and no application or petition for appointment is before the Court, the conservator may apply to exercise the powers and duties of a personal representative in order to be able to proceed to administer and distribute the decedent's estate. Upon application for an order granting the powers of a personal representative to a conservator, after notice to any person nominated personal representative by any will of which the applicant is aware, the Court may grant the application upon determining that there is no objection and endorse the letters of the conservator to note that the formerly protected person is deceased and that the

conservator has acquired all of the powers and duties of a personal representative. The making and entry of an order under this section has the effect of an order of appointment of a personal representative [as provided in Section 3–308 and Parts 6 through 10 of Article III], but the estate in the name of the conservator, after administration, may be distributed to the decedent's successors without prior re-transfer to the conservator as personal representative.

§5–425. [Enlargement or Limitation of Powers of Conservator.]

Subject to the restrictions in Section 5–407(c), the Court may confer on a conservator at the time of appointment or later, in addition to the powers conferred by Sections 5–423 and 5–424, any power that the Court itself could exercise under Sections 5–407(b)(2) and 5–407(b)(3). The Court, at the time of appointment or later, may limit the powers of a conservator otherwise conferred by Sections 5–423 and 5–424 or previously conferred by the Court and may at any time remove or modify any limitation. If the Court limits any power conferred on the conservator by Section 5–423 or Section 5–424, or specifies, as provided in Section 5–419(a), that title to some but not all assets of the protected person vest in the conservator, the limitation or specification of assets subject to the conservatorship must be endorsed upon the letters of appointment.

§5–426. [Preservation of Estate Plan; Right to Examine.]

In (i) investing the estate, (ii) selecting assets of the estate for distribution under subsections (a) and (b) of Section 5–424, and (iii) utilizing powers of revocation or withdrawal available for the support of the protected person and exercisable by the conservator or the Court, the conservator and the Court shall take into account any estate plan of the protected person known to them, including a will, any revocable trust of which the person is settlor, and any contract, transfer, or joint ownership arrangement originated by the protected person with provisions for payment or transfer of benefits or interests at the person's death to another or others. The conservator may examine the will of the protected person.

§5–427. [Claims Against Protected Person; Enforcement.]

(a) A conservator may pay or secure from the estate claims against the estate or against the protected person arising before or after the conservatorship upon their presentation and allowance in accordance with the priorities stated in subsection (c). A claim may be presented by either of the following methods:

(1) The claimant may deliver or mail to the conservator a written statement of the claim indicating its

basis, the name and mailing address of the claimant, and the amount claimed; or

(2) The claimant may file a written statement of the claim, in the form prescribed by rule, with the clerk of Court and deliver or mail a copy of the statement to the conservator.

(b) A claim is deemed presented on the first to occur of receipt of the written statement of claim by the conservator or the filing of the claim with the Court. A presented claim is allowed if it is not disallowed by written statement mailed by the conservator to the claimant within 60 days after its presentation. The presentation of a claim tolls any statute of limitation relating to the claim until 30 days after its disallowance.

(c) A claimant whose claim has not been paid may petition the [appropriate] Court for determination of the claim at any time before it is barred by the applicable statute of limitation and, upon due proof, procure an order for its allowance, payment, or security from the estate. If a proceeding is pending against a protected person at the time of appointment of a conservator or is initiated against the protected person thereafter, the moving party shall give notice of the proceeding to the conservator if the proceeding could result in creating a claim against the estate.

(d) If it appears that the estate in conservatorship is likely to be exhausted before all existing claims are paid, the conservator shall distribute the estate in money or in kind in payment of claims in the following order:

(1) costs and expenses of administration;

(2) claims of the federal or state government having priority under other laws;

(3) claims incurred by the conservator for care, maintenance, and education, previously provided to the protected person or the protected person's dependents;

(4) claims arising prior to the conservatorship;

(5) all other claims.

(e) No preference may be given in the payment of any claim over any other claim of the same class, and a claim due and payable is not entitled to a preference over claims not due; but if it appears that the assets of the conservatorship are adequate to meet all existing claims, the Court, acting in the best interest of the protected person, may order the conservator to give a mortgage or other security on the conservatorship estate to secure payment at some future date of any or all claims in class 5.

§5–428. [Personal Liability of Conservator.]

(a) Unless otherwise provided in the contract, a conservator is not personally liable on a contract properly entered into in fiduciary capacity in the course of administration of the estate unless the conservator fails to reveal the representative capacity and identify the estate in the contract.

(b) The conservator is personally liable for obligations arising from ownership or control of property of the estate or for torts committed in the course of administration of the estate only if personally at fault.

(c) Claims based on (i) contracts entered into by a conservator in fiduciary capacity, (ii) obligations arising from ownership or control of the estate, or (iii) torts committed in the course of administration of the estate, may be asserted against the estate by proceeding against the conservator in fiduciary capacity, whether or not the conservator is personally liable therefor.

(d) Any question of liability between the estate and the conservator personally may be determined in a proceeding for accounting, surcharge, or indemnification, or other appropriate proceeding or action.

§5–429. [Termination of Proceedings.]

The protected person, conservator, or any other interested person, may petition the Court to terminate the conservatorship. A protected person seeking termination is entitled to the same rights and procedures as in an original proceeding for a protective order. The Court, upon determining after notice and hearing that the minority or disability of the protected person has ceased, shall terminate the conservatorship. Upon termination, title to assets of the estate passes to the formerly protected person or to successors. The order of termination must provide for expenses of administration and direct the conservator to execute appropriate instruments to evidence the transfer.

§5–430. [Payment of Debt and Delivery of Property to Foreign Conservator without Local Proceedings.]

(a) Any person indebted to a protected person or having possession of property or of an instrument evidencing a debt, stock, or chose in action belonging to a protected person may pay or deliver it to a conservator, guardian of the estate, or other like fiduciary appointed by a court of the state of residence of the protected person upon being presented with proof of appointment and an affidavit made by or on behalf of the fiduciary stating:

(1) that no protective proceeding relating to the protected person is pending in this State; and

(2) that the foreign fiduciary is entitled to payment or to receive delivery.

(b) If the person to whom the affidavit is presented is not aware of any protective proceeding pending in this State, payment or delivery in response to the demand and affidavit discharges the debtor or possessor.

§5–431. [Foreign Conservator; Proof of Authority; Bond; Powers.]

If a conservator has not been appointed in this State and no petition in a protective proceeding is pending in this State, a conservator appointed in the state in which the protected person resides may file in a Court of this State in a [county] in which property belonging to the protected person is located, authenticated copies of letters of appointment and of any bond. Thereafter, the domiciliary foreign conservator may exercise as to assets in this State all powers of a conservator appointed in this State and may maintain actions and proceedings in this State subject to any conditions imposed upon nonresident parties generally.

PART 5

DURABLE POWER OF ATTORNEY

Adoption of Uniform Durable Power of Attorney Act

§5–501. [Definition.]

A durable power of attorney is a power of attorney by which a principal designates another his attorney in fact in writing and the writing contains the words "This power of attorney shall not be affected by subsequent disability or incapacity of the principal, or lapse of time," or "This power of attorney shall become effective upon the disability or incapacity of the principal," or similar words showing the intent of the principal that the authority conferred shall be exercisable notwithstanding the principal's subsequent disability or incapacity, and, unless it states a time of termination, notwithstanding the lapse of time since the execution of the instrument. As amended in 1984.

§5–502. [Durable Power of Attorney Not Affected By Lapse of Time, Disability or Incapacity.]

All acts done by an attorney in fact pursuant to a durable power of attorney during any period of disability or incapacity of the principal have the same effect and inure to the benefit of and bind the principal and his successors in interest as if the principal were competent and not disabled. Unless the instrument states a time of termination, the power is exercisable notwithstanding the lapse of time since the execution of the instrument. As amended in 1987.

§5–503. [Relation of Attorney in Fact to Court Appointed Fiduciary.]

(a) If, following execution of a durable power of attorney, a court of the principal's domicile appoints a conservator, guardian of the estate, or other fiduciary charged with the management of all of the principal's property or all of his property except specified exclusions, the attorney in fact is accountable to the fiduciary as well as to the principal. The fiduciary has the same power to revoke or amend the power of attorney that the principal would have had if he were not disabled or incapacitated.

(b) A principal may nominate, by a durable power of attorney, the conservator, guardian of his estate, or guardian of his person for consideration by the court if protective proceedings for the principal's person or estate are thereafter commenced. The court shall make its appointment in accordance with the principal's most recent nomination in a durable power of attorney except for good cause or disqualification.

§5–504. [Power of Attorney Not Revoked Until Notice.]

(a) The death of a principal who has executed a written power of attorney, durable or otherwise, does not revoke or terminate the agency as to the attorney in fact or other person, who, without actual knowledge of the death of the principal, acts in good faith under the power. Any action so taken, unless otherwise invalid or unenforceable, binds successors in interest of the principal.

(b) The disability or incapacity of a principal who has previously executed a written power of attorney that is not a durable power does not revoke or terminate the agency as to the attorney in fact or other person, who, without actual knowledge of the disability or incapacity of the principal, acts in good faith under the power. Any action so taken, unless otherwise invalid or unenforceable, binds the principal and his successors in interest.

§5–505. [Proof of Continuance of Durable and Other Powers of Attorney by Affidavit.]

As to acts undertaken in good faith reliance thereon, an affidavit executed by the attorney in fact under a power of attorney, durable or otherwise, stating that he did not have at the time of exercise of the power actual knowledge of the termination of the power by revocation or of the principal's death, disability, or incapacity is conclusive proof of the nonrevocation or nontermination of the power at that time. If the exercise of the power of attorney requires execution and delivery of any instrument that is recordable, the affidavit when authenticated for record is likewise recordable. This section does not affect any provision in a power of attorney for its termination by expiration of time or occurrence of an event other than express revocation or a change in the principal's capacity.

ARTICLE VI

NONPROBATE TRANSFERS ON DEATH (1989)

PART 1

PROVISIONS RELATING TO EFFECT OF DEATH

Section

6–101. Nonprobate Transfers on Death.

PART 2
MULTIPLE-PERSON ACCOUNTS

SUBPART 1
DEFINITIONS AND GENERAL PROVISIONS

SUBPART 2
OWNERSHIP AS BETWEEN PARTIES AND OTHERS

SUBPART 3
PROTECTION OF FINANCIAL INSTITUTIONS

PART 3
UNIFORM TOD SECURITY REGISTRATION ACT

PART 1
PROVISIONS RELATING TO EFFECT OF DEATH

§6–101. Nonprobate Transfers on Death.

(a) A provision for a nonprobate transfer on death in an insurance policy, contract of employment, bond, mortgage, promissory note, certificated or uncertificated security, account agreement, custodial agreement, deposit agreement, compensation plan, pension plan, individual retirement plan, employee benefit plan, trust, conveyance, deed of gift, marital property agreement, or other written instrument of a similar nature is nontestamentary. This subsection includes a written provision that:

(1) money or other benefits due to, controlled by, or owned by a decedent before death must be paid after the decedent's death to a person whom the decedent designates either in the instrument or in a separate writing, including a will, executed either before or at the same time as the instrument, or later;

(2) money due or to become due under the instrument ceases to be payable in the event of death of the promisee or the promisor before payment or demand; or

(3) any property controlled by or owned by the decedent before death which is the subject of the instrument passes to a person the decedent designates either in the instrument or in a separate writing, including a will, executed either before or at the same time as the instrument, or later.

(b) This section does not limit rights of creditors under other laws of this State.

PART 2
MULTIPLE-PERSON ACCOUNTS

SUBPART 1
DEFINITIONS AND GENERAL PROVISIONS

§6–201. Definitions.

In this part:

(1) "Account" means a contract of deposit between a depositor and a financial institution, and includes a checking account, savings account, certificate of deposit, and share account.

(2) "Agent" means a person authorized to make account transactions for a party.

(3) "Beneficiary" means a person named as one to whom sums on deposit in an account are payable on request after death of all parties or for whom a party is named as trustee.

(4) "Financial institution" means an organization authorized to do business under state or federal laws relating to financial institutions, and includes a bank, trust company, savings bank, building and loan association, savings and loan company or association, and credit union.

(5) "Multiple-party account" means an account payable on request to one or more of two or more parties, whether or not a right of survivorship is mentioned.

(6) "Party" means a person who, by the terms of an account, has a present right, subject to request, to payment from the account other than as a beneficiary or agent.

(7) "Payment" of sums on deposit includes withdrawal, payment to a party or third person pursuant to check or other request, and a pledge of sums on deposit by a party, or a set-off, reduction, or other disposition of all or part of an account pursuant to a pledge.

(8) "POD designation" means the designation of (i) a beneficiary in an account payable on request to one party during the party's lifetime and on the party's death to one or more beneficiaries, or to one or more parties during their lifetimes and on death of all of them to one or more beneficiaries, or (ii) a beneficiary in an account in the name of one or more parties as trustee for one or more beneficiaries if the relationship is established by the terms of the account and there is no subject of the trust other than the sums on deposit in the account, whether or not payment to the beneficiary is mentioned.

(9) "Receive," as it relates to notice to a financial institution, means receipt in the office or branch office of the financial institution in which the account is established, but if the terms of the account require notice at a particular place, in the place required.

(10) "Request" means a request for payment complying with all terms of the account, including special requirements concerning necessary signatures and regulations of the financial institution; but, for purposes of this part, if terms of the account condition payment on advance notice, a request for payment is treated as immediately effective and a notice of intent to withdraw is treated as a request for payment.

(11) "Sums on deposit" means the balance payable on an account, including interest and dividends earned, whether or not included in the current balance, and any deposit life insurance proceeds added to the account by reason of death of a party.

(12) "Terms of the account" includes the deposit agreement and other terms and conditions, including the form, of the contract of deposit.

§6–202. Limitation on Scope of Part.

This part does not apply to (i) an account established for a partnership, joint venture, or other organization for a business purpose, (ii) an account controlled by one or more persons as an agent or trustee for a corporation, unincorporated association, or charitable or civic organization, or (iii) a fiduciary or trust account in which the relationship is established other than by the terms of the account.

§6–203. Types of Account; Existing Accounts.

(a) An account may be for a single party or multiple parties. A multiple-party account may be with or without a right of survivorship between the parties. Subject to Section 6–212(c), either a single-party account or a multiple-party account may have a POD designation, an agency designation, or both.

(b) An account established before, on, or after the effective date of this part, whether in the form prescribed in Section 6–204 or in any other form, is either a single-party account or a multiple-party account, with or without right of survivorship, and with or without a POD designation or an agency designation, within the meaning of this part, and is governed by this part.

§6–204. Forms.

(a) A contract of deposit that contains provisions in substantially the following form establishes the type of account provided, and the account is governed by the provisions of this part applicable to an account of that type:

UNIFORM SINGLE-OR MULTIPLE-PARTY
ACCOUNT FORM
PARTIES [Name One or More Parties]:

——————————————— ———————————————

OWNERSHIP [Select One And Initial]:
————— SINGLE-PARTY ACCOUNT
————— MULTIPLE-PARTY ACCOUNT
Parties own account in proportion to net contributions unless there is clear and convincing evidence of a different intent.
RIGHTS AT DEATH [Select One And Initial]:
————— SINGLE-PARTY ACCOUNT
At death of party, ownership passes as part of party's estate.

————— SINGLE-PARTY ACCOUNT WITH POD (PAY ON DEATH) DESIGNATION
[Name One Or More Beneficiaries]:

——————————————— ———————————————

At death of party, ownership passes to POD beneficiaries and is not part of party's estate.
————— MULTIPLE-PARTY ACCOUNT WITH RIGHT OF SURVIVORSHIP
At death of party, ownership passes to surviving parties.
————— MULTIPLE-PARTY ACCOUNT WITH RIGHT OF SURVIVORSHIP AND POD (PAY ON DEATH) DESIGNATION
[Name One Or More Beneficiaries]:

——————————————— ———————————————

At death of last surviving party, ownership passes to POD beneficiaries and is not part of last surviving party's estate.

————— MULTIPLE-PARTY ACCOUNT WITHOUT RIGHT OF SURVIVORSHIP
At death of party, deceased party's ownership passes as part of deceased party's estate.
AGENCY (POWER OF ATTORNEY) DESIGNATION [Optional] Agents may make account transactions for parties but have no ownership or rights at death unless named as POD beneficiaries.

[To Add Agency Designation To Account, Name One Or More Agents]:

_____   _____

[Select One And Initial]:

_____ AGENCY DESIGNATION SURVIVES DISABILITY OR INCAPACITY OF PARTIES

_____ AGENCY DESIGNATION TERMINATES ON DISABILITY OR INCAPACITY OF PARTIES

(b) A contract of deposit that does not contain provisions in substantially the form provided in subsection (a) is governed by the provisions of this part applicable to the type of account that most nearly conforms to the depositor's intent.

§6–205. Designation of Agent.

(a) By a writing signed by all parties, the parties may designate as agent of all parties on an account a person other than a party.

(b) Unless the terms of an agency designation provide that the authority of the agent terminates on disability or incapacity of a party, the agent's authority survives disability and incapacity. The agent may act for a disabled or incapacitated party until the authority of the agent is terminated.

(c) Death of the sole party or last surviving party terminates the authority of an agent.

§6–206. Applicability of Part.

The provisions of Subpart 2 concerning beneficial ownership as between parties or as between parties and beneficiaries apply only to controversies between those persons and their creditors and other successors, and do not apply to the right of those persons to payment as determined by the terms of the account. Subpart 3 governs the liability and set-off rights of financial institutions that make payments pursuant to it.

SUBPART 2
OWNERSHIP AS BETWEEN PARTIES AND OTHERS

§6–211. Ownership During Lifetime.

(a) In this section, "net contribution" of a party means the sum of all deposits to an account made by or for the party, less all payments from the account made to or for the party which have not been paid to or applied to the use of another party and a proportionate share of any charges deducted from the account, plus a proportionate share of any interest or dividends earned, whether or not included in the current balance. The term includes deposit life insurance proceeds added to the account by reason of death of the party whose net contribution is in question.

(b) During the lifetime of all parties, an account belongs to the parties in proportion to the net contribution of each to the sums on deposit, unless there is clear and convincing evidence of a different intent. As between

parties married to each other, in the absence of proof otherwise, the net contribution of each is presumed to be an equal amount.

(c) A beneficiary in an account having a POD designation has no right to sums on deposit during the lifetime of any party.

(d) An agent in an account with an agency designation has no beneficial right to sums on deposit.

§6–212. Rights at Death.

(a) Except as otherwise provided in this part, on death of a party sums on deposit in a multiple-party account belong to the surviving party or parties. If two or more parties survive and one is the surviving spouse of the decedent, the amount to which the decedent, immediately before death, was beneficially entitled under Section 6–211 belongs to the surviving spouse. If two or more parties survive and none is the surviving spouse of the decedent, the amount to which the decedent, immediately before death, was beneficially entitled under Section 6–211 belongs to the surviving parties in equal shares, and augments the proportion to which each survivor, immediately before the decedent's death, was beneficially entitled under Section 6–211, and the right of survivorship continues between the surviving parties."

(b) In an account with a POD designation:

(1) On death of one of two or more parties, the rights in sums on deposit are governed by subsection (a).

(2) On death of the sole party or the last survivor of two or more parties, sums on deposit belong to the surviving beneficiary or beneficiaries. If two or more beneficiaries survive, sums on deposit belong to them in equal and undivided shares, and there is no right of survivorship in the event of death of a beneficiary thereafter. If no beneficiary survives, sums on deposit belong to the estate of the last surviving party.

(c) Sums on deposit in a single-party account without a POD designation, or in a multiple-party account that, by the terms of the account, is without right of survivorship, are not affected by death of a party, but the amount to which the decedent, immediately before death, was beneficially entitled under Section 6–211 is transferred as part of the decedent's estate. A POD designation in a multiple-party account without right of survivorship is ineffective. For purposes of this section, designation of an account as a tenancy in common establishes that the account is without right of survivorship.

(d) The ownership right of a surviving party or beneficiary, or of the decedent's estate, in sums on deposit is subject to requests for payment made by a party before the party's death, whether paid by the financial institution before or after death, or unpaid. The surviving party or beneficiary, or the decedent's estate, is liable to the payee of an unpaid request for payment. The liability is limited to a proportionate share of the amount transferred under this section, to the extent necessary to discharge the request for payment.

As amended in 1991.

§6–213. Alteration of Rights.

(a) Rights at death under Section 6–212 are determined by the type of account at the death of a party. The type of account may be altered by written notice given by a party to the financial institution to change the type of account or to stop or vary payment under the terms of the account. The notice must be signed by a party and received by the financial institution during the party's lifetime.

(b) A right of survivorship arising from the express terms of the account, Section 6–212, or a POD designation, may not be altered by will.

§6–214. Accounts   and   Transfers   Nontestamentary.

Except as provided in Part 2 of Article II (elective share of surviving spouse) or as a consequence of, and to the extent directed by, Section 6–215, a transfer resulting from the application of Section 6–212 is effective by reason of the terms of the account involved and this part and is not testamentary or subject to Articles I through IV (estate administration).

§6–215. Rights of Creditors and Others.

(a) If other assets of the estate are insufficient, a transfer resulting from a right of survivorship or POD designation under this part is not effective against the estate of a deceased party to the extent needed to pay claims against the estate and statutory allowances to the surviving spouse and children.

(b) A surviving party or beneficiary who receives payment from an account after death of a party is liable to account to the personal representative of the decedent for a proportionate share of the amount received to which the decedent, immediately before death, was beneficially entitled under Section 6–211, to the extent necessary to discharge the claims and allowances described in subsection (a) remaining unpaid after application of the decedent's estate. A proceeding to assert the liability may not be commenced unless the personal representative has received a written demand by the surviving spouse, a creditor, a child, or a person acting for a child of the decedent. The proceeding must be commenced within one year after death of the decedent.

(c) A surviving party or beneficiary against whom a proceeding to account is brought may join as a party to the proceeding a surviving party or beneficiary of any other account of the decedent.

(d) Sums recovered by the personal representative must be administered as part of the decedent's estate. This section does not affect the protection from claims of the personal representative or estate of a deceased party provided in Section 6–226 for a financial institution that makes payment in accordance with the terms of the account.

As amended in 1991.

§6–216. Community Property and Tenancy by the Entireties.

(a) A deposit of community property in an account does not alter the community character of the property or community rights in the property, but a right of survivorship between parties married to each other arising from the express terms of the account or Section 6–212 may not be altered by will.

(b) This part does not affect the law governing tenancy by the entireties.

SUBPART 3
PROTECTION OF FINANCIAL INSTITUTIONS

§6–221. Authority of Financial Institution.

A financial institution may enter into a contract of deposit for a multiple-party account to the same extent it may enter into a contract of deposit for a single-party account, and may provide for a POD designation and an agency designation in either a single-party account or a multiple-party account. A financial institution need not inquire as to the source of a deposit to an account or as to the proposed application of a payment from an account.

§6–222. Payment on Multiple-Party Account.

A financial institution, on request, may pay sums on deposit in a multiple-party account to:

(1) one or more of the parties, whether or not another party is disabled, incapacitated, or deceased when payment is requested and whether or not the party making the request survives another party; or

(2) the personal representative, if any, or, if there is none, the heirs or devisees of a deceased party if proof of death is presented to the financial institution showing that the deceased party was the survivor of all other persons named on the account either as a party or beneficiary, unless the account is without right of survivorship under Section 6–212.

§6–223. Payment on POD Designation.

A financial institution, on request, may pay sums on deposit in an account with a POD designation to:

(1) one or more of the parties, whether or not another party is disabled, incapacitated, or deceased when the payment is requested and whether or not a party survives another party;

(2) the beneficiary or beneficiaries, if proof of death is presented to the financial institution showing that the beneficiary or beneficiaries survived all persons named as parties; or

(3) the personal representative, if any, or, if there is none, the heirs or devisees of a deceased party, if proof of death is presented to the financial institution showing that the deceased party was the survivor of all other persons named on the account either as a party or beneficiary.

§6–224. Payment to Designated Agent.

A financial institution, on request of an agent under an agency designation for an account, may pay to the agent sums on deposit in the account, whether or not a party is disabled, incapacitated, or deceased when the request is made or received, and whether or not the authority of the agent terminates on the disability or incapacity of a party.

§6–225. Payment to Minor.

If a financial institution is required or permitted to make payment pursuant to this part to a minor designated as a beneficiary, payment may be made pursuant to the Uniform Transfers to Minors Act.

§6–226. Discharge.

(a) Payment made pursuant to this part in accordance with the type of account discharges the financial institution from all claims for amounts so paid, whether or not the payment is consistent with the beneficial ownership of the account as between parties, beneficiaries, or their successors. Payment may be made whether or not a party, beneficiary, or agent is disabled, incapacitated, or deceased when payment is requested, received, or made.
(b) Protection under this section does not extend to payments made after a financial institution has received written notice from a party, or from the personal representative, surviving spouse, or heir or devisee of a deceased party, to the effect that payments in accordance with the terms of the account, including one having an agency designation, should not be permitted, and the financial institution has had a reasonable opportunity to act on it when the payment is made. Unless the notice is withdrawn by the person giving it, the successor of any deceased party must concur in a request for payment if the financial institution is to be protected under this section. Unless a financial institution has been served with process in an action or proceeding, no other notice or other information shown to have been available to the financial institution affects its right to protection under this section.
(c) A financial institution that receives written notice pursuant to this section or otherwise has reason to believe that a dispute exists as to the rights of the parties may refuse, without liability, to make payments in accordance with the terms of the account.
(d) Protection of a financial institution under this section does not affect the rights of parties in disputes between themselves or their successors concerning the beneficial ownership of sums on deposit in accounts or payments made from accounts.

§6–227. Set-Off.

Without qualifying any other statutory right to set-off or lien and subject to any contractual provision, if a party is indebted to a financial institution, the financial institution has a right to set-off against the account. The amount of the account subject to set-off is the proportion to which the party is, or immediately before death was, beneficially entitled under Section 6–211 or, in the absence of proof of that proportion, an equal share with all parties.

PART 3
UNIFORM TOD SECURITY REGISTRATION ACT

§6–301. Definitions.

In this part:
(1) "Beneficiary form" means a registration of a security which indicates the present owner of the security and the intention of the owner regarding the person who will become the owner of the security upon the death of the owner.
(2) "Register," including its derivatives, means to issue a certificate showing the ownership of a certificated security or, in the case of an uncertificated security, to initiate or transfer an account showing ownership of securities.
(3) "Registering entity" means a person who originates or transfers a security title by registration, and includes a broker maintaining security accounts for customers and a transfer agent or other person acting for or as an issuer of securities.
(4) "Security" means a share, participation, or other interest in property, in a business, or in an obligation of an enterprise or other issuer, and includes a certificated security, an uncertificated security, and a security account.
(5) "Security account" means (i) a reinvestment account associated with a security, a securities account with a broker, a cash balance in a brokerage account, cash, interest, earnings, or dividends earned or declared on a security in an account, a reinvestment account, or a brokerage account, whether or not credited to the account before the owner's death, or (ii) a cash balance or other property held for or due to the owner of a security as a replacement for or product of an account security, whether or not credited to the account before the owner's death.

§6–302. Registration in Beneficiary Form; Sole or Joint Tenancy Ownership.

Only individuals whose registration of a security shows sole ownership by one individual or multiple ownership by two or more with right of survivorship, rather than as tenants in common, may obtain registration in beneficiary form. Multiple owners of a security registered in beneficiary form hold as joint tenants with right of survivorship, as tenants by the entireties, or as owners of community property held in survivorship form, and not as tenants in common.

§6–303. Registration in Beneficiary Form; Applicable Law.

A security may be registered in beneficiary form if the form is authorized by this or a similar statute of the state of organization of the issuer or registering entity, the location of the registering entity's principal office, the office of its transfer agent or its office making the registration, or by this or a similar statute of the law of the state listed as the owner's address at the time of registration. A registration governed by the law of a jurisdiction in which this or similar legislation is not in force or was not in force when a registration in beneficiary form was made is nevertheless presumed to be valid and authorized as a matter of contract law.

§6–304. Origination of Registration in Beneficiary Form.

A security, whether evidenced by certificate or account, is registered in beneficiary form when the registration includes a designation of a beneficiary to take the ownership at the death of the owner or the deaths of all multiple owners.

§6–305. Form of Registration in Beneficiary Form.

Registration in beneficiary form may be shown by the words "transfer on death" or the abbreviation "TOD," or by the words "pay on death" or the abbreviation "POD," after the name of the registered owner and before the name of a beneficiary.

§6–306. Effect of Registration in Beneficiary Form.

The designation of a TOD beneficiary on a registration in beneficiary form has no effect on ownership until the owner's death. A registration of a security in beneficiary form may be canceled or changed at any time by the sole owner or all then surviving owners without the consent of the beneficiary.

§6–307. Ownership on Death of Owner.

On death of a sole owner or the last to die of all multiple owners, ownership of securities registered in beneficiary form passes to the beneficiary or beneficiaries who survive all owners. On proof of death of all owners and compliance with any applicable requirements of the registering entity, a security registered in beneficiary form may be reregistered in the name of the beneficiary or beneficiaries who survive the death of all owners. Until division of the security after the death of all owners, multiple beneficiaries surviving the death of all owners

hold their interests as tenants in common. If no beneficiary survives the death of all owners, the security belongs to the estate of the deceased sole owner or the estate of the last to die of all multiple owners.

§6–308. Protection of Registering Entity.

(a) A registering entity is not required to offer or to accept a request for security registration in beneficiary form. If a registration in beneficiary form is offered by a registering entity, the owner requesting registration in beneficiary form assents to the protections given to the registering entity by this part.

(b) By accepting a request for registration of a security in beneficiary form, the registering entity agrees that the registration will be implemented on death of the deceased owner as provided in this part.

(c) A registering entity is discharged from all claims to a security by the estate, creditors, heirs, or devisees of a deceased owner if it registers a transfer of the security in accordance with Section 6–307 and does so in good faith reliance (i) on the registration, (ii) on this part, and (iii) on information provided to it by affidavit of the personal representative of the deceased owner, or by the surviving beneficiary or by the surviving beneficiary's representatives, or other information available to the registering entity. The protections of this part do not extend to a reregistration or payment made after a registering entity has received written notice from any claimant to any interest in the security objecting to implementation of a registration in beneficiary form. No other notice or other information available to the registering entity affects its right to protection under this part.

(d) The protection provided by this part to the registering entity of a security does not affect the rights of beneficiaries in disputes between themselves and other claimants to ownership of the security transferred or its value or proceeds.

§6–309. Nontestamentary Transfer on Death.

(a) A transfer on death resulting from a registration in beneficiary form is effective by reason of the contract regarding the registration between the owner and the registering entity and this part and is not testamentary.

(b) This part does not limit the rights of creditors of security owners against beneficiaries and other transferees under other laws of this State.

§6–310. Terms, Conditions, and Forms for Registration.

(a) A registering entity offering to accept registrations in beneficiary form may establish the terms and conditions under which it will receive requests (i) for registrations in beneficiary form, and (ii) for implementation of registrations in beneficiary form, including requests for cancellation of previously registered TOD beneficiary designations and requests for reregistration to effect a change of beneficiary. The terms and conditions so established may provide for proving death, avoiding or resolving any problems concerning fractional shares, designating primary and contingent beneficiaries, and substituting a named beneficiary's descendants to take in the place of the named beneficiary in the event of the beneficiary's death. Substitution may be indicated by appending to the name of the primary beneficiary the letters LDPS, standing for "lineal descendants per stripes." This designation substitutes a deceased beneficiary's descendants who survive the owner for a beneficiary who fails to so survive, the descendants to be identified and to share in accordance with the law of the beneficiary's domicile at the owner's death governing inheritance by descendants of an intestate. Other forms of identifying beneficiaries who are to take on one or more contingencies, and rules for providing proofs and assurances needed to satisfy reasonable concerns by registering entities regarding conditions and identities relevant to accurate implementation of registrations in beneficiary form, may be contained in a registering entity's terms and conditions.

(b) The following are illustrations of registrations in beneficiary form which a registering entity may authorize:

(1) Sole owner-sole beneficiary: John S Brown TOD (or POD) John S Brown Jr.

(2) Multiple owners-sole beneficiary: John S Brown Mary B Brown JT TEN TOD John S Brown Jr.

(3) Multiple owners-primary and secondary (substituted) beneficiaries: John S Brown Mary B Brown JT TEN TOD John S Brown Jr SUB BENE Peter Q Brown or John S Brown Mary B Brown JT TEN TOD John S Brown Jr LDPS.

[§6–311. Application of Part.

This part applies to registrations of securities in beneficiary form made before or after [effective date], by decedents dying on or after [effective date].]

ARTICLE VII
TRUST ADMINISTRATION

PART 1
TRUST REGISTRATION

Section

PART 2
JURISDICTION OF COURT CONCERNING TRUSTS

PART 3
DUTIES AND LIABILITIES OF TRUSTEES

PART 4
POWERS OF TRUSTEES

PART 1
TRUST REGISTRATION

§7–101. [Duty to Register Trusts.]

The trustee of a trust having its principal place of administration in this state shall register the trust in the Court of this state at the principal place of administration. Unless otherwise designated in the trust instrument, the principal place of administration of a trust is the trustee's usual place of business where the records pertaining to the trust are kept, or at the trustee's residence if he has no such place of business. In the case of co-trustees, the principal place of administration, if not otherwise designated in the trust instrument, is (1) the usual place of business of the corporate trustee if there is but one corporate co-trustee, or (2) the usual place of business or residence of the individual trustee who is a professional fiduciary if there is but one such person and no corporate co-trustee, and otherwise (3) the usual place of business or residence of any of the co-trustees as agreed upon by them. The duty to register under this Part does not apply to the trustee of a trust if registration would be inconsistent with the retained jurisdiction of a foreign court from which the trustee cannot obtain release.

§7–102. [Registration Procedures.]

Registration shall be accomplished by filing a statement indicating the name and address of the trustee in which it acknowledges the trusteeship. The statement shall indicate whether the trust has been registered elsewhere. The statement shall identify the trust: (1) in the case of a testamentary trust, by the name of the testator and the date and place of domiciliary probate; (2) in the case of a written inter vivos trust, by the name of each settlor and the original trustee and the date of the trust instrument; or (3) in the case of an oral trust, by information identifying the settlor or other source of funds and describing the time and manner of the trust's creation and the terms of the trust, including the subject matter, beneficiaries and time of performance. If a trust has been registered elsewhere, registration in this state is ineffective until the earlier registration is released by order of the Court where prior registration occurred, or an instrument executed by the trustee and all beneficiaries, filed with the registration in this state.

§7–103. [Effect of Registration.]

(a) By registering a trust, or accepting the trusteeship of a registered trust, the trustee submits personally to the jurisdiction of the Court in any proceeding under Section 7–201 of this Code relating to the trust that may be initiated by any interested person while the trust remains registered. Notice of any proceeding shall be delivered to the trustee, or mailed to him by ordinary first class mail at his address as listed in the registration or as thereafter reported to the Court and to his address as then known to the petitioner.

(b) To the extent of their interests in the trust, all beneficiaries of a trust properly registered in this state are subject to the jurisdiction of the court of registration for the purposes of proceedings under Section 7–201, provided notice is given pursuant to Section 1–401.

§7–104. [Effect of Failure to Register.]

A trustee who fails to register a trust in a proper place as required by this Part, for purposes of any proceedings initiated by a beneficiary of the trust prior to registration, is subject to the personal jurisdiction of any Court in which the trust could have been registered. In addition, any trustee who, within 30 days after receipt of a written demand by a settlor or beneficiary of the trust, fails to register a trust as required by this Part is subject to removal and denial of compensation or to surcharge as the Court may direct. A provision in the terms of the trust purporting to excuse the trustee from the duty to register, or directing that the trust or trustee shall not be subject to the jurisdiction of the Court, is ineffective.

§7–105. [Registration, Qualification of Foreign Trustee.]

A foreign corporate trustee is required to qualify as a foreign corporation doing business in this state if it maintains the principal place of administration of any trust within the state. A foreign co-trustee is not required to qualify in this state solely because its co-trustee maintains the principal place of administration in this state. Unless otherwise doing business in this state, local qualification by a foreign trustee, corporate or individual, is not required in order for the trustee to receive distribution from a local estate or to hold, invest in, manage or acquire property located in this state, or maintain litigation. Nothing in this section affects a determination of what other acts require qualification as doing business in this state.

PART 2
JURISDICTION OF COURT CONCERNING TRUSTS

§7–201. [Court; Exclusive Jurisdiction of Trusts.]

(a) The Court has exclusive jurisdiction of proceedings initiated by interested parties concerning the internal affairs of trusts. Proceedings which may be maintained under this section are those concerning the administration and distribution of trusts, the declaration of rights and the determination of other matters involving trustees and beneficiaries of trusts. These include, but are not limited to, proceedings to:

(1) appoint or remove a trustee;

(2) review trustees' fees and to review and settle interim or final accounts;

(3) ascertain beneficiaries, determine any question arising in the administration or distribution of any trust including questions of construction of trust instruments, to instruct trustees, and determine the existence or nonexistence of any immunity, power, privilege, duty or right; and

(4) release registration of a trust.

(b) Neither registration of a trust nor a proceeding under this section result in continuing supervisory proceedings. The management and distribution of a trust estate, submission of accounts and reports to beneficiaries, payment of trustee's fees and other obligations of a trust, acceptance and change of trusteeship, and other aspects of the administration of a trust shall proceed expeditiously consistent with the terms of the trust, free of judicial intervention and without order, approval or other action of any court, subject to the jurisdiction of the Court as invoked by interested parties or as otherwise exercised as provided by law.

§7–202. [Trust Proceedings; Venue.]

Venue for proceedings under Section 7–201 involving registered trusts is in the place of registration. Venue for proceedings under Section 7–201 involving trusts not registered in this state is in any place where the trust properly could have been registered, and otherwise by the rules of civil procedure.

§7–203. [Trust Proceedings; Dismissal of Matters Relating to Foreign Trusts.]

The Court will not, over the objection of a party, entertain proceedings under Section 7–201 involving a trust registered or having its principal place of administration in another state, unless (1) when all appropriate parties could not be bound by litigation in the courts of the state where the trust is registered or has its principal place of administration or (2) when the interests of justice otherwise would seriously be impaired. The Court may condition a stay or dismissal of a proceeding under this section on the consent of any party to jurisdiction of the state in which the trust is registered or has its principal place of business, or the Court may grant a continuance or enter any other appropriate order.

§7–204. [Court; Concurrent Jurisdiction of Litigation Involving Trusts and Third Parties.]

The Court of the place in which the trust is registered has concurrent jurisdiction with other courts of this state of actions and proceedings to determine the existence or nonexistence of trusts created other than by will, of actions by or against creditors or debtors of trusts, and of other actions and proceedings involving trustees and third parties. Venue is determined by the rules generally applicable to civil actions.

§7–205. [Proceedings for Review of Employment of Agents and Review of Compensation of Trustee and Employees of Trust.]

On petition of an interested person, after notice to all interested persons, the Court may review the propriety of employment of any person by a trustee including any attorney, auditor, investment advisor or other specialized agent or assistant, and the reasonableness of the compensation of any person so employed, and the reasonableness of the compensation determined by the trustee for his own services. Any person who has received excessive compensation from a trust may be ordered to make appropriate refunds.

§7–206. [Trust Proceedings; Initiation by Notice; Necessary Parties.]

Proceedings under Section 7–201 are initiated by filing a petition in the Court and giving notice pursuant to Section 1–401 to interested parties. The Court may order notification of additional persons. A decree is valid as to all who are given notice of the proceeding though fewer than all interested parties are notified.

PART 3
DUTIES AND LIABILITIES OF TRUSTEES

§7–301. [General Duties Not Limited.]

Except as specifically provided, the general duty of the trustee to administer a trust expeditiously for the benefit of the beneficiaries is not altered by this Code.

§7–302. [Trustee's Standard of Care and Performance.]

Except as otherwise provided by the terms of the trust, the trustee shall observe the standards in dealing with the trust assets that would be observed by a prudent man dealing with the property of another, and if the trustee has special skills or is named trustee on the basis of representations of special skills or expertise, he is under a duty to use those skills.

§7–303. [Duty to Inform and Account to Beneficiaries.]

The trustee shall keep the beneficiaries of the trust reasonably informed of the trust and its administration. In addition:

(a) Within 30 days after his acceptance of the trust, the trustee shall inform in writing the current beneficiaries and if possible, one or more persons who under Section 1–403 may represent beneficiaries with future interests, of the Court in which the trust is registered and of his name and address.

(b) Upon reasonable request, the trustee shall provide the beneficiary with a copy of the terms of the trust which describe or affect his interest and with relevant information about the assets of the trust and the particulars relating to the administration.

(c) Upon reasonable request, a beneficiary is entitled to a statement of the accounts of the trust annually and on termination of the trust or change of the trustee.

§7–304. [Duty to Provide Bond.]

A trustee need not provide bond to secure performance of his duties unless required by the terms of the trust, reasonably requested by a beneficiary or found by the Court to be necessary to protect the interests of the beneficiaries who are not able to protect themselves and whose interests otherwise are not adequately represented. On petition of the trustee or other interested person the Court may excuse a requirement of bond, reduce the amount of the bond, release the surety, or permit the substitution of another bond with the same or different sureties. If bond is required, it shall be filed in the Court of registration or other appropriate Court in amounts and with sureties and liabilities as provided in Sections 3–604 and 3–606 relating to bonds of personal representatives.

§7–305. [Trustee's Duties; Appropriate Place of Administration; Deviation.]

A trustee is under a continuing duty to administer the trust at a place appropriate to the purposes of the trust and to its sound, efficient management. If the principal place of administration becomes inappropriate for any reason, the Court may enter any order furthering efficient administration and the interests of beneficiaries, including, if appropriate, release of registration, removal of the trustee and appointment of a trustee in another state. Trust provisions relating to the place of administration and to changes in the place of administration or of trustee control unless compliance would be contrary to efficient administration or the purposes of the trust. Views of adult beneficiaries shall be given weight in determining the suitability of the trustee and the place of administration.

§7–306. [Personal Liability of Trustee to Third Parties.]

(a) Unless otherwise provided in the contract, a trustee is not personally liable on contracts properly entered into in his fiduciary capacity in the course of administration of the trust estate unless he fails to reveal his representative capacity and identify the trust estate in the contract.

(b) A trustee is personally liable for obligations arising from ownership or control of property of the trust estate or for torts committed in the course of administration of the trust estate only if he is personally at fault.

(c) Claims based on contracts entered into by a trustee in his fiduciary capacity, on obligations arising from ownership or control of the trust estate, or on torts committed in the course of trust administration may be asserted against the trust estate by proceeding against the trustee in his fiduciary capacity, whether or not the trustee is personally liable therefor.

(d) The question of liability as between the trust estate and the trustee individually may be determined in a proceeding for accounting, surcharge or indemnification or other appropriate proceeding.

§7–307. [Limitations on Proceedings Against Trustees After Final Account.]

Unless previously barred by adjudication, consent or limitation, any claim against a trustee for breach of trust is barred as to any beneficiary who has received a final account or other statement fully disclosing the matter and showing termination of the trust relationship between the trustee and the beneficiary unless a proceeding to assert the claim is commenced within [6 months] after receipt of the final account or statement. In any event and notwithstanding lack of full disclosure a trustee who has issued a final account or statement received by the beneficiary and has informed the beneficiary of the location and availability of records for his examination is protected after 3 years. A beneficiary is deemed to have received a final account or statement if, being an adult, it is received by him personally or if, being a minor or disabled person, it is received by his representative as described in Section 1–403(1) and (2).

PART 4
POWERS OF TRUSTEES

ARTICLE VIII
EFFECTIVE DATE AND REPEALER

§8–101. [Time of Taking Effect; Provisions for Transition.]

(a) This Code takes effect on January 1, 19 _____ .

(b) Except as provided elsewhere in this Code, on the effective date of this Code:

(1) the Code applies to governing instruments executed by decedents dying thereafter;

(2) the Code applies to any proceedings in Court then pending or thereafter commenced regardless of the time of the death of decedent except to the extent that in the opinion of the Court the former procedure should be made applicable in a particular case in the interest of justice or because of infeasibility of application of the procedure of this Code;

(3) every personal representative including a person administering an estate of a minor or incompetent holding an appointment on that date, continues to hold the appointment but has only the powers conferred by this Code and is subject to the duties imposed with respect to any act occurring or done thereafter;

(4) an act done before the effective date in any proceeding and any accrued right is not impaired by this Code. If a right is acquired, extinguished or barred upon the expiration of a prescribed period of time which has commenced to run by the provisions of any statute before the effective date, the provisions shall remain in force with respect to that right;

(5) any rule of construction or presumption provided in this Code applies to governing instruments executed before the effective date unless there is a clear indication of a contrary intent;

(6) a person holding office as judge of the Court on the effective date of this Act may continue the office of judge of this Court and may be selected for additional terms after the effective date of this Act even though he does not meet the qualifications of a judge as provided in Article I.

As amended in 1993.

GLOSSARY

A-B trust (also called bypass trust, credit shelter trust, exemption equivalent trust, or residuary trust) An estate planning device whereby a portion of a deceased spouse's estate passes to a trust rather than to the surviving spouse, thereby reducing the likelihood of the surviving spouse's estate being taxed. Typically, the surviving spouse is given a life estate in the trust.

abate To diminish, decrease, or reduce.

abatement The process of determining the order in which gifts made by the testator in a will shall be applied to the payment of the decedent-testator's debts, taxes, and expenses, which may cause the reduction or elimination of the gifts.

abode A person's principal place of residence or home.

accelerated remainder In the event the income or the preceding beneficiary fails, the property passes to the remainderman.

acceleration Hastening the enjoyment of an estate that was otherwise postponed to a later period.

accounting A formal written report of all items of property, income produced by the property, and expenses, prepared by a personal representative, trustee, or guardian and given to heirs, beneficiaries, and the probate court.

accrue Either a debt that has become due or a right a person becomes entitled to receive, but the debt has not yet been paid or the right received.

accumulated income The part of the income from a trust that is kept in the account.

active trust A trust that imposes on the trustee the duty of being active in the execution of the trust and performing management and administrative duties.

adeem To take away; to revoke a gift made in a will.

ademption The intentional act of the testator to revoke, recall, or cancel a gift made through the will.

adjusted gross estate The value of the decedent's estate after administration expenses, funeral expenses, creditors' claims, and casualty losses have been subtracted from the value of the gross estate. The value of the adjusted gross estate is used for computing the federal estate tax.

adjusted taxable gifts All taxable lifetime gifts made after December 31, 1976.

ad *litem* Meaning "for the suit"; "for the purposes of a lawsuit" (see **Guardian *ad litem***).

administration expenses The costs of managing the decedent's estate, e.g., filing fees, attorney's fees, and the commission of the personal representative.

administration of an estate The management of an estate by a personal representative that includes collecting estate assets, valuing them, paying decedent's taxes and debts, and distributing the remainder to beneficiaries and devisees.

administrator A male personal representative appointed by the probate court to administer the decedent's estate when there is no will. Also, an administrator can be a corporation, e.g., a bank.

administrator(-trix) *cum testamento annexo* Also called administrator C.T.A. (administrator with the will annexed). The personal representative appointed by the court in two situations: where the maker of the will does not name an executor or executrix, or where the maker of the will does name an executor or executrix but the latter cannot serve due to a deficiency in qualification or competency.

administrator(-trix) *de bonis non* Also called administrator D.B.N. (administrator of goods not administered). A court-appointed personal representative who replaces a previous administrator who has begun but failed to complete the administration of an intestate estate for any reason, including death.

administratix A female personal representative appointed by the probate court to administer the decedent's estate when there is no will.

adoption A formal legal process of establishing a relationship of parent and child between persons who are not so related by nature.

adoptive parent A person who legally adopts another individual, usually a child.

ad valorem taxes Taxes assessed in proportion to the value of the property.

advance directives (also called medical directives) Written statements in which individuals specify the kind of medical treatment they desire if they become incapacitated or terminally ill.

advancement Money or property given by a parent while living to a child in anticipation of the share that child will inherit from the parent's estate and in advance of the proper time for receipt of such property. It is intended to be deducted from the share of the parent's estate that the child receives.

affiant The person who makes, subscribes, and files an affidavit.

affidavit A sworn written statement of facts affirmed before a notary public.

affinity Relationship by marriage.

after-acquired property All property obtained by the maker of a will after the date of the formal execution of a will.

after-born child A child born after the parent's will has been executed.

agency An account in which the title to the property constituting the agency remains in the owner of the property and does not pass to the trust institution, and in which the agent is charged with certain duties regarding the property.

agent A person authorized by another person—called the principal—to act in place of the principal. The distinguishing characteristics of an agent are (1) that he or she acts on behalf of and subject to the control of his or her principal, (2) that he or she does not have title to the property of his or her principal, and (3) that he or she owes the duty of obedience to his or her principal's orders.

alienability Transferability.

alienation In the law of real property, alienation is the conveyance or transfer of property from one person to another.

allocation The crediting of a receipt or the charging of a disbursement in its entirety to one account, as to the principal account or the income account.

allowance The sum awarded by the court to a fiduciary as compensation for its services.

alternate valuation date For federal estate tax purposes, the personal representative may elect to value all the assets of a decedent at a date six months after the decedent's death rather than at the date of death.

ambulatory Revocable or subject to change.

ambulatory will A will subject to being revoked or changed, the phrase merely denoting the power a testator or testatrix possesses of altering the will during his or her lifetime.

amendment A change in a legal document by an addition, deletion, or correction.

American Bar Association (ABA) A national association of attorneys in the United States that sets the ethical standards and guidelines that apply to the legal profession.

amortization The operation of paying off an indebtedness by installments or by a sinking fund.

anatomical gift A donation of all or a part of a body after death.

ancestor Also ascendant. The person from whom one is descended. Also, the claimant to an intestate's share related to the decedent in an ascending lineal bloodline.

ancillary administration Additional administration used to dispose of and distribute that portion of the decedent's estate located in a state other than the decedent's domicile state.

ancillary administrator(-trix) The personal representative appointed by the court to distribute that part of a decedent's estate located in a jurisdiction (state) other than the decedent's domicile state.

annual exclusion The purpose of the annual exclusion is to eliminate the administrative inconvenience of taxing numerous small gifts by excluding the gifts to each donee during the calendar year below a certain amount, e.g., $10,000.

annuitant One who is entitled to an annuity, a beneficiary.

annuity A fixed sum to be paid at regular intervals, such as annually, for a certain or indefinite period, as for a stated number of years or for life.

antenuptial (prenuptial) contract A contract made by a man and woman before their marriage or in contemplation of that marriage whereby the property rights of either or both the prospective husband or wife are determined.

antilapse statutes Statutes that prevent or minimize the effects of a lapse in a will.

appointee The person who is to receive the benefit of a power of appointment.

apportionment A division, partition, or distribution of property into proportionate parts.

apportionment clause Clause in a will that allocates the tax burden among the residuary estate and the beneficiaries of the will.

appraisal (appraisement) A monetary valuation placed on property by a recognized expert.

appreciation Increase in value of an asset by the mere passing of time (normally due to market conditions).

approved list A list of authorized investments that a fiduciary may acquire. It may or may not be a statutory list.

ascendant Also ancestor. Claimant to an intestate's share related to the decedent in an ascending lineal bloodline.

assets All property of the deceased, real or personal, tangible or intangible, legal or equitable, that can be made available for or appropriated to payment of debts.

assignee The person to whom an assignment (transfer) is made.

assignment A transfer from one person to another of the whole of any property, real or personal, or of any estate or right therein.

assignor The person making a transfer.

attachment In property law, the act by a sheriff of seizing property from a judgment debtor by virtue of a judicial order or summons, thereby bringing the property under the jurisdiction of the court as security for payment of the debt.

attest To witness the making of the final draft of a will.

attestation clause Witnesses to a will state that they have attested the maker's signature. Ordinarily, they sign a clause to this effect.

attorney-client privilege A rule that confidential communications in the course of professional employment between attorney and client may not be divulged by the attorney without the client's consent.

attorney in fact Someone, not necessarily an attorney, who is given authority by a power of attorney to do a particular nonlegal act.

audit The review of financial records by an outside party, e.g., the Internal Revenue Service.

augmented estate The augmented estate consists of the value of all of the property, whether real or personal, tangible or intangible, wherever situated, that consists of the sum of four components (1) the decedent's net probate estate; (2) the decedent's nonprobate transfers to others; (3) the decedent's nonprobate transfers to the surviving spouse; (4) the surviving spouse's net assets and nonprobate transfers to others, reduced by funeral and administration expenses, homestead allowance, family allowance, exempt property, and enforceable creditors' claims.

bailment The delivery of goods or personal property by one person to another for some specific purpose but without passing title to the property or goods. The person delivering the goods is known as the *bailor,* the person receiving it is the *bailee.*

basis Original basis is usually an asset's cost, which may be adjusted later when improvements are made to the asset, e.g., the addition of a new roof to a home. Basis is important in tax calculations since capital gain or loss is the excess or loss of selling price compared to basis.

beneficial title See **Equitable title.**

beneficiary In the terminology of wills, a person to whom the decedent's property is given or distributed; or the orthodox term for a person or institution to whom the maker of a will gives personal property through the will.

beneficiary of a trust During the existence of the trust, the person or institution holding equitable title to whom the trustee distributes the income earned from the trust property. When the trust terminates, the trustee conveys legal title to the property held in trust to the beneficiary or to some other person designated by the settlor (grantor) by a deed (*inter vivos* trust) or by a will (testamentary trust).

bequest A gift of personal property, other than money, through a will.

boilerplate Standard and identical language used in legal documents of a like nature.

bona fide In good faith.

bond A certificate whereby a surety company promises to pay money if the personal representative of a deceased fails to faithfully perform the duties of administering the decedent's estate.

bonds A debt of a corporation or government that it acknowledges and agrees to pay to the holder of the bond a certain fixed sum of money on a specific date and interest on that sum in the interim.

budget (1) A statement of estimated receipts and expenditures. (2) A statement of funds available and needed for the payment of claims, taxes, and cash bequests in an estate.

buy-sell agreement An agreement among co-owners of a business promising to buy out one of their number upon death, disability, or retirement.

bypass trust An estate planning device whereby a portion of a deceased spouse's estate passes to a trust rather than to the surviving spouse, thereby reducing the likelihood of the surviving spouse's estate being taxed. Typically, the surviving spouse is given a life estate in the trust. Also, a testamentary trust established for the benefit of a surviving spouse.

canons of ethics General rules or principles regarding behavior and professional responsibilities that apply to lawyers in their practice of law.

capacity (or testamentary capacity) The legal power and ability to make a valid will, e.g., being sane and of adult age.

capital gain The profit realized by the sale or exchange of capital assets, e.g., assets owned for more than one year.

capital gains tax An income tax on profits from the sale or exchange of a capital asset at a lower rate than the rates applied to ordinary income.

case law The law created by judges' decisions. See also **Common law.**

cash surrender value In ordinary (straight) life insurance, the cash reserve that increases (builds) each year the policy remains in force as a minimum savings feature. After the policy has been in force for a period specified by the insurer (company), the policyholder may borrow an amount not to exceed the cash value.

casualty loss The destruction of property caused by a sudden, unexpected destructive force, e.g., flood, fire, vandalism, etc.

causa mortis In contemplation of approaching death.

cause of action The right of a person to commence a lawsuit.

caveat "Let him beware."

caveator An interested party who gives a formal notice or warning to a court or judge against the performance of certain acts within his or her power and jurisdiction. This process may be used in the proper courts to prevent (temporarily or provisionally) the proving of a will.

certified copy An authoritative endorsement or guarantee that the copy is accurate, i.e., the same as the original.

cestui que trust The beneficiary of a trust, the person having the enjoyment of property (real or personal) of which a trustee has the legal title. The beneficiary is said to hold equitable title to the trust property.

charitable deduction A deduction allowed in computing "net gifts" for the full value of all gifts made to public, religious, charitable, scientific, literary, and educational institutions that meet the specified tests in the statute.

charitable remainder annuity trust Trust in which a fixed amount of income is given to a beneficiary at least annually for life and after death, the remainder is given to charity.

charitable remainder trust Trust in which the settlor or a beneficiary retains the income from the trust for a time period (usually for life) after which the remainder is given to charity.

charitable remainder unitrust Trust in which a fixed percentage of not less than 5 percent of the fair market value of the trust property is determined annually and is given to a beneficiary for life, and after death, the remainder is given to charity.

charitable trust A charitable (public) trust is an express trust established for the purpose of accomplishing social benefit for the public or the community. Also, it is the only type of trust that can last indefinitely.

chattel Generally, any item of personal property.

chose in action A right to recover something through a civil lawsuit.

citation The reference to legal authorities such as constitutions, statutes, case decisions, etc., in arguments made to a court or in legal textbooks to identify the source of the authority. Also, the legal form, used in some states, that is the court's order fixing a date, time, and place for hearing the petition to prove a will or for administration, and that the petitioner is required to give notice of the hearing to all interested persons including creditors who must now timely file their claims against the decedent's estate.

civil action A lawsuit brought to remedy a private, individual wrong, such as a breach of contract or tort.

civil court Civil matters, i.e., breach of contract and personal injury (tort) cases, must be brought before a civil court. A civil court has no power to hear criminal cases.

class gift A gift of an aggregate sum to a body of persons, uncertain in number, as, for example, the class consisting of the children of the same parents.

"clean hands" doctrine Equitable relief may be denied to a person who has been guilty of unjust or unfair conduct.

clerk An officer of the court who receives and files documents and keeps records of court proceedings.

closely held corporation A corporation whose shares of stock are not traded on any recognized stock exchange, and are thus said to be "closely held."

closing statement An affidavit by the personal representative at the end of informal probate proceedings to close the estate and to be discharged.

code A collection or revision of laws scientifically arranged by table of contents, chapters, subheads, and index and passed and published by legislatures.

codicil A written amendment to a will that may modify or revoke provisions in the will but does not cancel (invalidate) the will. A codicil must be executed with the same formalities as a will.

codification A systemization. One of the common features of probate codes.

collateral heir A person not in a direct line of lineal ascent or descent tracing a kinship relationship to an intestate decedent through a common ancestor (e.g., brothers, sisters, aunts, uncles, nieces, nephews, cousins), forming a collateral line of relationship.

collaterals of the half-blood Persons related to an intestate through only one common ancestor. Example: Having the same father or mother, but not both parents, in common.

commingling Combining community and separate property, e.g., into the same account or by using both to acquire a different item of property. Also when a fiduciary (trustee) combines the money from the sale of trust property with his own funds instead of placing the money in the trust account.

commission Compensation a fiduciary receives for its services, based on a percentage of the principal or of the income or both.

common disaster clause A clause used in a will to avoid an undesirable result where the order of death of two or more persons cannot be established by proof. Simultaneous deaths (e.g., in an automobile accident) are deaths in a common disaster.

common law Common law is based on the unwritten principles of law that had their origin in England. These principles were developed according to the customs and traditions of the community or on what was "equitable," "fair," or "just."

common law state The 41 states of the United States that take their marital property law from the English common law; they are not community property states.

common probate procedure An informal or independent probate. Referring to one of the two probate procedures established by common law and included and modified in the Uniform Probate Code and called informal probate; the other procedure is solemn probate or the U.P.C. procedure called formal probate.

community property All property, other than property received by gift or inheritance, acquired by either spouse during marriage is considered to belong to both spouses equally in the nine community property states.

competent witness A person who is legally capable and suitable to act as a witness to a will.

complaint In a civil action, the written pleadings or claims the person suing (plaintiff) lists against the defendant and has served on him.

concurrent ownership One of the various forms of property ownership. Concurrent ownership is a situation where two or more persons share rights as co-owners.

conditional gift A gift of property that is subject to the performance of a condition specified in a will or trust.

condition precedent A condition or specific event that must occur before an agreement or obligation becomes binding.

condition subsequent A condition that will continue or terminate an existing agreement once the condition does or does not occur. See also **Defeasible.**

conflict of interest Divided loyalties (it would be a conflict of interest for an attorney to represent both sides in the dispute).

consanguinity Relationship by blood through at least one common ancestor.

conservator An individual or a trust institution appointed by a court to care for and manage property, specifically, the property of an incompetent person or minor.

consideration (1) In contract terminology, the benefit requested and received by a person making a promise in return for that promise. The benefit may be an act, forbearance, or return promise given to the original promisor (person making the promise). In sales contracts, the consideration for each party is either the price or the delivery of the goods; however, initially the consideration is the exchange of promises. (2) The cause, motive, impelling influence (i.e., something of value) that induces two or more contracting parties to enter into a contract.

constructive trust A remedial device invoked by courts of equity to obtain legal title from a person who obtained title by fraud or other wrongdoing and force him to convey that title to the one who should have it.

contingent remainder A remainder is contingent if the right to possession is dependent or conditional on the happening of some event in addition to the termination of the preceding estate.

contract for deed An agreement or contract to sell real property on an installment basis. On payment of the last installment, the title to the property is transferred by delivery of the deed to the purchaser.

convey To give or sell property to another.

conveyance Any transfer by deed or will of legal or equitable title to real property from one party to another, e.g., from one person to another person, a corporation, or the government.

copyright A government grant to an author of an exclusive right to publish, reprint, and sell a manuscript for a period of the life of the author plus 50 years after the author's death for works written after January 1, 1978.

corpus See **Trust estate or Trust property.**

court of equity The court that administers justice according to the rules of equity and fairness. Examples of remedies from this court include a court order forbidding the person sued (defendant) from doing some act, i.e., an injunction, or a reforming of a contract by the court to conform the contract to the parties' intentions.

court of law The court that administers justice according to the rules and practices of both statutory law and common law. An example of a remedy that a court of law grants is damages (money) as compensation for personal injury or breach of contract.

covenant A promise of two or more parties, incorporated in a trust indenture or other formal instrument, to perform certain acts or to refrain from the performance of certain acts.

creditor One who is owed money by another.

creditor's claim A document that must be filed by the creditors of a decedent in order to be paid from the assets of the decedent's estate.

creditor's notice In probate proceedings, the notice that is published stating the decedent's death and the name of the executor or the administrator to whom claims should be presented for payment.

credits Subtractions made directly from a tax that is owed; credits are more beneficial than deductions.

Crummy trust An irrevocable life insurance trust that permits premiums to be paid by the settlor with dollars given to the trust free of gift tax.

curator A court-appointed individual or a trust institution to care for the property of a minor or an incompetent person. In some states, a curator is the same as a temporary administrator or a temporary guardian.

curtesy In common law, the right of the surviving husband to a life estate in all of the real property left by his deceased wife. A husband was entitled to curtesy only if the married couple had a child born alive.

custodian A person who has charge or custody of property for the benefit of another, usually a minor.

custodianship An alternative to a trust or guardianship that allows a person to be appointed by the court to manage property for the benefit of a minor.

cy-pres doctrine *Cy-pres* means "as near as possible." Where a testator or settlor makes a gift to a charity or for a charitable purpose and subsequently it becomes impossible or impractical to apply the gift to that particular charity, the equity court may order it applied to another charity "as near as may be possible" to the one designated by the settlor.

damages The monetary remedy from a court of law that can be recovered by the person who has suffered loss or injury to her person, property, or rights by the unlawful act, omission, or negligence of another.

death benefits Monetary payments from agencies such as Social Security and the Veterans' Administration payable to the decedent's estate.

death certificate A document signed by a physician evidencing the death of a person.

death transfer taxes A government levy (rate or amount of taxation) on property transferred to others by an individual on his or her death. Such taxes include estate, inheritance, and/or gift taxes.

decedent The deceased person, referred to as having died testate or intestate.

declaration of trust The act or document by which the settlor who holds legal title to property or an estate acknowledges and declares that she retains the title to the property as trustee in a trust for the benefit of another person or for certain specified purposes.

decree The written judgment (decision) of a court of equity.

decree of distribution A decree whereby the court determines the persons entitled to the estate, names the heirs or devisees, states their relationship to the decedent, describes the property, determines the property to which each person is entitled, and gives other findings of fact.

deductions Items that may be subtracted from taxable income, the taxable estate, or taxable gifts, thereby lowering the amount on which the tax is due.

deed A written, signed document that transfers title or ownership of real property, such as land.

deed of trust An instrument in writing duly executed and delivered by which the legal title to real property is placed in one or more trustees.

defeasible Capable of being defeated, annulled, revoked, or undone upon the happening of a future event or the performance of a condition subsequent, or by a conditional limitation, as a defeasible title to property.

degree of kinship The relationship of surviving blood relatives to a decedent who dies intestate.

degree of relationship A method of determining which collateral relatives or heirs will inherit from an intestate.

demand To assert and file a claim for payment based on a legal right.

demandant Any person who has a financial or property interest in a decedent's estate and who files with the court a demand for notice of any order or filing pertaining to the estate.

demonstrative gift (legacy) A gift or bequest of a specific monetary amount to be paid from the sale of a particular item of property or from some identifiable fund.

dependent One who derives support from another; to be distinguished from one who merely derives a benefit from the earnings of the deceased.

deposition A written declaration of a witness, under oath and before a qualified officer, to be used in place of the oral testimony of the witness at a trial or other hearing, e.g., a hearing to validate a will.

depreciation A decline in value of an asset due to its increase in age. Also, a deduction allowed against the income produced by property in the amount of the property's original cost divided by its estimated useful life.

descendant Claimant to an intestate's share related to the decedent in a descending lineal bloodline.

descent Succession to the ownership of an estate by inheritance.

descent and distribution See **Laws of descent and distribution.**

devest See **Divest.**

devise A gift of real property through a will. In U.P.C. terminology, "devise" refers to gifts of both real and personal property.

devisee The recipient of a devise.

devolution The passing of property by inheritance, including both descent of real property and distribution of personal property.

direct heir In the direct line of ascent or descent of the decedent, such as father, mother, son, or daughter.

direct skip A generation-skipping transfer of an interest in property that is transferred to a skip person; a direct skip is subject to the federal estate tax.

disciplinary rules Statements of minimum professional conduct that, if violated, lead to sanctions against the offending attorney.

disclaimer A document that will allow an heir or beneficiary to give up the right to inherit or receive property without any adverse tax consequences. Also, the right a person has to refuse or reject appointment as trustee of a trust.

discretionary trust A trust that provides the trustee with direction as to the management of the fund. This entitles the beneficiary to only as much of the income or principal as the trustee in her discretion shall see fit to give the beneficiary or to apply for his use. It is also called a sprinkling trust.

disposition The parting with, transfer of, or conveyance of property.

dissent Refusal to agree with something already stated or to an act previously performed. For example, a widow asserting her rights under the law and refusing to take the share provided for her in her husband's will is known as her "dissent from the will."

distributee or next-of-kin The person to whom personal property of the intestate decedent is distributed (orthodox terminology).

distribution The apportionment and division, under authority of a court, of the remainder of the estate of an intestate, after payment of the debts and charges, among those who are legally entitled to share in the same. Also, the transfer of property to the beneficiaries of a trust.

distributive share A recipient's portion of property left by a decedent who died intestate, as determined by state intestate succession laws.

divest or devest "To take away." Usually referring to an authority, power, property, or title, as to take away a vested right.

dividend The share of profits or property to which the owners of a business are entitled, e.g., stockholders are entitled to dividends authorized by a corporation in proportion to the number of shares they own.

domicile The legal home where a person has a true, fixed, and permanent place of dwelling and to which the person intends to return when absent. A temporary residence, such as a summer home, is not a domicile. A person may have only one domicile but could have more than one residence. Domicile and residence are frequently used interchangeably, but they are distinguished in that domicile is the legal home, the fixed permanent place of habitation, while residence is a transient place of dwelling. Domicile, not residence, determines venue.

domiciliary administration Administration in the state where a person was domiciled at the time of death.

donee One to whom a gift is made or a bequest given.

donee (of a power of appointment) The person to whom a power of appointment is given, also called the holder, who selects the appointee to receive an estate or income therefrom.

donor One who makes a gift or who creates a trust.

donor (of a power of appointment) The testator or settlor who creates a power or authority upon another (the donee) to appoint, that is, to select the person(s) (the appointee) to receive an estate or an income therefrom after the testator's or donee's death.

double indemnity Payment of double the face amount of a life insurance policy if the death of the insured (policyholder) is caused by an accident.

dower At common law, the wife's right to a life estate in one-third of the real property her husband owned during the marriage. Most states (except community property states) have replaced common law dower with statutes that give one spouse (wife or husband) the right to an "elective" or "forced" share of the other spouse's property. The spouse may renounce the will and "elect" to take the statutory share.

durable power of attorney for health care A document that gives an agent, as a substitute for the principal (the patient), the power and authority to make all medical and health care decisions when the patient is disabled and unable to make such decisions, including the authority to direct the withholding or withdrawal of life sustaining treatment.

duress Coercion; acting under the pressure of a threat.

ejectment In the law of real property, a civil action (a lawsuit brought in a court) for the recovery of the possession of land and for damages for the unlawful detention of its possession.

elective share See **Forced share statute.**

eleemosynary Relating to the distribution of charity, as an eleemosynary institution.

emergency provision The provision of a will or trust agreement that gives the trustee power to pay over or apply principal or accumulated income to meet emergencies in the life of the beneficiary due to unforeseeable events.

employee stock ownership plan (ESOP) A special category of a qualified benefit plan that is funded with the employer's own stock.

employer identification number See **Federal employer identification number.**

encumbrance (incumbrance) A claim or lien against real property, e.g., mortgages, easements, or a judgment, tax, or mechanic's lien.

endowment insurance An insurance contract in which the insurance company agrees to pay a stipulated amount when the policyholder reaches a specified age or upon the policyholder's death if that occurs earlier.

equitable title The right of the party to whom it (equitable or beneficial title) belongs to the benefits of the trust. The party can have the legal title transferred to her; e.g., a person in possession of real property such as a home who has equitable title while that person pays off the installment (on a mortgage) on the home to the legal title owner, e.g., the bank. Once the last payment is made, legal title will be transferred to the possessor by the delivery of a deed.

equity A system of laws or judicial remedies granted by certain courts, called courts of equity (chancery), distinct from the common law courts. Examples of such judicial remedies, granted when no adequate remedy from a court of law is available, are injunctions, reformation of contracts, and specific performance.

escheat The passage of property to the state when an intestate decedent leaves no surviving blood relatives or a spouse entitled to inherit the intestate's estate.

estate The whole of the property, real and personal, owned by any person. Also called the *gross estate*.

estate administration See **Administration of an estate.**

estate checking account A checking account established by the personal representative to hold the decedent's monetary assets.

estate equalization Rearranging property ownership of total estate assets owned by the spouses so that each spouse's individual estate has approximately the same value.

estate for years An estate for a fixed and determinate period of time, e.g., a lease for ten years.

estate plan An arrangement using the law of wills, trusts, tax, insurance, and property to gain maximum financial benefits for the disposition of a person's assets during life and at death.

estate tax (or transfer tax) A tax imposed on the privilege of passing an estate at death. The rate of tax is ordinarily based on the size of the estate and does not depend on the shares of the individual beneficiaries or their relationship to the decedent. To be distinguished from an inheritance tax.

estoppel Words or acts that prohibit a person from alleging or denying certain facts.

ethical considerations Ideals of professional conduct that attorneys should strive to achieve.

exculpatory provision A clause in favor of a trustee in a will or trust instrument that implies that the trustee has the power he purports to execute and clears him of all responsibility where this power is exercised in good faith. Sometimes called an immunity provision.

execution The completed or finished product, e.g., an executed (written and signed) will.

execution of a valid will The writing and signing by the testator and the attesting and signing by two or more witnesses of the will to establish its validity.

executor A man named in the will by the maker to be the personal representative of the decedent's estate and to carry out the provisions of the will. Also can be a corporation, e.g., a bank.

executrix A woman named in the will by the maker to be the personal representative of the decedent's estate and to carry out the provisions of the will.

exempt property The decedent's personal property up to a specific dollar amount that is given to the surviving spouse and/or minor children and is exempt from creditors' claims.

exemption equivalent Immunity from paying estate tax for decedents' estates currently valued to a maximum of $600,000.

exordium clause The beginning preamble or introductory clause of a will.

express trust A trust established by voluntary action and represented by a written document or an oral declaration.

face value The dollar amount appearing on a document, e.g., a life insurance policy.

fair market value The monetary amount that an item of property, e.g., a house, would bring if sold on the open market. Generally, the price agreed to by a willing seller and willing buyer, neither party being compelled to offer a price above or below the average price for such an item.

family allowance A statute that allows the court to award to the surviving spouse and/or minor children some of the personal property of the deceased and a monthly cash allowance for their maintenance and support before any debts are paid or distribution made under a will or without a will.

family conference A meeting of surviving family members to discuss the decedent's will or the intestate statute and the administration of the estate.

federal employer identification number A number that must be obtained from the I.R.S. for each individual estate or trust.

federal estate tax A tax imposed on the transfer of the taxable estate and not on any particular legacy, devise, or distributive share. It is neither a property tax nor an inheritance tax and is imposed solely on the "testamentary transfer or a transfer by intestate succession."

fee simple estate A freehold estate that is absolute and unqualified; an estate that is the largest, best, and most extensive estate that can be enjoyed in real property. It is not limited in duration or in the owner's method of disposition. Also known as a fee simple absolute, an estate in fee, or simply a fee.

fiduciary A person who is appointed to serve in a position of trust and who controls and manages property exclusively for the benefit of others. An example would be a trustee acting for the benefit of a trust beneficiary. Other examples would be a guardian or conservator acting for a minor, a partner acting for fellow partners, and a personal representative acting for beneficiaries of an estate.

fiduciary capacity The legal capability of a person or institution such as a bank to act as a fiduciary.

fiduciary duty A duty or responsibility required of a fiduciary that arises out of a position of loyalty, trust, and confidence. In the law of trusts, it is a duty that a trustee owes to the beneficiary of a trust.

final account The personal representative's notarized written account that shows all changes in the assets of the estate during his administration and discloses the balance of property available for distribution to the will's devisees or to the decedent's heirs.

fixture Real property that may have once been personal property but now is permanently attached to land or buildings.

forced share statute Forced heirship or elective share. The spouse's statutory right to choose a share of the decedent spouse's estate instead of inheriting under the provisions of the decedent's will.

foreclosure The termination of all rights in property of the person (the mortgagor) who, in writing, pledges the property for the purpose of securing a debt.

foreign state Any state other than the decedent's domicile state.

formal probate A probate proceeding conducted by the probate court in the administration of a decedent's estate, with or without a will, that requires notice to interested persons. See also **Solemn probate.**

fraud in the execution Fraud occurs when the testator is deceived about the character or contents of the document he is signing.

fraud in the inducement In this case, the testator makes the will or provision relying on a false representation of a material fact made to her by one who knows it to be false.

freehold estate A right of title to land; an estate in land or other real property of uncertain duration. There are three freehold estates: fee simple, fee tail, and life estate.

future estate or interest Any fixed estate or interest, except a reversion, in which the privilege of possession or enjoyment is future and not present.

garnish Make a claim against.

garnishment A three-party statutory proceeding in which a judgment creditor may demand that an employer who owes wages to an employee (the judgment debtor) pay these wages to the creditor to satisfy the creditor's claim against the employee (debtor).

general legacy A gift of a fixed amount of money from the general assets of the estate.

general power of appointment The right to pass an interest in property to whomever a donee (the one who is given the power) chooses, including herself or her estate, creditors, or creditors of the estate.

generation-skipping transfer tax A federal tax on the transfer of property valued over $1,000,000 to a person who is two or more generations below the generation of the grantor-transferor, e.g., a grandparent transferring property to a grandchild thereby skipping a child.

generation-skipping transfer trust A trust whereby property or benefits transferred by a grantor are split between persons (beneficiaries) from two or more generations that are younger than the generation of the grantor of the trust. Also, a trust that partially avoids federal gift and estate taxes on large sums of money or other valuable assets between generations of family members.

gift A transfer of property without payment or an expectation of receiving anything in return for it.

gift *causa mortis* A gift of personalty made in expectation of death, completed by actual delivery of the property, and effective only if the donor dies.

gift *inter vivos* Gifts between the living. To be effective, there must be actual delivery of the property during the lifetime of the donor and without reference to the donor's death.

gift splitting For gift tax purposes, an election by spouses to make a gift by one of them to a third party as being made one-half by each spouse.

gift tax A graduated tax imposed by the federal government on transfers of property by gift during the donor's lifetime.

gift tax exclusion A donor can give $10,000 annually to a donee or a like amount to each of any number of donees free from federal gift tax.

grantee The person to whom a conveyance of real property is made.

grantor The person who makes a conveyance (transfer) of real property to another. Also, the trustor, settlor, or donor who creates a trust.

gross estate All of a person's property before deductions (debts, taxes, and other expenses or liabilities) that is subject to the federal estate tax. See **Estate.**

guardian The person or institution named by the maker of a will or appointed by the court when there is no will to care for the person and/or property of a minor or a handicapped or incompetent person.

guardian *ad litem* A person appointed by the court to defend or bring a lawsuit on behalf of a minor or an incompetent person.

guardian of the person A person who is responsible for the care and custody of a child.

guardian of the property A person who is responsible for managing a child's property until the child becomes an adult.

half-blood A term denoting the degree of relationship that exists between those who have the same mother *or* the same father, but not both parents in common.

health care proxy A document in which a patient designates a proxy or surrogate who has legal authority to make medical and health care decisions if the patient is too incapacitated to do so personally.

heir or heir-at-law In orthodox terminology, a person including a spouse, who is entitled by statute to the real property of an intestate decedent. Also, a person who is entitled by intestate succession statutes to inherit property from the decedent's estate.

hereditament Things capable of being inherited, be they corporeal or incorporeal, real, personal, or mixed, and including not only lands and everything thereon, but also heirlooms and certain furniture that by custom may descend to the heir together with the land.

holographic will A will drawn and signed entirely in the maker's own handwriting that requires no witnesses. State laws establish the conditions for a valid holographic will.

homestead The house and the adjoining land (within statutory limits) where the head of the family lives; the family's fixed place of residence.

homestead allowance A statute that provides a modest cash award for the benefit of a surviving spouse or minor children; it is a priority payment to them and is not subject to creditors' claims. Also, a deduction allowed on a state death tax return for the surviving family members.

homestead exemption A statute that protects a family from eviction from their home by creditors.

homicide or slayer statute A person who is convicted of murdering another person cannot inherit from the victim's estate.

"hose and spray" power The power of a trustee to sprinkle the trust income among various persons and decide how much to distribute to each (only someone other than the grantor can have this power as trustee).

householder (also called head of household) A person who is entitled to the homestead exemption.

illegitimate child See **Nonmarital child.**

implied trust Implied trusts are trusts imposed on property by the courts when trust intent is lacking. These trusts are subdivided into resulting and constructive trusts. Both types are also passive trusts and are said to be created by "operation of law."

inchoate Incomplete, partial, unfinished; begun but not completed.

inchoate dower At common law, the wife's interest in the property owned by her husband during his life while the husband is still alive. It is a claim contingent on the wife surviving her husband.

incidents of ownership The right of the insured or her estate to the economic benefits of the insurance policy. Also, an element or right of ownership or degree of control over a life insurance contract. This right includes the options to change the beneficiary, to surrender or cancel the policy, to assign the policy, to pledge the policy for a loan, or to obtain a loan from the insurer (insurance company) against the cash surrender value of the policy. The retention by the insured of an incident of ownership in the life insurance policy will cause the policy proceeds to be included in the decedent's gross estate.

income Interest, dividends, or other return from money that has been invested.

income beneficiary The beneficiary who is entitled to receive the income produced from trust property.

incompetent person A person under legal disability, e.g., a mentally incapacitated person.

incorporation by reference A reference in a will to another existing document that makes the other document a part of the will itself.

incorporeal hereditament Anything inheritable and not tangible or visible, such as a right to rent or a promise to pay money.

increment An increase; that which is gained or added.

indefeasible That which cannot be defeated, revoked, or made void.

indemnify To reimburse someone for property that was lost, damaged, or stolen.

indenture A deed to which two or more persons are parties and in which these persons enter into reciprocal and corresponding grants or obligations toward each other.

individual retirement accounts (IRAs) Retirement funds allowed to any wage earner who can contribute up to $2,000 per year as an income tax deduction or $2,250 per year if a nonworking spouse joins in the account. For some taxpayers, the 1986 Tax Reform Act has terminated the tax deduction.

informal probate An unsupervised probate proceeding in which notice to interested persons is not required. See **Common probate.**

inherit To receive property from the estate of an ancestor.

inheritance tax (or "succession tax") A tax on the right to receive property from a decedent at death. Usually determined by the size of the share of the particular beneficiary and her relationship to the decedent. To be distinguished from an estate tax.

inheritance tax waiver A notice from a state taxing authority indicating that either no inheritance tax is due on certain property (so that ownership to it may be transferred) or that the tax on the property has been paid.

injunction A remedy from a court of equity that consists of a court order forbidding the performance of some act.

in loco parentis In the place of a parent; with a parent's rights, duties, and responsibilities.

***in personam* jurisdiction** The authority of the court over the individual against whom a lawsuit is brought, i.e., the defendant.

***in rem* jurisdiction** The authority of the court over things ("res"), i.e., the property of the decedent. A probate court is empowered to hear cases concerning decedents' wills, instruments by which decedents direct the transfer of property or "things." Therefore, the jurisdiction of a probate court is basically *in rem*.

insane delusion A person with a disordered mind who imagines facts to exist for which there is no evidence.

insolvent estate The estate of a decedent that has more debts than assets.

insurable interest An interest in the life of an individual or in property by which there will be financial loss if the insured dies or, in the case of property, if it is damaged, lost, or destroyed. Such an interest will entitle the person possessing the interest to obtain insurance on it.

intangible personal property A personal property interest that cannot be touched or moved, such as a right to sue another person, cash, stocks, bonds, and the like. Also called a **Chose in action.**

interest-free loan A popular method of shifting income taxes to lower-bracket taxpayers.

interested party (person) A person including heirs, devisees, children, spouses, personal representatives, creditors, beneficiaries, and any others having a property right in or claim to the estate of the decedent.

interested witness A person who is a beneficiary and a witness of the same will.

interlineation The act of writing between the lines of an instrument, e.g., a will. This could void the will.

***in terrorem* clause** A clause in a will that states that if a beneficiary of the will objects to probate or challenges the will's distributions, the contestant forfeits all benefits of the will.

inter vivos "Between the living."

***inter vivos* gift** A voluntary transfer of property by a living person, called the donor, to a recipient, called the donee. Consideration is not required for an *inter vivos* gift, as it would be in the case of a contract.

***inter vivos* (living) trust** A trust created by a maker (settlor) during the maker's lifetime. It becomes operative during the lifetime of the settlor. A "living trust."

intestacy Death without a valid will.

intestate As an adjective, meaning "without a will"; as a noun, meaning a person who died without a valid will.

intestate succession The manner in which a decedent's property will be distributed when death occurs without a valid will, determined by state law.

intestate succession statutes Laws passed in each state establishing the manner in which a decedent's property will be distributed when death occurs without a valid will.

inventory A complete physical check of all the assets of the decedent and a listing of said assets and their value at the time of the decedent's death on the forms provided for the inventory.

irrevocable life insurance trust A living trust that cannot be revoked or amended that is established by a settlor who assigns the ownership of a new or existing life insurance policy on her life to the trust and contributes money annually to the trustee to pay the premiums.

irrevocable trust A trust that may not be revoked by the settlor after its creation.

issue All persons who have descended from a common ancestor; a broader term than "children." Includes lineal descendants of any degree (children, grandchildren, etc.), natural, legitimate issue only, excluding adopted or illegitimate children.

joint tenancy Ownership of real or personal property with the right of survivorship, by two or more persons (called the joint tenants) by gift, sale, or inheritance. Joint tenants have the same interest, acquired by the same conveyance, commencing at the same time, held by the same undivided possession, and each has the *right of survivorship* by which a deceased joint tenant's interest in the property automatically goes to the surviving joint tenant or tenants.

joint will A will written on a single piece of paper and executed by two or more persons as the wills of both or all of them.

judgment The official decision of a court of justice establishing the rights and claims of parties in a lawsuit submitted to the court for determination.

jurisdiction The authority by which a particular court is empowered by statute to decide a certain kind of case and to have its decision enforced.

"kiddie" tax The net unearned income (i.e., investment income) of minor children under age 14 is taxed as if it were the parent's income.

kin Relationship by blood.

kindred Family; relatives; individuals related by blood.

lapsed devise A devise that fails, or takes no effect, by reason of the death, unwillingness, or incapacity of the devisee during the testator's lifetime.

lapsed legacy When the legatee dies before the testator, or before the legacy is payable, the bequest is said to lapse, as it then falls into the residuary fund of the estate.

lapse Failure to distribute a gift in a will because the legatee, beneficiary, or devisee dies before the testator.

last will and testament A legally enforceable declaration of one's intention to dispose of one's property, both real and personal, after death. It is revocable or amendable by means of a codicil up to the time a person dies or loses the mental capacity to make a valid will.

laws of descent and distribution Rules by which inheritances are regulated. These laws govern the *descent* of real property from ancestor to heirs and the *distribution* of personal property to beneficiaries.

leasehold estate One of the categories into which the law of real property divides the rights of ownership, the other being a freehold estate. The categories are distinguished by the extent and duration of the individual's interest or according to how long and how much an interest a person has in realty.

ledger A book of account in which a record of monetary transactions is made.

legacy A gift of money through a will.

legal description of real estate A description recognized by law that definitely (specifically) locates real property by reference to government surveys or recorded maps.

legal entity Something having legal existence, e.g., a natural or artificial person (corporation) that can sue or be sued.

legal investments Investments by trustees and other fiduciaries governed by statutes.

legal life estate A life estate created by operation of law and not directly by the parties themselves.

legal title In trust law, the form of ownership of trust property held by the trustee giving the trustee the right to control the property. Legal title is the antithesis of equitable title.

legatee The person who receives a gift of personal property under a will.

Letters of Administration The formal instrument of authority and appointment given to a personal representative (administrator) by the proper court to carry out the administration of the decedent's estate according to the proper state intestate succession statute.

Letters of Authority Certificates of appointment called Letters Testamentary, when there is a will, or Letters of Administration, when there is no will.

Letters Testamentary The formal instrument of authority and appointment given to a personal representative (executor) by the proper court to carry out the administration of the decedent's estate according to the terms of a will.

lien A claim or charge on property for payment of some debt. An estate in real property includes the right to possession and enjoyment of it, while a lien on real property is the right to have it sold or otherwise applied in satisfaction of a debt.

life estate A freehold estate in which a person, called the life tenant, holds an interest in land during her own or someone else's lifetime.

life in being A phrase used in the common law and statutory rules against perpetuities, meaning the remaining duration of the life of a person who is in existence at the time the deed or will takes effect.

life insurance A contract, a legally binding agreement, by which one party (the insurance company) promises to pay another (the policyholder or the designated beneficiary) a certain sum of money if the policyholder sustains a specific loss (i.e., death or total disability). For this protection, the policyholder makes a payment, called a premium, to the insurance company on a regular basis, such as annually.

life insurance trust See **Irrevocable life insurance trust.**

life interest A claim or interest not amounting to ownership and limited by a term of life, either that of the person in whom the right is vested or that of another.

life tenant The person holding a life estate in property.

limited or special power of appointment Power of appointment is limited when it can be exercised only in favor of persons or a class of persons designated in the instrument creating the power.

lineal A lineal is a person related to an intestate decedent in a direct line of kinship either upward in an ascending bloodline (e.g., parents, grandparents, or great-grandparents) or downward in a descending bloodline (e.g., children, grandchildren, or great-grandchildren).

lineal ascendants or lineal ancestors Persons with whom one is related in the ascending line—one's parents, grandparents, great-grandparents, etc.

lineal descendants Persons with whom one is related in the descending line, one's children, grandchildren, great-grandchildren, etc.

liquidate To turn assets into cash by their sale.

living trust A trust that is created and becomes operative during the lifetime of the settlor. The same as an *inter vivos* trust.

living will A document, separate from a will, that expresses a person's wish to be allowed to die a natural death and not be kept alive by artificial means.

lucid interval A temporary restoration to sanity during which an incompetent person has sufficient intelligence and judgment to make a valid will.

maintenance allowance An allowance provided by state statutes from the decedent's estate to the surviving spouse and minor children, which gives them reasonable maintenance during the administration of the decedent's estate for a statutory time period, e.g., 12 to 18 months. In some states, maintenance is also called the family allowance.

malfeasance Doing an act that a personal representative should not do at all; a wrongful act or mismanagement.

marital deduction An unlimited amount of the decedent's gross estate, which may be given to the surviving spouse without becoming subject to the federal estate tax levied against the decedent's estate.

marital deduction trust A trust that is designed to make the most financially advantageous use of the marital deduction against the federal estate tax.

marshaling of assets The arrangement or ranking of testamentary assets in a certain order to be used for the payment of debts, taking into consideration which claims have priority over others.

minor A person who is under the legal age of majority, usually eighteen.

Model Rules of Professional Conduct Standards of conduct written by the ABA to establish ethical guidelines for the practice of law.

Model Code of Professional Responsibility Rules of conduct governing the legal profession written by the ABA and adopted by many states.

mortgage A contract by which a person pledges property to another as security in order to obtain a loan.

mortgagee The person who takes, holds, or receives a mortgage from the borrower; the creditor.

mortgagor The person who gives a mortgage to the lender; the debtor.

mutual wills Separate and identical wills usually made by spouses containing reciprocal provisions and an agreement that neither spouse will change his or her will after the death of the other.

natural guardian The father of the child, or the mother if the father is dead or vice versa.

natural objects of the testator's bounty Family members and other friends and institutions, e.g., charitable or religious organizations, for whom the testator has affection.

necessaries Necessary items that supply the personal needs of an individual or family, such as food, clothing, or shelter.

negative will A will that specifically disinherits a named person or class of persons.

net estate Under estate tax statutes, "net estate" means that which is left of the gross estate after various deductions allowed by statute in the course of settlement.

next-of-kin In the law of descent and distribution, this term properly denotes the persons nearest of kindred to the decedent, those who are most nearly related to him by blood.

no contest clause See *In terrorem* **clause.**

nomination The act of suggesting or proposing a person for an office, position, or duty; to be distinguished from appointment. Thus, the testator nominates, but the court appoints, the executor under a will.

nonadverse party Any person having a substantial beneficial interest in the trust that would be adversely affected by the exercise or nonexercise of the power that he possesses respecting the trust.

nonmarital (illegitimate) child A child born to parents who are not married.

nonprobate asset This type of property will pass by operation of law.

non-skip person Any transferee of a direct skip who is not a skip person.

notary public A person authorized by the state whose function is to administer oaths, certify documents and deeds, and attest to the authenticity of signatures.

notice to creditors A written notice posted in public places or by notice in newspapers to creditors of an estate to present their claims for what the executor or administrator owes them from the estate assets. It is also a notice to debtors to come in and pay what they owe the estate.

notice to surviving spouse Notification to a surviving spouse or minor children regarding the allowances of personal property from the decedent's estate to which they are entitled. In addition, a renunciation and election rule applying only to the spouse who has not consented to the will, giving him or her the right to file a statement in writing renouncing and refusing to accept the provisions of such a will.

nuncupative will An oral will spoken in the presence of a witness or witnesses that is valid only under exceptional circumstances, such as the impending death of the person "speaking" the will. Nuncupative wills are prohibited in some jurisdictions.

olographic (or holographic) testament See **Holographic will.**

omitted child See **Pretermitted child or heir.**

operation of law Rights pass to a person by the application of the established rules of law, without the act, knowledge, or cooperation of the person.

operative Taking effect, e.g., when a will becomes operative, the maker of the will has died, and the will is now in operation.

opinions Statements issued by the ABA and state bar associations interpreting and applying their codes and rules that establish ethical guidelines for the practice of law.

ordinary (whole or straight) life insurance Life insurance that combines protection with a minimum savings feature called cash surrender value. Premium payments are required throughout the policyholder's lifetime. The cash value slowly increases until it equals the face amount of the policy. The policyholder may surrender the policy at any time and take out the money (cash value) for his own use or retain the policy until death for the benefit of the named beneficiary.

orphan's court   Another name for the probate court in some states.

orthodox terminology   Traditional definitions of words relating to wills and probate matters, used universally before the adoption into law of the Uniform Probate Code.

parol evidence   Oral or written evidence.

parol evidence rule   A general rule of contract law that oral or written evidence (testimony) is not allowed to vary, change, alter, or modify any terms or provisions of a written contract (agreement).

partition   The division of real property held by joint tenants or tenants in common into distinct portions so that they may hold the property in severalty, i.e., in single ownership. It does not create or convey a new or additional title or interest, but merely severs the unity of possession.

passive trust   An implied, resulting, constructive trust, or a trust that does not give oral or written affirmative powers and duties to a trustee to perform discretionary acts of management or administration for the benefit of named beneficiaries. A passive trust commissions the trustee to perform only minor acts of a mechanical or formal nature and often creates no administrative duties at all.

patent   A government grant to an inventor of an exclusive right to make, use, and sell an invention for a nonrenewable period of 17 years.

pecuniary bequest or legacy   A bequest of a sum of money or of an annuity.

per capita   "Individually." When all heirs entitled to a portion of an intestate decedent's estate are related to the deceased in the same degree of relationship (same-generation ascendants or descendants), each receives an identical portion, all sharing equally. Also, a distribution of property based on giving equal shares to all those entitled to the intestate's estate.

perpetuity   Any limitation or condition that may take away or suspend the power of alienation for a period beyond a life or lives in being and 21 years thereafter plus the usual period of gestation.

personal guardian   An individual or trust institution appointed by a court to take custody of and care for the person of a minor or an incompetent.

personal property   Also referred to as "chattels personal" or movable property. Everything subject to ownership that is not real estate; includes such items as clothing, household furnishings, stocks, money, contract rights, life insurance, and similar holdings.

personal representative   A person who administers the decedent's estate and either carries out the terms of the will or follows the appropriate intestate succession statute in distributing the estate. If the personal representative has been named in the will to carry out such liaison duties, he is called an executor (a woman is an executrix); if the court appoints the personal representative because no valid will exists, he is an administrator (administratrix, in the case of a woman). Generally, the executor and administrator perform similar duties, face similar liabilities, and hold similar powers. In sum, the court that has jurisdiction over the estate of the decedent manages this estate through the personal representative.

per stirpes   By "representation." When heirs entitled to a portion of an intestate decedent's estate are related to the deceased in different degrees of relationship (intergenerational ascendants or descendants) with some heirs having predeceased the intestate, the descendants of such persons receive their shares through the predeceased heirs. Also, a distribution of property that depends upon the relationship to the intestate of those entitled to the estate.

petition for probate or administration   An application to the proper court (probate court) from the person (called the petitioner) seeking to validate a will or to administer an intestate's estate asking the court to grant the request sought in the application.

posthumous child   A child born after the death of its father or, when a caesarean operation is performed, after that of the mother.

postmortem   After death; pertaining to matters occurring after death.

postnuptial contract or agreement   A contract made by spouses after marriage whereby the property rights of either or both spouses are determined.

pour-over   A "pour-over" provision refers to the transfer of property from an estate or trust to another estate or trust upon the happening of an event as provided in the instrument. Also, a provision in a will that directs the residue of the estate into a trust.

power in trust   A power that the donee (the trustee) must exercise in favor of the beneficiary of the trust.

power of appointment   A power or authority conferred by one person (called the donor) by deed or will on another (called the donee) to select and nominate the person or persons (called the appointees) who are to receive and enjoy an estate or an income therefrom or from a fund, after the testator's death or the donee's death, or after the termination of an existing right or interest.

power of attorney A document, witnessed and acknowledged, authorizing another to act as one's agent or attorney.

precatory trust A trust created by certain words, which are more like words of entreaty and permission than words of command or certainty. Examples of such words are "hope, desire, wish, and request," "have fullest confidence," "heartily beseech," and the like.

precatory words Words such as hope, desire, request, ask, beseech, wish, or recommend.

predecease To die before another.

prenuptial agreement See **Antenuptial contract.**

present interest An immediate and unrestricted interest in real or personal property including the privilege of possession or the enjoyment of the property.

present value In the law of trusts, the present value is the value of the trust property to the beneficiaries for gift tax purposes. The present value varies with the length of time the trust runs and is a percentage of the full value of the trust property.

pretermitted (omitted) child or heir A child or other descendant omitted in a parent's will.

prima facie At first sight; on the face of it. A fact presumed to be true unless disproved by evidence to the contrary.

primary beneficiary The person selected by the policyholder of a life insurance contract who is given a superior claim to the benefits of the insurance over all others.

primogeniture The state of being the firstborn among several children of the same parents; seniority by birth in the same family.

principal The capital or property of an estate or trust, as opposed to the income, which is the fruit of the capital. Also, a person who authorizes another (called the agent) to act on the person's behalf.

private trust A trust established or created for the financial benefit of a certain designated person or class of persons, clearly identified or capable of being identified by the terms of the trust.

probate The procedure by which a document is presented to the court to confirm it as a valid will. The process by which a proper court declares the will to be a valid testamentary disposition, or the system provided by law for transferring property of a decedent to successors.

probate administration See **Probate proceedings.**

probate assets (or probate property) Property passed by will or descended as intestate property.

probate court The court that has jurisdiction over the probate of wills, the grant of administration, and supervision of the management and settlement of the estates of decedents, including the collection of assets, the allowance of claims, and the distribution of the estate. In some states, probate courts (also called surrogate courts, orphan's courts, or courts of chancery) have jurisdiction over the estates of minors, including the appointment of guardians and the settlement of their accounts, and the estates of incompetents, habitual drunkards, and spendthrifts.

probate estate This includes the decedent's assets that are solely owned, that are property held as tenants in common, and that are subject to administration by the personal representative.

probate in common form An informal proceeding in court without notice to the interested parties. Probate in common form is revocable.

probate in solemn form A formal probate proceeding that requires court supervision and notice to all interested parties.

probate proceeding The process of distributing the estate of a person who died testate or intestate; includes all other matters over which probate courts have jurisdiction.

promissory note A promise in writing to pay a specified sum of money to the order of a named payee or to the bearer of the note.

property Anything subject to ownership.

property guardian An individual or trust institution appointed by a court to care for and manage the property of a minor or an incompetent. The same individual can be both personal and property guardian and is then called simply the guardian.

proponent The petitioner who presents a will to the court for approval.

pro rata According to a certain rate or percentage.

prorate To divide, share, or distribute proportionally.

prudent-person rule for trust investment This rule is used in states that have statutes governing investments by trustees. Originally stated in 1830 by the Supreme Judicial Court of Massachusetts, it says that, in investing, all that is required of trustees is that they conduct themselves faithfully and exercise a sound discretion and observe how people of prudence, discretion, and intelligence manage their own affairs not in regard to speculation but in regard to the permanent disposition of their funds, considering the probable income as well as the probable safety of the capital to be invested. This rule is also used in states where there is no statute governing investments.

publication In the law of wills, the formal declaration made by a testator at the time of signing a will that it is her last will and testament.

public administrator A public official appointed by the court to administer an estate of an intestate when no interested persons, including family members, are available.

public (charitable) trust   A trust established for the social benefit either of the public at large or the community.

pur autre vie   An estate lasting for the life of a person other than the life tenant.

purchase-money resulting trust   A resulting trust in which property is purchased and paid for by one person, and at his direction, the seller transfers possession and title to another person.

qualified small estate   A decedent's estate that consists entirely of statutory exempt property or allowances, funeral and administration expenses, and is within a certain limited monetary value.

QTIP trust (Qualified Terminable Interest Property Trust)   A type of trust that will qualify for the marital deduction in which the surviving spouse receives all the income for life but is not given a general power of appointment. Generally, the marital deduction (for gift and estate tax purposes) is not available if the interest transferred will terminate upon the death of the transferee spouse and pass to someone else. For example, if a husband places property in trust for his wife for life, and the remainder to their children when his wife dies, this is a terminable interest that does *not* qualify as a marital deduction for the husband or for the husband's estate. If, however, the QTIP election is made so that the property transferred into the trust is treated as qualified terminable interest property, the terminable interest restriction is waived, and the marital deduction is allowed. In exchange for this deduction, the surviving spouse's (wife's) gross estate must include the value of the QTIP election assets, even though she has no control over the ultimate disposition of these assets, i.e., she has no general power of appointment. Terminable interest property qualifies for this election if the donee or heir (the wife in this example) is the only beneficiary of the asset during her lifetime, and she receives income distributions from the trust property at least annually. If the trust property is transferred as a gift, the donor spouse (the husband) is the one who makes the QTIP election. If the trust property is transferred by death, the personal representative (executor) of the estate of the deceased spouse (the husband) has the right to make the election on schedule M of Form 706, the United States Estate Tax Return (see Form 96 in Appendix A).

quasi-community property   Property that is acquired outside a community property state and then moved into it or that is owned by spouses who have moved into a community property state.

ratification   The confirmation, approval, or sanction of a previous act done either by persons themselves or by another.

real property   Realty or real estate. Land and generally whatever is built or growing on or affixed (permanently attached) to land. It includes land, buildings, and fixtures. A fixture is real property that may once have been personal property but now is permanently attached to land or buildings. An example of a fixture on land is a tree. In a building, a fixture could be the carpeting nailed to a floor, a built-in dishwasher, and the like.

receivables   Debts (promissory notes and the like) established in the course of business, due from others at present or within a certain time period.

receiver   An indifferent person between the parties to a cause, appointed by the court to receive and preserve the property or fund in litigation, receive its rents, issues, and profits, and apply or dispose of them at the direction of the court when it does not seem reasonable that either party should hold them or where a party is incompetent to do so, as in the case of an infant.

reciprocal wills   See **Mutual wills.**

reformation of contracts   Equitable remedy to conform a written agreement to the actual intention of the contracting parties.

registrar   The judge of the court or, most often, the person designated by the judge to perform the functions on behalf of the court in informal proceedings.

relationship by affinity   A connection by ties of marriage.

relationship by consanguinity   Blood relationship; the relationship of persons descended from the same common ancestor.

remainder   In the law of wills, the remainder is the balance of an estate after all the other provisions of the will have been satisfied. Also referred to as "rest" and "residue." Also, a future estate in real property that takes effect on the termination of a prior estate created by the same instrument (document) at the same time.

remainderman   A person entitled to the remainder of an estate, e.g. a future fee simple estate, after a particular smaller estate, e.g., a life estate, has expired.

renounce   To reject, disclaim, abandon. To divest oneself of a right, power, or privilege.

renunciation   The act by which a person abandons a right acquired without transferring it to another, e.g., to refuse to accept a gift in a will.

representation   See **Right of representation.**

republication   The reexecution, revival, or restoration by a testator of a will that had previously been revoked.

republish   Reestablish; as to reestablish a will.

res   A thing; an object. The phrase "trust res" means trust property. Everything that may form an "object" of rights.

residence   The dwelling in which one temporarily lives or resides. "Residence" is not always synonymous with "domicile," although the terms are frequently interchanged. "Residence" may imply a temporary dwelling, whereas "domicile" always denotes a permanent dwelling.

residual devise A gift of all the testator's estate not otherwise effectively disposed of by a will.

residuary or residue clause A clause in a will that disposes of the remaining assets (residue) of the decedent after all debts and gifts in the will are satisfied.

residuary estate (also called the residue of the estate) The remaining assets (residue) of the decedent's estate after all debts have been paid and all other gifts in the will are distributed.

Restatement of Trusts In 1935, recognizing the need to simplify and clarify the law of trusts, a group of trust experts working for the American Law Institute set forth the existing rules of law affecting trust creation and administration and included illustrations and comments. The complete work was called the Restatement of the American Law of Trusts. In 1957, the original Restatement was revised and the revisions were incorporated into the Restatement of Trusts, Second. In 1992, another revision was completed. Throughout the trust chapters of this book, relevant sections of the Restatement (Second) or (Third) of Trusts will be cited.

resulting trust Resulting trusts are based on presumed or implied intent. These trusts arise by operation of law rather than as the result of any intentional act by the trustor where it appears that the trustor, in conveying away the property, did not make an effective disposition of the beneficial interest or did not intend that the person taking or holding title should have the beneficial interest.

reversion or reversionary interest The interest in real property that a grantor retains when a conveyance of the property by deed or by will transfers an estate smaller than what the grantor owns. At some future time, the real property reverts back to the grantor.

revocable Susceptible of being revoked, annulled, or made void by canceling, rescinding, repealing, or reversing.

revocable living trust A trust that the creator (settlor) has a right or power to revoke (cancel). Generally, such a power must be expressly reserved by the settlor in the trust instrument.

revocation of will Recalling, annulling, or rendering inoperative an existing will by some subsequent act of the testator or testatrix.

revocatory clause A clause or statement in a will that revokes all prior wills and codicils.

revoke To cancel.

right of election The right of a surviving husband or wife to choose to take, under the decedent's state law, his or her statutory share in preference to the provision made in the deceased spouse's will.

right of representation The right of a child to receive the share of an intestate's property that the child's deceased parent would have received if the parent was still living.

right of succession The right of an heir or successor to share in a decedent's estate, determined by degree of kinship.

right of survivorship An important characteristic of a joint tenancy that, upon the death of one joint tenant, passes the decedent's interest in the property by operation of law to the surviving joint tenants, with the last joint tenant entitled to the whole property.

right to die laws Statutes that allow a dying person to refuse medical treatment to prolong life.

royalty A payment made to an author, composer, or inventor by a company that has been licensed to either publish or manufacture the manuscript or invention of that author, composer, or inventor.

Rule Against Perpetuities A rule that fixes the time within which a future interest must vest (pass). The estate must vest (pass) within a time limited by a life or lives then in being and 21 years thereafter, together with the period of gestation. The rule applies only to private trusts, not to public trusts.

safe deposit box A locked box in a bank vault to which only the renter of the box has access.

savings bank trust See **Totten trust.**

secondary beneficiary The person selected by the policyholder as a successor to the benefits of a life insurance policy whenever the proceeds of the policy are not paid to the primary beneficiary.

securities Stocks, bonds, and other documents issued by corporations.

seisin (or seizin) Actual possession, where the possessor intends to claim the land as a fee simple or life estate. Seisin is not the same as legal title. The difference between legal title and seisin is that the person who holds seisin over the land does not necessarily hold legal title to it.

self-proved will A statutory procedure that provides for proving of a will by an acknowledgment of the testator and with an affidavit of witnesses made before a notary public.

separate property Property one person owns free from any rights or control of others; as the property that the husband or wife owned prior to their marriage or acquired during marriage by inheritance, will, or gift.

settlement The final distribution of an estate by an executor or an administrator.

settlement option One of a number of alternatives that parties to an insurance contract agree to follow to discharge their agreement.

settlor A person who creates a trust; also called donor, grantor, creator, or trustor.

severalty Property in severalty is that owned and held by one person only, without any other person having an interest or right in the property.

severance Act of severing, separating, or partitioning; with respect to joint tenancy, severance is the destruction of any one of the four essential unities accomplished by one of the joint tenants transferring *inter vivos* the interest in real property to another person by deed, thereby creating a tenancy in common for the new owner with the other remaining joint tenants.

short-term trust An irrevocable trust running for at least 10 years or more, or for the life of the beneficiary, in which the income is payable to a person other than the settlor. The income from a trust of this kind is taxable to the income beneficiary and not to the settlor. Also known as a Clifford, come-back, give and keep, and reversionary trust. Such trusts have been severely limited by the 1986 Tax Reform Act.

simultaneous death clause A clause in a will that determines the distribution of property in the event there is no evidence as to the priority of time of death of the testator and another, usually the testator's spouse.

skip person An individual (such as a grandchild) who is two or more generations below the generation of the transferor (grantor). A trust can also be a skip person.

small estate A decedent's estate with few assets and a limited monetary value.

soldiers' and sailors' wills Several states have statutes relaxing statutory requirements for wills of soldiers and sailors. They usually require that the will be made by soldiers in actual military service or sailors while at sea. These wills are usually limited to disposing of personalty.

solemn probate procedure Formal probate. Probate proceedings that require court supervision and notice to interested persons.

sound mind Having the mental capacity to make a will.

sovereign (governmental) immunity A common law rule that exempts or frees the government from tort liability. Many states have limited or abolished this immunity.

special administrator An administrator appointed by the court to take over and safeguard an estate pending the appointment of an executor or general administrator.

special power of appointment A power of appointment that cannot be exercised in favor of the donee or her estate, but only in favor of an identifiable person(s) other than the donee.

specific bequest or legacy A gift, by will, of a particular item of personal property or a gift of a class of personal property in a will.

specific devise A gift, by will, of real property.

specific performance A remedy from a court of equity requiring the parties to a contract to do what they promised, e.g., perform their contract according to its terms.

spendthrift One who spends money unwisely and wastefully.

spendthrift clause A clause in a will that prevents the beneficiary from having the power to transfer his interest in the principal or income of a trust in any manner, preventing such interest from being subject to the claims of his creditors, attachment, execution, or other process of law.

spendthrift trust A trust created to provide the income but not the principal from a fund for the maintenance of a beneficiary and at the same time to secure it against his improvidence or incapacity.

spouse's allowance Allowance made by the court to the surviving husband or wife for the purpose of providing him or her with funds for living expenses during the period of settlement of the estate.

sprinkling trusts A trust in which the income or principal is distributed among the members of a designated class in amounts and proportions determined by the discretion of the trustee. Also called spraying trusts.

standing A person who stands to lose a pecuniary interest in a decedent's estate if a will is allowed.

stare decisis The practice of following previous court decisions. A Latin term meaning "to stand by previous decisions."

statute A law passed by a state or federal legislature. Statutory law is one source of law, i.e., state statutes, federal statutes. State and federal governments publish books of law that are called statutes.

Statute of Frauds State laws that provide that no suit or civil action shall be maintained on certain classes of oral contracts unless the agreement is put in writing and signed by the party to be charged, i.e., the person being sued, or by an authorized agent of that person. Each state has its own Statute of Frauds patterned on the medieval English statute of the same name.

statute of limitations Each state has its own statute of limitations that bars suits on valid claims after the expiration of a specific period of time. The period varies for different kinds of claims.

Statute of Uses An English statute enacted in 1536 directed against the practice of creating "uses" in land. It converted the purely equitable title of persons (beneficiaries) entitled to a use into a legal title or absolute ownership with right of possession. The statute is said to "execute the use," that is, it turned equitable estates into legal estates.

statutes of descent Statutes that govern the descent of real property under intestacy.

statutes of distribution   Laws prescribing the manner of the distribution of personal property under intestacy.

statutes of mortmain   As far back as the thirteenth century, various English statutes were enacted that restricted or forbade charitable and religious societies or corporations from holding property. *Mortmain* means "dead hand." These statutes were intended to prevent land from becoming perpetually controlled by one dead hand, that of the charitable entity. Many states have "mortmain"-type statutes, which limit the power of a testator to make charitable gifts. Modern mortmain statutes are usually for the purpose of protecting the family of a decedent from disinheritance by deathbed gifts to charity.

statutory investment   An investment that a trustee is specifically authorized to make under the terms of the statutes governing investments by trustees.

statutory lists   Lists of conservative investments set forth by statute in which a trustee is to invest. These statutes are of two types: (1) "permissive," where the trustee may invest outside the list but has the burden of justifying any investments not on the list; (2) "mandatory," where the trustee is liable for any investment not on the list. These lists are also known as "legal lists."

statutory will   A fill-in-the-blank type of will that is authorized by statute in a few states.

stepped-up basis   A provision whereby the heir's basis in inherited property is equal to its value at the date of the decedent's death.

stock dividend   A dividend of shares of stock distributed to stockholders.

stocks   Fractional shares (certificates) representing an ownership in a corporation.

stock split   One share of stock is split into a larger number of shares resulting in a proportional change in the number of shares owned by each stockholder.

stock transfer   The transfer of stock from one person to another by sale or gift handled by a party designated by the corporation called a transfer agent (often a bank).

straw man   A person used to create a joint tenancy of real property between the existing owner of the property and one or more other persons. The owner transfers a deed to the straw man, and the straw man immediately reconveys, by a second deed, the property back to the original owner and the new co-owner as joint tenants.

subject matter jurisdiction   The power a court must have to render the kind of judgment requested by a party to an action-at-law.

subrogation   The substitution of one person in the place of another with reference to a lawful claim, demand, or right. An equitable remedy borrowed from civil law to compel the ultimate discharge of a debt or obligation by a person who in good conscience should pay it.

subscribe   To sign a will.

subscribing witness   One who sees a writing executed, or hears it acknowledged, and at the request of the party thereupon signs her name as a witness.

subscription   The act of signing one's name to a written document.

succession   The act of acquiring property of a deceased person, whether by operation of law upon the person's dying intestate or by taking under a will.

succession tax   A tax imposed on the privilege of receiving property from a decedent by devise or inheritance. It is imposed on each legacy or distributive share of the estate as it is received.

successive beneficiary   One who takes the place of another beneficiary by succession. For example, under a will in which property is left to A for life, then to B for life, and then to C outright, B and C are successive beneficiaries.

successors   An all-inclusive U.P.C. term meaning those persons, other than creditors, who are entitled to real or personal property of a decedent either under the will or through intestate succession.

summary proceeding   Any proceeding by which a controversy is settled, a case is disposed of, or a trial is conducted in a prompt and simple manner without the aid of a jury, without presentment or indictment, or in other respects out of the regular course of common law. An example would be a process used to settle an estate without the probate procedure.

summons   In a civil action (lawsuit), the notification to a defendant that he is being sued and that he must answer it at a time or place named in the notice document.

supernumerary witnesses   Where more than the required number of witnesses attest a will (e.g., three sign instead of the required two) and it turns out that one of them is "beneficially interested," that witness is regarded as supernumerary.

support trust   A trust containing a direction that the trustee shall pay or apply only so much of the income and principal as is necessary for the education and support of the beneficiary and to spend the income only for that purpose. This type of trust can be used where spendthrift trusts are not recognized.

surcharge   An overcharge beyond what is just and right, e.g., an amount the fiduciary is required by court decree to make good because of negligence or willful failure of duty.

surety   An individual or company that, at the request of another, such as a personal representative, agrees to pay money in the amount of a bond in the event that the personal representative fails to faithfully perform his duties. An example would be the surety on an administrator's or guardian's bond.

surrogate The name given in some of the states to the judge or judicial officer who has the authority to act concerning the administration of probate matters, guardianships, etc.

surrogate court See **Probate court.**

tangible personal property Property that can be touched, e.g., furniture, jewelry, or a car.

taxable distribution Any distribution of income or principal from a trust to a skip person.

taxable estate The balance of an estate after the various expenses, claims, and deductions allowed by statute are subtracted from the gross estate.

taxable gift A transfer of property that is both voluntary and complete by an individual for less than an adequate and full consideration in money or money's worth.

taxable termination Any termination of an interest in property held in trust; however, a termination is not a taxable termination if (1) immediately afterward any non-skip person has an interest in the trust property or (2) distribution can never thereafter be made to a skip person.

tax waiver A written consent from the state tax department allowing the withdrawal of property belonging to the estate of a decedent by the administrator or the executor for the purpose of assembling the assets and to permit distribution.

tenancy An interest in or ownership of property by any kind of legal right or title. Not necessarily limited to the more restricted meaning of one (called a tenant) who has temporary use and possession of real property, e.g., an apartment, owned by another (called the landlord).

tenancy at sufferance A person who has tenancy at sufferance has come into possession of land by lawful title and continues to hold the property even after her title or interest has terminated.

tenancy at will A person who has tenancy at will holds possession of premises by permission of the owner or landlord but without a fixed term. The person has no sure estate because he is at the will or pleasure of the owner.

tenancy by the entirety A form of joint tenancy with the right of survivorship available only to a husband and wife. It is essentially a *joint tenancy* modified by the common law theory that husband and wife are one person, but it is distinguished from the usual joint tenancy in that it cannot be terminated by one joint tenant's *inter vivos* conveyance of his or her interest. Neither one of the tenants by the entirety can convey (transfer) the property or sever the tenancy by the entirety without the consent of the other spouse. The predominant and distinguishing feature of both joint tenancy and tenancy by the entirety is the "right of survivorship."

tenancy (estate) for years The temporary use and possession of lands or tenements not one's own, for a determinate period of time, as for a year or a fixed number of years.

tenancy in common The ownership of an undivided interest of real or personal property by two or more persons without the right of survivorship. Each person has the right to hold or occupy the whole property in common with the other co-tenants, and each is entitled to share in the profits derived from the property. Unlike a joint tenancy, when a tenant in common dies, the decedent's interest goes to an heir or as directed in a will.

tenants in common Two or more persons who own property in a tenancy in common.

terminable interest An interest in property that terminates upon the death of the holder or upon the occurrence of some other specified event.

term insurance Life insurance that is pure protection without savings (cash value). It is also the cheapest insurance. It requires the insurance company to pay the face amount of insurance, i.e., the proceeds, to the beneficiary if the policyholder dies within a given time period (term).

territorial jurisdiction A court has authority only over matters affecting persons and property within the geographic limits assigned to the court by statute.

testacy Death with a valid will.

testament A will. In early English law, a will of personal property.

testamentary capacity Age and sanity (sound mind) requirements for a person to make a will. That measure of mental ability that is recognized in law as sufficient for the making of a will.

testamentary devise In orthodox terminology, a transfer of real property through a will.

testamentary disposition A disposition of property by way of gift that is not to take effect unless or until the grantor dies.

testamentary guardian A guardian of a minor or an incompetent person appointed in the decedent's last will.

testamentary trust A trust created in a will. It becomes operative only after death.

testate As an adjective, having made a valid will; as a noun, one, either a man or a woman, who has made a valid will.

testator A man who makes and/or dies with a will.

testatrix A woman who makes and/or dies with a will.

testimonium clause A clause in a will in which the maker states that she has freely signed and dated the will and requests the proper number of witnesses to do the same.

"tickler" system A chronological list of all the important steps and dates in the stages of the administration of the decedent's estate.

title The right to or legal ownership of property.

Torrens title proceeding A judicial proceeding for the registration of title to real property in which all interests, encumbrances, and estates in the property are determined and entered on the record and on the legal document called the certificate of title, which is used to transfer ownership.

tort A private or civil wrong or injury independent of contract law.

Totten trust A trust created by the deposit by one person of his own money in his own name as a trustee for another. It is a tentative trust revocable at will until the depositor dies or completes the gift in his lifetime by some unequivocal act or declaration, such as a delivery of the passbook or notice to the beneficiary. The depositor may withdraw all or any part of the funds during his lifetime, and on death, the beneficiary may enforce the trust as to any part remaining on deposit at the death. The word "Totten" refers to a famous case establishing this principle.

transfer An act of the parties (e.g., individuals, corporations, or the government) by which the title to property is conveyed from one party to another.

transfer agent The party designated by a corporation (usually a bank) to be contacted whenever a stock transfer, e.g., a sale or gift of stock, occurs. The bank records changes in the ownership of the stock and keeps the list of stockholders of the corporation.

transferee The party to whom the title to property is conveyed.

transferor The party who transfers or conveys the title to property. Also, the decedent or donor who creates a generation-skipping trust.

transfer tax A tax on the passing of the title to property or a valuable interest out of or from the estate of a decedent by inheritance, devise, or bequest.

trust A right of property, real or personal, held by one person (trustee) for the benefit of another (beneficiary). The trustee holds legal title to the property; the beneficiary holds equitable title.

trust account This general term includes all types of accounts in a trust department, such as agencies, guardianships, and estates.

trust capital All extraordinary receipts, such as proceeds from the sale or the exchange of assets, and settlement of claims for injury to trust property.

trust corpus See **Trust property** or **Trust estate.**

trustee The person or institution named by the maker of a will to administer property for the benefit of another according to provisions in a testamentary trust or by the maker of a trust in an *inter vivos* trust.

trust estate The property that is the subject matter of the trust.

trust fund All the property held in trust in a given account. See also **Trust property.**

trust income All ordinary receipts from use or investment of the trust property, such as interest, rents, and dividends.

trust instrument Any writing under which a trust is created, such as a will, trust agreement, declaration of trust, or court order.

trust investments A broad term that includes not just securities but all kinds of property in which trust funds are invested.

trustor A person who intentionally creates a trust. Also known as a settlor, grantor, or testator.

trust powers The authority to engage in the trust business.

trust property Also called the trust corpus, res, fund, estate, or subject matter of the trust. The property interest that the trustee holds subject to the right of someone else.

trust res See **Trust property.**

ultra vires Acts beyond the express and implied powers of a corporation.

unauthorized practice of law Engaging in any legal work that involves exercising professional judgment or advice usually reserved for a lawyer.

undivided interest A right to an undivided portion of property that is owned by one of two or more tenants in common or joint tenants before the property is divided (partitioned).

undue influence The influence one person exerts over another person to the point where the latter is overpowered and induced to do or forbear an act that she would not do or would do if left to act freely.

unified credit The credit given against the federal estate tax after death, or credit against the gift tax for certain transfers prior to death.

Uniform Anatomical Gift Act Any individual who is competent and of legal age may give all or a part of her body to any hospital, surgeon, physician, accredited medical or dental school, college or university, or any bank or storage facility for education, research, advancement of medical or dental science, therapy or transplantation, or to any specified individual for therapy or transplantation. The gift of all or part of the body may be made by a document other than a will, e.g., a card designed to be carried on the person that must be signed by the donor in the presence of witnesses, who in turn must sign the card in the presence of the donor.

Uniform Gift to Minors Act A law that enables a gift of specified types of property to be given to a custodian or guardian and held for a minor until the minor reaches adulthood.

Uniform Probate Code (U.P.C.) A uniform law available for adoption by the states to modernize and improve the efficiency of estate administration. To help alleviate the confusion of having 50 states with different procedures for handling decedents' estates, the National Conference of Commissioners on Uniform State Laws and the American Law Institute prepared model uniform statutes and recommended their adoption by the states. The Uniform Probate Code is one such model. These codes are not the law of a particular state until that state adopts them.

Uniform Simultaneous Death Act An act that provides that where the inheritance of property depends on the priority of death of the decedents and where there is no sufficient evidence that the decedents have died other than simultaneously, the property of each decedent involved shall be distributed as if each had survived the other.

unity of possession One of the essential elements of concurrent forms of ownership, i.e., ownership involving two or more persons. It requires that concurrent owners must hold the same undivided possession of the whole property and that each owner has the right to share proportionately in profits derived from it, e.g., cultivated crops, livestock, and the like.

unsupervised administration A method of administering an estate without court action unless requested by an interested person.

uses The early medieval English forerunner of a trust (specifically, a passive trust) based on the principle of separation of the legal title to an estate from the equitable (beneficial) title. The person who legally owned the estate (i.e., had legal title) did not have the right to gain benefits from it (a considerable right in the Middle Ages), and the person who had the right to the benefits did not legally own it. In feudal society, uses were valuable to landowners as means of assigning or avoiding the responsibilities of landowners, e.g., their obligations to their lords for military support, for payment of a portion of their crops, and the like. Consequently, many landowners abused this practice by creating uses. The Statute of Uses abolished "uses," which were equivalent to modern-day passive trusts, and put an end to the practice described above.

venue The particular place, county or city, where a court having jurisdiction may hear and decide a case.

vested interest An interest in which there is a present fixed right in real or personal property although the right of possession and enjoyment may be postponed until some future date or until the happening of some event.

vested remainder An estate by which a present interest passes to the party, with the right of possession and enjoyment postponed until the termination of the prior estate.

voluntary trust A trust created by the voluntary act of the settlor and not conditioned upon his death. The actual title passes to a *cestui que trust* while the legal title is retained by the settlor, to be held by him for the purposes of the trust.

voucher A bank voucher that contains a check and a ledger or voucher that allows for a documented record of the use, date, and amount of the business transaction, e.g., a payment of a decedent's debt.

waste Any act or omission that does permanent damage to real property or unreasonably changes its character or value.

whole life insurance See **Ordinary (straight) life insurance.**

widow's allowance An allowance consisting of personal property made by the court to a widow to cover her immediate needs after her husband's death.

widow's exemption For the purpose of computing the state inheritance tax, a certain amount is allowed as a deduction on the widow's share of her husband's estate. This is known as the widow's exemption.

will The legally enforceable written declaration of a person's intended distribution of property after death.

will contest Litigation to overturn a decedent's will.

work product privilege Work of an attorney for a client that includes private memoranda prepared in anticipation of litigation or for trials does not have to be disclosed (given to the opposing party).

younger-generation beneficiary Any beneficiary who is assigned to a generation younger than the grantor's generation.

INDEX